THE OXFORD HANDBOOK OF

HEALTH
ECONOMICS

THE OXFORD HANDBOOK OF

HEALTH

ECONOMICS

Edited by

SHERRY GLIED

and

PETER C. SMITH

OXFORD

UNIVERSITY PRESS

OXFORD

UNIVERSITY PRESS

Great Clarendon Street, Oxford, OX2 6DP,
United Kingdom

Oxford University Press is a department of the University of Oxford.
It furthers the University's objective of excellence in research, scholarship,
and education by publishing worldwide. Oxford is a registered trade mark of
Oxford University Press in the UK and in certain other countries

© Oxford University Press 2011

The moral rights of the author have been asserted

First published in 2011
First published in paperback 2013

Published in the United States of America by Oxford University Press
198 Madison Avenue, New York, NY 10016, United States of America

British Library Cataloguing in Publication Data
Data available

Library of Congress Cataloging in Publication Data
Data available

ISBN 978-0-19-967540-1

Acknowledgements

THE editors would like to thank all those who contributed their expertise to this volume. At Oxford University Press, the handbook was commissioned by Sarah Caro, who guided the early development of the volume, and brought to a successful conclusion by Georgia Pinteau. We also greatly appreciated the help of the publisher's editorial team, which included Chris Champion, Emma Lambert, Rachel Platt, and Aimee Wright. Great thanks are due to Vanessa Windass, who provided unfailing secretarial support throughout the project, and to Dahlia Rivera. Finally, we should like to thank the authors, whose scholarship is evident throughout these pages, and who responded to editorial suggestions with great wisdom and patience.

Contents

LIST OF FIGURES

LIST OF TABLES

LIST OF BOXES

LIST OF CONTRIBUTORS

Gerard F. Anderson, Ph.D., is a professor of health policy and management, professor of international health, and professor of medicine at Johns Hopkins University. Dr. Anderson is currently conducting research on chronic conditions, comparative health care systems, health care payment reform, and technology diffusion. He has authored two books, published over 200 peer-reviewed articles, testified in Congress over forty times as an individual witness, and serves on multiple editorial committees. Prior to his arrival at Johns Hopkins, Dr. Anderson held various positions in the Office of the Secretary, US Department of Health and Human Services.

Laurence Baker is Professor of Health Research and Policy at Stanford University, and Research Associate of the National Bureau of Economic Research. His research includes extensive analysis of managed care and its effects on health care delivery, costs, and outcomes. He received his Ph. D. in Economics from Princeton University in 1994.

Michael Baker is a professor of economics and public policy at the University of Toronto and a research associate of the NBER. His recent research focuses on how public policies affect mothers' decisions to return to work after giving birth, and thereby their children's health and development.

Till Bärnighausen is Assistant Professor of Global Health at the Harvard School of Public Health and Senior Epidemiologist at the Africa Centre for Health and Population Studies, University of KwaZulu-Natal. He has published widely on health systems in developing countries, HIV epidemiology, and HIV services, systems and economics. Till is a medical specialist in Family Medicine. He holds doctoral degrees in International Health Economics (Harvard) and History of Medicine (Heidelberg), and master degrees in Financial Economics (SOAS) and Health Systems Management (LSH&TM).

Pedro Pita Barros is Professor of Economics at Universidade Nova de Lisboa. His research focuses on health economics and on regulation and competition policy. His work covers topics such as health expenditure determinants, waiting lists, and bargaining in health care, among others. He has served as Member of the Board of the Portuguese Energy Regulator.

Åke Blomqvist a native of Sweden, received his Ph.D. from Princeton in 1971. He was with UWO, Canada, until 2002 when he moved to the National University of Singapore. He is currently Professor in the China Center for Human Capital and Labor Economics Research, CUFE, Beijing, a post which he has held since 2009. His research interests include international comparisons of health care systems and reform, most recently in China.

David E. Bloom is Clarence James Gamble Professor of Economics and Demography and Chair of the Department of Global Health and Population, Harvard School of Public Health. Bloom has worked in development, health, labor economics, and demography. His current research focuses on theoretical and empirical links among health, demography, and economic growth.

Karen Bloor is a senior research fellow in the Department of Health Sciences at the University of York. Her main research interests are in the economics of health policy, particularly relating to the medical workforce.

Kristian Bolin is Professor of Economics at Lund University. His research is mainly within health economics. He has performed both theoretical and empirical work, focusing on the areas of individual health and health-related behavior. He has also performed research applying health economics to other areas, for instance, economic micro-simulation.

John Brazier is a Professor of Health Economics at the School of Health and Related Research and the University of Sheffield. He has more than twenty years' experience of conducting economic evaluations for policy makers and has served as a member of the National Institute of Health and Clinical Excellence Appraisal Committee.

James F. Burgess, Jr., Ph.D., is an associate editor at *Health Economics* and is on the editorial board of *Health Services Research*. He has appointments at the US Department of Veterans Affairs Center for Organization, Leadership, and Management Research, and as a Professor of Health Policy and Management at the Boston University School of Public Health.

Michael E. Chernew, Ph.D., is a professor of Health Care Policy in the Department of Health Care Policy at Harvard Medical School. He is a member the Medicare Payment Advisory Commission (MedPAC), which is an independent agency established to advise the US Congress on issues affecting the Medicare program. He is also a member of the Congressional Budget Office's Panel of Health Advisors and Commonwealth Foundation's Commission on a High Performance Health Care System.

Jon B. Christianson, Ph.D., is the James A. Hamilton Chair in Health Policy and Management in the School of Public Health, University of Minnesota. His research interests include the effects of financial incentives in health care, insurance benefit design, and public reporting of provider performance.

Karl Claxton is a professor in the Department of Economics and Related Studies and the Centre for Health Economics at the University of York. His research interests encompass the economic evaluation of health technologies and he serves as a member of the National Institute for Health and Clinical Excellence Appraisal Committee.

Douglas A. Conrad, Ph.D., is Professor of Health Services and Adjunct Professor of Business and Economics at the University of Washington, and Director of the Center for

Health Management Research (CHMR) of the Health Research and Educational Trust. He has an MHA (1973) from the University of Washington, and an MBA (1976) and Ph.D. (1978; Economics and Finance) from the Graduate School of Business of the University of Chicago.

David M. Cutler is the Otto Eckstein Professor of Applied Economics in the Department of Economics and Kennedy School of Government. Cutler's work in health economics and public economics has earned him significant academic and public acclaim. Cutler is the author of *Your Money or Your Life: Strong Medicine for America's Health Care System*, published by Oxford University Press. This book, and Professor Cutler's ideas, were the subject of a feature article in the *New York Times Magazine*, "The Quality Cure," by Roger Lowenstein. Cutler is a research associate at the National Bureau of Economic Research and a member of the Institute of Medicine.

Patricia M. Danzon, Ph.D., is Professor of Health Care Management at The Wharton School, University of Pennsylvania. She received a B.A. from Oxford and a Ph.D. in Economics from the University of Chicago. She has held faculty positions at Duke and the University of Chicago. Professor Danzon is a member of the Institute of Medicine and the National Academy of Social Insurance. She has published widely in scholarly journals on a broad range of subjects related to pharmaceuticals and health economics and consults widely for public and private organizations.

Michael Drummond, B.Sc., M.Com., D.Phil., is Professor of Health Economics and former Director of the Centre for Health Economics at the University of York. His research interest is the economic evaluation of health care treatments and programs, and he has undertaken evaluations in a wide range of medical fields. Drummond is the author of two major textbooks and more than 500 scientific papers. He has been President of the International Society of Technology Assessment in Health Care and of the International Society for Pharmacoeconomics and Outcomes Research, and he is currently a member of the Guidelines Review Panels of the National Institute for Health and Clinical Excellence (NICE) in the UK.

Jose-Luis Fernandez is Deputy Director at the Personal Social Services Research Unit, London School of Economics. A health and social care economist, Dr. Fernandez specializes in the analysis of funding systems, service productivities, and the interaction between health and social care. Other interests include the study of variability in local care services provision, and of equity and efficiency in the allocation of social services.

Julien Forder is Professor of the Economics of Social Policy and Deputy Director of Personal Social Services Research Unit at the University of Kent, a senior research fellow at the London School of Economics and a senior associate of the King's Fund. He is an economist and conducts research in social and health care.

Richard G. Frank, Ph.D., is the Margaret T. Morris Professor of Health Economics in the Department of Health Care Policy at Harvard Medical School. He is also a research associate with the National Bureau of Economic Research. Currently he is serving as Deputy Assistant Secretary for Planning and Evaluation in the US Department of Health and Human Services. In 1997, Frank was elected to the Institute of Medicine, and has been awarded the Georgescu-Roegen prize from the Southern Economic Association, the Carl A. Taube Award from the American Public Health Association, and the Emily Mumford Medal from Columbia University's Department of Psychiatry. He is Co-Editor of the *Journal of Health Economics*.

Bianca K. Frogner is an assistant professor in the Health Services Management and Leadership Department in the School of Public Health and Health Services at the George Washington University. She is a health economist with expertise in industrialized health systems, health labor force dynamics, and welfare economics.

Sherry Glied, Ph.D., is a professor in the Department of Health Policy and Management of Columbia University's Mailman School of Public Health. She is a member of the Institute of Medicine. She is the author of *Chronic Condition* (1998) and, with Richard Frank, *Better But Not Well, Mental Health Policy in the US since 1950* (2006).

Susan Griffin is a Senior Research fellow at the Centre for Health Economics, University of York. Her research interests include decision-analytic models in cost-effectiveness analysis and value of information analysis. In 2008, Susan became a Research Council UK academic fellow in Health Economics and Public Health.

Jane Hall is the Director of the Centre for Health Economics Research and Evaluation, and Professor of Health Economics in the Faculty of Business, University of Technology Sydney, Australia. She is a fellow of the Academy of Social Sciences in Australia.

Peter S. Hussey is a policy researcher at the RAND Corporation. He holds a Ph.D. in Health Policy and Management from the Johns Hopkins Bloomberg School of Public Health. Prior to joining RAND, Dr. Hussey worked in health policy at the Organization for Economic Cooperation and Development in Paris, France.

Tor Iversen is Professor of Health Economics at the University of Oslo, Norway. He is also Scientific Director of the Health Economics Research Program at the University of Oslo (HERO). His research interests include the role of economic incentives in health care and comparative health system research.

William Jack is Associate Professor of Economics at Georgetown University in Washington, DC. His research interests include applied microeconomic theory, empirical development, and public finance. He has worked at the IMF, the US Congress, the University of Maryland, the Australian National University, and Sydney University. He is a member of the UNAIDS/World Bank Economics Reference Group, and has taught at the African Economic Research Consortium in Nairobi, Kenya. He holds a D.Phil. and an M.Phil. in Economics from Oxford University, where he was a Rhodes Scholar; and a B.Sc. in Mathematics and Physics from the University of Western Australia.

Stephen Jan is a senior health economist at the George Institute for International Health, University of Sydney. His interests are health systems research and evaluation, institutionalist economics, equity and international and indigenous health issues.

Andrew M. Jones is Professor of Economics at the University of York, UK, where he is head of the Department of Economics and Related Studies. He is the Research Director of the *Health, Econometrics and Data Group* (HEDG) at the University of York and Visiting Professor at the University of Bergen. He is Joint Editor of *Health Economics* and of *Health Economics Letters* and serves on the editorial boards of *Cuadernos Economicos de ICE* and *Population Health Metrics*. He researches and publishes in the area of microeconometrics and health economics, with emphasis on the determinants of health, the economics of addiction, and socioeconomic inequalities in health and health care.

Donald S. Kenkel is a professor in the Department of Policy Analysis and Management at Cornell University and a research associate of the National Bureau of Economic Research. He received his Ph.D. in Economics from the University of Chicago. His research focuses on the economics of health promotion and disease prevention.

Martin Knapp is Professor of Social Policy at the London School of Economics and Professor of Health Economics at King's College London, Institute of Psychiatry. He directs two research centers, and recently became inaugural Director of the new NIHR School for Social Care Research.

Ramanan Laxminarayan is Director and Senior Fellow Director at the Center for Disease Dynamics, Economics, and Policy, and a research scholar and lecturer at Princeton University. He has an Undergraduate Degree in Engineering from the Birla Institute of Technology and Science in Pilani, India; a Master's in Public Health (Epidemiology); and a Doctorate in Economics from the University of Washington. His research deals with the integration of epidemiological models of infectious diseases and drug resistance with economic analysis of public health problems. He has worked to improve understanding drug resistance as a problem of managing a shared global resource.

George Leckie, Ph.D., is a research associate at the Centre for Multilevel Modelling and an associate member of the Centre for Market and Public Organisation, Department of Economics at the University of Bristol (UK). Leckie's research interests surround the application of multilevel modelling in social research, especially health and education.

Adriana Lleras-Muney is an associate professor in the Economics Department at UCLA and a research associate of the NBER. She received her Ph.D. from Columbia University and was an assistant professor at Princeton University. Her research examines the relationships between socio-economic status and health and the effect of disease on economic development.

Anup Malani is a professor of Law and the Aaron Director Research Scholar at the University of Chicago. He is also an editor of the *Journal of Law and Economics*, a faculty research fellow at the National Bureau of Economic Research, a university fellow at Resources for the Future, and a senior fellow at the Center for Disease Dynamics, Economics, and Policy. He holds both a J.D. and Ph.D. in Economics from the University of Chicago. Malani's research focuses on health economics, law and economics, and corporate law and finance. His recent work in health economics has focused on infection control and the pharmaceutical industry.

Dustin May is pursuing a Doctorate of Osteopathic Medicine (D.O.) at Nova Southeastern University. Previously, he served on the health care staff of the US Senate Finance Committee, the US House of Representatives Commerce Committee, and as a research assistant, Harvard Medical School, Department of Health Care Policy.

Alan Maynard is Professor of Health Economics in the Department of Health Sciences and Hull York Medical School at the University of York. His main research interests are in the economics of health policy with particular reference to workforce, competition and the pharmaceutical industry.

Thomas G. McGuire is Professor of Health Economics at Harvard Medical School. Two papers received "best paper of the year" awards for 2008, from Academy Health for work on physician–patient interaction and from the National Institute for Health Care Management for work on incentives in managed care plans. McGuire is a member of the Institute of Medicine, and an editor of the *Journal of Health Economics*.

Anne Mills is Professor of Health Economics and Policy, Head of the Faculty of Public Health and Policy, and Director of the Health Economics and Financing Programme at the London School of Hygiene and Tropical Medicine. She has over 35 years' experience of health economics research in Africa and Asia.

Pau Olivella (Ph.D., Northwestern University, 1989) is Associate Professor at the Universitat Autonoma de Barcelona, CODE member, Barcelona GSE affiliated professor, and MOVE research fellow. He specializes in insurance and health economics. He has served as Associate Editor of the *Spanish Economic Review* and is currently Associate Editor of the *Journal of Health Economics*.

Jan Abel Olsen is Professor in Health Economics and Health Services Research at the University of Tromsø, Norway, and part-time Professor at the University of Oslo, Norway, and at Monash University, Australia. His research interests include health policy and international health issues.

Mark V. Pauly is Bendheim Professor in the Department of Health Care Management, Professor of Health Care Management, Insurance and Risk Management, and Business and Public Policy at the Wharton School, and Professor of Economics in the School of Arts and Sciences at the University of Pennsylvania. He currently serves on the national advisory committees for the NIH National Center for Research Resources, the National Academy of Sciences' Committee to Study the Veterinary Workforce, and the National Vaccine Advisory Commission, and is an active member of the

Institute of Medicine. Dr. Pauly is a co-editor-in-chief of the *International Journal of Health Care Finance and Economics* and an associate editor of the *Journal of Risk and Uncertainty*.

Carol Propper is Professor of Economics at Imperial College and Professor of the Economics of Public Policy at the University of Bristol. Her interests are in the economics of health care markets, in particular the effect of competition, incentives, targets, and pay on performance of hospitals.

Nigel Rice is Professor of Health Economics at the Centre for Health Economics, University of York. He directs the Health, Econometrics and Data Group (HEDG), a research group focused on the use of quantitative methods to inform health and health care policy. Professor Rice is an editor of the *Journal of Health Economics*.

Donna Rowen is a research fellow at the School of Health and Related Research (ScHARR) at the University of Sheffield. Her main research interest is measuring and valuing health and quality of life with a particular focus on mapping between outcome measures and the methodology of developing condition-specific preference-based measures of health.

Erik Schokkaert is currently Research Director at CORE (Université Catholique de Louvain). He is Full Professor of Public Economics and Health Economics at the KULeuven. His main research topics are the modelling of different concepts of distributive justice and their application to health insurance and social security.

Frederik T. Schut is a professor of Health Economics at the Institute for Health Policy and Management (iBMG) at the Erasmus University Rotterdam. His research focuses on competition and regulation and the role of consumer behavior in health care and health insurance markets.

Anthony Scott is an ARC future fellow, and directs the Health Economics Research Program at the Melbourne Institute of Applied Economic and Social Research at the University of Melbourne. Professor Scott's research interests are in the economics of primary care, incentives and performance of health care providers, and health professionals' labor markets.

Mark Sculpher is Professor of Health Economics at the Centre for Health Economics, University of York, where he is Director of the Programme on Economic Evaluation and Health Technology Assessment. He has over 160 peer-reviewed publications and is a co-author of two major text books in the area. Sculpher has been a member of the National Institute for Health and Clinical Excellence (NICE) Technology Appraisal Committee and currently sits on the NICE Public Health Interventions Advisory Committee. He chaired NICE's 2004 Task Group on methods guidance for economic evaluation. He is also a member of the Commissioning Board for the UK NHS Health Technology Assessment program and the UK Medical Research Council's Methodology Research Panel.

Louise Sheiner is a senior economist at the Federal Reserve Board of Governors. Her research covers topics such as the variation of health spending by age and by geographic region, and the effects of growth in health spending on individual and government budgets. She received her Ph.D. in Economics from Harvard University.

Luigi Siciliani is a reader at the Department of Economics and Related Studies and is affiliated to the Centre for Health Economics at the University of York. His research includes the design of incentive schemes with altruistic providers, the role of quality competition in healthcare markets, and waiting times.

Jody Sindelar, Ph.D., is Professor and Chair of the Division of Health Policy at Yale's School of Public Health and is appointed to the National Bureau of Economics Research. She was President of the American Society of Health Economics and serves on several editorial boards. Her primary research area is the economics of substance abuse.

Peter C. Smith is Professor of Health Policy at the Imperial College Business School and co-director of the Centre for Health Policy. He is a mathematics graduate from the University of Oxford, and was formerly Director of the Centre for Health Economics at the University of York. He has published widely on the financing and performance of health systems, and has a special interest in the links between research evidence and policy. He has worked with and advised many ministries and international agencies, including the World Health Organization, the International Monetary Fund, the World Bank, the European Commission, and the OECD.

Mark Stabile is Director of the School of Public Policy and Governance and Associate Professor of Economics and Public Policy at the Rotman School of Management, University of Toronto. He is also a research associate at the National Bureau of Economic Research, Cambridge, Massachusetts, and a fellow at the Rimini Centre for Economic Analysis, Italy.

Andrew Street is a professor of Health Economics; Director of the Health Policy team in the Centre for Health Economics; and an editor of the *Journal of Health Economics*. Andrew's research covers measurement of health system productivity, evaluation of activity based funding mechanisms, and analysis of organizational efficiency.

Jack E. Triplett has been with the Brookings Institution since 1997, currently as nonresident Senior Fellow. Before joining Brookings, he was Chief Economist at the US Bureau of Economic Analysis; Associate Commissioner for Research and Evaluation at the Bureau of Labor Statistics; and Assistant Director for Price Monitoring, US Council on Wage and Price Stability. He has a Ph.D. from the University of California (Berkeley) and has published widely on productivity analysis and price index and national accounts measurement. He is a member of the American Economic Association's Committee on Economic Statistics and he has advised government statistical agencies and international organizations.

Carolyn Hughes Tuohy, FRSC, is Professor Emeritus of Political Science and Senior Fellow in the School of Public Policy and Governance, University of Toronto. Her publications include *Accidental Logics: The Dynamics of Change in the Health Care Arena in the United States, Britain and Canada* (Oxford University Press, 1999).

Wynand P. M. M. van de Ven is Professor of Health Insurance at the Erasmus University Rotterdam. His teaching and research focus on managed competition in health care. He has experience as a governor and adviser in health care. He is one of the founding fathers of the European Risk Adjustment Network.

Carine Van de Voorde is Researcher at the Department of Economics at the Catholic University of Leuven and senior economist at the Belgian Health Care Knowledge Centre. Her main research interests are in health insurance with a focus on risk adjustment of health plans and financial access to health services.

Eddy van Doorslaer, Ph.D., is a professor of Health Economics at the Department of Applied Economics of the Erasmus School of Economics and at the Department of Health Policy and Management of the Erasmus University Rotterdam. He is also an Associate Editor of the journals *Health Economics* and *Journal of Health Economics*.

Tom Van Ourti has been Assistant Professor at the Erasmus University in Rotterdam since 2006. His main research interest is the measurement of inequalities in health and health care.

Tom Vogl is a Ph. D. Candidate in Economics at Harvard University and a doctoral fellow of the Multidisciplinary Program on Inequality and Social Policy at the Harvard Kennedy School.

Simon Walker is a member of the Team for Economic Evaluation and Health Technology Assessment in the Centre for Health Economics, University of York. He joined in October 2006 after completing an M.Sc. in Health Economics at York. He had previously graduated from Clare College, Cambridge, with a B.A. in Economics.

Peter Zweifel is a professor of economics at the Socioeconomic Institute, University of Zurich. From 2001 to 2008, he was Co-editor-in-chief (with Mark Pauly, Wharton School) of the *International Journal of Health Care Finance and Economics*. His main research interests are health economics, insurance economics, energy economics, and regulation, topics on which he has published widely.

CHAPTER 1

....

INTRODUCTION

....

SHERRY GLIED AND PETER C. SMITH

HEALTH policy is a central concern of most economies. In the developed world, the proportion of gross domestic product attributed to health services is growing rapidly, and traditional methods of financing health care are coming under strain. Increasing life expectancies are giving rise to new challenges for the long-term management of chronic disease. Health disparities, caused mainly by factors outside the health system, remain a policy issue in many countries, but there is a shortage of evidence on how to address them. The health care industry and providers of health care have delivered astonishing technological advances, but are also uniquely powerful interest groups, and there are often formidable pressures to adopt new technologies before proper evaluation is possible.

In low income settings an additional set of considerations applies. The problems of infectious diseases remain profound, yet there are also predictions of an imminent epidemic of non-communicable disease, driven by behavioral changes and increased life expectancy. Many countries continue to rely on out-of-pocket expenditure to finance most health care services, giving rise to widespread exposure to catastrophic health-care-related expenditure. The size and quality of the health workforce is a growing concern, driven by increased migration of skilled workers. Health system financing is often fragile, with many countries operating with very limited budgets and highly reliant on donor funds.

The discipline of health economics builds on the insights of microeconomic theory and has, over the decades, developed a substantial empirical basis. It has contributed significantly to addressing and understanding the profound health issues confronted in almost all countries, and has had a large impact on the development, implementation, and evaluation of health systems policy. As the chapters in this handbook attest, the discipline continues to investigate and shed light upon areas of interest to policymakers.

Any organizational scheme for a volume such as this will be to some extent arbitrary and contested. We have chosen to arrange the chapters into seven broad topic areas: the organization of health systems, determinants of health, institutions and problems of health care finance, institutions and problems of health care supply, assessing performance, fairness, and more general overviews of the field. In this chapter, we provide an introduction to the contents by discussing four critical health policy questions, in particular highlighting novel insights and connections amongst the chapters.

1.1 WHY ARE SOME PEOPLE HEALTHY AND OTHERS NOT?

A fundamental and enduring question facing any student of health is why some people are healthy and others not. Medical science suggests that heredity, environment, behaviors, and fortune all play a part in determining underlying health. For policymakers, the question is what policy can and should do to address these differences. The consequent policy questions mainly concern the prevention of poor health (primarily by influencing behavior and environmental factors) and compensating for the consequences of health differences.

Perhaps surprisingly, economics has a played central role in improving our understanding of health determinants. The chapter by Kristian Bolin (Chapter 6) presents the economic theory of health production, originally developed by Michael Grossman, which envisions health as a capital stock, akin to a machine or, as Bolin points out, to education or human capital. Bolin emphasizes the similarities between health capital and human capital and the policy implications of this relationship. The theme of a connection between education and health surfaces again in the chapter by David Cutler, Adriana Lleras-Muney, and Tom Vogl (Chapter 7), who highlight the role of education, both as a direct input into health production, and as a measure of social rank. Cutler, Lleras-Muney, and Vogl note the co-evolution of education and health through the life-course. This idea is further elaborated in the chapter by Michael Baker and Mark Stabile (Chapter 8), who describe the determinants and role of investments in child health on later outcomes. Together, these three chapters provide a summary of the scholarly underpinnings—and remaining areas of uncertainty—underlying the recent policy focus in many countries on investments in early childhood.

Of course, investments in good health do not end in childhood. What people do—and do not do—as adults also has substantial effects on subsequent health. Overeating, smoking, and failing to exercise, or not making appropriate use of preventive medical interventions, can cause serious damage to outcomes. Observers are often perplexed by the evidence that people continue to indulge in unhealthy behavior, even when they understand the consequences of this behavior. Likewise, many people complain that policymakers and health systems place an inadequate emphasis on prevention, over-spending on treatments for diseases that could have been avoided altogether at lower cost. The chapter by Donald Kenkel and Jody Sindelar (Chapter 10) takes on the first of these questions, describing how traditional and behavioral economics, and new empirical studies, have improved our understanding of the decision to engage in dangerous behaviors. Kenkel and Sindelar's chapter devotes considerable attention to new econometric methodologies that have been used to assess the causal determinants of dangerous behavior. These methodologies are further explored in the chapter on health care econometrics by Andrew Jones and Nigel Rice (Chapter 37) at the end of the volume. Jane Hall (Chapter 23) addresses the complementary question about prevention policy decisions, often in very similar terms. She explains the continued skepticism among health economists about the maxim that an ounce of prevention is worth a pound of cure. Hall points out that questions about who benefits, and when, are critical determinants of decision-making about investment in prevention.

Infectious diseases remain a central preoccupation in many countries, and a global pandemic is an ever-present risk that transcends national borders. Ramanan Laxminarayan and Anup Malani (Chapter 9) set out the economic issues that arise in this highly complex domain. They point to the need to consider the often perverse incentives that occur when seeking to put in place mechanisms to control infectious disease. Careful policy design is needed to avoid the tendency for individuals, organizations and nations to "free-ride" on the preventive efforts of others.

The likelihood that, as these chapters suggest, some disease is a consequence of individual decisions to take risks or to under-invest in prevention, or education, raises challenges for the distribution of health care resources. Jan Abel Olsen (Chapter 34) takes on the question of which inequities in health outcomes are properly the scope of government policy. He argues that inequity can only be understood and addressed once the cause of the inequality is known.

All these questions, in turn, depend on having an understanding of what constitutes health. While clinical indicators for specific diseases are well-established, determining the optimal balance of resource allocation between prevention and treatment, or among persons whose illnesses arose for different reasons, requires health status measures that are comparable across conditions. Donna Rowen and John Brazier (Chapter 33) assess the current state of health utility measurement, closing with a discussion of the question of whose assessment of a health state should be used in economic evaluation.

1.2 What is the Best Way to Organize and Compensate Health Care Providers?

Medical care is, in large measure, a service industry, with services provided by highly skilled and well-compensated professionals. All health care systems—in developed and developing countries—struggle with the question of how best to deliver medical services. The health economics literature approaches these questions at three levels. One set of studies focuses on the supply and compensation of individual workers; a second set examines the design of intermediary organizations, including hospitals and insurers; a third set examines the question of optimal organization at the level of the system itself.

The first element of a health care system is the skilled workforce that provides treatment. Consistent with the centrality of the health care worker in the system, workforce planning was one of the earliest problems addressed by health economists. Till Bärnighausen and David Bloom (Chapter 21) trace the evolution of the economic approach to this question in their chapter, also addressing the role of the workforce in achieving health goals in developing country contexts.

Once health care workers have been trained, they must be compensated. Three chapters, by Thomas McGuire; Anthony Scott and Stephen Jan; and Jon Christianson and Douglas Conrad explore aspects of this compensation problem. McGuire (Chapter 25) addresses the economic literature on physicians as agents, illustrating this concept through reference to the situation where policymakers would like a primary care physician to provide a "medical home" for the patient. He concludes that certain forms of mixed payment systems are most likely to achieve this goal. Scott and Jan (Chapter 20) expand on this idea, examining the role of primary care providers in the health system. Scott and Jan emphasize the dual agency role of primary care doctors—as agents for their patients and, in many models, as agents for payers. These dual roles can create conflicting incentives. Both McGuire and Scott and Jan emphasize the role of incentives in affecting the volume of services. Christianson and Conrad (Chapter 26) turn attention to the question of how incentives might affect the quality of care. This chapter summarizes the growing literature on "pay for performance" schemes in a range of countries, noting the rather ambiguous results of many of these efforts.

In many contexts within the health care system, health workers operate as part of teams, in conjunction with one another, or with other types of workers. These situations are considered in the chapters by Pedro Pita Barros and Pau Olivera; Jose-Luis Fernandez, Julien Forder, and Martin Knapp; and Laurence Baker. Barros and Olivella (Chapter 19) describe the economics literature on the operation of hospitals using a framework based on the notion of "teams." They note both the distinction between ownership of hospitals (which may be public or private) and control of operations within hospitals (often the domain of health care professionals). They then turn to examining how teams operate within hospitals. Fernandez, Forder and Knapp (Chapter 24) consider the very different context of long-term care, where the care team often combines formal and informal workers. They highlight the complexities of incentives and financing in such situations. Baker (Chapter 18) turns to managed care organizations, which formally integrate different provider types. A focus of Baker's chapter is on the potential spillover effects of these arrangements on patients and providers who are not themselves part of the arrangements.

As the discussion above suggests, there are almost always multiple providers or multiple provider organizations within a health system. A basic insight of microeconomic theory is that, in situations of incomplete information, which are rampant in health care, competition among providers may lead to adverse selection, with better and worse risks sorted to different providers or insurance plans. This insight provides the basis of three chapters that explore what happens when multiple providers co-exist. Wynand van de Ven and Frederik Schut (Chapter 17) discuss alternative strategies for addressing selection, and conclude that a system of risk-adjusted subsidies paid to insurers is likely to be most effective. Carol Propper and George Leckie (Chapter 28) scrutinize the empirical literature on competition between providers and, as selection theory suggests, find that the outcomes are highly varied, and that competition generates winners and losers among patients as well as providers. Richard Frank (Chapter 11) notes that problems of incomplete information are particularly salient in the context of mental health. He examines how different health systems have addressed the difficulties of allocating care between different types of providers and different types of patients.

Together, supply levels, payment incentives, and organizational structures determine much of the micro functioning of health systems. Two chapters consider how to compare the functioning of different health systems. Jim Burgess and Andrew Street (Chapter 29) describe econometric approaches to comparing the efficiency of health care organizations (at the level of the hospital, the insurer, or the system). Jack Triplett (Chapter 30) considers approaches to tracking changes in the productivity of a health care system over time. We do not yet have methods that allow a clear determination of system efficiency, but these chapters describe both the progress that has already been made and the steps that need to be taken to bring us closer to such an assessment.

1.3 How Much Should Society Spend on Health Care and Where Should Resources be Focused?

Given the manifest imperfections in the market for health services, and the heavy reliance in many countries on government funding, the question of determining the optimal level and mix of health services is a central policy issue. Michael Chernew and Dustin May (Chapter 14) describe the rapid growth in expenditure in most developed countries, and discuss the factors that have driven the growth, such as population aging, general economic growth, and the adoption and use of new medical technologies. They consider a range of strategies for slowing cost growth, including economic evaluation of technologies. Chernew and May also note the increased reliance on government funding. This gives rise to the particularly important issue of intergenerational equity, addressed by Louise Sheiner (Chapter 36). To what extent should the increasing health expenditure on (current) older people be funded by the current (younger) workforce, and will the current funding arrangements be sustainable in the future?

A particularly influential approach to cost containment developed by economists has been the application of cost-effectiveness analysis (CEA) to health technologies, as described by Simon Walker, Mark Sculpher, and Mike Drummond (Chapter 31). CEA is intended to help collective purchasers of health care (governments and insurers) to determine which interventions to prioritize, by ranking them according to the cost of each unit of "health benefit" they produce. In implementing this principle, uncertainty has become a central concern, and Susan Griffin and Karl Claxton (Chapter 32) describe current approaches to handling the uncertainty inherent in all cost-effectiveness estimates.

The pharmaceutical industry plays a key entrepreneurial role in health systems, and has contributed to some major advances in health care. It has an unusual cost structure, resulting from very long, costly, and uncertain research and development processes, and policy instruments such as health technology assessment rules, patent rights, and safety regulations have a key influence on profitability and investment strategy. Patricia Danzon (Chapter 22) summarizes the literature, and considers the question of who should guide and pay for research and development.

Given the size of the health sector, policy decisions that affect it can have important macroeconomic consequences. William Jack (Chapter 5) summarizes a complex evidence base on the impact of health on income and well-being. There is strong evidence of a potentially strong impact of improved health on the productivity and well-being of individual workers. However, this "promise" of health interventions can be fully effective only if delivered efficiently and aligned (*inter alia*) with properly functioning education services and labor markets. Furthermore, the extent to which the individual benefits of improved health necessarily feed through to improved macroeconomic performance remains an open question.

Ultimately, many of the crucial decisions that affect national health spending are taken by politicians, and therefore reflect political as well as economic concerns. There is a rich tradition of economists exploring the many political influences on public policy decisions, including powerful interest groups, bureaucratic power, and electoral concerns. Carolyn Hughes Tuohy and Sherry Glied (Chapter 4) explore the relevance of this literature to the health domain, and confirm the powerful influence of politics on the shape of the health system.

1.4 How Should Health Care Services be Financed and Distributed?

There is a widespread belief that the design and operation of the health system can have a profound impact on the efficiency of health services and the health outcomes they secure. However, health systems arise for multiple reasons, not always consistent with economic theory. There is therefore a striking diversity in the organization of health systems around the world, with no clear consensus on many fundamental design issues. Bianca Frogner, Peter Hussey, and Gerard Anderson (Chapter 2) summarize patterns amongst developed countries, and Anne Mills (Chapter 3) describes the even greater diversity found amongst developing countries.

In practice, virtually all health systems rely in part on public financing. Åke Blomqvist (Chapter 12) describes what economics can tell us about the share of expenses that should be covered by the public plan and how those revenues should be raised. Peter

Zweifel (Chapter 13) challenges the economic role of public financing in health care, and asks whether a purely private insurance system, with redistributive income-based subsidies only, could satisfy policy goals. Mark Pauly (Chapter 16) describes the implications of third party financing, whether public or private. The key issue is that—in the absence of direct user payment for services—there is an incentive for inefficient moral hazard, or excess use of services.

Insurers—private and public—therefore seek to control moral hazard through the use of co-payments and other rationing devices. Erik Schokkaert and Carine Van de Voorde (Chapter 15) consider how user charges or co-payments are used in both developed and developing countries. There is a fundamental tension between controlling moral hazard and assuring access to needed services, especially amongst the very poor. Many health systems therefore seek to ration access to care using other instruments. In particular, Iversen and Siciliani (Chapter 27) examine the implications of using waiting times, rather than co-payments, as a rationing device.

Most systems of publicly funded health care, offering universal access to at least some subset of services, have been implemented with redistributive goals very much in mind. Eddy van Doorslaer and Tom Van Ourti (Chapter 35) examine how the success of this redistributive function can be measured, describing strategies used for measuring the inequality of the outcomes of a health care system in terms of use of care.

In concluding the volume, Alan Maynard and Karen Bloor (Chapter 38) survey the successes and lacunae of the health economics research endeavor. They point to the key role that funding agencies have historically had in directing research attention towards particular domains, but argue that the discipline has in recent years become more balanced in seeking to offer policy advice on most of the important elements of the health system. Without question, health economics has had some notable successes in influencing public policy for the good, for example in the design of payment mechanisms, the measurement of performance, and the assessment of health technology. It is to be hoped that such successes will be replicated and extended in the future.

CHAPTER 2

....

HEALTH SYSTEMS IN INDUSTRIALIZED COUNTRIES

....

BIANCA K. FROGNER, PETER S. HUSSEY, AND GERARD F. ANDERSON

2.1 OVERVIEW

THIS chapter focuses on the health systems of the industrialized countries that are members of the Organization for Economic Co-operation and Development (OECD)*. It begins with an overview of the various ways to finance health systems in industrialized countries. The chapter then explores the variation in health spending cross-sectionally and over time. The chapter concludes with a discussion of factors contributing to health spending and the tradeoffs to consider when controlling rising health care spending versus increasing productivity, improving health outcomes and producing quality care.

2.2 COMPARING HEALTH SYSTEMS

Health systems in industrialized countries differ on many levels. This section focuses on two important levels for health economists: (1) how health insurance revenues are pooled and (2) who provides health care services. While this typology is commonly used to group health systems into broad categories, it ignores the fact that all countries' health systems are unique, and most countries health systems are the result of historical evolution, political compromises, and many other factors.

---

* We will focus on 30 industrialized countries and exclude recent members: Chile, Estonia, Israel, and Slovakia due to the lack of historical data.

2.2.1 Pooling

Most health systems can be divided into one of two different financing arrangements: some have a single health insurance pool (single-payer) while others use multiple health insurance pools (multi-payer) (Hussey and Anderson 2003). With exception of the US, Turkey, and Mexico, OECD countries with either single- or multi-payer health systems are able to provide universal coverage (discussed further below). Within this broad rubric of single-payer vs. multi-payer systems there are many variations. Single-payer systems can be national in scope. Single-payer systems can be decentralized, with separate health insurance pools for different geographic regions such as provinces or states. However, these systems can be still classified as single-payer since all beneficiaries within each region are covered by a single regional insurance pool. The single-payer systems can be government-operated or operated by the private sector with regulations and oversight provided by the government.

Most multi-payer systems allow for some beneficiary choice of insurer; however, the entities establishing the insurance companies can have varying levels of private sector and government involvement. For example, the Netherlands mandates all individuals that work or live there to purchase a basic government-defined benefit package from a private insurance company after major reform in 2006. On the other end, Germany has several government-regulated, not-for-profit Sickness Insurance Funds that cover the majority of the population. In the US, individuals may qualify for public and/or private health insurance, with most individuals choosing from a long list of for-profit and not-for-profit insurance companies. Historically, the insurance pools in most multi-payer systems were organized by employer or other population subgroup.

Advocates of both systems identify distinct advantages of their system. Single-payer systems generally offer greater government control over the provision of care, since the insurance pool is able to exercise monopsony power within the region over the prices paid for services, which services are available, and other aspects of insurance design. These systems tend to emphasize equity and do not have to confront risk selection in insurance. Multi-payer systems, on the other hand, generally allow for consumer choice of insurer, which can drive innovation and competition. In multi-payer systems, the emphasis is on efficiency and choice. Multi-payer systems could also have the same monopsony paid as a single-payer system if they negotiate collectively.

Many countries have some combination of single- and multi-payer insurance. Single-payer systems typically have secondary private insurance providing one of three types of coverage: substitutive, supplementary, or complementary. Substitutive private insurance can replace single-payer insurance coverage for eligible individuals. Eligibility can be based on income, employment status, or occupation. Supplementary private health insurance provides additional coverage for services also covered by the single-payer insurer. An example of a country with supplementary insurance is Australia, where the government has encouraged the purchase of private insurance to reduce public expenditures. Complementary private insurance covers services not included in the single-payer insurance benefits. An example of a country with complementary insurance is Canada, where complementary insurance covers outpatient pharmaceutical costs and other services that are not covered under most provincial single-payer plans.

2.2.2 Provision of Services

Health systems can also be divided into direct or indirect provision of services (Abel-Smith 1992; Hsiao 2007). In systems with direct provision, a single integrated entity both finances and delivers health services. Providers are generally paid through budgets or some other type of resource allocation such that there is a large degree of public control over the provision of services. The amounts paid to providers and invested in capital and staff is also determined publicly. In systems with indirect provision, independent providers contract with purchasers. A government agency may act as the purchaser, or may use private intermediaries (Hsiao 2007). An indirect provision system allows for more competition between providers but provides less control over the provision of services.

2.2.3 Major Types of Health Systems

There are four main types of systems representing specific combinations of pooling and provision. While no country adopts any of these systems exactly, many countries do follow the models loosely.

1. *Social Insurance*. Public multi-payer systems with indirect provision are known as Social Insurance systems. (The prototypical Social Insurance is that of Germany.) Typically, Social Insurance systems rely primarily on payroll taxes as their primary source for health care revenues. Social Insurance was the first form of health insurance developed by Bismarck in the 1880s.
2. *National Health Service*. Centralized single-payer systems with direct provision are known as a National Health Service. (The prototypical National Health Service has been that of the United Kingdom although it has added more private sector and decentralization components recently.) Typically, National Health Service systems rely primarily on general taxation for health care revenues and control provision at the central government level.
3. *National Health Insurance*. Centralized single-payer systems with private provision of medical services are known as National Health Insurance. (The prototypical National Health Insurance system is that of Canada.) Typically, National Health Insurance systems rely on federal and state taxation to fund mostly private hospitals, physicians and other clinicians, and institutions.
4. *Private Insurance*. Some countries have private multi-payer systems with indirect provision. One example is the private insurance system is the US, but it is a unique case in many ways. Other primarily private insurance systems, such as Switzerland, have greater government control over pooling and purchasing than the US. In most industrialized countries with private insurance, insurance coverage is mandatory, the government provides premium subsidies for low-income individuals and cross-subsidization between insurance pools based on patient risk, and insurers are heavily regulated to prevent risk selection by insurers in areas such as the prices that are paid to providers for health services, minimum benefits, premium rating, and so forth.

2.3 COVERAGE

Most of the OECD countries obtained near full coverage (95 percent and above) of the population through public sources in 2008. The exceptions were Germany (89%), Turkey (67%), Mexico (71%), and the US (29%). In 2008, the Netherlands had 62 percent of the population covered by public sources with the remainder covered by private sources; under the Health Insurance Act of 2006, 98.5 percent of the population were now covered by private sources with the remainder uninsured (Westert et al. 2008). The remainder of the population in Germany is insured through private health insurance. Despite a combination of public and private insurance, the US continued to have 15.9 percent of population left without insurance coverage (DeNavas-Walt et al. 2006). This gap is expected to close under the Patient Protection and Affordable Care Act of 2010, which requires nearly all US citizens and residents to have health insurance by 2014 through expansion of employer sponsored coverage, federal insurance programs, or private markets with the help of tax credits. The remainder of the population in Turkey and Mexico were also uninsured. In 2003, Mexico passed a reform measure to provide universal health insurance by 2010 (Knaul and Frenk 2005).

2.4 TRENDS IN HEALTH CARE SPENDING

This section surveys the differences in health care spending across the OECD countries followed by a closer look at demand and supply factors, including the role of health insurance.

The two measures commonly used to compare levels of health care spending across countries are health care spending as a percentage of the Gross Domestic Product (GDP) and health care spending per capita, adjusted for costs of living using purchasing power parities (PPP). Health care spending as a percentage of GDP employs an opportunity cost perspective—if more dollar resources are dedicated to the health sector, then less becomes available to other sectors.

Health care spending has been capturing a growing share of the GDP in all OECD countries between 1970 and 2008. In the median OECD country, health care spending was 5.1 percent of GDP in 1970 and increased to 9.1 percent by 2008 (Table 2.1). A persistent outlier in health care spending has been the US, where health care spending increased from 7.0 percent of the GDP in 1970 to 16.0 percent in 2008. The concern is that the US is allocating more dollars to health care but is receiving fewer real resources (Anderson, 2003). Denmark was also an early outlier, actually spending a greater percentage of its GDP on health than the US (7.9%) in 1970. By 2008, Denmark had similar health care spending levels as the median OECD country, the result of a very slow rate of growth in health care spending between 1970 and 2008. In 2008, France had the second highest level of spending in the OECD in terms of health care spending as share of the GDP (11.2%), even though it started around the median OECD level in 1970 (5.4%), the result of rapid growth in health care spending during this time period.

Table 2.1 Health Care Spending in OECD Countries, 2008

	Total health spending per capita (US$ PPP)	Total health spending, % GDP	Average annual growth, 1970–2008	Public spending, % THE	Private spending (excluding out-of-pocket), % THE	Out-of-pocket spending, % THE
Australia	3353	8.5	3.4 d	67.5	14.5	18.0
Austria	3970	10.5	4.3	76.9	8.0	15.1
Belgium	3995	11.1	5.0	a	a	20.5
Canada	4079	10.4	3.0	70.2	15.1	14.7
Czech Republic	1781	7.1	a	82.5	1.8	15.7
Denmark	3540	9.7	2.5 d	84.5	1.7	13.8
Finland	3008	8.4	3.7	74.2	6.4	19.4
France	3696	11.2	3.9	77.8	14.8	7.4
Germany	3737	10.5	3.1	76.8	10.2	13.0
Greece	2687	9.7	3.8 e	60.3	a	a
Hungary	1437	7.3	a	71.0	5.1	23.9
Iceland	3359	9.1	4.5	83.2	1.5	15.3
Ireland	3793	8.7	5.5	76.9	8.7	14.4
Italy	2870	9.1	a	77.2	3.3	19.5
Japan	2729	8.1	3.9 e	81.9	3.5	14.6
Korea	1801	6.5	a	55.3	9.7	35.0
Luxembourg	4237	6.8	a	84.1	3.5	12.4
Mexico	852	5.9	a	46.9	3.8	49.3
Netherlands	4063	9.9	3.1 f	a	a	5.7
New Zealand	2685	9.9	2.9	80.4	5.7	13.9
Norway	5003	8.5	4.6	84.2	0.7	15.1
Poland	1213	7.0	a	72.2	5.3	22.4
Portugal	2151	9.9	6.6 g	71.5	5.6	22.9
Slovak Republic	1770	8.0	a	67.8	7.0	25.2
Spain	2902	9.0	4.9	72.5	6.8	20.7
Sweden	3470	9.4	2.6	81.9	2.5	15.6
Switzerland	4627	10.7	2.9	59.1	10.1	30.8
Turkey	818	6.2	a	71.2	a	21.8
United Kingdom	3129	8.7	3.9	82.6	6.3	11.1
United States	7538	16.0	4.2	46.5	41.4	12.1
OECD median	3241	9.1	3.9	75.5	6.0	15.6

a Data not available b 2007 c 2006 d 1971 to 2007 e 1970 to 2007 f 1972 to 2008 g 1970 to 2006
THE = Total Health Expenditure

In the median OECD country, per-capita health care spending increased from $191 in 1970 to $3,241 per capita in 2008. However this does not adjust for inflation.[1] Again, the US has been a persistent outlier in terms of health care spending per capita, spending $351 in 1970 and $7,538 in 2008. Denmark was an early outlier spending $356 per capita on health in 1970, but by 2008 Denmark was spending at levels similar to the OECD median level ($3,540).

A limitation to the use of PPP-adjusted per-capita spending in international comparisons of health care spending growth is that any changes may reflect a change in the market basket of goods used to create the PPP index rather than true changes in the level of health care spending. Growth rates in health care spending are better compared using the average annual growth rates of health care spending adjusted for inflation and population growth. Using this measure, the average annual rate of health care spending growth was 3.9 percent in the median OECD country from 1970 to 2008 (Table 2.1).[2] The rate of health care spending growth was higher than inflation in every OECD country during the overall time period. Among the OECD countries, Denmark had the slowest growth at 2.5 percent (1971–2007) while Portugal had the fastest growth at 6.6 percent per year over the thirty-eight-year period. There is some evidence of convergence with the countries starting with higher initial spending levels growing slower than countries which initially spent relatively little on health care (Okunade et al. 2004).

2.4.1 Public vs. Private Spending

Health care spending can be divided into public and private spending. In 2008, approximately three-quarters of the health spending was from public funds in the median OECD country, while the remaining quarter was from private funds. Only in the US and Mexico did private health care dollars represent over half of the health care spending. Of the private health care dollars in the median OECD country, 72 percent were out-of-pocket expenses in 2008. Private health insurance is responsible for a small proportion of health spending in most OECD countries.

2.4.2 Specific Health Care Sectors

Three sectors of health care represent over half of the total health care spending in most OECD countries: inpatient hospital care, outpatient medical services, and

---

[1] A price deflator is not available when using purchasing power parities.

[2] The implicit price deflator was used to control for inflation (2000 = 100), which allows for changes in expenditures in response to changes in prices. The implicit price deflator is not based on a fixed basket of goods such as with the Consumer Price Index (CPI). Over the thirty-five-year time period, the implicit price deflator and the CPI closely follow each other, and eventually converge as the methodology to compute CPI has become more precise. Either could be used, but the CPI requires assumptions about a changing market basket of goods which may not be useful in international comparisons. The medical CPI could also be used, but given the limited availability of medical CPI deflators for other countries, this

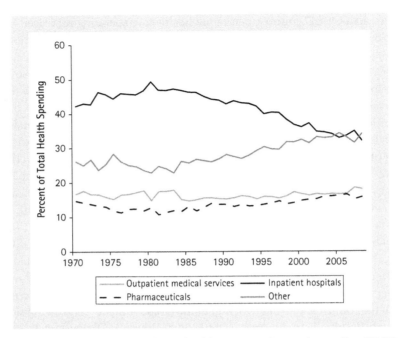

FIGURE 2.1 Health care sector share of total health care spending in the median OECD country, 1970–2008

Source: OECD 2007.

Notes: Category of pharmaceuticals includes other medical non-durables. "Other" includes day health care, dental services, other outpatient care, home health care, ancillary services, medical goods, therapeutic appliances and other medical durables, prevention and public health, health administration and insurance, and investment on medical facilities.

pharmaceuticals (Figure 2.1).[3] Inpatient hospital spending declined rapidly during this period from a median of 48.5 percent in 1970 to 32.3 percent in 2008. Medical services have maintained a fairly constant share of health care spending from 1970 to 2008. The median OECD country has seen a slight increase in the share of pharmaceutical expenditures from 17.5 percent in 1970 to 13.8 percent in 2008.

2.4.3 What Has Driven Health Spending Growth?

Researchers have attempted to identify the primary driving forces underlying the growth of health spending, and to account for difference in growth rates across countries. Per-capita incomes and population aging are commonly cited drivers. The remainder of the increase is often called excess health expenditures.

was not used. According to Triplett and Bosworth, economists believe that the CPI medical price index overstates the inflation of medical care, but believe that PPI (produce price index) may provide a better picture though it is hard to adjust for changes in the efficacy of treatment.

  [3] Inpatient hospital care includes curative, rehabilitative, and long-term nursing care. Pharmaceuticals include over-the-counter medicines and other medical non-durables.

This section takes a closer look at each of the major demand and supply factors that could account for the increase in health spending. The discussion draws upon the typology used by Newhouse (1992) in which he identified demand and supply factors that were well-studied in the health care literature to account for the increase in health spending over time within the US. His paper has been replicated with more recent data (Cutler 1995; Smith et al. 2000) to help US policymakers understand the historical growth and project future growth of health spending. A similar analysis for other countries could not be identified within the literature. This type of comparison could provide a common baseline to better understand the differences in the rate of increase in health spending among industrialized countries, and to inform policymakers in other OECD countries. First, health spending growth is decomposed into the components attributable to per-capita income, population aging, and other factors ("excess"). Then the potential factors contributing to the "excess" portion of growth are examined.

2.5 DEMAND FACTORS OF HEALTH CARE SPENDING

2.5.1 Income

Rising incomes have been one major driver of the demand for health care. Countries with higher incomes typically spend more on health care. National income can be approximated using real GDP per capita. Real GDP per capita increased by 120 percent from 1970 to 2008 in the median country of the OECD. During this time period, health spending per capita increased by 314 percent in the median OECD country, after controlling for inflation and population growth (Table 2.2). Health spending grew an average of 1.8 percent per year faster than GDP in the median OECD country, ranging from 0.7 percent faster in Denmark and 4.1 percent faster in Portugal (Figure 2.2).

The income elasticity of demand (e) is a measure of the impact of GDP growth on health care spending. The health economics literature has generally concluded that there is a strong positive relationship between GDP growth and health spending (Culyer 1989; Hitiris and Posnett 1992; Roberts 1999, 2000; Gerdtham and Jonsson 2000). However, consensus does not exist regarding whether a percentage increase in income results in a larger percentage increase in health care consumption, which would make health care a luxury good ($e > 1$); a smaller percentage increase, which would make health care a necessary good ($e < 1$); or the same percentage increase, which would make health care unit elastic ($e = 1$). The empirical estimate depends on many factors including the functional form, countries included in the analysis, choice of independent variables, and time frame. While there is disagreement, most recent studies using aggregate national data from industrialized countries have concluded that health care is a luxury good. Estimated

Table 2.2 Percentage Change in Health Spending and GDP, 1970–2008

	Real health spending per capita	Real GDP per capita	Scenario 1: income elasticity, e=1.2	Scenario 2: income elasticity, e=1.4
Australia	238% a	90%	108%	126%
Austria	389%	140%	169%	197%
Belgium	540%	125%	150%	175%
Canada	212%	107%	128%	149%
	b	b	b	b
Czech Republic	b	b	b	b
Denmark	141% a	97%	117%	136%
	b	b	b	b
Finland	299%	163%	196%	228%
France	323%	104%	125%	146%
Germany	220%	82%	98%	115%
Greece	297% c	126%	151%	176%
Hungary	b	b	b	b
Iceland	433%	177%	213%	248%
Ireland	662%	341%	410%	478%
	b	b	b	b
Italy	b	110%	132%	155%
Japan	314% c	132%	158%	185%
Korea	b	682%	818%	955%
Luxembourg	b	b	b	b
Mexico	b	91%	110%	128%
Netherlands	195% d	115%	138%	161%
New Zealand	199%	59%	70%	82%
Norway	449%	183%	220%	256%
Poland	b	b	b	b
Portugal	904% e	157%	188%	220%
Slovak Republic	b	b	b	b
	b	b	b	b
Spain	526%	144%	173%	202%
Sweden	169%	94%	113%	132%
Switzerland	195%	48%	57%	67%
Turkey	b	b	b	b
United Kingdom	334%	124%	149%	174%
United States	375%	112%	134%	156%
OECD median	314%	120%	143%	167%

[a] 1971 to 2007 [b] Data not available [c] 1970 to 2007 [d] 1972 to 2008 [e] 1970 to 2006

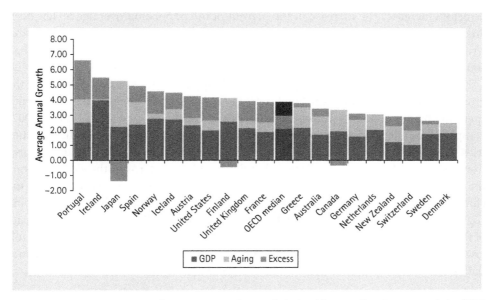

FIGURE 2.2 Decomposition of average annual growth in health spending into growth in GDP, aging, and excess in OECD countries, 1970–2008

Source: OECD 2010; White 2007.

Note: Data not available for Belgium, Czech Republic, Hungary, Italy, Korea, Mexico, Poland, Slovak Republic, and Turkey, Luxembourg.

values of *e* have ranged from 1.2 to 1.4 (Hitiris and Posnett 1992; Gerdtham and Jonsson 2000; Getzen 2000; Di Matteo 2003).[4]

Using the range of income elasticity values (1.2–1.4), the contribution of the growth in GDP to the growth in health spending is calculated in Table 2.2 (percentage change in GDP growth multiplied by the income elasticity value). This suggests that 143 to 167 percentage points, or approximately half, of the 314 percent growth in health spending over time was attributable to GDP growth in the median OECD country.[5]

2.5.2 Aging

The percent of the population over the age 65 increased in all countries from 1970 to 2008, increasing 40 percent in the median OECD country. The increase in population aging clustered around the median in most countries, although Ireland was an exception with almost no change in the proportion of elderly, and Korea and Japan had a near

---

[4] Studies using micro-data, usually in an analysis of only one country, tend to find elasticity values below 1. Thomas E. Getzen (2002), "Health Care Is an Individual Necessity and a National Luxury: Applying Multilevel Decision Models to the Analysis of Health Care Expenditures," *Journal of Health Economics*, 19(2): 259–70.

[5] Authors' best estimate with acknowledgement that the range is sensitive to choice in elasticity values.

threefold increase. The increase in the percent of the population over age 65 has been due mainly to a combination of increasing life expectancy and declining fertility rates (Anderson and Hussey 2000). Life expectancy increased by 8.8 years in the median country from 1970 to 2008, while fertility rates declined by 31 percent.

However, the growth in the proportion of elderly population is a crude proxy for the growth of health spending attributable to the elderly. Unfortunately, data on health spending by age cohorts is limited among OECD countries. One study (White 2007) compared the effects of aging on health care spending among twenty-one OECD countries. He calculated an index of health care spending by age using an US data source from 1970 to 2002 and then assumed that the spending patterns of the elderly among the countries was similar across countries.[6] The pattern of health spending among the elderly relative to a working population (18 to 64 years old) in the US has been declining slightly over time (Hartman et al. 2008).[7] When examining White's findings, the impact of the growth in aging populations relative to health care spending growth does not follow a clear pattern. However, the simplifying assumptions used in the calculation reduce the variation in the data and thus could be underestimating the effect of aging.

2.5.3 Possible Reasons for the Excess Growth

After accounting for growth in an aging population and income, the health care literature refers to the residual growth of health spending as "excess" growth (White 2007).[8] Figure 2.2 decomposes the average annual growth in health spending in each OECD country into growth from GDP, aging and excess, adjusted for inflation from 1970 to 2008. The excess growth rate in the median OECD country was 0.9 percent, and ranged from −1.4 percent in Japan up to 2.5 percent in Portugal. Three countries experienced negative excess growth (Canada, Finland, Japan, and the Netherlands) such that the combined effect of GDP and aging growth more than explains the growth in health spending.

There is no consensus on the sources of excess growth; however, the remaining sections discuss possible contributing factors. The factors listed in the health economics literature (Newhouse 1992; Cutler 1995) include: spread of insurance, supplier-induced demand and defensive medicine, factor productivity, and technology.

2.5.4 Spread of Insurance

The median OECD country had almost no change in the prevalence of health insurance coverage between 1970 and 2008 given that the majority of countries had universal coverage in

---

[6] Australia, Austria, Belgium, Canada, Denmark, Finland, France, Germany, Greece, Iceland, Ireland, Japan, Luxembourg, the Netherlands, Norway, Portugal, Spain, Sweden, Switzerland, the UK, and the US.

[7] The analysis uses data from 1987 to 2004.

[8] Also, accounting for inflation and population growth.

1970. In the 1970 to 2008 period several countries (Australia, Greece Italy, Portugal, Spain, and Switzerland) that in 1970 did not have full insurance coverage moved toward 100 percent public coverage of their population and this could contribute to higher spending. Also, benefit packages could have expanded over time. The limited data suggests an increase in the prevalence of private health insurance supplementing or complementing basic public coverage in some countries.[9] Increased health insurance benefits through the expansion of private insurance coverage could have contributed to health spending growth by increasing demand. In spite of this expansion of coverage we do not see any evidence that the spread of public or private insurance is a major reason for rising health spending across the OECD countries.

2.6 Supply Factors of Health Care Spending

2.6.1 Supplier-induced Demand and Defensive Medicine

Supplier-induced demand—the ability of providers to generate demand for their services—is a concept that has both advocates and skeptics. Numerous studies have found a positive association between per-capita spending and the supply of health care resources in the area (Welch et al. 1993; Fisher et al. 2003). Every OECD country had an increase in the number of physicians per 1000 capita between 1970 and 2008, although the rate of increase varied. The median OECD country had a 223 percent increase. As the supply of physicians has increased over time, it is possible that they have increased demand to expand their incomes. However, the relationship between growth in the supply of physicians (or other providers) and health spending growth depends on payment systems and other factors and has proven difficult to quantify (Labelle et al. 1994).

Often discussed in relation to supplier-induced demand is an increase in defensive medicine where a physician provides more services than necessary to prevent malpractice lawsuits. Measuring defensive medicine is difficult to confirm and quantify because determining which health services are "defensive" is difficult to determine. One study of the US Medicare system found that patients hospitalized for two diagnoses (acute myocardial infarction and ischemic heart disease) had lower hospital spending in states with certain types of tort reform (Kessler and McClellan 1996). However, the US Congressional Budget Office (CBO) was unable to replicate Kessler and McClellan's results using a broader set of diagnoses (Beider and Hagen 2004). Additionally, the CBO found mixed evidence for defensive medicine in the published literature. These divergent conclusions underscore the uncertainty around the contribution of defensive medicine to health spending.

---

[9] From 1995 to 2008, Australia went from 33% to 50% of the population with supplementary or complementary private health insurance, Canada from 56% to 68%, Denmark from 0% to 17.8%, Germany from 7% to 19%.

Assuming that defensive medicine contributes to health spending, determining how the practice of defensive medicine has changed over time within a country is difficult to assess. Similarly, determining how the practice of defensive medicine differs between countries that have very different legal systems is complex. A possible measure is the growth in malpractice claims and payments. One study compared growth in the malpractice payments over a four year period (1997–2001) among four OECD countries—Australia, Canada, the United Kingdom, and the US. The average annual real growth in total malpractice payments ranged from 5 to 28 percent (Anderson et al. 2005). The average payment per claim (including claims that were dropped or decided for the defendant) ranged from $4 to $16 per capita when averaged over the entire population. Given these factors, defensive medicine is unlikely to have been a major driver of health spending growth in the median OECD country.

2.6.2 Factor Productivity

The service sector, of which health care is a part, has been capturing a growing share of the economy in all industrialized countries, comprising approximately 70 percent to 80 percent of the total labor force. At the same time, the agricultural and manufacturing sectors have been shrinking. The "Baumol Cost Disease" theory (1967) separates the economy into two sectors, agricultural and manufacturing, which are progressive sectors—they rapidly adopt productive technologies and requires less labor input over time to produce the same material output—while services such as health care are stagnant sectors—they do not adopt productive technologies as rapidly and often require a human touch (Baumol 1993). With less labor required in the progressive sector of the economy, it is possible to shift labor into the less productive sectors.

Pauly (1993) interpreted "Baumol's Cost Disease" theory in the context of health care to say that a significant component of health care costs is due to the difference in productivity a person could have obtained in an industry other than health care. Thus, when comparing health care spending across countries, the differences in productivity of their manufacturing and agricultural industries should be compared. Based on a cross-sectional analysis, Pauly concluded that differences in the productivity in the agricultural and manufacturing sectors are not different across countries, and hence Baumol's theory does not explain the differential rates of growth of health care spending across the OECD countries. However, recent evidence analyzing long-run labor trends across sectors in OECD countries suggests that the shifts in labor due to changes in productivity could explain some of the differences in the rate of growth of health care spending (Hartwig 2008).

Another method to measure change in factor productivity is to compare changes in inflation. The US has a medical price index (MPI), which supposedly measures changes in the prices of services and goods related to health care. The MPI can be compared with a general price inflator (e.g., implicit price deflator) to see how much faster prices in the health care industry have been growing, and hence why health care spending has been capturing a growing share of countries' economies. However, price indices such as the MPI assume a fixed basket of goods. This does not provide an accurate representation of health care markets, where the goods provided are constantly evolving. The result is a tendency for the MPI to overstate changes in costs of goods (Newhouse, 2001). Also, a comparable MPI is not available internationally. There is no consensus in the literature regarding the role factor productivity plays in rising health spending.

2.7 TECHNOLOGY

The general conclusion among health economists is that a major factor influencing the growth of health spending is technology (Newhouse 1992; Cutler 1995; Fuchs 2000). However there is disagreement concerning whether technology is endogenous (a result of increased health spending) or exogenous (where new technologies lead to increased health spending). One camp (Getzen 2000; Glied 2003) believes technology is endogenous through logical reasoning that health spending propels the investment into new technologies, which results in more health spending. Another camp believes technology is exogenous to health spending based on empirical analysis (Okunade and Murthy 2002). International studies suggest that the incentives created by the payment systems vary from country to country and this could influence whether technology is endogenous or exogenous and how it contributes to health care spending.

In economic analyses, technology is classified into several different types: (1) physical capital investment, which is the facilities and equipment used to provide health care; (2) human capital investment, which is knowledge translated into skills gained from education; and (3) labor augmenting technology, which makes labor more efficient.[10] In this section, we compare these three types of technology across OECD countries.

2.7.1 Physical Capital

Investment in physical capital is often measured as the number of advanced medical equipment such as MRIs and CT scanners (spending or depreciation data on capital equipment, which would reflect the value as well as amount of equipment, is typically not available). The number of MRIs and CT scanners varies widely among OECD countries, and the rate of adoption of these technologies has varied widely as well (Table 2.3). An alternative measurement is of investment in physical structures such as hospitals

---

[10] Here "efficient" refers to productive efficiency which is when the economy is operating at its production possibility frontier curve. In a simplified two good economy, the curve represents the maximum output given a combination of the inputs (goods) based on the technology and factors of production available at the lowest cost. Other common definitions of efficiency include Pareto efficiency whereby given a set of goods, the allocation is such that no individual can be made better off without making another worse off. Allocative efficiency is when a set of goods are allocated such that the net benefit of the individual has been maximized. Distributive efficiency is the allocation of goods such that the aggregate utility of the society is maximized, in other words the goods are allocated to those with the greatest need.

Table 2.3 Number of CT Scanners and MRI Units per Million Persons, 2008

	CT scanners per million persons	MRI units per million persons
Australia	56.0	5.6
Austria	29.9	18.0
Belgium	b	b
Canada	12.7	6.7
Czech Republic	13.5	5.1
Denmark	21.5	b
Finland	16.5	16.2
France	b	b
Germany	b	b
Greece	30.7	19.6
Hungary	7.1	2.8
Iceland	31.3	18.8
Ireland	15.1	9.4
Italy	31.0	20.0
Japan	97.3	43.1
Korea	36.8	17.6
Luxembourg	27.6	12.7
Mexico	4.2	1.5
Netherlands	10.3	10.4
New Zealand	12.4	9.6
Norway	b	b
Poland	10.9	2.9
Portugal	26.0	8.9
Slovak Republic	13.7	6.1
Spain	b	b
Sweden	b	b
Switzerland	32.0	b
Turkey	10.2	6.9
United Kingdom	7.4	5.6
United States	34.3	25.9
OECD median	19.0	9.5

[a] 2006 [b] Data not available [c] 2007

and other medical facilities. Generally, the percentage of health care spending devoted to this type of physical capital investments has declined in the median OECD country between 1970 and 2008.[11]

[11] France is the only country that increased the percentage of their total health care spending by one percentage point with physical capital investments. Physical capital investments are defined as gross capital formation.

2.7.2 Human Capital

In the labor economics literature, human capital is commonly proxied using years of education or wages estimated as a function of years of education, experience, and rate of return to investment in schooling. This form of technology is not commonly discussed in the literature on health care spending. However, the role of human capital is evident—as new procedures and techniques become available, more skilled workers (e.g. technicians and technologists) are needed to use the new technologies. Physical capital and human capital can also be considered complements, whereby technological advances are accompanied by increases in skilled labor with the necessary knowledge to operate the technologies (Goldin and Katz 1998). The number of skilled workers beyond nurses and physicians is not tracked reliably in OECD or other international data sources. However, limited evidence suggests that higher spending levels in the US may be due to a more skilled workforce than in other industrialized countries, but on the whole, healthcare wages does not drive health spending growth (Frogner, 2010).

2.7.3 Labor Augmenting Technology

In the macroeconomic literature, labor augmenting technologies improve productivity because fewer workers are required to produce the same or more output (Baumol 1967). An example of a labor augmenting technology that makes health care employees more efficient is the adoption of health IT systems. Health IT is only recently achieving widespread adoption among the industrialized countries with Canada, Germany, and Norway making significant investments in technology and infrastructure. While health IT systems have been operational for over a decade, the productivity benefits of these technologies have not been carefully studied (Anderson et al. 2006). Two studies in the US reached conclusions that health IT could, potentially, result in an annual net savings of approximately 4 percent but the Congressional Budget Office review of the evidence could find little evidence of cost savings in the programs that were operating (Walker et al. 2005; CBO 2008; Girosi et al. 2008).

2.7.4 Research and Development (R&D)

Underlying the discovery and development of the various forms of technology is investment into health R&D. For example, a MRI unit is a result of a culmination of discoveries by scientists and engineers about biology, computer imaging, nuclear physics, and basic mechanics. Another example of the role of health R&D is investment into higher education and creation of new knowledge embodied in human capital. The investment in health R&D is what Newhouse (1992) refers to as the "march of science" driving health spending. However, accounting for the influence of the health R&D investment on health spending is debated; the exogenous technology argument is that health R&D

investment levels are determined by external policy decisions while the endogenous technology argument is that as health spending increases, more money is invested into health R&D. Empirical studies of the role of R&D in health spending is difficult given the large lag time between the discovery of new ideas into the development of new technology; instead, the current literature uses proxies of health R&D such as MRI units and CT scanners.

2.8 OTHER POSSIBLE FACTORS

2.8.1 Chronic Disease

Chronic disease is creating a growing burden on health care spending. The cost impact of these chronic diseases on the growth of health spending is not available for most OECD countries, however, within the US, 85 percent of health spending was attributable to people with chronic diseases in 2006 (Anderson 2007). Measures of risk factors of chronic disease such as obesity, smoking, and drinking levels could provide insight into the future incidence of chronic disease and the burden on the health care spending. However, assessing the impact of these pathways on the historical growth of health care spending in all thirty OECD countries is beyond the scope of this chapter. Studies in the United States and elsewhere suggest that these factors are associated with a high percentage of the increasing prevalence of chronic disease.

Five of the most common chronic diseases (diabetes mellitus, chronic lower respiratory disease, cerebrovascular disease, ischemic heart disease, and malignant neoplasm) were estimated to contribute in a range of 19 percent and 28 percent of the change in overall nominal health care spending in the US between 1987 and 2000 (Thorpe et al. 2004).[12] When these five chronic diseases in the US were compared to a pooled group of ten European countries in 2004, the US had consistently higher prevalence and treated prevalence rates (Thorpe et al. 2007).[13] Given the prevalence and treated prevalence rates are lower in the European countries and the declining mortality rates (Table 2.4) as sign of improved health outcomes, the impact of these five diseases on health care spending levels in the typical OECD country is most likely lower than the contribution for the US as determined by Thorpe and colleagues (2004), although the impact is still likely to be significant. Historical information on changes in chronic disease prevalence and treated

---

[12] Based on authors' calculation of the contribution of heart disease, pulmonary conditions, cancer, cerebrovascular disease, and diabetes. The study included a total of 15 most costly conditions including mental disorders, hypertension, trauma, arthritis, back problems, skin disorders, pneumonia, infectious disease, endocrine and kidney. The sum contribution to change in total health care spending was 43% to 61%.

[13] Austria, Denmark, France, Germany, Greece, Italy, the Netherlands, Spain, Sweden, Switzerland. Treated prevalence is the product of physician-diagnosed prevalence and the proportion of individuals taking medication for the disease.

Table 2.4 Percentage Change in Mortality per 100,000 Persons for Five Common Chronic Diseases, 1970 to 2007

	Malignant neoplasms	Diabetes mellitus	Cerebro-vascular disease	Ischemic heart disease	Chronic lower respiratory disease	Five combined conditions
Australia	−18% a	−36% a	−79% a	−79% a	−91% a	−64%
Austria	−31%	28%	−80%	−50%	−71%	−51%
Belgium	b	b	b	b	b	b
Canada	b	b	b	b	b	b
Czech Republic	b	b	b	b	b	b
Denmark	−1% a	44% a	−51% a	−76% a	−89% a	−45%
Finland	−31%	−60%	−74%	−57%	−95%	−56%
France	−13%	−27%	−79%	−52%	−76%	−42%
Germany	−24% a	−49% a	−76% a	−41% a	−92% a	−48%
Greece	17%	−67%	−33%	4%	−99%	−16%
Hungary	9%	160%	−49%	−10%	−20%	−13%
Iceland	0%	68%	−66%	−68%	−67% e	−47%
Ireland	−9%	−12%	−76%	−59%	−95%	−52%
Italy	−12%	−32%	−68%	−59%	−91%	−46%
Japan	−12%	−49%	−84%	−54%	−81%	−59%
Korea	b	b	b	b	b	b
Luxembourg	−31% a	−42% a	−58% a	−67% a	−86% f	−52%
Mexico	6%	175%	−28%	52%	−66%	25%
Netherlands	−16%	−4%	−67%	−76%	−87%	−51%
New Zealand	−15% a	2% a	−69% a	−65% a	−93% a	−53%
Norway	−4%	41%	−73%	−70%	−74%	−50%
Poland	18%	16%	40%	28%	−95%	10%
Portugal	b	b	b	b	b	b
Slovak Republic	b	b	b	b	b	b
Spain	−1% c	13% d	−71% c	−21% c	−92% c	−38%
Sweden	−15%	−8%	−56%	−69%	−74%	−49%
Switzerland	−28%	−60%	−76%	−43%	b	−48%
Turkey	b	b	b	b	b	b
United Kingdom	−16%	−30%	−69%	−65%	−95%	−53%
United States	−10% d	−2% d	−71% d	−70% d	−69% d	−53%
OECD median	−12%	−8%	−69%	−59%	−88%	−49%

a 1970 to 2006 b Data not available c 1971 to 2005 d 1970 to 2005 e 1971 to 2007 f 1971 to 2006 prevalence is not available to make conclusions about its relation to differences in health spending growth among industrialized countries.

2.8.2 Other Supply Factors

The availability of the supply and utilization of health care resources may affect health care spending. A study of trends in the growth of various resources and utilization (e.g. acute care beds, hospital admissions, length of stay, acute care hospital days) over the last thirty-eight years suggests two notable changes in most OECD countries. The number of physicians per 1000 capita in the median OECD country has increased by about 220 percent, or an additional 1.7 physicians per 1000 capita. During the same time period, the length of stay for inpatient care has fallen by approximately 58 percent. While the data is limited in scope, the increase in the supply of physicians accompanied by a decrease in utilization of hospital care may be a reflection of efforts by health systems to shift care from costly inpatient settings to lower cost outpatient settings.

2.8.3 Waiting Lists/Rationing Care

Some believe that rationing care through supply control policies is another alternative to control spending (See Siciliani and Iverson in this volume for further discussion). The result of these supply constraints has been waiting lists in some countries. The impact of using waiting lists as a method to reduce or sustain health care spending is debatable. An OECD study showed that the health spending was greater in the seven countries without waiting lists versus twelve countries with waiting lists (Anderson et al. 2005). While there was a difference, many factors besides waiting lists could explain the spending difference ($330). Another study found that waiting lists are largely constituted by elective procedures; these elective procedures represent only a small proportion of total health spending in most countries (Anderson et al. 2005).

2.8.4 Quality of Care

Comparisons of health care spending do not reflect the quality of health care delivered. Higher quality care could be related to higher health spending; although, in some cases higher quality could be cost-decreasing (e.g., a poorly performed surgical procedure could result in a costly complication). Different OECD countries are likely delivering very different "products" of health care, but these differences are difficult to measure. International comparisons of the quality of health care are limited, but available evidence shows that quality is mixed, with no clear relation to the level of health spending (Hussey et al. 2004; Davis et al. 2007). No information is available on how the rate of change in health care quality compares in different OECD countries.

2.9 Summary and Conclusion

As OECD countries address the increasing level of health care spending they will need to examine the factors contributing to the increasing levels of health care spending. This chapter provides an overview of the factors generally considered to be the major factors contributing to rising health care spending and the variation in the levels of health care spending across the OECD countries. Each country will need to examine the list in terms of their own circumstances and evaluate which policy solutions are most appropriate for their own unique circumstances. However, many of the fundamental drivers of health spending growth are shared across countries: most notably, technological diffusion and the shift of the disease burden toward chronic diseases. Determining successful approaches to managing these drivers of spending while improving the quality and outcomes achieved should be a priority for OECD countries.

References

ABEL-SMITH, BRIAN (1992), "Cost Containment and New Priorities in the European Community," *The Milbank Quarterly*, 70(3): 393–416.

ANDERSON, GERARD F. (2008), "Chronic Conditions: Making the Case for Ongoing Care," <http://www.fightchronicdisease.org/pdfs/ChronicCareChartbook_FINAL.pdf>, accessed June 24, 2010.

—— and HUSSEY, PETER S. (2000), "Population Aging: A Comparison Among Industrialized Countries," *Health Affairs*, 19(3): 191–203.

—— FROGNER, BIANCA K., and WATERS, HUGH R. (2005), "Health Spending in the United States and the Rest of the Industrialized World," *Health Affairs*, 24(4): 903–14.

—— FROGNER, BIANCA K., JOHNS, ROGER A., and REINHARDT, UUE E. (2006), "Health Care Spending and Use of Information Technology in OECD Countries," *Health Affairs*, 25(3): 819–31.

—— REINHARDT, UUE E., HUSSEY, PETER S., and PETROSYAN, VARDUHI (2003), "It's the Prices, Stupid: Why the United States Is So Different from Other Countries," *Health Affairs*, 22(3): 89–105.

BAUMOL, WILLIAM J. (1967), "Macroeconomics of Unbalanced Growth: The Anatomy of Urban Crisis," *American Economic Review*, 57(3): 415–26.

—— (1993), "Health Care, Education and the Cost Disease: A Looming Crisis for Public Choice," *Public Choice*, 77(1): 17–28.

BEIDER, P. and HAGEN, S. (2004), "Limiting Tort Liability for Medical Malpractice," *Congressional Budget Office Issue Brief* (Washington, DC: Congressional Budget Office).

CBO (CONGRESSIONAL BUDGET OFFICE) (2008), "Evidence on the Costs and Benefits of Health Information Technology," a CBO Paper. <http://www.cbo.gov/ftpdocs/91xx/doc9168/05-20-HealthIT.pdf>, accessed September 16, 2008.

CULYER, ANTHONY J. (1989), "The Normative Economics of Health Care Finance and Provision," *Oxford Review of Economic Policy*, 5(1): 34–58.

CUTLER, DAVID M. (1995), "Technology, Health Costs, and the NIH," *National Institutes of Health Economics Roundtable on Biomedical Research* (Bethesda, MD: National Institutes of Health).

DAVIS, KAREN, SCHOEN, CATHY, SCHOENBAUM, STEPHEN C., DOTY, MICHELLE M., HOLMGREN, ALYSSA L., KRISS, JENNIFER L., and SHEA, KATHERINE K. (2007), "Mirror, Mirror on the Wall: An International Update on the Comparative Performance of American Health Care" (Washington, DC: Commonwealth Fund), 1–30.

DENAVAS-WALT, CARMEN, PROCTOR, BERNADETTE D., and LEE, CHERYL HILL (2006), "Income, Poverty, and Health Insurance Coverage in the United States: 2005," *Current Population Survey* (Washington, DC: US Census Bureau), 76.

DI MATTEO, LIVIO (2003), "The Income Elasticity of Health Care Spending: A Comparison of Parametric and Nonparametric Approaches," *The European Journal of Health Economics*, 4(1): 20–9.

FISHER, ELLIOTT S., WENNBERG, DAVID E., STUKEL, THERESE A., GOTTLIEB, DANIEL J., LUCAS, F. L., and PINDER, ETOILE L. (2003), "The Implications of Regional Variations in Medicare Spending. Part 1: The Content, Quality, and Accessibility of Care," *Annals of Internal Medicine*, 138(4): 273–87.

FROGNER, BIANCA K. (2010), "The Missing Technology: An International Comparison of Human Capital Investment," *Applied Health Economics and Health Policy*, 8(6): 361–371.

FUCHS, VICTOR R. (2000), "The Future of Health Economics," *Journal of Health Economics*, 19(2): 141–57.

GERDTHAM, ULF-G. and JONSSON, BENGT (2000), "International Comparisons of Health Expenditure: Theory, Data and Econometric Analysis," in Anthony J. Culyer and Joseph P. Newhouse (eds.), *Handbook of Health Economics* (1st edn.) (Amsterdam: Elsevier Science B.V.), 11–53.

GETZEN, THOMAS E. (2000), "Health Care Is an Individual Necessity and a National Luxury: Applying Multilevel Decision Models to the Analysis of Health Care Expenditures," *Journal of Health Economics*, 19(2): 259–70.

GIROSI, FEDERICO, MEILI, ROBIN, and SCOVILLE, RICHARD (2005), *Extrapolating Evidence of Health Information Technology Savings and Costs* (Santa Monica: RAND Corporation), 1–108.

GLIED, SHERRY (2003), "Health Care Costs: On the Rise Again," *Journal of Economic Perspectives*, 17(2): 125–48.

GOLDIN, CLAUDIA and KATZ, LAWRENCE F. (1998), "The Origins of Technology-Skill Complementarity," *Quarterly Journal of Economics*, 113(3): 693–732.

HARTMAN, MICAH, CATLIN, AARON, LASSMAN, DAVID, CYLUS, JONATHAN, and HEFFLER, STEPHEN (2008), "US Health Spending By Age, Selected Years Through 2004," *Health Affairs*, 27(1): w1–w12.

HARTWIG, JOCHEN (2008), "What Drives Health Care Expenditure? Baumol's Model of 'Unbalanced Growth' Revisited," *Journal of Health Economics*, 27(3): 603–23.

HITIRIS, THEO and POSNETT, JOHN (1992), "The Determinants and Effects of Health Expenditure in Developed Countries," *Journal of Health Economics*, 11(2): 173–81.

HSIAO, WILLIAM C. (2007), "Why Is a Systemic View of Health Financing Necessary?" *Health Affairs*, 26(4): 950–61.

HUSSEY, PETER and ANDERSON, GERARD F. (2003), "A Comparison of Single- and Multi-payer Health Insurance Systems and Options for Reform," *Health Policy*, 66(3): 215–28.

—— OSBORN, ROBIN, FEEK, COLIN, MCLAUGHLIN, VIVIENNE, MILLAR, JOHN, and EPSTEIN, ARNOLD (2004), "How Does the Quality of Care Compare in Five Countries?" *Health Affairs*, 23(3): 89–99.

KESSLER, DANIEL and MCCLELLAN, MARK B. (1996), "Do Doctors Practice Defensive Medicine?" *The Quarterly Journal of Economics*, 111(2): 353–90.

KNAUL, FELICIA MARIE and FRENK, JULIO (2005), "Health Insurance in Mexico: Achieving Universal Coverage Through Structural Reform," *Health Affairs*, 24(6): 1467–76.

LABELLE, ROBERTA, STODDART, GREG, and RICE, THOMAS (1994), "A Re-examination of the Meaning and Importance of Supplier-induced Demand," *Journal of Health Economics*, 13(3): 347–68.

NEWHOUSE, JOSEPH P. (1992), "Medical Care Costs: How Much Welfare Loss?" *Journal of Economic Perspectives*, 6(3): 3–21.

—— (2001), "Medical Care Price Indices: Problems and Opportunities/The Churg-Hua Lecturs," National Bureau of Economic Research Working Paper No. 8168.

OECD (ORGANIZATION FOR ECONOMIC CO-OPERATION AND DEVELOPMENT) (2010), "OECD Health Data 2010," October (Paris: OECD).

OKUNADE, ALBERT A. and MURTHY, VASUDEVA N. R. (2002), "Technology as a 'Major Driver' of Health Care Costs: A Cointegration Analysis of the Newhouse Conjecture," *Journal of Health Economics*, 21(1): 147–59.

—— KARAKUS, MUSTAFA C., and OKEKE, CHARLES (2004), "Determinants of Health Expenditure Growth of the OECD Countries: Jackknife Resampling Plan Estimates," *Health Care Management Science*, 7(3): 173–83.

PAULY, MARK V. (1993), "US Health Care Costs: The Untold True Story," *Health Affairs*, 12(3): 152–9.

ROBERTS, JENNIFER (1999), "Sensitivity of Elasticity Estimates for OECD Health Care Spending: Analysis of a Dynamic Heterogeneous Data Field," *Health Economics*, 8(5): 459–72.

—— (2000), "Spurious Regression Problems in the Determinants of Health Care Expenditure: A Comment on Hitiris," *Applied Economics Letters*, 7(5): 279–83.

SMITH, SHEILA, HEFFLER, STEPHEN K., and FREELAND, MARK S. (2000), "The Impact of Technological Change on Health Care Cost Increases: An Evaluation of the Literature," Working Paper. Centers of Medicare and Medicaid Services, Baltimore.

THORPE, KENNETH E., FLORENCE, CURTIS S., and JOSKI, PETER (2004), "Which Medical Conditions Account for the Rise in Health Care Spending?" *Health Affairs*, July–Dec. (Supplemental Web Exclusives), W4: 437–45.

—— HOWARD, DAVID H., and GALACTIONOVA, KATYA (2007), "Differences in Disease Prevalence as a Source of The US–European Health Care Spending Gap," *Health Affairs*, 26(6): w678–w686.

TRIPLETT, JOCK E., and BOSWORTH BANY P., (2004), "*Productivity int he US Service Sector: New sources of Economic Growth.*" The Bookings Institution: Washington, DC. 401p.

WALKER, JAN, PAN, ERIC, JOHNSTON, DOUGLAS, ADLER-MILSTEIN, JULIA, BATES, DAVID W., and MIDDLETON, BLACKFORD (2005), "The Value of Health Care Information Exchange and Interoperability," *Health Affairs*. <http://content.healthaffairs.org/cgi/reprint/hlthaff. w5.10v1>, accessed September 16, 2008.

WELCH, W. PETE, MILLER, MARK E., WELCH, H. GILBERT, FISHER, ELLIOTT S., and WENNBERG, JOHN E. (1993), "Geographic Variation in Expenditures for Physicians' Services in the United States," *New England Journal of Medicine*, 328(9): 621–27.

WESTERT, G. P., VANDENBERG, M. J., KOOLMAN X., VERKLEIJ, H., (2008), "Dutch Health Care Performance Report 2008." <http://www.rivm.nl/vtv/object_binary/o6118_Dutch%20 Healthcare%20Performance%20Report%202008.pdf>, accessed September 8, 2008.

WHITE, CHAPIN (2007), "Health Care Spending Growth: How Different is the United States from the Rest of the OECD?" *Health Affairs*, 26(1): 154–61.*

CHAPTER 3

....

HEALTH SYSTEMS IN LOW- AND MIDDLE-INCOME COUNTRIES*

....

ANNE MILLS

3.1 INTRODUCTION

....

Low- and middle-income countries (LMICs)—the focus of this chapter—comprise all countries in the world outside the sixty high-income countries. They number in total 149, and not surprisingly represent an enormous range of country and health system contexts. They account for 84 percent of the world's population, 90 percent of the world's 2001 disease burden (Lopez et al. 2006), 24 percent of the world's GDP, and only 13 percent of global health expenditure. The health systems of the very poorest countries—say Democratic Republic of Congo or Nepal—differ enormously from those in high-income countries, but at the other end of the LMIC range, countries such as Mexico or Malaysia share many features and concerns in common with high-income countries.

This chapter is the only one in this volume which focuses exclusively on LMICs, and given the limited attention paid to economic dimensions of LMIC health systems relative to those in high-income countries, and the restricted evidence base, coverage in other chapters inevitably favors high-income countries. The aim of this chapter is to provide an economic analysis of LMIC health systems and policy implications, and to assist readers to interpret the relevance to LMIC settings of the more in-depth material in other chapters.

More specifically, the chapter aims to:

- Analyze the economic dimensions of health systems in low- and middle-income countries, including how they differ from those of high-income countries

* Many thanks to Yoel Lubell for producing the data for Tables 3.1–3.4, and Figures 3.2, 3.4, and 3.5.

- Identify distinctive characteristics of low- and middle-income countries that affect the policy recommendations that can be derived from the application of economic thinking to their health systems
- Identify key areas of debate that remain unresolved.

Given the diversity and number of LMICs, some structure for aggregation is needed in order to summarize their key features. One of the most commonly used classifications is that of the World Bank which is reflected in the chapter structure here: a grouping by income level into low income, lower middle income, upper middle income, and high income.

Geographical region is another common classification, recognizing that regions and geographically contiguous countries have some defining characteristics in common, such as a common broad cultural and historical identity and roughly similar economic structures, even if there may also be great differences such as those between South Africa and much of the rest of Sub-Saharan Africa. It also has the advantage that regions are widely used in common parlance (witness the current focus on Africa). The World Bank recognizes six regions to which LMIC are allocated: East Asia and the Pacific, Europe and Central Asia, Latin America and the Caribbean, the Middle East and North Africa, South Asia, and Sub-Saharan Africa. The World Health Organisation (WHO) uses a country classification based on the WHO regional governance structure, but sub-dividing WHO regions into two or three sub-regions based on stages of health development in terms of levels of child and adult mortality, producing a total of fourteen sub-regions.

Finally, political or institutional characteristics are commonly used to distinguish specific sub-sets of countries. For example, until recently countries in transition from planned economies were singled out as a group (e.g. countries of the former Soviet Union, China, and Vietnam). Most recently the term "fragile states" has entered the vocabulary, to indicate states that are weak in their institutional capacity, control of territory and ability or willingness to provide services to their people.[1] Low-income Countries Under Stress (LICUS) is another, similar classification, which can be broken down into four categories: countries experiencing prolonged political crisis; LICUS in fragile transition; LICUS with weak governance/slow progress; and LICUS with deteriorating governance.

All of these categorizations have value in understanding health systems and appropriate policies: income level is vital as reflecting the resources available to invest in health; geography reflects a broader range of factors which influence health conditions and affect how health systems function; level of health development highlights the health conditions which health systems must tackle; and institutional characteristics are important, as this chapter argues later, for defining which policies are relevant and understanding how particular policies might work in particular institutional settings.

This chapter hence presents data in two ways: by income level and by World Bank geographical region. These are both the most widely used classifications and those of the highest relevance for economic analysis. It should be noted that the averages presented are country-weighted not population-weighted, since a health system is a national entity,

---

[1] <http://www.gsdrc.org/go/topic-guides/fragile-states/terms-and-definitions> accessed January 4, 2008.

and the country average gives a better representation of experience across countries than a population-weighted average which is dominated by countries with large populations. To illustrate the key features of the countries that are the concern of this chapter, Table 3.1 provides summary information on selected health indicators and per capita Gross Domestic Product (GDP). It shows that average life expectancy ranges from 53 years for males and 55 for females in low-income countries to 76 and 81 in high-income countries. Infant mortality shows a more than fourteen-fold difference between low- and high-income countries, and TB a more than twenty-one-fold difference. In terms of regions, SSA consistently shows the worst health-related indicators. GDP per capita in US dollars differs nearly seventy-fold between low- and high-income countries.

Since purchasing power is poorly represented by exchange rate conversions of country financial indicators, GDP per capita is also shown adjusted for purchasing power parity, namely in international dollars, which adjusts the value of GDP to reflect more accurately the basket of goods and services it can be used to purchase within each country. Such an adjustment reduces the distance between GDP per capita, from a thirteen-fold difference between high-income countries and LMICs, to a six-fold difference.

3.2 Economic Dimensions of LMIC Health Systems

A health system comprises all the organizations, institutions, and resources that are devoted to producing health actions whose primary purpose is to improve health (WHO 2000). It can be analyzed in various ways, but here the prime focus is on the economic dimensions of health systems. Figure 3.1 enables these to be explored in terms of four key actors (the population, providers, financing agents, and government/professional bodies), five functions (revenue collection, pooling, resource allocation, service provision, and regulation) and the associated relationships and incentives. This section presents summary data and evidence to characterize the dimensions of the performance of the five functions.

3.2.1 Revenue Collection

Revenue can be classified by source (government taxes, social security payments, out-of-pocket payments, external grants and loans), whether these are public or private, and their level (Table 3.2). The lower the country income level, the higher tends to be the share of out-of-pocket payments (Figure 3.2) and the lower the share of revenue (e.g. tax, insurance premiums) which flows through financing agents. At the most extreme (e.g. highly fragile states such as those where government barely functions), virtually all revenue for health services may flow in the form of direct payments. Even in a country

Table 3.1 Selected Health Indicators and GDP Per Capita

Indicator	Life expectancy at birth: males	Life expectancy at birth: females	Infant mortality rate (per 1000 live births)	Tuberculosis prevalence (per 100,000)	GDP per capita US$ (2005)	GDP per capita (international $)
Low income	52.7	55.4	85.9	431	383	2499
Lower middle income	63.8	68.3	39.0	191	1686	6442
Upper middle income	66.7	72.9	21.3	104	4842	11,174
Low & middle income	60.3	64.6	52.3	262	2085	5245
High income	75.8	81.0	5.8	20	26,590	32,725
East Asia & Pacific	64.3	68.6	36.6	258	1779	6052
Europe & Central Asia	65.8	73.5	24.3	93	3038	9290
Latin America & Caribbean	68.7	73.8	24.5	94	3099	8410
Middle East & North Africa	65.7	70.4	38.9	130	2850	6126
South Asia	60.6	62.6	65.1	230	929	3137
Sub-Saharan Africa	49.4	51.6	91.3	482	1058	1994

Source: Health indicators from WHO data: <http://www.who.int/whois/database/core/core_select_process.cfm?countries=all&indicators-nha> accessed November 1, 2008. GDP data and country classification from World Bank: <http://ddp-ext.worldbank.org/ext/DDPQQ/member.do?method=getMembers> accessed January 11, 2008.

Note: Means weighted by country.

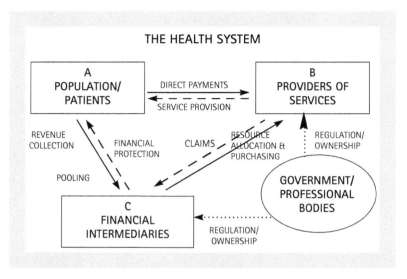

FIGURE 3.1 The health system
Source: Mills (2000).

like India, 83 percent of total expenditure on health is from private sources, and of this 94 percent is from out-of-pocket payments.[2]

External resources feature as an important element of total health expenditure in low-income countries, making up on average 23 percent. Despite this, per capita public expenditure is still extremely low—$12 in low-income countries on average, and $23 for per capita total health expenditure. Adjusting these values for purchasing parity does increase them, but even so total public health expenditure is far below the amount needed to finance a basic package of health services (WHO 2001).

3.2.2 Revenue Pooling

Pooling concerns the aggregation of pre-paid revenues. Prepayment (whether via insurance premiums or tax) allows for payment of health care costs in advance, though there may be some copayments required at the time of service use. Pooling means that members of the pool collectively share risks of needing health care.

The data in Table 3.2 on out-of-pocket payment demonstrate the very limited pooling in LMICs. In addition, pooling is limited by the fragmentation of risk pools, which is common in many countries. For example, there may be different risk pools for those people entitled to access Ministry of Health (MOH) services, those who are members of a compulsory social insurance scheme (or there may be multiple schemes for different industries), those who join voluntary private insurance schemes, and those who are

[2] WHO core indicators accessed January 4, 2008.

Table 3.2 Health System Financing

Indicator	THE as % of GDP	GHE as % of THE	Private expenditure on health as % of THE	GHE as % of total government expenditure	External resources for health as % of THE	Social security health expenditure as % of GHE	Out-of-pocket expenditure as % of PHE	Private prepaid plans as % of PHE	Per capita THE at average exchange rate (US$)	Per capita THE at international dollar rate	Per capita GHE at average exchange rate (US$)
Low income	5.2	43.9	56.1	9.0	22.5	6.1	85.0	3.0	23	79	12
Lower middle income	6.2	58.2	41.8	10.5	9.0	19.5	81.5	8.5	106	271	65
Upper middle income	6.4	63.0	37.0	11.3	2.2	35.8	80.5	15.5	346	639	220
Low & middle income	5.9	54.2	45.8	10.2	12.2	19.4	82.5	8.2	137	294	85
High income	7.6	70.8	29.2	13.9	0.2	36.6	75.6	20.1	2414	2288	1758
East Asia & Pacific	5.9	63.0	37.0	10.3	19.0	14.3	82.1	3.5	110	252	86
Europe & Central Asia		56.7	43.3	10.6	6.1	43.9	88.3	1.9	223	478	149
Latin America & Caribbean	6.6	55.5	44.5	12.7	3.0	28.2	79.9	19.3	210	458	119
Middle East & North Africa	5.9	54.6	45.4	7.6	4.8	17.7	88.5	9.3	164	326	83
South Asia	4.6	37.4	62.6	6.5	7.4	4.4	93.7	1.4	41	130	24
Sub-Saharan Africa	5.3	50.6	49.4	9.6	20.8	2.9	77.8	8.7	67	133	40

Source: Health indicators from WHO data: <http://www.who.int/whois/database/core/core_select_process.cfm?countries=all&indicators=nha> accessed January 11, 2008.

Notes: THE = Total Health Expenditure; GHE = Government Health Expenditure; PHE = Private Health Expenditure. Means weighted by country.

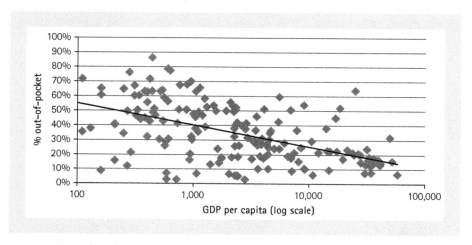

FIGURE 3.2 Out-of-pocket share of total health expenditure in relation to GDP per capita

Notes: Calculated using WHO data from <http://www.who.int/whosis/database/core/core_select_process.cfm?countries=all&indicators=nha> accessed November 1, 2008.

members of community-based insurance arrangements. Such fragmentation maintains gross inequities in access to health care and quantity and quality of services received. There are ways of addressing such inequities—notably through risk equalization funds, financed by contributions from the various risk pools, which compensate pools with higher than average risks. However, there are relatively few examples of such funds in LMICs, with some considerable concern on how well they function. For example, in Colombia, reforms introduced competition between insurers, with the insured being allowed to select their preferred insurer. To ensure that high risk individuals are not discriminated against by insurers, a redistribution fund receives contributions and distributes them to insurers as risk-adjusted capitation payments. However, Gottret and Schieber (2006: 264) argue that it is highly unlikely that the risk adjustment mechanism works well enough to prevent selection behavior by insurers. Public subsidies can also be used to compensate for inequities, but not unusually do so to an inadequate degree or even may accentuate inequities. Thailand, for example, ensures universal coverage of health care through a tripartite arrangement where civil servants have their own non-contributory scheme, those employed in the formal sector belong to the social security scheme, and the rest of the population are entitled to register for the universal coverage scheme. Per capita public funding in 2002 amounted to B1947 for civil servants and B1217 for the social security scheme (which cares only for workers not their dependents), whereas that for the rest of the population, which includes significant proportions of those with greater health care needs, notably children and the elderly, was only B1202. More generally, in countries where a substantial proportion of the population does not have physical access to public health services, public subsidies to existing risk pools may be at the expense of not devoting these funds to those who have no access.

Given the inequities which tend to be maintained by multiple pools (as well as the problems they create for health providers), and the difficulties of ensuring that what might in theory be desirable competition between insurers does not produce undesirable consequences such as cream-skimming, some countries have chosen to create a single risk pool—for example, Costa Rica merged its general tax-funded national health service and its payroll tax-funded social health insurance in the mid-1990s, and Korea recently merged industry-related sickness funds and schemes for public sector workers (Kwon 2003). Entrenched interests can, however, make this politically difficult to achieve, as in Thailand where legislation permits the merging of schemes but politically it is not currently being pursued.

3.2.3 Resource Allocation and Purchasing

Ideally LMIC health systems should be characterized in terms of patterns of expenditure—for example, relative shares allocated to areas of spending such as primary care, hospitals, pharmaceuticals, public health, and administration. However, such information is unavailable in an aggregated form. An increasing number of countries are implementing National Health Accounts (Powell-Jackson and Mills 2007) but variations in expenditure breakdowns make it difficult to aggregate. In general, a high proportion of government health expenditure goes on hospitals, and within that a high share is absorbed by higher level hospitals (Hensher et al. 2006). Barnum and Kutzin found that all levels of public hospitals in developing countries absorbed a mean of 60 percent of recurrent public health expenditures, and across five countries (Belize, Indonesia, Kenya, Zambia, Zimbabwe) tertiary hospitals accounted for 45–69 percent of total public expenditure on hospitals (Barnum and Kutzin 1993). A more recent study, in South Africa, found that tertiary and regional hospitals accounted for nearly 60 percent of total public hospital expenditure, and tertiary hospitals alone accounted for nearly one-fifth of total public expenditure (Thomas and Muirhead 2000).

In terms of total health expenditure, pharmaceuticals account for a major share given their dominance in private out-of-pocket payments and in turn the dominance of such payments in total health expenditure. WHO data suggest that pharmaceutical expenditure accounts for 19 percent of total health expenditure in low-income countries and 25 percent in middle-income countries, in contrast to 14 percent in high-income countries (WHO 2004).

Few LMICs have well-developed arrangements for purchasing services. The language of purchaser/provider splits has permeated health sector reform discussions (Mills et al. 2000), but change has been slow on the ground. Most MOH funded and provided services remain hierarchical in their structure, though a number of countries have increased the degree of decentralized management (e.g. Tanzania, India, Indonesia, Philippines). Purchasing arrangements have been most explicit where donor-funded contracts—often with NGOs—have been employed to provide services in countries emerging from conflict such as Cambodia, Afghanistan, and the Democratic Republic of Congo.

Social insurance schemes in LMICs historically either were integrated (owning their own facilities—common in Latin America) or paid fee-for-service to providers.

Poor performance of the integrated form, and cost escalation encouraged by fee-for-service payment, has encouraged innovations in payment systems and especially experimentation with case-based payment and capitation in countries that have recently implemented universal coverage such as Taiwan, Korea, and Thailand (Mills 2007).

3.2.4 Service Provision

Service provision is easiest to characterize by inputs (beds, health workers) and by levels of utilization and coverage (percent of a target population receiving an intervention). However, only very crude data are available for LMICs on inputs, and data on utilization and coverage are extremely limited other than for some high priority services for children and mothers such as treatment of common illnesses, immunization and skilled birth attendance, where information is available as well on distribution by socioeconomic status.

Table 3.3 demonstrates that the density of health workers is very low, with for example, only 0.3 physicians and one nurse per 1000 people in low-income countries. SSA has the lowest density of physicians (one doctor for every 5000 people), and South Asia of nurses (one nurse for every 1430 people). There is an almost seven-fold difference in physicians per 1000 people between low- and upper-middle-income countries, and a nearly four-fold difference in nurses.

Figure 3.3 shows median coverage levels for key services amongst the sixty-eight countries which bear the world's highest burdens of child and maternal mortality. While immunization coverage levels are reasonably high given recent efforts and increased funding, many children and mothers are not receiving lifesaving interventions—for example, less than half of children with suspected pneumonia are taken to an appropriate health facility, and only 32 percent of children with suspected pneumonia receive antibiotics. Within overall low coverage levels, there are considerable within-country inequalities by socioeconomic group (Table 3.4). In low-income countries, children from the highest wealth quintile have double the measles immunization coverage of the lowest wealth quintile, and there is a seven-fold difference between highest and lowest wealth quintiles in presence of a skilled birth attendant at birth.

In many countries a very substantial share of utilization is in the private sector (as suggested by the high share of out-of-pocket payments in total health expenditure, though some part of these are to public providers). In low-income countries use of the informal private sector is especially common—outlets such as general stores, often unlicensed drug shops, and market traders. In the absence of a widespread network of public services, such outlets are often the nearest and cheapest source of treatment. Figure 3.4 shows that private sources of care were as frequently used for sick children in twenty-two SSA countries as public sources. While availability of drugs can be better in the private sector than in the public sector, there are also problems of inappropriate and poor quality drug sales (Goodman et al. 2004).

Table 3.3 Health System Inputs

Indicator	Physicians per 1000 population	Nurses per 1000 population	Midwives per 1000 population	Hospital beds per 1000 population
Low income	0.3	1	0.2	16.5
Lower middle income	1.2	2.6	0.3	25.3
Upper middle income	2	3.7	0.3	41.8
Low & middle income	1.1	2.3	0.3	27.4
East Asia & Pacific	0.5	1.8	0.2	22.3
Europe & Central Asia	2.9	6.1	0.4	63.7
Latin America & Caribbean	1.6	2.1	0.1	18.9
Middle East & North Africa	1.1	1.8	0.1	18.4
South Asia	0.4	0.7	0.3	12.6
Sub-Saharan Africa	0.2	1.2	0.2	15

Source: Health indicators from WHO data: <http://www.who.int/whois/database/core/core_select_process.cfm?countries=all&indicators-nha> accessed January 15, 2008. Country classification from World Bank: <http://ddp-ext.worldbank.org/ext/DDPQQ/member.do?method=getMembers> accessed January 15, 2008.

Note: Means weighted by country.

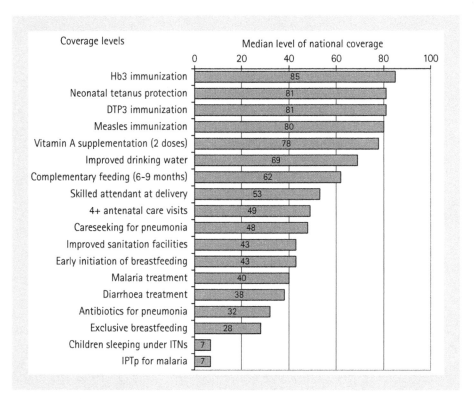

FIGURE 3.3 Median coverage levels for priority maternal, neonatal and child health interventions (68 priority countries)
Source: UNICEF 2008.

3.2.5 Regulation

Regulation in LMICs tends to be both partial and weakly enforced (Mills and Ranson 2005). The range of regulation tends to be similar to that in high-income countries, including control of professions, of facilities, and of pharmaceuticals. However, it is common for new developments in the private sector to remain unregulated (for example, private laboratories and other diagnostic technologies), and the information, systems and staffing to ensure regulations are followed are usually grossly inadequate, especially in low-income countries. Moreover, boundaries between public and private roles are commonly blurred— for example, many publicly employed doctors also do private practice, and even Ministers of Health may have commercial interests in health care or health insurance. Hence regulatory capture can be a major problem leading to weak enforcement (Mills et al. 2001).

3.2.6 Categorization and Evolution of LMIC Health Systems

High-income-country health systems have been categorized in terms of number of insurance pools, whether insurance is public or private, and whether provision is

Table 3.4 Inequalities Within Country Groupings

	Measles immunization coverage among 1-year-olds: ratio of highest-lowest wealth quintile	Births attended by skilled health personnel: ratio of highest-lowest wealth quintile*
Low income	2	7.2 (30)
Lower middle income	1.2	3.6 (13)
Upper middle income	1.2	1.4 (7)
Low & middle income	1.7	5.5 (50)
East Asia & Pacific	1.6	2.4 (2)
Europe & Central Asia	1.1	1.4 (5)
Latin America & Caribbean	1.3	4.8 (10)
Middle East & North Africa	2.3	1.5 (2)
South Asia	2.1	10.3 (4)
Sub-Saharan Africa	1.8	6 (27)

Sources: Health indicators from WHO data: <http://www.who.int/whosis/database/core/core_select_process.cfm?countries=all&indicators=nha> accessed January 15, 2008. Country classification from World Bank: <http://ddp-ext.worldbank.org/ext/DDPQQ/member.do?method=getMembers> accessed January 15, 2008.

Notes: *Limited data: in brackets are the number of countries for which data were available in each group; †Data combined from World Development Indicators 2007 and UNICEF Global Database on Treatment of Pneumonia; ‡<http://www.childinfo.org/areas/ari/countrydata.php> accessed January 18, 2008.

public or private (see Chapter 16); or historically in terms of whether they are a "Beveridge" system (national health service funded from general tax and with public ownership of providers) or a Bismarck system (compulsory social insurance financed by employers and employees financing a combination of public and private providers).

Such models in general do not characterize well the health systems of LMICs, which on the whole are marked by fragmentation—of sources of revenue, risk pools, and provider organizations. Moreover, inadequate resources to finance universal coverage of a reasonable range of health services mean that access to services is highly unequal between groups covered by different arrangements.

Countries frequently have co-existing at the same time:

- A publicly funded, publicly provided health service, either officially free at the point of use (but often in low-income countries involving informal payment), or charging subsidized user fees; in many African countries church-run services effectively form a substantial component of this public network.
- Compulsory social insurance arrangements for some or all of those employed in the formal sector, often a minority of the labor force, and financing services either

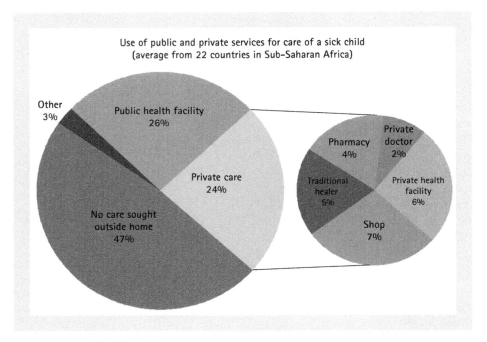

FIGURE 3.4 Use of public and private services
Source: Data from T. Marek et al. 2005.

though its own facilities (still common in Latin America) or through purchase of services (most common in Asia outside India)

- Special arrangements for specific population groups—for example, publicly funded services specifically for the armed forces, and employer-funded services for major industrial and mining enterprises
- Extensive private sector services, both more and less formal, funded through out-of-pocket payment.

Other features, less widely found, include:

- Private insurance arrangements, especially in upper-middle-income countries (in South Africa, private insurance arrangements cover approximately 18 percent of the population: 60 percent of the wealthiest quintile but only 2 percent of the poorest); some areas have seen a rapid expansion in private insurance, for example, the Middle East and North Africa (Gottret and Schieber 2006)
- High quality private hospitals serving foreigners (e.g. in India, Thailand)
- Community financing schemes, involving a great diversity of financing and provision arrangements ranging from integrated schemes (a hospital running its own pre-payment scheme) to NGOs which run an insurance scheme reimbursing some of the health care costs of its members.

The exceptions to this pattern are a few wealthier middle-income countries which have merged and re-organized funding and provision arrangements in the process of providing for universal coverage. Even with these countries, however, inadequate resources tend to mean that arrangements are either not fully universal (for example, a substantial proportion of Colombia's population is still not encompassed by the compulsory and subsidized insurance regimes, and falls back on a publicly funded safety net), or co-exist with still substantial levels of exposure to out-of-pocket payments. Such payments can arise for three main reasons: copayments may be required to obtain services within the benefit package; the benefit package may be quite narrow, excluding certain services which then have to be paid for; or the quality of care of the providers available to the insured may not satisfy their preferences, leading them to patronize other providers for whom they must pay.

The data in Table 3.2 and Figures 3.1 and 3.2 suggest that as countries grow richer, the public share of revenue increases, and the out-of-pocket share falls, though at any given income level countries can exhibit very different patterns. With the exception of Thailand, virtually all countries that recently established universal coverage have done so on the basis of merging fragmented schemes and expanding compulsory social insurance arrangements, using general tax revenues to subsidize the inclusion of sections of the population outside the formal labor force (Mills 2007). Social insurance was also the chosen means to reform the financing of health systems in East and Central Europe following the collapse of the USSR, in part because these countries had a large formal employment sector making payroll taxes feasible and wished to move away from the state domination implicit in use of general tax revenues (Gottret and Schieber 2006). While achieving universal coverage with reasonable depth of service provision is heavily dependent on a country's income level, political and social factors must be supportive to increasing the government's role in health (Mills 2007).

There is some evidence from developing countries to suggest that while the public share of revenue may increase as countries grow richer, the public share of provision shrinks (Hanson and Berman 1998). This may in part be a response of private investors to demand from a growing middle class for medical care that is not satisfied by public services, and subsequent opening of access to private facilities to patients covered by public insurance. For example, Asian countries with universal coverage which until recently were classed as upper-middle-income (e.g. Korea, Taiwan) have a very substantial share of utilization which is catered for in the private sector. In Thailand, employees in the social security scheme must choose a hospital at which to register and have free choice between public and private accredited hospitals; over the first ten years of the scheme the share of private hospitals increased from 17 percent in 1991 to 49 percent in 2001.

3.3 DISTINCTIVE CHARACTERISTICS OF LMICs

LMICs share to a considerable degree some features in common which are likely to affect the policy recommendations that are derived from the application of economic thinking to health systems. These features are discussed here and their relevance drawn out. They concern the economic structure of countries; the strength of political and social institutions including governance structures; management capacity in the public sector; and the influence of agencies external to the country. There is of course a spectrum of these features in LMICs, with some demonstrating highly under-developed markets and institutions, and others having institutions much closer to those in high-income countries. But it is important that these aspects of the country context are taken into account in policy prescriptions.

Many of these dimensions have been brought together under the general heading of "capacity" (Hilderbrand and Grindle 1994), which is considered to have internal and external dimensions. Internal aspects of capacity include human resources (skills and numbers), resource availability, the appropriateness of organizational structures and systems, and coordination between agencies involved in any particular task. External factors include the public sector institutional context such as civil service rules and regulations, and the broader societal context including the macroeconomic situation, government stability, and the richness of civil society institutions. This framework draws attention to the wider institutional factors that may hamper the effective functioning of health systems; it also indicates what types of reforms might be relevant in what types of settings.

3.3.1 Economic Structure

Four aspects of the economic structure of countries are important. First, the degree of poverty has a pervasive effect on health systems. At the household level, there is now a substantial body of evidence showing that for poorer groups, illness can readily lead to levels of cost that are catastrophic for household welfare, or alternatively the potential costs discourage households from seeking necessary care. Even a sequence of minor illnesses in children can be catastrophic in terms of diverting cash from other basic needs especially food, or putting households in debt to local money lenders. In one study, typical of many, around one-third of urban and rural households in an area on the Kenyan coast incurred monthly health-related costs exceeding 10 percent of household expenditure, half of these households were in the two lowest socioeconomic groups, and borrowing and gifts were the main strategies used to cope with costs (Chuma et al. 2007). In a similar, earlier study in Sri Lanka, Russell found that low but frequent illness burdens, often suffered by households with a chronically sick member or several young children, were a persistent shock to vulnerable households' income and assets, undermining attempts to save and invest or gradually pushing them into poverty (Russell 2007). He also found that low-income households had weaker social networks and could access fewer financial resources than better-off households. Hence in low-income countries, even more so than in the rich world, a strong case can be made for the provision of protection against financial costs and especially against the consequences of chronic illness. In the case of Sri Lanka, free hospital care appeared an especially important safety net: on the whole, primary care was affordable and often purchased in the private sector, whereas private hospital care was far more costly, leading people to use the public sector.

At the systems level, the poverty of a country severely affects its ability to collectively finance adequate access to health care. Historically it has been argued that a set of simple interventions would cost only a few dollars per capita per year. However, more recent costings of a package of high priority interventions, which allow for adequately funding both the package itself and the necessary support costs at higher levels, suggest that such costs are a substantial share of per capita income. For example, the costs of high coverage of the package of forty-nine interventions prioritized in the report of the Commission on Macroeconomics and Health amounted to $38 per year in low-income countries or 6 percent of GNP (WHO 2001). For least developed countries the latter would be 11.4 percent. These amounts greatly exceed current levels of government health expenditure and even total health expenditure, and do not include any allowance for expenditure on services outside the essential package—such as much hospital care. It is telling that those countries which have seen most rapid progress to universal coverage are the South-East Asian "tigers" which have experienced very rapid economic growth in recent decades. No country can afford all the health care it would like, but budget constraints in the developing world are of an order of magnitude different from those in high-income countries.

At the systems level, poverty has another consequence, which is that health worker remuneration reflects local income levels. Historically doctors and nurses have always been internationally mobile (for example, in the Caribbean—Walt et al. 2002), but the processes of globalization have made it easier for trained health workers to migrate to where salaries are higher and conditions of work better. Certain countries, such as Ghana and Malawi, have been especially affected by migration (Hongoro and McPake 2004). This issue has a number of consequences not just for human resource management policies within the health systems of low- and middle-income countries, but also for the health care delivery system. Task-shifting to lower levels of health workers, for example, is inevitable if the number of people on antiretroviral treatment is to be increased, and the scope for using community health workers is again the focus of attention (Haines et al. 2007). The issue of the health workforce is examined in greater depth in Chapter 21.

The second aspect of the economic structure of a country that is important, affecting especially health system financing, is the nature of the labor force. Developing countries, especially the poorest, are characterized by a small share of working age adults in the formal sector, and a large share in the informal economy. In some Latin American countries the informal share of the labor market is even growing (Gottret and Schieber 2006). A large informal sector makes it impossible to use payroll taxes as a major source of health care finance, and also hampers the government's ability to raise general tax revenue. Moreover, although the introduction of social health insurance in a country is usually accompanied by plans to extend it to the informal sector on a voluntary basis, the reality is that this proceeds extremely slowly (Mills 2007). Some see community-based insurance as the interim solution (Preker et al. 2002), but even here there are very few examples of schemes of any size emerging. Thus the structure of the labor force greatly affects the options available for collective financing. In addition, the informal nature of much income generation makes it difficult to target subsidies or exemptions to low-income groups since these cannot be easily identified.

The third aspect of the economic structure is income inequality. This is especially pronounced in middle-income countries, and has two consequences for health systems. One is that the buying power of the richer groups, given low quality public services, is focused on the private health sector, which then grows and attracts scarce physical resources such as doctors and nurses away from the public sector, further increasing disparities in quality between public and private services. The second consequence is that when different income groups use different services of different quality, this makes it very difficult to move towards universal arrangements. Leveling down is not an option, but leveling up is very costly. Moreover, large income inequalities may prevent the emergence of the social solidarity necessary to finance a universal system.

The fourth aspect is an under-developed private sector. This has a number of consequences. For example, it limits the scope for competition as a driver of efficiency and low prices in market arrangements. While this may be less relevant with respect to facilities such as hospitals, where a number of factors limit price competition in countries at all levels of development, it is certainly relevant to pharmaceuticals, and to the efficiency of the myriad suppliers of inputs to the health sector. Goodman has found in Tanzania, for example, that despite the apparent number of drug sellers in rural markets, there is a high degree of concentration, and high price mark-ups (Goodman et al. 2009). Another consequence is that limited private sector capacity limits the scope for deriving increased efficiency from contracting out services to the private sector. In a number of countries, attempts to contract out ancillary services such as security, cleaning, and laundry have been hampered by the very limited capacity of the private sector to respond (Mills 1997). More broadly, a small private sector is unable to serve as a source of financial and management expertise to the public sector—a strategy often used in rich countries when public institutions are considered to be in need of reform or of specific business skills such as financial management.

3.3.2 Political and Social Institutions

By definition, the less developed a country, the weaker tend to be its political, economic, and social institutions. These include the institutions of democracy and representation, of civil society, and of professional groupings. While these institutions do not function perfectly in the rich world, and indeed their very long history can inhibit change, nonetheless they form the backdrop to the relationships within health systems that help promote efficiency and equity. This argument is best justified through examples of where common health sector policies or reform prescriptions do not work as expected.

One common reform policy is that of hospital autonomy. Comparing public hospitals in the developing and developed world, the management of the former tends to be much more centralized. Given evidence of considerable inefficiencies, a standard policy prescription has been to increase the degree of autonomy, especially financial autonomy (Mills et al. 2001). However, there is some evidence that the introduction of such policies has harmed the access of the poor, since increased fees have been imposed without proper implementation of exemptions arrangements (Hanson et al. 2001). In general, despite efforts to strengthen the governance structure of hospitals, the interests of the poor, and indeed of users in general, are not well reflected in the decision-structures of hospitals and there is little pressure on them to be seen to be serving the public interest.

Another example is that of capitation payment. It is well recognized that while capitation payment provides an incentive to keep expenditure within a budget, it also runs the risk of limiting quantity and quality of care to an undesirable extent, especially with capitation payment to commercial providers with incentives to maximize profits and select healthier patients. In high-income countries this has not been found to be a major concern given professional ethics and self-regulation. A study in Thailand—where capitation is the mode of payment used in the social health insurance scheme for all levels of care—found some evidence that private hospitals limited the quantity and quality of inputs for insured patients (Mills et al. 2000). In some instances—for example, use of generic drugs—this may have reduced costs with no harmful effects on quality of care. In other instances—for example, providing shorter courses of drugs to hypertensive patients—this may have increased non-compliance because of the need for more frequent visits. There was also some evidence of dumping more costly patients by discouraging them from registering the following year. Monitoring focused on structural quality, with no attention to process indicators or to encouraging the supportive broader institutional environment required to ensure ethical behavior. This would include quality assurance programs, and active medical councils ensuring high standards of medical ethics. In Thailand, at the time of the study, it was left to an active media to detect and publicize problems of medical care quality.

A third example is that of risk protection. The essential argument for insurance is that it reduces financial risk. However, Wagstaff and Lindelow (2008) found in China that health insurance appeared to increase out-of-pocket payment and the risk of catastrophic and large expenses. Given their data, they were not able to determine the precise reasons for this. However, other studies point to the very strong drivers to generate revenue in Chinese hospitals (Liu and Mills 2003, 2005), and thus as Wagstaff and Lindelow suggest, it is likely that at least part of the increased payment was due to providers exploiting their informational advantage and providing expensive medical care that the individual would not necessarily have chosen knowing its costs and benefits. In this case, although hospitals were ostensibly "public" they functioned in practice as income generating enterprises, without the normal checks and balances that professional self-regulation and a relatively informed patient population provide in a more developed setting.

More broadly, Schick (1998) has criticized the relevance of developed world public sector reforms to the institutional setting of developing countries. He argued, for example, that "in New Zealand, formal contracts and internal markets were feasible because the country had a robust market sector and established mechanisms for enforcing contracts" whereas in a developing country context, "it would be foolhardy to entrust public managers with complete freedom over resources when they have not yet internalized the habit of spending public money according to prescribed rules."

3.3.3 Management Capacity

Within the context of weak institutions, management limitations impose a major barrier to the capacity of the health system in developing countries to raise money for health and to translate inputs into outputs. Such limitations go well beyond simple numbers of managers or levels of education and training, to encompass information and financial management systems, for example.

Efficient performance of revenue collection systems is a major problem for tax authorities and social insurance agencies alike, though some forms of tax are less difficult to collect than others. It is common for enrollment in social health insurance schemes to fall well below the size of the target population, and in addition for non-payment to be a major problem. In Kazakhstan, for example, premium collection amounted to only 9–52 percent of expected revenues in different oblasts (Gottret and Schieber 2006), and in Colombia, evasion in the contributory scheme was the equivalent of 2.75 percent of GDP in 2000 (Escobar and Panopolou 2003). It can be argued that public care free at the point of use and funded by general tax revenues is a less costly and less managerially intensive way of collecting and spending money for the provision of health care than insurance arrangements, since the former avoids the need for enrollment, premium collection, eligibility checks at facilities and monitoring compliance with insurance regulations. Tax collection brings with it its own difficulties, though reform of tax administration has been one of the better performing programs of the World Bank (World Bank 2008).

Management capacity has also been shown to be a major problem in the implementation of policy changes (Mills et al. 2001). While most attention has focused on the adoption of appropriate policies, many of the reasons for poor health system performance have their roots in implementation problems rather than policy design deficiencies. For example, the commonly recommended policy of user fees with exemptions for the poor is stymied by the inability of virtually all countries to implement an effective exemption system, even when exemption criteria are simple—for example, children under 5. While it is true that lack of incentives to give fee waivers is a major problem, the solution, of reimbursing facilities for lost user fee revenue, depends on effective financial management—which was problematic in Ghana, for example, when this solution was tried (Witter et al. 2007). Poor performance of contracting out arrangements is another area where management capacity has been a limiting factor, explaining why anticipated benefits may be less than expected. In South Africa, for example, the government authorities relied on the contractor itself (a commercial company) to draw up the contract, and then failed to effectively monitor its performance (Broomberg et al. 1997). Most recently, the introduction in low-income countries of conditional cash transfers, where financial incentives are given to households and often also providers to encourage specific behaviors (for example, delivery in a health facility), have hit problems of implementation. Evidence of their success originates from middle-income countries, especially in Latin America, where management capacity is greater. Preliminary evidence from Nepal, for example, indicates as in Ghana, that weak financial management is the critical bottleneck in effective implementation (Powell-Jackson et al. 2008).

In addition to poor financial management, weak information systems have a pervasive effect on the functioning of the health system (Mills et al. 2001). Table 3.5 summarizes the findings from a four-country study (Ghana, Zimbabwe, India, Sri Lanka) on how weak information systems affected specific policies, namely increased autonomy for public hospitals, use of user fees (with exemptions) as a source of health financing, contracting out services to the private sector, and adequate regulation of the private sector. In all cases, poor information was a binding constraint on the operation of these policies.

The overall consequences of weak institutions and management capacity is indicated by analysis of the relationship between health outcomes and the World Bank's CPIA (Country Policy and Institutional Assessment) index, which assesses how conducive a country's policy and institutional framework is to encouraging poverty reduction, sustainable growth, and the effective use of development assistance. Analysis of the elasticity of health outcomes to government health spending found that spending had a larger effect on health outcomes in countries with higher CPIA scores (Wagstaff and Claeson 2004). Of the four elements in the CPIA index, public sector management was the weakest and had improved least over time (the others being economic management, structural policy, and policy for social inclusion) (Gottret and Schieber 2006).

While it is undoubtedly true that problems of institutions and management capacity demonstrate a gradient from low- to high-income countries, rather than there being two distinctly different groups of types of country, nonetheless the differences are such that policy prescriptions appropriate to high-income country settings may fail in low capacity settings.

3.3.4 External Dependence for Health Financing

External dependence is primarily a problem of low-income countries. Table 3.2 showed that 22.5 percent of total health expenditure came from external sources in low-income countries. The great majority of this (around 70 percent in an analysis by Greco et al. 2007) flows through governments (most of the remainder going to the private sector), suggesting that on average around 36 percent of government health expenditure is from external sources. This share can be much higher in certain favored countries—for example, probably over 70 percent in Uganda, Mozambique, and Cambodia. While flows of aid are an important income stream for health, they bring with them some major complications which can affect the performance of the overall health system.

Firstly, there is the problem of predictability. Aid finances activities which are usually not short-term, but commitments are time limited. Hence countries do not know whether funding is available in the long term, and flows of funds can vary considerably from year to year. Figure 3.5 shows the change over time in external resources for health in nine African countries. Such variation poses major planning difficulties, and is one of the reasons why absorptive capacity is a constant problem. It can also inhibit sensible policy change—for example, one reason why the shift to an effective antimalarial combination

Table 3.5 The Impact of Weak Information Systems

Policy	Identified weakness in information system	Impact of weakness
Autonomous hospitals	Cost accounting systems poorly developed and returns generally late and incomplete	Difficult to move towards performance-based budgeting without first strengthening systems
User fees and exemptions	Limited financial data available (e.g. revenues generated, exemptions given, spending profiles)	Weakens monitoring of: collection mechanisms, effectiveness of exemptions, and appropriateness of spending decisions
	Non-compliance with new financial information systems (Ghana)	
Contracting-out	Limited data on public sector costs or performance	Makes it difficult to evaluate wisdom of contracting-out service
Regulation	Absence of complete database on private providers	No list to use for conducting inspections of private providers
	Inadequate systems for collecting information on case load in private sector	Difficult to compile complete picture of health service provision and hence to develop policies towards the private sector
	Inadequate records kept by private sector providers	Difficulty of proving or disproving cases of medical malpractice

Source: Adapted from Mills et al. 2001.

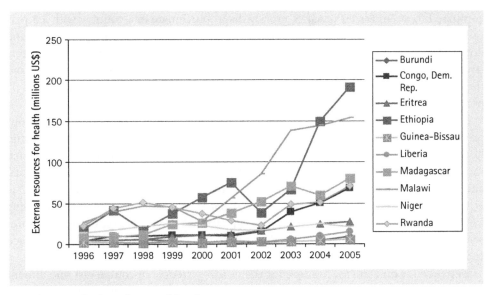

FIGURE 3.5 Volatility of external funding

Notes: Calculated from NHA data on % THE from external resources, available at <http://www.who.int/nha/country/en/> accessed December 1, 2008.

was delayed in Africa, despite a failing drug, was that the replacement drug was far more expensive and it was not clear how a switch would be financed in the longer term.

A second major problem is the fragmentation of aid flows. Despite the 2005 Paris Declaration on aid effectiveness, which agreed improvements in country ownership and harmonization of arrangements, progress has been slow in improving coordination of flows of funds. Acharya et al., for example, pointed out that Vietnam, a fairly representative aid recipient with aid flows of around 5 percent of GDP, had twenty-five official bilateral donors, nineteen official multilateral donors, and about 350 international NGOs in 2002 (Acharya et al. 2006). They collectively accounted for over 8000 projects, or about one project per 9000 people. Such fragmentation has pervasive system effects, over-burdening limited planning and management capacity, skewing incentives amongst managers and health providers in terms of where to direct their effort, and producing both duplication and neglect in service delivery, depending on which areas are favored by donors.

The third main problem is the effects of the politics of donor countries, which are an important influence on the type of aid, what it is for and who receives it. Recent years have seen massive attention given especially to HIV/AIDS, though also to other diseases such as TB, malaria, and polio. The disease specific concerns of key donors have clearly skewed resource allocation within countries—for example, a Rwanda government report stated that $18m was earmarked for malaria (the biggest cause of mortality and morbidity) and just $1m for the integrated management of childhood illnesses, compared to $47m for HIV/AIDS, grossly disproportionate in a country with a 3 per-cent infection rate (MOH 2006). Moreover some 27 percent of total Government and donor expenditure was absorbed in administration, reflecting the proliferation of actors (twenty-one donors and over forty NGOs), the large number of discrete projects, and the perpetual need to re-negotiate in a situation of very short donor pipelines, with 55 percent of donor projects due to end within a year.

More broadly, health need often does not appear to figure large in donor decisions on which countries to support. An analysis of donor funding for maternal and child health showed that a number of very needy countries—for example, with maternal mortality rates over 1000 per 100,000 live births—received less funding for maternal and neonatal health per livebirth than countries with lower rates (see Figure 3.6; Powell-Jackson et al. 2006). Regression analysis of the determinants of this funding averaged over the period 2003–6 showed no relationship with degree of need as repre-sented by disability adjusted life years lost due to maternal and neonatal deaths (Greco et al. 2008).

Dependence on external funding for the health system is of course just one dimen-sion of a broader vulnerability of low-income countries, who have much fewer resources to cope with economic vicissitudes, and who face difficulties in competing in increas-ingly global markets for physical and human capital. The problems of outmigration of skilled health personnel, discussed earlier, is another manifestation of how this vulnera-bility affects the health system.

3.4 Unresolved Debates

Given the numerous challenges of financing and organizing the health systems of LMICs, and the weakness of information such as that available for high-income coun-tries that would enable uncontroversial conclusions to be drawn on health systems per-formance and how this relates to different patterns of health system arrangements, it is not surprising that there are many unresolved debates.

Out-of-pocket payments and user fees remain a continuous cause of controversy. While the evidence is strong that payments discourage use of health care by the poorest (Palmer et al. 2004), and user fees at public hospitals can readily give rise to catastrophic payments where exemptions systems do not function (Patcharanarumol et al. 2009), on pragmatic grounds they are a contribution to health financing, and they are one of the more feasible sources of domestic funding for low-income countries where the contri-bution of social insurance is limited by the structure of the workforce and tax mobilization is weak. It is clearly more desirable to increase tax mobilization and devote more to health, but countries may not choose to spend increased tax revenues in this way, given the many competing demands on their budgets.

Universal arrangements versus targeting public assistance to the poor also remains a source of considerable controversy. Strong arguments can be put in favor of the

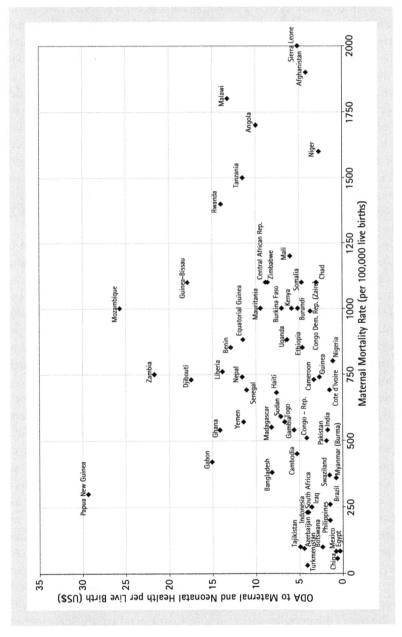

FIGURE 3.6 External funding for maternal and neonatal health in relation to need

Source: Powell-Jackson et al. 2006

Note: ODA = Official Development Assistance

importance of a well-funded, publicly led, and universal health system (Gilson et al. 2007), and indeed these arguments now appear well-accepted in middle-income countries such as Thailand. In low-income countries, however, resource limitations make it difficult to provide universally even a limited package of high priority interventions, despite the increase in external funding seen recently. The commonly recommended solution is to target resources on the poorest, but there is little evidence so far that such targeting can be done effectively, or that it is cost-effective relative to broader approaches to service provision (Hanson et al. 2007).

In LMICs with a reasonably substantial formal sector workforce, an interesting debate is developing on whether social health insurance or tax funding should be the basis for the financing of a universal health system (Mills 2007). In recent years, social health insurance has been the preferred financing source. However, Wagstaff (2007) recently argued that for a number of reasons, not least implications for the cost of labor, general tax revenues were a preferable source. Arguments seen historically in Europe between these two main sources of financing are being played out in the arena of LMICs, with the creation of a consortium to promote social health protection involving ILO, WHO, the World Bank, France and Germany.

As in high-income countries, pay for performance experiments are now happening in low- and middle-income countries on quite a wide scale, from conditional cash transfers to vouchers for specific services or products (e.g. insecticide treated mosquito nets), performance contracts for NGOs, and indeed performance contracts for individual health workers. While there is evidence from middle-income countries that pay for performance can stimulate use of preventive services, for example, the evidence base for low-income countries is extremely thin, and there have been no studies on whether it is more cost-effective to introduce these arrangements rather than, for example, strengthen more conventional approaches to service delivery (Lagarde et al. 2007).

Within service delivery, a key area of controversy is the role of the private sector. The private sector is a reality which many people use, either because they prefer it or because there is no alternative. It can be a useful source of care close to people's homes, but also can be a source of very poor quality care and can generate catastrophic payments, especially for the poorest. Recent initiatives have sought to explore how promotion of the private sector can benefit the poor in Africa (IFC 2007), but the evidence remains very weak to justify emphasizing either private finance or provision as the main solution to the health needs of the poorest. More broadly, the appropriate role of the private sector as a complement to the public sector is also controversial. On the one hand it can be argued that it provides a safety valve for the less poor, enabling public services to focus on serving the poor; on the other hand it can be argued that in the context of extremely limited human and financial resources, a private sector serving a reasonably substantial share of the population absorbs more than its fair share of resources and makes these unavailable to the rest of the population, in contrast to universal arrangements where all population groups share the same services.

Finally, perhaps the greatest challenge with respect to health system design lies in fragile states, where by definition governments lack the capability to play a leadership role. Issues such as sources of financing, decisions on priority health services, who should provide services, and trade-offs between seeking short terms gains versus creating longer term sustainable systems, are even more difficult in this context. But there is a gross lack of evidence in this area to guide public policy.

REFERENCES

ACHARYA, A., DE LIMA, A. T. F., and MOORE, M. (2006), "Proliferation and Fragmentation: Transactions Costs and the Value of Aid," *Journal of Development Studies*, 42(1): 1–21.

BARNUM, H. and KUTZIN, J. (1993), *Public Hospitals in Developing Countries: Resource Use, Cost, Financing* (Baltimore, MD: Johns Hopkins University Press).

BROOMBERG, J., MASOBE, P., and MILLS, A. (1997), "To Purchase or to Provide? The Relative Efficiency of Contracting Out Versus Direct Public Provision of Hospital Services in South Africa," in S. Bennett, B. McPake, and A. Mills (eds.), *Private Health Providers in Developing Countries: Serving the Public Interest?* (London: Zed Press).

CHUMA, J., GILSON, L., and MOLYNEUX, C. (2007), "Treatment-seeking Behaviour, Cost Burdens and Coping Strategies Among Rural and Urban Households in Coastal Kenya: An Equity Analysis," *Tropical Medicine & International Health*, 12(5): 673–86.

ESCOBAR, M.-L. and PANOPOLOU, P. (2003), "Columbia: The Economic Foundation of Peace," in M. Giugale, O. Lafourcade, and C. Luff (eds.), *Health* (Washington, DC: World Bank), 653–707.

GILSON, L., DOHERTY, J., LOEWENSEN, R., et al. (2007), "Challenging Inequity Through Health Systems. Final Report Knowledge Network on Health Systems" (Geneva: WHO Commission on the Social Determinants of Health).

GOODMAN, C., NJAU, J. D., et al. (2004), "Retail Supply of Malaria-related Drugs in Rural Tanzania: Risks and Opportunities," *Tropical Medicine and International Health*, 9(6): 655–63.

—— KACHUR, P., ABDULLA, S., BLOLAND, P., and MILLS, A. (2009), "Concentration and Drug Prices in the Retail Market for Malaria Treatment in Rural Tanzania," *Health Economics*, 18(6): 727–42.

GOTTRET, P. and SCHIEBER, G. (2006), *Health Financing Revisited* (Washington, DC: World Bank).

GRECO, G., POWELL-JACKSON, T., BORGHI, J., and MILLS, A. (2010), "Countdown to 2015: The Financing Gap for Scaling up Child, Newborn and Maternal Health Between 2003 and 2006." London School of Hygiene and Tropical Medicine: Health Economics and Financing Programme, Draft, May.

HAINES, A., SANDERS, D., LEHMANN, U. et al. (2007), "Achieving Child Survival Goals: Potential Contribution of Community Health Workers," *Lancet*, 369(9579): 2121–31.

HANSON, K. and BERMAN, P. (1998), "Private Health Care Provision in Developing Countries: A Preliminary Analysis of Levels and Composition," *Health Policy Plan*, 13(3): 195–211.

—— ARCHARD, L., and McPAKE, B. (2001), "Creating Markets in Hospital Care: The Adoption of Developed Country Health Sector Reforms by Developing Countries. Is It Appropriate?," *Tropical Medicine and International Health*, 6(10): 747–8.

—— WORRALL, E., and WISEMAN, V. (2007), "Targeting Services Towards the Poor: A Review of Targeting Mechanisms and Their Effectiveness," in S. Bennett, L. Gilson, and A. Mills (eds.), *Health, Economic Development and Household Poverty: From Understanding to Action* (London: Routledge).

HENSHER, M., PRICE, M., and ADOMAKOH, S. (2006), "Referral Hospitals," in D. T. Jamison, A. R. Measham, J. B. Breman, et al. (eds.), *Disease Control Priorities in Developing Countries* (2nd edn.; Washington DC: World Bank and Oxford University Press).

HILDERBRAND, M. E. and GRINDLE, M. S. (1994), *Building Sustainable Capacity: Challenges for the Public Sector* (Cambridge, MA: UNDP and HIID, Harvard University).

HONGORO, C. and McPAKE, B. (2004), "How to Bridge the Gap in Human Resources for Health," *Lancet*, 364(9443): 1451–6.

IFC (INTERNATIONAL FINANCE CORPORATION) (2007), *The Business of Health in Africa International Finance Corporation* (Washington, DC: IFC).

KWON, S. (2003), "Payment System Reform for Health Care Providers in Korea," *Health Policy Plan*, 18(1): 84–92.

LAGARDE, M., HAINES, A., and PALMER, N. (2007), "Conditional Cash Transfers for Improving Uptake of Health Interventions in Low- and Middle-income Countries: A Systematic Review," *Jama*, 298(16): 1900–10.

LIU, X. and MILLS, A. (2003), "The Influence of Bonus Payments to Doctors on Hospital Revenue: Results of a Quasi-experimental Study," *Applied Health Economics and Health Policy*, 2(2): 91–8.

——(2005), "The Effect of Performance-related Pay of Hospital Doctors on Hospital Behaviour: A Case Study From Shandong, China," *Human Resources for Health*, 3: 11.

LOPEZ, A. D., MATHERS, C. D., EZZATI, M., et al. (2006), *Global Burden of Disease and Risk Factors* (Washington DC: Oxford University Press and the World Bank).

MAREK, T., O'FARRELL, C., YAMAMOTO, C., and ZABLE, I. (2005), "Trends and Opportunities in Public–Private Partnerships to Improve Health Services Delivery in Africa." SARA Project. World Bank, Washington, DC.

MILLS, A. (1997), "Contractual Relationships Between Government and the Commercial Private Sector in Developing Countries," in S. Bennett, B. McPake, and A. Mills (eds.), *Private Health Providers in Developing Countries: Serving the Public Interest?* (London: Zed Press).

—— (2007), "Strategies to Achieve Universal Coverage: Are There Lessons from Middle Income Countries?" A literature review commissioned by the Health Systems Knowledge Network, Commission on Social Determinants of Health (Geneva: WHO).

—— and RANSON, K. (2005), "The Design of Health Systems," in M. H. Merson, R. E. Black, and A. Mills (eds.), *International Public Health: Diseases, Programs, Systems and Policies*, 2nd edn. (Boston: Jones and Bartlett Publishers).

——BENNETT, S., SIRIWANARANGSUN, P., et al. (2000), "The Response of Providers to Capitation Payment: A Case-study from Thailand," *Health Policy*, 51(3): 163–80.

——, BENNETT, S., and RUSSELL, S. (2001), *The Challenge of Health Sector Reform: What Must Governments Do?* (Oxford: Macmillan Press).

MOH (MINISTRY OF ECONOMICS AND FINANCE AND MINISTRY OF HEALTH) (2006), "Scaling Up to Achieve the Health MDGS in Rwanda." A background study for the High-level Forum Meeting in Tunis 2006.

PALMER, N., MUELLER, D. H., GILSON, L., et al. (2004), "Health Financing to Promote Access in Low Income Settings: How Much Do We Know?" *Lancet*, 364(9442): 1365–70.

PATCHARANARUMOL, W., MILLS, A., and TANGCHAROENSATHIEN, V. (2009), "Dealing With the Cost of Illness: The Experience of Four Villages in Lao PDR," *Journal of International Development*, 21: 212–30.

POWELL-JACKSON, T. and MILLS, A. (2007), "A Review of Health Resource Tracking in Developing Countries," *Health Policy Plan*, 22(6): 353–62.

—— BORGHI, J., MUELLER, D. H., et al. (2006), "Countdown to 2015: Tracking Donor Assistance to Maternal, Newborn, and Child Health," *Lancet*, 368(9541): 1077–87.

POWELL-JACKSON, T., MORRISON, J., TIWARI, S., NEUPANE, B. D., and COSTELLO, A. M. (2008), "The Experiences of Districts in Implementing a National Incentive Programme to Promote Safe Delivery in Nepal," *BMC Health Service Research*, 9: 97.

PREKER, A. S., JAKAB, M., and SCHNEIDER, M. (2002), "Health Reforms in Central and Eastern Europe and the Former Soviet Union," in E. Mossialos, A. Dixon, J. Figueras, et al. (eds.), *Funding Health Care: Options for Europe*. European Observatory on Health Care Systems Series (Buckingham, UK: Open University Press).

RUSSELL, S. (2007), "Coping with the Costs of Illness: Vulnerability and Resilience Among Poor Households in Urban Sri Lanka," in S. Bennett, L. Gilson, and A. Mills (eds.), *Health, Economic Development and Household Poverty: From Understanding to Action* (London: Routledge).

SCHICK, A. (1998), "Why Most Developing Countries Should Not Try New Zealand's Reforms," *The World Bank Research Observer*, 13(1): 123–31.

THOMAS, S. and MUIRHEAD, D. (2000), "National Health Accounts Project." The Public Sector Report, University of Cape Town, Cape Town, South Africa.

UNICEF (2008), "Tracking Progress in Maternal, Newborn & Child Survival: The 2008 Report." Countdown to 2015: Maternal, Newborn & Child Survival, UNICEF.

WAGSTAFF, A. (2007), "Social Health Insurance Reexamined" (Washington, DC: World Bank).

—— and CLAESON, M. (2004), "The Millennium Development Goals for Health: Rising to the Challenges" (Washington, DC: World Bank).

—— and LINDELOW, M. (2008), "Can Insurance Increase Financial Risk? The Curious Case of Health Insurance in China," *Journal of Health Economics*, 27(4): 990–1005.

WALT, G., ANTONIUS, R., DOKOUI, S. et al. (2002), "The Historical Development of Human Resources Policies in the Health Sector of Four Caribbean Territories: Imitated or Created?" *Health Policy*, 62(1): 85–101.

WORLD BANK (IEG) (2008), "Public Sector Reform: What Works and Why? An IEG Evaluation of World Bank Support" (Washington, DC: World Bank).

WHO (2000), "The World Health Report 2000. Health Systems: Improving Performance" (Geneva: WHO).

—— (2001), "Macroeconomics and Health: Investing in Health for Economic Development. Report of the Commission on Macroeconomics and Health" (Geneva: WHO).

—— (2004), "World Pharmaceutical Situations Report 2004," (Geneva: WHO).

WITTER, S., ARHINFUL, D. K., KUSI, A., et al. (2007), "The Experience of Ghana in Implementing a User Fee Exemption Policy to Provide Free Delivery Care," *Reproductive Health Matters*, 15(30): 61–71.

CHAPTER 4

....

THE POLITICAL ECONOMY
OF HEALTH CARE

....

CAROLYN HUGHES TUOHY AND SHERRY GLIED

GOVERNMENT is everywhere deeply involved in health and health care. The large government role exists, in part, as an efficiency-enhancing response to the market failures described elsewhere in this volume. Government is also important in health care because of the importance accorded to the redistribution of health resources for equity reasons, also described in the volume. Regardless of why government is involved, the presence of government as an actor in the system introduces a distinctive set of forces on how it operates.

There is a substantial literature on political economy in economics but it is only sporadically applied to health care (Mueller 2003). The political economy of health and health care is also of interest to political scientists, but in this literature, too, its presence is less than proportional to the size of health care in government activities.

This chapter describes the role of government in the health care system and the factors and forces that determine how that role is played. In so doing, it examines how theories of political economy drawn from both economics and political science have been and can be applied to this sector. It first describes the scope of government in health care, and then examines how theories of political economy can be applied to the sector. The chapter then examines the implications of these theories for political choices under three headings: interest groups, voting behavior, and institutions.

4.1 SCOPE OF GOVERNMENT INVOLVEMENT
IN HEALTH CARE

....

Governments play several roles in the health care system. Here, we focus on four broad categories of government action in health care markets, linked to corresponding market failures: health care as a merit good; information gaps; infrastructure as a public good; and externalities.

4.1.1 Health Care as a Merit Good

The first of these roles deals with health care as a merit good, which should be distributed among the population through some concept of equity (essentially, some version of the view that access to health care should depend upon need—see Olsen, Chapter 34, this volume). While the distribution of health care delivery varies considerably, every developed country, and most developing countries, implement policies to redistribute resources designed in some way to increase the equity of distribution of health care. Moreover, public redistribution of resources associated with health care has long historical precedent (e.g., Dutch almshouses, the English 1601 Poor Law, poor relief for the sick, etc.). Redistribution in health care may focus on providing a minimum standard to those with low incomes (Pauly 1971). A substantial literature argues, however, that health care redistribution seeks not only to maintain minimum standards but also to "limit the domain" of inequality in health care receipt (Tobin 1970). This focus on reducing inequality calls for government to play a role both in determining the optimal level of subsidy for lower income groups and also, potentially, in constraining the health care purchasing decisions of those with higher income (Lindsay 1969; Glied 1998).[1] Governmental constraints on those with higher incomes may also result from short- to medium-term considerations of potential feedback effects. For example, under conditions of constrained supply of health care providers and facilities, allowing higher income consumers unlimited choice of services may limit the provision of more essential care to those with lower incomes. Governments may therefore deem it necessary to constrain choice, at least until the supply constraint can be relaxed.

The redistributive "work" done through public insurance or in-kind health care benefits reduces income inequality over and above the effect of cash transfers. However, once actual utilization over the full life-cycle is taken into account, the redistributive impact of government health care programs is reduced, though not eliminated (Garfinkel et al. 2006; Glied 2008b).

4.1.2 Information Gaps

A second longstanding function of government in health care is to redress information gaps through regulatory action. The complexity of biological processes means that consumers face very high information costs in assessing the health implications of various goods and services, and may be vulnerable to undue influence from providers. Initially, government regulation of health care focused on protecting the safety of consumers. Many of the earliest incursions of government into the regulation of product quality were in the sphere of health (for example, the regulation of food and drugs

---

[1] In Canada, for example, private insurance for publicly provided services is either banned or effectively tightly constrained. The degree of constraint varies by province (Flood and Archibald 2001; Tuohy 2009).

dates back to the 1920s). This protection also extended to licensure and regulation of the health care professions. The information gap between providers and consumers of health care services means that consumers must enter into an "agency relationship" with providers, trusting them to act in the consumer's best interest, as discussed in Chapter 25, in this volume. The typical mode of regulating this agency relationship has been for the state to recognize the authority of professional self-regulatory bodies and progressively integrate them into the governance apparatus of the state (Starr 1982). In effect, this establishes a "second-level" agency relationship between the state and the professional body.

From an economic perspective, much of this regulatory function has an explicit or implicit redistributive component. In many arenas, private organizations offer complementary systems of quality validation (the "Good Housekeeping" seal of approval; specialty society certifications; and hospital quality approval organizations such as the Joint Commission on the Accreditation of Healthcare Organizations). The requirement that purveyors of health care associated goods and services meet minimal government standards in order to practice seeks to protect those who would be unaware of, or unwilling to pay a premium price for, privately accredited goods and services.

The regulatory functions of government extend beyond ex ante development and enforcement of quality standards. Governments also develop and maintain the legal infrastructure that enforces ex post quality standards through liability regimes. The rules governing the liability of health care goods and services providers (products liability and malpractice litigation, in particular), have been a focus of economic study, especially in contexts where these systems are very costly (see Chapter 22 in this volume).

Government regulatory efforts to address information gaps also extend to the health insurance market. The existence of asymmetric information between purchasers and sellers of health insurance provides a rationale for many forms of government intervention. To address the possibility that purchasers of coverage are unable to assess the viability of insurers, most countries regulate the solvency and financial practices of insurance companies. The existence of private information about health risks raises the possibility of adverse selection in health insurance markets, which could lead to the disintegration of markets for private insurance (Rothschild and Stiglitz 1976; Newhouse 1996).

Even observable information about health risks poses difficulties in health insurance markets. Rational consumers would presumably wish to be protected against the financial consequences of future deteriorations in health states. It is, however, problematic even in theory, and apparently unworkable in practice, to create viable long-term health insurance contracts (see Cochrane 1995 for discussion of the theory). Government regulation of private health insurance markets may offer a proxy for such long-term contracts by forcing the pooling of people with differing health risks. Finally, under many social welfare functions, society would also benefit from insuring people against bad health endowments (for example, being born with a genetic defect), and this is a role only governments are able to perform.

4.1.3 Infrastructure as a Public Good

A third set of functions of government involves making direct or indirect investments in health and health care infrastructure. This category includes investments in public health, such as the construction of water and sewage infrastructure; investments in health care facilities, such as hospitals and clinics (Hill-Burton funding in the United States); investments in the education of health care personnel; investment in information technology and communications infrastructure; and investments in health care research. Government makes indirect investments through conferring patents in the pharmaceutical and device sectors (Cutler and Miller 2005).

The tremendous importance of knowledge and technological development in generating improvements in health outcomes (Deaton 2004) implies that investment in such public goods is a critical government function. New health care knowledge that is not embodied in tradeable goods is a public good, whose benefits redound to those alive today throughout the world as well as to future generations. Without government subsidy, these goods will likely be under-produced in private markets (Glied 2008a). Certain investments in health care service delivery, particularly the eradication of infectious disease or of drug resistant organisms, also convey enormous benefits to future generations and are likely to be under-produced without public intervention (Philipson 2000).

4.1.4 Externalities

A final set of government functions involves the regulation and taxation of goods and behaviors that generate externalities. Both positive externalities—such as immunization practices—and negative externalities—such as second-hand smoke—arise in health care. In situations where transactions costs exist, the private market is unlikely to choose the right level of behavior to control externalities (Coase 1960). Governments can intervene through the direct regulation of such behaviors, and through Pigouvian subsidies and taxes.

Together, these functions mean that the government plays a very significant role in the health care sector. Across the OECD, government funds about 73 percent of total health care expenditures, and about two-thirds of expenditures on infrastructure (see Figure 4.1). As the discussion above suggests, even the share that is not directly financed by the government is heavily shaped by government regulatory and investment policy. No country has—and few have ever had—a purely market-driven health care system completely devoid of government influence.

Conversely, health care is an increasingly important component of the function of government. Across the OECD, about 15 percent of all tax revenue is devoted to health care—a proportion that is steadily increasing. Moreover, the distribution of tax revenue through health care requires much more regulation—of provider prices, organizations, quality—than many other forms of redistribution. It is, thus, likely that

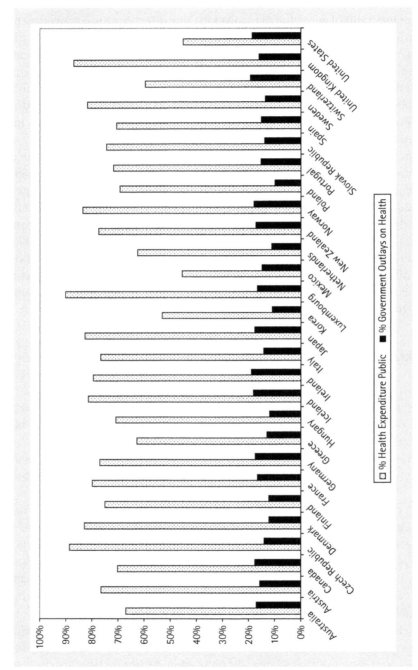

FIGURE 4.1 Government health expenditures and as a share of all government outlays, 2005

Source: OECD 2008.

a much greater share of the real work of modern governments is related to the health care sector.

4.2 POLITICAL ECONOMY THEORIES APPLIED TO HEALTH CARE

Economic theory suggests that the government's role in the health care system is a response to the various market failures described above. In most theoretical models, government is characterized as a benevolent and omniscient social planner that puts to right the failures of the market. In reality, of course, government, and the individuals working within government, are themselves actors facing incentives and constraints of their own. The particular nature of the incentives and constraints facing policymakers depends on details of institutional and policy design. A parliamentary government differs in its scope of action from a presidential one; a constitution places limits on the actions of either; proportional representation creates different incentives than does single-member-district representation; federalism creates a new set of interactions. The inherent structural differences of various governments create meaningful variations in how they respond to a more universal set of market failures. Furthermore, once particular policy frameworks are adopted, they subsequently channel the behavior of government as well as other actors. While economic theories of government behavior may have substantial and broad explanatory power, the actual form of government's role in a specific health care system can only be understood by taking account of the interaction of several key groups of actors within this institutional context.

Economists from Adam Smith on have considered the role of government as that of an actor in itself. The modern economics literature on political economy stems from the contributions of George Stigler, who developed the capture theory of regulation (1971), George Buchanan and Gordon Tullock, who developed the theory of rent-seeking behavior (1962), and William Niskanen, whose theories of bureaucratic behavior are noted below (1971). These and subsequent theories of government action do not map onto the framework of market failure delineated above. Rather, they describe how governments respond to the incentives and constraints they face, independent of the nature of the underlying economic problem.

The political science literature takes a different starting point, seeking to understand the distribution of power in the health care arena. Early studies focused on organized groups, principally the medical profession, as further discussed below. More recently, the role of institutions in shaping behavior has come to dominate the political science literature, much of which takes a comparative, cross-jurisdictional approach. Whether from an economics or a political science viewpoint, political economists seek to understand government policy toward health care as the outcome of the behavior of actors pursuing interests in the face of institutional incentives and constraints.

Very broadly speaking, there are four categories of interests in the health care arena: health care providers (including health care professionals and suppliers of goods, notably pharmaceuticals), recipients of care (patients and potential patients), third-party private payers for care (insurers) and governments. Theories about the interactions of those groups, and the implications of those interactions for the role of government, fall under three general headings, depending upon their principal explanatory focus: interest group organization, institutions, and the electoral system.

4.2.1 Theories Focusing on Interest Groups

These theories look at the capacity of each of the four broad sets of actors in the health care field (including government actors) to mobilize collectively in pursuit of their own interests. This approach dominated the early literature on the political economy of health care, focusing on the asymmetrical political and economic power enjoyed by certain interests in the area, especially the medical profession and later private insurers. This advantage arises from imbalances in the control of certain key resources and in the distribution of costs and benefits. As noted above, the acquisition of specialized knowledge gives health care providers control of a key information resource. The medical profession was, as Moran puts it, "the first great interest in health care to achieve effective organization; and as mass consumption of health care developed in the wake of the transformation of the curative efficacy of medicine, [doctors] emerged as the managers of the consumption process" (Moran 1999:186–7). As private insurance spread, private insurers came to acquire economic and political influence through their control of very large pools of private capital, both from premiums and by participating in equity markets. This was especially true in countries such as the United States in which government did not move early to occupy the field and rather adopted public insurance programs limited to certain groups within the population. Their key roles on the supply and demand side of the health care market respectively give doctors and insurers both strong incentives and substantial resources to mobilize for political action.

Various theories of the political economy of health care have addressed different dimensions of interest group organization and behavior: the asymmetric distribution of benefits and costs; capture; and oligarchy and policy networks.

4.2.1.1 Concentrated Benefits and Diffuse Costs

Economists are often disappointed to discover that legislatures rarely allocate resources on strict cost-effectiveness criteria. Rather, the legislative process appears to be disproportionately influenced by interest groups. Mancur Olson's (1971) theory of collective action, first published in 1965, suggests that interest groups are able to exert such influence because the benefits of action accrue to a narrow, well-organized group, whilst the costs are dispersed broadly across a diffuse group. The narrow, well-organized group can effectively monitor the behavior of its members to discourage free-riding. The substantial benefits of legislative action to each member further encourage the membership to exert effort to gain legislative ends. By contrast, the dispersed, disorganized group who will pay the costs of the new legislation often cannot even identify the other members of their group, let alone compel their participation in efforts to stop the legislation. Each member of the group will incur only a minuscule cost because of the new legislation, so it is not in any individual's self-interest to exert much effort.

This theory suggests that disease specific interest groups may be able to expand public funding for a particular health condition, at the expense of the diffuse group of taxpayers.

Carpenter (2002) shows that FDA drug approval times are shorter for drugs with more active and wealthier disease-interest groups. Some evidence suggests that patterns of public research funding may also be influenced by interest groups. In particular, the composition of US Congressional committees with jurisdiction over the budget of the National Institutes of Health has been shown to influence the cross-state allocation of research funding (Hegde and Mowery 2008; Hegde, 2009).

This theory of the political economy of government action also provides an explanation of why governments often fail to devote sufficient attention to areas, such as public health, where their contributions may be most valuable. Mobilizing to protect public health requires costs that generate benefits—public goods—of service to the entire population. But these public health activities enhance efficiency most when they address issues where no-one can effectively be excluded from the benefits of government action. Indeed, public health is most useful when the potential beneficiaries of public health actions are unknown and may not even yet be born. Thus public health, by design, has no clear apparent constituency to support it (Glied 2008a).

4.2.1.2 *Capture*

A second theory of government behavior focuses on the interactions between interest groups and regulators. In the economics literature, interest groups are seen as "capturing" the regulatory power of the state (Stigler 1971). The economics literature on capture in health care has focused on the behavior of hospitals and physicians. Friedman and Kuznets (1945) call attention to the government-legitimated role of organized medicine as a factor explaining the exceptionally high earnings of physicians relative to other professionals. There is a continuing flow of empirical studies examining the role of licensure on earnings (see, for example, Kleiner and Kudrle 2000; Kugler and Sauer 2005; Timmons and Thornton 2008). Similarly, hospitals may use the regulatory process to control competition. This type of capture has been studied in the context of the "certificate of need" programs under which US states seek to regulate the level and nature of hospital capacity (Salkever and Bice 1978). Capture theory has also been invoked to explain the presence of mandated health insurance benefits (Jensen and Morrisey 1999). The strongest empirical study of benefit mandates (for psychologists' services) finds some evidence of regulatory capture, but also finds evidence that the mandate addressed the public interest (Lambert and McGuire 1990).

Much of the early literature in political science (and to some extent sociology) on professional regulation either implicitly or explicitly treated the incorporation of professional self-regulatory bodies into the regulatory apparatus of the state as a case of the capture of the regulatory process by the regulated group (Gilb 1966). Somewhat later, the dominance of health care providers within various health care planning bodies established at the local and regional levels in a number of jurisdictions was also treated as a case of capture by (principally medical) professionals as a result of their information advantage and local elite status (see for example Marmor and Morone 1980). In the United States, the powerful role of the American Medical Association in the development and administration of the Resource-Based Relative Value Scale for the remuneration of physicians under the Medicare program has been portrayed as the effective capture of that process within the Health Care Financing Administration in the 1980s and 1990s (Vladek 1999).

More recently, changes in health care technology have created opportunities for other interest groups to capture key niches within the state. In particular the development of influential health technology assessment agencies, such as the National Institute for Health and Clinical Excellence (NICE) in England, offers considerable scope for capture by pharmaceutical and device manufacturers, and patient interest groups. A particular problem for such agencies is the need to find sources of expert advice that do not have direct or indirect links to interested parties. Even NICE, generally viewed as an international leader among such agencies in its analytic techniques and consultation models (Culyer 2006; Drummond and Sorenson 2009), has come under some criticism in this regard (Birch and Gafni 2007; House of Commons Health Select Committee 2008; Schandler 2008).

4.2.1.3 *Oligarchy and Policy Networks*

Another theme within the interest group approach to understanding the political economy of health care relates to shifts in the relative influence of different groups within the policy process over time. Broadly speaking, the political science literature moved from a focus on single interest groups to a focus on tightly linked oligarchies of private and public elites. The concept of "iron triangles" linking economic interests, bureaucratic actors, and politicians (another version of theories of capture) arose to describe and analyze these oligarchies. Increasingly, however, alongside this literature there emerged another line of analysis arguing that the concept of an iron triangle is incomplete and dated, failing to take account of the fluidity of the political process and the fracturing and re-alignment of interest groups. These analysts propose a concept of the issue network or policy network as a framework in which to map and understand the shifting alliances and balances of power over time (Heclo 1978). Yet others argue that there has been no general temporal shift from iron triangle to policy network, and that it is an empirical question as to which concept best describes a given arena (Marsh and Rhodes 1992).

The health care literature reflects this debate. The early literature focused almost exclusively on the disproportionate influence of the medical profession—as a cartel in the market (Kessel 1957) and a hegemon in the political arena (Garceau 1941; Hyde and Wolff 1954; Eckstein 1960). As other suppliers and private insurers assumed powerful roles as well, the emphasis came to be on the oligarchic nature of the health care arena, marked by tight alliances of medical, hospital, and business interests with privileged access to and predominant influence over bureaucratic and political decision-makers (Alford 1975; Starr 1982; Wilsford 1991). As changing technology has given rise to new groups and sub-groups, the political economy of health care has become more and more complex, leading some observers (at least in the US) to remark on the factionalization of previously dominant groups and the rise of challenging interests. The result has been the emergence of policy networks within which these multiple groups compete and form shifting alliances (Peterson 1993). Some observers went so far as to describe this phenomenon as "hyperpluralism" (Schick 1995). In Britain, however, some see the persistence of "professionalized networks"—looser than an iron triangle but still exhibiting concentrations of professional power (Wistow 1992). Moran, observing both countries, sees a stronger role for the state than is implied by either the triangle or the network model:

> In a nutshell, closely integrated hierarchies dominated by professional and corporate interests, operating with a substantial degree of independence from the core institutions of the state, are being replaced: by looser, more open, more unstable networks; by networks in which professional and corporate elites still exercise great power but in a more contested environment than hitherto; and by an institutional setting in which the core institutions of the state exercise much tighter surveillance and control than hitherto.... [T]he turn to new modes of government has actually strengthened the core institutions of the state, and accentuated one of the defining features of the health care state—the intertwining of the institutions of the health care system and the state itself. (Moran 1999: 178–9)

4.2.2 Theories Focusing on Voting Behavior

In general, health care services delivered to individuals are private goods. The apparent interest in redistribution of health care resources, and perhaps in maintaining a level of equity in the distribution of these resources, means that governments have a role to play in the financing or direct delivery of these otherwise private goods. The economic theory of public provision of private goods focuses on how governments make determinations about the size of this redistributive function (Epple and Romano 1996).

In democracies, decisions about the size of the health care sector will be influenced by the behavior of voters. Suppose people vote on the level of health care services that should be provided by the public system. The level of health spending chosen will correspond to that selected by the median voter (where median reflects level of preference for such spending). If there is a distribution of demand for health care services, some voters will demand more health care services than the median and will, at the median choice, have an unmet demand for health care services (Epple and Romano 1996).

This unmet demand will consist, in part, of people with exceptionally poor health status and a correspondingly high need for public health care services. This group will prefer that the form of overall redistribution be shifted toward health care services. This focused demand for increased health care redistribution is likely to be manifest through lobbying and capture, as described above.

Another portion of this excess demand is likely to reflect the positive income elasticity of health care demand. Numerous studies at both the individual, regional, and national levels suggest that the income elasticity of demand for health care services is positive—higher income people demand more health care services than do lower income people. Estimates of the elasticity range from 0.22 in individual analyses (Manning and Marquis 1996) to more than one in cross-national estimates (Newhouse 1977). The positive elasticity likely reflects a willingness (and ability) to pay more for a given *level* of health outcomes, as well as greater demand for health, medical quality, convenience, and amenities.

The positive income elasticity of demand for health care services suggests that a segment of unsatisfied voters will be higher income people who will be willing and able to purchase supplemental coverage to meet their excess demand. The existence of this contingent of voters may explain the surprisingly high prevalence of private health insurance within health care systems that devote substantial public resources to meeting the demand for equity in health care delivery (Colombo and Tapay 2004).

The public choice model of public provision of private goods (Epple and Romano 1996) suggests that allowing supplemental private purchase will generally lead to a reduction in public expenditures. The logic of this argument is that under a system that permits private purchase, higher income voters will prefer a lower level of public health care spending than otherwise, choosing to top up public spending with private purchases. Permitting private purchase will move the winning median voter down the distribution of health care service demand. The empirical evidence on private spending is consistent with this theoretical result. Tuohy, Flood, and Stabile (2004) find that the existence of private insurance tends to be associated with future reductions in public spending in analyses across the OECD.

A further implication of reduced public spending when private provision is permitted is that systems with mixed public and private payment will spend more on health care services (in aggregate) than will purely publicly funded systems. Mean income—which influences how much supplemental private insurance is purchased—is generally higher (often much higher) than median income—which, in voting models affects the amount of public provision. This pattern implies that the demand for privately purchased services will rise faster than public provision falls (Epple and Romano 1996). This increase in overall spending and reduction in public spending generally increases overall social welfare in voting models. Both private purchasers and some public purchasers—those with low demand for health care services—are better off in the scenario where some private purchase is permitted. Those who do not value health care highly will prefer the scenario with less public provision (and correspondingly lower taxes or higher spending on other programs). Public purchasers with low demand for health care will benefit as services are reduced and either taxes fall or social spending is diverted to programs they value more highly. However, to the extent that equity in the distribution of health care resources is, itself, a contributor to social welfare (a possibility that is not incorporated in existing voting models), private purchase may diminish social welfare.

4.2.3 Theories Focusing on Institutions

All of the approaches discussed so far deal with incentives resulting from inherent characteristics of health care, and would seem to suggest that the actions of governments should be fairly similar across nations. But in practice we observe a good deal of cross-national variation in health policy. In fact, the behavior of interest groups and voters can be understood only in terms of the institutional context in which they occur.

Early work on the importance of the incentive structures embedded in institutions as a way of understanding the behavior of actors came from economics. Institutional economists such as Tullock (1965) and Niskanen (1971) viewed bureaucrats as akin to decision-makers within private firms, with the substitution of budget maximization for the profit-maximization motive, and paid relatively little attention to the relationship between bureaucrats and other actors in the system other than to view the latter as homogeneous "sponsors." The focus of these models is on the interests of "bureaucrats" in maximizing their influence on the level and nature of government output, where the concept of the bureaucrat is interpreted broadly to embrace all public sector actors with significant influence over the allocation of resources (Goddard et al. 2006). The essence of this approach is the belief that bureaucrats receive power and remuneration in proportion to the size of their enterprise, and will therefore seek to implement policies that maximize the size of their own enterprises and to undermine activities that are outside their direct control. They are able to do so because they have an informational advantage over their political counterparts.

It is not easy to find direct applications of this model to the priority setting process in the health care sector. However, the tendency for bureaucracies to maximize their own budgets and sphere of influence at the expense of other considerations is readily observed in the health sector, in which health ministries often find it difficult to persuade bureaucrats in other ministries, such as education, to adopt policies designed to improve health, because of the reluctance of each sector to relinquish control. It has also been argued that "street-level bureaucracy" plays a powerful role in the way in which policy is implemented (Lipsky 1980). The considerable degree of discretion accorded to health care workers ("street-level bureaucrats") in determining the nature, amount, and quality of benefits provided by their agencies has a powerful impact on the rationing of resources, and the factors governing their decisions may not be those based on cost-effectiveness principles (Hudson 1997).

Recent political science literature on the political economy of health broadens the focus to consider the importance of institutions in shaping the behavior not only of government actors but of all actors in the health care arena. Much of this literature draws comparisons across nations, in order to demonstrate the importance of different institutional structures and policy frameworks in shaping political and economic behavior. Three principal and inter-related themes emerge: relations among branches of government; relations among levels of government; and historical institutionalism and path dependency.

4.2.3.1 *The Role of Institutions in Concentrating Authority—Relations Among Branches of Government*

Some institutional structures elevate the role of government actors, giving them the capacity and the incentive to make decisions and take action accordingly. Other structures make government much more open and vulnerable to the influence of particular actors whose interests are in promoting or thwarting different courses of action. The contrast typically made in this regard is between parliamentary systems, which strengthen the executive, and congressional systems marked by separation of powers and "checks and balances," providing multiple routes of access and multiple "veto points" for interest groups. Britain and post-1958 France are examples of parliamentary systems with strong executives. (In the French case the executive is strengthened by the existence of a political-bureaucratic elite with common training and similar career paths and a weak judiciary; in the British case it is strengthened by the "Westminster" model of executive control of the legislature reinforced by party discipline.) The United States, on the other hand, is the principal example of a separation-of-powers congressional model. Many political scientists have explored the role of such institutional differences in explaining cross-national variation in the pattern of development and the content of health policy. For example, studies of French health care policy (Wilsford 1991; Immergut 1992) show how the institution of a strong executive under the constitution adopted in 1958 enabled government to enact controls on doctors and hospitals that had been impossible under previous constitutional regimes. Numerous studies of American health care policy show how the existence of multiple veto points stymied attempts to adopt national health insurance throughout the twentieth century (see for example Steinmo and Watts 1995). And Britain provides the classic example of the ability of a unitary state with a Westminster parliamentary system to take decisive action in initially establishing the National Health Service in 1948 and then drastically altering its formal institutional structure in the early 1990s (Hacker 1998; Klein 2006).

It should be noted that the concentration of authority has several flip-sides. The concentration of authority also concentrates accountability—it makes it difficult for governments to deflect or spread the blame for unpopular decisions and may therefore make government actors particularly risk-averse (Pierson 1994: 33). It can drive opposition into protest movements and "direct action," as in the case of France (Wilsford 1991). Or it can shift opposition to the implementation rather than the legislative phase of policymaking, as in the case of the "internal market" reforms of the 1990s in Britain (Tuohy 1999).

4.2.3.2 *The Role of Institutions in Concentrating Authority—Relations Among Levels of Government*

Many health care systems rely on multiple levels of governance. The Canadian, Australian, German, Italian, Swedish, and Swiss health insurance systems all make extensive use of subsidiary levels of government in both the financing and delivery of services. In the United States, the Federal Medicaid program involves both Federal and State governments. Even more unitary systems, such as the UK health service, use regional authorities, who are at financial risk, for some functions.[2] The introduction of multiple systems of governance adds further complexity to the political economy of health care provision, and multiplies the routes of access for interest groups and the veto points available to them.

Economists have developed a substantial literature on the topic of decentralized public services, usually referred to under the banner of "fiscal federalism" (Oates 1999). This literature focuses on the optimal administrative level at which to vest powers of finance and purchasing of public services, and examines the consequences of alternative distributions of responsibilities. It therefore seems very germane to recent debates on decentralization in health care, though to date there have been few English language analyses of the implications of the fiscal federalism literature for health system design (see Petretto 2000 for an exception).

While fragmentation of public funding between levels of government is very likely to affect variations in spending, the direction and magnitude of these effects are likely to depend on the specific arrangements. In theory, there are a number of possible effects. Under some circumstances, the existence of multiple levels may generate over-provision or inefficiency of services. A system in which sub-national governments make decisions about the quality and level of care, provider payment, and eligibility, and the national government pays a share of costs, as exists in the US Medicaid program, is likely to generate "moral hazard" and escalating spending. Furthermore, local jurisdictions often jealously guard local capital infrastructure such as hospitals, which can be considered symbols of local municipal prestige. A decentralized system might therefore lead to a system of dispersed facilities that fails to secure the economies of scale and scope offered by more concentrated patterns of infrastructure (Levaggi and Smith 2005).

Under other circumstances, however, multiple levels of government may lead to under-provision. A system where national governments provide a fixed payment to sub-national governments which then pay the full marginal dollar (such as Canada for physician and hospital services and Australia for hospital services) may lead to under-funding at the sub-national level, particularly if there is competition for taxpayers among sub-national governments. A further possibility under decentralization is that

---

[2] In the UK, moreover, substantial authority has been delegated to sub-national governments in Scotland, Wales, and Northern Ireland since 1999 (Greer 2004).

there is an under-provision of certain "public goods" such as medical training and research, as jurisdictions seek to free-ride on the efforts of others. Under either set of circumstances, no level of government can claim full credit for spending increases but each level can "pass the buck" and shift blame for spending cuts to the other, making it more likely that federal systems will reduce spending in times of general fiscal constraint, other things being equal (Pal and Weaver 2003: 12). Finally, if sub-national governments systematically compare their performance to one another, competition among governments may lead to improved performance. Empirical evidence for each of these hypothetical effects is mixed: In practice, which of these dynamics pertain at sub-national levels depends upon the institutional structures at each level, and the resulting relationship between government and interest group actors (France 2008; Tuohy 2009).

4.2.3.3 *Historical Institutionalism and Path Dependency*

The most recent trend in institutionalist analysis is to recognize the importance of institutions and policy frameworks in shaping government action not only at a given point in time but *over time* (Oliver et al. 2005). The argument here is that government actions taken at Time T establish the context for subsequent decisions made at Time T+1. Once a policy has been established, various groups come to have a stake in that policy, and interest structures therefore become embedded in it in ways that make it difficult to change. In other words, because the costs of exit from a particular course of action rise as actors invest in that course, policy becomes set along a particular path of development with relatively few branches (Pierson 2000). Only large and relatively rare conjuctures of forces external and internal to the health care arena are sufficient to shift the line of development onto a different path. These moments of major change are marked by the "high politics" of ideological and partisan conflicts and swings, and cannot be understood by focusing on the health care sector alone. The policy frameworks established during these moments shape the subsequent behavior of actors and effectively determine the repertoire of policy options available.

Several studies (Barer et al. 1995; Oliver et al. 2005; Klein 2006) apply this approach to single-nation studies to show how changes in health policy were brought about at different points in time and how they affected subsequent behavior. Others extend this mode of analysis by employing comparisons across nations. Tuohy (1999), for example, shows how the varying health policy experiences of Britain, the United States, and Canada in the 1990s can be traced to the "logics" of the health care systems established during propitious moments for large reform in each nation in 1948, 1965, and 1966, respectively. Wilsford (1994) combines a path-dependency argument with a "veto points" analysis as discussed above. He argues that systems with multiple veto points such as that of the US require much greater (and more rare) conjunctures of forces to shift paths, whereas systems with more concentrated state authority, such as that of Britain, require less extraordinary occurrences to enable new paths to be chosen.

4.3 CONCLUDING COMMENTS

Health care now represents an important focus for political discourse in many countries, and policymaking is therefore frequently subject to forces that classical economic analysis fails to recognize. This chapter has sought to highlight the important dimensions along which political influences occur, and has therefore addressed territory that lies at the interface between economics and political science.

Models of political economy offer a formal and structured way of considering some of the wide range of influences on policymaking, and offer a rich and challenging research agenda in both low- and high-income settings. Approaches that consider the organizational context within which policy is made, and that broaden the range of incentives considered when applying the concept of "rational behavior" to relevant interested actors, may offer useful insights into how policy decisions emerge in the health care context.

Among the insights offered by these politico-economic approaches are the following. Inherent features of health care, such as highly complex and specialized knowledge bases, the high value placed on health, and the concentration of benefits and diffusion of costs under health insurance, give certain groups not only high stakes but also competitive advantages in influencing policy outcomes. Some groups control resources that are fundamental to the functioning of the system. Health providers, especially physicians, enjoy a hefty information advantage. The prevalence of insurance, both public and private, creates large pools of capital and gives those who control those pools substantial influence. Other groups, such as those suffering from life-threatening illnesses, may have a strong claim on public attention and sympathy. But institutional features affect the ability of interested actors to deploy these advantages to affect policy outcomes. For example, federal structures and congressional systems allow more points of access and, conversely, more veto points than do unitary structures and Westminster parliamentary systems. Moreover, institutions establish incentive structures in themselves by giving those who hold institutional positions a stake in defending and enhancing those positions. Depending on the details of their design, federal structures may create incentives that lead either to over-provision or to under-provision of health services. Finally, incentives are embedded not only in broad institutional structures but in specific policy frameworks themselves, which therefore become resistant to change. Broadly speaking, single-payer systems forge a tight axis between health care providers and governments, social insurance systems create networks of intermediary organizations, and systems based on private markets make coalition-building a much more complex process.

Despite several decades of advances in the application of economics to health and health care, described elsewhere in this handbook, the discipline has sometimes had less impact on policy and practice than might be expected if decision-makers were to operate according to the assumptions of traditional economic theory. Hitherto this terrain has been under-researched by economists. We argue that it is nevertheless an important area of study for all those interested in the context within which health policy is set, and the forces that give rise to policy outcomes.

REFERENCES

ALFORD, ROBERT R. (1975), *Health Care Politics: Ideological and Interest Group Barriers to Reform* (Chicago: University of Chicago Press).

BARER, MORRIS L., MARMOR, THEODORE R., and MORRISON, ELLEN M. (1995), "Health Care Reform in the United States: On the Road to Nowhere Again?" *Social Science and Medicine*, 41(4): 453–60.

BIRCH, STEPHEN and GAFNI, AMIRAM (2007), "Economists' Dream or Nightmare? Maximizing Health Gains from Available Resources Using the NICE Guidelines," *Health Economics, Policy and Law*, 2: 193–202.

BUCHANAN, G. and TULLOCK, G. (1962), *The Calculus of Consent: Logical Foundations of Constitutional Democracy* (Ann Arbor, MI: Ann Arbor Paperbacks).

CARPENTER, DANIEL P. (2002), "Groups, the Media, Agency Waiting Costs, and FDA Drug Approval," *American Journal of Political Science*, 46(3) (July): 490–505.

COASE, RONALD H. (1960), "The Problem of Social Cost," *Journal of Law and Economics*, 3(1): 1–44.

COCHRANE, JOHN (1995), "Time-consistent Health Insurance," *Journal of Political Economy*, 103 (June): 445–73.

COLOMBO, FRANCESCA and TAPAY, NICOLE (2004), "Private Health Insurance in OECD Countries: The Benefits and Costs for Individuals and Health Systems." OECD Health Working Papers No. 15, OECD, Paris.

CULYER, A. J. (2006), "NICE's Use of Cost Effectiveness as an Exemplar of a Deliberative Process," *Health Economics, Policy and Law*, 1: 299–318.

CUTLER, DAVID and MILLER, GRANT (2005), "The Role of Public Health Improvements in Health Advances: The Twentieth-Century United States," *Demography*, 42(1): 1–22.

DEATON, ANGUS (2004), "Health in an Age of Globalization," in Susan Collins and Carol Graham (eds.), *Brookings Trade Forum* (Washington, DC: The Brookings Institution), 83–130.

DRUMMOND, M. F. and SORENSON, C. (2009), "Nasty or Nice? A Perspective on the Use of Health Technology Assessment in the United Kingdom," *Value in Health*, 12(Supp. 2): S8–S13.

ECKSTEIN, HARRY (1960), *Pressure Group Politics: The Case of the British Medical Association* (Stanford: Stanford University Press).

EPPLE, D. and ROMANO, R. E. (1996), "Public Provision of Private Goods," *Journal of Political Economy*, 104(1): 57–84.

FLOOD, C. and ARCHIBALD, T. (2001), "The Illegality of Private Health Care in Canada," *Canadian Medical Association Journal*, 164(6): 825.

FRANCE, GEORGE (2008), "The Form and Context of Federalism: Meanings for Health Care Financing," *Journal of Health Politics, Policy and Law*, 33: 649–705.

FRIEDMAN, MILTON and KUZNETS, SIMON (1945), *Income from Independent Professional Practice* (New York: National Bureau of Economic Research).

GARCEAU, OLIVER (1941), *The Political Life of the American Medical Association* (Cambridge, MA: Harvard University Press).

GARFINKEL, IRWIN, RAINWATER, LEE, and SMEEDING, TIMOTHY M. (2006), "A Re-examination of Welfare. States and Inequality in Rich Nations: How In-kind Transfers and Indirect Taxes Change the Story," *Journal of Policy Analysis and Management*, 25(4): 897–919.

GILB, CORINNE LATHROP (1966), *Hidden Hierarchies: the Professions and Government* (New York: Harper and Row).

GLIED, SHERRY (1998), *Chronic Condition: Why Health Reform Fails* (Boston: Harvard University Press).

GLIED, S. (2008a), "Public Health and Economics: Externalities, Rivalries, Excludability, and Politics," in James Colgrove, Gerald Markowitz, and David Rosner (eds.), *The Contested Boundaries of American Public Health* (New Brunswick: Rutgers University Press), 15–31.

—— (2008b), "Health Care Financing, Efficiency, and Equity," in Colleen Flood, Mark Stabile, and Carolyn Hughes Tuohy (eds.), *Exploring Social Insurance: Can A Dose of Europe Cure Canadian Health Care Finance?* (Montreal: McGill-Queen's University Press).

GODDARD, M., HAUCK, K., PREKER, A., and SMITH, P. (2006), "The Economics of Priority Setting in Health: A Critical Perspective," *Health Economics, Policy and Law*, 1(1): 79–90.

GREER, SCOTT (2004), *Territorial Politics and Health Policy* (Manchester and New York: Manchester University Press).

HACKER, JACOB S. (1998), "The Historical Logic of National Health Insurance: Structure and Sequence in the Development of British, Canadian and US Medical Policy," *Studies in American Political Development*, 12 (Spring): 57–130.

HECLO, HUGH (1978), "Issue Networks and the Executive Establishment," in Anthony King (ed.), *The New American Political System* (Washington, DC: American Enterprise Institute).

HEGDE, DEEPAK (2009), "Political Influence Behind the Veil of Peer Review: An Analysis of Public Biomedical Research Funding in the US," *Journal of Law and Economics*, November, 52(4): 665–90.

—— and MOWERY, DAVID C. (2008), "Research Funding: Politics and Funding in the US Public Biomedical R&D System," *Science*, December 19, 322(5909): 1797.

HOUSE OF COMMONS HEALTH SELECT COMMITTEE (2008), *National Institute for Health and Clinical Excellence* (London: The Stationery Office).

HUDSON, B. (1997), "Michael Lipsky and Street Level Bureaucracy: A Neglected Perspective," in M. Hill (ed.), *The Policy Process: A Reader* (Essex: Prentice-Hall).

HYDE, D. R. and WOLFF, P. (1954), "The American Medical Association: Power, Purpose and Politics in Organized Medicine," *Yale Law Journal*, May, 63: 938–1022.

IMMERGUT, ELLEN M. (1992), *Health Politics, Interests and Institutions in Western Europe* (New York: Cambridge University Press).

JENSEN, GAIL A. and MORRISEY, MICHAEL A. (1999), "Employer-sponsored Health Insurance and Mandated Benefit Laws," *The Milbank Quarterly*, 77(4): 425–59.

KESSEL, REUBEN (1957), "Price Discrimination in Medicine," *Journal of Law and Economics*, October, 1: 20–53.

KLEIN, RUDOLF (2006), *The New Politics of the NHS: From Creation to Reinvention* (Abingdon, UK: Radcliffe).

KLEINER, MORRIS M. and KUDRLE, ROBERT T. (2000), "Does Regulation Affect Economic Outcomes? The Case of Dentistry," *The Journal of Law and Economics*, 43(2): 547–82.

KUGLER, ADRIANA D. and SAUER, ROBERT M. (2005), "Doctors Without Borders? Relicensing Requirements and Negative Selection in the Market for Physicians," *Journal of Labor Economics*, 23(3): 437–65.

LAMBERT, DAVID A. and McGUIRE, THOMAS G. (1990), "Political and Economic Determinants of Insurance Regulation in Mental Health," *Journal of Health Politics Policy and Law*, 15: 169–89.

LEVAGGI, R. and SMITH, P. (2005), "Decentralization in Health Care: Lessons from Public Economics," in P. Smith, L. Ginnelly, and M. Sculpher (eds.), *Health Policy and Economics: Opportunities and Challenges* (London: Open University Press).

LINDSAY, C. M. (1969), "Medical Care and the Economics of Sharing," *Economica*, XXXVI: 351–62.

LIPSKY, M. 1980. *Street-level Bureaucracy: Dilemmas of the Individual in Public Services* (New York: Russell Sage Foundation).

MANNING, W. G. and MARQUIS, M. S. (1996), "Health Insurance: The Tradeoff Between Risk Pooling and Moral Hazard," *Journal of Health Economics*, 15(5): 609–39.

MARMOR, THEODORE R. and MORONE, JAMES (1980), "Representing Consumer Interests: Imbalanced Markets, Health Planning and the HSAs," *The Milbank Memorial Fund Quarterly*, 58(1): 125–65.

MARSH, D. and RHODES, R. A. W. (1992), "Policy Communities and Issue Networks: Beyond Typology," in D. Marsh and R.A.W. Rhodes (eds.), *Policy Networks and British Government* (Oxford: Oxford University Press), 249–68.

MORAN, MICHAEL (1999), *Governing the Health Care State: A Comparative Study of the United Kingdom, the United States and Germany* (Manchester: Manchester University Press).

MUELLER, D. C. (2003), *Public Choice III* (Cambridge, UK: Cambridge University Press).

NEWHOUSE, JOSEPH P. (1977), "Medical Care Expenditure: A Cross-national Survey," *Journal of Human Resources*, 126(1): 115–25.

—— (1996), "Reimbursing Health Plans and Health Providers: Efficiency in Production Versus Selection," *Journal of Economic Literature*, 34(3) (Sept.): 1236–63.

NISKANEN, WILLIAM A. (1971), *Bureaucracy and Representative Government* (Chicago: Aldine, Atherton).

OATES, W. (1999), "An Essay on Fiscal Federalism," *Journal of Economic Literature*, 37: 1120–49.

OECD (ORGANISATION FOR ECONOMIC CO-OPERATION AND DEVELOPMENT) (2008), *OECD Health Database* (Paris: OECD).

OLIVER, ADAM, MOSSIALOS, ELIAS, and WILSFORD, DAVID (guest eds.) (2005), "Legacies and Latitude in European Health Policy," *Journal of Health Politics, Policy and Law*, 30(1–2).

OLSON, MANCUR (1971), *The Logic of Collective Action : Public Goods and the Theory of Groups* (rev. edn.) (Cambridge, MA: Harvard University Press).

PAL, LESLIE A. and KENT WEAVER, R. (2003), "The Politics of Pain," in Leslie A. Pal and R. Kent Weaver (eds.), *The Government Taketh Away: the Politics of Pain in the United States and Canada* (Washington DC: Georgetown University Press), 1–40.

PAULY, M. V. (1971), *Medical Care at Public Expense* (New York: Praeger).

PETERSON, MARK A. (1993). "Political Influence in the 1990s: From Iron Triangles to Policy Networks," *Journal of Health Politics, Policy and Law* 18(2): 395–438.

PETRETTO, A. (2000), "On the Cost–Benefit of the Regionalisation of the National Health Service," *Economics of Governance*, 1: 213–32.

PHILIPSON, TOMAS (2000), "Economic Epidemiology and Infectious Diseases," in A. J. Culyer and J. P. Newhouse (eds.), *Handbook of Health Economics*, 1: 1761–99.

PIERSON, PAUL D. (1994), *Dismantling the Welfare State? Reagan, Thatcher and the Politics of Retrenchment* (Cambridge, UK: Cambridge University Press).

—— (2000). "Increasing Returns, Path Dependence, and the Study of Politics," *American Political Science Review*, 94(2): 251–67.

ROTHSCHILD, MICHAEL and STIGLITZ, JOSEPH (1976), "Equilibrium in Competitive Insurance Markets: An Essay on the Economics of Imperfect Information," *The Quarterly Journal of Economics*, 90(4) (Nov.): 629–49.

SALKEVER, DAVID S. and BICE, THOMAS W. (1978), "Certificate of Need Legislation and Hospital Costs," in M. Zubkoff, I, Raskin, and R. Hanft (eds.), *Hospital Cost Containment: Selected Notes for Future Policy* (New York: Prodist-Milbank Memorial Funds), 429–60.

SCHANDLER, M. (2008). "The Use of Cost-effectiveness by the National Institute for Health and Clinical Excellence (NICE): Not Yet an Exemplar of a Deliberative Process," *Journal of Medical Ethics*, 34: 534–9.

SCHICK, ALLEN (1995). "How a Bill Did Not Become Law," in Thomas E. Mann and Norman J. Ornstein (eds.), *Intensive Care: How Congress Shapes Health Policy* (Washington, DC: AEI/ Brookings), 227–72.

STARR, PAUL (1982), *The Social Transformation of American Medicine* (New York: Basic Books).

STEINMO, SVEN and WATTS, JON (1995), "It's the Institutions, Stupid! Why Comprehensive National Health Insurance Always Fails in America," *Journal of Health Politics, Policy and Law*, 20(2) (Summer): 329–72.

STIGLER, GEORGE (1971), "The Theory of Economic Regulation," *Bell Journal of Economics and Management Science*, 3: 3–18.

TIMMONS, EDWARD J. and THORNTON, ROBERT J. (2008), "The Effects of Licensing on the Wages of Radiologic Technologists," *Journal of Labor Research*, 29(4): 333–46.

TOBIN, JAMES (1970). "On Limiting the Domain of Inequality," *Journal of Law and Economics*, 13(2) (Oct.): 263–77.

TULLOCK, G. (1965), *The Politics of Bureaucracy* (Washington, DC: Public Affairs Press).

TUOHY, CAROLYN HUGHES (1999), *Accidental Logics: the Dynamics of Change in the Health Care Arena in the United States, Britain and Canada* (New York: Oxford University Press).

—— (2009), "Single Payers, Multiple Systems: The Scope and Limits of Subnational Variation under a Federal Health Policy Framework," *Journal of Health Politics, Policy and Law*, 34(4) (August): 453–96.

—— FLOOD, C. M., and STABILE, M. (2004), "How Does Private Finance Affect Public Health Care Systems? Marshaling the Evidence from OECD Nations," *Journal of Health Politics, Policy and Law*, 29(3): 359–96.

VLADEK, BRUCE (1999), "The Political Economy of Medicare," *Health Affairs*, 18(1) (Jan.–Feb.): 22–36.

WILSFORD, DAVID (1991). *Doctors and the State: the Politics of Health Care in France and the United States* (Durham, NC: Duke University Press).

—— (1994). "Path Dependency, or Why History Makes it Difficult But Not Impossible to Reform Health Care Systems in a Big Way," *Journal of Public Policy*, 14(3): 251–83.

WISTOW, G. (1992). "The Health Service Policy Community: Professionals Pre-eminent or Under Challenge?" in D. Marsh and R.A.W. Rhodes (eds.), *Policy Networks and British Government* (Oxford: Oxford University Press), 51–74.

CHAPTER 5

....

THE PROMISE OF HEALTH: EVIDENCE OF THE IMPACT OF HEALTH ON INCOME AND WELL-BEING

....

WILLIAM JACK

5.1 INTRODUCTION

....

THE correlation between health status and income across individuals, over time, and among countries is undeniable: being healthy is part of being rich, although it is not just access to material resources that links socioeconomic status to health. As Cutler et al. show in Chapter 7 of this volume, other dimensions of SES, including education, social rank, and ethnicity, are also associated with better health. Nonetheless, the link between health and income has been the focus of much interest, as researchers have examined the mechanisms that underlie these associations, asking if income is the driver of health differences, if health improvements lead to economic growth, or if other factors influence both.

The ensuing debate has, broadly speaking, pitted economists against public health specialists, however intriguingly they have tended to occupy different sides of the discussion depending on the context. Within the rich countries of the OECD, economists have tended to focus on health as a source of human capital, and hence economic output, while members of the public health community have argued that a causal link from income to health is grounds for redistribution. Conversely, in the context of the developing world, health specialists, as represented for example by the views espoused by the World Health Organization, have argued in favor of expanded public spending on health care and prevention as a means of providing a route out of poverty, while others have questioned the returns to such spending and focused instead on the imperative of fostering economic growth to improve the lives, and the health, of the world's poor.

Many debates are fueled by heroic but ultimately imperfect analyses, themselves the results of attempts to use data and techniques that are not up to the task at hand. Examination of the health–income nexus, which has had to confront significant measurement and identification problems, has indeed been prone to these forces, and has not been helped by the fact that both directions of causality are likely operative.

This chapter addresses just one side of this debate, and reviews recent evidence that has been gathered regarding the link from health to income. As identification strategies have improved, and as better data have been collected, estimates of the causal impact of health on economic output have been refined. These estimates of the income-augmenting effects of health improvements are a necessary, although still insufficient input in the formulation of public policies, as they provide more comprehensive data on the return to improved health. The challenge of discovering and implementing cost-effective policies that do in fact improve health remains however, and is beyond the scope of this chapter.

The next section outlines a number of mechanisms by which health innovations can affect incomes. Section 5.3 presents empirical evidence that speaks to this issue, much of it produced over the last decade. Section 5.4 concludes.

5.2 Mechanisms

Better health comes in many forms and at different stages of life. The life-cycle patterns of human capital and other investments, of labor market participation and income generation, and of fertility decisions, mean that the effects of health improvements are likely to vary depending on when, and by whom, they are experienced. This section outlines the various routes by which improved health can plausibly lead to increases in measured incomes, taking account of the expected wide range of heterogeneity in effects.

We classify health improvements loosely into three categories, corresponding to improved nutrition, reduced morbidity, and reduced mortality. These categories clearly are not mutually exclusive, as better nourished individuals fall sick less often, and death is often, but not always, portended by illness. Nonetheless, with this classification in mind, we set out the routes by which improved health can affect income—namely direct productivity effects, effects on incentives to accumulate human and physical capital, and aggregation effects, which are important to assess in extrapolating the effects of improvements at the individual level to improvements in population health.

5.2.1 Direct Effects

The obvious route from health to income is a direct productivity link. Higher levels of nutrition and energy intake can likely increase the productivity of both manual work and tasks that require concentration. Fogel (2004) traces increases in economic growth to surges in agricultural productivity, and the impact this had on hunger and nutrition. Using historical records, he proposes that there simply were not enough calories consumed to exhaust the productive capacity of workers in nineteenth-century Europe, and that increases in food availability led directly to increases in the size and stature, strength, and effort of the workforce. As reviewed by Strauss and Thomas (1998), the historical evolution of height, attributed in large part to nutritional improvements, provides a useful proxy for health status, and is closely linked to economic development.

Nutrition does not only increase physical strength, but it provides protection against both chronic and infectious disease. Fogel develops the concept of physiological capital to denote the biological capacity of an individual to learn, acquire skills, and work, and focuses on the impact of *in utero*, infant, and early childhood nutrition and parental behaviors (such as smoking and drinking) that can lead to impairment of the nervous system and neurological damage. Longer term health effects of low birth-weight and malnutrition early in life include increased risk of heart disease, stroke, hypertension, and diabetes.

Lower morbidity can similarly affect both the productivity of a worker's time spent on the job, but also the length of time devoted to work, and absenteeism. In countries in which children contribute to household income, often by undertaking domestic and farm chores such as cleaning, fetching water, and guarding livestock, reductions in morbidity and increases in nutrition can have direct impacts on total, if not always market, income. And reductions in mortality have to be (weakly) good for a given individual's output. Total, if not per capita, output is also likely to rise in the presence of mortality reductions, unless congestion costs are especially large.

Alternatively, health improvements of one individual can directly increase the incomes of others. When parents and grandparents who tend to sick children are relieved of this task, their measured incomes may rise as they (re-)enter the labor market. The same is true for children who would otherwise be working if not for the fact that they have to tend to a sick parent. In both these cases, one person's health improvement increases the labor supply, and hence the income, of another. To the extent that *both* individuals enter the labor market, measured incomes will increase further. However, even if health improvements for one individual do not free up time of another, they could nonetheless increase the productivity of both, for example due to the existence of either task complementarity or increasing returns in household production.

Finally, improvements in one person's health can lead to improvements in the health of others, with direct or indirect effects on their incomes. This mechanism appears most likely to be operational in the context of reducing the transmission of communicable and infectious diseases, in which either behavioral change is important (such as the use of insecticide-treated bed nets to prevent malaria, or condoms to prevent transmission of HIV and other STIs), or when public goods such as water and sanitation facilities are used. There could well be increasing returns to improved health associated with network externalities in such cases, which require that a certain critical mass of individuals adopt preventive behaviors or gain access to public goods before the health (and incomes) of the broader community can improve.

5.2.2 Effects on Capital Accumulation

Grossman (1972) was among the first to model health improvements as investments in human capital, and indeed, the direct economic impacts of better health at early ages tend to show up later in life, if only for life-cycle reasons. But improvements in health, as well as adding directly, by definition, to the stock of human capital, can also strengthen incentives of individuals to increase the rate of human capital investment, particularly in the form of education, either because the effective price falls, or because the returns to education increase.

Healthier children may well attend school more regularly, learn more efficiently while there, and perform better on tests, all of which increase their acquisition and maintenance of human capital for a given level of effort and cost. The incentive to invest in education therefore increases when the effective price falls, increasing the number of years, the quality of the education sought, and the willingness (most often of parents) to pay for that education. Although a similar mechanism could affect the incentive of those who are past school age to invest in training, we expect that better health among adults is unlikely to have as large an effect on human capital investment and future income.

However, the *prospect* of better health in adulthood may well induce greater levels of human capital investment, among those of school age or older. Even if the effective price of education or training does not fall, better health in adulthood can increase both the length of time over which the returns to education are earned because of a longer working life, and the length of time over which these returns are consumed, as life expectancy increases. Again, the effects of morbidity declines among adults, which are likely to affect adult labor supply, and the impact of reduced adult mortality rates, which might affect life expectancy more, could have similar impacts on human capital investment, but for different reasons.

We note one important difference between health improvements that reduce the price of human capital investment or the direct return to it, and those that simply affect life expectancy. In principle, the first kind of health improvement increases the incentive to invest in *human* capital, while the second, which simply affects the return to saving, induces an increase in investment in *all* forms of capital. The difference may be difficult to observe in practice however, given that a majority of individuals hold a large share of their total asset base in the form of human capital, while credit market imperfections, which are particularly acute in developing countries, could limit the ability of individuals to invest in any capital other than through on-the-job training. On the other hand, Bloom et al. (2003) develop a model in which increases in life expectancy lead to higher savings rates at every age, and present some cross-country evidence in support of this result.

5.2.3 Aggregate Effects

Most of the mechanisms by which health improvements increase income described above involve changes in inputs to the production process—for example, through increases in the quantity or quality of labor supply in the short term, and changes in the stock of human and possibly other capital over the longer term. If income generation depends on other inputs that are in fixed supply, such as land, then the per capita effects of population-wide health improvements might be much smaller than those experienced by a single individual who enjoys a similar health improvement. These general equilibrium effects limit the extent to which studies at the micro-level can be extrapolated, and can also account for at least some of the relatively weak cross-country empirical evidence on the impact of health on income.

Similarly, undisputedly positive health improvements can nonetheless reduce per capita income if they adversely alter the dependency ratio. This seems particularly likely for a number of interventions that directly target mortality: in rich countries mortality rates have recently fallen most among the elderly, while in the developing world infant (under one year) and child (under 5 years) mortality rates have been reduced through expansions of immunization and nutrition programs, and improved sanitation. The short run impacts of such health improvements on per capita income are almost certainly negative, as neither group contributes significantly to measured GDP.

Some authors have even suggested that the impact on total income of reductions in mortality rates among adults of working age may not be large enough to offset the population effect, thereby reducing per capita income. Conversely, high-mortality epidemics can have ambiguous effects on per capita income. The Black Death in fourteenth-century Europe, and the HIV/AIDS epidemic in southern Africa, both led in the short run to reductions in the labor force without offsetting reductions in the capital stock, leading to higher labor productivity and greater incomes for those lucky enough to be spared. The expansion of antiretroviral therapy (ART) across Africa in the last five years, which has increased survival rates among HIV-infected individuals, many in the prime of working life, could thus have lowered per capita income.

How should we interpret these arithmetic consequences of changes in population structure and size? The natural implication is that a focus on per capita incomes is not necessarily well-placed, and that it is important to adopt meaningful welfare measures that reflect the obvious social costs of mortality. One straightforward adjustment is to divide total income produced by the total number of people, living and dead, who were once alive and who would be now if not for a given mortality risk. Let's call this per nata income. Higher mortality thus decreases total income (the numerator) but not the denominator.

This measure is not entirely satisfactory, of course, as it implicitly assumes fixed fertility rates. It can thus be argued that in calculating the income effects of reductions in child mortality rates that lead women to have fewer children, the denominator *should* in any average measure indeed fall. In fact, even health improvements that reduce morbidity among children can induce parents to move along the quality–quantity frontier (Becker 1981), reducing the desired number of births, and the denominator in a meaningful measure of mean welfare.

5.3 EMPIRICAL EVIDENCE

Perhaps the starkest differences in health and income are apparent in cross-country comparisons. While the identification challenges that must be overcome in estimating the impact of improved health on income and economic activity in such settings are manifold, they have nonetheless not deterred researchers from addressing the issue at this level of aggregation. A sizeable empirical literature has thus focused on using national-level data to investigate the relationships between health and income.

Alternatively, researchers have used natural or quasi-experiments, in which arguably exogenous shocks to health status, associated with either sudden disease outbreaks or discrete policy-driven improvements in the health environment, to identify the impact of health on income. At a more micro-level, randomized control trials have been employed to improve nutrition or health, and the impacts on schooling, labor supply, and income measured. Of course, as identification has become more reliable with these methods, the parameters of interest have focused on progressively narrower relationships.

5.3.1 Cross-country Studies

Cross-country correlations between population health (as measured by life expectancy) and income per capita, as exemplified by the Preston Curve (Preston 1975), are strong and have remained so over the last hundred years (Pritchett and Viarengo 2010). Figure 5.1 uses 2007 data from the United Nations Development Programme's Human Development Report database[1] to illustrate this relationship. While advances in technology and its diffusion have shifted the relationship between income and health, the cross-country correlation between the variables has proven robust over time. One strand of the literature thus employs cross-country regression techniques in an attempt to identify a causal link from health to income at the national level. These studies have had to make strong identifying assumptions that are sometimes difficult to sustain.

A number of authors have used cross-country regression analysis to isolate the impact of improvements in population health on macroeconomic performance, in particular per capita GDP, that could underlie the correlations observed in the Preston curve. Pritchett and Summers (1996) were among the first to address this issue, using infant and child mortality rates as measures of population health. As instruments for economic growth, they employed terms of trade shocks, the investment to GDP ratio, the black market premium for foreign exchange, and the deviation of the official exchange rate from its purchasing power parity level, all of which were argued to be correlated with income, but would not directly affect health. While their estimates

---

[1] <www.undp.hdr.org>.

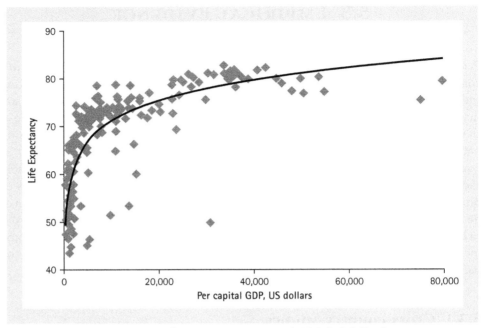

FIGURE 5.1 Life expectancy per capital GDP (US dollars)

provide evidence that income growth does drive health improvement, they do not rule out the reverse effect.[2]

Gallup and Sachs (2001) showed that better health was correlated with larger subsequent changes in income, suggesting that health could affect not only the level, but the growth rate of income. Obvious endogeneity problems plague this strand of the literature, as omitted variables that determine health could explain future income growth. They noted, however, that the geographic concentration of infectious diseases in tropical regions of the world suggested a plausible instrument for health status, namely distance from the equator, and found a strong impact of health on income growth using this approach.

Geography as a proxy for health has however been challenged by a number of authors (e.g. Acemoglu, Johnson, and Robinson 2001; Easterly and Levine 2003; Rodrik, Subramanian, and Trebbi 2004), who point out that geographic location may well influence economic growth either directly or through historical patterns of institutional development and adoption. Once the impact of geography on the choice of institutions is accounted for, there remains no independent link from geography (and thus health) to income. The most acute problem these studies face is simply the availability of reliable

---

[2] Pritchett (2010: 8) notes that "[o]ur point is only that the relationship between health and income cannot by fully accounted for by 'reverse causation' as estimates that account for this potential channel show equally strong associations."

historical data.[3] However, even with reasonable data, a remaining methodological problem is that both health and institutional choice are potentially endogenous, and a single instrument cannot identify the contribution of each to growth. In response, McArthur and Sachs (2001) note the relatively small sample size employed in that study, and its limited geographic diversity, and present evidence on a wider sample of countries and claim that *both* institutions and the disease environment—in particular the prevalence of malaria—influence future economic growth. Sachs (2003) attempts to further identify the specific impact of malaria by constructing an index of "malaria ecology" and a separate instrument for institutional choice based on mortality rates of colonial settlers. He finds both affect future income, suggesting again that both health and institutions matter for growth. But since malaria ecology could easily be associated with the conditions encountered by early settlers, and hence the choice of institutions, the validity of the estimates remains in question.

Bloom, Canning, and Sevilla (2004) present results from thirteen cross-country analyses that complement or refine the Gallup and Sachs methodology, all of which report large effects of health on income growth. The authors themselves try to resolve the problem of omitted variables by regressing income growth on *changes* in health, and other lagged variables. This general approach does not find significant support in the wider macroeconomic literature, however (Mankiw 1995; Weil 2007).

Acemoglu and Johnson's (2007) study is probably the most innovative recent cross-country analysis of the impact of health on income. It uses the international epidemiological transition of the 1940s, associated with the discovery and diffusion of penicillin and sulfa drugs, vaccines, insecticides, and the creation of the World Health Organization, as an exogenous source of health improvements. Specifically, the authors use variation in the *potential* health improvement associated with full adoption of these innovations, which they argue are uncorrelated with future income growth, as an instrument for actual health improvements. They find that population growth rates increased in response to the innovations, as did aggregate income, but per capita income fell.

Acemoglu and Johnson's methodology—using potential health improvements as an instrument for actual changes in health status—has been used in a number of other studies on the impact of malaria on income (see below). However, some commentators have questioned the mechanisms underlying the empirical results. In particular, while capital constraints may well bind in the short run, reducing the potential for increases in per capita income, over the forty-year period of their analysis one would expect the capital stock, including the productivity of land, to increase accordingly, and for fertility rates to adjust. Focusing instead on the effect of *higher* mortality on economic outcomes, Young (2005) uses micro-data to calibrate a model of the AIDS epidemic in South Africa. He incorporates fertility effects and the impact of adult mortality on the intergenerational transmission of human capital, but still finds that the increase in

---

[3] Indeed, Albouy (2008) has questioned the usefulness of much of the settler mortality data used by Acemoglu, Johnson, and Robinson.

capital–labor ratios associated with the disease leads to higher per capita income, consistent with Acemoglu and Johnson's macro-analysis.

Weil (2007) uses microeconomic estimates of the effect of health on individual incomes (some of which are reviewed below) to calibrate a model of production which is then used to estimate the share of cross-country variation in per capita GDP that is attributable to variations in health indicators. That is, per capita output differs across countries because of differences in physical capital assets, worker skills (or educational capital), the capacity of workers to work hard and long, and to think clearly (health capital), and other factors. Using this methodology, he finds that between about 10 and 30 percent of the variation of log GPD per capita across countries can be attributed to differences in health human capital. His preferred estimate (23%) is "roughly the same as the share accounted for by human capital from education, and larger than the share accounted for by physical capital."

The strength of Weil's approach is that it relies on well-identified microeconomic estimates of the causal impact of health on income. One limitation, recognized by the author, is that it is difficult to use the framework to estimate the "full" contribution of differences in health to cross-country variation in incomes. Allocating national output as the return to various factors becomes problematic when one factor (say health) determines investment in others (say education). While many microeconomic studies of the effect of health on income examine this and other similar routes, Weil's analysis focuses on the proximate effect of health on income—that which arises due to the physical and mental capacity of workers. That is, his analysis can be thought of as providing an estimate of the impact of removing health differences across countries, while holding all other factors, including physical and educational capital, fixed. Allowing those factors to endogenously respond to improvements in health would likely lead to somewhat larger income responses.

5.3.2 Micro-level Evidence

The labyrinth of channels from health to income and back, the time lags between innovations in one and effects on the other, and the dependence of these effects on a range of other complementary institutional and environmental factors, all suggest the debates surrounding macro-level empirical analyses using aggregate data will continue for some time. An alternative approach has been to investigate the individual mechanisms by which health affects income using quasi-experimental data, and randomized control trials.

Nutrition is perhaps most important for human growth and development, and so has been heavily studied among children. However, nutritional intake in adulthood can directly affect economic output, as reviewed by Thomas and Frankenberg (2002). They summarize their findings as indicating that "[w]hile the establishment of this link is not straightforward, the weight of evidence points to nutrition, and possible other dimensions of health, as significant determinants of economic productivity."

For example, Thomas et al. (2004) report the results of a large-scale iron supplementation intervention in Indonesia that covered over 17,000 adults. They find that iron supplements had significant effects on men who were otherwise anemic, and who experienced increased energy levels, better work attendance, and up to 20 percent higher productivity.[4] There was however no discernible effect for women.

On the other hand, the physiological benefits of better nutrition do not always show up in greater measured output. For example, Thomas and Frankenberg report the results of randomized experiments in which iron supplementation improved energy use on the job, but did not lead to higher measured incomes. For example, in a study of female Chinese cotton workers, Li et al. (1994) found iron supplements were effective in increasing energy levels and that they reduced energy expenditure per work task completed. However, the subjects did not increase output in their primary jobs, but spent more time on non-work activities.[5] This could have been due to constraints in the work-place that made it difficult to increase output (reliance on other workers, technology constraints), or simply to the fact that optimizing individuals chose to spend the additional energy on non-work activities.

In contrast to iron supplementation, the impact of increases in caloric intake is less clear, with some randomized experiments showing no effect, and others a small impact. Observational studies (i.e. those with non-random variation in caloric intake) have shown positive correlations between calories and productivity, but suffer from problems of unobserved heterogeneity.[6] For example, Foster and Rosenzweig (1994) report that caloric intake is correlated with hourly productivity, but the causality is likely in the opposite direction, as the variation they exploit rests in the strength of effort incentives—higher powered incentives lead to more effort, higher income, and higher caloric consumption. Croppenstedt and Muller (2000), however, estimate a positive impact of health and nutritional status on the productivity of peasant farmers in Ethiopia.

Childhood nutrition can affect future incomes either through a direct effect on future productivity or by inducing improved attendance and performance at school. Some studies can estimate only the net impact of these two channels, while others have been able to isolate the effect of the link through education from the more direct effect.

Hoddinott et al. (2008) report results from a long-term study of the impact of child nutrition in Guatemala, in which children in two villages were offered a highly nutritious dietary supplement, while those in two comparison villages were offered a supplement of minimal nutritional value. Sixty percent of village residents, by then aged between 25 and 42, were tracked more than twenty years later. Wages rates of those from the treatment villages were found to be 46 percent higher than those of control villages, but they nonetheless did not have significantly higher earned incomes.

---

[4] A high attrition rate (about 50%) weakened the robustness of these results. If those who quit the study were less likely to benefit from iron supplements, then the estimated effect is biased upward.

[5] The second study, Edgerton et al. (1979) studied Sri Lankan tea plantation workers.

[6] Deolalikar 1988; and Haddad and Bouis 1991.

Case and Paxson (2008) find that the labor market pays a wage premium to individuals of greater height, itself a robust indicator of childhood nutrition. They go further and argue that the premium is not a reward for height itself, either due to discrimination or the productivity that height might portend, but that height serves as a marker for cognitive ability, which is rewarded by the market. Similarly, Behrman and Rosenzweig (2004) use data on twins and find that fetal growth is associated with future height and years of completed schooling in adulthood. These studies suggest that *in utero* and early childhood health can have important effects on the efficiency with which children learn while at school, and hence their future economic performance.

In a similar vein, Case, Fertig, and Paxson (2004) control for parental income, education, and social class and find that children who experience poor health attain lower education, worse health, and lower social status in adulthood. Poor health in childhood thus acts as a mechanism of inter-generational poverty transmission.

In the developing world, childhood malnutrition and morbidity not only can reduce returns on the intensive margin by compromising learning efficiency at school, but they can have large effects on the extensive margin by reducing school enrollment and attendance. In a field experiment in western Kenya, Miguel and Kremer (2004) assigned simple and cheap de-worming treatment to randomly selected students across randomly selected schools. They found that absenteeism in treated schools was reduced by one-quarter, and that by reducing transmission of the infection the intervention also improved the health and school participation of untreated students in both treated and nearby untreated schools. However, despite the impact on school participation, the intervention did not have a significant effect on test scores, so the contribution to human capital and future economic activity remains unknown.

In contrast, Field et al. (2009) use temporal and geographic variation in the implementation of intensive iodine supplementation in Tanzania to study the impact on schooling of reductions in iodine deficiency syndrome. They find that children treated *in utero* attain between one-third and one-half a year more education relative to their (untreated) siblings and peers, and that this effect is particularly great for girls. They also infer from the data that this increase in years of schooling attained is driven in part by better performance while in school, and the associated higher likelihood of passing tests which allow grade progression, and that the program did not affect the age at which children begin formal education. Thus iodine supplementation can be interpreted as reducing the price of completed school grades, and hence the demand for education.

Like iodine deficiency syndrome, anemia can impact childhood educational attendance and attainment. Bobonis et al. (2006) report the results of a field experiment in which iron supplements were randomized across 2–6-year-old children in Delhi slums, where the pre-intervention rate of anemia was 69 percent. This study focused on very young children, for whom test score data were of little relevance. They find that child weight increased, and that pre-school participation rates rose, at least in the short run. On the other hand, the longer run impacts of the intervention were harder to interpret, due to sample attrition and non-random sorting of new cohorts.

Following a similar strategy to that employed by Field et al., Bleakley (2007a and 2007b) uses two specific historical health interventions—hookworm eradication in the southern United States and malaria eradication campaigns in selected countries in the Americas (US, Brazil, Colombia, and Mexico)—to estimate the effect of health on income. In his study of the impact of hookworm eradication efforts under the Rockefeller Sanitary Commission in the American South in the early twentieth century, Bleakley measures pre-existing infection rates in 1913 by location (on average, 40 percent of school-aged children were infected prior to the intervention). In a similar fashion to the approach adopted by Acemoglu and Johnson (2007), the author uses variation in infection rates by location, which reflect the potential benefits from eradication, to identify the impact of changes in the health environment on economic outcomes. He finds that areas with higher pre-existing infection rates saw greater increases in school enrollment, attendance, and literacy after the intervention. For example, he finds that before 1910 the impact of infection rates in 1913 on school attendance is negative, but that by 1920 there is no impact of 1913 infection rates on attendance. That is, those areas that had the most to gain from the eradication saw enrollment rates increase more. Similar results are found for literacy.

There may have been other changes in the economic environment that could have led to similar trends over this period, but it is argued that these should have affected adults in different areas in a similar way. However, no similar pattern is found among adults across the affected areas, who, by the nature of the disease, had virtually no pre-existing infection.

A similar exercise is performed using the malaria eradication campaigns in the United States c.1920 and in Brazil, Colombia, and Mexico c.1955 (Bleakley 2006). Pre-existing prevalence rates provide the exogenous variation permitting him to identify the impact of childhood exposure to malaria on future adult literacy and incomes. He finds that for individuals born well before the relevant eradication campaign, those born in more malarious regions had lower wages and literacy later in life, but for those born well after the campaigns, pre-eradication malaria prevalence had little effect on future wages and literacy. He concludes that "persistent childhood malaria infection reduces adult income by 40 to 60 percent."

Interestingly, Bleakley is able to differentiate between the impact of morbidity and mortality on future income. He finds that eradication of *vivax* malaria (which causes high morbidity, but relatively few deaths) leads to significant increases in human capital formation and future income, but that eradication of *falciparum* malaria (which is relatively fatal) produces no such gains. His preferred rationalization of this result is that reductions in mortality rates increase the marginal benefit of human capital acquisition (as there are more years in which to earn a return on human capital investments), but this might have little impact on the level of investment if marginal costs are increasing steeply.[7]

---

[7] An alternative reason that reductions in malaria mortality rates did not appear to affect human capital acquisition could be that the large share of deaths due to this cause are suffered by children, before the marginal schooling decisions have been made. See the discussion below of Jayachandran and Lleras-Muney's (2009) study in Sri Lanka.

On the other hand, a reduction in morbidity makes it easier to attend school and to learn while there, thereby flattening the marginal cost curve, and leading to significant increases in human capital acquisition.

Bleakley uses his estimates to extrapolate across countries, and estimates that malaria can account for about 10–16 percent of the income gap between the US and Latin America. For the Americas at least then, this evidence suggests that eradicating malaria would modestly narrow the cross-country income gap by inducing higher growth in Latin America. He concludes that "…while reducing malaria could bring substantial income gains to some countries, the estimated effect is approximately an order of magnitude too small to be useful in explaining the global income distribution" (2006: 26). According to this research, improving health could be important for growth, but is unlikely to be a panacea.

Using a similar approach, Cutler et al. (2007) examine the impact of a malaria eradication program across Indian states during the 1950s and find that the program increased literacy and primary school completion by ten percentage points, accounting for about half the observed gains in these measures over the period spanning the intervention in malarious regions. Hong (2007) and Lucas (2009) both find significant affects of either exposure to malaria or its eradication on a variety of economic outcomes such as schooling, literacy, labor force participation, and/or wealth.

Almond (2006) uses a negative historical health innovation as opposed to a policy-driven improvement to again estimate the link from *in utero* health to economic performance later in life. In particular, he studies the effects of the 1918 influenza epidemic, which was harsh and short, and whose incidence varied geographically. In comparing cohorts exposed *in utero* to the flu with those who were born just before or conceived just after, he found the former had "reduced educational attainment, increased rates of physical disability, lower income, lower socioeconomic status, as well as accelerated adult mortality compared with other cohorts." Similarly, those born in states where the pandemic was less severe fared better than those in other states.

The role of health on the incentive to invest in education has attracted both theoretical and empirical attention of researchers. For example, Kalemli-Ozcan et al. (2000) and Soares (2005) incorporate both education and fertility choices in models of demographic transition and the impact of health on growth. The essential feature of these models is that longer life expectancy increases the returns to investment in general, including education. Those cross-country analyses above that assess the impact of life expectancy on income are unable to identify a large effect partly because much of the improvement in life expectancy over the twentieth century was associated with reductions in infant and child mortality, which occurs before most educational decisions are made.

Jayachandran and Lleras-Muney (2009) present evidence that reductions in adult mortality, which increase the life expectancy of school-aged children, can have important effects on educational attainment. They exploit a sharp fall in maternal mortality, from 1.8 to 0.5 maternal deaths per hundred live births over a short seven-year period in Sri Lanka that translated into a 4.1 percent increase in life expectancy of 15-year-olds, and find that female literacy increased 2.5 percent and years of schooling rose by 4.0 percent. Their empirical strategy is strengthened by a number of unique features of the environment: first, as well as occurring after education decisions have been made, maternal mortality affects relatively young adults, and reducing it saves potentially many future years (and hence induces a stronger human capital acquisition response); second, the authors are able to compare outcomes for women across districts (in which the reductions in maternal mortality rates varied); and third, the outcomes for both women and men (whose mortality rates and life expectancy changed less over the same period) can be usefully compared.

At the cross-country level, Fortson (2007) uses data from Demographic and Health Surveys in southern Africa to assess the effect of adult mortality on the incentive to invest in human capital. She finds that living in an area with higher HIV prevalence, and hence a higher perceived risk of premature death, is associated with lower educational attainment and slower grade progression. This effect is not observed just for orphans, but for non-orphans as well. Reduced life expectancy appears to dampen the incentive to invest in human capital.

Most often it is adults who make education decisions on behalf of their children, so reductions in adult mortality can increase the incentive to invest in human capital simply because those who would finance it are alive to do so. For example, Case, Paxson, and Ableidinger (2004) find that orphanhood reduces the school enrollment of children compared with other children with whom they live, suggesting that biological ties seem to matter in the allocation of investment.

5.4 Conclusions

This chapter has outlined a number of mechanisms by which improvements in health could lead to increases in income, and has documented a growing body of empirical evidence that assesses the strength of these links. From a policy perspective, it is not necessarily useful to dwell on the question of whether health determines income or vice versa as both directions of causality are likely to be operative. The more useful question is, "Are the income returns to some health improvements likely to be enough to tip the balance in favor of interventions that would otherwise not pass a cost–benefit test?" It remains very difficult to address this question in general, the answer to which depends on the nature of the health improvement, the intervention itself, and the economic and institutional environment.

Basic public economics suggest that policymakers first investigate the prevalence of market failures that inhibit the adoption of the kinds of interventions that might otherwise have large health, and income, effects. Obvious candidates are public goods (e.g. vector control), and perhaps goods that exhibit increasing returns to scale in production, such as in the provision of some private goods including e.g. iodized salt, which might be best provided, financed, or simply mandated by government.

Alternatively, the correlation between health and income suggests that health policy should be an integral part of social policy in general and of redistributional policies in particular. First, independent of any causation between the two, either (poor) health status can be used as a marker of (low) income, so income transfers in the form of tax credits and subsidies might be directed to the sick and infirm; or publicly provided health-improving goods and services, of little value to those who are not sick, could serve as an efficient self-targeted means of redistributing to the poor. However, the scope for errors of both inclusion and exclusion is wide, and some health conditions concentrated particularly among the poor, and some services valued particularly by them, might have better targeting properties than others.

Second, absent issues of targeting efficiency, the causal link from health to income, and the fact that income does not fully explain health outcomes, suggests that the provision of health services to the poor could be an efficient means of improving their well-being. There is a taste of a merit–good argument to this reasoning: the fact that education, itself correlated with income, is an important independent determinant of health, suggests that demand for certain health services among the poor might not be as high as it could be. Whether this means the poor should be provided with health services or education is not clear—perhaps both?

In the poorest regions of the world, the potential gains to health improvement can only be realized if complementary institutions such as schools with effective teachers and well-functioning labor and credit markets exist. The promise of health, however, is matched by the challenges of delivering health services, an issue that we have not addressed here but which must be incorporated into any policy choice involving public provision or financing of health interventions. In these environments especially, the mobilization of resources to finance improved health, and the income gains it promises, must go hand in hand with the design of incentives for effective service delivery, embedded in responsive and well-governed institutions.

References

ACEMOGLU, DARON and JOHNSON, SIMON (2007), "Disease and Development: The Effect of Life Expectancy on Economic Growth," *Journal of Political Economy*, 115(6): 925–85.

—— and ROBINSON, JAMES A. (2001), "The Colonial Origins of Comparative Development: An Empirical Investigation," *American Economic Review*, 91(5): 1369–401.

ALBOUY, DAVID (2008), "The Colonial Origins of Comparative Development: An Investigation of the Settler Mortality Data," NBER working paper No. 14130.

ALMOND, DOUGLAS, JR. (2006), "Is the 1918 Influenza Pandemic Over? Long-term Effects of *In Utero* Influenza Exposure in the Post-1940 US Population," *Journal of Political Economy*, 114 (Aug.): 672–712.

BECKER, G. (1981), *A Treatise on the Family*. Cambridge, MA: Harvard University Press.

BERHMAN, JERE and ROSENZWEIG, MARK R. (2004), "Returns to Birthweight," *Review of Economics and Statistics*, 86 (May): 586–601.

BLEAKLEY, HOYT (2006), "Malaria in the Americas: A Retrospective Analysis of Childhood Exposure." Documento CEDE 2006–35, September.

—— (2007a), "Disease and Development: Evidence from Hookworm Eradication in the American South," *The Quarterly Journal of Economics*, February, 122(1): 73–117.

—— (2007b), "Spillovers and Aggregate Effects of Health Capital: Evidence from Campaigns Against Parasitic Disease in the Americas." Unpublished manuscript, University of Chicago.

BLOOM, DAVID, CANNING, DAVID, and GRAHAM, BRYAN (2003), "Longevity and Life-cycle Savings," *Scandinavian Journal of Economics*, 105(3): 319–38.

—— and SEVILLA, JAYPEE (2004), "The Effect of Health on Economic Growth: A Production Function Approach," *World Development*, 32(1): 1–13.

BOBONIS, G., MIGUEL, E., and SHARMA, C. (2006), "Iron Deficiency, Anemia, and School Participation," *Journal of Human Resources*, 41(4): 692–721.

CASE, ANNE and PAXSON, CHRISTINA (2008), "Stature and Status: Height, Ability, and Labor Market Outcomes," *Journal of Political Economy*, 116(3): 499–532.

—— and ABLEIDINGER, JOSEPH (2004), "Orphans in Africa: Parental Death, Poverty, and School Enrollment," *Demography*, 41(3): 483–508.

CASE, A., FERTIG, A., and PAXSON, C. (2004), "The Lasting Impact of Childhood Health and Circumstances." Center for Health and Wellbeing Discussion Paper, Princeton.

CROPPENSTEDT, ANDRE and MULLER, CHRISTOPHE (2000), "The Impact of Farmers' Health and Nutritional Status on Their Productivity and Efficiency: Evidence from Ethiopia," *Economic Development and Cultural Change*, 48(3): 475–502.

CUTLER, DAVID, FUNG, WINNIE, KREMER, MICHAEL, and SINGHAL, MONICA (2007), "Mosquitoes: The Long-term Effects of Malaria Eradication in India." Unpublished working paper, Harvard University.

DEOLALIKAR, ANIL (1988): "Nutrition and Labor Productivity in Agriculture: Estimates for Rural South India," *Review of Economics and Statistics*, 70(3): 406–13.

EASTERLY, WILLIAM and LEVINE, ROSS (2003), "Tropics, Germs and Crops: How Endowments Influence Economic Development," *Journal of Monetary Economics*, 50(1): 3–39.

EDGERTON, V. R., GARDNER, G., OHIRA, Y., GUNAWARDENA, K. A., and SENEWIRATNE, B. (1979), "Iron-deficiency Anemia and its Effect on Worker Productivity and Activity Patterns," *British Medical Journal*, 2: 1546–9.

FIELD, ERICA, ROBLES, OMAR, and TORERO, MAXIMO (2009), "Iodine Deficiency and Schooling Attainment in Tanzania," *American Economic Journal: Applied Economics*, 1(4): 140–69.

FOGEL, ROBERT (2004), "Health, Nutrition, and Economic Growth," *Economic Development and Cultural Change*, 52(3): 643–58.

FORTSON, JANE (2007), "Mortality Risk and Human Capital Investment: The Impact of HIV/AIDS in Sub-Saharan Africa." Mimeo, Becker Center on Chicago Price Theory. (To be published in *Review of Economics and Statistics*, posted online in MIT Press Journals July 2010.)

FOSTER, ANDREW and ROSENZWEIG, MARK (1994), "A Test for Moral Hazard in the Labor Market: Contractual Arrangements, Effort, and Health," *The Review of Economics and Statistics*, LXXVI(2): 213–27.

GALLUP, JOHN L. and SACHS, JEFFREY D. (2001), "The Economic Burden of Malaria," *American Journal of Tropical Medicine and Hygiene*, 64(1,2)S: 85–96.

GROSSMAN, MICHAEL (1972), "On the Concept of Health Capital and the Demand for Health," *Journal of Political Economy*, 80(2): 223–55.

HADDAD, LAWRENCE J. and BOUIS, HOWARTH E. (1991). "The Impact of Nutritional Status on Agricultural Productivity: Wage Evidence from the Philippines," *Oxford Bulletin of Economics and Statistics* (Department of Economics, University of Oxford), February, 53(1): 45–68.

HODDINOTT, JOHN, MALUCCIO, JOHN A., BEHRMAN, JERE R., FLORES, RAFAEL, and MARTORELL, REYNALDO (2008), "Effect of a Nutrition Intervention During Early Childhood on Economic Productivity in Guatemalan Adults," *The Lancet*, 371(9610): 411–16.

KALEMLI-OZCAN, S., RYDER, H., and WEIL, D. (2000), "Mortality Decline, Human Capital Investment, and Economic Growth," *Journal of Development Economics*, 62(1): 1–23.

LI, R., CHEN, X., YAN, H., DEURENBERG, P., GARBY, L., and HAUTVAST, J. G. (1994), "Functional Consequences of Iron Supplementation in Iron-deficient Female Cotton Workers in Beijing, China," *American Journal of Clinical Nutrition*, 59(4): 908–13.

LUCAS, ADRIENNE (2009), "Malaria Eradication and Educational Attainment: Evidence from Paraguay and Sri Lanka," *American Economic Journal: Applied Economics*, 2(2): 46–71.

MANKIW, N. GREGORY (1995), "The Growth of Nations," *Brookings Papers on Economic Activity*, 26(1995-1): 275–326.

MCARTHUR, JOHN W. and SACHS, JEFFREY D. (2001), "Institutions and Geography: Comment on Acemoglu, Johnson and Robinson 2000," NBER Working paper No. W8114.

MIGUEL, EDWARD and KREMER, MICHAEL (2004), "Worms: Identifying the Impacts on Education and Health in the Presence of Treatment Externalities," *Econometrica*, 72(1): 159–217.

PRESTON, S. H. (1975), "The Changing Relation Between Mortality and Level of Economic Development," *Population Studies*, 29(2): 231–48.

PRITCHETT, LANT and SUMMERS, LAWRENCE H. (1996), "Wealthier is Healthier," *Journal of Human Resource*, 31: 841–68.

RODRIK, DANI, SUBRAMANIAN, ARVIND, and TREBBI, FRANCESCO (2004), "Institutions Rule: The Primacy of Institutions over Geography and Integration in Economic Development," *Journal of Economic Growth*, 9(2): 131–65.

SACHS, JEFFREY D. (2003), "Institutions Don't Rule: Direct Effects of Geography on Per Capita Income," NBER Working Paper No. W9490.

SOARES, RODRIGO (2005), "Mortality Reductions, Educational Attainment and Fertility Choice," *American Economic Review*, 95(3): 580–601.

STRAUSS, JOHN and THOMAS, DUNCAN (1998), "Health, Nutrition, and Economic Development," *Journal of Economic Literature*, XXXVI: 766–817.

THOMAS, DUNCAN and FRANKENBERG, ELIZABETH (2002), "Health, Nutrition and Prosperity: A Microeconomic Perspective," *Bulletin of the World Health Organization*, 80(2): 106–13.

—— FRIEDMAN, JED, et al. (2004): "Iron Deficiency and the Well-Being of Older Adults: Early Results from a Randomized Nutrition Intervention," *American Economic Review*, 93(2): 107–11.

WEIL, DAVID (2007), "Accounting for the Effect of Health on Economic Growth," *Quarterly Journal of Economics*, 122(3): 1265–306.

YOUNG, ALWYN (2005), "The Gift of the Dying: The Tragedy of AIDS and the Welfare of Future African Generations," *Quarterly Journal of Economics*, CXX(2): 423–66.

CHAPTER 6

....

HEALTH PRODUCTION

....

KRISTIAN BOLIN

IN this chapter, I will, first, provide a comprehensive, but not too technical, account of the dominating theoretical model of individual health-related behavior: the demand-for-health model (the Grossman model, or the health-production model). Then, I will discuss the large body of both theoretical and empirical work that Michael Grossman's seminal contribution to health economics has inspired (without performing a systematic literature review). In the second part of the chapter, I will present and briefly discuss some of the theoretical extensions of the model. Then, I turn to empirical evidence with regard to the demand-for-health model, and identify relevant areas in which additional empirical research is indispensable for the success of public policy efforts in the health area. Particular interest will be paid to the relation between the two main components of human capital—educational and health capital. The fourth part of the chapter will be devoted to policy issues that arise from the research discussed in the preceding sections. The policy section begins with a theoretical discussion which seeks to identify potential policy target-variables and the effect of those variables on individual health and health-related behavior. The chapter ends with a discussion of what lessons for the shaping of public health policies can be drawn from the demand-for-health model and the empirical estimates of it, and of what future developments are required. General conclusions end the chapter.

Michael Grossman's demand-for-health model laid the foundation for much of what nowadays is labeled Health Economics. Today, many economics articles that are published in peer-reviewed journals in the research fields of health, and most articles focusing on individual health-related behavior, refer to Grossman's (1972) *Journal of Political Economy* article. In health economics textbooks, the demand-for-health model, and the ideas and research that have sprung from it, has an obvious role to play. It is hard to assess the influence that the model has exerted on research within other disciplines and on the way in which, for instance, public policymakers conceptualize health and health-related behavior. It seems safe to say, though, that the concept of human capital has spread from initially being used exclusively by highly specialized economists, to being used by a broad variety professions and by politicians and policymakers. It is doubtful if human capital would have been that widespread in its use today had it not been for the extension of the human capital theory into incorporating an explicit theory of health. The significance of this is highlighted by health, along with education, being the principal human capital component that may be influenced through individual decisions, and the fact that health-related policies account for a great share of all public policies.

Since the publication of the demand-for-health model, several extensions and alternative formulations have been developed and published. I deal briefly with most of these below, in the section "Theoretical Extensions." My account of the demand-for-health model in the section "Theoretical Outline of the Demand-for-health Model" takes into account neither the criticism of the model nor the extensions of it. My version of the model presented below is not identical to Grossman's initial formulation, although it incorporates the core features of his model. I deviate from the original formulation mainly (1) by using a continuous-time formulation, and (2) by not *explicitly* treating household production.

6.1 INTRODUCTION

To a health economist the individual is the obvious unit of study when it comes to analyzing decisions pertaining to individual health and health-related behavior, which is consistent with the individualistic paradigm generally applied in economic theory. Although individual health-related behavior cannot fully explain the realized amount of health it is certainly true that the individual faces a vast range of possibilities to influence his or her health. Beyond the influence of own health that the individual exercises, his or her health is also determined (a) by decisions made by others, over which the individual may or may not have any influence, (b) by entirely exogenous variables, such as the environment in which the individual lives, and (c) by genes.

Activities that have long-term consequences for the individual are, in economics, typically regarded as investments. The attributes in which investments are made are referred to as capital. The fundamental economic-theoretical framework for thinking about human capital investment activities includes a wide range of behaviors: for instance, financial savings and health-related activities can both be analyzed within basically the same apparatus. For our purposes, the theory of human capital is an essential point of departure. Even though our prime interest is in health we are also interested in other, and maybe competing, interests that the individual may harbor. For instance, a great number of empirical studies have shown that education (measured as attained education or years of schooling) is one of the most important correlates of health, and it is a question of immense policy importance whether or not health—and educational—capital are causally linked or if the correlation between them, which have been observed in several studies, is explained by a third variable which influences both education and health.

6.1.1 Utility and Household Production

Now, I will present the demand-for-health model, and explain its key features. In doing so, I need to introduce a set of economic-theoretical concepts. I begin by explaining those. *Third*, the concept of *utility* is essential to all economic theories which are built on individual choices. I will use the one good case, i.e. utility is derived from a single good, which is bought on the market. The *utility function* assigns a specific number to each amount of that commodity. Usually, in consumer theory the utility function represents the individual's *preference order* of each conceivable amount of the good—this means that any function that always increases when its argument increases may be used to represent the individual's preferences. When there are two or more goods from which the individual derives utility, the utility function is assumed to provide a measure of the extent to which the individual is willing to substitute the one good for the other. This willingness together with (relative) market prices partly determines his or her demand for each of the goods. Formally, in this chapter, I will assume that the individual derives utility from H (health capital) and Z (consumption), according to the utility function:

$$U(H, Z). \tag{1}$$

I assume that positive and diminishing marginal utilities of health and consumption, i.e., $\frac{\partial u}{\partial H} > 0$ and $\frac{\partial^2 u}{\partial H^2} < 0$ (and similarly for Z). For simplicity, I also assume that the commodity Z is a market good, which distinguishes it from health, since investments in health (I) is produced by the individual. The individual's "production capability" is a significant source of influence of the demand for market-produced goods.

Second, in *household production* market goods and own time (τ) is transformed into commodities (Lancaster, 1966).[1] In this approach to consumer theory a distinction is made between fundamental objects of choice—commodities—and market goods (for instance, different kinds of food are market goods, while a meal is a commodity). Market goods are bought on the market using monetary resources obtained through labor (or wealth). This means that each unit of time that is not sold as labor has an opportunity cost that can be readily expressed in terms of forgone earnings (or in their market goods equivalents). The extent to which the individual is willing to accept this depends on his or her relative abilities of using market goods and own time in this process. This is reflected by the household production function.[2] In principle, we are able to answer the question of how the individual allocates his or her own time, in a single-period model, using this framework (see Becker 1965).

---

[1] The theory of household production is a key component in Becker's (1964) formulation of his human capital theory.

[2] The household may be comprised of different constellations—one person or several persons. In the text, I refer to the one-person household in the section *Theoretical Extensions*.

6.2 Theoretical Outline of the
Demand-for-Health model

Michael Grossman's extension of the human capital theory (Grossman 1972a and b) builds on traditional neoclassical capital theory, the human capital theory (developed focusing on education, Becker 1964), the theory of allocation of time (Becker 1965), and Lancaster's approach to consumer theory (Lancaster 1966). In Grossman's (1972) paper he emphasized (a) that health is a durable capital stock, (b) that health capital differs from other forms of human capital in that its main impact is on the total amount of time a person can spend producing money earnings and commodities rather than on his or her wage rate, and (c) that the demand for health care must be derived from the more fundamental demand for good health.

The original demand-for-health model comprises two types of human capital: educational (E) and health (H); health is determined within the model (endogenous) whereas the stock of education is taken as given (exogenous). As mentioned above, the distinguishing feature of health capital is that it determines the amount of productive time that the individual can use freely. Educational capital is determinant for the productivity of that time. Each individual is born with a certain amount of health capital, which depreciates with age, and is assumed to produce investments (I) in health in order to align the realized amount of health with the demanded amount.[3]

6.2.1 Cost of Household Production

In order to reduce the degree of complexity, I will restrain from modeling household production explicitly, and instead use the household's cost function which corresponds to the particular production technology used.[4] All relevant information concerning the allocation choices that the individual makes is comprised in the cost function.[5] Technically, the cost function is obtained by, *first*, solving the problem of how to produce a given quantity at the lowest cost, for a given set of prices, which yields the individual's demand functions for own time and market goods. *Second*,

---

[3] I distinguish between the stock of education and education as in schooling. Schooling is used for investing in educational capital. Depending on the nature of the specific technologies used for this there is a certain correlation between schooling and the stock of educational capital.

[4] Grossman's (1972) original formulation of the demand-for-health model did model household production explicitly.

[5] For instance, the (conditional) demand functions regarding the inputs to production (own time and a market good) can be obtained by Sheppard's lemma, which states that the partial derivate of the cost function with respect to the price of a good equals the (compensated) demand for that good.

these demand functions are multiplied with their respective unit cost and summed. The cost function thus obtained provides the lowest cost of producing each quantity of health investments from household production. Even though Grossman's original formulation of his model incorporated *medical care goods* and own time inputs, nothing forbids a broader interpretation of the original formulation of the model.[6] Thus, I will assume that market goods used in the production of health investments may include also, for instance, wholesome food and exercise equipment (but assume that there is no joint production).[7] Further, some goods and actions may be hazardous to health and might, hence, be thought of as representing negative investments in health, for instance, smoking.[8]

Educational capital has two properties that are relevant for our purposes: (1) it increases market productivity and, hence, the wage rate, and (2) it determines the individual's efficiency in combining time and goods in order to produce health investments. I assume that the cost function associated with the production of health investments may be expressed as follows:

$$C = C(w(E), \bar{p}; E) \cdot I = \pi(w(E), \bar{p}; E) \cdot I, \qquad (2)$$

Where w is the wage rate, $\bar{p}$ is the vector of prices of market goods used in health production, and π is the one-unit cost of producing I. Further, I assume that the individual's market productivity is increasing in educational capital; and the individual's capacity to produce gross investments in health capital is increasing in the actual amount of educational capital. Formally, this means that:

$$\frac{\partial w}{\partial E} \geq 0, \text{ and}$$

$$\frac{\partial C}{\partial E} = \frac{\partial \pi}{\partial E} \cdot I \leq 0. \qquad (3)$$

6.2.2 Depreciation of Health

The stock of health depreciates at each point in time; the rate of depreciation is denoted $\delta(t)$. It is assumed that the rate of depreciation increases with age: $\delta'(t) > 0$. That is, given the health stock, H_t, at time t, the amount with which health depreciates at time t is equal to $\delta(t) \cdot H_t$

---

[6] Grossman (1972a: 226) noted this. He also pointed out that allowing for other goods that affect health—for instance, diet and cigarette smoking—leads to joint production in the household.

[7] See Grossman (1972a: 226).

[8] The effect of hazardous consumption may also be regarded as part of the inputs used in the production of gross health investments; op. cit.

6.2.3 The Benefits of Good Health

Good health is demanded for two reasons in the demand-for-health model. *First,* health is welfare enhancing per se. This is the consumption aspect of health. There are also complementarities between ordinary consumption and the consumption of good health, that is, the benefits that are accruing from the "consumption" of a certain amount of health depend on the consumption of other goods (formally, the cross-derivative of the utility function is non-zero). *Second,* health determines the amount of time available for productive purposes—the investment aspect of health. We assume that the amount of healthy time is increasing in the stock of health, but that the effect of the stock on healthy time is diminishing in the size of the stock. In other words, the larger is the size of the health stock, the more healthy time becomes available, but each additional amount of health capital produces less healthy time than the units preceding it (for an illustration see Figure 6.1). Formally, the investment aspect of health is reflected by the relationship between sick time, τ^s, and the stock of health:

$$\tau_t^s(H_t) \ \partial\tau_t^s/\partial H_t < 0; \text{ and } \partial^2\tau_t^s/\partial H_t^2 > 0 \tag{4}$$

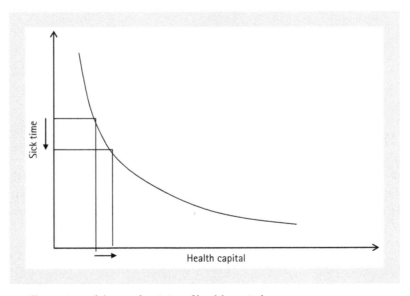

FIGURE 6.1 Illustration of the productivity of health capital

Notes: At the vertical axis the amount of sick time is measured, while the horizontal axis measures the amount of health capital. At small amounts of health capital an increase in the stock means that sick time is reduced by a large amount, and at large amounts of health capital an additional unit of health has a small impact on the amount of sick time. This means that the productivity of health capital in producing healthy time is diminishing.

6.2.4 The Life-cycle Perspective and Time Preferences

One essential feature of the demand-for-health model is missing in the model outlined above: the life-cycle perspective. It is assumed that the individual allocates his or her resources—own time and financial resources—so as to attain the highest possible sum of utilities over the life-cycle. Moreover, the individual is assumed to value current utility different than future utility—this is reflected by the individual's *time preferences*, which indicate the relative value of current utility in relation to future utility.[9, 10]

Formally, it is assumed that the individual allocates his or her resources *as if* solving a deterministic dynamic optimization problem and adhering to its solution (uncertainty is discussed below, in the section *Theoretical Extensions*). The solution to this problem provides an optimal time-path of health investments and, hence, of health capital, over the life-cycle (and, also, optimal time-paths for all other choices that the individual makes and which are parts of the model). Taking time preferences into account, the *current* value of utility accruing at time *t*, is:

$$e^{-\rho t} \cdot U(H_t, Z_t), \tag{5}$$

where ρ is the rate of time preferences.

It should be emphasized, though, that the plan that results from the solution to the optimization problem is not unchangeable: changes in market good prices, the opportunity cost of own time, education or in some of the other parameters which enter the individual's optimization problem will induce the individual to revise his or her plan for how to allocate available resources.[11] Thus, the health-related behavior that the individual chooses will vary between different contexts. In particular, different institutional settings, for instance, the organization of the health care sector, determine the cost that the individual meets for producing health investments.

6.2.5 The Equations of Motions for Health and Wealth

The individual possesses three stocks—the stock of educational capital, health capital (human capital), and physical capital. Grossman's original formulation of the model

---

[9] The concept of time preferences has been used in economics for a long time; see Fredrick et al. (2002).

[10] In Grossman's original formulation of the model, time preferences were implicitly present in the inter-temporal utility function. Several of the extensions of the model are formulated in continuous time using utility functions that permit that utilities from different points in time are added (time-additive utility functions); see, for instance, Jabobson (2000); and Bolin et al. (2001b).

[11] We assume that the individual acts as if having perfect knowledge. However, should new information emerge he or she has to re-calculate the optimization problem faced at the beginning of the life-cycle. Thus, the individual may end up solving a sequence of optimization problems over the life-cycle.

demanded that lifetime resources equals lifetime outlays and, hence, allowed the accumulation of physical capital to be negative for some periods. Notice that since health capital cannot be sold, gross investments cannot be negative. Investments and depreciation, in respective stock, means that changes in the stocks of health and wealth can be described by the following equations:

$$\dot{H}_t = I_t - \delta_t \cdot H_t, \text{ and} \tag{6}$$

$$\dot{W}_t = rW_t + w_t \cdot (T - \tau_t^s) - C_t - p \cdot Z_t. \tag{7}$$

The first equation is the equation of motion of health capital, and the second equation is the equation of motion of wealth; p is the price of the consumption commodity; total resources (R), are total time (T) times the wage rate $(R = w \cdot T)$.

6.2.6 The Individual's Optimization Problem

The individual is assumed to allocate his or her limited resources over the life-cycle in order to maximize life-cycle utility. This means that health-improving activities compete with other activities which also improve the individual's welfare. The balance between the individual's different preferences determines the individual's demand for health, which, in turn, determines his or her demand for health care.

The individual faces the following optimization problem:

$$\max \int_0^T e^{-\rho t} U(H_t, Z_t) \, dt$$

subject to:

$$\dot{H}_t = I_t - \delta_t \cdot H_t;$$

$$\dot{W}_t = rW_t + w_t \cdot (T - \tau_t^s) - C_t - Z_t \cdot p.$$

In the case when both stocks are given at the outset (at $t = 0$) and at time T we have:[12]

$$H_0 = H_0; H_T \geq H_{\min}; \text{ and } W_0 = W; W_T \geq 0,$$

[12] In addition to the equations of motion, the problem may also contain information concerning the amount of respective stock at the outset and at the final point in time. Certain types of problems have no given end-time, that is, T is an endogenous variable to be decided by the solution to the problem. Obviously, such a formulation is useful when analyzing the problem of *optimal length of life*; see, for instance, Erlich and Chuma (1990); and, for a discussion of the optimal-length-of-life problem, Grossman (2000).

where H_0 is the inherited amount of health capital;[13] H_T is the amount of health capital at time T; H_{min} is the lowest possible amount of health capital (W at time $t = 0$ and $t = T$ have analogous interpretations).

6.2.7 The Optimality Condition

Using optimal control theory (Seierstad and Sydsæter 1987; Chiang 1992) in order to solve the problem above results in the following optimality condition regarding the demand for health capital:[14]

$$\frac{e^{-(p-r)t}}{\lambda_0^W} \frac{\partial U}{\partial H_t} - w_t(E) \cdot \frac{\partial \tau_t^s}{\partial H_t} = (r + \delta_t^H - \frac{\pi_t(E)}{\pi_t(E)}) \cdot \pi_t^H(E), \tag{8}$$

where λ_0^W is the marginal life-cycle utility of wealth at the outset (at $t = o$). The optimality condition is explained below.

6.2.8 Interpretation

The left-hand side of (8) constitutes the marginal benefits of health capital, which equals the discounted marginal consumption utility of health capital (the first term), and the monetary value of one additional unit of health capital (the second term). Similarly, the right-hand side constitutes the marginal cost of an additional unit of health capital: the term r reflects the opportunity cost of investing in health rather than in the capital market; the depreciation term reflects the fact that each unit of health capital depreciates by a certain amount at each point in time, making it more expensive to add an additional unit of health capital to the stock; the last term reflects that the one-unit cost of producing gross investments in health may vary over time and, hence, if the one-unit cost is on a rising trajectory the cost of one additional unit of health capital is lower today than in the future, in which case the incentives for making investments in health today rather than tomorrow are strengthened.

Below, I will in some detail reproduce the core predictions that can be derived from the model that has been outlined above.

---

[13] Clearly, the individual is not an autonomous individual at birth. Thus, the inherited amount of health capital should be thought of as the amount that results when the individual starts making his or her own health-related decisions, i.e. the amount that results from inheritance and upbringing.

[14] Chiang (1992) is a medium advanced textbook, while Seierstad and Sydsæter (1987), and Kamien and Schwartz (1991), respectively, are more advanced. The condition (8) can be derived by, first, formulating the Hamiltonian function for the problem above and, then, applying the maximum principle. For a solution to maximization problems similar to that above see, for instance, Grossman (1972b: appendix); Wagstaff (1986); Bolin et al. (2001b).

6.3 Predictions: The Demand for Health and the Demand for Health Investments

The most important predictions concern those that pertain to time (age), the opportunity cost of time, and the efficiency in household production—age, wage, and education. Grossman (1972, 2002) conducted his analysis separately in two parts of his model—the investment model and the consumption model. In the investment model, there are no consumption motives for being healthy, and vice versa. In my treatment below, I will focus on the investment part of the model, even though the optimality condition (8) pertains to the mixed model. Ultimately, we are interested not only in the demand for health, but also in the demand for gross health investments, and in the demand for inputs used in the production of those investments, that can be derived from the underlying demand for good health. In what follows, However, I will focus on the demand for health and changes in that demand induced by changes in exogenous variables. Grossman (see Grossman 1972b; and 2002: 369–77) provides a comprehensive treatment of the effects of the demand for health, health investments, and goods used in the production of investments, in the investment and consumption models, respectively.

In summary, these results are that, under certain not too far-fetched conditions: (a) age would be negatively correlated with health capital but positively correlated with expenditures on health care; (b) the individual's wage rate would be positively correlated both with the demand for health and with the demand for health care; and (c) education would be positively correlated with health capital but negatively correlated with expenditures on health care. The demand-for-health model explains variations in health status (besides the exogenously given initial levels of health) and health care utilization among individuals.

Intuitively, when the demand for health capital increases so will also the demand for gross investments in health, and the demand for the different inputs used in the production of those investments. I want to stress that this intuition may be inconsistent with the theoretical predictions, which is the case when the effect of age is analyzed (remember that it is assumed that the rate of depreciation increases with age). The reason why our first intuition may be wrong in the age case is that *both* the demand for health, and the supply of health capital from a given amount of gross investments decreases with age. The supply of health capital decreases since each unit of gross investment is offset by a larger depreciation of the health stock and, hence, a smaller fraction of each produced amount of gross health investments transforms into health capital.

The marginal benefits—and costs—of health capital are illustrated in Figure 6.2. The figure illustrates the individual's demand or marginal benefits—and costs (supply) of health capital—as given by equation (8). I will make use of this diagram, and variations of it, when illustrating the effects of changes in exogenous variables on the demand for health.

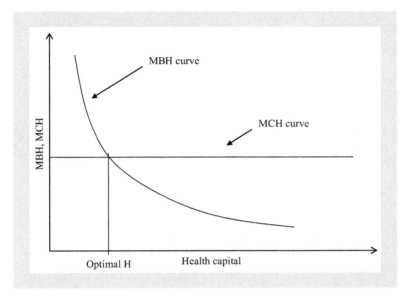

FIGURE 6.2 Illustration of the demand for health capital

Notes: The downward sloping curve illustrates the marginal benefit of health capital, MBH (the right hand side of equation 8). The horizontal line illustrates the marginal cost of health capital, MCH (supply of health capital), which is infinitely elastic since the marginal cost of health capital is independent of the stock.

Next, I will present the core prediction that can be derived from the demand-for-health model.

6.3.1 Age

Age affects the demand for health by making the possession of a certain level of health capital more expensive. This is so since the rate of depreciation increases over time and, hence, increasing resources have to be deployed in order to keep the stock of health at a certain level. Thus, the model predicts that health decreases with age.

As regards the effect of age on the demand for gross health investments, matters are slightly more complicated: the demand for health decreases, implying a reduced demand for gross health investments. At the same time, however, the supply of health capital from a given amount of gross health investments decreases as the rate of depreciation increases. The joint effect of these two forces can be shown to be to increase the demand for gross health investments with age under plausible conditions (see Grossman 1972b: 238–9; or Grossman 2000: 367–70).

In Figure 6.3 two different aged, but otherwise identical, individuals are compared. Age will not influence the MBH curve, but the supply curve will shift upwards, because of the higher rate of depreciation. Thus, the equilibrium amount of health for the old individual is lower than for the young individual.

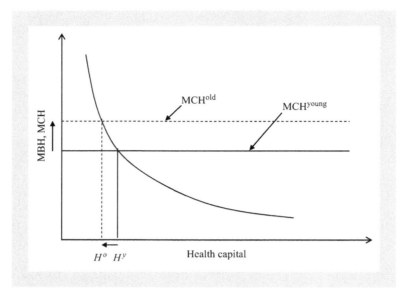

FIGURE 6.3 Illustration of the effect of age on the demanded amount of health capital

Notes: The dotted supply curve illustrates the marginal cost of health capital for an individual of high age, while the lower supply curve illustrates the marginal cost for an individual of low age. The individuals are otherwise identical. In the first case the demand for health is H^y, and in the second case H^o. This analysis could also illustrate a situation in which two individuals of the same age are compared, but where their rates of depreciation differ for some other reason. Notice that the steeper the MBH curve the less health is affected by age.

6.3.2 Wage (Market Productivity)

A higher wage rate has two effects in the demand-for-health model: (1) it increases the value of available healthy time and, hence, strengthens the incentives for being healthy (to hold health capital); and (2) makes own time used for producing gross investments in health more expensive. A higher unit cost of own time will increase the marginal cost of health capital which, in turn, will tend to decrease the demanded amount of health capital. However, as long as gross health investments are not produced solely by own time, it can be shown that the net effect of these two opposite forces is to increase the demand for health (see Grossman 1972b: 240–3; or Grossman 2000: 371–2). In the version of the demand-for-health model that I use, the consumption commodity is not produced using own time and, hence, the relative price of health will increase with the wage rate. Consequently, in this case the investment and consumption parts produce counteracting prediction regarding the wage rate effect on the demand for health.

Figure 6.4 illustrates the effects of a wage rate increase on the demand for health. For simplicity, the analysis in the figure ignores the consumption aspects of health.

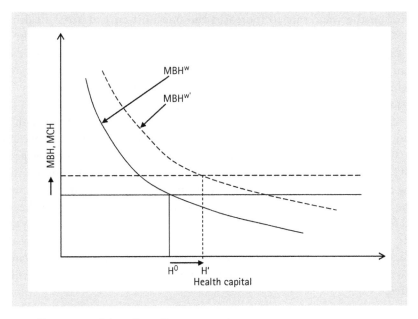

FIGURE 6.4 Illustration of the effect of a wage rate increase

Notes: The dotted curves illustrate the marginal benefit and cost of health capital after the wage rate increase. It can be shown that if gross health investments are not produced solely by own time, the shift in the MBH curve is always larger than the shift in the supply (MCH) curve.

6.3.3 Education[15] (Human Capital Other Than Health Capital)

I will assume that education (or the stock of educational capital) has both market and non-market effects. In particular, knowledge (educational capital) influences the demand for health in two ways: (1) it improves household production efficiency (the *efficiency effect*); and (2) it makes each unit of own time used in household production more expensive—the *time-price effect* (education increases also market productivity and, hence, the wage rate). The efficiency effect reflects the fact that fewer resources are needed in order to produce a given quantity of gross health investments, which decreases the one-unit cost of investments and, hence, increases the demand for health.[16] The time-price effect works through the positive effect of

[15] Grossman (1972, 2000) analyzed market and non-market effects separately, i.e. wage rate (market) effects were derived separately from the effects of education (non-market).

[16] Thus, education is assumed to influence productivity through the production process itself. This is referred to as productive efficiency. Alternatively, one could have assumed that education enables individuals to improve on the allocation of resources in the production process, implicitly assuming that the allocation was inefficient from the beginning.

education on the wage rate to increases the one-unit cost of gross health investments. Notice that the time-price effect of education cannot outweigh the market
effect—through a higher wage rate—of education. For the exact same reasons as
above, an increase in education will lead to an increase in the demand for health, as
long as health investments are not produced using own time as the only input to
production.

Now, let us illustrate the effects on the demand for health of an increase in the educational stock using Figure 6.5. First, an increase in the amount of educational capital will
increase the marginal benefits of health capital, through the effect on the wage rate, i.e.
the MBH curve will shift upwards. Second, an increase in the educational stock will
affect the marginal cost of health capital. If the efficiency effect dominates the time-price
effect the marginal cost curve will make a downward shift. Obviously, in this case the
demand for health will increase when the educational stock increases. When the time-
price effect dominates, however, the marginal cost curve shifts upward, but by a smaller
percentage than the MBH curve. Thus, in this case, changes in the marginal benefits and
marginal costs of health capital are counteracting, but the net effect on health will always
be positive.

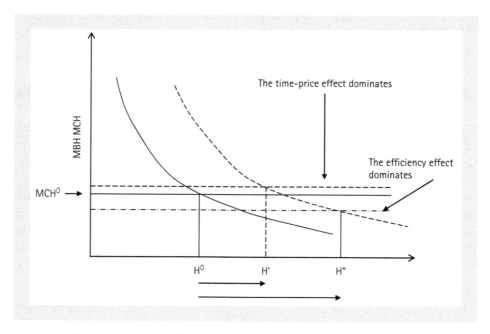

FIGURE 6.5 Illustration of the effect of an increase in educational capital on the demanded
amount of health capital

Notes: The uppermost dotted horizontal line illustrates the supply of health capital in the case when the time-price
effect outweighs the efficiency effect of educational capital, while the lower dotted line illustrates the supply of health capital in the case when the efficiency effect dominates.

6.4 Theoretical Extensions

The demand-for-health model, as Michael Grossman developed it some thirty-five years ago, comprises a number of simplifying assumptions. The most important ones are (1) the assumption of the single individual, (2) the assumption of constant returns to scale in the production of gross health investments, (3) the assumption of an exogenous rate of depreciation, (4) the assumption of no uncertainty as regards the rate of depreciation of the health stock, and (5) the assumption that the other components of the stock of human capital are exogenous. Theoretical research efforts that extend Grossman's original model in the directions of (1), (2), (3), and (4) have certainly been made. However, no theoretical model, which treats both health and the other principal component of human capital—educational capital—as endogenous has (to the best of my knowledge) to date been published in a peer-reviewed journal. This is somewhat paradoxical, since this may be the most important line of development of the demand-for-health model that can be undertaken. A theoretical model of simultaneous individual choices of investments in educational and health capital is fundamental for the capability of analyzing the relationship between these two primary human capital components, and will, facilitate the formulation of more efficient health policies.

The demand-for-health model has been extended in order to take account of (1) the family as the producer of health investments (Jacobson 2000; Bolin, Jacobson, and Lindgren 2001b, 2002c) and the employer as the producer of health (Bolin, Jacobson, and Lindgren, 2002a); (2) decreasing returns to scale and the demand for longevity (Ehrlich and Chuma 1990), (3) an endogenous rate of depreciation (Muurinen 1982; and Liljas 1998); and (4) uncertainty (Liljas 1998; and Laporte and Furguson 2007).[17]

The Elsevier *Handbook of Health Economics* chapter on the human capital model of the demand for health, Grossman (2000), provides a comprehensive survey of the theoretical extensions of the demand-for-health model. Here I will focus on the contributions that have been published since then, which are mainly work that relax the single individual assumption. In a recent paper, though, Laporte and Furguson (2007) incorporated uncertainty in the demand-for-health model, by applying stochastic dynamic optimization methods. A discussion of this would be too technical and lies outside the scope of this chapter—the interested reader is referred to the article by Laporte and Furguson.

---

[17] Similar models for analyzing individual health behavior when health status is uncertain and governed by a stochastic process have been developed by, for instance, Dowie (1975), Cropper (1977, 1981), Dardanoni and Wagstaff (1987, 1990), Selden (1993), Chang (1996), Zweifel and Breyer (1997: 62–88), and Picone, Uribe, and Wilson (1998).

6.4.1 The Relaxation of the Single-individual Household Assumption

It seems obvious that the context in which we live influences the choices that we make. Along that line Gary Becker developed an economic theory for how decisions are made within a family (Becker 1991). This field of research has expanded since then and nowadays includes a variety of different economic-theoretical approaches to the family. Becker's approach assumed cooperation between the family members which, obviously, need not be the case. There are several plausible reasons for why cooperation may break down at certain occasions. For instance, at divorce the spouses may interact strategically. Game theory has been used to model family decisions in such cases (for a survey of those theories see Bergstrom 1997).

Jacobson (2000) was the first to extend Grossman's model in order to comprise the *family*. She did so by means of (1) a common utility function for the family's utility, and (2) family-specific household production functions using the different family members' time as inputs into production. Bolin et al. (2001b) made the more general assumption of different utility functions for husband and wife, and applied the Nash-bargaining solution to the family's problem of how to allocate its members' time and resources.

Both these extensions of the demand-for-health model assume that the family members cooperate and follow the decisions that have been made by the family. However, since, for instance, agreements concerning how to allocate household time are not legally enforceable, existing incentives held by one spouse to improve upon a given allocation, given that the other spouse has made irreversible commitments, may lead to non-cooperation. Health-related decisions and the subsequent realized conducts are not immune against this and, hence, strategic interaction within the family may significantly influence health and health investment. Bolin et al. (2002a) applied non-cooperative game theory in order to analyze the family's demand for health and health investments. This strategic family model was further extended by Bolin et al. (2002c) in order to include also the labor market and employer incentives for investing in employee health. The assumption of constant returns to scale and, hence, a constant marginal cost of gross health investments, in household production were maintained in all of the extensions of the original demand-health model mentioned above (the situation when household production exhibits decreasing returns to scale is discussed below).

The fundamental conclusions from these analyses are (a) that the family will not try to equalize the health capital of different family members but, rather, the family will allocate the investments in health capital so that the ratio of marginal benefits and marginal cost of health capital is equalized between the family members, (b) that the family's decision-making process influences the allocation of health investments, (c) that, since there are no legally enforceable contracts regarding the allocation of time, the individual family member may act strategically, in which case the equilibrium will, in general, be inefficient, and (d) that labor market relations are important for the family's health-related behaviors. The extensions of the demand-for-health model, in order to incorporate more than one individual, which I have presented in this section provide the necessary tools for deriving predictions concerning the effects of different family policy variables on health and health-related behavior.

More generally, the family structure is important for the time allocation decisions that comprise investments in all types of human capital. Becker has explained the existence of the family (see, for instance, Becker 1991) as a way of exploiting the gains created by specialization according to comparative advantages. Thus, gains from specialization achieved in a two-person family's allocation of time and money create resources in excess of those that would have been created by two single households. So, Becker's theory of the family predicts that individuals that live together are wealthier than those that live as singles. Consequently, a testable proposition is: living together (either in cohabitation or in marriage) is associated with higher stocks of health capital, provided that health is a normal good. The effect on goods and time used for producing health investments is ambiguous, since the increase in the demand for health might be outweighted by increased productivity, induced by marriage, in the production of gross investments.

6.4.2 Introducing Uncertainty

Perhaps the most common way of formalizing illness in economic-theoretical models is to think of it as being the result of a low amount of health capital. A number of published extensions of the demand-for-health model treat the stock itself as a stochastic variable (see, e.g., Liljas 1998; and footnote 17 provides additional examples). A fundamentally different—and more consistent with the stock-concept of health—way of conceptualizing illness is offered by considering the rate of depreciation of the stock of health capital as inherently stochastic. For instance, assume that an individual fall ill with cancer. At the moment when the cancer commences the stock of health is still unaffected by the illness, but starts to depreciate at a higher rate than what was previously the case. The same way of reasoning applies in other cases of illness too; the time from when the depreciation rate takes on a higher value to the point in time when the health stock would be significantly affected varies, though. Thus, using the demand-for-health framework it seems natural to think of illness as connected primarily to the rate of depreciation of health capital, and only indirectly to the stock of health.

The initial formulation of the demand-for-health model precluded uncertainty. Grossman, however, recognized that the individual does not have perfect foresight regarding his or her length of life. His suggestion as to how uncertainty should be included into the demand-for-health model was to let the individual face a probability distribution of depreciation rates at each point in time. This means that at each point in time the rate of depreciation may deviate (more or less) from its expected value.

Liljas (1998) extended the Grossman model by assuming that the *health stock* at each point in time is given as the realization from a probability distribution. In this way he avoids a technical-modeling difficulty, but at the same time deviates from the fundamental notion of the demand-for-health model for how to perceive illness: changes in health are realized through gross investments and depreciation. By assuming that health-related uncertainty operates directly on the health stock, without taking the way through net investments, he avoids the difficulty that one would face if instead following Grossman's notion of uncertainty: how are depreciation rates connected over time? In other words, if the rate of depreciation makes a sudden jump, what does this imply for its value at the next point in time?

6.5 Empirical Estimations of Health

In this section, I present empirical studies of health. I begin by dealing with studies that are directly or indirectly based on the demand-for-health model, and move on to studies that focus on the relationship between education and health.

The stock of empirical studies that have focused on testing the predictions of the demand-for-health model is, to date, relatively small compared to the attention paid to certain other areas of empirical research in economics. No doubt, this owes to the fact that suitable data has not been available for long. In particular, additional empirical testing of the demand-for-health model needs to employ longitudinal data and panel data methods in order to capture the dynamic properties of the model. One specific correlate of health has received more attention than the others: education. The relationship between health and educational capital is particularly important since these two human capital components are the most important targets for public policy initiatives in the area of individual welfare.

6.5.1 The Demand-for-Health Model

Several empirical studies of the demand for health, and the demand for health investments, refer to Grossman's ideas, but few have actually been based on empirical counterparts to Grossman's formal model. Empirical estimations of the demand-for-health model comprise: Grossman's own study on US data (Grossman 1972a); Muurinen (1982) on Finnish data; Wagstaff (1986, 1993) on Danish data; and Sundberg (1996), Gerdtham et al. (1999), and Gerdtham and Johannesson (1999) on Swedish data. The results of these empirical studies have not unambiguously supported the demand-for-health model. This may be explained by most of the studies having used cross-sectional data, which cannot capture the dynamic features of the theoretical demand-for-health model.

Thus, Wagstaff (1993) claimed that the early empirical formulations were inappropriate since they failed to capture the inherently dynamic character of the model and proposed an alternative formulation apparently more consistent with Grossman's theoretical model. However, Wagstaff introduced dynamics in his empirical formulation without any development of a formal, theoretical model. Grossman (2000: 388–92) derived a dynamic empirical demand-for-health model, and showed that at least three data points would be required in order to compute unbiased estimates. An empirical model which takes the dynamic properties of the demand-for-health model into account has been developed, building on Grossman (2000), by Bolin, Jacobson, and Lindgren (2001a, 2002b). Bolin and Lindgren (2002), Bolin, Lindgren, Lindström, and Nystedt (2003) and Bolin, Lindgren and Rössner (2006) utilized this empirical model and panel data in order to estimate the demand-for-health model, taking into account the effects of specific chronic conditions and social interactions, respectively. The main results in these more recent studies concerning the effects of age, wage, and education on health largely confirm the theoretical predictions derived above.

Several other studies comprise analyses of health and health-related behavior, although not in a strict demand-for-health framework. For instance, Gerdtham (1993) examined the impact of aging on health care expenditures; Gerdtham (1997) examined equity in health care utilization; and Gerdtham and Johannesson (2000), Gerdtham and Johannesson (2003), Van Doorslaer and Gerdtham (2003), and Lauridsen et al. (2004) examined determinants of inequality in health.

The extensions of the theoretical demand-for-health model in order to include the family, have an empirical counterpart: Wilson (2002) studied the correlation between spouses' health status. He found that, controlling for a number of explanatory variables, the family and the decision-making process it conveys lead to correlation between health levels of spouses. The processes that are behind this are assortive mating according to dimensions related to health and health-related behavior (i.e., education, diet, smoking, exercise) and the direct effect of the health between spouses.[18]

6.5.2 The Correlation and Possible Causality Between Education and Health

There is a strong positive correlation between education (measured as years of formal schooling completed) and good health. This empirical finding seems to be independent of the chosen indicator of health (or bad health) such as self-assessed health, physiological indicators of health, or morbidity and mortality rates. It also emerges whether the units of observation are individuals or groups. The correlation between the two human capital components have been reported in studies dating back at least thirty-five years—Auster et al. (1969), Grossman (1972a), Newhouse and Friedlander (1980), Shakotko et al. (1981), and Fuchs (1982) are some examples of early studies. There are three possible, but not mutually exclusive, explanations to the observed correlation: (1) more education improves health, (2) better health leads to more education, and (3) there is no direct causality between health and education—instead the

---

[18] Baker and Stabile (2009) provide a review of the determinants of child health.

positive correlation is explained by some third variable, such as genetic characteristics, parental background, or time preferences, which affects both health and education.[19] From a public health policy perspective it is obviously important to be able to distinguish among these three possible explanations and to obtain quantitative estimates of their relative importance. Resources risk being put to use inefficiently without such knowledge. For instance, policy efforts targeted on health improvements, and grounded on the erroneous assumption that education causes health, will not achieve its goals.

A number of studies have been concerned with whether or not education and health are causally linked. Grossman (1975), Wagstaff (1986), Kemna (1987), and van Doorslaer (1987) all found that education influences self-assessed health, while Berger and Leigh (1989) found that education improves working ability. There are also empirical studies which report evidence of causality from health to education; see, for instance, Edwards and Grossman (1979), Perri (1984), Wolf (1985), and Chaikind and Corman (1991). The third variable hypothesis, though, is less convincingly supported in the empirical literature. It has been tested by Farrell and Fuchs (1982), Fuchs (1982), Berger and Leigh (1989), Sander (1995a, 1995b), and Leigh and Dhir (1997). The results obtained by Farrell and Fuchs (1982) corroborated the time preference hypothesis, while the results of the other studies were inconsistent with the time preference hypothesis. Grossman and Kaestner (1997) performed an extensive review of this literature and concluded that the empirical evidence for causality from schooling to health is convincing, while the empirical support for causality in the opposite direction is somewhat weaker.[20]

More recent empirical work corroborates the conclusion that education has a causal impact on health (see, for instance, Adams 2002; Spasojevic 2003; Arkes 2004; Arendt 2005; Lleras-Muney 2005; Kenkel et al. 2006; Oreopoulos 2006; de Walque 2007a; and Grimard and Parent 2007).

Häkkinen et al. (2006) distinguished between direct and indirect effect of education on health. They found that education has a positive influence on health, and that this effect works both through direct and indirect channels. The direct effect of education on health was estimated as the productive effect of education, while the indirect effect was estimated as the allocative effect of education. That is, education has both an effect on the technology that is used for producing investments in health—the direct or productive effect—and an effect on the ability of the individual to combine inputs into the production of health more efficiently. In other words: education influences the amount of health that the individual is able to produce from any given combination of inputs as well as the ability to choose the inputs efficiently.

---

[19] Becker and Mulligan (1997) developed a model in which time preferences are determined endogenously. Thus, they argue that education could lower the discount rate.

[20] A recent survey of the effects of education on non-market outcomes is provided by Grossman (2003).

6.6 POLICY

The main lesson to be learned from economic theory is that incentives matter for decisions made by individuals. So, in as far as health is influenced by individual decisions, the context in which these decisions are taken, and the incentives that are created by that context, should be at focus when discussing health-related policy issues.

More to the point, public policy efforts in the health area must take individual health-related decisions into account in order to achieve the intended effect and to do it efficiently. Thus, a comprehensive toolbox for policymakers would comprise theoretical models and empirical findings that are applicable to a large variety of health-related policy situations. To some extent this knowledge exists, but significant additional research efforts are called for. From an (health) economist's point of view, the Grossman model is the obvious point of departure both for theoretical research and for research aiming at refining estimates concerning relationships between exogenous variables and endogenous health-related variables. In particular, more refined estimates that can shed light on the question of causality between, on the one hand, individual health and, on the other, individual characteristics, living conditions and potential policy targets are needed. Public policy measures aiming at improving health should target variables that influence the incentives held by individuals to invest in health. Possible targets are not only prices on goods used for producing investments in health, but also prices on goods used for the production of investments in educational capital.

At the core of a "demand-for-health model view" of public health policy is the individual making decisions about how to allocate health investments over the life-cycle. So, policy initiatives bearing the touch of the model discussed in this chapter should focus on influencing individual incentives, for instance, through price policies or efforts that aim at improving health-related knowledge. Even though individuals make decisions concerning how to invest (or disinvest) in health with the purpose of maximizing lifetime utility, they may end up with health and/or health-related behavior that can be improved upon, both from the perspective of the individual as well as from a societal perspective. Apart from bad genes and some environmental factors which cannot be influenced by health policies, such situations may be the result of lacking financial resources, and/or inadequate knowledge for how to efficiently combine and make the most out of available resources. In addition, individual health-related decisions may be impaired by imperfect information concerning the health risks involved when consuming certain goods. The demand-for-health model and its current extensions can serve as analytical tools when formulating policy incentives in the health area.

So, what particular health policy initiatives are possible to analyze within the demand-for-health framework in its current degree of development? Obviously, one has to confine to policy targets which are parameterized within the theoretical model. The parameters in the optimality condition (8) correspond to polices that (1) influence prices of goods and own time used to produce health investments; (2) shift taxes on labor incomes; (3) affect wages (labor market policies); and (4) affect educational levels. I will focus on discussing policy initiatives that target prices on goods and own time, and policies that seek to enhance health levels through educational efforts.

6.6.1 A Subsidy on Market Goods

A formal analysis of the health effect of a policy measure which targets the price of the market good used as an input into production of investments may proceed like this: introduce a subsidy, s ($0 < s < 1$). Then, the one-unit cost of health investments becomes:

$$\pi(E) = \pi(w, (1-s) \cdot p; E). \tag{9}$$

In the diagram which illustrates the optimal amount of health capital (Figure 6.2), this means that the supply curve of health capital will shift down (more health capital to a lower marginal cost). The assumptions we have made regarding (1) the productivity of health capital ($\frac{\partial^2 t_t^s}{\partial H^2} > 0$) and (2) the marginal utility of health ($\frac{\partial^2 U}{\partial H^2} > 0$), assures that the MBH curve has a negative slope and, hence, the demanded amount of health capital will increase when the subsidy is increased. Although it is possible to analyze this situation entirely by means of mathematical analytical methods, I use the same diagram as before to illustrate the effects of a subsidy on the demand for health.[21]

From Figure 6.2 it is obvious that the impact on health that a subsidy might have depend on the relative slopes of the supply and MBH curves. We have already assumed that the supply of health capital is infinitely elastic (a horizontal line in the price–capital plane). Consequently, the effect of the health policy which targets the prices of, for instance, health care goods, depends on the elasticity of the MBH curve: when the MBH schedule is relatively elastic (a flat MBH curve), the shift in supply will induce a large change in demand; when the MBH schedule is relatively inelastic (a steep MBH curve) the shift in supply will induce a small change in demand. Thus, a subsidy policy is likely to have the largest health effects on those that are on the relatively flat part of their MBH curves, that is, on those that are relatively healthy.

---

[21] For two persons of the same age the formal analysis is as follows: differentiating equation (8) (and assuming that $\frac{\pi_t^{Hi}(E)}{\pi_t^H(E)} \approx 0$), yields: $\dfrac{dH_t}{ds} = - \dfrac{(r+\delta) \cdot \frac{\partial \pi}{\partial p} \cdot p}{\frac{e^{-(p-r)t}}{\lambda_0^W} \cdot \frac{\partial^2 U}{\partial H_t^2} - W_t(E) \cdot \frac{\partial^2 \tau_t^s}{\partial H_t^2}}$. Since the one-unit cost increases

in the price of the market good ($\frac{\partial \pi}{\partial p} > 0$), the marginal product of health diminishes as the stock increases ($\frac{\partial^2 t_t^s}{\partial H_t^2} > 0$), and the marginal utility of health diminishes as the stock increases ($\frac{\partial^2 U}{\partial H_t^2} > 0$) this expression is positive, predicting that a subsidy increase will increase the demand for health.

It should come as no surprise that consumers change their consumption patterns in response to changes in relative prices. Nevertheless, in a recent study Smed et al. (2007) found that, indeed, food consumption patterns may be influenced by taxes and subsidies. This suggests that policymakers are able to influence health indirectly by taxing unhealthy and/or subsidizing healthy food-consumption.

6.6.2 Educational Capital

Public policies that target the level of educational capital may be a tool for achieving improved health levels. Theoretically, the mechanism that lies behind this is the efficiency enhancing effect of educational capital in the production process that is utilized for producing health investments. This, and available empirical evidence, suggest that there is a positive causal link from educational capital to health capital and, hence, that educational capital is a potential target for health policymakers. The version of the demand-for-health model that I formulated above incorporates causality between the two stocks to the extent that the individual's demand for health depends on educational capital. The sign and magnitude of this causality depends on the effects of educational capital on household production (the relative strength of the time–price and the efficiency effects) and on the market effects of educational capital (the wage rate). In Figure 6.5 the effect of an increase in the stock of education on health was analyzed. We concluded that more educational capital would lead to improved health.[22] For policy purposes, however, more detailed knowledge concerning the relationship between inputs and the production of educational capital is needed.

Also, there are specific aspects of the content of the stock of education and the effects of it that are important in the health context: the ability to make decisions that are consistent with the objectives that the individual strives to achieve, depends heavily on fundamental knowledge concerning the characteristics of the outputs that are produced by specific consumption patterns and behaviors. For instance, consumption decisions based on erroneous assumptions concerning the caloric content of foods may lead to overweight or obesity; erroneous assumptions concerning the health-related output

---

[22] A formal analysis of the effects of educational capital on the demand for health can be performed in the same way as in the previous case. Differentiate equation (8) with respect to E, and solve for

$$\frac{dH_t}{dE_t} : \frac{dH_t}{dE_t} = \frac{\frac{\partial W}{\partial E} \cdot \frac{\partial \tau_t^s}{\partial H} + (r+\delta) \cdot \frac{\partial \pi}{\partial p}}{e^{-(p-r)t} \cdot \frac{\partial^2 U}{\partial H_t^2} - W_t(E) \cdot \frac{\partial^2 \tau_t^s}{\partial H_t^2}}$$. The total effect of educational capital on the one-unit cost of

health investment, $\frac{\partial \pi}{\partial E}$, will be positive (negative) if the efficiency effect of educational capital outweighs (is outweighed by) the time–price effect. However, if health investments are not produced solely by own time the expression above will be positive.

produced by consumption will lead to health levels that differ from the demanded health levels, etc.

Clearly, even though close to complete knowledge concerning the health effects of markets goods and health-related behaviors may, in principle, be available, individuals may face a cost of information inducing health investment decisions to be based on less than complete information. In this case, information will induce shifts in the perceived supply of health capital curve so that the perceived curve coincides with the true curve. Thus, when the virtues of physical exercise, for instance, are not fully appreciated, information will induce increased investments in health (this is so since less resources than previously assumed are needed in order to produce each unit of gross health investments, which means that the supply curve shifts downward). The study by de Walque (2007b) illustrates the potential benefits of policy measures in which health-related information is disseminated.

6.6.3 Uncertainty

In reality, however, the health effects of goods and behaviors are uncertain. That is, we may know what can be *expected* from a given good or behavior and also the probabilities attached with a set of outcomes, but cannot be absolutely certain that a particular outcome will be realized. Provided that the individuals are neutral in their attitudes towards risk, information about expected outcomes will make them adjust their health investment activities in accordance with the expected effects of inputs (goods and behaviors). Formally, this amounts to little more than applying the expected value operator to all relevant variables entering the individual's maximization problem, which will result in an optimality condition like equation (8), but where relevant variables are replaced by their expected values.

Some of the market goods that are used as inputs into the production of health investments may produce other commodities that provide utility and, hence, a rational consumer may accept some potentially adverse health effects in order to achieve consumption utility. Different consumption pattern may produce health outcomes that are costly to society and call for policy measures in order to reduce health care costs. For instance, certain eating habits, tobacco smoking, and heavy alcohol consumption may entail serious health consequences for the individual. However, unless the individual meets the full consequences of his or her choices, as regards future health care needs, too large quantities of, for instance, unhealthy food will be consumed.

A rational individual chooses his or her consumption of potentially hazardous goods (and of potentially hazardous behavior) taking into account both consumption benefits and health risks. The balance between benefits provided and risks faced ensure that chosen consumption patterns are optimal from the individual's point of view. However, since the individual may not bear the total cost accruing in case of adverse health effects, too large quantities of such consumption will result. Thus, as regards health risks there are two main issues: (1) true risks may not be known, and (2) the individual's willingness to accept health risks may lead to inefficient risk-taking for the society at large. Moreover, if individuals exhibit hyperbolic discounting when making their health-related decision the problem of inefficient risk-taking may be aggravated.

What can a policymaker do about this situation? The obvious answer is to provide information about health risks and to make individuals face their own health risks. The first of these measures may be problematic: when information about the true risks involved in hazardous consumption or potentially hazardous behavior is disseminated (smoking, drug abuse, alcohol consumption, sexual contacts, etc.) individual health-related behavior will accommodate it accordingly. Thus, if risks are over-estimated, information about true risks may induce increased potentially hazardous consumption (Lundborg and Lindgren 2002). As regards the task of making individuals face their own health risks: there is, in most existing health care systems, a limit as to the extent to which individuals bear the full consequences of their health-related behavior and, hence, moral hazard is a problem which is fundamental to policymakers in the health area.

6.7 CONCLUDING REMARKS

In this chapter, I have presented the part of the human capital theory that treats health as an endogenously decided component of the stock of human capital: the demand-for-health model, formulated by Michael Grossman some thirty-five years ago. The notion that individuals are able to influence their own health and the development of a theoretical model of individual demand for health and health investments marks a significant point in human capital theory development. There is empirical evidence suggesting that the stocks of educational and health capital are causally inter-related. Thus, the next step in the development of the human capital theory should be to develop a theoretical model in which both education and health investments are choice variables.

I have presented several of the extensions of the demand-for-health model that have been developed: for instance, as regards the family as a maker of health-related decisions. The early empirical estimations were not unanimously supportive of the predictions produced by the model. However, more recent empirical studies provide stronger support for the theoretical predictions. The explanation for this may be that the earlier studies mostly employed cross-section data, while longitudinal data has been increasingly used in more recent studies.

The policy relevance of the demand-for-health model is increasing. The reason for this is that, first, it is the only theoretical model of individual health-related behavior with a solid foundation in economic theory and, second, improvements in the supply of data during the last decades have facilitated the application of the model to different empirical questions. Finally, there are several highly policy-relevant areas—for instance, tobacco and alcohol consumption, drug abuse, and obesity—that have been studied "in the spirit" of the demand-for-health model, but to which the full dynamic features of the model have not yet been applied.[23] Empirical developments in that direction have the potential to provide important insights.

REFERENCES

ADAMS, S. J. (2002), "Educational Attainment and Health: Evidence from Sample of Older Adults," *Education Economics*, 10: 97–109.

ARENDT, J. N. (2005), "Does Education Cause Better Health? A Panel Data Analysis Using School Reform for Identification," *Economics of Education Review*, 24: 149–60.

ARKES, J. (2004), "Does Schooling Improve Adult Health?" Working paper, RAND Corportion.

AUSTER, R., LEVESON, I., and SARACHEK, D. (1969), "The Production of Health: An Exploratory Study," *Journal of Human Resources*, 4 (Fall): 411–36.

BECKER, G. (1965), "A Theory of Allocation of Time," *Economic Journal*, 75: 493–517.

BECKER, G. S. (1964), *Human Capital* (New York: Columbia University Press for the National Bureau of Economic Research).

—— (1991), *A Treatise on the Family* (Cambridge, MA: Harvard University Press).

—— and MULLIGAN, C. B. (1997), "The Endogenous Determination of Time Preference," *Quarterly Journal of Economics*, 112 (Aug.): 729–58.

BERGER, M. C. and LEIGH, J. P. (1989), "Schooling, Self-selection, and Health," *Journal of Human Resources*, 24 (Summer): 433–55.

BERGSTROM, THEODORE (1997), "A Survey of Theories of the Family," in M. R. Rosenzweig and O. Stark (eds.), *Handbook of Population and Family Economics* (Amsterdam: Elsevier).

BOLIN, K, and LINDGREN, B. (2002), "Asthma and allergy—The significance of chronic conditions for individual health behaviour," *Allergy*, 57: 115–22.

—— JACOBSON, L., and LINDGREN, B. (2001a), "How Stable Are the Empirical Results of the Grossman Model-testing: Different Indicators of Health Capital and Health Investments in Sweden 1980/81, 1988/89 and 1996/97," Studies in Health Economics Working Paper No. 36. Lund University Centre for Health Economics.

—— —— —— (2001b), "The Family as the Health Producer: When Spouses are Nash-bargainers," *Journal of Health Economics*, 20: 349–62.

—— —— —— (2002a) "Employer Investments in Employee Health: Implications for the Family as Health Producer," *Journal of Health Economics*, 21: 563–83.

—— —— —— (2002b) "The Demand for Health and Health Investments in Sweden 1980/81, 1990/91 and 1996/97," in Björn Lindgren (ed.), *Individual Decisions for Health* (London: Routledge), 93–112.

—— —— —— (2002c) "The Family as the Health Producer: When Spouses Act Strategically," *Journal of Health Economics*, 21: 475–95.

—— LINDGREN, B., LINDSTRÖM, M., and NYSTEDT, P. (2003), "Investments in Social Capital: Implications of Social Interactions for the Production of Health," *Social Science and Medicine*, 56: 2379–90.

---

[23] Kenkel and Sindelar (2009) provide a review of the economics of health behaviors and addiction.

—— —— and RÖSSNER, S. (2006), "The Significance of Overweight and Obesity for Individual Health Behaviour: An Economic Analysis Based on the Swedish Surveys of Living Conditions 1980/81, 1988/89, and 1996/97. Population Based Study," *Scandinavian Journal of Public Health*, 34: 422–31.

CHAIKIND, S. and CORMAN, H. (1991), "The Impact of Low Birthweight on Special Education Costs," *Journal of Health Economy*, 10: 291–311.

CHANG, F. (1996), "Uncertainty and Investment in Health," *Journal of Health Economics*, 15: 369–76.

CHIANG, A. C. (1992), *Elements of Dynamic Optimization* (Singapore: McGraw-Hill).

CROPPER, M. L. (1977), "Health, Investment in Health, and Occupational Choice," *Journal of Political Economy*, 85: 1273–94.

—— (1981), "Measuring the Benefits from Reduced Morbidity," *American Economic Review*, 71: 235–40.

DARDANONI, V. and WAGSTAFF, A. (1987), "Uncertainty, Inequalities in Health and the Demand for Health," *Journal of Health Economics*, 6: 283–90.

—— —— (1990), "Uncertainty and the Demand for Medical Care," *Journal of Health Economics*, 9: 23–38.

DE WALQUE, D. (2007a), "Does Education Affect Smoking Behaviour? Evidence Using the Vietnam Draft as an Instrument for College Education," *Journal of Health Economics*, 26: 877–95.

—— (2007b), "How Does the Impact of an HIV/AIDS Information Campaign Vary with Educational Attainment? Evidence from Rural Uganda," *Journal of Development Economics*, 84: 686–714.

DOWIE, J. (1975), "The Portfolio Approach to Health Behaviour," *Social Science & Medicine*, 9: 619–31.

EDWARDS, L. N. and GROSSMAN, M. (1979), "The Relationship Between Children's Health and Intellectual Development," in S. J. Mushkin and D. W. Dunlop (eds.), *Health: What is it Worth?* (Elmsford: Pergamon Press).

EHRLICH, I. and CHUMA, H. (1990), "A Model of the Demand for Longevity and the Value of Life Extensions," *Journal of Political Economy*, 98 (Aug.): 761–82.

FARRELL, P. and FUCHS, V. R. (1982), "Schooling and Health: The Cigarette Connection," *Journal of Health Economics*, 1: 217–30.

FREDRICK, S., LOEWENSTEIN, G., and O'DONOGHUE, T. (2002), "Time Discounting and Time Preferences: A Critical Review," *Journal of Economic Literature*, 40: 351–401.

FUCHS, V. R. (1982), "Time Preferences and Health: An Exploratory Study," in V. R. Fuchs (ed.), *Economics Aspects of Health* (Chicago: University of Chicago Press for the National Bureau of Economic Research).

GERDTHAM, U. (1993), "The Impact of Aging on Health Care Expenditure in Sweden," *Health Policy*, 24: 1–8.

—— (1997) "Equity in health care utilization: further tests based on hurdle models and Swedish micro data," *Health Economics*, 6: 303–19.

—— and JOHANNESSON, M. (1999), "New Estimates of the Demand for Health: Results Based on a Categorical Health Measure and Swedish Micro Data," *Social Science & Medicine*, 49: 1325–32.

—— —— (2000), "Income-related Inequality in Life-years and Quality-adjusted Life-years," *Journal of Health Economics*, 19: 1007–26.

GERDTHAM, U. and JOHANNESSON, M. (2003), "Absolute Income, Relative Income, Income Inequality and Mortality," *Journal of Human Resources*, XXXIX: 228–47.

—— —— LUNDBERG, L., and ISACSON, D. (1999), "The Demand for Health: Results from New Measures of Health Capital," *European Journal of Political Economy*, 15: 501–21.

GRIMARD, F. and PARENT, D. (2007), "Education and Smoking: Were Vietnam Draft Avoiders Also More Likely to Avoid Smoking?" *Journl of Health Economics*, 26: 896–926.

GROSSMAN, M. (1972a), *The Demand for Health: A Theoretical and Empirical Investigation* (New York: Columbia University Press for the National Bureau of Economic Research).

—— (1972b), "On the Concept of Health Capital and the Demand for Health," *Journal of Political Economy*, 80: 223–55.

—— (1975), "The Correlation Between Health and Schooling," in N. E. Terleckyj (ed.), *Household Production and Consumption* (New York: Columbia University Press for the National Bureau of Economic Research).

—— (2000), "The Human Capital Model of the Demand for Health," in A. J. Culyer and J. P. Newhouse (eds.), *Handbook of Health Economics* (Amsterdam: Elsevier).

—— (2003), "Education and Nonmarket Outcomes," in E. Hanushek and F. Welch (eds.), *Handbook of the Economics of Education* (Amsterdam: Elsevier).

—— and KAESTNER, R. (1997), "Effects on Education on Health," in J. R. Behrman and N. Stacey (eds.), *The Social Benefits of Education* (Ann Arbor, MI: N. University of Michigan).

HÄKKINEN, U., JÄRVELIN M. R., ROSENQVIST, G., and LAITINEN, J. (2006), "Health, Schooling and Lifestyle Among Young Adults in Finland," *Health Economics*, 15: 1201–16.

JACOBSON, L. (2000), "The Family as Producer of Health: An Extension of the Grossman Model," *Journal of Health Economics*, 19: 611–37.

KAMIEN, M. I., and SCHWARTZ, N. L. (1991), *Dynamic Optimization: The Calculus of Variations and Optimal Control in Economics and Management* (Amsterdam: North-Holland).

KEMNA, H. J. M. I. (1987), "Working Conditions and the Relationship Between Schooling and Health," *Journal of Health Economics*, 6: 189–210.

KENKEL, D., LILLIARD, D., and MATHIOS, A. (2006), "The Roles of High School Completion and GED Receipt in Smoking and Obestity," *Journal of Labor Economics*, 24: 635–60.

LANCASTER, K. J. (1966), "A New Approach to Consumer Theory," *Journal of Political Economy*, 74: 132–57.

LAURIDSEN, J., CHRISTIANSEN, T., and HAKKINEN, U. (2004), "Measuring inequality in self-reported health. Discussion of a recently suggested approach using Finnish data," *Health Economics*, 13(7): 725–32.

LEIGH, J. P. and DHIR, R. (1997), "Schooling and Frailty Among Seniors," *Economics of Education Review*, 16: 45–57.

LILJAS, B. (1998), "The Demand for Health with Uncertainty and Insurance," *Journal of Health Economics*, 17: 153–70.

LLERAS-MUNEY, A. (2005), "The Relationship Between Education and Adult Mortality in the United States," *Review of Economic Studies*, 72: 189–221.

LUNDBORG, P. and LINDGREN, B. (2002), "Risk Perceptions and Alcohol Consumption Among Young People," *Journal of Risk and Uncertainty*, 25: 165–83.

MICHAEL, R. T. (1972), *The Effect of Education on Efficiency in Consumption* (New York: Columbia University Press for the National Bureau of Economic Research).

MUURINEN, J. M. (1982), "An Economic Model of Health Behaviour: With Empirical Applications to Finnish Health Survey Data." Ph.D. thesis, Department of Economics and Relatd Studies, University of York, UK.

NEWHOUSE, J. P. and FRIEDLANDER, L. J. (1980), "The Relationship Between Medical Resources and Measures of Health: Some Additional Evidence," *Journal of Human Resources*, 15 (Spring): 200–18.

OREOPOULOS, P. (2006), "Estimating Average and Local Average Treatment Effects of Education When Compulsory Schooling Laws Really Matter," *American Economic Review*, 96: 152–75.

PERRI, T. J. (1984), "Health Status and Schooling Decisions of Young Men," *Economics of Education Review*, 3: 207–13.

PICONE, G., URIBE, M., and WILSON, R. M. (1998), "The Effect of Uncertainty on the Demand for Medical Care, Health Capital, and Wealth," *Journal of Health Economics*, 17: 171–85.

SANDER, W. (1995a), "Schooling and Quitting Smoking," *Review of Economic Statistics*, 77: 191–9.

—— (1995b), "Schooling and Smoking," *Economics of Education Review*, 14: 23–33.

SEIERSTAD, A. and SYDSÆTER, K. (1987), *Optimal Control Theory with Economic Applications* (Amsterdam: North-Holland).

SELDEN, T. (1993), "Uncertainty and Health Care Spending by the Poor: The Health Capital Model Revisited," *Journal of Health Economics*, 12: 109–15.

SHAKOTKO, R. A., EDWARDS, L. N., and GROSSMAN, M. (1981), "An Exploration of the Dynamic Relationship Between Health and the Cognitive Development in Adolescence," in J. van der Gaag and M. Perlman (eds.), *Contributions to Economic Analysis: Health, Economics, and Health Economics* (Amsterdam: North-Holland).

SMED, S., JENSEN, J. D., and DENVER, S. (2007), "Socio-economic Characteristics and the Effect of Taxation as a Health Policy Instrument," *Food Policy*, 32: 624–39.

SPASOJEVIC, J. (1996), "Effects of Education on Adult Health in Sweden: Results from a Natural Experiment." Ph.D. dissertation, City University of New York Graduate Center.

SUNDBERG, G. (1996), "The Demand for Health and Medical Care in Sweden. Essays on Health Economics." Economic Studies 26. Ph.D. thesis, Department of Economics, Uppsala University, Uppsala, 13–77.

VAN DOORSLAER, E. K. A. (1987), "Health, Knowledge and the Demand for Medical Care." Ph.D. thesis. Assen, Maastricht, The Netherlands.

WAGSTAFF, A. (1986), "The Demand for Health: Some New Empirical Evidence," *Journal of Health Economics*, 5: 195–233.

—— (1993), "The Demand for Health: An Empirical Reformulation of the Grossman Model," *Health Economics*, 2: 189–98.

WILSON, S. (2002), "The Health Capital of Families: An Investigation of the Inter-spousal Correlation in Health Status," *Social Science & Medicine*, 55: 1157–72.

WOLF, D. M. (1985), "The Influence of Health on School Outcomes: A Multivariate Approach," *Medical Care*, 23: 1127–38.

ZWEIFEL, P. and BREYER, F. (1997), *Health Economics* (New York and Oxford: Oxford University Press).

CHAPTER 7

....

SOCIOECONOMIC STATUS AND HEALTH: DIMENSIONS AND MECHANISMS*

....

DAVID M. CUTLER, ADRIANA LLERAS-MUNEY, AND TOM VOGL

7.1 INTRODUCTION

IN societies, rich and poor, those of greater privilege tend to enjoy better health. Among older adults in Britain and the United States, a move from the top education or income tercile to the bottom is associated with an increase of at least fifteen percentage points in the likelihood of reporting fair or poor health (Banks et al. 2009). The Mexican elderly share this pattern, with the poorest and least educated terciles reporting poor health at least ten percentage points more often than the richest and most educated terciles (Smith and Goldman 2007). Mortality differences are just as striking. For the United States and six European countries, Figure 7.1 shows the increase in mortality risk associated with having less than upper-secondary education (according to the International Standard Classification of Education). Compared with their better educated compatriots, those with less than upper-secondary education are at least 20 percent more likely to die in a given year. Figure 7.1 reveals some variation across countries, but this variation appears to have little to do with differences in health care systems. For example, the mortality differentials for the United States, which favors market-based health care (at least for the non-elderly), and Austria, where the government provides universal health care, are virtually identical.

* We thank Sherry Glied, Peter Smith, and Elizabeth Ty Wilde for comments. T. Vogl thanks the National Science Foundation for research support.

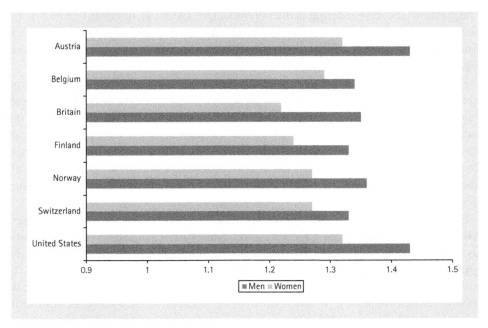

FIGURE 7.1 Education and mortality among adults over 40, US and Europe

Sources: The estimates for European countries are drawn from Huisman et al. (2005), while those for the US are from Cox proportional hazards regressions using the 1990 National Health Interview Survey (NHIS) with mortality follow-up until 2002. Section 7.2 provides further details on the NHIS sample.

Notes: The bars represent the increase in annual mortality risk associated with having less than upper-secondary education (compared with at least upper-secondary education). All hazard ratios are adjusted for age. The Swiss sample is representative of only German-speaking regions of Switzerland; the British sample includes only England and Wales.

The scientific study of this relationship (commonly referred to as the "gradient") between socioeconomic status (SES) and health dates back at least as far as the nineteenth century, when researchers investigated differences in health outcomes among royalty, the landed elite, and the working class in Europe.[1] Since then, measures of SES have come to appear regularly in analyses of the determinants of health and mortality. Given that a variety of socioeconomic variables—including income, education, occupation, race, and ethnicity, among others—exhibit similar associations with health, many researchers have come to agree that "a broader underlying dimension of social

---

[1] See Antonovsky (1967) for a review of the pre-1960 literature on the SES–health gradient. This literature generally documents a positive correlation between SES and health holding environmental conditions constant. However, during historical eras of urbanization, the tendency of the wealthy to locate in urban areas increased their exposure to unsanitary conditions, obfuscating the gradient in analyses that pooled individuals living in urban and rural areas (Mosk and Johansson 1986; Haines 2001). Similarly, members of British ducal families did not enjoy a mortality advantage over the common population until about 1750, perhaps because of the dispersal of the common population across sparsely populated rural areas (Harris 2004) or because of the unhealthy (albeit copious) diets of the peerage (Fogel 1986).

stratification or social ordering is the potent factor" (Adler et al. 1994: 15), so that the various SES variables primarily serve as indicators, or "markers," of this underlying dimension.[2] This view emphasizes the broad influence of SES, rather than the effects of specific resources and hierarchies.

However, recent evidence suggests that treating SES as a unified concept is not correct. SES consists of not one but many dimensions, which relate to health in diverse ways.[3] Different measures of SES may operate through different mechanisms, and it is useful to explore these mechanisms precisely. For example, short-term positive fluctuations in income appear to reduce health, whereas long-term measures of income and wealth are correlated with better health. Education tends to remain stable throughout adulthood, so these patterns would not be observed if one used education as a measure of SES.

For those interested in designing policies to address the gradient, an understanding of this diversity of mechanisms is indispensable. Some dimensions of socioeconomic status may be more susceptible to manipulation than others—income transfers, for example, are more easily designed than policies that affect occupational choices. The multiplicity of mechanisms also raises questions about cost-effectiveness. If policymakers wish to improve health, are public funds better spent on income transfers, education, or public health programs? Furthermore, if for some dimensions of SES the gradient runs primarily from health to SES, then policy manipulations of these dimensions will have no impact on health. In fact, in these cases, policies that improve health may, as a side effect, boost access to certain resources. Policy efforts to affect health through SES will similarly be fruitless when the SES–health correlation reflects an underlying "third factor" that we do not observe.

In this chapter, we review the past two decades of research on the SES–health gradient, paying particular attention to how the mechanisms linking health to each of the dimensions of SES diverge and coincide. We divide the concept of SES into four domains—education, financial resources, rank, and race and ethnicity—arguing that each of these deserves attention in its own right. After laying out some basic facts about the SES–health gradient (section 7.2), we devote a separate section to each of these socioeconomic correlates of health. In sections 7.3 and 7.4, which treat education and financial resources, we concentrate on conceptual approaches that view the individual in isolation, as is commonplace in economics (Grossman 1972; Bolin, Chapter 6, this volume). The section on rank (section 7.5) is situated in a more sociological setting, paying attention to the interplay between the individual and society. The links between occupation and health are the focus of this section, but we also revisit the gradients in education and financial resources, now viewing them through the lens of social rank. Section 7.6 then summarizes the evidence on racial and ethnic differences in health, and in section 7.7 we provide some concluding remarks.

---

[2] See also Link and Phelan (1995) on SES as a "fundamental" (and unidimensional) cause of disease.

[3] Deaton and Paxson (2004), Geyer et al. (2006), and Torssander and Erikson (2008) similarly argue for greater emphasis on the multidimensional nature of SES.

Two themes surface repeatedly in the discussion. Throughout, we emphasize that the extent to which socioeconomic advantage *causes* good health varies, both across these four dimensions and across the phases of the life-cycle. Circumstances in early life play a crucial role in determining the co-evolution of socioeconomic status and health throughout adulthood. We also periodically comment on the inter-disciplinary nature of research on the SES–health gradient. The literature we review features contributions from economics, sociology, demography, epidemiology, psychology, and endocrinology, among others. We take note of what economists have learned from other disciplines and, more relevantly for this volume, how the concepts and methods of economics have advanced the state of knowledge on socioeconomic status and health. In the last two decades, economists' most substantial contributions to this literature have involved untangling causal mechanisms.

Although the SES–health gradient is observed in societies at all phases of economic development, in order to contain the discussion, we focus on the evidence pertaining to the contemporary industrialized world. When appropriate, we touch upon the evidence from poorer countries, commenting on how it squares with the evidence from their wealthier counterparts. A detailed discussion of the gradient in developing settings is beyond the scope of this chapter. However, given the harshness of the binding economic constraints in such settings, the SES–health gradient and its underlying mechanisms demand further attention in poor countries.[4]

To conclude each section, we remark on the lingering puzzles. In the late 1980s and early 1990s, researchers from various disciplines called for renewed emphasis on disentangling the relationship between SES and health (Marmot et al. 1987; Feinstein 1993; Adler et al. 1994). Whatever gains the literature has made since then, much remains to be learned. This chapter is as much an overview of the current knowledge as it is a call for future research.

7.2 Socioeconomic Status and Health: Some Facts

In this section, we motivate the discussion by describing the relationship between SES and health in the United States, an institutional setting with which we are familiar. Given the similar mortality–education relationships across countries in Figure 7.1, an in-depth look at a single country may also illuminate the gradients in other countries. Moreover, the methods we use here are easily applied to data from other settings.

We use data from the National Health Interview Surveys of 1986 through 1995, and we consider two commonly used measures of health: mortality, an objective but blunt

---

[4] For an overview of the socioeconomic determinants of health in developing countries, see Strauss and Thomas (1998).

measure of health, and self-reported health status (SRHS), which captures quality of life and has been shown to be highly correlated with objective measures of health, including mortality (Idler and Benyamini 1997). SRHS can take five values; a value of 1 corresponds to excellent health and 5 to poor health. We restrict our attention to these waves of the NHIS because more recent five-year mortality follow-up data are not available.

We start by plotting the relationship between education and five-year mortality for ten year age groups. Figure 7.2a shows that those with more then sixteeen years of school have substantially lower mortality rates than those with less than eight years of school, and the relationship is more or less monotonic in between.

To interpret the age patterns in the figure, one must first decide whether to concentrate on absolute or relative differences in mortality risk. In absolute terms, the gradient steepens as individuals age. However, because the elderly have high mortality rates at all levels of education, the *relative* effect of education is weakest among individual's ages 65 and over. As shown in Figure 7.2b, more education is also associated with better self-reported health. Among all age groups, each additional year of schooling is associated with a clear and consistent improvement in SRHS. As in the case of relative mortality risk, the effect of education is smallest among those aged 65 and over.

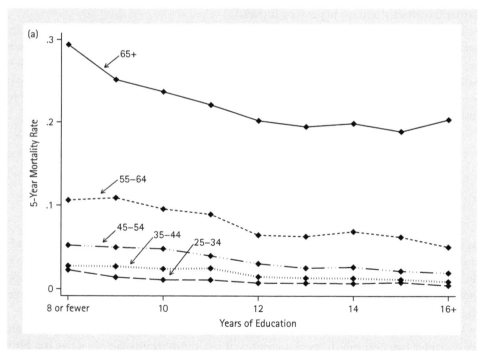

FIGURE 7.2a Education and mortality, US adults over 25

Source: NHIS 1986–95.

Notes: The estimated mortality rates are weighted using the survey weights provided by the NHIS. 5-year mortality is defined as death before the start of the sixth year following the survey year.

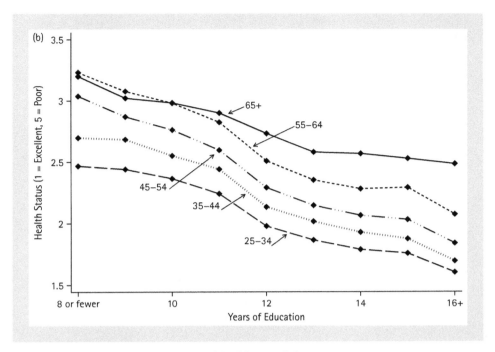

FIGURE 7.2b Education and self-reported health, US adults over 25
Source: NHIS 1986–95.
Notes: The means are weighted using the survey weights provided by the NHIS.

In Figures 7.3a and 7.3b, we repeat the exercise using household income instead of education. For mortality (Figure 7.3a), we use local logistic regression, a semi-parametric method that allows for flexible estimation of relationships with binary dependent variables (Fan et al. 1998). We see that income is protective for all age groups, with the association strongest at lower levels of household income. Figure 7.3b then applies local linear regression, a non-parametric smoother similar to the method used in Figure 7.2a (Fan 1992), to estimate the relationship between income and SRHS. Income is also associated with better self-reported health. We note a clear pattern in the SRHS results, first documented by Case et al. (2002): the profile becomes steeper with age until age 64 and then flattens among the elderly. The income gradient among children, whose health status is reported by parents, also steepens with age (results not shown). Already these results suggest that the effect of income and that of education may be independent: for most age groups, the effect of education on either outcome does not appear to decrease at high levels of education, whereas the effect of income does.[5]

---

[5] Formally, this fact does not rule out the possibility that education and income work through the same channel. In particular, the earnings–schooling relationship has become convex (Mincer 1997;

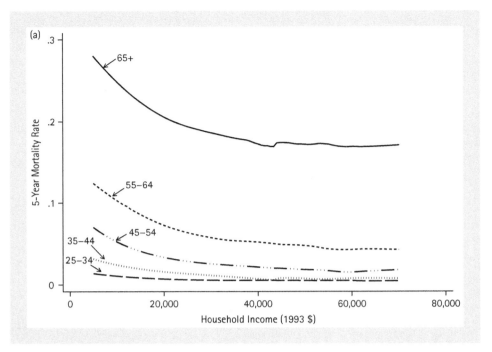

FIGURE 7.3a Income and mortality, US adults over 25

Source: NHIS 1986–95.

Notes: The curves are local logistic regression estimates. The regressions are weighted using the survey weights provided by the NHIS. Household income is reported in income brackets in the NHIS; it is imputed here from the March CPS of the same year as the mean income in the income bracket and education cell of the household head.

To document the health gradient in rank, our third dimension of SES, Figure 7.4 shows occupational patterns of mortality among working age adults. The populations within age groups are standardized to the age and sex structure of the United States in the 2000 census, so that they are directly comparable across occupation categories. The categories are ordered to reflect decreasing "rank." They include (1) managerial, professional, and executive occupations; (2) technical, sales, and administrative occupations; (3) service occupations, which consist of protective services, household services, and precision production, among others; and (4) manual labor, which includes machine operators, fabricators, and various other laborers. While the groupings are obviously arbitrary (they are the NHIS's, not ours), mortality rates appear to rise with each incremental decrease in occupational rank.

Deschênes 2001; Lemieux 2006). If education and income affect health through the same channel, then the combination of a convex income–schooling profile and a concave health–income profile admits any shape for the health-education profile, as long as health is increasing in education. Nonetheless, the sharp differences between Figures 7.2a, 7.2b, 7.3a, and 7.3b give reason to doubt that education and income affect health in an identical way.

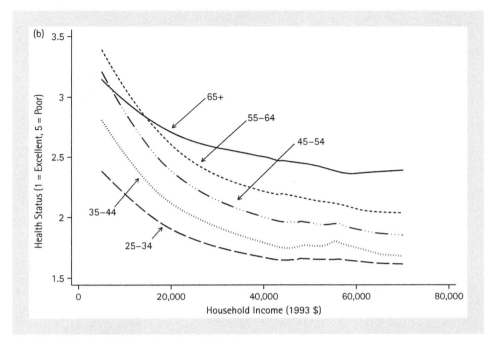

FIGURE 7.3b Income and self-reported health, US adults over 25

Source: NHIS 1986–95.

Notes: The curves are local linear regression estimates. The regressions are weighted using the survey weights provided by the NHIS. Household income is reported in income brackets in the NHIS; it is imputed here from the March CPS of the same year as the mean income in the income bracket and education cell of the household head.

Figures 7.5a and 7.5b then look at differences in mortality and SRHS by ethnicity and race. We split the sample into three categories: non-Hispanic whites, non-Hispanic blacks, and Hispanics. At every age, blacks experience higher mortality than whites or Hispanics, and the gap widens as people age. Hispanics exhibit a very different pattern, with higher mortality than whites at younger ages but lower mortality after roughly age 50. Since our sample is not restricted to the native born, changes in the composition of migrants over time could explain the age pattern. Nevertheless, the health advantage of this otherwise relatively disadvantaged population, at least among some age groups, is interesting. Surprisingly, SRHS does not show the same pattern. Across all ages, blacks report themselves to be in worse health than Hispanics, and Hispanics report worse health than whites.[6] Again, however, black–white differences remain largest among older individuals.

---

[6] Bzostek et al. (2007) assess the reasons for this contradictory evidence on ethnic differences in mortality and SRHS. They argue that language barriers, educational differences, and the somatization of emotional distress by Hispanics explain some of the divergence, but much remains to be learned on this issue.

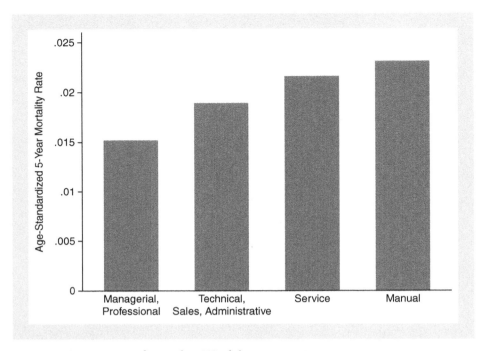

FIGURE 7.4 Occupation and mortality, US adults ages 25–65

Source: NHIS 1986–95.

Notes: The mortality rates are age- and sex-standardized using the 2000 population structure of the United States. See text for a description of the occupations in each category.

Overall, these figures suggest differences across SES measures; each measure may relate to health through a different set of mechanisms. We explore this further in Table 7.1, which uses data from the 1990 NHIS to estimate the relationships described in Figures 7.1–7.4, now with a focus on working age adults.

We limit the analysis to the 1990 wave of the survey in order to take advantage of the rich set of covariates available for that sample. In the left-hand panel, we estimate the relationship between ten-year mortality and each SES measure using logistic regression; in the right-hand panel, we repeat this exercise for self-reported fair or poor health. We report marginal effects estimated at the means of all independent variables. We multiply all estimates by 100 in order to express the marginal effects in percentage point units. These results are of course meant to illustrate the gradients, but one should be cautious in interpreting them as causal.

In the first column, we report the marginal effects from models that include each SES variable *by itself* in addition to basic demographic controls (age, gender, region and size of metropolitan area, marital status and family size). The results reproduce the results in Figures 7.1–7.4 and those commonly found in the literature. Education (measured in years) is associated with lower mortality, as is higher income. Workers in lower status

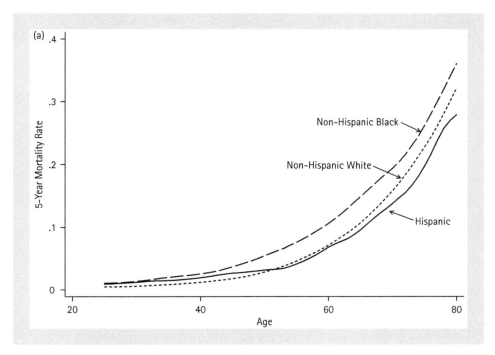

FIGURE 7.5a Race and mortality, US adults over 25

Source: NHIS 1986–95.

Notes: The curves are local logistic regression estimates. The regressions are weighted using the survey weights provided by the NHIS.

occupations face significantly higher mortality rates than their higher status counterparts. Workers in all four categories enjoy better survival rates than individuals not in the labor force. Finally, we find that African-Americans have higher mortality than whites. Hispanics, too, are more likely to die than non-Hispanic whites in this sample, but the difference in mortality risk is considerably smaller than the black–white difference.

Column (2) reports results from a model that include all SES measures together. Comparing columns (1) and (2), several conclusions emerge. The associations of education and income with mortality fall in magnitude but remain significant. In other words, an extra year of schooling reduces mortality among those with identical income, occupation, race, and ethnicity. Similarly, an increase in household income is associated with lower mortality even controlling for other SES characteristics. However, occupational status is no longer significantly related to the probability of dying, except that those out of the labor force have higher mortality rates than those that are employed.[7] Furthermore,

---

[7] For the specifications in columns (2)–(5), F-tests of joint significance fail to reject the hypothesis that all occupation coefficients (excluding the coefficient on labor force participation) equal zero.

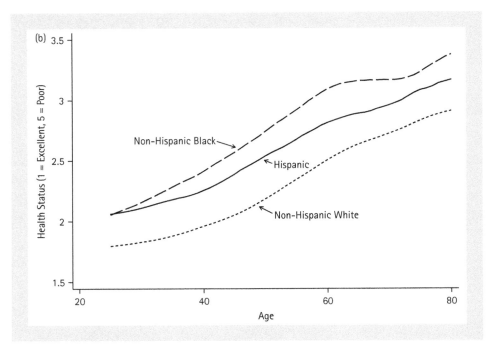

FIGURE 7.5b Race and self-reported health, US adults over 25

Source: NHIS 1986–95.

Notes: The curves are local linear regression estimates. The regressions are weighted using the survey weights provided by the NHIS.

while blacks still face significantly higher mortality rates than whites, Hispanic mortality is statistically indistinguishable from white mortality.

Columns (3)–(5) consider several popular explanations for these associations.[8] The first possibility we explore involves lower SES individuals leading unhealthier lives. Column (3) reruns the model that includes all SES measures, now controlling for an array of behavioral variables, including smoking, alcohol use, physical fitness, and seatbelt use. Adjustment for health behaviors flattens the gradients in education and income, though these gradients are still present. Strikingly, the racial gap in mortality is *larger* after holding health behaviors constant. Columns (4) and (5) then consider instead whether health knowledge (measured with a series of questions about tobacco, alcohol,

---

[8] The notes to Table 7.1 describe the variables used for this exercise in more detail than the ensuing paragraphs. We do not address the access to health insurance as a potential explanation for the gradient because the 1990 NHIS does not include questions on health insurance coverage. However, in results from the 2000 NHIS (not shown), controlling for health insurance access reduces estimates of the SRHS gradient only negligibly. Since we do not observe long enough mortality follow-up for this sample, we focus on the 1990 NHIS here.

Table 7.1 Socioeconomic Status and Health, NHIS 1990, Ages 25–64

	10-year mortality						Fair/poor self-reported health			
	(1)	(2)	(3)	(4)	(5)	(6)	(7)	(8)	(9)	(10)
Education										
Years of Education	-0.33	-0.18	-0.11	-0.17	-0.18	-1.45	-0.82	-0.66	-0.82	-0.77
	[0.03]**	[0.04]**	[0.04]**	[0.04]**	[0.04]**	[0.06]**	[0.06]**	[0.05]**	[0.06]**	[0.05]**
Household Income (Ref. < $15,000)										
$15,000 - $24,999	-0.95	-0.48	-0.31	-0.46	-0.45	-2.58	-1.31	-1.1	-1.31	-1.04
	[0.27]**	[0.26]	[0.25]	[0.27]	[0.26]	[0.40]**	[0.36]**	[0.34]**	[0.36]**	[0.33]**
$25,000 - $49,999	-2.17	-1.25	-0.89	-1.22	-1.21	-7.18	-3.82	-3.2	-3.82	-3.32
	[0.25]**	[0.26]**	[0.24]**	[0.26]**	[0.26]**	[0.39]**	[0.37]**	[0.35]**	[0.37]**	[0.34]**
$50,000+	-2.96	-1.66	-1.17	-1.64	-1.63	-11.94	-6.15	-5.2	-6.15	-5.56
	[0.32]**	[0.33]**	[0.31]**	[0.33]**	[0.33]**	[0.54]**	[0.54]**	[0.52]**	[0.53]**	[0.50]**
Occupation (Ref. Managerial & Professional)										
Tech., Sales, Admin. Support	-0.01	-0.53	-0.65	-0.54	-0.49	3.02	0.67	0.5	0.67	0.86
	[0.35]	[0.35]	[0.33]*	[0.35]	[0.35]	[0.63]**	[0.57]	[0.54]	[0.57]	[0.53]
Service	0.77	-0.29	-0.51	-0.32	-0.22	6.16	1.36	0.93	1.36	1.71
	[0.32]**	[0.34]	[0.31]	[0.34]	[0.33]	[0.56]**	[0.55]*	[0.51]	[0.55]*	[0.50]**
Operators, Fabricators, Laborers	1.18	0.02	-0.38	-0.02	-0.10	6.82	1.6	0.99	1.6	2.01
	[0.38]**	[0.40]	[0.37]	[0.40]	[0.20]	[0.64]**	[0.62]*	[0.58]	[0.62]*	[0.58]**
Out of labor force	3.26	2.01	1.55	2.00	2.03	12.93	7.29	6.5	7.29	7.11
	[0.31]**	[0.32]**	[0.29]**	[0.32]**	[0.31]**	[0.52]**	[0.52]**	[0.49]**	[0.52]**	[0.48]**

(continued)

Table 7.1 Continued

	10-year mortality					Fair/poor self-reported health				
	(1)	(2)	(3)	(4)	(5)	(6)	(7)	(8)	(9)	(10)
Race/ethnicity (Ref. Non–Hispanic White)										
Non-Hispanic Black	1.47	0.67	0.95	0.66	0.71	5.5	2.28	2.34	2.28	2.53
	[0.29]**	[0.29]*	[0.27]**	[0.29]**	[0.29]*	[0.47]**	[0.39]**	[0.38]**	[0.40]**	[0.37]**
Hispanic	0.88	-0.06	0.40	-0.06	-0.01	4.29	-0.58	0.08	-0.57	0.06
	[0.42]*	[0.42]	[0.39]	[0.41]	[0.41]	[0.64]**	[0.57]	[0.53]	[0.57]	[0.52]
Controls for:										
Demographic Variables	X	X	X	X	X	X	X	X	X	X
Other SES Variables		X	X	X	X	X	X	X	X	X
Behavioral Variables			X					X		
Knowledge Variables				X					X	
Stress Variables					X					X
Observations	25,752	25,752	25,752	25,752	25,752	25,894	25,894	25,894	25,894	25,894

Notes: The estimates represent marginal effects from logit estimations, evaluated at the means of the independent variables. All estimates are multiplied by 100, in order to reflect marginal effects in percentage points. Brackets contain robust standard errors.

* $p < 0.05$; ** $p < 0.01$.

Mean 10-year mortality is 5.59%, and mean fair/poor health is 9.22%. Demographic variables include age, sex, region, size of metropolitan area, marital status, and family size. Behavioral variables include current smoker, ever smoker, number of cigarettes per day, obesity, regular exercise, and use of a seat-belt always. Knowledge variables include the number of correct responses to health questions about smoking, drinking, and heart disease, with one tally for each of these three domains. Stress variables include self-reports of "a lot of stress" over the past week and over the past year. The race specifications also include a dummy for "other" race.

and heart disease) or stress (self-reported incidence over the past week or year) explain the gradient. These are rough proxies of hard-to-measure concepts, but at any rate, they fail to account for any of the observed SES differences in health.

Columns (6)–(10) present the same set of models using SRHS instead of mortality, and the results lead to similar conclusions. Education and income exhibit strong, significant gradients, in part explained by behaviors and (to a lesser extent) stress. Blacks report themselves in worse health than whites, and Hispanics are statistically indistinguishable from whites once other SES measures are added. In the case of occupations, we now find that relative to professional occupations, individuals in all other occupations report themselves in worse health; with the exception of one category, this holds true when controlling for income, education, and race. The addition of health behavior covariates substantially diminishes differences by occupation, but knowledge and stress do not.

Our quick look at the NHIS suggests three facts that are important for the subsequent discussion. First, gradients exist for all measures of SES and health, with the measures of SES somewhat but not totally related. Income, education, occupation, and race are all correlated, and the common component explains a good part of the SES gradient in health. But each variable acts on its own as well. Second, the gradients vary across age groups, with many gradients initially steepening as people age and then flattening at age 65. Whether this is due to differential impact of resources at older ages or differential mortality by SES is not entirely clear. Finally, the impact of SES is partly behavioral. At least one reason that higher SES people enjoy better health is that they are less likely to smoke, drink heavily, or be obese—although it is not clear why this is the case (Cutler and Lleras-Muney 2007b). Our results leave open the issue of exactly how much of the SES gradient is attributable to these individual factors.

7.3 EDUCATION

A proper starting point for any discussion of the SES–health gradient is education. In their pioneering work on the socioeconomic determinants of mortality in the United States, Kitagawa and Hauser (1973) used educational attainment as their primary indicator of SES, and since then, education has played a central role in analyses of the SES–health gradient. The focus on education has two rationales: education can be obtained for both working and non-working individuals, and education is more plausibly exogenous than income and occupation to the production of adult health (Elo and Preston 1996). Adult health may have direct morbidity effects on labor market performance, whereas any simultaneity in the education–health gradient would have to operate indirectly.

Of course, the case for reverse causality in the education–health gradient is also plausible. If good health allows children to attain more schooling and also makes them more likely to become healthy adults then the relationship between education and adult health will in part reflect the effect of health on education (see, e.g., Case et al. 2005). Similarly, if the expectation of a longer, healthier life induces increased investment in human capital, as standard economic models of human capital accumulation predict, then the education–health gradient may be a sign of health affecting education. Nonetheless, the earlier literature deemed hypotheses of this sort less likely than those involving the direct impact of health on labor market outcomes.

Although they are difficult to interpret, non-experimental estimates of the relationship between education and health measures abound.[9] As shown in section 7.2, more educated individuals in the United States report better health and face lower mortality risk. They also suffer less anxiety and depression, endure fewer functional limitations, and face decreased probabilities of being diagnosed with heart conditions, stroke, hypertension, high cholesterol, emphysema, diabetes, asthma, or ulcer—even after conditioning on background characteristics such as race, age, and income.[10] These differences by education also hold in a wide range of European countries (see Mackenbach 2006 and references therein).

In contrast to research on the other dimensions of SES, where evidence on causality is sparser and less consistent, analyses of natural experiments have produced evidence that schooling causes better health.[11] To our knowledge, these analyses derive exclusively from the economics literature. Lleras-Muney (2005) examines US cohorts affected by compulsory schooling laws in the early twentieth century, finding that individuals born in states that forced them to remain in school longer enjoyed significantly higher survival rates in adulthood.[12] Analyses of the effects of compulsory schooling legislation in Europe suggest similar conclusions.[13] Other evidence from the United States uses local economic conditions during the teenage years and military draft avoidance to instrument for educational attainment. Arkes (2004) takes advantage of the fact that high unemployment rates lower the opportunity cost of staying in school, finding that individuals exposed to higher unemployment rates as teenagers attain higher levels of education and are less likely to suffer from conditions that limit work or require personal care. De Walque (2004) and Grimard and Parent (2007) use the effect of draft avoidance

---

[9] The results reported in this paragraph derive from Cutler and Lleras-Muney (2007a).

[10] Interestingly, Cutler and Lleras-Muney (2007a) find *positive* education gradients for being diagnosed with cancer, smallpox, or hay fever. However, their dataset is based on self-reports, and they note that reporting of hay fever and certain types of cancer may reflect differential disease knowledge. For cancer, they also point out that the better-educated have a greater tendency to display risk factors such as late childbearing, that they may be more likely to survive the disease, and that they may face lower competing risks, allowing them to live long enough to be diagnosed with cancer.

[11] Grossman (2006) describes these studies in detail.

[12] Mazumder (2007) shows that the inclusion of state-specific trends across cohorts renders Lleras-Muney's mortality result statistically insignificant, although the coefficients remain large and negative. Mazumder's estimate of the effect of education on self-reported health status is robust to the inclusion of these trends.

[13] See Oreopolous (2007) on England and Ireland; Arendt (2005) on Denmark; and Spasojevic (2004) on Sweden.

behavior on college enrollment during the Vietnam War to identify the impact of education on smoking behavior. Both studies show that education decreases the probability that an individual currently smokes or ever smoked.[14]

The health benefits of education also flow inter-generationally. Better-educated parents—and especially mothers—have healthier children (Meara 2001; Currie and Moretti 2003), and these children grow up to be healthier adults (Case et al. 2005).[15] Currie and Moretti (2003) use college openings in mothers' localities to identify plausibly exogenous variation in maternal college-going, finding positive effects on birth weight and negative effects on smoking during pregnancy. Unlike the effects of parental income, described in the next section, the effects of parental education on child health do not appear to vary systematically with the child's age (Case et al. 2002).

In their review of the literature on the education–health gradient, Cutler and Lleras-Muney (2007a) point out several shortcomings of these quasi-experimental studies. First, the studies concentrate solely on the quantity of education, providing no insight into how its quality or content affect health. Nor, second, do they shed a great deal of light on the mechanisms mediating the causal relationship. Finally, as in any instrumental variables setting, the estimates correspond to local average treatment effects; they identify the effect of schooling among individuals on the margin of dropping out of high school (in the case of compulsory schooling laws and local unemployment rates) or on the margin of attending college (in the case of draft avoidance).[16] The average effect of education on health among these individuals may differ substantially from the average effect across the population. As such, the magnitudes of the quasi-experimental estimates may lack external validity.

Although these studies support the hypothesis that education improves health, another body of evidence indicates that health also affects education. Again, methodological advances in economics have played a key role in identifying this direction of causation. The evidence on contemporary industrialized countries derives primarily from non-experimental but data-rich longitudinal studies on both individuals and twins. In Britain, adolescents who were born with low birth weight or suffered health insults in childhood have worse schooling outcomes (Case et al. 2005). Among twin pairs in the United States and Norway, those born with lower birth weight than their twins stay in school commensurately fewer years (Behrman and Rosenzweig 2004; Black et al. 2007). Further confirmation is available from natural experiments in the histories of industrialized countries. Almond (2006), studying the long-run effects of the 1918 influenza

[14] However, De Walque (2004) and Grimard and Parent (2007) find mixed results for smoking cessation (among individuals who started smoking in high school).

[15] The literature on developing countries has long observed that maternal education is positively related to child health, starting with Caldwell (1979). Recent estimates based on increases in educational attainment following a massive school construction project in Pakistan confirm that this relationship is causal (Breirova and Duflo 2004).

[16] For a discussion of this issue as it pertains to the *economic* returns to schooling, see Card (2001). Also see Imbens and Angrist (1994) for an introduction to the concept of the local average treatment effect.

epidemic in the United States, shows that cohorts exposed to the epidemic *in utero* arrived at adulthood with lower educational attainment. Similarly, Bleakley (2007) examines the impact of hookworm eradication in the American South, finding significant effects on education and literacy.

Not surprisingly, these results are consistent with evidence from many developing countries, where the constraining effects of poor childhood health are likely to be stronger than in industrialized countries. Miguel and Kremer (2004) present the results of a randomized, controlled trial that administered de-worming pills to school-age children in Kenya. These results are in line with Bleakley's long-run results, showing a sizeable, positive impact on school attendance. Bobonis et al. (2006), also evaluating a randomized trial, find that iron supplementation increases pre-school attendance in India. These randomized experiments also square with the quasi-experimental evidence from developing countries. Retrospective evaluations of malaria eradication campaigns in several countries indicate that these campaigns increased literacy, and sometimes schooling attainment, among individuals exposed to them in childhood (Lucas 2005; Bleakley 2007). Likewise, iodine supplementation programs have been found to boost schooling attainment among individuals exposed to them *in utero* (Field 2007), as would be expected in light of the importance of iodine in fetal brain development.

These studies seem to imply that health affects schooling attainment either through its effects on morbidity—with ill children unable to attend school often and unable to concentrate when they do attend—or through its effects on cognitive development. Another hypothesis, with support in recent work by Jayachandran and Lleras-Muney (2009), suggests that the expectation of a longer life induces greater investment in human capital. How these mechanisms weigh against one another is an open research question.

Although little experimental or quasi-experimental evidence exists on the mechanisms linking education and health, the theories and evidence on this issue are worthy of discussion. Income mediates some of the relationship between education and health, but it would appear not to be the whole story. As shown in section 7.2, in simple (and perhaps miss-specified) OLS regressions, the protective effect of education remains even after controlling for income. Further, estimates of the effect of education on income and of the effect of income on health are too small for income to account for all of the health differences across education groups. Controlling for occupation, race, and ethnicity also fails to eliminate the education gradient. Thus, differences in health by education do not seem to stem only from differences in the labor market outcomes of more and less educated individuals. Note, however, that because income is noisy and measured with error, as well as possibly endogenous (see section 7.4), the effect of education may still be entirely due to the resulting differences in permanent income.

The remaining health differences have significant behavioral antecedents.[17] The better educated are less likely to smoke (as already noted), drink excessively, carry excess

---

[17] The results reported in this paragraph again draw on Cutler and Lleras-Muney (2007a).

weight, or use illegal drugs. In the sense that these patterns reflect *lower* spending on certain goods by people with more education, they challenge income-based explanations for the gradient—these posit that the greater wealth of the better educated allows them to spend *more* on goods, but we instead observe them consuming less.[18] Those with more education also obtain more preventive care (e.g. flu shots and mammograms), manage existing conditions more effectively (e.g. diabetes and hypertension), and make more use of safety devices such as seat belts and smoke detectors. In our sample of non-elderly American adults, a subset of these differences in health behaviors account for over 40 percent of the relationship between education and mortality (Table 7.1).[19]

Even if we were able to convincingly explain away all of the effect of education on mortality using behaviors, an important question would remain: Why do more educated individuals behave more healthily? An obvious explanation for these differences in behaviors is that more educated individuals are better informed. However, the results presented here (and elsewhere) show that only a small fraction of the education gradient can be attributed to information alone. The literature examining the drivers of unhealthy behavior, which Kenkel and Sindelar (Chapter 10, this volume) review, may also shed light on this question.

Part of the answer may lie in cognitive ability, which differs from knowledge per se. Cutler and Lleras-Muney (2007b) find suggestive evidence that education affects cognition, which in turn affects the ability to process information regarding healthy behaviors.[20] For example, better educated people perform better on cognitive tests, and this seems to explain some of the behavior–education gradient.

Relatedly, more educated individuals are more likely to take advantage of new medical technologies. Holding income and health insurance status fixed, more educated individuals have higher take-up of medications recently approved by the FDA (Lleras-Muney and Lichtenberg 2002). The effect is driven by medications that involve long-term use by the patient, suggesting a role for learning and self-management. Accordingly, the survival benefits of education accrue disproportionately to individuals with chronic diseases (Lakdawalla and Goldman 2001; Case et al. 2005), which involve self-management and learning, as well as diseases for which treatment technologies have advanced most rapidly (Glied and Lleras-Muney 2008). These patterns of technology adoption are consistent with the mediating role of cognitive ability. More broadly, they support Link and Phelan's (1995) premise that individuals of higher education (and higher SES generally)

---

[18] However, these patterns are consistent with an income-based explanation if tobacco, alcohol, excess weight, and illegal drugs are inferior goods.

[19] Measurement error and unobserved heterogeneity may bias the estimated share of the education–mortality association attributable to behavior. The direction of this bias is most likely towards zero, although it is theoretically ambiguous.

[20] Cutler and Lleras-Muney (2007b) also consider the possibility that heterogeneity in discount rates and risk aversion jointly determine educational attainment and health investments, but they find no evidence that this is so.

are better equipped to recognize, understand, and access new disease knowledge and medical technologies.[21]

Other theories emphasize differences in preferences and differences in the ability of individuals to change their behavior. In the case of preferences, differences in how individuals discount the future or react to risk may jointly determine educational attainment and health investments. For example, less patient individuals may be less willing to stay in school to boost future earnings, as well as being less willing to forgo smoking to avoid future disease. Furthermore, more educated individuals may have more control over their lives, or be less depressed. Although patience, depression, and a sense of control over one's life affect health behaviors, Cutler and Lleras-Muney (2007b) find that these theories cannot explain behavioral differences between more and less educated individuals. A final, prominent theory emphasizes the effect of stress. We will review this theory in more detail below. At this juncture, we simply note that we did not find here or in previous work evidence that stress can account for education gradients. Nonetheless, these hypotheses are difficult to test, and the concepts that underlie them elude precise measurement.

In sum, education is strongly related to health, with both reverse causality and direct effects. However, the extent to which the correlation between education and health reflects direct causality, reverse causality, or omitted factors is not known. Although the mechanisms by which health affects educational attainment are well-understood, how education affects health is not. We suspect that cognitive ability represents a significant part of the link between education and health, but other factors may also be at work. Furthermore, it seems unlikely that any one mechanism alone can explain the effect of education on health.

7.4 FINANCIAL RESOURCES

Both income and wealth have strong independent correlations with health, net of education and other measures of SES. Assessing causality is difficult, however. Income and wealth improve access to health inputs (such as medical care and food), but health improves one's ability to participate in the labor market and earn a decent wage. Illness also raises health care spending, thus reducing wealth. Additionally, "third factors"—such as education—may determine both financial resources and health status. Despite these caveats, many public health researchers have attributed the health–income gradient to a causal effect running from income to health. Some have even gone as far as labeling income "one of the most profound influences on mortality" (Wilkinson 1990: 412). Initial research seemed to support this view—in one such study, McDonough et al.

---

[21] Cutler et al. (2006) emphasize Link and Phelan's hypothesis in their review of the determinants of mortality.

(1997) estimated that a move from a household income of $20,000–$30,000 to a household income greater than $70,000 (in 1993 dollars) was associated with a halving of the odds of adult mortality. It was difficult to fathom that an association so large could be entirely due to omitted variables or reverse causality. However, more recent studies suggest that the direction of causality is far from clear and, furthermore, that it varies considerably by age.

Among adults, the negative impact of poor health on income and wealth appears to account for a sizeable part of the correlation between financial resources and health. In samples of middle-aged and elderly Americans, Smith (1999) finds that the onset of a new illness reduces household wealth by far more than the household's out-of-pocket health expenditures, even among households with health insurance. A large share of this reduction in wealth is attributable to a decline in labor earnings. Negative health shocks strongly predict retirement and reduced labor force participation (Smith 1999, 2004, 2005; Case and Deaton 2003).

Careful studies that look for the effect of income on health find little evidence to support this causal link in samples of older individuals in developed countries. In regressions that use panel data (unlike those in section 7.2) and control for education, wealth, and lagged income do not exhibit consistent relationships with the onset of new health conditions (Adams et al. 2003; Smith 2007). Evans and Snyder (2006) analyze the health effects of the Social Security "notch," which resulted in sharp changes in the benefit structure of US Social Security in the 1970s. Their results indicate that reductions in social security income if anything *increased* longevity among recipients.[22]

Alternative sources of evidence weigh similarly against the hypothesis that income protects adult health. Ruhm (2000, 2005) finds that recessions improve adult health, arguably because individuals engage in healthier lifestyles during downturns—they exercise more, drink less, and smoke less, for example. These patterns probably reflect some combination of job stress and the increased opportunity cost of time during economic booms.[23] Ruhm's findings challenge the accepted wisdom that income exerts a strong protective effect on health, although his results only pertain to short-term fluctuations in income rather than changes in permanent income. Also, Ruhm documents these effects in developed countries, where social insurance is available; the results may not apply in all settings. Another test for the accepted wisdom arises from a comparison of mortality trends in the United States and Britain over the past fifty years (Deaton and Paxson 2004). Trends in adult mortality were highly correlated in the two countries,

[22] The Evans and Snyder (2006) results contrast those of Case (2004) and Jensen and Richter (2003), who use similar strategies to analyze the health effects of income in a developing economy (South Africa) and a transitional economy (Russia), respectively. Both find evidence that income from pension receipts improves health.

[23] Sullivan and von Wachter (2006) find that lay-offs increase mortality risk, contrasting Ruhm's results. However, the psychosocial effects of being laid off may differ from the general effects of an economic downturn.

even when their income paths diverged. Instead of income, the major driver of mortality decline appears to have been medical technology.

For children, however, parental income has strong protective effects on health. Case et al. (2002) document stark associations between family income and various measures of child health. As they note, child health is less likely than adult health to affect family income, so they are somewhat more liberal in interpreting the association as causal.[24] The association remains large after the authors control for household composition, race, parental education, and parental labor force status. Moreover, it does not appear to reflect genetic confounders, health insurance access, or health behaviors. As observed in section 7.2, the income gradient in children's health status (reported by their parents) steepens as they grow older. Part of this steepening reflects the accumulation of health insults, especially chronic conditions, as children age. Similar results have been found in Canada (Currie and Stabile 2003).

This accumulation may continue into adulthood. A rapidly growing literature demonstrates that healthier children become healthier, wealthier adults, much in the way that they attain more schooling (see section 7.3). The same papers that have looked at the impact of *in utero* and early childhood disease on schooling also document effects on labor market outcomes (e.g., Behrman and Rosenzweig 2004; Almond 2006; Black et al. 2006; Bleakley 2007). This finding has potentially profound consequences. If household economic resources protect children's health, and their health influences their potential for economic success later in life, then child health may play a part in the inter-generational transmission of socioeconomic status. The evidence indeed suggests this is so. In Britain, for example, the number of chronic conditions endured in childhood predicts employment and occupational grade in adulthood, even after adjustment for parental socioeconomic characteristics, maternal smoking during pregnancy, birth weight, and a range of other covariates (Case et al. 2005).

Once more, these results are consistent with the evidence from developing economies. In several countries in the Americas, earnings in adulthood increased as a result of childhood exposure to malaria eradication (Bleakley 2007). Likewise, among Chinese adults, birth year exposure to China's Great Famine lowered labor force participation by seven percent (Meng and Qian 2006). And in rural Indonesia, women born during years with good rainfall (and presumably good crop yields) own more assets in adulthood (Maccini and Yang 2007).[25] Taken together, these studies lay bare the profound effects of early-life conditions on later-life economic status.

The fact that income and resources appear to affect health in early developmental stages but not later in life poses some interesting questions. What are the mechanisms by which income protects children's health, and why do they stop operating (or become less

---

[24] As corroborating evidence, Case et al. (2002) show that low birth weight babies do not reduce their mothers' labor force participation. However, Fertig (2007) finds that low birthweight children are more likely to experience family dissolution in the United States (but not in Britain). This suggests that poor child health may in fact affect a family's economic circumstance.

[25] Interestingly, Maccini and Yang (2007) do not find evidence of this effect for men.

important) later in adulthood? Perhaps as individuals age, their health is best thought of as a stock that is relatively impervious to small changes in circumstance, whereas the same does not hold for children. Whether income affects adult health remains an open question. However, a preponderance of evidence suggests that in developed countries today, income does not have a large causal effect on adult health, whereas adult health has a large effect on adult income.

7.5 RANK

Sections 7.3 and 7.4 formulated the gradient as an individual-level phenomenon. In that framework, education, income, and wealth characterize individuals who are separated from the society in which they live. The relationships of these variables with health operate through individuals' preferences and their capacities to purchase health inputs, process information, and participate in economic life. As Bolin (Chapter 6, this volume) emphasizes, setups of this sort have informed much of the economic approach to health, perhaps because of their appealing simplicity; the utility function, the health production process, and the budget set all coincide with the individual, making the problem conceptually tractable.

A separate set of theories views the gradient as inherently social. Individuals of greater wealth and education enjoy better health not because of some process affecting the individual in isolation but rather because of the individual's position in a social hierarchy.[26] These theories posit that low SES in any of a number of dimensions—including education, financial resources, and occupation—produces psychosocial stress due to feelings of subordination and lack of control. Health deteriorates as a result of this stress (Brunner and Marmot 1999; Wilkinson 1999). While the education and income gradients have received a good deal of attention from economists, the specific role of rank remains primarily in the domain of other disciplines.

The key mechanism in this framework is the fight-or-flight response, a chain of biochemical and physiological reactions to threats that occurs in most vertebrates. The physiological reactions, which in humans include a heightened heart rate and a redistribution of blood away from essential organs and towards the skeletal muscles, prepare the animal to protect itself against immediate danger. However, repeated exposure to the biochemical events associated with fight-or-flight takes its toll on the body, resulting in what is known as "allostatic load" among humans. Increases in allostatic load raise mortality risk and cardiovascular disease risk, hasten cognitive and physical decline, and suppress the immune system (McEwen 1998; Seemen et al. 2001). Repeated exposure to

---

[26] Of course, the distribution of resources also matters in the theories already discussed, due to its effects on the prices of goods and knowledge. But this is different from positing that distribution *directly* affects health.

stress is also associated with the shortening of special clusters of DNA at the ends of chromosomes, called telomeres (Epel et al. 2004). Telomere shortening is thought to be an integral part of the aging process; it is associated with heightened mortality from all causes, cardiovascular disease and infectious disease (Cawthon et al. 2003).

Much of the motivation for the literature on social hierarchies and health comes not from humans but from monkeys. A well-known example is Sapolsky's (1993, 2004) research on baboons, which finds that subordinate males display higher levels of gluco-cortoids, hormones that are secreted in response to stress. The subordinates also per-form poorly on a range of health measures, including blood pressure, cholesterol levels, and body fatness. When researchers induce changes in baboons' social standing, the same patterns occur, implying that this is not merely the result of genetic sorting. The adverse effects of subordinate social position are most visible in animals with stable social hierarchies, like baboons and humans.

In humans, the bulk of the research on the link between social hierarchies and health has concentrated on occupational measures of rank. The leading examples, the two Whitehall studies of British civil servants (Marmot et al. 1978; Marmot et al. 1991), doc-ument that civil servants with lower prestige jobs experience higher rates of mortality from cardiovascular causes and from all causes. As in the case of education, these mor-tality differences have behavioral precursors; higher ranking officials display a lower obesity rate, a lower propensity to smoke, and higher propensities to exercise and eat fruits and vegetables. Employment grade also associates positively with a sense of con-trol over one's health and one's work, job satisfaction, social support, and the absence of stressful life events. Studies relating the work environment and health in settings across Europe and the United States yield comparable results.[27] Given that most subjects of these studies enjoy a high degree of job security and have access to adequate earnings, common interpretations of their results place more weight on psychosocial factors than on material considerations.

A nascent body of research considers subjective measures of social status, generating findings that complement the occupation-based studies. Researchers provide subjects with a drawing of a ladder, asking them to mark the rung that best describes their posi-tion in society. Using data from the second of the Whitehall studies, Singh-Manoux et al. (2005) show that compared with occupational grade, subjective social status more strongly predicts composite scores of physical and mental health, as well as changes in these scores. Researchers have uncovered similar patterns in the United States (Operario et al. 2004) and Taiwan (Collins and Goldman 2008). Of course, the degree to which these associations reflect causal relationships remains an open question.

Many have extended these psychosocial theories to explain the gradients in educa-tion and financial resources. In these theories, education, income, and wealth influ-ence health through their effects on an individual's place in a social hierarchy. The

---

[27] Marmot et al. (1999) review the literature examining the relation between the work environment and health. For a more recent illustration, see Erikson and Torssander (2008), who show occupational gradients in mortality for the majority of the 65 causes of death they consider.

rank-based explanation for the education gradient has not undergone much rigorous testing, although the literature cites it widely (Adler et al. 1994). It finds some support in the negative correlations between education and negative emotions, which themselves predict health status (Gallo and Matthews 2003). However, little is known about the causal mechanisms underlying these associations.

In contrast, hierarchy-based explanations for the income gradient are the subject of a voluminous literature. In this framework, a person's income matters only insofar as it distinguishes him from his neighbor. Many analysts, perhaps most notably Wilkinson (1996), couple this with the idea that subordination worsens health more than domination improves it, leading to the prediction that inequalities in income and wealth are detrimental to population health. A similar hypothesis, also argued by Wilkinson (2000), posits that inequality affects health by insulting humans' innate sense of fairness. These theories have motivated a large literature to closely examine the correlation of income inequality and health, which has been observed since the influential cross-country work of Rodgers (1979).[28] Rodgers noted that among countries with equal average incomes, those with greater income inequality had lower life expectancy. He interpreted this fact in a way that contradicted much of the subsequent literature, arguing that the health–income profile was concave at the individual level, so that an extra dollar given to a poor person influences his health far more than the same dollar would affect a rich person's health. As a result, countries with more income inequality—and therefore more poor people—would experience worse population health outcomes. In this setup, the negative correlation between inequality and health is an artifact of aggregation; inequality per se does not affect an individual's health.

Over the ensuing years, the literature in social epidemiology downplayed this explanation, choosing instead to emphasize the role of relative income. No longer was one's absolute income the primary determinant of health, as in the Rodgers framework; rather, the more popular models saw income as a marker of relative social status. Several studies documented the correlation between income inequality and health at varying levels of geographic aggregation—ranging from countries (Wilkinson 1992), to US states (Kaplan et al. 1996; Kennedy et al. 1996a, 1996b), to US metropolitan areas (Lynch et al. 1998)—all understood through the lens of relative income.

However, recent economic research has cast doubt on this interpretation.[29] Across US states and cities, much of the association between income inequality and health disappears when analyses control for racial composition—areas more heavily inhabited by African-Americans exhibit poorer health and higher income inequality, but the latter explains very little of the former holding racial composition constant (Mellor and Milyo 2001; Deaton and Lubotsky 2003). Furthermore, the results of studies at the individual level, which consider whether regional income inequality predicts an individual's health after controlling for the individual's income, have generated mixed and fragile results (e.g.

---

[28] For a sampling of the literature on income inequality and health, see the volume edited by Kawachi et al. (1999).

[29] See Deaton (2003) for a review of the literature on income inequality and health.

Mellor and Milyo 2002). Finally, Deaton and Paxson's (2004) analysis of mortality trends in the US and Britain finds that changes in income inequality explain little, if any, of the mortality decline in those two countries during the second half of the twentieth century.

Given such weak evidence, Deaton concludes: "The raw correlations that exist in (some of the) data are most likely the result of factors other than income inequality, some of which are intimately linked to broader notions of inequality or unfairness" (2003: 115). Notably, this does not shut the door on the relative income hypothesis. Eibner and Evans (2005) show that relative income deprivation predicts subsequent mortality at the individual level. The effects of such deprivation are likely to accumulate over the course of a lifetime, so cross-sectional comparisons of current mortality and current relative income are likely to understate the true relationship. But whether or not relative income matters for health, there is little evidence that it drives aggregate correlations between income inequality and population health.

Although these theories of rank, relative deprivation, and inequality are appealing—and find support in biological theory and animal experiments—they present some challenges when applied to humans. First, in large human modern societies, an individual's rank or relative position is difficult to assess. The theory emphasizes how one fares relative to some reference group. Outside of special settings like Whitehall, the relevant reference group is not clear: do individuals compare themselves to their parents? Their friends? Their neighbors? One cannot infer from the data which reference groups are important (Manski 1993; Deaton and Paxson 2004), nor is it clear that they are unique. Additionally, an individual's rank possibly varies depending on the group—a poorly paid employee of the civil service, for example, might also be the leader of a church. Another difficulty with the study of the effects of rank, as an economic model of group interaction would highlight, is that individuals have control over their rank. As emphasized by Frank (1985) and by Falk and Knell (2004), individuals to some extent choose the groups to which they belong (and thus their rank in those groups).[30] Furthermore, even if an individual's reference group is given (for example, one's unit in the military), the individual can affect his or her rank in that group over time through behavior. In either case—endogenous group formation or endogenous ranking—the observed correlation between rank and health is difficult to interpret. Finally, the literature has yet to come to a consensus on whether rank alone matters, or whether the distance across ranks matters as well.

The policy implications of these theories are also unclear. If rank alone determines health, what policies should be implemented to increase health? Given that individuals can choose their reference groups and affect their ranks, policies affecting rank alone would be unlikely to diminish rank-based health gradients. However, one possible policy prescription is to put in place programs that help individuals to mitigate the health consequences of lower rank. In his studies of animals, Sapolsky (2004) reports several factors that can mitigate the effects of stressors. The presence of social supports, the pres-

---

[30] However, individuals may be unable to accurately predict within-group rank (Lowenstein et al. 2003).

ence of outlets for frustration, the perception that an individual's situation is improving, the predictability of stressors, and an individual's perceived ability to control the onset of the stressor are a few of the factors that can allay the health effects of identical stressors. Although these mitigating factors do not point to obvious policy prescriptions, they would seem to hold the key to addressing the rank-related gradient in humans, if sufficient evidence supported the idea that low rank is an important cause of poor health.

7.6 RACE AND ETHNICITY

A final social source of health disparities in many societies involves stratification along racial and ethnic lines. Racial and ethnic differences in health are common in many parts of the world, but their causes vary substantially from country to country. Due both to spatial limitations and to the literature's disproportionate treatment of the US case, we focus exclusively on the US.

In the United States, black adults are significantly more likely than white adults to die from a variety of causes. To give a stark example, in 1980, male residents of Harlem were less likely than male Bangladeshis to survive past age 40 (McCord and Freeman 1990). African-American adults suffer from disproportionately high rates of mortality from all causes—cardiovascular causes and cancer, diabetes and strokes, and they face a higher hazard of homicide than their white counterparts (Sorlie et al. 1992; Howard et al. 2000).[31] In accordance with section 7.2, the literature shows that adjustment for other dimensions of SES (such as education and income) only partially offsets these differences. As with education and income, racial differences are smaller among the oldest age groups. Also as with these other dimensions of SES, the differences are especially striking in children. African-American infants are significantly more likely to die in their first year of life than their white counterparts (Luke and Brown 2006), and they are also more likely to be born pre-term or with low birth weight (Paneth 1995). In fact, white infants born in the United States' poorest counties have superior survival to non-white infants born in the nation's wealthiest counties (Krieger et al. 2008). As shown in section 7.2, however, the health burden faced by black Americans does not carry to other disadvantaged ethnic groups in the United States, most notably individuals of Hispanic descent (Franzini et al. 2001).

Explanations for the patterning of health along racial and ethnic lines vary. To explain the black–white health disparities that remain after accounting for differences in education and income, many appeal to racial bias (including discrimination), difficulties in patient–provider communication, residential segregation, and the legacy of history.[32] Of course, these are intertwined, but we can gain some insight by focusing on each separately.

---

[31] Black Americans are far less likely than white Americans to commit suicide, however (Howard et al. 2000).

[32] See Williams and Collins (1995) for an overview of racial disparities in health in the United States.

In recent years, the medical literature has emphasized accounts based on racial bias, with a focus on racial differences in access to health care. After adjustment for income, black Medicare beneficiaries are less likely than whites to receive mammograms and to visit physicians for ambulatory care, as well as being more likely to be hospitalized, to be amputated, and to die at any given age (Gornick et al. 1996).[33] This may suggest that elderly African-Americans may receive or seek too little preventive care, leading to increased reliance on desperate measures (like amputation) and decreased survival probabilities. But conditional on seeking treatment, there are large racial differences in quantity and quality of treatment received. Peterson et al. (1997) show that blacks with coronary heart disease are less likely than whites to undergo invasive heart surgery, a difference that observable disease characteristics cannot explain. Both before and after adjustment for these disease characteristics, black patients are more likely to die than white patients. Racial differences in treatment account for the lion's share of this mortality gap.

Importantly, racial differences in both preventive and acute care may stem from African-American mistrust of the medical system (Whittle et al. 1997)—a mistrust that dates back at least as far as the Tuskegee Syphilis Study, which purposely left syphilis untreated in a group of poor and largely illiterate black men despite known effective treatments (Gamble 1997). The legacy of the Tuskegee Study provides one example of the long reach of history, which we discuss in greater detail below. However, while mistrust may account for some part of racial differences in care, it is unlikely to be the entire explanation.

Evidence suggests racial bias among physicians as another element of the story. In a study by Schulman et al. (1999), physicians watched videos of black and white actors complaining of chest pains and then inspected charts with clinical data for these hypothetical patients. Conditional on these clinical disease features, physicians referred white patients to cardiac catheterization with significantly higher probability than they did black patients. Of course, this result may reflect physicians using race as a signal of unobserved clinical features, rather than racism or racial bias. However, there is scant evidence to suggest that the patient's race provides information to physicians over and above the clinical data that were provided to them in the study.[34] Another explanation for differential referral by race involves the obstacles to effective communication between white physicians and black patients (Cooper-Patrick et al. 1999; Johnson et al. 2004).[35] But racial bias remains a strong candidate for explaining the findings of Schulman et al.

---

[33] Differential rates of amputation are partly attributable to African-Americans' high prevalence of diabetes, which can lead to gangrene, the most common cause of adult amputation in industrialized countries. Nonetheless, the disproportionate burden of diabetes on blacks is not large enough to account for the entire difference in amputation.

[34] Research does suggest that coronary catheterization may have different effects on men and women (e.g. Loop et al. 1983). However, the referral differences in the Schulman et al. (1999) study were in fact *larger* among women.

[35] The hypothesis that obstacles to communication hinder the care of African-American patients harks back to the work of Bourdieu (1986) on cultural capital, often cited in the sociology literature.

Although physician bias may account for part of the racial disparity in access to health care in the United States, recent economic research suggests that geography may play a larger role. This research underscores racial differences between, rather than within, hospitals or provider groups. African-Americans tend to reside in areas where hospitals and physicians provide lower quality care, which can explain a reasonably large share of racial differences in treatments and outcomes (Chandra and Skinner 2004). For instance, Skinner et al. (2005) examine hospital-level patterns in mortality among patients admitted for heart attacks, separating hospitals into ten deciles according to the proportion of their clientele that was black. After adjustment for observable risk factors and an array of patient and hospital characteristics (including the patient's race and the average income in the patient's zip code), patients admitted to hospitals with the greatest proportion of black patients were 18 percent more likely to die within ninety days than patients admitted to hospitals with a disproportionately white clientele. The geography of health care plays an important part in producing racial differences in health. However, it cannot entirely explain these differences; for example, the Peterson et al. (1997) study of racial differences in the treatment of coronary heart disease took place in a single hospital.

The new focus on geography also relates to a more established literature on the health effects of residential segregation and concentrated urban poverty. Concentrated poverty is thought to erode social support, cause neglect of the physical environment, and increase crime, all of which have been hypothesized to affect mental and physical health. Sociologists Collins and Williams (1999) report that, among African-Americans, increased residential isolation from whites is associated with increased mortality risk, and the association is robust to adjustment for black poverty rates. This might in part reflect the geography of health care, but the same pattern is observed for homicide, for which health care is unlikely to play a role. Nevertheless, as with any observational study, the estimates should be interpreted with caution. In particular, the analysis does not fully control for where people decide to live. Experimental evidence from the Moving to Opportunity program (Kling et al. 2007) is therefore instructive. The program offered housing vouchers to a randomized subset of poor households, leading these households to move to lower poverty areas. The results indicate that moving to lower poverty areas induced improvements in mental health, but the estimates for physical health and youth risk behavior are mixed. Especially disturbing are the results for young males, whose health and engagement in risky behaviors (such as drug and alcohol use) deteriorated after moving to lower poverty areas. These findings may imply that the negative psychosocial effects of residential disruption outweigh positive neighborhood effects among adolescent males, but at any rate, they do not weigh in favor of neighborhood-based explanations for racial health disparities.

Black–white differences in health have a long history in the United States. In 1900, a full thirty-five years after the abolition of slavery, roughly three black children died for every two deceased white children (Ewbank 1987). Although racial differences in mortality narrowed in the first half of the twentieth century, especially among infants (Troesken 2004), the infant mortality gap remained stubbornly large over the subsequent fifty years, even as income-based differences in infant mortality diminished

(Krieger et al. 2008). Some have speculated that the contemporary disparities may have historical origins. One theory along these lines posits that the circumstances surrounding the capture of slaves in Africa, the transatlantic slave voyage, and slavery in the United States led to selective survival among Africans genetically predisposed to conserve salt and water (Wilson and Grim 1991). These genetic traits are associated with high blood pressure, thus offering an explanation for the high rates of hypertension and cardiovascular disease today. This theory is still being debated (Jackson 1991; Curtin 1992; Barghaus et al. 2007). Another historical theory involves the early-twentieth-century rise in African-Americans' propensities to smoke and abuse alcohol, which accompanied the Great Northern Migration. Williams and Collins (1995) attribute this shift to the centrality of drinking taverns to Northern social life and the alienation of blacks in Northern cities, suggesting that these had persistent effects on substance use among African-Americans. Still other work on the legacy of history draws on the 1960s desegregation of hospitals in the US South, which improved the health of black infants (Almond et al. forthcoming). The healthier infant girls grew up to be healthier women, who now mother healthier infants of their own (Almond and Chay 2006). The injustices of the past may thus affect those born in the present.

Black–white mortality differences are especially salient because the US Hispanic population, though currently facing socioeconomic disadvantage of a magnitude similar to that of black America, enjoys survival rates that are on par with, or even slightly higher than, survival rates among non-Hispanic whites (Sorlie et al. 1993; Liao et al. 1998; Elo et al. 2004). This phenomenon is known as the "Hispanic Paradox." As shown in section 7.2, Hispanics are slightly more likely to die than non-Hispanic whites in early adulthood, but they are also less likely to die in old age (Liao et al. 1998). Compared to the infants of non-Hispanic whites, the infants of Hispanic women face similar rates of low birth weight and infant mortality (Paneth 1995).

Selection mechanisms and data problems may explain some of this pattern. First, the mortality statistics for Hispanics may suffer from age misreporting (Elo and Preston 1997) and undercounts of deaths (Smith and Bradshaw 2006). Second, Latino immigrants may return home to die in their countries of origin, thus disappearing from US mortality data and creating what is known as "salmon bias." However, this is not true of all Hispanic groups; Cuban immigrants to the United States, who for geopolitical reasons are unlikely to return home, enjoy a survival advantage that is comparable to that of their counterparts from elsewhere in Latin America and the Caribbean (Abraído-Lanza et al. 1999). A third selection-based explanation for the Hispanic Paradox posits that those who choose to migrate to the United States may be inherently healthier than their non-migrating compatriots (Marmot et al. 1984). Jasso et al. justify this proposition by noting that "because the health of the US native born is so far in excess of those in most migrant sending countries, if migrants to the US have better health than the US native born, they surely have better health than those who stayed in the sending countries" (2004: 234–5). This line of reasoning rests on the rather strong assumption that the health of migrants would have been similar had they remained in their sending countries. More careful analyses cast doubt on this theory. In Mexico, for example, health is at most a weak predictor of subsequent migration (Rubalcava et al. 2008). Among urban women, those with better health exhibit a slightly higher propensity to immigrate to the United States, but this pattern does not hold among rural women or among men.[36] While this does not necessarily disprove the "healthy migrant hypothesis," neither does it weigh in its favor.

As in the cases of education and rank, behavioral differences can take us some of the remaining distance in explaining the Hispanic Paradox. Compared to non-Hispanic whites, Latinos of both sexes are less likely to drink excessively, and Latina women are less likely to smoke (Pérez-Stable et al. 1994). These differences are especially large for recent immigrants. Several risk behaviors increase in prevalence with the length of residence in the United States, as well as across generations, a process known as "acculturation." Compared to their more acculturated counterparts, newcomers consume more fiber, breastfeed more, and are less likely to abuse alcohol, tobacco, and illicit drugs (Vega and Amaro 1994; Lara et al. 2005). Furthermore, children of first generation women are less likely than children of second generation women to be born with low birth weight or to die in the first year of life. This is partially because second generation mothers have a higher propensity to smoke and drink (Landale et al. 1999). Notably, these patterns may reflect changes in the composition of immigrant cohorts over time, rather than actual acculturation. To our knowledge, researchers have yet to sort out this issue.

To some extent, race and ethnicity are markers of genetic differences across groups. But the usefulness of race as a marker of genetic susceptibility to disease is unclear and is the subject of much debate. Even if genetics alone play some role, the current consensus is that the interaction of genes and environment is much more important in explaining outcomes—thus, racial and ethnic differences in health likely result in part from non-genetic sources, such as differences in behavior, access to care, social and cultural norms, and discrimination. The task of unraveling the mechanisms that lead to racial and ethnic inequalities is important for policy. If racial differences are driven by genetic differences, policy should encourage research that identifies genes associated with particular diseases or predisposition to disease, in addition to investment in genetic screening technologies.[37] If the differences arise due to other causes, then more direct action might be more appropriate. For example, if differences in health are driven by differences in access to quality care hospitals, then one might seek to increase access to those hospitals or to improve quality across hospitals. Some of the explanations for racial and ethnic differences bring us back to debates about education, income, and rank. Others do not. If prejudice plays a large role, then policy might appropriately emphasize laws intended to minimize unequal treatment.

---

[36] In fact, Rubalcava et al. (2008) find that Mexican men who self-report better health are *less* likely to migrate. They advise against attaching too much significance to this finding, however, due to confusion over the meaning of the health status question.

[37] See Hall (Chapter 23, this volume) for a discussion of genetic screening.

7.7 Conclusion: Towards a Unified Theory

The literature we review shows clearly that socioeconomic status and health are strongly related, in both industrialized and developing countries, in both welfare states and liberal democracies. That said, the mechanisms linking the various dimensions of SES to health are diverse. Some dimensions of SES cause health, some are caused by health, and some are mutually determined with health; some fall into all three categories at once.

These differential patterns of causality make a single theory of socioeconomic gradients in health difficult to imagine. We suspect, though, that the right theory will emphasize the life-cycle, much as Baker and Stabile (Chapter 8, this volume) suggest. In childhood, parental resources—education and income, for example—have a potent effect on health. Parental membership in a disadvantaged racial or ethnic group may also influence health, in part through its impact on parental resources and in part outside of that. Parenting behaviors, which themselves are influenced by SES, play some role in the determination of child health (Case and Paxson 2002).

Once childhood health is set, the effect of economic resources on health diminishes. In most of adulthood, income and wealth no longer appear to have a large effect on health. Education continues to be a powerful determinant of health, but to a great extent because of its impact on behaviors rather than its association with resources. Exactly why education affects health behaviors remains unclear, but much of the story seems to hinge on the ability to process new information and to take advantage of new technologies. The lasting impact of childhood circumstance also begins to emerge, as healthier children obtain more education.

Feedbacks appear in adulthood as well. Unhealthy adults earn less, spend less time in the labor force, and retire earlier. Insults to child health may persist into adulthood, constraining adults in the labor market. Similarly, the detrimental effect of childhood illness on schooling leaves some adults deficient in human capital, and their children worse off as well. Thus emerges the inter-generational element of the theory; poor childhood health begets limited means in adulthood, which in turn beget poor childhood health for the next generation.

Low social status—whether through membership in a disadvantaged racial group or through low rank in a hierarchy—may also cause poor health in adulthood, but the mechanisms here remain poorly understood. In some cases, broader societal forces are at work: for example, when geographic sorting prohibits one group from living in the vicinity of quality health care facilities, or when direct discrimination leads to poor outcomes. In others, the legacies of historical discrimination and injustice loom large, possibly affecting even the genetic makeup of historically disadvantaged groups. In still other cases, current position in society may influence an individual's health through a range of psychosocial mechanisms.

Apart from the substantive findings of the literature we review, we have also remarked on its inter-disciplinary nature. Economists have made substantial contributions empirically and theoretically, using the tools of modern economics. This has been possible in part because economists have focused on each component of SES separately, an approach which is more suitable to finding causal relationships and also to implementing policy. However, several aspects of the SES–health gradient remain understudied by economists—for example, health differences by rank. Group dynamics are inherently harder to understand than individual behavior. And economists need to look to other disciplines for an understanding of the biology behind the findings we observe.

Because the exact mechanisms underlying the link between socioeconomic status and health are not completely clear, the optimal policy response is difficult to determine. One appealing strategy is to enact policies focused on children. Improving childhood health may lead to superior socioeconomic outcomes later in life in addition to current health improvements. Additionally, if the effect of education operates primarily through cognition and higher order thinking, then government efforts would be better directed at general schooling, rather than health-specific information campaigns. As one component of research on socioeconomic status and health, it would be valuable to experiment with policies targeted along these lines.

REFERENCES

ABRAÍDO-LANZA, A. F., DOHRENWEND, B. P., NG-MAK, D. S., and TURNER, J. B. (1999), "The Latino Mortality Paradox: A Test of the 'Salmon Bias' and Healthy Migrant Hypotheses," *American Journal of Public Health*, 89: 1543–8.

ADAMS, PETER, HURD, MICHAEL D., McFADDEN, DANIEL, MERRILL, ANGELA, and RIBEIRO, TIAGO (2003), "Healthy, Wealthy, and Wise? Tests for Direct Causal Paths between Health and Socioeconomic Status," *Journal of Econometrics*, 112(1): 3–56.

ADLER, N. E., BOYCE, T., CHESNEY, M. A., COHEN, S., FOLKMAN, S., KAHN, R. L., and SYME, S. L. (1994), "Socioeconomic Status and Health: The Challenge of the Gradient," *American Psychologist*, 49(1): 15–24.

ALMOND, D. (2006), "Is the 1918 Influenza Pandemic Over? Long-term Effects of *in utero* Influenza Exposure in the Post-1940 US Population," *Journal of Political Economy*, 114: 562–712.

—— and CHAY, K. (2006), "The Long-run and Intergenerational Impact of Poor Infant Health: Evidence from Cohorts Born During the Civil Rights Era." Mimeo, Columbia University.

—— —— and GREENSTONE, M. (forthcoming), "Civil Rights, the War on Poverty, and Black–White Convergence in Infant Mortality in the Rural South and Mississippi," *American Economic Review*.

ANTONOVSKY, AARON (1967), "Social Class, Life Expectancy and Overall Mortality," *Milbank Memorial Fund Quarterly*, 45: 31–73.

ARENDT, J. N. (2005), "Does Education Cause Better Health? A Panel Data Analysis Using School Reform for Identification," *Economics of Education Review*, 24: 149–60.

ARKES, JEREMY (2003), "Does Schooling Improve Adult Health?" RAND Working Paper, Santa Monica, CA.

BANKS, J., MARMOT, M., OLDFIELD, Z., and SMITH, J. P. (2009), "The SES Health Gradient on Both Sides of the Atlantic," in D. A. Wise (ed.), *Developments in the Economics of Aging* (Chicago: University of Chicago Press).

BARGHAUS, K. M., CUTLER, D. M., FRYER, R. G., and GLAESER, E. L. (2007), "Understanding Racial Differences in Health." Mimeo, Harvard University.

BEHRMAN, J. R. and ROSENZWEIG, M. R. (2004), "Returns to Birthweight," *Review of Economics and Statistics*, 86(2): 586–601.

BLACK, S. E., DEVEREUX, P. J. and SALVANES, K. G. (2007), "From the Cradle to the Labor Market? The Effect of Birth Weight on Adult Outcomes," *Quarterly Journal of Economics*, 122(1): 409–39.

BLEAKLEY, H. (2007), "Disease and Development: Evidence from Hookworm Eradication in the American South," *Quarterly Journal of Economics*, 122(1): 73–117.

—— (2010), "Malaria Eradication in the Americas: A Retrospective Analysis of Childhood Exposure," *American Economic Journal: Applied Economics*, 2(2): 1–45.

BOBONIS, G. J., MIGUEL, E., and SHARMA, C. P. (2006), "Iron Deficiency, Anemia and School Participation," *Journal of Human Resources*, 41(4): 692–721.

BOURDIEU, P. (1986), "The Forms of Capital," in J. G. Richardson (ed.), *Handbook for Theory and Research for the Sociology of Education* (Westport, CT: Greenwood Press), 241–58.

BREIEROVA, LUCIA and DUFLO, ESTHER (2004), "The Impact of Education on Fertility and Child Mortality: Do Fathers Really Matter Less than Mothers?" NBER Working Paper No. 10153.

BRUNNER, E., and MARMOT, M. G. (1999), "Social Organization, Stress, and Health," in M. Marmot and R. G. Wilkinson (eds.), *Social Determinants of Health* (Oxford: Oxford University Press), 17–43.

BZOSTEK, S., GOLDMAN, N., and PEBLEY, A. (2007), "Why Do Hispanics in the USA Report Poor Health?" *Social Science and Medicine*, 65(5): 990–1003.

CALDWELL, JOHN (1979), "Education as a Factor in Mortality Decline: An Examination of Nigerian Data," *Population Studies*, 3(3): 395–413.

CARD, DAVID (2001), "Estimating the Return to Schooling: Progress on Some Persistent Econometric Problems," *Econometrica*, 69(5): 1127–60.

CASE, ANNE (2004), "Does Money Protect Health Status? Evidence from South African Pensions," in David Wise (ed.), *Perspectives on the Economics of Aging* (Chicago: University of Chicago Press), 287–311.

—— and PAXSON, C. (2002), "Parental Behavior and Child Health," *Health Affairs*, 21(2): 164–78.

—— LUBOTSKY, D., and PAXSON, C. (2002), "Economic Status and Health in Childhood: The Origins of the Gradient," *American Economic Review*, 92(5): 1308–34.

—— FERTIG, A., and PAXSON, C. (2005), "The Lasting Impact of Childhood Health and Circumstance," *Journal of Health Economics*, 24: 365–89.

CAWTHON, R. M., SMITH, K. R., O'BRIEN, E., SIVATCHENKO, A., and KERBER, R. A. (2003), "Association Between Telomere Length in Blood and Mortality in People Aged 60 Years or Older," *Lancet*, 361(1): 393–5.

CHANDRA, A. and SKINNER, J. (2004), "Geography and Health Disparities," in N. B. Anderson, R. Bulatao, and B. Cohen (eds.), *Critical Perspectives on Racial and Ethnic Differences in Health in Late Life* (Washington, DC: National Research Council of the National Academies), 604–40.

COLLINS, A. L. and GOLDMAN, N. (2008), "Perceived Social Position and Health in Older Adults in Taiwan," *Social Science and Medicine*, 66(3): 536–44.

COLLINS, C. A. and WILLIAMS, D. R. (1999), "Segregation and Mortality: The Deadly Effects of Racism?" *Sociological Forum*, 14(3): 495–523.

COOPER-PATRICK, L., GALLO, J. J., GONZALES, J. J., VU, H. T., POWE, N. R., NELSON, C., and FORD, D. E. (1999), "Race, Gender, and Partnership in the Patient–Physician Relationship," *Journal of the American Medical Association*, 282: 583–9.

CURRIE, JANET and MORETTI, ENRICO (2003), "Mother's Education and the Intergenerational Transmission of Human Capital: Evidence from College Openings," *Quarterly Journal of Economics*, 118(4): 1495–532.

—— and STABILE, M. (2003), "Socioeconomic Status and Health: Why is the Relationship Stronger for Older Children?" *American Economic Review*, 93(5): 1813–23.

CURTIN, P. D. (1992), "The Slavery Hypothesis for Hypertension Among African Americans: The Historical Evidence," *American Journal of Public Health*, 82: 1681–6.

CUTLER, D. M. and LLERAS-MUNEY, A. (2007a), "Education and Health: Evaluating Theories and Evidence," in J. S. House, R. F. Schoeni, G. A. Kaplan, and H. Pollack (eds.), *The Health Effects of Social and Economic Policy* (New York: Russell Sage Foundation).

—— and LLERAS-MUNEY, A. (2007b), "Understanding Differences in Health Behaviors by Education." Mimeo, Princeton University.

—— DEATON, A., and LLERAS-MUNEY, A. (2006), "The Determinants of Mortality," *Journal of Economic Perspectives*, 20(3): 97–120.

—— FUNG, W., KREMER, M., SINGHAL, M., and VOGL, T. (2010). "Early-Life Malaria Exposure and Adult Outcomes: Evidence from Malaria Eradication in India," *American Economic Journal: Applied Economics*, 2(2): 72–94.

DE WALQUE, D. (2007), "Does Education Affect Smoking Behaviors? Evidence Using the Vietnam Draft as an Instrument for College Education," *Journal of Health Economics*, 26(5): 877–95.

DEATON, A. (2003), "Health, Inequality, and Economic Development," *Journal of Economic Literature*, 41(1): 113–58.

—— and LUBOTSKY, D. (2003), "Mortality, Inequality and Race in American Cities and States," *Social Science and Medicine*, 56(6): 1139–53.

—— and PAXSON, C. (2004), "Mortality, Income, and Income Inequality Over Time in Britain and the United States," in D. A. Wise (ed.), *Perspectives on the Economics of Aging* (Chicago: University of Chicago Press), 247–79.

DESCHÊNES, O. (2001), "Unobserved Ability, Comparative Advantage and the Rising Return to Education in the United States: A Cohort-based Approach." Industrial Relations Section Working Paper No. 465, Princeton University.

EIBNER, C. and EVANS, W. N. (2005), "Relative Deprivation, Poor Health Habits, and Mortality," *Journal of Human Resources*, 40(3): 592–620.

ELO, I. T. and PRESTON, S. H. (1996), "Educational Differentials in Mortality: United States, 1979–85," *Social Science and Medicine*, 42(1): 47–57.

—— —— (1997), "Racial and Ethnic Differences in Mortality at Older Ages," in L. Martin and B. Soldo (eds.), *Racial and Ethnic Differences in the Health of Older Americans* (Washington, DC: National Academy Press), 10–42.

—— TURRA, C. M., KESTENBAUM, B., and FERGUSON, B. R. (2004), "Mortality Among Elderly Hispanics in the United States: Past Evidence and New Results," *Demography*, 41: 109–28.

EPEL, E. S., BLACKBURN, E. H., LIN, J., et al. (2004), "Accelerated Telomere Shortening in Response to Life Stress," *Proceedings of the National Academy of Sciences*, 101(49): 17312–15.

ERIKSON, R. and TORSSANDER, J. (2008), "Social Class and Cause of Death," *European Journal of Public Health*, 18(5): 473–8.

EVANS, W. N. and SNYDER, S. (2006), "The Impact of Income on Mortality: Evidence from the Social Security Notch," *Review of Economics and Statistics*, 88(3): 482–95.

EWBANK, DOUGLAS C. (1987). "History of Black Mortality and Health before 1940," *Milbank Quarterly* 65(S1): 100–28.

FALK, ARMIN and KNELL, MARKUS (2004), "Choosing the Joneses: On the Endogeneity of Reference Groups," *Scandinavian Journal of Economics*, 106(3): 417–35.

FAN, J. (1992), "Design-adaptive Nonparametric Regression," *Journal of the American Statistical Association*, 87: 998–1004.

—— FARMEN, M., and GIJBELS, I. (1998), "Local Maximum Likelihood Estimation and Inference," *Journal of the Royal Statistical Society: Series B (Statistical Methodology)*, 60(3): 591–608.

FEINSTEIN, J. S. (1993), "The Relationship Between Socioeconomic Status and Health: A Review of the Literature," *Millbank Quarterly*, 71: 279–320.

FERTIG, A. (2007), "Healthy Baby, Healthy Marriage? The Effect of Children's Health on Divorce." Mimeo, University of Georgia.

FIELD, E., ROBLES, O., and TORERO, M. (2009), "Iodine Deficiency and Schooling Attainment in Tanzania," *American Economic Journal: Applied Economics*, 1(4): 140–69.

FOGEL, R. (1986), "Nutrition and the Decline in Mortality Since 1700: Some Preliminary Findings," in S. Engerman and R. Gallman (eds.), *Long Term Factors in American Economic Growth* (Chicago: Chicago University Press), 439–555.

FRANK, R. H. (1985), *Choosing the Right Pond* (New York: Oxford University Press).

FRANZINI, L., RIBBLE, J. C., and KEDDIE, A. M. (2001), "Understanding the Hispanic Paradox," *Ethnicity and Disease*, 11(3): 496–518.

GALLO, L. C. and MATTHEWS, K. A. (2003), "Understanding the Association Between Socioeconomic Status and Physical Health: Do Negative Emotions Play a Role?" *Psychological Bulletin*, 129(1): 10–51.

GAMBLE, V. N. (1997), "Under the Shadow of Tuskegee: African Americans and Health Care," *American Journal of Public Health*, 87(11): 1773–8.

GEYER, S., HEMSTROM, O., PETER, R., and VAGERO, D. (2006), "Education, Income, and Occupational Class Cannot Be Used Interchangeably in Social Epidemiology: Empirical Evidence Against a Common Practice," *Journal of Epidemiology and Community Health*, 60: 804–10.

GLIED, S. and LLERAS-MUNEY, A. (2008), "Health Inequality, Education, and Medical Innovation," *Demography*, 45(3): 741–61.

GORNICK, M. E., EGGERS, E. W., REILLY, T. W., et al. (1996), "Effects of Race and Income on Mortality and Use of Services Among Medicare Beneficiaries," *New England Journal of Medicine*, 335(11): 791–9.

GRIMARD, F. and PARENT, D. (2007), "Education and Smoking: Were Vietnam War Draft Avoiders Also More Likely to Avoid Smoking?" *Journal of Health Economics*, 26(5): 896–926.

GROSSMAN, M. (1972), *The Demand for Health—A Theoretical and Empirical Investigation* (New York: National Bureau of Economic Research).

—— (2008), "Education and Non-market Outcomes," in E. Hanushek and F. Welch (eds.), *Handbook of the Economics of Education* (Amsterdam: North-Holland, Elsevier Science), 577–633.

HAINES, M. R. (2001), "The Urban Mortality Transition in the United States: 1800–1940," *Annales de Demographie Historique*, 101: 33–64.

HARRIS, B. (2004), "Public Health, Nutrition, and the Decline of Mortality: The McKeown Thesis Revisited," *Social History of Medicine*, 17(3): 379–407.

HOWARD, G., ANDERSON, R. T., RUSSELL, G., HOWARD, V. J., and BURKE, G. L. (2000), "Race, Socioeconomic Status, and Cause-specific Mortality," *Annals of Epidemiology* 10(4): 214–23.

HUISMAN, M., KUNST, A., BOPP, M., et al. (2005), "Educational Inequalities in Cause-specific Mortality in Middle-aged and Older Men and Women in Eight Western European Populations," *Lancet*, 365(9458): 493–500.

IDLER, E. L. and BENYAMINI, Y. (1997), "Self-rated Health and Mortality: A Review of Twenty-seven Community Studies," *Journal of Health and Social Behavior*, 38(1): 21–37.

IMBENS, G. W., and ANGRIST, J. D. (1994), "Identification and Estimation of Local Average Treatment Effects," *Econometrica*, 62(2): 467–75.

JACKSON, F. L. C. (1991), "An Evolutionary Perspective on Salt, Hypertension, and Human Genetic Variability," *Hypertension*, 17(1, S1): 129–32.

JASSO, G., MASSEY, D. S., ROSENZWEIG, M. R., and SMITH, J. P. (2004), "Immigrant Health: Selectivity and Acculturation," in N. B. Anderson, R. Bulatao, and B. Cohen (eds.), *Critical Perspectives on Racial and Ethnic Differences in Health in Late Life* (Washington, DC: National Research Council of the National Academies), 227–66.

JAYACHANDRAN, S. and LLERAS-MUNEY, A. (2009), "Life Expectancy and Human Capital Investment: Evidence from Maternal Mortality Declines," *Quarterly Journal of Economics*, 124(1): 349–97.

JENSEN, R. T. and KASPAR, R. (2004). "The Health Implications of Social Security Failure: Evidence from the Russian Pension Crisis," *Journal of Public Economics*, 88(1–2): 209–36.

JOHNSON, R. L., ROTER, D., POWE, N. R., and COOPER, L. A. (2004), "Patient Race/Ethnicity and Quality of Patient–Physician Communication During Medical Visits," *American Journal of Public Health*, 94(12): 2084–90.

KAPLAN, G. A., PAMUK, E. R., LYNCH, J. W., COHEN, R. D., and BALFOUR, J. L. (1996), "Inequality in Income and Mortality in the United States: Analysis of Mortality and Potential Pathways," *British Medical Journal*, 312: 999–1003.

KAWACHI, I., KENNEDY, B. P., and WILKINSON, R. G. (1999), *The Society and Population Health Reader: Volume 1: Income Inequality and Health* (New York: New Press).

KENNEDY, B. P., KAWACHI, I., and PROTHROWSTITH, D. (1996), "Income Distribution and Mortality: Cross-sectional Ecological Study of the Robin Hood Index in the United States," *British Medical Journal*, 312: 1004–7.

KITAGAWA, E. M. and HAUSER, P. M. (1973), *Differential Mortality in the United States: A Study in Socioeconomic Epidemiology* (Cambridge, MA: Harvard University Press).

KLING, J., LIEBMAN, J. B., and KATZ, L. F. (2007), "Experimental Analysis of Neighborhood Effects," *Econometrica*, 75(1): 83–119.

KRIEGER, N., REHKOPH, D. H., CHEN, J. T., WATERMAN, P. D., MARCELLI, E., and KENNEDY, M. (2008), "The Fall and Rise of US Inequalities in Premature Mortality: 1960–2002," *PLoS Medicine*, 5(2): 227–41.

LAKDAWALLA, D. and GOLDMAN, D. (2001), "Understanding Health Disparities Across Education Groups." NBER Working Paper No. 8328.

LANDALE, N. S., OROPRESA, R. S., and GORMAN, B. K. (1999), "Immigration and Infant Health: Birth Outcomes of Immigrant and Native-born Women," in D. J. Hernandez (ed.), *Children of Immigrants* (Washington, DC: National Academy of Sciences Press), 244–85.

LARA, M., GAMBOA, C., KAHRAMANIAN, M. I., MORALES, L. S., and BAUTISTA, D. H. (2005), "Acculturation and Latino Health in the United States: A Review of the Literature and its Sociopolitical Context," *Annual Review of Public Health*, 26: 367–97.

LEMIEUX, T. (2006), "The Mincer Equation Thirty Years After *Schooling, Experience, and Earnings*," in S. Grossbard-Shechtman (ed.), *Jacob Mincer, A Pioneer of Modern Labor Economics* (New York: Springer), 127–48.

LIAO, Y., COOPER, R. S., CAO, G., DURAZO-ARVIZU, R., KAUFMAN, J. S., LUKE, A., and McGEE, D. L. (1998), "Mortality Patterns Among Adult Hispanics: Findings from the NHIS, 1986 to 1990," *American Journal of Public Health*, 88(2): 227–32.

LINK, B. G. and PHELAN, J. (1995), "Social Conditions as the Fundamental Causes of Disease," *Journal of Health and Social Behavior*, 35(Extra Issue): 80–94.

LLERAS-MUNEY, A. (2005), "The Relationship Between Education and Adult Mortality in the United States," *Review of Economic Studies*, 72: 189–221.

——— and LICHTENBERG, F. (2006), "The Effect of Education on Medical Technology Adoption: Are the More Educated More Likely to Use New Drugs?" *Annales d'economie et statistique*, 79(80).

LOOP, F. D., GOLDING, L. R., MacMILLAN, J. P., COSGROVE, D. M., LYTLE, B. W., and SHELDON, W. C. (1983), "Coronary Artery Surgery in Women Compared with Men: Analyses of Risks and Long-term Results," *Journal of the American College of Cardiology*, 1: 383–90.

LOWENSTEIN, G., O'DONOGHUE, T., and RABIN, M. (2003), "Projection Bias in Predicting Future Utility," *Quarterly Journal of Economics*, 118(4): 1209–48.

LUCAS, A. M. (2010), "Malaria Eradication and Educational Attainment: Evidence from Paraguay and Sri Lanka," *American Economic Journal: Applied Economics*, 2(2): 46–71.

LUKE, B. and BROWN, M. B. (2006), "The Changing Risk of Infant Mortality by Gestation, Plurality, and Race: 1989–1991 versus 1999–2001," *Pediatrics*, 118: 2488–97.

LYNCH, J. W., KAPLAN, G. A., and PAMUK, E. R. (1998), "Income Inequality and Mortality in Metropolitan Areas of the United States," *American Journal of Public Health*, 88: 1074–80.

MACCINI, S. and YANG, D. (2007), "Under the Weather: Health, Schooling and Socio-economic Consequences of Early Life Rainfall." Mimeo, University of Michigan.

MACKENBACH, J. P. (2006), *Health Inequalities: Europe in Profile* (London: UK Department of Health).

MANSKI, C. F. (1993), "Identification of Endogenous Social Effects: The Reflection Problem," *Review of Economic Studies*, 60(3): 531–42.

MARMOT, M. G., ROSE, G., SHIPLEY, M., and HAMILTON, P. J. S. (1978), "Employment Grade and Coronary Heart Disease in British Civil Servants," *Journal of Epidemiology and Community Health*, 32: 244–9.

——— ADELSTEIN, A. M., and BULUSU, L. (1984), "Lessons from the Study of Immigrant Mortality," *Lancet*, 2: 1455–7.

——— KOGEVINAS, M., and ELSTON, M. A. (1987), "Social-economic Status and Disease," *Annual Review of Public Health*, 8: 111–35.

——— SIEGRIST, J., THEORELL, T., and FEENEY, A. (1999), "Health and the Psychosocial Environment at Work," in M. Marmot and R. G. Wilkinson (eds.), *Social Determinants of Health* (Oxford: Oxford University Press), 105–31.

——— SMITH, G. D., STANSFIELD, S., et al. (1991), "Health Inequalities Among British Civil Servants: The Whitehall II Study," *Lancet*, 337(8754): 1387–93.

MAZUMDER, B. (2008), "Does Education Improve Health? A reexamination of the Evidence from Compulsory Schooling Laws," *Federal Reserve Bank of Chicago Economic Perspectives*, Q2: 2–16.

McCORD, C. and FREEMAN, H. P. (1990), "Excess Mortality in Harlem," *New England Journal of Medicine*, 322: 173–7.

McDONOUGH, P., DUNCAN, G. J., WILLIAMS, D., and HOUSE, J. (1999), "Income Dynamics and Adult Mortality in the United States, 1972 through 1989," *American Journal of Public Health*, 87(9): 1476–83.

McEWEN, B. S. (1998), "Protective and Damaging Effects of Stress Mediators," *New England Journal of Medicine*, 338(3): 1771–9.

MELLOR, J. M. and MILYO, J. (2001), "Reexamining the Evidence of an Ecological Association Between Income Inequality and Health," *Journal of Health Politics, Policy, and Law*, 26: 487–522.

—— —— (2002), "Income Inequality and Health Status in the United States: Evidence from the Current Population Survey," *Journal of Human Resources*, 37(3): 510–39.

MENG, X. and QIAN, N. (2006), "The Long Run Health and Economic Consequences of Famine on Survivors: Evidence from China's Great Famine." IZA Discussion Paper 2471.

MIGUEL, E. and KREMER, M. (2004), "Worms: Identifying Impacts on Education and Health in the Presence of Treatment Externalities," *Econometrica*, 72(1): 159–217.

MINCER, J. (1997), "Changes in Wage Inequality, 1970–1990," *Research in Labor Economics*, 16: 1–18.

MOSK, C. and JOHANSSON, S. R. (1986), "Income and Mortality: Evidence from Modern Japan," *Population and Development Review*, 12(3): 415–40.

OPERARIO, D., ADLER, N. E., and WILLIAMS, D. R. (2004), "Subjective Social Status: Reliability and Predictive Utility for Global Health," *Psychology and Health*, 19(2): 237–46.

OREOPOULOS, P. (2007), "Do Dropouts Drop Out Too Soon? Wealth, Health and Happiness from Compulsory Schooling," *Journal of Public Economics*, 91(11–12): 2213–29.

PANETH, N. (1995), "The Problem of Low Birthweight," *Future of Children*, 5: 19–34.

PÉREZ-STABLE, E. J., MARÍN, G., and MARÍN, B. V. (1994), "Behavioral Risk Factors: A Comparison of Latinos and non-Latino Whites in San Francisco," *American Journal of Public Health*, 84: 971–6.

PETERSON, E. D., SHAW, L. K., DeLONG, E. R., et al. (1997), "Racial Variation in the Use of Cardiac Revascularization Procedures," *New England Journal of Medicine*, 336: 480–6.

RODGERS, G. B. (1979), "Income and Inequality as Determinants of Mortality: An International Cross-section Analysis," *Population Studies*, 33(3): 343–51.

RUBALCAVA, L. N., TERUEL, G. M., THOMAS, D., and GOLDMAN. N. (2008), "The Healthy Migrant Effect: New Findings from the Mexican Family Life Survey," *American Journal of Public Health*, 98(1): 78–84.

RUHM, C. J. (2000), "Are Recessions Good for Your Health?" *Quarterly Journal of Economics*, 115(2): 617–50.

—— (2005), "Healthy Living in Hard Times," *Journal of Health Economics*, 24(2): 341–63.

SAPOLSKY, R. M. (1993), "Endocrinology Alfresco: Psychoendocrine Studies of Wild Baboons," *Recent Progress in Hormone Research*, 48: 437–68.

—— (2004), *Why Zebras Don't Get Ulcers. An Updated Guide to Stress, Stress-related Diseases, and Coping* (3rd edn.; New York: Freeman).

SCHULMAN, K. A., et al. (1999), "The Effect of Race and Sex on Physicians' Recommendations for Cardiac Catheterization," *New England Journal of Medicine*, 340: 618–26.

SEEMAN, T. E., McEWEN, B. S., ROWE, J. W., and SINGER, B. H. (2001), "Allostatic Load as a Marker of Cumulative Biological Risk: MacArthur Studies of Successful Aging," *Proceedings of the National Academy of Sciences*, 98(8): 4770–5.

SINGH-MANOUX, A., MARMOT, M. G., and ADLER, N. E. (2005), "Does Subjective Social Status Predict Health and Change in Health Status Better than Objective Status?" *Psychosomatic Medicine*, 67: 855–61.

SKINNER, J., CHANDRA, A. STAIGER, D., LEE, J., and McCLELLAN, M. (2005), "Mortality After Acute Myocardial Infarction in Hospitals that Disproportionately Treat Black Patients," *Circulation*, 112: 2634–41.

SMITH, D. P. and BRADSHAW, B. S. (2006), "Rethinking the Hispanic Paradox: Death Rates and Life Expectancy for US Non-Hispanic White and Hispanic Populations," *American Journal of Public Health*, 96: 1686–92.

SMITH, J. P. (1999), "Healthy Bodies and Thick Wallets: The Dual Relation Between Health and Economic Status," *Journal of Economic Perspectives*, 13(2): 145–66.

—— (2004), "Unraveling the SES–health Connection," *Population and Development Review*, 30(Suppl.): 108–32.

—— (2005), "Consequences and Predictors of New Health Events, in D. A. Wise (ed.), *Analyses in the Economics of Aging* (Chicago: University of Chicago Press), 213–37.

—— (2007), "The Impact of Social Economic Status on Health Over the Life-Course," *Journal of Human Resources*, 42: 739–64.

SMITH, K. V. and GOLDMAN, N. (2007), "Socioeconomic Differences in Health Among Older Adults in Mexico," *Social Science and Medicine*, 65: 1372–85.

SORLIE, P., ROGOT, E., ANDERSON, R., JOHNSON, N. J. and BACKLUND, E. (1992), "Black–white Mortality Difference by Family Income," *Lancet*, 340: 346–50.

SORLIE, P. D., BACKLUND, E., JOHNSON, N. J., and ROGOT, E. (1993), "Mortality by Hispanic Status in the United States," *Journal of the American Medical Association*, 270: 2464–8.

SPASOJEVIC, J. (2003), "Effects of Education on Adult Health in Sweden: Results from a Natural Experiment." Ph. D. dissertation, City University of New York Graduate Center, New York.

STRAUSS, J. and THOMAS, D. (1998), "Health, Nutrition, and Economic Development," *Journal of Economic Literature*, 36(2): 766–817.

SULLIVAN, D. and VON WACHTER, T. (2006), "Mortality, Mass-Layoffs, and Career Outcomes: An Analysis Using Administrative Data." Mimeo, Columbia University.

TORSSANDER, J. and ERIKSON, R. (2009). "Stratification and Mortality—A Comparison of Education, Class, Status, and Income," *European Sociological Review*, 26: 465–74.

TROESKEN, W. (2004), *Water, Race, and Disease* (Cambridge, MA: MIT Press).

VEGA, W. A. and AMARO, H. (1994), "Latino Outlook: Good Health, Uncertain Prognosis," *Annual Review of Public Health*, 15: 39–67.

WHITTLE, J. C., GOOD, C. B., and JOSWIAK, M. (1997), "Do Patient Preferences Contribute to Racial Differences in Cardiovascular Procedure Use?" *Journal of General Internal Medicine*, 12(5): 267–73.

WILKINSON, R. G. (1990), "Income Distribution and Mortality: A 'Natural' Experiment," *Sociology of Health and Illness*, 12: 391–412.

—— (1992), "Income Distribution and Life Expectancy," *British Medical Journal*, 304: 165–8.

—— (1996), *Unhealthy Societies: The Affliction of Inequality* (London: Routledge).

—— (1999), "Health, Hierarchy and Social Anxiety," *Annals of the New York Academy of Sciences*, 896: 48–63.

—— (2000), *Mind the Gap: Hierarchies, Health, and Human Evolution* (London: Weidenfeld Nicolson).

—— and COLLINS, C. (1995), "US Socioeconomic and Racial Differences in Health: Patterns and Explanations," *Annual Review of Sociology*, 21: 349–86.

WILSON, T. W. and GRIM, C. E. (1991), "Biohistory of Slavery and Blood Pressure Differences in Blacks Today," *Hypertension*, 17(1) (S1): 122–8.

CHAPTER 8

......

DETERMINANTS OF HEALTH IN CHILDHOOD

......

MICHAEL BAKER AND MARK STABILE

8.1 INTRODUCTION

......

ECONOMIC researchers have long recognized the interplay between health and economic outcomes at both the macro and micro levels. Researchers have documented the associations between health and wealth (see Chapter 7 in this volume) of both individuals and states and have explored extensively how improvements in health affect several outcomes of economic interest such as human capital, labor market success, social programs, and aggregate GDP, to name a few. While the relationship between health and economic outcomes takes place over all periods of the human life-cycle, an increasing body of literature has focused on the economic determinants and economic consequences of health in childhood, based on an increasingly accepted notion that broad investments in children produce returns over the entire life-cycle.

Evidence from the epidemiology literature argues for strong linkages between early child health and adult health. The work by David Barker, commonly referred to as the "fetal origins hypothesis," suggests that poor fetal health is related to higher adult risk of disease, particularly coronary heart disease and type 2 diabetes (Barker 1998; Gluckman and Hanson 2006) and has served as a starting point for much of the economic research in this area. In her recent review of the child health literature, Currie (2009) notes that this research can been seen in the broader context of research which explores the interactions between genes and their environment where individuals may be genetically predisposed to certain health problems, but interactions with various environmental factors lead to the manifestation of the health conditions. Work by Heckman and colleagues (2007) extends this argument beyond childhood health and lays out a dynamic model of the effects of past health and human capital stock on the ability to accumulate current health and human capital (outlined in Cunha, Heckman, and Schennach 2006) to the broader notion that early childhood investment lays a foundation for the success of future investments and therefore future economic payoffs.

The notion that health acts as an input into the human production of other valuable goods and that the "health stock" itself is a function of current and past investments is based on the well-known theoretical work of Grossman (1972). Grossman's notion of health as an input into the production of both work and leisure, and investments in the health stock having long-run payoffs can easily be extended back to childhood to provide an organizing framework for much of the literature reviewed in this chapter.

Children are born with a stock of health, H_0. Children receive insults to their health in the form of chronic conditions (both mental and physical), diseases, injuries, etc. The health stock can also be augmented with parental investments of both time and money so that the health stock next period is a function of the health stock in the previous period, investments made to health, and any realized insults to the child's health. A simple representation of this function would then be:

$$H_t = f(H_{t-1}, I_t, P_t, \Omega),$$

where I_t represents insults to the child's health at time t, P_t represents parental investments of time and money at time t, and Ω denotes parental endowments (such as IQ, education, income, genes, etc.).

This health stock, while providing utility to a child, will also serve as an input into a variety of other goods and stocks. Importantly, health will be a key input into human capital accumulation. At the most basic level, a child must be well enough to go to school, with a health stock of, say, $H(min)$. However, beyond this, variation in the stock of physical and mental health will affect the child's ability to learn and participate at school and acquire human capital, E. Human capital, therefore, is a function of, among other things, the health stock at time t, or $Et(H_t, X_t, \Omega)$, where Xt represents other inputs (parental and otherwise) into the ability to acquire human capital. This, in turn, will affect future economic outcomes such as labor market earnings. We would expect that children from families with more resources would have, on average, a higher level of health stock ($\partial H/\partial I > 0$). We would also expect that insults to health are not completely exogenous, but rather depend in part on the child's environment (housing stock, neighborhoods, etc) such that children from families with fewer resources would have lower health ($\partial H/\partial \Omega > 0$), and may receive more shocks to their health ($\partial I/\partial \Omega > 0$). It may be the case that children from families with more resources will be able to mitigate the effects of health shocks more than families without resources (through better information, or better medical treatment).

Heckman (2007) describes the notion of "dynamic complementarity" in the case of human capital accumulation as arising when "stocks of capabilities acquired in the previous period make investment in the [current] period more productive. Such complementarity explains why returns to educational investments are higher at later stages of the child's life-cycle for more able, more healthy, and more motivated children" (Heckman 2007: 13253). In this simple representation, health stocks in previous periods contribute to the current health stock, which then contributes to current human capital accumulation.[1]

The empirical studies reviewed in this chapter broaden the general ideas presented above to examine the validity of the notion that health in childhood has both short-term and longer-term economic consequences, and that childhood health is itself a function of a broader set of policies, investment decisions and parental choices, and a function of parental health stock and economic background. While these areas are not solely explored by economists, economists have made significant contributions over the past decade or so by focusing on large sample analysis, and pressing on the identification of causal relationships. This review focuses on examples of recent economic research that have made such contributions to this literature.

While Grossman left the definition of health to be broadly defined, the empirical research reviewed here uses a broad set of survey and administrative instruments to construct a set of health measures over the life of the child across several dimensions. Childhood health at birth is measured using birth weight, gestational length, and Apgar scores (which measure the overall health of the child both five minutes and ten minutes after birth). As children age, several surveys and screeners are used to capture the development of cognitive ability, behavioral development, and physical health and development. Test scores probe picture recognition and vocabulary in early years, advancing to more standard tests of math and reading comprehension. Behavioral screeners are used to capture symptoms of common mental illnesses such as attention deficit hyperactivity disorder, aggression disorders, depression, and others at various stages of the child's development. Measures of illnesses, chronic conditions, injuries, and measure of height and weight are used to examine physical health problems, acute health shocks, and physical growth and development.

The literature reviewed here strongly suggests that influences on the child, from pre-birth to adolescence, have important implications for both health and other markers of success such as education. Socioeconomic indicators and environmental shifts influence these relationships, and various studies with plausible causal identification suggest that the effects can be quite large. The extent to which policy levers can and do have large impacts on these relationships varies. Some, such as maternal leave policies and tax and subsidy policy appear to affect various margins of behavior and health, while others have proven less effective. Overall, there remains considerable scope for research on the effects of child health on the life-course and the plausible policy levers that can improve well-being.

---

[1] In Heckman's (2007) representation, health is one of these early capabilities, as would be cognitive and non-cognitive abilities.

8.2 Infant and Early Childhood Health

8.2.1 Health at Birth and Childhood Well-being

It seems evident that fetal health and health in early infancy would have significant effects on later infant health outcomes. But, since fetal health and health in early infancy, as well as later health, depend on family environment, socioeconomic status (SES), and other factors that may not be observed by researchers, it has been challenging to estimate the causal elements in this link. Several recent papers have examined the role of early infant health on survival and early infant health outcomes.

Many of these studies use large administrative samples and track children from birth onward. The studies seek to estimate causal relationships between infant health and future outcomes using variation within families and within twins in order to control for omitted variables common across families, or between twins, that may be related to both poor health and poor outcomes such as various aspects of socioeconomic status. The most common measures of health at birth found in the literature are birth weight, Apgar scores, and gestational length. In general these measures are considered more objective than survey measures of infant health. Weight at birth is considered low if it is below 2500 grams, and very low below 1500 grams. Gestational periods are considered premature if they are below 37 weeks. Apgar scores are based on five items and scored out of 10. Scores below 7 are considered poor.[2]

One set of economic studies have examined the effects of poor infant health on short-term survival. For example, Almond, Chay, and Lee (2005) examine the relationship between low birth weight, low Apgar scores, and mortality in the first year of life. Using a large sample of twin births from the National Center for Health Statistics (US data), they show that, while both birth weight and Apgar scores are strongly related to infant mortality across families, the relationship between birth weight and infant mortality significantly decreases when differences between twins are examined. In contrast, the relationship between Apgar scores and infant mortality remains strong both across families and within twin pairs.

A second stream of social science literature has used twin studies to examine the longer-term effects of birth weight on health and education. Behrman and Rosenzweig (2004) use twin data from the Minnesota Twins Registry to examine the effects of low birth weight on the educational attainment and adult health of women. They find that increasing birth weight increases schooling attainment by about one third of a year and that this effect is stronger within twins than across children of different families.

---

[2] The Apgar score summarizes five vital sign conditions at birth. Heath care providers assess an infant's heart-rate, respiration, muscle tone, reflex, and color and assign values of zero, one, or two for each category, with the best possible total score equaling ten. A score less than seven often triggers additional action to stabilize conditions. A score of seven to ten is considered normal.

Conley, Strully, and Bennett (2003) examine the effects of low birth weight on high school graduation and placement in special education using the Panel Study of Income Dynamics. They find that the effects of low birth weight on timely high school graduation are more pronounced among siblings than across families. This suggests that the within-family differences, that is the differences in birth weight between siblings, account for much of the relationship between birth weight and educational attainment. Differences in birth weight between families account for less of this relationship. The study does not look at other measures of infant health (Apgar and gestation) nor does it explore the potential non-linear effects of low birth weight on infant health.

Evidence using data from other nations extends many of the findings in the United States. Currie and Hyson (1999) show that, conditional on many measures of family background and circumstances, low birth weight children from the 1958 British birth cohort have lower test scores, educational attainments, wages, and probabilities of being employed as of age 33. Black et al. (2007) use a sample of Norwegian twins to examine the long-run consequences of low birth weight. Their evidence confirms that low birth weight is not a good predictor of infant death within twin pairs. However, they do find long-term effects of low birth weight on cognitive outcomes, educational outcomes, and on earnings. In particular, birth weight has long-term effects on height, IQ, earnings, and education. Oreopoulos et al. (2008) use administrative data from the Canadian province of Manitoba and find both low birth weight and low Apgar scores to be strong predictors of both high school completion and welfare take-up and length.

The evidence that early infant health matters in both the short and longer term is large and fairly consistent. What is less clear is how these early measures of health affect longer term health—whether they are early indicators of future health problems, whether they trigger environmental responses within or outside the family that have longer-term consequences, or whether there is some other explanation for the observed linkage between health at birth and outcomes throughout the life-course. Understanding these mechanisms, and further research into the role of economic inputs into child health over the life-course are both important next steps for research and key elements for policymakers seeking to improve population outcomes.

8.2.2 Environmental Factors and Infant Health

Environmental contamination such as pollution is commonly thought to have particularly strong effects on the old and very young. Some recent research attempts to investigate a relationship between air pollution and health in infancy and childhood.

Chay and Greenstone (2003a) use variation in pollution induced by the 1980–82 US recession to examine its effect on child hood health. They report that reductions in total suspended particulates lead to reductions in infant mortality, primarily in the neonatal period. The recession is estimated to have reduced infant deaths by 2500 in this period. Supporting evidence that uses variation in pollution induced by the 1970 US Clean Air Act is provided by Chay and Greenstone (2003b).

Neidell (2004) examines the impact of pollution on childhood asthma exploiting seasonal variation in pollution levels within place. Carbon monoxide is found to affect asthma, with a greater impact for children of lower SES. Clearly environmental factors play a contributing role in development of childhood health, both on their own, and through interactions with SES. These relationships, with plausible causal pathways, are informative to policymakers looking to prevent longer term health problems through focusing on the socioeconomic circumstances and living environment of the child.

8.2.3 Maternal Employment

A prominent focus of economic research on child health and development is the roles of maternal employment and parental and non-parental care, including interventions that provide early childhood education. An important economic dimension of this research is the mother's decision to work in the period following giving birth.

Klerman and Leibowitz (1997) outline a static model of the decision to work post-birth. Employers may voluntarily choose to offer a maternity leave out of a desire to preserve match or job specific human capital. Mothers choose between whatever leave is offered and the option of quitting. An optimal duration of post-birth absence from the labor market is chosen in light of the difference in wages between the current and best alternative jobs and a reservation wage that declines with each month post-birth.

In most developed countries governments intervene in this private transaction by mandating a minimum period of job protected, and perhaps compensated, maternity leave. Interestingly, Klerman and Leibowitz point out that the predicted impact of such legislation on time at home post-birth is ambiguous, as some mothers choose to stay home longer in the presence of a mandate while others will stay home a shorter period.[3]

An important issue in empirical research investigating the impact of maternal employment on children's health is omitted variables bias. The problem is that variables that are not included as covariates in the estimating equation that are correlated both with a mother's decision to work and the outcomes of her children. These variables may not be available because they simply were not collected in the survey data, or they may be fundamentally unmeasurable. There are two common approaches to this problem in this literature. The first is to seek out data sets with extensive arrays of information about mothers and their families, and to include these variables as controls in the estimating equation. The hope here is, in effect, that there are no omitted variables once all these

[3] The empirical evidence of the impact of maternity leave mandates on mothers' labour supply is mixed. Studies based on the introduction of the Family and Medical Leave Act in the US show impacts that are sometimes small or sensitive to specification (e.g. Waldfogel 1999; Baum 2003a, 2003b; Han et al. 2009). Research based on Canadian policies suggests short mandates do not increase the time spent at home while longer ones do (Baker and Milligan 2008a).

covariates have been included. The second is to exploit variation in maternal employment induced by maternity leave mandates, or other public policies that affect the labor market decisions of mothers with young children. In this case the assumption is that this variation in employment is not correlated with the omitted variables in the error term of the estimating equation. A noted limitation of this approach is that the result is usually a local average treatment effect specific to the sub population whose behavior is affected by the policy.[4]

At the very beginning of a child's life maternal employment will interrupt the first months of maternal care. During this period mothers recover from giving birth, bond with their children and importantly have the opportunity to breastfeed. Perhaps the strongest advice for childhood nutrition is that babies initially be breastfed. The World Health Organization recommends 6 months of exclusive breastfeeding, counsel echoed by many public health and medical associations. In many countries there is further guidance to include breast milk in children's diets up to age 2.

Many benefits are attributed to breast milk including reduced rates of mortality, respiratory ailments, gastro-intestinal diseases and allergies for children and lower incidence of ovarian and premenopausal breast cancer for mothers. Many reviews of the literature note, however, that the supporting evidence is almost exclusively observational and the contribution of confounding factors may be important (e.g. Horta et al. 2007). There appears to be only one study of the benefits of breastfeeding that adopts a randomized design (Kramer et al. 2001).

Although breastfeeding data is not collected systematically in many countries, there appears to be a consensus that practice falls well short of the desired behavior (e.g. UNICEF 2008). Promotion of breastfeeding targets both initiation and duration. Surveys of mothers in developed countries reveal physical and technical difficulties lead the reasons for ending breastfeeding at short durations while work related issues are the leading reason at longer durations (Hamlyn et al. 2002, Lansinoh Laboratories 2005; see also Schwartz et al. 2002). It is therefore not surprising that the very small economic literature on breastfeeding focuses on the mother's decision to return to work post-birth.

A number of studies have documented the association between shorter breastfeeding duration (although not incidence) and the return to work (surveyed in Dennis 2002). A caution for much of this evidence is that some omitted factor may drive both breastfeeding and work behavior.

Roe et al. (1999) use an instrumental variables (IV) approach to sort out the causality assuming that mother's occupation affects the return to work decision but not breastfeeding decisions. They conclude that causality flows from work to breastfeeding and longer periods at home post-birth are associated with longer breastfeeding durations.

Chatterji and Frick (2005) use a family fixed effects framework to control for unobserved family background factors. They report that return to work within three months of birth reduces the probability of initiating breastfeeding by 16–18 percent and a

---

[4] See Imbens and Angrist (1994) on local average treatment effects.

reduction in duration (among those who initiate) of 4 to 5 weeks. Complementary evidence is reported by Berger et al. (2005) who, using propensity score matching, report return to work within the first three months reduces the incidence of breastfeeding by 13 percent and the duration by 4.5 weeks.

An alternative approach to the omitted variables problem is to use policy induced changes in behavior. Haider et al. (2003) examine the impact of the work requirements of recent welfare reform in the US on breastfeeding rates. They estimate that these reforms reduced national breastfeeding rates at six months post-birth by over 5 percent.

Baker and Milligan (2008a) use a recent legislated increase in job protected maternity leave (in Canada) from six months to one year to explore the relationship between time at home post-birth and breastfeeding. They report little impact on the incidence of breastfeeding, but an increase in the number of months babies were breastfed in their first year of life of one month. This can be compared to the increase of over three months in the amount of time mothers were at home post-birth as a result of the reform. The increase in the proportion of mothers exclusively breastfeeding at six months was over 39 percent. They also examine a collection of parent reported measures of their children's health, focusing on respiratory ailments, finding the increases in breastfeeding had little impact.

It is clear that the recent economic studies in this area depart from most of the breastfeeding literature in that the question of causality if not answered is at least actively pursued. This is a welcome development given the central role breastfeeding is thought to play in infant health.

What other outcomes might be affected by a mother's decision to work? One focus of research is childrens's cognitive development. Older studies in this area offer mixed results and more recent contributions do not completely resolve the uncertainty. A notable feature of this research is the number of studies that use the same data set (the National Longitudinal Survey of Youth, NLSY).

A starting point is Ruhm's (2004) study using NLSY data that measures cognitive development using the Peabody vocabulary, reading and math tests. His empirical strategy is to regress child outcomes on an indicator of mother's employment controlling for a large number of observable child, mother and household characteristics to account for differences across mothers who do and do not choose to work. He finds maternal employment in the first three years has a small negative effect on the verbal abilities of 3–4-year-olds and a larger negative effect on the math and reading abilities of 5–6-year-olds. For example, an additional twenty hours of work in the first three years is estimated to reduce PIAT reading scores by 0.11 standard deviations and PIAT math scores by 0.08. Any work in the first year is estimated to reduce these scores by 0.08 standard deviations.

Complementary evidence for work in the first year, using the same data and test scores, is provided by Baum (2003c). Berger et al. (2005), using the same data, estimate a negative impact on PPVT of returning to work with twelve weeks of birth but most of the estimates are not statistically significant.[5] Using a similar empirical approach, Hill

---

[5] They use a propensity score approach.

et al. (2005) report full time work before eighteen months has small negative effects on cognitive development measured at ages 4–7 in the UK.

Alternative approaches to the omitted variable problem lead to both supportive and dissenting conclusions. James-Burdumy (2005), again using NLSY data and a family fixed effects estimator, finds that first year employment only negatively affects PIAT reading scores, and work in the second or third years has either no or positive impacts on test scores.[6] Bernal (2008) estimates a dynamic model of women's labor supply and child care decisions post-birth and finds a year of maternal full time employment in the first five years of life leads to a reduction in the NLSY cognitive scores of 1.8 percent (0.13 standard deviations).

It is important to note that there is a large complementary body of research by sociologists and developmental psychologists among others that is frequently cited in economic studies and often uses similar methods. Waldfogel (2006) provides a summary of the results of much of this research concluding maternal employment in the first year of life negatively affects cognitive development while work at later ages does not.

A majority of this research adopts an observational approach, relying on a battery of control variables to account for mothers' decisions to work. Given the persistent disagreement in the conclusions of these studies a priority for future research should be the development of alternative empirical strategies.

A very related although not identical literature investigates the impacts of different types of non-parental care on child development. For many families, however, maternal employment and non-parental care go hand-in-hand, and in many data sets the detail on the type of non-parental care is limited, so the difference between the two literatures is practically (although not conceptually) of small significance.

An ongoing area of research here is the impact of the US Head Start program for disadvantaged children.[7] Currie and Neidell (2007) attempt to discover what characteristics of the program have the strongest beneficial effects. They find that children in areas with higher Head Start spending have better reading and vocabulary scores and grade retention is lower in areas where a higher proportion of expenditures are on child centered (health and education) activities.

There are also studies of various types of pre-school programs. Loeb et al. (2007), using an array of observable characteristics to control for selection into these centers, report that they raise language, pre-reading, and math skills by 10 percent of a standard deviation, with the largest gains for children from the lowest income families. Magnuson et al. (2007) report on the impacts of pre-kindergarten, pre-school, Head Start, and other non-parental care.[8] They find that both pre-kindergarten and pre-school raise kindergarten reading and math scores although the effects largely dissipate by grade 1.

---

[6] Ruhm (2002) also reports family fixed effects estimates that are negative but mostly statistically insignificant.

[7] Currie (2001) reviews some of the earlier evidence on this program.

[8] They use teacher fixed effects, propensity scores and IV (using the fraction of state spending on pre-kindergarten and the fraction of young children attending pre-kindergarten as instruments) to control for omitted variables.

A study of more generic non-parental care turns up negative impacts. Bernal and Keane (2008) exploit US welfare reform in the 1990s for identification, and find for the children of single mothers the use of childcare leads to a 2.9 percent reduction in the NLSY cognitive scores, a result that is driven by informal (e.g. family childcare) rather than formal childcare. Informal daycare, while used by many parents, has not been a focus of past research and deserves greater attention in the future.

As noted by Ruhm (2004) the mechanisms for these cognitive effects are not well understood. In a recent study, Cawley and Liu (2007) use time use data to shed light on this question. Using state unemployment rates as an instrument for mothers' employment, they report working mothers are less likely to read to their children or help them with their homework, or spend less time in these activities if they do them. Likewise they expend less time playing with and supervising their children. The average age of the children in this study is 7. Baker and Milligan (2010) provide some evidence of the impact of mothers' time at home in the first year of life based on an expansion of Canada's mandated maternity leave from six to twelve months. They report a large increase (50%) in the amount of time mothers were at home in the first year, but no corresponding impacts on children's temperament, motor and social skills or the amount of activities (e.g. reading, play) with their mothers, up to 29 months of age.

Another child outcome that has been associated with mothers' employment is children's mental health and behavioral development. This literature took a turn with the publication of findings from the National Institute of Child Health and Human Development (NICHD) Study of Early Child Care (e.g. NICHD 2003). This observational analysis indicated that the amount of time through the first 4.5 years of life that a child spends away from his or her mother is a predictor of assertiveness, disobedience, and aggression.[9]

Confirmations of these negative effects are offered in a number of economic studies in this area. In a nationally representative US sample, Loeb et al. (2007) finds that detrimental effect of centre based non-parental care on behavior is increasing in the hours of exposure, and is particularly pronounced when entry into care is before the age of 1. Using the NLSY, Berger et al. (2005) find that the children of mothers who returned to work within twelve weeks of birth displayed more externalizing behavior problems at age 4 as measured by the Behavior Problems Index.

Baker et al. (2008b) study the introduction of subsidized universal childcare in the Canadian province of Quebec. Using comparisons of Quebec children to children in other provinces, they find a sharp increase in the use of non-parental care is matched by negative impacts on measures of behavior (aggressiveness, anxiety) as well as motor social development.

Another source of evidence is from studies of the effects of pre-kindergarten and pre-school programs. Magnuson et al. (2007) report that attendance in either a

---

[9] This finding had been previously been reported most prominently in the research of Belsky (e.g. 2001).

pre-kindergarten program or a pre-school is associated with elevated levels of externalizing behavior and lower levels of self control in kindergarten, with larger impacts for pre-kindergarten. Unlike the impacts on cognitive development reported above, these impacts on behavior persist into first grade.

The increasing number of studies that find these negative behavioral effects of maternal employment/non-parental care provide a challenge for future research in this area. Integrating these findings with evidence of the positive cognitive effects of some programs is one priority. Perhaps more important is that they highlight the limitations of focusing on only a single dimension of child health and development in program evaluations.

A final focus of recent research in this area are effects of maternal employment on the medical care of children and the incidence of specific ailments. Gordon et al. (2007) examine the impact of maternal employment and non-maternal care on the health of children aged 12–36 months using NICHD-SECC data and a mother–child fixed effects specification. They find little effect on the incidence of either infectious disease or injury. However, time in centre based care increases the rates of ear infections for children aged 12–24 months and the rates of respiratory illness for children aged 12–36 months. Baker et al. (2008) provide evidence that non-parental care increases the odds of both ear infections and nose/throat infections among Canadian children, and their results by age (0–2 years, 3–4 years) suggest the effect is present in both centre based and family child care. Berger et al.'s (2005) study finds a link between early return to work post-birth (within twelve weeks) and lower rates of medical checkups and lower rates of immunizations for diptheria, pertussis, tetanus and (oral) polio. Ruhm (1998) and Tanaka (2005) report that maternity leave mandates, presumably acting through an effect on maternal employment, lower post-neonatal mortality in a sample of primarily European countries.

8.2.4 Socioeconomic Status

Whether money matters for children is a wide-ranging question, but certainly one important dimension is whether it matters for children's health. An effect of socioeconomic status (SES) on child health could arise because wealthier families can afford better health care and healthier environments for their children to be born and grow up in. A separate chapter of this volume is dedicated to the relationship between SES and health, but it's worth briefly highlighting here some of the contributions of economists to the study of this issue for children.

Recent research documents a correlation between parents' SES and children's health outcomes. While the measures of SES and health vary by study, the message of this research is that lower SES is associated with lower health outcomes. This association is present at young ages. Evidence presented in Currie's (2009) review of the subject, drawing on studies by Case et al. (2002), Currie and Stabile (2003), and Currie, Shields, and Price (2004), shows a negative correlation between the reported health of children under 4 and family income in the US, Canada, and the UK.

Further support is offered by studies of health shocks and specific illnesses and ailments. Case et al. (2002), Currie and Stabile (2003), Currie, Shields, and Price (2004), and Currie and Lin (2007) all find higher rates of chronic conditions (e.g. asthma, poor mental health) among poor children. Currie (2009) provides comparisons of the incidence of a substantial list of chronic conditions, illnesses, birth outcomes, and activity limitations for US children aged 2–17 living in poor and non-poor families. In almost all instances those in poor families have worse outcomes. Berger et al. (2005) report low-income children in the US have lower cognitive scores and worse behavior. Interestingly, Dooley and Stewart (2007) present dissenting evidence on this specific point for Canada, reporting little relationship between income and children's emotional behavioral outcomes. Finally, Propper et al. (2004) present related evidence for children in the UK. They report that low-income children exhibit worse health by a maternal reported summary measure, and a high number of symptoms of poor health.

What it is about low SES that has a negative impact on children's health is an area of continuing research? An important alternative hypothesis is that some other, typically unobserved, factor determines both SES and children's health outcomes. The number of studies associating poor child outcomes with low SES far exceeds the number that make substantive progress on this difficult question of causality.

One area in which there has been progress is a good example of economists' contribution to this literature. One common marker of families' SES is the educational attainment of parents. There is burgeoning literature in economics estimating the returns to education that provides an array of instruments for educational attainment that could be used in this context.

One strategy from this literature is to exploit exogenous variation in the costs of attending university, proxied by distance to a post-secondary institution.[10] Currie and Moretti (2003) use the geographical expansion of colleges in the US as an instrument for university attendance. They find that the increase in educational attainment resulting from the opening of a local college improves pre-natal factors (less smoking, greater use of pre-natal care), birth weight and gestational age. Carneiro et al. (2007) use a related strategy instrumenting maternal education with the presence (rather than the opening) of a college locally at age 14. They report consequent improvements on children's cognitive scores and reductions in their behavioral problems.

Another strategy adapted from this literature is geographic variation in school entry ages and compulsory schooling laws.[11] McCrary and Royer (2006) use this approach finding an impact on educational attainment that has little consequence for the health of offspring. In a related paper Chou et al. (2010) study the impact of an increase in the length of compulsory schooling in Taiwan. In this case the length of compulsory schooling was increased (by three years). The resulting increase in educational attainment is

---

[10] See for example Card (1995) on the use of this strategy to estimate the returns to education.

[11] See Angrist and Krueger (1991) for an application of this approach to estimating the returns to schooling.

found to be linked to lower rates of low birth weight and infant mortality (both neonatal and post-neonatal).

These approaches have limitations. First, as in any instrumental variables strategy we must convince ourselves that the instruments are legitimate. Second, if an increment in education has different effects on different people, we must recognize that we are estimating local average treatment effects. Most properly this is evidence for the types of individuals whose educational investment decisions react to college proximity or compulsory schooling laws. Nevertheless, in a literature that is much stronger on observation than on causality, these types of studies represent a step forward.

8.3 ACCESS TO MEDICAL CARE

Researchers have used expansions and contractions in public insurance coverage to examine the relationship between improved access to health care, the utilization of health care, and health status in several contexts. In the US there is a considerable body of evidence examining the Medicaid expansions through the 1980s and 1990s. Currie and Grogger (2002) note that an important goal of these changes is to improve health by encouraging low income and children to seek appropriate care.

Beginning in 1984 states were first permitted and then required to extend Medicaid coverage to other groups of children. By 1992 States were required to cover children below age 6 in families with incomes up to 133 percent of the poverty line and had the option of covering families up to 185 percent of the poverty line. For further review of the expansions see Cutler and Gruber (1996).

Several studies have examined the effects of the expansions on health care utilization and child health. Currie and Gruber (1996a, 1996b) found that many eligible women did not take up the coverage that was made available to them. However, their findings do indicate that despite these low take-up rates, the expansions targeted at low income families with children did increase the probability of going to a doctor for *preventative* care (measured as yearly check-ups as a measure of preventative care) by 9.6 percent. They also find large effects on the relationship between increased access to care through insurance expansions and child mortality. Their results suggest that for every ten percentage point increase in the fraction of children eligible for Medicaid, child mortality drops by 0.128 percentage points or 3.4 percent.

Currie and Gruber (2001) examine the effects of the Medicaid expansions on the medical treatment at child birth and on infant mortality. Among teen mothers and mothers with less than a high school education, enhanced eligibility resulted in increased utilization of a variety of obstetric procedures. The authors find less evidence of reductions in infant mortality (conditional on infant health) but do find significant reductions for mothers for whom the nearest hospital had a NICU.

Kaestner, Joyce, and Racine (1999) and Dafny and Gruber (2005) examine the nature of the increase in utilization. Their findings suggest that eligibility leads to fewer "avoidable" hospitalizations. Kaestner, Joyce, and Racine (1999) find no evidence of Medicaid expansions and increases in utilization on improvements in self-reported health status.

Research examining the Canadian experience of moving to a single, publicly funded payer also provides evidence on the relationship between increased access to care and utilization. In her 1996 paper, Hanratty investigates the effects of Canada's move to national health insurance through the 1960s on infant health. Her findings suggest that the introduction of national health insurance in Canada is associated with a 4 percent decline in the infant mortality rate and a decrease in the incidence of low birth weight of, on average, 1.3 percent for all births and by 8.9 percent for births to single, lower income mothers.

Overall, evidence on the relationship between increased access to care, primarily through expansions in public health insurance and health care utilization suggests that improved access to medical care does result in increase in the use of preventative care, particularly among expectant mothers, with small but significant improvements in child health. The magnitude of the relationship between increased access to care and improved health is a function of two things: first, whether individuals and families use the increased access made available to them, and, second, whether the increased utilization is effective in improving health. Clearly, simply improving access to care is not sufficient to ensure take-up of care. Information barriers and SES gradients remain. A second question is whether, conditional on accessing the care, the care is effective in improving health. Here, the evidence reviewed suggests that access to preventative care, particularly among expectant mothers and children, can be effective in improving health. There is little evidence beyond these groups however, to draw broader conclusions on the role of increased utilization on health.

8.4 Health and Behavior Post-Early-Years

The last decade or so has seen a considerable amount of research on the economics of health related behaviors at older ages, with considerable focus specifically on the economic factors that affect health at young ages. We focus here on the key literature regarding smoking, drinking, and obesity. We then examine some of the new research on the economics of mental health and childhood behavior.

8.4.1 Smoking

Several studies have examined the relationship between prices, regulation and smoking across both adults and youths. The literature up to the last decade is reviewed in a paper by Chaloupka and Warner (2000) and Chapter 10 in this volume by Kenkel and Sindelar provides a comprehensive review of the economics of "bads." Here we provide a brief update on the literature on youth smoking over the past few years. Chaloupka and

Warner review several studies of smoking that rely mainly on cross sectional estimates of the effects of prices and regulation on smoking behavior. As more longitudinal data have become available in the US and elsewhere, several recent studies have re-estimated the relationship between price, regulation, and smoking behavior, using variation across jurisdictions over time to identify this relationship.

Gruber and Zinman (2000) and Gruber (2001) use variation in state cigarette taxes as instruments for state prices and state laws over time to estimate models of youth smoking, and in particular to try and explain the rise in youth smoking in the US over the 1990s. They show that prices are "powerful determinants" of smoking for high school seniors (Gruber and Zinman 2000) although price does not appear to be as important for younger teens. Gruber (2001) finds less evidence of the efficacy of laws that make it more difficult to smoke, other than small effects of age restrictions for the purchase of cigarettes.

Glied (2003) examines whether changes in prices which lead to declines in youth smoking result in fewer youths smoking when they are older by tracking individuals using panel data from the NLSY. Glied examines the relationship between taxes and smoking behavior when individuals are young and then tracks their smoking behavior into adulthood. Understanding whether helping price sensitive youths avoid smoking during their teenage years results in fewer adult smokers, or whether it simply delays the onset of smoking is an important element in understanding the efficacy of tax policy in reducing the number of long term smokers in the population and therefore the significant health consequences of long-term smoking. Glied finds that the reductions in youth smoking are partially offset in adulthood, suggesting that estimates of the effects of price on youth smoking overstate the life-course effects of price as a tobacco control strategy.

DeCicca et al. (2002) and DeCicca et al. (2008) use a complementary US data set longitudinal data set, the National Educational Longitudinal Study, to re-examine the relationship between youth smoking participation and state taxes and find little evidence that taxes affect smoking behavior once state fixed effects and differences in smoking attitudes across states over time are properly accounted for. They do, however, find some evidence on the responsiveness to price among youths conditional on being a smoker.

Carpenter and Cook (2008) use repeated cross-sections from the Youth Risk Behavior Surveys, to re-examine the relationship between cigarette taxes and smoking behavior among youths. These data survey nearly 750,000 young adults and are designed to be representative of the local area sampled. The authors find evidence consistent with earlier studies (cf. Gruber 2001) that found negative effects of higher state taxes on youth smoking behavior.

In sum, there has been considerable new research on the role for public policy on youth smoking behavior that has resulted in a variety of results. The bulk of the evidence suggests that prices do affect youth behavior and have stronger effects on cessation than initiation but some recent studies call into question whether these effects are permanent or simply delay smoking initiation until later in life.

8.4.2 Obesity

Research examining the increase in obesity in North America, and more recently across the OECD has grown considerably over the past decade.[12] The literature has focused on two broad areas, the causes of obesity, both at a point in time and over longer periods of time, and the consequences of obesity. While the medical literature has examined the genetic and metabolic determinants of obesity, the economic literature has focused on external and environmental causes. One strand of the literature argues that technological change has changed the nature of work, making market work more sedentary. Technological change has also resulted in lowered costs of calories through more efficient food production (cf. Philipson and Poser 2003; Lakdawalla and Philipson 2009). A second strand of the literature claims that the change in obesity is due to caloric intake (increased eating) and not a decrease in the number of calories burned (cf. Cutler, Glaeser, and Shapiro 2003; Bleich, Cutler, Murray, and Adams 2008). Declines in the time cost of food production and technological advances in firm level food preparation are cited as the primary causes of increased caloric intake. A third strand of literature examines household work decisions and childhood obesity and find evidence that increased labor participation among women is correlated with increases in childhood obesity (Anderson, Butcher, and Levin 2003; Chia 2008).

New research has also examined the relationship between obesity and school outcomes. Evidence suggests that obese children in US miss more school than non-obese children but there is little evidence that obesity results in poorer outcomes on test scores (Schwimmer et al. 2003; Chia 2007). On the other hand, evidence from Canada suggests that overweight children (not included in the obese category) fare poorer on math test scores. These differences are not driven by observable differences in the populations, leaving open the question of why health consequences differ across populations (Chia 2007).

8.4.3 Mental Health

Currie and Stabile (2009, 2006) note the large numbers of children who have some form of mental health problem. The MECA Study cited in the 1990 US Surgeon General's Report on Mental Health states that 20 percent of children have some form of impairment from a mental or behavioral disorder and 5 percent suffer extreme functional impairment. Given these large numbers of children, researchers have recently begun to investigate the relationship between mental health in childhood and a variety of human capital and labor market outcomes later in life.

Economic research on the relationship between child mental health and economic outcomes falls into three categories. There are a series of studies that look at the longer

---

[12] This review draws on a Ph.D. thesis at the University of Toronto by Yee Fei Chia. See Chia (2007) for a more detailed discussion of this literature.

term consequences of behavior problems in large samples (cf. Farmer 1993, 1995; Kessler et al. 1995; Gregg and Machin 1998; Caspi et al. 1998; Miech et al. 1999; and McLeod and Kaiser 2004). Findings here suggest that children with either a mental health diagnosis, or high survey scores of aggregated mental health problems are less likely to complete schooling, lower earnings and lower probabilities of employment at early stages of their working careers.

A second stream of the literature focuses on particular "externalizing" mental health conditions such as attention deficient hyperactivity disorders (ADHD) and behavior problems. Mannuzza and Klein (2000) review three studies of the long-term outcomes of children with ADHD and find that the ADHD children consistently have worse outcomes in adolescence and young adulthood than control children. Also, the studies do not address the possibility that the negative outcomes might be caused by other factors related to a diagnosis of ADHD, such as poverty, the presence of other learning disabilities, or the fact that many people diagnosed with ADHD end up in special education.

Currie and Stabile (2006) address these problems by examining the effects of ADHD in sibling fixed effects models using longitudinal data from both the United States and Canada. In a follow-up paper (Currie and Stabile 2008) they consider several other mental health conditions as well as aggregate measure of child mental health. The authors find that behavior problems have a large negative effect on future educational outcomes. The most consistent effects across the two countries are found for ADHD. In models that include sibling fixed effects, anxiety/depression is found to increase grade repetition but has no effect on the other outcomes we examine (such as test scores), suggesting that depression acts through a mechanism other than decreasing cognitive performance. Conduct disorders are also found to have broadly negative effects in the US, while in Canada, they reduce the probability that 16–19-year-old youths are in school but do not have significant effects on other outcomes. They find little evidence that these effects are modified by socioeconomic status.

A third recent strand of research examines the importance of "non-cognitive skills" such as hyperactivity, anxiousness, and self-esteem (cf. Blanden, Gregg, and Macmillan 2006; Heckman et al. 2006) in human capital formation, and later on income and income inequality. The findings suggest that such non-cognitive skills are important determinants of academic and economic success.

8.4.4 Maternal Behavior and Child Health and Behavior

A related area of research is the role that maternal behavior plays in the development of child health and behavior. A number of papers have approached these issues from various angles. We focus on a handful of representative papers here.

Chatterji and Markowitz (2001) examine the relationship between maternal substance abuse and child mental health as measured by a Behavioral Problems Index. The Behavioral Problems Index (also used in some of the mental health studies cited above) consists of a series of questions, answered by a child's mother, on the child's behavior and mental health, including hyperactivity, anxiety, anti-social behavior, and depression. The authors use data from the National Longitudinal Survey of Youth to examine whether there is evidence of a causal relationship between maternal use of alcohol and drugs and concurrent child behavioral problems for children ages 4 through 15. Fixed effects results suggest that there is some evidence of a link between maternal risky behavior and higher scores on the behavioral problems index. Results are stronger for drug use than for alcohol use.

Perry (2008) investigates the link between maternal depression and the management of childhood health—in particular childhood asthma. She analyzes how treatment of maternal depression affects child outcomes. To address the possibility of some unobserved factor that drives both the decision to seek treatment and the management of the child's asthma, treatment is instrumented with a measure of the variation in the propensity of primary care physicians to treat depression. The results indicate the treatment of mothers' depression leads to better management of the child's condition and thus asthma care related costs.

A study by Hango and Houseknecht (2005) again uses the NLSY to examine the role that marital disruptions play on child health. In this case, the authors look at the effects of divorce/separation on children's likelihood of suffering medically treated injuries. The measure of injuries is from a question in the NLSY that asks about whether the child had an injury in the past year that required medical attention. They distinguish between the direct effects of the marital disruption on injury—direct harm, usually emotional, caused by the parent—and potential mediating effects which might come through altering the relationship between the parent and child, or secondary effects such as financial changes, which could then lead to an increase in injuries. Overall there is little evidence which shows that marital disruption affects the likelihood of child injury for boys, either directly or indirectly. They find some evidence that marital disruption reduces the likelihood of injuries to girls. Overall, the authors conclude that there does not appear to be any significant mediating effect at work and only weak evidence of direct effects for girls.

8.5 Conclusions

Empirical research on child health spans many disciplines. What distinguishes economists' contributions to the field? At one time it may have been econometric tools, but anyone who reads widely in this area realizes that these methods are quickly gaining currency in other disciplines.

Some of the research reviewed in this chapter identifies another possibility. Looking behind the economic correlates of child health to the individual choices that determine them has provided new insights and offered new empirical strategies. A good example is use of the instrumental variables strategies from the literature on the returns to education in research on maternal education and child health. Relating breastfeeding and the non-parental care of children to mothers' decisions to work has identified labor market policies as a source of identifying variation for investigating child outcomes. This economic approach has in some areas caused researchers to revisit conventional wisdom. In others, it has helped to gauge the magnitude of long-understood associations. More generally it brings a heightened appreciation of the importance of causality to a literature that seems too often content with correlation.

New data sets are providing opportunities for wider application of this approach. Particularly exciting are administrative data form birth records, hospital admissions and medical records that paint a much richer portrait of the health outcomes of people of all ages, and can permit analyses of how events in childhood are related to later outcomes. The burgeoning literature on the long run consequences of low birth is a good example of this point. This relationship between health in childhood and at older ages is an important contribution of health economics to the larger research project on how investments in children pay off across the life-cycle. New findings from this wider field are transforming how we view the importance of childhood.

Our review of this literature also identifies some priorities for future research. First, there are many areas in which we are growing more confident that causal relationships exist, but remain ignorant of the mechanisms that underlie them. For example, what exactly is it about being born low birth weight, or its correlates, that leads to poor labor market outcomes in later life and what role do economic inputs play along the way? Second, attracted by the empirical design of social experiments for disadvantaged children, we sometimes neglect the health of more heterogeneous populations of children. More advantaged children, however, will be the majority clients of universal public policies. Third, as noted above follow up study of findings from infancy and childhood will make a fundamental contribution to the portrait of life-cycle health. Finally, while the field of child health is very broad, economists' contributions are not, and there would appear to be many areas that might benefit from attention from economists.

REFERENCES

ALMOND, DOUGLAS, CHAY, KENNETH Y., and LEE, DAVID S. (2005), "The Costs of Low Birth Weight," *Quarterly Journal of Economics*, 120(3): 1031–83.

——— EDLUND, LENA, LI, HONGBIN, ZHANG, JUNSEN (2007), "Long-term Effect of the 1959–1961 China Famine: Mainland China and Hong Kong." NBER Working Paper 13384.

ANDERSON, PATRICIA, LEVINE, PHILLIP, and BUTCHER, KRISTIN (2003), "Maternal Employment and Overweight Children," *Journal of Health Economics*, 22(3): 477–504.

ANGRIST, JOSHUA D. and KRUEGER, ALAN (1991), "Does Compulsory School Attendance Affect Schooling and Earnings?" *Quarterly Journal of Economics*, 106(4): 979–1014.

BAKER, MICHAEL and MILLIGAN, KEVIN (2008a), "How Does Job-Protected Maternity Leave Affect Mothers' Employment and Infant Health?" *Journal of Labor Economics*, 26: 655–92.

———(2008b), "Maternal Employment, Breastfeeding and Health: Evidence from Maternity Leave Mandates," *Journal of Health Economics*, 27: 871–87.

——————(2010), "Evidence From Maternity Leave Expansions of the Impact of Maternal Care on Early Child Development," *Journal of Human Resources*, 45(1): 1–32.

—— GRUBER, J., and MILLIGAN, K. (2008), "Universal Childcare, Maternal Labour Supply and Child Well-being," *Journal of Political Economy*, 116: 709–45.

BARKER, DAVID (1998), *Mothers, Babies and Health in Later Life*, 2nd edn. (Edinburgh: Churchill Livingstone).

BAUM II, CHARLES L. (2003a), "The Effect of State Maternity Leave Legislation and the 1993 Family and Medical Leave Act on Employment and Wages," *Labour Economics*, 10(5): 573–96.

—— (2003b), "The Effects of Maternity Leave Legislation on Mothers' Labor Supply after Childbirth," *Southern Economic Journal*, 69(4): 772–99.

—— (2003c). "Does Early Maternal Employment Harm Child Development? An Analysis of the Potential Benefits of Leave-Taking," *Journal of Labor Economics*, 21(2): 409–48.

—— and FORD, WILLIAM F. (2004), "The Wage Effects of Obesity: A Longitudinal Study," *Health Economics*, 13(9): 885–99.

BEHRMAN, JERE R. and ROSENZWEIG, MARK R. (2004), "Returns to Birthweight," *Review of Economics and Statistics*, 86(2): 586–601.

BELSKY, JAY (2001), "Developmental Risks (Still) Associated with Early Child Care," *Journal of Child Psychology and Psychiatry*, 42: 845–59.

BERGER, LAWRENCE M., HILL, JENNIFER, and WALDFOGEL, JANE (2005), "Maternity Leave, Early Maternal Employment and Child Health and Development in the US," *The Economic Journal*, 115(501): F29–F47.

BERNAL, RAQUEL (2008), "The Effect of Maternal Employment and Child Care on Children's Cognitive Development," *International Economic Review*, 49(4): 1173–209.

—— and KEANE, MICHAEL (2010), "Quasi-Structural Estimation of a Model of Child Care Choices and Child Cognitive Ability Production," *Journal of Econometrics*, 156(1): 164–89.

BLACK, SANDRA E., DEVEREUX, PAUL J., and SALVANES, KJELL G. (2007), "From the Cradle to the Labor Market? The Effect of Birth Weight on Adult Outcomes," *Quarterly Journal of Economics*, 122(1): 409–39.

BLANDEN, JO, GREGG, PAUL, and MACMILLAN, LINDSEY (2006), "Explaining Intergenerational Income Persistence: Non-cognitive Skills, Ability and Education." Centre for Market and Public Organisation Working Paper 06/146.

BLEICH, SARA, CUTLER, DAVID, MURRAY, CHRISTOPHER, and ADAMS, ALYCE (2008), "Why is the Developed World Obese?" *Public Health*, 29: 273–95.

BROOKS-GUNN, JEANNE and DUNCAN, GREG J. (1997), "The Effects of Poverty on Children," *The Future of Children*, 7(2): 55–71.

CARD, DAVID (1995), "Using Geographic Variation in College Proximity to Estimate the Return to Schooling," in Louis N. Christofides, E. Kenneth Grant and Robert Swindinsky (eds.), *Aspects of Labour Market Behaviour* (Toronto: University of Toronto Press).

CARNEIRO, PEDRO, MEGHIR, COSTAS, and PAREY, MATTHIAS (2008), "Maternal Education, Home Environments and the Development of Children and Adolescents." Institute for Fiscal Studies Working Paper W07/15.

CARPENTER, CHRISTOPHER and COOK, PHILIP J. (2008), "Cigarette Taxes and Youth Smoking: New Evidence from National, State, & Local Youth Risk Behavior Surveys." *Journal of Health Economics*, 27(2): 287–99.

CASE, ANNE, LUBOTSKY, DARREN, and PAXSON, CHRISTINA (2002), "Economic Status and Health in Childhood: The Origins of the Gradient," *American Economic Review*, 92(5): 1308–34.

CASPI, AVSHALOM, WRIGHT, BRADLEY, MOFFITT, TERRIE, and SILVA, PHIL (1998), "Early Failure in the Labor Market: Childhood and Adolescent Predictors of Unemployment in the Transition to Adulthood," *American Sociological Review*, 63: 424–51.

CAWLEY, JOHN (2004), "The Impact of Obesity on Wages," *Journal of Human Resources*, 39(2): 451–74.

—— and LIU, FENG (2007), "Mechanisms for the Association Between Maternal Employment and Child Cognitive Development." NBER Working Paper 13609.

—— and DANZIGER, SHELDON (2005), "Obesity as a Barrier to the Transition from Welfare to Work." Journal of Policy Analysis and Management, 24(4): 727–43.

CHALOUPKA, FRANK J. and WARNER, KENNETH E. (2000), "The Economics of Smoking," *Handbook of Health Economics*, 1st edn., Vol. 1, No. 1 (Amsterdam: Elsevier), 1539–627.

CHATTERJI, PINKA and FRICK, KEVIN D. (2005), "Does Returning to Work After Childbirth Affect Breastfeeding Practices?" *Review of Economics of the Household*, 3(3): 315–35.

—— and MARKOWITZ, SARA (2001), "The Impact of Maternal Alcohol and Marijuana Use on Children's Behavioral Problems," *Journal of Health Economics*, 20(5): 703–31.

CHAY, KENNETH and GREENSTONE, MICHAEL (2003a), "The Impact of Air Pollution on Infant Mortality: Evidence from Geographic Variation in Pollution Shocks Induced by a Recession," *Quarterly Journal of Economics*, 118(3): 1121–67.

—— (2003b), "Air Quality, Infant Mortality, and the Clean Air Act of 1970." NBER Working Paper No. 10053.

CHIA, YEE FEI (2007), "Weighty Issues: An Examination of Childhood Weight and School Outcomes During Puberty." Mimeo, University of Toronto.

—— (2008), "Maternal Labour Supply and Childhood Obesity in Canada: Evidence from the NLSCY," *Canadian Journal of Economics*, 41(1): 217–42.

CHOU, SHIN-YI, LIU, JIN-TAN, GROSSMAN, MICHAEL and JOYCE, THEODORE J. (2007), "Parental Education and Child Health: Evidence from a Natural Experiment in Taiwan." *American Economic Journal: Applied Economics*, 2(1): 33–61.

CONLEY, D., STRULLLY, K., and BENNETT, NEIL (2003), *The Starting Gate: Birth Weight and Life Chances* (Berkeley, CA: University of California Press).

CUNHA, FLAVIO, HECKMAN, JAMES, and SCHENNACH, SUSANNE (2008), "Estimating the Elasticity of Intertemporal Substitution in the Formation of Cognitive and Non-Cognitive Skills." Mimeo, University of Chicago.

CURRIE, ALISON, SHIELDS, MICHAEL A., and PRICE, STEPHAN WHEATLEY (2004), "Is the Child Health/Family Income Gradient Universal? Evidence from England." IZA Discussion Paper 1328.

CURRIE, J. (2009), "Healthy, Wealthy, and Wise: Socioeconomic Status, Poor Health in Childhood, and Human Capital Development." *Journal of Economics Literature*, 47(1): 87–122.

—— and HYSON, ROSEMARY (1999), "Is the Impact of Health Shocks Cushioned by Socioeconomic Status? The Case of Low Birth Weight," *American Economic Review* 2 (May): 19–22.

—— and MORETTI, ENRICO (2003), "Mother's Education and the Intergenerational Transmission of Human Capital: Evidence From College Openings," *Quarterly Journal of Economics*, 118(4): 1495–532.

——and GROGGER, JEFFREY (2002), "Medicaid Expansions and Welfare Contractions: Offsetting Effects on Prenatal Care and Infant Health?" *Journal of Health Economics*, 21(2): 313–35.

—— and GRUBER, JONATHAN (1996a), "Health Insurance Eligibility, Utilization of Medical Care, and Child Health," *Quarterly Journal of Economics*, 111(2): 431–66.

————(1996b), "Saving Babies: The Efficacy and Cost of Recent Changes in the Medicaid Eligibility of Pregnant Women," *Journal of Political Economy*, 104(6): 1263–96.

—— (2001), "Public Health Insurance and Medical Treatment: The Equalizing Impact of the Medicaid Expansions," *Journal of Public Economics*, 82(1): 63–89.

—— and STABILE, MARK (2003), "Socioeconomic Status and Health: Why is the Relationship Stronger for Older Children?" *American Economic Review*, 93(5): 1813–23.

—— (2006), "Child Mental Health and Human Capital Accumulation: The Case of ADHD," *Journal of Health Economics*, 25(6): 1094–118.

—— (2009), "Mental Health in Childhood and Human Capital." In Jonathan Gruber (ed.), *An Economic Perspective on the Problems of Disadvantaged Youth* (Chicago: University of Chicago Press for NBER).

—— and NEIDELL, MATTHEW (2007), "Getting Inside the 'Black Box' of Head Start Quality: What Matters and What Doesn't," *Economics of Education Review*, 26(1): 83–99.

—— and HYSON, ROSEMARY (1999), "Is the Impact of Health Shocks Cushioned by Socioeconomic Status? The Case of Low Birthweight," *American Economic Review*, 89(2): 245–50.

—— and LIN, WANCHUAN (2007), "Chipping Away at Health: More on the Relationship Between Income and Child Health," *Health Affairs*, 26(2).

CUTLER, DAVID M. and GRUBER, JONATHAN (1996), "The Effect of Medicaid Expansions on Public Insurance, Private Insurance, and Redistribution," *American Economic Review*, 86(2): 378–83.

—— GLAESER, EDWARD L., and SHAPIRO, JESSE M. (2005), "Public Insurance and Child Hospitalizations: Access and Efficiency Effects," Journal of Public Economics, 89(1): 109-29.

DAFNY, LEEMORE and GRUBER, JONATHAN (2005), "Public Insurance and Child Hospitalizations: Access and Efficiency Effects," *Journal of Public Economics*, 89(1): 109–29.

DECICCA, PHILIP, KENKEL, DONALD, and MATHIOS, ALAN (2002), "Putting Out the Fires: Will Higher Taxes Reduce the Onset of Youth Smoking?" *Journal of Political Economy*, 110(1): 144–69.

—— and SHIN, JUSTINE (2008), "Youth Smoking, Cigarette Prices and Anti-smoking Sentiment," *Health Economics*, 17(6): 733–49.

DENNIS, CINDY-LEE (2002), "Breastfeeding Initiation and Duration: A 1990–2000 Literature Review," *Journal of Obstetric, Gynecologic, & Neonatal Nursing*, 31(1).

DOOLEY, MARTIN and STEWART, JENNIFER (2007), "Family Income, Parenting Styles and Child Behavior: Emotional Outcomes," *Health Economics*, 16(2).

FARMER, ELIZABETH M. Z. (1993), "Externalizing Behavior in the Life Course: The Transition from School to Work," *Journal of Emotional and Behavioral Disorders*, 1: 138–48.

—— (1995), "Extremity of Externalizing Behavior and Young Adult Outcomes," *Journal of Child Psychology and Psychiatry*, 36. (Fiscal Studies Working Paper No. 15/07. Sept. 2007.)

GLIED, SHERRY (2003), "Is Smoking Delayed Smoking Averted?" *American Journal of Public Health*, 93(3): 412–16.

GLUCKMAN, P. D. and HANSON, M. A. (2006), "Adult Disease: Echoes of the Past," *European Journal of Endocrinology*, 155(Suppl. 1): 47–50.

GORDON, RACHEL A., KAESTNER, ROBERT, and KORENMAN, SANDERS (2007), "The Effects of Maternal Employment on Child Injuries and Infectious Disease," *Demography*, 44(2): 405–26.

GREGG, PAUL and MACHIN, STEVEN (1998) "Child Development and Success or Failure in the Youth Labour Market." Center for Economic Performance, London School of Economics Discussion Paper 0397, July.

GRUBER, JONATHAN (2001), "Youth Smoking in the 1990s: Why Did It Rise and What Are the Long-Run Implications?" *American Economic Review*, 91(2): 85–90.

—— and ZINMAN, JONATHAN (2000), "Youth Smoking in the US: Evidence and Implications." NBER Working Paper 7780.

HAIDER, STEVEN J., JACKNOWITZ, ALISON, and SCHOENI, ROBERT F. (2003), "Welfare Work Requirements and Child Well-Being: Evidence from the Effects on Breast-Feeding," *Demography*, 40(3): 479–97.

HAMLYN, BECKY, BROOKER, SUE, OLEINIKOVA, KARIN, and WANDS, SARAH (2002), *Infant Feeding 2000* (Norwich: The Stationery Office).

HAN, W.-J., RUHM, C., and WALDFOGEL, J. (2007), "Parental Leave Policies and Parents' Employment and Leave-Taking," *Journal of Policy Analysis and Mangement*, 28(1): 29–54.

HANGO, DARCY W. and HOUSEKNECHT, SHARON K. (2005), "Marital Disruption and Accidents/Injuries Among Children," *Journal of Family Issues*, 26(1): 3–31.

HANRATTY, MARIA J. (1996) "Canadian National Health Insurance and Infant Health," *American Economic Review*, 86(1): 276–84.

HECKMAN, JAMES (2007), "The Economics, Technology and Neuroscience of Human Capability Formation," *Proceedings of the National Academy of Sciences*, 104(33): 13250–5.

—— STIXRUD, JORA, and URZUA, SERGIO (2006), "The Effects of Cognitive and Noncognitive Abilities on Labor Market Outcomes and Social Behavior," *Journal of Labor Economics*, 24(3): 365–89.

HILL, JENNIFER L., WALDFOGEL, JANE, BROOKS-GUNN, JEANNE, and HAN, WEN-JUI (2005), "Maternal Employment and Child Development: A Fresh Look Using Newer Methods," *Developmental Psychology*, 41(6): 833–50.

HORTA, B., BAHL, R., MARTINES, J. C. and VICTORIA, C. G. (2007), *Evidence on the Long-Term Effects of Breastfeeding, Systematic Reviews and Meta-Analysis* (Geneva: World Health Organization).

IMBENS, GUIDO W. and ANGRIST, JOSHUA D. (1994), "Identification and Estimation of Local Average Treatment Effects," *Econometrica*, 62(2): 467–75.

JAMES-BURDUMY, SUSANNE (2005), "The Effect of Maternal Labor Force Participation on Child Development," *Journal of Labor Economics*, 23(1): 176–7.

KAESTNER, ROBERT, JOYCE, THEODORE, and RACINE, ANDREW (1999), "Does Publicly Provided Health Insurance Improve the Health of Low-Income Children in the United States." NBER Working Paper 6887.

KESSLER, R. C., FOSTER, C. L., SAUNDERS, W. B., and STANG, P. E. (1995), "Social Consequences of Psychiatric Disorders, I: Educational Attainment," *American Journal of Psychiatry*, 152(7): 1026–32.

KLERMAN, JACOB ALEX and LEIBOWITZ, ARLEEN (1997), "Labor Supply Effects of State Maternity Leave Legislation," in Francine D. Blau and Ronald G. Ehrenberg (eds.), *Gender and Family Issues in the Workplace* (New York: Russell Sage Foundation).

KRAMER, MICHAEL S., CHALMERS, BEVERLEY, HODNETT, ELLEN D., et al. (2001), "Promotion of Breastfeeding Intervention Trial (PROBIT): A Randomized Trial in the Republic of Belarus," *Journal of the American Medical Association*, 285(4): 463–4.

LAKDAWALLA, DARIUS and PHILIPSON, TOMAS (2009), "The Growth of Obesity and Technological Change," *Economics and Human Biology*, 7(3): 283–93.

LANSINOH LABORATORIES (2003), "Lansinoh National Breastfeeding Survey Results." Press Release. <http://www.corporatenews.net/cgi-bin/pc201v3.php?source=pc200v3.php&pr=11&pccl=24610> accessed March 22, 2007.

LOEB, SUSANNA, BRIDGES, MARGARET, BASSOK, DAPHNA, FULLER, BRUCE, and RUMBERGER, RUSSEL W. (2007), "How Much is Too Much? The Influence of Preschool Centers on Children's Social and Cognitive Development," *Economics of Education Review*, 26(1): 52–66.

MAGNUSON, KATHERINE A., RUHM, CHRISTOPHER, and WALDFOGEL, JANE (2007), "Does Prekindergarten Improve School Preparation and Performance?" *Economics of Education Review*, 26(1): 33–51.

MANNUZZA, SALVATORE and KLEIN, RACHEL G. (2000), "Long-term Prognosis in Attention-Deficit/Hyperactivity Disorder," *Child and Adolescent Psychiatric Clinics of North America*, 9(3): 711–26.

McCRARY, JUSTIN and ROYER, HEATHER (2006), "The Effect of Female Education on Fertility and Infant Health: Evidence from School Entry Policies Using Exact Data of Birth." NBER Working Paper 12329.

McLEOD, JANE D. and KAISER, KAREN (2004), "Childhood Emotional and Behavioral Problems and Educational Attainment," *American Sociological Review*, 69(5): 636–58.

MIECH, RICHARD A., CASPI, AVSHALOM, MOFFITT, TERRI E., ENTNER WRIGHT, BRADLEY R. and SILVA, PHIL A. (1999), "Low Socioeconomic Status and Mental Disorders: A Longitudinal Study of Selection and Causation during Young Adulthood," *American Journal of Sociology*, 104(4): 1096–131.

NEIDELL, MATTHEW J. (2004), "Air Pollution, Health, and Socio-economic Status: The Effect of Outdoor Air Quality on Childhood Asthma," *Journal of Health Economics*, 23(6): 1209–36.

NICHD (NATIONAL INSTITUTE OF CHILD HEALTH AND HUMAN DEVELOPMENT; EARLY CHILDCARE RESEARCH NETWORK) (2003), "Does Amount of Time Spent in Childcare Predict Socioemotional Adjustment During the Transition to Kindergarten?" *Child Development*, 74(4): 976–1005.

OREOPOULOS, PHILIP, STAIBLE, MARK, WALLD, RANDY, and ROOS, LESLIE L. (2008), "Short-, Medium-, and Long-Term Consequences of Poor Infant Health: An Analysis Using Siblings and Twins," *Journal of Human Resources*, 43(1): 88–138.

PERRY, CYNTHIA D. (2008), "Does Treating Maternal Depression Improve Child Health Management? The Case of Pediatric Asthma," *Journal of Health Economics*, 27(1): 157–73.

PHILIPSON, TOMAS J. and POSNER, RICHARD A. (2003), "The Long-Run Growth in Obesity as a Function of Technological Change," *Perspectives in Biology and Medicine*, 46(3): 87–108.

PROPPER, CAROL, BURGESS, SIMON, and RIGG, JOHN (2004), "The Impact of Low Income on Child Health: Evidence from a Birth Cohort Study." Leverhulme Centre for Market and Public Organization, Working Paper 04/098.

ROE, BRIAN, WHITTINGTON, LESLIE A., FEIN, SARA BECK, and TEISL, MARIO F. (1999), "Is there Competition between Breast-Feeding and Maternal Employment?" *Demography*, 36(2): 157–71.

RUHM, CHRISTOPHER J. (1998), "The Economic Consequences of Parental Leave Mandates: Lessons From Europe," *Quarterly Journal of Economics*, 113(1): 285–317.

—— (2004), "Parental Employment and Child Cognitive Development," *Journal of Human Resources*, 39(1): 155–92.

SCHONBERG, UTA and LUDSTECK, JOHANNES (2007), "Maternity Leave Legislation, Female Labor Supply, and the Family Wage Gap." IZA Discussion Paper 2699.

SCHWARTZ, KENDRA, D'ARCY, HANNAH J. S., GILLESPIE, BRENDA, BOBO, JANET, LONGEWAY, MARYLOU, and FOXMAN, BETSY (2002), "Factors Associated with Weaning in the First 3 Months Postpartum," *Journal of Family Practice*, 51(5): 439–44.

SCHWIMMER, JEFFREY B., BURWINKLE, TASHA M., and VARNI, JAMES W. (2003), "Health-Related Quality of Life of Severely Obese Children and Adolescents," *Journal of the American Medical Association*, 289(14): 1851–3.

TANAKA, SAKIKO (2005), "Parental Leave and Child Health across OECD Countries," *The Economic Journal*, February, 115(501): F7–F28.

UNICEF (2008) "The Breastfeeding Initiatives Exchange," <http://www.unicef.org/ programme/breastfeeding/> accessed June 10, 2008.

WALDFOGEL, JANE (1999), "The Impact of the Family and Medical Leave Act," *Journal of Policy Analysis and Management*, 18(2): 281–302.

—— (2006), *What Children Need* (Cambridge: Harvard University Press).

CHAPTER 9

....

ECONOMICS OF INFECTIOUS DISEASES

....

RAMANAN LAXMINARAYAN AND ANUP MALANI

INFECTIOUS diseases remain an important cause of poor health in developing countries (Lopez et al. 2006). Hygiene, sanitation, vaccination, and treatment access have improved and thus reduced the burden of infections in developed countries, but these continue to pose barriers to similar reductions in low- and middle-income countries. Even in developed countries, influenza and HIV/AIDS remain challenges that demand attention from public health authorities. From an economist's perspective, infectious diseases are distinguished from many other health issues by the central role played by externalities.[1] Control of infectious diseases yields both positive externalities (prevention and treatment can delay or reduce spread of infection to uninfected individuals) and negative externalities (overuse of treatment can lead to drug resistance, which has global consequences for treatment effectiveness).

In this chapter, we review four main strands of literature on the economics of infectious diseases. First is the economic impact of infectious diseases, discussed in section 9.1. Although there are direct impacts on life years, there are also important impacts on labor productivity and perhaps investment decisions. These impacts have been studied in contexts ranging from hookworm eradication in the United States and malaria control in India, Africa, and Vietnam to HIV/AIDS epidemics in Africa.

A second strand focuses on the interplay between disease prevention or treatment and individual risk-taking behavior, discussed in section 9.2. Much of this literature builds upon Peltzman's idea of risk compensation, which holds that people adjust their behavior to a regulation in ways that counteract the intended effect of the regulation (Peltzman 1975). For example, when the government passes a seatbelt

---

[1] To be sure, externalities also play a role in designing interventions against tobacco, where secondhand smoke is an issue, and alcohol, where drunk driving imposes costs on others.

law, some drivers may respond by driving less safely. In the case of infectious diseases, individuals respond to greater risk of disease by taking greater protective measures. Conversely, a reduction in the expected cost from disease due to the availability of treatment could disincentivize self-protection measures (Philipson and Posner 1993). Another theme in this literature is that vaccination, an important tool in the prevention of infectious diseases, presents a classic public goods problem. Society gains from individual vaccination because of herd immunity, but this value is not recognized by individuals, who have an incentive to free-ride on vaccination by other individuals.

A third strand of literature relates to incentives faced by institutions and nations to respond to the emergence and spread of infectious diseases, discussed in section 9.3. Disease reporting and eradication efforts are also global public goods. Individual countries may fail to internalize the benefits of prompt reporting on the global spread of disease. Likewise, the benefits for the last country to eliminate a disease are much less than the benefits that accrue to all countries when the disease is permanently wiped out from the planet. Policies relying on prompt reporting of disease outbreaks or domestic eradication of disease must recognize the incentives that individual countries face.

A fourth strand of literature is on the optimal design of and allocation of resources for prevention and treatment programs, discussed in section 9.4. These programs are based on epidemiological models of disease spread that present significant mathematical challenges. Section 9.5 concludes the chapter.

9.1 Economic Impact of Infectious Diseases

The primary cost of infectious disease is loss of life. According to Lopez et al. (2006), five infectious diseases (lower respiratory infections, HIV, diarrheal diseases, tuberculosis, and malaria) were among the top ten global causes of death in 2001. Because onset is earlier in life than other top causes, such as ischemic heart disease, their impact is magnified when the outcome is not merely death but loss of life years. Together, all infectious diseases account for more than 25 percent of premature death globally.

A secondary impact of infectious disease is reduction in income and thus consumption. There is a large literature on the impact of disease, and health generally, on income. Although much of this literature studies infectious diseases, it does not identify any impacts of contagious disease that differ from impacts of non-contagious disease and infectivity is treated as having little economic consequence. This is surprising, as one might suspect that infectious diseases may have important consequences for the location or dispersion of economic activity.[2]

Focusing broadly on the effects of health on income and development, it is useful to distinguish partial equilibrium and general equilibrium effects. Bleakley (2010) offers a theoretical framework to think about partial equilibrium effects. Health has both a direct effect and an indirect effect on discounted lifetime income: $Y(H, E(H))$. The direct effect is increased productivity during working years and increased number of working years. The indirect effect is changes in the level of investment in human capital $E(H)$ and thus income.

Although a number of prominent papers (e.g. Miguel and Kremer 2004; Bobonis et al. 2006) focus on the effect of disease or disease control interventions on human capital investments, there are strong theoretical reasons to suspect that the indirect effects of disease are only of second-order importance. First, improvements in childhood health have theoretically ambiguous effects on, say, years of schooling. Health improves both the returns to schooling (the investment pays off over a longer working life) as well as the opportunity costs of schooling (the loss of wages during days in school).[3] This trade-off does not work against improvements in adult health. An increase in anticipated health after schooling increases the return to schooling without increasing the loss of wages during school. The effect of adult health on human capital investment is dampened, however, if improvements in longevity are associated with a reduction in hours worked per year (Bleakley and Lange 2009).

There is a second reason to think the indirect effect is minor: the envelope theorem. An individual chooses the level of human capital investment such that marginal benefit is equal to marginal cost. Even if health increases marginal benefit, the marginal cost is so high that the overall marginal return is likely to be small. This may explain conflicting results on the effect of disease control on education (compare Lucas 2010 with Cutler et al. 2007 on the effects of malaria eradication) and why Bleakley (2007a, 2007b), Cutler et al. (2007), and Behrman (2009) find that health seriously affects income but not human capital accumulation.[4] Further (indirect) support comes from

[2] Another area ripe for research is the impact of development on infectious disease. Again according to Lopez et al. (2006), infectious diseases account for five of the top ten causes of death in low- and middle-income countries but only one (lower respiratory infections) of the top ten in high-income countries. Two papers that examine this disparity in the context of HIV are Oster (2005) and (2007). The latter asks the interesting question: Why is the elasticity of risk taking to HIV prevalence so high in the United States but low in Africa? The answer is that the utility of a disease-free life is greater in the United States, and thus the benefit of infection control is greater there. This is a theme that we will revisit in section 9.3.

[3] It is possible, however, that improvements in health increase the productivity of inframarginal investment in human capital. This might explain why Bleakley (2007a, 2007b) finds that US hookworm eradication programs and malaria control in the United States and certain Latin American countries substantially improved adult literacy among children born after those diseases were controlled.

[4] The envelope theorem argument may extend to macro investments in physical capital. Improvements in complementary labor productivity may have only second-order effects on investment in physical capital, given that investment, if set optimally, recently had zero net marginal return.

papers that find a significant effect of improvements in adult health on labor productivity (e.g. Thomas et al. 2003; Larson et al. 2004; Russell 2004; Ashraf et al. 2009).

A contrary view is given by Corrigan et al. (2004, 2005) and Bell et al. (2006). These papers argue that parents transmit human capital to their children and that increases in (young) adult mortality reduce this transmission. Simulation exercises based on over-lapping generation models incorporating this mechanism suggest both larger and longer duration effects from HIV epidemics. For example, Bell et al. (2006) predict that the 20 percent HIV prevalence in South Africa could shrink that economy by half in as little as four generations.

Finally, we turn to the general equilibrium effects of improvements to health (see also Chapter 5 in this volume). As Bleakley and Lange (2009) highlight, the central issue here is the fixed factor problem. Although investment in labor and physical capital can respond to health-induced improvements in labor productivity, land may be a fixed factor. If improvements in health increase population and thereby labor supply,[5] then there may be less land per worker. This will offset the positive effect of health on labor productivity and may even reduce income per capita. This effect is less significant in developed countries, where urbanization and trade have reduced the importance of the fixed factor land. But it may explain why cross-sectional comparison regressions frequently find insignificant effects of disease on per capita income (e.g. Bloom and Mahal 1997; Acemoglu and Johnson 2006). Calibrated general equilibrium models that also find modest effects of health on income include Young et al. (2005) and Ashraf et al. (2009).

9.2 INDIVIDUAL INCENTIVES

The literature on the role that individual incentives play in infectious disease dynamics and control can usefully be sorted into three categories. The first includes papers that examine the impact of disease prevalence on self-protection and, in return, the effect of self-protection on prevalence. The main conclusion here is that self-protection both slows the spread of infections and reduces the return from public interventions to slow disease. The second category comprises papers that examine the demand for treatment and vaccines. These papers conclude that both treatment for the infected and vaccination to prevent infections have positive externalities on population prevalence. The challenge is how to solve this public goods problem, especially given that treatment or vaccination and other forms of self-protection are substitutes. The third set of papers

---

[5] The effect on population is a combination of the direct reduction in mortality and the indirect response of fertility rates. The direction of the fertility effect may depend on whether health improvement is seen as a reduction in the price of quantity of children (Acemoglu and Johnson 2006; Jayachandran and Lleras-Muney 2009) or in the price of quality of children (Bleakley and Lange 2009).

examines the demand for information on one's infection state—that is, on testing. For diseases such as HIV/AIDS, testing is important because it is a prerequisite for treatment, and the availability of treatment may reduce the cost of risky behavior. Below we review these three subsets of the literature in order.

9.2.1 Prevalence and the Demand for Risk

Initially, models and simulations of disease dynamics in the mathematical epidemiology literature assumed that individual risk taking was exogenous (e.g. Anderson and May 1991).[6] An increase in disease prevalence accelerated the spread of disease and thus its consequences. These models also suggested that interventions to reduce prevalence—either treatment for the infected or vaccination that prevented infections—actually had significant effects on prevalence.

More sophisticated analyses introduced sensitivity analysis that examined the effects of interventions while varying the degree of risk taking by individuals. Although risk taking was still exogenous (it did not decrease *because* of prevalence), these analyses demonstrated that high levels of risk taking could swamp the efficacy of treatments and vaccines (Blower and McLean 1994; see also Hadeler and Castillo-Chavez 1995; Blower et al. 2002; Bogard and Kuntz 2002; Stover et al. 2002; Blower et al. 2003; Gray et al. 2003; Smith and Blower 2004; Anderson and Hanson 2005).

In the late 1980s and early 1990s, biologists (Liu et al. 1986, 1987; Blythe et al. 1991; Hethcote et al. 1991; Brauer et al. 1992; Velasco-Hernandez and Hsieh 1994; Gubbins and Gilligan 1997a, 1997b) and economists (e.g. Philipson and Posner 1993; Geoffard and Philipson 1996; Kremer 1996) began endogenizing risk taking in infectious disease models (mainly susceptible-infected, or SI, categorical models). The economic models posited a formal demand for risky behavior, such as sex, and assumed that the cost of risky behavior included infections. Since disease prevalence increased the chance of infection, it reduced demand for sex. The notion of prevalence-response elasticity was born. The important implication was a feedback loop that slowed the spread of disease without any public health intervention: growth in prevalence reduced risk taking, which in turn reduced growth in prevalence. Indeed, it is theoretically possible that self-protection alone could reduce steady-state levels of prevalence and even lower the basic reproductive rate of infection (R_0)—the number of persons whom one infected individual infects—below one and thus extinguish a disease. Subsequent models expanded upon this insight by considering such variations as heterogeneity in the levels of risk taking

---

[6] Risk taking is the opposite of self-protection. For HIV, for example, risk taking is measured by condom use or number of sexual partners. For influenza, self-protection is largely the avoidance of public spaces. Following the literature, we will examine the demand for medical treatment and vaccinations separately from other self-protection measures, though there is no strong theoretical reason for doing so.

across individuals (Kremer 1996) and the role of individuals' expectations about the future epidemics on current levels of risk taking (Auld 2003).

9.2.2 Demand for Treatment and Prevention

For infectious disease, both vaccines and treatment have positive externalities. By getting treated or vaccinated, one enters and expands the population of uninfected or resistant individuals. The larger this population, the lower the risk of infection for other individuals. Because individuals do not internalize this external benefit, however, there is a socially insufficient demand for treatment and vaccines, though in practice it is assumed the private benefit of treatment is sufficient to induce universal demand. The natural implication is that vaccination should be subsidized (e.g. Vardavas et al. 2007).[7]

The concept of prevalence–response elasticity, however, complicates this conclusion. Because public health interventions reduce prevalence, they also reduce self-protection (e.g. Lakdawalla et al. 2006). As a result, public subsidies and self-protection are substitutes (Philipson 1996). Indeed, if vaccination is voluntary, not even subsidies will be able to achieve universal coverage. As the fraction of the population that gets vaccinated approaches one, the demand for vaccination falls to zero unless the subsidy is greater than the private cost of the vaccine (Bauch and Earn 2004). Even a mandatory vaccination program may fall short if it does not cover the entire population: the mandatory program will reduce demand among the exempt population (Geoffard and Philipson 1997; Bauch et al. 2003).

Some analyses have gone further and suggested that treatment and vaccination could cause so much risk taking that the epidemic would actually grow (Blower and McLean 1994; Blower et al. 2000). Indeed, Auld (2003) speculates that this risk may have contributed to the decision not to release then-existing, semi-efficacious HIV vaccines.

The above intuition, and indeed much of the literature on demand for risk taking and vaccination, can be described with a simple model. An individual engages in greater self-protection or vaccination if the benefit outweighs the costs: $[p_0 - p_1]D > c$. The benefits are calculated as the difference between the probability of infection if an individual does not self-protect or vaccinate (p_0) and the probability if he does (p_1), all times the health cost of infection (D). The cost (c) is the utility from risk-taking or the monetary price and health risk from vaccination. Obviously, the risk of infection will *inter alia* increase with the number of individuals who are infected: $p_1(I), p_1'(I) < 0$. Since the level of infection falls with vaccination subsidies ($I'(s) < 0$), so does the benefit from and demand for individual vaccination.

A large strand of the literature focuses on the role of fatalism or competing risks on incentives. The probability of infection is capped at one. If there are two factors that cause infection, then we may write $p_1 = \max\{p_{11} + p_{12}, 1\}$, where p_{11} is the immediate probability

---

[7] The mirror image of this conclusion is that risk taking has a negative externality and should be subject to a Pigouvian tax.

of infection if under self-protection or vaccination this period, and p_{12} is another unavoidable source of risk. If p_{12} is high, then p_{11} will generate little demand for self-protection or vaccination (because p_{12} either closes the gap between p_1 and p_0 or makes the cap bind). For example, if p_{12} is a competing cause of death for survivors of an initial infection, then they will have less incentive to take a vaccine (Dow et al. 1999).[8] If individuals expect a serious epidemic in the next period (p_{12}), then they have less incentive to reduce risk-taking in this period (p_{11}) (Auld 2003). If life without the disease is not very pleasant (L), the demand for self-protection may be low. Oster (2007) suggests this may explain why prevalence elasticity may be lower in Africa than in the United States.

Indeed, our model captures the intuition behind an interesting paper by Heal and Kunreuther (2005) that challenges the conventional notion of individuals free-riding on public vaccination programs. Their paper relaxes the assumption that vaccines are effective against infection through contact with other humans and assumes that vaccines confer some protection against infection through contact with the environment. Our model can account for this by making $p_{12}(I(s))$ rather than p_{11} a function of the prevalence. Now, an increase in vaccination subsidies will lower I but will decrease a *competing* cause of death. This will increase the marginal utility of vaccination (p_{11}). Vaccination by others is not a substitute for self-vaccination because it is ineffective at protecting against contact with other humans.

9.2.3 Demand for Testing

The third topic that has garnered substantial attention in the literature on individual incentives is the demand for information on one's disease state. Information is important for two reasons. First, it may be a prerequisite for obtaining treatment. For example, one cannot get a script for an antiretroviral without a test result confirming that one is HIV+. Second, aggregate data on prevalence may depend on voluntary testing. In this case, the data will report prevalence only among the population that chooses to test.

Because information is costly, either because tests are costly or because there is a stigma to being sick, demand for information is not universal. People will demand information only if they expect it may materially change their prior beliefs. Low-risk individuals who are fairly certain they are not infected will not demand testing. Nor will high-risk individuals who are fairly certain they are, unless testing is necessary for treatment. It is mainly individuals who have priors around, say, a one-half probability of infection, who will test (Boozer and Philipson 2000).

The public health community thought quite differently about testing for HIV/AIDS. The conventional view was that testing was necessary for people to obtain treatment, and that treatment saved lives. Philipson and Posner (1993) questioned this logic. They

---

[8] The flip side, of course, is that if the government lowers the risk from a competing cause (p_{12}), then the individual may take greater efforts to self-protect or vaccinate (p_{11}).

noted that if information was a conduit for treatment and if treatment increased demand for risky behavior, then information obtained through mandatory testing could increase the demand for risky behavior after a positive test and possibly *worsen* an epidemic. Survey data collected by epidemiologists suggested that individuals were more cautious after testing positive for HIV.[9] Mechoulan (2004) uses a simulation model to show that a small number of altruists could ensure that testing does not exacerbate an epidemic.

What if testing is not mandatory? Mechoulan (2007) considers the effect of treatment on demand for risky behavior when testing is voluntary (and individuals are selfish). Among inframarginal testers, treatment increases risk taking, as in prior models. However, treatment also increases the return to testing, so marginal non-testers start obtaining tests. Together, these increase prevalence, but this triggers the usual prevalence response feedback, reducing all individuals' risk-taking behavior. If prevalence-response elasticity is very high, it is possible that risk taking could even fall, on balance.

9.3 INSTITUTIONAL AND NATIONAL INCENTIVES

Institutional incentives for control of infectious diseases operate in ways similar to those of individual incentives but with important contextual differences. Take the example of hospital incentives to control infectious disease outbreaks. Often, patients are colonized with disease-carrying bacteria in one health care institution and carry these to another institution. Investment in infection prevention at any single institution therefore benefits both that institution as well as others, which would have fewer incoming infected patients (Smith et al. 2005). Interestingly, incentives to control infections strongly depend on the number of incoming patients who are colonized with disease-causing bacteria. If the number increases, it would be in a hospital's interests to ramp up its infection control. However, if too many incoming patients are colonized, it would be hopeless for the hospital to try to control the epidemic on its own without the cooperation of other institutions, and its optimal infection control expenditure should decline.

---

[9] Testing is frequently accompanied by counseling. Individuals who received both testing and counseling also report greater condom use (Kamenga et al. 1991; Bhave et al. 1995; Deschamps et al. 1996; Jackson et al. 1997; Bentley et al. 1998; Levine et al. 1998; Voluntary HIV-1 Counseling and Testing Efficacy Study Group 2000), lower rates of unprotected intercourse (Deschamps et al. 1996; Voluntary HIV-1 Counseling and Testing Efficacy Study Group 2000). Surveys also suggest that testing and counseling are associated with lower HIV incidence (Bhave et al. 1995; Celentano et al. 2000) and rates of sexually transmitted disease (Jackson et al. 1997; Levine et al. 1998; Celentano et al. 2000). There are important caveats to these studies. First, intervention involves testing and counseling, not just testing. Second, the studies do not control for selection and thus do not demonstrate causation (Mechoulan 2004).

At the level of countries, incentives related to infectious diseases operate on similar principles. Control of malaria in South Africa, for instance, is possible if its neighbors, particularly Zimbabwe and Mozambique, were also willing to fight malaria within their borders. Returns to investment in control are diminished if a large number of patients carry these diseases across borders. Thus, a country's incentives to control a freely moving disease like malaria are determined as much by its ability to stop the inflow of infected individuals as by the ability to control the disease within its own borders. Reducing malaria in a country could have transboundary benefits by incentivizing infection control in its neighboring countries as well.

This principle also applies more generally to the challenge of global disease eradication. The elimination of disease in all forms anywhere on the planet is a global public good, since it theoretically suggests that countries can cease all control measures and vaccination programs.[10] Eradication is a binary public good: the maximum benefits are achieved when the disease is completely gone. However, incentives for the last country to eliminate the disease may be insufficient for two reasons. First, the benefits that accrue to the entire world when the last country achieves eradication are almost certainly much larger than the costs of eradication as well as the benefits of eradication in that country alone. Second, the benefits in the last country may be small because the disease has been eliminated everywhere else and there is no risk of importation.

Diseases that have already been eliminated in high-income countries are the best candidates for eradication in the rest of the world. Indeed, it may be in the financial interests of high-income countries to finance global eradication so that they can reduce their expenditures on prevention and control. In general, disease eradication, which requires simultaneous elimination in many countries, calls for strong international institutions that can enforce a cooperative optimum even when the Nash equilibrium is for no country to eliminate the disease. Economic conditions are not sufficient. The disease must have a relatively low basic reproductive number (the number of secondary cases generated by a single infected individual in a fully susceptible population), should not have a non-human reservoir, and should be easily identifiable so that the last few cases can be eliminated. However, even with favorable epidemiological conditions and a high benefit-cost ration of eradication (believed to be about 90:1 in the case of smallpox) (Fenner et al. 1988), disease eradication is, at best, a fortuitous event and by no means inevitable, as the experience with smallpox showed.

Disease eradication represents one end of the spectrum of dealing with an infectious pathogen. The emergence and spread of pathogens from animals to humans represent the other. The global spread of zoonoses (as these diseases are known) like swine flu and SARS highlights the difficult decision governments face when presented with evidence of a local outbreak. Reporting the outbreak may bring medical assistance but is also likely to

---

[10] In practice, this has been true for smallpox, but here too, vaccinations have resumed for military and emergency personnel because of the threat of bioterrorist attacks using the smallpox virus. For a highly infectious disease like measles, it may never be feasible to stop vaccinations because the stock of immunity to measles is itself a global public good that is relatively expensive to replace in a short time, should the disease ever be reintroduced either accidentally or by malfeasance.

trigger trade sanctions by countries hoping to contain the disease. Suppressing the information may avoid trade sanctions but increases the likelihood of widespread epidemics. Malani and Laxminarayan (2010) model the government's decision as a signaling game in which a country has private but imperfect evidence of an outbreak. The first important conclusion is that not all sanctions discourage reporting. Sanctions based on fears of an undetected outbreak (false negatives) encourage disclosure by reducing the relative cost of sanctions that follow a reported outbreak. Second, improving the quality of detection technology may not promote the disclosure of an outbreak because the forgone trade from reporting truthfully is that much greater. Third, informal surveillance is an important channel for publicizing outbreaks and functions as an exogenous yet imperfect signal that is less likely to discourage disclosure. In sum, obtaining accurate information about potential epidemics is as much about reporting incentives as it is about detection technology.

A final example of a global public good in the context of infectious disease is drug effectiveness. Take the case of drugs to treat malaria. The use of antimalarials places selection pressure on parasites to evolve resistance to these drugs. Moreover, resistance is bound to arise when these drugs are misused and could have adverse consequences for all malaria-endemic countries. Efforts to manage resistance across national borders would have to rely on international agreements and regulations (Walker et al. 2009) or on tax or subsidy instruments (Arrow et al. 2004). In the absence of such agreements and regulation, countries are unable to commit themselves to an optimal use of antibiotics, which would be in all countries' interest. At the macroeconomic level, a too-intensive use of antibiotics as an input in a country's production results (Cornes et al. 2001). A supranational authority would have to consider both the externality benefits of antibiotic use, in terms of reducing infections, and the costs, in terms of resistance (Rudholm 2002). Whether antibiotic consumption should be taxed or subsidized to reach the first-best outcome then depends on the relative magnitude of the externalities.

A relatively new class of antimalarial drugs, called artemisinins, requires a different way of thinking about optimal subsidies to manage resistance. When chloroquine, a once-powerful antimalarial drug, became obsolete, the public health world was left with the challenge of using the last remaining effective drug class, artemisinins, in an effective manner. The World Health Organization (2001) has recommended that artemisinins be used in combination with a partner drug that is unrelated in its mechanism of action and genetic bases of resistance, so that a single mutation cannot encode resistance to both components. Artemisinin combination treatments (ACTs), if used instead of monotherapies of either artemisinin or the partner drug, should slow the emergence of antimalarial resistance. However, the WHO guidelines are routinely flouted because monotherapies are much less expensive than ACTs. In response to this problem, an Institute of Medicine report (Arrow et al. 2004) recommended establishing an international fund to buy ACTs at producer cost and resell them at a small fraction of that cost.

On economic efficiency grounds there is a second-best case for subsidizing ACTs, because the ideal policy—taxing monotherapies and other antimalarials according to the marginal external cost from the elevated risk of resistance evolution—is infeasible, given their widespread use in the informal sector. The efficiency argument is further strengthened by the positive externality to the extent that effective treatment of one individual reduces the risk of infection transmission to other individuals. Laxminarayan et al. (2010) show that it is possible to determine the optimal subsidy in a dynamic disease modeling framework. Bioeconomic analysis has been helpful for determining whether the social benefit from the subsidy, in terms of delayed resistance and saved lives, exceeds the social cost of resistance because of increased use of ACTs (Laxminarayan et al. 2006). It was also instrumental in turning an idea into the Affordable Medicines Facility for malaria, a global financing system launched in early 2009.

9.4 Optimal Allocation of Resources to Fight Infectious Diseases

Recent papers have examined the optimal allocation of resources to fight infectious disease, especially in the context of disease treatment. Given the inevitable constraint of limited treatment resources, there is not enough money to treat all infected individuals, even for a disease like HIV with unprecedented resources made available for treatment. For instance, in Zambia, a country with one of best-funded malaria control programs in Sub-Saharan Africa, only 13 percent of children with malaria receive effective treatment. Questions of optimal allocation of resources across different populations are not just of academic interest. International policy makers at the World Health Organization and the Global Fund for AIDS, TB, and Malaria, as well as national ministries of health, are charged with allocating limited treatment resources across different populations that have different prevalence levels of infection. Although the stated objective of these agencies is to reduce the burden of disease, the focus is on populations with the highest burden of disease.

There is a long literature of applying optimal control theory in the context of epidemiological models. ReVelle et al. (1967) analyzed how best to allocate treatment resources to contain tuberculosis. Sanders (1971) and Sethi (1974) evaluated the socially optimal level of treatment under the assumption of linear treatment costs in an optimal control framework but disagreed on whether the optimal treatment level followed a bang-bang path or was singular.

Choosing the best policy calls for a combination of epidemiological and economic insights, an approach that has been taken in recent papers in both economics and epidemiology (Goldman and Lightwood 1997; Rowthorn and Brown 2003; Smith et al. 2005). Other papers have examined the optimal allocation of resources in a dynamic setting. Gersovitz and Hammer (2004, 2005) evaluate the optimal allocation of resources between prevention and treatment by a social planner and compare this decision with that made by representative individuals who ignore disease externalities.

The allocation of scarce financial resources for disease treatment between geographical regions is usually guided by disease burden, but this basis does not recognize the dynamic nature of infections. Treating a single infected individual not only cures that individual but also prevents other healthy individuals who are in close proximity from getting infected. Rowthorn et al. (2009) address the question of optimal allocation of treatment resources across two connected populations when there is a period-by-period constraint on the number of treatments available to the social planner. Such a constraint is realistic and relevant from the perspective of most health authorities, which are given annual budgets and cannot transfer funds inter-temporally. Rowthorn et al. find that the optimal solution is to preferentially treat the population with low prevalence of infection before allocating remaining resources to the higher-prevalence population. Whereas the usual policy is to provide a larger treatment budget for the more highly afflicted district, they find that, from an economic perspective, disease burden may be a poor criterion to use for allocating treatment resources. However, the paper by Rowthorn et al. relies on a simulation model and cannot conclusively prove that a corner solution is always optimal. This result is shown analytically in a paper by Anderson et al. (2010). The intuition underlying this finding is that the economic value of treatment is greater in this population because of the lower probability of re-infection. From a methodological perspective, the proof depends on the concavity of the cost function. We show that with just a single group, the minimized cost function in every period is weakly concave in the overall wealth allocation. Given this concavity, it is then straightforward to show that with two groups, the health authority will allocate all wealth to a single group.

Optimal allocation of resources has also been examined for the effect of de-worming treatments on school performance in Kenya. Miguel et al. (2001) find that school-based mass de-worming drug treatment for children significantly reduced school absenteeism, a finding that escaped earlier studies in which treatment was randomized among some children in a school. De-worming only some students had few lasting benefits, since treated students were likely to be quickly re-infected by untreated students. However, when treatment was administered to all students in a single school, the externality benefits from treatment (reducing infections of other students) were found to be large.

9.5 Conclusions

The emergence and spread of infectious diseases is strongly influenced by the behavior of individuals, institutions, nations, and international organizations. At the individual level, beliefs about the likelihood of infection and the consequences of being infected drive both the decision to prevent disease in the first place, whether through vaccination or self-protection, and the decision to test for infection after exposure. Greater levels of vaccination in the community are likely to reduce incentives for vaccination for any single individual because of the ability to free-ride. Indeed, because community-level protection and individual protection are substitutes, vaccination campaigns may increase the level of individual risk taking, subverting those very campaigns. These basic principles also operate at the level of institutions and countries, and the problems remain the same: insufficient incentives to prevent and control disease (including through vaccination), and insufficient incentives to provide information on disease outbreaks. Disease eradication and the effectiveness of drugs to treat infections are global public goods that require international cooperation and strong international institutions to ensure that they are provided at a socially appropriate level; the challenges remain.

The extent to which infectious disease control, whether at the individual level or at the international level, involves incentives and behavior accounts for the growing literature on the economics of infectious disease. When done well, papers in this field have paid close attention to the specific dynamics of diseases, consistent with scientific understanding, to ensure the validity of conclusions drawn by economic models. We have learned much from modeling disease dynamics and control by scaling up from individual infections to epidemics in populations; these models include such factors as the spatial structure and heterogeneity of host populations and the topology of contacts between infected and susceptible individuals. Incorporating this epidemiological complexity into economic models both enriches the quality and robustness of conclusions drawn and informs the work of the vast community of global health professionals, many of whom are not economists.

REFERENCES

ACEMOGLU, D. and JOHNSON, S. (2006), "Disease and Development: The Effect of Life Expectancy on Economic Growth." NBER Working Paper 12269. Cambridge, MA: NBER.

ANDERSON, R. and HANSON, M. (2005), "Potential Public Health Impact of Imperfect HIV Type 1 Vaccines," *Journal of Infectious Diseases*, 191(suppl. 1): S85–96.

ANDERSON, R. M. and MAY, R. M. (1991), *Infectious Diseases of Humans: Dynamics and Control* (New York: Oxford University Press).

ANDERSON, S. T., LAXMINARAYAN, R., and SALANT, S. W. (2010), "Diversify or Focus? Spending to Combat Infectious Diseases When Budgets Are Tight, Resources for the Future." RFF Discussion Paper 10-15. Resources for the Future, Washington, DC.

ARROW, K. J., PANOSIAN, C. B., and GELBAND, H. (eds.) (2004), *Saving Lives, Buying Time: Economics of Malaria Drugs in an Age of Resistance* (Washington, DC: Institute of Medicine, Board on Global Health).

ASHRAF, Q. H., LESTER, A., and WEIL, D. (2009), "When Does Improving Health Raise GDP?" *NBER Macroeconomics Annual*, 23(1): 157–204.

AULD, M. C. (2003), "Choices, Beliefs, and Infectious Disease Dynamics," *Journal of Health Economics*, 22(3): 361–77.

BAUCH, C. T. and EARN, D. J. (2004), "Vaccination and the Theory of Games," *Proceedings of the National Academy of Sciences USA*, 101(36): 13391–4.

—— GALVANI, A. P., and EARN, D. J. (2003), "Group Interest Versus Self-Interest in Smallpox Vaccination Policy," *Proceedings of the National Academy of Sciences USA*, 100(18): 10564–7.

BEHRMAN, J. R. (2009), "Early Life Nutrition and Subsequent Education, Health, Wage, and Intergenerational Effects," in M. Spence and M. Lewis (eds.), *Health and Growth* (Washington, DC: Commission on Growth and Development and the World Bank), 167–83.

BELL, C., DEVARAJAN, S., and GERSBACH, H. (2006), "The Long-Run Economic Costs of AIDS: A Model with an Application to South Africa," *World Bank Economic Review*, 20(1): 55–89.

BENTLEY, M. E., SPRATT, K., SHEPHERD, M. E., GANGAKHEDKAR, R. R., THILIKAVATHI, S., BOLLINGER, R. C., and MEHENDALE, S. M. (1998), "HIV Testing and Counseling Among Men Attending Sexually Transmitted Disease Clinics in Pune, India: Changes in Condom Use and Sexual Behavior Over Time," *AIDS*, 12(14): 1869–77.

BHAVE, G., LINDAN, C. P., HUDES, E. S., DESAI, S., WAGLE, U., TRIPATHI, S. P., and MANDEL, J. S. (1995), "Impact of an Intervention on HIV, Sexually Transmitted Diseases, and Condom Use Among Sex Workers in Bombay, India." *AIDS*, 9(Suppl. 1): S21–30.

BLEAKLEY, H. (2007a), "Disease and Development: Evidence from Hookworm Eradication in the American South," *The Quarterly Journal of Economics*, 122(1): 73–117.

—— (2007b), "Spillovers and Aggregate Effects of Health Capital: Evidence from Campaigns against Parasitic Disease in the Americas." Unpublished manuscript, University of Chicago, Chicago, IL.

—— (2010), "Health, Human Capital, and Development," *Annual Review of Economics*, 2(1).

—— and LANGE, F. (2009), "Chronic Disease Burden and the Interaction of Education, Fertility, and Growth," *The Review of Economics and Statistics*, 91(1): 52–65.

BLOOM, D. and MAHAL, A. (1997), "Does the AIDS Epidemic Threaten Economic Growth?" *Journal of Econometrics*, 77(1): 105–24.

BLOWER, S. M. and MCLEAN, A. R. (1994), "Prophylactic Vaccines, Risk Behavior Change, and the Probability of Eradicating HIV in San Francisco," *Science*, 265(5177): 1451–4.

—— GERSHENGORN, H. B., and GRANT, R. M. (2000), "A Tale of Two Futures: HIV and Antiretroviral Therapy in San Francisco," *Science*, 287(5453): 650–4.

—— KOELLE, K., and MILLS, J. (2002), "Health Policy Modeling: Epidemic Control, HIV Vaccines, and Risky Behavior," in E. Kaplan and R. Brookmeyer (eds.), *Quantitative Evaluation of HIV Prevention Programs* (New Haven, CT: Yale University Press), 260–89.

—— SCHWARTZ, E. J., and MILLS, J. (2003), "Forecasting the Future of HIV Epidemics: The Impact of Antiretroviral Therapies & Imperfect Vaccines," *AIDS Review*, 5(2): 113–25.

BLYTHE, S. P., COOKE, K., and CASTILLO-CHAVEZ, C. (1991), "Autonomous Risk-Behavior Change, and Non-Linear Incidence Rate, in Models of Sexually Transmitted Diseases." Biometrics Unit Technical Report B-1048-M, Cornell University, Ithaca, NY.

BOBONIS, G. J., MIGUEL, E., and PURI-SHARMA, C. (2006), "Anemia and School Participation," *Journal of Human Resources*, 41(4): 692–721.

BOGARD, E. and KUNTZ, K. M. (2002), "The Impact of a Partially Effective HIV Vaccine on a Population of Intravenous Drug Users in Bangkok, Thailand: A Dynamic Model," *Journal of Acquired Immune Deficiency Syndrome*, 29(2): 132–41.

BOOZER, M. and PHILIPSON, T. (2000), "The Impact of Public Testing for Human Immunodeficiency Virus," *Journal of Human Resources*, 35(3): 419–46.

BRAUER, F., BLYTHE, S., and CASTILLO-CHAVEZ, C. (1992), "Demographic Recruitment in Sexually Transmitted Disease Models." Biometrics Unit Technical Report BU-1154-M, Cornell University, Ithaca, NY.

CELENTANO, D. D., BOND, K. C., LYLES, C. M., EIUMTRAKUL, S., et al. (2000), "Preventive Intervention to Reduce Sexually Transmitted Infections: A Field Trial in the Royal Thai Army," *Archives of Internal Medicine*, 160(4): 535–40.

CORNES, R., VAN LONG, N., and SHIMOMURA, K. (2001), "Drugs and Pests: Intertemporal Production Externalities," *Japan and the World Economy*, 13(3): 255–78.

CORRIGAN, P., GLOMM, G., and MENDEZ, F. (2004), *AIDS, Human Capital and Growth* (Bloomington, IN: Indiana University).

—— (2005), "AIDS Crisis and Growth," *Journal of Development Economics*, 77(1): 107–24.

CUTLER, D., FUNG, W., KREMER, M., and SINGHAL, M. (2007), "Mosquitoes: The Long-Term Effects of Malaria Eradication in India." Working paper 13539. NBER Working Paper Series. National Bureau of Economic Research, Cambridge, MA.

DESCHAMPS, M. M., PAPE, J. W., HAFNER, A., and JOHNSON, W. D. (1996), "Heterosexual Transmission of HIV in Haiti," *Annals of Internal Medicine*, 125(4): 324–30.

DOW, W. H., PHILIPSON, T., and SALA-I-MARTIN, X. (1999), "Longevity Complementarities under Competing Risks," *American Economic Review*, 89(5): 1358–71.

FENNER, F., HENDERSON, D., ARITA, I., JEZEK, Z., and LADNYI, I. (1988), *Smallpox and Its Eradication* (Geneva: World Heath Organization).

GEOFFARD, P. Y. and PHILIPSON, T. (1996), "Rational Epidemics and Their Public Control," *International Economic Review*, 37(3): 603–24.

—— (1997), "Disease Eradication: Private Versus Public Vaccination," *American Economic Review*, 87(1): 222–30.

GERSOVITZ, M. and HAMMER, J. S. (2004), "The Economical Control of Infectious Diseases," *Economic Journal*, 114(492): 1–27.

—— (2005), "Tax/subsidy Policies Toward Vector-borne Infectious Diseases," *Journal of Public Economics*, 89(4): 647–74.

GOLDMAN, S. M. and LIGHTWOOD, J. (1997), "Cost Optimization in the SIS Model of Infectious Disease with Treatment." Working paper 97-245. Economics Working Papers. University of California at Berkeley, Berkley, CA.

GRAY, R. H., LI, X., WAWER, M. J., et al. (2003), "Stochastic Simulation of the Impact of Antiretroviral Therapy and HIV Vaccines on HIV Transmission; Rakai, Uganda," *AIDS*, 17(13): 1941–51.

GUBBINS, S. and GILLIGAN, C. A. (1997a), "Biological Control in a Disturbed Environment," *Philosophical Transactions of the Royal Society of London. Series B: Biological Sciences*, 352(1364): 1935–49.

—— —— (1997b), "A Test of Heterogeneous Mixing as a Mechanism for Ecological Persistence in a Disturbed Environment," *Proceedings of the Royal Society of London. Series B: Biological Sciences*, 264(1379): 227–32.

HADELER, K. P. and CASTILLO-CHAVEZ, C. (1995), "A Core Group Model for Disease Transmission," *Mathematical Bioscience*, 128(1–2): 41–55.

HEAL, G. and KUNREUTHER, H. (2005). "The Vaccination Game." Working paper, Columbia Business School and The Wharton School, New York.

HETHCOTE, H. W., VAN ARK, J. W., and KARON, J. M. (1991), "A Simulation Model of AIDS in San Francisco: II. Simulations, Therapy, and Sensitivity Analysis," *Mathematical Bioscience*, 106(2): 223–47.

JACKSON, D. J., RAKWAR, J. P., RICHARDSON, B. A., et al. (1997), "Decreased Incidence of Sexually Transmitted Diseases Among Trucking Company Workers in Kenya: Results of a Behavioural Risk-Reduction Programme," *AIDS*, 11(7): 903–9.

JAYACHANDRAN, S. and LLERAS-MUNEY, A. (2009) "Life Expectancy and Human Capital Investments: Evidence from Maternal Mortality Declines," *Quarterly Journal of Economics*, 124(1): 349–97.

KAMENGA, M., RYDER, R. W., JINGU, M., et al. (1991), "Evidence of Marked Sexual Behavior Change Associated with Low HIV-1 Seroconversion in 149 Married Couples with

Discordant HIV-1 Serostatus: Experience at an HIV Counselling Center in Zaire," *AIDS*, 5(1): 61–8.

KREMER, M. (1996), "Integrating Behavioral Choice into Epidemiological Models of AIDS," *Quarterly Journal of Economics*, 111(2): 549–73.

LAKDAWALLA, D., GOLDMAN, D., and SOOD, N. (2006), "HIV Breakthroughs and Risky Sexual Behavior," *Quarterly Journal of Economics*, 121(3): 1063–102.

LARSON, B., HAMAZAKAZA, P., KAPUNDA, C., HAMUSIMBI, C., and ROSEN, S. (2004), *Morbidity, Mortality, and Crop Production: An Empirical Study of Smallholder Cotton Growing Households in the Central Province of Zambia* (Boston, MA: Center for International Health and Development, Boston University School of Public Health).

LAXMINARAYAN, R., OVER, M., and SMITH, D. L. (2006), "Will a Global Subsidy of New Antimalarials Delay the Emergence of Resistance and Save Lives?" *Health Affairs*, 25(2): 325–36.

—— PARRY, I. W. H., SMITH, D. L., and KLEIN, E. Y. (2010), "Should New Antimalarial Drugs Be Subsidized?" *Journal of Health Economics*, 29(3): 445–56.

LEVINE, W. C., REVOLLO, R., KAUNE, V., et al. (1998), "Decline in Sexually Transmitted Disease Prevalence in Female Bolivian Sex Workers: Impact of an HIV Prevention Project," *AIDS*, 12(14): 1899–906.

LIU, W. M., LEVIN, S. A., and IWASA, Y. (1986), "Influence of Nonlinear Incidence Rates upon the Behavior of SIRS Epidemiological Models," *Journal of Mathematical Biology*, 23(2): 187–204.

—— HETHCOTE, H. W., and LEVIN, S. A. (1987), "Dynamical Behavior of Epidemiological Models with Nonlinear Incidence Rates," *Journal of Mathematical Biology*, 25(4): 359–80.

LOPEZ, A. D., MATHERS, C. D., EZZATI, M., JAMISON, D. T., and MURRAY, C. J. L. (eds.) (2006), *Global Burden of Disease and Risk Factors* (New York: Oxford University Press).

LUCAS, A. M. (2010), "Malaria Eradication and Educational Attainment: Evidence from Paraguay and Sri Lanka," *American Economic Journal: Applied Economics*, 2(2): 46–71.

MALANI, A. and LAXMINARAYAN, R. (2011), "Incentives for Surveillance and Reporting of Infectious Disease Outbreaks," *Journal of Human Resources*, 46(1): 176–202.

MECHOULAN, S. (2004), "HIV Testing: a Trojan Horse?" *Topics in Economic Analysis & Policy*, 4(1): Art. 18.

—— (2007), "Risky Sexual Behavior, Testing, and HIV Treatments," *Forum for Health Economics & Policy*, 10(2): Art. 5.

MIGUEL, E. and KREMER, M. (2004), "Worms: Identifying Impacts on Education and Health in the Presence of Treatment Externalities," *Econometrica*, 72(1): 159–217.

—— and NBER (NATIONAL BUREAU OF ECONOMIC RESEARCH) (2001), "Worms: Education and Health Externalities in Kenya." Working Paper 8481, NBER, Cambridge, MA.

OSTER, E. (2005), "Sexually Transmitted Infections, Sexual Behavior, and The HIV/AIDS Epidemic," *Quarterly Journal of Economics*, 120(2): 467–515.

—— (2007), "HIV and Sexual Behavior Change: Why Not Africa?" Working Paper W13049, NBER, Cambridge, MA.

PELTZMAN, S. (1975), "The Effects of Automobile Safety Regulation," *Journal of Political Economy*, 83(4): 677–725.

PHILIPSON, T. (1996), "Private Vaccination and Public Health: An Empirical Examination for US Measles," *Journal of Human Resources*, 31(3): 611–30.

—— and POSNER, R. (1993), *Private Choices and Public Health: The AIDS Epidemic in an Economic Perspective* (Cambridge, MA: Harvard University Press).

ReVelle, C. S., Lynn, W. R., and Feldmann, F. (1967), "Mathematical Models for the Economic Allocation of Tuberculosis Control Activities in Developing Nations," *American Review of Respiratory Diseases*, 96(5): 893–909.

Rowthorn, R. and Brown, G. (2003), "Using Antibiotics When Resistance Is Renewable," in R. Laxminarayan (ed.), *Battling Resistance to Antibiotics and Pesticides: An Economic Approach* (Washington: DC: Resources for the Future), 42–62.

—— Laxminarayan, R., and Gilligan, C. A. (2009), "Optimal Control of Epidemics in Metapopulations," *Journal of the Royal Society Interface*, 6(41): 1135–44.

Rudholm, N. (2002), "Economic Implications of Antibiotic Resistance in a Global Economy," *Journal of Health Economics*, 21(6): 1071–83.

Russell, S. (2004), "The Economic Burden of Illness for Households in Developing Countries: A Review of Studies Focusing on Malaria, Tuberculosis, and Human Immunodeficiency Virus/Acquired Immunodeficiency Syndrome," *American Journal of Tropical Medicine and Hygiene*, 71(2 Suppl.): 147–55.

Sanders, J. L. (1971), "Quantitative Guidelines for Communicable Disease Control Programs," *Biometrics*, 27(4): 833–93.

Sethi, S. P. (1974), "Quantitative Guidelines for a Communicable Disease Program: A Complete Synthesis," *Biometrics*, 30(4): 681–91.

Smith, D. L., Levin, S. A., and Laxminarayan, R. (2005), "Strategic Interactions in Multi-Institutional Epidemics of Antibiotic Resistance," *Proceedings of the National Academy of Sciences USA*, 102(8): 3153–8.

Smith, R. J. and Blower, S. M. (2004), "Could Disease-Modifying HIV Vaccines Cause Population-Level Perversity?" *Lancet Infectious Diseases*, 4(10): 636–9.

Stover, J., Garnett, G., Seitz, S., and Forsythe, S. (2002), "The Epidemiological Impact of an HIV/AIDS Vaccine in Developing Countries." Policy Research Working Paper 2811, World Bank, Washington, DC.

Thomas, D., Frankenberg, E., Friedman, J., et al. (2003), "Iron Defciency and the Well-Being of Older Adults: Early Results from a Randomized Nutrition Intervention." Unpublished manuscript.

Vardavas, R., Breban, R., and Blower, S. (2007), "Can Influenza Epidemics Be Prevented By Voluntary Vaccination?" *PLoS Computational Biology*, 3(5): e85.

Velasco-Hernandez, J. X. and Hsieh, Y. H. (1994), "Modelling the Effect of Treatment and Behavioral Change in HIV Transmission Dynamics," *Journal of Mathematical Biology*, 32(3): 233–49.

Voluntary HIV-1 Counseling and Testing Efficacy Study Group (2000). "Efficacy of HIV-1 Counselling and Testing in Individuals and Couples in Kenya, Tanzania, and Trinidad: A Randomised Trial," *Lancet*, 356(9224): 103–12.

Walker, B., Barrett, S., Polasky, S., et al. (2009), "Looming Global-Scale Failures and Missing Institutions," *Science*, 325(5946): 1345–6.

WHO (World Health Organization) (2001), "Antimalarial Drug Combination Therapy. Report of a WHO Technical Consultation." WHO/CDS/RBM/2001/35, World Health Organization, Geneva.

Young, G. J., White, B., Burgess, Jr, J. F., et al. (2005), "Conceptual Issues in the Design and Implementation of Pay-for-Quality Programs," *American Journal of Medical Quality*, 20(3): 144–50.

CHAPTER 10

···

ECONOMICS OF HEALTH BEHAVIORS AND ADDICTIONS: CONTEMPORARY ISSUES AND POLICY IMPLICATIONS

···

DONALD S. KENKEL AND JODY SINDELAR

10.1 INTRODUCTION

··

SOME of the most important health-related decisions take place outside the health care sector, including when we choose to consume substances that are bad for our health. Worldwide, there are an estimated 1.2 billion smokers, two billion users of alcohol, and 185 million users of drugs such as marijuana, cocaine, and heroin. While not all use of alcohol and other drugs is harmful, the WHO estimates that there were ninety-one million people negatively affected by their own alcohol use disorders and another fifteen million by drug use disorders in 2002 (<http://www.who.int/mental_health/en/=>). The WHO also attributes more than five million deaths each year to tobacco use, about two million deaths each year to alcohol use, and 200,000 deaths each year to drug use. These excess deaths, and-related morbidity, reflect the increased risks of chronic illnesses and accidents related to substance use. In its burden of disease calculations, the WHO estimates that tobacco use accounts for about 4 percent of the disability-adjusted life years (DALYs) lost worldwide, alcohol use accounts for another 4 percent of lost DALYs, and drug use accounts for about 1 percent of lost DALYs.

Smoking, alcohol, and drug abuse and dependence are not only unhealthy for the individual consumers, but have broader consequences for others as well. Deaths and DALYs lost due to substance use include the victims of second-hand tobacco smoke, victims of crime and drunk drivers. Substance use and the policies to combat it create societal costs beyond health consequences. For example, it is estimated that in 2002 the US spent about $25 billion to arrest and imprison drug offenders and another $6 billion in efforts to reduce the supply of illicit drugs (NIDA). In the US private payers and the public sector jointly fund substance abuse treatment. A national survey found that 59 percent of substance abuse treatment facilities received federal, state, or local government funds (Substance Abuse and Mental Health Services Administration 2007).

In different times and places policymakers have used wide ranging approaches to reduce the consumption and societal harms of unhealthy choices. The list includes approaches such as: information, taxation, regulation, prohibition, and litigation. Mass media and school-based campaigns to inform consumers of the health consequences of smoking, alcohol abuse, and drug use are a mainstay of modern public health policy that focuses on prevention. What were once called "sin taxes" on cigarettes and alcohol are now widely supported as public health measures. Cigarette and alcohol sales are also often subject to special regulatory efforts including advertising bans and limits on the number of licensed outlets and their hours of operation. Most countries totally prohibit the sale, possession, and consumption of certain substances. Because of their almost universal, blanket prohibitions, marijuana, cocaine, heroin, and other drugs are known as "illegal drugs," as distinguished from legal substances like tobacco and alcohol and pharmaceutical products that treat medical conditions. Many countries also enact targeted prohibitions of generally legal substances in specific circumstances; common examples include restaurant smoking bans, driving while intoxicated, and restrictions on youth through drinking age minimums. The most notable example of litigation as a public health measure is the Master Settlement Agreement (MSA) between the tobacco industry and forty-eight US states. The MSA resulted in a tax-like hike in cigarette prices, new anti-smoking media campaigns, and new restrictions on cigarette advertising and other tobacco industry practices.

In addition to public policies, medical treatments are available to help substance users and abusers. Smokers are more likely to quit successfully if they use a pharmaceutical smoking cessation product such as a nicotine replacement therapy (Fiore et al. 2000). In the US alone, the cessation product industry's estimated retail sales are nearly $1 billion annually (MarketResearch 2005). In 2006 there were 1.8 million annual admissions to US facilities that provide treatment for alcohol and drug abuse (Substance Abuse and Mental Health Services Administration 2008).

Understanding the unhealthy consumption of substances creates intertwined challenges and opportunities for the field of economics. Addiction to harmful substances appears to challenge the standard neoclassic assumption that consumers make rational, utility-maximizing choices. The simple answer—that people derive enough utility from the consumption of the substances that they willingly accept the health consequences— seems an unsatisfactory explanation for many people's struggles with addiction. As will be discussed in more detail below, economists' efforts to understand addictive behavior have led to the theory of rational addiction as well as behavioral economics models that incorporate hyperbolic discounting and cue-triggered addiction.

The consumption of unhealthy substances has also been a fertile source for empirical research questions and controversies. Estimates of basic economic concepts like the price-elasticity of demand take on policy relevance. For example, a cigarette tax hike might be an attractive policy tool to reduce smoking if the price-elasticity of demand for cigarettes is −0.5, but not if the price-elasticity is −0.05. Another body of econometric research at the intersection of health and labor economics explores the labor market consequences of substance abuse, including lost human capital, lowered productivity, and lost jobs. The fundamental problem for these empirical studies is to identify causal effects, either of public policies on substance use outcomes, or of substance use on labor market outcomes. Economics offers a systematic conceptual framework and a set of sophisticated econometric tools to take on these difficult empirical challenges.

This chapter attempts to provide an overview of how economic research on unhealthy substances responds to these challenges and opportunities. In the following sections we introduce models which economists use to understand consumers' use of unhealthy substances, discuss the economic approach to substance use policy, and provide an overview of some of the interesting questions being asked in modern empirical research. The scope of our review is admittedly limited. In particular, we do not attempt to provide a comprehensive review or meta-analysis of empirical findings. Numerous reviews of that sort already exist, especially for policy relevant findings such as the price-elasticity of the demand for cigarettes and alcohol (Gallet and List 2003; Wagenaar, Salois, and Komro 2009). We hope this chapter will complement such reviews and offer a critical perspective on the research challenges behind empirical estimates of even apparently simple economic concepts.

10.2 ECONOMIC MODELS OF SUBSTANCE USE

Economists have developed a rich set of theoretical analyses to explore consumers' decisions to use unhealthy substances or bads. A useful starting place is to consider a simple model of health-related consumption (Grossman 1972). The consumer is assumed to make choices about substance use and other consumer goods to maximize her utility. Her choices are constrained by the amount of income and time she has available, and by a health production function that shows how her choices to smoke, drink, and so on are related to health consequences. The mathematical condition for the optimization problem is the commonsense rule that the consumer should use the substance until the expected marginal benefits just equal the expected marginal costs. Importantly, the marginal costs of substance use include the monetary price of the substance as well as the health costs. "Corner solutions," where the consumer chooses to consume a zero quantity, are common for many substances. Indeed, many or most consumers would probably be deterred from the use of substances like tobacco or heroin just by the health costs, even if they were available free of charge.

10.2.1 Rational Addiction

The simple economic model of consumer behavior just sketched above is a static or "timeless" model that does not explore how consumption decisions are related over time. This is an obvious limitation, particularly for the study of addictive substances. In the theory of rational addiction the consumer is assumed to make choices about substance use to maximize her lifetime utility (Becker and Murphy 1988). The consumer's preferences for consumption are related over time through the assumption that people who consumed the substance in the past and have an addictive capital stock enjoy a higher marginal utility of consuming the addictive substance today. The rational addiction model incorporates features of addiction such as tolerance and withdrawal that are used in clinical diagnostic criteria (e.g. the Diagnostic Statistical Manual of the American Psychiatric Association). However, in other ways this economics approach to addiction departs from the way many clinicians approach addiction. According to the theory of rational addiction, addictions can be healthy (e.g. exercise), unhealthy (e.g. cocaine) or unrelated to health (e.g. opera). The rational addiction model thus does not make or require strong distinctions between addictions and habits, or even between substance addictions and learning to appreciate opera. The key is that the rational addict is forward-looking and recognizes that her choices to consume today will affect her marginal utility of consuming in the future. This can be contrasted with a myopic addict who fails to look forward and ignores the future consequences of today's consumption decisions.

Becker and Murphy (1988) argue that their model of rational addiction can explain many features of addictive consumption, and generates new predictions. The model's dynamics involve two unstable steady states, one with low and one with a high level of consumption. This fits a general pattern for addictive substances, where many consumers are not addicted (at the low consumption steady state) but a minority consumes very high levels. Moreover, for a given person, a life-cycle shock such as losing a job can move the consumer from the low- to the high-consumption state. The model can explain other features of addiction such as "cold turkey" quitting. The model can be extended to allow consumers to learn about, and make mistakes regarding, their propensity to become addicted (Orphanides and Zervos 1995).

10.2.2 Time Inconsistency

Like other dynamic models in economics, the model of rational addiction assumes that when a consumer makes tradeoffs between her current and future utility, she systematically discounts the future. This preference is captured by the discount rate, which indicates the consumer's marginal rate of substitution between today's utility and future utility. However, based on research in psychology and behavioral economics, Gruber and Koszegi (2001) propose modifying the rational addiction model to incorporate hyperbolic discounting. The mathematical formulation of hyperbolic discounting means that the consumer displays a taste for immediate gratification: at any given moment, the person has an extra bias for the present period over the future. This is termed a "present bias." This results in time inconsistency: the marginal rate of substitution between periods $t+1$ and $t+2$ is different from the perspective of time t (when both $t+1$ and $t+2$ are in the future) than it will be from the perspective of time $t+1$, when period $t+1$ is the present period. The taste for immediate gratification seems to fit many addictions, and empirical estimates from the rational addiction model that do not allow for hyperbolic discounting tend to yield implausibly high discount rates. The hyperbolic discounting model also predicts that the consumer might use a self-control or commitment device to overcome her time inconsistency. For example, Hersch (2005) provides empirical evidence that smokers who plan to quit are more likely to support laws that ban smoking in public places, perhaps because these laws serve as a commitment device that will help them carry through their plans to quit.

Smoking, over-eating, and excessive drinking can be explained in part by a strong bias for consumption in the present over in the future beyond the standard discounting. Smoking, over-consuming alcohol, and over-eating are all activities that produce short-term satisfaction but longer term negative consequences. The impulsivity of present-bias leads to "time-inconsistent preferences." In the present moment persons choose to consume the substance which they later regret. This is sometimes construed as "being of two minds": the present-oriented mind wants to binge, while the future-oriented mind knows it will regret it and wishes it could exercise more self-control. There is some evidence that different parts of the brain are active in the short-term versus long-term planning activities.

10.2.3 Cue-triggered Addiction

Bernheim and Rangel (2004) develop yet another inter-temporal model of addiction that focuses on cue-triggered addiction. In their model the consumer operates in either a cold or hot mode of decision-making. In the cold mode, properly functioning decision processes lead consumers to choose their most preferred alternatives. In the hot mode, the consumers' decision-making processes are dysfunctional so their decisions and preferences may diverge from that which result from decision-making in their cold period. Making decisions in the hot period can result in use of an addictive substance, e.g. even when a person would resist alcohol in the cold period, she would consume in the hot period. Similar to the idea of an addictive stock, in this model the probability of entering the hot mode is assumed to depend upon the consumer's history of substance use, as well as choice of lifestyle and random events. The addict knows that she makes bad decisions while in the hot mode, so she chooses lifestyles accordingly. For example, a recovering addict might avoid places or people associated with her former use. This feature of the model is somewhat similar to the idea of a commitment device in the hyperbolic discounting model.

10.2.4 Empirical Tests of Models of Addiction

The preceding brief overview illustrates advances in theoretical economic models to better understand addictive behavior. It is also useful at this point to provide a very brief overview of empirical tests of the different economic models of substance use. A large body of empirical work estimates the extent to which consumer demand for various substances responds to prices and public policies. Although the empirical specifications used are not necessarily tightly linked to a specific theoretical model, the empirical results provide general support for the economic approach to substance use. For example, as Grossman (2005) argues: "in my view, Becker and Murphy's main contribution is to suggest that it is a mistake to assume that addictive goods are not sensitive to price. Even if one does not accept all the aspects of their model, one can examine this proposition in the context of the standard theory of consumer behavior." Some empirical work provides more formal empirical tests, particularly of testable predictions that distinguish rational from myopic addiction. These tests provide evidence for rational (forward thinking) addiction to cigarettes, alcohol, cocaine, and coffee. However, the same empirical approach also yields evidence of rational addiction to milk, eggs, and oranges, which suggests the empirical tests as implemented to date may be problematic (Auld and Grootendorst 2004). Future empirical tests might usefully focus on other implications of the rational addiction model, including predictions that price hikes will have different impacts on demand depending upon whether they are temporary or permanent, and whether they are anticipated or unanticipated. To date, empirical tests have also not been able to test the rational addiction model against a model with hyberbolic discounting. For example, both the rational addiction and the hyperbolic model suggest that future prices matter for today's consumption and there is little empirically to select one model over the other (Gruber and Koszegi 2001). However, there may be additional tests to distinguish the models; for example, the hyperbolic discounting model predicts that consumers will invest in self-commitment devices. Similarly, evidence of behavior aimed at avoiding cues would be consistent with a cue-based model but not rational addiction.

10.3 Economic Approach to Substance Use Policy

Economics offers two types of insights into public policy towards substance use. First, welfare economics yields normative propositions about when public policies that reduce substance use will improve social welfare. Second, empirical economics provides evidence about which policies will be effective in reducing substance use and improving substance use-related outcomes. This section focuses on the welfare economics of substance use policy; the next section discusses empirical studies. Neoclassical welfare economics underlies many policy recommendations. Behavioral economics is being used more recently to forge resolutions to problems of addiction.

10.3.1 Neoclassical-based Policies

According to neoclassical welfare economics, when markets work fairly well goods and resources are allocated efficiently. Thus, the government should not intervene unless there are critical market failures. Provision of information, corrective taxes, and regulations are three broad classes of public policy approaches that address market failures relating to addictive goods. In the framework of neoclassical welfare economics, prohibition could be justified only when the market failures are so extreme that it is optimal to allocate no resources to producing the substance in question.

10.3.1.1 *Provision of Information*

In the case of addictions, one market failure could be lack of information on the long-term health costs of present consumption. Provision of information is a (neo-)classic role for government for several reasons. Accurate, accessible, and ample information can help individuals to make utility-maximizing decisions. Further, economies of scale in the development and distribution of the information make it such that a single supplier of information would be most efficient. In addition, because information is a public good, the private sector would tend to under-supply health information. Also, the possibility that private sellers might provide misleading information extends the role of the government to addressing misinformation. According to the neoclassical view, once individuals are provided with the information (and assuming no other critical market failures), they (not the government) are most capable of deciding the utility-maximizing consumption levels.

A prime example of the provision of information on the health harms of addictive substances occurred with the landmark 1964 US Surgeon General Report on smoking and health and similar reports in other countries, which publicized some of the health hazards of smoking. Mandated warning labels on tobacco and alcohol products are more recent examples of the role of the government in providing information.

10.3.1.2 *Corrective Taxation*

If a substance user imposes external costs on others, then there is a role for government to align the costs incurred by the user so that she considers the full cost to society of consumption when she decides, say, to smoke or drive drunk. Through corrective (Pigovian) excise taxes, the external costs are, in effect, internalized. The price the individual faces when buying the substance includes not only the market price, but also the tax which reflects the marginal harm imposed on society. Thus taxes on cigarettes and alcohol can help to correct the health harms of passive smoking and the risk of drunk driving that are imposed on others.

The standard neoclassical economic criteria for determining the optimal tax on a substance is that the tax should be levied to reflect the marginal negative externalities. However, it can be difficult not only to empirically estimate the size of the negative externality, but also to determine the full and appropriate range of factors to include as external costs. Attempts to quantify the external costs of smoking illustrate these challenges. An early landmark study suggested that the then prevailing tax on cigarettes was higher than the marginal negative impact imposed on society (Manning et al. 1989). This study recognized that while smokers have higher health care costs that are shared due to group health insurance coverage, they die earlier than non-smokers and are thus less likely to draw their actuarially full share from financially pooled pension plans. This "benefit" to others from the shared financial programs helped to offset the other negative externalities of smoking.

The Manning et al. study was a relatively early study and did not include a number of negative externalities that have since received more attention. These include impacts of: (1) smoking mothers on the fetus and infants; (2) passive smoke on others at home, at work, and in pubic places; (3) teen smoking on their peers; (4) family smokers on others' propensity to smoke (Falba and Sindelar 2008); and (5) the impact of other regulations such as smoking bans.

In a more recent study, Sloan et al. (2004) provide estimates of the marginal per pack social cost imposed by smokers. They estimate that the external costs typically measures are valued at $2.20 per pack. However, to the extent that current life insurance plans charge a premium for smokers, the externalities are dramatically reduced. Sloan et al. (2004) also values the impact on family members other than the smoker and terms these "quasi-external" costs. They estimate that these quasi-externalities borne by family members (e.g. second-hand smoke and harm to the fetus of pregnant women smoking) are relatively large. When these are also considered, Sloan et al. find that current tobacco taxes are not high enough to reflect the full set of external effects.

In addition to the challenges of correctly estimating the external costs of substance use, there are additional challenges to implement optimal corrective taxes. Because taxation is often a blunt instrument, it can be difficult to levy a tax that exactly matches the marginal social cost to each drink or cigarette. Deadweight loss can occur with alcohol taxation because only some drinkers impose negative externalities on others (Pogue and Sgontz 1989; Kenkel 1996). Drunk drivers pose a risk to others on the road while an individual having a glass of wine at home at dinner may not. In contrast, most smokers impose harm on others through second-hand smoke, risk of fire, and collectively financed medical care.

Regressivity and revenue also come into play in discussions of the optimal taxes on substances (e.g. Remler 2004; Colman and Remler 2008). The revenues from tobacco and alcohol excise taxes are appealing to the government. They provide a steady stream of funds. However, theses taxes are regressive as low education individuals spend a disproportionate percentage of their income on tobacco (Busch et al. 2004a). In addition, smokers in the US are likely to have lower levels of education and are more likely than average to have a mental health problem, thus the tax is likely to fall most heavily on these disadvantaged groups. On the other hand, to the extent that these populations are suffering the most harm to their health, if the tax encourages them to stop smoking, their health will benefit the most as well (Warner 2000). Colman and Remler (2008) find that while low-income smokers are somewhat more price-elastic, they are also so much more likely to smoke that the tax is nonetheless regressive.

In determination of the optimal tax, distributional issues sometimes have to be balanced against efficiency gains. For example, revenue raised through the tobacco taxes could, in theory, be used to compensate poor smokers. However, while policymakers, public health advocates, and others suggest that the revenues from sin taxes should be earmarked for addressing the "sins," economists believe that sources and uses of revenue should be separate issues. Economists argue that funds should be used to maximize the marginal societal gain, regardless of their source.

Negative externalities can alternatively be mitigated by subsidizing a good or service that reduces the externality. For example, federal and state governments subsidize drug and alcohol treatment and tobacco quit lines. Treatment for illicit drugs helps the drug user as well as victims of drug-related crime. Treatment for alcoholism can reduce drunken driving crashes that hurt others. Smoking cessation services and medications can reduce passive smoke, cigarette-related fires and the peer effect of smoking.

10.3.1.3 *Regulation*

Regulations are an alternative policy approach to address market failures. Youths are often restricted from use of addictive substances on several grounds including that they underestimate the negative impact of use. Many countries ban cigarette advertisements in most or all media (Saffer and Chaloupka 2000); alcohol advertising bans are also fairly common (Saffer 1991). Regulations that restrict the number of retailers licensed to sell alcohol and their hours of operation may help reduce the negative externalities of alcohol abuse. Regulations can target the sources of external costs such as drunken driving laws reduce externalities (Kenkel 1993). Similarly, as noted above, regulating or banning smoking in public places targets an important source of external costs from smoking. Calculations of the optimal tax on alcohol or cigarettes should take into account other public policies, for example Kenkel (1996) finds that with tough drunk driving laws, the optimal tax on alcohol is lower. Regulations can also require, rather than prohibit, certain behavior. For example, drug offenders and drunk drivers sometimes must seek treatment.

10.3.1.4 *Prohibition*

Prohibiting use is a more stringent form of regulation which has been used over time, for youths and specific drugs. The federal government has made the sale and use of some drugs illegal for all ages and in all circumstances. For instance, in the United States the sale and use of cocaine and heroin is illegal and punishable by prison and sentencing. Morphine and oxycotin, by contrast, are sold legally when prescribed by a physician; in other cases, sale and use are illegal. Methadone can be provided by licensed clinics, but black market and street market sales are illegal. The welfare impact of the criminalization of drugs is a hotly debated policy issue with many suggesting that the negative externalities associated with this prohibition outweigh the gains.

10.3.2 Behavioral Economics and Public Policy

The relatively new field of behavioral economics, which combines psychology and economics, provides insights into addictive behavior and helps provide the basis for policies to combat addiction and adverse health habits. The new view advocated in the field of behavioral economics is that government can use knowledge of the addicted individuals' predictable misperceptions, errors in judgment and lack of will-power to design effective interventions that improve welfare.

Instead of assuming that individuals are strictly rational, psychologists and behavioral economists have documented that individuals sometimes behave in seemingly irrational, but still often predictable, ways. Pouring out a bottle of alcohol to prevent drinking but then going out to buy another would be one example. Further, a person's willingness and ability to make the full set of calculations necessary to maximize lifetime utility are bounded. This concept is termed "bounded rationality" (Kahneman and Tversky 2000). Daniel Kahneman, psychologist, shared the Nobel Prize in Economics in 2002 with Vernon Smith, an economist, for work in this area. Bounded rationality implies that people cannot always make decisions in their own best interest, even using their *own* criteria as to what would be best for them.

Further, lack of will-power to follow through on decisions is also thought to affect behavior, especially with regard to addictive substances. Lack of will-power leads individuals to seek ways to "pre-commit" to certain behavior, such as abstaining from smoking or drinking. This may explain why smokers support restrictions on smoking in worksites and public places (Hersch 2005); the restrictions may deter their consumption even though they suffer from low will-power. Gamblers, for example, will put themselves on black ball list at casinos because they know that they cannot control their own gambling obsession.

Behavioral economists include other elements of psychology as well as economics in analyzing issues and formulating solutions. For example framing of decisions and the salience of impacts of decisions have been found to affect decision-making. Consequently, these factors have been used in forging policy solutions. For example, it is thought that it is not only the content of information that affects decisions, but also how the information is framed and presented. Some countries, e.g. Canada and Singapore, require graphic warning labels to be put on cigarette packs rather than simply providing factual information.

The behavioral economics perspective provides an expanded view of the role of government in affecting individual decision-making, especially with respect to addictions and health habits. The government can identify and address situations in which the individual systematically makes "irrational" or biased decisions and could benefit from improved self-control. This expanded role of government contrasts to the neoclassical perspective which contends that government should not interfere in individual decisions because individuals know best their preferences, and even if individuals make mistakes, the government would not do better on average. From the neoclassical perspective, expanding beyond the realm of correcting market failures would be paternalistic and counterproductive. However, according to behavioral economics, helping people make and implement decisions is not always paternalistic, can be unavoidable, and should be done by addressing systematic biases (see for instance Camerer et al. 2003.) Asymmetric policies that help those who most need and want help while not distorting choices of others may be best at maximizing overall welfare (O'Donoghue and Rabin 2003).

The behavioral economic view is that systematic biases can be harnessed to develop effective policies and interventions. For example, if the present-bias always results in failed attempts to quit, then the solution may be to make the decision to abstain more attractive to counterweight the present bias. One example discussed below is to pay people to abstain from substance use. Another example might be drug courts that allow an arrested drug user to avoid jail by getting treatment and abstaining from drug use. Lack of will-power may also systematically occur in predictable situations, for example, when addicted individuals see cues that arouse their desires to smoke, drink, or use drugs. Smoking bans may help indirectly people stop smoking by preventing smokers from seeing others smoke in public places thus enabling them to more easily avoid cues that arouse their own desire to smoke.

10.3.3 Welfare Effects of Public Policies

The alternative models of addiction have different welfare predictions and policy prescriptions. For example, taxing cigarettes could be welfare enhancing if it is correcting for externalities and/or if it is serving as a pre-commitment device. However, the optimal level of taxation might be different under each model of behavior. The standard neoclassical model suggests that the optimal tax on addictive negative habits should depend only on externalities. In contrast, the time-inconsistent (e.g. present biased or hyperbolic discounting) model would suggests that "internalities" that users impose on themselves could be considered as well in calculating the optimal tax level as well (Gruber 2002). For example, Gruber and Koszegi (2000) found that under the time-inconsistent model, internalities are about $30 per pack of cigarettes, which is 100 times the size of the estimated externalities from smoking. However, using cues-based model of addiction, one would conclude that taxes in excess of externalities would distort "cold state" choices without reducing problematic "hot state" usage by much.

Whether provision of information would be a welfare-enhancing policy and how to provide the information would also depend on the assumed model. If individuals lack will-power, not information, then additional information will not likely improve welfare. Similarly, if it is not strictly availability of information but rather ability to accurately perceive information, provision of information per se will not enhance welfare. Individuals may perceive information in a biased way (Viscusi 1992; Sloan et al. 2004).

While people sometimes overestimate the risks of smoking for the average smoker, smokers inaccurately report that their personal risks are lower than the average smoker, and only slightly above the risks of non-smokers. Youths inaccurately report that they will be able to stop smoking when they want. Alternatively, even a highly knowledgeable addict may make poor choices in hot mode.

Time-inconsistency, cue-based model, and lack of will-power all suggest that some regulations that restrict access could enhance welfare. For instance, increasing the difficulty of obtaining an addictive substance on short notice while in "hot state" could enhance welfare. Example of restrictions on access include: hours and age restrictions on access to alcohol and tobacco; smoking bans; and making the use and sale of certain drugs illegal. All of these policies may be particularly important for reducing substance use during hot periods. In contrast, if the demand for addictive substances is rational, then such restrictions would reduce the welfare of users, even though they would address some negative externalities.

Whether a policy is welfare enhancing depends in part on the underlying model of addictive behavior and health habits. However, as indicated above, empirical analysis has been unable to identify which model is the most appropriate and compelling.

10.4 EMPIRICAL RESEARCH INTO THE ECONOMICS OF SUBSTANCE USE

In addition to developments in theoretical approaches and the welfare economics of substance use, there is a large and growing body of empirical research into the economics of substance use. Our intent here is to highlight important issues in several strands of empirical research, including: the impact of cigarette taxes and other tobacco control policies on smoking; the relationships between alcohol consumption and adverse health and social outcomes; and behavioral economic research on substance abuse interventions. The discussion is intended to showcase interesting research and issues, but is far from comprehensive. Space constraints preclude discussion of many additional empirical studies that explore a variety of fascinating questions about the economics of substance use.

10.4.1 Cigarette Taxes and Smoking Bans

Federal, state, and some city governments have implemented policies to reduce smoking and to mitigate the impact of smoking on non-smokers. The arsenal of policies to reduce tobacco use is broad and drawn largely (but not exclusively) from the areas discussed above: provision of information, regulation and taxation. Most of the empirical research relates to taxation, so we focus primarily on the impact of taxation. There is a smaller literature on smoking bans which we discuss briefly. Taxation and bans on smoking are considered to be two of the more powerful public policies to address tobacco use.

10.4.1.1 *Taxation*

Typically, empirical economic research does not address the normative questions from welfare economics about the proper role of government in tobacco control. Instead, the research attempts to answer apparently simpler and more practical questions such the extent to which tobacco taxes reduce the number of smokers and the quantity of cigarettes smoked. The answers to these depend on the price-elasticity of demand. The more price-elastic the demand, the more likely smokers are to quit smoking and cut back in quantity, and the less likely non-smokers are to initiate smoking or relapse after quitting. A consensus about the price-elasticity would aid policymaking, however, research in this area is evolving.

With that caveat in mind, the large body of empirical studies on cigarette demand are often seen as reaching a consensus that the overall price-elasticity of demand is in the relatively narrow range of −0.3 to −0.5 (Manning et al. 1989; Viscusi 1992; Chaloupka and Warner 2000; Gallet and List 2003). According to this consensus, cigarette demand is inelastic, but not perfectly so. As a result, tax increases would be expected to modestly reduce smoking and yield increased revenues. This combination is attractive to public health policymakers. Research on the price-elasticity of cigarette demand in population sub-groups is thinner. Some reviews claim that there is also a consensus that youth smoking is substantially more price-elastic than adult smoking (e.g. Chaloupka and Warner 2000). However, a number of recent studies that use longitudinal data find evidence that higher prices increase cessation but have little or no impact on smoking initiation in the US (Douglas and Hariharan 1994; Douglas 1998; DeCicca, Kenkel, and Mathios 2002, 2008), Britain (Forster and Jones 2001), and Spain (Nicolas 2002). These findings suggest that taxes may not be as effective as previously thought in preventing initiation and, in general, protecting youths. Studies have also analyzed price-elasticity differences by education, income, gender, and race/ethnicity (e.g. Farrelly et al. 1998; Stehr 2007; Colman and Remler 2008). The results of these studies are more often conflicting about which population sub-groups have more or less price-elastic cigarette demand.

There have been several important developments in empirical economic research on the price-elasticity of smoking. First, there has been steady progress in the available data. Instead of national or state-level aggregate sales data, increasingly researchers use individual-level data from either cross-sectional or longitudinal surveys. Second, appropriate econometric modeling has progressed as richer data have become available. The analysis of aggregate data only provides estimates of how total cigarette sales vary with the average price of cigarettes. With cross-sectional data, the standard econometric approach often uses a two-part model. The two-part model provides separate estimates of the price-elasticity of smoking participation, and the price-elasticity of daily cigarette consumption, conditional on participation. With longitudinal data, it is possible to decompose smoking participation into two separate processes—the decision to start smoking and the decision to quit—in which each are possibly governed by different factors (DeCicca, Kenkel, and Mathios 2008). For youths, both decisions are critical; for adults, the decision process differs. As almost no adults initiate smoking for the first time, their participation relates more closely to the decision to quit and the ability to remain smoke-free without relapse (Ayyagari and Sindelar 2008).

In 2000, an estimated 70 percent of smokers said they wanted to quit, and 41 percent had tried to quit during the preceding year; however, only some quit successfully and a large number of these relapse. Becker and Murphy (1988: 693) point out that rationality does not rule out the possibility that smokers may have to experiment and fail before they learn a successful method to quit. Alternatively, this behavior might be better understood in terms of behavioral economics with its emphasis on self-control problems, relapse in response to cues, and the consequent demand for pre-commitment devices. With regard to cues of a different sort, Avery et al. 2007 found that advertising of smoking cessation products encouraged smokers to quit both directly because they bought and used these products and indirectly, possibly as reminders or cues to stop smoking.

As in other areas of empirical microeconomics, recent empirical research also increasingly focuses on estimating the causal effect of cigarette prices on smoking. Much of the variation in cigarette prices stems from variation in cigarette tax rates across jurisdictions or over time. Cigarette tax rates are not randomly set, but arise from political processes: for example, across US states and European countries, cigarette taxes tend to be low in tobacco-producing regions. Thus, cigarette tax levels may be aligned with hard-to-observe factors such as anti-smoking sentiment, confounding the relationship between taxation and smoking rates. Some recent studies address this concern by relying on repeated cross-sections (Farrelly et al. 2001; Gruber and Zinman 2001). Such studies can then include state fixed effect variables to control for hard-to-observe influences such as state anti-smoking sentiment. This general approach faces a dilemma. On the one hand, there may be insufficient within-state variation in taxes or prices to allow precise estimates. On the other hand, the within-state variation that does exist may itself be associated with changes in unobserved influences. As another approach, DeCicca et al. (2008) develop a direct measure of state anti-smoking sentiment, and include it as a control variable in their models of youth smoking.

10.4.1.2 Smoking Bans

In addition to cigarette taxes, empirical economic research investigates the impact of many other tobacco control policies on smoking. Cities, states, and countries around the world have passed clean indoor air laws in increasing numbers (USDHHS 2000). The Adda and Cornaglia (2006) study stands out among health economic studies for its use of a direct measure of passive smoke. Their study examined cotinine (a metabolite of nicotine) and showed that on average, smoking bans have no impact on the exposure of non-smokers. However, by evaluating smoking bans by setting they found that laws that ban smoking in shopping malls, schools, and public transportation reduce exposure, while bans in recreational public places increase exposure. Their interpretation is that recreational bans drive smokers to smoke in private places, thus increasing family members', especially children's, exposure to environmental tobacco smoke. Other indirect effects / unintended consequences of bans have been shown to include: (1) more intensive (compensatory) smoking by smokers (Adda and Cornaglia 2007); (2) a reduction in the demand for alcohol, a potential complement to smoking (Picone et al. 2004; Gallet and Eastman 2007); and (3) an increase in alcohol-related traffic fatalities following bans on smoking in bars, perhaps due to increased miles driven by drivers wishing to smoke and drink (Adams and Cotti 2008).

The precursor to public bans was private bans in the workplace. In one of the first national evaluations of workplace smoking bans, Evans et al. 1999 found that workplace bans reduced smoking prevalence as well as the number of cigarettes smoked by those who continued to smoke. While they found that workplace bans were more likely to be adopted in firms where workers had better health habits, their results were largely robust to this potential endogeneity of the bans. A similar selection bias may apply to public bans as well as tobacco taxes, as indicated above.

10.4.2 Alcohol Consumption and Adverse Health and Social Outcomes

Alcohol consumption presents more complex analytical problems as compared to smoking because most drinking is without negative consequences, while some has adverse externalities and internalities. In the US and many other countries, most adults drink alcoholic beverages, and most drinking is not harmful. In fact, it is increasingly well-established that moderate consumption of alcohol reduces cardiovascular health risks (NIAAA 2003). At the same time, alcohol abuse and dependence pose major health risks (NIAAA 2000). In the US, alcohol is involved in about 40 percent of traffic fatalities. Long-term alcohol abuse exerts harmful effects on many of the human body's organ systems, including the liver and the immune, cardiovascular, and skeletal systems.

An active line of empirical economic research focuses on the relationships between alcohol consumption and health-related outcomes such as traffic fatalities and unsafe sexual activity, as well as social outcomes including unemployment, reduced earnings, lowered schooling attainment, and criminal activity. Empirical research has addressed two types of questions about the relationships between alcohol and adverse outcomes. First, some studies focus on the policy question of whether alcohol control policies such as excise taxes reduce adverse outcomes. Second, other studies focus on the related social science question of whether excessive alcohol consumption plays a causal role as a determinant of adverse outcomes.

Making sense of the complex empirical relationships between alcohol control policies, alcohol consumption, and various outcomes requires careful and sophisticated econometric analysis, guided by an appropriate conceptual framework. Economic models of household production provide an appropriate conceptual framework for the analysis of many alcohol-related outcomes. For example, econometric studies of drunk driving conceptualize alcohol consumption as an input with a negative marginal product in the household production of traffic safety. Similarly, the commonsense idea that alcohol has a negative marginal product in the production of human capital motivates studies of the impact on drinking on schooling. Bray (2005) specifies a model of alcohol's impact on wages through its effect on the formation and accumulation of human capital.

The conceptual framework implies a simple structural econometric model consisting of two equations: a demand function that shows drinking as a function of alcohol taxes and other policies; and a production function that shows an outcome (such as traffic safety or human capital formation) as a function of drinking. Studies that focus on policy questions often substitute the demand function into the production function, to yield a reduced-form equation that shows an outcome like traffic safety as a function of alcohol taxes and other policies. This approach is useful for policy analysis, because it provides a direct estimate of the impact of a policy-manipulable variable like taxes on outcomes of interest. Studies that focus on social science questions also use the structural approach to estimate a structural equation that shows a causal effect of alcohol consumption on the outcome in question.

Policy-focused studies in health economics have contributed useful estimates of links between various alcohol control policies and various outcomes. Saffer and Grossman (1987) spell out the reduced-form approach in their study of the impact of beer taxes and the legal drinking age on youth traffic fatalities. Their estimates imply that a combination of a uniform drinking age of 21 and a beer tax increase could have reduced youth traffic fatalities by 54 percent. Examining the same policies but another outcome, in their reduced-form work Cook and Moore (1993) estimate that higher drinking ages and higher beer taxes increase the probability that adolescents eventually graduate college. Carpenter (2005) estimates the reduced-form relationship between underage drunk driving laws (known as zero tolerance laws) and the rate of sexually transmitted diseases. He finds that these laws reduce the gonorrhea rate among white male teenagers by about 14 percent. The plausibility of this reduced-form relationship is supported by previous research suggesting alcohol abuse is a risk factor for unsafe sexual activity, and by Carpenter's (2004) previous finding that zero tolerance laws reduce heavy episodic drinking by young males by 13 percent.

Most recent empirical studies that take a more structural approach use the method of instrumental variables (IV) to estimate the causal treatment effects of drinking on outcomes. The IV method is necessary because observed statistical associations between excessive alcohol consumption and adverse outcomes do not necessarily reflect causation. One problem is that important unobservable factors might jointly determine drinking and outcomes, so the associations are spurious, not causal. For example, Kenkel and Ribar (1994) suggest that deficient childhood backgrounds or personality disorders might be important unobservable factors driving the negative relationship between alcoholism and earnings. The IV method exploits the exogenous variation in the IVs as natural or quasi-natural experiments that create variation in drinking that is uncontaminated by unobserved individual factors that jointly drinking and outcomes. Since 1990 or so the economics profession has made important advances in understanding the properties of the IV method in practical applications. Much of the attention has focused on the problem of establishing the validity of the instrument and on the weak IV problem (Murray 2006). Another line of econometric research extends the IV approach to applications with heterogeneous treatment effects (Auld 2006). Yet another active line of econometric research focuses on the application of the IV method to inherently nonlinear models (Angrist 2001; Bhattacharya, Goldman, and McCaffery 2006; Terza, Bradford, and Dismuke 2008). These applied econometric problems—the suitability and strength of the IVs, heterogeneous treatment effects, and non-linearities—are often relevant for IV studies of alcohol-related problems. Recent econometric advances open up some important lines of inquiry for future studies of alcohol-related problems.

Although some econometric issues remain, the IV method is especially well-established in US studies of the impact of problem drinking on labor market outcomes such as earnings and unemployment (Kenkel and Ribar 1994; Mullahy and Sindelar 1996; Terza 2002). More recently, this line of research has been extended to study the labor market consequences of problem drinking in other countries, including the UK (MacDonald and Shields 2001, 2004), the Netherlands (van Ours 2004), and Finland (Johansson et al. 2007). The method has also been applied to study other outcomes including the consequences of underage drinking, such as delayed high-school graduation (Renna 2007) and delinquency and criminal activity (French and Maclean 2006). Taken together, this body of econometric research supports a general consensus that problem drinking has serious labor market consequences.

Empirical research also sheds light on the complexity of the relationships between alcohol consumption and labor market consequences. The complexity is partly but not entirely due to the distinction between moderate and abusive alcohol consumption. For example, the negative relationships between alcoholism and earnings appear to vary by gender and across the life-cycle (Mullahy and Sindelar 1991, 1993). More surprisingly, a series of studies provide evidence that drinkers earn more than their non-drinking peers (Berger and Leigh 1988; French and Zarkin 1995; Zarkin et al. 1998; MacDonald and Shields 2001; and van Ours 2004). These findings suggest that while abusive alcohol consumption might be penalized in the labor market, moderate drinkers might earn more than non-drinkers because they are healthier.

Although empirical economic studies of alcohol-related problems explicitly or implicitly refer to models of individual behavior, it should be kept in mind that the observed data are equilibrium outcomes. For example, alcohol's impact on wages reflects not only alcohol's impact on the individual's productivity, but also the extent to which the labor market penalizes low productivity. This leads to the testable prediction that problem drinkers will tend to face larger wage losses in flexible labor markets than in labor markets with long-term union contracts or other rigidities. The importance of equilibrium behavior is not confined to labor markets. Traffic safety provides a non-market example. Because they expect many impaired drives to be on the road after New Year's Eve parties, many non-drinkers refrain from driving or drive especially cautiously on New Year's Eve. These endogenous responses will tend to mask the true structural relationship between an individual's drinking and driving ability. Similarly, the observed relationship between alcohol consumption and crime reflects the endogenous behavior of both criminal offenders and their potential victims. Alcohol-abusing potential victims may take fewer precautions, making them more vulnerable. In this situation there are two channels for alcohol control policies to reduce crime through reducing excessive alcohol consumption: by reducing criminal behavior; and by increasing precautionary behavior among potential crime victims.

10.4.3 Alcohol Taxes

Assessing the optimal tax for alcohol is complicated by the fact that most drinking is not harmful and thus a tax on alcohol will engender both deadweight losses and as well as gains from the reduction in externalities. A first step in assessing the welfare impact is to estimate the overall impact of taxes on alcohol demand and then to estimate the heterogeneity by groups. There is considerable range in estimates of the price-elasticity of demand for alcohol with variation likely attributable to data type (aggregated or individual) and source (national, cross-sectional), age groups (often youths), measure of consumption, price (beer, wine or spirits, separately or an average), use of tax rate versus price, econometric methods and other factors. Wagenaar et al. (2009) conduct a formal meta-analysis and review of 1003 estimates of the price and tax elasticities of demand for alcohol from 112 studies. See also Leung and Phelps (1993) for an earlier review. Grossman et al. (1998) review the evidence for youths specifically. Wagenaar et al. conclude that alcohol prices and tax rates significantly reduce consumption of alcohol. Using the simple mean effect across all of the studies, they find price-elasticities for beer, wine, and spirits to be respectively: $-.46, -.69,$ and $-.80$. Using more-sophisticated meta-analysis techniques, including weighting the study outcomes by the precision of the estimates, they find smaller estimates of the elasticities. Specifically they find the elasticities for beer, wine, and spirits to be respectively: $-.17, -.30$ and $-.29$. They estimate the overall price-elasticity for alcohol to be $-.44$ based on studies using aggregate level data and $-.03$ for studies using individual level data. For heavy drinkers, the elasticity is estimated to be $-.28$.

While these meta-estimates are extremely useful benchmarks, there is potential heterogeneity by age, race, and tax versus price of alcohol that are masked. For example using data from the 1993 NHIS and self-reported number of days with five or more drinks, Kenkel (1996) finds the elasticity of $-.5$ for men and more than double this for women (-1.3). For youths, while most studies find that the initiation of use of alcohol, the amount consumed conditional on drinking and the overall drinking rate are sensitive to price, statistically significant effects are not always found (Chaloupka and Wechsler 1996). Manning et al. (1995) find that the price-elasticity of demand for alcohol varies by consumption levels. They use a two-part model and find that the price-elasticity for the number of drinks, conditional on being a drinker is insignificantly different from zero while price significantly affects the decision to drink (elasticity of $-.55$). Using quantile regression they find that the most price responsive drinkers are the moderate drinkers. The median drinker has a price-elasticity of -1.19. The lowest quan-

tile drinker has a price-elasticity of −0.55 while the heaviest two quantiles have elasticities of −0.49 and 0.12 respectively; all but the latter are significant. Manning et al.
conclude that there is heterogeneity in the price-elasticities and that failure to differentiate these groups could conceal important policy-relevant information.

Using both the Panel Study of Income Dynamics (PSID) and the Health and
Retirement Study (HRS), Dave and Saffer (2007) find the drinking participation elasticity to be between −.05 and −.04 for younger individuals in the PSID, and −.22 to −.11 for
HRS participants over age 55. Conditional on being a drinker, the tax elasticity of conditional demand (measured as the average number of drinks per day) is estimated to be
between −.08 to −.27 depending on the specification. Chronic drinkers have a tax elasticity on this intensive margin of −.27 indicating that even heavy drinkers are at least as,
if not more, price sensitive than other drinkers. This contrasts to the findings of Manning
et al. above in which the moderate drinkers were found to be the most price sensitive.
Also using the HRS, Ayyagari et al. 2009, find heterogeneity in the price-elasticity across
latent groups-based using finite mixture models. One latent group is significantly
responsive to price but the other is unresponsive. Differences between these two groups
can be explained in part by the behavioral factors of risk aversion, financial planning
horizon, forward looking, and locus of control.

10.4.4 Behavioral Economic Research and Substance Abuse Interventions

10.4.4.1 *Present-bias and Small Incentives Change Behavior*

Present-bias can explain why smokers who want to quit do not and why individuals who
want to restrain their alcohol intake, say at a party, fail to do so. Behavioral economics
suggests that by changing the incentives to give extra incentives to resist harmful behavior, the present-bias may be at least partially overcome.

A large number of studies have shown that an incentive system designed to give small
payments conditional on abstaining from smoking or using illicit drugs can help users
abstain. Immediate payments conditional on the "pro-social" behavior of abstaining is
used to align the consequences of long-term behaviors with the consequences for current behaviors. One line of research analyzes the effectiveness of reducing drug use by
paying drug users to abstain from using drugs (for a review, see Lussier et al. 2006). This
strategy, in which small but escalating payments are given conditional on objective
measures of abstaining, is known as contingency management (Petry et al. 2005;
Sindelar, Elbel, et al. 2007; and Sindelar, Olmstead, et al. 2007). It is surprising that such
small payments can make a big difference given that the real gains to quitting are much
higher. Drug users are at higher risk of death from overdose, contracting HIV/AIDS and
sexually transmitted disease, losing their job, experiencing family disruptions, and being
arrested. That such small payments are effective at improving cessation when such huge
potential health and social benefits are not can be explained better by behavioral

economics than by neoclassical economics. The small payment bolsters will-power and tips the scales in favor of short-term abstaining to gain the long-run goal of permanent abstinence. Other studies indicate the effectiveness of similar incentive payments in smoking cessation (Volpp et al. 2006; Finkelstein et al. 2007).

10.4.4.2 *Lack of Will-power and Pre-commitment Mechanisms*

Even if individuals make utility-maximizing decisions carefully, they may not have the will-power to follow through on their own decisions. Self-control is needed to enact utility-maximizing decisions; however, self-control is in short supply. Although economists model self-control through use of discount rates, psychologists conceive self-control problems as a lack of will-power (Baumeister and Vohs 2003). Smokers who are trying to quit often start smoking again when they see cues, even cues as small as an ash tray, which arouse their desire to smoke. Cues trigger emotional states and make resisting temptation more difficult. In cold periods, individuals may decide they will no longer indulge. But when triggered by situational cues, e.g. in a hot state, the person drinks more than she had planned. This lack of self-control dooms attempts to quit smoking, using drugs, and abusing alcohol.

Pre-commitment devices are demanded in so-called "cold" periods so that the person does not succumb to the addiction in the later "hot" periods of arousal. Individuals who give in to cues in hot periods repeatedly may realize the same problem is going to happen again and again. In a "cold" period, they may choose to enroll in a treatment program or may take advantage of "pre-commitment devices." In the behavioral economics literature, the smokers, drinkers, and drug users who realize that they are going to succumb to the addictive substance are called "sophisticates" because they realize their tendencies and take preventive steps. In contrast, so-called "naives" are oblivious of this failing of theirs and cannot plan ahead to address the inevitable use of drugs.

Moving to a dry county in which alcohol is not sold may serve as a pre-commitment device that reduces the opportunity to drink on short notice. Similarly, finding a job in smoke-free environment would aid smoking cessation. A surprising number of smokers have been found to favor higher taxes on cigarettes—across a number of state polls on average 38 percent of smokers favored higher cigarette taxes (Campaign for Tobacco Free Kids 2008)—and bans on smoking in public places (Hersch 2005). The smoking ban not only makes it more difficult for the smoker to light up, it also reduces environmental cues as others cannot smoke either. This smokers' support for constraints on smoking is harder to explain in a neoclassic framework because the option to smoke has value and self-control is not considered to be an issue. The support for such restraints is perhaps better understood as a pre-commitment device for smokers would who like to quit but find it difficult. This could be consistent with the "dual self" model, hyperbolic discounting and cues hot and cold model. Smokers, drinkers, and drug users who want to quit or cut back, and also know that they may lose the self-control to do so in response to certain cues and situations, may seek to avoid situations and/or take advantage of pre-commitment devices.

10.5 SUMMARY

Smoking, alcohol abuse, and use of illicit drugs are critical social problems. Economists have addressed these issues through modeling of addictive behaviors, positing policies, analyzing responses to policies, and assessing the welfare implications of policies. Taxation of tobacco and alcohol has been a frequent topic of empirical studies in economics in part because taxation addresses negative externalities, an important market failure. Relatively recently, behavioral economics has added new dimensions to the role of taxation including incorporation of "internalities" and considering taxation as a pre-commitment devices and addressing "internalities" as well. Other forms of government intervention have also been suggested based on models of addiction that supplement or replace the neoclassical decision-making model as applied to addictive substances. Smoking bans and other restrictions may deter individuals from obtaining substances in so-called "hot" periods in which their decision-making abilities may be reduced. Empirical evidence on public policies, especially the tax elasticity of demand paves the way for more precise welfare evaluations. Literature in these areas is getting more sophisticated in terms of econometric approaches (in particular in addressing causality) and also in assessing the heterogeneity of impacts. Future research could also apply these approaches and findings to other addictions such as over-eating, gambling, and misuse of prescription drugs. These areas are ripe for theoretical, empirical, and policy-related research.

REFERENCES

ADAMS, SCOTT and COTTI, CHAD (2008), "Drunk Driving After the Passage of Smoking Bans in Bars," *Journal of Public Economics*, 92: 1288–305.

—— BERLINSKY, S., and MACHIN, S. (2007), "Short-run Economic Effects of the Scottish Smoking Ban," *International Journal of Epidemiology*, 36(1):149–54. (*IJE* Advance Access originally published online on December 14, 2006.)

ADDA, J. and CORNAGLIA, F. (2010), "The Effect of Taxes and Bans on Passive Smoking," *The American Economic Journal: Applied Economics*, January, 2(1): 1–32.

ANGRIST, J. (2001), "Estimation of Limited Dependent Variable Models with Dummy Endogenous Regressors: Simple Strategies for Empirical Practice," *Journal of Business & Economic Statistics*, 19(1): 2–16.

AULD, M. C. (2006), "Using Observational Data to Identify the Causal Effects of Health-related Behavior," in A. M. Jones (ed.), *The Elgar Companion to Health Economics* (Cheltenham, UK: Edward Elgar Publishing).

—— and GROOTENDORST, P. (2004), "An Empirical Analysis of Milk Addiction," *Journal of Health Economics*, 23(6): 1117–33.

AVERY, ROSEMARY, KENKEL, DONALD, LILLARD, DEAN, and MATHIOS, ALAN (2007), "Private Profits and Public Health: Does Advertising Smoking Cessation Products Encourage Smokers to Quit?" *Journal of Political Economy*, 115(3): 447–81.

AYYAGARI, PADMAJA and SINDELAR, JODY L. (2008), "Smoking, Stress and Self-control." Working Paper Series rwp08-018.

AYYAGARI, P., DEB, P., FLETCHER, J., GALLO, W. T., and SINDELAR, J. L. (2009), "Sin Taxes: Do Heterogeneous Responses Undercut Their value?" NBER Working Paper w15124.

BAUMEISTER, R. F. and VOHS, K. D. (2003), "Time and Decision: Economic and Psychological Perspectives on Intertemporal Choice. Will-power, Choice, and Self-control," in G. Lowenstein, D. Read, and R. F. Baumeister (eds.), *Time and Decision: Economic and Psychological Perspectives on Intertemporal Choice* (New York: Russell Sage Foundation Press).

BECKER, G. S. and MURPHY, K. M. (1988), "A Theory of Rational Addiction," *Journal of Political Economy*, 96(4): 675–700.

BERGER, M. and LEIGH, J. P. (1988). "The Effect of Alcohol Use on Wages," *Applied Economics*, October, 20: 1343–51.

BERNHEIM, DOUGLAS, B., and RANGEL, ANTONIO (2004), "Addiction and Cue-triggered Decision Processes," *American Economic Review*, 94(5) (Dec.): 1558–90.

BHATTACHARYA, J., GOLDMAN, D., and McCAFFREY, D. (2006), "Estimating Probit Models with Self-Selected Treatments," *Statistics in Medicine*, 25: 389–413.

BRAY, J. W. (2005), "Alcohol Use, Human Capital, and Wages," *Journal of Labor Economics*, 23(2): 279–312.

BUSCH, S., JOFRE-BONET, M., FALBA, T., and SINDELAR, J. L. (2004a), "Burning a Hole in the Budget: Tobacco Spending and its Crowd-Out of Other Goods," *Applied Health Economics and Health Policy*, 3(4): 263–72.

—— FALBA, T., DUCHOVNY, N., JOFRE-BONET, M.,O'MALLEY, S., and SINDELAR, J. L. (2004b). "Value to Smokers of Improved Cessation Products: Evidence from a Willingness-to-Pay Survey," *Nicotine and Tobacco Research*, 6(4): 631–9.

CAMERER, C., ISSACHAROFF, S., LOEWENSTEIN, G., O'DONOGHUE, T., and RABIN, M. (2003), "Regulation for Conservatives: Behavioral Economics and the Case for 'Asymmetric Paternalism,'" *University of Pennsylvania Law Review*, 151(3): 1211–54.

CAMPAIGN FOR TOBACCO FREE KIDS (2008), "Voters in All States Support Significant Increases in State Cigarette Taxes." <www.tobaccofreekids.org> accessed Aug. 25, 2009.

CARPENTER, C. (2004), "How do Zero Tolerance Drunk Driving Laws work?" *Journal of Health Economics*, 23: 61–83.

—— (2005), "Youth Alcohol Use and Risky Sexual Behavior: Evidence from Underage Drunk Driving Laws," *Journal of Health Economics*, 24: 613–28.

CHALOUPKA, F. J. and GROSSMAN, M. (1996), "Price, Tobacco Control Policies and Youth Smoking." Working paper 5740, National Bureau of Economic Research, New York.

—— (1997), "Price, Tobacco Control Policies and Smoking Among Young Adults," *Journal of Health Economics*, 16: 359–73.

—— and WARNER, KENNETH E. (2000), "The Economics of Smoking," in J. P. Newhouse and A. J. Culyer (eds.), *Handbook of Health Economics*, Vol. 1B (Amsterdam: North-Holland).

—— and WESCHLER, H. (1996), "Binge Drinking in College: The Impact of Price, Availability, and Alcohol Control Policies," *Contemporary Economic Policy*, 14(4): 112–24.

COLMAN, G. J. and REMLER, D. K. (2008), "Vertical Equity Consequences of Very High Cigarette Tax Increases: If the Poor are the Ones Smoking, How Could Cigarette Tax Increases be Progressive?" *Journal of Policy Analysis and Management*, 27(2): 376–400.

COOK, P. J. and MOORE, M. J. (1993), "Drinking and Schooling," *Journal of Health Economics*, 12(4): 411–30.

DAVE, D. and SAFFER, H. (2007), "Risk Tolerance and Alcohol Demand among Adults and Older Adults." NBER Working Paper No. 13482.

DECICCA, P., KENKEL, D., and MATHIOS, A. (2002), "Putting Out the Fires: Will Higher Taxes Reduce the Onset of Youth Smoking?" *Journal of Political Economy*, 110(1): 144–69.

—— (2008), "Cigarette Taxes and the Transition from Youth to Adult Smoking: Smoking Initiation, Cessation, and Participation," *Journal of Health Economics*, 27(4): 904–17.

—— SHIN, Y.-J., and LIM, J.-Y. (2008), "Youth Smoking, Taxes, and Anti-smoking Sentiment," *Health Economics* 17(6): 733–49.

DOUGLAS, S. (1998), "The Duration of the Smoking Habit," *Economic Inquiry*, 36(1):49–64.

—— and HARIHARAN, G. (1994), "The Hazard of Starting Smoking: Estimates from a Split Population Duration Model," *Journal of Health Economics*, 18: 429–41.

EVANS, W. N., FARRELLY, M. C., and MONTGOMERY, E. (1999), "Do Workplace Smoking Bans Reduce Smoking?" *The American Economic Review*, 89(4): 728–47.

FALBA, T. A. and SINDELAR, J. L. (2008), "Spousal Concordance in Health Behavior Change," *Health Services Research*, 43(1): 96–116.

FARRELLY, M. C., BRAY, J. W., PECHACEK, T., and WOOLLERY, T. (2001), "Response by Adults to Increases in Cigarette Prices by Sociodemographic Characteristics," *Southern Economic Journal*, 68(1): 156–65.

FINKELSTEIN, E. A., LINNAN, L. A., TATE, D. F., and BIRKEN, B. E. (2007), "A Pilot Study Testing the Effect of Different Levels of Financial Incentives on Weight Loss Among Overweight Employees," *Journal of Occupational and Environmental Medicine*, 49: 981–9.

FORSTER, M. and JONES, A. M. (2001), "The Role of Tobacco Taxes in Starting and Quitting Smoking: Duration Analysis of British Data," *Journal of the Royal Statistical Society*, 164 (Series A): 517–47.

FRENCH, M. T. and MACLEAN, J. C. (2006), "Underage Alcohol Use, Delinquency, and Criminal Activity," *Health Economics*, 15: 1261–81.

—— and ZARKIN G. (1995), "Is Moderate Alcohol Use Related to Wages? Evidence from Four Worksites," *Journal of Health Economics*, 14: 319–44.

GALLET, C. and EASTMAN, H. (2007). "The Impact of Smoking Bans on Alcohol Demand," *Social Science Journal*, 44(4): 664–76.

—— and LIST, J. A. (2003) "Cigarette Demand: A Meta-analysis of Elasticities," *Health Economics*, 12: 821–35.

GROSSMAN, MICHAEL (2005), "Individual Behaviors and Substance Use: The Role of Price," in B. Lindgren and M. Grossman (eds.), *Advances in Health Economics and Health Services Research*, Vol. 16 (Amsterdam: Elsevier), 15–40.

GROSSMAN, MICHAEL, CHALOUPKA, FRANK J., and SIRTALAN, ISMAIL (1998), "An Empirical Analysis of Alcohol Addiction: Results from the Monitoring the Future Panels," *Economic Inquiry*, January, 36(1): 39–48.

GRUBER, J. (2002) "Smoking's 'Internalities,'" *Regulation*, 25(4): 25–57.

—— and KOSEGI, BOTOND (2001), "Is Addiction 'Rational'? Theory and Evidence," *Quarterly Journal of Economics*, 116(4): 1261–303.

—— and ZINMAN, JONATHAN (2001), "Youth Smoking in the US: Evidence and Implications," in Jonathan Gruber (ed.), *Risky Behavior Among Youth: An Economic Analysis* (Chicago: University of Chicago Press), 69–120.

HERSCH, J. (2005), "Smoking Restrictions as a Self-Control Mechanism," *Journal of Risk and Uncertainty*, 31(1): 5–21.

JOFRE-BONET, M. and SINDELAR, J. L. (2001), "Drug Treatment as a Crime Fighting Tool," *Journal of Mental Health Policy and Economics*, 4(4): 175–8.

JOHANSSON, E., ALHO, A., KIISKINEN, U., and POIKOLAINED, K. (2007), "The Association of Alcohol Dependency with Employment Probability: Evidence from the Population Survey 'Health 2000 in Finland,'" *Health Economics*, 16: 739–54.

KAHNEMAN, D. and TVERSKY, A. (eds.) (2000) *Choices, Values and Frames* (New York: Cambridge University, Russell Sage Foundation).

KENKEL, DONALD (1993), "Drinking, Driving, and Deterrence: The Effectiveness and Social Costs of Alternative Policies," *Journal of Law and Economics*, 36(2): 877–913.

—— (1996), "New Estimates of the Optimal Tax on Alcohol" *Economic Inquiry*, 34: 296–319.

—— and Ribar, David (1994), "Alcohol Consumption and Young Adults' Socioeconomic Status." Brookings Papers on Economic Activity-Micro, pp. 119–61.

LEUNG, S. F. and PHELPS, C. E. (1993), "My Kingdom for a Drink...? A Review of Estimates of the Price Sensitivity of Demand for Alcoholic Beverages," in M. E. Hilton and G. Bloss (eds.), *Economics and the Prevention of Alcohol-Related Problems*. NIAAA Research Monograph No. 25, NIH Pub. No. 93-3513 (Bethesda, MD: National Institute on Alcohol Abuse and Alcoholism), 1–32.

LUSSIER, J. P., HEIL, S. H., MONGEON, J. A., BADGER, G. J., and HIGGINS, S. T. (2006), "A Meta-analysis of Voucher-based Reinforcement Therapy for Substance Use Disorders," *Addiction*, 101: 192–203.

MACDONALD, Z. and SHIELDS, M. A. (2004), "Does Problem Drinking Affect Employment? Evidence from England," *Health Economics*, 13: 139–55.

—— (2001), "The Impact of Alcohol Use on Occupational Attainment in England," *Economica*, 68: 427–53.

MANNING, W. G., KEELER, E. B., NEWHOUSE, J. P., SLOSS, E. M., and WASSERMAN, J. (1989), "The Taxes of Sin: Do Smokers and Drinkers Pay Their Way?" *Journal of the American Medical Association*, 261(11): 1604–9.

—— BLUMBERG, L., and MOULTON, L. H. (1995), "The Demand for Alcohol: The Differential Response to Price," *Journal of Health Economics*, 14(2):123–48.

MULLAHY, J. and SINDELAR, J. L. (1991), "Gender Differences in Labor Market Effects of Alcoholism," *American Economic Review*, 81(2): 161–5.

—— (1993), "Alcoholism, Work and Income Over the Life Cycle," *Journal of Labor Economics*, 11(3): 494–520.

—— (1994), "Alcoholism and Income: The Role of Indirect Effects," *Milbank Quarterly*, 72(2): 359–75.

—— (1995), "Health Capital, Risk Aversion, and the Variance of Income: Assessing Some Welfare Costs of Alcoholism and Poor Health," *Journal of Human Resources*, 30(2): 439–59.

—— (1996), "Employment, Unemployment, and Problem Drinking," *Journal of Health Economics*, 15(4): 409–34.

MURRAY, M. P. (2006), "Avoiding Invalid Instruments and Coping with Weak Instruments," *Journal of Economic Perspectives*, 20(4): 111–32.

NIAAA (NATIONAL INSTITUTE ON ALCOHOL ABUSE AND ALCOHOLISM) (2000), *Tenth Special Report to the US Congress on Alcohol and Health* (Washington, DC: NIAAA).

—— (2003), *State of the Science Report on the Effects of Moderate Drinking* (Washington, DC: NIAAA).

NICOLAS, A. L. (2002), "How Important are Tobacco Prices in the Propensity to Start and Quit Smoking? An Analysis of Smoking Histories from the Spanish National Health Survey," *Health Economics*, 11: 521–35.

O'DONOGHUE, T. and RABIN, M. (2003), "Studying Optimal Paternalism, Illustrated with a Model of Sin Taxes," *AER Papers and Proceedings*, 93(2): 191.

ORPHANIDES, A. and ZERVOS, D. (1995), "Rational Addiction with Learning and Regret," *Journal of Political Economy*, 103(4): 739–58.

PICONE, G., SLOAN, F., and TROGDON, J. (2004), "The Effect of the Tobacco Settlement and Smoking Bans on Alcohol Consumption," *Health Economics*, 13: 1063–80.

POGUE, T. F. and SGONTZ, L. C. (1989), "Taxing to Control Social Costs: The Case of Alcohol," *American Economic Review*, March, 79(1): 235–43.

REMLER, D. K. (2004), "Poor Smokers, Poor Quitters, and Cigarette Tax Regressivity," *American Journal of Public Health*, 94(2): 225–9.

RENNA, F. (2007), "The Economic Cost of Teen Drinking: Late Graduation and Lowered Earnings," *Health Economics*, 16: 407–19.

PETRY, N. M., PEIRCE, J., STITZER, M. L. et al. (2005), "Prize-based Incentives Improve Outcomes of Stimulant Abusers in Outpatient Psychosocial Treatment Programs: A National Drug Abuse Treatment Clinical Trials Network Study," *Archives of General Psychiatry*, 62: 1148–56.

SAFFER, H. (1991), "Alcohol Advertising Bans and Alcohol Abuse: An International Perspective," *Journal of Health Economics*, 10(1): 65–79.

—— and CHALOUPKA, F. (2000), "The Effect of Tobacco Advertising Bans On Tobacco Consumption," *Journal of Health Economics*, 19(6): 1117–37.

—— and GROSSMAN, M. (1987), "Beer Taxes, the Legal Drinking Age, and Youth Motor Vehicle Fatalities," *Journal of Legal Studies*, 16: 351–74.

SINDELAR, J. L., ELBEL, B., and PETRY, N. M. (2007), "What Do We Get For Our Money? Cost-Effectiveness of Adding Contingency Management," *Addiction*, 102(2): 309–16.

—— OLMSTEAD, T., and PEIRCE, J. (2007), "Cost-effectiveness of Prize Based Contingency Management in Methadone Maintenance Treatment Programs," *Addiction*, 102(9): 1463–71.

SLOAN, F. A., OSTERMAN, JAN, PICONE, GABRIEL, CONOVER, CHISTOPHER, and TAYLOR, DONALD H. (2004), *The Price of Smoking* (Cambridge, MA: The MIT Press).

Substance Abuse and Mental Health Services Administration, Office of Applied Studies (2007), "National Survey of Substance Abuse Treatment Services (N-SSATS): 2006. Data on Substance Abuse Treatment Facilities." DASIS Series: S-39, DHHS Publication No. (SMA) 07-4296, Rockville, MD.

Substance Abuse and Mental Health Services Administration, Office of Applied Studies (2008), "Treatment Episode Data Set (TEDS). Highlights—2006." National Admissions to Substance Abuse Treatment Services, DASIS Series: S-40, DHHS Publication No. (SMA) 08-4313, Rockville, MD.

TERZA, J. V. (2002), "Alcohol Abuse and Employment: A Second Look," *Journal of Applied Econometrics*, 17: 393–404.

—— BRADFORD, W. D., and DISMUKE, C. E. (2008), "The Use of Linear Instrumental Variables Methods in Health Services Research and Health Economics: A Cautionary Note," *Health Services Research*, 43(3): 1102–20.

USDHHS (US Department of Health and Human Services) (1986), *The Health Consequences of Smoking: The Changing Cigarette. A Report of the Surgeon General* (Washington, DC: US Department of Health and Human Services, Public Health Service, Centers for Disease

Control, Center for Health Promotion and Education, Office on Smoking and Health, DHHS Publication No. (CDC) 87-8398).

—— (2000), *Reducing Tobacco Use: A Report of the Surgeon General* (Atlanta, GA: US Department of Health and Human Services, Centers for Disease Control and Prevention, National Center for Chronic Disease Prevention and Health Promotion, Office on Smoking and Health).

—— (2004), *The Health Consequences of Smoking: A Report of the Surgeon General* (Atlanta, GA: US Department of Health and Human Services, Centers for Disease Control and Prevention, National Center for Chronic Disease Prevention and Health Promotion, Office on Smoking and Health).

VAN OURS, J. C. (2004), "A Pint a Day Raises a Man's Pay; But Smoking Blows that Gain Away," *Journal of Health Economics*, 23: 863–86.

VISCUSI, W. K. (1992), *Smoking: Making the Risky Decision* (New York: Oxford University Press).

VOLPP, K., LEVY, A. ASCH, A., et al. (2006), "A Randomized Controlled Trial of Financial Incentives for Smoking Cessation," *Cancer Epidemiology: Biomarkers and Prevention*, 15(1): 12–8.

WAGENAAR, A. C., SALOIS, M. J., and KOMRO, K. A. (2009), "Effects of Beverage Alcohol Price and Tax Levels on Drinking: A Meta-Analysis of 1003 Estimates from 112 Studies," *Addiction*, 104: 179–90.

ZARKIN, G., FRENCH, M., MROZ, T., and BRAY, J. (1998), "Alcohol Use and Wages: New Results from the National Household Survey on Drug Abuse," *Journal of Health Economics*, 17: 53–68.

CHAPTER 11

··

ECONOMICS AND MENTAL HEALTH: AN INTERNATIONAL PERSPECTIVE[*]

··

RICHARD G. FRANK

11.1 INTRODUCTION

THE aspirations for mental health delivery in most Organization of Economic Cooperation and Development (OECD) member countries have been lofty and surprisingly similar. Western nations are typically committed to inclusion of and support for people with mental illness in the mainstream of society; to community oriented treatment for mental disorders; and to greater integration of mental health care into the health care system (USDHHS 1999; European Commission 2005). Each society also recognizes a duty to provide for the safety of the public and this means taking account of the disturbed and disturbing behavior that can arise in connection with mental disorders. Western nations must therefore deal with the conflicting impulses of community orientation and protection of the public. These aspirations are held in common across nations despite the fact that nations take very different approaches to organizing and financing health care. Nearly all OECD countries have wrestled with several common questions regarding how to provide mental health care to their citizens. They include

* I am grateful to the John D. and Catherine T. MacArthur Foundation for financial support of this research. I am grateful to Sherry Glied and Peter Smith for helpful comments on an earlier draft, and to Tara Tai for research assistance.

- What resources get allocated to treatment and care of people with mental disorders?
- What is the role of government, and which level of government (local/central), in the financing and provision of mental health care?
- To what extent should mental health care and general medical care be integrated?
- What should the mix of inpatient and community-based care be for specialty mental health care?

Answers to these questions are tied up with basic conceptions of mental health "exceptionalism," each nation's basic commitments to its citizens, its approach to the control of health care costs and promotion of efficiency. It is commonly observed in mental health policy analyses that in most OECD countries too little is being spent on mental health care, that mental health care is not sufficiently integrated into the health care system and that the balance between institutional and community-based services is not right.

In choosing how to answer fundamental questions about policy towards mental health care, each nation must come to terms with some key economic forces. In this chapter, I consider how different nations address economics and mental health in the formulation of mental health policy. I focus on three key economic phenomena that are central to understanding the allocation of resources to the treatment of mental disorders. These are externalities, methods for efficient rationing of health resources, and incentives for allocating funds across different types of mental health services. The chapter is organized into four sections. The next section provides some background on mental disorders and how mental health care is organized in different OECD countries. The third section considers how mental health spending is determined as part of health care rationing schemes in various nations. The section also discusses the role of government and how each country aligns its financing arrangements with stated policy goals of reducing reliance on institutional care for people with mental illnesses. The last section offers some concluding observations on mental health policy.

11.2 BACKGROUND

Recent estimates of the prevalence of mental disorders in select European and North American countries suggest that the twelve-month prevalence of DSM-IV diagnosable mental disorders ranges from about 20 percent in Canada to 29 percent in the USA (Bijl et al. 2003).[1] Mental disorders are frequently impairing conditions that disrupt the ability of affected individuals to function in their usual roles as worker, community and household member (Kessler et al. 1995, 1998; Frank and Koss 2005).

---

[1] The other European countries were Germany and the Netherlands.

Table 11.1 Spending on Health and Mental Health as share of GDP

	Health	Mental health
Australia (2002)	9.1%	0.71%
Canada (2004)	9.9%	0.67%
France (2003)	10.4%	0.99%
Germany (2002)	10.8%	1.00%
United Kingdom (2002)	7.7%	1.05%
United States (2003)	15.2%	0.91%

Sources: Knapp et al. 2007 and 2008; Frank and Glied 2006.

Notes: OECD, OECD Health Data 2006:<www.oecd.org/health/heatlhdata>

As a result higher income (OECD) nations commonly spend between 5 percent and 14 percent of their health dollar on mental health care (Kuno and Asukai 2000; Knapp et al. 2007). This implies that OECD countries devote between 0.3 percent and 1.1 percent of their national incomes to treatment of mental disorders.[2] Most spend over 0.6 percent of GDP on mental health with Italy, Japan and Portugal being exceptions (Kuno and Asukai 2000; McDaid et al. 2007). It is important to note that the patterns of spending on mental health care are different from those observed in international comparisons of health care spending. Table 11.1 reports the shares of GDP for health and mental health care for a select set of nations. The data show that there is more variation in mental health spending levels across nations than there is for health care. However, the United States is not an outlier in mental health spending as it is in general health care.

All higher income nations deliver mental health care to their residents through a mix of the nation's general health care delivery system and specialized institutions that attend to the needs of people with mental disorders. The structure of health care delivery and financing in each nation is therefore of central importance. The reliance on different institutions for organizing, paying for, and rationing health and mental health care can be expected to produce different results. These may be reflected in spending levels on health and mental health care reported above, the different mix of mental health services delivered and the priority given to caring for different sub-populations of people with mental disorders. Most OECD countries have national policies that establish universal access to health care where low income households are guaranteed access to health care through publicly financed subsidies. The United States has until recently been a prominent exception.

The main approaches to organizing health care access and financing are through competitive insurance markets (US, Netherlands), budgeted systems of direct service

---

[2] These numbers are not entirely comparable because different nations allocate mental health expenditures in different parts of their national accounts. However, careful comparative analyses (Triplett 2001) comparing the US, Australia, and the United Kingdom finds mental health spending in the region of 1 percent of GDP.

provision (UK) and social health insurance systems with budgets (Canada, France and Germany). Within each of these approaches to organizing and paying for health services are specific rationing arrangements for mental health care. Rationing tools applied to mental health care include insurance benefit design (cost sharing, limits and exclusions from coverage); access restrictions on levels of care; capacity constraints on treatment resources; and payment arrangements including prospectively set budgets. All of these rationing methods are typically used by OECD countries, although they are applied in very different combinations. Providing a comprehensive review of all mental health delivery for all OECD countries is beyond the scope of this review. I will therefore focus the discussion on a few examples of nations that take different approaches to health and mental health care delivery.

Government always plays a central role in the organization, financing and delivery of mental health care. In Western Europe, government accounts for between 65 percent and 90 percent of all health spending (OECD 2006).[3] In Canada and the United States about 69 percent and 44 percent of health care expenditures were made by government respectively (OECD 2006). In the United States government pays for about 59 percent of all mental health care (Frank and Glied 2006). In some cases treatment of mental disorders becomes a matter of public safety and thus all high income nations have laws in place that allow the state to involuntarily treat people for mental disorders. Acting to involuntarily treat people requires individuals to be likely to harm themselves or be a threat to others. The commitment by OECD countries to promote community-based treatment and inclusion of people with mental disorders into the mainstream of society while also accepting the responsibility for public protection creates a policy tension that is a persistent source of passionate debate in all these nations and thus shapes public mental health spending.

Public mental health care is frequently organized, paid for and managed by local government institutions in Western Europe, Canada, and the US.[4] In Germany states carry primary responsibility for paying for and overseeing the delivery of mental health care. In Canada provinces organize mental health care. France uses a system of specialty catchment areas for governance of the mental health system while the UK makes use of National Health Service (NHS) trusts and local social service departments, to pay for and deliver mental health care. The US makes use of private specialty managed care organizations known as behavioral health care carve-outs to manage and pay for mental health care under private and some public insurance arrangements. State governments also play an important role in organizing, providing and paying for mental health care (Frank and McGuire 2000). Decentralization of the governance of mental health care offers flexibility in allocating treatment resources so as to attend to local conditions and needs. It can also create local policies that conflict with national policy goals for mental health care and may lead to horizontal inequity; that is, people in similar circumstances

---

[3] Two exceptions are Greece (53%) and Switzerland (45%).
[4] This is the case even when most financing comes from central government and when local governments contribute significantly to financing of mental health care.

in different locations having different opportunities with respect to the amount and type of treatment resources available (Bindman et al. 2000).

Since the 1960s all higher income nations have been engaged in a re-alignment of the mix of hospital (and residential) care and community-based mental health care. Determining the "right mix" of institutional and community mental health services creates a highly charged debate involving competing economic, political, ethical and legal ideas and interests. Concerns over the rights of psychiatric patients, alongside the high costs of maintaining treatment oriented psychiatric hospitals and the emergence of ever more effective community-based treatments have generally persuaded policy makers to emphasize treatments in less restrictive environments (Rogers and Pilgrim 1996; Grob 2001). The US experienced an era of deinstitutionalization that began in the 1960s and extended into the 1980s. Most European nations began reducing their reliance on hospital-based care during the late 1970s and early 1980s and continued into the beginning of the twenty-first century (McCaid et al. 2008). The result is that there have been notable reductions in the inpatient psychiatric capacity in virtually all OECD countries.

Table 11.2 reports the stock of psychiatric beds per 100,000 population in six western European and North American countries. The table shows that there have been reductions in the stock of beds in all nations between 1990 and 2006. The 1990 bed stock figures reflect considerable variation in each nation's capacity to treat mental disorders in hospitals. The observed pattern reflects differences in the timing of when nations started to reduce their psychiatric bed stock and also different policy choices regarding mental health spending, the method of paying for mental health care and the role of psychiatric hospitals in delivery of mental health care. The data on hospital beds for 2006 shows that all six nations reduced their bed capacity. It also reflects growing variation in how each society sees the function of the psychiatric hospital. These choices are also reflected in the share of mental health spending devoted to hospital care. For example, in France and the United States, two countries that spend similar shares of GDP on mental health care, France allocates roughly 80 percent of mental health spending on inpatient care (Verdoux 2007) and the United States about 36 percent (Mark et al. 2007). Thus basic resource allocation choices are made differently. We will focus on the economic forces that affect such allocations.

Table 11.2 Psychiatric Beds per 100,000 Population*

	1990	2006
Canada	193.4	
France	180.0	90.0
Germany	167.4	153.0
Netherlands	161.3	136.1
UK	131.8	59.1
US	111.6	73.3

Sources: WHO Atlas; NCHS, Health US, OECD Health Data.

Note: *Includes residential treatment beds for children

11.3 Moral Hazard, Externalities, and Rationing

11.3.1 Moral Hazard

Every high income society insulates all or most of its residents from the costs of treating mental disorders through insurance mechanisms. Nearly all nations make use of cost sharing mechanisms in recognition of the inefficiencies stemming from *moral hazard* (Arrow 1963). Control of moral hazard has often resulted in mental health care being treated differently than are other forms of health services. For example, in Canada many classes of licensed mental health care providers are excluded from direct reimbursement under the Canadian national health insurance system (Romanow and Marchildon 2003). French health insurance excludes psychotherapy provided by psychologists from public health insurance. France and Germany exclude all psychoanalysis from reimbursement under health insurance schemes (Verdoux 2007; Salize, Rossler, and Becker 2007). The US has long debated the differential treatment of mental health care within its private and public health insurance schemes (Frank and McGuire 2000). In the US private health insurance plans have typically had limits on the number of inpatient days (typically thirty per year) and outpatient visits (usually twenty per year) that are covered by private health insurance (Barry et al. 2003). In addition, until recently many private health insurance plans and the Medicare program that insures elderly Americans carried higher cost sharing for ambulatory mental health services than do other outpatient health services.[5]

The special treatment of mental health care in health insurance has been justified on efficiency grounds by a presumption that demand for mental health services is more responsive to the terms of insurance coverage than are other health services (McGuire 1981). In particular the demand response to cost sharing has been viewed as greater for mental health services (psychotherapy especially) than for other ambulatory medical services. The direct evidence on the demand response for mental health services comes mostly from studies conducted in the United States (Frank and McGuire 2000). There is however, indirect evidence available from Australia, Canada, Germany and the Netherlands (Bijl et al. 2003; and Williams and Doessel 2008).

Evidence on the demand response for mental health care in the US is based on econometric research that began appearing in the 1980s. That research made use of cross-sectional data from national surveys of households and providers (McGuire 1981; Horgan 1986; Taube, Kessler, and Burns 1986; Watts, Scheffler, and Jewell 1986). Those

---

[5] In July of 2008 the US Congress enacted legislation that equalized cost sharing for psychotherapy and other outpatient visits to providers. In October of 2008 the Congress passed private insurance parity legislation as part of economic rescue legislation.

papers used variation in observed ambulatory cost sharing arrangements and utilization of ambulatory mental health care across health insurance plans to estimate the
demand response to insurance. The models were based on simple assumptions about the
demand function for mental health care. That is, it was assumed that consumers faced a
linear price schedule based on average coinsurance and had perfect foresight. The annual
number of visits was assumed to be the relevant product being purchased. The two part
model (Manning et al. 1981) was used to analyze the survey data because most people
do not use mental health services so the survey data exhibited a concentration of observations at a value of zero mental health visits. Thus in the first part a logit or probit model
of whether any mental health care was used was estimated. The second part consisted of
an ordinary least squares model of the number of annual mental health visits (usually
after applying a logarithmic transformation to visits) conditional on having used some
mental health care.

The estimated demand response parameters were very consistent across studies,
indicating that ambulatory mental health services were more responsive to cost sharing provisions than were general health services. These results were called into question for two main reasons. First, the results were based on non-experimental
assignment of people to insurance arrangements raising the possibility of selection
bias. Selection bias is likely because in the US many people can choose among multiple
competing health plans. Thus it is likely that those anticipating use of mental health
services would choose plan with more generous coverage provisions for mental health
services (i.e. low coinsurance rates). Only the McGuire (1981) study among the first
generation research attempted to address the possible selection into coverage. The second concern about the first generation research findings relates to the presence of
deductibles, coinsurance and coverage limits noted above. These provisions in most
US insurance imply that consumers face a non-linear price schedule that can be characterized by three sets of block prices (Manning and Frank 1992). The three blocks for
ambulatory care include a deductible (e.g. $150); a segment of coverage with a coinsur-
ance rate (e.g. 50%) and then coverage limits of perhaps twenty visits after which consumers pay the full price of care. Such a block pricing scheme builds in a relation
between service use and average price unrelated to demand response. That is, a declining block price schedule will create a negative relation between the average
out-of-pocket price and service use.

The RAND Health Insurance Experiment (HIE) was designed to address the selection issues that were prevalent in observational data from US health insurance markets
(Newhouse and the HIE Group 1993). The HIE addressed the selection issue by randomly assigning households to different insurance designs. The HIE also improved the
measurement of key variables by essentially running its own insurance program and
measuring exactly what services were used and when. Provider prices were directly
observed and measured. Finally, great innovations were made in the measurement of
health and mental health status along with other factors that can affect the demand for
mental health services. Random assignment and improved measurement did not
address all the issues noted above because the issue of non-linear price schedules was

still present.[6] This resulted in an analysis of episodes of mental health care that took account of the non-linear price schedules (Manning et al. 1989). The estimates obtained by the RAND HIE showed an arc elasticity of coinsurance of −0.80 for ambulatory mental health compared to −0.30 for ambulatory health services. Thus in the fee for service context of US insurance prevalent prior to the 1990s, mental health services were considerably more responsive to insurance provisions than were general medical services.

Since the advent of managed care a series of studies of insurance benefit expansions for mental health services show much smaller increases in utilization and spending than would be expected if price elasticity estimates on the order of −0.8 were operating (Goldman, McCulloch, and Sturm 1998; Huskamp 1999; Goldman et al. 2006; Lu, Frank, and McGuire 2008). These studies in the US show that the use of non-price rationing methods can alter the observed price response of demand for mental health care.

Outside of the United States most evidence of moral hazard is indirect. Comparative epidemiological studies have estimated the percentage of people with a diagnosable disorder that get treatment (Bijl et al. 2003). Epidemiological studies in the US, Canada, and elsewhere have shown that only a modest portion of the population with a diagnosable mental disorder gets treatment. Similarly, among Canadians, Germans, and Dutch residents with a serious mental disorder 52.3 percent, 67 percent, and 66.3 percent respectively get treated each year (Bijl et al. 2003). This suggests significant levels of under-treatment. The same study however, shows that among people without a diagnosable disorder 3.4 percent of Canadians, 14.1 percent of Germans, and 7.6 percent of the Dutch receive mental health treatment and roughly half of that treatment is provided by mental health specialists. These figures need to be interpreted cautiously because considerable psychiatric distress can occur at levels of symptoms that are below diagnostic thresholds. Also, people that are successfully receiving maintenance treatment for a disorder like depression may not meet diagnostic criteria at a point in time. Nevertheless, the substantial levels of treatment among people without diagnosable conditions raise the possibility of moral hazard in service use. Given the evidence on moral hazard, it is not surprising that all nations that provide for financial protection against the costs of treating mental disorders put into place a set of mechanisms to control costs and utilization of mental health services.

11.3.2 Rationing and Budgets for Mental Health Care

It is frequently observed that mental health is underfunded and this is often described in terms of stricter rationing of mental health care relative to general medical care (USDHHS 1999). In assessing the rationing of mental health care we first consider how an efficient rationing system would allocate resources between health and mental health

---

[6] The HIE rather than having limits on covered services featured a stop loss that meant that after $1000 or less in out-of-pocket expenses were incurred all subsequent care was free to the consumers. Thus the HIE featured a set of declining block price schedules.

services. We will then examine how actual health systems make such allocations and consider the forces that shape these outcomes. We go on to discuss how rationing occurs within the mental health care system. We begin by assuming that the health benefits to a population (B) are produced by a mix of general health (g) and mental health services (m) conditional on characteristics and habits of the population (X). That is mental health is part of health and mental health care contributes to overall health in a variety of complicated ways.[7] These include direct effects of mental health care on alleviating mental disorders, indirect effects through improved adherence to medical treatment and also by creating greater resilience to health shocks (Conti, Berndt, and Frank 2008). So the production function for health benefits can be expressed as

$$B = B(g, m; X). \qquad (1)$$

A hypothetical social planner that seeks to maximize population health subject to a budget $I = r_g g + r_m m$; where the r_is are prices of general medical care and mental health care.[8] Maximization of population health subject to the budget results in the well known equilibrium condition that mental health care and general medical care will be purchased until the marginal health product of each type of care per dollar is equal:

$$B_m/r_m = B_g/r_g \qquad (2)$$

The subscripts indicate a partial derivative of B and r with respect to the subscripted argument. To arrive at an efficient allocation of health and mental health services each nation would establish rationing methods that would steer the health and mental health systems towards the service levels implied by the efficient equilibrium condition.

In practice students of mental health delivery and policy regularly argue that mental health services are underfunded and misallocated (Burnam and Escarce 1999; Knapp and Mangalore 2007; Knapp et al. 2007). The argument is founded on several key observations. First, the social costs of mental illness are high and touch on general health, child development, criminal justice and labor markets (WHO 2001). Second, there have been great advances in the ability to treat most major mental illnesses thereby offering the potential to reduce the social costs of the mental illnesses through treatment (USDHHS 1999; Frank and Glied 2006).[9] Third, rates of treatment for the mental disorders, with some of the strongest effectiveness of care evidence, such as depression and anxiety disorders, are quite low (Bijls et al. 2003; Kessler et al. 2005). The implication is that by spend-

---

[7] Viewing mental health as part of health is widespread. US Surgeon General David Satcher wrote: "We recognize that the brain is the integrator of thought, emotion, behavior and health. Indeed, one of the foremost contributions of contemporary mental health research is the extent to which it has mended the destructive split between 'mental' and 'physical' health" (DHHS 1999).

[8] The budget might be set either at a first best level or some other level. This will not affect the basic point about efficient (second best) allocation conditions.

[9] For a detailed discussion about the conditions that must be in place to make more spending on mental health and substance abuse problems efficient, see Meara and Frank (2005).

ing more on mental health care, the social returns would exceed the extra costs. This line of argument has been forcefully set out for the case of Great Britain by Sir Richard Layard (2004). While the full case is difficult to systematically establish (Meara and Fran 2005) there is evidence of important gains in the productivity of mental health spending in recent times (Berndt et al. 2002; Layard 2004; Cutler 2005; Frank and Glied 2006; McCaid et al. 2008). The degree to which these returns would exceed the incremental returns of spending on general medical care has also not been systematically established—again there are clues suggesting that reallocation of spending in many nations toward mental health would improve welfare (Layard 2004; Cutler 2005; Knapp et al. 2008). Moreover, it has been observed that even in systems where funds are directed towards mental health care by central government agencies or other payers the resulting allocations to actual treatment are frequently below the targeted levels (Finch et al. 1992; Bindman et al. 2000). Given the suggestion that actual allocations to mental health care are inefficiently low we turn to the question of the economic forces that might drive that result.

11.3.2.1 *National Approaches to Rationing of Mental Health Care*

Most OECD countries use prospectively set budgets to ration some or all mental health services. How these budgets are set and administered differs in important ways across high income countries. A few examples follow. In Western Europe and Canada all residents are covered by insurance or another type of health care financing scheme (e.g. National Health Service). Canada uses prospectively set budgets for hospitals under its National Health Insurance plan (Arnett 2006) and for provincially funded community-based mental health services that do not involve inpatient and office-based physician services (which are part of the National Health Insurance plan). Spending decisions on mental health and other services that are not part of the fee for service arrangements for physicians in Canada are most often made by regional health authorities within Provinces. Arnett (2006) observes that this requires mental health care needs to compete with other health problems for budget shares, often to the disadvantage of mental health care.

In Germany health care is mostly paid for through a universal health insurance system that is based on private health insurance companies. Health insurers directly pay for hospital care and medications on a fee for service basis. Hospitals also provide outpatient mental health services that are primarily aimed at people with severe and persistent mental disorders (Salize et al. 2007). Outpatient physician services are financed through a system of delegation from health insurers to medical management organizations that organize networks of physicians through contractual arrangements. Health insurers pay these networks of physicians from a prospectively set global budget for all outpatient services. Pension funds, disability coverage, and the Federal Bureau of Labor also have a role in paying for rehabilitation services. Finally, a variety of community-based mental health services (supported employment, housing, psycho-social rehabilitation) and health and mental health services for people that are not covered by private insurance or pension plans are paid for by the social welfare system. Recent data suggests that roughly 66 percent of mental health care is paid for by private health insurance and 34 percent by the social welfare system (Salize et al. 2007).

France also relies mostly on private health insurers that are organized by a combination of employers, unions and the government (Rodwin 2003). Public hospitals dominate the French health care system, accounting for about two-thirds of all beds. France pays for hospital services through a set of prospectively set regional budgets that are administered by regional agencies that are expected to adhere to national policy priorities (Verdoux 2007). Individual hospitals in turn are given prospective budgets. Outpatient mental health care provided by psychiatrists in private offices or in community mental health centers is purchased via fee for service payments and no limits on the number of visits are imposed, although psychoanalysis is, in principle, excluded from coverage.[10] Planning for community-based mental health services is done through a network of 839 mental health catchment areas.

England funds and provides most health care through the National Health Service (NHS). Local health care delivery is administered by NHS trusts. At the center of this system is the primary care trust that receives a prospective budget from the NHS to serve the population of a specified geographic area. There are about 150 primary care trusts that serve an average of 400,000 people. The NHS sets budgets according to the size and age of the population, local costs, and indicators of need for general and acute medical care, psychiatric care (acute and community-based) and general community health (Bindman et al. 2000). Thus there is an implied allocation for mental health care based on a psychiatric need index. Beyond this basic allocation there are special funds designated for mental health care based on the number of former long stay public mental hospital residents in an area. There are also some other smaller special budget lines for mental health. In addition, social care is delineated from health care and is managed and paid for separately. Social care includes a variety of human services that are used by people with severe and persistent mental disorders such as personal care, social worker services, and supported housing services.

The primary care trust is charged with the responsibility of serving the population either through direct provision of care or by contracting with specialty trusts. Most localities rely on specialized mental health trusts or community mental health teams to deliver mental health care to those in need. Because people with disabling mental and medical conditions are served by both the NHS and the social care sector, specialty care trusts that can provide both health care and social care services have been established in some areas. In all cases entry into specialized trusts requires referrals from primary care providers.

The United States most often delivers mental health services under prospectively set budgets in the context of competitive health insurance arrangements (this is the case for most private insurance and most Medicaid enrollees). In addition, the US states also set local mental health budgets that serve low income and uninsured populations (Mazade and Glover 2007). In the US private insurance health plans frequently compete to enroll people (competition for enrollees) that are covered by employer sponsored insurance

---

[10] Psychiatry is one of the few specialties where patients can directly access care without a referral from a primary care practitioner.

plans. In some cases Medicaid programs mimic such arrangements. This most often involves a two-step process. Health insurers offer employers price bids and descriptions of the services and coverage to be provided. Employers then choose a set of health plans (e.g. 3–5) that will be offered to their employees and dependants. Consumers then choose among the selected competing health plans.

Most health plans in the US make use of so-called managed behavioral carve-out arrangements to organize and pay for mental health care for plan enrollees. Behavioral health care carve-out arrangements involve separating the insurance function for mental health and substance abuse care and contracting separately for management of those services with an organization that specializes in managing mental health and substance abuse services (Frank, McGuire, and Newhouse 1995). The majority of carve-out contracts originate from health plans although a significant minority of carve-out arrangements involves direct contracts between payers (employers or state Medicaid programs) and specialty carve-out vendors.[11] The most common form of payment in a carve-out contract involves a capitation payment (e.g. per person per month). Therefore at any given time the carve-out organization must manage the specialty mental health care for a population under a budget (the capitation payment × the number of enrollees). Spending on prescription drugs and mental health delivered by primary care are usually excluded from the carve-out contract. These are most often paid for by fee for service payments.

Public mental health systems that serve people without either public or private insurance are usually funded by prospectively set budgets based in large part on historical allocations. In those systems most states directly finance and manage a set of public mental hospitals. The majority of states separate the public mental hospital budget from the budgets given to local mental health authorities (Frank and Gaynor 1995).[12] Mental health spending in the US as a share of total health spending has declined from nearly 11 percent in the 1970s to 6.2 percent in 2003 (Mark et al. 2007).

11.3.3 Incentives and Rationing of Mental Health Care

Consider global budgets like those used for outpatient care in Germany, primary care trusts in the United Kingdom; hospital care and community-based mental health care in Canada; and private health plans in the United States. In each case observers have noted that actual spending for mental health services frequently falls short of either what is implied by a funding formula or by what might be considered a fair or efficient allocation. In Germany psychiatrists have fared poorly within the global budget for outpatient

---

[11] Since the economic dynamics for these contracts are quite different from the majority of arrangements these will be briefly discussed later in this paper. For a more complete discussion, see Frank and McGuire 2000; and Frank and Garfield 2007.

[12] There are important exceptions to this approach that have been adopted by state such as Ohio and California where local mental health programs are financially responsible for all or part of the cost of using public mental hospitals.

physician services (Salize et al. 2007). That is, the share of the outpatient physician spending claimed by psychiatrists has been declining and is reported to be limiting the ability to supply high quality mental health care (Salize et al. 2007). Canadian hospital systems appear to disproportionately reduce mental health services as general hospital budgets have tightened. In recent testimony mental health advocates claimed that (presumably both federal and provincial) government funding allocations favor biomedical investments at the expense of mental health services (Kirby and Keon cited in Arnett 2006).

In the United Kingdom, a study by Bindman and colleagues showed that underspending relative to allocations for mental health care to primary care trusts was greatest in areas that are economically deprived. Finally, in some prominent markets for health plans, spending on mental health care has consistently eroded. Under the Federal Employees Health Benefit Program in the US mental health spending declined from roughly 9 percent of total spending to under 3 percent between 1978 and 1999 (Goldman et al. 2006).

What forces might produce departures from the efficiency condition in equation (2)? The economics behind the budgets in each nation are somewhat different. In Canada, Germany, and the United Kingdom actual spending choices for the "health budget" are made within bureaucratic systems and are not influenced by the types of market forces that affect budgets of private insurers in the US. How might a public or private organization charged with managing health resources to serve the health care needs of a population make choices that appear to depart from optimal use of resources? Some reasons include misperceptions of the benefits of effective treatment for mental disorders, misperception of the productivity of spending on mental health care, opportunities for cost shifting and mental health providers holding a weak political position in competition for budget dollars.

In Canada, France, Germany, and the UK and in some cases the US, central governments or more centralized payers delegate decisions about spending public or quasi-public funds to local entities.[13] In each case a central authority (central government, public insurance scheme) establishes some national priorities for health and mental health care and delegates the implementation to sub-national institutions to manage the supply of services. The resulting allocations appear to often result in "under-provision" of mental health care.

One can view the vertical relation between a central government and local delivery of health care as a principal–agent problem (Ferris and Winkler 1990; McGuire and Riordan 1995). Both central and local health authorities may be assumed to value the health and mental health and be constrained by the budgets. However, the weights central and local authorities place on various activities that promote health may differ. In addition, local authorities make their choices based on the fiscal and regulatory rules set out by payers such as government and centralized insurers. These include the incentives contained in health care financing arrangements, service mandates and priority

---

[13] In this case the term quasi-public refers to funds that are obtained through private premiums (France and Germany) that are mandated and regulated by central government policy.

populations that are identified in policy. The local health authority will usually have more information about local conditions than the central authority a classic feature of the principal–agent problem. The implication of this is that local health authorities may not strictly pursue the central government's policy agenda. One question then is: why do local and central government health policy objectives diverge?

Local health systems may undervalue the benefits of mental health care for several reasons. Mental disorders carry a social stigma. The stigma frequently is intertwined with notions that mental disorders are less clearly identified and less treatable than are other medical conditions (USDHHS 1999). In addition, since mental disorders are stigmatized, people with those illnesses tend to be reluctant to seek treatment thereby making demand and local need for care appear lower than it might actually be. Most OECD countries recognize such stigma and have mounted anti-stigma campaigns (Angermayer et al. 2004).

The general public and public officials may not perceive spending on mental disorders to carry the same pay-offs as do other forms of health care spending. This may in part be due to the fact that there have been important recent developments in the understanding of mental illnesses and the ability to treat them. The clinical science of treating mental disorders has advanced notably in the last twenty years (USDHHS 1999; WHO 2001; Frank and Glied 2006). Cutler (2005) documents important gains in the treatment of depression, one of the most prevalent of the mental disorders. Frank and Glied (2006) describe the recent advances that have been made in the treatment of anxiety disorders, the most prevalent of mental illnesses. Other important innovations have improved treatment of schizophrenia and childhood mental disorders (USDHHS 1999). Cost-effectiveness evaluations of evidence-based treatments for depression suggest that they produce gains in Quality Adjusted Life Years (QALYs) at levels comparable to other medical treatments (Glied et al. 2008; Knapp et al. 2008). The ability to restore functioning in people suffering from schizophrenia has improved more slowly. The rapid advances in treatment capabilities alongside stigma may imply that political and bureaucratic allocation systems integrate findings into decision making slowly over time.

Public health care systems rely on specialized bureaucracies to allocate resources. At the heart of the political economy literature is the consideration of whether government functions in the public interest (as reflected by voters) or whether government actions reflect the interests of sub-sets of individuals with their own agendas (Besley 2006). The allocation of resources among competing health interests can be seen as a case where public allocation methods may be influenced by special interests. In England there are primary care trusts, in Germany there are physician management organizations that allocate outpatient health care funds, and in Canada provincial health authorities construct allocations to various health care programs. In these types of organizations various groups of physicians and citizens compete in the bureaucratic and political arena for a share of the treatment resources. In these cases the political power of advocacy groups and medical sub-specialty groups are important in determining budget allocations. Organized advocacy by mental health care consumers and their families is a relatively recent phenomenon (Tomes 2006). The influence of these groups typically remains weak relative to disease-specific interest groups focused on illnesses such as cancer or heart disease. Psychiatry is typically one of the less influential specialty societies in most OECD countries and thus often fares poorly in budget competition (Mechanic 1999). [14]

Finally, mental health services are frequently funded and/or supplied by several bureaucratic departments all operating under fixed budgets. Thus in the UK both the NHS and social care have responsibility for the care of people with severe mental disorders. There may therefore exist opportunities for cost shifting. That is, strict rationing of mental health services may be seen as an opportunity to expand monies available for general medical care while allowing people with mental disorders to obtain care from the social care sector. Matching grants are sometimes used to encourage local supply of a public service. Britain has in the past experimented with matching grants (Yellowlees 1990) which appeared not to result in the desired allocation of resources for mental health services. More recently the creation of combined trusts (mental health and social care) has tried to use organizational design to blunt incentives to cost shift created by fragmentation in financing.

In countries that rely on competition between profit-maximizing health insurers like the US, the nature of market competition can create incentives to under-supply mental health care (Frank and McGuire 2000). In the US private health insurance plans, Medicaid managed care plans and health plans operating under the Medicare Advantage program are paid capitation rates (per person per month prospective payments) to insure and manage care. The majority of these plans "carve-out" mental health care which means that they manage the insurance risk of mental and addictive disorders separately through the use of specialized managed behavioral health care organizations under capitation contracts. As noted earlier, these contracts typically cover specialty mental health and substance abuse care but not prescription drugs or mental health services delivered in primary care.

The hallmark of managed care is that it relies less on demand side prices to consumers to ration care than do traditional fee for service insurance plans. We noted above that the evidence on moral hazard in health care suggests that under fee-for-service arrangements the demand response to cost sharing for ambulatory mental health services was significantly greater than that for ambulatory medical services generally. The implication of that was that under fee-for-service insurance plans it may have been efficient to cover health and mental health services differently. Consider now imposing a set of managed care arrangements that make use of non-price-rationing methods such as provider network design, provider payment incentives, utilization review, and feedback of performance information to providers. These activities can be viewed as setting shadow prices for rationing health and mental health services (Keeler, Carter, and Newhouse 1998; Frank and McGuire 2000). The presumption is that these policies are set "as if" there were a price that reflected the value of the incremental service to the consumer.

[14] While this is somewhat of a chicken–egg problem, histories of mental health care suggest that psychiatry has long been on the edge of the medical profession and has often been marginalized with respect to influence and professional standing (Grob 1994).

Thus all services that generate benefits that are valued at or above the "shadow" price are provided and those services valued at less than the shadow price are not supplied.

The implications of rationing by shadow prices instead of demand prices are profound. That mental health services are more price-elastic than general medical care does not imply a differential shadow price. There are however important impacts on quantity determination (Frank and McGuire 1998). The model of rationing by shadow price is illustrated in Figure 11.1.

The figure reflects the demand curves for health and mental health services respectively. The demand for mental health care reflects the empirical evidence and is more responsive than that for general medical care. Let q represent an initial shadow price that is used to ration both health and mental health care. The corresponding quantities of health and mental health services are h and m. Now consider raising the shadow price from q to q' so as to impose stricter rationing on both services, the new quantities implied are h' and m'. Note that the reduction from m and m' is larger than the reduction from q to q'. This means that the same shadow price results in greater cutbacks for mental health care than for general medical care. The figures also highlight that shadow prices are equal for the two services even though the quantity responses are different. Frank and McGuire (2000) show that equal shadow prices represent an efficient (second best) outcome. That is, the same rationing standards should be applied to all services. Thus each dollar spent on services generates the same benefits across different types of services. This corresponds to the condition set out in equation (2).

Rationing by shadow prices might be expected to improve the insurance coverage for mental health care. There is evidence showing that some cost-sharing provisions for mental health care have become more generous but that many special rationing features for mental health care remain (Barry et al. 2003). In the context of competitive insurance markets, the economic incentives for the individual health plan may be not

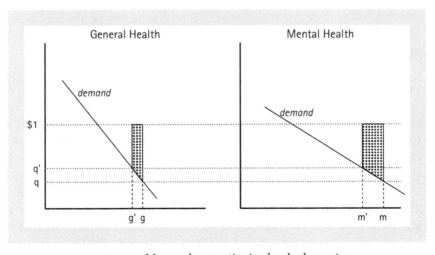

FIGURE 11.1 Managed care rationing by shadow prices

to use a common set of shadow prices to ration care. This is because it is thought that people with mental health care needs tend to gravitate to health plans with more generous coverage for mental health services. Moreover, people with mental disorders tend to have higher costs both because they use mental health services and because they carry higher health care costs (Frank and McGuire 2000; and Ellis and McGuire 2007). Therefore, people with mental disorders have higher total health care spending because they are more likely to use mental health services than the average insured person and because people with mental disorder also use more general medical services than average. Users of mental health care are therefore predictably more costly than other potential enrollees. Profit maximizing health plans therefore have an economic incentive to avoid enrolling people with mental health problems unless premiums paid to insurers can be adjusted to reflect the elevated risk through a risk adjustment mechanism. Extant evidence suggests that risk adjusters can attenuate the selection incentives but strong incentives remain (Ettner et al. 1998). Increasing the shadow price for mental health services has two effects: (1) it reduces moral hazard, and (2) it discourages one set of relatively costly people from enrolling in the plan. It is the second selection-related incentive that drives a wedge between social and private efficiency. Hence competitive insurance plans have an economic incentive to be "too restrictive" in rationing mental health care from a social efficiency perspective. Evidence from the US on this point includes Deb, Rubin, and Wilcox-Gok 1996. One study of Swiss health insurance markets also reports evidence of selection related behavior for mental health care (Perneger et al. 1995).

This discussion highlights that there are special features of mental illnesses and mental health delivery that result in resource allocations that are socially inefficient. What is striking is that even though countries like Canada, Germany, the United Kingdom, and the United States differ in the institutions that govern their health care financing and delivery systems all have institutional structures that may drive mental health care to sub-optimal levels.

11.3.4 Rationing of Hospital Care

In the previous section I addressed the efficiency of aggregate spending level on mental health care in OECD countries. We now turn to the policy issue of the mix of inpatient psychiatric care and community-based mental health services. This issue has challenged every OECD health care system at different times in recent history. Recall that nearly every OECD nation is committed to a policy of inclusion in the community for people with mental disorders. Table 11.2 summarizes recent changes in the availability of psychiatric beds in key OECD countries. The table reports notable variation in the resources devoted to inpatient care across nations and striking reductions in the number of psychiatric beds in some nations (France and the UK especially). The US had many fewer psychiatric beds per capita than the other OECD nations in 1990 because there had been important reductions in the number of psychiatric beds between 1970 and 1980

(Frank and Glied 2006). As already noted each nation pays for mental health services differently. The observed allocation of beds and utilization of inpatient psychiatric care frequently reflects the economic incentives of the health care financing system. I now present a framework for considering several major national approaches to allocation of treatment resources within the mental health sector.[15]

I first consider the case of a local mental health program (region, provincial, state) that faces a fixed budget for provision of mental health care to a homogeneous population of people with mental health problems (Frank and Gaynor 1991, 1995). I also assume for simplicity that the budget is set at the first best optimal thereby abstracting from the discussion in the previous section. The mental health in a population is posited to be produced by combining inpatient psychiatric care (H) and community-based treatment (C). A financing mechanism such as that in the UK involves a fixed budget for mental health (as might occur in a mental health trust). The local mental health system faces a set of providers to which it must allocate funds to obtain services. The local program might be assumed to maximize social utility and would, given the productivity of each type of service and its cost, choose the utility maximizing combination of inpatient and community-based mental health care. Figure 11.2 illustrates such equilibrium.

The line $B_0 B_1$ represents the mental health program's budget. Note that B_1 can be thought of as the inpatient capacity constraint. The curve $U_0 U_0$ is the indifference curve that is tangent to the budget line at E_1, implying the utility maximizing combination of

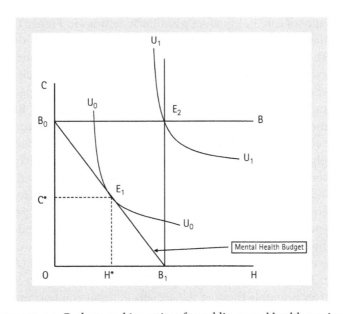

FIGURE 11.2 Budgets and incentives for public mental health services

[15] This section reflects ideas based on my joint research with Martin Gaynor and Thomas McGuire.

community- and hospital-based care (C^*, H^*). Because we assume that the budget constrain was set optimally C^* and H^* represent socially efficient levels of community-based and hospital care.

Now consider a case that resembles the economic incentives in Germany. That is, assume that psychiatric inpatient care is paid on a fee-for-service basis and community-based services are funded via a prospectively set budget. Thus the community-based programs will view hospital services as a "free good" in that they are off-budget and they will spend their entire budget allocation on community-based care. Thus the equilibrium choice of community- and hospital-based services will be B_0 and B_1 the maximum of both inpatient and outpatient services. This is because the effective budget constraint becomes $0B_0 E_2 B_1$ and the utility maximizing indifference curve for the local program is $U_1 U_1$. This result suggests that mental health spending will be driven higher than the socially efficient level and utilization of inpatient care will also be high relative to the socially efficient level. We in fact observe that Germany has among the highest level of inpatient use in Europe.

Most nations separate hospital and community-based budgets and payment arrangements. In France hospitals in a region are allocated a fixed mental health budget and community programs are paid on a fee-for-service basis. Hospital budgets are established based on negotiation and historical allocations (Rodwin 2003). This means that hospitals have an incentive to keep their beds full as a means of resisting budget cuts (McCaid et al. 2007). One can thereby view the incentives of the hospital as maximizing the quantity of care delivered subject to a budget constraint. There has been pressure to improve the quality of care in inpatient psychiatric settings in France (Verdoux 2007). One recent initiative is for the decreased use of restraints through design of special patient rooms. The result is likely upward pressure on the cost of treatment. Cost control for inpatient psychiatric care in France has mostly relied on capacity reductions in government-owned psychiatric hospitals. Table 11.2 shows a 50 percent reduction between 1990 and 2006. France continues to spend a high share of its mental health budget on inpatient care, even though there are incentives to use community-based services. France also uses local planning bodies to coordinate and plan services and they control the supply of professional staff. This effectively imposes capacity constraints on community-based services which serves to constrain community-based spending.

The Netherlands and many parts of the US have attempted to bring together community and inpatient mental health budgets. Within the Medicaid and private insurance capitated carve-out contracts serve as one such mechanism (Frank and Garfield 2007). In state mental health systems in the US a number of states now make community programs pay the average cost of each day of public mental hospital use (Arkansas, Ohio, and California). This links the community and inpatient budgets so that community program incentives resemble those of the socially efficient equilibrium in Figure 11.2. Frank and Gaynor (1995) examined the change in payment arrangements in Ohio. In that case the state government gave each community program a block grant equal to the historical average state hospital costs of residents of the county that the community program serves. The community program in turn was required to purchase public mental hospital care at the per diem costs of care. By raising the cost of hospital care to the community program the policy was a step towards aligning social and private costs of different mental health resources. The result was a large decline in the use of public mental hospital care that was attributable to the new payment incentives (Frank and Gaynor 1994).

Thus far I have assumed that there is only one type of psychiatric patient. I now consider the possibility of two types of patients. One type has severe and persistent mental illnesses while the other has less disabling and impairing types of disorders (see Frank and Gaynor 1995 for a detailed treatment of this issue). This distinction is important because people with severe and persistent mental disorders having complex treatment needs are frequently less adherent to recommended treatments (Bachrach 1982) and can have run-ins with the criminal justice system. This makes these patients difficult and costly to treat. They are also less professionally rewarding (Grob 1994). For these reasons treatment programs have often displayed a tendency to avoid engaging such patients into treatment (US GAO 1977). The implication is that community treatment programs may have preferences over the patients they treat which may not align with the social benefits of treating different types of patients. Hence merely aligning payments with the pecuniary costs of treatment will not result in incentives for efficient allocation of therapeutic effort toward people with severe mental disorders (Figure 11.2). Instead efficiency requires additional subsidies that compensate for the disutility of treating difficult patients in community-based mental health programs. The State of Texas implemented such a subsidy scheme in the late 1980s by paying community-based programs a daily bonus based on their ability to engage a severely mentally ill client and keep them out of public institutions (Ganju and Bouchard 1990). The result was an increase in supply of services to people with severe mental disorders and a reduction in the use of public mental hospitals. Together these experiences show that local delivery systems respond to financial incentives and that obtaining efficient allocations of mental health spending may require Pigouvian tax and subsidy schemes.

11.4 CONCLUDING OBSERVATIONS

It is impressive how the fundamental vision for mental health care delivery is widely shared among higher income countries. A politics of inclusion towards people with mental illness is practiced across higher income nations. This means an expanded reliance on community-based treatment and a recognition that the stigma associated with mental illness poses a challenge to effective mental health delivery. Given these shared values and the vastly different approaches to financing and managing health care delivery taken by different OECD member countries, most nations appear to have great difficulty in making progress towards their goals for mental health care. Our review suggests that embedded in each nation's health care rationing system are institutions that appear to disadvantage the efficient allocation of resources towards mental health care. The mix of delegation of micro-spending decisions to sub-national institutions and the fragmentation of mental health financing and delivery are common to nearly all OECD countries. In addition bureaucratic competition in Canada, France, Germany, and the UK and market competition in the US may result in excessively restrictive rationing of mental health services. In the US separation of mental health care from other health risks has been proposed as a mechanism for more efficient spending levels for mental health care in the context of competitive insurance markets. Nevertheless, it has been the expansion of general health insurance (public and private) in the US that has resulted in expanded spending levels on mental health care. Most countries create some specialized institutions for the financing and delivery of mental health care. In practice, despite rhetoric lauding full integration of health and mental health care, no nation fully integrates these two areas. However, more separation does not appear to produce efficient levels of mental health spending.

Finally, given the more expansive approach to social services in most of Western Europe compared to the United States, it is puzzling that efforts to reduce reliance on psychiatric institutions have lagged behind those of the US. A key ingredient in the ability to reduce the use of psychiatric hospitals in the US was the creation of new income support and health insurance mechanisms that allow community-based support for people with severe and persistent mental illnesses (Frank and Glied 2006). Thus one would have expected a greater level of mainstreaming in Europe. It appears that most European societies would be less tolerant of the types of neglect that has been experienced by an important minority of people with severe mental illnesses in the US (Grob 1994; Frank and Glied 2006). The result may therefore be a more cautious paternalistic approach to deinstitutionalization and also a slower pace of change found in Western Europe.

References

Angermeyer, M. C., Beck, M., Dietrich, S. and Holzinger, A. (2004), "The Stigma of Mental Illness: Patients' Anticipations and Experiences," *International Journal of Social Psychiatry*, 50: 153–62.

Arnett, J. L. (2006), "Health and Mental Health in Canada," in R. Olson (ed.), *Mental Health Systems Compared: Great Britain, Norway, Canada and the United States* (Springfield, IL: Charles C. Thomas).

Arrow, K. J. (1963), "Uncertainty and the Welfare Economics of Medical Care," *American Economic Review*, 53: 941–69.

Bachrach, L. (1982), "Assessment of Outcomes in Community Support Systems: Results, Problems And Limitations," *Schizophrenia Bulletin*, 8(1): 39–61.

Barry, C. L. et al. (2003), "The Design of Mental Health Benefits: Still Unequal After All These Years," *Health Affairs*, 22(5): 127–37.

Berndt, E. R. et al. (2002), "The Medical Treatment of Depression 1991–1996: Productive Inefficiency, Expected Outcome Variation and Price Indexes," *Journal of Health Economics*, 27(3): 373–96.

BESLEY, T. (2006), *Principled Agents?* (Oxford: Oxford University Press).

BIJL, R.V., DE GRAAF, R., HIRIPI, E., et al. (2003), "The Prevalence of Treated and Untreated Mental Disorders in Five Countries," *Health Aff*airs, 22: 122–33.

BINDMAN, J., GLOVER, G., GOLDBERG, D., and CHISOLM, D. (2000), "Expenditure on Mental Health Care by English Health Authorities: A Potential Cause of Inequity," *British Journal of Psychiatry*, 177: 267–74.

BURNAM, M. A. and ESCARCE, J. J. (1999), "Equity in Managed Care for Mental Disorders," *Health Affairs*, (Sept./Oct.), 18(5): 22–31.

CONTI, R. M., BERNDT, E. R., and FRANK, R. G. (2008), "Early Retirement and Public Disability Insurance: Exploring the Impact of Depression," in D. Culter and D. Wise (eds.), *Health At Older Ages: The Causes And Consequences Of Declining Disability Among The Elderly* (Chicago: University of Chicago Press).

CULTER, D. M. (2005), *Your Money or Your Life: Strong Medicine for America's Health Care System* (Cambridge, MA: Harvard University Press).

DEB, P., RUBIN, J., and WILCOX-GOK, V. (1996), "Choice of Health Insurance by Families of the Mentally Ill," *Health Economics*, 5(1): 61–76.

ELLIS, R. P. and MCGUIRE, T. G. (2007), "Predictability and Predictiveness in Health Care Spending," *Journal of Health Economics*, 26(1): 25–48.

ETTNER, S. L., FRANK, R. G., MCGUIRE, T. G., NEWHOUSE, J. P., and NOTMAN, E. H. (1998), "Risk Adjustment of Mental Health and Substance Abuse Payments," *Inquiry*, 35(2): 223–39.

EUROPEAN COMMISSION (2005), "Improving the Mental Health of the Population: Towards a Strategy on Mental Health for the European Union." EC Health and Consumer Protection Directorate Green Paper COM, 484, Brussels, Belgium.

FERRIS, J. M. and WINKLER, D. R. (1990), "Agency Theory and Intergovernmental Relations," in R. Prudhomme (ed.), *Public Finance with Several Levels of Government* (The Hague: Foundation Journal of Public Finance).

FINCH, M. et al. (1992), "The Treatment of Alcohol and Drug Abuse Among Mentally Ill Medicaid Enrollees: The Utilization of services in Pre-paid Plans versus Fee for Service Care," in R. Frank and W. Manning (eds.), *Economics and Mental Health* (Baltimore: Johns Hopkins University Press).

FRANK, R. G. and GARFIELD, R. (2007), "Managed Behavioral Health Care Carve-Outs: Past Performance and Future Prospects," *Annual Review of Public Health*, 28: 303–20.

—— and GAYNOR, M. (1991), "Incentives in Intergovernmental Transfers: Mental Health Services in the US," in R. Prud'homme (ed.), *Public Finance with Several Levels of Government* (The Hague: Foundation Journal of Public Finance).

———— (1994), "Organizational Failure and Government Transfers: Evidence From and Experiments in the Financing of Mental Health Care," *Journal of Human Resources*, 29(1):108–25.

———— (1995), "Incentives, Optimality and Publicly Provided Goods: The Case of Mental Health Services," *Public Finance Quarterly*, 23(2): 167–92.

—— and GLIED, S. A. (2006), *Better But Not Well: Mental Health Policy in the United States Since 1950* (Baltimore: Johns Hopkins University Press).

—— and KOSS, C. (2005), "Mental Health and Labor Markets Productivity Loss and Restoration." Paper for the World Health Organization, WHO, Geneva.

—— and MCGUIRE, T. G. (2000), "Parity for Mental Health and Substance Abuse Care under Managed Care," *The Journal of Mental Health Policy and Economics*, 1: 153–9.

FRANK, R. G. and McGUIRE, T. G. (2000), "Economics and Mental Health," in J. Newhouse and A. Culyer (eds.), *Handbook of Health Economics* (Amsterdam: North Holland Press).

———— and NEWHOUSE, J. P. (1995), "Risk Contracts in Managed Mental Health Care," *Health Affairs*, 14(3): 50–64.

GANJU, V. and BOUCHARD, C. (1990), "Funding Incentives for Community Based Programs: The Impact on Local Services of the Texas $35.50 Program." Working Paper, Texas Department of Mental Health and Mental Retardation, Austin, Texas.

GLIED, S. A. et al. (2008), "Cost Benefit Analysis of Depression Management in Primary Care." Working Paper, Department of Health Policy and Management, Columbia University, New York.

GOLDMAN, H. H., FRANK, R. G., BURNAM, M. A., et al. (2006), "Behavioral Health Insurance Parity for Federal Employees," *New England Journal of Medicine*, 354(13) (March): 36–44.

GOLDMAN, W., McCULLOCH, J., and STURM, R. (1998), "Costs and Utilization of Mental Health Services Before and After Managed Care," *Health Affairs*, 17(2): 40–52.

GROB, G. N. (1994), *The Mad Among Us: A History of the Care of America's Mentally Ill* (New York: Free Press).

—— (2001), "Mental Health Policy In 20th-Century America," in Ronald W. Manderscheid and Marilyn J. Henderson (eds.), *Mental Health, United States, 2000* (USDHHS Pub No. (SMA) 01-3537. Washington, DC: Superintendent of Documents, US Government Printing Office).

HORGAN, C. M. (1986), "The Demand for Ambulatory Mental Health Services from Specialty Providers," *Health Services Research*, 21(2): 291–320.

HUSKAMP, H. A. (1999), "Episodes of Mental Health and Substance Abuse Treatment Under a Managed Behavioral Health Care Carve-Out," *Inquiry*, 36(2): 147–61.

INMAN, R. (1978), "The Fiscal Performance of Local Governments: An Interpretive Review," in P. Miezkowski and M. Straszheim (eds.), *Current Issues in Urban Economics* (Baltimore: Johns Hopkins University Press).

KEELER, E., CARTER, G., and NEWHOUSE, J. P. (1998), "A Model of the Impact of Reimbursement Schemes on Health Plan Choice," *Journal of Health Economics*, 17(3): 297–320.

KESSLER, R. C. et al. (1995), "The Social Consequences of Psychiatric Disorders, I Educational Attainment," *American Journal of Psychiatry*, 152(7): 1026–32.

—— et al. (1998), "The Social Consequences of Psychiatric Disorders. III: Marital Instability," *American Journal of Psychiatry*, 155(8): 1092–6.

—— et al. (2005), "Prevalence and Treatment of Mental Disorders 1990–2003," *New England Journal of Medicine*, 352(24): 2515–23.

KNAPP, M. (1990), "Economic Barriers to Innovation in Mental Health Care: Community Care in the United Kingdom," in I. Marks and R. Scott (eds.), *Mental Health Care Delivery* (Cambridge, UK: Cambridge University Press).

—— and MANGALORE, R. (2007), "Mental Health: Continuing Challenges," in *The Commonwealth Ministers Book 2007* (London: Commonwealth Secretariat), 1–4.

—— et al. (2007), "Economics, Mental Health and Policy: Summary of MHEEN Seminar." Personal Social Services Research Unit, London School of Economics, London.

—— et al. (2008), "Cost Effectiveness and Mental Health." MHEEN Policy Briefing 2.

KUNO, E. and ASUKAI, N. (2000), "Efforts Toward Building a Community-Based Mental Health System in Japan," *International Journal of Law and Psychiatry*, 23(3–4): 361–73.

LAYARD, R. (2004), "Mental Health: Britain's Biggest Social Problem." Working Paper.

LU, C. L., FRANK, R. G., and MCGUIRE, T. C. (2008), "Demand Response of Mental Health Services to Cost Sharing Under Managed Care," *Journal of Mental Health Policy and Economics*, 11(3): 113–26.

MANNING, W. G. and FRANK, R. G. (1992), "Econometric Issues in the Demand for Mental Health Care under Insurance," in R. Frank and W. Manning (eds.), *Economics and Mental Health* (Baltimore: Johns Hopkins University Press).

—— et al. (1981), "The Two-Part Model of the Demand for Medical Care: Preliminary Results from the Health Insurance Study," in J. Van der Gaag and M. Perlman (eds.), *Health, Economics and Health Economics* (Amsterdam: North Holland).

—— WELLS, K. B., BUCHANAN, J. L., KEELER, E. B., VALDEZ, E. B., and NEWHOUSE, J. P. (1989), "Effects of Mental Health Insurance: Evidence from the Health Insurance Experiment." RAND Working Paper No. R-3015-NIMH/HCFA, Santa Monica, CA.

MARK, T. L. et al. (2007), "Mental Health Treatment Expenditure Trends, 1986–2003," *Psychiatry Services*, 58 (Aug.): 1041–8.

MAZADE, N. and GLOVER, R. W. (2007), "State Mental Health Policy: Critical Priorities Confronting State Mental Health Agencies," *Psychiatric Services*, 58(9): 1148–50.

MCCAID, D., KNAPP, M., MEDEIROS, H. et al. (2007), "Mental Health and Economics in Europe: Findings from the MHEEN Group," *EuroHealth*, 13(3): 1–6.

MCCAID, D. et al. (2008), "Making the Economic Case for the Promotion of Mental Well Being and the prevention of Mental Health Problems." MHEEN Policy Briefing 2.

MCGUIRE, T. G. (1981), *Financing Psychotherapy: Costs, Effects and Public Policy*. Cambridge, MA: Ballinger.

MCGUIRE T. G. and RIORDAN, M. H. (1995), "Contracting for Community Based Public Mental Health Services," in A. Rupp and T. Ha (eds.), *Economics and Mental Health* (Greenwich, CT: JAI Press).

MEARA, E. and FRANK, R. G. (2005) "Spending on Substance Abuse Treatment: How Much is Enough?" *Addiction*, 100(9) (Sept.): 1240–8.

MECHANIC, D. (1999), *Mental Health and Social Policy* (Boston: Allyn and Bacon).

MICHAEL, R. J. (1980), "Bureaucrats, Legislators and the Decline of the State Mental Hospital," *Journal of Economics and Business*, 32(3): 198–205.

NEWHOUSE, J. P. and the HIE GROUP (1993), *Free for All: Lessons from the RAND Health Insurance Experiment* (Cambridge, MA: Harvard University Press).

OECD (2006), *OECD Health Data 2006*. Available at: <www.oecd.org/health/healthdata>.

PERNEGER, T. V., ALLAZ, A. F., ETTER, J. F., and ROUGEMONT, A. (1995), "Mental Health and Choice between Managed Care and Indemnity Health Insurance," *American Journal of Psychiatry*, 152(7): 1020–5.

RODWIN, V. (2003), "The Health Care System Under French NHI: Lessons for US Health Care Reform," *American Journal of Public Health*, 93(1): 30–7.

ROGERS, A. and PIGRIM, D. (1996), *Mental Health Policy in Britain* (New York: St Martins Press).

ROMANOW, R. J. and MARCHILDON, G. P. (2003), "Psychological Services and the Future of Health Care in Canada," *CanadianPsychology*, 44(4): 283–95.

SALIZE, H. J., ROSSLER, W., and BECKER, T. (2007), "Mental Health Care in Germany: Current State and Trends," *European Archives of Clinical Neuroscience*, 257: 92–103.

TAUBE, C. A., KESSLER, L. G., and BURNS, B. J. (1986), "Estimating the Probability and Level of Ambulatory Mental Health Services Use," *Health Services Research*, 21(2): 321–40.

Tomes, N. (2006), "The Patient as a Policy Factor: A Historical Case Study of the Consumer/ Survivor Movement in Mental Health," *Health Affairs*, 25(3): 720–9.

Triplett, J. (2001), "What's Different about Health? Human Repair and Car Repair in National Accounts and in National Health Accounts," in D. Cutler and E. Berndt (eds.), *Medical Care Output and Productivity* (Chicago: University of Chicago Press), 15–96.

USDHHS (United States Department of Health and Human Services) (1999), *Mental Health: A Report of the Surgeon General* (Washington, DC: USDHHS).

US GAO (United States General Accounting Office) (1977), "Returning the Mentally Disabled to the Community: Government Needs to do More" (Washington D.C.: US Government Printing Office).

Verdoux, H. (2007), "The Current State of Adult Mental Health Care in France," *European Archives of Clinical Neuroscience*, 257: 64–70.

Watts, C. A., Scheffler, R. M., and Jewell, N. P. (1986), "Demand for Outpatient Mental Health Services in a Heavily Insured Population: The Case of the Blue Cross and Blue Shield Association's Federal Employees Health Benefits Program," *Health Services Research*, 21(2): 267–90.

Williams, R. F. G. and Doessel, R. P. (2008), "The Australian Mental Health System: An Economic Overview and Some Research Issues," *International Journal of Mental Health Systems*, 2(4): 1–12.

WHO (World Health Organization) (2001), *World Health Report: Mental Health: New Understanding, New Hope* (Geneva: WHO).

Yellowlees, H. (1990), "Administrative Barriers to Implementation and Diffusion of Innovative Approaches to Mental Health Care in the United Kingdom," in I. M. Marks and R. A. Scott (eds.), *Mental Health Care Delivery: Innovations, Impediments and Implementation* (Cambridge, UK: Cambridge University Press).

CHAPTER 12

PUBLIC-SECTOR HEALTH CARE FINANCING[*]

ÅKE BLOMQVIST

12.1 INTRODUCTION

SERIOUS illness requiring costly treatment can have devastating financial consequences for individuals and families. Because illness strikes randomly, risk pooling through various kinds of insurance arrangements can reduce the impact of illness-related financial shocks: Through risk pooling, the potentially devastating financial impact on the few unlucky enough to be stricken by illness is converted into a predictable smaller cost shared both by those who fall ill and those who don't. Economic analysis can be used to show that, under reasonable circumstances, such arrangements are efficient in the sense that on average, members of a community in which there is risk pooling are better off than if there is none. In principle, risk pooling for this purpose can be accomplished via the market mechanism, through private health insurance. However, as has long been recognized in the literature, reliance on private markets in this context may produce outcomes that are both inefficient (in a microeconomic sense) and inequitable. This, of course, is the reason why the public sector has become heavily involved in financing health care in most countries in the world.

With respect to efficiency, a particularly intractable problem is that of adverse selection (further discussed in Chapters 13, 15, and 16 in this volume). Adverse selection arises when different consumers are subject to different risks of illness, especially in situations when it is impossible or costly for insurers to identify those who are at high risk. There is then a tendency for those at low risk of illness to want to escape from insurance plans that they share with individuals who are at higher risk (since the presence of latter increases the expected payouts per person for such insurance plans, and

* I would like to thank Sherry Glied and Peter Smith for helpful comments on an earlier draft.

therefore tends to increase their premium cost). If insurance markets are allowed to let individuals sort themselves in this manner, the result may be that those at low risk forgo insurance or end up in plans that only offer limited protection, while those at high risk end up in plans with very high premiums; alternatively, the only plans that survive in the market may be low-quality plans that only offer limited protection.[1] Neither kind of outcome is economically efficient. An outcome under which those at high risk of illness have to pay very high premiums, or cannot get insurance at all, can also not be considered equitable, at least not if those at high risk are in this category through no fault of their own (because of inherited risk factors, past illness, and so on). Note that, contrary to the adverse selection problem, the equity issue arises whether or not the insurers can identify those at high risk on the basis of observable factors.[2]

While it is possible for society to address the problems of inefficiency and inequity of private insurance markets through various forms of regulation, the experience in the countries that have tried to do so has not been particularly encouraging. In most advanced countries, therefore, the route that has been taken instead has been to reduce or eliminate the problems with private insurance by offering, or requiring, membership in publicly funded (or publicly organized) insurance plans. The question that will be considered in this chapter is: How should such public plans be designed and funded?

The chapter is divided into three main sections, each dealing with a fundamental question that must be addressed in a system where government takes a major role in health care financing. The first one is what the relative importance of the public plan and private payments as sources of funding should be (where private sources are understood to include both out-of-pocket payments by patients and private insurance). The second question is how the revenue to pay for public spending on health care should be raised. How does financing through general revenue compare with various forms of social insurance? If financing is through general revenue, how should responsibility be divided between different levels of government? If it is through social insurance, should there be several funds among which individuals can choose, or a single fund for all? A related issue is how health care for the elderly should be financed in a social insurance system. The third fundamental question, finally, concerns the way the money should be spent. Should the public insurance plan also be the service provider (as in the national health insurance model) or should health services be supplied by independent providers? In the latter case, what should be the nature of the contracts between providers and the public plan? In particular, what methods should be used to pay providers (doctors and hospitals)?

---

[1] The classic analysis of adverse selection is Rothschild and Stiglitz (1976). Two papers that demonstrate its empirical significance in different ways are Marquis (1992) and Cutler and Reber (1998). Cutler and Zeckhauser (2000) provides a useful summary.

[2] An early paper that stresses the equity motive for government provision of health insurance is Blomqvist and Horn (1984).

12.2 What Share of Health Expenditures Should the Public Plan Cover?

Even though the public sector dominates the financing of health care in most countries, part of the expenditures conventionally classified as related to health is privately paid for in all countries. Private payments can be classified in three categories. The first includes spending on health-related goods and services that are not covered by insurance, public or private. Examples would be many kinds of cosmetic surgery, over-the-counter (non-prescription) drugs, eye glasses in most countries and dental services in some. The second category consists of the consumers' share of the cost of partially insured services. Consumer cost-sharing in this sense is common in private insurance plans, but it is considerable in the public insurance plans in some countries as well. A third source of private funding is private insurance; its share in total cost is largest in the US, but it accounts for a substantial share in many other countries as well.

12.2.1 Consumer Cost-Sharing in Public Plans

Requiring consumers to pay a share of the cost of insured services under public plans serves two purposes: To reduce the amount of revenue that the government has to raise in order to finance the publicly funded plan, and to reduce the losses in economic efficiency that may result from over-utilization of health services when consumers are insured. At the same time, of course, a higher degree of consumer cost-sharing implies a reduction in the degree of protection from the financial consequences of serious illness (or equivalently, a reduction in what economists refer to as the "gains from insurance").

The problem of finding the degree of consumer cost-sharing that best balances the objectives of more complete insurance protection against the tendency for insurance to cause an inefficiently high level of health expenditures has been extensively analyzed in the literature;[3] it is further discussed in Chapters 15 and 16 in this volume. In general, it can be shown to be efficient for the consumer's cost-share to be lower when he or she incurs large health care costs, but higher with relatively low costs. This can be accomplished via a plan with an initial deductible (under which consumers are responsible for 100 percent of their health care costs in a given period of time, up to the limit of the deductible), followed by one or more intervals of partial cost-sharing, perhaps up to some maximum (a "stop-loss provision") beyond which the plan pays 100 percent of any additional costs.[4]

---

[3] Influential early contributions are Pauly (1968) and Zeckhauser (1970). The empirical work in the Rand Health Insurance study showed quantitatively the importance of striking an appropriate tradeoff; see Newhouse et al. (1993). For an alternative exposition, and a critique of some of the earlier analysis, see Nyman (2003).

[4] Blomqvist (1997) provides a formal analysis.

The theoretical analysis of the efficient degree of consumer cost-sharing has focused on the trade-off between the gain from more complete insurance against the associated inefficiency of over-utilization, but in practice, the appropriate degree of cost-sharing should also depend on certain other factors, in particular, on the relative costs of administering plans with different degrees of cost-sharing. It is sometimes argued that one of the major advantages of a public insurance system with no patient cost-sharing (as in Canada and the UK) is that it avoids costs associated with billing and collection of patient payments.

On the other hand, the public finance literature has long recognized that in making choices between private and government funding of various activities, account should be taken of the fact that the explicit and implicit cost of collecting taxes to finance public spending may be quite high: The total cost to the economy of collecting one dollar of government revenue is well above one dollar. One reason for this is the cost incurred in paying the expenditures of the government bureaucracy that administers the tax system, and to the taxpayers that must do the tax-related record-keeping. In addition, taxation has an implicit cost because it causes distortions in the economy as resources are shifted to non-taxed activities when prices change in response to increased taxes. Recognition of the high real cost of raising tax revenue strengthens the case for making consumers pay a larger share of their health care costs.

Patient cost-sharing as a means of controlling health services utilization and aggregate health care costs is an example of what in the health economics literature is called "demand-side incentives" (that is, incentives that affect the patients who use health services). A prominent theme in the health economics literature in recent years has been that services utilization and total health care spending in a given population also depend strongly on the incentives on the *providers* of health services who treat the patients and advise them on what services they should utilize ("supply-side incentives"). If utilization can be effectively controlled through supply-side incentives, the case for high user fees is less strong. Supply-side incentives are briefly discussed in the final section.[5]

12.2.2 Private Insurance in Countries with Public Funding of Health Care

Even in systems where much of the financial risks associated with major illness has been socialized via government funding or social insurance, private insurance may retain a significant role. The amount of government revenue that must be raised to pay for the government's share obviously depends in part on the extent and form that this role is

---

[5] Specific forms of supply-side incentives are discussed in Chapters 19, 25, and 26 of this volume. Useful earlier surveys are in Ellis and McGuire (1993), and Glied (2000).

allowed to take; conversely, the rules under which the public sector finances its insurance plan(s) can influence the scope and extent of private insurance.

Statistics on the relative importance of private health insurance as a share of total health care financing show a great deal of variability across countries.[6] Among developed countries, the one where it accounts for the largest share is the US where a recent estimate shows it paying for 35 percent of total health care spending. By the same token, the public sector's share, at 44 percent, is lower in the US than in any other developed country. Another country in which the share of private insurance has been relatively large is the Netherlands, where it accounted for as much as about 15 percent of total spending before 2006. Part of the reason was that until reforms implemented that year, individuals with an income above a certain threshold were not allowed to enroll in the publicly organized sickness fund system. Private insurance also accounts for a substantial portion of total health expenditure (7–13%) in Australia, Canada, France, Germany, and Switzerland, but in other countries (those of Scandinavia, Italy) its share is very small or negligible (less than 1%).[7]

The large variation in the share of private insurance in total health care funding mirrors the wide differences across countries in the regulations that govern the interaction between publicly funded plans and private insurance. The main explanation for the large role of private insurance in the US, of course, is that publicly funded plans in that country only cover some 25 percent of the population (essentially those over 65, who are eligible for the Medicare plan, and those meeting the low-income criteria necessary to qualify for state Medicaid plans). Thus for the remaining 75 percent of the population, protection against the financial consequences of ill health can only be acquired via a private insurance plan. In Germany, the rules allowed people with incomes above a certain level to opt out of the government-organized insurance system and sign up with a private plan instead, until the reforms of 2007 (see below).

12.2.2.1 *Supplementary and Complementary Private Insurance*

In most developed countries, public-sector plans are universal, meaning that every citizen is covered (or at least has the option of being covered) by them. However, even in countries with a universal public plan, private insurance may play a major role. When significant categories of health spending are excluded from public-plan coverage (for example, outpatient pharmaceuticals or dental care), individuals may sign up for private insurance plans that cover these expenditures. In the terminology used by the OECD,[8]

---

[6] The material in this and the next few paragraphs draws heavily on Colombo and Tapay (2004).

[7] The figure for Switzerland does not include the costs paid by private plans for the expenditures of those Swiss citizens who have chosen to obtain the compulsory insurance required under Swiss law from a private insurer; Colombo and Tapay (2004), Table 12.1, note d. Under the new rules in the Netherlands, enrollment in the publicly funded health insurance system is now compulsory for all citizens. However, the individual insurance plans in which citizens are enrolled are classified as private. It is not clear, therefore, whether the share of private insurance in the Netherlands should now be given as zero, or as 100 percent!

[8] See Colombo and Tapay 2004: 14.

this is described as private insurance being a *supplement* to the public plan. Major examples of this kind of arrangement are Canada and the US Medicare plan before 2007. In both cases, a main reason why many people in the public plan also had private insurance was that the public plans did not cover outpatient pharmaceuticals.[9] In countries where the public plan requires a significant degree of patient cost-sharing, private insurers may also be allowed to offer plans that cover the share that patients are responsible for under the public plan. The OECD uses the term *complementary* to refer to such plans. The foremost example of a country where private insurance plays this role is France where it has been estimated that as many as 85 percent of the population have complementary private coverage. Another example is, again, the US Medicare plan in which many enrollees have signed up for private "Medigap" plans that cover the patient co-payments under the basic plan (and that, until 2007, often covered most of the cost of outpatient pharmaceuticals as well).

Complementary private insurance is controversial, since it can be interpreted as working at cross-purposes with the cost-sharing provisions in the public plan. Generally, the intention of cost-sharing is to give patients an incentive to reduce the extent of over-utilization of health services (in comparison with the economically efficient level) that tends to result when consumers are insured, by making the implicit subsidy to health services utilization less than 100 percent. Private complementary coverage nullifies this incentive, since it makes the consumer "fully insured" (that is, provides a 100 percent subsidy to the cost of health care). Moreover, private plans of this kind are effectively subsidized by the public plan. For example, suppose consumers in the public plan are required to pay 50 percent of their health care costs in a particular expenditure range. If they acquire a complementary private plan that pays the consumers' share and, as a result, increase their utilization of health services, only half of the cost of the additional services will be paid for by the private plan: The other half will be paid for by the public plan. Because the public plan pays 50 percent of the extra cost, the premiums for the private plans are effectively subsidized by those who pay for the public plan (taxpayers or payers of social insurance contributions).[10] Because of this effect, a system in which complementary private insurance of this type is allowed makes it artificially cheap for consumers to become fully insured, which in turn reinforces the incentive to over-utilize health services. For this reason, complementary private insurance is not allowed, or at least not encouraged, in some countries where the public plan requires patient cost-sharing (Japan, Sweden).

12.2.2.2 Duplicate vs. Substitute Private Insurance: Opting Out

While supplementary and complementary private insurance plans extend the coverage in the public plan, they do not duplicate or substitute for it. In a few countries,

---

[9] In Canada, many provinces have government plans that cover pharmaceuticals for specific population groups; in the US, Medicare now covers a substantial portion of outpatient pharmaceutical costs.

[10] For a formal analysis of this point, see Blomqvist and Johansson (1997).

however, private insurers can offer plans that cover the same types of services as those covered by the public plan. In cases such as the UK and Sweden, those who sign up for such plans effectively have double coverage: If they fall ill and need care, they can choose to have it paid for either through the public plan or through their private plan. Not surprisingly, those who are privately insured in these countries tend to be persons with high income, and often receive their care in private hospitals and clinics that do not provide services under the public plan, or (as in the UK) from specialists who work both as salaried hospital employees in the public plan but also practice privately in outside clinics. In other cases, however, the private plans cover persons who have *opted out* of their public-plan coverage. That is, they have agreed to not claim reimbursement, or receive services, from the public plan if they fall ill, but to rely on their private plan instead.

In a true opting out system, those who opt out derive some financial advantage from doing so. In Germany before 2007, for example, employees (and retirees) whose income exceeded a certain threshold level were allowed to opt out of the sickness fund plan; if they did, they and their employers did not have to pay the contributions (in the form of payroll deductions) that finance most of the cost of the sickness fund system. Similarly, in the US Medicare system, enrollees are allowed to opt for coverage through a private managed-care insurance plan, instead of staying with the basic Medicare plan. If they do, the Medicare plan transfers a specified sum to the private insurance plan they have enrolled in.[11] In such systems, therefore, there is an effective opportunity for choice between the public and competing private plans, in contrast to the case where those who sign up for a private plan remain insured by the public plan, and still have to pay the taxes or contributions that finance it.

An interesting case of this kind is Australia, where the public plan provides universal access to hospital and outpatient care, as well as to a range of pharmaceuticals. However, private hospital insurance is common, with 44 percent having such coverage in the early 2000s.[12] In the Australian case, private coverage constitutes duplicate insurance in the sense that it does not prevent enrollees from receiving any of the benefits to which they are entitled under the public plan (including care with zero patient cost-sharing in public hospitals). However, in recognition of the fact that those with private insurance often seek treatment in private hospitals (which are not publicly funded), or are treated as "private patients" in public hospitals (which means that their insurance plans will be paying some or all of their hospital fees), the Australian government provides a 30 percent subsidy for the cost of private insurance. This subsidy is similar to what applies in a true opting out system in which those who obtain private insurance are given relief from at least some of the contributions they otherwise would have to make to the public plan.

---

[11] A useful description of the Medicare plan and the options available under it is in "Medicare: A Primer," Kaiser Family Foundation (2008a), available at <www.kff.org/medicare/>.

[12] Colombo and Tapay (2003) contains a detailed description of the Australian system.

12.3 How Should Revenue Be Raised
to Pay for the Public Plan?

As in the previous section, we define as a "public plan" any arrangement that provides publicly organized risk pooling for all or some population groups. Under such arrangements, revenues must be raised to pay for the plan's share of the cost of the health services that are produced for its enrollees. Again, widely different methods are used for this purpose in different countries. In this section we describe some common ones and discuss how they can be evaluated from the conventional viewpoints of economic efficiency and equity.

12.3.1 General Tax Revenue

In some countries, government funding of health care is not separated from funding of other kinds of government expenditure: Health care costs under the public plan are paid for out of general revenue. Countries in this category include the United Kingdom where health care is largely paid for out of general revenue raised by the central government. Other examples are Canada, where health care costs are paid out of provincial government revenue, the US Medicaid plans which are funded by American state governments, and Sweden where county governments are responsible for managing the local health care system and pay for it by charging a proportional income tax on the same base as that used by the central government to collect the progressive income tax. In some cases (the UK, certain Canadian provinces), governments also may collect levies designated as health insurance premiums (or something similar), but since they are compulsory and collected together with general income taxes, these premiums are functionally equivalent to taxes.

When public-plan health costs are paid for from general government revenue, the equity and efficiency properties of the mechanism used to raise this revenue can be analyzed using the methods that are described in the literature on public finance (taxation).[13] Although "equity" is not an unambiguous concept, in practice it refers to the notion that those with low income should be taxed less than the rich; that is, the system should be *progressive* to a reasonable degree. Efficiency, on the other hand, refers to the fact (briefly discussed above) that the total cost to the economy of raising a certain amount of revenue exceeds the amount raised; the difference is sometimes called the *collection costs* of the tax system. As already noted, collection costs arise not only because resources have to be used to administer the tax system, but also because different forms of taxation cause distortions in the economy as individuals and firms change their behavior in response to various taxes. While some degree of distortion is inevitable, especially if the

---

[13] A classic exposition is Atkinson and Stiglitz (1980); see also Auerbach and Feldstein (1985).

tax system is highly progressive, different kinds of taxation cause different degrees of distortion and collection costs, so that, loosely speaking, an efficient system is one that minimizes the collection costs for a given degree of income redistribution.

While the public finance literature deals with the question how to assess the equity and efficiency properties of a country's entire tax system (that is, the system through which *all* public sector revenue is raised, to pay for all kinds of government expenditures), attempts have sometimes been made in the literature to assess the efficiency and (especially) equity of the way countries raise revenue to finance a *specific kind* of expenditure (such as health or education). Such attempts may be reasonable if it is possible to clearly associate the expenditures involved with specific revenue sources. However, it is often not clear that such an association is meaningful. Consider, for example, a hypothetical country that spends equal amounts of money on two items only (say, defence and education), and collects equal amounts of revenue from two kinds of taxes only (say, an income tax and a sales tax). Suppose that an analysis of the two kinds of taxation led to the conclusion that the income tax was more progressive than the sales tax. Since there is no meaningful way to say which source of revenue pays for which category of expenditure, it can also not be meaningful to claim, for example, that the revenue to pay for education is raised in a more equitable way than that to pay for defence (or vice versa). Although this may seem an obvious point, a failure to recognize it has caused a certain amount of confusion in the health policy debate in some countries. The problem only becomes even more ambiguous when there are many different sources of revenue and categories of spending. Analysis of equity issues such as those relating to health services access, or to the distribution of the burden of private health care costs do not suffer from this conceptual problem, but attempts at estimating who bears the burden of the government's share of health care funding are inherently arbitrary and therefore of limited usefulness.[14]

12.3.1.1 *Cost-sharing Between Several Levels of Government*

As noted above, in countries like Canada, the US, and Sweden, management and funding of the health care system has to a large extent been delegated to state and local governments, that is, governments at a level below the central (federal) ones. There are good reasons for this: When making expenditure decisions, sub-national governments can be more sensitive to local conditions and preferences than central-government decision makers would be likely to be.

If spending decisions are decentralized, one may argue that responsibility for funding should be as well, so that the decisions about how much to spend are ultimately made by the same politicians who have to raise the taxes to pay for them. However, in countries where responsibility for health system funding has been decentralized, there is typically a significant degree of cost-sharing under which the central level of government contributes part of the total cost of publicly funded health care. This raises two questions.

---

[14] A survey of the research on equity in health care is in Wagstaff and van Doorslaer (2000). See also Wagstaff et al. (1999), and this volume, Chapter 35.

First, when two levels of government share the responsibility for funding health care, how should the equity and efficiency properties of the revenue-raising process be assessed? Second, do the rules of the cost-sharing system put the proper incentives on the political actors whose decisions shape the publicly funded health care system?

With respect to the first question, the equity and efficiency properties of funding health care through cost-sharing of this type obviously depends on the methods of taxation and revenue collection that are used at both levels of government. From an individual tax payer's point of view it is a matter of indifference whether a particular tax is paid to the central or local government, so the relevant equity and efficiency properties are those of the combined system of taxation by both levels of government. (This point is sometimes summarized in the maxim that states that even when there are many governments, "there is only one taxpayer.") Moreover, it is (as in the single-government case) not possible to identify any particular revenue sources as being those used for funding health care specifically. For a lower level government (state or provincial), therefore, the relevant problem should be to design a system of taxation that efficiently and equitably (from the viewpoint of its own population) raises enough revenue to pay for *all* expenditures that it is responsible for, taking the taxes imposed by the higher level of government as given. The central government, in turn, must take into account the taxes that lower-level governments will impose when deciding on what forms of taxation to use in order to pay for those expenditure that *it* is responsible for, as well as whether it should use its powers of taxation to bring about a more equitable distribution of after-tax income across lower level jurisdictions.[15]

The rules that apply to cost-sharing between higher and lower governments may also have an impact on the process whereby spending decisions are made. If cost-sharing takes the form of matching grants under which the transfers from the central government are based on the amounts actually spent by the lower-level government, the result may be a tendency toward inefficiently large amounts of health care spending in comparison with spending on activities that are not cost-shared. (In weighing benefits of incremental health care to their constituents against their costs, state and local politicians do not have sufficient incentive to take into account the share of the cost that is borne by the central government, since that part is shared among all taxpayers in the country, not just those in the state, province, or county where the spending decisions are made.) Partly in reflection of this problem, cost-sharing arrangements today typically are governed by different and more complicated rules than those in a straight system of matching grants. For example, they make take the form of block grants (transfers of fixed sums of money).[16]

---

[15] A general reference on fiscal federalism is Ahmad and Brosio (2006); the chapter by Boadway deals specifically with equity-related transfers.

[16] From an accounting point of view, confusion may arise in systems of cost-sharing when the lower-level government spends money on many different programs and the central government makes general-purpose transfers as well as ones that are "ear-marked" for specific purposes. In Canada, for example, there is endless debate over the question what percentages of health care costs are paid by the central and provincial governments, respectively. In this debate, the central government tries to take credit for a large share of this politically popular form of spending by stating that a large part of the transfers to the provincial governments are "for health," not "general-purpose transfers."

12.3.2 The Social Insurance Model

The main alternative to general taxation as the method for funding government-organized health insurance plans is what is known as the social insurance model. While there are substantial differences in the way it is organized in different countries that use this model, its backbone almost always is a system of income-related contributions to health insurance plans for employees. Among developed countries, it is probably the most widely used model. In Europe, it is used in France, Germany, and the Netherlands; other large countries that follow it are Japan and the US (for the Medicare plan). It is also being introduced in a number of the world's middle and low-income countries, including China.[17]

In most countries that use it today, the roots of the social insurance model are in earlier voluntary systems, in which employees in particular industries or crafts (typically through their labor unions) organized voluntary insurance through sickness funds, to which all contributed, and from which the cost of members' health care were paid. As governments gradually took a more active role in transforming the sickness fund system into a social insurance model, they built on the existing system but strengthened it, for example, by making membership compulsory. Further extensions of coverage to other population categories than employees (the retired, the self-employed, the unemployed) were sometimes accomplished through the creation of separate funds for the respective population groups. In some countries, the system has attained universal coverage (France, Japan), while in others certain population groups are excluded (the US) or allowed to opt out (in Germany before 2007).[18] However, even in countries where most of the population is covered by social insurance, a distinguishing feature remains that insurance is through a system of multiple funds, not a single one. I will return to this point below.

In comparing the equity and efficiency properties of the social insurance model of funding health care with the general-revenue financing model, the first point that should be made is that, for those population groups for which membership in the public plan is compulsory (which may be the entire population), the contributions that the insured are required to pay toward funding the plan (as a percentage of their salary, or on some

---

[17] A review of the process of health policy reform in China is Blomqvist and Qian (2008). Hsiao and Shaw (2007) review the experience of several other low- and middle-income countries that have introduced social health insurance plans.

[18] As noted above, persons with an income above a certain threshold level were excluded from social insurance in the Netherlands before the 2006 reform. The French, German, and Dutch social insurance systems are described in detail in the volumes published by the World Health Organization on behalf of the European Observatory on Health Systems and Policies: Sandier, Paris, and Polton (2004), Busse and Riesberg (2004), den Exter et al. (2004); for updates describing the Dutch and German reforms in 2006–7, see van de Ven and Schut (2008) and Lisac (2006). The Japanese system is described in Campbell and Ikegami (1998); an update is Imai (2002). Descriptions of the US Medicare system can be found in any of the standard US textbooks in health economics; a useful summary is in Kaiser Family Foundation (2008a).

other basis) are equivalent to a tax. This is most obviously the case in countries such as France and Japan in which everyone automatically is a member of the publicly organized plan, but the principle also applies to cases where membership is compulsory only for certain population groups (as in the US): For those who must belong to the plan, the amounts that they are required to pay are equivalent to a tax.

This equivalence has two important consequences. First, it means that the equity and efficiency properties of the social insurance system can only meaningfully be analyzed as part of the overall system of raising government revenue for all purposes: As previously argued, it is not meaningful to separately analyze the equity and efficiency properties of the revenue raised for some particular purpose. In this sense, therefore, social insurance funding of health care involves the same issues as those arising when funding is from general revenue. Second, once it is recognized that the contributions paid into the social insurance system is only one of many sources of government revenue, it becomes clear that it is not in general efficient to match the revenues raised from this source with a particular kind of spending (health care). If one wants to explain why many countries still try, at least to some extent, to match health care expenditure under their public plans to specific types of revenue (such as social insurance contributions), one must appeal to other factors (such as the history of the health insurance system, or political considerations), not economic efficiency or equity.

As countries broadened their social insurance systems to encompass population groups such as the self-employed, those on welfare, and the retired, additional revenue had to be raised from sources other than employer–employee contributions in order to finance the funds that were given the responsibility to cover these population groups. Various methods have been used. For the self-employed, contributions proportional to income (rather than salaries) have sometimes been required. For the unemployed and those on welfare, direct premium subsidies from the government have been paid to the relevant funds. As will be further discussed below, a particularly important issue is how to extend social insurance to cover the elderly, whose health care costs on average are large. In some countries, the fund or funds covering them have not only been directly subsidized out of general government revenue, but have also received transfers (referred to as cross-subsidies) from the funds covering employees.

12.3.2.1 *Social Insurance and Horizontal Equity*

Even though most countries have systems of extensive direct and indirect subsidies to sickness funds in which members are at high risk of illness, or have low income, in many cases it still remains the case that members of some funds have to pay contributions at higher rates than in other funds, in order for the funds to break even as they are supposed to. For example, in Japan there are still substantial differences in the required contribution rates across funds in different industries, or across the municipal funds through which the self-employed and retired people are covered. As a result, workers in different industries or retirees in different municipalities may have to pay very different amounts for the same health insurance benefits even if they have the same income. To most people, such differences are inconsistent with the way they would define an equitable system. In particular, they conflict with what is known in the public-finance literature as the principle of *horizontal equity*: That taxpayers in similar circumstances (with the same level of income) should be taxed at the same rate.

12.3.2.2 *Efficiency Properties of Social Insurance Contributions*

Although the equity and efficiency properties of the tax system depend on the combined effects of all taxes together, one can identify certain characteristics that a particular revenue source (such as social insurance contributions) tends to have when viewed by itself. If financing is through employment-related contributions that are proportional to a person's salary, there are efficiency effects similar to those of an income tax. That is, a worker has less incentive to raise his/her income through means such as working overtime, accepting positions with more responsibility in return for higher pay, or undergoing further education and training, and so on, since part of a gross salary increase "leaks away" into higher social insurance contributions. In a competitive labor market, this effect will apply both to the employer's and the employee's share in systems where both contribute. While a system of income-related contributions of course is motivated by a concern for equity, the efficiency effects should also be taken into account when designing the system, and are especially likely to be severe in a country where workers also are subject to a proportional or progressive income tax. Moreover, because social insurance contributions are levied on labor income only, they implicitly discriminate against job creation and labor-intensive industries, in favor of capital intensive production, an issue that has raised concern in those European countries that have suffered from persistently high unemployment rates.[19]

One way to reduce the incentive effects is to make the contributions income-dependent only up to a ceiling, something that will at least partially reduce the incentive effects of payroll deductions since for those at the ceiling the contribution is equivalent to a lump-sum tax. While this makes the system regressive from an equity point of view, the trade-off of more efficiency for less equity may be justifiable if the tax system as a whole is progressive.

12.3.3 Social Insurance: A Single Fund vs. Multiple Funds?

The arrangements that countries with social insurance systems have used to equalize contribution rates across different employment-related funds, and to share the cost of covering those who are not employed, have sometimes become quite complex. This naturally raises the question whether it wouldn't be simpler to reorganize the system into a single fund that covered all those eligible for the public insurance plan. Doing so would obviously eliminate the problem of different contribution rates for people in similar

---

[19] In France, salary-related contributions from employees now have been replaced by a system under which contributions are paid also on capital income and (at a reduced rate) on pensions and social benefits as well; see Sandier, Paris, and Polton (2004: 36–8).

circumstances as a source of horizontal inequity and would be easier to administer than a system of multiple funds, especially if the latter involves complicated arrangements for risk pooling and cross-subsidization.

The standard argument in economics against offering insurance through a single public plan would be that this plan would constitute a monopoly, and economic analysis suggests that monopolies tend to produce socially inefficient outcomes. Even if the monopoly is prevented from charging high prices and earning high profits (through regulation or because it is operated by government), the fact that it lacks competition may give it insufficient incentives to control costs or to improve the quality of its services.

Whether or not these arguments apply in the context of social health insurance depends on several things. First, in a situation where those covered by the public plan cannot choose in which fund to enroll (as is the case in Japan and France), there is no real competition among funds; effectively, each one is a monopoly. Second, even if eligible individuals are free to choose among funds (as in Germany), there may still be little effective competition if each fund is constrained by regulation to offer exactly the same package of benefits (including an unrestricted freedom for enrollees to choose among providers). In such cases, the only ways that a fund can try to control costs and become more competitive is by reducing its own administrative costs (which are not likely to be very large to begin with), or by trying to attract healthy low-risk enrollees (raising the possibility of adverse selection, something that is inconsistent with the plan's objective of an equitable distribution of the burden of illness).

The situation is different, however, if individuals are free to choose in which sickness fund to enroll, *and funds are allowed to compete by offering benefit packages that differ in some dimensions*. Among the countries that use the social insurance model, many have systems that incorporate this feature at least to some extent: Belgium, Germany, the Netherlands, Switzerland, Israel, and the US (in the Medicare plan). In the Netherlands, for example, individual insurers (the term "sickness fund" is no longer used) are now allowed to offer plans under which coverage is restricted to treatment by doctors with whom the fund has negotiated regarding fees and other aspects of care. In order to compete for enrollees, each fund therefore has an incentive to negotiate with providers for a set of fees and treatment practices that represents the best possible combination of cost and quality. That is, choice and competition among funds gives them an incentive to be cost-effective, along the lines that standard economic theory suggests.[20]

While the arguments for these advantages of competition are persuasive, whether the competitive model ultimately is an acceptable one depends very much on whether it can be designed in such a way that adverse selection problems remain limited. As before,

[20] The competing-funds model was also part of the proposals for universal health insurance in the US advanced by the Clinton administration in the early 1990s. Flood (2000: ch. 3, pp. 41–126) has good descriptions of both that and the Dutch reform models, both of which originated with the work of Enthoven (see Enthoven 1988, 1993, 1994; and Enthoven and van de Ven 2007). Other countries that have used it include Israel and Switzerland, and it is being introduced in Germany as well; for a review see van de Ven et al. (2007).

funds have an incentive to compete not just by being efficient in providing care for a given population, but also by trying to attract individuals whose expected treatment costs are low relative to the amount of money they bring into the fund.[21] The consequences of this incentive are likely to be particularly severe if the system is set up so that the fund receives the same amount from the central revenue pool for every individual. In such a situation, it is easy to identify those with low expected treatment costs: the young and healthy. By the same token, the risk of severe adverse selection can be reduced if the system is set up so that the fund receives larger amounts for those with high expected cost of illness (the old, persons with disabilities or known chronic conditions). In the Netherlands, the system has been set up with an elaborate set of risk adjustments under which the amount the insurance plan that a person chooses is paid from the central pool reflects his or her expected cost as closely as possible.[22] As this version of the Dutch model has only operated for a few years, it is still too early to tell to what extent the risk adjustment system has been able to overcome the adverse selection problem.

12.3.4 Social Insurance and the Retired

One issue that must be addressed in social insurance systems dominated by employment-related funding is how to pay for insurance covering the elderly. It is a particularly important problem for two reasons. First, older people on average have much higher health care expenditures than those in younger age groups. Second, because most of them are retired, their health care costs (as well as their other consumption expenditure) cannot be financed out of their current labor earnings, but must be paid for either out of past savings (private or public), or via transfers from the non-elderly.

Different countries have used different methods to deal with this issue. In France, Germany, and Holland, the elderly are members of the same insurance pool as employees are. Since their contribution rates (as a percentage of their public or private pensions) are the same as, or lower than, the percentage that employees contribute from their salaries, while their average health care costs are higher, the systems in these countries provide *implicit* transfers from the young to the old. Typically, the insurance funds also receive some direct subsidies from the government.[23] In Japan, the elderly are

---

[21] For a clear exposition of the issues involved, see Newhouse (1996). Van de Ven et al. (2007) describe practical approaches that have been used to deal with them.

[22] When an individual joins one of the Dutch plans, it receives two premiums: one risk-rated one from the central pool, and one that is paid directly by the person who joins; the latter may differ from fund to fund, but must be the same for every individual in a given fund.

Various methodologies and issues relevant to risk-rating are discussed in van de Ven and Ellis (2000), Ellis (2008), and also in Chapter 17 of this volume.

[23] The total contribution on behalf of employees to health insurance in all these countries also includes a portion that is paid by the employer. In Germany, the contributions paid by pensioners are supplemented by additional payments from the government, so the total percentage contribution rate of pensioners is similar to that for employees. In France, however, there is no such supplement, so the total percentage contribution rate from pensioners is much lower than from employees.

covered through a separate system of municipally administered funds. The revenues of these funds come partly from premium payments by the elderly themselves, but mostly from *explicit* transfers from the funds through which younger individuals (employees) are insured, as well as from direct government subsidies.

In one sense, the subsidies from the young to the old in social insurance systems can be interpreted simply as an extension of the basic idea that publicly funded health insurance should pool risk *and* redistribute resources from those with low expected health care expenditures and high income, to those with higher expected costs and lower income. From this perspective, the elderly are just people who, on average, fall in the latter category, and the relevant public finance problem remains that of designing a tax and contribution system that raises the total revenue required for government spending in an equitable and efficient manner. However, when designing such a system, society must take into account that today's young are tomorrow's old, so that changes in transfers and taxes affecting the old can have a significant influence on labor supply and savings decisions of the young as well. Efficiency and equity implications of intergenerational transfers have been most extensively analyzed in the context of social insurance programs that provide retirement income security, but they are equally relevant to transfers in the form of subsidizing the cost of health insurance for the elderly. Logically, therefore, the question of how health insurance for the elderly should be paid for must be analyzed in a framework that considers both types of programs.[24]

One question to which intergenerational issues are relevant is whether social insurance programs should be financed through a system of prior contributions to a fund, or according to the pay-as-you-go principle (that is, through a system in which all benefits are financed from current contributions and there is no prior build-up of a fund). The European systems are based on the latter principle, while in the US Medicare system there is a "Medicare Trust Fund" which, in principle, represents accumulated past contributions out of which future health care costs of the population covered by Medicare will be paid.[25] Those who advocate funded programs sometimes do so because they see prior funding as a device for reducing the extent of intergenerational transfers and the tax burden on the young.

However, the difference between the two types of systems should not be exaggerated. As economic analysis makes clear, in a population with a stable age structure, fully-funded and pay-as-you-go systems can be essentially equivalent in the long run, the only difference being that the latter implies a large one-time transfer from the young to the generation that is old at the time when the social insurance program is introduced. Moreover, the burden of dealing with the high health care costs of a temporary bulge in the old

[24] The discussion of retirement income security in the US is summarized in Feldstein (1996) or Gramlich (1996). Feldstein (1999) considers the specific issue of funding health care in an aging population, which is also discussed in Chapter 36 of this volume.

[25] At present, this fund has a substantial positive balance. However, projections indicate that if contribution rates and health care expenditures of those eligible for Medicare continue along present trends, the funds will gradually diminish and may disappear completely over the next ten or twenty years.

population (of the type that will be seen in countries that experienced pronounced baby booms) must be borne by society whether or not it is paid for out of an existing fund, and can be distributed fairly over time even if there is no accumulated fund (for example, by allowing the public plan to finance a deficit by borrowing from the government).

The Social Security and Medicare Trust Funds in the US system[26] are *collective* funds, so even though they reflect the contributions of past generations of workers toward the funding of benefits to be paid out after retirement, there is not a tight connection between the contributions of individual workers and their subsequent entitlement to benefits: In the case of the Medicare fund, there is *no* connection as everyone over 65 is entitled to the same coverage. For this reason, payments into the Medicare fund have incentive effects that are equivalent to a tax: Reducing the contributions does not reduce future benefits. The proposals advanced by the Bush administration to modify the Social Security system by introducing individual retirement accounts were designed to modify its incentive effects by creating closer links between contributions and future benefits. In Singapore, the social insurance system is actually built around the principle of individual accounts, not only for retirement income, but also (through required contributions to Medical Savings Accounts) for health care and health insurance. That is, workers have to pay certain percentages of their income into funds that they can draw on to pay for health care costs (or health insurance) or retirement income, and the amounts that they can draw depend on the amounts that they have put into their individual accounts.[27]

Contributions to individual accounts do have the advantage of reducing the negative incentive effects of program funding in comparison with a system of contributions to collective funds under which there is a weak connection between past contributions and benefit entitlements. However, unless the contributions are subsidized, they do so by reducing the degree of redistribution between individuals with high or low life-time incomes, since poor individuals only are able to accumulate relatively small balances in their accounts before retirement. Thus in a society that cares both about economic efficiency *and* equity, individual accounts are not a direct substitute for collective funding: Balancing equity against efficiency requires a mix of collective and individual funding of retirement income and the cost of health care in old age.[28]

---

[26] The term "Social Security" in the US refers to the government retirement income security program.

[27] For descriptions of the Singapore system see Lim (2002) and Chia (2002); Asher and Nandy (2006) give a critical view.

[28] Individual Medical Savings Accounts as instruments for financing health care also have the disadvantage that they don't imply any risk pooling, as (private or public) health insurance does. In the Singapore system, however, the funds in individuals' MSAs can be used to pay for health *insurance*, not just for health services. For younger workers, insurance premiums are generally much lower than the amounts they have to put into their MSAs, so that by the time they retire, most workers have substantial account balances that can be used to pay for health insurance after retirement.

In the North American discussion about MSAs, they are typically not seen primarily as instruments to help finance health insurance in a person's old age. Instead they are seen as a device that can be used to reduce the tendency for insured persons to over-utilize health services. For a detailed (but critical)

12.3.4.1 *Health Insurance for the Elderly When Opting Out is Allowed*

In social insurance systems that allow some individuals to opt out of the public plan, the rules that govern opting out have to be carefully specified when the funding system involves working-age people subsidizing health insurance for the old. In systems such as the German one before 2007, working-age people who opted out of the public plan were exempt from the payroll deductions that provide most of the revenue for the public plan. Since this payroll deduction is set at a rate that is high enough not only to pay for the expected health care costs of the working-age people themselves, but also to subsidize part of the cost of the health insurance for retirees, the implied short-term incentive to opt out could be quite strong: The actuarially fair premium cost of a private insurance plan for a healthy working-age person is likely to be low compared to the social insurance plan contribution, at least for people with high income.

To compensate for this incentive, the German system used an elaborate set of regulations on private insurance, including a surcharge on private insurance premiums payable to the social insurance plan, and rules that required private insurers to "set aside savings for old age from the insurance premiums when the insured are young";[29] individuals who opted out of the public plan were also not allowed to rejoin it later (something that would have been attractive for older people, since the public plan is heavily subsidized for them). Given this very complicated system, it is not surprising that major reforms were implemented in 2007 under which everyone must contribute at the same rate to the public system; see Lisac (2006).

In the Netherlands, and in the US Medicare plan, opting-out in the sense of choosing not to pay the contribution to the public social insurance plan, is not allowed, but in both cases individuals are given some choice between what can be thought of as different versions of the public plan. (In Holland, individuals are free to choose among many insurance plans, which may offer different versions of the basic plan and have contracts with different providers; in the US, those enrolled in the Medicare plan may choose from one of many approved managed-care options, as a substitute for the basic plan.) In both cases, competing plans may require individual premiums, but most of their revenue for enrolling an opted-out member of the basic public plan is a transfer from that plan. In order to provide the different private insurers with a level playing field, these transfers are set so as to reflect the expected health care costs of the individuals who join; as discussed above, in Holland, it is adjusted for factors such as gender, age, disability status, region of residence, certain types of previous illness history and so on. Risk adjustments along Dutch lines could be used in order to reduce the risk of adverse selection in the context of the US Medicare plan as well.

survey of their usefulness for this purpose, and of the experience with MSAs in different countries, see Hurley and Guindon (2008).

[29] Busse and Riesberg (2004: 78).

12.4 How Should Providers Be Paid
Under the Public Plan?

The preceding sections have dealt with the questions how countries with public health insurance plans combine public and private funding of health care expenditures, and how they raise the funds to pay for the public plan. Public (and private) insurance plans also must consider the issue of what the relationship between the plans and the provider of health services will be, including what methods will be used to pay the providers.

Early analysis of these issues proceeded from consideration of two polar cases of system organization. In the first, health services under the public plan were provided in hospitals and clinics owned by the government, and by doctors who were government employees; the prevailing payment methods were negotiated annual budgets for hospitals, and fixed salaries for health services personnel. This was the "public integrated" model.[30] Examples often cited of this model include the UK and the Scandinavian countries. The other polar case was what is referred to as the "public reimbursement" model, in which most services are provided in privately owned hospitals and by privately practicing doctors, and payment by the public plan to the providers was on the basis of fee for service, or (in the case of hospitals) "itemized billing." Countries that have used various versions of this model include France, Japan, and the US Medicare plan.

As health systems gradually changed over time, a number of countries developed institutional arrangements that did not fit either of these polar cases very well. In the literature on comparative health system organization, an intermediate category referred to as "public contract" systems was introduced to describe various countries that didn't fall in either of the pure categories. The models in these countries differed from the two polar cases in two important respects. First, unlike the public integrated model, health services in countries with the public contract model are not produced in government-owned hospitals or by doctors who are salaried government employees. Instead, they are produced by independent (often privately owned) hospitals or by independently practicing doctors, under *contracts* with the public plan. Second, unlike in the public reimbursement model, in the public-contract model payment of providers is not usually on the basis of "retrospective" fee for service, but instead on the basis of some form of "prospective" payment such as capitation for primary care providers, or Diagnosis-Related Groups for hospitals (these methods are briefly discussed below).

The fact that various versions of the public-contract model tend to experiment with different methods to pay service providers is one possible reason why their cost-effectiveness may ultimately prove superior to that of either the public integrated model or the public reimbursement model: Different payment methods imply different incentives on providers, and these incentives can be designed to improve the system's cost-effectiveness. The fact that health system reform in a number of countries has moved the

---

[30] The terminology here follows that in the survey by Gerdtham and Jönsson (2000).

system away from centrally managed versions of the public integrated model (the UK) or from the pure public reimbursement model (the US, Switzerland) is consistent with this suggestion.[31] In addition, however, the relationship between health service providers and public plans may also differ in another important dimension, namely in the way providers compete for the patients covered by the public plan. In some countries, there has at times been almost no such competition (in the Swedish system before the 1990s, for example), as patients covered by the public plan were assigned to specific providers based on factors such as residential address or the like. In others (such as Japan or Canada), providers compete directly for individual patients, since patients covered by the public plans in those countries are free to obtain care from whichever licensed provider they want.[32] But in a number of other countries, competition for patients has taken an indirect form, in that providers have had to compete for funding *contracts* with entities (such as district health authorities or sickness funds) that have been responsible for negotiating the conditions of service provision on behalf of their client populations. Opening up the system to competition of this type may also influence its cost-effectiveness, and an interesting question to consider is which form of provider competition (for patients directly, as under the public reimbursement model, or indirectly through a system of contracts with "purchasing agents") is most likely to promote efficient operation of the health care system. I will briefly discuss both the importance of payment methods, and of the nature of provider competition, in the remaining pages.

12.4.1 Payment Methods

In health economics, the analysis of the methods used by insurers and patients to compensate the providers of health services focuses on the ways doctors are paid, on the one hand, and on the way the costs of hospital treatment are covered, on the other.[33]

As noted above, in public integrated systems, doctors have sometimes been directly employed by the government and compensated through straight salaries. Although the

---

[31] In their review of the international literature on aggregate health care spending, Gerdtham and Jönsson (2000) report evidence suggesting that other things equal, per capita spending in countries using the *public reimbursement* model is lower than in those using the public-contract model. However, this finding appears to be based principally on a regression in which dummy variables for payment methods such as capitation, and for gatekeeping in primary care, were included as well (col. 1, table 4, p. 34). These payment methods, which are typically not used in public reimbursement systems, are shown as having strong negative effects on cost; either one is strong enough to swamp the apparent advantage of the public reimbursement model if it is used in a public-contract country. Moreover, the apparent advantage of the public reimbursement model disappears in other specifications.

[32] Note that "competition" in these cases does not refer to price competition (since providers' fees in both cases are strictly regulated); however, doctors and hospitals can still compete by trying to raise the *quality* of the services they offer.

[33] For more extensive discussion of payment methods in primary and hospital care see Chapters 19, 20, 25, and 26 in this volume. Useful surveys of the relevant literature are also in Dranove and Satterthwaite (2000) and, more recently, in Léger (2008), and Busse, Schreyögg and Smith (2006).

salary method has the advantage of simplicity, a potential disadvantage is that it does not imply an incentive on doctors to see many patients or produce a large volume of services, something that will tend to increase the number of doctors that are required for a given population, or lead to longer waiting times before patients can see a doctor. Similarly, the method used to finance the operation of the hospitals that treat patients in public integrated systems has often been to give them an annual budget fixed at a level corresponding to their anticipated costs; this method has been used in countries with public-contract systems as well (Canada). Like salary for doctors, an annual budget implies little or no incentive on hospitals to be productive in either the sense of treating many patients or of raising the quality of care. As before, this may in the end raise the cost of caring for a given population, or cause waiting lists to develop for certain kinds of treatment.

In countries that have been classified as having public reimbursement systems (US, Japan), the method that has typically been used to compensate doctors in outpatient care has been fee for service. In contrast to the straight salary method, fee for service implies an incentive on doctors to be productive in the sense of supplying a large volume of services, since this raises their income. For hospitals, public reimbursement systems have historically also paid them on the basis of fee for service ("itemized billing"). As in the case of fee for service for doctors, itemized billing implies an incentive for hospitals to be productive in the sense of supplying a large volume of services.

To some economists, fee for service (that is, payment in accordance with the amount of output produced) seems an appealing method of payment because per-unit service fees most closely resemble the prices that regulate supply and demand in markets for most other goods and services. However, health economics has long emphasized certain special characteristics of health services that make it less likely that competitive markets will be able to perform their normal allocative function in this sector. One is the extreme degree of information asymmetry between buyers and sellers in this market: Patients on average do not have the medical expertise to know what ails them, let alone what treatment methods are available or how helpful they are likely to be. Moreover, health services must sometimes be produced urgently, on short notice, and exactly what an individual patient needs can often not be established until the process of diagnosis and treatment has begun. For both these reasons, individual patients cannot effectively compare, in advance, the prices and treatment approaches offered by competing providers, for many kinds of health services.[34] This in turn means that competition among providers *for individual patients* will not be very effective in keeping down the prices that doctors and hospitals may charge for treatment episodes. Not surprisingly, therefore, the fees paid under most public reimbursement plans are regulated by the government when fee for service is the method of payment. This is the case for both physician and hospital services in Japan, and for physician services in the basic US Medicare plan, and in

---

[34] Moreover, when insurance pays most of the cost, patients also don't have an *incentive* to be concerned about the fee the doctor charges, making the market even less competitive.

Canada.[35] Although fee regulation of this kind can help keep costs down, it also gives rise to other problems of the kind economic theory predicts from price controls, such as long waiting lists for certain kinds of services (an indication of excess demand), and physician shortages in locations (such as rural areas) where physicians are reluctant to practice unless they can charge higher fees.

While salary for doctors and negotiated budgets for hospitals have been used in some public integrated systems and fee for service (itemized billing) in public reimbursement systems, a different principle referred to as "prospective payment" has been employed in some countries that are classified as following the public contract model. The most illustrative examples of this principle are *capitation* for physician services, and *Diagnosis-Related Groups* (DRG) for hospital services. Under capitation (which mostly is used in primary care), a doctor agrees to provide services as necessary to all patients registered on the practice's list, in return for a fixed monthly payment per patient; this fixed amount *does not depend on the volume of services actually produced*. Similarly, the basic idea of a DRG system is that the amount a hospital will be paid for a given treatment episode should largely depend on the diagnostic category in which the patient was placed, not on the actual cost of treating him or her. Thus from the point of view of the doctors and hospitals, their payment for a given patient or treatment episode is predetermined ("prospectively" determined), and does not depend on the volume or cost of the services actually produced for given patient categories. This contrasts with the fee for service method, under which provider payments are determined "retrospectively" (after the actual volume of services is known). Clearly, the incentives inherent in a system of capitation and DRGs are quite different from those in either a salary/budget system or under fee for service. Under capitation, doctors have an incentive to take responsibility for a large number of patients, but not to produce a high volume of services for each one. Similarly, under the DRG model of hospital reimbursement, a hospital has an incentive to treat a large number of cases, but to treat each case at the lowest possible cost.[36]

12.4.2 Payment Methods: Which is the Best?

Because they have different incentives on providers, different payment systems will produce outcomes with different patterns of medical care and aggregate costs. Can we

---

[35] Note that even though Canada's health care system is classified in the "public contract" category by Gerdtham and Jönsson (2000), it pays its doctors via fee for service.

[36] In some cases, a patient's diagnostic classification will be made as soon as he/she arrives at the hospital. In other cases, the classification may be modified after further diagnosis or treatment, and may depend on what procedure is used, etc. However, the principle is that the payment should depend on the classification of the patient's illness, not on the cost of the services the doctors chose to use for a patient in a given category. Early theoretical and empirical discussions of the incentive properties of the DRG model can be found in Newhouse (1983), Dranove (1987), and Newhouse and Byrne (1988). For an extensive discussion of the way they have been used in Europe, see Busse, Schreyögg and Smith (2006).

answer the question: Which of the payment methods will yield the best (most cost-effective) outcome?

The answer, not surprisingly, is that it depends on how one defines cost-effectiveness. From the viewpoint of the government, the advantage of a system of salaried doctors and hospitals funded by annual negotiated budgets is that, at least in principle, it facilitates control over aggregate costs. However, from the viewpoint of patients, the lack of direct incentives on providers to take care of many patients and produce high volumes of service will be a disadvantage if it leads to long waiting times and less favorable medical outcomes. Fee for service, on the other hand, can be very expensive (depending on whether or not the fees are regulated), but has the advantage from a patient's point of view that doctors and hospitals are willing to treat each patient and illness episode intensively (as more services produce higher income). Prospective payment methods such as capitation or DRGs give providers an incentive to keep aggregate costs low (since each doctor has an incentive to take responsibility for many patients, and each hospital has an incentive to treat many patients but spend as little as possible on each one), but by the same token, might lead to a lower average quality of care and less favorable health outcomes.

Choosing among payment methods, therefore, can in part be interpreted as a balancing between the conflicting objectives of cost control, on the one hand, and the desire of risk-averse patients for a high level of care when they are ill, on the other. Given that societies may differ in terms of their relative valuations of these two objectives, it may not be surprising that different countries have chosen somewhat different systems in this respect, and that in many countries mixed systems are used that combine prospective and retrospective elements. However, the trend in recent decades has been for the differences to become somewhat narrower. In particular, the "polar cases" of straight salary/global budgets and fee for service/itemized billing have become less common, and various forms of prospective payment (such as capitation and DRGs) have become somewhat more common. This has been particularly true in the US where private-sector managed care plans that pay doctors and hospitals through various forms of prospective payment have increased their market share relative to conventional plans based on fee-for-service reimbursement.[37] But the trend toward prospective payment has also been present in public plans. For example, in many European countries, hospital financing is now through some form of DRG-based system,[38] and those in the US Medicare system who have chosen insurance through

---

[37] According to data in Kaiser Family Foundation (2008b: chart 5.1), in 1988, less than 20 percent of employees were covered by the types of managed-care plans that typically pay providers on a prospective basis (such as HMOs or Point of Service Plans); by 2008, the share of such plans was 32 percent. While plans that typically pay providers on the basis of fee for service have increased their share in the last ten years, the increase is due mostly to the growth of Preferred Provider Organizations in which doctors have agreed to negotiated fees.

[38] Busse, Schreyögg, and Smith (2006). The version used in England, referred to as Payment by Results (PbR) is briefly described in Maybin (2007).

a managed-care option are often treated by physicians who are paid through capitation.[39]

12.4.2.1 *Payment Methods and Consumer Choice in Public Plans*

In an earlier section, I argued that in certain circumstances, it might be advantageous to offer consumers covered by a social insurance plan a choice among different versions of the plan (for example, among competing approved plans in the Dutch system). Other things equal, it is efficient to allow consumers to choose among plans with benefit packages that differ in various dimensions: When this is allowed, the system will gradually come to reflect consumers' preferences to the greatest possible extent.

In particular, giving consumers a choice among versions of the basic plan provides an opportunity of revealing which method of paying providers is most efficient (in the eyes of patients), in the sense of best balancing the objectives of cost control and quality of care. For example, some funds may pay their doctors via capitation, while others use fee for service. With the cost-saving incentives in a capitation system, funds using that method could charge somewhat lower premiums. Indirectly, therefore, consumers in such a system would be given the option to choose a less expensive plan in which doctors (and other providers) had strong incentives to save costs, or to choose a more expensive plan in which providers were not subject to such incentives, so that they might, for example, spend more time on diagnosis and treatment of each patient and be more liberal in ordering diagnostic tests. More risk-averse patients might prefer the latter option, while less risk-averse ones might choose the less expensive plan.

12.5 LESSONS LEARNED?

In this essay, I have considered three issues that have been hotly debated in countries with major government funding of health care. First, what share of total health care costs should the government pay for, and what, if any, should be the roles of user fees and private insurance in such a system? Second, should public health care funding be from general tax revenue, or through some form of social insurance? Third, how should the government pay providers: through fee for service (typical of the public reimbursement model), through salaries and global budgets (as in earlier public integrated models), or on a prospective basis (such as under capitation and DRGs, used in some public contract models)? The next few paragraphs summarize what I consider some useful lessons that

---

[39] While the choice of payment method in the past has been associated with the choice between the different fundamental models of health service production (public integrated, public reimbursement, and public contract), the correlation has not been perfect. For example, capitation (rather than straight salary) has long been the principal method used in paying for primary care in the UK, and DRGs (rather than itemized billing) were first introduced in the US Medicare plan, even though the UK and US health care systems are usually classified as examples of the public integrated and public reimbursement systems, respectively.

can be learned from past experience in different countries that have grappled with these issues, and how these lessons may influence future health policy.

With respect to the balance between public and private funding, the question of user fees remains controversial. Most countries require some degree of patient co-payment (US Medicare, France, Japan), but others (the UK, Canada) stick to the principle of essentially zero user charges. To the extent one can discern a trend in the importance that the issue has been given over time, it is probably in the direction of less emphasis on user fees as a tool for containing costs, as evidence has accumulated that supply-side incentives are relatively more effective in accomplishing this. Similarly, countries vary a great deal with respect to the role that private insurance is allowed to play alongside the public plans. Perhaps the most important development in this respect has been the increasing role of private insurance plans in a "subcontracting" role in publicly funded systems such as US Medicare, and in the social insurance systems in countries such as Germany, Holland, and Switzerland: *Funding* of the insurance plans is largely through public sources, but private insurers have been allowed an increasing role as health services *purchasers* who arrange for the delivery of health services for their clients by contracting with providers.

On the question of what are appropriate methods for raising public funds to pay for health care, there may be increasing recognition that tax financing and social insurance should just be regarded as different methods of raising government revenue, and that there is no conceptual basis for trying to identify certain forms of government expenditure with particular revenue sources. While this principle is simple, historical patterns of health care funding has created vested interests that get in the way of the political decisions that are necessary to translate it into reforms that make the system more equitable and efficient. The high cost of providing health care for an aging population, and the question how the burden of doing this should be distributed between the young and the old, make the issue even more complicated.

Finally, with respect to the methods that are used to pay for publicly funded health care, there has been a clear trend in the direction of prospective funding methods and "public contracting." DRG-based funding was developed and used in the US Medicare system several decades ago, but has become widely used in Europe as well (including in the UK under the name of "payment by results" during the last several years); conversely, full or partial capitation in primary care has been used in Europe (the UK, the Netherlands) for a long time, but is now more commonly used in the managed-care plans under which many US Medicare and Medicaid beneficiaries are covered.

References

Ahmad, Ehtisham and Brosio, Giorgio (eds.) (2006), *Handbook of Fiscal Federalism* (Cheltenham, UK: Edward Elgar).

Asher, Mukul and Nandy, Amarendu (2006), "Health Financing in Singapore: A Case for Systemic Reforms," *International Social Security Review*, 59: 75–92.

ATKINSON, ANTHONY B. and STIGLITZ, JOSEPH E. (1980), *Public Economics* (New York: McGraw-Hill).

AUERBACH, ALAN J. and FELDSTEIN, MARTIN (eds.) (1985), *Handbook of Public Economics* (Amsterdam: North Holland).

BLOMQVIST, ÅKE G. (1997), "Optimal Non-linear Health Insurance," *Journal of Health Economics*, 16: 313–21.

—— and HORN, HENRIK (1984), "Public Health Insurance and Optimal Income Taxation," *Journal of Public Economics*, 24: 353–73.

—— and JOHANSSON, PER-OLOV (1997), "Economic Efficiency and Mixed Public/private Insurance," *Journal of Public Economics*, 66: 505–16.

—— and QIAN, JIWEI (2008), "Health System Reform in China: An Assessment of Recent Trends," *Singapore Economic Review*, 53: 1–22.

BOADWAY, ROBIN (2006), "Intergovernmental Redistribution: Efficiency and Equity," in E. Ahmad and G. Brosio (eds.), *Handbook of Fiscal Federalism* (Cheltenham, UK: Edward Elgar).

BUSSE, REINHARD and RIESBERG, ANNETTE (2004), *Health care systems in transition: Germany* (Copenhagen: WHO Regional Office for Europe on behalf of European Observatory on Health Systems and Policies).

—— SCHREYÖGG, JONAS, and SMITH, PETER C. (2006), "Editorial: Hospital Case Payments Systems in Europe," *Health Care Management Science*, 9: 211–13.

CAMPBELL, JOHN C. and IKEGAMI, NAOKI (1998), *The Art of Balance in Health Policy: Maintaining Japan's Low-cost Egalitarian System* (Cambridge, UK: Cambridge University Press).

CHIA, NGEE CHOON (2002), "Health for All: Financing and Delivery Issues," in Koh Ai Tee, Lim Kim Lian, Hui Weng Tat, Bhanoji Rao, and Chng Meng Kng (eds.), *Singapore Economy in the 21st Century: Issues and Strategies* (Singapore: McGraw-Hill Education), 164–87.

COLOMBO, FRANCESCA and TAPAY, NICOLE (2003), "Private Health Insurance in Australia: A Case Study." OECD Health Working Papers, No. 8.

—— —— (2004), "Private Health Insurance in OECD Countries: The Benefits and Costs for Individuals and Health Systems." OECD Health Working Papers No. 15.

CULYER, ANTHONY J. and NEWHOUSE, JOSEPH P. (eds.) (2000), *Handbook of Health Economics*, Vols. 1A and 1B (Amsterdam: North-Holland).

CUTLER, DAVID M. and REBER, S. J. (1998), "Paying for Health Insurance: The Tradeoff Between Competition and Adverse Selection," *Quarterly Journal of Economics*, 113: 433–66.

—— and ZECKHAUSER, RICHARD J. (2000), "The Anatomy of Health Insurance," in A. J. Culyer and J. P. Newhouse (eds.), *Handbook of Health Economics* (Amsterdam: North-Holland), 563–643.

DRANOVE, DAVID (1987), "Rate Setting by Diagnosis Related Groups and Hospital Specialization," *RAND Journal of Economics*, 18: 417–27.

—— and SATTERTHWAITE, MARK A. (2000), "The Industrial Organization of Health Care Markets," in A. J. Culyer and J. P. Newhouse (eds.), *Handbook of Health Economics* (Amsterdam: North-Holland), 1093–140.

ELLIS, RANDALL P. (2008), "Risk Adjustments in Health Care Markets: Concepts and Applications," in Mingshan Lu and Egon Jonsson (eds.), *Financing Health Care: New Ideas for a Changing Society* (Weinheim: Wiley-VCH), 177–222.

—— and MCGUIRE, THOMAS (1993), "Supply-side and Demand-side Cost Sharing in Health Care," *Journal of Economic Perspectives*, 7: 135–51.

ENTHOVEN, ALAIN C. (1988), *Theory and Practice of Managed Competition in Health Care Finance* (Amsterdam: North Holland).

—— (1993), "The History and Principles of Managed Competition," *Health Affairs*, 12 (Suppl.): 24–48.

—— (1994), "On the Ideal Market Structure for Third-party Purchasing of Health Care," *Social Science and Medicine*, 39: 1413–24.

—— and VAN DE VEN, WYNAND P. M. M. (2007), "Going Dutch: Managed-competition Health Insurance in the Netherlands," *New England Journal of Medicine*, 357: 2421–3.

DEN EXTER, ANDRÉ, HERMANS, HERBERT, DOSLJAK, MILENA, and BUSSE, REINHARD (2004), *Health Care Systems in Transition: Netherlands* (Copenhagen: WHO Regional Office for Europe on behalf of European Observatory on Health Systems and Policies).

FELDSTEIN, MARTIN (1996), "The Missing Piece in Policy Analysis: Social Security Reform (The Richard T. Ely Lecture)," *American Economic Review Papers and Proceedings*, 86: 1–14.

—— (1999), "Prefunding Medicare," *American Economic Review Papers and Proceedings*, 89: 222–7.

FLOOD, COLLEEN M. (2000), *International Health Care Reform: A Legal, Economic and Political Analysis* (London: Routledge).

GERDTHAM, ULF G. and JÖNSSON, BENGT (2000), "International Comparisons of Health Expenditure," in A. J. Culyer and J. P. Newhouse (eds.), *Handbook of Health Economics* (Amsterdam: North-Holland), 11–54.

GLIED, SHERRY (2000), "Managed Care," in A. J. Culyer and J. P. Newhouse (eds.), *Handbook of Health Economics* (Amsterdam: North-Holland), 707–45.

GRAMLICH, EDWARD M. (1996), "Approaches for Dealing with Social Security," *Journal of Economic Perspectives*, 10(3): 55–66.

HSIAO, WILLIAM C. and SHAW PAUL, R. (eds.) (2007), *Social Health Insurance for Developing Nations* (Washington, DC: The World Bank).

HURLEY, JEREMIAH E. and GUINDON, G. EMMANUEL (2008), "Medical Savings Accounts: Promises and Pitfalls," in Mingshan Lu and Egon Jonsson (eds.), *Financing Health Care: New Ideas for a Changing Society* (Weinheim: Wiley-VCH), 125–47.

IMAI, YUTAKA (2002), "Health Care Reform in Japan." OECD Economics Department Working Paper 321.

KAISER FAMILY FOUNDATION (2008a), "Medicare: A Primer." <www.kff.org/medicare/>.

—— (2008b), "2008 Kaiser/HRET Employer Health Benefits Survey." <http://ehbs.kff.org/>.

LÉGER, PIERRE-THOMAS (2008), "Physician Payment Mechanisms," in Mingshan Lu and Jonsson Egon (eds.), *Financing Health Care: New Ideas for a Changing Society* (Weinheim: Wiley-VCH), 149–76.

LIM, KIM LIAN (2002), "Enhancing the Financial Security of Older Singaporeans," in Koh Ai Tee, Lim Kim Lian, Hui Weng Tat, Bhanoji Rao, and Chng Meng Kng (eds.), *Singapore Economy in the 21st Century: Issues and Strategies* (Singapore: McGraw-Hill Education), 66–94.

LISAC, MELANIE (2006), "Health Care Reform in Germany: Not the Big Bang," *Health Policy Monitor* (Nov.), <http://www.hpm.org/survey/de/b8/2>.

LU, MINGSHAN and JONSSON, EGON (eds.) (2008), *Financing Health Care: New Ideas for a Changing Society* (Weinheim: Wiley-VCH).

MARQUIS, M. S. (1992), "Adverse Selection with a Multiple Choice Among Health Insurance Plans: A Simulation Analysis," *Journal of Health Economics*, 11: 125–53.

MAYBIN, JO (2007), "Payment by Results." King's Fund Briefing (Oct.), <www.kingsfund.org>.

NEWHOUSE, JOSEPH P. (1983), "Two Prospective Difficulties with Prospective Payment for Hospitals, or, it's Better to be a Resident than a Patient with a Complex Problem," *Journal of Health Economics*, 2: 269–74.

—— (1996), "Reimbursing Health Plans and Health Providers: Efficiency in Production vs. Selection," *Journal of Economic Literature*, 34: 1236–63.

—— and BYRNE, D. J. (1988), "Did Medicare's Prospective Payment Cause Lengths of Stay to Fall?" *Journal of Health Economics*, 7: 413–26.

—— and THE INSURANCE EXPERIMENT GROUP (1993), *Free For All? Lessons from the Rand Health Insurance Experiment* (Cambridge, MA.: Harvard University Press).

NYMAN, JOHN (2003), *The Theory of Demand for Health Insurance* (Stanford, CA: Stanford University Press).

PAULY, MARK V. (1968), "The Economics of Moral Hazard: Comment," *American Economic Review*, 58: 531–6.

ROTHSCHILD, MICHAEL and STIGLITZ, JOSEPH E. (1976), "Equilibrium in Competitive Insurance Markets: An Essay on the Economics of Imperfect Information," *Quarterly Journal of Economics*, 90: 630–49.

SANDIER, SIMONE, PARIS, VALÉRIE, and POLTON, DOMINIQUE (2004), *Health Care Systems in Transition: France* (Copenhagen: WHO Regional Office for Europe on behalf of European Observatory on Health Systems and Policies).

SCHREYÖGG, JONAS, STARGARDT, TOM, TIEMANN, OLIVER, and BUSSE, REINHARD (2006), "Methods to Determine Reimbursement Rates for Diagnosis Related Groups (DRG): A Comparison of Nine European Countries," *Health Care Management Science*, 9: 215–23.

VAN DE VEN, WYNAND and ELLIS, RANDALL P. (2000), "Risk Adjustment in Competitive Health Plan Markets," in A. J. Culyer and J. P. Newhouse (eds.), *Handbook of Health Economics*, Vol. 1A (Amsterdam: North-Holland), 755–846.

—— and SCHUT, FREDERIK T. (2008), "Universal Mandatory Health Insurance in the Netherlands: A Model for the United States?" *Health Affairs*, 27: 771–81.

—— BECK, KONSTANTIN, VOORDE, CARINE VAN DE, WASEM, JÜRGEN and ZMORA, IRIT (2007), "Risk Adjustment and Risk Selection in Europe: 6 Years Later," *Health Policy*, 83: 162–79.

WAGSTAFF, A. and VAN DOORSLAER, E., (2000), "Equity in Health Care Finance and Delivery," in A. J. Culyer and J. P. Newhouse (eds.), *Handbook of Health Economics*, Vol. 1B (Amsterdam: North-Holland), 1803–62.

—— et al. (1999), "Equity in the Finance of Health Care: Some Further International Comparisons," *Journal of Health Economics*, 18: 263–90.

ZECKHAUSER, RICHARD (1970), "Medical Insurance: A Case Study of the Tradeoff Between Risk Spreading and Appropriate Incentives," *Journal of Economic Theory*, 2: 10–26.

CHAPTER 13

··

VOLUNTARY PRIVATE
HEALTH INSURANCE

··

PETER ZWEIFEL

13.1 INTRODUCTION

··

THE purpose of this chapter is to examine how voluntary private health insurance works. This task is complicated by the reality that we do not observe large-scale fully voluntary private individual health insurance markets. Rather, voluntary health insurance exists, and has existed, in three more limited forms. First, we observe individual health insurance markets, such as those in Switzerland, the Netherlands, and many of the states of the United States, where insurers compete but the pricing of policies is very heavily regulated. Second, in the United States (as well as in Canada and several other countries in the past, and in some developing countries), we observe voluntary private coverage through large pre-existing groups, typically employment-based, often supported by tax policy though with limited regulation of pricing. Finally in many countries with universal public health insurance, we observe voluntary private health insurance that is auxiliary to this public system.

While empirical evidence on the functioning of voluntary private individual health insurance markets is lacking, there is a large and well-developed theoretical literature describing the functioning of private insurance markets in other sectors. This chapter begins by summarizing this extensive literature and describing how such markets would work if they existed in the health sector. Next, the chapter considers the functioning of the three common forms of voluntary insurance described above. Finally, the chapter proposes a political economy based explanation for why the theoretically optimal market does not exist. The chapter concludes with areas for future research.

13.2 THE THEORY OF VOLUNTARY PRIVATE INDIVIDUAL HEALTH INSURANCE

13.2.1 Demand for Voluntary Private Individual Health Insurance

There is a well-developed theory of the demand for private health insurance (Pauly and Herring 1999; Pauly 2000; Zweifel and Manning 2000; Nyman 2003; Zweifel, Breyer, and Kifmann 2009: ch. 6). The basic result is unambiguous: Risk-averse individuals are predicted to opt for an "actuarially fair" insurance contract rather than bearing the financial risk themselves. An actuarially fair contract is one that charges a premium just equal to the expected value of the loss, without any so-called loading, i.e. surcharges for administrative expense, risk bearing, and profit on the part of the insurer. This means that insurance coverage is provided free of charge at least on expectation, causing the first-best solution to be full coverage. As one would expect from the theory of demand, when the loading (and hence the net price of coverage) increases, the quantity demanded decreases, possibly to zero (no coverage or 100 percent co-payment). Since insurers have influence over the loading, supply-side considerations are crucial, as explained below.

This still leaves open issues of optimal design of a health insurance contract when departures from the basic model have to be taken into account. I consider these under five headings: health loss, *ex ante* moral hazard, *ex post* moral hazard, asymmetric information about health risks, and risk of deterioration in health status.

13.2.1.1 *Health Loss*

In the standard model of insurance, losses occur exclusively in terms of wealth. Health insurance is different because the insured first of all suffers a health loss. This may modify the demand for health insurance depending on whether the marginal utility of wealth is greater or smaller when sick or healthy (Cook and Graham 1977). In panel (a) of Figure 13.1, the risk utility function runs flatter in the healthy than the sick state, indicating a lower marginal utility of wealth.

Since wealth should optimally be reshuffled until its marginal utility is the same regardless of health status, this case calls for higher wealth in the sick than the healthy state ($W_s^* > W_h^*$) and hence compensation for pain and suffering. Conversely, in panel (b), marginal utility of wealth is higher when healthy than when sick. Accordingly, wealth optimally is lower in the sick state ($W_s^* < W_h^*$), calling for co-payment in health insurance.

This ambiguity can be resolved by appealing to the Eeckhoudt–Schlesinger (2006) result that risk-averse individuals wish to avoid the accumulation of losses (here in terms of health and wealth, due to medical expenditure). Therefore, the utility difference between "healthy" and "sick" must be large when wealth is low and small when wealth is high. Accordingly, the marginal utility of (risky) wealth is higher at a given wealth level

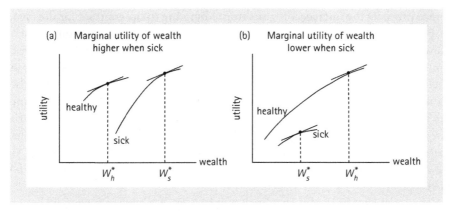

FIGURE 13.1 Optimal wealth levels depending on the state of health

in the "sick" than in the "healthy" state. If this is the case, panel (a) will obtain. Note that the theoretical argument is couched in terms of risky wealth, which makes empirical testing difficult. Using an indicator of permanent wealth, Finkelstein et al. (2008) find evidence supporting the case of panel (b). Their evidence suggests that consumers might wish to spend more rather than being made to save as much for the retirement period (when the probability of being sick is much higher).

13.2.1.2 Ex Ante *Moral Hazard*

If insurance coverage causes consumers to reduce preventive effort, resulting in an increased probability of illness, the optimal contract may require a non-zero rate of co-payment. This implies a need for less than full coverage, in order to alleviate the tendency to such *ex ante* moral hazard (Zweifel and Manning 2000; Nyman 2003; and see Chapter 16, this volume). However, when *ex ante* moral hazard exists in combination with the case of panel (a) of Figure 13.1, full or even more than full coverage may still be optimal.

13.2.1.3 Ex Post *Moral Hazard*

In this case, the insured opts for treatment in excess of optimal levels once the "loss" (i.e. illness) has occurred. This suggests the need for a non-zero rate of co-payment. But again, this may be counter-balanced by a very high marginal utility of wealth in the sick state (see panel (a) of Figure 13.1).

13.2.1.4 *Asymmetric Information about Health Risks*

If some aspects of health risks are not costlessly observable to the insurer, prices will not fully reflect private expectations about health risks. Rothschild and Stiglitz (1976) show that, assuming no moral hazard effects, this affects optimal contract design in the following way. Unfavorable risks first are offered a full coverage contract at a high but fair premium. The basic model predicts that they will opt for it. Next, favorable risks are offered a partial coverage contract calling for some co-payment at a low (fair) premium. Partial coverage prevents the unfavorable risks from migrating to the contract for the favorable ones, pretending they are favorable risks. This is a so-called separating equilibrium.

However, a separating equilibrium can be challenged by a competing insurer offering more coverage to favorable risks at slightly better terms. As soon as the potential challenger has a planning horizon of more than one period and operates in a fairly concentrated market, such an attack becomes less likely because it will attract the incumbent's unfavorable risks later (Wilson 1977). Also, learning from past loss experience, insurers have the possibility of refining this sorting mechanism, offering favorable risks successively higher coverage on favorable terms (Dionne and Doherty 1994). Under these circumstances, optimal contracts are likely of the experience-rating (or *bonus-malus*) type.

13.2.1.5 *Risk of Deterioration of Health Status*

Consumers may demand coverage based not only on their current health status but also on a requirement that a future deterioration of their health status will be covered as well. As shown by Cochrane (1995), this so-called guaranteed renewability calls for a "front-loading" of premiums to make the insured pre-finance their higher future expected health care expenditure. According to Herring and Pauly (2006), this front-loading may attain up to 150 percent of the low-risk premium at age 18, assuming a high-inflation scenario.

13.2.2 Supply of Voluntary Private Individual Health Insurance

On the supply side, private health insurance can be characterized by at least four aspects, viz. (1) the loading (i.e. the net price of health insurance), (2) the amount of risk selection effort, (3) the degree of vertical integration (integrating health care providers mainly in the guise of so-called Managed Care options), and (4) market structure. It should be noted that while the theory of insurer behavior in general is fairly well developed (Cummins 1991; Cummins and Sommer 1996), there is little empirical research into the behavior of private health insurers, let alone not for profit mutuals. The following theoretical considerations therefore are highly tentative (for more details, see Zweifel, Krey, and Tagli 2007).

13.2.2.1 *Loading*

The total premium is given by the "net" or "actuarially fair" premium plus the loading,

$$P(I) = net\, premium + loading$$
$$= \pi(V) \cdot (1-c) \cdot I + \mu \cdot \pi(V) + \lambda \cdot \pi(V) \cdot (1-c) \cdot I. \qquad (1)$$

The net premium is equal to the net expected claim falling on the health insurer. Equation (1) states that π, the probability of loss (the probability of illness, respectively), depends on preventive effort V in a negative way such that $\pi'(V) < 0$; however, it will always be true that $\pi > 0$. Of the health care expenditure covered I, only the fraction $(1 - c)$ falls on the insurer, since c is the rate of co-insurance ($c < 1$). Turning to the loading, there are two components. First, μ is the loading factor for variable administrative costs, which occur with probability π. Second, λ symbolizes the loading factor for acquisition cost, risk bearing, and profit, which is charged on the expected benefits to be paid net of co-payment.

The more complete is coverage I the weaker in general are the insured's incentives for prevention V. Taking into account this *ex ante* moral hazard effect, the amount of loading can be written as

$$Amount\ of\ loading = \Lambda = \mu \cdot \pi[V(I)] + \lambda \cdot (1-c) \cdot \pi[V(I)]\pi\ [V(I)]\cdot I. \qquad (2)$$

The following determinants of the amount of loading are of importance.

Reinsurance Insurers shift the risk of incurring very high claims to specialized reinsurance companies. Generally, the associated premium is an expense that causes the loading to increase (Doherty and Tinic 1981). However, it also improves the solvency of the insurer, permitting a lower value of the loading factor λ. Its net effect therefore is ambiguous.

Pool size A large number of insured of similar type allows insurers to estimate parameters π and I with increased precision, enabling them to reduce reserves per unit risk to attain a given level of solvency (Dror and Preker 2002: 135). However, a large pool may also mean that individual consumers are shielded from social control by other members of the pool, which encourages moral hazard effects that in turn serve to increase π and I and hence the amount of loading (see below).

Benefit package An extension of the benefit package enlarges the universe of health care services that may give rise to a claim. Therefore, the probability of loss π increases even without any behavioral modification on the part of the insured. For the same reason, payments I increase as well. According to equation (2), the amount of loading must increase.

Co-payments and limits on coverage Co-payments and limits on coverage have two effects on the amount of loading. First, co-payments increase the net price of medical care to consumers, lowering the quantity demanded, while limits increase the net price to its full marginal value when the limit is exceeded. Therefore, payments I decrease on average and with them, the amount of loading (see equation (2) again). In addition, caps exclude very high values of I, reducing the variance of I and hence the loading coefficient λ. Finally, an increase in the rate of co-insurance c serves to reduce the amount of loading through lowering the part of the loss to be paid by the insurer.

Moral hazard effects Focusing on *ex ante* moral hazard first, an increase in I is associated with a higher amount of total loading. Partially differentiating equation (2), one obtains

$$\Lambda'(I) = \underset{(-)}{\mu} \cdot \underset{(-)}{\pi'(V)} \cdot V'(I) + (1-c) \cdot \lambda \cdot \underset{(-)}{\pi'(V)} \cdot \underset{(-)}{V'(I)} \cdot I + \pi \cdot (1-c) \cdot \underset{(+)}{\pi} \big[V(I) \big] > 0. \qquad (3)$$

Ex ante moral hazard means that the probability of loss π increases with coverage I. This occurs because preventive effort decreases ($V'(I) < 0$ in equation (3)), which in turn causes π to increase ($\pi'(V) < 0$). Therefore, the first term of equation (3) is positive. For the same reason, the second term is positive as well, while the third term is positive by definition. Therefore, *ex ante* moral hazard unambiguously causes the loading to increase.

Turning to *ex post* moral hazard effects, let I now become the amount of benefits actually claimed (rather than promised in the contract). This depends on the net price of medical care and hence the rate of co-insurance. Therefore, I must be replaced by $I(c)$ in equation (2). Partial differentiation w.r.t. c yields

$$\Lambda'(c) = -\lambda \cdot \pi \cdot I + \lambda \cdot (1-c) \cdot \pi \cdot I'(c) < 0. \qquad (4)$$

Therefore, the higher the rate of co-insurance, the lower the amount of loading and conversely, the lower the rate of co-insurance the higher the net price of insurance.

Quality and proximity of health care services Health care services of high quality have a direct effect on the total loading because the benefits actually claimed will typically be more expensive (see the effect of a high value of I in equation (2)). Increasing the proximity of services decreases the cost of access and hence the total cost of utilizing medical care to consumers. Therefore, both the probability π of utilization and the amount of services claimed I are likely to increase, and therefore the amount of loading (see equation (4)).

Regulatory framework Both premium and product regulation are relevant in this context. If designed to guarantee solvency, premium regulation leads to an increase in the safety loading, reflected in λ. According to equation (2), this causes the amount of loading to increase. Turning to product regulation, the objective may be consumer protection through improved transparency. This might enhance demand, leading to a greater risk pool. In this case, reserves per unit risk can be reduced, resulting in a decrease λ. On the other hand, product regulation might also drive up the cost of doing business and hence the administration loading factor μ. Therefore, the overall effect of regulation on the loading is ambiguous. In the case of US auto liability insurance regulation, Frech and Samprone (1980) found that regulation had a demand-decreasing effect, pointing to a positive relationship between regulation and amount of loading.

Fraud and abuse Fraud and abuse are an extreme of moral hazard. In the case of *ex ante* moral hazard, preventive effort V could be said to turn negative, implying that the insured actively seek to cause losses in order to obtain benefits. This causes $V'(I)$ in equation (3) to become strongly negative. Thus, the amount of loading increases rapidly with any increase in I when fraud is present. It also has an effect on *ex post* moral hazard. For example, service providers and patients may collude to overstate medical bills, which might be encouraged by a low rate of co-insurance. As soon as the insured has to pay an important part of the medical bill out of pocket, he or she has an incentive to resist fraudulent overbilling. In terms of equation (4), the relationship between benefits claimed I and the degree of cost sharing ($I'(c)$) is particularly strong in this case. This indicates that the amount of loading must increase markedly with any decrease in co-payment when fraud is prevalent.

13.2.2.2 Risk Selection Effort

Most policymakers and even many economists believe that "skimming the cream" i.e. seeking to attract favorable risks and deter unfavorable risks, is typical of private (health) insurers. If insurers were entirely free to set their premiums according to risk and could costlessly observe all elements of risk, they would have no incentive to invest in such risk selection (Pauly 1984). Under these circumstances, an unfavorable risk would be charged a high premium whereas a favorable risk would demand and obtain a low premium. Insurers would adjust premiums to equalize the expected contribution margin over "cost" across risk groups, with "cost" equal to future expected value of future health care expenditure to be paid (Zweifel and Breuer 2006). The incentive to cream-skim arises either because premiums are regulated, or because observation of risk factors is costly. The marginal cost to the insurer of selection effort then enters premium-setting calculations (for a theoretical treatment, see Zweifel 2007).

Risk aversion of insurer It is sometimes argued that insurers avoid high risk cases because the insurer itself is risk averse. The relevance of risk aversion for the behavior of insurers has been the subject of continued debate (Greenwald and Stiglitz 1990). The Capital Asset Pricing Model developed in financial economics suggests that risk diversification by the insurer is in the interest of (fully diversified) shareholders only if it serves to lower the company's value of β, where β is the regression parameter linking the company's individual rate of return to the general rate of return on the capital market. This would generally imply that insurers should not behave in a risk averse fashion. However, insurance managers have a personal interest in diversification of their own, since their human capital is heavily invested in the company. Given that governance usually is imperfect, they may be able to impose their risk aversion on the insurance company by avoiding costly cases.

Seller concentration Wilson (1977) shows that, if there are only two companies (A and B) in the market, risk selection would not make much sense, provided the companies' planning horizon extends beyond the current period. Initially, suppose A is able to filter out the favorable risks. Noticing the surge in its number of unfavorable risks, B in turn will resort to risk selection in period 2. Thus, in period 3 the unfavorable risks would again seek coverage with A, causing both A and B to lose by investing in risk selection. As a general rule, in line with this theory, risk selection effort is seen to be low in concentrated health insurance markets.

13.2.2.3 *Vertical Integration*

If private insurance markets were competitive, what would the companies look like? Would they be limited to the sale of reimbursement insurance (like traditional indemnity insurers)? Or would they contract directly with providers or manage care (like managed care plans)? In general, the boundaries of an enterprise such as an insurance company are not predetermined; for instance, a manufacturer can decide to perform the distribution of its products itself (as the major petroleum companies have). Under competitive pressure, this vertical integration is likely to occur only if it serves to increase the overall efficiency of the enterprise. However, it may be seen as potentially anti-competitive since the number of independent units (the distributors in the example) decreases. Consistent with this anti-competitive view, in many countries, the initiative for vertical integration within the health care sector has come not from health insurers but from service providers. For example, the Blue Cross / Blue Shield scheme was founded by US hospitals in the 1930s, who integrated the insurance function (for more details, see Zweifel, Krey, and Tagli 2007). Focusing on insurer-driven vertical integration (resulting in Managed Care Organizations such as Health Maintenance Organizations or Preferred Providers' Organizations), one can distinguish the following influences on the nature and strength of vertical integration. Factors contributing to the likelihood of vertical integration include:

Market power of the insurer Market power amounts to a necessary condition for the imposition of vertical restraints (or vertical integration in the limit). If one of many competing health insurers were to seek to impose vertical restraints, the service provider might strike a contract with a competitor that does not seek to impose such constraints unless the loss of autonomy is offset by financial benefits. Therefore, the greater market power of insurers, the more likely is vertical integration.

System efficiency gains to be realized: double marginalization One potential source of efficiency that can be realized through vertical integration will occur if providers are organized as cartels or constitute regional monopolies, and insurers also have market power. This situation can give rise to the so-called "double marginalization problem" (Waldman and Jensen 2001: 468f.). If providers have monopoly power, the marginal cost curve facing a purchaser is increasing rather than constant. The quantity of services purchased from health care providers who are organized as cartels or constitute regional monopolies will be lower than the competitive level. The second marginalization follows when the insurer (who also has some market power) offers insurance coverage for sale. Once more, there is an incentive to keep volume low because additional insurance can be only sold at a reduced premium. In this context, vertical integration can eliminate one of these monopoly mark-ups and increase the overall margins available to the insurer.

System efficiency gains to be realized: reputational effects Integrated insurers can monitor provider behavior. This may give them an advantage in developing and maintaining reputations for the provision of high quality. It may also allow them to establish whether a provider's treatment recommendation is justified (Ma and McGuire 1997).

System efficiency gains to be realized: medical arms race Vertical integration can help to deal with the medical technology race. Given almost complete insurance coverage, health care providers must compete on the basis of service and location rather than price. This causes medical technology to become an important competitive parameter, triggering a race. By way of contrast, the insurer reaps an efficiency gain by having a few specialized providers offering the most advanced technology for diagnosis and treatment.

Management know-how of insurer The effectiveness of vertical integration will depend crucially on the ability of managers successfully to negotiate and monitor vertical restraints. This is especially so in the case of full vertical integration, which requires the insurer to know how to run provider facilities efficiently.

Potential to increase entry barriers to competitors One motivation for vertical restraints and integration can be to keep potential entrants out of the insurance market (Preker, Harding, and Dravis 2000). Incumbent insurers can do this by tying up scarce health care services, which are not available to potential entrants who seek to establish contractual relationships to build an integrated system. For instance, they may strike an exclusive contract with the only hospital in the area performing open heart surgery. Given the complexity of health care services, controlling a part of medical and hospital supply can constitute a more effective barrier than closing the health insurance market itself. Admittedly, an outsider can overcome this barrier by offering compensation high enough to make health care providers leave the vertical arrangement, but such compensation tends to be above the level an entrant is prepared to pay (Carlton and Perloff 1999: 357).

There are several factors impeding vertical integration. Especially in low-income countries, the first two of the (partial) list below are of importance:

Lack of capital on the part of the insurer Full vertical integration (vertical restraints to a lesser degree) often requires a capital investment on the part of the firm acquiring control. If internal finance is available, management enjoys some leeway in deciding about such an investment, monitoring by the firm's owners (i.e. shareholders) being incomplete. Lacking internal finance, management has to convince banks and investors that vertical integration enhances profitability and that the debt can be repaid.

Opportunistic behavior and fraud on the part of insurers Insurers with a reputation for opportunistic and fraudulent behavior have difficulty in having contractual partners accept vertical restraints. By engaging in opportunistic behavior, insurers inflict damage on providers, who lose credibility with their patients. This damage in turn reduces the insurer's chances of successfully arranging vertical restraints with providers.

Cartelization of service providers Cartelization of health care providers makes the imposition of vertical constraints difficult. First, the cartel is a means for providers to jointly increase their incomes. An insurer seeking to negotiate vertical restraints must pay at a level exceeding the cartel price. Second, a cartel must impose discipline on its members to be successful, i.e. getting them to restrict output in spite of a high sales price. Restrictions on output, however, conflict with the integrating firm's desire to avoid double marginalization (see above) which may result in the imposition of a minimum volume of sales. Providers may want to maintain a low volume of services provided in order to support higher fees. However, an insurer may want to contract for a minimum volume of services at a fixed fee to avoid an upward pressure on premiums.

Legislation prohibiting vertical restraints Restraints can be impossible when legislation prohibits vertical restraints or vertical integration in the health care sector. The requirement that only individuals with a medical degree can own medical practices in many industrial countries limits the extent of insurer ownership of such facilities.

13.2.2.4 *Market Structure*

Market structure has several dimensions, among the more important being the number of buyers and sellers and the amount of product differentiation (Carlton and Perloff 1999: ch. 1). The number of buyers (consumers, employers) has not been an issue in health insurance markets. With regard to product differentiation, it can be said that its degree increases with the number of sellers unless economics of scope are very marked (see below).

One particular aspect of market structure that will be touched upon only in passing exposition is the legal form of the insurance company. Originally, most health insurers were mutuals, perhaps because a reasonable degree of homogeneity of risks could be attained in this way, permitting them to hold less reserves per unit risk while holding the probability of insolvency constant (Cummins 1991). While the homogeneity of their membership give them a comparative advantage when it comes e.g. to controlling moral hazard, they are at a disadvantage when it comes to raising capital for expanding their risk pool because they do not issue tradable ownership shares. For this reason, the preferred legal form of insurers has become the publicly traded stock company in industrial countries. Yet, the mutual form is alive and even thriving in the guise of community-based health insurance in low-income countries. In the wake of development, with increasing demand for capital to finance expansion, these schemes may change their legal form to become stock companies (for additional discussion of community-based schemes, see Zweifel, Krey, and Tagli 2007).

Focusing on the degree of concentration as the main descriptor of market structure, some important factors influencing it are listed below.

Diversity of preferences With greater diversity of preferences, a larger set of differentiated insurance products is necessary for matching supply and demand. This creates potential for niche products written by specialized insurers, and therefore a greater number of companies, ceteris paribus. However, the theory of consumer demand also says that diversity of preferences becomes effective only if incomes are sufficiently high. With a very small income, the set of viable insurance products is too restricted to permit choices that lie far apart. Therefore, the number of profitable product varieties (and usually firms) is low when income is low.

Economies of scale The size of the risk pool may be the source of economies to scale, defined as decreasing unit cost as a function of the number of individuals insured. A larger pool size enables the insurer to reduce its reserves per unit risk without increasing its risk of insolvency. This means that the premiums of a large insurer contain a smaller amount of loading (see item (1) above), which results in a lower premium for a given amount of expected benefits paid. A large insurer could therefore gain even more market share, with a natural monopoly as a possible outcome.

However, increasing the number insured within a given country may require that the insurer accept less favorable risks, with the consequence of a rise in the expected value of the benefit to be paid. Also, a larger pool can be associated with a loss of social control among the insured, encouraging moral hazard. According to equation (4) above, both effects cause the amount of loading to increase, thus counteracting economies of scale. There does not seem to be very much empirical evidence on this issue in the domain of insurance generally, let alone health insurance. However, the available evidence points to constant rather than increasing returns to scale (see e.g. Fecher, Perelman, and Pestieau 1991). In the absence of economies of scale, there is no reason to expect a particularly high degree of concentration in private insurance markets.

Economies of scope Economies of scope prevail in insurance if the cost of providing an extra unit of coverage in one line of business decreases as a function of the volume written in some other line. In the context of health insurance, economies of scope may operate at two levels. First, the health insurance line may benefit from other business activities of the same firm. For instance, it may be possible to market health insurance through the existing distribution network for selling e.g. banking services. The limited available empirical evidence suggests that economies of scope at this level are not important (see e.g. Suret 1991).

Second, however, health insurers A and B may realize that while their products are differentiated, the expenses for marketing and administering those of A increase less than proportionately when the quantity of B's products is increased as well. The amount of loading hence would increase less than proportionately with the expected volume of benefits combined, providing a powerful motive for a merger of the two companies. With economies of scope (often also called synergies) of this second type, there is a tendency towards concentration, which however does not have to be accompanied with a smaller number of product varieties. More generally, the number of product varieties sold in the market does not vary in step with the number of firms in this case.

Barriers to entry High barriers to entry exist when a newcomer to the market must make large investments that cannot be recuperated if entry fails (high sunk costs). Barriers to entry thus cause the degree of concentration to be higher than otherwise. They are clearly relevant in the case of health insurance markets, where a newcomer usually needs to launch an extensive advertising campaign to gain even a small share of the market. This investment cannot be recuperated if the newcomer should decide to withdraw later in time. High barriers to entry serve to reinforce collusive agreements, which would be undermined by the emergence of an additional competitor.

Barriers to exit   When challenged by a newcomer, one or several of the incumbents may consider exiting from the market rather than defending their position. However, exit is not an attractive alternative if it entails the loss of investments that cannot be recuperated (i.e. constituting sunk costs). For instance, a sales force specialized in health insurance is not an asset anymore once the firm leaves the market; even with economies of scope, it has a reduced value e.g. in selling life insurance. Barriers to exit thus keep the degree of concentration lower than it would otherwise be. However, through their stabilizing effect, they help to preserve collusive agreements.

Anti-trust policy   In many countries, merger projects must be submitted to anti-trust authorities. Mergers that would result in a notable increase in the level of concentration are subject to scrutiny according to the rules followed both by the US Federal Trade Commission and the Commission of the European Union. Up to this point, few mergers of health insurers have been blocked. This does not mean that anti-trust policy does not have an impact on concentration. Indeed, the mere risk of having a merger proposal rejected may well keep concentration at a lower level than would otherwise obtain.

Contestability of health insurance markets   Insurance markets need not include many suppliers at a point in time to act in a competitive fashion. When insurance markets are and remain contestable (meaning they are characterized by low barriers to entry), incumbent insurers will not be able to exploit their market position, as they will be concerned with ensuring their economic survival in a competitive market. In addition, when insurers have to compete because barriers to entry are low, their profitability is driven down to the level of competitive returns.

In sum, there is no strong reason to expect private health insurance markets to tend towards a "natural monopoly" due to economies of scale or scope.

13.3 PRIVATE HEALTH INSURANCE MARKETS IN PRACTICE

This section examines how private health insurance has been used in practice. Private health insurance often appears in markets where primary coverage is provided through a social health insurance system. In some cases (Netherlands, Switzerland, the United States) primary coverage is mainly provided through private health insurers in the absence of social health insurance as a backstop. In almost all such cases insurance providers are heavily regulated. One exception may have been South Africa prior to the downfall of Apartheid. The government of that time considered the white minority capable of choosing between differentiated health insurance products (Khunoane 1993). The private primary health insurance market that is generally observed is typically characterized by substantial regulation.

13.3.1 Premium Regulation

In most countries that use primary private health insurance, health insurance premiums are regulated. Concern that insurers would charge high premiums to unfavorable risks if left unregulated has gained the upper hand. As the preceding discussion suggests, however, from an efficiency perspective, unfavorable risks should pay higher premiums. The most important component of a health insurer's marginal cost is the expected future health care expenditure to be paid for an additional enrollee, and "price equals marginal cost" is one of the basic conditions for economic efficiency. In the context of health insurance, high premiums for unfavorable risks (with their high future health care expenditure) are entirely justified.

The neoclassical policy recommendation to address the equity consequences of allowing premiums to vary is to subsidize those who cannot pay the price rather than creating inefficiencies by artificially limiting price variation associated with health risk. In practice, however, this prescription is not heeded. While Switzerland (and to some extent the Netherlands) do have targeted premium subsidization, premiums are still not allowed to reflect risk.

Regulating premium variation, as shown in section 13.2.2.2, shows, can induce risk selection effort on the part of competitive insurers. This effect is especially pronounced in at least two cases.

13.3.1.1 *Diversity of Risks*

The greater the differences between risk types, the more premium regulation will usually induce excess variance in the underwriting result of the insurer unless there is a good risk adjustment scheme in place (see below). Private health insurers are predicted to counter this increase by stepping up risk selection effort.

13.3.1.2 *Access to Risk Information*

Improved risk information (such as genetic profiling) may permit the insurer to predict future health care expenditure with greater precision. Once such information is publicly available, failure to voluntarily provide it would itself suggest that the person might constitute a high risk. Regulations prohibiting its use by insurers, which exist in many countries, could lead to adverse selection by those who knew their risks were unfavorable. Therefore, improved access to risk information greatly enhances the effectiveness and hence amount of risk selection efforts (Zweifel 2007).

13.3.2 Regulation Designed to Counteract Risk Selection

Insurers' incentive to "skim the cream" (in good part in response to premium regulation) has been counteracted by the implementation of risk adjustment schemes (see Van de Ven and Ellis (2000) and Chapter 17 in this volume for surveys). The idea is to bring price and marginal cost back in line by making insurers with an above-average share of favorable risks pay into the scheme, which subsidizes insurers with an above-average share of unfavorable risks. The design of such risk adjustment schemes can be complex and may not encompass all the factors that determine insurer decisions. For example, in order to fully neutralize incentives, the regulator would have to know the rate of discount an insurer used to calculate present value of future revenue and cost streams, which could require regulator access to strategic business information in a managed care context (Zweifel and Breuer 2006). Of course, payments into the risk adjustment scheme are ultimately borne by the favorable risks (analogous to an indirect tax), who in their turn have an interest in seeking out an insurer offering a contract with a premium more in line with their true risk. The purpose of the risk adjustment scheme in a competitive market is to create a level playing field that prevents insurers offering such premiums.

13.3.3 Regulation Designed to Encourage Private Primary Health Insurance: Employer-based Schemes

Historically, health insurance coverage was offered as a fringe benefit by unions or employers. With the Bismarck reform of 1881, this benefit became compulsory in Germany for all wage earners below a certain income limit; in return, sick funds became institutions of social insurance. The government of the United States (but also of several low-income countries) have used the fact that group insurance sold through employers is less loaded with acquisition expense to encourage (e.g. through tax treatment) or mandate employment-based health insurance. Insuring groups formed through employment is also thought to reduce incentives for risk selection in contexts where prices do not perfectly reflect underlying risks (see Gruber 2000).

Tying insurance coverage to employment groups in this way has two related problems. One is that structure and extent of coverage does not fully correspond to consumer preferences because the employer is an imperfect agent of workers. The other is that workers now can choose only combinations of jobs and health insurance, which may cause them to remain with the "wrong" job because the alternative does not offer the preferred insurance contract. In the case of the United States, the evidence is mixed on both scores (see Morrisey 2001).

More generally, to the extent that expanding private health insurance through employment goes along with premium regulation (typically in the guise of community rating), it again triggers risk selection effort on the part of insurers. This can be countered by imposing open enrollment, i.e. mandating insurers to accept any member of a firm's workforce. Still, favorable risks may cluster in a contract especially tailored to their preferences.

13.3.4 Private Insurance as Auxiliary to Public Health Insurance

In many countries with public health insurance, private health insurance is available to those who can afford it. Some governments (notably that of Australia in 1999/2000) have offered subsidies to purchasers of private health insurance with the aim of reducing demand pressure on public hospitals (see Hopkins and Zweifel 2005 for an evaluation).

As shown by Dahlby (1981) and Zweifel (2007), private voluntary health insurance can improve expected welfare of both risk types under more general conditions if there is compulsory (but not full) coverage provided by a social insurer or the government. The reason is that a compulsory public package serves to relax the rationing constraint that hurts favorable risks. Smith (2007) introduces another distinction, between rich and poor. He shows that a first-best outcome can be implemented by allowing complementary private insurance for the rich. If private insurance is allowed to substitute for the statutory package however, the tax base used for financing the statutory package typically is eroded, thus constraining the planner's ability to implement a preferred outcome.

13.4 Why is Social Health Insurance So Preponderant?

In most developed countries, the bulk of health insurance is provided either by a social insurance scheme (usually characterized by mandatory membership, open enrollment, and community rating) or a national health service (usually tax-financed). Private health insurance has a very small market share in these countries. As has been shown in section 13.2, risk selection and a high loading charged might be responsible for this. More generally, there may be efficiency reasons for the preponderance of social/public insurance (SHI). However, equity and public choice considerations may be as important.

13.4.1 Efficiency Reasons

13.4.1.1 *Adverse Selection*

As explained in section 13.2.1.4, the only possible Rothschild-Stiglitz equilibrium is a separating one in which only unfavorable risks are offered complete coverage. Favorable risks are rationed in terms of coverage because more coverage (at their favorable terms) would make their contract attractive to the high risks. Compared to such an equilibrium, SHI may achieve a Pareto improvement by forcing everyone into a pooling contract with partial coverage, complemented by private health insurance at actuarially fair terms (Dahlby 1981; Newhouse 1996; Zweifel 2007). High risks are made better off because they pay a lower contribution for the mandated part of their coverage, whereas low risks benefit from the relaxation of the rationing constraint, resulting in total (social plus complementary private) coverage. However, it is unclear to what extent asymmetric information concerning health risks is really a problem. First, medical exams can be used to determine the risk of an applicant—albeit at a cost. Second, premiums of existing contracts can be adjusted in response to past health care expenditure (Dionne and Doherty 1994).

13.4.1.2 *Altruism and Free-riding*

Altruistic rich members of society who are more interested in the health than the subjective well-being of the poor may be willing to subsidize their health care (Pauly 1970). However, donations would increase the utility not only of the donors but also of other altruistic members of society. Therefore, donors would have to fear free-riding by others. The solution can be SHI with compulsory membership and contributions according to ability to pay or a tax-financed national health service. Still, this advantage has to be weighed against the problem that SHI typically imposes a uniform contract, which may impose a great deal of efficiency loss on the population if preferences are heterogeneous (for experimental evidence to this effect, see Zweifel, Telser, and Vaterlaus 2006). Complementary private insurance cannot remedy this entirely because only the coverage not embraced within the SHI is available to citizens for expressing heterogenous preferences.

13.4.1.3 *Optimal Taxation When Health and Income are Correlated*

A related justification of SHI is derived from the theory of optimal taxation (Cremer and Pestieau 1996). If abilities cannot be observed by tax authorities, the extent to which income taxation can be used for redistribution from the high-skilled to the low-skilled is limited because the high-skilled can always pretend to be low-skilled by reducing their labor supply. However, if the high-skilled also have a low risk of illness, a mandatory SHI with a uniform contribution redistributes income from them to the low-skilled, i.e. in the desired fashion. It must be emphasized that this justification departs from traditional Paretian welfare economics by postulating a specific distributional goal.

13.4.2 Equity Reasons

A further justification, also known as the "principle of solidarity," relates to the achievement of equality of opportunity. Even at birth, individuals are endowed with different health risks. Moreover, with the rapid progress of genetic diagnostics and the spreading of tests during pregnancy, the ability to measure newborns' health risks will increase. In private health insurance, these differences in risk immediately translate into differences in premiums, causing individuals endowed with a high health risk to be additionally disadvantaged by having to pay a higher premium (Sinn 1996). Behind the veil of ignorance, one would want to have at least the financial cost of such pre-existing illness distributed across society.

13.4.3 Public Choice Reasons

In private health insurance, redistribution occurs purely by chance, from consumers who do not suffer a loss during a given period of time to those who do. In contrast, SHI mixes in elements of systematic redistribution. On the contribution side, uniformity serves to systematically redistribute wealth from high to low risks. On the benefits side, the redistributive effect of SHI is more ambiguous. To the extent that favored officials or social groups are high users of medical care, or have preferential access to services, SHI may be pro-rich by granting them access (almost) free of charge. In general, citizens may have to wait for a long time—possibly up to their death—to find out whether SHI was advantageous to them or not. This lack of transparency makes social health insurance an ideal means for politicians who seek office (or re-election) by catering to the interests of groups who are sufficiently organized to have an effect on the election outcome (Gouveia 1997; Hindriks and De Donder 2003; Tullock 2003). The redistributive effects of SHI can be detailed as follows.

13.4.3.1 *Redistribution of Wealth*

Using SHI as a vehicle for systematic redistribution has the important advantage from a political perspective that net payers have considerable difficulty determining the systematic component of redistribution. For example, when the contribution to social health insurance amounts to a payroll tax (as e.g. in Germany), high wage earners pay more for their health insurance. However, they are uncertain about the systematic redistribution component contained in their contribution because the expected value of their benefits might also be higher than average.

13.4.3.2 *Redistribution of Medical Care*

SHI has two redistributive effects. First, SHI has an income effect because some individuals who would have demanded less or no medical care without insurance coverage now demand a positive amount (Nyman 2003). Indeed there is (macro) evidence suggesting that medical care is (at least) a normal good (if not a luxury good) (Gerdtham et al. 1992; Miller and Frech 2004; Zweifel, Steinmann, and Eugster 2005). Insurance coverage then amounts to an in-kind redistribution from the rich to the poor if the supply of medical services is not infinitely elastic and if the price elasticity of demand for medical care is at least as high for the rich as the poor (for evidence, see Newhouse and the Insurance Group 1993: ch. 11). However, there is also a price effect because health insurance boosts the "true" willingness-to-pay (WTP) for medical care depend-ing on the rate of co-insurance (Zweifel, Breyer, and Kifmann 2009: ch. 12). For exam-ple, if "true" WTP is 100 and the rate of co-insurance is 25 percent, observed WTP is 400. Again, the redistributive effects depend on whether the price elasticity of demand for medical care is higher among the poor than among the rich.

13.4.3.3 *Redistribution of Health*

Altruism with regard to health probably is more marked than with regard to income, although evidence seems to be lacking (the methodology for measuring distributive preferences for health is still in its infancy, see Olsen 2000). Therefore, politicians can claim to have a mission when seeking to guarantee "Health for All" (the famous slogan of the World Health Organization). Equal access to health insurance then may be seen as an important factor (Culyer and Wagstaff 1993) for securing equal access to medical care, and for securing equal health status. The link between the two hinges on the mar-ginal effectiveness of health care (for which there is some evidence, see e.g. Miller and Frech 2004; Lichtenberg 2004; Martin, Rice, and Smith 2008).

If SHI indeed contributes to winning votes and increasing the chance of (re-)election of a democratic government, one would expect public expenditure for it to increase around election time. One piece of evidence relates to two types of public expenditure by the Dutch government, expressed as GDP shares, between 1956 and 1993, viz. health (such as subsidies to hospitals) and general social insurance. Van Dalen and Swank (1996) find that transfers in favor of social insurance are systematically higher during the years prior, concurrent with, and after an election. The estimated effect is 13 percent, e.g. an increase from 15 to 17 percent of GDP. The evidence thus is compatible with gov-ernments proposing or extending SHI to benefit pivotal voter groups.

13.5 FUTURE CHALLENGES

Both private and social public health insurance are facing important future challenges (see e.g. Lindbeck 1995; Jacobs and Goddard 2002).

13.5.1 Cost of Dying

It is well-known by now that much of an individual's lifetime health care expenditure occurs during the last two years of life (Lubitz and Riley 1993; Zweifel, Felder, and Meier 1999; Seshamani and Gray 2004; Zweifel, Steinmann, and Eugster 2005). This fact has spurred a debate on rationing based on age as a criterion within SHI. However, rationing through the public sector means disregard of individual preferences. A more efficient alternative would be a contract design (e.g. increased cost sharing for end of life care) that induces self-rationing by the insured. Private health insurers may develop such contracts and make them available to individuals who will accept such restrictions in exchange for lower premiums. Contract designs of this type are less likely under SHI reform because of the need to appeal to majorities through the political process.

13.5.2 Multiple Risks

Health risks are not the only risks confronting individuals during their lifetime. From their point of view, it would be efficient to combine weakly or even better negatively cor-related risks in one contract in order to achieve a degree of risk diversification that the insurer could honor through a lower combined premium (Zweifel 2000). For example, for females auto liability risks are lower but financial health risks higher than for males, and combining the two would result in a reduced total premium. Private insurers are in a position to write such "umbrella" policies. They are at present offering them to expats who are not subject to national line-specific regulation that renders such combinations virtually unfeasible (see e.g. global.insurance.com). "Umbrella" policies are also facili-tated by business in several countries resulting in international risk diversification. By way of contrast, social insurance typically is financed by specific contributions (to unem-ployment insurance, SHI, etc.) that fail to take correlations into account, and it has been confined to the domestic population (Zweifel and Eugster 2008). However, the possible gain in efficiency could be wiped out if insurers writing "umbrella" policies were to take advantage of the reduced overall premium elasticity of consumers for increasing their monopolistic markup.

13.5.3 International Purchasing

Vertically integrated private health insurers may act as "wholesale" purchasers of health-care services on behalf of their clients, who then choose a particular provider in the event of illness. Traditionally, public social insurers were legally bound to purchase domestically, with exceptions within the European Union (Hermans and Berman 1998; Hatzopoulos 2008). This limits the choice of contractual partners considerably, espe-cially in small countries. Once more, private health insurers are more inclined to pur-chase internationally than SHI schemes, which have to cater to politicians who seek to protect domestic providers from international competition.

13.5.4 Technological Change in Medicine

New therapies are continually being developed since there is demand for almost all of them, their price to patients being close to zero once they are included in the insurer's list of benefits. When deciding about their inclusion, health insurers are challenged to weigh the additional benefits against the additional costs (weighted by the probability of use) on behalf of their clients. SHI programs do this through cost-effectiveness calculations (typically, money spent per Quality-Adjusted Life Year, QALY) provided by a central institution such as the National Institute for Cost Effectiveness (NICE) of the United Kingdom. These calculations do not take into account variation in individual preferences for health and willingness to pay. Again, private health insurers could develop contracts offering more (or less) restrictive benefits and make them available to individuals who will accept such restrictions in exchange for lower (or higher) premiums (see Havighurst 1977).

For example, in discrete choice experiments, which expose respondents to repeated choices between a status quo and an alternative featuring a different mix of attributes of the product in question, Telser and Zweifel (2002) had elderly respondents hypothetically choose between the status quo and hip protectors that lowered the probability of breaking the femur, had a certain ease of handling and wearing comfort, but also an out-of-pocket price (net of health insurance). They found that the average willingness to pay for the existing variants of the product were negative.

In sum, while important challenges are confronting health insurers regardless of type, economic theory and empirical investigations combine to suggest that private health insurers may be comparatively well-prepared to meet them—provided that they are subject to competition in contestable markets.

REFERENCES

CARLTON, D. W. and PERLOFF, J. M. (1999), *Modern Industrial Organization* (3rd edn.; Reading, MA: Addison-Wesley).

COCHRANE, J. H. (1995), "Time-consistent Health Insurance," *Journal of Political Economy*, 103(3): 445–73.

COOK, P. J. and GRAHAM, D. A. (1977), "The Demand for Insurance and Protection: The Case of Irreplaceable Commodities," *Quarterly Journal of Economics*, 91(1): 143–56.

CREMER, H. and PESTIEAU, P. (1996), "Redistributive Taxation and Social Insurance," *International Tax and Public Finance*, 3: 281–95.

CULYER, A. J. and WAGSTAFF, A. (1993), "Equity and Equality in Health and Health Care," *Journal of Health Economics*, 12(4): 431–57.

CUMMINS, D. (1991), "Capital Structure and Fair Profits in Property-liability Insurance," in J. D. Cummins and R. A. Derrig (eds.), *Managing the Insolvency Risk of Insurance Companies* (Boston: Kluwer), 295–308.

—— and SOMMER, D.W. (1996), "Capital and Risk in Property-liability Insurance Markets," *Journal of Banking and Finance*, 20: 1069–92.

DAHLBY, D. G. (1981), "Adverse Selection and Pareto Improvements Through Compulsory Insurance," *Public Choice*, 31(3): 547–58.

DIONNE, G. and DOHERTY, N. A. (1994), "Adverse Selection, Commitment, and Renegotiation: Extension and Evidence from Insurance Markets," *Journal of Political Economy*, 102(2): 209–35.

DOHERTY, N. A. and TINIC, S. M. (1981), "Reinsurance Under Condition of Capital Market Equilibrium: A Note," *Journal of Finance*, 36(4): 949–53.

DROR, D. M. and PREKER, A. S. (eds.) (2002), *Social Reinsurance: A New Approach to Sustainable Community Health Financing* (Washington DC: World Bank).

EECKHOUDT, L. and SCHLESINGER, H. (2006), "Putting Risk in its Proper Place," *The American Economic Review*, 96(1): 280–9.

FECHER, E., PERELMAN, S. D., and PESTIEAU, P. (1991), "Scale Economies and Performance in the French Insurance Industry," *Geneva Papers on Risk and Insurance, Issues and Practice*, 60 (July): 315–26.

FINKELSTEIN, A., LUTTMER, E. F. P., and NOTOWIDIGDO, M. J. (2008), "What Good is Wealth Without Health? The Effect of Health on the Marginal Utility of Consumption." Working Paper, NBER 14089.

FRECH, H. E. and SAMPRONE, J. C. (1980), "The Welfare Loss of Excessive Non-price Competition: The Case of Property/liability Insurance Regulation," *Journal of Law and Economics*, 21: 429–40.

GERDTHAM, U. G., JÖNSSON, B., and SØGAARD, J. (1992), "An Econometric Analysis of Health Care Expenditure: A Cross Section Study of OECD Countries," *Journal of Health Economics*, 11: 63–84.

GOUVEIA, M. (1997), "Majority Rule and the Public Provision of a Private Good," *Public Choice*, 93: 221–44.

GREENWALD, B. C. and STIGLITZ, J. E. (1990), "Asymmetric Information and the New Theory of the Firm," *American Economic Review: Papers and Proceedings*, 80(2): 160–5.

GRUBER, J. (2000), "Health Insurance and the Labor Market," in A. J. Culyer and J. P. Newhouse (eds.), *Handbook of Health Economics* (Amsterdam: North Holland), 645–706.

HATZOPOULOS, V. (2008), "Public Procurement and State Aids in Public Health Care Systems," *Euro Observer*, 10(3): 3–4.

HAVIGHURST, C. C. (1977), "Controlling Health Care Costs by Strengthening the Private Sector's Hand," *Journal of Health, Politics, Policy and Law*, 1(4): 471–98.

HERMANS, H. E. G. M. and BERMAN, P. C. (1998), "Access to Health Care and Health Services in the European Union: Regulation 1408/71 and the E111 Process," in R. Leidl (ed.), *Health Care and Its Financing in the Single European Market* (Amsterdam: IOS Press), 324–43.

HERRING, B. and PAULY, M. V. (2006), "Incentive Compatible Guaranteed Renewable Health Insurance Premiums," *Journal of Health Economics*, 25(3): 395–417.

HINDRIKS, J. and DE DONDER, P. (2003), "The Politics of Redistributive Social Insurance," *Journal of Public Economics*, 87: 2639–60.

HOPKINS, S. and ZWEIFEL, P. (2005), "The Australian Health Policy Changes of 1999 and 2000," *Applied Health Economics and Health Policy*, 4(4): 229–38.

JACOBS, R. and GODDARD, M. (2002), "Trade-offs in Social Health Insurance Systems," *International Journal of Social Economics*, 29: 861–75.

KHUNOANE, B. (2003), *Consultative Forum on Risk Equalization: The Context of Health Financing Reform in South Africa* (Pretoria: Department of Health).

LICHTENBERG, F. R. (2004), "Sources of US Longevity Increase, 1960–2001," *Quarterly Review of Economics and Finance*, 44: 369–89.

LINDBECK, A. (1995), "Hazardous Welfare State Dynamics," *American Economic Review*, 85(2): 9–15.

LUBITZ, J. B. and RILEY, G. F. (1993), "Trends in Medicare Payments in the Last Year of Life," *New England Journal of Medicine*, 328: 1092–96.

MA, A. and MCGUIRE, T. G. (1997), "Optimal Health Insurers and Provider Payment," *American Economic Review*, 87: 685–704.

MARTIN, S., RICE, M. S., and SMITH, P. (2008), "Does Health Care Spending Improve Health Outcomes? Evidence from English Programme Budgeting Data," *Journal of Health Economies*, 27: 826–42.

MILLER, R. D., JR., and FRECH III, H. E. (2004), *Health Care Matters. Pharmaceuticals, Obesity, and the Quality of Life* (Washington, DC: AEI Press).

MORRISEY, M. A. (ed.) (2001), "Why Do Employers Do What They Do? Studies of Employer Sponsored Health Insurance," *International Journal of Health Care Finance & Economics*, 1 (3/4) (special issue).

NEWHOUSE, J. P. (1996), "Reimbursing Health Plans and Health Providers: Efficiency in Production versus Selection," *Journal of Economic Literature*, 34: 1236–63.

—— and INSURANCE EXPERIMENT GROUP (1993), *Free for All? Lessons From the RAND Health Insurance Experiment, A RAND Study* (Cambridge, MA: Harvard University Press).

NYMAN, J. A. (2003), *The Theory of Demand for Health Insurance* (Stanford, CA: Stanford University Press).

OECD (2004), *The OECD Health Project: Towards High-performing Health Systems* (Paris: OECD).

OLSEN, J. A. (2000), "A Note on Eliciting Distributive Preferences for Health," *Journal of Health Economics*, 19: 541–50.

PAULY, M. V. (1970), "The Efficiency in the Provision of Consumption Subsidies," *Kyklos*, 23: 33–57.

—— (1984), "Is Cream Skimming a Problem for the Competitive Medical Market?" *Journal of Health Economics*, 3: 87–95.

—— (2000), "Insurance Reimbursement," in A. J. Culyer and J. P. Newhouse (eds.), *Handbook of Health Economics*, Vol. 1A (Amsterdam: Elsevier).

—— and HERRING, B. (1999), *Pooling Health Insurance Risks* (Washington, DC: American Enterprise Institute).

PREKER, A., HARDING, A., and DRAVIS, P. (2000), "Make or Buy Decisions in the Production of Health Care Goods and Services: New Insights from Institutional Economics and Organizational Theory," *Bulletin of the World Health Organization*, 78(6): 779–90.

ROTHSCHILD, M. and STIGLITZ, J. E. (1976), "Equilibrium in Competitive Insurance Markets: An Essay on the Economics of Imperfect Information," *Quarterly Journal of Economics*, 90: 630–49.

SESHAMANI, M. and GRAY, A. (2004), "A Longitudinal Study of Effects of Age and Time to Death on Hospital Costs," *Journal of Health Economics*, 23: 217–35.

SINN, H.-W. (1996), "Social Insurance, Incentives and Risk Taking," *International Tax and Public Finance*, 3: 259–80.

SMITH, P. C. (2007), "Provision of a Public Benefit Package Alongside Private Voluntary Health Insurance," in A. Preker et al. (eds.), *Private Voluntary Health Insurance in Development* (Washington, DC: World Bank).

SURET, M. (1991), "Scale and Scope Economies in the Canadian Property and Casualty Insurance Industry," in *Geneva Papers on Risk and Insurance, Issues and Practice*, 59 (April): 236–56.

TELSER, H. and ZWEIFEL, P. (2002), "Measuring Willingness-to-pay for Risk Reduction: An Application of Conjoint Analysis," *Health Economics*, 11: 129–39.

TULLOCK, G. (2003), "The Origin of the Rent-seeking Concept," *International Journal of Business and Economics*, 2: 1–8.

Van Dalen, H. P. and Swank, O. A. (1996), "Government Spending Cycles: Ideological or Opportunistic?" *Public Choice*, 89: 183–200.

Van de Ven, W. P. M. M. and Ellis, R. P. (2000), "Risk Adjustment in Competitive Health Plan Markets," in J. P. Newhouse and A. J. Culyer (eds.), *Handbook of Health Economics*, Vol. 1A (Amsterdam: Elsevier).

Waldman, D. and Jensen, M. (2001), *Industrial Organization*, (New York: Addison Wesley).

Wilson, C. A. (1977), "A Model of Insurance Markets with Incomplete Information," *Journal of Economic Theory*, 16: 167–207.

Zweifel, P. (2000), "The Division of Labor Between Private and Social Insurance," in G. Dionne (ed.), *Handbook of Insurance* (Boston: Kluwer).

—— (2007), "The Theory of Social Health Insurance," *Foundations and Trends in Microeconomics*, 3(3): 183–273.

—— and Breuer, M. (2006), "The Case for Risk-based Premiums in Public Health Insurance," *Health Economics, Policy and Law*, 1(2): 171–88.

—— and Eugster, P. (2008), "Life-cycle Effects of Social Security in an Open Economy: A Theoretical and Empirical Survey," *Zeitschrift für die Gesamte Versicherungswissenschaft* (German Journal of Risk and Insurance), 97(1): 61–77.

—— and Manning, W. G. (2000), "Moral Hazard and Consumer Incentives in Health Care," in A. J. Culyer and J. P. Newhouse (eds.), *Handbook of Health Economics*, Vol. 1A (Amsterdam: Elsevier).

—— Felder, S. and Meier, M. (1999), "Aging of Population and Health Care Expenditure: A Red Herring?" *Health Economics*, 9: 485–96.

—— Steinmann, L., and Eugster, P. (2005), "The Sisyphus Syndrome in Health Care Revisited," *International Journal of Health Care Finance and Economics*, 5: 127–45.

—— Telser, H., and Vaterlaus, S. (2006), "Consumer Resistance Against Regulation: The Case of Health Care," *Journal of Regulatory Economics*, 29(3): 21–39.

—— Krey, B. B., and Tagli, M. (2007), "Supply of Private Voluntary Health Insurance in Low-income Countries," in A. Preker et al. (eds.), *Private Voluntary Health Insurance in Development* (Washington, DC: World Bank).

—— Breyer, F., and Kifmann, M. (2009), *Health Economics* (2nd edn.; Boston, MA: Springer).

CHAPTER 14

···

HEALTH CARE COST GROWTH

···

MICHAEL E. CHERNEW AND DUSTIN MAY

The nation's long-term fiscal balance will be determined primarily by the future rate of health care cost growth.
Peter Orszag, Director, Congressional Budget Office (Orszag 2007)

14.1 INTRODUCTION

···

14.1.1 Background

EXPENDITURES on health care have risen consistently over the past century. The share of gross domestic product devoted to medical spending in countries belonging to the Organisation for Economic Co-operation and Development (OECD) increased from 5.1 percent in 1970 to 8.9 percent in 2006 (OECD 2008). With 70 percent of total health care spending for OECD countries financed through public funds (Docteur and Oxley 2003), such continued growth is a central issue for policymakers. A myriad cost containment strategies designed to address health care cost growth have been implemented.

Health care cost growth is an international problem; most developed countries have experienced a high rate of growth in health care costs irrespective of system structure (CBO 2008). This growth has been tied to several factors, including population aging, general economic growth, and the adoption and use of new medical technologies (White 2007). From 1985 to 2002, the top five OECD spenders were the United States, Switzerland, Portugal, Iceland, and Norway. Notably, the United States stands alone as the only OECD country without a publicly integrated or publicly contracted health care system and, by some estimates, significantly higher rates of health care cost growth than any other OECD country, although this conclusion remains far from clear (OECD

2007; White 2007). Conclusions about relative cost growth are sensitive to the years being examined and whether purchasing power parity adjustments are made. If, following much of the literature, one uses purchasing power parity adjustments, data from 1960 through 2004 suggests that the rate of cost growth in the US has been comparable to that of the other OECD countries (Figure 14.1) (OECD 2007). However, comparable figures starting in 1975 or using local price indices without purchasing power parity adjustments would suggest somewhat faster cost growth in the US.

More importantly, regardless of how other countries compare to the United States, many major industrialized countries have experienced more rapid growth in health care than in GDP. As a result, the share of GDP devoted to health care has been growing (Figure 14.2). Of course cost growth may not be welfare diminishing, but the rising share of GDP devoted to health care raises public financing challenges in all countries.

Projections for the United States suggest that if health care costs continue to grow at similar rates, about 90 percent of the increase in American GDP between 2010 and 2050 will be devoted to health care. In contrast, during the 1980s and 1990s, health care consumed, at most, about 25 percent of American GDP growth (Chernew et al. 2003). The impact of costs on health insurance coverage will disproportionately affect low income individuals, exacerbating existing health disparities (Keenan et al. 2006). If future spending growth exceeds GDP by even 1 percentage point, millions of Americans will lose coverage over the next decade (Chernew et al. 2005) and benefits will likely diminish for those with coverage. This will further strain public payers and the entire health care sector by increasing the demand for services by the uninsured and, at the same time, increasing the costs of subsidizing their treatment/coverage.

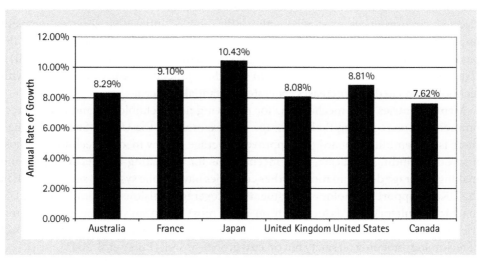

FIGURE 14.1 Cost growth in OECD countries
Source: OECD Health Data 2007.

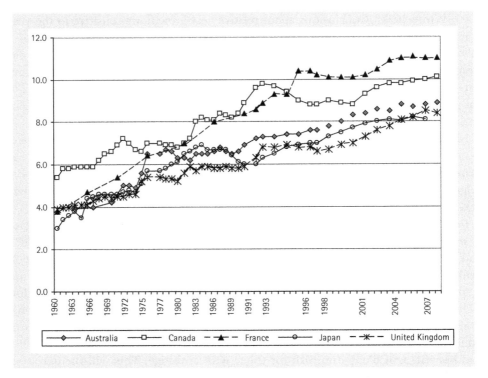

FIGURE 14.2 Total health expenditures as a share of gross domestic product, 1960–2007
Source: OCED Health Data 2009.

The dominant factor contributing to rising spending is the development and diffusion of new medical technology (Newhouse 1992; Fuchs 1996; Chernew 1998). While selected circumstances exist where the utilization of innovative services may not improve health (i.e. inappropriate care), there is little debate that on balance, over the past half-century, medical technology has yielded clinical benefit (Cutler 2001). Irrespective of these desirable gains in health, financial pressures associated with technology-related cost increases generate substantial concern.

Many countries have mechanisms for reviewing new technologies and making recommendations regarding their coverage. For example, in the United States, although there is no centralized board that approves coverage of new medical technology, most insurers, including Medicare, have mechanisms for evaluating new technologies and making coverage determinations. Other countries have public systems, such as NICE in the UK, to support technology assessment and coverage decisions. In contrast to the US, in which regulatory boards focus only on safety, most European and other OECD countries, by contrast, have standardized system-wide approaches for dealing with the impact of technology not only on safety but on cost growth as well (Busse et al. 2002).

In addition to cost containment strategies focused explicitly on new technologies, a number of strategies have been used (or proposed) in the US and other countries to contain the rise in health care cost growth. These include demand side interventions such as greater patient cost sharing at the point of service, supply side initiatives such as managed care / managed competition, provider competition and supply restrictions, pricing reforms, and initiatives such as disease management and pay for performance, which are designed to improve health and hopefully, as a result, lower expenditures.

Unlike the United States, most OECD countries adopted national health programs during the 1950s and 1960s or earlier. The programs, which continue to evolve, vary in their structure and in the mechanisms they use to address cost growth in ways that are fundamentally different from the American experience. Specifically, several approaches are used to contain costs: (1) budget-setting (most commonly for hospitals, but also done at the national, sectoral, and institutional levels), (2) price and payment regulation (on e.g. pharmaceutical prices or physician wages), (3) supply side restrictions (e.g. limits on medical school entry or number of hospital beds), and (4) non-monetary provider incentives (e.g. clinical guidelines, use of standardized evidence-based treatments). These strategies are not mutually exclusive and are implemented in different ways.

The similar rates of cost growth among other countries when compared with the United States demonstrate that there is no "magic bullet" for limiting cost growth. Evidence suggests that supply-side reforms appear to produce shorter term savings in the level of spending, but not sustained reductions in the growth rate of medical costs (Cutler 1999). Ultimately, political systems may succumb to public demand for access to new technologies and modern styles of medical practice (Cutler 1999).

14.1.2 General Issues Relating to Cost Growth

In examining the potential for various strategies to contain cost growth, several concepts are important.

14.1.2.1 *Evidence Relating Technology to Cost Growth*

As noted above, technology is commonly considered to be the primary driver of cost growth. The process by which technology increases costs is complex. Certainly technology may alter the price of care, but the more salient driver of the relationship between technology and costs is related to how technology alters the patterns of care. While in some cases technology may be manifest in new services which substitute for other services, in many cases technology leads to proliferation of new services without replacing existing services. Moreover, in many cases the use of technology generates increased use of pre-existing services. For example, new diagnostic tests generate additional treatments (e.g. prostate cancer screening leads to more prostatectomies) and new treatments generate greater diagnostic testing (e.g. new treatments for osteoporosis generate demand for bone mineral density tests).

Finally, new technology can alter care patterns in complex ways. If technology improves health, we would expect reductions in spending in any given period. However, it is possible that improved health induces consumption of health care services that might otherwise not have been used. For example, better management of congestive heart failure may induce demand for services that improve quality of life in other ways, such as hip replacement. Moreover, any technology-related reduction in mortality will increase spending in the period of extended life. Such spending may be relatively low, if individuals are in good health, but if technology extends the lives of individuals with complex and expensive chronic disease, the fiscal consequences of reduced mortality could be significant. The relationship between technology and cost growth is ultimately an empirical question.

The conclusion that technology is a primary driver of cost growth is based on a wide body of literature, classified by Chernew et al. (1998) into two broad categories. The first category, labeled "residual studies," examines aggregate cost growth and attempts to adjust for changes in factors other than technology that might generate cost growth (Schwartz 1987; Newhouse 1992, 1993; Peden and Freeland 1995). These factors are typically aging, medical price changes, income growth, and the spread of insurance. The remaining unexplained cost growth is attributed to technology, though no specific technologies are identified. In this strand of the literature the definition of technology is very broad. Specifically, "technology" is the set of factors related to cost growth that the study did not explicitly measure.

The second category of literature, labeled "affirmative studies," is based on examination of specific health care services considered to be new technology (Scitovsky and McCall 1976; Showstack et al. 1982; Scitovsky 1985; Cutler and McClellan 1996). These studies define technology in a much more tangible way, but are inherently limited in their ability to capture the totality of the manner in which technology influences cost growth. However, in some cases, these affirmative studies focus on specific diseases or specific provider types, thereby allowing identification of the broad impact technologies have had on treatment patterns.

The affirmative studies indicate that the technologies driving cost growth have likely changed over time. Scitovsky (1985) and Scitovsky and McCall (1976), for example, studied selected diseases and concluded that between 1951 and 1971, increasing costs were related to increased use of "little ticket" technologies such as laboratory tests and X-rays (Scitovsky and McCall 1976; Scitovsky 1985). However, increasingly throughout the 1970s, big ticket items such as intensive care units, followed by cesarean sections, revascularization for heart disease, and radiation and chemotherapy therapy for cancer accounted for a substantial portion of cost growth. Cutler and McClellan (1996) confirm the importance of big ticket items in the 1980s, emphasizing the importance of catheterization and revascularization in driving cost growth for treating heart attacks. In many cases, new tests were additive rather than substitutive (Showstack et al. 1982; Cutler and McClellan 1996).

In the 1990s, different types of new technology contributed to cost growth, particularly prescription drugs. Many new and costly drugs became standard treatment for chronic diseases, such as statins for heart disease. Combined with the rise in third party payment for such new treatments, pharmaceutical sales grew at an average pace of 11.9 percent from 1987–1994 and 12.8 percent from 1994–1999. Four-fifths of the latter period's growth was attributable to increases in utilization (Berndt 2001).

What seems clear is that while the type of new technology may change, the preponderance of evidence suggests that new treatment patterns, driven by new services and new knowledge changing the application of old services, is a fundamental driver of cost growth.

14.1.2.2 *Population Expenditures vs. Unit Costs or Disease-/Service-specific Spending*

Alarm over health care cost growth is typically centered on the rise in health care expenditures at the population level. Expenditures reflect both unit costs (prices) and utilization patterns (quantities). Some interventions may reduce unit prices, but, because of the utilization response, may not reduce expenditures. For example, the introduction of laparoscopic cholecystectomy in the United States resulted in increased spending because of the rapid increase in utilization associated with the new technology, despite a 25 percent lower per unit cost (Legoretta et al. 1993).

This helps explain why innovative technology often raises expenditures in the health care sector, even though it is perceived to lower costs in other industries. The perception of reduced costs associated with technology in other sectors often reflects reduced unit costs, not reduced expenditures. For example, as technology reduced unit costs in the information technology sector, spending growth in the overall sector increased 26 percent annually from 1982 to 1996 (Haimowitz 1997).

Expenditures are also not limited to any particular disease. Individuals cured of one disease inevitably get another. It is possible that reductions in expenditures on one disease may increase overall spending if competing conditions are more expensive. Finally, cost growth at the population level may not reflect trends in cost growth for particular services. Efforts to constrain spending in one area may simply generate greater spending in other areas. For example, in the United States, as inpatient sending growth slowed following implementation of prospective payment systems (PPS), outpatient spending soared (Miller and Sulvetta 1992).

14.1.2.3 *Level vs. Rate of Change in Costs*

In assessing cost containment strategies, it is crucial to distinguish between those interventions that affect the trajectory of cost growth versus those that affect the level. While the variation in the level of costs is important, the more serious fiscal challenge faced by health care systems is cost growth. For example, if health care costs continue to grow in the US at historic rates (about 4–5% per person, per year, inflation adjusted, since 1965), it would only take three to four years for costs to return to current levels following a 15 percent reduction in costs. Interventions that lower the level of spending may reduce spending by a considerable amount, which is important, but will not resolve the cost crisis unless they also reduce the trajectory of spending growth.

This distinction is important in assessing the ability of systems which are more conservative in their adoption of new technology to control cost growth. A system that adopts new technology more slowly than another system may have the same rate of cost growth if the baseline level of costs is lower. For example, if a given country has a base spending rate that is 20 percent below that of another country, it will experience the same cost growth if it utilizes a new technology 20 percent less frequently.

14.1.2.4 *Past Experience vs. Future Potential*

When assessing the impact of cost containment strategies on the trajectory of spending, it is important to recognize the difference between past experience and potential effects. While few existing strategies have demonstrably reduced the rate of cost growth to sustainable levels, many cost containment strategies would have the potential to do so if implemented in a stronger manner. For example, if payment rates for health care services are set low enough, it is likely health care cost growth would slow. Physicians would have no incentive to offset lower payments with greater volume. A strong system of capitation could also, by definition, control health care cost growth. The challenge is whether such systems are sustainable politically. In many cases, systems which in theory could control spending, such as capitation or the use of a system to restrict the growth in physician payments in the US Medicare system, have not succeeded in limiting cost growth because purchasers or legislators have been unwilling to maintain caps on spending (Cutler 1999; Chernew et al. 2000).

14.2 COST CONTAINMENT APPROACHES

14.2.1 Cost Sharing at the Point of Service

14.2.1.1 *Background*

Today, most health care systems employ some method of cost sharing as a means to reduce health care utilization (see Chapter 15, "User Charges," by Schokkaert and van de Voorde, this volume). Though cost sharing can have many permutations, the most common methods used are copayments (fixed payments for a given service), coinsurance (a percentage of the total cost), and deductibles (a fixed amount of out-of-pocket spending that patients must incur before coverage is provided). In some systems, cost-sharing levels vary with income. The most common approach is to provide lower cost sharing to vulnerable populations (OECD 2007). Some countries, such as the Netherlands, Sweden, and Germany, place a ceiling on cost sharing as a percentage of income; if cost sharing exceeds that threshold, it is refunded (Ros et al. 2000). Recently in the United States, policymakers have implemented various "means tested" cost sharing and premium structures into the Medicare program, which provides universal coverage to those with a disability or over 65 years of age (Medicare Prescription Drug Improvement and Modernization Act 2003).

In the private market in the US, a greater reliance on patient cost sharing at the point of service (i.e. when they seek care) is proliferating. This is particularly the case with the emergence of "high deductible" health insurance plans. These plans typically require patients to pay out-of-pocket for the first several thousand dollars of health care expenses. Patients are then fully (or nearly fully) covered for "catastrophic" illness exceeding that initial deductible up to a coverage limit. Typically, these plans are offered in conjunction with an option for consumers to set up a health savings account, in which funds may be set aside to pay for out-of-pocket medical expenses at any time. Consumers or their employers may contribute to these accounts with pretax income. Increases in both availability and enrollment in high-deductible health insurance plans have been observed in recent years. Although these plans represent only 1.7 percent of the private health insurance market in the United States, enrollment has grown considerably from 438,000 in 2004 to over three million by January of 2006 (GAO 2006). However, 8.5 million persons with a high enough deductible to qualify for tax-deferred contributions do not currently have such an account (EBRI, CMWF 2006).

14.2.1.2 Evidence

Seminal work by Newhouse et al. (1993) in the RAND Health Insurance demonstrated that patient cost sharing reduced the consumption of health care services (see also Phelps and Newhouse 1974). The elasticity of spending with respect to health care was estimated to be −0.2 (Manning et al. 1987; Keeler and Rolph 1988). Subsequent studies that involved mental health care and dental care demonstrated reductions in utilization in response to price and in the types of services utilized (Keeler et al. 1988; Mueller and Monheit 1988). Recent evidence has shown varying elasticity (from −0.1 to −0.4) for particular prescription drugs based upon the type of chronic condition they are used to treat (Goldman et al. 2004).

However, the decreased utilization associated with cost sharing does not disproportionately impact necessary care, as proponents of cost sharing would hope and standard economic theory would predict. Patients apparently reduce use of appropriate and inappropriate care in similar proportions (Siu et al. 1986). Consistent with this view, many recent studies suggest patients reduce use of prescription drugs when faced with modestly higher copayments (Huskamp et al. 2003; Goldman et al. 2004; Goldman et al. 2007; Landon et al. 2007). With regard to emergency care, though, cost sharing is associated with decreases in repeat and low severity visits (Selby et al. 1996; Wharam et al. 2007).

On average, the results from the RAND health insurance experiment did not find a strong impact of cost sharing on health (Newhouse 1993). However, cost sharing has been demonstrated to have disproportionately negative effects on the quality and delivery of health care among low-income populations (Brook et al. 1983; Wright et al. 2005). The effect of cost sharing on elderly and those with chronic illness has also been extensively studied (Heisler et al. 2004; Piette et al. 2004). Adverse events, lower adherence, and decreased management of illness are all associated with increased patient cost sharing (Tamblyn et al. 2001). Despite evidence that points toward cost sharing as way to lower costs, the longer term consequences on health associated with lower utilization of high value services have yet to be fully evaluated.

Because cost sharing is associated with lower costs, many health care payers view cost sharing as a means to reduce cost growth in health care (Chernew 2004). Yet there is virtually no evidence examining the impact of cost sharing on cost growth. It is possible higher cost sharing lowers spending, but does not alter the trajectory of spending growth.

14.2.1.3 Potential

In the extreme, one would expect that greater cost sharing would constrain spending growth as patients face more binding budget constraints. Yet, this potential has yet to be demonstrated. If patients place enough value on health, health spending could rise to a very high share of income (Hall and Jones 2007). At current levels of cost sharing, significant segments of the population may be able to afford substantial cost growth.

14.2.2 Managed Care/Managed Competition

14.2.2.1 *Background*

At the most basic level, managed care plans integrate the financing and delivery of care. However, there is incredible diversity in the extent that this integration occurs, ranging from staff model Health Maintenance Organizations (HMOs), in which a limited network of physicians are employed by the health plan, to PPO plans, which generally negotiate a discounted fee-for-service price schedule and provide access to a broad provider network. Across the spectrum of managed care plans, different tools are used to affect care and/or costs. These include utilization review/management programs,[1] changes in the way physicians are paid, education programs, and restrictions on provider networks. The theoretical foundation of managed care posits that once financing and delivery are integrated, plans will optimally balance costs and quality and will have the tools to eliminate inefficiencies that arise when provision of care is separated from financing care.

The success of managed care depends on the environment in which managed care plans operate. Proponents of managed care contend that a regulated environment is needed to generate the beneficial effects of competition among managed care plans (Enthoven 2003). Under a system of "managed competition" managed care plans (or other health plans) compete under a set of rules, such as uniform benefit structure and incremental pricing, which promote competition and, in theory, would control costs and cost growth.

14.2.2.2 *Evidence*

The influence of managed care on cost growth has been studied using either a "plan comparison" or "market comparison" approach. In the plan comparison approach, measures of aggregate expenditure growth, such as premium increases, are compared between plans. Evidence from these studies suggests that there were no significant differences in cost growth between different types of systems (Ginsburg and Pickreign 1996; Chernew 1998).

In contrast, the market comparison approach, which compares markets with different levels of managed care penetration, typically indicates that the level of HMO penetration in a particular market is inversely proportional to the rate of cost growth in a market (Chernew 1998). However, even in these studies, the rate of cost growth in high managed care penetration markets still exceeded GDP growth (Chernew 1998). For example, Melnick and Zwanziger (1995) report that in markets with significant managed

---

[1] Utilization review is an internally performed review by a health insurer of how certain medical services are requested and performed. The review typically involved pre-review, or pre-authorization; concurrent review, or inpatient evaluation of care and needs; and retrospective review, or the larger historical picture of how physicians, labs, or hospitals handle their patient populations.

care penetration, cost growth still exceeded income growth by 1.5 percentage points. The stronger market level effect may reflect spillovers from the managed care sector. Health care providers may treat patients similarly irrespective of their insurance status (Chernew 1998) and, as a result, HMO-induced practice patterns spill over into other weakly managed systems. The spillover may also reflect changes in the infrastructure of the health care market place (such as reduced capacity) which may have an effect on the non-managed care population.

14.2.2.3 *Potential*

Although managed care has demonstrated the potential to slow cost growth at the market level, the magnitude of the effect has not appeared to be substantial enough to stabilize the share of GDP devoted to health care. The primary challenge facing managed care plans seems to be the difficulty for any one plan to influence the behavior of health care providers. Plans appear to be able to succeed by maintaining cost growth in line with their competitors, and thus the cost of plans of more strongly managing providers may be significant, given the influence providers have with patients (Chernew 2004; Figueras et al. 2005). Historically, consumers were not attracted to stricter plans. Justified or not, negative perceptions of managed care have grown and enthusiasm for a managed care-based system of delivery and financing of care has waned (Mechanic 2001; Peterson 2002). It remains to be seen whether tolerance of stronger managed care restrictions will increase as cost pressures rise.

14.2.3 Payment Reforms

14.2.3.1 *Background*

The impact of payment changes on expenditures reflects both the direct impact of changes in price on expenditures and the indirect effect of payment changes on utilization (see Chapter 15, "User Charges," by Schokkaert and van de Voorde, this volume). Considerable evidence suggests that physicians respond to financial incentives (Hellinger 1998; Hillman et al. 1999). Two aspects of payment matter: the form of payment (e.g. fee-for-service, capitation, salary) and the level of payment. For example, fee-for-service payment encourages utilization and capitation discourages use (Enthoven and Vorhaus 1997; Chernew et al. 2000). Within any given form of payment, the generosity may matter. For example, the incentives to increase volume under a fee-for-service system rise as payment rates rise, although because of income effects, individual physicians may respond to rate increases by lowering volume and rate cuts by increasing volume (Rice 1983). Under capitation, the incentive to constrain use may be insensitive to the level of capitation, although competition may create a relationship between the level of capitation and utilization.

Current reform proposals include efforts to move to an episode based payment system (Davis 2007). This extends earlier trends toward prospective payment for many health care services. Episode based payment redefines the product away from specific services and towards a defined care period. This in some ways resembles a capitation per episode.

14.2.3.2 *Evidence*

Evidence suggests that payment reform can change the level of spending. Cutler et al. (2000) report that managed care plans were able to achieve savings primarily through reduced payment rates. Chernew et al. (2000) report that when physicians in a capitated plan bear increasing risk for the pharmaceutical expenditures of their patients, they prescribe fewer and less expensive medications. During the implementation of Medicare prospective payment, the cost of a Medicare hospital day declined one-third from 1984 to 1994, even as the number of days used by Medicare beneficiaries fell by about one-fifth (Scanlon 2006). The Medicare PPS has also led high-cost hospitals to lower their costs (Hadley et al. 1989).

Evidence of the impact of payment on expenditure growth rates is more scant. States with DRG-based Medicaid payments experienced lower growth in spending on hospital services (Hellinger 1986), but spending on other services may have risen to offset this. It is certainly instructive that, although Medicare has prospective payment for many services, inflation adjusted, per beneficiary cost growth in Medicare has risen 5.6 percent annually since 2000 and 4.3 percent annually since 1990 (CMS 2007). Even capitation may not control cost growth. In an examination of an insurer that used capitation as its payment strategy, Chernew et al. (2000) note that physicians were able to obtain higher capitation rates over time and eventually the capitation plan studied collapsed.

14.2.3.3 *Potential*

Payment reform could undoubtedly control both costs and cost growth. In the extreme, very low payments discourage supply, and hence utilization. For this reason payment systems designed to control costs run the risk of impeding access. Understanding how payment reforms affect costs, cost growth, and quality in a decentralized system of competing providers and payers is a central challenge for the health economics community.

14.2.4 Competition among Providers/Supply Restrictions

14.2.4.1 *Background*

Policymakers generally believe that competition among providers is an integral element to reducing cost growth (Norwalk 2007). Philosophically, this reflects economic models (and experience from other markets) that competition lowers prices (though importantly, those models do not predict the effects of competition on spending). In health care, the theoretical relationships are more complex. Some researchers have posited a "Medical Arms Race" model of competition in the hospital market in which hospitals compete for physicians by offering more expensive services and, therefore, competition drives up costs (Luft et al. 1988). It is literature of this type which supports a range of health planning interventions, such as "Certificate of Need" Programs, which limit entry but are intended to control expenditures.

In the physician market, some researchers have advocated models of supplier-induced demand, in which greater entry of physicians induces other physicians to induce greater utilization by their patients, negating any cost saving effects of entry (Fuchs 2003). Some researchers have been focused not simply on the number of physicians, but on their characteristics. Specifically, some researchers believe that greater reliance on primary care physicians will lower costs, while greater reliance on specialty physicians will increase costs (Starfield 2003).

Internationally, a range of competition inducements and supply restrictions have been tried, particularly as costs rose during the 1990s and later as "market reforms" gained fashion among policymakers. During the 1990s, OECD countries had varying success regulating the supply of physicians, hospital beds, health workforce wages, and direct supply-side means like changing care delivery/utilization patterns (Saltman and Figueras 1998). Following the rise of managed care in the United States during that time, OECD countries have been experimenting with competition among providers them-selves with similarly mixed success, though these arrangements tend more toward a "public/private" administration than a purely private system of competing providers or insurers like the United States (Saltman 2002).

14.2.4.2 Evidence

Empirical evidence from the 1970s supports the predictions of the Medical Arms Race model, suggesting that more competitive markets have higher costs (Luft et al. 1988). More recent evidence suggests that this relationship may have diminished in the 1990s as managed care penetration grew (Devers et al. 2003). Specifically, markets with both a competitive hospital market *and* considerable penetration by managed care plans expe-rienced slower cost growth (Zwanziger et al. 2000). However, cost growth in high man-aged care markets still exceeded rates of income growth (Bamezai et al. 1999). More recently, the Medical Arms Race may have returned as managed care has weakened (Devers et al. 2003). Thus competition may again be associated with higher costs, and perhaps, higher cost growth.

Evidence from merger studies suggest that merged hospital systems can increase prices and, given inelastic demand, this likely translates to higher expenditures (Gaynor and Vogt 2003). This result creates a paradox in the literature: Markets with more pro-viders tend to have higher costs, but mergers among hospitals also seem to increase costs. Clearly more work on the causal pathways underlying the relationship between costs and competition is needed.

Another source of evidence related to competition and costs comes from Certificate of Need (CON) laws in the United States. These laws have historically restricted the supply of health facility beds, but can also restrict the adoption of medical technology. This evi-dence is useful because it may illuminate the potential impact of policies related to supply of hospital services. Existing results suggest that the impact of CON laws on spending has been modest (Grabowski et al. 2003). This may not reflect the effect of competition on costs as much as the modest effects of CON on competition.

Similar complexity exists when analyzing the physician market. Evidence supports the association between more physicians and higher costs (Bodenheimer 2005). This seems to be driven by specialist physicians because research also supports the contention that more primary care physicians are associated with lower spending. These associations may not be causal. For example, advocates of supplier-induced demand theory argue that a greater number of physicians cause greater use. Yet, work by Dranove and Wehner (1994) demonstrates that a greater supply of obstetricians/gynecologists is associated with greater fertility, suggesting that physician supply may reflect, rather than cause, demand.

Although the debate about the relationship between physician and hospital supply and spending and costs will continue, it is important to note that much of this literature is related to the level of costs, not the trajectory. The limited evidence on cost growth suggests that even in the most successful settings (significant managed care penetration and hospital competition) the share of GDP devoted to health care still rises, albeit at a somewhat slower rate than in other markets.

14.2.4.3 *Potential*

Assessing the extent to which competition could control cost growth in the future is complicated and undoubtedly dependent on the institutional details of the health care environment. Even advocates of greater competition are likely to agree that, in the current system, increasing the number of providers (which is often a proxy for competition) is unlikely to be an effective way of controlling spending growth. Yet we have little experience in settings more conducive to competition. Competition may work well in some instances (when services are easier to evaluate and information problems less severe), and work less well in other settings, where market imperfections are more difficult to overcome.

14.2.5 Disease Management/"Pay for Performance" Initiatives/Wellness Programs

14.2.5.1 *Background*

Many observers have noted that the health care expenditures of individuals with chronic disease are much greater than expenditures of individuals without such disease (Thorpe and Howard 2006). Moreover, conditions related to individual behaviors, such as obesity, are correlated with higher spending and, some have argued, important drivers of health care cost growth. The share of obese Medicare beneficiaries increased from 9.4 percent in 1987 to 22.5 percent in 2002 (Thorpe and Howard 2006).

For this reason, some believe that initiatives aimed at improving health will save money. There are many such programs including disease management programs (which use a range of techniques to improve patient management of chronic disease), pay for performance (P4P) programs (which pay physicians for meeting targets related to the percentage of their patients that comply with recommended prevention and chronic disease standards), and wellness programs (which include activities such as risk assessment programs, often online, for nutrition, weight management, stress management, smoking cessation, etc.).

14.2.5.2 *Evidence*

Disease management, pay for performance, and wellness programs will only save money if the services they promote are cost-saving. That is not always the case (Fireman et al. 2004). For example, Neumann et al. (2005) suggest that most preventive services are not cost saving from a societal perspective. A key issue is the baseline risk of adverse consequences and the ability of these services to reduce that risk. Access to certain chronic disease services may be cost saving for individuals at significant risk of adverse outcomes. For example, Rosen et al. (2005) indicate that free provision of anti-hypertensive medications to Medicare patients with diabetes may result in cost savings. In general, however, evidence of these savings associated with disease management and pay for performance programs is weak (Weingarten et al. 2002; Rosenthal and Dudley 2007). There is some evidence in the literature suggesting that wellness programs can save money and even slow cost growth (Naydeck et al. 2008), but concerns about study design preclude any definitive conclusions. Even if these programs lower costs at a point in time, it is even less clear what their impact would be on the trajectory of spending if the healthier beneficiaries lived longer lives, increasing the number of people in the population and potentially the share with chronic diseases.

The impact of obesity reduction initiatives is even more uncertain. While the share of the population that is obese has grown, a simple re-weighting of spending to reflect the greater share of obese individuals accounted for less than 2 percent of the overall increase in health care spending in the USA between 1987 and 2001. Most of the growth related to obesity stems from more rapid cost growth among obese individuals as opposed to an increase in the prevalence of obesity. This may reflect the distribution of technical progress across diseases as opposed to any causal factor related to the changing number of obese Americans. While anti-obesity programs may be able to save money at a point in time, their impact on the trajectory of spending remains speculative at best.

14.2.5.3 *Potential*

Health improvement initiatives may be an important component of the health care system. Better health is an important policy goal. Yet, it is likely too optimistic to assume that better health will substantially lower the trajectory of health care spending. Health care costs were growing rapidly well before the epidemic of obesity and health care cost growth among the healthy persists. For example, Chernew et al. (2005) find faster rates of cost growth among the least disabled Medicare beneficiaries, relative to the more disabled beneficiaries. Because healthier beneficiaries live longer, and may demand a range of quality of life improving services, it would not be prudent to assume that better health, as desirable as it is, will substantially slow cost growth.

14.2.6 Information interventions

14.2.6.1 *Background*

Several popular policy proposals incorporate information-related interventions to contain costs. These include proposals to expand comparative effectiveness research (CER) or information technology (IT) (Gingrich 2006; Clinton 2007; Obama 2009). The theory behind both of these types of proposals is that there is substantial waste in the American health care system, including duplicate tests and use of unnecessary or wasteful services. Proponents of these strategies contend that if the knowledge base was larger and information managed more efficiently, substantial savings could accrue.

Many countries support a centrally coordinated CER structure, typically financed with public funds. For example, the United Kingdom's National Institute for Health and Clinical Excellence (NICE) analyzes both the clinical effectiveness and cost-effectiveness of technologies and provides guidance on appropriate treatments for specific diseases or types of patients. Unlike the United States, many countries with an existing CER infrastructure routinely use CER data to determine coverage and, sometimes, payment rates (Orszag 2008). In the United States, federally funded agencies such as NIH and AHRQ support CER as a part of their established practices, and several for-profit and not-for-profit entities currently engage in CER to varying degrees. However, these efforts are modest when compared to the $2 trillion spent on health care annually. Current proposals call for expanded CER efforts in the US. There is also considerable momentum behind increasing adoption of IT. Political and policy leaders from both parties have urged the adoption of health IT (Manos 2007).

14.2.6.2 *Evidence*

Evidence of cost savings associated with CER is scant. Chernew and Fendrick (2007) argue that CER may provide the foundation for cost containment, facilitating systems that promote value and discourage waste, but without other system reforms CER is unlikely to save substantial amounts. A recent estimate found that CER would have a net increase on direct federal outlays by $1.1 billion over ten years; savings to private and public payers would total $6 billion over the same period. While a modest estimate, this study suggested that CER would need a substantial amount of time to develop a widely accepted body of effectiveness research. If CER was effective at gaining acceptance by providers, the analysis suggested that it could result in substantial health care savings in the future (Orszag 2008).

Estimates of savings from IT have been very controversial. One estimate suggests savings of $78 billion per year for adoption of electronic health records (Hillestad et al. 2005). Other observers note the heavy investment IT will require and question the potential for savings (Powner 2005). Like CER, IT is a tool. Estimates of the financial impact hinge on assumptions about how this tool will change practice.

14.2.6.3 *Potential*

In the future, the health care system, however configured, will need to use information more wisely. CER and IT will likely prove valuable, maybe even indispensable, to a well-functioning health care system. However, costs have been growing for decades even as IT and CER have been improving. Each allows the system to reduce waste, but cost growth was not driven primarily by increasing waste. Neither CER nor IT address the underlying reasons for cost growth, namely, new medical technology and knowledge, thus it is unlikely that these initiatives, as important as they are, will be the foundation, as opposed to a component, of cost containment strategies.

14.3 Conclusions

Health care cost growth is among the most important issues facing the United States and other developed countries. Past experience suggests a consistent increase in health care spending per capita. It is unclear how high health care spending can go. As Hall and Jones (2007) note, the limits depend in part on how much we value the health that medical care provides relative to other goods and services that we might purchase. Institutional details also matter. If insurance shields individuals from much of the cost at the point of service, the appetite for greater use of health care may expand beyond the point where the benefits justify the costs.

The public financing aspect of health care spending adds an additional dimension to assessing the impact of rapid health care cost growth. Specifically, the tax burden associated with greater spending could have important macro-economic consequences. In the US, for example, financing promised Medicare Part A (largely hospital and skilled nursing facilities) benefits through 2080 would require more than a doubling of the payroll tax. Further tax increases would likely be required to support physician, outpatient, and prescription drug services. While there is no well defined threshold above which health care cost growth is unsustainable, public and private payers are increasingly feeling the strain of greater spending.

Any effort to reduce the rate of cost growth will entail restricting the rate of growth of utilization of health care services and may entail reducing the level (or rate of growth) of prices for health care services. Because all expenditures are revenue to some individual or organization, efforts to slow expenditure growth are synonymous with efforts to restrain revenue growth. Thus, such efforts are inherently political. Issues of efficiency, equity, and control will all be important as society faces these important choices.

"Feel good" approaches to cost containment, such as more prevention, better chronic disease management, IT or CER, are important, but evidence is not strong that they will alter the rate of cost growth.

Changes in patient incentives or provider payment have a greater potential to control costs, but we have not demonstrated the political will to implement them in a strict fashion. Moreover, the market mechanisms we have devised have not yet indicated consumers are willing or able to accept the changes in the system that would be needed to control cost growth. However, as costs grow, pressures to control spending will grow and distributional issues will become even more salient. Private and public decision makers may show a new willingness to adopt strategies that in the past have not been accepted.

REFERENCES

BAMEZAI, A., ZWANZIGER, J., MELNICK, G. A., and MANN, J. M. (1999), "Price Competition and Hospital Cost Growth in the United States (1989–94)," *Health Economics*, 8(8): 233–43.

BERNDT, E. R. (2001), "The US Pharmaceutical Industry: Why Major Growth in Times of Cost Containment?" *Health Affairs (Millwood)*, 20(2): 100–14.

BODENHEIMER, T. (2005), "High and Rising Health Care Costs. Part 3: The Role of Health Care Providers," *Annals of Internal Medicine*, 21(142): 996–1002.

BROOK, R. H., WARE, J. E., ROGERS, W. H., et al. (1983), "Does Free Care Improve Adults' Health? Results from a Randomized Controlled Trial," *New England Journal of Medicine*, 309(23): 1426–34.

BUSSE, R. C., ORVAIN, J., VELASCO, M., et al. (2002), "Best Practice in Undertaking and Reporting Health Technology Assessments," *International Journal of Technology Assessment in Health Care*, 18(2): 361–422.

CENTER FOR MEDICARE AND MEDICAID SERVICES (CMS) (2007), "Annual Report of the Boards of Trustees of the Federal Hospital Insurance and Federal Supplementary Medical Insurance Trust Funds." <http://www.cms.hhs.gov/reportstrustfunds/downloads/tr2007.pdf>.

CHERNEW, M. E. (1998), "Managed Care, Medical Technology, and Health Care Cost Growth: A Review of the Evidence," *Medical Care Research and Review*, 55(3): 259–88.

—— (2004), "Barriers to Constraining Health Care Cost Growth," *Health Affairs*, 23(6): 122–8.

—— (2005), "Disability and Health Care Spending among Medicare Beneficiaries," *Health Affairs*, W5: R42–52.

—— and FENDRICK, A. M. (2007), "A Business Case for Comparative Effectiveness Research. A Commissioned Analysis," *Learning What Works Best: The Nation's Need for Evidence on Comparative Effectiveness in Health Care. IOM Roundtable on Evidence-Based Medicine* (London: Institute of Medicine).

—— COWEN, M. E., KIRKING, D. M., et al. (2000), "Pharmaceutical Cost Growth Under Capitation: A Case Study," *Health Affairs*, 19(6): 266–76.

—— HIRTH, R. A., and CUTLER, D. M. (2003), "Increased Spending on Health Care: How Much Can The United States Afford?" *Health Affairs*, 22(4): 15–25.

—— CUTLER, D. M., and KEENAN, S. (2005), "Increasing Health Insurance Costs and the Decline in Insurance Coverage," *Health Services Research*, 40(4): 1021–39.

CLINTON, H. (2007), "Hillary Clinton Campaign Website." <http://www.hillaryclinton.com/feature/healthcareplan/americanhealthchoicesplan.pdf> accessed September 18, 2008.

CBO (CONGRESSIONAL BUDGET OFFICE) (2008), "Geographic Variation in Health Care." <http://www.cbo.gov/ftpdocs/89xx/doc8972/MainText.3.1.shtml#1077748> accessed March 31, 2008.

CUTLER, D. M. (1999), "Equality, Efficiency, and Market Fundamentals: The Dynamics of International Medical Care Reform." Unpublished Manuscript.

—— (2001), "Is Technological Change In Medicine Worth It?" *Health Affairs*, 20(5): 11–29.

—— and MCCLELLAN, M. (1996), "The Determinants of Technological Change in Heart Attack Treatment." NBER Working Paper 5751.

—— —— and NEWHOUSE, J. P. (2000), "How Does Managed Care Do It?" *RAND Journal of Economics*, 31(3): 526–48.

DAVIS, K. (2007), "Paying for Care Episodes and Care Coordination," *New England Journal of Medicine*, 356(11): 1166–68.

DEVERS, K. J., BREWSTER, L. R., and CASALINO, L. P. (2003), "Changes in hospital competitive strategy: a new medical arms race?" *Health Service Research*, 38(1) (pt 2): 447–69.

DOCTEUR, E. and OXLEY, H. (2003), "Health-Care Systems: Lessons from the Reform Experience." OECD Health Working Paper: OECD.

DRANOVE, D. and WEHNER, P. J. (1994), "Physician-induced Demand for Childbirths," *Health Economics*, 13(1): 61–73.

EBRI (EMPLOYEE BENEFIT RESEARCH INSTITUTE) and CMWF (COMMONWEALTH FUND) (2008), "Issue Brief No. 300, 2nd Annual Consumerism in Health Care Survey."<http://www.ebri.org/pdf/briefspdf/EBRI_IB_12-20061.pdf> accessed February 8, 2010.

ENTHOVEN, A. C. (2003), "Employment-based Health Insurance is Failing: Now What?" *Health Affairs Supplement: Web Exclusives*, W3: 237–49.

—— and VORHAUS, C. B. (1997), "A Vision of Quality in Health Care Delivery," *Health Affairs*, 16(3): 44–57.

FIGUERAS, J., JAKUBOWSKI, E., and ROBISON, R. (2005), "Purchasing to Improve Health Systems Performance. European Observatory on Health Systems and Policy Series." <http://www.euro.who.int/Document/E86300.pdf>.

FIREMAN, B., BARTLETT, J., and SELBY, J. (2004), "Can Disease Management Reduce Health Care Costs By Improving Quality?" *Health Affairs*, 23(6): 63–75.

FUCHS, V. R. (1996), "Economics, Values, and Health Care Reform," *American Economic Review*, 86(1): 1–24.

—— (2003), "Floridian Exceptionalism," *Health Affairs (Millwood)*, W3: 357–62.

GAO (GOVERNMENT ACCOUNTABILITY OFFICE) (2006), "Consumer-Directed Health Plans Early Enrollee Experiences with Health Savings Accounts and Eligible Health Plans," Report to the Ranking Minority Member, Committee on Finance, US Senate.

GAYNOR, M. and VOGT, W. B. (2003), "Competition Among Hospitals," *RAND Journal of Economics*, 34(4): 764–85.

GINGRICH, N. (2006), *Testimony to the Committee on Government Reform, House of Representatives* (Washington, DC: House of Representatives).

GINSBURG, P. B. and PICKREIGN, J. D. (1996), "Tracking Health Care Costs," *Health Affairs (Millwood)*, 15(3): 140–9.

GOLDMAN, D. P., JOYCE, G. F. ESCARCE, J. J., et al. (2004), "Pharmacy Benefits and the Use of Drugs by the Chronically Ill," *Journal of the American Medical Association*, 291: 2344–50.

—— ——, and ZHENG, Y. (2007), "Prescription Drug Cost Sharing: Associations with Medication and Medical Utilization and Spending and Health," *Journal of the American Medical Association*, 298(1): 61–9.

GRABOWSKI, D. C., OHSFELD, R. L., and MORRISEY, M. A. (2003), "The Effects of CON Repeal on Medicaid Nursing Home and Long-term Care Expenditures," *Inquiry*, 40(2): 146–57.

HADLEY, J., ZUCKERMAN, S., and FEDER, J. (1989), "Profits and Fiscal Pressure in the Prospective Payment System: Their Impacts on Hospitals," *Inquiry*, 26(30: 354–65.

HAIMOWITZ, J. (1997), *Has the Surge in Computer Spending Fundamentally Changed the Economy?* Kansas City, MO: Federal Reserve Bank of Kansas City.

HALL, R. E. and JONES, C. I. (2007), "The Value of Life and the Rise in Health Spending," *The Quarterly Journal of Economics*, 122(1): 39–72.

HEISLER, M., LANGA, K. M., EBY, E. L., et al. (2004), "The Health Effects of Restricting Prescription Medication Use Because of Cost," *Medical Care*, 42(7): 626–34.

HELLINGER, F. J. (1986), "Reimbursement Under Diagnosis-related Groups: the Medicaid Experience," *Health Care Financing Review*, 8(2): 35–44.

—— (1998), "Regulating the Financial Incentives Facing Physicians in Managed Care Plans," *American Journal of Managed Care*, 4(5): 663–74.

HILLESTAD, R., BIGELOW, J., BOWER, A., et al. (2005), "Can Electronic Medical Record Systems Transform Health Care? Potential Health Benefits," *Health Affairs (Millwood)*, 24(5): 1103–17.

HILLMAN, A. L., ESCARCE, J. J., RIPLEY, K., et al. (1999), "Financial Incentives and Drug Spending in Managed Care," *Health Affairs*, 18(2): 189–200.

HUSKAMP, H. A., DEVERKA, P. A., EPSTEIN, A. M., et al. (2003), "The Effect of Incentive-Based Formularies on Prescription Drug Utilization and Spending," *New England Journal of Medicine*, 349(23): 2224–32.

KEELER, E. B. and ROLPH, J. E. (1988), "The Demand for Episodes of Treatment in the Health Insurance Experiment," *Journal of Health Economics*, 7(4): 337–67.

KEELER, E. B., MANNING, W. G., and WELLS, K. B. (1988), "The Demand for Episodes of Treatment in the Mental Health Services," *Journal of Health Economics*, 7: 369–92.

KEENAN, P., CUTLER, D. M., and CHERNEW, M. E. (2006), "The 'Graying' of Group Health Insurance," *Health Affairs (Millwood)*, 25(6): 1497–506.

LANDON, B. E., ROSENTHAL, M. B., NORMAND, S. L., et al. (2007), "Incentive Formularies and Changes in Prescription Drug Spending," *American Journal of Managed Care*, 13(6) (pt 2): 360–9.

LEGORETTA, A. P., SILBER, J. H., CONSTANTINO, G. N., et al. (1993), "Increased Cholecystectomy Rate after the Introduction of Laparoscopic Cholecystectomy," *Journal of the American Medical Association*, 270(12): 1429–32.

LUFT, H. S., GARNICK, D. W., HUGHES, R. G., et al. (1988), "Hospitals Competition, Cost, and Medical Practice," *Journal of Medical Practice Management*, 4(1): 10–15.

MANNING, W. G., NEWHOUSE, J. P., DUAN, N., et al. (1987), "Health Insurance and the Demand for Medical Care: Evidence from a Randomized Experiment," *The American Economic Review*, 77(3): 251–77.

MANOS, D. (2007), "Healthcare IT Gains Traction in Congress." <http://www.healthcareitnews.com/story.cms?id=7165> accessed September 18, 2007.

MECHANIC, D. (2001), "The Managed Care Backlash: Perceptions and Rhetoric in Health Care Policy and the Potential for Health Care Reform," *Milbank Quarterly*, 79(1): 35–54.

Medicare Prescription Drug Improvement and Modernization Act of 2003 (2008), *Public Law* 108–173. <http://www.ustreas.gov/offices/public-affairs/hsa/pdf/pl108-173.pdf> accessed February 08, 2010.

MELNICK, G. A. and ZWANZIGER, J. (1995), "State Health Care Expenditures under Competition and Regulation, 1980 through 1991," *The American Journal of Public Health*, 85: 1391–6.

MILLER, M. E., and SULVETTA, M. B. (1992), "Medicare Hospital Outpatient Services and Costs: Implications for Prospective Payment," *Health Care Finance Review*, 14(2): 135–49.

MUELLER, C. D., and MONHEIT, A. C. (1988), "Insurance Coverage and the Demand for Dental Care. Results for Non-aged White Adults." *Journal of Health Economics*, 7(1): 59–72.

NAYDECK, B. L., PEARSON, J. A., OZMINKOWSKI, R. J., et al. (2008), "The Impact of the Highmark Employee Wellness Programs on 4-Year Healthcare Costs," *Journal of Occupational and Environmental Medicine*, 50(2): 146–56.

NEUMANN, P. J., ROSEN, A. B., and WEINSTEIN, M. C. (2005), "Medicare and Cost-Effectiveness Analysis," *New England Journal of Medicine*, 353: 1516–22.

NEWHOUSE, J. P. (1992), "Medical Care Costs: How Much Welfare Loss?" *Journal of Economic Perspectives*, 6(3): 3–21.

—— (1993), *Free-For-All: Health Insurance, Medical Costs, and Health Outcomes: The Results of the Health Insurance Experiment* (Cambridge, MA: Harvard University Press).

NORWALK, L. (2007), "The President's FY 2008 Budget: Medicare and Medicaid," *House Ways and Means Subcommittee on Health Hearing on Department of Health and Human Services* (Washington, DC: Centers for Medicare & Medicaid Services).

OBAMA, B. (2009), "Plan for a Healthy America: Obama & Biden's Plan." <http://www.barackobama.com/issues/healthcare> accessed February 10, 2009.

OECD (ORGANIZATION FOR ECONOMIC COOPERATION AND DEVELOPMENT) (2007), *Towards High Performing Health Systems: Policy Studies*. The OECD Health Project (Paris: OECD).

—— (2008), "Growth in Health Spending Slows in Many OECD Countries, According to OECD Health Data 2008." <http://www.oecd.org/document/27/0,3343,en_2649_34631_4 0902299_1_1_1_1,00.html>.

ORSZAG, P. R. (2007), *Testimony on Health Care and the Budget: Issues and Challenges for Reform* (Washington, DC: Committee on the Budget, United States Senate).

—— (2008), "Research on the Comparative Effectiveness of Medical Treatments: Issues and Options for an Expanded Federal Role." <http://www.cbo.gov/ftpdocs/88xx/doc8891/Frontmatter.1.2.shtml> accessed May 29, 2008.

PEDEN, E. A., and FREELAND, M. S. (1995), "A Historical Analysis of Medical Spending Growth, 1960–1993," *Health Affairs (Millwood)*, 14(2): 235–47.

PETERSON, M. A. (2002), "Editor's Note: Managed Care Redux," *Journal of Health Politics, Policy and Law*, 27(3): 345–51.

PHELPS, C. E. and NEWHOUSE, J. P. (1974), "Coinsurance, the Price of Time, and the Demand for Medical Services," *The Review of Economics and Statistics*, 56(3): 334–42.

PIETTE, J., WAGNER, T., and POTTER, M., et al. (2004), "Health Insurance Status, Cost-Related Medication Underuse, and Outcomes Among Diabetes Patients in Three Systems of Care," *Medical Care*, 42(2): 102–109.

POWNER, D. (2005), "Letter to The Honorable Jim Nussle, Chairman, Committee on the Budget, House of Representatives from David Powner: HHS's Estimate of Savings from Health IT." Government Accountability Office, Washington, DC.

RICE, T. H. (1983), "The Impact of Changing Medicare Reimbursement Rates on Physician-Induced Demand," *Medical Care*, 21(8): 803–15.

ROS, C. C., GROENEWEGEN, P. P., and DELNOIJ, D. M. (2000), "All Rights Reserved, or Can We Just Copy? Cost Sharing Arrangements and Characteristics of Health Care Systems," *Health Policy*, 52(1): 1–13.

ROSEN, A. B., HAMEL, M. B., WEINSTEIN, M. C., et al. (2005), "Cost-Effectiveness of Full Medicare Coverage of Angiotensin-Converting Enzyme Inhibitors for Beneficiaries with Diabetes," *Annals of Internal Medicine*, 143(2): 89–99.

ROSENTHAL, M. B. and DUDLEY, R. A. (2007), "Pay-for-Performance: Will the Latest Payment Trend Improve Care?" *Journal of the American Medical Association*, 297(7): 740–4.

SALTMAN, R. B. (2002), "Regulating Incentives: The Past and Present Role of the State in Health Care Systems," *Social Science and Medicine*, 54(11): 1677–84.

—— and FIGUERAS, J. (1998), "Analyzing the Evidence on European Health Care Reforms," *Health Affairs (Millwood)*, 17(2): 85–108.

SCANLON, W. J. (2006), "Medicare Hospital Outpatient Services and Costs: Implications for Prospective Payment," *Health Affairs*, 25(1): 70–80.

SCHWARTZ, W. B. (1987), "The Inevitable Failure of Current Cost-containment Strategies. Why They Can Provide Only Temporary Relief," *Journal of the American Medical Association*, 257(2): 220–4.

SCITOVSKY, A. A. (1985), "Changes in the Costs of Treatment of Selected Illnesses," *Medical Care Research and Review*, 23(2): 1245–57.

—— and McCALL, N. (1976), *Changes in Treatment Costs for Selcted Illnesses, 1951–1964–1971* (Washington, DC: US Department of Health Education and Welfare, National Center for Health Services Research).

SELBY, J. V., FIREMAN, B. H., and SWAIN, B. E. (1996), "Effect of a Copayment on Use of the Emergency Department in a Health Maintenance Organization," *New England Journal of Medicine*, 334(10): 635–41.

SHOWSTACK, J. A., SCHROEDER, S. A., and MATSUMOTO, M. F. (1982), "Changes in the Use of Medical Technologies, 1972–1977," *New England Journal of Medicine*, 15: 124–33.

SIU, A. L., SONNENBERG, F. A., MANNING, W. G., et al. (1986), "Inappropriate Use of Hospitals in a Randomized Trial of Health Insurance Plans," *New England Journal of Medicine*, 20(315): 1259–66.

STARFIELD, B. (2003), "Primary Care and Specialty Care: A Role Reversal?" *Medical Education*, 37(9): 756–7.

TAMBLYN, R., LAPRISE, R., HANLEY, J. A., et al. (2001), "Adverse Events Associated with Prescription Drug Cost-Sharing Among Poor and Elderly Persons," *Journal of the American Medical Association*, 285(4): 421–9.

THORPE, K. E. and HOWARD, D. H. (2006), "The Rise in Spending Among Medicare Beneficiaries: The Role of Chronic Disease Prevalence And Changes in Treatment Intensity," *Health Affairs*, 25(5): w378–88.

WEINGARTEN, S. R., HENNING, J. M., BADAMGARAV, E., et al. (2002), "Interventions Used in Disease Management Programmes for Patients with Chronic Illness: Which Ones Work? Meta-analysis of Published Reports," *British Medical Journal*, 325: 925.

WHARAM, J. F., LANDON, B. E., GALBRAITH, A. A., et al. (2007), "Emergency Department Use and Subsequent Hospitalizations Among Members of a High-deductible Health Plan," *Journal of the American Medical Association*, 297(10): 1093–102.

WHITE, C. (2007), "Health Care Spending Growth: How Different Is The United States From The Rest of the OECD?" *Health Affairs (Millwood)*, 26(1): 154–61.

WRIGHT, B. J., CARLSON, M. J., EDLUND, T., et al. (2005), "The Impact of Increased Cost Sharing on Medicaid Enrollees," *Health Affairs (Millwood)*, 24(4): 1106–16.

ZWANZIGER, J., MELNICK, G. A., and BAMEZAI, A. (2000), "The Effect of Selective Contracting on Hospital Costs and Revenues," *Health Service Review*, 35(4): 849–67.

CHAPTER 15

....

USER CHARGES

....

ERIK SCHOKKAERT AND
CARINE VAN DE VOORDE

15.1 INTRODUCTION

....

WE define "user charges" or "user fees" for health care as official payments charged by the providers to the patients at the point of delivery. From the economic point of view, they can simply be seen as consumer prices. The term "user charges" is mainly (but not exclusively) used in tax-financed systems. To denote the cost-sharing by patients in systems of (private or social) health insurance, one speaks about co-payments (a fixed amount per service), co-insurance (when patients have to pay a fixed percentage of the cost) and deductibles (where patients only are reimbursed above a certain minimum cost ceiling). The economic effects of these forms of cost sharing are very similar to those of user charges, because they can also be interpreted as consumer prices.[1] From an analytical point of view, it therefore makes sense to treat the two together. We will do so in this chapter. We will mainly focus on public systems, however, and only refer to empirical results for private insurers, when they give insights about patient or provider behavior that are also relevant to the public systems. We will use the term "co-payments" to indicate cost-sharing in health insurance systems and the term "user charges" for the official payments in tax-financed systems. We will also use the term "user charges" if we want to encompass both situations.

Both user charges and co-payments refer to *official* payments for health care items that are provided by the public sector or are covered by the prevailing system of health

---

[1] A deductible is then interpreted as a non-linear pricing scheme in which patients have to pay the full cost below the deductible and a zero price above the deductible.

insurance. In some countries, providers are allowed to raise excess fees on top of the offi-cial fees, or patients cannot avoid unofficial payments if they want to get treated. Moreover, patients obviously have to pay themselves for health care items that are not covered by the public system nor by health insurance. To indicate the sum of all the own payments of the patients, we will use the term "out-of-pocket payments." This is the most relevant concept from an equity point of view.

There is a large literature both on moral hazard and co-payments in insurance and on the effects of user charges in low- and middle-income countries (further LMICs), but these two streams of literature are hardly integrated. More integration could improve both. The literature on moral hazard in developed insurance systems is analytically rig-orous and has implemented sophisticated econometric techniques to correct e.g. for self-selection (Zweifel and Manning 2000). It sometimes is rather casual about the influ-ence of the broader institutional context, however. The literature on LMICs has convinc-ingly shown that this broader context does matter: professional ethics and patterns of decision-making by providers, the availability of alternatives (such as OTC-medicines or supplemental insurance) for the patients, the pre-existing socioeconomic inequali-ties, the working of intermediate organizations all have an influence on the effects of user charges. There is no reason why such features would be less important in developed countries than in LMICs. On the other hand, the literature on LMICs is not always analytically rigorous, with a focus on simple case studies (see, e.g., the critical evaluation in Palmer et al. 2004) and with sometimes a hidden presupposition that the traditional behavioral models of economics do not work well in a setting with huge transaction costs and under-developed markets and political institutions. There are no good reasons to accept this presupposition, however.

A partial explanation for the differences in emphasis is that the literature on LMICs is often more policy-oriented and tends to evaluate a whole policy package, of which user fees are only a part (Gilson and Mills 1995). The latter may have desirable effects in one situation, and may be detrimental in another situation, e.g. depending on who is decid-ing about what to do with the proceeds. From an analytical point of view, however, it is essential to distinguish carefully the effects of the different components of the package. To give an example: even if user fees can go together (or not) with an increase in the quality of the services delivered, it is important to try to distinguish carefully the price effect and the quality effect from each other.

In the second section, we first give a brief overview of the importance of out-of-pocket payments in the world. In the following sections, we discuss the allocative effects of user charges, their implementation as a revenue-raising mechanism, and their effects on equity. We will spend relatively little attention on case studies or on studies based on interviews, and focus on the quantitative information derived from surveys. We then go briefly into a few theoretical papers on optimal user charges. Finally, we have a digression on two related phenomena: informal (even illegal) pay-ments to providers and extra (or balance) billing, i.e. charging additional fees on top of the official fee schedule that is used for reimbursement. We will show that these raise the same issues as user charges in general.

15.2 THE IMPORTANCE OF OUT-OF-POCKET PAYMENTS IN THE WORLD

Table 15.1 gives an overview of the importance of out-of-pocket payments in different regions of the world (source: World Health Statistics 2008). Table 15.2 shows the countries where the share of out-of-pocket payments in total expenditures on health was more than 60 percent in 2005. Out-of-pocket payments play a dominant role in LMICs where they cover about 50 percent of health care expenditures. They are also important in some transition economies and former republics of the Soviet Union, where the collapse of the existing state-driven system led to huge financing problems (Balabanova et al. 2004).

Out-of-pocket expenditures are less important in the high-income countries where health care financing is based on taxes and/or social insurance. Yet even in these countries, they are far from negligible. According to the same WHO source (World Health Statistics 2008), in 2005 they covered 22.5 percent of total health expenditures in a social

Table 15.1 Out-of-pocket Payments in Different Regions of the World

	Total expenditure on health as % of GDP		Per capita total expenditure on health (PPP international $)		General government expenditure on health as % of total expenditure on health		Out-of-pocket expenditure as % of total expenditure in health	
	2000	2005	2000	2005	2000	2005	2000	**2005**
African region	5.8	5.9	88	112	43.7	45.3	29.1	**26.5**
Region of the Americas	11.3	12.7	1 961	2 675	45.8	46.8	18.4	**16.3**
South-East Asia region	3.5	4.0	63	100	30.1	29.0	61.4	**64.2**
European region	8.0	8.6	1 215	1 649	73.4	74.3	18.2	**17.6**
Eastern Mediterranean region	4.5	4.9	168	242	44.8	51.4	48.7	**42.7**
Western Pacific region	5.7	5.8	359	529	59.6	56.8	35.6	**35.8**
Low income	4.2	4.6	56	84	28.0	25.9	65.0	**67.4**
Lower middle income	4.6	4.8	183	295	43.4	44.9	51.7	**46.8**
Upper middle income	6.2	6.6	505	705	52.5	53.2	32.9	**30.2**
High income	10.0	11.2	2 744	3 712	59.7	60.1	15.7	**14.4**
Global	8.0	8.6	579	790	56.0	56.0	23.3	**22.5**

Source: WHO, World Health Statistics 2008.

Table 15.2 Countries with Out-of-Pocket Expenditures
>60% of Total Health Expenditures in 2005

Myanmar	88.9	Dem. Rep. Congo	65.4
Guinea	87.7	Vietnam	64.0
Pakistan	80.9	Singapore	63.9
Afghanistan	77.9	Azerbaijan	63.6
Georgia	77.0	Togo	63.1
India	76.1	Bangladesh	62.6
Tajikistan	74.6	Nepal	62.6
Laos	73.6	Nigeria	62.5
Burundi	71.4	Senegal	61.7
Ivory Coast	68.9	Sudan	61.3
Cameroon	68.1	Cambodia	60.1

Source: WHO, World Health Statistics 2008.

insurance country like Belgium, 20.3 percent and 20.9 percent in NHS-type countries like Italy and Spain respectively and even 30.5 percent in a private insurance country like Switzerland. Moreover, there seems to be a tendency toward an increase of patient cost-sharing in countries where it traditionally has played a minor role, such as the UK or the Netherlands. This is not only explained by a concern to fight moral hazard and overconsumption, but it also reflects the increasing pressure on the public financing part of the system.

Similar arguments have been used to advocate user charges in LMICs. While they have always existed in these countries, their use was strongly stimulated by the World Bank in the 1980s. It has been said that two "models" of user charges were applied in Africa (Gilson and Mills 1995): the "World Bank" model with national user fees (mainly present in Anglophone countries), and the "Bamako Initiative" model of community financing (mainly in Francophone countries). The revenue and quality effects of the user charges were less positive than hoped, however, and the distributional effects turned out to be worse. More recently, therefore, the World Bank changed its position and the WHO also argued strongly against user charges. Countries like Uganda and South Africa introduced a policy of removing user fees again.

15.3 User Charges and Efficiency:
The Price Effect

From an economic point of view, the rationale of user charges is to improve allocative efficiency. Assume a world without uncertainty and without externalities and in which the government can redistribute incomes in a lump sum way. In such a first-best world, prices of private goods optimally should be set equal to their marginal cost. In the health sector, externalities or merit good considerations offer arguments for subsidizing prices. More importantly, the pervasive uncertainty creates a need for insurance, and hence for the (partial) reimbursement of health care costs. All this does not imply, however, that optimal consumer prices are zero. In the insurance setting, the moral hazard problem suggests that some cost sharing is optimal. There is a trade-off between better insurance on the one hand and the welfare losses due to the price distortions on the other hand—yet, if the price elasticity of health care demand is not zero, the optimal level of cost sharing is not zero either. A similar logic can be applied to the design of a system of tax-financing (Jack 1999). Taxes paid are similar to the premiums in an insurance system and price subsidies mimic the reimbursement of costs. User charges are then the equivalent of the cost-sharing arrangements in health insurance, and a priori, they should *not* be zero.

The traditional welfare approach evaluates outcomes on the basis of subjective consumer preferences. This is not generally accepted in all societies, and even among health economists there is a deep ideological divide between those who accept the traditional approach and those who argue that willingness-to-pay as revealed by market demand has no obvious welfare meaning in a situation with poorly informed patients. We will sidestep this issue and focus on the empirical results as such. The first question then is whether user charges have an effect on health care consumption. If there is a price effect, this raises a second issue: is it true that zero prices induce less efficient ("frivolous") consumption, and that the introduction of positive user charges leads mainly to a cut of these less efficient treatments?

The literature gives an unambiguous answer to the first question. User charges do have a negative effect on health care consumption. The evidence is overwhelming for co-payments in the developed insurance systems. The authoritative Rand-experiment revealed that in the United States the price elasticity of health care demand was significantly different from zero, although small in absolute terms. Estimates were between −.15 and −.20 (Manning et al. 1987). Similar findings have been reported in a large number of papers using non-experimental techniques (Cutler and Zeckhauser 2000; Zweifel and Manning 2000). The evidence is almost equally strong for the effects of user charges in LMICs. Introducing or increasing user fees has almost always and everywhere led to a decrease of utilization (Gertler and Hammer 1997; Sepehri and Chernomas 2001; Palmer et al. 2004; James et al. 2006). Particularly interesting is the finding that the recent abolition of user fees led to a significant increase in utilization in South Africa and Uganda (Gilson and McIntyre 2005).

In this respect, one should not be misled by the fact that some case studies found a positive effect on utilization after the introduction of user fees.[2] This positive result

---

[2] Among others, positive effects on utilization after the introduction of user fees have been reported for Benin and Guinea (Soucat et al. 1997), Cameroon (Litvack and Bodart 1993), India (Rao and Peters 2007), Mali (Mariko 2003), Mauritania (Audibert and Mathonnat 2000), Niger (Chawla and Ellis 2000) and the Philippines (Hotchkiss 1998).

reflects the effect of other variables that changed simultaneously, most often that of a quality improvement. To evaluate the overall policy, it is of course necessary to consider the net effect of all these simultaneous changes, but from an analytical point of view it is essential to distinguish carefully the different variables, e.g. to get good estimates of the magnitude of the (negative) price effect on the one hand and the (positive) quality effect on the other hand. It is not surprising that different case studies yield conflicting results if they do not sufficiently control for these confounding factors. Sepehri and Chernomas (2001) and Palmer et al. (2004) rightly emphasize the importance of methodological refinements in the analysis of utilization data for LMIC.

The answer to our second question (does the decrease in utilization mainly affect inefficient and "frivolous" treatment?) is less clear-cut. Still, both in developed health insurance systems and in LMICs, the evidence suggests that the decrease in utilization may have negative effects on the quality of care and hence even on the health situation of the patients. Since it is not easy to draw the boundary line between "efficient and necessary" and "frivolous or unnecessary" health care, the most interesting insights are obtained when looking at specific interventions.

The use of prescription drugs in the US offers an interesting example (Gibson et al. 2005; Goldman et al. 2007; Wagner et al. 2008; Austvoll-Dahlgren et al. 2008). Most studies find that cost sharing leads to a decrease in the utilization of essential medication, defined as medication that is necessary to maintain or improve health. Often adherence to a regimen of maintenance medication goes down with patients skipping doses or stretching out refills. With a few exceptions (Pilote et al. 2002), higher cost-sharing for, and therefore lower utilization of, prescription drugs, has led to greater use of inpatient and emergency medical services by chronically ill patients (patients with congestive heart failure, lipid disorders, diabetes, and schizophrenia).

Given the importance of non-financial costs in many LMIC, it would be highly surprising if there were much frivolous health care use there. Simply mentioning some specific empirical results may illustrate what is at stake. A fee increase in Swaziland led to reduced utilization among the users of essential services for the management of diarrheal diseases, sexually transmitted diseases, acute respiratory infections, and infant immunizations rather than among patients suffering from less important conditions (Yoder 1989). Borghi et al. (2006) argue that the removal of user fees might be a crucial step to improve maternal health in LMICs. Souteyrand et al. (2008) review the literature on AIDS and conclude that user fees are currently the main barrier to adherence to antiretroviral therapy and that their abolition would be associated with increased survival rates. Finally, combining the available evidence in a simulation study, James et al. (2005) calculate that the elimination of user fees could prevent between 150,000 and 300,000 deaths annually among children aged under 5 in twenty African countries.

Although until now we focused on the own price effect, i.e. the effect of an increase in user charges for a given item on the utilization of that same item, cross-price effects are also significant. Again, the evidence for the developed countries and the LMICs goes in the same direction. Two- or three-tier plans for prescription drugs in the US, introducing differentiated cost sharing for different categories of drugs, have clear effects on the pattern of drug consumption. Preferred brand-name drugs are substituted for non-preferred drugs if the level of cost sharing is different and there is also some (albeit weaker) evidence for a switch from brand-name to generic drugs (Gibson et al. 2005). The switch from drugs or outpatient doctor visits to inpatient and emergency care (without cost sharing) can also be seen as a cross-price effect (Gaynor et al. 2006; Chandra et al. 2007). These offset effects are concentrated in the most ill populations, particularly those who had a chronic illness or who had high previous medical spending.

There is less formal evidence on cross-price effects for LMICs, but it goes in the same direction. In general, there has been a shift from services with user charges to services that are free of charge (Gilson and Mills 1995; Sepehri and Chernomas 2001). An interesting case is that of direct conditional cash transfers, which can be interpreted as direct price subsidies, i.e. as negative prices. In Mexico, Honduras, and Brazil, their introduction had a positive effect on the use of preventive health services and on the coverage of prenatal care and health checkups for children (Palmer et al. 2004).

These findings on cross-price effects are particularly relevant. Some of the described shifts are undesirable from the point of view of health or welfare, but others go clearly in the "right" direction. A cleverly designed system of differentiated user charges (and subsidies) should then no longer be seen as a blunt instrument to raise revenue and to cut frivolous expenditures, but may become an important tool for influencing behavior (both of patients and of providers) and for increasing micro-efficiency. We will come back to this issue later in this chapter.

A final word of caution. It is obvious that health care providers exert a large influence on final utilization. The effects of introducing user charges are therefore the result of a combination of behavioral changes at both the demand and the supply side. A short-run decrease in utilization because of the introduction of co-payments may be counteracted in the long run by providers aiming at protecting their incomes (see, e.g., the evidence for Belgium during the 1990s in Van de Voorde et al. 2001). And also for designing a differentiated system, e.g. for prescription drugs, it is important to know whether and to what extent providers will change their prescribing behavior. It is very possible that providers adjust their behavior, more specifically their fees, to the economic power or the degree of illness of their patients. The interaction between patient and provider decisions is a crucial topic for further research.

15.4 User Charges as a Revenue-raising Mechanism

While allocative efficiency is the main issue from the point of view of economic theory, the move to user charges has been driven in many LMICs by the need to increase the revenue available for health care. With limited finance (and limited supply of services) available, the introduction of health care free of charge leads to excess demand

and to the necessity of non-price rationing mechanisms. These non-price rationing mechanisms are often highly inefficient with many individuals denied health care for which they are willing and able to pay. It has even been argued that non-price rationing would mainly harm the poor and weak groups in society: if personal connections and/or informal payments start playing an important role, this is most probably to the advantage of the relatively rich and powerful. We will return to these equity issues in the next section.

The basic point on revenue constraints can be made in a traditional economic model, without even introducing any insurance issues. Consider Figure 15.1 (Thobani 1984). Suppose externalities or merit good considerations drive a wedge between private demand for health care D_p and social demand D_s. Suppose also for simplicity that the marginal cost (MC) is constant. The optimum amount would then be given by OV. Suppose we start now in a situation without user charges and with health care free of charge. The government has resources $OP_{mc}AF$ to finance the subsidies. The amount of health care demanded would then be OZ—and there would be excess demand FZ. Hence the need for non-price rationing with the resulting inefficiencies (Griffin 1992). In the "best" scenario where this non-price rationing allocates the health care to the individuals with the largest willingness to pay, the social surplus would be given by $P_{mc}KLA$. The optimal situation (with utilization OV) could in principle be obtained by a subsidy P_sP_{mc}, leaving a "user charge" OP_s. However, in that situation total subsidies would be $P_{mc}BCP_s$. This is more than the fixed budget $OP_{mc}AF$ available for the government. Therefore, this optimal situation cannot be reached. The points that can be reached are given by the iso-subsidy curve FS (a rectangular hyperbola). More specifically it is possible to reach E, with an amount consumed of OU, a subsidy per unit P_uP_{mc}, a user charge OP_u and total subsidies equal to $P_{mc}WEP_u$, by construction equal to $OP_{mc}AF$. The welfare gain in moving from OF to OU is given by the trapezoid $LGWA$. Introducing positive user charges is welfare improving compared to a situation in which the services are provided free of charge. More strikingly, in this situation the user charge OP_u is larger than the "optimal" user charge OP_s. In a situation with fixed government resources, this lower user charge OP_s would induce excess demand TV, a lower utilization level OT and a welfare loss $HGWR$.

Uncertainty and insurance aspects are neglected in the figure. However, if we reinterpret the figure so that P_s becomes the "optimal" co-payment (evidently lower than the marginal cost because of the welfare increase due to the reduction of the financial risk), it still is true that in a situation with fixed government resources, raising user charges above P_s would be better than having health care free of charge. Another way to extend the interpretation of Figure 15.1 is by introducing quality considerations. Until now we assumed that the limitation on government resources puts a constraint on the quantity of services provided. It is also possible that this limitation leads to a deterioration of the quality of the services—in which case FZ reflects the excess demand for good quality services. The move from OF to OU can then be reinterpreted as reflecting an increase in the quality of the services provided.

This whole reasoning of course depends on (1) the fact that the government subsidy remains fixed when user charges are introduced, so that the total amount of available

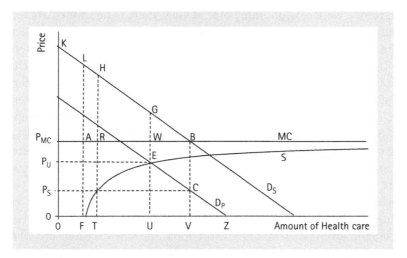

FIGURE 15.1 Optimality of user charges as a revenue-raising device

resources increases, and (2) that the additional revenues from the user charges are used to increase the quantity and/or the quality of the services provided. These assumptions are not self-evident, as the increase in administration costs may crowd out part of the increase in revenues (Creese 1991). Moreover, for central governments with financing problems it is tempting to use the revenues from user charges to cut down subsidies. Therefore the effects of user charges on supply and on quality are more likely to be positive if the revenues are kept at the local level—within local communities, or even within groups of providers or hospitals. Even then, however, the quality and quantity increases crucially depend on the decision structure and on the provider incentives that are in place. Complementary reforms at other stages of the decision process may be needed. In this respect, in most LMICs, the availability of medicines at the local level is a crucial issue, which will not be solved by introducing user charges for physician visits.

It is not surprising therefore that the empirical evidence on the supply effects of user charges is mixed. While in some (mainly West-African) countries the quality of local services seems to have improved in the wake of the Bamako initiative, other experiences have been much less successful (Gilson and Mills 1995). In any case, the simple world depicted in Figure 15.1, in which user charges quasi-automatically improve the provision of services, is oversimplified. It is always necessary to investigate carefully the microeconomic incentives for the providers. As Jack (1999: 205) puts it: "The idea that individuals will be better-off because they are paying higher prices certainly strikes one as disingenuous at best, and mildly nuts at worst. It is the use of these resources that is important, and there is no particular reason that they should be provided by users."

In fact, from a welfare economic point of view, there is no immediate reason why tax revenues should be earmarked for specific purposes. Nor is it a priori obvious that the financing of health care services should come mainly from the users of these services. There is a gap in the theoretical reasoning here. To evaluate user charges as a revenue-raising mechanism, we need a better insight into the basic causes of the limitations put on the health care budget, i.e. on the explanation for the existence of the curve *FS*. This calls for a public choice approach. How do central governments take their decisions on the allocation of the overall budget? What are the main obstacles to setting up a more formal system of health insurance? What is the relative importance of tax distortions, transaction costs, and mere considerations of uneven political power?

Once we have a better insight into these political questions, we can return to the optimality issue. How to finance health care given the distortions caused by different financing sources, and given what we have learnt about the way decisions are taken? Some decentralization is desirable if the rules set by the central government must be implemented at the local level by individuals who may have their own objectives. If the latter are better placed to take decisions which are in line with local needs, decentralization could lead to an increase in trust among the citizens and to an increase in their tax compliance—or, more generally, their willingness to pay. On the other hand, while offering "richer" people the opportunity to supplement the subsidized system with their own private payments of course increases the available revenue, it may at the same time increase feelings of inequity and decrease trust in the system among poorer groups of the population.

The revenue argument for user charges has been put forward mainly for LMICs. Yet, also in the developed countries, the move towards larger user charges has partly been driven by revenue considerations in a situation of increasing pressure on the public budget. There is a growing feeling that a larger part of the financial burden should be borne by the patients themselves in order to cope with the expected rapid increase in health care costs (Murphy and Topel 2006; Hall and Jones 2007). However, transaction costs considerations related to under-developed markets and administrative systems play a minor role in the richer countries. The focus is rather on priority setting, i.e. on the choice of treatments to take up in the collective financing arrangements. There is a continuum here: from provision free of charge, over various cost-sharing arrangements, to fully private financing, where the latter implies that those services are not taken up in the collective system. While there is a need for non-price rationing within the collective system, outside that system, the price mechanism will work. This raises obvious equity issues. In many countries, there is a socioeconomic bias in the take-up of supplemental insurance covering the treatments, which are not covered in the collective system (Colombo and Tapay 2004). Moreover, in a globalizing world with international markets, the rich and well-educated have growing possibilities to escape the non-price rationing in the collective system. Expensive medicines can be bought on the Internet. From an equity point of view then, private markets are perhaps working too well.

15.5 User Charges and Equity

Equity issues have popped up already a couple of times in the previous sections. They are essential for a full evaluation of user charges. Equity comes in different forms and can be interpreted in many different ways. We will not go into this philosophical discussion and mainly focus on two aspects: first equity in finance, then equity in delivery and equality of access. Finally, we discuss the working of social exemption mechanisms. Overall, in the context of equity, the focus is less on user charges as such and more on total out-of-pocket expenses.

15.5.1 User Charges and Equity in Finance

In most societies there is a widespread conviction that health care is not a commodity like other commodities, because health care expenditures are largely imposed on individuals, rather than freely chosen. It follows that the financial burden should not disproportionately rest on those who suffer from illness, i.e. that it should be largely independent of the health risks. User charges, i.e. prices paid at the point of service, by definition go against this basic ethical intuition. In fact, this explains why so many are opposed to them on the basis of principle.

A more demanding (and less generally accepted) requirement is that the financing of health care should be according to ability to pay. A financing structure is then called progressive if health care expenditures take a larger part of income for the rich than for the poor. If the absolute level of health care expenditures is about the same for the poor and the rich (which seems a conservative assumption, given the available evidence on socioeconomic inequalities in health), then by construction these expenditures will take up a larger fraction of income for the poorer households. User charges can only be "progressive" if the rich consume disproportionately more health care, or if there is a system of exemptions for poor households.

The empirical evidence is in line with these a priori predictions. The most interesting insights are obtained from comparative studies based on large-scale household surveys. It turns out that user charges are a strongly regressive component in the health care financing structure of developed countries (van Doorslaer et al. 1999; De Graeve and Van Ourti 2003). The same finding of regressivity is reported by Cissé et al. (2007) who analyze 1998–1999 household surveys for the capitals (Abidjan, Bamako, Conakry, and Dakar) of four francophone West-African countries that have increased the importance of user charges at the end of the eighties. The results for thirteen Asian territories in O'Donnell et al. (2008) show that care is needed. They find that out-of-pocket payments for health care are regressive only in Japan and Taiwan, that they are proportional to ability to pay in China, Hong Kong, Korea, Kyrgyz, and the Punjab, and that they are even progressive in Bangladesh, Indonesia, Nepal, the Philippines, Sri Lanka, and

Thailand. However, this mainly reflects that the poor in the so-called "progressive" countries receive less health care since they simply cannot afford to pay and therefore forgo
treatment.

A more revealing approach is to focus explicitly on the income consequences of health
care financing for the poor. Two possible approaches and the main empirical results are
reviewed in Wagstaff (2008). A first approach is to look at so-called "catastrophic expenditures," defined as health spending that exceeds a predefined share of the household's
income or expenditures. In their country comparisons Xu et al. (2003, 2007) define catastrophic health care expenditures to be more than 40 percent of household's non-
subsistence spending, which is total spending minus the food spending of the household
having the median food share in total household spending in the country. They estimate
(based on surveys in eighty-nine countries covering 89 percent of the world population)
that 150 million people globally suffer financial catastrophy according to that definition.
The relative importance of user charges in total health care financing is the most important explanatory factor for the inter-country differences. In their study for Asia, van
Doorslaer et al. (2007) define catastrophic payments in terms of the share of OOP-
payments in total household expenditure and in non-food expenditure—and they show
results for a range of "threshold" values. More than 5 percent of the households have a
share of health care expenses larger than 10 percent of total household expenditures in
Hong Kong, Kyrgyz Republic, Nepal, Taiwan—and more than 10 percent of the households have catastrophic expenditures in Bangladesh, China, India, Korea, and Vietnam.
Again, unsurprisingly, the relative importance of user charges is the main explanation
for the inter-country differences. The number of households with catastrophic expenditures is much smaller in the richer countries, even if co-payments are relatively important (like in France and Belgium). This is an almost mechanical consequence of the
larger average household incomes, but it is also partly due to the existence of relatively
effective exemption systems.

A second approach defines households as having catastrophic health expenditures if
they fall below the poverty line when health care expenditures are taken into account
but would not be poor without them—the so-called "medical poverty trap." Case studies
show that, even if one considers only direct health care expenditures—and not the productive time losses due to illness—user charges may push large number of households
into poverty (Whitehead et al. 2001). A convincing set of results is reported in van
Doorslaer et al. (2006) for eleven Asian countries. They calculated that an additional 2.7
percent of the population under study (not less than seventy-eight million people)
ended up below the $1-a-day poverty line due to their health care expenditures. Again,
the problem is similar, but quantitatively much less important in the richer countries
that have user charges or a large degree of cost sharing.

Let us make two final remarks. First, most studies assume that health care expenditures are paid out of current income or out of current non-medical expenditures.
Households may also resort to other coping strategies such as borrowing or selling a
part of their stock of financial and physical assets (McIntyre et al. 2006; Wagstaff
2008). Taking these strategies into account may seriously change the poverty picture

(Flores et al. 2008). However, a complete evaluation would then require the use of a full inter-temporal model that also takes into account the long-run consequences of the depletion of assets.

Second, simple generalizations should be avoided. In their detailed study of Uganda, Xu et al. (2006) conclude that the incidence of catastrophic expenditures among the poor did not fall significantly after the removal of the user fees. They suggest that the unavailability of drugs may have forced patients to purchase drugs from the private sector—and that informal payments may have returned or increased to compensate the providers for the revenue lost from user fees. This again illustrates the importance of distinguishing carefully between user charges on the one hand and total out-of-pocket expenses on the other hand.

15.5.2 User Charges and Equality of Access

Certainly for the LMICs, the position has been defended that introducing user charges would at the end benefit rather than harm the poor, despite the financial consequences described before. The argument is based on the idea that in many situations the only alternative to user charges is a huge under-supply of good-quality services, leading to a black market with informal payments and the implementation of non-price rationing mechanisms, which would be "exploited" more efficiently by the rich and powerful. For an overall evaluation, it is then necessary to take into account both supply and demand effects.

The empirical results do not support this theoretical argumentation. A large majority of studies suggest that user charges lead to a stronger reduction in utilization among the poor than among the rich (James et al. 2006). As an example, Schneider and Hanson (2006) find that health spending had a small impact on the socioeconomic situation of uninsured and insured households in Rwanda. However, this is at the expense of inequity in utilization of care, since those who have to pay user fees report significantly lower visit rates.

The evidence is overwhelming in the studies that focus on the price effect per se. Standard economic theory predicts that an increase in health care prices should lead to a larger reduction in consumption for those households, which spend a larger part of their income on health care. These are most probably the poor (and the chronically ill). The empirical evidence for LMICs strongly supports this theoretical hypothesis (Sepehri and Chernomas 2001).[3] The evidence for the richer countries goes in the same direction. Thomson et al. (2003) summarize a long list of case studies for many European countries suggesting that the weaker groups in society are more responsive to price changes and that the poor in some cases postpone necessary health care consumption. Lexchin and

---

[3] Different price elasticities for the poor and the rich have been reported by, among others, Kim et al. (2005) for South Korea, Asfaw et al. (2004) for Ethiopia, Hotchkiss (1998) and Ching (1995) for the Philippines, and Sauerborn et al. (1994) for Burkina Faso.

Grootendorst (2004) review the literature on the effects of cost sharing for prescription drugs in North America. With the necessary caveats about the quality of some of the studies, they conclude that virtually every article they reviewed supports the view that cost sharing decreases the use of prescription drugs by the poor and the chronically ill, i.e. the prediction that the larger the share of income spent on drugs, the higher the price sensitivity. Similar results about the effects of user charges on the use of prescription medicines have been reported for Sweden (Lundberg et al. 1998).

These results suggest that user charges may threaten equality of access. Can exemption mechanisms help to alleviate the problem?

15.5.3 Exemption Mechanisms

In the developed health care systems, exemption mechanisms have been introduced to mitigate the social consequences of user charges (Thomson et al. 2003). The very diverse arrangements (sometimes differentiated for different categories of health care) broadly fall into two categories. First, for some groups (either the chronically ill or the economically weak or both), user charges can be lowered (for some or all health care services)—or households from these groups can even be totally exempted. Second, for some or all households, a possibly income-related ceiling can be introduced, limiting the total amount of user charges to be paid. Both arrangements can be justified theoretically. The former exploits the difference in price elasticities between different social groups. The latter is in line with Arrow's basic "theorem of the deductible," suggesting that an optimal policy involves full insurance above a deductible (Arrow 1970; Gollier and Schlesinger 1996). We will come back to these theoretical issues in the next section.

The effectiveness of these exemption mechanisms can only be evaluated with the specific institutional features of the country concerned in mind. Moreover, it is not easy to estimate their behavioral effects, given that they may lead to highly non-linear budget constraints. A complete evaluation requires the use of micro-simulation techniques. Although there are only a few such studies available, it seems fair to say that in the richer countries the exemption mechanisms have been relatively successful in protecting the poor. This hypothesis is to some extent confirmed by the low percentage of households with catastrophic health care expenditures in these economies (Xu et al. 2003).

Even sophisticated exemption mechanisms cannot fully solve the problem of catastrophic expenditures, however. For the very poor, third-payer arrangements are necessary, as the simple fact of having to advance the user charges may be sufficient reason to postpone perhaps necessary health care. The chronically ill raise special problems. Directly defining a list of chronic illnesses giving right to a complete exemption from user charges is to some extent arbitrary, and such a list may also create moral hazard and coding effects. The alternative approach of introducing a differentiated ceiling for the chronically ill can only be efficient if it takes into account that (by definition) their expenditures are highly correlated over time. This is not easily implementable within common procedures like, e.g., a yearly ceiling, and requires the collection of rich information at the individual level. Moreover, there is a trade-off between protecting the chronically ill and protecting the poor. Chronically ill patients can also be found among the very rich—while among the weaker socioeconomic groups some households may not need much protection.

As the experience in the developed economies shows that the implementation of social exemption mechanisms requires administrative sophistication, it is not surprising that in the LMICs the experience with such mechanisms has been disappointing. Who is to grant the exemptions (and possibly perform the necessary means testing) in a situation with weak governments and weak intermediate social structures? Often the exemption criteria are only vaguely defined—or the necessary information, e.g. about incomes, is missing and extremely hard to collect. Available evidence suggests that in actual practice numerous exemptions are unrelated to income or to morbidity, but go to e.g. civil servants, police and students (Willis and Leighton 1995).[4] There are also some positive experiences. In an experimental setting in Sudan, exemptions from user fees for malaria treatment were granted to a high risk group of pregnant women and children under 5 years (Abdu et al. 2004). The criteria were well-defined and the targeted group was specific and easily identifiable, and as a result utilization increased significantly. In Zambia, the introduction of discount cards, i.e. a set of coupons to cover episodes of care at a discount, facilitated access for lower income groups (Kondo and McPake 2007).[5] In their study about Asia, van Doorslaer et al. (2007) point to the relative efficiency of the social protection mechanisms in Indonesia and Thailand, where a system of health cards for the poor has been introduced. Exemption mechanisms can work, if the political and administrative obstacles for their implementation can be overcome.

15.6 TOWARDS A THEORY OF OPTIMAL USER CHARGES?

Many considerations play a role in setting "optimal" user charges. First, there is the trade-off between insurance against financial risk versus fighting moral hazard. Second, a system of differential user charges can be designed to influence the behavior of patients and providers in a "better" direction. Third, there is a danger that the poor are hit more severely by the user charges. This may require differential treatment of different

---

[4] Detailed case studies show that exemption systems did not work in China (Meng et al. 2002), Ghana (Nyonator and Kutzin 1999), Kenya (Mbugua et al. 1995), Niger (Meeuwissen 1992), Sierra Leone (Fabricant et al. 1999) and Zaire (Haddad and Fournier 1995).

[5] The discount cards were less efficient than a prepayment scheme, however, and the authors emphasize the importance of finding solutions for the implementation problems related to such schemes.

individuals through the design of social exemption mechanisms. Fourth, in some situations user charges may be seen as a necessary instrument for the government to raise additional revenue. We are then facing the problem of priority setting.

An integrated model capturing all these considerations is not yet available in the literature—and most probably would not be very informative either. The existing papers focus on various aspects of the overall problem. Not surprisingly, the same basic variables appear in most of them. Reformulating the previous ideas in theoretical terms, the optimal structure of reimbursements (or of user charges) will depend on (a) the degree of risk aversion of the agents; (b) the price elasticity of health care demand; (c) the specification of the social welfare function and the distribution of health care expenses over the population; (d) the possible constraints on the government budget. The optimal user charges (or the optimal structure of cost sharing) will reflect the trade-offs between these different effects.

In the insurance context, the trade-off between insurance and fighting moral hazard has been analyzed extensively (Pauly 1968; Arrow 1970; Zeckhauser 1970). This literature is covered in other chapters in this volume. A part of it is relevant for the specific issue of social exemption mechanisms. Indeed, economic theory suggests that an optimal insurance plan should have a stop-loss of some sort. However, using data from the Rand Health Insurance Experiment, Manning and Marquis (1996) conclude that the optimal stop-loss would be extremely high and that plans with a combination of first dollar cost sharing and stop-loss perform much better than pure stop-loss plans. Yet, as they emphasize themselves, their results crucially depend on their assumptions of a low risk aversion parameter and of a constant price elasticity. If the price elasticity of demand were to fall toward zero at the upper end of the distribution, the conclusions would definitely be different.

Things get more complicated when we introduce the possibility of differentiating the degree of cost sharing for different health care items. In a seminal paper, Besley (1988) applied the theory of Ramsey taxation to the optimal structure of health insurance reimbursements. Again, the same basic variables appear. In a setting with a single individual, the crucial determinants are (1) the covariance between the marginal utility of income in different health states and the expenditures on the health good, i.e. the insurance effect; and (2) the expected distortions from an out-of-pocket price less than the market price. In general, the optimal rate of insurance coverage is a decreasing function of the compensated price elasticity of demand. In a more realistic setting with heterogeneous individuals, it becomes important to check whether consumers of a particular medical service have high or low distributional weights. In a similar but simpler model, Hoel (2005) shows that introducing equity considerations does not necessarily lead to lower co-payments. Suppose severity is rather homogeneous in the population, but incomes vary. Suppose also that the initial user charges are such that some individuals choose to be treated while others choose not to be treated. Then an increased concern for equity *increases* the optimal user charge provided a sufficiently large number of persons who choose treatment get reduced welfare weights.

Besley (1988) emphasized that in evaluating the risk-sharing and distortive effects of health care reimbursements for different health commodities, it is important to take into account the whole structure of cross-price effects. Recently, this idea has been taken up again in the literature, partly because of the empirical findings on the cross-price effects of the increased (and differentiated) co-payments for prescription drugs (Goldman and Philipson 2007). Suppose that the price elasticity for drug demand is large and that the financial risks are small. Then a single-good approach would advocate a high co-payment for this drug. Let us now add the information that this increased co-payment leads to larger hospital spending in the future. In that case it may even be optimal to raise no or a very low co-payment for that drug. Designing an optimal system of co-payments or user charges requires a careful consideration of the substitution patterns between the different commodities.

Going one step further, one could ask whether it is not worthwhile to design the system of user charges so as to stimulate the "best" treatments from a health point of view. As we have seen, there is much evidence suggesting that a linear increase in user charges does not only lead to a cut in "frivolous" expenditures, but also to a cut in medically necessary health care. Given this evidence, it may seem advisable, e.g., to lower user charges for medically valuable services, or to grant exemptions for specific treatments to patients with selected clinical diagnoses. Instead of focusing on the price elasticity of demand, one then focuses on the benefit-cost ratio of the various treatments. At first sight, this so-called "value based insurance design" (Chernew et al. 2007) requires so much information that it is difficult to implement in the health care systems of LMICs. Nevertheless, this view is too pessimistic. Partial steps can easily be taken. Conditional cash transfers to households who use preventive health services are a (perhaps primitive) example of value-based design. To give another example, Holloway et al. (2001) show that in rural Nepal a clever design of user fees led to a marked reduction in the number of unnecessary drug items prescribed per patient.

The idea of "value-based design" confronts us again with the discussion about the basic welfare foundations of health care policy. Should we accept consumer sovereignty or not? Pauly and Blavin (2008) show that the traditional welfare approach leads to the same conclusions as the value-based approach if patient demands are based on correct information about benefits and costs. Is it then better to improve the information of the patients—or to restructure the system of financial incentives?

The paper that is most explicitly directed to the optimality of user charges in LMICs is very much in this spirit (Smith 2005). Smith takes the position of a benevolent decision-maker seeking to maximize health gains (and not utilities) subject to a fixed budget constraint. This decision-maker has to decide for each technology about the proportion of the full market price to be subsidized. User charges are then a way of augmenting the available budget. His conclusions are striking. Other things equal, government subsidies should be directed at interventions that have high benefit-cost ratios, have high price elasticities of demand, particularly among the poor, and have relatively high incidence among the poor. The first conclusion is perfectly in line with the idea of "value-based insurance design." The second conclusion is opposite to the conclusion that is derived within the traditional welfare framework. The intuition in Smith's paper is that one should avoid raising user charges when these at the margin deter a significant number of (mainly poor) patients from seeking necessary care. Maximizing health gains clearly leads to different conclusions than maximizing a welfarist social welfare function.

Until now, the theoretical literature kept to the assumption of a benevolent decision-maker. In reality, decisions are taken through a complex political process by often poorly informed decision-makers that are confronted with all kinds of pressure groups. The experience with user charges (and with exemptions) shows that policy measures, introduced with the best of intentions, can have unexpected and undesirable side effects. Introducing public choice considerations into the normative analysis therefore remains a difficult but important challenge.

15.7 Official and Unofficial User Charges

If we see official user charges as prices, they are closely related to two other phenomena: informal payments and balance (or extra) billing. Sometimes it is even difficult to distinguish sharply between them. In any case, evaluating user charges (and social exemption mechanisms) requires careful consideration of the possible interactions between these different "prices."

15.7.1 Informal Payments

Although it is understandably difficult to get reliable data about the importance of unofficial payments, they are certainly not negligible in many health care systems, mainly in LMICs and transition economies. Balabanova et al. (2004) estimate that in the former Soviet Union 36.7 percent of the patients make use of personal connections to get treated and 28.5 percent informally offer money to health professionals. In some cases, these informal payments are necessary to cover the cost of care in a situation of regulated (non-equilibrium) quantities and prices; in other cases, they simply reflect abuse of power by quasi-monopolistic providers. The effects on equity and on quality will obviously differ depending on the specific circumstances of the country concerned, and so will the adequate regulatory response (Ensor 2004).

The most detailed information about the distributional effects of informal payments is available for those countries where relatively large surveys have been organized. It turns out that the equity effects differ from country to country. In Hungary (Szende and Culyer 2006) and in Greece (Liaropoulos et al. 2008), all income groups pay about the same amount of informal payments, which of course implies that they are highly regressive. In other countries, such as Bulgaria (Balabanova and McKee 2002), the providers seem to treat high and low-income patients differently: wealthier, younger, and better-educated patients pay relatively more. This latter finding is less positive than it may seem at first sight, however, since the quality, or even the sheer availability of care, may depend on paying informally. Moreover, informal payments are much less transparent than official user fees, for patients as well as for regulators and researchers. This lack of transparency adds to the uncertainty and possibly the vulnerability of patients. It also complicates the task of devising adequate social exemption mechanisms.

It has been suggested that the introduction of official user charges may be one way to reduce the importance of informal payments. A shift from unofficial to official user fees is more than a simple substitution of one price for another. Official user fees are less uncertain for the patients and there is a better chance that their revenues will go to the hospitals rather than to the private doctors. There is evidence that in Cambodia the introduction of user fees led to a significant improvement in the quality of the hospital services, also for low-income users (Akashi et al. 2004). Yet this does not always work in practice. In Bulgaria, the official (formal) user charges seem to have come simply on top of the informal payments (Balabanova and McKee 2002). And in their detailed analysis of different health centers in Uganda, McPake et al. (1999) sketch a differentiated picture. In some facilities, formal charges replaced the formerly existing informal charges, in other facilities there were no informal user charges so that the introduction of formal charges led to a direct price increase, in still other facilities formal charges did not change the ability of health workers to charge informally. Evaluating the effects of introducing official user charges requires a detailed investigation of the microeconomic incentives and of the social norms and structures of political decision-making that are in place.

15.7.2 Extra Billing

In some insurance systems the providers can ask fees on top of the official fees that are agreed upon in the official reimbursement scheme, i.e. on top of the sum of reimbursed fees and official co-payments. This practice is called balance billing in the US terminology, while in other countries one talks about "extra billing" or about "supplementary fees." Contrary to the informal payments discussed before, extra billing is not illegal. Yet its effects are very similar. Extra billing may reflect a need to cover costs, if, e.g., official hospital budgets are not sufficient—or it may simply follow from the use of market power. It often leads to a less transparent pricing structure for the patients, and it increases the uncertainty about out-of-pocket payments. Although there sometimes is some protective regulation (e.g. in the form of restrictions on supplementary fees for patients in common rooms), in general the extra costs are not included in the social exemption mechanisms. Therefore, the working of these mechanisms may be to some extent undermined.

The theoretical arguments formulated in favor of extra billing are remarkably similar to the arguments put forward in favor of user charges. This is especially clear in the debate about the restrictions on balance billing for Medicare beneficiaries in the US, introduced from the late 1980s onwards. There were concerns that restricting balance billing would lower the quality of care provided. In a theoretical model with monopolistically competitive physicians, Glazer and McGuire (1993) derive the conclusion that with balance billing (a form of price discrimination), quality is set at a higher level both for patients paying the supplemental price and for those not paying that price. They recommend the introduction of a fee policy in which physicians would be paid a higher (official) fee for patients for which they do not raise a supplement, i.e. agree to accept the official fee as the full payment. However, Glazer and McGuire are careful to point out that this efficiency result must be weighed against distributional considerations.

The empirical evidence on the effects of the balance billing restrictions is limited. In her interesting study, McKnight (2007) finds that balance billing restrictions led to a 9 percent reduction in overall spending on medical services among elderly households. Higher income households benefited more than lower income households, suggesting that physicians were more inclined to balance bill higher income households. She also shows that the restrictions had few, if any, consequences for the quality of care received by Medicare beneficiaries. The number of doctor visits did not change and there was no significant impact on the duration of the visits or on the likelihood of certain tests. The only negative impact was on the likelihood of planning a follow-up telephone call. She therefore concludes that the primary impact of the restrictions on balance billing was simply a transfer from physicians to the elderly patients. The absence of strong quality effects is in line with the results on user charges, as described before.

15.8 CONCLUSION

Different arguments have been put forward in favor of or against user charges in health care. The available research yields some robust insights on the empirical relevancy of these arguments, and there is a reassuring convergence in the findings for different health care systems. User charges may be useful to fight moral hazard and overconsumption—yet it turns out that not only frivolous overconsumption will be cut, but also medically necessary care. They may help to raise sufficient revenue for financing an adequate package of good quality health care in a context of large unmet needs or rapid technological progress—yet a health care system with user charges as the dominating financing mechanism will put a heavy burden on the poor and the sick. While insurance and equity considerations therefore point to the crucial importance of risk sharing mechanisms, either through a system of health insurance or through tax financing, user charges may still have a role to play within such a broader system.

A clever design of the system of user charges may help a lot to soften the trade-offs that policymakers have to face. Differentiated user charges can induce the choice of a more efficient health care package. Social exemption mechanisms may help mitigating the distributional issues. Yet, to fine-tune the system detailed information about the behavior of providers and of patients from different socioeconomic groups is necessary. Moreover, introducing a sophisticated system of user charges requires well-developed administrative institutions. This leads to a paradox. User charges are better acceptable in developed health care systems, in which they can be designed in a more efficient and equitable way. The financing problem is less acute in these systems, however. Because in many LMICs it is difficult to set up an adequate system of insurance or of tax financing, user charges will have to play a more important role. At the same time, there is a good chance that they will not be designed in a sophisticated way, or that the social exemption mechanisms will not work. User charges are then the most problematic where they are most needed.

At the end, the trade-offs between less insurance and more overconsumption, less revenue and a less equitable financing structure, less patient sovereignty and a less efficient pattern of health care consumption, reflect ethical choices. Where to draw the boundary between individual and social responsibility? The issue of the optimal level and structure of user charges therefore confronts us with the broader issues of social justice and of priority setting in a public health care system.

REFERENCES

ABDU, Z., Z. MOHAMMED, I. BASHIER, and B. ERIKSSON 2004. The impact of user fee exemption on service utilization and treatment seeking behaviour: the case of malaria in Sudan. *International Journal of Health Planning and Management* 19: S95–106.

AKASHI, H., T. HUOT, E. YAMADA, K. KANAL, and T. SUGIMOTO. 2004. User fees at a public hospital in Cambodia: effects on hospital performance and provider attitudes. *Social Science and Medicine* 58(3): 553–64.

ARROW, K. 1970. *Essays in the Theory of Risk Bearing.* Amsterdam: North-Holland.

ASFAW, A., J. VON BRAUN, and S. KLASEN. 2004. How big is the crowding-out effect of user fees in the rural areas of Ethiopia? Implications for equity and resources mobilization. *World Development* 32(12): 2065–81.

AUDIBERT, M. and J. MATHONNAT. 2000. Cost recovery in Mauritania: initial lessons. *Health Policy and Planning* 15(1): 66–75.

AUSTVOLL-DAHLGREN, A., M. AASERUD, G. VIST, C. RAMSAY, A. OXMAN, H. STURM, J. KÖSTERS, and A. VERNBY. 2008. Pharmaceutical policies: effects of cap and co-payment on rational drug use. *Cochrane Database of Systematic Reviews* 1: CD007017. DOI: 10.1002/14651858. CD007017.

BALABANOVA, D. and M. MCKEE. 2002. Understanding informal payments for health care: the example of Bulgaria. *Health Policy* 62: 243–73.

——J. ROSE R. POMERLEAU, and C. HAERPFER. 2004. Health service utilization in the former Soviet Union: evidence from eight countries. *Health Services Research* 39: 1927–50.

BESLEY, T. 1988. Optimal reimbursement health insurance and the theory of Ramsey taxation. *Journal of Health Economics* 7: 321–36.

BORGHI, J., T. ENSOR, A. SAMANATHAN, C. LISSNER, and A. MILLS. 2006. Mobilising financial resources for maternal health. *The Lancet* 368: 1457–65.

CHANDRA, A., J. GRUBER, and R. MCKNIGHT. 2010. Patient cost-sharing and hospitalization offsets in the elderly. *American Economic Review* 100(1): 193–213.

CHAWLA, M. and R. ELLIS. 2000. The impact of financing and quality changes on health care demand in Niger. *Health Policy and Planning* 15(1): 76–84.

CHERNEW, M., A. ROSEN, and M. FENDRICK. 2007. Value-based insurance design. *Health Affairs*, 30 (Jan.): w195–w203.

CHING, P. 1995. User fees, demand for children's health care and access across income groups: the Philippine case. *Social Science and Medicine* 41(1): 37–46.

CISSE, B., S. LUCHINI, and J. P. MOATTI. 2007. Progressivity and horizontal equity in health care finance and delivery: what about Africa? *Health Policy* 80(1): 51–68.

COLOMBO, F. and N. TAPAY. 2004. Private health insurance in OECD countries: the benefits and costs for individuals and health systems. Health Working Paper 15, OECD, Paris.

CREESE, A. 1991. User charges for health care: a review of recent experience. *Health Policy and Planning* 6(4): 309–19.

CUTLER, D. and R. ZECKHAUSER. 2000. The anatomy of health insurance. In A. Culyer and J. Newhouse (eds.), *Handbook of Health Economics* (New York: Elsevier), 563–643.

DE GRAEVE, D. and T. VAN OURTI. 2003. The distributional impact of health financing in Europe: a review. *The World Economy* 26: 1459–79.

ENSOR, T. 2004. Informal payments for health care in transition economies. *Social Science and Medicine* 58: 237–46.

FABRICANT, S., C. KAMARA, and A. MILLS. 1999. Why the poor pay more: household curative expenditures in rural Sierra Leone. *International Journal of Health Planning and Management* 14(3): 179–99.

FLORES, G., J. KRISHNAKUMAR, O. O'DONNELL, and E. VAN DOORSLAER. 2008. Coping with health-care costs: implications for the measurement of catastrophic expenditures and poverty. *Health Economics* 17(12): 1393–12.

GAYNOR, M., J. LI, and W. VOGT. 2006. Is drug coverage a free lunch? Cross-price elasticities and the design of prescription drug benefits. Working Paper 12758, NBER.

GERTLER, P. and J. HAMMER. 1997. Strategies for pricing publicly provided health services. Policy Research Working Paper 1762, World Bank, Washington, DC.

GIBSON, T., R. OZMINKOWKI, and R. GOETZEL. 2005. The effects of prescription drug cost sharing: a review of the evidence. *American Journal of Managed Care* 11(11): 730–40.

GILSON, L. and D. McINTYRE. 2005. Removing user fees for primary care in Africa: the need for careful action. *British Medical Journal* 331: 762–5.

GILSON, M. and A. MILLS. 1995. Health sector reforms in sub-Saharan Africa: lessons of the last 10 years. *Health Policy* 32: 215–43.

GLAZER, J. and T. McGUIRE. 1993. Should physicians be permitted to "balance bill" patients? *Journal of Health Economics* 11: 239–58.

GOLDMAN, D., G. JOYCE, and Y. ZHENG. 2007. Prescription drug cost sharing: associations with medication and medical utilization and spending and health. *Journal of the American Medical Association* 298(1): 61–9.

——— and T. PHILIPSON. 2007. Integrated insurance design in the presence of multiple medical technologies. *American Economic Review (Papers and Proceedings)* 97(2): 427–32.

GOLLIER, C. and H. SCHLESINGER. 1996. Arrow's theorem on the optimality of deductibles: a stochastic dominance approach. *Economic Theory* 7: 359–63.

GRIFFIN, C. 1992. Welfare gains from user charges for government health services. *Health Policy and Planning* 7(2): 177–80.

HADDAD, S. and P. FOURNIER. 1995. Quality, cost, and utilization of health services in developing countries: a longitudinal study in Zaire. *Social Science and Medicine* 40(6): 743–53.

HALL, R. and C. JONES. 2007. The value of life and the rise in health spending. *Quarterly Journal of Economics* 112: 39–72.

HOEL, M. 2005. Concerns for equity and the optimal co-payments for publicly provided health care. Working Paper No 1620, CESifo.

HOLLOWAY, K., B. GAUTAM, and B. REEVES. 2001. The effects of different kinds of user fees on prescribing quality in rural Nepal. *Journal of Clinical Epidemiology* 54(10): 1065–71.

HOTCHKISS, D. 1998. The tradeoff between price and quality of services in the Philippines. *Social Science and Medicine* 46(2): 227–42.

JACK, W. 1999. *Principles of Health Economics for Developing Countries*. Washington, DC: World Bank, WBI Development Studies.

JAMES, C., K. HANSON, B. McPAKE, et al. 2006. To retain or remove user fees? Reflections on the current debate in low- and middle-income countries. *Applied Health Economics and Health Policy* 5(3): 137–53.

—— S. MORRIS, R. KEITH, and A. TAYLOR. 2005. Impact on child mortality of removing user fees: simulation model. *British Medical Journal* 331(7519): 747–9.

KIM, J., S. KO, and B. YANG. 2005. The effects of patient cost sharing on ambulatory utilization in South Korea. *Health Policy* 72(3): 293–300.

KONDO, M. and B. McPAKE. 2007. Making choices between prepayment and user charges in Zambia. What are the results for equity? *Health Economics* 16(12): 1371–87.

LEXCHIN, J. and P. GROOTENDORST. 2004. Effects of prescription drug user fees on drug and health services use and on health status in vulnerable populations: a systematic review of the evidence. *International Journal of Health Services* 34(1): 101–22.

LIAROPOULOS, L., O. SISKOU, D. KAITELIDOU, M. THEODOROU, and T. KATOSTARAS. 2008. Informal payments in public hospitals in Greece. *Health Policy* 87(1): 72–81.

LITVACK, J. and C. BODART. 1993. User fees plus quality equals improved access to health care: results of a field experiment in Cameroon. *Social Science and Medicine* 37(3): 369–83.

LUNDBERG, L., M. JOHANNESSON, D. ISACSON, and L. BORGQUIST. 1998. Effects of user charges on the use of prescription medicines in different socio-economic groups. *Health Policy* 44(2): 123–34.

MANNING, W. and S. MARQUIS. 1996. Health insurance: the tradeoff between risk pooling and moral hazard. *Journal of Health Economics* 15: 609–39.

—— J. NEWHOUSE, N. DUAN, E. KEELER, A. LEIBOWITZ, and M. MARQUIS. 1987. Health insurance and the demand for medical care: evidence from a randomized experiment. *American Economic Review* 77(3): 251–77.

MARIKO, M. 2003. Quality of care and the demand for health services in Bamako, Mali: the specific roles of structural, process and outcome components. *Social Science and Medicine* 56(6): 1183–96.

MBUGUA, J., G. BLOOM, and M. SEGAL. 1995. Impact of user charges on vulnerable groups: the case of Kibwezi in rural Kenya. *Social Science and Medicine* 41(6): 829–35.

MCINTYRE, D., M. THIEDE, G. DAHLGREN, and M. WHITEHEAD. 2006. What are the economic consequences for households of illness and of paying for health care in low- and middle-income country contexts? *Social Science and Medicine* 62: 858–65.

MCKNIGHT, R. 2007. Medicare balance billing restrictions: impacts on physicians and beneficiaries. *Journal of Health Economics* 26: 326–41.

MCPAKE, B., D. ASIIMWE, F. MWESIGYE, M. OFUMBI, L. ORTENBLAD, P. STREEFLAND, and A. TURINDE. 1999. Informal economic activities of public health workers in Uganda: implications for quality and accessibility of care. *Social Science and Medicine* 49: 849–65.

MEEUWISSEN, L. 2002. Problems of cost recovery implementation in district health care: a case study from Niger. *Health Policy and Planning* 17(3): 304–13.

MENG, Q., Q. SUN, and N. HEARST. 2002. Hospital charge exemptions for the poor in Shandong, China. *Health Policy and Planning* 17: S56–63.

MURPHY, K. and R. TOPEL. 2006. The value of health and longevity. *Journal of Political Economy* 114(5): 871–904.

NYONATOR, F. and J. KUTZIN. 1999. Health for some? The effects of user fees in the Volta region of Ghana. *Health Policy and Planning* 14(4): 329–41.

O'DONNELL, O., E. VAN DOORSLAER, R. RANNAN-ELIYA, et al. 2008. Who pays for health care in Asia? *Journal of Health Economics* 27: 460–75.

PALMER, N., D. MUELLER, L. GILSON, A. MILLS, and A. HAINES. 2004. Health financing to promote access in low income settings: how much do we know? *The Lancet* 364 (Oct. 9): 1365–70.

PAULY, M. 1968. The economics of moral hazard: comment. *American Economic Review* 58: 531–7.

——— and F. BLAVIN. 2008. Moral hazard in insurance, value-based cost sharing, and the benefits of blissful ignorance. *Journal of Health Economics* 24(27): 1407–17.

PILOTE, L., C. BECK, H. RICHARD, and M. EISENBERG. 2002. The effects of cost-sharing on essential drug prescriptions, utilization of medical care and outcomes after acute myocardial infarction in elderly patients. *Canadian Medical Association Journal* 167: 246–52.

RAO, D. and D. PETERS. 2007. Quality improvement and its impact on the use and equality of outpatient health services in India. *Health Economics* 16(8): 799–813.

SAUERBORN, R., A. NOUGTARA, and E. LATIMER. 1994. The elasticity of demand for health care in Burkina Faso: differences across age and income groups. *Health Policy and Planning* 9(2): 185–92.

SCHNEIDER, P. and K. HANSON. 2006. Horizontal equity in utilisation of care and fairness of health financing: a comparison of micro-health insurance and user fees in Rwanda. *Health Economics* 15(1): 19–31.

SEPEHRI, A. and R. CHERNOMAS. 2001. Are user charges efficiency- and equity-enhancing? A critical review of economic literature with particular reference to experience from developing countries. *Journal of International Development* 13: 183–209.

SMITH, P. 2005. User charges and priority setting in health care: balancing equity and efficiency. *Journal of Health Economics* 24(5): 1018–29.

SOUCAT, A., T. GANDAHO, and D. LEVY-BRUHL. 1997. Health seeking behaviour and household health expenditures in Benin and Guinea: the equity implications of the Bamako initiative. *International Journal of Health Planning and Management* 12(Suppl. 1): S137–63.

SOUTEYRAND, Y., V. COLLARD, J.-P. MOATTI, I. GRUBB, and T. GUERMA. 2008. Free care at the point of service delivery: a key component for reaching universal access to HIV/AIDS treatment in developing countries. *AIDS* 22(Suppl. 1): S161–68.

SZENDE, A. and A. CULYER. 2006. The inequity of informal payments for health care: the case of Hungary. *Health Policy* 75(3): 262–71.

THOBANI, M. 1984. Charging user fees for social services: education in Malawi. *Comparative Education Review* 28(3): 402–23.

THOMSON, S., E. MOSSIALOS, and N. JEMIAI. 2003. *Cost Sharing for Health Services in the European Union*. London: London School of Economics, LSE Health and Social Care.

VAN DE VOORDE, C., E. VAN DOORSLAER, and E. SCHOKKAERT. 2001. Effects of cost sharing on physician utilization under favourable conditions for supplier-induced demand. *Health Economics* 10: 457–71.

van Doorslaer, E., A. Wagstaff, H. van der Burg, et al. 1999. The redistributive effect of health care finance in twelve OECD countries. *Journal of Health Economics* 18: 291–313.

—— O. O'Donnell, R. Rannan-Eliya, et al. 2006. Effect of payments for health care on poverty estimates in 11 countries in Asia: an analysis of household survey data. *The Lancet* 368(Oct. 14): 1357–64.

———————— et al. 2007. Catastrophic payments for health care in Asia. *Health Economics* 16: 1159–84.

Wagner, T., M. Heisler, and J. Piette. 2008. Prescription drug co-payments and cost-related medication underuse. *Health Economics, Policy and Law* 3(1): 51–67.

Wagstaff, A. 2008. *Measuring financial protection in health*. World Bank: Policy Research Working Paper 4554.

Whitehead, M., G. Dahlgren, and T. Evans. 2001. Equity and health sector reforms: can low-income countries escape the medical poverty trap? *The Lancet* 358: 833–6.

WHO (World Health Organization). 2008. *World Health Statistics* (Geneva: WHO Press).

Willis, C. and C. Leighton. 1995. Protecting the poor under cost recovery: the role of means testing. *Health Policy and Planning* 10(3): 241–56.

Xu, K., D. Evans, K. Kawabata, R. Zeramdini, J. Klavus, and C. Murray. 2003. Household catastrophic health expenditure: a multicountry analysis. *The Lancet* 362: 111–17.

—— D. Evans, P. Kadama, J. Nabyonga, P. Ogwal, P. Nabukhonzo, and A. Aguilar. 2006. Understanding the impact of eliminating user fees: utilization and catastrophic health expenditures in Uganda. *Social Science and Medicine* 62: 866–76.

—————— G. Carrin, A. Aguilar-Rivera, P. Musgrove, and T. Evans. 2007. Protecting households from catastrophic health spending. *Social Science and Medicine* 26(4): 972–83.

Yoder, R. 1989. Are people willing and able to pay for health services? *Social Science and Medicine* 29: 35–42.

Zeckhauser, R. 1970. Medical insurance: a case study of the tradeoff between risk spreading and appropriate incentives. *Journal of Economic Theory* 2: 10–26.

Zweifel, P. and W. Manning. 2000. Moral hazard and consumer incentives in health care. In A. Culyer and J. Newhouse (eds). *Handbook of Health Economics*, Vol. 1 (Amsterdam: Elsevier), 409–59.

CHAPTER 16

··

INSURANCE AND THE DEMAND FOR MEDICAL CARE

··

MARK V. PAULY

16.1 INTRODUCTION

INSURANCE coverage of the cost of or spending on medical goods and services will often change the quantities, qualities, types, or prices of the care patients receive, relative to what would have happened had they not had insurance. Among those with some insurance, differences in the form or extent of coverage can also affect use. Research directed at understanding when and why health insurance affects the demand for medical care (and therefore the price or quantity of what is demanded) is extensive. If one views this research (as we shall suggest below) as tracing out the consumer or market demand function for care, this too has been one of the most intensively investigated demand curves in all of applied microeconomics. This chapter will discuss what is known about this phenomenon and how economic theory interprets what is known.

There are two different policy questions which information on the relationship between insurance and demand may help to answer. The one that has been the primary focus of the bulk of such research has concerned the effect of insurance on the demand for *care* (called moral hazard in the insurance literature). A second question takes the analysis a step further and explores the impact of any insurance-care demand connection on the voluntary demand for insurance. The first line of inquiry is relevant in countries with both voluntary and mandatory health insurance, since it deals with the impact of variations in insurance design and coverage on the use of care. The second issue has been more extensively treated in settings in which insurance coverage is (to some extent) voluntary, but (as I will argue) it is also relevant to the choice of optimal insurance design. (This health economics research is not relevant in countries where public policy specifies that insurance must fully cover all services with no cost sharing or opportunities for out-of-pocket payment for non-covered services.)

Models of the demand for health insurance almost always incorporate analysis of the effect of insurance on demand for care, called "moral hazard" in the insurance literature.[1] In many (though, as we shall see, by no means all) cases, a larger potential or actual impact of coverage on demand (compared to a small or zero impact) reduces the buyer's demand for insurance. The possibility of moral hazard in which insurance affects behavior which in turn alters expected losses or claims poses a potential tradeoff between moral hazard and risk protection in private or public insurance demand.

Strong demand effects potentially have negative effects on welfare when insurance is voluntary and the person's use of medical care and health only affects the person's utility. But for at least some populations in developed countries, insurance is either heavily subsidized or mandated primarily because of a desire to change the demand for care (as well as to provide financial protection). In this case, the policy question and social goal (and potential efficiency improvement) involves creating *more* moral hazard than would otherwise exist, and harnessing it in ways that achieve social goals.

In what follows I will initially use the voluntary insurance purchasing model to frame the discussion of demand effects because that is the model used extensively in the literature. But I will (much) later raise the alternative social goals model (though it is much less definitively and rigorously specified than the voluntary purchase model), and also use this to interpret insurance effects on demand.

16.2 Introduction to Moral Hazard in Insurance Economics

Voluntary insurance for any kind of risk works best and most efficiently in cases when there is a chance that a loss-producing event may occur, but when both the amount of the loss and the chance that it will happen are fixed, regardless of the behavior of the insurance purchaser. Medical expense insurance often does not quite fit this case. There is no doubt that illnesses occur to some extent randomly, and that some medical spending may be desirable to pay for treatment of the illness. But both the chances of getting sick and the amount of medical care and medical spending associated with the illness are to some extent under the control of the consumer, so the consumer (on the demand side) may choose to change both the illness probability and the amount of medical spending to different levels with and without insurance coverage. On the supply side, the possibility of variation in treatment means that provider recommendations for treatment (and cost) may also vary with the presence of insurance and the way in which providers are paid. When such moral

---

[1] Pauly 1968.

hazard is possible, the consumer faces a tradeoff: more protection against risk may cause the consumer to behave differently, in ways that increase money losses or make given losses more likely to happen, and which in turn raise the cost of insurance (Zeckhauser 1970). There are therefore two main questions about voluntary insurance design for individual consumers—both positive as describing the insurance people will choose and normative as defining the insurance they should choose for efficiency: (1) under a given form of insurance, what risk protection of what type should be sacrificed to control moral hazard? (2) How might insurance be configured best in view of the tradeoff between risk protection and moral hazard? For the most part, analysis of the effect of insurance on patient demand has taken that demand as determined by the patient's illness state, preferences, and insurance. I will consider possible effects on supplier recommendations or advice for treatment (induced demand), although the effect of insurance on supply is really a different (and less extensively investigated) topic. The classic treatment of that subject is by Ma and McGuire (1997). I will not deal extensively with that subject here.

16.3 THE (PROBABLY INFEASIBLE) BENCHMARK INDEMNITY MODEL

Is there a setting in which insurance would have no effects on demand? One might imagine that there could be health insurance which would make dollar payments of a predetermined amount, depending on the person's health state. Conditional on the occurrence of a given illness, the consumer (with advice from the physician) will choose a level of use of medical services and products and an associated level of spending so that consumption of all types of medical care is set at the point where the marginal "health and welfare" benefit of care equals the marginal cost of that care in a competitive market. The level of spending thus determined will then be the dollar amount the consumer will want the insurance to pay if the illness strikes.

To make this idea concrete, first think of a patient-consumer who knows everything that is known about the effectiveness of treatment of various amounts, types, and costs for a given illness, and about the effectiveness of treatment of different illnesses of different degrees of severity. Suppose there is just one illness of a uniform severity that might affect this person with probability p. Without insurance, this person would choose how much to spend (S^*) on medical care by comparing the marginal benefits from additional spending with the cost of that spending for each type of medical care; call that package of care X^*. Finally, suppose the person could buy insurance that would make a payment when the illness hits and not otherwise, and whose premium is equal to the expected value of claims payments (actuarially fair). When premiums are actuarially fair, insurance will be demanded by all risk-averse people, and they will demand the same level of coverage regardless of the strength of risk aversion. But even if premiums are fair variations in risk aversion will affect insurance demand when moral hazard is present. What payment (or benefit level) would the person most prefer?

It is easy to see that it is approximately S^*. If the person gets a check for S^*, he will then want to choose X^*, the quantity of care at which marginal benefit equals marginal cost. Setting aside (for the present) some usually small income effects, that will be the level of spending at which marginal benefit originally (without insurance) equaled marginal cost. If we ignore insurance administrative cost, the premium will then be p dollars per dollar of benefit to be paid; at that unit premium a risk-averse person will choose the benefit level B as equal to S^*, and therefore choose to pay a total premium $P = pS^*$. Not only will that coverage eliminate financial risk (in the sense that the amount the consumer will have available to spend on other consumption will be the same whether ill or not), but the quantity of care the consumer will want to have will be the quantity whose cost can be covered by the insurance payment. That is, at $B = S^*$, the consumer will want to consume just S^* worth of care. Consuming more will be unattractive because the expected benefit will fall short of the additional cost, and consuming less (while pocketing some of the insurance payment) will also not happen because the consumer will value the care more than the money.

As an alternative to paying the dollar amount S^*, insurers might offer a "managed care" insurance contract, which takes the form of promising a certain amount and type of care conditional on the occurrence of each illness. It is clear that the optimal managed care benefit in this simple model is care that costs $\$S^*$ and is the same as X^*. This makes the point that in a world of perfect information there is no intrinsic advantage to managed care, since it produces a final result that is identical to that of optimal indemnity insurance.

16.4 Necessary Conditions for Indemnity Insurance to be Feasible and Optimal

In this simple model there was only one illness and one level of severity, so it might be plausible to assume that the insurer could tell if the insured was sick or not. If there are multiple illnesses and multiple levels of severity for a given illness, the theoretically ideal indemnity insurance would be one that made payments conditional on the existence, type and severity of illness, at the level of benefit S^* for that illness, severity, and type. While I believe that there is more scope for the use of pure indemnity contracts than now exists, there are limitations to them. The most obvious one is that the insurer may not be able to know precisely what illness and severity level occurs. Suppose at some severity level L the person would want S^* spent on medical care, and at some more severe level L' the person would want to spend S'. However, in the absence of any additional out-of-pocket cost, the person may prefer S' even in the state L because the additional spending provides positive marginal benefit.

It is now easy to see what the problem is. The consumer will claim to be at severity level L' regardless, and the average or expected value of care with insurance will therefore be higher than without insurance: moral hazard will occur. Moral hazard is one of the distinguishing features of health insurance. It is also easy to see that moral hazard leads to consumption of care worth less than its benefit: in state L with insurance the person consumes $S' - S^*$ additional care, but we know that this additional care is not worth what it costs. Yet it will cause the premium to rise from $p(L) S^* + p(L')S'$ to $(p(L) + p(L'))S'$, a larger number (where $p(L)$ is the probability of getting the illness at the severity level L and $p(L')$ is the probability of getting it at the higher severity level L').

More generally, moral hazard arises when the insurer cannot tell exactly how sick the person is, and therefore does not know which of many marginal benefit curves is applicable to the situation in question (Pauly 2008). The mirror image of this statement is also illuminating: moral hazard need not occur if the insurer can tell what the person's illness condition is. There has been some discussion of cases in which the insurer is assumed to have this knowledge, and suggesting that managed care rules or value-based cost sharing should then be applied (Chernew, Rosen, and Fendrick 2007). But note that in the perfect information case, managed care rules would say that the person should receive S^* units of care, while value based insurance should pay the full cost of the S^* amount of care. That is, there should be no positive cost sharing at all: insurance should pay in full for the amount of care appropriate to the patient's condition, and not pay for any other course of treatment.

In the more realistic case when the insurer cannot know precisely the state of health, the optimal benefit payment (or managed care treatment package) will be a compromise between the benefit payment if L occurs and the benefit payment if L' occurs. If S and S' would represent the optimal spending levels corresponding to each state, in the world with moral hazard the insurance might pay something between S and S', with the result that in the truly more sick state S' there will be positive patient cost sharing, and consequently exposure to financial risk. The greater the degree of risk aversion, the higher the payment, other things equal. If the insurance requires that the full amount of any benefit be spent on medical care, there will also be over-use of care (relative to that at which marginal benefit equals marginal cost) in the less severe illness state. Alternatively, the managed care policy might specify a treatment package between the two ideal levels; there will be no financial risk, but there will be the risk of under-provision of care in the S' state, and possible over-provision in the S state if patients always adhere to the specified treatment package. Financial risk will be replaced by health outcome risk.

16.5 INCOME EFFECTS WITH MORAL HAZARD

The purpose of insurance is to change the household's level of wealth in different states of the world, compared to a situation with no insurance. Wealth is increased in "high loss" states where benefits exceed premiums, and reduced in "low loss" states where premiums exceed benefits. If insurance is actuarially fair, expected wealth is left unchanged, and if the buyer is risk averse, expected utility is increased. However, it is likely that the amount of medical spending at which the household's marginal willingness to pay (amount of other consumption sacrificed for medical care) will be larger in a high loss state with insurance benefit payment received than without insurance because the benefit payment will affect the level of wealth or income. In the indemnity case, although much of the benefit payment will be used to pay for the medical services that would have been bought in the absence of insurance, some of what would have been a reduction in consumption of other goods without insurance may also be diverted to medical services if the higher wealth raises the person's willingness to pay for additional wealth. That is, rather than return to the level of consumption spending that would have occurred in the absence of a loss, the person may choose to cut into consumption to some extent. There may well then be positive income or wealth effects on spending in the high loss case; by the same argument, there should be negative effects on medical spending in the low loss case.

Will this change in the pattern of use with insurance mean that overall medical spending will rise or fall? There are two potential channels for income effects. One is from the premium. If, on the one hand, the insurance is subsidized, that will increase expected wealth compared to a world with no insurance and no subsidy. On the other hand, if the insurance premium rises, either because of higher loading or because of higher medical care prices, that will reduce wealth, other things equal. Of course the risk-averse person gets a gain in expected utility from insurance even if the premium has a loading.

The other channel concerns the relationship between the premium and the insurance payout in the particular health state that occurs. If the benefit payment exceeds the premium, wealth is increased in that state. If the payment is below the premium, wealth is reduced. The net effect of coverage on use obviously depends on whether the income effects in the high loss states cancel out the income effects in the low loss states. Generally they will not cancel out; rather, the net income effect on average spending per insured person (compared to average spending per uninsured person) will be positive as Nyman (1999) following de Meza (1983) has shown most clearly. If there is a uniform income elasticity of demand and if there is positive health care spending in all states, and if the premium is close to fair, it is easy to see that the percentage change in wealth from insurance in high loss states, weighted by the probability of being in those states, will approximately equal the weighted percentage change in wealth in low loss states (or fall a little short if there is insurance loading). For example suppose that the probability of the high loss state is 0.1, the person's wealth is 100, the uninsured expense in the high loss state is 50 and in the low loss state is 5. The premium is assumed to be actuarially fair at 9.5. Thus wealth is increased in the high loss state (compared to no insurance) by 40.5, and is reduced in the low loss state by 4.5. The percentage change in wealth (relative to the base of 100) is thus ten times greater (in the opposite direction) in the high loss state compared to the low loss state. But while the percentage changes in wealth are approximately offsetting, the amounts of spending are different: a given percentage change in spending is obviously much greater in a high spending state than in a low spending state. So the overall impact of changes in *ex post* wealth on the quantity of care demanded and on spending is highly likely to be positive.

The possibility of a disproportionately larger change in spending in the case of a rare high cost illness is plausible. One reason is the household's wealth acts as a limit on total spending (actually wealth minus minimum subsistence); in the example spending cannot exceed 100. But the household clearly would not violate its budget constraint if it bought insurance that paid 200 in the high loss state, since the premium for such insurance (24.5) fits within the wealth constraints of either state.

There is thus a modest difference between the theory of insurance as applied to risks that only reduce money wealth (where the monetary value of the reduction in wellbeing cannot exceed uninsured wealth) compared to insurance that pays directly for higher consumer spending when adverse events occur. But this alone is not a major distinguishing feature between health insurance and other insurance markets thought to function in a more satisfactory way.

In the first case, suppose a person has wealth of $\$W$ and a risk of a loss with probability p. It seems obvious that the worst thing that can happen to that person is that his wealth is driven to zero. It therefore follows that the person will never demand insurance that pays a benefit (in any state of the world) that is greater than W, because that kind of insurance would leave his wealth higher in states where that payment occurred, something he would not desire if he was risk-averse.

If W represents cash or liquid assets, this model is correct; the worst thing that could happen to someone is to lose all their wealth. If the person owns a physical asset, it is possible for a lawsuit associated with harm related to that asset to render a judgment greater than the value of the asset. The person will then declare bankruptcy, so in that sense cannot lose more than the wealth represented by what the physical asset is worth. But as many models of business demand for insurance note, there are non-monetary (or at least non-current-period) downsides to bankruptcy: time costs, shame costs, costs in terms of future career prospects. The person might then buy insurance to cover the cost of losses in excess of the value of the asset, if paying for that additional insurance coverage was preferred to experiencing these extra-wealth reductions in welfare. But note that the expected value of the insurance benefits will then exceed pW; observed payments will be greater with insurance than without, even though the insurer can perfectly distinguish the loss state of the world from the no loss state of the world.

The same sort of thing can happen with medical insurance. Suppose that there is small probability q that I may contract liver cancer, and I have wealth W. Without treatment, liver cancer is fatal within a short time period, but two treatments are possible: one treatment (say, chemotherapy) costs X, an amount which is less than W, and has a survival probability of p, and the other treatment (say, liver transplant) costs X' which is greater than both X and W, but has a higher survival probability p'. So my insurance choices are to buy a policy which pays X, costs qX, gives me expected survival probability of $(1-q)+pq$, and leaves my wealth at $W-qX$, while another policy costs qX', gives higher survival probability of $(1-q)+qp'$, and leaves me with smaller wealth $W-qX'$. I may prefer the second policy to the first, if the value of the increase in survival probability $q(p'-p)$ is greater than the value of the forgone consumption $q(X'-X)$. With no income effects, if insurance were unavailable, I would be forced to choose the treatment X, and have expected expense qX. With insurance possible, I would choose insurance that pays for the treatment X', and would have the larger expected expense qX'. There would be an observed positive effect on spending but (as in the wealth case in the previous paragraph) it would not come either from distorted incentives or from income effects, but from the fact that money wealth does not perfectly proxy all the things that go into a person's lifetime utility.

16.6 Moral Hazard and Optimal Health Insurance with Single-period Independent Demand

The classic model of moral hazard assumes a single period with households facing identical risks of different illness states. Relative to a benchmark "average health" state, some of the other possible health states represent the exogenous occurrence of illness for which there are costly but effective treatments available. Across a range of types of medical care, the marginal health product of some or all of them is higher when a person is sicker; medical care (usually but not always) does you more good when you are sicker. More generally, the person is assumed to have a demand for medical care of the form:

$$D = D(P', Y-R, H'(H), Z)$$

Where P' is the marginal user price (the additional amount paid out of pocket) for a unit of a composite medical care, Y is disposable compensation (including the value of benefits), R is the health insurance premium, $H'(H)$ is the marginal health product (marginal benefit in terms of some indicator of health, such as healthy days), which depends on the person's health status H, and Z is a vector of other influences on the demand for medical care such as education, family size, etc. (I do not insert age in the demand function (in contrast to Grossman 1972, because I assume the effect of age is included in health status.)

The two variables in this demand expression that are influenced by health insurance (in the short run) are P' and R. The premium R is assumed to depend on the expected benefits from the coverage provided in the insurance policy, the insurer's "loading" for administrative expenses and profits, and any taxes, tax subsidies, or explicit subsidies for the insurance. In the US employment based health insurance system, R is often paid in two parts, as an explicit employee premium ("worker share"), and as a component of total compensation ("employer share").

The specification of P' can be complex. The simplest case is one in which insurance covers all components of the composite medical service, subject to a constant coinsurance rate c to be paid by the consumer as cost sharing. Then P' is just cP, where P is the gross unit price paid to the provider of the medical good or service. In more complex insurance designs some medical services may be excluded from coverage entirely, and there may be deductibles and upper limits on benefit payments for covered services. In what immediately follows we will ignore these complexities and assume that, in theory and in empirical estimation, the "quantity of insurance" will be represented solely by the co-insurance rate c.

The premium R will then depend on c, but it will also depend on the person's expected spending on medical care at any given level of P' (or c), and so on all of the variables that enter the medical care demand function. If the level of insurance coverage and the amount the person must pay for it is predetermined, one can then ask about the effect of various levels of c on the quantity of medical care demanded, and the great bulk of the literature treats the cost-sharing problem in this way. If the household has a choice of what insurance to buy, then both D and P' are obviously determined simultaneously (at least in an expectational sense), and so both D and P' are endogenous.

If income effects are zero, one can think of the effect of P' on D (given the assumption of a given gross price P that is large enough so that providers would make any quantities available) as equivalent to the quantities that would be read off a conventional (Marshallian) demand curve (that incorporates income effects) of price changes. To be sure, the larger the quantity of care a given person demands, the higher the premium if premiums depend on expected benefits. But if the size of the pool of persons among whom the insurer is spreading the risk is reasonably large, the effect of this change on R (and hence on the person's demand for care) is negligible. However, the effect of changing P' on everyone's demand (or on the average insured person's demand) will be taken into account in determining the market premium for different levels of c. That is, the insurer will notice that, other things equal, the total amount of medical care demanded will be higher for people with lower values of C, and therefore price insurance coverage (and calculate the marginal premium for changing c) while taking this into account.

Given this type of effect on the use of medical care, how much and/or what type of insurance would the person choose? Let us take the simple case in which the insurance premium is actuarially fair. It is clear that potential insurance purchasers would prefer insurance that did not increase demand, or at least limited the increase in demand. One method of doing so is to increase the co-insurance proportion c. The other way of doing so is to have managed care that constrains the amount of care that will be covered to something less than what the person would demand with c equals zero, or some low level of c. In either case limiting moral hazard has a cost as noted, either in a greater risk of out of pocket cost or in a greater risk of not getting optimal care in the case of an illness of great but unobservable severity.

If only cost sharing can be used, it should be clear that, other things equal, the optimal limit on use will be greater the larger the responsiveness of use to insurance coverage. This is the "Zeckhauser proposition" (Zeckhauser 1970) that has been much discussed in the literature. In the case of linear demand curve, the key parameter turns out to be the slope of the demand curve; in the case of constant elasticity curves, it is the elasticity. In absolute value, the higher the slope or the elasticity, the higher the optimal level of co-insurance.

In the more general case, it will generally be preferable to use a combination of patient and provider "cost sharing" to limit moral hazard, rather than rely entirely on one or the other strategy (Ellis and McGuire 1993; Pauly and Ramsey 1999). The reason is that maximum quantity limits, even if imperfect, may be preferable to cost sharing in situations of high total spending, but cost sharing may work better to control moral hazard at lower levels of spending. The intuition is that limits constrain (high) spending close to the limit, while cost sharing offers incentives to control spending when spending is low. In addition, managed care which is limited to imposing upper limits on cost may be a good way to control moral hazard when demand responsiveness is high, but cost sharing may work better when demand responsiveness is low—thus reversing the Zeckhauser proposition about the relationship between optimal cost sharing and demand responsiveness.

16.7 INTERRELATED DEMANDS

In reality there is no single or simple composite medical good or service. Instead, different types of care are used in different health states. Different services can be either close complements or close substitutes, which means that changes in the user price of one medical good can affect demand for other goods, conditional on their user prices. Sometimes these interrelationships are virtually contemporaneous, but sometimes the effect operates with a lag. In the lagged case, a medical good whose consumption now reduces my demand for some other medical goods in the future would generically be labeled "preventive care," even though it may not be traditional preventive care. Other than issues of uncertainty and discounting, discussed below, such cost offsets capture what is sometimes called "dynamic moral hazard" (Zweifel and Manning 2000). The mechanism by which a good consumed in the present affects demand for a good in the future is usually through affecting the probability of future health states. This relationship is sometimes called "ex ante moral hazard" although it really can be viewed (for insurance purposes) as a special case of interrelated demands.

One difference between interrelated demands that occur within a short time period (like allergy shots and allergy attacks) versus those where the consequences are far in the future (like blood pressure medicine) is that in the latter case the size of the real discount rate is important. It is important for determining socially optimal coverage (at high real interest rates blood pressure control makes less sense) and in explaining patient behavior. As Newhouse (2006) has suggested, consumers may have irrationally high (hyperbolic) discount rates, higher than true real rates, making them less likely to see interaction effects as beneficial even if they have perfect information about the effectiveness of preventive care.

Once we consider the situation in which there are different kinds of medical goods and services, we need also consider the possibility that there are other goods, services, or activities not traditionally labeled "medical" which nevertheless affect health and therefore affect the demand for medical care. Exercising at gym or health club, for example, is a good which often has a positive price but which affects future health and therefore future demand for medical care.

The general proposition in this non-independent case is that insurance should cover a given type of medical care more generously, other things equal including the coverage of other medical services, the larger is the extent of substitution or cost offset. Conversely, the more generous the coverage of the "offset" services, the lower the optimal coverage of the offsetting service. Complementarity in demand will usually imply lower levels of coverage. Even activities not usually thought of as medical, like the cost of access to exercise facilities, might appropriately be covered, and coverage of a service with low or zero risk (like an annual preventive service that happens with certainty every year) might be covered by insurance if it generates cost offsets. Generally it will be preferable to deal with cost offsets against a type of care initially generously covered by providing coverage to the offsetting service rather than by reducing coverage for the offset service, since the former provides more risk protection.

16.8 Insurance Coverage with Imperfect Supply-side Competition

The standard theory of insurance and moral hazard assumes that medical services are competitively supplied at prices that equal marginal cost, usually also assumed constant. If supply is not competitive and cannot construct average cost, then insurance effects on demand may translate into price changes. One simple case is that of a linear demand curve for care provided by a (constant marginal cost) monopolist; the lower the co-insurance rate, the higher will be the monopolist's profit maximizing price. In partial contrast, if the monopoly market demand curve were constant elasticity, then increases in the generosity of insurance coverage would leave the price unaffected since the monopolist's markup rule only contains the (assumed constant) values of marginal cost and demand elasticity; the only effect of insurance is to increase the quantity that the monopolist will sell at the given marked-up price.

That the monopoly quantity with moral hazard may be below the competitive quantity with moral hazard has raised the question of whether such over-pricing might offset the over-consumption that is associated with moral hazard. For a given exogenous value of insurance coverage there will be an offsetting effect of monopoly pricing. But Gaynor, Haas-Wilson, and Vogt (2000) have shown that if the insurance demander selects the level of coverage optimally, altering the product market from competitive to monopoly can never be welfare increasing. The intuition is that consumers will set cost sharing in the competitive case where the marginal welfare cost of changes in coverage just equals the marginal risk reduction benefit. Moving the market to monopoly at that co-insurance rate will lead to a sufficiently great increase in price that the consumer will choose to become exposed to more financial risk, and this increase in risk exposure more than offsets any savings from reduced consumption of medical care. That is, the optimal level of coverage at the higher monopoly price will leave cost sharing amount at a higher level than if the price were competitive, so that monopoly will mean both higher premiums and less risk protection.

16.9 Moral Hazard and Patterns of Voluntary Insurance Coverage: Theory and Practice

The forgoing discussion implies that consumers will demand the most generous insurance coverage against types of care or types of illnesses for which demand responsiveness is low, the probability of illness is low, and the cost of treatment is high. Conversely, coverage will be less generous if demand is price responsive and the illness is common and relatively inexpensive to treat.

If administrative expense were a fixed proportion of expected benefits, there would be positive amounts of insurance coverage for all uncertain medical services, but the generosity of coverage would vary as described above. If there is a fixed cost associated with initiating coverage for some new class of services, the presence of low risk and high price responsiveness may mean that no positive level of coverage is optimal.

This theory implies that, unless administrative costs inhibit and in the absence of adverse selection, there should be variation in the level of insurance coverage across services and illnesses, and there is some such variation, though it would be an exaggeration to say that there is as much variation in coverage as there is probable variation in price responsiveness and risk. One implication is that parity in coverage across different types of services or illnesses may be generally inefficient, and laws and regulations requiring parity may be welfare reducing.

In the theory just discussed, insurance coverage should not be uniform. Instead, cost sharing should vary with demand responsiveness and with administrative costs. In the voluntary market in the United States, and in other countries, coverage has historically varied across services. The general pattern is that inpatient care (both hospital and doctor) are almost completely covered. Outpatient care (in a doctor's office, hospital outpatient department, or clinic has modest cost sharing—for some reason, usually 20%). Prescription drugs, dental care, outpatient mental health care, and home health care are less well-covered, with average cost sharing in the 30 to 50 percent range. Nursing home care is barely covered by private insurance. Finally, very high (catastrophic) expenses usually have zero or minimal marginal cost sharing regardless of the type of service.

Part of the reason for this pattern in the United States is historical: Both hospitals and hospital-oriented physicians started what became the dominant insurance plans to cover their own services (Blue Cross and Blue Shield, respectively). Commercial companies typically offered "major medical" catastrophic coverage which was uniform across services with a high total cost (above a deductible). Commercial firms also pioneered coverage of prescription drugs, home health care, and long-term care.

As a broad generalization (except for nursing home care), it does appear that the pattern of coverage matches the theory; coverage varies directly with the size of the loss and inversely with demand responsiveness. However, until recently, insurances that used fine variations in the level of coverage to affect demand for specific services or in the case of specific illnesses had not occurred because of high administrative cost, but those costs have been lowered in recent years by electronic processing. This is especially the case for coverage of prescription drugs which often had prohibitively high claims processing costs with paper-based methods, but which has taken the lead in electronic pharmacy claims-submission methods (Danzon and Pauly 2002).

The absence of voluntary coverage for nursing home or residential care is largely explained by crowd-out from the public Medicaid program (Brown and Finkelstein 2007, 2008). This program pays for nursing home care, but only after beneficiaries have spent their wealth and incomes. In other countries, long-term care is provided by a combination of social insurance, social services, and housing policy. There is no country with a large market in voluntary long-term care insurance. However, there are often continued disputes with the social insurance plan or trust about what will be paid, and consequent use of private funds if public support is thought to be inadequate. Requirements to use private wealth (including housing wealth, at some point) are common in other countries as well. In addition, the concentration of such expenses in a part of the lifecycle and health states where the marginal utility of other consumption is low may have depressed demand.

16.10 EMPIRICAL EVIDENCE ON THE EFFECT OF INSURANCE ON THE DEMAND FOR MEDICAL CARE

There has been extensive empirical investigation of the effect of changing cost sharing on consumer demand for medical care including, but not limited to, information from one of the most costly and most famous social experimental interventions, the Rand Health Insurance Experiment. It may not be an exaggeration to say that we know more about the elasticity of demand for medical services than for almost any other commodity in household budgets. With the amount of effort devoted to investigating this question, it is not surprising that we do have some definitive conclusions, but there are also some serious puzzles remaining, and more interesting new research continues to emerge.

The two main empirical findings from research to date are these: (1) the aggregate or average consumer demand curve, whether Marshallian (uncompensated) or Hicksian (compensated), slopes downward and to the right. (2) Demand curves are significantly price responsive at all consumer income levels. These conclusions are at variance with common perceptions of medical care demand by non-economists who traditionally have asserted that non-poor consumers only use medical care when they have to do so because they are sick or are ordered to do so by their physician, and that only lower income households would restrain their demand for needed care because of cost sharing. But there are also two serious questions which remain: (1) Does the effect of cost sharing just impact the consumer's decision to initiate care for an episode of illness, or does it also influence the rate at which care is used once a physician has been involved in the process; and (2) is the impact of changing cost sharing for an individual consumer the same as the impact of a similar change for a large share of the population in a market? These two questions are related, because their answers depend on how physicians behave in response to patient cost sharing.

The question of the effect of insurance coverage of various types and amounts on the demand for medical services at various gross prices is obviously important to private or public insurance plans: it is crucial to understanding the benefits costs of changing coverage and, if combined with information on the value of coverage, is necessary (though not sufficient) for judging whether a change in coverage is efficiency improving and/or desirable to consumers or taxpayers. The most economically obvious way to set up the problem is to envision insurances with various levels of proportional co-insurance (including "no coverage" at 100%). The impact of a change in coverage which changes co-insurance would be expected to be very similar to the impact of a single change in gross price. That is, we might assume that the effect of change in the price of a doctor visit from $100 to $50 on the quantity of care demanded with no insurance is the same as the effect of going from no coverage to 50 percent co-insurance with the gross price of a visit remaining at $100 (except for the possible income effect of paying the premium in the latter case). Moral hazard in this sense is nothing more than movement along an ordinary demand curve.

There has been extensive investigation of the impact of changing insurance coverage on quantities of specific medical services and on total medical care spending; there has been much less investigation of any effects on the quality of care (except as captured by a movement to higher priced and presumably higher quality services). Finally, there has been some investigation of the effect of changes in insurance coverage on health outcomes.

It will be useful to use as a benchmark the most discussed and most expensive empirical estimates of medical care demand elasticities, those from the Rand health insurance experiment (Newhouse and The Insurance Experiment Group 1993). That experiment, conducted in the United States in the early 1980s, was a social experiment that randomly assigned samples of the US population under the age of 65, non-institutionalized, and with incomes below an upper income cutoff to a variety of different health insurance plans, ranging from "free care" (coverage without cost sharing for medical, dental, and eye care) to plans with varying levels of co-insurance and deductibles. The experiment did not include a subpopulation with no insurance. While I will provide some more details below, the key parameter values generated by the experiment were estimates of demand elasticity that were statistically significantly different from zero, and in the range of −0.1 to −0.2.

While the experiment has never been repeated, more recent estimates of demand elasticity generated by natural variation in coverage that have tried to deal with the problem of endogeneity, have confirmed the Rand result of a negatively sloped demand curve for almost all populations in almost all settings. Generalizations are difficult here, but it is my impression that these more recent studies have rarely found point estimates lower than those from the experiment. The best current consensus estimate of the elasticity is at or above the Rand estimate.

Before discussing the actual estimates of demand elasticity, I consider the key issue of endogeneity of coverage that has figured so strongly in empirical modeling strategies. To begin with, one of the main rationales for the Rand experiment was that it was a design which should automatically avoid problems of endogeneity by the use of the clinical trial model with random assignment. The rationale for this was that earlier observational studies may have yielded biased estimates. While bias is a potential problem any time there is consumer choice, it is helpful to think about what the nature and direction of the bias might be in order to interpret estimates where there is potential bias and to judge whether it is worthwhile to go to greater effort to avoid bias. Early estimates of the relationship between insurance coverage and medical care use or spending generally used cross sectional data where observations were households or geographic areas. Particularly in the former case, if adverse selection was likely, the observed relationship between coverage and use or spending would be biased upwards in magnitude as an estimate of moral hazard alone. High risks would have more insurance (away from zero), and the high spending by the well-insured could be caused by their higher risk as well as by their generous coverage. (Indeed, a recent spate of econometric studies intended to estimate adverse selection have had to deal with moral hazard as a possible contaminating influence (Cardon and Hendel 2001; Town 2008).) The implication here is that the bias will be greater the greater is adverse selection. Adverse selection will bias downward (toward zero) estimates of the relationship between coverage and health outcomes, because the higher risks who selected coverage would probably have had worse health outcomes than the average risks (Pauly 2005).

In contrast, if insurers are able to identify high risks (thus avoiding adverse selection) and charge them higher premiums, this might cause high risks (at least, low-income high risks) to forgo coverage or to buy less generous coverage. Or, as some recent research indicates, people with higher levels of financial risk aversion have lower levels of current health risk because they have avoided risk taking behavior and consumption items that threaten health. In these cases, the observed relationship between coverage and spending would be a downward biased estimate of moral hazard and the observed relationship between coverage and health outcomes would be biased away from zero. As will be discussed in more detail below, there is evidence of both kinds of selection in voluntary insurance markets.

The early studies that did not control for endogeneity did indeed sometimes get empirical estimates of demand elasticity which were sometime much larger than the Rand range, but they also sometimes got estimates below −0.1 (especially when they looked at household data when adverse selection was most likely). If one takes the Rand estimates as an unbiased benchmark, it is hard to generalize about the direction or magnitude of bias in these earlier studies.

I now briefly review the results of the Rand experiment and subsequent discussions of interpretation of those results. The experiment assigned people to insurance plans with varying levels of co-insurance (0, 25, 50, and 95%) with stop-losses at a predetermined percentage of household income. As noted, use and expenditures on medical care were significantly higher under the free care (0% co-insurance) plan than under the cost sharing plans; the increment in average expense from replacing cost sharing with free care was as high as 46 percent. All types of medical care spending were higher in the free care setting: inpatient care, outpatient care, preventive care, prescription drugs, and dental care. The elasticity was less than average in magnitude for inpatient care, especially for children, and was higher than average for dental care, preventive care, and outpatient mental health care. (Since the plans generally imposed uniform co-insurance, Rand results cannot provide estimates of the effect of changing co-insurance for one type of care while holding the others constant—except for an outpatient deductible plan which was found to discourage both outpatient and inpatient care, implying that they were gross complements.) The response to cost sharing did not differ by household income or other household characteristics, although there was a small income effect on the use of care. It appears that the primary impact of cost sharing was on the rate of initiation of episodes of care; expense per episode did not differ across plans. That is, once care is initiated and is being guided by a physician, variations in individual patient cost sharing appear to have little impact: doctors treat everyone the same.

The experiment also looked at a set of indicators of health outcomes that were supposed to be sensitive in the short run to the use of care. The only indicators that were affected by cost sharing for all population groups were measures of oral health and vision correction. For the low-income group originally at high risk, free care was associated with better blood pressure control, but there were no significant effects for middle income households or for low-income households at average or better risk. The pattern of minimal effects on health was not always consistent with professional judgments about the effectiveness of care. People with cost sharing did use emergency room care less frequently for causes that were not true emergencies (compared to those that were true emergencies), but there was no differential effect of cost sharing on other ambulatory or inpatient care labeled as medically necessary or appropriate; cost sharing discouraged care to the same extent whether it was thought to be effective for health outcomes or not. There was no investigation of the use of care characterized as having positive but low effectiveness (in absolute terms or relative to cost). Since there is no theoretical expectation in demand theory that people will use care that is ineffective or harmful, even if it is free, the mixed results for health effects remain puzzling. One would have to invoke supplier-induced demand that got stronger as cost sharing fell to explain these results.

Empirical work since the experiment has been of four types: estimates of the impact of no insurance relative to typical insurance coverage; attempts to replicate the experiment using other methods for assuring exogeneity of coverage; explorations of cost sharing in plans that also contain managed care features, and research on settings in which coverage was varied for a large fraction of the consumers in a market, rather than just for a handful as in the experiment.

A recent survey article by Buchmueller et al. (2005) looked at the US literature regarding the effect of having some insurance versus having no insurance on use of outpatient and inpatient care. If we assume that insurance on average covered 80 percent of outpatient care cost and 90 percent of inpatient care cost, the implied elasticities are −0.4 to −0.8 for outpatient care, and −0.25 to −0.5 for inpatient care. The general pattern is thus one of elasticities that are definitely negative and significant with numerical values somewhat higher than those for the experiment.

An example of the second kind of study is an analysis by Matthew Eichner (1998) that used as the instrument for lowered cost sharing the exogenous impact of care for a family member's accident in insurance plans with family deductibles. The goal was to examine how care was used after the deductible was covered (implying zero or low cost sharing for any additional care) compared to households with positive expected cost sharing because they were still liable for some of the deductible. This work found a statistically significant effect of free care on use and spending; the point estimate of the elasticity was in the range of −0.7.

A third set of studies look at the effects of cost sharing that differ from the uniform co-insurance, fee-for-service model of the Rand experiment. One study by Hillman et al. (1999) looked at the effect of different levels of drug co-payment per prescription in two kinds of managed care settings: one was a fee-for-service IPA model where physicians were at risk for the cost of their own services but not for the cost of drugs they prescribed, and the other a network model where doctors were at risk (collectively) for their prescription drug costs. Drug co-payments varied as cost sharing for other services held constant. One might have expected some supply-side restraint on prescribing compared to non-managed care fee-for-service even in the first case, since physician visits and drug prescriptions are complements, but one would have expected more restraint in the second case. This was indeed the outcome: the frequency of cost of prescriptions was lower at higher co-payments than at lower co-payments, but the patient responsiveness to cost sharing was much greater in the first setting than in the second. The point estimate of elasticity in the fee-for-service setting was a little more than −0.2, but was much smaller in the second setting.

Other studies of drug cost sharing have looked at the effect of so called "triple tier" design where cost sharing is highest for non-preferred brand name drugs. The almost universal finding is that such cost sharing shifted prescribing and use away from the higher co-pay drugs. Its impact on overall drug spending depends on the comparator: if the comparator is a plan with a closed formulary (so no coverage at all for non-preferred drugs) it led to higher spending (Rector et al. 2003); but if the comparator was lower and uniform across the board set of co-payments there was a reduction in total use as well, not just a shift in patterns of use.

The behavior observed in these first three kinds of studies obviously depends on more than just consumer choice, since the consumer needs a physician prescription or order to obtain a prescription drug or many other non-emergency services. The broader issue of how physician behavior seems to change in response to changes or variation in patient cost sharing is just now beginning to be examined. Some older hypotheses about physician behavior suggested that physicians try to achieve a target income, or at least try to offset the impact of external changes which reduce their income (Evans 1974). Simple versions of this hypothesis are obviously inconsistent with the finding that cost sharing reduces the use of physician services or services from which physicians benefit; if the target income hypothesis were literally true, doctors would increase patient demand enough by inducement to offset the effects of cost sharing. But there is some evidence for physician inducement especially in response to exogenous reductions in the gross price for their services (Yip 1998). Probably both inducement and cost sharing affect the quantity that ends up being provided. But how the exchange of information, physician orders, and patient psychology interact to produce this blended result is unknown.

Another insight that incorporates physician behavior notes that physicians may well respond differently to changes in their patients' cost sharing when the change occurs for a large number of patients (as often happens in real markets) rather than for just a tiny fraction of patients (as in the Rand experiment and the cross sectional studies using individual data). A plausible assumption is that physicians would prefer to treat all of their patients with a given illness of a given severity approximately the same; this is less costly (in monetary and effort terms) than paying attention to each patient's insurance coverage (Glied and Zivin 2002). There are costs to "pattern of practice" differentiation in a physician practice as in other markets. And it may be ethically uncomfortable to treat differently based on insurance rather than on illness state only. Both of these reasons have been offered as explanations for the Rand finding that cost sharing did not affect the cost per treated episode (although a censoring story, in which people with high sharing only seek treatment for severe illness, could also explain that result). There is evidence that the care a given patient gets may depend on the insurance coverage of others in the local market as well as on that person's insurance status (Pauly 1979; Pagán and Pauly 2006, 2005). The strongest evidence that demand response is greater for a large-scale change is offered by a recent study by Finkelstein (2007) that looked at the effect of the introduction of Medicare in the United States (which dramatically lowered average cost sharing); the estimated response in terms of both use and spending was much greater than would have been implied by the Rand experiment elasticities. The response was especially large for newer technologies which would have needed a large total market to be profitable.

16.11 INSURANCE DEDUCTIBLES AND THE USE OF MEDICAL CARE

Public and private health insurance frequently contains deductibles—money amounts per time period (or, occasionally, per illness) that must be paid out of pocket before any insurance benefits are paid. In the pure theory of insurance, Arrow (1963) showed that, with proportional administrative loading, optimal coverage is full coverage above a deductible. The intuition behind this conclusion is that the marginal risk premium for losses relative to the mean becomes vanishingly small as the size of the loss shrinks, and therefore becomes less than the marginal loading, which remains positive. This rationale for a deductible is only strengthened if the administrative cost structure also has a positive marginal cost per claim; insurance will not be worthwhile for a set of small claims amounting to a small total amount.

When the consumer has price-sensitive demand for care, the influence of deductibles on spending is complex because a deductible in effect faces the consumer with a two part block tariff: full price up to a certain level of total spending, and then low or zero marginal price. Since the marginal price is different depending on whether the deductible is covered or not, the consumer has to consider the distribution of expected expenses (See Zweifel and Manning 2000 for a discussion of such models). While the actual analytics of demand responsiveness are complicated by a deductible—since the relevant empirical price depends on the (expected) distribution of expenses over the different ranges of marginal prices—the main intuitive finding is obvious: the lower the deductible the higher the demand for care, other things equal.

There has been some policy interest in the effects of deductibles on spending because of the controversy about high deductible health plans/health savings accounts arrangements in the United States and their supposedly large effects on demand. One issue is the impact of a deductible when the cost of a treated illness is sure to exceed the deductible. Some critics of high deductible plans point out that, regardless of the size of the deductible, the *ex post* marginal price will be zero, and conclude that there should be little effect on demand from high deductibles and that they would expose people to higher financial risk. However, this argument only follows if the realized zero marginal price is the only one facing all potential buyers of high cost treatment. Somewhat surprisingly, the Rand experiment showed that this conjecture is empirically incorrect and that cost sharing does matter for the use of high-cost treatment. The reason is probably because cost sharing affects the consumer/patient's decision to initiate treatment that will turn out to be high cost. Think of an inpatient hospital admission for some illness; any inpatient care in the United States is virtually certain to have a high cost that exceeds the maximum permitted deductible in tax subsidized high deductible health plans. But the higher the deductible, the higher the out of pocket cost of initiating that episode of care. An increase in the deductible does not have to discourage many admissions to save a lot (although the Rand experiment does say that low deductibles have the strongest marginal effect on total medical spending). A more correct analysis would exempt hospital admissions known to be virtually non-discretionary (like care following a heart attack or serious burn accident) from high deductibles.

The other controversial issue concerns the impact of high deductibles on the use of prevention and early treatment. The conventional wisdom is that high deductibles or exclusions will thereby discourage their use. Some high deductible plans, in response to this concern, exempt a small number of highly effective preventive services from the deductible. The higher user price from a high deductible would, in isolation, discourage the use of preventive or early care that might have reduced the cost of some illness. But a key question is the extent of patient cost sharing should the illness occur. If the deductible is high enough that a large portion of the cost of the potential illness is also under the deductible, there should be an offsetting and potentially strong incentive to pay out of pocket for prevention or early care, since it avoids yet higher out of pocket payments later on. (If the cost of an episode of flu will still be under the deductible, it will pay for me to get a flu shot even if it is also not covered.) Conversely, if most of the cost of the illness is above the deductible, there will be a weaker incentive to use preventive care. So one cannot generalize a priori.

16.12 MORAL HAZARD AND VALUE-BASED COST SHARING: THEORY AND EVIDENCE

There are many interesting threads introduced by consideration of physician–patient interactions. One particular issue concerns the level of patient knowledge of marginal benefit from care. A conventional demand model (as applied to medical care or anything else) assumes that the buyer makes some estimate of the (marginal) benefit from various quantities of various goods in deciding how much to demand. In principle one could specify a level of information that is less than complete as an additional demand influence; in simple modeling consumers are usually assumed to be as well-informed as is possible, and to behave according to their well-informed demand curves.

If patients do not have correct perceptions of the marginal benefit from consumption of medical care, they may make incorrect decisions. There may therefore be scope for altering cost sharing away from the level that would have been ideal with correct information and toward the level that would push people to the right choice. An alternative is to provide them with correct information. There are three reasons why a consumer/patient may not have correct perception of the marginal benefit from some care: (1) the patient may be deciding whether or not to initiate an episode of care based on symptoms and knowledge that do not allow the patient to know whether treatment of the symptoms or illness is beneficial, or beneficial enough relative to cost; (2) having initiated an episode of treatment by contacting a physician, the physician may not have been able to convey or convince the patients about the marginal benefit from care; (3) if use of care has interaction effects on demands for other kinds of care, insurance coverage of the costs of those other kinds of care may disguise the expected total correct marginal cost of close substitutes or complements.

Let us consider the third case in the context of preventive care which causes cost offsets (reductions) in the use of other medical care. Assume that the patient is correctly informed about the health benefits (in terms of reduced future probability of illness). If there was no insurance coverage for either "prevention" or "treatment" (say, because the cost of either or both fell below the deductible on a policy), then the patient would face optimal incentives: pay for the preventive care if the combination of the value of improved future health and future treatment cost savings is greater than the cost of the preventive service. In contrast, if insurance covered all of the cost of treatment but none of the cost of prevention, in deciding on consumption of preventive care the patient would ignore the cost savings. One way to improve incentives would be to offer treatment coverage at reduced premiums for those who had already bought preventive care, but another way would be to have insurance cover some of the cost of preventive care. The ideal incentive would reduce the price of the preventive treatment by the expected value of the cost offset.

So far, the issue of the demand for prevention has not arisen. If the preventive service is binary—you either get a flu shot or you do not—the shape of the demand curve for prevention from a given population of people insured for treatment depends on the distribution of reservation prices for prevention. This in turn will depend on any nonmonetary cost for the preventive service—values consumers place on pain, time, or inconvenience, and the value they place on avoiding the adverse health outcome, given the treatment they would expect to consume. If reservation prices are all above the value of the improved health outcome, there is no gain from lowering the user price of preventive care, since all would use it anyway. If some reservation prices are below the full cost of the preventive service, there will be a larger gain at any level of coverage the more price responsive is demand; this is the benign moral hazard discussed by Pauly and Held (1990). Gain is maximized at any level of demand elasticity by setting the incentive at the optimal level, but the amount of gain (and therefore the offset against any transactions cost from a subsidy) is greater the higher the price responsiveness.

Now let us consider the case in which there is no cost offset but patients have not been correctly informed about marginal benefit (or the discount rate for future benefits). With correct information, the more elastic the schedule of marginal benefit, the higher is the optimal level of co-insurance. If marginal benefit is uniformly under-estimated, Pauly and Blavin (2008) show that co-insurance rates should be lower than under correct estimation, but should still vary inversely with demand elasticity or price responsiveness. In the case of over-estimation of marginal benefit, co-insurance should be higher than in the correct information case but also vary inversely with responsiveness. One additional finding of interest: if it is costly to correct under-estimation of marginal benefit, it may be preferable to use lower co-insurance (which also provides better risk protection) to move use closer to the optimal point than to provide information. The reason is that reducing co-insurance increases risk protection, and so has a negative cost, whereas information provision has a positive cost.

16.13 Moral Hazard and New Technology

Medical care spending rises in developed countries largely because of changes in technology which improve the quality of care but at a higher net cost. Higher levels of cost sharing reduce cost and use when they are implemented, but have no theoretically predictable effect of the rate of growth of spending. This is because, without more specific assumptions, we should assume that they reduce the rate of use of any new technology by the same proportional amount as they reduce the base of use of older technology; with equiproportional reductions in base and increment, the rate of growth remains the same.

Empirical evidence on techniques to reduce moral hazard in new technology has not yet produced definitive results. Aggressive managed care, such as that embodied in staff or group model HMOs, seems to reduce use and spending below fee-for-service counterparts with the same (very small or zero) cost sharing, but not compared to coverage with typical cost sharing, and it does not seem to reduce the rate of growth in spending across the board. There is some evidence from US aggregate data that lower overall proportions of out of pocket payment are associated with higher rates of growth of spending (Peden and Freeland 1998). A complete model which determines the rate of investment in technological change, the rate and form of introduction of new technology, and the ideal level or pattern of insurance cost sharing has yet to be determined. Insurers could potentially use cost sharing and coverage to select different rates of growth in spending and technology, especially if insurers retain the power to refuse to cover (set co-insurance below 100%) for new technologies whose adoption under lower levels of co-insurance might make insured populations worse off (Goddeeris 1984a and 1984b). Definitive results on the actual or ideal relationship between insurance coverage and spending growth have yet to be established.

16.14 Beneficent Moral Hazard in Social Insurance

While the bulk of the normative economic theory dealing with the impact of insurance on the use of care views such an impact as having a negative effect both on welfare and the demand for insurance, health policy discussion by policymakers and health advocates frequently views patient cost sharing with considerable apprehension, and not just because it is a necessary evil to control spending. Instead, public policy in all countries views both health insurance and the increase in use (or "improvement in access") associated with such insurance as positively desirable. Obviously there is not a large volume of economic research consistent with this view, but are there economic interpretations and theories (beyond the cost offset or patient adherence considerations) that would conclude that cost sharing lower than that suggested by insurance theory is socially desirable?

One approach that leads to such a conclusion begins with the observation or assumption that there may be external benefits at the margin from the use of medical services and goods in excess of that which uninsured consumers would choose. Externalities can come from two main sources: contagious disease (Phelps 2003) and altruistic concern for others' health or care use (Pauly 1971). Given the relatively small share of spending attributable to preventable or treatable contagious disease in developed countries, the second rationale is of potentially greater quantitative significance. The fundamental model can be described in words: add the demand or marginal valuation of care by others in the community to that of each individual, equate the summed marginal evaluation to marginal cost to define the optimal quantity, determine the user price (below market price) at which demand equals the optimal quantity, and use subsidies, mandates, or regulations to make sure that insurance lowers user price to at least this level. For the well-off, the insurance and care they would demand without subsidies is likely to display little or no external benefit at the margin—they use "enough" care—but especially for low-income households the level of coverage may well be determined at the margin by this care-specific altruistic externality (Folland, Goodman, and Stano 2009).

Despite the obvious importance of social insurance in determining the insurance coverage people have and the obvious importance of this theory in specifying the optimal form of social insurance, there is relatively little research on it. The rationale for social insurance is sometimes specified instead as dealing with market failure, especially the possibility of adverse selection (Zweifel, Breyer, and Kiffmann 2009), or as a version of optimal taxation theory (Petretto 1999); in these cases the more traditional moral hazard theory would apply. In a study to present the case for universal health insurance, the Institute of Medicine (2003) measured benefit by human capital (discounted future earnings attributed to health improvements associated with insurance), rather than appealing to any social benefits.

There has been some work relating choice of generosity of coverage to taxpayer demand based on altruism (Grannemann 1980; Holahan and Chang 1989) but no direct test of the connection between coverage, private demand, and public demand. One implication of this theory is that a necessary condition for optimal coverage is that the medical care use induced by lower cost sharing is still cost effective at the margin, where the value of health is the sum of the patients' and society's willingness to pay. There have been some attempts to monetize the societal willingness to pay but the distinction between private benefits (I want to pay taxes for Medicare because I will value my improved health outcomes when I am on Medicare) and social benefits (I want to pay taxes for Medicare because I will value improved health outcomes for old people other than myself) is usually not made.

One possible explanation for the lack of attention to the design of insurance in this context is that the most prominent target population, poor households, would demand socially suboptimal levels of care even when there is no cost sharing and coverage is complete. In US Medicaid, for example, cost sharing is usually zero or nominal at best. Any limitation on volume of care is produced by changing the level of provider fees or other influences on access, rather than by manipulating buyer demand. When income rises high enough for cost sharing to be relevant, perhaps social concern at the margin (except for very high risk people) is close to zero. Or more generally, social insurance systems may prefer to use supply side incentives to affect quantities rather than insurance coverage per se.

16.15 Conclusion

Insurance coverage does affect the use and cost of medical care, and so potentially can play a role in assuring that spending comes closer to the (second best) optimum. (The first best optimum requires so-far infeasible indemnity insurance.) But the information for making judgments about the value of care whose use is discouraged by cost sharing has so far not proven universally definitive and not even persuasive where it is reasonably definitive. Disentangling the intricate web of insurance coverage for medical services with interrelated demands and with demand subject to different levels and types of misinformation is a daunting challenge, but one worth accepting.

References

Austvoll-Dahlgren, A., Aaserud, M., Vist, G., Ramsay, C., Oxman, A., Sturm, H., Kösters, J., and Vernby, A. (2008). Pharmaceutical policies: effects of cap and co-payment on rational drug use. *Cochrane Database of Systematic Reviews*, 1: Art. No. CD007017, DOI:10.1002/14651850.CD 007017.

Arrow, K. J. (1963). Uncertainty and the welfare economics of medical care. *American Economic Review*, 53(5), 941–73.

Brown, J. R., and Finkelstein, A. (2007). Why is the market for long-term care insurance so small? *Journal of Public Economics*, 91(10), 1967–91.

—— (2008). The interaction of public and private insurance: Medicaid and the long-term care insurance market. *American Economic Review*, 98(3), 1083–102.

Buchmueller, T. C., Grumbach, K., Kronick, R., and Kahn, J. G. (2005). Book review: the effect of health insurance on medical care utilization and implications for insurance expansion: A review of the literature. *Medical Care Research and Review*, 62(1), 3–30.

Cardon, J. H., and Hendel, I. (2001). Asymmetric Information in health Insurance: evidence from the National Medical Expenditure Survey. *RAND Journal of Economics*, 32(3), 408–27.

CHERNEW, M. E., ROSEN, A. B., and FENDRICK, M. A. (2007). Value-based insurance design. *Health Affairs*, 26(2), w195–w203.

DANZON, P., and PAULY, M. V. (2002). Health insurance and the growth in pharmaceutical expenditures. *The Journal of Law and Economics*, XLV(2, Part 2), 587–613.

DE MEZA, D. (1983). Health insurance and the demand for medical care. *Journal of Health Economics*, 2(1), 47–54.

EICHNER, M. J. (1998). The demand for medical care: what people pay does matter. *American Economic Review*, 88(2), 117–21.

ELLIS, R. P., and MCGUIRE, T. G. (1993). Supply-side and demand-side cost sharing in health care. *Journal of Economic Perspectives*, 7(4), 135–51.

EVANS, R. G. (1974). Supplier-induced demand: some empirical evidence and implications. In M. Perlman, ed., *The Economics of Health and Medical Care* (pp. 162–73). Edinburgh: Macmillan.

FINKELSTEIN, A. (2007). The aggregate effects of health insurance: evidence from the introduction of Medicare. *Quarterly Journal of Economics*, 122(1), 1–37.

FOLLAND, S., GOODMAN, A., and STANO, M. (2009). *Economics of health and health care*, 6th edition (pp. 392–94). Upper Saddle River, NJ: Prentice Hall.

GAYNOR, M., HAAS-WILSON, D., and VOGT, W. B. (2000). Are invisible hands good hands? Moral hazard, competition, and the second-best in health care markets. *Journal of Political Economy*, 108(5), 992–1005.

—— LI, J., and VOGT, W. (2006). Is drug coverage a free lunch? Cross-price elasticities and the design of prescription drug benefits. NBER Working Paper No. 12758.

GLIED, S., and ZIVIN, J. G. (2002). How do doctors behave when some (but not all) of their patients are in managed care? *Journal of Health Economics*, 21(2), 337–53.

GODDEERIS, J. H. (1984a). Insurance and incentives for innovation in medical care. *Southern Economic Journal*, 51(2), 530–39.

—— (1984b). Medical insurance, technical change and welfare. *Economic Inquiry*, 22(1), 56–67.

GRANNEMANN, T. (1980). Reforming national health: Programs for the poor. In Mark Pauly, ed., *National Health Insurance: What Now? What Later? What Never?* Washington, DC: American Enterprise Institute.

GROSSMAN, M. (1972). On the concept of health capital and the demand for health. *Journal of Political Economy*, 80(2), 223–55.

HILLMAN, A. L., ESCARCE, J. J., RIPLEY, K., GAYNOR, M., CLOUSE, J., and ROSS, R. (1999). Financial incentives and drug spending in managed care. *Health Affairs*, 18(2), 189–200.

HOLAHAN, J., and CHANG, D. (1989). *Medicaid Spending in the 1980s*. Washington, DC: Urban Institute Press.

INSTITUTE OF MEDICINE (2003). *Hidden costs, value lost: uninsurance in America*. Washington, DC: Committee on the Consequences of Uninsurance, Institute of Medicine.

MA, C.-T., and MCGUIRE, T. (1997). Optimal health insurance and provider payment. *The American Economic Review*, 87(4), 685–704.

NEWHOUSE, J. P. (2006). Reconsidering the moral hazard–risk avoidance tradeoff. *Journal of Health Economics*, 25(5), 1005–14.

—— and THE INSURANCE EXPERIMENT GROUP (1993). *Free for all? Lessons for the Health Insurance Experiment*. Cambridge, MA: Harvard University Press.

NYMAN, J. (1999). The economics of moral hazard revisited. *Journal of Health Economics*, 18(6), 811–24.

PAGÁN, J. A., and PAULY, M. V. (2005). Access to conventional medical care and the use of complementary and alternative medicine. *Health Affairs*, 24(1), 255–62.

—— —— (2006). Community-level uninsurance and the unmet medical needs of insured and uninsured adults. *Health Services Research*, 41(3, Pt 1), 788–803.

PAULY, M. V. (1968). The economics of moral hazard. *American Economic Review*, 58(3), 531–37.

—— (1971). *Medical Care at Public Expense: A Study in Applied Welfare Economics*. New York: Praeger Publishers, Inc.

—— (1979). *Doctors and Their Workshops*. Chicago: University of Chicago Press.

—— (2005). Effects of health insurance on use of care and outcomes for young women. *The American Economic Review*, 95(2), 219–23.

—— (2008). Adverse selection and moral hazard: implications for insurance markets. In F. A. Sloan and H. Kasper, eds., *Incentives and Choice in Health and Health Care* (pp. 103–29). Cambridge, MA: MIT Press.

—— and BLAVIN, F. E. (2008). Moral hazard in insurance, value-based cost sharing, and the benefits of blissful ignorance. *Journal of Health Economics*, 27(6), 1407–17.

—— and HELD, P. J. (1990). Benign moral hazard and the cost effectiveness of insurance coverage. *Journal of Health Economics*, 9(4), 447–61.

—— and RAMSEY, S. D. (1999). Would you like suspenders to go with that belt? An analysis of optimal combinations of cost sharing and managed care. *Journal of Health Economics*, 18(4), 443–58.

PEDEN, E. A., and FREELAND, M. S. (1998). Insurance effects on US medical spending (1960–1993). *Health Economics*, 7(8), 671–87.

PETRETTO, A. (1999). Optimal social health insurance with supplementary private insurance. *Journal of Health Economics*, 18(6), 727–45.

PHELPS, C. E. (2003). *Health Economics*, 3rd edition. New York: Pearson Addison-Wesley.

RECTOR, T. S., FINCH, M. D., DANZON, P. M., PAULY, M. V., and MANDA, B.S. (2003). Effect of tiered prescription copayments on the use of preferred brand medications. *Medical Care*, 41(3), 398–406.

THOMSON, S., MOSSIALOS, E., and JEMIAI, N. (2003). *Cost Sharing for Health Services in the European Union*. London: London School of Economics, LSE Health and Social Care.

TOWN, R. J. (2008). Adverse selection, welfare and the optimal pricing of employer-sponsored health plans. Paper presented at Leonard Davis Institute Research Seminar, December 3, 2008, Wharton School, University of Pennsylvania, Philadelphia, PA.

WAGSTAFF, A. (2008). Measuring financial protection in health. World Bank Policy Research Working Paper No. 4554.

YIP, W. C. (1998). Physician response to Medicare fee reductions: changes in the volume of Coronary Artery Bypass Graft (CABG) surgeries in the Medicare and private sectors. *Journal of Health Economics*, 17(6), 675–99.

ZECKHAUSER, R. (1970). Medical insurance: A case study of the tradeoff between risk spreading and appropriate incentives. *Journal of Economic Theory*, 2(1), 10–26.

ZWEIFEL, P. J., and MANNING, W. G. (2000). Moral hazard and consumer incentives in health care. In A. J. Culyer and J. P. Newhouse, eds., *Handbook of Health Economics*, Volume 1A (pp. 409–59). Amsterdam: Elsevier.

—— BREYER, F., and KIFMANN, M. (2009). *Health Economics*, 2nd Edition. New York: Springer-Verlag New York, LLC.

CHAPTER 17

··

GUARANTEED ACCESS TO AFFORDABLE COVERAGE IN INDIVIDUAL HEALTH INSURANCE MARKETS*

··

WYNAND P. M. M. VAN DE VEN AND
FREDERIK T. SCHUT

17.1 INTRODUCTION

··

IN a competitive health insurance market insurers have to charge a sufficient premium for each contract to cover the expected costs (claims as well as loading costs). Given the huge variation in predicted health expenses among individuals, this pricing strategy would clearly make health insurance unaffordable to most high-risk individuals.

A straightforward way to guarantee universal access to health insurance is to eliminate competition. Indeed, quite a number of countries have introduced a social health insurance scheme that is administered by a single payer or non-competing insurers, i.e. multiple insurers without any consumer choice of insurer (e.g. Canada, France, Italy, Japan). An important drawback of such a scheme, however, is that effective incentives for efficiency and innovation are difficult to arrange. For that reason, an increasing number of countries have introduced competition among health insurance carriers within the context of a social health insurance scheme (e.g. Belgium, Czech Republic, Germany, Israel, Netherlands, Slovakia, Switzerland, and USA-Medicare).

---

* Parts of this chapter have been presented at the Workshop "The Structure of Health Plan Competition" (May 3–4, 2007) as a part of the project "FRESH-thinking" directed by Ezekiel J. Emanuel and Victor R. Fuchs (see <http://www.fresh-thinking.org/>). The authors thank the workshop participants, Sherry Glied and Peter Smith for their comments on a previous draft.

Since universal access is the rationale of having a social health insurance scheme, the key question is: *How to guarantee access to affordable coverage for the high risks in the individual insurance market?* This is the central question of this chapter.

In this chapter we deal with individual insurance, and not with group insurance, which is the dominant form of private health insurance in e.g. the USA (for the advantages and disadvantages of employer group health insurance, see e.g. Enthoven and Fuchs 2006; and Pauly et al. 1999). The only way to make individual health insurance affordable for the high risks is to organize implicit or explicit cross-subsidies from low-risk to high-risk individuals. Both the type of subsidies and the organization of the payment of subsidies can differ, however, and may have different welfare effects. In this chapter we provide a taxonomy of the various types of subsidies and discuss the welfare effects for each of these types. Furthermore, for the theoretically preferred type of subsidy we discuss the implications of the way the subsidy payments are organized.

This chapter is organized as follows. In section 17.2 we will discuss three different strategies health insurers can employ to achieve equivalence of premiums and expected costs per insurance contract. In section 17.3 we examine the various types of subsidies. Section 17.4 discusses the advantages and disadvantages of community-rated premiums, being a popular way of rate regulation in many countries. In section 17.5 we point out the implications of the different ways of organizing the payment flows of risk-adjusted subsidies. Section 17.6 concludes.

17.2 EQUIVALENCE OF PREMIUMS AND RISKS

A competitive insurance market tends towards *equivalence* between the premium and the expected costs (claims as well as loading costs) for each contract. That is, insurers must charge a sufficient premium for each contract to cover the expected costs. They cannot compensate predictable losses on the contracts with the high risks by making predictable profits on the low risks, because competition minimizes predictable profits. An insurer can use three different strategies to achieve equivalence of premiums and expected costs per contract:

1. *risk rating*: adjusting the premium for each product to the individual's risk;
2. *risk segmentation*: adjusting the product (e.g. coverage, benefits design) to attract different risk groups per product and charge premiums accordingly;
3. *risk selection*: adjusting the accepted risk to the stated premium of a given product.

If insurers pursue only the first strategy (risk rating), they would have to charge widely varying premiums to different individuals, since the individual variation in expected health care costs is tremendous. Only adjusting for age, the highest premium would already be more than ten times the lowest one (ranging from less than €500 per year at the age of 15 to over €5000 at the age of 85). Moreover, the age-related variation in health care expenditure is increasing over time (Buchner and Wasem 2006). In addition to age, insurers can easily identify other risk factors, such as whether the individual suffers from a severe chronic disease. For instance, the expected medical costs of people suffering from renal failure, lymphatic cancer or spinal cord injury are about €80,000 per year (Stam 2007). Clearly, in a competitive insurance market health insurance would be unaffordable for many high-risk individuals if health insurers fully adjust premiums to the individuals' risk.

In practice, even in quite competitive health insurance markets we do not observe such a wide premium variation (Van de Ven et al. 2000; Herring and Pauly 2001). Health insurers do not fully adjust premiums to the underlying individual risk because the necessary information may not be available or only at very high cost, or because insurers fear that this may harm their reputation (Newhouse 1996). Moreover, to some extent cross-subsidies among different risk groups may be sustainable, because consumers are not perfectly informed about their risk type and face non-trivial switching costs (Van de Ven and van Vliet 1995).

In addition to risk rating, health insurers typically also pursue the other two strategies (risk segmentation and risk selection). First, by offering different insurance products, insurers can encourage self selection (e.g. by offering a high-deductible plan to attract low risk individuals, see e.g. Tollen et al. 2004). Under certain conditions self-selection may result in a separating equilibrium in which the market is segmented according to risk type (Rothschild and Stiglitz 1976; Wilson 1977). In the extreme, each risk type buys a separate coverage at an actuarially fair premium. This outcome differs from risk rating in the sense that low-risk groups are forced to signal their risk by purchasing less than full coverage. Second, by medical underwriting, refusing high-risk applicants or by excluding treatments for pre-existing conditions from coverage, health insurers can select risks directly (Schut 1995).

Risk segmentation and risk selection may be attractive because these strategies may be less expensive than refined risk-rating and are likely to be less visible than charging extremely high premiums. Whereas risk rating makes coverage *less affordable* for the high risks, risk segmentation and risk selection make full coverage *less available*, either to low risks in case of self-selection (in which case the high risks may have an affordability problem) or to high risks in case of selective underwriting. In both ways, guaranteed access to affordable coverage for the high risks is jeopardized. In fact, in a competitive market health insurers can only provide protection against *unpredictable* variation of costs *during the contract period* (usually a year). If a healthy person gets a serious disease and becomes a high risk, the insurer may either raise the premium in the next contract period, or may refuse to renew the contract. To prevent such premium shocks and loss of insurance Cochrane (1995) proposed insurance contracts with state-contingent severance payments. Based on such a contract a person who is diagnosed with a long-term illness would receive from his insurer a lump sum equal to the increased present value of future premiums. This lump sum would allow the consumer to pay the future higher premiums. Although elegant in theory, in practice such insurance against rises in future premiums is not offered. A reason may be that, given the uncertainty about future new medical technologies, insurers are not able to make an accurate actuarial calculation of the present discounted value of someone's future *life-long* additional expenses and/or their calculations may give rise to a lot of dispute with their consumers. Cochrane (1995: 465) admits that "contracts contingent on undreamed-of inventions are obviously impractical" and suggests that some "disinterested third party" should decide "how much health expenses should adapt to unexpected changes in technology." At best such a third party could only partly solve the problem, and to enforce the premium surcharges would require substantial regulation, which seems at odds with Cochrane's plea for deregulation. In addition, time-consistent insurance contracts would require a mechanism to pay and receive severance payments (e.g. a special account for each consumer) that can be enforced and is understandable to both consumers and courts. This does not seem likely, and even Cochrane seems skeptical about the prospects that courts will understand these contracts and will be prepared to enforce the necessary severance payments. So in practice a major market failure is that there is no insurance against the financial risk of becoming a future high risk (Newhouse 1984; Pauly 1992).

17.3 CROSS-SUBSIDIES

To simplify our analysis, we assume that health insurers are bound to an *open enrollment* (or *guaranteed issue*) requirement. This implies that insurers must accept each applicant for a *standard coverage*. In practice, open enrollment is required in all countries with a competitive social health insurance market. As long as insurers are free in setting premiums, this assumption is non-restrictive, because insurers are allowed to risk-adjust the premium for each applicant and can offer each type of policy in addition to the policy with the standardized coverage. By this assumption the problem of unavailability that would occur in case of rejection or coverage restrictions is essentially transformed into a problem of *unaffordability* (high premiums for high-risk individuals) to be solved by cross-subsidies from low-risk to high-risk individuals.

We distinguish two main categories of subsidies to make individual health insurance affordable for the high risks: *explicit* premium subsidies and *implicit* cross-subsidies. These two categories of subsidies can be used on their own or in combination.

17.3.1 Explicit Subsidies

Explicit subsidies involve transfers of money to high-risk individuals in order to enable them to buy health insurance. Examples of *explicit* subsidies are vouchers, tax deductions, tax credits, and employers' contributions to an employee's individual health insurance. The subsidy system can be organized by a *sponsor* (e.g. government, a large employer, or a coalition of employers) such that high-risk persons who are confronted with unaffordable premiums receive a premium subsidy from a subsidy fund, which is filled by mandatory contributions. The subsidies may be earmarked for the purchase of specified insurance coverage. In this chapter we do not focus on how the subsidy fund is filled. For different ways of financing the subsidy fund and related distributional issues see Blomqvists' Chapter 12 in this volume.

17.3.1.1 Risk-adjusted vs. Premium-based Subsidies

Two types of explicit premium subsidies can be distinguished: (1) *premium-based subsidies*, which depend on the level of the premium paid (Van de Ven 2006; Zweifel and Breuer 2006); (2) *risk-adjusted subsidies*, which depend on the risk factors that the insurers use in a free market, such as age and health status.

Premium-based subsidies are not optimal for the following three reasons. First, they reduce the incentive for high-risk consumers to shop around for the lowest premium, and thereby reduce the insurers' incentive for efficiency. They reduce the competitive advantage of the most efficient insurers and reduce overall price competition. Second, they stimulate the high-risk consumers to buy more (complete) insurance than they would have done in case of no subsidy at the margin, resulting in a welfare loss due to additional moral hazard caused by over-insurance. Third, premium-based subsidies create a misallocation of subsidies. The magnitude of the premiums is determined by many factors, not all of which the sponsor may want to use for determining the subsidies. Assume that the total set of factors that determine insurers' premiums can be divided into two subsets: those factors for which cross-subsidies are desired by the sponsor, the S(ubsidy)-type factors; and those for which cross-subsidies are not desired, the N(on-subsidy)-type factors (Van de Ven and Ellis 2000: 768–9). In most countries age, gender, and health status will probably be considered as S-type risk factors, at least to a certain extent. But the sponsor could decide that the differences in premiums that are caused by other factors, should not be reflected in the subsidies. Potential N-type factors that may result in premium variation are, for example, differences in efficiency among health insurers, regional differences in supply and prices, variations in practice style of contracted health care providers, and differences in individual consumer characteristics such as lifestyle, health behavior, preventive behavior, and taste. If subsidies for health insurance premiums are given *irrespective of the cause of the premium differences*, as is the case with premium-based subsidies, they most likely result in a misallocation of subsidies. The relevance of the distinction between S-type and N-type factors can be illustrated by the decision of the Belgian government that regional variation in supply (e.g. the per capita number of providers and hospital beds) is explicitly considered an N-type risk factor, for which the subsidies should not be adjusted. Schokkaert and Van de Voorde (2003: table 2) illustrate the non-trivial impact of this political decision on the subsidies.

Risk-adjusted subsidies do not suffer from the above mentioned problems. First, risk-adjusted subsidies can be specifically based on S-type risk factors that insurers use in their premium setting. To the extent that a risk factor (e.g. region) reflects S-type (e.g. health) as well as N-type (e.g. over-supply, high prices, inefficiency) factors, the sponsor must decide to what extent premium increases due to this risk factor will (not) be subsidized. Second, in case of risk-adjusted subsidies consumers are fully price sensitive at the margin. This avoids the other two problems of premium-based subsidies. The sponsor has to decide about the cost level of the services, including the quality and the intensity of treatment, which it considers to be acceptable to be subsidized.

Risk-adjusted subsidies can make health insurance affordable *every new contract period*. If a person's health status deteriorates over time and consequently the insurer has to increase the person's premium to cover the higher expected costs, the future subsidy value will be adjusted to the change in the individual's risk characteristics. In this sense risk-adjusted subsidies provide protection against the financial risk of becoming a future high-risk.

If consumers would receive a risk-adjusted subsidy based on the same risk factors that insurers use, the differences in out-of-pocket-premiums (i.e. premium minus subsidy) would be minimal and would primarily reflect differences in quality, taste, loading fee or efficiency.

The effectiveness of risk-adjusted subsidies to reduce the differences in out-of-pocket-premiums depends on the one hand on the risk factors that the sponsor uses for calculating the risk-adjusted subsidies; and on the other hand on the risk factors that the insurers use for calculating the risk-adjusted premiums and the other tools they have to segment the market.

As pointed out in Box 17.1 for several reasons risk-adjusted subsidies might be insufficient, at least in the short run. Therefore, although premium-based subsidies are not

---

Box 17.1 Reasons Why Risk–adjusted Subsidies may be Insufficient to Guarantee Affordable Coverage for all High–Risk Individuals, at Least in the Short Run

1. In a dynamic insurance market, where insurers develop new risk factors for setting their premiums, it may take some time before the sponsor includes these new risk factors in the subsidy formula.
2. Insurers and the sponsor may use slightly different definitions of certain (new) risk factors or risk classes, which may result in too low subsidies for certain groups.
3. To prevent incentives for inefficiency, the sponsor may not want to (fully) subsidize certain risk factors. For example, an insurer may classify an applicant as a diabetes patient because of the prior use of insulin, which cost €500 per year. If diabetes patients on average have €3500 above average expenses, the insurer will charge a premium that is €3500 above average. If the sponsor would "reward" this type of risk classification with an additional subsidy of €3500, it would give a perverse incentive to the insurers for unnecessarily classifying applicants as a diabetes patient. However, if the sponsor does not subsidize these risk factors because of these perverse incentives, risk-adjusted payments will be insufficient for the concerned risk group.
4. The sponsor's transaction costs may be too high to find out what all the relevant risk factors are that insurers use in practice (see section 17.3.1.2).
5. Certain groups of high-risk individuals are too small, so that the law of the large numbers is not applicable (see section 17.3.1.2).

optimal, they may provide a (temporary) complement to risk-adjusted subsidies for certain (income-)groups. Alternatively, the sponsor may create a safety-net such that nobody pays more for health insurance than a certain percentage of income.

The transaction costs of giving risk-adjusted subsidies directly to consumers are high. Each consumer must inform the sponsor about his or her risk factors, such as age, gender, prior health care utilization, and health status. These transaction costs can be substantially reduced by giving the subsidies to the insurers, who in a transparent competitive market are forced to reduce each consumer's premium with the per capita subsidy they receive for this consumer. By giving risk-adjusted subsidies to the insurers the different risks that consumers represent for the insurers are equalized. We therefore refer to this way of organizing the risk-adjusted subsidies as *"risk equalization"* (see Box 17.4). In practice, all countries that apply risk-adjusted subsidies do this in the form of risk equalization (see section 17.5).

17.3.1.2 *Excess-loss Compensations*

A problem may occur if insurers are not able to accurately adjust the premium to a consumer's risk, either because it is too costly to collect sufficient information or because the group of applicants is too small, so that the law of the large numbers is not applicable. This may be particularly relevant in the case of high-risk applicants with a rare disease. Insurers can reduce this problem by exchanging information about an individual's risk factors, if a consumer decides to switch to another insurer. In addition, insurers can develop a nation-wide standard rating model based on statistical information of all insurers. This will increase the accuracy of risk rating. (Although a standard rating model provides the nation-wide predicted per capita health expenses per risk category, in a competitive market it is essential that *each individual insurer sets its own premium rates.*) If, nevertheless, it is impossible or too costly for an insurer to risk-rate an applicant, the insurer may ask an extremely high premium if it is the case that he cannot reject the applicant because of an open-enrollment requirement (as we assume in this chapter).

If insurers cannot calculate a risk-adjusted premium for certain groups of high-risk applicants, most likely the sponsor cannot calculate risk-adjusted subsidies either. To solve this problem the sponsor can provide the insurers with a subsidy for high-risk subscribers in the form of *excess-loss compensations* (or *outlier payments*). For example, the insurers can be fully or partly compensated by the subsidy fund for an individual's expenses in excess of a certain annual threshold. (Excess-loss compensations can be considered as a form of mandatory reinsurance with community-rated reinsurance premiums.) These subsidies will substantially reduce the insurers' expenditures for consumers in the long right tail of the frequency distribution of health expenses. This will help the insurers to calculate a risk-adjusted premium for the high-risk applicants. In case of full compensation above the threshold, the threshold amount effectively functions as the maximum premium (excluding loading fees) for all insurers. The high risks clearly benefit more from this type of subsidy than the low risks. Excess-loss compensations are applied in several countries, for instance in Australia and the Netherlands

(Colombo and Tapay 2003). The advantages of excess-loss compensations have to be weighted against the disadvantage of reducing the insurers' incentive for efficiency.

17.3.2 Implicit Subsidies

A complementary or alternative strategy to make individual health insurance affordable for the high-risks in a competitive insurance market with open enrollment is to enforce regulations that *implicitly* result in cross-subsidies from low-risk to high-risk individuals. Two types of regulation to enforce implicit cross-subsidies can be discerned: (1) a *guaranteed renewability* requirement; and (2) *universal premium-rate restrictions*.

17.3.2.1 Guaranteed Renewability

In general a *guaranteed renewability* requirement obliges the insurers at the end of each contract period to renew the contract with their enrollees at the "standard premium and standard conditions" (see e.g. Pauly et al. 1995; Herring and Pauly 2006). To understand what this means, let us assume that we start with a homogeneous group of individuals who all have the same risk of developing a (new) serious disease during the contract period in question. All individuals have to pay an additional "guaranteed renewability fee" on top of their actuarially fair premium (i.e. a premium equal to the individual's expected costs during the contract period). This "guaranteed renewability fee" equals the present discounted value of the cost of protection against the risk that future premiums will be higher than the standard premium because of the onset of a chronic condition in the current contract period. The "guaranteed renewability fee" should be sufficient to allow the insurer to ask for all following contract periods a "standard premium" to his insured individuals, who during the contract period in question develop a serious disease and thereby become a high risk for the rest of their life (even if all others would switch to another insurer). The "guaranteed renewability fee" can be considered an implicit cross-subsidy from those whose risk remains unchanged towards the unlucky ones, who develop a serious disease in the contract period in question and will be a high risk for the following contact periods.

Given our assumption that insurers are obliged to enroll all applicants for a certain standard coverage, a guaranteed renewability requirement imposes a premium-rate restriction on insurers with respect to renewing the contract of their own enrollees, but not with respect to new applicants, who were previously insured with another insurer. A more stringent form of regulation is to universally impose premium-rate restrictions with respect to all potential applicants (see section 17.3.2.2). Whereas the aim of a guaranteed renewability clause is to create implicit cross-subsidies in the *future* periods towards those who during the current contract period become a high risk, the goal of applying universal premium-rate restrictions to all applicants is to create implicit cross-subsidies from the low-risks to the high-risks in the *current* contract period.

Guaranteed renewability has some major limitations (see Box 17.2). For example, guaranteed renewability cannot be combined with a free choice of health insurer *for the*

Box 17.2 Limitations of Guaranteed Renewability

Guaranteed renewability has several limitations (for some, see Pauly 1992 and Pauly et al. 1995):

1. A guaranteed-renewability requirement substantially reduces competition, since the high risks are "married with their insurer." This "lock-in" is a serious problem, if the chronically ill are dissatisfied with the quality of care or the benefits package offered by their insurer. They cannot switch at an affordable premium to another insurer, because the other insurers will ask them a much higher premium than the standard premium. In other words, *guaranteed renewability cannot be combined with a free consumer choice of health insurer for the high risks.*

2. The fact that high-risk individuals cannot switch to another insurer reduces insurers' incentives for efficiency, in particular after the low risks have left the pool.

3. A guaranteed-renewability clause cannot make health insurance affordable for those who at the start of the guaranteed-renewability requirement are already a high risk (and previously had no guaranteed-renewability contract).

4. Given the uncertainty about future new medical technologies, insurers most likely are not able to make an accurate actuarial calculation of the present discounted value of the future *life-long* additional expenses of those who in the contract period will become a high risk. For example, in 1960 it was nearly impossible to make a reliable estimate of the level of health expenses in 2010. In other words, it is highly questionable whether a guaranteed-renewability clause does really guarantee a "standard premium" fifty years later.

5. It is impossible to define the relevant standard policy conditions for a period of twenty to fifty years. Due to the development of new diagnostic tests, new treatments, new drugs and medical technology, the current benefit package is likely to be largely irrelevant fifty years later. This problem is particularly serious if the low risks leave the original pool and buy new products. This is very likely since the insurer has an incentive to open a new pool and attract healthy risks at lower premium than the standard premium. In other words, it is highly questionable whether a guaranteed-renewability clause does really guarantee a "standard coverage" fifty years later.

6. A guaranteed-renewability clause does not protect parents for the lifelong health care cost of new-born children with serious birth defects.

7. A guaranteed-renewability clause does not give a financial incentive for health-risk reducing behavior (which would exist in case of risk-adjusted premiums).

8. Finally, a guaranteed-renewability requirement provides insurers with an incentive to select against those applicants who have an above-average probability of becoming a future high-risk. One way to do so would be to exclude from coverage the drugs and providers who have the best reputation of dealing with diseases, for which a relatively large proportion of the incidence is genetically predictable.

high-risks because the "high risks are married with their insurer." This "lock-in" is a serious problem if the chronically ill are dissatisfied with the quality of care or the benefits package offered by their insurer. They cannot switch at an affordable premium to another insurer, because the other insurers will ask them a much higher premium than the standard premium. Another problem is that it is highly questionable whether a guaranteed-renewability clause can really guarantee a "standard coverage" and a "standard premium" fifty years later. These problems can be countered by implementing *universal* premium-rate restrictions.

17.3.2.2 *Universal Premium-rate Restrictions*

Universal premium-rate restrictions hold with respect to *all* applicants, i.e. not only those who want to renew a contract with the same insurer, but also those who were previously insured with another insurer. Universal premium-rate restrictions can take several forms: community rating, a ban on certain rating factors (e.g. health status, genetic information, duration of coverage, or claim experience) or rate-banding (i.e. a minimum and maximum premium). Community rating usually has the form of a requirement that insurers must charge the same premium (in case of risk-equalization: the same out-of-pocket-premium) for the same product to each enrollee, independent of the enrollee's risk. The goal of such regulation is to create implicit cross-subsidies from the low-risks to the high-risks who are in the same pool, in the *current* contract period. However, pooling of people with different risks creates predictable profits and losses for certain subgroups, and thereby provides insurers with incentives for risk selection, which can have several unfavorable effects, as explicated in Box 17.3.

An effective way to reduce the incentives for risk selection is to implement a good risk equalization scheme (for terminology see Box 17.4). In such a scheme insurers with a

---

Box 17.3 Unfavorable Effects of Risk Selection

1. Health plans have a disincentive to respond to the preferences of high-risk consumers. For example, health plans with a good reputation for chronic care would attract many unprofitable patients and would be the victim of their own success. For example, Beaulieu et al. (2006) discuss the case of an HMO with a successful Diabetes Management Program, resulting in improved health outcomes and lower costs, that eventually lost money because the program attracted a disproportionate share of diabetics. Therefore, health plans may structure their coverage such that the plan is unattractive for the high risks, or they may choose not to contract with providers who have the best reputation for treating chronic illnesses. This in turn discourages physicians and hospitals to acquire such a reputation, which would be an unfavorable outcome of a competitive market. Although systematic evidence is lacking, several studies give rise to concern about insurer behavior in the presence of strong financial incentives to be unresponsive to the preferences of the chronically ill (Ware et al. 1996; Nelson et al. 1997; Riley et al. 1997; Davis and Schoen 1998; Miller 1998).

Box 17.3 Continued

2. Efficient health plans, which do not engage in risk selection, may lose market share to inefficient risk-selecting plans, resulting in a welfare loss to society.
3. In case of large predictable profits resulting from selection, selection will be more profitable than improving efficiency in health care production. At least in the short run, when an insurer has limited resources available to invest in cost-reducing activities, it may prefer to invest in selection rather than in improving efficiency. Moreover, for unfavorable risk groups insurers are likely to be only interested in cost minimization and not in improving quality (or an optimal benefit/cost ratio).
4. To the extent that some health plans are successful in attracting the low-risk persons, these selection activities result in risk segmentation, whereby the high risks pay a higher premium than the low risks. Alternatively, insurers could specialize in excellent integrated care for chronic diseases and offer contracts at very high community-rated premiums if there are sufficient chronically ill people who are willing and able to buy such a contract. Such a market segmentation conflicts with the goal of community rating.
5. Selection may induce instability in the insurance market, since low-risk people have a permanent incentive to break the pooling of heterogeneous risks by switching to lower-priced (new) health plans.
6. Finally, resources are wasted, since investments that are purely aimed at attracting low-risks by risk segmentation or selection, produce no net benefits to society (zero-sum game among health plans).

Box 17.4 Risk Equalization: Risk–adjusted Compensations to Insurers

We define *risk equalization* as "risk-adjusted compensations to insurers."

Risk equalization can be used with or without premium rate restrictions. *Without* premium rate restrictions the goal of risk equalization is to make health insurance affordable for the high risk individuals (see section 17.3.1). Insurers then reduce each consumer's premium with the per capita compensation (subsidy) they receive for this consumer. *With* premium rate restrictions the goal of risk equalization is to reduce the incentives for selection (see section 17.3.2). In that case the per capita compensation that an insurer receives for a high-risk individual reduces the predictable loss on this high-risk individual.

Sometimes the term *risk adjustment* is used rather than risk equalization (see e.g. Van de Ven and Ellis 2000). However, risk adjustment is a broader concept than our definition of risk equalization, because risk adjustment can be applied not only to premium subsidies, but also to e.g. provider payments or outcome measures. We use the term *risk equalization* to denote the specific case of "risk-adjusted compensations to (the consumers via) the insurers."

relative large share of predictably high risks receive more compensation than insurers with a relative large share of low risks. If risk equalization were perfect, it would eliminate all predictable profits and losses for all subgroups that insurers can distinguish. In that case, the initially imposed premium rate restrictions would be superfluous.

In practice perfect risk equalization does not (yet) exist. However, to eliminate risk selection, perfect risk equalization is not required, since risk selection is not costless to health insurers and may harm their reputation (Van de Ven and van Vliet 1995). If the predictable losses and profits after risk equalization are sufficiently small, this may not be a problem, because an insurer has to take into account the costs of selection and the (statistical) uncertainty about the net benefit of selection. Simulation results indicate that the extent to which the size of the potential selection problem is over-estimated by not ignoring small predictable losses and profits, increases the better the risk equalization formula is (Van Barneveld et al. 2000). Hence, the risk equalization formula should be refined to such an extent that insurers expect that the costs of selection outweigh the benefits. By making the risk groups in the equalization more homogeneous, the costs of selection increase while on average the profits fall. But still an unanswered question is how much "imperfection" is sufficient to prevent risk selection.

17.3.3 Conclusion

We have discussed the following strategies to make individual health insurance affordable for the high-risk individuals in a competitive market with open enrollment: *explicit* subsidies, either risk-adjusted or premium-based, and excess-loss compensations; and *implicit* cross-subsidies enforced by either a guaranteed-renewability requirement or by universal premium-rate restrictions for a specified insurance coverage. We use the term *risk equalization* if the risk-adjusted subsidies are given to the insurer, who reduces the consumer's premium with the subsidy. Table 17.1 summarizes the potential effectiveness and market distortions of the above-mentioned strategies.

The conclusion that can be derived from this table is that (currently) none of the strategies is both fully effective *and* without any market distortion. So policymakers have to choose the most appropriate (strategy or) blend of strategies given the weights that society attaches to affordability, efficiency and the potential effects of selection. To the extent that *risk-adjusted subsidies* or *equalization payments* insufficiently subsidize some high-risk consumers, they can be complemented by one or more of the other strategies. The choice among these complementary strategies confronts policy makers with a tradeoff between affordability, efficiency and selection. The better the equalization payments are adjusted for relevant risk factors, the less severe is this tradeoff. If policy makers choose to use the strategy of *premium-based subsidies* or *excess-loss compensations*, they are confronted with a tradeoff between affordability and efficiency. In case they choose to enforce implicit cross-subsidies by *universal premium rate restrictions*, they are confronted with a tradeoff between affordability and (the unfavorable effects of) selection.

Table 17.1 Effectiveness and Market Distortions of Different Strategies to Make Individual Health Insurance Affordable for High Risks in a Competitive Insurance Market with Open Enrollment

Strategy	Effectiveness	Market distortions
Risk-adjusted subsidies or (equivalently) risk equalization	Depends: • on the one hand on the risk factors that the sponsor uses for calculating the equalization payments; • and on the other hand on the risk factors that the insurers use for calculating the risk-adjusted premiums and the other tools they have to segment the market.	Dependent on the quality of the chosen risk adjusters (e.g. prior utilization may reduce incentives for efficiency) (see Van de Ven et al. 2000: 323–5)
Premium-based subsidies	Yes, to any desired extent.	• Reduction of price competition because of the reduction of the consumers' incentive to shop around for the lowest premium; • Over-insurance resulting in additional moral hazard; • Misallocation of subsidies (also subsidy for N-type factors)
Excess-loss compensation	Yes, to any desired extent.	Reduction of incentives for efficiency
Guaranteed renewability	• No solution for those who at the start of the guaranteed-renewability requirement are a high risk. • Highly questionable whether in the long run the insurers can guarantee "standard premium and standard coverage." • Questionable whether a guaranteed-renewability clause is effective with respect to new-borns with birth defects.	• No consumer choice of insurer for the high risks. • Limited competition resulting in reduced insurers' incentives for efficiency with respect to the high-risks' expenses. • Consumers have no financial incentive for health-risk reducing behavior. • Selection against applicants with an above average probability of genetically predictable diseases.
Universal premium-rate restrictions	• Yes, except for good quality care for chronically ill. • No, to the extent that selection results in market segmentation.	• Insurers have a disincentive to be responsive to the high-risks' preferences; • Reduction of the insurers' incentives to contract good quality care for high-risks. • Potential failure of efficient insurers with disproportionate shares of high-risk enrollees. • A reduction of the insurers' incentives for efficiency (at least in the short run). • Instability of the insurance market.

The insurers' incentives for selection can be reduced by implementing a system of risk equalization among the insurers, or by making the premium rate restrictions less restrictive (which makes health insurance less affordable for the high risks) or by providing the insurers with ex post compensations (which reduces the insurers' incentives for efficiency). Again the sponsor or policymaker is confronted with a tradeoff between affordability, efficiency and selection.

We conclude that risk-adjusted subsidies or (equivalently) risk equalization in principle is the preferred strategy to guarantee universal access to affordable coverage in the individual health insurance market. In the case of no or imperfect risk equalization policymakers are confronted with a complicated tradeoff between affordability, efficiency, and selection. The better the risk equalization is, the less severe is this tradeoff. In the (theoretical) case of perfect risk equalization there is no need for any of the other strategies and the tradeoff no longer exists. Each of the other strategies alone inevitably confronts policymakers with a tradeoff. Therefore, *good risk equalization offers the only effective means of addressing the tradeoff between affordability, efficiency and selection.*

17.4 COMMUNITY RATING: DOES ONE PREMIUM FIT ALL?

In contrast with this conclusion many (if not all) countries with a competitive health insurance market use premium-rate restrictions and an open enrollment requirement as the major tool to make health insurance affordable for the high risks. Mostly the premium-rate restrictions have the (extreme) form of community rating per insurer per product. Community rating usually has the form of a requirement that insurers must charge the same premium for the same product to each enrollee, independent of the enrollee's risk. (For a review of community rated private health insurance in several countries, see Gale 2007.) In spite of its social objective, it turns out that this type of regulation has several adverse effects.

17.4.1 Drawbacks of Community Rating

A first drawback of community rating is that it induces strong incentives for selection, which may threaten good-quality care for the chronically ill, may result in failure of efficient health insurers, may induce wasteful investments in selection efforts, and may reduce the stability of the insurance market. These adverse effects are most pronounced in competitive health insurance markets where community rating is implemented without risk equalization (e.g. in Australia, South Africa, and some States of the USA). Since the early 1990s many States in the USA have implemented regulation such as open enrollment and premium-rate restrictions (often in the form of community rating) for health insurance offered to individuals (US-GAO 1997) and small employers (US-GAO 1995). In the 1990s there has been a gradual trend toward tighter rating reforms in the US small-group market (Curtis et al. 1999). In none of these cases has the regulation been combined with risk equalization. The effects of these regulations have been a shift in composition of insured people from lower to higher risks, a rise in the cost of coverage, an increase in the number of uninsured people, in some instances a reduction in the choice of plans available, and a reduction of the supply of insurers willing to grant coverage (Astorino et al. 1996; Lo Sasso and Lurie 2003; Pauly and Herring 2007).

Next, in contrast to risk-adjusted premiums, community rating does not provide incentives for risk-reducing behavior and cannot discriminate between risk factors for which a sponsor would want to cross-subsidize (e.g. differences in health status) and those for which he would not (e.g. variations in supply). Moreover, in contrast to explicit subsidies, community rating cannot restrict cross-subsidization to low-income people only.

Finally, if direct premium differentiation is forbidden, product differentiation may result in indirect premium differentiation. Insurers may offer special products for various risk groups, e.g. depending on life-stage, life-style or health status. Such risk segmentation across the product spectrum can be observed in e.g. Australia, Ireland, and South Africa, where premiums must be community rated (Colombo and Tapay 2003; Gale 2005; Armstrong 2010; McLeod and Grobler 2010). In this way "community rating per product" results in low premiums for low risks and (unsubsidized) high premiums for high risks, which conflicts with the goal of community rating.

17.4.2 Why is Community Rating so Popular?

This raises the question: Why is community rating so popular among policy makers? In many countries community rating seems to be an indisputable axiom, without any debate whether there are better tools to achieve the goal of "affordable health insurance."

Besides the above mentioned disadvantages community rating also has some advantages. First, it increases transparency. If insurers risk-rate premiums, it is more difficult for the consumer to make an informed choice of insurer than in the case of community-rated premiums. However, if community rating results in extensive product differentiation, the advantage of a transparent premium structure may be largely forgone. A second advantage of community rating is the low transaction costs. Explicit premium subsidies as well as premium setting and underwriting activities by insurers require administration and transaction costs. Of course, this advantage holds only when community rating is *not* complemented with other strategies, such as risk equalization, to counteract incentives for risk selection. Another advantage is that community rating requires no public finance, whereas explicit subsidies require a system of mandatory contributions (to the subsidy fund), which may be considered to be a part of public finance. Since most governments are under pressure to restrain public finance, community rating may be politically advantageous.

Finally, many people believe that community rating offers a better guarantee of making health insurance affordable than a risk equalization system, which needs to be complemented with additional subsidies. However, as discussed above, if selection is successful and results in a market segmentation where the low-risk and high-risk consumers are no longer in the same pool, and therefore do not pay the same premium (as is the case in e.g. Australia, Ireland, South Africa, and Switzerland), this argument may hold only in the short run.

The popularity of community rating as observed in practice indicates that policymakers or the majority of the people attach a higher value to the (perceived) benefits than to the (potential) disadvantages of community rating. This may be partly due to the fact that the direct effect of community rating on affordability is immediately visible, while potential indirect effects such as poor-quality care or high premiums for chronically ill patients may only show up after some years. Obviously, in the short run community rating provides a more effective strategy to guarantee affordability than risk equalization. This may at least explain the preference for starting with community rating in combination with poor risk equalization. The preference for community rating may also be partly due to a general unawareness of the fact that community rating implies cross-subsidies also for types of non-health related risk factors, for which most people may not want cross-subsidies. Finally, policymakers may hold the view that in practice risk selection is not a serious problem. One reason for this may be that they ignore or underestimate the forgone opportunities of good-quality, well-coordinated care that would occur if chronically ill people would be the preferred clients, rather than non-preferred "predictable losses."

All in all, the justification of mandatory community-rating, i.e. the most extreme form of premium-rate restrictions, is less straightforward than its popularity in practice suggests.

17.5 How to Organize the Subsidy Payments?

Not only the type of subsidy matters, but also the way the subsidy payments are organized. There are at least three modalities to organize the subsidy payment flows (see Figure 17.1).

In *modality A*—the *"voucher model"*—the subsidy goes directly to the consumer and the consumer pays the premium partly with the subsidy and partly out-of-pocket. As far as relevant, consumers pay their contribution to the subsidy fund. (For several ways of financing the subsidy fund, see Blomqvist's Chapter 12 in the volume.) So far, however, the voucher model has not been applied in practice. In all countries using *risk-adjusted*

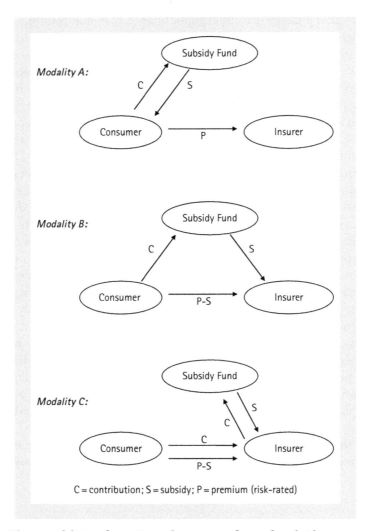

FIGURE 17.1 Three modalities of organizing the payment flows of a subsidy system

subsidies, the subsidy is given directly to the insurer (risk equalization, see Box 17.4). In a transparent competitive market the insurers are forced to reduce the consumers' premium with the per capita subsidy they receive for this consumer. *Modality B* depicts one form of risk equalization in which the consumer pays the mandatory contribution *directly* to the subsidy fund. In *modality C* the consumer pays the mandatory contribution to the subsidy fund *indirectly via* the insurer. In that case each insurer and the subsidy fund clear the net difference of all the contributions to the subsidy fund and the subsidies of the relevant clients. Modality B is applied in Belgium, Israel, the Netherlands (till 2006), Russia, and in Medicare in the USA, and modality C is used for risk equalization in Colombia, Czech Republic, Germany (till 2009), Ireland and Switzerland. Since 2006 the Dutch risk equalization system is a mixture of the modalities B and C, and in Germany the government aims at a transformation of equalization scheme from modality C to B in 2009. A fourth modality (not depicted in Figure 17.1) is that the sponsor collects both the premium and the contributions and transfers the premium and the subsidies to the insurers (*Modality D*). This alternative is applied by some employer purchasing coalitions in the USA.

In practice there can be a whole continuum of models between modalities B and C, dependent on how the equalization payments (= subsidies) are calculated. A straightforward way is to let an individual's equalization payment be equal to the predicted health expenses based on the individual's risk factors and the equalization formula, minus a fixed amount X. Negative equalization payments imply payments from the insurer to the subsidy fund. If we assume that the net average premium P (excluding loading fee) equals the average predicted health expenses, the national average of the consumers' out-of-pocket-premiums (i.e. premium minus subsidy) equals X. In countries such as Russia and Israel $X = 0$. In countries such as Switzerland and Ireland X equals the average predicted per capita expenses. The Netherlands has an intermediate position, with X equal to 45 percent of the average predicted per capita expenses. A brief description of the Dutch risk equalization scheme is included in Box 17.5.

Although at first glance modality A (the "voucher model") and modalities B and C (the "risk-equalization models") may seem to be quite different, the way the premium subsidies and the contributions to the subsidy fund are calculated can in principle be the same. Nevertheless, in practice the way the subsidy payments are organized, has important implications. As explained below the different modalities each have specific advantages and disadvantages, which are summarized in Table 17.2.

Based on the criteria enlisted in Table 17.2 the following important differences between the three modalities can be observed:

1. Under modality A it is possible to restrict the payment of risk-adjusted subsidies to low-income people only. In the case of risk equalization (modalities B or C) this is practically not feasible. In modalities B and C there are also cross-subsidies from low-income low-risk individuals to high-income high-risk individuals. In that case income transfers across income groups have to be organized separately.
2. Income-related contributions can be more easily combined with modalities A and B than with modality C, because insurers, who collect the contributions in modality C, generally do not know the consumer's income. The German government decided to replace modality C by modality B in 2009.
3. Another advantage of the separate contributions under modalities A and B is that universal access can be guaranteed by making *contributions* mandatory rather than the take-up of *insurance*. The advantage of not having a mandate for high-income people to purchase standard basic coverage is that it may reduce moral hazard, if these people choose to purchase less coverage than standard basic coverage. Notice that for high-income people, in contrast to low-income people, free-

Box 17.5 Risk Equalization in the Netherlands, 2009

In 2009, the risk equalization in the Netherlands is based on the following risk-adjusters: age/gender (38 groups), Pharmacy-based Cost Groups (PCG) (20 groups), Diagnostic Cost Groups (DCG) (13 groups), source of income/age (4×4=16 groups), social economic status (SES)/age (4×3=12 groups), and region (10 groups). (For further background information on the Dutch risk equalization, see e.g. Van de Ven et al. 2004.)

The risk-adjusted equalization payments are calculated by means of an additive model that uses these risk-adjusters. A simplified example (with less risk groups) is as follows:

Age/gender	Payment	PCG	Payment	DCG	Payment
Men, 0	€2000	No PCG	−€300	No DCG	−€100
Men, 1–54	€1000	Asthma/COPD	€1000	Brain injury	€2000
Men, 55–69	€2000	Heart disease	€1500	Liver disorder	€3000
Men, > = 70	€3000	Stomach disease	€2000	Neurological disorder	€5000
		Diabetes (insulin)	€3500	Pulmonary fibrosis	€10,000
Women, 0	€2000	Transplantation	€4000		
Women, 1–54	€1300	Cancer	€5000		
Women, 55–69	€1800	HIV/AIDS	€10,000		
Women, > = 70	€2800	Kidney problems	€20,000		

Source of income	Payment	SES	Payment	Region	Payment
Disability payment	€1000	SES 1	€400	Region 1	€100
Other social security payments	€500	SES 2	€300	Region 2	€20
Self-employed	−€200	SES 3	€0	Region 3	−€30
Other	−€100	SES 4	−€200	Region 4	−€100

Examples of risk equalization payment per person:

1. Woman 43, no PCG, no DCG, self-employed, SES 4, and Region 4:
   €1300 − €300 − €100 − €200 − €200 − €100 = €400
2. Man 87, diabetes (insulin), cancer, kidney problems, pulmonary fibrosis, other social security payments, SES 1, Region 1:
   €3000 + €3500 + €5000 + €20,000 + €10,000 + €500 + €400 + €100 = €42,500

In addition to the risk equalization payments the insurers receive a community-rated premium per adult enrollee (ranging from about €900 to about €1100 per person (of 18 years and older) per year, dependent of the insurer).

Table 17.2 Criteria to Compare 3 Modalities (see Figure 17.1) of Organizing the Payment Flows of Risk-adjusted Subsidies

Criterion	Modality A	Modality B	Modality C
1. Subsidies can be restricted to low-income people only	*		
2. Contribution to the subsidy fund can be income-related	*	*	
3. Subsidies can be enforced without a mandate to buy health insurance	*	*	
4. Low transaction costs of organizing the subsidies		*	*
5. High responsiveness of consumers to premium differences		*	
6. Low chance of default of premium payments		*	
7. Requires small transfer of payments via the subsidy fund			*
8. Acceptability for insurers	*	*	

Note: *Indicates which modality best satisfies the criterion.

riding behavior and lack of foresight are no relevant arguments to enforce a mandate, as long as they pay the needed health care out-of-pocket. Thus, the modalities A and B can be more easily combined with a voluntary health insurance scheme than modality C, because in the case of voluntary insurance modality C has to be supplemented with a mechanism to ensure that low-risk individuals who do not buy insurance, pay a contribution to the subsidy fund.

4. The transaction costs of providing the risk-adjusted subsidies are higher under modality A, because the subsidy fund has to deal with every individual consumer, instead of a limited number of insurers as in modalities B and C. For instance, for each individual consumer an exchange of relevant information about the current value of the risk factors has to be organized, which is likely to be very expensive. This is likely to be a major reason why the voucher model has not been applied in practice as yet.

5. The direct individual payment to the insurer under modality B (premium minus subsidy) is considerably less than under modalities A and C. Hence, cost savings by insurers will have a much larger proportional effect on the level of direct payments under modality B than under modalities A and C. This is likely to result in stronger consumer responses (Buchmueller and Feldstein 1997).

6. Another advantage of modality B is that the low direct payments from consumers to insurers reduce the chance that individuals, for whatever reason, do not pay their premium and become uninsured because of default of premium.

7. In modality C the subsidy fund and each insurer clear the net difference over all individuals. So in modality C only insurers with an over-representation of

high-risk insured receive a subsidy from the subsidy fund and only insurers with an under-representation of high-risk insured pay a contribution to the subsidy fund. Consequently, the actual amount of money passing via the subsidy fund under modality C is relatively small as compared with modalities A and B. Modality C can be considered a system in which there is an internal equalization *within* each insurer, complemented with an equalization system *among* the insurers to compensate for differences in risk portfolios among the health insurers. If all insurers would have an identical risk portfolio, there would be no equalization *among* the insurers, and consequently the net payments to and from the subsidy fund would be zero. This argument is relevant for countries where the government is unable or unwilling to collect contributions to the subsidy fund e.g. because of limited taxation capacity.

8. Finally, modality C is likely to encounter more resistance from insurers than modality B for psychological reasons. Under modality B all insurers receive a per capita subsidy from the subsidy fund. It is easy to explain the fairness of the system whereby insurers receive a low payment for a low-risk consumer and a high payment for a high-risk consumer. Under modality C, however, insurers may have the perception of being "winners" or "losers," depending on whether the net balance of their payments to the subsidy fund is positive or negative. This "winner–loser" image might not be beneficial for the acceptance of the risk equalization system.

17.6 CONCLUSION AND DISCUSSION

A competitive health insurance market with free consumer choice provides health insurers with incentives for efficiency, but also with incentives for risk rating, risk segmentation and/or risk selection. Since universal access is a major goal of social health insurance schemes, a key question is: *How can we guarantee access to affordable coverage for the high risks in the individual health insurance market?*

The conclusion from our analysis is that a system of *risk-adjusted subsidies* is the preferred form of subsidy to make individual health insurance affordable in a competitive insurance market with free consumer choice of insurer. Under this approach insurers are free to ask risk-rated premiums. The preferred way of organizing the payment flows of risk-adjusted subsidies depends on political, economic and pragmatic arguments. In practice, all countries that apply risk-adjusted subsidies, give the subsidy to the insurer who reduces the consumers' premium with the per capita subsidy they receive for this consumer. We refer to this way of organizing the risk-adjusted subsidies as *risk equalization*. In most of these countries age and gender are used as risk-adjusters, sometimes supplemented with indicators of disability and institutional and welfare status (see Van de Ven and Ellis 2000; Van de Ven et al. 2003, 2007). So far, health related risk-adjusters have only been implemented in the Netherlands and the USA (Medicare).

Recent results indicate that the Dutch equalization formula-2007 compensates the over-whelming majority (92%) of the population reasonably well for differences in health status; but that for a hard-core group of high risks (8%) the out-of-pocket premiums would be quite substantial (Van de Ven et al. 2008).

To the extent that some high-risk consumers are insufficiently subsidized, the risk-adjusted subsidies or equalization payments can be complemented by premium-based subsidies, excess-loss compensations, and/or implicit cross-subsidies enforced by premium rate restrictions for a specified insurance coverage.

We explained that the choice among these complementary strategies confronts policy makers with a complicated tradeoff between affordability, efficiency, and the negative effects of selection, notably low quality care for the chronically ill. The better the premium subsidies are adjusted for relevant risk factors, the less these complementary strategies are needed, and the less severe is the tradeoff.

In practice, however, in most countries a careful weighing of alternative complementary strategies does not take place. We find that policymakers appear to have a strong preference for a particular complementary strategy: community rating. Although community rating has some important short-term advantages, it also may have serious negative effects in the long run, particularly as a result of the disincentives to provide good quality care to the chronically ill.

Furthermore, we find that many countries do not use the preferred form of subsidy to guarantee universal access to health insurance. At least half of the OECD countries have chosen to provide some type of tax subsidies to encourage the purchase of private health insurance (OECD 2004). Deductions from taxable income are the most common form of incentives offered to purchasers. These subsidies can be quite significant, such as Australia's 30 percent premium tax rebate, and the about 35 percent tax subsidization of employees' health insurance in the USA (Pauly 1986; Selden and Gray 2006). Based on our analysis, we conclude that substantial improvements in efficiency could be achieved, if these premium-based subsidies would be replaced with risk-adjusted subsidies.

We conclude that in a competitive market for individual health insurance good risk equalization is the only effective strategy to resolve the tradeoff between affordability, efficiency, and selection. Given that the current risk equalization schemes in most countries are highly imperfect, further investments in improving risk equalization are essential. Investments should not only be made in better data, but also in research and development of better risk-adjusters. New research efforts should particularly focus on the individuals who belong to the top 1 percent or top 4 percent with the highest expenses over a series of years. On the one hand, these persons are responsible for a substantial part of the total expenses and, on the other hand, the risk equalization formulas that are currently used, perform worst for these groups.

References

Armstrong, J., 2010, Risk equalization and voluntary health insurance markets: the case of Ireland, *Health Policy*, 98(1): 15–26.

ASTORINO, A., V. C. BUNCE, P. HUNDEE, J. J. JAKELIS, D. LACK, M. LITOW, R. TURNER and J. WHELAN, 1996, State health insurance reform: experience with community rating and guaranteed issue in the small group and individual markets. Report, April 1996, The Council for Affordable Health Insurance, Alexandria, VA.

BEAULIEU, N., D. M. CUTLER, K. HO, G. ISHAM, T. LINDQUIST, A. NELSON, and P. O'CONNOR, 2006, The business case for diabetes disease management for managed care organizations, *Forum for Health Economics & Policy* 9(1): 1–36.

BUCHMUELLER, T. C., and P. J. FELDSTEIN, 1997, The effect of price on switching among health plans, *Journal of Health Economics* 16(2): 231–47.

BUCHNER, F., and J. WASEM, 2006, "Steeping" of health expenditure profiles, *The Geneva Papers* 31(4), 581–99.

COCHRANE, J. H., 1995, Time-consistent health insurance, *Journal of Political Economy*, 103(3): 445–73.

COLOMBO, F. and N. TAPAY, 2003, Private health insurance in Australia: case study. OECD Health working paper no. 8, October 30.

CURTIS, R., S. LEWIS, K. HAUGH, and R. FORLAND, 1999, Health insurance reform in the small-group market, *Health Affairs*, 18(3): 151–60.

DAVIS, K. and C. SCHOEN, 1998, Assuring quality, information, and choice in managed care, *Inquiry* 35 (Summer): 104–14.

ENTHOVEN A. C. and FUCHS, V. R., 2006, Employment-based health insurance: past, present, and future, *Health Affairs* 25(6): 1538–47.

GALE, A. P., 2005, What price health? Private health insurance cost pressures and product pricing. The Institute of Actuaries of Australia. Paper presented to the Institute of Actuaries of Australia 2005 Biennial Convention, Melbourne, Australia, May 8.

—— 2007, One price fits all. Paper presented to the Institute of Actuaries of Australia Biennial Convention, Christchurch, New Zealand, September 23–7.

HERRING, B. and M. V. PAULY, 2001, Premium variation in the individual health insurance market, *International Journal of Health Care Finance and Economics*, 1: 43–58.

—— —— 2006, Incentive-compatible guaranteed renewability health insurance premium, *Journal of Health Economics*, 25: 395–417.

LO SASSO, A. and I. Z. LURIE, 2003, The effect of State policies on the market for private non-group health insurance. Institute for Policy Research, Northwestern University Working Paper Series 04–09, October 20.

McLEOD, H. and P. GROBLER, 2010, Risk equalization and voluntary health insurance: the South Africa experience, *Health Policy*, 98(1): 27–38.

MILLER, R. H., 1998, Healthcare organizational change: implications for access to care and its measurement, *Health Services Research* 33(3): 653–80.

NELSON, L., R. BROWN, M. GOLD, A. CIEMNECKI, and E. DOCTEUR, 1997, Access to care in Medicare HMOs 1996, *Health Affairs*, 16(2): 148–56.

NEWHOUSE, J. P., 1984, Cream skimming, asymmetric information, and a competitive insurance market, *Journal of Health Economics*, 3(1): 97–100.

—— 1996, Reimbursing health insurers and health providers: efficiency in production versus selection, *Journal of Economic Literature* 34: 1236–63.

OECD, 2004, *Private Health Insurance in OECD Countries*. Paris: OECD.

PAULY, M. V., 1986, Taxation, health insurance, and market failure in the medical economy, *Journal of Economic Literature*, 24(2) (June): 629–75.

—— 1992, Risk variation and fallback insurers in universal coverage insurance plans, *Inquiry* (29): 137–47.

—— and B. HERRING, 2007, Risk Pooling and regulation: policy and reality in today's individual health insurance market, *Health Affairs* 26(3): 770–9.

—— H. KUNREUTHER, and R. HIRTH, 1995, Guaranteed renewability in insurance, *Journal of Risk and Insurance*, 10: 143–56.

—— A. PERCY, and B. HERRING, 1999, Individual versus job-based health insurance: weighing the pros and cons, *Health Affairs* 18(6): 28–44.

RILEY, G. F., M. J. INGBER, and C. G. TUDOR, 1997, Disenrollment of medicare beneficiaries from HMOs, *Health Affairs*, 16(5): 117–24.

ROTHSCHILD, M., and J. STIGLITZ, 1976, Equilibrium in competitive insurance markets: an essay on the economics of imperfect information, *Quarterly Journal of Economics*, 90(4): 629–49.

SCHOKKAERT, E. and C. VAN DE VOORDE, 2003, Belgium: risk adjustment and financial responsibility in a centralized system, *Health Policy*, 65(1): 5–19.

SCHUT, F. T., 1995, Competition in the Dutch health care sector. Dissertation, Erasmus University Rotterdam, Rotterdam.

SELDEN, T. M. and B. M. GRAY, 2006, Tax subsidies for employment-related health insurance: estimates for 2006, *Health Affairs*, 25(6): 1568–79.

STAM, P. J. A., 2007, Testing the effectiveness of risk equalization models in health care. Ph.D. Dissertation, Erasmus University Rotterdam, Rotterdam.

TOLLEN, L. A., M. N. ROSS, and S. POOR, 2004, Risk segmentation related to the offering of a consumer-directed health plan: a case study of Humana Inc., *Health Services Research* 39(S1): 1167–88.

US-GAO, 1995, Health insurance regulation; variation in recent state small employer health insurance reforms. GAO/HEHS-95-161FS, General Accounting Office, Washington, DC.

—— 1997, Private health insurance; millions relying on individual market face cost and coverage trade-offs. GAO/HEHS-97-8, General Accounting Office, Washington, DC.

VAN BARNEVELD E. M., L. M. LAMERS, R. C. J. A. VAN VLIET, and W. P. M. M. VAN DE VEN, 2000, Ignoring small predictable profits and losses: a new approach for measuring incentives for cream skimming, *Health Care Management Science*, 3(2): 131–40.

VAN DE VEN, W. P. M. M., 2006, The case for risk-based subsidies in public health insurance, *Health Economics, Policy and Law* 1(3): 171–88.

—— and R. P. ELLIS, 2000, Risk adjustment in competitive health insurance markets. In A. J. Culyer and J. P. Newhouse (eds.), *Handbook of Health Economics* (chapter 14). Amsterdam, Elsevier, 755–845.

—— and R. C. J. A. VAN VLIET, 1995, Consumer information surplus and adverse selection in competitive health insurance markets: An empirical study, *Journal of Health Economics*, 14(2): 149–69.

—— R. C. J. A. VAN VLIET, F. T. SCHUT, and E. M. VAN BARNEVELD, 2000, Access to coverage for high-risk consumers in a competitive individual health insurance market: via premium rate restrictions or risk-adjusted premium subsidies? *Journal of Health Economics* 19: 311–39.

—— K. BECK, F. BUCHNER, et al., 2003, Risk adjustment and risk selection on the health insurer market in five European countries, *Health Policy* 65(1), 75–98.

—— R. C. J. A. VAN VLIET, and L. M. LAMERS, 2004, Health-adjusted premium subsidies in the Netherlands, *Health Affairs*, 23(3): 45–55.

—— K. BECK, C. VAN DE VOORDE, J. WASEM, and I. ZMORA, 2007, Risk adjustment and risk selection in Europe: six years later, *Health Policy*, 83: 162–79.

—— P. J. A. Stam, R. C. J. A. van Vliet, and F. T. Schut, 2008, Does one premium fit all? Risk equalization as an alternative to community rating. (As yet) unpublished paper, Erasmus University Rotterdam, May.

Ware, J. E., M. S. Bayliss, W. H. Rogers, M. Kosinski and A. R. Tarlove, 1996, Differences in 4-year health outcomes for elderly and poor, chronically ill patients treated in HMO and fee-for-service systems, *Journal of the American Medical Association*, 276(13): 1039–47.

Wilson, C., 1977, A model of insurance markets with incomplete information, *Journal of Economic Theory*, 16(2): 167–207.

Zweifel, P. and M. Breuer, 2006, The case for risk-based premiums in public health insurance, *Health Economics, Policy and Law*, 1(2): 171–88.

CHAPTER 18

MANAGED CARE

LAURENCE BAKER

18.1 INTRODUCTION

THE latter half of the twentieth century saw many important changes in health care systems around the world. In the United States, one of the most important trends was a shift in the structure of health insurance arrangements. Early on, insurance was commonly provided under traditional indemnity insurance arrangements characterized by generous coverage for patients; generous, usually fee-for-service, payment for providers; and little insurer oversight of utilization decisions. These features gave rise to concerns about moral hazard and a perceived lack of incentives for providing high quality care. As insurers, prodded by insurance purchasers alarmed by steadily increasing health care costs, sought to address the shortcomings of traditional indemnity insurance arrangements, they turned to a set of new arrangements that collectively came to be known as "managed care." Managed care, in the broadest sense, encompasses a range of activities, organizational structures, and financial incentives designed to better integrate health insurance and health care delivery in order to more effectively "manage" the delivery of health care and achieve goals such as lower costs, increased quality, and improved efficiency. These "managed care practices" can include organizing and tightening control over provider networks, increasing the amount of insurer oversight of health care utilization, and using financial incentives that encouraged more efficient use of resources.

Managed care practices are used by many health insurers. While most insurers have come to use at least some practices associated with managed care in their plans, some particular plan structures have become more closely associated with managed care than others, because they tend to embrace a relatively broad range of managed care practices and because they became more prominent during the time that managed care ideas were expanding in influence. These types of plans are often referred to as "managed care plans," and include health maintenance organizations (HMOs), which stereotypically adopt a number of managed care practices and implement them relatively aggressively, and preferred provider organizations (PPOs), which stereotypically use a number of managed care practices but tend to be less aggressive than HMOs.

Growth in managed care is strongly associated with the 1980s and 1990s in the United States, a time sometimes referred to as the managed care revolution. This time period saw significant change in health insurance arrangements in the United States, and it was during this time that the term "managed care" became established. At the same time, the concepts associated with managed care are found much more broadly. Managed care practices and plans have been found in the United States in one form or another since the early 1900s. Practices associated with managed care are also found in most health care systems around the world, and in some cases have been effectively used over longer periods of time outside of the United States.

With the changes it has brought about, growth of managed care has raised important questions about its impact on health care. The majority of the interest has centered on the effect that enrolling in a managed care plan, as opposed to a less restrictive type of health plan, has on the health care delivered to an individual. Advocates of managed care argue that managed care practices can foster improvements in quality and reductions in costs, restraining waste and inefficiency associated with traditional indemnity insurance arrangements and thereby improving the efficiency of health care delivery. Opponents, though, argue that aggressive use of managed care practices risks putting cost cutting front and center, displacing concerns about quality and health outcomes and running the risk of under-producing valuable health care. Various versions of this debate have been carried out in the popular press and in academic journals over recent decades, producing volumes of research and writing (see, for example, Luft 1981; Miller and Luft 1994; Miller and Luft 1997; Chernew, Hirth et al. 1998; Dudley et al. 1998; Glied 2000).

Managed care could also have impacts on the health care system more broadly, beyond effects on just those patients who enroll in managed care plans. By shifting the incentives that drive the activities of health care producers, growth in managed care could lead to fundamental changes in the structure and functioning of the entire health care system, ultimately producing "spillover effects" even on patients not enrolled in managed care plans (Baker 1997; Baker 2003).

This chapter discusses effects of managed care on patients and on the health care system, including the characteristics and history of managed care plans in more detail and evidence on the impacts of managed care on enrolled patients and on the health care system. While the focus is on the US experience, the results will be of relevance to almost all health systems seeking to manage demand for services.

18.2 Managed Care Practices and Managed Care Plans

18.2.1 Characteristics of Managed Care Plans

Managed care is to a large degree defined by efforts to increase the degree to which health insurance and health care delivery are vertically integrated. Managed care plans can use different combinations of specific activities, but a central feature of many managed care activities is their intended ability to better align health care delivery with the goals of the health insurer. The activities associated with managed care plans can fall into a number of groups, including defining and managing provider networks, increasing the amount of insurer influence in utilization decisions, changing provider financial incentives, targeting the set of covered services, and varying patient cost sharing requirements (Landon et al. 1998; Flynn et al. 2002).

18.2.1.1 *Selective Contracting and Provider Organization*

In traditional health insurance arrangements, covered beneficiaries may select physicians, hospitals, and other health care providers more or less at their own discretion, subject to little influence from the health insurer. Managed care plans, by contrast, commonly engage in "selective contracting," identifying and contracting with a subset of the available providers to develop a network to care for their enrollees. Controlling the size of the provider network and carefully selecting the included providers can give health plans a valuable tool for influencing care delivery. Defining networks also creates an opportunity for plans to invest in targeted efforts to manage and influence the behavior of the selected providers.

There are several approaches plans use when forming physician networks. Some managed care plans, referred to as "staff-model" HMOs, hire physicians directly. Other organizations, called "group-model" HMOs, develop a physician network by entering into exclusive contracts with one or more, typically large, physician groups, who agree to care for the plan members. In both of these cases, the insurer gets a considerable amount of control over which physicians will be included in the network. These arrangements also tend to foster a close relationship between the physicians and the insurer, which can reduce agency problems, enhancing the ability of insurers to work with physicians to define and achieve goals for health care delivery.

Group-model and staff-model HMOs were among the earliest types of managed care organizations, but over time other network arrangements have become more common. "Network-model" HMOs build physician networks by contracting on a non-exclusive basis with multiple, typically larger, physician groups. IPA-model HMOs build physician networks by contracting with "independent practice associations" (IPAs),[1] entities that assemble networks of physicians by contracting with individual physician practices, stereotypically solo or small-group practices that elect to join the IPA on a non-exclusive basis. In network-model or IPA-model HMOs, the network physicians agree to see patients from the insurer under defined terms, but remain independent from the insurer in the sense that they may also continue to do business with other insurers. These types of arrangements are often quite flexible for insurers and can be used to create very large networks relatively quickly. The relatively weak relationship between contracted physicians and the insurer can, however, lead to agency problems and a need for aggressive oversight of physician activities.

Evidence about contracting of physicians is relatively scarce. As might be expected, group and staff model HMOs appear to have smaller networks than IPA and network model HMOs, and have physician-to-enrollee ratios lower than the US overall average (e.g. Feldman, Chan et al. 1990; Feldman, Kralewski et al. 1990; Weiner 2004). Evidence on whether plans use selective contracting with physicians to pursue cost or quality goals is sparse, though some evidence does suggest that managed care plans attempted to select physicians with lower costs (Robinson 1993) and higher quality (Mukamel et al. 2000; Mukamel et al. 2002).

Managed care plans also typically define a network of hospitals that their enrollees may use. Some HMOs, such as Kaiser Permanente, a prominent group-model HMO, own and operate their own hospitals. More commonly, managed care plans contract non-exclusively with existing hospitals. The effects of selective contracting with hospitals have been extensively discussed and analyzed. As a general proposition, selective contracting could offer important advantages, since individual patients may have a difficult time acquiring and interpreting information about costs or quality when choosing a hospital. Ultimately, though, the effects of selective contracting depend on the extent to which plans devote resources to careful selection of hospitals and the objective function the plans use in the selection process. Selective contracting could drive higher quality but, if plans focus primarily on finding low-cost hospitals, their networks may end up inefficiently under-providing quality (e.g. Pauly 1989). Whether and when this might occur has been the source of lively discussion. Studies that have examined hospital behavior around times that selective contracting became more widely used, primarily in the context of the legalization of selective contracting for hospital services in California in the early 1980s, provide evidence that selective contracting is associated with lower prices for hospital services, lower price-cost margins, and slower growth in hospital costs and revenues ((Zwanziger and Melnick 1988; Robinson 1991; Melnick et al. 1992; Dranove et al. 1993; Zwanziger et al. 1994).

Another way to learn about the effects of selective contracting is to look at the hospitals plans choose to include in their networks. Some work suggests that HMOs try to contract with lower cost hospitals (Gaskin et al. 2002), though another study found that HMOs seemed to prefer contracting with hospitals in the middle of the cost distribution (Zwanziger

---

[1] Sometimes also referred to as "independent physician associations."

and Meirowitz 1997). From the perspective of quality, some work suggests that HMOs do appear to contract based on quality and outcomes (e.g. Gaskin et al. 2002), but the majority of the evidence is more equivocal. Some surveys of plan personnel suggest plans care about quality but often end up relying on loose measures such as reputation or accreditation (e.g. Schulman et al. 1997; Rainwater and Romano 2003). A couple of studies have reported evidence of HMO patients being treated at higher quality hospitals than non-HMO patients (e.g. (Chernew et al. 1996; Chernew, Scanlon et al. 1998)), but other work finds no relationship (Escarce et al. 1997) or reaches the opposite conclusion (e.g. Erickson, Torchiana et al. 2000; Erickson, Wise et al. 2000).

Once plans define their provider networks, in most cases enrollees are required to use network providers. In these arrangements, often called "closed panel" arrangements, the insurer will only pay for care delivered by network providers. Patients who seek care from out-of-network providers in non-emergency situations would typically be required to pay the associated charges out of their own pockets. Some managed care plans have used "open-panel" arrangements, in which the plan encourages enrollees to use network providers, perhaps providing more generous cost sharing for care obtained from network providers, but still allows enrollees to see non-network providers in return for paying a higher share of the bill.

18.2.1.2 *Overseeing and Influencing Utilization*

There are a variety of mechanisms that insurers can use to directly oversee and influence the utilization decisions of physicians and patients. One set of efforts to directly control utilization falls under the umbrella of "utilization review" programs. These are frequently applied to hospital care, where they can take several forms. One common form is "preadmission review," also referred to as "prior authorization" or "pre-approval," in which plans impose a requirement that hospital stays be approved in advance if the associated costs are to be reimbursed by the plan. Another is "concurrent review" programs in which plans review and evaluate hospital stays as they are ongoing, allowing opportunities to act if plans identify resource use they deem inappropriate. Utilization review can also be imposed on outpatient services, where plans might impose pre-approval requirements for services that are costly or that the plan views as subject to overuse, such as the use of high-cost diagnostic tests or high-cost brand name drugs (e.g. Sullivan and Rice 1991; Mullins et al. 2006). Some plans may require a second physician's opinion before approving coverage for some services like non-urgent surgeries (Lindsey and Newhouse 1990; Scheffler et al. 1991). Research on utilization review programs suggests that they can have significant impacts on care in many, but not all, situations (e.g. Wickizer 1990; Scheffler et al. 1991; Wickizer et al. 1991; Khandker and Manning 1992; Wickizer 1995; Wickizer and Lesser 1998a and 1998b; Wickizer et al. 1999; Lessler and Wickizer 2000).

Formularies and coverage limitations are another form of direct limitation on service use. Most insurers have developed formularies for pharmaceuticals. In the simplest cases, patients and physicians are restricted to using pharmaceutical products included on the formulary. Most plans today use more sophisticated formularies that organize pharmaceuticals into different groups and provide different levels of patient cost sharing across the groups, with patients facing the most favorable cost sharing when they use the drugs most favored by the plan (e.g. Claxton et al. 2009). Beyond formularies, many plans voice support for limiting coverage of services that appear to be cost-ineffective or have other undesirable characteristics, though in practice the unfavorable publicity that can be associated with limiting coverage in competitive markets has meant that few plans have successfully lived up to their announced goals.

Plans can influence care through the use of case management or disease management programs, aimed at identifying potentially high-cost patients early on and developing tailored care approaches for them. Plans may also use discharge planning, aimed at ensuring that appropriate care is delivered to patients after their discharge from the hospital.

Many plans have also developed institutional structures that limit the use of some kinds of services. Perhaps the most common is the gatekeeper arrangement, under which plans require enrollees to sign up with a primary care physician (the "gatekeeper"), make all initial consultations for care with that physician, and obtain a referral from the primary care physician before specialist services will be reimbursed. This holds out the promise of improving care coordination and quality, as well as reducing costs of care. Early evidence suggested that gatekeeper requirements could have important effects, including reduced spending and improved coordination (e.g. Lubeck et al. 1985; Hurley et al. 1989; Hurley et al. 1991). More recent evidence suggests that in the presence of other managed care practices, adding or removing gatekeeper requirements need not produce strong changes in utilization and spending (Kapur et al. 2000; Escarce et al. 2001; Ferris et al. 2001), though it may be associated with more use of recommended screening (Phillips et al. 2004).

Finally, plans can pursue many different activities designed to influence the care decisions of providers, increasing the chances that they will act in ways desired by the plan. Many plans work to directly educate physicians in their networks about developments and treatments of interest, issue clinical practice guidelines, or use reminder systems to prompt to providers and patients about desired behaviors. Along with these efforts, plans may monitor the practice patterns of physicians to track things such as compliance with quality goals or other utilization rates, such as the use of specialist referrals or diagnostic tests. The information compiled can be shared with providers in efforts to influence their activities, and used as an input into payment programs and network management activities.

18.2.1.3 *Financial Incentives*

Managed care is often associated with two types of changes in provider payment: reductions in the level of provider payments, and changes in the mechanisms used to pay providers. Traditional indemnity insurance, as it developed in the United States, typically did not act aggressively to restrain increases in provider payments, and generous provider payments were one of the factors underlying rapid growth in healthcare spending during the latter part of the 1900s. Many managed care plans worked to limit provider payments. It appears that managed care plans had some market power vis-à-vis physicians and hospitals, particularly early in the time period when managed care was growing, and they used this to extract price concessions (Rosenthal, Landon et al. 2001). A study comparing HMOs and traditional insurance in Massachusetts reported that both types of plans had similar treatment patterns, but that HMOs paid 30 to 40 percent less primarily because of lower unit prices (Cutler et al. 2000). Studies also suggest that physician earnings, particularly those of specialists, were reduced by managed care activity (e.g. Simon and Born 1996; Simon et al. 1998; Hadley and Mitchell 1999).

Many managed care plans have also tried, with varying degrees of success, to move away from fee-for-service payment systems that can create incentives for inefficient use of health care (Pauly 1970, 1980) toward payment mechanisms like capitation that can provide incentives to reduce utilization (Ma 1994; Newhouse 1996). Some plans augment standard capitation or fee-for-service payment arrangements with the use of other financial incentives, often targeted at encouraging providers to meet specific plan goals. Plans may directly pay bonuses for performing services of interest like immunizations. "Withhold pools" are another example, in which some of the funds due to each provider at various points during a year are withheld by the plan and retained in a pool. At the end of the year, the contents of the pool holding withholds from many physicians are released to individual physicians based on their performance on some set of metrics. Physicians who meet utilization, quality, or other targets might receive their full due payments along with an additional bonus from the pool, while physicians not meeting targets might receive less.

Plans may vary the payment mechanisms used for different physicians, for example paying primary care physicians using capitation, but other types of physicians using fee-for-service arrangements. Plans may also use different payment mechanisms for different services, such as using capitation payments for the majority of primary care services but also incorporating fee-for-service payments for specific sets of preventive services. Payment approaches may also vary across the levels of multi-tiered relationships. For example, a plan that contracts with an IPA to use the IPA's network may compensate the IPA for physician services using capitation, but the IPA may use the funds received to pay individual physicians in its network using different arrangements such as fee-for-service (Gold et al. 1995; Conrad et al. 1998; Rosenthal et al. 2002). As a general rule, plans are much more likely to use capitation with larger provider groups than with smaller practices (Rosenthal, Frank, et al. 2001). One important reason for this is that smaller practices can have difficulty effectively managing the financial risks associated with capitation.

Managed care payments to hospitals are typically structured in one of two ways. Many plans use prospective payment systems based on diagnosis related groups (DRGs), which can create incentives to reduce utilization akin to those created by capitation payments for physicians. Others may use "per-diem" payment systems, which are associated with incentives to hospital managers similar to those of fee-for-service payments for physicians. Where managed care plans own and operate their own hospitals, they may use other cost-based or budget-based hospital payment systems.

There is a large body of evidence showing that payment incentives influence physician behavior (e.g. Hickson et al. 1987; Hemenway et al. 1990; Kralewski et al. 1999; Kralewski et al. 2000; Gosden et al. 2001), though there are some studies that find small or no effects in some particular situations (e.g. Hutchison et al. 1996; Hillman et al. 1998). Evidence also suggests that hospitals respond to incentives such as those associated with DRG payments (e.g. Zwanziger and Melnick 1988).

Over time, patterns of provider payment have varied. The use of capitation in particular has ebbed and flowed. As managed care generally expanded in the late 1980s and early 1990s, many health insurers attempted to implement payment mechanisms emphasizing capitation for providers and more prospective payments for hospitals. In the latter part of the 1990s, providers became increasingly dissatisfied with capitation and DRG payments, the problems caused by shifting significant amounts of risk to providers became clearer, and managed care plans became less aggressive in general, and as a result the use of capitation and prospective payment receded (Robinson 2001).

18.2.1.4 Covered Services

Both managed care plans and traditional insurance plans normally cover a broad range of outpatient and inpatient services that are determined to be medically necessary for the care of their enrollees. However, managed care plans do sometimes differ in their coverage of particular types of services. Many HMOs have adopted coverage policies that encourage the use of preventive care by providing generous coverage for it. This may be related to the history of group and staff model HMOs as organizations that would retain populations over long periods of time, such that strong prevention activities would clearly pay off. It may also be related to strategic efforts to attract healthier, more prevention-oriented, patients, which may be advantageous for HMOs (Frank et al. 2000). In some other cases, managed care plans can be more restrictive. For example, managed care plans have tended to be more aggressive than indemnity plans in the use of formularies to restrict the use of costly new pharmaceutical products.

18.2.1.5 Patient Cost Sharing

Managed care plans can also differ from indemnity insurers in their use of patient cost sharing. Indemnity insurance plans, lacking strong supply-side constraints on inefficient utilization, typically relied heavily on patient cost sharing as a demand side incentive to reduce moral hazard. Substantial deductibles and coinsurance requirements were common features of indemnity plans. Many managed care practices can be viewed as supply-side attempts to influence health care utilization. With stronger supply-side controls, managed care plans have less need to rely on demand-side controls. Some early HMOs used no cost sharing at all, seeing little reason to burden patients when they believed their supply side constraints were sufficient. Over time, though, small copayments have been shown to further improve efficiency and so are now common (Cherkin et al. 1989; Gabel 1997), with many HMOs imposing copayments for the use of most services, for example $10 or $20 per visit. PPOs frequently use stronger demand-side incentives than HMOs (e.g. Claxton et al. 2009).

18.2.2 The Development of Managed Care and Types of Managed Care Plans

Managed care has evolved over time, coming to be associated primarily with several different types of plans with stereotypical features. Group and staff model HMOs have perhaps the longest history of managed care plans in the United States. As early as the 1930s, there were vertically integrated organizations that provided insurance against health-related risks and had a network of providers to deliver care to enrolled individuals. Referred to early on as pre-paid group practices (PGPs), these organizations grew into some of the most prominent group and staff model HMOs. Examples include Kaiser Permanente, which has now grown to become the largest group-model HMO in the United States, and the Group Health Cooperative of Puget Sound, operating today as a large staff model HMO.

Though the details of plan arrangements vary from one plan to another, group and staff model HMOs generally share a set of common features that distinguish them from other types of plans (Figure 18.1). They are characterized by well-defined and highly organized provider networks, usually directly employing physicians. They almost always operate on a closed-panel basis, and typically require enrollees to work with a primary care physician who acts as a gatekeeper. Care decisions can be subject to relatively strong controls, but because of the typically close relationship between physicians and the plan, many efforts to monitor and control utilization can be developed with some collaboration between physicians and the insurer and implemented using peer-review approaches. Because these plans impose strong supply-side controls on utilization, they tend to exert little effort on the demand side, often using only relatively small copayments at the point of service use. Most group and staff model HMO physicians are paid using mechanisms that include significant salary components.

While group and staff model HMOs have existed for many years, for much of their history they operated in a limited niche. Many physicians, along with national physician organizations like the American Medical Association, preferred practice models that emphasized physician independence and autonomy. As a result, they disapproved of PGPs and encouraged the creation of regulatory barriers to their spread. Many patients were also apparently wary of PGPs, and their growth remained quite slow even after some of the early restrictions were relaxed. As of the early 1970s, there were a number of PGPs in operation, but only a few percent of the US population had enrolled in one.

By that time, though, persistent cost growth had become an important issue and was perceived to be fueled, at least in part, by the prevalent traditional indemnity insurance arrangements. The search for new models of health insurance that could better cope with rising costs drew attention to PGPs and managed care approaches. One key turning point was passage of the HMO Act of 1973, which enacted important legal changes favorable to managed care plans. Between 1970 and 1975, the number of HMOs operating in the United States increased from 37 to 183 and HMO membership doubled (Gruber et al. 1988). Growth in managed care accelerated further in the 1980s with the relaxation of restrictions on selective contracting. Prior to that time, many states had required that insurance plans offer enrollees a choice of any qualified provider, restricting one of the core tools of managed care plans. Changes to these rules ushered in an era of rapid growth in managed care (Gabel et al. 1986).

		Traditional Indemnity Insurance	Group or Staff Model HMO	IPA or Network Model HMO	Preferred Provider Organization (PPO)
Patient Perspective	Network	Enrollee may see any provider; some plans place basic restrictions on provider choice (e.g. basic accreditation)	Enrollee must see network providers; out-of-network care not covered	Enrollee must see network providers; out-of-network care not covered	Enrollee encouraged to see network providers (e.g. with more favorable cost sharing); out-of-network care sometimes covered with less favorable cost sharing
	Utilization Review	Limited	Can be strong; peer-review common	Can be strong; more often arm's-length review	Some, typically less aggressive than HMOs
	Gatekeeper	None	Required	Required	None
	Cost Sharing	Higher deductibles and coinsurance	Minimal; typically small copayments	Minimal; typically small copayments	Higher deductibles and coinsurance
Provider Perspective	Network	Any provider can see covered patients	Providers employed by the plan (staff model) or have exclusive contract with the plan (group model)	Providers maintain independent practices; non-exclusively contract with the plan	Providers maintain independent practices; non-exclusively contract with the plan
	Utilization Review	Limited	Can be strong; peer-review common	Can be strong; more often arm's-length review	Some, typically less aggressive than HMOs
	Financial Incentives	Fee-for-service payments, commonly based on fee schedules	Mixed financial incentives; salary common	Mixed financial incentives; some capitation; can include withhold pools or bonus arrangements	Mixed financial incentives; commonly fee-for-service using fee schedules; can include withhold pools or bonus arrangements

FIGURE 18.1 Characteristics of 4 stereotypical types of health insurance plans

Some of this growth occurred as group and staff model HMOs expanded, but rapid expansion of group and staff models proved difficult and much of the new growth during this time period was in new plan types. Two of the most important were network model and IPA model HMOs. From the patient perspective, the main features of these plans are similar to those of group and staff model HMOs. From the provider perspective, however, they look quite different. Network model HMOs construct their physician network by contracting non-exclusively with multiple, typically larger, physician groups. In IPA-model HMOs, the physician network is created by contracting with an IPA, which in turn contracts with many, typically smaller, independent practices. Physicians who are part of an organization that has a relationship with a network-model or IPA-model HMO typically retain significant shares of their practice from other sources, so these models typically allow a large degree of flexibility for physicians. These organizational forms could also be quickly developed and expanded in a period of more flexible, faster growth. At the same time, they also face some organizational challenges. The affiliation between the health insurer and its network physicians is much looser, which can create agency problems for the insurer. The insurer, or the entity that operates the network on behalf of the insurer, may thus feel the need to go to greater lengths to monitor physician behavior and impose restraints on utilization. Given the lack of a close relationship between the plan and physicians, these controls are more often imposed on physicians than developed and implemented collaboratively with physicians. Network-model and IPA-model plans can use a variety of compensation mechanisms, but are the types of plans more commonly associated with the use of capitation, withhold pools, and other financial incentives to manage the agency challenges that can arise.

The other important form of managed care plan that came to prominence during the expansion of managed care is the Preferred Provider Organization (PPO). One way of thinking about PPOs is as plans that fill the conceptual space between IPA-model HMOs and traditional indemnity insurers. From the perspective of the patient, PPOs have a network of physicians to choose from (the "preferred providers"), but typically only encourage use of network providers though financial incentives, rather than requiring it. PPOs do not typically use gatekeepers. PPOs often exert some effort to oversee and control utilization, but stereotypically these efforts are less aggressive than those used by HMOs. With weaker supply-side restraints on utilization than HMOs, PPOs often incorporate more demand side incentives—higher deductibles and coinsurance requirements are common.

As managed care plans expanded rapidly in the 1980s and 1990s, often touting their ability to control health care costs, consumer concerns that plans were over-emphasizing cost reduction and de-emphasizing the quality of health care delivered grew. The resulting "managed care backlash" (Blendon et al. 1998) slowed the push toward strongly managed plans. Many employers responded to the demands of their employees and moved toward plans making less aggressive use of managed care practices, such as PPOs. Many plans, responding to changes in the preferences of their customers, moderated their use of managed care practices.

Managed care continues to evolve. New plans, such as point-of-service (POS) plans that meld components of HMOs and PPOs, have developed, and interest in managed care techniques seems likely to continue to ebb and flow in coming years. As of this writing, managed care as used in the US private sector contains a mix of different types of plans. Conventional indemnity insurance has essentially disappeared, falling to 2 percent of the privately insured market in 2008. PPO plans are the most prominent, with about 60 percent of private insurance plans. Private sector enrollment in HMOs and POS plans is between 30 and 40 percent. In the public sector, there remains a significant amount of conventional insurance in the Medicare program, but there have been increases in the use of managed care in both the Medicare and Medicaid programs over time.

18.3 MANAGED CARE AND SELECTION

The potential for biased selection can have important implications for health insurance markets, and the role of managed care in selection has received quite a bit of attention. Relative to indemnity insurance plans, managed care plans are usually expected to receive favorable selection. Managed care plans often emphasize prevention in their coverage decisions, and thus may attract individuals with preferences for preventive care, who are often thought to be healthier than average. On the other end of the health spectrum, many individuals with significant health issues have developed strong relationships with specific providers and managed care plans with restrictions on provider choices may threaten these relationships, leading less healthy individuals to favor plans with less management. Individuals interested in using expensive services, such as those with significant health conditions or those who simply have preferences for specialist consultations or the consumption of advanced services, may also perceive utilization review, gatekeeper requirements, or other care management efforts as undesirable. There are some potentially countervailing incentives—managed care plans often require fewer out-of-pocket payments than other types of plans, which could be advantageous to individuals who use a large amount of medical care, and people with significant health needs may prefer to work with a health plan that they perceive to have carefully selected providers and can thus help them navigate complex care choices—but these forces appear to be weaker. The most common expectation is that incentives leading to favorable selection into managed care plans will prevail. For similar reasons, one might expect more restrictive plans, such as HMOs, to receive more favorable selection than less restrictive plans such as PPOs.

Dozens of studies have examined selection and managed care. Patterns of selection could easily vary with the specific characteristics of the health plans being studied, but in practice most studies are constrained by data availability to study selection into HMOs. These studies take a variety of approaches to measuring selection, but for the most part they focus on measures of health status or prior medical spending of individuals enrolled in HMOs and those who are not. Study designs also vary. Some use cross-sectional comparisons of individuals in and out of HMOs. Other studies focus on individuals who are newly offered a choice of health plans, examining the characteristics of those who choose different types of plans, or examine individuals who elect to switch from one type of plan to another.

Several reviews summarize results from studies of selection into HMOs published by the late 1990s (Hellinger 1987; Hellinger 1995; Glied 2000; Hellinger and Wong 2000). For the most part, these studies report results consistent with the view that HMOs receive favorable selection, though they do note that the extent, and even existence, of favorable selection can vary from case to case. For example, some studies focused on just maternity care found that HMOs tended to receive adverse selection relative to other types of plans.

More recent studies generally concur. Medicare HMO enrollees had lower mortality rates, used fewer hospital days, and tended to score better on many (though not all) measures of health status than those in traditional Medicare (Call et al. 1999; Call et al. 2001; Maciejewski et al. 2001; Mello et al. 2003; Dhanani et al. 2004). A set of studies also suggests favorable selection into HMOs in private markets. Two studies found substantial favorable selection into an HMO among state government employees in Massachusetts (Cutler and Zeckhauser 1998, Altman et al. 2003). Nicholson and colleagues found that people who switched into a private HMO used 11 percent fewer resources in the year before switching than people who stayed in a non-HMO (Nicholson et al. 2004) (though these results are not unanimous; see for example Polsky and Nicholson 2004).

Whether or not selection into HMOs is problematic or not may vary from case to case. In principle, selection could improve the ability of insurance markets to function and pool risk, or it could impede it. Managed care plans, by selecting for healthier patients, may lead to market equilibria in which healthy individuals tend to pool together, leaving less healthy individuals pooled in less managed or indemnity plans. Less complete pooling could be inefficient. On the other hand, allowing healthier and sicker people to select into different insurance plans may be required for insurance plans to exist at all. In the presence of sufficiently divergent risks and asymmetric information about preferences, selection of individuals with different levels of risk into different plans may be the only way to achieve a stable equilibrium in insurance markets. If this is the case, trying to pool people of broadly divergent types together would result in unstable insurance arrangements that would fail to function effectively in the long run. In this sense, selection and market segmentation induced by managed care may have desirable features (Rothschild and Stiglitz 1976; Pauly 1985; Glied 2000).

Some experiences with managed care and selection suggest the potential for inefficient effects on pooling. In particular, situations have been reported in which the introduction of managed care plans led to selection that appeared to destabilized formerly stable pooling equilibria, putting other plans in "adverse selection spirals" and even ultimately driving other plans out of business (e.g. Feldman et al. 1993; Cutler and Reber 1997).

18.4 Effects of Managed Care on Health Care for Enrollees

Taken individually, any particular activity of a managed care plan may influence health care delivery. Taken together, the collected set of practices embodied in a managed care plan will generate an aggregate impact on health care that reflects the net effect of the individual practices and interactions between them. A considerable amount of effort has been devoted to studying these types of effects, asking about the impacts that joining managed care plans has on health care delivery, costs, and outcomes.

These can be difficult questions to address. In the first place, the effect of joining a managed care plan is likely to be quite variable. Different types of plans can have very different features. Individual plans of the same general type may use different specific practices and place emphasis in different areas. The same insurance company may offer multiple specific policies, each with different specific characteristics. It can be difficult to find out the specific arrangements that are in place in a given plan, and they may vary over time. As noted by Glied (2000), plans also vary in their other characteristics. Plans may be for-profit or not-for-profit, operate in areas with many or few hospitals, providers, or other plans, have long experience or be new market entrants, or vary on any number of other characteristics that can complicate inferences and be difficult to measure.

Selection bias can also raise challenges. Cross sectional comparisons of health care delivered to patients in different plans can encounter considerable difficulties effectively accounting for variations in health status, preferences, and other characteristics of patients in different plans. Many studies therefore examine situations in which the plan choices offered to individuals change or individuals switch plans for other reasons. Though they can ameliorate the most prominent challenges facing cross-sectional analyses, these kinds of studies can also suffer from selection-related challenges, for example if the characteristics of individuals who elect to switch plans differ from those of individuals who do not.

One common hypothesis is that joining a managed care plan would result in less utilization of expensive inpatient services, potentially replaced with more outpatient care. Other hypotheses are that managed care plans would reduce the use of expensive, potentially overused, tests and procedures, generate higher quality of care, and lower costs. These have been tested in many studies, and several reviews have collected and summarized this evidence (Miller and Luft 1994; Miller and Luft 1997; Dudley et al. 1998; Glied 2000; Miller and Luft 2002). For a variety of reasons, most of the work in this area has focused on differences between HMOs and non-HMO plans.

The early evidence on hospital use suggested that HMO enrollees had fewer admissions and shorter lengths of stay than non-HMO enrollees (Miller and Luft 1994), but more recent evidence suggests less clear differences—some studies have reported that HMO patients use less hospital care in some cases, but others suggest small or no differences, or even higher rates in HMO patients (Miller and Luft 1997; Miller and Luft 2002; Dhanani et al. 2004). One important feature of these comparisons seems to be changes in hospitalization patterns in non-HMO plans, which may have come to more closely approximate those of HMOs. For physician use, early evidence suggested the same or more physician visits by HMO enrollees (Miller and Luft 1994). More recent studies also often show more physician use by HMO patients (e.g. Deb et al. 2006), but differences have become less clearly delineated over time (e.g. Miller and Luft 1997; Miller and Luft 2002). Evidence does tend to suggest less use of high cost services in HMOs, and more use of preventive care (Miller and Luft 2002).

Studies that have explicitly examined costs of care for HMO enrollees are relatively scarce. Given the ambiguity in recent results on hospitalization and physician use, it is not clear that HMOs will neccassarily have significantly lower costs than other types of plans, though the results suggesting less use of expensive tests and procedures might suggest at least some effect on overall costs. Some direct evidence on costs does suggest that overall costs per enrollee are lower in HMOs than other types of plans, though this effect is not found in all studies (Miller and Luft 2002). In practice, many HMOs have lower premiums than other types of plans, which may suggest lower costs.

Results on quality of care are mixed. A large subset of the evidence on quality of care in HMOs has focused on care for patients with cardiac conditions or cancer. Miller and Luft, in their 2002 review, report that in nineteen published findings on quality of cardiac care in HMOs, seven of the findings were predominantly favorable for HMOs and seven were predominantly unfavorable, with the others inconclusive. They reported similar results for cancer care and studies of other conditions. Over the last several years, this pattern has generally persisted. Some results suggest that some managed care patients receive better care than other patients (e.g. Xu and Jensen 2006; Zeng et al. 2006) while other studies suggest no difference or even the opposite (e.g. Every et al. 1998; Luft 2003).

Some related work has examined measures of access to care, such as patient reported measures of the ease of contacting their usual provider, ease of getting an appointment, or whether they have any unmet needs for care. Miller and Luft (2002) reviewed several studies of these kinds of measures and found mixed results, with a slight tilt toward findings unfavorable to HMOs. Other studies have examined patient reported satisfaction with care, which tends to be lower among HMO patients, particularly for things such as patient–physician communication and quality of services. HMO patients were sometimes more satisfied with costs of care and prevention than other patients.

18.5 Area-level Effects of Managed Care

Beyond impacts on enrolled individuals, growth in managed care may also have broader influences on the structure and functioning of the entire health care system. These could lead to "spillover effects" in which managed care activity ends up influencing care for patients outside of managed care plans. Two previous reviews have examined this type of effect of managed care (Chernew, Hirth et al. 1998; Baker 2003).

There are a handful of mechanisms by which managed care could influence the health care system as a whole. First, managed care could influence physician practice patterns (Glied and Zivin 2002). The notion that physicians often adopt patterns of practice that they apply to most or all of their patients is commonly accepted. Changes in physician practice patterns may thus lead to generalized changes in care delivery (Phelps 1992). Highly managed plans like HMOs often devote considerable resources to influencing the physicians who practice in their panels, doing things like disseminating literature and information and providing feedback on the treatments given to their patients, which could lead to the development of more conservative practice styles that these physicians apply even to their non-HMO patients. Moreover, physicians practicing in areas with high levels of managed care activity, even if they themselves do not take care of many managed care patients, may frequently encounter physicians who do and may thus be influenced by their more conservative practice styles. A related effect could occur at the health plan level. As managed care activity increases in an area, the competitive pressure felt by traditional insurers may increase. Some studies argue that traditional insurers adopted some of the practices of managed care plans once their value in achieving cost savings was demonstrated (Goldberg and Greenberg 1979; Goldberg and Greenberg 1980; Frank and Welch 1985; Feldman et al. 1986; Baker and Corts 1996), although this literature is not unanimous (e.g. McLaughlin 1988a).

Second, shifts in structures and incentives could change decisions that health care providers make about the kinds of services they will offer. This argument is often made around shifts in demand. If managed care reduces demand for some types of technologies or services, either directly from their own patients or indirectly by influencing overall practice patterns, offering those technologies or services will become less profitable, which will reduce the extent to which those technologies or services become available. A commonly encountered belief is that managed care would slow the adoption of new technologies. This may be correct in some cases, but it need not always be the case. Managed care plans may encourage the diffusion of new technologies and services that they view as cost-effective. These kinds of effects could also extend beyond technologies. For example, growth in managed care could attract generalist physicians and discourage others, or spur the growth of outpatient surgery centers.

Managed care could influence the health care system by driving changes in provider organization. Physicians may find it advantageous to practice in larger groups as the prevalence of managed care grows. Hospital–physician integration may be promoted by the presence of managed care in an area. Managed care may also lead to changes in patient expectations, knowledge, or behavior. Managed care activities to educate patients or promote health practices may contribute to the generalized spread of information in high managed care areas, perhaps prompting changes in the behavior of other area patients.

That managed care could have broad effects on the structure and functioning of the health care system through the mechanisms outlined above is quite plausible. Whether or not these effects exist and, if so, how important they are, is a matter for empirical research. There have been a number of studies that have attempted to look at these issues. Most studies attempt in one way or another to compare measures of health care system capabilities, treatments, costs, or outcomes across areas with varying levels of managed care activity. Studies adopt a variety of designs, including cross-sectional analyses and analyses of changes in area managed care activity over time. Studies of these issues face some important challenges. Perhaps the most important is the fact that managed care activity is not randomly distributed across areas, but rather is related to health care spending and health care delivery patterns, which can raise the potential for endogeneity. Many studies make serious attempts to deal with this challenge, but it has often proven difficult to fully address.

18.5.1 Studies of Health Expenditures

If managed care activity does drive area-level changes in health care delivery, one place to find an effect would be in area-level measures of spending, and many studies have focused in this area. Within this group, one large subgroup of studies focuses on hospital utilization and spending. Most of the earliest studies of managed care spillovers, reviewed by Frank and Welch (1985), fall into this category. Some of these earlier studies supported the view that managed care activity would drive down hospital use (Chiswick 1976; Goldberg and Greenberg 1979; Dowd 1987: part I), but most work found no effect or even the opposite (e.g. McLaughlin et al. 1984; Feldman et al. 1986; Luft et al. 1986; Hay and Leahy 1987; McLaughlin 1987; McLaughlin 1988b). More recent work has tended to suggest that increases in HMO market share are associated with reductions in hospital spending (e.g. Noether 1988; Robinson 1991; Robinson 1996; Gaskin and Hadley 1997). Some studies have gone beyond hospital spending to examine broader measures of spending. For example, Cutler and Sheiner (1998) studied the relationship between state-level HMO market share and total health care expenditures, reporting reductions in hospital spending associated with higher HMO market share that was partly offset by higher physician spending. A number of studies have also examined spending among traditional Medicare (fee-for-service) beneficiaries for evidence of spillover effects. This is a strong population to examine in that it is covered by a stable, essentially non-managed health insurance program. Relative to studies of hospital spending, many of which pool spending by managed care plan enrollees and patients in other plans, analysis of the traditional Medicare market offers a clearly defined opportunity to obtain estimates of the relationship between area HMO market share and spending by non-managed-care plan enrollees. Evidence from these studies frequently, but not unanimously, suggests that increases in managed care activity are associated with lower levels of spending by traditional Medicare enrollees (Clement et al. 1992; Welch 1994; Rodgers and Smith 1995; Baker 1997; Baker and Sharkarkumar 1998; Baker 1999).

Another way to study effects of managed care on spending is to look at premiums. Although insurance premiums reflect many things, including profit margins for insurance companies and the under-writing cycle, the presence of lower spending levels should tend to be reflected in lower premiums. A couple of studies report that higher levels of HMO market share are associated with lower premiums overall or for non-HMO plans (Feldstein and Wickizer 1995; Wickizer and Feldstein 1995; Baker et al. 2000), though two other studies do not find strong and consistent associations (Baker and Corts 1996; Hill and Wolfe 1997).

One question that arises in interpretation of these studies is whether the effects on spending arise through changes in price or changes in quantity. This is hard to determine in some of the studies, but others suggest that variations in quantity play an important role. Medicare hospital expenditures, for example, should not be strongly subject to variation in price since the Prospective Payment System centrally determines prices. Hence, the most natural interpretation of studies that show reductions in Medicare inpatient spending associated with higher managed care activity is that practice patterns have shifted so that patients receive fewer hospitalizations and fewer intensive tests and procedures. Outside of Medicare, it is more plausible that increased managed care activity led to reductions in the prices charged by hospitals and other providers, which could contribute to reductions in overall expenditures in some of these studies. Some studies suggest that increased competition between hospitals can reduce expenditures (Chernew, Hirth et al. 1998), and that the presence of managed care plans can enhance competition (Feldman, Chan et al. 1990; Kessler and McClellan 2000).

18.5.2 Studies of Infrastructure and Capabilities

In a number of studies, area managed care activity is associated with the number and types of providers, the capabilities of the health care system, and the ways the system is organized. Chernew (1995) reports that areas with higher HMO market share had fewer hospital beds in the mid- and late 1980s. Studies of physician workforce suggest that high managed care areas have attracted and retained fewer physicians, particularly specialists (Escarce et al. 1998; Escarce et al. 2000; Polsky et al. 2000). Evidence also tends to suggest that physicians in high managed care areas work less, have lower incomes (particularly specialists), and report lower satisfaction (Simon and Born 1996; Hadley and Mitchell 1997; Simon et al. 1997; Simon et al. 1998; Hadley et al. 1999; Hadley and Mitchell 1999). Analyses of organizations suggest an association between managed care activities and consolidation and integration in some provider markets (Burns 1997; Baker and Brown 1999; Morrisey et al. 1999; Dranove et al. 2002). Evidence also tends to support the view that managed care has slowed the adoption of many technologies, particularly high cost, infrastructure-intensive new technologies such as MRI, NICUs, and cardiac revascularization (Cutler and McClellan 1996; Baker and Wheeler 1998; Cutler and Sheiner 1998; Baker 2001; Baker and Phibbs 2002), though not all studies find effects (e.g. Hill and Wolfe 1997; Baker and Spetz 1999).

18.5.3 Studies of Treatments, Quality, and Health Outcomes

Some area level studies show relationships between managed care activity and treatment patterns. Patients with acute myocardial infarction tend to receive less intensive treatment in areas with more HMOs, as do some cancer patients (Baker and McClellan 2001; Heidenreich et al. 2002; Bundorf et al. 2004). Cancer screening rates appear to be higher in areas with higher HMO market shares (Phillips et al. 1998). Quality measures appear related to overall managed care activity in one study (Rogowski et al. 2007), and some work reports fewer preventable hospitalization rates associated with increasing managed care (Backus et al. 2002; Zhan et al. 2004). Some work also associates high managed care areas with lower mortality for some groups, though the associations may vary from place to place (e.g. Mukamel et al. 2001; Escarce et al. 2006). On the other hand, Baker and Brown (1999) examined breast cancer stage at diagnosis and mortality rates in high and low managed care areas and found no significant differences, and Heidenreich et al. (2002) did not find effects on mortality rates in their study of treatments for AMI patients.

18.6 Aggregate Spending Patterns Since the Rise of Managed Care

Some additional evidence on the effects of managed care can come from analysis of overall spending patterns in the United States. Newhouse and colleagues looked at spending in fee-for-service and HMO plans over 1976–1981 and found that they grew at comparable rates (Newhouse et al. 1985). This followed earlier work by Luft that also showed comparable growth rates from the 1960s into the early 1970s (Luft 1981). Both suggested little effect of managed care on overall spending patterns.

Evidence from the mid- and late 1990s, however, does suggest the possibility of an effect. After rising at an annual rate of more than 10 percent between 1980 and 1990, annual growth in spending slowed to a rate of 4 percent to 5 percent per year between 1994 and 1997, about the time when managed care had grown to the point where it could plausibly be a force in US health expenditures. The slowdown was most pronounced in hospital spending, where annual growth rates fell to just above 3 percent during this time period, consistent with research suggesting that managed care has particularly targeted hospital use. Other areas of spending that do not seem to have been as strong a focus of managed care plans, like prescription drugs, maintained high growth rates during this time period. More recently, however, rates of increase in total spending have picked up. Starting in about 1998, as many managed care plans began to act less aggressively, annual growth in total health care spending accelerated and has remained relatively high in recent years. The mid-1990s slowdown is consistent with the power of managed care to reduce aggregate spending, but as it focuses on the entire population, is not clear evidence of a generalized effect on spending. Its apparently transitory nature also suggests a one-time effect on costs rather than an effect on long term growth rates.

18.7 Conclusion

Managed care and the insurance practices it embodies have important economic implications, both conceptually and in practice. Changes in provider payment, patient cost sharing, care oversight and management, provider networks, and covered services appear to influence care delivered to managed care plan enrollees and, more broadly, to be able to affect the structure and operation of the health care system more broadly. While available information provides important insights into managed care and its effects, important things remain to be studied and continual evolution in health plans will likely demand ongoing attention to the effects of health plans and managed care on health care delivery, costs, and efficiency.

REFERENCES

ALTMAN, D., D. M. CUTLER, and R. J. ZECKHAUSER (2003). "Enrollee mix, treatment intensity, and cost in competing indemnity and HMO plans." *Journal of Health Economics* 22: 23–45.

BACKUS, L., M. MORON, P. BACCHETTI, L. C. BAKER, and A. B. BINDMAN (2002). "Effect of managed care on preventable hospitalization rates in California." *Medical Care* 40(4): 315–24.

BAKER, L. C. (1997). "The effect of HMOs on fee-for-service health care expenditures: Evidence from Medicare." *Journal of Health Economics* 16(4): 453–82.

—— (1999). "Association of managed care market share and health expenditures for fee-for-service Medicare patients." *Journal of the American Medical Association* 281(5): 432–7.

—— (2001). "Managed Care and Technology Adoption in Health Care: Evidence from Magnetic Resonance Imaging." *Journal of Health Economics* 20(3): 395–421.

—— (2003). "Managed Care Spillover Effects." *Annual Review of Public Health* 24: 435–56.

—— and M. L. BROWN (1999). "Managed care, consolidation among health care providers, and health care: Evidence from mammography." *RAND Journal of Economics* 30(2): 351–74.

—— and K. S. CORTS (1996). "HMO penetration and the cost of health care: market discipline or market segmentation?" *American Economic Review* 86(2): 389–94.

—— and M. B. MCCLELLAN (2001). "Managed care, health care quality, and regulation." *Journal of Legal Studies* 30(2, part 2): 715–42.

—— and C. S. PHIBBS (2002). "Managed care, technology adoption, and health care: the adoption of neonatal intensive care." *RAND Journal of Economics* 33(3): 524–48.

—— and S. SHARKARKUMAR (1998). "Managed care and health care expenditures: evidence from Medicare, 1990–1994." In A. M. Garber (ed.), *Frontiers in Health Policy Research*, Vol. 1. Cambridge, MA, MIT Press, 117–52.

—— and J. SPETZ (1999). "Managed care and medical technology growth." In A. M. Garber (ed.), *Frontiers in Health Policy Research*, Vol. 2. Cambridge, MA, MIT Press, 27–52.

—— and S. K. WHEELER (1998). "Managed care and technology diffusion: the case of MRI." *Health Affairs* 17(5): 195–207.

—— J. C. CANTOR, S. LONG, and M. S. MARQUIS (2000). "HMO Market Penetration and Costs of Employer-Sponsored Health Plans." *Health Affairs* 19(5): 121–8.

BLENDON, R. J., M. BRODIE, J. M. BENSON, D. E. ALTMAN, L. LEVITT, T. HOFF, and L. HUGICK (1998). "Understanding the managed care backlash." *Health Affairs* 17(4): 80–94.

BUNDORF, M. K., K. A. SCHULMAN, J. A. STAFFORD, D. J. GASKIN, J. G. JOLLIS, and J. J. ESCARCE (2004). "Impact of managed care on the treatment, costs, and outcomes of fee-for-service Medicare patients with acute myocardial infarction." *Health Services Research* 39(1): 7–12.

BURNS, L. R., G. J. BAZZOLI, L. DYNAN, and D. R. WHOLEY (1997). "Managed care, market stages, and integrated delivery systems: is there a relationship?" *Health Affairs* 16(6): 204–18.

CALL, K. T., B. DOWD, R. FELDMAN, and M. MACIEJEWSKI (1999). "Selection Experiences in Medicare HMOs: Pre-Enrollment Expenditures." *Health Care Financing Review* 20(4): 197–209.

———————— N. Lurie, A. M. McBean, and M. Maciejewski (2001). "Disenrollment from Medicare HMOs." *American Journal of Managed Care* 7(1): 37–51.

Cherkin, D. C., L. Grothaus, and E. Wagner (1989). "The effect of office visit copayments on utilization in a health maintenance organization." *Medical Care* 27(11): 1036–45.

Chernew, M. (1995). "The impact of non-IPA HMOs on the number of hospitals and hospital capacity." *Inquiry* 32(2): 143–54.

—— R. Hayward, and D. Scanlon (1996). "Managed care and open-heart surgery facilities in California." *Health Affairs* 15(1): 191–201.

—— D. P. Scanlon, and R. Hayward (1998). "Insurance type and choice of hospital for coronary artery bypass graft surgery." *Health Services Research* 33: 447–66.

—— E., R. A. Hirth, S. S. Sonnad, R. Ermann, and A. M. Fendrick (1998). "Managed care, medical technology, and health care cost growth: a review of the evidence." *Medical Care Research and Review* 55(3): 259–88.

Chiswick, B. R. (1976). "Hospital utilization: an analysis of SMSA differences in occupancy rates, admission rates, and bed rates." *Explorations in Economic Research* 3(3): 326–78.

Claxton, G., B. DiJulio, B. Finder, et al. (2009). Employer health benefits; 2008 Annual survey, Kaiser Family Foundation and HRET.

Clement, D. G., P. M. Gleason, and R. S. Brown (1992). *The Effects of Risk Contract HMO Market Penetration on Medicare Fee-For-Service Costs: Final Report.* Princeton, NJ, Mathematica Policy Research.

Conrad, D. A., C. Maynard, A. Cheadle, et al. (1998). "Primary care physician compensation method in medical groups: does it influence the use and cost of health services for enrollees in managed care organizations." *Journal of the American Medical Association* 279(11): 853–8.

Cutler, D. and M. McClellan (1996). "The determinants of technological change in heart attack treatment." NBER Working Papers 5751.

—— and S. Reber (1997). "Paying for health insurance: the tradeoff between competition and adverse selection." NBER Working Paper 5796.

—— and L. Sheiner (1998). "Managed care and the growth of medical expenditures." In A. M. Garber (ed.), *Frontiers in Health Policy Research*, Vol. 1. Cambridge, MA, MIT Press, 77–116.

—— and R. J. Zeckhauser (1998). "Adverse selection in health insurance." In A. M. Garber (ed.), *Frontiers in Health Policy Research*, Vol. 1. Cambridge, MA, MIT Press, 1–32.

—— M. McClellan, and J. P. Newhouse (2000). "How does managed care do it?" *RAND Journal of Economics* 31(3): 526–48.

Deb, P., C. Li, P. K. Trivedi, and D. M. Zimmer (2006). "The effect of managed care on use of health care services: results from two contemporaneous household surveys." *Health Economics* 15: 743–60.

Dhanani, N., J. F. O'Leary, E. Keeler, A. Bamezai, and G. Melnick (2004). "The effect of HMOs on the inpatient utilization of Medicare beneficiaries." *Health Services Research* 39(5): 1607–27.

Dowd, B. E. (1987, part I). "HMOs and twin cities admission rates." *Health Services Research* 21(2): 177–88.

Dranove, D., M. Shanley, and W. White (1993). "Price and concentration in local hospital markets: the switch from patient-driven to payer-driven competition." *Journal of Law and Economics* 36: 179–204.

—— C. J. Simon, and W. D. White (2002). "Is managed care leading to consolidation in health care markets?" *Health Services Research* 37(3): 573–94.

DUDLEY, R. A., R. H. MILLER, T. Y. KORENBROT, and H. S. LUFT (1998). "The impact of financial incentives on quality of health care." *Milbank Quarterly* 76(4): 649–86.

ERICKSON, L. C., D. F. TORCHIANA, E. C. SCHNEIDER, J. W. NEWBURGER, and E. L. HANNAN (2000). "The relationship between managed care insurance and use of lower-mortality hospitals for CABG surgery." *Journal of the American Medical Association* 283(15): 1976–82.

—— P. H. WISE, E. F. COOK, A. BEISER, and J. W. NEWBURGER (2000). "The impact of managed care insurance on use of lower-mortality hospitals by children undergoing cardiac surgery in California." *Pediatrics* 105(6): 1271–8.

ESCARCE, J. J., J. A. SHEA, and W. CHEN (1997). "Segmentation of hospital markets: where do HMO enrollees get care?" *Health Affairs* 16(6): 181–92.

—— M. V. PAULY, and P. R. KLETKE (1998). "HMO penetration and the practice location choices of new physicians: a study of large metropolitan areas in the US." *Medical Care* 36(11): 1555–66.

—— D. POLSKY, G. D. WOZNIAK, and P. R. KLETKE (2000). "HMO growth and the geographical redistribution of generalist and specialist physicians, 1987–97." *Health Services Research* 35(4): 825–48.

—— K. KAPUR, G. F. JOYCE, and K. A. VAN VORST (2001). "Medical care expenditures under gatekeeper and point-of-service arrangements." *Health Services Research* 36(6): 1037–57.

—— A. K. JAIN, and J. A. ROGOWSKI (2006). "Hospital competition, managed care, and mortality after hospitalization for medical conditions: evidence from three states." *Medical Care Research and Review* 63(6 (Suppl.)): 112S–140S.

EVERY, N. R., C. P. CANNON, C. GRANGER, et al. (1998). "Influence of insurance type on the use of procedures, medications, and hospital outcomes in patients with unstable angina: results from the GUARANTEE registry." *Journal of the American College of Cardiology* 32(2): 387–92.

FELDMAN, R., B. DOWD, D. MCCANN, and A. JOHNSON (1986). "The competitive impact of health maintenance organizations on hospital finances: An exploratory study." *Journal of Health Politics, Policy, and Law* 10(4): 675–98.

—— H.-C. CHAN, J. KRALEWSKI, B. DOWD, and J. SHAPIRO (1990). "Effects of HMOs on the creation of competitive markets for hospital services." *Journal of Health Economics* 9: 207–22.

—— J. KRALEWSKI, J. SHAPIRO, and H. C. CHAN (1990). "Contracts between hospitals and health maintenance organizations." *Health Care Management Review* 15(1): 47–60.

—— B. DOWD, and G. GIFFORD (1993). "The effect of HMOs on premiums in employment-based health plans." *Health Services Research* 27(6): 779–811.

FELDSTEIN, P. J. and T. M. WICKIZER (1995). "Analysis of private health insurance premium growth rates: 1985–1992." *Medical Care* 33(10): 1035–50.

FERRIS, T. G., Y. CHANG, D. BLUMENTHAL, and S. D. PEARSON (2001). "Leaving gatekeeping behind: effects of opening access to specialists for adults in a health maintenance organization." *New England Journal of Medicine* 345(18): 1312–17.

FLYNN, K. E., M. A. SMITH, and M. K. DAVIS (2002). "From Physician to Consumer: The Effectiveness of Strategies to Manage Health Care Utilization." *Medical Care Research and Review* 59(4): 455–81.

FRANK, R. G. and W. P. WELCH (1985). "The competitive effects of HMOs: A review of the evidence." *Inquiry* 22: 148–61.

—— J. Glazer, and T. G. McGuire (2000). "Measuring adverse selection in managed health care." *Journal of Health Economics* 19: 829–54.

Gabel, J. R. (1997). "Ten ways HMOs have changed during the 1990s." *Health Affairs* 16(3): 134–45.

—— D. Ermann, and G. De Lissovoy (1986). "The emergence and future of PPOs." *Journal of Health Politics, Policy & Law* 11(2): 305–22.

Gaskin, D. J., and J. Hadley (1997). "The impact of HMO penetration on the rate of hospital cost inflation, 1985–1993." *Inquiry* 34(3): 205–16.

—— J. J. Escarce, K. A. Schulman, and J. Hadley (2002). "The determinants of HMOs' contracting with hospitals for bypass surgery." *Health Services Research* 37(4): 963–84.

Glied, S. (2000). "Managed care." In A. J. Culyer and J. P. Newhouse (eds), *Handbook of Health Economics*, Vol. 1A. Amsterdam, North Holland, 707–53.

—— and J. G. Zivin (2002). "How do doctors behave when some (but not all) or their patients are in managed care?" *Journal of Health Economics* 21(2): 337–53.

Gold, M. R., R. Hurley, T. Lake, T. Ensor, and R. Berenson (1995). "A national survey of the arrangements managed-care plans make with physicians." *The New England Journal of Medicine* 333(25): 1678–83.

Goldberg, L. G. and W. Greenberg (1979). "The competitive response of Blue cross and Blue shield to the growth of health maintenance organizations in northern California and Hawaii." *Medical Care* 17(10): 1019–28.

—— —— (1980). "The competitive response of Blue Cross to the health maintenance organization." *Economic Inquiry* 18(1): 55–68.

Gosden, T., F. Forland, I. S. Kristiansen, et al. (2001). "Impact of payment method on behaviour of primary care physicians: a systematic review." *Journal of Health Services Research and Policy* 6(1): 44–55.

Gruber, L. R., M. Shadle, and C. L. Polich (1988). "From movement to industry: the growth of HMOs." *Health Affairs* 7(3): 197–208.

Hadley, J. and J. Mitchell (1997). "Effects of HMO market penetration on physicians' work effort and satisfaction." *Health Affairs* 16(6): 99–111.

—— —— (1999). "HMO penetration and physician's earnings." *Medical Care* 37(11): 1116–27.

—— —— D. Sulmasy, and M. Bloche (1999). "Perceived financial incentives, HMO market penetration, and physicians' practice styles and satisfaction." *Health Services Research* 34(April): 307–21.

Hay, J. W. and M. J. Leahy (1987). "Competition among health plans: some preliminary evidence." *Southern Economic Journal* 11: 831–46.

Heidenreich, P. A., M. B. McClellan, C. Frances, and L. C. Baker (2002). "The relation between managed care market-share and the treatment of elderly fee-for-service patients with myocardial infarction." *American Journal of Medicine* 112(3): 176–82.

Hellinger, F. J. (1987). "Selection bias in health maintenance organizations: Analysis of recent evidence." *Health Care Financing Review* 9(2): 55–63.

—— (1995). "Selection bias in HMOs and PPOs: A review of the evidence." *Inquiry* 32(2): 135–42.

—— and H. S. Wong (2000). "Selection bias in HMOs: A review of the evidence." *Medical Care Research and Review* 57(4): 405–39.

Hemenway, D., A. Killen, S. B. Cashman, C. L. Parks, and W. J. Bicknell (1990). "Physicians' responses to financial incentives: Evidence from a for-profit ambulatory care center." *New England Journal of Medicine* 322(15): 1059–63.

HICKSON, G. B., W. A. ALTEMEIER, and J. M. PERRIN (1987). "Physician reimbursement by salary or fee-for-service: effect on physician practice behavior in a randomized prospective study." *Pediatrics* 80(3): 344–50.

HILL, S. C. and B. L. WOLFE (1997). "Testing the HMO competitive strategy: an analysis of its impact on medical resources." *Journal of Health Economics* 16(3): 261–86.

HILLMAN, A. L., K. RIPLEY, N. I. GOLDFARB, I. NUAMAH, J. P. WEINER, and E. LUSK (1998). "Physician financial incentives and feedback: Failure to increase cancer screening in Medicaid managed care." *American Journal of Public Health* 88(11): 1699–701.

HURLEY, R. E., D. A. FREUND, and D. E. TAYLOR (1989). "Emergency room use and primary care management: Evidence from four Medicaid demonstration programs." *American Journal of Public Health* 79: 843–7.

———— and B. J. GAGE (1991). "Gatekeeper effects on patterns of physician use." *Journal of Family Practice* 32: 167–74.

HUTCHISON, B., S. BIRCH, J. HURLEY, J. LOMAS, and F. STRATFORD-DEVAI (1996). "Do physician payment mechanisms affect hospital utilization? A study of health service organizations in Ontario." *Canadian Medical Association Journal* 154(5): 653–61.

KAPUR, K., G. F. JOYCE, K. A. VAN VORST, and J. J. ESCARCE (2000). "Expenditures for physician services under alternative models of managed care." *Medical Care Research and Review* 57(2): 161–81.

KESSLER, D. P. and M. B. McCLELLAN (2000). "Is Hospital Competition Socially Wasteful?" *Quarterly Journal of Economics* 115(2): 577–615.

KHANDKER, R. K. and W. G. MANNING (1992). "The impact of utilization review on costs and utilization." *Developments in Health Economics and Public Policy* 1: 47–62.

KRALEWSKI, J. E., W. WALLACE, T. D. WINGERT, D. J. KNUTSON, and C. E. JOHNSON (1999). "The effects of medical group practice organizational factors on physicians' use of resources." *Journal of Healthcare Management* 44(3): 167–81.

———— E. C. RICH, R. FELDMAN, et al. (2000). "The effects of medical group practice and physician payment method on costs of care." *Health Services Research* 35(3): 591–613.

LANDON, B. E., I. B. WILSON, and P. D. CLEARY (1998). "A conceptual model of the effects of health care organizations on the quality of medical care." *Journal of the American Medical Association* 279(17): 1377–82.

LESSLER, D. S. and T. M. WICKIZER (2000). "The impact of utilization management on readmissions among patients with cardiovascular disease." *Health Services Research* 34(6): 1315–29.

LINDSEY, P. A. and J. P. NEWHOUSE (1990). "The cost and value of second surgical opinion programs: A critical review of the literature." *Journal of Health Politics, Policy & Law* 15(3): 543–70.

LUBECK, D. P., B. W. BROWN, and H. R. HOLMAN (1985). "Chronic disease and health care service performance: Care of osteoarthritis across three health services." *Medical Care* 23: 266–77.

LUFT, H. S. (1981). *Health Maintenance Organizations: Dimensions of Performance*. New York, NY, John Wiley and Sons.

———— (2003). "Variations in patterns of care and outcomes after acute myocardial infarction for Medicare beneficiaries in fee-for-service and HMO settings." *Health Services Research* 38(4): 1065–79.

———— S. C. MAERKI, and J. B. TRAUNER (1986). "The competitive effects of health maintenance organizations: Another look at the evidence from Hawaii, Rochester, and Minneapolis/St. Paul." *Journal of Health Politics, Policy, and Law* 10: 625–58.

Ma, C. A. (1994). "Health care payment systems: cost and quality incentives." *Journal of Economics and Management Strategy* 3(1): 93–112.

Maciejewski, M. L., B. Dowd, K. T. Call, and R. Feldman (2001). "Comparing mortality and time until death for Medicare HMO and FFS beneficiaries." *Health Services Research* 35(6): 1245–65.

McLaughlin, C. G. (1987). "HMO growth and hospital expenses and use: A simultaneous-equation approach." *Health Services Research* 22(2): 183–205.

—— (1988a). "The effect of HMOs on overall hospital expenses: Is anything left after correcting for simultaneity and selectivity?" *Health Services Research* 23(3): 421–41.

—— (1988b). "Market responses to HMOs: Price Competition or Rivalry?" *Inquiry* 25: 207–18.

—— J. C. Merrill, and A. J. Freed (1984). "The impact of HMO growth on hospitalization costs and utilization." In R. M. Scheffler and L. F. Rossiter (eds), *Advances in Health Economics and Health Services Research*, Vol. 5. Greenwich, CT, JAI Press, 57–93.

Mello, M. M., S. C. Stearns, E. C. Norton, and T. C. Ricketts (2003). "Understanding biased selection in Medicare HMOs." *Health Services Research* 38(3): 961–92.

Melnick, G. A., J. Zwanziger, A. Bamezai, and R. Pattison (1992). "The effects of market structure and bargaining position on hospital prices." *Journal of Health Economics* 11(3): 217–33.

Miller, R. H. and H. S. Luft (1994). "Managed care plan performance since 1980. A literature analysis." *Journal of the American Medical Association* 271(19): 1512–19.

—— —— (1997). "Does managed care lead to better or worse quality of care?" *Health Affairs* 16(5): 7–25.

—— —— (2002). "HMO plan performance update: an analysis of the literature 1997–2001." *Health Affairs* 21(4): 63–86.

Morrisey, M. A., J. Alexander, L. R. Burns, and V. Johnson (1999). "The effects of managed care on physician and clinical integration in hospitals." *Medical Care* 37(4): 350–61.

Mukamel, D. B., A. I. Mushlin, D. L. Weimer, J. Zwanziger, T. Parker, and I. Indridason (2000). "Do quality report cards play a role in HMOs' contracting decisions? Evidence from New York state." *Health Services Research* 35: 319–32.

—— J. Zwanziger, and K. J. Tomaszewski (2001). "HMO penetration, competition, and risk-adjusted hospital mortality." *Health Services Research* 36(6, part 1): 1019–35.

—— D. L. Weimer, J. Zwanziger, and A. I. Mushlin (2002). "Quality of cardiac surgeons and managed care contracting practices." *Health Services Research* 37(5): 1129–43.

Mullins, C. D., D. C. Lavallee, F. G. Pradel, A. R. DeVries, and N. Caputo (2006). "Health plans strategies for managing outpatient specialty pharmaceuticals." *Health Affairs* 25(5): 1332–9.

Newhouse, J. P. (1996). "Reimbursing health plans and health providers: efficiency in production versus selection." *Journal of Economic Literature* 34(3): 1236–63.

—— W. B. Schwartz, A. P. Williams, and C. Witsberger (1985). "Are fee-for-service costs increasing faster than HMO costs?" *Medical Care* 23(8): 960–6.

Nicholson, S., M. K. Bundorf, R. M. Stein, and D. Polsky (2004). "The magnitude and nature of risk selection in employer-sponsored health plans." *Health Services Research* 39(6): 1817–38.

Noether, M. (1988). "Competition among hospitals." *Journal of Health Economics* 7(3): 259–84.

Pauly, M. V. (1970). "Efficiency, incentives, and reimbursement for health care." *Inquiry* 7(1): 115–31.

—— (1980). *Doctors and their Workshops: Economic models of physician behavior.* Chicago, IL, University of Chicago Press.

PAULY, M. V. (1985). "What is adverse about adverse selection?" *Advances in Health Economics and Health Services Research.* 6: 281–6.

—— (1989). "Is medical care different? Old questions, new answers." *Journal of Health Politics, Policy and Law* 13(2): 227–37.

PHELPS, C. E. (1992). "Diffusion of information in medical care." *Journal of Economic Perspectives* 6(3): 23–42.

PHILLIPS, K. A., K. KERLIKOWSKE, L. C. BAKER, S. W. CHANG, and M. L. BROWN (1998). "Individual, practitioner, and environmental factors associated with adherence to screening mammography guidelines." *Health Services Research* 33(1): 29–53.

—— J. S. HAAS, S.-Y. LIANG, et al. (2004). "Are gatekeeper requirements associated with cancer screening utilization?" *Health Services Research* 39(1): 153–78.

POLSKY, D., P. R. KLETKY, G. D. WOZNIAK, and J. J. ESCARCE (2000). "HMO penetration and the geographic mobility of practicing physicians." *Journal of Health Economics* 19(5): 793–809.

—— and S. NICHOLSON (2004). "Why are managed care plans less inexpensive: risk selection, utilization, or reimbursement?" *Journal of Risk and Insurance* 71(1): 21–40.

RAINWATER, J. A. and P. S. ROMANO (2003). "What data do California HMOs use to select hospitals for contracting?" *American Journal of Managed Care* 9(8): 553–61.

ROBINSON, J. C. (1991). "HMO market penetration and hospital cost inflation in California." *Journal of the American Medical Association* 266(19): 2719–23.

—— (1993). "Payment mechanisms, nonprice incentives, and organizational innovation in health care." *Inquiry* 30(3): 328–33.

—— (1996). "Decline in hospital utilization and cost inflation under managed care in California." *Journal of the American Medical Association* 276(13): 1060–4.

—— (2001). "The end of managed care." *Journal of the American Medical Association* 285(20): 2622–8.

RODGERS, J. and K. SMITH (1995). *Do Medicare HMOs Reduce Fee-For-Service Costs?* Washington, DC, Price Waterhouse LLP.

ROGOWSKI, J. A., A. K. JAIN, and J. J. ESCARCE (2007). "Hospital competition, managed care, and mortality after hospitalization for medical conditions in California." *Health Services Research* 42(2): 682–705.

ROSENTHAL, M. B., R. G. FRANK, J. L. BUCHANAN, and A. M. EPSTEIN (2001). "Scale and structure of capitated physician organizations in California." *Health Affairs* 20(4): 109–19.

—— B. E. LANDON, and H. A. HUSKAMP (2001). "Managed care and market power: physician organizations in four markets." *Health Affairs* 20(5): 187–93.

—— —— J. L. BUCHANAN, and A. M. EPSTEIN (2002). "Transmission of financial incentives to physicians by intermediary organizations in California." *Health Affairs* 21(4): 197–205.

ROTHSCHILD, M. and J. E. STIGLITZ (1976). "Equilibrium in competitive insurance markets: an essay on the economics of imperfect information." *Quarterly Journal of Economics* 90: 626–49.

SCHEFFLER, R. M., S. D. SULLIVAN, and T. H. KO (1991). "The impact of Blue Cross and Blue Shield plan utilization management programs, 1980–1988." *Inquiry* 28(3): 263–75.

SCHULMAN, K. A., L. E. RUBENSTEIN, D. M. SEILS, M. HARRIS, J. HADLEY, and J. J. ESCARCE (1997). "Quality assessment in contracting for tertiary care services by HMOs: a case study of three markets." *Joint Commission Journal for Quality Improvement* 23(2): 117–27.

SIMON, C. J. and P. H. BORN (1996). "Physician earnings in a changing managed care environment." *Health Affairs* 15(3): 124–33.

—— D. D. Dranove, and W. D. White (1997). "The impact of managed care on the physician marketplace." *Public Health Reports* 112(3): 222–30.

—— —— —— (1998). "The effect of managed care on the incomes of primary care and specialty physicians." *Health Services Research* 33(3 part 1): 549–69.

Sullivan, C. B. and T. Rice (1991). "The health insurance picture in 1990." *Health Affairs* 10(2): 104–15.

Weiner, J. P. (2004). "Prepaid group practice staffing and US physician supply: lessons for workforce policy." *Health Affairs* W4: 43–59.

Welch, W. P. (1994). "HMO market share and its effect on local Medicare costs." In H. S. Luft (ed.), *HMOs and the Elderly*. Ann Arbor, MI, Health Administration Press, 231–49.

Wickizer, T. M. (1990). "The effect of utilization review on hospital use and expenditures: a review of the literature and an update on recent findings." *Medical Care Review* 47(3): 327–63.

—— (1995). "Controlling outpatient medical equipment costs through utilization management." *Medical Care* 33(4): 383–91.

—— and P. J. Feldstein (1995). "The impact of HMO competition on private health insurance premiums, 1985–1992." *Inquiry* 32(3): 241–51.

—— and D. Lesser (1998a). "Do treatment restrictions imposed by utilization management increase the likelihood of readmission for psychiatric patients?" *Medical Care* 36(6): 844–50.

—— —— (1998b). "Effects of utilization management on patterns of hospital care among privately insured adult patients." *Medical Care* 36(11): 1545–54.

—— J. R. C. Wheeler, and P. J. Feldstein (1991). "Have hospital inpatients cost containment programs contributed to the growth in outpatient expenditures?" *Medical Care* 29(5): 442–51.

—— D. Lessler, and J. Boyd-Wickizer (1999). "Effects of health care cost-containment programs on patterns of care and readmissions among children and adolescents." *American Journal of Public Health* 89(9): 1353–8.

Xu, X. and G. A. Jensen (2006). "Health effects of managed care among the near-elderly." *Journal of Aging and Health* 18(4): 507–33.

Zeng, F., J. F. O'Leary, E. M. Sloss, M. S. Lopez, N. Dhanani, and G. Melnick (2006). "The effect of Medicare health maintenance organizations on hospitalization rates for ambulatory care sensitive conditions." *Medical Care* 44(10): 900–7.

Zhan, C., M. R. Miller, H. Wong, and G. S. Meyer (2004). "The effects of HMO penetration on preventable hospitalizations." *Health Services Research* 39(2): 345–61.

Zwanziger, J. and A. Meirowitz (1997). "Strategic factors in hospital selection for HMO and PPO provider networks." In M. A. Morrisey (ed.), *Managed Care and Changing Health Care Markets*. Washington, DC, AEI Press, 77–94.

—— and G. A. Melnick (1988). "The effects of hospital competition and the Medicare PPS program on hospital cost behavior in California." *Journal of Health Economics* 7(4): 301–20.

—— —— and A. Bamezai (1994). "Cost and price competition in California Hospitals, 1980–1990." *Health Affairs* 13: 118–26.

CHAPTER 19

HOSPITALS: TEAMING UP[1]

PEDRO PITA BARROS AND PAU OLIVELLA

19.1 INTRODUCTION

HOSPITALS are one of the main institutions operating in health care markets. It is of no surprise that considerable research has been devoted to understand how they work, both in the economics literature and in other fields. Previous summaries of the more important findings are reported in the *Handbook of Health Economics* (Culyer and Newhouse 2000) and in the *Elgar Companion to Health Economics* (Jones 2006).

The present chapter presents two distinctive features with respect to these other surveys. The first one is that we emphasize the separation of ownership and control in hospitals. In other words, the day-to-day actions and decisions taken within a hospital are often far from the direct control of the hospital's ruling body. As we will see, this view is not new, and can be traced back to the seminal work of Pauly and Redisch (1973), who views the hospital as a "physician's cooperative." Once this separation is recognized, performance may be equally related to ownership as to internal organizational features like individual as well as group incentives or hierarchical design. This observation paves the way to the other distinctive feature of this chapter, namely, to look at hospitals through the lens of teams. Hospitals are entities that have an internal organization characterized by team work. Hospitals also have to "team up" with special partners, namely payers of health care provided to patients and patient-referring agents.

[1] We have benefited from the comments and suggestions of Kurt Brekke, Pablo Colorado, Paula González, Inés Macho-Sadler, Xavier Martinez-Giralt, Andrew Street, Artur Vaz, and especially from the editors, Sherry Glied and Peter Smith. Olivella acknowledges financial support from ECO2009-7616, Consolider-Ingenio CSD2006-16, 2009SGR-169, and Barcelona Economics-Xarxa CREA. The usual disclaimer applies.

Some countries rely mainly on private hospitals, while in other countries a majority of public hospitals is present. In the first group, we have the United States and the Netherlands, for example, while in the latter group, we find countries with national health services (such as the UK, Italy and Spain, among others). However, one implication of our view of hospitals is that the existing differences of the relative prevalence of each possible ownership structure may in fact have less importance than that deemed in the received literature. Hence, rather than provide an exhaustive treatment of these differences, our approach allows us to focus on common—internal organization—aspects.

The chapter is structured as follows. We will dedicate the next two sections to introduce the reader to the more classical approach to hospital, first as a producer and then as an agent endowed with preferences. Hence, in section 19.2 we address technology issues like output measurement, as well as economies of scale and scope. In section 19.3 we briefly overview different theories on how the ruling body of the hospital chooses between the different technologically feasible options, and on how its preferences over these options are formed. These theories are based on the usual observation that many hospitals are non-profit organizations, and propose that the hospital maximizes some other "utility function." Also in this chapter, we depart from this view and explain the notion of the separation of ownership and control, through the approaches of physician agency (Pauly and Redisch 1973), and the hospital as an internal market (Harris 1977). In the latter, equilibrium of demand and supply of resources is achieved without resorting to explicit prices. Rather, explicit as well as implicit contracts are used to govern decision-making and resource allocation, i.e. to govern incentives. We will however argue that the procedure by which contracts themselves are negotiated and chosen within the hospital, amongst those that are efficient, has received little attention. These approaches motivate our interest on incentives within the hospital, which we develop in section 19.4. We focus on the framework where two or more agents interact. There, the issues of observability (the measurement of each team member's contribution), team incentives, and optimal hierarchical design become crucial. In section 19.5 we show that the idea of team interactions can be extended beyond the limits of the hospital in two main areas. We first address the relationship of hospitals with third-party payers. In most countries, we find health insurance mechanisms, be they private or public, which assume the responsibility to pay for care provided to patients. Most models addressing payment rules assume a single payer. Often, this is not the case, and the degree of economies of scale may matter to the payment rule. Second, we notice that patients arrive at hospital referred by other agents, namely general practitioners (GP). Therefore, hospitals also have to "team" with GPs, and hospital preferences will determine how these two parties interact. In section 19.6, we turn to the existing empirical evidence on two important issues discussed in the previous sections. The first issue is that of the optimal size of the hospital, which is intimately related to economies of scale and scope. The second issue is whether ownership really matters in reference to observed performance, where we update the evidence provided by Gaynor (2006). Finally, In section 19.7 we discuss and propose challenges for future research.

19.2 Technology: What Does
a Hospital Do?

According to the neoclassical view, a hospital uses resources (inputs) ranging from medical equipment to pharmaceutical products, nurses, and doctors. Combining those resources according to current knowledge and technology, patients are treated (output). The utilization of resources entails costs and different combinations of resources may be used to treat similar clinical conditions. Treating patients, on the other hand, leads to revenues. Therefore, even if several particularities do exist, hospitals can be studied using the traditional economic apparatus. Namely, issues about size and diversification advantages can be addressed. The only difficulty lies in the precise definition and measurement of hospitals' output. Let us address this latter issue first, as it is one of the most challenging.

To answer the simple question "What does a hospital do?," we need to observe the sequence of events that take place: The patient arrives at the hospital either by advice of some health professional (directed in from outpatient visits, referred by primary care organizations, etc.) or from the patient's own initiative (mainly, through a decision to go to the emergency room services). When the patient arrives at the hospital he or she brings a certain initial condition and likely evolution of health status, which may depend on her own characteristics. Then, the hospital (the doctor) makes an assessment of the situation and decides on how many resources to spend on the patient. The resources the doctor uses include her own time, nurses and other non-medical personnel, medical equipment, and pharmaceutical products. The hospital must be organized in such a way that these resources are available when needed. Sickness evolves, given the initial condition and the resources dedicated to treatment, and a final health outcome emerges. In this respect, the most distinguishing characteristic of a hospital is the objective of providing *acute* illness treatment. This implies that hospitals have to deliver a service tailored to the specific condition of each patient. In order to tailor treatment, the doctor gathers information about the patient's condition, processes it, and takes a decision about the therapeutic path to be followed. This makes the operation of a hospital quite distinct from that of traditional business units, where, like in the treatment of chronic illness, needs are identified well in advance. We believe that the existing literature has not addressed this distinction in a complete way.

From this brief description, several notions of output may be constructed. However, almost all studies consider physical measures of activity as the hospital output. This is done for practical reasons. A closer look at the hospital shows that a different approach to empirical modeling may be appropriate, when feasible. Still, more often than not empirical studies are forced to rely upon the simple output measures. The most popular (and easy to measure empirically) is the number of patients treated, and we may refine that by considering different types of output. A common approach is to divide output into three activities: inpatient treatments (or discharges),[2] outpatient visits (that is, visits to specialists), and emergency room episodes. In line with these observations, the classic view of the hospital sees it, naturally, as a multiproduct unit.

We may also define hospital output according to the type of illness involved in the case of admissions. The need to set a measure of output, essential to compare performance of hospitals, has led to the creation and development of patient classification systems, like the Diagnosis Related Groups (DRG), which are homogeneous episodes of sickness treatment that group similar clinical situations demanding roughly the same amount of resources.[3] They also provide a tool to organize payments to hospitals. The information system provided by DRGs could even allow for a characterization of hospital outputs that takes each DRG as a different output, although the number of outputs resulting from such a classification would make a full economic analysis too complex.

The main advantage of these hospital output definitions is the ability to measure them, even in a crude way. However, a more demanding definition of the hospital's output is to see it as a change in the probability distribution over possible health states of the patient. This measure, in contrast to the proceeding ones, conveys more a notion of quality than of quantity, and follows directly from the path the patient takes within the hospital. Its main difficulty is with observation, as detailed information regarding the health status of the patient when leaving the hospital is usually unknown, except for the coarse distinction of live discharge versus death, which leads directly to the notion of mortality rate as an output measure. When the patient enters the hospital with a clinical condition, he or she may receive care at the hospital. Despite the efforts and resources used, the patient may not survive. However, the resources used by the hospital were not useless, as they have increased the probability of survival of the patient compared to doing nothing. They changed the odds of survival. Thus, the contribution of the hospital is this change in survival probability. The death of the patient is a possible outcome even after committing resources to treatment. Aggregating over patients, the higher likelihood of survival will translate into a lower mortality rate.[4]

Besides mortality rates, whenever appropriate data is collected, output of the hospital can be defined as the expected health gain resulting from treatment. Additional QALYs (quality-adjusted life-years) as a measure of output, for example, contemplates both extensions in life and improvements in quality of life.

The survival probability is, of course, one of the dimensions of interest. Ideally, one would like to measure the difference in health status with and without treatment. This is a hard issue, requiring further developments on both data available and analytic tools.

---

[2] Technological change has reduced the hospital stay for several interventions, which in some cases means patients return home in the same day of intervention.

[3] Different countries use different names for patient classification systems. We keep here the term DRG for expositional purposes.

[4] This approach also has the advantage of interpreting death as an output equal to live discharge—they are just different realizations from the same probability distribution—thus avoiding the somewhat ad hoc procedure of treating death within a hospital episode as an undesirable output (Dismuke and Sena 2001; Yawe and Kavuma 2007).

Castelli et al. (2007) propose an approach taking into account increases in life, weighted by quality, and adjusting for waiting time until intervention. The approach is demanding in terms of the information required, however.

Another characteristic of hospitals' operation is randomness of demand. Daily, weekly and monthly variance in demand for hospital services is considerable. Since hospital care should not be denied to those in need, excess capacity, on the one hand, and rationing/waiting lists, on the other hand, accommodate variations in demand. The natural response to demand variance is to hold some excess capacity to satisfy peak demand (Joskow 1980; Friedman and Pauly 1981; Gal-Or 1994; Carey 1998).

Let us now turn to the classical issues of optimal size and diversification advantages. Size advantages can be summarized on the simple notion of having a lower unit cost the larger the hospital is. This leads to the economic notion of economies of scale. In simple terms, a hospital has economies of scale if, by increasing its activity level by some scalar larger than one (e.g. doubling activity), costs increase less than proportionately (less than double). If costs increase in line with (more than) activity, with constant (increasing) average costs, the hospital has constant (decreasing) returns to scale.

Another important concept is economies of scope. A hospital has economies of scope whenever producing several outputs entails lower costs than producing each of them alone. In the case of hospital activity, there are economies of scope if, for example, having inpatient treatment and emergency room episodes in the same organization has lower costs than providing the same levels of care through independent organizations.

The two concepts, economies of scale and economies of scope, are relevant to delineate the size and range of services provided by hospitals. If economies of scale were never exhausted, one should observe only a few and very large hospitals. In other words, analysis of economies of scale provides guidance with regard to the optimal size of the hospital. Since we observe that hospitals of very different size do survive over time in the same geographic area, this could mean that economies of scale vanish at some level of activity.

Similarly, economies of scope express the advantages of combining different types of services. Real world observation suggests that emergency room, outpatient visits and inpatient activities have economies of scope, as they are regularly performed by the same organization. Perhaps emergency room has less pronounced economies of scope with respect to the other two activities, since we do sometimes observe hospitals with only inpatient care and outpatient visits. On the other hand, primary care activities and/or long-term recovery seem to have dis-economies of scale with respect to inpatient care as they tend to be performed by separate organizations.

As for the empirical measurement of economies of scale and scope, which we review in sub-section 19.6.1, this is usually done by considering the three broad aggregates that we outlined above: total number of discharges, outpatient visits and emergency room episodes. An alternative could be to estimate economics of scale and/or scope by taking each DRG as a distinct output. This could be quite a difficult task since, typically, a patient classification system may have more than 500 DRGs. In contrast, when our interest lies in the detail within the hospital, then focusing at the DRG level may be a fruitful way to go.[5]

Economies of scale and economies of scope are not a choice of the hospital. They are determined by medical knowledge and technology. However, an important role exists for "management" choices on which resources to use and how to combine them to achieve the desired outcome (activity level). The choices made can be seen at the light of three concepts of efficiency. First, a good decision process leads to technological efficiency, defined as a situation where no waste of resources exists. That is, reducing the amount of any of the inputs used results in not achieving the desired level of activity. Different combinations of resources for a given objective may have this characteristic of being efficient from a technological viewpoint. It now becomes the second layer of efficiency: from the technologically efficiency combinations of inputs, valuation of resources at their (opportunity) cost will reveal which combination(s) have the minimum cost to achieve the desired objective for hospital activity. The crucial element added in this step is the set of input prices. The third, and final, step is the definition of the desired level of activity (output). This implies defining the objective function of the hospital: what is valued and which trade-offs are present. The definition of the objective function of the hospital is addressed in more detail in the next section.

Let us finally stress one of our main messages. The literature has failed to fully tackle the main distinctive feature of a hospital relative to other health care providers: the ability to treat acute illness in a way that accounts for the uncertainty in the treatment process.

19.3 Preferences: What Does a Hospital Want?

The previous section addressed the definition of hospital technology. The next step is to define what the hospital wants to do. It implies defining the objective function of the hospital, an issue intertwined with ownership. We look first at utility-maximizing hospitals in a general way, and then at the implications of different ownerships.

19.3.1 Models of Hospital Behavior

The objective function of the hospital can be defined in several different ways and existing literature reflects those possibilities. Departures from simple profit maximization have been justified in various manners, including altruism in physician preferences (taking physicians to be the crucial decision-makers), reduced-form representation of

---

[5] The recent work of Olsen and Street (2008) is a good example of this approach.

interaction between hospital managers (who care about costs and revenues) and physicians (who care about benefits to patients), etc. Making explicit the objective function of the hospital allows for determination of the optimal/desired output level.

A traditional discussion about choosing the "right" (desired) hospital output is associated with the role of quality and the trade-off between lower costs and higher quality. This trade-off is based on the assumption that higher quality implies more costs. This is likely to be so in efficient hospitals. However, inefficient hospitals may have room to improve simultaneously in both dimensions.

Quality is also an issue when comparing public and private (for-profit) ownership structures, with the usual presumption being that private hospitals will degrade (non-observable) quality of care to save on costs. This view, however, ignores the role that quality may have in attracting patients. Whenever, due to health insurance arrangements (be it voluntary, mandatory, social or public insurance) patients become relative insensitive to price but are still reacting to quality differences, then private (for profit) hospitals will use quality as a competitive tool. Quality in for-profit hospitals may then be higher than in public hospitals, namely in those dimensions that influence more consumers' decisions. Differences in objective functions are not neutral to the desired level of activity for the hospital. Whenever a trade-off between quality and quantity exists, different preferences generate distinct outcomes.

The quantity–quality model of Newhouse (1970) focuses on the role of hospital administrators. As Newhouse noted, even if the profit maximization objective is removed, the hospital still faces a trade-off between quantity and quality. Indeed, for a given budget, greater quantities of care can only come at the expense of a decrease in quality of care, and vice-versa. We refer to this trade-off as "the budget constraint." She then proposes that the hospital will pursue some balance between quality within this budget constraint, and that this balance will be determined by the preferences of the ruling body of the hospital, to which we will refer simply as "the board." Phelps (2002) offers us an overview of the determinants of these preferences. The basic idea is that a median voter exists in the board, that is, a voter whose preferences are such that an equal number of board members are on the "more quality and less quantity side" and on the "more quantity and less quality" side. The median voter will win any vote over the choice within the budget constraint.

A deeper question is where a particular composition of the board in terms of these preferences comes from. Phelps propose that this depends on some (exogenous) initial conditions (the rules of the game and perhaps the preferences of donors), and on how new board members are elected (again the rules of the game). If new board members are chosen by the board itself, the composition of board preferences should show some stability.

Several other models of hospital behavior can be found in the literature. For example, Weisbrod (1988) describes non-profit hospitals, assuming decision-makers that aim at both quality and quantity. They are not fundamentally different from for-profit hospitals, as technological efficiency and allocative efficiency are equally important to achieve.

A problem with these views is that any conflict of objectives between the board and the many different groups that actually take the decisions within the hospital (managers, clinicians, and so on) is assumed away. We now describe the different attempts in the literature to address this important issue.

19.3.2 The Separation of Governance and Control

Pauly and Redisch (1973) are the first authors to offer us a different view of the hospital. They assume that clinicians, who take many of the important decisions, will disregard the objectives of the board and will maximize their own welfare.[6] This is the view of the hospital as a "physicians' cooperative." Inasmuch as physicians may be able to capture a proportion of the hospital's profits (receipts of all kinds minus operation costs), the two views may seem truly antithetical. Indeed, the budget balance constraint assumed by Newhouse is tantamount to a zero profit condition, while the physicians' cooperative will strive at maximizing profits. However, the advertent reader will quickly realize that the two views in fact converge in their predictions if (i) hospitals compete against each other and (ii) free entry is guaranteed by the authorities. Indeed, long run competition among profit maximizing hospitals (or among any for profit organization for that matter) will drive profits down to zero. It is well-known, however, that this conclusion breaks down in industries where large economies of scale and scope are present, and where entry is heavily regulated. Hospital care is one such industry. Moreover, the time horizon for the usual decision-maker in a hospital (not to speak of emergency admissions) and that of the board could be very different. In a nutshell, budget considerations are most surely ignored by a clinician taking life and death decisions.

This debate is, in any case, enlightening. It casts doubt into the difference between profit maximizing and non profit organizations, and redirects the attention from board politics to the separation between "ownership" (in the sense of governance) and control in organizations. It also cast doubts on whether it is relevant to perform the usual distinction between publicly owned, independent non-profit organizations, and for-profit hospitals. To put it bluntly, why should a physician who is paid on a fee-per-service basis in a publicly owned hospital and a physician who is paid on the same basis in a non-profit hospital behave any different? It then all boils down to the choice of incentive structure and organizational design.

In light of this, one is faced with the difficulty of making sense of the observed diversity with respect to ownership structure. Indeed, within and across countries we often find co-existence of the following three ownership structures: public, private for-profit,

---

[6] One direct way to perhaps reconcile the two views is to assume that the median voter in the board is a clinician. However, the classical view looks at choices within the budget constraint, while Pauly and Redisch take a different view, where the quantity/quality pair falls short of the budget and the difference is pocketed by the clinicians.

and private not-for-profit, with distinct shares in each case. For example, Belgium and the Netherlands have a majority of private hospitals, France has mainly public hospitals (⅔ of the total), Denmark and Sweden mainly public hospitals but owned locally, while the UK has a majority of public hospitals owned by the National Health Service. Germany has a slight majority (53%) of public hospitals, but financing is done at the regional level and rules apply equally to all. For-profit hospitals can be owned by corporations or by cooperatives (associations) of doctors. Not-for-profit hospitals may be owned by foundations or by churches, for example. Public hospitals belong to governments, though in some countries this occurs at the city/county level while in others hospitals are controlled by the central government.

In any case, the central question is whether the performance of each of these structures is any different. We will address this empirical question in sub-section 19.6.2. If there is a difference, is it due to differences in ownership structure or to the way in which the diverging objectives (physicians', nurses', managers') are aligned through implicit and explicit contracts?

A further advance concerning the separation between ownership and control within the hospital is that of Harris (1977). She introduces the idea that we should see the hospital as a non-market way of organizing demand and supply of a certain type of health care. On the demand side, we have medical staff whose objective is to acquire the necessary resources to treat patients. On the supply side, we have the administration who is in charge of the management decisions, making sure that these resources are available and also balancing them across the diverse internal demands within the hospital. Another important contribution from Harris (1977) is the explicit recognition that a double hierarchy exists within the hospital, each one associated to one side of the market. More importantly, she argues that the equilibrium in this market is reached not by a price mechanism but by negotiation. This original view has had only a partial impact on the economic analysis of the hospital. We propose a possible explanation for this below.

Once the market ceases to be the mechanism to allocate resources, one needs to study what is the alternative procedure by which the actual players within the organization choose amongst the different options. In this respect, economists have distinguished between two phases. The first phase is the determination of the set of efficient alternatives. The second is the choice of alternatives within this set. Notice that, by the first fundamental theorem of welfare economics, both phases can be achieved, by price magic, in a completely decentralized fashion. However, when the first fundamental theorem is not applicable due to externalities, economies of scale and scope, or asymmetric information then one needs to resort to contracts and negotiation. In this sense, one could view Phelps's approach to board politics as one attempt to address this second phase of the analysis. However, notice that the rules of the game in the day-to-day interaction among hospital staff are much less clear than in the board. Defining such rules for each possible such interaction becomes a difficult task, given the specificity of each patient's case. Hence, on-the-spot negotiation and a general lack of commitment will dominate these interactions.

As for the first phase, the determination of optimal contracts in the hospital, agency and team theory have made important contributions, which we review in section 19.4. On theory grounds, we identify there several attempts to address the specific nature of the hospital as a decision-making unit.

In contrast, the second phase—how and which allocation is chosen among the efficient—has received little attention. This is despite the fact that there exist well-established tools in cooperative game theory and in its non-cooperative underpinning (bargaining theory) that could in principle be applied. Why is it then that we seldom see this done?[7] In our opinion, the fundamental reason is the fact that certain aspects of the environment can only be observed by one of the parties. For instance, consider a clinician asking a hospital administrator to purchase some high-tech piece of equipment. The administrator may be more knowledgeable about the financial costs, about whether this equipment is available in other hospitals in the area, or about the true magnitude of its cost offsets; whereas the doctor may have privileged information on the health benefits and diagnostic accuracy that the equipment would bring in for each particular patient. Unobservable differences in objectives (e.g. altruism, career concerns, and so on) among the negotiating parties would play the same role. Such a situation is what Game Theory refers to as an asymmetric information setting. Unfortunately, available theory (or we should say theories) provides very partial insights on how such a manager and clinician would (or should be allowed to) arrive at a decision. The reason is that current theories of bargaining under asymmetric information are plagued by the curse of multiple equilibria. In other words, even if one agrees that a certain theory is the appropriate one, that single theory is in many cases unable to pin down a unique prediction. What is worse, the particular set of equilibria that may be obtained depends on the bargaining procedure itself (who starts making offers, the existence of outside options, and so on).

19.4 INCENTIVES WITHIN THE HOSPITAL

19.4.1 General Elements

Before we enter the discussion of incentives, let us point out the three most important factors that give rise to a (non-trivial) incentive problem in the hospital context. The first factor is the existence of a conflict of objectives.

Here are some examples that will allow us to set some terminology. As pointed out above, even if the (median voter of) the board may have decided on a particular balance between quantity and quality, the agents actually taking decisions may have conflicting objectives with that particular mandate. The doctor may be more inclined to either save

---

[7] An exception is Galizzi and Miraldo (2008).

on her own diagnostic effort or to improve the evidence about her skills by ordering extra tests, or by overstaffing. Similarly, hospital managers may want to secure good results by installing state of the art technical equipment that may be unneeded given the existence of similar resources nearby. In this example, the board acts as "the principal" in the relationship, while we refer to doctors and managers as "agents." As another example, the institution that pays for hospital care but does not enjoy it directly (be it the government, an insurance company, or even a donor) may desire to contain costs more than the board. In this case the board is the agent of the paying institution, who acts now as the principal. These two examples point out that the actual chain of command from the payer to the doctor is much longer than just a two-tier principal–agent relationship. Hence, the hierarchy will have several concatenated principal–agent relationships, where the agent of a given pair is the principal of the next. The payer is the principal vis-à-vis the board and the board is the principal vis-à-vis the doctor. In fact, the actual structure of the hierarchy constitutes an important subject of study as will be seen below.

The second factor is the presence of asymmetric information. Asymmetric information may arise for two reasons. One is the impossibility that the principal observe and scrutinize all the actions taken by its agents. Doctors—and not the board—decide over admission, testing and treatment while managers—and not the board—decide over equipment and resource inventories. The other is the impossibility that the principal perfectly observe the environment in which these actions were taken. For instance, the doctor may have privileged information on the present health conditions of the potential population of patients.

The third and final factor is the existence of risk. Risk blurs the link between what is observable by the principal and either the actions of the agents or the environment. The health status of patient may worsen despite the fact that the correct course of action was taken by the doctor in charge. The average length of stay may increase because of reasons that lie beyond the responsibility of the team in charge of the floor. Although procedures exist to gain information about the agent's actions or the environment, these procedures will at most yield partial information. Examples of such procedures are external and internal audits and reports or questionnaires filled in by patients.

Such asymmetric information problems as well as how remuneration systems can palliate these problems, are issues treated elsewhere in this volume (on agency, see Chapter 25; and on provider payment and incentives, see Chapter 26). However, we will argue here that the hospital environment adds new aspects to the usual single-principal/single-agent relationship.[8] Most of these aspects arise from our view of the hospital as a team (e.g. doctors and nurses, hospital administrators and specialists). This view naturally leads to issues like the availability of measures of each team member's performance,

---

[8] Some single-principal/single-agent problems become particularly relevant in the context of the hospital. Among others, see Brekke and Kuhn (2006) on marketing to doctors by pharmaceutical firms (detailing); Gonzalez (2004), Biglaiser and Ma (2007), and Brekke and Sorgard (2007) on physicians' dual practice; and Neary (2001) on resource hoarding.

the convenience to provide group incentives, and hierarchical design (should some decisions be delegated? who contracts with whom?).

19.4.2 Group Incentives

The first question that arises when looking at team performance and remuneration is with what accuracy can one observe each individual's contribution. This depends on the particular measure of performance that one uses. Take the example of a doctor and a nurse, an example that we will exploit further below. If one assesses the performance of the nurse as simply the amount of visits that the nurse makes to any given patient, then such performance measure could be deemed to be the nurse's individual responsibility. In contrast, if one looks at the difference between the patient's initial and final health status, then this will be a complex function of the efforts of both the doctor and the nurse. We will formalize this distinction below. Another issue is whether the pay of these two agents should be based on such complex signals, i.e. on whether each agent's pay should be linked to the other's actions and decisions. One more example illustrates this point. Suppose, as it is typically in US hospitals, that the doctor is paid on a fee-for-service basis whereas the nurse is salaried.[9] Even if the improvement in patient's health can be regarded as joint production, neither remuneration system is taking into account the fact that such improvement is in fact the result of the interaction between doctor and nurse. If instead one would reward these professionals on the basis of some measure of health improvement, we would indeed be observing team pay.

This example notwithstanding, it is true that team incentives are more the exception than the rule in the real world. This is despite the fact that paying individuals according to individual performance measures only may lead to uncooperative behavior and inefficiencies. To better understand where and when these inefficiencies arise, we provide a more formal analysis of this issue.

The theory of team incentives has dealt with two different frameworks. Whether we are in one or the other framework depends on whether individual signals carrying information on each and all parties' decisions are available or not. The simplest example of each in the context of a hospital would be the following. Suppose that one keeps track of most of the actions that a nurse and a physician have taken when treating an inpatient. This information would include number of bedside visits, medication dispensed, or even questionnaires filled in by the patient on her appraisal of the performance of each. We then would be in a context of individualized signals. Consider now a situation in which we know only the number of days before the patient is discharged, or her condition at the time of discharge. We then have a single signal that is the result of the interaction of nurse and physician.[10]

---

[9] In US hospitals, medical staff hold a loose contractual relationship with the hospital while nurses are hospital employees.

[10] For an empirical analysis of the effects of financial rewards on team incentives in the collection of indirect tax in the UK, see Burgess et al. (2007).

The issues involved in each of these two frameworks are very different. In the first framework one wonders whether the contract of one agent should be based not only on her own signal but also on the other agent's signal as well. In the second framework one is concerned about free-riding. Notice also that whether we are in one or the other framework is not exogenous, as one can design protocols, monitoring and auditing, or even adjust the physical location of each player, in order to better distinguish one player's contribution from the other's.

As for the individualized signal's framework, the main insight is offered by Holmstrom (1982). It is only in very special circumstances that the third-party payer should *not* make one team member's contract depend on the other's performance. In fact, the needed mathematical property is somewhat obscure.[11] It includes, though, an intuitive case: the situation where team members performances (signals) are completely independent. Notice, however, that such a restrictive assumption leads to an extremely degenerate case of a "team." It is very likely that useful indicators of a nurse's performance will indeed depend on the actions taken by the team's doctor. Taking as a rather extreme example, the number of visits by the nurse will increase as a consequence of a shirking doctor.

In the absence of any informational asymmetries amongst team members and the third-party payer, the previous discussion implies that it is optimal to centralize contracts. We return to this issue in sub-section 19.4.2. To sum up, we should see team incentives that are based on every team member's performance.

A second contribution of Holmstrom (1982) is to formalize the very intuitive but often forgotten idea that one should not punish a team member for some other member's inappropriate action. This is not a fairness issue only. Take the example of a team composed of an oncologist, who chooses her diagnostic effort, and a manager, who decides upon the quality of a computed tomography scanner to be installed. Suppose that if the manager installs a very low quality CT scanner, the performance measure of the doctor (say, length of stay) becomes independent of the doctor's diagnostic effort. Then the contract of the doctor should not depend on the length of stay. Suppose on the contrary that, if the manager has installed a high quality scanner, then the length of stay becomes a good signal of doctor's effort.[12] In other words, the probability of a long length of stay diminishes when the doctor exerts the needed level of care. In that case the doctor's contract should indeed depend on the length of stay.

To sum up, it should be the case that the incentives contained in the doctor's contract depend on the manager's performance. The doctor's pay should depend heavily on the length of stay when there is indication that the manager performed well, whereas it should not depend on the length of stay otherwise. This not only provides the right

---

[11] The property is that team member A's signal (say signal a) be a sufficient statistic for team member B's signal (say signal b) when one is trying to infer A's actions. In that case, A's contract is independent of B's signal. One says that a is a sufficient statistic for b if one can express the joint distribution of a and b as a product of two functions, one that depends only on a and b, and one that depends only on a and on A's actions.

[12] We are assuming that the advantages of that signal together with the improved efficacy of the scanner more than compensate the higher cost of the better quality scanner.

incentives to the doctor, but also leads to the right risk-sharing between manager and doctor. Nothing in this discussion relates to fairness.

Admittedly, this points toward a quite sophisticated system of incentives. Indeed, it is also perhaps the case that one cannot directly observe the manager's actions and one needs to look at, say, running costs as a proxy for these actions. But these running costs surely depend on doctors' actions, and so on. Failure to recognize these interdependencies would lead to an incentive system that does not promote the right decisions, makes team members bear unnecessary compensation risks, and may even undermine overall morale.

As a caveat for the reader, one should not think only of monetary incentives. It has been shown that non-pecuniary rewards are as important: improved facilities and amenities, promotion, recognition by the other members of the team, and so on are good examples.[13] In general, the literature has converted these incentives into money equivalents, a simplification that is not free of criticism. It has been argued that psychological and behavioral factors like team morale or altruism could be undermined when financial incentives come in.[14]

Let us turn to the single team signal framework. Although there are ways to organize a hospital so that individual accountability to the board is possible, there are some instances where it is just impossible to disentangle each team members' performance. Take for instance emergency admissions, where there is just no time to produce individual indicators. Perhaps only extremely imperfect indicators can be obtained ex-post. Then, the only signal available is the health condition of the patient in subsequent periods. How should the team members' performance be influenced? As mentioned above, it is the free-rider problem that is central in this context. The general literature has produced quite a negative result here: there exists no mechanism that solves the free-riding problem, unless some outside party "breaks the budget." In other words, if the team enjoys the net benefit of the relationship and shares it among its members, there does not exist a sharing rule that provides the right incentives. The idea is the following: In order to motivate each member of the team, it is necessary that, in case of under-performance, some group penalty be levied. This group penalty then implies a reduction in whatever net revenue has been accomplished. This in turn will decrease the shares of the net revenue enjoyed by each of the team members. Provided that the group penalty is sufficiently harsh, individuals will behave. This mitigates the free-rider problem that originates when the full net benefit is to be shared. Take for example a health authority that provides incentives to a hospital by allocating extra funds. This health authority acts as the outside party that breaks the budget balance. If the hospital performs under some standard, it will not enjoy that extra fund. More importantly, the health authority keeps the

---

[13] Ratto et al. (2001) discuss how non-pecuniary rewards may foster team incentives in the context of the National Health System in the UK.

[14] As Seabright (2002) poses it, "civic virtue may, on this view, be crowded out by the introduction of explicit incentives." See this work for a way to endogenize this result by means of a standard screening model under asymmetric information.

undistributed funds. This serves as a commitment device. It is easy to see why it is diffi-cult to sustain threats of group penalties that would be purely wasteful in the absence of such a third party. Once team performance is low, the team members have all the incen-tives to renegotiate the contract. Why self-inflict a wasteful punishment? However, if team members foresee such a renegotiation before deciding what to do, the free-rider problem reappears—full force.

The main lesson that springs from the previous discussion is that one should ensure that no such renegotiation is possible. Namely, one should keep distance between the payer (whoever bears the performance bonuses, be it the hospital manager, the insurer, or the Board of Trustees), and the team members. Put more bluntly, the payer should not be one more team member. She should benefit from any reduction in pay that is levied on the under-performing team.

Another possibility would be to introduce competition between teams. This would be tantamount to having the winning team collecting the bonus. Some experiments in this area have been performed, but never within the hospital, where each team provides such a different service from the other that any comparison becomes impossible. In other words, competition could be beneficial only if teams are whole hospitals that compete in providing a similar set of services to similar populations.

19.4.2.1 Doctors and Nurses

One of the issues addressed in Chapter 22 is that of the shifting of skills between profes-sions. Tavares (2005) analyzes the particular case of the shift of responsibilities from doc-tors to nurses. Her main insight is that such a shift may in fact require a larger overall budget for incentive compensation. This author uses a model of the doctor–nurse team in which there is a single, overall indicator (patient is either cured or requires new treatment). The main intuition is that free-riding incentives on the part of doctors are reinforced if nurses' effort becomes more productive. She uses this model to discuss how failure by the health authorities to recognize this effect can lead to equilibrium actions within the team that not only harm overall welfare, but also may lead to resentment on the part of nurses. Therefore, she can also use this model to explain both the demand by doctors for higher pay and the demand by nurses of a recognition of their change in status.

19.4.2.2 Centralization vs. Decentralization and the Provision of Incentives

When we consider the hospital as a cascade of contracts we are already assuming a spe-cial hierarchical form. Indeed, one could imagine a hospital where all contracting is cen-tralized, so that a single decision-maker—possibly the third-party payer—chooses the contracts of all team members. Abstracting from communication costs, several authors have studied the advantages of delegated contracting. Jelovac and Macho-Stadler (2002) propose a model of a hospital where two agents, let us refer to them as a manager and a doctor, decide on separate production inputs. Let us say that the first input is investment in equipment and the second one is diagnostic effort. These authors illustrate a subtle idea: when two agents interact, the contract for one of the agents can also be used to discipline the other. With this in mind, assume that the third-party payer can observe neither the manager's investment nor the doctor's effort. Consequently, an important piece of information is lost when all contracting is in the hands of the third-party payer. More specifically, the third-party payer cannot make the contract for the doctor contingent on the manager's investment decision, because the third-party payer cannot observe this decision. Hence, that contract, which could be used to govern the manager, loses this functionality. In contrast, if we allow the manager to design the doctor's contract, this specific function of the doctor's contract is restored. Of course, delegating contracting also has a disadvantage. The manager can manipulate the doctor's contract to her own benefit. When is it then that decentralization fares better from the third-party payer's point of view? Take the case when investment and diagnostic effort are complements of production. Then decentralizing is better, since the manager can, by providing incentives to the doctor, enhance her own incentives. Therefore, it all depends on the degree of complementarity. For instance, it could be argued that, for treatments that are not high-tech, the doctor's productivity is quite independent of the hospital equipment. Centralization would be the better choice there.

Admittedly, and despite the theoretical appeal of the preceding discussion, it is not easy to find real world instances where these issues have been pondered in the context of hospital organization. In contrast, they have originated much debate in the managerial science literature.

Macho-Stadler and Perez-Castrillo (1998) study the delegation of contract design in the presence of collusion amongst team members. Although their analysis is very general, their insights can be readily applied to hospital management. Take the same example as before. If the third-party payer delegates to the manager the contracting of a specialist, this is equivalent to the third-party payer centralizing all contracts and then the manager and the specialist colluding in their decisions. Formally, if the third-party payer is to find the optimal coalition-proof set of contracts, this is equivalent to finding the best manager's contract from the point of view of the payer whilst taking into account that the manager will behave opportunistically when providing incentives to the doctor.

This has important implications for the organization of a hospital. Suppose that, in the absence of coalition formation, it was better to centralize contracts. Then, the policy of separating management and medical decisions (the double hierarchy, as seen by Harris 1977) is indeed beneficial if such separation limits the extent to which managers and doctors can collude.

Finally, Boadway et al. (2004) also recognize the distinctive role that managers and doctors play in the hospital. The main issue addressed is the asymmetry of information: doctors have better information about patient needs (high- versus low-tech treatments and equipment) than hospital managers do. Managers, in turn, have better information on case mix than the payer (which is taken here to be a public authority, like the NHS). They show that a cascade of contracts should be aimed at eliciting the private information of these agents at the least cost. The main implication is that high-tech equipment and high-tech services are over-promoted in comparison to a situation where information is symmetric.

19.5 The Hospital and the Outside World

19.5.1 Contracting with Payers

Recent decades have witnessed important changes in the way hospitals relate with payers of health care. The managed care trend, initiated in the early 1970s in the United States, and the movement toward activity based payments in many other countries have changed the way hospitals are financed (see Chapter 26 in this volume for a discussion of provider payment rules). We take here a different view, looking at other issues, like the existence of multiple payers and the (potential) role of economies of scale in their presence.

The creation of DRGs has made possible the use of more sophisticated payment schedules. From simply invoicing payers for the health care provided, many hospitals around the world now have to negotiate in advance how payments will be made and how much it will receive for each type of care.

Third-party payers, be they commercial health insurance companies, sickness funds or national health services, faced with ever-increasing health costs look at ways to induce more efficient health care delivery. Over time, payment rules to hospitals became a tool for third-party payers to influence hospital behavior, not just a mere transfer of funds. It is worth pointing out the most important transformation that took place: payment mechanisms are now seen as a way to influence indirectly hospitals' organization. From a traditional cost reimbursement system, in which hospitals invoiced their costs to third-party payers, payment mechanisms evolved to prospective payment, with prices set for treatment episodes. This change resulted from the recognition that cost reimbursement gives too few incentives for efficiency. Moving to prospective payments, characterized by more aggregate units of care provided (treatment episode, for example), leads to stronger incentives for efficiency. The downside of this change is that it also creates incentives for risk selection and for misclassification of patients.

The change in payment rules, and the existence of asymmetric information between payers and hospitals, opens the door for hospitals to "game" against payment schedules. The traditional, simple, relationship of cost invoicing of cost reimbursement has been replaced. The new relationships have now to balance two different objectives: to provide incentives for efficiency of health care delivery within the hospital, and avoid incentives for cream-skimming (risk selection) by hospitals. The basic trade-off that needs to be solved in the definition of payment schedules to hospitals has given rise to an extensive literature, which is reviewed in Chapter 26.

Some related issues are less well-understood: the role of economies of scale (and scope), and the role of large third-party payers, both of which are associated with an often neglected feature—hospitals can be funded by more than one payer. This is generally true in health systems where a multiplicity of health insurers co-exist. Also in countries where a national health service is the preferred mode of health insurance, it is often the case that voluntary health insurance covering hospital care is present.

The existence of multiple payers leads to new issues in the definition of payment schedules, especially if one of the payers is significantly larger than the others. These large payers negotiate with hospitals, and are usually able to obtain different prices. Volume typically gains lower prices to the payer.

Suppose a hospital is already operating at a volume range where diseconomies of scale exist, after contracting an activity level with a third-party payer. Then, another third-party payer wishes to contract with the hospital. The basic question is: how should the price be set?

In this simple sequential description, the price set for the second, smaller, third-party payer must reflect its impact on costs, and therefore, will exceed the average cost (per patient treated). If there are diseconomies of scale, the incremental average cost of extra patients treated will be higher than the average costs in the main contractual relationship. Under economies of scale, the reverse possibility occurs: the marginal third-party payer benefits from dilution of fixed costs, and the incremental average cost will be less. Therefore, for a constant batch of potential patients that it brings to the hospital, the exact payment schedule that the hospital is willing to accept can be quite different according to whether economies, or diseconomies, of scale prevail.

A related question is whether, in the presence of a strong component of fixed costs, the smaller third-party payers should contribute to cover the fixed cost. How should this contribution be set? For example, one may think that smaller third-party payers should pay only the incremental cost that the care provided to their beneficiaries creates. Another approach would be to set a payment by each third-party payer equal to the average cost. The difference between the two alternatives may be significant. First, in the presence of diseconomies of scale, having the smaller third-party payer paying according to the average cost shifts some cost to the larger payer. Second, in a more subtle way and following from the first effect, third-party payers may offer a more generous coverage to their beneficiaries and induce higher use of hospital services. Both effects suggest that marginal third-party payers should pay more than the average cost, though the question of how to determine the identity of the marginal payer is not easy to answer.

Another (disputed) effect in the relationship of the hospital with large payers is the cost shifting behavior. Cost shifting has been defined as the practice of hospitals increasing prices to one group of third-party payers following price decrease associated with payments from another group enforced by some large payer, typically large government-based programs (like Medicare or Medicaid, in the US). The existence of cost shifting behavior naturally requires the ability of the hospital to set prices for the care it provides. An initial explanation for cost shifting behavior required market power of hospitals and that prior to a change in prices paid by large payers such market power was not fully exploited by the hospital (although no rationale is presented why market power was not exercised to full extent before, and why that changes). Morrisey (2003) addresses the issue from the perspective of market power as the cause of cost shifting, to dismiss it as a relevant issue.[15] When faced with a price decrease forced by a large payer, hospitals face an alternative course of action, rather than cost shift: to look for savings resulting from economies of scale and/or from economies of scope, and to reduce inefficiencies.[16] Morrisey looks at the role of non-profit organizations (and provision of charitable care) as the reason why market power is not fully exploited in the first place, just to discard it. Under Morrisey's argument, having objectives other than pure profit maximization does not imply that payers do not negotiate to obtain the lowest price possible from providers. Providers also have an advantage in diversifying payers, to avoid becoming dependent on a single one. Improvement in the mix of patients from different payers can also be attempted by providers, namely through carefully crafting services offered. Thus, other strategies available to hospitals are superior to cost shifting. For public policy action, Morrisey (2003) proposes measures that increase market competition.

On the empirical side of cost shifting behavior, most works find small effects of cost shifting, and no particular pattern emerges. In some cases for-profit hospitals do not engage in cost shifting, while for-profit hospitals do. In other cases, both type of hospitals do cost shifting.[17] Cost shifting across different services is only possible if they are paid for by distinct third-party payers. More recently, Santerre (2005) performs an empirical analysis of cost shifting behavior, finding only a very minor efficiency loss, less than 1 percent of total private hospital expenditures (for 1992, US data). This corroborates an earlier discussion by Ginsburg (2003), who highlights that welfare costs associated with distortions with inelastic demands tend to be small. Only distribution issues remain.

A related problem is addressed in Ma and McGuire (1993), where the way to pay for fixed costs (joint costs, in their terminology) by third-party payers is discussed.[18] Their analysis takes into account that the level of fixed costs is endogenous with payment structures in the case of hospitals. The way the payment rules are set will determine the incentives for investment and technology adoption.[19]

In this context, the possibility of a reimbursement transfer to pay for the fixed cost (called pass-through in Ma and McGuire's (1993) discussion) may improve overall efficiency. In particular, if one of the third-party payers has the opportunity to use cost reimbursement and commit first to its payment schedule, it may use the payment system strategically. By first defining its payment rule, it forces the other providers to cover the remaining costs of the provider. In doing so, it also increases aggregate social welfare, although some fixed cost share is shifted from the largest to the smallest third-party payer.

In their paper, Ma and McGuire (1993) identify the larger third-party payer with a public payer, the federal Medicare program. Their most interesting result is that an

---

[15] See Morrisey (1994) for an earlier view on the issue.

[16] Note that prospective payment mechanisms aim at reducing inefficiencies as well.

[17] See Hadley and Feder 1985; Dranove 1988; Clement 1999; Zwanziger et al. 2000; Duggan 2002; Rosenman and Friesner 2002; Friesner and Rosenman 2004.

[18] Further discussion of hospital decisions in the presence of cost shifting is found in Glazer and McGuire (1994).

[19] Typically, payers refrain from paying innovation and tend to shift the innovation adoption risk to providers.

efficiency allocation of resources (investment decisions) is achieved in equilibrium if and only if the large payer moves first and commits to a reimbursement level of the joint costs. This commitment mitigates the incentive the large payer has to shift costs to small payers (through the different prices the hospital has to charge each payer).

There are, of course, other reasons for differential treatment of third-party providers, namely variation in bargaining power, which may be linked to the size of demand each third-party payer brings to the hospital.[20]

The great majority of discussions about payment schedules to hospitals implicitly assume a single third-party payer or identical third-party payers. We argue here that variation in third-party payer size, in terms of patients they bring to the hospital, can easily lead to different payment schedules, with non-trivial impact on the design of such payment schedules. Elements such as the degree of economies of scale, interaction amongst third-party payers mediated by the need to finance the hospital and bargaining positions will create variation in payment schedules across third-party payers.

This is potentially relevant for all health systems, irrespective of their funding organization being based on tax-funded national health services, sickness funds or private health insurance. Further research is needed to fully detail how these considerations are to be incorporated into activity-based payment rules and other contractual approaches using DRGs as the basic unit of payment.

19.5.2 Referrals

Typically, the analysis of hospitals starts with patients showing up at the door of the hospital, and not much is said about demand for hospital services. Either it is assumed to be randomly determined from the point of view of the hospital or that demand for hospital services is determined by quality of care and prices, both time and monetary ones (including here the prices resulting from agreements between third-party payers and the hospital).

Future demand is discussed usually with reference to waiting lists for surgery, which nonetheless result from hospital decisions. This common approach neglects the role of the interactions between the hospital and other health care providers that may refer patients for hospital treatment.

In this respect, a common observation one hears from hospital managers, specialists, and policymakers is that a large fraction of cases they see could have been resolved in primary care.[21] This issue is closely related to the discussion on payment structures. Whenever hospitals are funded by case payments they prefer to receive more patients for treatment while hospitals funded by capitation (to treat people in a defined

---

[20] For a summary of questions related to bargaining between hospitals and third-party payers, see Barros and Martinez-Giralt (2006) and the references therein.

[21] This concern was already voiced in the survey by Scott (2000), who mentioned the large differences observed in referral rates across GPs. See also Malcomson 2004.

catchment area) will invest more in keeping patients treated at primary care level when clinically feasible. In other words, these professionals are demanding a larger role of primary care in gatekeeping. In fact, several health systems make referral by a GP a necessary condition to visit a specialist. This is indeed the case in Italy, the Netherlands, Norway, Spain, and the United Kingdom. In contrast, the gatekeeping role of the GP is very limited in Belgium, Finland, France and Germany. The issue of whether referral by a GP should be made compulsory or not has deserved quite a lot of attention recently. Gatekeeping determines to a considerable extent the demand faced by the hospital. Moreover, referrals to the hospital depend on both the incentives faced by GPs and on the formal relationship between primary care and hospitals.[22]

This is true not only for a national health system where hospitals are public but also for managed care institutions. The latter also tend to value primary care as a screening device before people get admitted for hospital treatment. Therefore, the scarcity of literature regarding how this relationship is established and what its implications are is surprising. For example, in national health services, primary care centers are run separately from hospitals, while in health maintenance organizations a more integrated view of hospital care and primary care exists.

In many circumstances, referral decisions are the only connection and entail no financial transfer. The fund-holding GP's experience in the UK introduced a financial element into this relationship (GPs that were fund holders had to pay for the care of their patients out of the budget they received). Whenever no money is involved, we often see calls for cooperation between physicians at the hospital and at the primary care center. At the other extreme, we see managed care institutions vertically integrating the role of GPs in terms of referral to hospital care.

Some interesting questions arise in this relationship, since the decision to refer a patient to hospital treatment, and thus to create the hospital's demand, lies in the hands of the GP at primary care institutions. The relationship that is established between them will influence the referral flows and the overall efficiency of the health system.[23] From the point of view of the hospital, a closer relationship with primary care may be more or less valued according to the way its financing is set.

The more aggregated way of paying a hospital with a well-defined catchment area, namely within a national health service, is to pay by capitation—a fixed amount per year per member of the population in the relevant geographic area.[24] Under this capitation system, the hospital has a clear incentive to detect health problems early and to treat patients at primary care facilities whenever feasible. On the other

---

[22] For the reader interested in the issue, see, for example, Brekke et al. 2007; Garcia-Marinoso and Jelovac 2003; and Gonzalez 2006.

[23] For further discussion on this, see Barros and Martinez-Giralt (2003) for a theoretical approach and Kripalani et al. (2007) for a review of existing literature on the relationship between primary care and hospitals.

[24] Of course, capitation payments can also be defined with reference to groups formed in different ways, say, the beneficiaries of a given sickness fund or health insurer.

hand, if the hospital is paid mainly on the basis of how many patients it treats, it has the opposite incentive.

The balance between improving internal efficiency and improving referral decisions from primary care is clearly different to the hospital according to the way it is paid. Recent empirical research provides some information on the relevance of these mechanisms. Dusheiko et al. (2006) find that fund-holding in the UK reduced referral to elective surgery. Thus, an integrated view of hospital and primary care incentives may prove useful to better understand how the demand for the hospital is actually determined. Still, further work on the issue is welcome.[25]

19.6 Some Empirical Evidence

19.6.1 Technology

Since data on hospitals is often routinely collected, it is of no surprise that many studies related to scale and scope economies in hospitals have been produced, as well as studies addressing productive efficiency, using several statistical techniques (the most popular ones being stochastic frontier analysis and DEA: Data Envelopment Analysis).[26]

Typically, concern with economies of scale (and/or scope) arises from the search for the most efficient scale for a hospital to operate at. Knowledge about economies of scale and economies of scope is important to define the size of new hospitals, and range of services offered, when the hospital care is delivered directly by the Government (as in the case in countries where a national health service exists) and to assess hospital mergers, in countries where hospital provision is mainly private. The literature on hospital cost structures attempts to define the optimal hospital size, with most estimates putting it in the range 200–300 beds. The discussion of the optimal size and scope of hospitals has somewhat faded away in recent years.

From the recent studies, Preyra and Pink (2006) estimate a short-run cost function and extend from it to the long-term cost function, finding an optimal value of about 180 beds, using data from Ontario, for the period 1994/1996. This estimate is lower than previous conventional wisdom suggested, though it is in line with a general trend toward shorter hospitalization spells, which require fewer beds.[27]

---

[25] Windmeijer et al. (2005) is one of the few studies that address the relationship between hospitals and general practice, though they do not address the role of referral.

[26] See Chapter 26 in this volume for a more in-depth review of efficiency studies. See also the general reviews in Hollingsworth 2003; and Jacobs et al. 2006.

[27] For other recent evidence, see, among others, Ho and Hamilton 2002; Dranove and Lindrooth 2003; Gaynor and Vogt 2003; and Ray 2003.

One of the main issues in measuring economies of scale (productivity, in general) in hospitals is the role of quality. More efficient hospitals are more likely to have a lower marginal cost of providing quality, and accordingly they may supply a higher quality level in equilibrium (which is likely to raise costs and mask their efficiency advantage).

The way we look at the quantity–efficiency trade-off pointed out earlier needs to be reformulated in the presence of inefficiency. An inefficient hospital may actually improve on both dimensions, quality and quantity, when it moves closer to the efficiency frontier.

The question of how the efficient scale and the degree of economies of scope change with quality has not been addressed in recent literature. The explicit consideration of quality choice by the hospital has other implications as well, since the competitive environment of the hospital will affect such choices.

On the issue of quality, the recent review by Gaynor (2006) makes clear the ambiguities resulting from theory and concludes that there is mixed evidence. The regularities identified by Gaynor (2006) allow a distinction according to whether a regulated price regime or a free price regime prevails. In the first case, basically covering studies involving the US Medicare system, more competition seems to be associated with higher quality. In contrast, when considering privately insured patients and prices set by hospitals, no relationship between competition and quality exists. Both findings are in line with economic theory.

Under regulated prices, quality is the main "competitive tool" of hospitals and it is used intensively. Whenever both price and quality are available instruments to the hospital, the effort to attract patients is spread over both of them.[28] More competition may then be associated with either higher or lower quality, also depending on the intensity to which the hospital uses the price in its policy. Since the marginal gain from using price or quality to attract patients is also determined by the cost structure, not only is competition in the marketplace relevant, but also cost structures. Economies of scale will favor the use of the price vis-à-vis quality, for example.

In more recent research, the discussion on economies of scale has been set aside. Most empirical studies about hospital cost functions concentrate on efficiency measurement, in particular technological efficiency. They seldom report information on the optimal efficient scale of hospitals.

The issue of scale is being recovered somewhat at a different level. Given the increasing availability of micro data, exploration of scale effects becomes possible. An example is provided by Gaynor et al. (2005), who in a simple but effective way distinguish between economies of scale and learning by doing as motives for a better performance (meaning a lower rate for in-hospital mortality). There is a growing literature on the link between higher volume and higher quality for many surgical procedures.

Scale also brings bargaining power gains. Burgess et al. (2005) and Melnick and Keeler (2007) find that a group of hospitals is in a position to charge higher prices. Since

---

[28] This is true also when patients have insurance coverage, as most health insurers negotiate prices with providers.

location of care provided is not a main force, it is bargaining power that is driving the results. Thus, scale brings gains, compared to single units, though related to prices rather than technological opportunities. These gains are not social gains as prices just distribute surplus between agents.

A final area where scale does matter is teaching. Several empirical works have addressed the extra costs of teaching activities, usually by inclusion of a dummy variable for teaching hospital status (capturing different levels in costs in teaching hospitals, compared to non-teaching ones) or by separating samples according to teaching/non-teaching status. This is hardly satisfactory, as it ignores how teaching activities impact the cost function. Several studies found higher costs for teaching hospitals.[29] Teaching increases costs because it diverts effort from doctors and leads to use of more resources, but it can also reduce costs because medical students can be a cheaper substitute for some medical labor work.[30] A better understanding of how teaching hospitals operate should be sought in future research agendas.

The issue of random demand and its impact on hospital costs has received attention in several works.[31] More recently, Sharma et al. (2008) show that response to an unexpected demand surge for hospital services is more likely to be met by early discharges to free up capacity than rationing admissions.

19.6.2 Does Ownership Matter?

Most of the debate about ownership has been centered on empirical analysis of performance differences, namely cost efficiency. The main empirical hypothesis tested is based on the idea that as not-for-profit hospitals have a less well-defined residual claimant,[32] we should expect them to be less efficient, although related problems are that for-profit hospitals may more easily induce demand and charge higher prices. Differences in several performance indicators have been addressed: financial results, quality variables and "upcoding" behavior. By "upcoding" we have in mind that one way for hospitals to play against the payment system is to code patients in a payment category higher than the correct one (in order to obtain a higher transfer from the third-party payer).

The legal distinctions associated with each ownership form are reviewed in Sloan (2000) and will not be repeated here. The early evidence points to no systematic difference in either cost efficiency or quality levels between for-profit and not-for-profit hospitals, though most literature on the issue is related to US experience. The ambiguity resulting from earlier studies has not been solved by recent works.

Several explanations have been advanced to explain the inconclusive comparisons across ownership forms, namely measurement issues (especially the questions

[29] See, among others, Linna 1998; Grosskopf et al. 2001; Rosko 2001, 2004; Farsi and Filippini 2008.
[30] Barros and Machado 2010.
[31] See Gaynor and Anderson 1995; Keeler and Ying 1996; Carey 1998; and Baker et al. 2004.
[32] On this see section 19.4 on the consequences of the absence of a residual claimant.

associated with the appropriate definition of cost of capital in not-for-profit hospitals) and the hypothesis that market discipline is not strong enough to make for-profit hospitals sufficiently different from not-for-profit hospitals.

The ownership of a hospital is an issue only if it implies different objective functions or different constraints on behavior. With regard to the latter, it is often the case that not-for-profit organizations typically have constraints on how to distribute accounting surpluses. In particular, any surplus generated cannot be used to pay dividends, and it should, according to common provision in statutes, be re-invested in the activity (or in a closely related one). Surpluses may also be distributed to stakeholders (managers, employees, physicians, etc.), though usually not openly discussed as such.

The differences in objective functions may result from choice of boards. Whilst in for-profit institutions, shareholders select who runs the hospital, in not-for-profit institutions other means must be found, and self-perpetuation is easily achieved by entrenched directors. Moreover, exerting accountability is more difficult, presumably creating more room for managerial discretion. To control it, to some extent at least, compensation plans (involving stock options and bonuses) for executives in not-for-profit institutions are usually ruled out.

Distinct methodological approaches have been followed to make the comparisons, with unclear implications of the ambiguous results. Whether paired comparisons, regression analysis or stochastic frontier estimation is used, there is no clear supremacy of one ownership form over the other. Shen et al. (2005) conduct a meta-analysis for US hospitals (since 1990), finding that there are only minor differences between for-profit and not-for-profit hospitals.[33] Moreover, their analysis indicates that differences found in previous studies were attributed to methodological issues, such as functional forms, model specifications and definition of dependent variables in the empirical application.[34]

The debate about ownership has been less intense outside the US, although evidence has been gathered over the years in other countries. The focus has moved to management practice, with separation of ownership on the one side, and management rules on the other side. This is especially visible in countries with national health services that own and operate hospitals. Introduction of different governance and management rules, namely the use of trust or foundation status, is seen as a way to improve management efficiency without touching the usually delicate issue (at least, on political grounds) of ownership. Again, no strong differences in performance seem to be associated with ownership status.[35]

Sloan (2000) sets a research agenda about unsolved ownership issues: the role of other outputs associated with ownership (such as local control of the hospital), the need to

---

[33] See also Wong et al. 2005.

[34] See also, among others, Duggan 2000; Rosko 2001; Silverman and Skinner 2001; Picone et al. 2002; Rosenau and Linder 2003; Cremieux et al. 2005; Dafny 2005; Leone and van Horne 2005; Lindrooth and Weisbrod 2007; Wright 2007; and Eggleston et al. 2008.

[35] See Marini et al. (2008) on the UK; Herr (2008) on Germany; Milcent (2005) on France; Barbetta et al. (2007) on Italy.

have evidence from other countries, to look on differences other than performance (cost efficiency) alone, deeper knowledge of quality differences, better understanding of what constraints exist in each case, and how patient choice may affect the definition of ownership form. Except for more evidence from outside the US, little progress has been made in the other topics. The ambiguities regarding the comparison over ownership forms are still far from settled.

19.7 Discussion and Challenges for Future Research

For a long time, economic analysis treated hospitals differently in theory and in empirical applications. In the former, issues of physician agency, contracting of hospital services and team production have been at the heart of many studies. In contrast, empirical studies have treated the hospital as a black box, addressing mostly issues about efficiency and implications of different ownership forms (government-owned, private for-profit, and private not-for-profit). Bridging the gap of theory to empirical work is a major challenge for current empirical research. A potential line of future developments is to explore the empirical implications stemming from new theories on the internal organization of the hospital.

Even at a theoretical level, there are still many open questions. Many of them await the development of new tools. As mentioned in previous sections, a major shortcoming of present analyses is that the negotiation process that leads to the allocation of risk and expected surplus amongst the parties within the hospital has been overlooked. One advantage of focusing on hospitals in addressing this issue will be that technological aspects of the medical decision will constrain the set of possible bargaining procedures. As mentioned at the outset, Harris (1977) pointed out that medical care at the hospital has some peculiarities, urgency and specificity, that require a tailored decision-making process marked by a mixture of protocols and needed improvisation. Perhaps these peculiarities will guide the theorist in the specification of the "right" bargaining process.

Although it is true that the literature has studied the negotiation of the hospital with the third-party payer, the issue of how to incorporate economies of scale and scope (an therefore size), as well as the different objectives that ownership structure implies into these negotiations, has only recently received attention. Ownership issues alone, as envisaged by Sloan's (2000) agenda, present many opportunities for fruitful future research.

Still at the theoretical level, a thorough analysis of behavioral rather than fully rational and selfish decision-making is needed. Issues of altruism have only recently been introduced in the neoclassical paradigm of selfish utility maximization.[36]

---

[36] Biglaiser and Ma (2007) and Ma and Chone (2007) are examples of how one could integrate negotiation and altruism in the classical incentive model.

Finally, many studies have addressed the issue of hospital efficiency. Typically, efficiency scores are estimated and sometimes researchers attempt to find regularities between high efficiency scores and hospital characteristics. However, the internal organization of the hospital is not a common variable of interest, most likely due to obvious measurement problems. This may hinder development of a more thorough knowledge on how hospitals work.

One of the messages from our review is that hospital activities are better seen as performed by "teams." We interpret teams in a very broad sense, to include the joint effort of several economic agents, in order to achieve an outcome in the absence of a clear market mechanism (i.e. price) and where individual accountability is hard to obtain. If one considers the production of health and well-being of the system as a whole, this idea of team, or interaction, transcends the limits of the hospital. The interaction between acute treatment at the hospital and chronic treatment outside the hospital, and the interaction of primary care at the general practitioner and secondary care at the hospital specialist through referrals, are clear examples of this.

References

BAKER, L., C. PHIBBS, C. GUARMO, D. SUPINA and J. REYNOLDS, 2004, Within-year variation in hospital utilization and its implications for hospital costs, *Journal of Health Economics*, 23: 191–211.

BARBETTA, G. P., G. TURATI and A. ZAGO, 2007, Behavioral differences between public and private not-for-profit hospitals in the Italian National Health Service, *Health Economics*, 16: 75–96.

BARROS, P. P. and X. MARTINEZ-GIRALT, 2003, Preventive health care and payment systems, Topics in Economic Analysis and Policy, Berkeley Electronic Press, 3(1): Article 10.

———— 2006, Models of negotiation and bargaining in health care, pp. 242–9, in A. Jones, ed., *The Elgar Companion to Health Economics*. Cheltenham: Edward Elgar.

—— and S. R. MACHADO, 2010, Money for nothing? The net costs of medical training, *Health Care Management Science*, 13(3): 234–55.

BIGLAISER, G. and A. MA, 2007, Moonlighting: public service and private practice, *RAND Journal of Economics*, 38(4): 1113–33.

BOADWAY, R., M. MARCHAND, and M. SATO, 2004, An optimal contract approach to hospital financing, *Journal of Health Economics*, 23(1): 85–110.

BREKKE, K. and M. KUHN, 2006, Direct to consumer advertising in pharmaceutical markets, *Journal of Health Economics*, 25(1): 102–30.

—— and L. SORGARD, 2007, Public versus private health care in a national health service, *Health Economics*, 16(6): 579–601.

—— R. NUSCHELER, and O. R. STRAUME, 2007, Gatekeeping in health care, *Journal of Health Economics*, 26(1): 149–70.

BURGESS, JR., J. F., K. CAREY and G. YOUNG, 2005, The effect of network arrangements on hospital pricing behavior, *Journal of Health Economics*, 24(2): 391–405.

BURGESS, S., C. PROPPER, M. RATTO, S. SCHOLDER, and E. TOMINEY, 2007, Smarter task assignment or greater effort: What makes a difference in team performance? Mimeo.

CAREY, K., 1998, Stochastic demand for hospitals and optimizing "excess" bed capacity, *Journal of Regulatory Economics*, 14: 165–87.

CASTELLI, A., D. DAWSON, H. GRAVELLE, and A. STREET, 2007, Improving the measurement of health system output growth, *Health Economics*, 16: 1091–107.

CLEMENT, J., 1999, Dynamic cost shifting in hospitals: evidence from the 1980s and the 1990s, *Inquiry*, 34: 340–50.

CRÈMIEUX, P.-Y., P. OUELLETTE and F. RIMBAUD, 2005, Hospital cost flexibility in the presence of many outputs: a public–private comparison, *Health Care Management Science*, 8(2): 111–20.

CULYER, A. J. and J. P. NEWHOUSE, eds., 2000, *Handbook of Health Economics*, Vols. I–II. Amsterdam: Elsevier Science, B.V.

DAFNY, L., 2005, How do hospitals respond to price changes? *American Economic Review*, 95(5): 1525–47.

DISMUKE, C. and V. SENA, 2001, Is there a trade-off between quality and productivity? The case of diagnostic technologies in Portugal, *Annals of Operations Research*, 107: 101–16.

DRANOVE, D., 1988, Pricing by non-profit institutions: the case of hospital cost shifting, *Journal of Health Economics*, 7(1): 44–57.

—— and R. LINDROOTH, 2003, Hospital consolidation and costs: another look at the evidence, *Journal of Health Economics*, 22(6): 983–97.

DUGGAN, M.G., 2000, Hospital ownership and public medical spending, *Quarterly Journal of Economics*, CXV(4): 1343–73.

—— 2002, Hospital market structure and the behavior of not-for-profit hospitals, evidence from responses to California's disproportionate share program, *RAND Journal of Economics*, 33: 433–46.

DUSHEIKO, M., H. GRAVELLE, R. JACOBS and P. SMITH, 2006, The effect of financial incentive on gatekeeping doctors: evidence from a natural experiment, *Journal of Health Economics*, 25(3): 449–78.

EGGLESTON, K., Y.-C. SHEN, J. LAU, C. SCHMID and J. CHAU, 2008, Hospital ownership and quality of care: what explains the different results in the literature, *Health Economics*, 17(12): 1345–62.

FRIEDMAN, B. and M. PAULY, 1981, Cost functions for a service firm with variable quality and stochastic demand, *Review of Economics and Statistics*, 63: 610–24.

FRIESNER, D. and R. ROSENMAN, 2004, Inpatient–outpatient cost shifting in Washington hospitals, *Health Care Management Science*, 7(1): 17–26.

GALIZZI, M., and MIRALDO M., 2008, Optimal contracts and contractual arrangements within the hospital: bargaining vs. take-it-or-leave-it offers, Centre for Health Economics, University of York, RP37.

GAL-OR, E., 1994, Excessive investment in hospital capacities, *Journal of Economics and Management Strategy*, 3(1): 53–70.

GARCÍA-MARINOSO, B. and I. JELOVAC, 2003, GPs' payment contracts and their referral practice, *Journal of Health Economics*, 22: 617–35.

GAYNOR, M., 2006, Competition and quality in health care markets, *Foundations and Trends in Microeconomics*, 2(6), Hanover, MA: NowPublishers, 441–558.

—— and G. ANDERSON, 1995, Uncertain demand, the structure of hospital costs and the cost of empty beds, *Journal of Health Economics*, 14: 291–317.

—— and W. VOGT, 2003, Competition among hospitals, *RAND Journal of Economics*, 34(4): 764–85.

—— H. SEIDER and W. VOGT, 2005, The value-outcome effect, scale economies, and learning-by-doing, *American Economic Review*, 95(2): 243–7.

GINSBURG, P., 2003, Can hospitals and physicians shift the effects of cuts in Medicare reimbursement to private payers?, *Health Affairs*, W3: 472–9.

GLAZER, J. and T. G. McGUIRE, 1994, Payer competition and cost-shifting in health care, *Journal of Economics and Management Strategy*, 3(1): 71–92.

GONZÁLEZ, P., 2004, Should physicians' dual practice be limited? An incentive approach, *Health Economics*, 13(6): 505–24.

——2006, The gatekeeping role of general practitioners: does patients' information matter? Working paper ECON 06.09, Universidad Pablo de Olavide.

GROSSKOPF, S., D. MARGARITIS, and V. VALDMANIS, 2001, Comparing teaching and non-teaching hospitals: a frontier approach, *Health Care Management Science*, 4(1): 83–90.

HADLEY, J. and J. FEDER, 1985, Hospital cost-shifting and care for the uninsured, *Health Affairs*, 4: 67–80.

HARRIS, J., 1977, The internal organization of hospitals: some economic implications, *The Bell Journal of Economics*, 8(2): 467–82.

HERR, A., 2008, Cost and technical efficiency of German hospitals: does ownership matter? *Health Economics*, 17: 1057–71.

HO, V. and B. HAMILTON, 2002, Hospital mergers and acquisitions: does market consolidation harm patients? *Journal of Health Economics, 2000*, 19(5): 767–91.

HOLLINGSWORTH, B., 2003, Non-parametric and parametric applications measuring efficiency in health care, *Health Care Management Science*, 6(4): 203–18.

HOLMSTROM, B., 1982, Moral hazard in teams, *Bell Journal of Economics*, 13: 324–40.

JACOBS, R., P. SMITH and A. STREET, 2006, *Measuring Efficiency in Health Care: Analytic Techniques and Health Policy*. Cambridge, UK: Cambridge University Press.

JELOVAC, I. and I. MACHO-STADLER, 2002, Comparing organizational structures in health services, *Journal of Economic Behavior and Organization*, 49: 501–22.

JONES, A., ed., 2006, *The Elgar Companion to Health Economics*. Cheltenham, UK: Edward Elgar.

JOSKOW, P., 1980, The effects of competition and regulation on hospital bed supply and the reservation quality of the hospital, *Bell Journal of Economics*, 11: 421–47.

KEELER, T. E. and J. YING, 1996, Hospital costs and excess bed capacity: a statistical analysis, *Review of Economics and Statisticas*, 78: 470–81.

KRIPALANI, S., F. LeFEVRE, C. PHILLIPS, M. WILLIAMS, P. BASANAH, and D. BAKER, 2007, Deficits in communication and information transfer between hospital-based and primary care physicians: implications for patient safety and continuity of care, *Journal of the American Medical Association*, 297(8): 831–41.

LEONE, A. and R. VAN HORNE, 2005, How do nonprofit hospitals manage earnings? *Journal of Health Economics*, 24(4): 815–37.

LINDROOTH, R. and B. WEISBROD, 2007, Do religious non-profit and for-profit organizations respond differently to financial incentives? The hospice industry, *Journal of Health Economics*, 26(2): 342–57.

LINNA, M., 1998, Measuring hospital cost efficiency with panel data models, *Health Economics*, 7(5): 415–27.

MA, A. and CHONE, P. 2007, Optimal health care contracts under physician agency. Working Papers Series WP2007-004, Department of Economics, Boston University.

—— and T. McGUIRE, 1993, Paying for joint costs in health care, *Journal of Economics and Management Strategy*, 2(1): 71–95.

MACHO-STADLER, I. and D. PEREZ-CASTRILLO, 1998, Centralized and decentralized contracts in a moral hazard environment, *The Journal of Industrial Economics*, 46(4): 489–510.

MALCOMSON, J. M., 2004, Health service gatekeepers, *RAND Journal of Economics* 35: 401–21.

MARINI, G., M. MIRALDO, R. JACOBS, and M. GODDARD, 2008, Giving greater financial independence to hospitals: does it make a difference? The case of the English NHS trusts, *Health Economics*, 17(6): 751–75.

MELNICK, G. and E. KEELER, 2007, The effects of multi-hospital systems on hospital prices, *Journal of Health Economics*, 26(2): 400–12.

MILCENT, C., 2005, Hospital ownership, reimbursement systems and mortality rates, *Health Economics*, 14(11): 1151–68.

MORRISEY, M., 2003, Cost-shifting: new myths, old confusion, and enduring reality, *Health Affairs*, W3: 489–91.

—— 1994, *Cost-shifting in Health Care: Separating Evidence from Rethoric*. Washington, DC: The American Enterprise Institute Press.

NEARY, H. M., 2001, Dynamic consistency in incentive planning with a material input, *Journal of Economic Behavior & Organization*, 44: 315–32.

NEWHOUSE, J. P., 1970, Toward a theory of nonprofit institutions: an economic model of a hospital, *American Economic Review*, 60(1): 64–74.

OLSEN, K. and A. STREET, 2008, The analysis of efficiency among a small number of organizations: how inferences can be improved by exploiting patient-level data, *Health Economics*, 17(6): 671–81.

PAULY, M. and M. REDISCH, 1973, The not-for-profit hospital as a physicians' cooperative, *American Economic Review*, 63(1): 87–99.

PHELPS, C. E., 2002, *Health Economics*. Reading, MA: Addison-Wesley.

PICONE, G., C. SHIN-YI, and F. SLOAN, 2002, Are for-profit conversions harmful to patients and to Medicare? *RAND Journal of Economics*, 33(3): 507–23.

PREYRA, C. and G. PINK, 2006, Scale and scope economies through hospital consolidations, *Journal of Health Economics*, 25(6): 1049–68.

RATTO, M., S. BURGESS, B. CROXSON, I. JEWITT, and C. PROPPER, 2001, Team-based incentives in the NHS: An economic analysis. CMPO Working Paper Series No. 01/37.

RAY, S., 2003, Measuring scale efficiency from the translog multi-input, multi-output distance function, Dept. of Economics, University of Connecticut.

ROSENAU, P. and S. LINDER, 2003, Two decades of research comparing for-profit and nonprofit health provider performance in the United States, *Social Science Quarterly*, 84(2): 219–41.

ROSENMAN, R., and D. FRIESNER, 2002, Cost shifting revisited: the case of service intensity, *Health Care Management Science*, 5(1): 15–24.

ROSKO, M., 2001, Cost efficiency of US hospitals: a stochastic frontier approach, *Health Economics*, 10(6): 539–51.

—— 2004, Performance of US teaching hospitals: a panel analysis of cost inefficiency, *Health Care Management Science*, 7(1): 7–16.

SANTERRE, R. E., 2005, The welfare loss from hospital cost-shifting behavior: a partial equilibrium analysis, *Health Economics*, 14(6): 621–6.

SCOTT, A., 2000, The economics of general practice, chapter 22, pp. 1176–202, in A. J. Culyer and J. P. Newhouse, eds., *Handbook of Health Economics*, Vol. II. Amsterdam: Elsevier Science, B.V.

SEABRIGHT, P. 2002, Blood, Bribes and the crowding-out of altruism by financial incentives, mimeo IDEI, Université de Toulouse-1.

SHARMA, R., M. STANO and R. GEHRING, 2008, Short-term fluctuations in hospital demand: implications for admissions, discharge, and discriminatory behavior, *RAND Journal of Economics*, 39(2): 586–606.

SHEN, Y.-C., K. EGGLESTON, J. LAU and C. SCHMID, 2005, Hospital ownership and financial performance: a quantitative research review. NBER Working Paper 11662.

SILVERMAN, E. and J. SKINNER, 2001, Are for-profit hospitals really different? Medicare upcoding and market structure. NBER Working Paper 8133.

SLOAN, F., 2000, Not-for-profit ownership and hospital behavior, chapter 21, pp. 1142–74, in A. J. Culyer and J. P. Newhouse, eds, *Handbook of Health Economics*, Vol. I. Amsterdam: Elsevier Science, B.V.

TAVARES, A. I., 2005, The change of the doctor–nurse paradigm: some conditions and implications. Mimeo, Department of Economics, Universitat Autónoma de Barcelona.

WEISBROD, B., 1988, *The Nonprofit Economy*. Cambridge, MA: Harvard University Press.

WINDMEIJER, F., H. GRAVELLE, and P. HOONHOUT, 2005, Waiting lists, waiting times and admissions: an empirical analysis at hospital and general practice level, *Health Economics*, 14(19): 971–85.

WONG, H., C. ZHAN and R. MUTTER, 2005, Do different measures of hospital competition matter in empirical investigations of hospital behavior? *Review of Industrial Organization*, 26(1): 61–87.

WRIGHT, D., 2007, Specialist payment schemes and patient selection on private and public hospitals, *Journal of Health Economics*, 26(5): 1014–26.

YAWE, B. and S. KAVUMA, 2007, Technical efficiency in the presence of desirable and undesirable outputs: a case study of selected district referral hospitals in Uganda. Mimeo.

ZWANZIGER, J., G. MELNICK, and A. BANEZAI, 2000, Can cost shifting continue on a price-competitive environment? *Health Economics*, 9(3): 211–25.

....

CHAPTER 20

PRIMARY CARE

....

ANTHONY SCOTT AND STEPHEN JAN

20.1 INTRODUCTION

THE role of primary care systems and the way they are financed and organized varies greatly across countries. Thirty years since the Alma Ata declaration on the goal of primary care in health care systems in achieving "health for all," progress remains patchy (WHO 2008). At the broadest level, the variation in the development of comprehensive primary health care systems across countries has been determined by differences in economic and social development and the unique ways in which health care systems evolve. In turn, the historical development of health care systems determine more specific characteristics such as the extent of public versus private financing in the provision of primary care, whether there is an orientation toward hospital-based or community-based health care, the degree of autonomy of physicians, the role of incentives, and the extent of de-centralization in decision-making. Many of these features, once established, may be difficult to change. This explains why countries often at similar stages of economic development with mature health care systems can have vastly different systems of primary care.

For example, the US system is very much oriented toward hospital and specialist care and is generally seen to have a weak system of primary health care relative to other developed countries (Starfield 2008). Many other health systems have stronger primary health care sectors, including registered lists of patients and support by regional primary care organizations (Smith and Mays 2005; Scott and Coote 2007). On the other hand, the experience of rapid economic transition in China over the past three decades has seen its primary health care system change from being based around community health workers or "barefoot doctors," regarded as an exemplar for low-income countries, towards the emergence of a health care system heavily reliant on physician-based hospital care. This has significantly reduced access to affordable basic health care for much of the population, particularly the rural poor (Hu et al. 2008). Such experiences highlight the substantial challenges faced by countries of all stages of economic development in establishing comprehensive systems of primary health care.

Changing patterns of need and demand are also influencing how primary health care systems develop. In many low- and middle-income countries, issues such as infectious disease and maternal and child health remain priorities for primary care, where low-cost interventions can generate relatively large health gains. In other countries, the increasing burden of chronic disease suggests new roles for primary care workers in providing primary and secondary prevention and ongoing long-term care, rather than the treatment of acute episodic illness, and a greater emphasis on the delivery of psycho-social interventions (Beaglehole et al. 2008; Joshi et al. 2008). These changes have provided new challenges in terms of the roles, skills and incentive structures of the primary care workforce, and new models of integration, coordination and support as those with chronic disease move between different sectors of the health system. In addition, rising income and wealth increases the opportunity cost of attending primary care, and so demand for more accessible and flexible primary care services increase.

Many argue that the evidence-base for a strong system of primary health care is unequivocal, citing improved access to health care, lower health care costs, and higher population health (Starfield et al. 2005; Starfield 2008). Furthermore, it is argued that these benefits will only accrue if the many features of primary health care are implemented in their entirety (WHO 2008). Implementing only one or two features of primary health care, e.g. gatekeeping, is unlikely to work on their own (Forrest 2003). Furthermore, evidence-based guidance for how primary care should be developed, financed and organized across different settings remains weak.

Ideally, a health system would be designed in which the role of primary care relative to specialist care is determined by an assessment of the comparative costs and outcomes of treatment in the two settings, and their relationship to equity objectives such as access to health care. The interface between these two settings, including the role of gatekeeping and referral processes, is therefore important in determining the most efficient balance between the two settings. This balance is in turn influenced by institutional and incentive structures that determine who patients see at different points in their care. Primary care physicians often have a strong agency role on behalf of patients, acting as coordinators of their care, and most definitions of primary care are based around this role. The informational properties and dynamic nature of the contract between patients and primary care physicians and their teams is therefore a key driver of efficiency (Scott 2000). The out of hospital setting for primary care also has important implications for equity in health care systems.

The aim of this chapter is to review the evidence on the role of primary care in health care systems. This is not a systematic review of the literature, but will focus on the key issues and evidence from both developed and developing countries and from an economics perspective. The next section defines the main features of primary care and how these are evolving across countries. Section 20.3 provides an overview of the evidence on whether an expansion or strengthening of primary care improve health outcomes, reduce costs, and improve access. Section 20.4 addresses issues around the financing of primary care and remuneration of primary care workers. In the context of the labor market for primary care workers and global health workforce shortages, section 20.5 examines the most cost-effective ways to ensure the adequate supply of the primary care workforce. Finally, section 20.6 sets out some conclusions.

20.2 Defining Primary Care and its Role in the Health Care System

There are many definitions of primary health care. Most definitions include person-centredness, continuity of care, participation of patients, families and communities, comprehensiveness in terms of the range of health problems that can be addressed and integration with other providers and professionals (WHO 2008). These definitions are based around a desire for a strong agency role in primary care that addresses both the informational asymmetries in the doctor–patient relationship and the role of the primary care doctor as a gatekeeper. Starfield highlights a number "cardinal" characteristics of such care. These include provision of first point of contact, delivery of long-term patient-focused care, comprehensiveness in the range of services provided and coordination of all the other health care services received by the patient (Starfield and Shi 2007). The extent to which primary health care systems possess all of these features varies across countries. From an economic perspective, these characteristics have implications for market structure, incentive design, organization, and efficiency of services provided.

20.2.1 Gatekeeping

Gatekeeping implies that primary care acts as a filter or device where individuals with a wide range of health problems are required to use primary care as the first point of contact for their non-emergency health care needs, and are then diagnosed and/or treated in a primary care setting, and/or referred to more expensive specialist care if necessary. Gatekeeping is thought to avoid unnecessary and costly referrals to specialists. Although it is argued that gatekeeping can also lead to lower health care costs overall, the causal effect of gatekeeping has not yet been established. Evidence from the US suggests that gatekeeping as used in HMOs has been unsuccessful in lowering health care costs, even though there is a strong association between the existence of gatekeeping and lower costs from international comparisons. The likelihood is that countries with fewer health care resources have used gatekeeping and stronger supply-side regulation to assist with priority setting, and that these are therefore correlated with gatekeeping (Forrest 2003).

In terms of interventions to improve a key aspect of this gatekeeping role, the focus has been on referrals from primary care to specialist services. A recent systematic review found some evidence that educational programs for primary care physicians which entail the active involvement of specialists have influenced referral rates and appropriateness of referrals, whilst there was little strong evidence on the role of financial incentives (Akbari et al. 2008). However, more recent studies using difference-in-difference analysis on the impact of GP fundholding in the UK have revealed some effects. For example, Dusheiko showed that the abolition of GP fundholding in the UK increased hospital admissions by 5 percent, and that fundholding led to lower patient satisfaction with services provided (Dusheiko et al. 2006; Dusheiko et al. 2007). Other studies have shown that fundholding reduced waiting times for hospital care by 8 percent (Propper et al. 2002).

Gatekeeping suggests that health workers in primary care should be trained as generalists with the ability to offer diagnosis and treatment for conditions that they decide do not require specialist care. Generalism is concerned with the comprehensiveness of services provided and the breadth of education and training of primary care professionals. The definition of what falls within the boundaries of primary or specialist care however can vary and change over time. General practitioners with special interests are recognized in the UK, and in the US many of the services often conducted by specialists such as routine follow-ups, obstetrics, minor surgery and joint aspirations are more likely to be taken on by primary care physicians than in other industrialized countries (Starfield 2008).

The gatekeeping role and comprehensiveness of service provision also implies that keeping patients out of hospital requires a role for prevention, health promotion, screening and education for self-management. This requires a team approach of physicians, nurses, social care professionals, and allied health and dentistry, and skills in the provision of prevention and screening rather than treatment. The existence of teams does not necessarily imply co-location of team members or group practice; it implies that primary care sits within an effective network of other providers and therefore "good primary care" is associated with sound organization, infrastructure support and access to specialist, hospital and follow-up care when needed. This in turn introduces a complex set of informal contractual relationships between team and network members that will rely heavily on trust, information transmission, reciprocity, and social norms. Nevertheless, team-based incentives are likely to play a significant role in the performance of individuals within such teams, thus highlighting the need for design of efficient contracts (Holmstrom 1982). The issue of team incentives has been examined very little in health care and represents a major gap in the literature (Burgess et al. 2009).

20.2.2 Strong Agency Relationships

From the patients' perspective, gatekeeping and generalism suggest that primary care should act as a hub through which patients are guided through the health care system. Primary care professionals act as both agents for patients and the coordinators of their health care; and thus also acting as agents for the payers of health care. Given informational asymmetries between health professionals and patients, effective doctor–patient agency relationships include the two-way transfer of information, including primary care workers having knowledge of their patients' values and preferences, and being knowledgeable about patients' families and the local community (Lawn et al. 2008; Scott and Vick 1999). This can be achieved through a system that encourages regular contact and long-term agency relationships. In the UK and Norway for instance such relationships are formalized by registration or enrollment to a particular practice (Iversen and Lurås 2000). The concept of the "medical home" from the US also aims to strengthen ties with patients, which is important in the management of chronic disease (see Chapter 25 by McGuire). This can be viewed as encouraging continuity of care and the transfer of information through a stronger doctor–patient relationship but conversely, may inhibit patient choice of provider and competition, since patients can incur costs when switching providers. Nevertheless continuity of care is seen as an important means of encouraging participation of patients in decision-making, the transfer of information in the professional-patient relationship, and the building of trust; thus helping to reduce informational asymmetries and the transactions costs of seeing multiple providers (Saultz and Lochner 2005).

The closeness of contact with patients also suggests that primary care needs to be accessible. This implies an appropriate number and geographic distribution of primary care professionals aligned with population health needs for health care, and that costs to patients at the point of service should be minimized. An example of a successful initiative in this area has been the Family Health Program in Brazil. This program, which was tied in with a broader government agenda of decentralization, substantially expanded geographic access to primary care services to over 60 percent of the regional municipalities in that country (Peres et al. 2006). Such initiatives effectively improve access to care by reducing the indirect costs incurred by patients.

20.2.3 Comprehensiveness and Integration

Primary care as a provider of a comprehensive range of services encourages economies of scope as well as reducing the transactions costs of service provision through integration. The nature and extent of integration within primary care organizations (e.g. effective team working), between different primary care providers (e.g. the formation of networks and regional primary care organizations), and between primary care providers and other health organizations (e.g. hospitals, aged care facilities, social care services) can occur across a number of dimensions and is not easily comparable to traditional economic models of horizontal and vertical integration which focus on the production of a single good or service through a predictable supply chain (Simoens and Scott 2005). Economic models of integration emphasize the minimization of transaction or production costs. These criteria for integration are likely to influence the regulation of market structure in primary care, as well as primary care providers' own decisions to integrate. Primary care providers may also integrate due to individual personal and professional motives, such as professional support, improved information, or improvements in quality of care for patients.

In the context of low- and middle-income countries, the integration of health care services is viewed as a key imperative in primary care. It entails the bundling of services such as vaccination, child and maternal health and chronic disease prevention and management so that they can be delivered more efficiently and at a higher level of quality than otherwise through a fragmented model where individual services are delivered by specialist providers (WHO 1996). Integration is viewed as a means of encouraging economies of scale and scope through utilizing limited infrastructure and resources to provide a comprehensive range of services to a defined population.

There is little evidence at present on the effects of integrated models of care on costs and health outcomes. Very few studies have been conducted evaluating such models of care in high- or in low- and middle-income country settings in a conclusive manner and thus no clear evidence is available that they improve service delivery, health outcomes or costs (Simoens and Scott 2005; Briggs and Garner 2006; Powell Davies et al. 2008).

20.3 PERFORMANCE

What is the evidence that suggests such a comprehensive system of primary health care, or any elements of it, is efficient and equitable compared to alternative ways of organizing health services, such as hospital-based care? There are a number of ways of defining performance, and in this section we examine the evidence that takes a broad production function approach to relating primary care-related inputs of health care systems (e.g. the number of primary care physicians in an area) to health outcomes, costs, and access. We do not review specific clinical or public health interventions delivered within primary care.

There are a number of studies examining the impact of primary care in health care systems, having implications for the optimal mix between primary and hospital-based care, and whether primary care should be strengthened. The overall impact of primary care has been reviewed and examined extensively by Starfield and colleagues, including empirical work and an extensive review of the literature (Macinko et al. 2003; Starfield et al. 2005). The vast majority of studies, which have been conducted across different settings and time periods, with different measures of primary care, and different outcome measures, find strong positive associations between the "strength" of a primary care system and health, and that strong systems of primary care are associated with lower health disparities and costs. This includes studies examining the association of within-country and cross-country measures of the "strength" of primary care with various outcome measures. The "strength" of primary care is measured in a number of ways, including primary care physician to population ratios, measurements of the main characteristics of primary care, such as access and gatekeeping, and comparing individuals who have a primary care physician as their main point of contact with those that do not. Many of these studies inevitably used observational data and sought to control for the main observable confounding variables, although the causal effect of primary care on health,

health disparities, and costs cannot be definitively established. Furthermore, although these reviews of evidence are comprehensive, they are not systematic in their selection, or in the quality assessment, of included studies, and this may result in biased conclusions. Nevertheless, the strength of this evidence lies in its consistent results across a large number of datasets, contexts, countries, and time periods.

Evidence from the UK confirmed these findings whilst explicitly controlling for the endogeneity of primary care physician supply (Gravelle et al. 2008). They found that a higher number of GPs led to improvements in individuals' self-reported health status and EQ5D scores. This is in contrast to a study using an arguably stronger study design. Aakvik and Holmås, using sixteen years of data from Norway, use a dynamic panel data model that accounts for endogeneity and time persistence, and finds no statistically significant effect of the number of the GPs in an area on a range of mortality rates (Aakvik and Holmås 2006).

Most of the evidence on the impact of primary care cited above focuses largely on developed countries. The cost-effectiveness of primary care in low- and middle-income country settings, either at a system level or indeed in relation to specific interventions, has not been well addressed in the literature (Lewin et al. 2008; Rohde et al. 2008; Walker and Jan 2005). Rohde and colleagues provide additional, albeit far from conclusive evidence of the role of primary health care systems in promoting health, with a focus on low- to middle-income countries (Rohde et al. 2008). They examined the performance of primary health care systems internationally by firstly identifying a number of "overperforming" countries—countries that on the basis of life expectancy relative to national income and HIV prevalence are performing above what would be expected. Of the thirty low- and middle-income countries that fall into this category, all were noted as having achieved at least a scaled up selective primary health care system encompassing areas such as family planning and immunization; of these thirty well-performing health systems, fourteen furthermore had established comprehensive primary health care systems. A case study of success in this area is Thailand where initiatives traced to the early 1970s to prioritize primary health care have been associated with dramatic improvements in key health indicators of child and maternal mortality and HIV prevention and treatment (Rohde et al. 2008). These reforms were based on a model of primary care that was characterized by a number of key features: increased government investment in public health infrastructure based on a district health system; social health insurance reforms culminating in the achievement of universal coverage in 2001; the use of community volunteers to enable services to be brought closer to communities; and the increased collection and use of public health data (Rohde et al. 2008).

In an overview of systematic reviews conducted in primary care, Lewin critically appraises the types of interventions that could be effective in strengthening primary care in low- and middle-income countries (Lewin et al. 2008). They examine changes in governance, financial arrangements, delivery arrangements, and implementation strategies. This includes the minimization of user fees in order to extend access to care, which could potentially be facilitated through implementation of social health insurance or community based health insurance schemes. To achieve coverage for the most disadvantaged groups, a number of measure are suggested: (i) some external subsidy to ensure feasibility; (ii) promote a role for private for profit providers—recognizing though that the evidence regarding the quality of such services is mixed; (iii) the integration of primary health services as opposed to fragmentation of services on the basis of disease areas; (iv) task shifting—i.e. using nurses and lay (or community) health workers to take over tasks from physicians; and (v) ongoing monitoring and performance feedback to promote quality.

20.4 Financing Primary Care

The method of financing primary care is embedded within the system of financing for the whole health care system. Funds may come from tax-based finance, social insurance models, and private contributions through direct user fees or cost-sharing with third party public or private insurers. A strong system of primary care requires that the method and distribution of financing encourages access to care, and that the remuneration of primary care providers encourages the provision of an efficient mix of cost-effective services provided in community settings.

20.4.1 Financing and Access

Universal access to primary care may only be feasible in high- and some middle-income countries with significant taxation bases or established forms of social health insurance. Low- and lower-middle-income countries are more likely to rely on private contributions. Access to primary care in countries with a higher share of private contributions, either user fees or private health insurance premiums, is more likely to be based on ability to pay, thus reducing access for those on relatively low-incomes.

The evidence that user charges reduce the utilization of primary care, and that their removal increases utilization, is clear across countries of all income levels. There is some evidence that those who are most responsive are those on lower incomes and in poorer health, and that user charges may be associated with lower health outcomes (Zweifel and Manning 2000; Palmer et al. 2004; and Chapter 15, this volume). This may be ameliorated to some extent with exemptions, special schemes and safety nets for the poor and disadvantaged. However, these means-tested schemes are often subject to high transactions costs as they are administratively cumbersome and furthermore may not provide cover for disadvantaged groups who do meet eligibility requirements (Donaldson et al. 2004).

Financial access is dependent to a large extent on the level of fees and availability of insurance. This has particular relevance to low- and lower-middle-income countries where out of pocket payments for health care tend to comprise a larger component of funding than in high-income and some middle-income settings where government financing and pre-payment through some form of health insurance tends to be more prevalent. The evidence generally supports tax based systems of financing as being more progressive than mandatory social health insurance systems (e.g. Wagstaff 2009). The main reasons for this are that taxation tends to be a more progressive form of revenue generation than social health insurance premiums, social health insurance tends to have a higher rate of co-payment and social health insurance schemes often only cover those in the formal employment sector. On the other hand, voluntary systems of pre-payment, including community based health insurance schemes and private insurance, are less likely to achieve equity goals (Mills 2007; Wagstaff 2009).

In terms of evidence of effect, the studies that have been conducted on user fees have tended to be not well controlled and often the introduction of user fees in these studies has taken place alongside various other policy initiatives (Palmer et al. 2004). As a consequence it is difficult to make conclusions about the efficiency and equity of user fees in each of these contexts. Conversely, it has also been found that the removal of fees has been associated with increases in service use although it is not clear the extent to which these additional services are necessary (Lagarde and Palmer 2008; Lewin et al. 2008). Nevertheless evidence based on household level data has highlighted the significant barriers to care posed by user fees and that they encourage behaviors such as inappropriate self-treatment and partial medication dosing (Russell 2004). Although exemption from such fees for poorest groups can in theory address these concerns, in practice such policies have not worked well due to high transactions costs and inconsistency in the application of the criteria for these exemptions (Gilson and McIntyre 2005).

Despite evidence of the negative equity implications of user fees both in terms of access to care and the burden on households, initiatives to remove such fees—as have recently been introduced in public clinics South Africa and Uganda—need to proceed with caution. Without an offsetting increase in revenue from other sources such as taxation revenue, the removal of user fees could simply strip resources from the primary care sector while at the same time encourage an increase in demand (Gilson and McIntyre 2005). One of the key rationales for user fees is that they potentially provide a means of promoting a sustainable primary health care system through providing funding and resources. Significant reliance, for instance, on donor aid programs to prop up the primary care sector cannot be seen as a viable long-term proposition.

In many low- and middle-income countries, the conventional sources of payment are often augmented by informal payments to providers. Although generally illegal, informal payments can be a significant source of funding and a major burden on patients. It has been reported that such payments can as much as double the cost of an individual service in rural Uganda (McPake et al. 1999). However it is not only the scale of such payment but also their unpredictability and the impunity with which they are charged which can be a significant deterrent to treatment (Lewis 2007; McPake et al. 1999). In such instances the costs incurred by patients in accessing health care include significant transaction costs associated with the failure of providers to credibly commit to a price (Jan 2003; North 1993). It has been suggested that one means of reducing the ability of providers to charge such payments is to maintain sufficiently high levels of official charges to make informal payments less feasible; but these need to be backed by transparent exemption policies and some degree of insurance protection (Lewis 2007). Otherwise, this solution might well reduce informal payments per se, but would do little to overcome the more fundamental problem, namely, the cost barrier faced by the patient—simply replacing one form of payment with another. Conversely, it has been observed that initiatives to remove user charges to encourage better access to care are often hampered by the response of health workers to demand higher informal payments to offset the removal of these fees. Addressing the underlying causes of informal payments requires addressing the basic reasons for such payments by ensuring adequate remuneration to health workers, adequate resourcing for individual health facilities and establishing effective regulatory systems (Schokkaert and Van der Vorde, Chapter 15 in this volume).

20.4.2 Remuneration of Primary Care Providers

The payment of primary care professionals and their teams has been dominated from the mid-1990s by the growth of blended payment schemes, including pay for performance for primary care physicians and practices. The emphasis on performance management in health care systems has led to the linkage of remuneration to achieving pre-specified levels of activity, standards of care, or behaviors in specific disease areas based on guidelines of best practice. These programs usually complement existing remuneration methods such as fee-for-service or capitation, creating more complex blended payment systems that aim to re-orient the payment scheme away from structures, processes and volumes towards health outcomes. They have also largely been introduced in the areas of preventive services such as immunization and screening, and chronic disease management. These are areas where performance is most easily measurable (Christianson and Conrad, Chapter 26 in this volume).

Empirical evidence on the effects of remuneration has generally shown that financial incentives can influence behavior, but the magnitude of their effects is dependent on context (Christianson et al. 2008; Gosden et al. 2001; Petersen et al. 2006; Robinson 2001; Scott and Hall 1995; Christianson and Conrad, Chapter 26, and McGuire, Chapter 25 in this volume). Compared to salaried and capitation payment, FFS has consistently been shown to lead to a higher volume and intensity of care being provided. However, after many years of research, what this literature has yet to show is whether this improves welfare. The focus in the empirical literature is on the effects of changes in the level and type of remuneration on "process" measures rather than on health outcomes and quality of care (Christianson et al. 2008; Gosden et al. 2001). Capitation payment has been shown to lead to low levels of health care provision and a more conservative approach to treatment by doctor. Salaried payment has again been shown to lead to lower levels of treatment provided in comparison to FFS (Gosden et al. 1999), although there has been little empirical research on the role incentives contained within salary scales, careers and subjective performance appraisal (Gosden et al. 1999; Mavromaras and Scott 2005; Prendergast 1999). In order to avoid the more extreme incentives to provide too much or too little care, blended or mixed systems of remuneration have been advocated by many as the way forward (Robinson 2001; Eggelston, 2005; McGuire, Chapter 25 in this volume), although there are still many issues with regard to the most efficient blend of payment schemes. Furthermore the effect of such incentives can be influenced by broader institutional arrangements. For instance, anecdotal evidence from China highlights how the inherent moral hazard problem to over-treat associated with FFS is exacerbated by individual providers having a dual role in prescribing and dispensing medications and because providers' incomes derive directly from the profits from such sales (Hu et al. 2008).

A notably large scheme introduced in 2004 is the Quality and Outcomes Framework (QOF) that provides around 30 percent of income to GPs in the UK, in addition to capitation and other types of payment. The QOF is a performance pay scheme with a total of 146 performance targets across eleven diseases areas (Roland 2004). This was accompanied by a 38 percent increase in the total remuneration of GPs over two years, and a reduction in working average working hours per GP (Whalley et al. 2008). Evidence that behavior and quality of care has actually changed is only beginning to emerge. This is because the reform was implemented nationally and so there was no concurrent control group, and there were little comparable data before the QOF was introduced. Evidence is emerging that the achievement of targets in deprived areas grew faster than achievement in the most affluent areas (Doran et al. 2008a); that GPs' recording of risk factors in incentivized disease areas increased relative to unincentivized areas, and that there were positive effects on the recording of risk factors in non-incentivized disease areas (Sutton et al. 2010); and that a only small proportion of GPs "gamed" the system to reach higher targets (Doran et al. 2008b).

An earlier example is the Practice Incentive Program (PIP) for GPs in Australia, introduced in 1999. This is an example of a pay for performance program added on to a FFS payment scheme. In addition to the usual fee per consultation, the PIP provided capitation payments to improve practice infrastructure, and incentive payments to improve quality of care for patients with diabetes, asthma, mental health problems, and to improve coverage in cervical screening. These were linked to clinical guidelines and paid after a sequence of visits was completed. A recent evaluation found that in diabetes, the HbA1c test (blood glucose test) was around 20 percent more likely to be ordered by GPs in the PIP compared to GPs not in the PIP (Scott et al. 2009). The study controlled for a wide variety of patient and GP characteristics, and also controlled for the self-selection of GPs into the PIP using a bivariate probit model. The results suggest that modifications to the FFS scheme can have marked effects on quality of care.

There are also hundreds of such schemes in the US, mainly in private HMOs, but also being introduced by Medicare and Medicaid. One of the largest private schemes in the US, the Integrated Health Association's scheme in California, was recently evaluated using difference-in-difference methods, and found no impact of the scheme on a range of indicators of quality of care (Mullen et al. 2009). Weaknesses of schemes in the US include multiple payers and performance pay being a small proportion (typically around 5%) of physician revenue (Rosenthal et al. 2006).

Pay for performance schemes in primary care are also being advocated in low- and middle-income countries, and like many other empirical evaluations, results are limited by a lack of control groups and poor study designs (Eichler 2006; Eldridge and Palmer 2009; Oxman and Fretheim 2008).

The use of financial incentives is not without its potential problems. Prendergast (1999) summarizes the broader economic literature, argues that pay for performance schemes (piece rates) are usually only appropriate for relatively simply defined and easily measureable tasks, and argues that in complex working environments with multiple probabilistic outcomes, there is a risk that such schemes may reduce efficiency compared to other types of payment scheme due to multitasking concerns (Prendergast 1999). In terms of pay for performance, a key issue is the potential shift of effort towards the remunerated disease area and away from unremunerated disease areas. This relative price effect is inevitable where resources are scarce, yet it is unclear whether these shifts in activity are allocatively efficient, i.e. generate more health gains overall such that the additional health gains from the remunerated activity outweigh the health losses from other activities that are given up. This is especially difficult to manage in complex areas such as health care. Performance targets and levels may also generate myopia and there are incentives to "perform to target" and do no more once the target is reached (Goddard et al. 2000).

Remuneration systems, through their relative price effects, can potentially distort allocative efficiency. This is another consequence of multitasking. In many low- and middle-income countries the role of external donors has significantly altered the context in which primary health care sits within the health system. In the past decade or so there have been a number of global initiatives such as those funded by the Bill and Melinda Gates Foundation, the GAVI Alliance and the Global Fund to fight AIDS, Tuberculosis and Malaria in which the focus has been on the eradication of specific diseases. Such initiatives are commonly referred to as "vertical" or "top-down" programs as they are planned and implemented at a national or global level with a specific disease focus that cuts across primary care and hospital sectors. The problem this has created in many settings has been imbalances in funding and a distortion of priorities. For example, the whole government health budget of Zambia of $136 million in 2006 was similar in size to the $150 million from the President's Emergency Plan for AIDS relief for that country. As a consequence, individuals are able to access HIV care for free but need to pay for the basic treatment and prevention in other disease areas (De Maeseneer et al. 2008). One further consequence of such distortion is that salaries for donor funded programs are often more than double than those paid for local public health programs therefore making it difficult for local facilities delivering health care programs outside these initiatives to maintain and compete for staff (De Maeseneer et al. 2008).

It is this tension between the packaging of essential services (vertical) vs. general approach (horizontal) that has characterized much of the debate about how best to achieve the aims of Alma Ata and more generally, how to strengthen primary health care systems within low- and middle-income countries. Historically Alma Ata established primary care as the basis for attainment of health for all by 2000 through locally relevant and affordable technology. Following on there were some advocates of interim measures which involved packages of essential services in which there was a specific focus on treatments for certain disease in which there were known cost-effective interventions (growth monitoring, oral rehydration, encouragement of breast feeding, immunization) (Haines et al. 2007a; Walsh and Warren 1979). Some saw this apparent shift from a generalist approach through the emphasis on specific diseases as being at odds with the charter of Alma Ata (Cueto 2004). Recently, recognition that the lack of progress toward the goals of Alma Ata has led to the initiation of the "15by2015" campaign (<www.15by2015.org>) which has targeted the reallocation of 15 percent of the vertical budgets of international donors toward primary care by 2015 (De Maeseneer et al. 2008).

In theory at least, another form of unintended consequences of extrinsic financial incentives is that they can reduce and "crowd out" intrinsic motivation of professionals (Frey and Jegen 2001). Many theoretical models of physician behavior have included patients' health or utility as an argument in the doctors' utility function. There may therefore be less need for complex incentive schemes in health care (Mooney and Ryan 1993). Strong extrinsic incentives may shift the focus of physicians' motivation and behavior to be more dependent on the monetary reward than on intrinsic factors. This may be complementary and so reinforce behavioral effects, but in theory it is suggested that extrinsic rewards may sometimes reduce the level of activity rather than increase it as predicted by standard theory. In addition if the incentive is removed, the level of the activity may fall even though there may be good evidence supporting its effects on patients' health status. There is little empirical evidence about this.

Finally, the cost-effectiveness of alternative methods and amounts of financial incentives, and of alternative methods to change behavior, has been examined little in the literature. Fee-for-service schemes accompanied by complex fee schedules are more costly to administer and implement compared to, say, salaried payment. One randomized trial of fees versus education for dentists to apply fissure sealants to children's teeth found that the effect of the fee was to increase fissure sealants by almost 10 percent, whilst the educational intervention (and an arm with both fee and education) had little effect. The fee was also found to be the most cost-effective intervention (Clarkson et al. 2008). Further research on the relative cost-effectiveness of changes in remuneration schemes, and in comparing changes in remuneration with other behavior change interventions, is needed.

20.5 PRIMARY CARE WORKFORCE

A major barrier to achieving more primary care-focused and accessible health systems are shortages of primary health care workers (see Chapter 21, this volume). It has been estimated that there is a worldwide shortage of four million health workers—including doctors, nurses, and community health workers. Within Sub-Saharan Africa, there would need to be at least a tripling of the number of health workers, adding one million extra workers, to enable the achievement of the Millennium Development Goals for health (Chen et al. 2004).

Lengthy training of primary care physicians, and strong professional boundaries between primary care physicians and non-physicians, combined with the regulation of training and of the availability of training places, means that the labor market for primary workers is inflexible. Policies to address shortages can operate at a number of points in the career pathway, including entry (training and specialty choice), exit (drop outs, temporary exits, retirement), and productivity (hours of work, throughput, adherence to "best-practice" guidelines, technological change, skill mix). Competition in national (Elliott et al. 2007) and international labor markets can also influence recruitment and retention to primary care, and is a particular issue in low- to middle-income countries (Hongoro and McPake 2004). In addition, the global and within-country distribution of the primary care workforce across geographical areas is often not related to health care need, but can also be influenced by regulation and incentive schemes. This is important in ensuring access.

Most policies to influence supply operate at the entry point of training, where national workforce planning exercises are conducted in many countries to expand or contract supply through changing the number of funded training places. Given the long lags in training, especially for physicians, and major inaccuracies in forecasting demand and supply, the usefulness of these exercises in attempting to balance demand and supply is limited, as evidenced by the continuing cycles of shortages and surpluses (Bloor and Maynard 2003; Goodman 2005). In addition to the institutional context, the main drivers of supply in many countries are demographic cohort effects, such as the retirement of "baby boomers," and a gradual shift to part-time working amongst both men and women reflecting changing preferences for work–life balance amongst younger doctors. The impact of government policy on these demographic trends is much less clear cut.

At the early stages of medical careers, primary care is often regarded as providing lower earnings and status than other specialties, and so the number of specialists in many developed countries often grows faster than the number of primary care physicians. The allocation and control of funded specialty training places also favors the non-primary care specialties, and this is further exacerbated by growing sub-specialization. Evidence on specialty choice suggests that a number of factors play a role, including expected earnings, the level of educational debt, and predictable working hours (Bazzoli 1985; Nicholson 2002; Fox 2003; Thornton and Esposto 2003). All of these studies are from the US.

There have been few published studies examining the elasticities of labor supply (hours worked and participation) with respect to hourly earnings for primary care physicians and this is therefore a priority for further research. A systematic review and meta-analysis of the effect of financial incentives (including direct payments, scholarships, and loans) on recruitment into underserved areas was focused mainly on US literature and on medical students and physicians (Bärnighausen and Bloom 2009). Study designs were generally of a low quality and suffered from selection bias. They find that financial incentives were associated with movement to underserved areas in the short term, and in retaining health workers in underserved areas in the longer term.

A review of interventions to improve motivation and retention of health professionals in developing countries indicated that financial incentives alone were inadequate and that they needed to be backed by non-financial motivators such as career development, professional recognition, adequate infrastructure support and resource availability. There was not enough evidence available in the literature to make any firm conclusions as to whether the impact of these motivational factors on international migration was different across different types of health care providers, or which of these were the most important factors. One key limitation of these studies however was that they were generally small and their findings based on self-reported motivations (Willis-Shattuck et al. 2008).

The importance of non-pecuniary factors has been tackled in a number of discrete choice experiments that examine the job choices of primary care physicians, and also that of nurses in low-income countries (Gosden et al. 2000; Scott 2001; Wordsworth et al. 2004). These have found that income as well as non-pecuniary factors influence job choices. Some DCEs have also examined preferences and willingness to pay for doctors and nurses working in underserved areas and low-income countries (Chomitz et al. 1998; Gosden et al. 2000; Hanson and Jack 2008; Kolstad 2008; Mangham and Hanson 2008). For example in Ethiopia, higher wages, housing, equipment, and drugs were predicted to substantially increase supply (Hanson and Jack 2008).

Persistent shortages of primary care physicians create an environment for increased roles for other primary care professionals, such as nurses and physician assistants. This is motivated not only by an increased capacity of primary care services to improve access, but also by a belief that other health workers provide more cost-effective care. Areas of common overlap between the skills of doctors and nurses include preventive services, ongoing management of long-term conditions, and first contact care for minor illness (Sibbald et al. 2006). Systematic reviews of the role of nurses in primary care and other contexts have concluded that although the research evidence was limited, there were few differences in health outcomes and quality of care between nurses and doctors, and no evidence that nurses provided lower quality of care. In some instances patient satisfaction with nurses was higher and nurses provided longer consultations than doctors. The effects on costs depended on whether nurses are substitutes or complements. Provision of care may be increased as nurses take on some tasks of doctors but doctors do not reduce their workload, or where nurses or doctors identify unmet need (Richardson et al. 1998; Horrocks et al. 2002; Laurant et al. 2004). Doctors may also be able to focus on more complex tasks. Although the cost of a nurse is lower than a doctor, there was some evidence that this was offset by longer consultations and more repeat visits and test ordering (Horrocks et al. 2002).

Physician assistants represent a more highly trained professional, who carry out many similar task to doctors whilst working with doctors but not independently of them. They have been used in the US to increase access in primary care settings for disadvantaged populations, and evidence suggests they provided similar quality of care at a similar cost to physicians (Mittman et al. 2002).

In low-and middle-income countries, there are often major and sometimes over-whelming constraints on workforce supply and skills. Although physicians do exist in varying degrees, non-physician based primary care is closer to the norm. These cover various categories of health workers including: nurses, auxiliary health workers such as nurses' aids and clinical officers with basic training in specific medical tasks, and community (or lay) health workers who are generally selected from the community and are provided very basic training (Hongoro and McPake 2004). Their responsibilities are typically restricted to very specific activities such as providing immunizations, health education or DOTS supervision.

Historically, the ability of low- and middle-income countries to train and retain health workers has been hampered by the lack of training capacity, the economic interests of professional groups, poor working conditions and remuneration and the opportunities that exist through emigration (Hongoro and McPake 2004).

In terms of international migration of primary care workers (and others) a solution posited for addressing the shortage of human resource capacity in low- and middle-income countries has been to establish global agreements to restrict the migration of health workers. A number of high-income countries, such as the UK for instance, have established policies that set out ethical standards for recruitment of staff. Despite this, loopholes exist in the UK and elsewhere and there is evidence that health worker migration still occurs at a significant level (Stilwell et al. 2003; Hongoro and McPake 2004). Such failures highlight the difficulty in achieving collective action on this issue at a global level. The ineffectiveness of such sanctions highlight the importance of addressing the deeper causes of this skills migration—specifically the lack of professional and economic opportunities that exist for health care workers in their own countries. Higher remuneration is one obvious solution although it is unlikely to be feasible or indeed sustainable in many low-income settings. One option may be to provide training to enable the extended use of lower level health workers in areas which may traditionally have been carried out by technically trained staff. Although the evidence on the use of community health workers is in general mixed, there is some evidence that supports a wider role for community health workers (Walker and Jan 2005; Haines et al. 2007b). For instance, in rural Nepal, the use of community health workers in a primary health care setting has been found to be highly effective and cost effective in the delivery of maternal and infant health promotion (Borghi et al. 2005).

Another solution for retaining health workers within country is to encourage income opportunities offered through dual practice. Dual practice occurs when public sector health care worker hold second jobs in private practice. It is often viewed pejoratively as it is sometimes associated with unscrupulous behavior such as the misappropriation of public sector resources and the channeling of patients attending public clinics into private practice. As a consequence it is sometimes banned or restricted. Such sanctions, however, invariably fail in the face of often weak monitoring and enforcement systems and strong secular interests resulting in regulatory capture (Stigler 1971). However a pragmatic approach recognizes the severe human resource and funding constraints that operate in many of these settings—and thus the solution offered by dual practice is that, with appropriate regulation, it enables highly resource constrained public sector facilities to maintain their staff (Jan et al. 2005).

20.6 Conclusions

There is significant and growing evidence that health care systems with strong and well-functioning primary care sectors are likely to perform better in terms of effectiveness, cost-effectiveness, and access, compared to health systems with relatively weak primary care sectors. The strength of this evidence lies not in its definitive analysis of causal effects (as most studies examine associations rather than causal effects), but through the breadth of different studies across different settings and with different data, that show coherent and positive results about the value of primary care. In the context of ever-growing demands on resources based on raised consumer expectations, demographic change, increasing technology and the growing burden of chronic disease, primary care systems with their multiple roles as gatekeeper, provider and coordinator of services are likely to be crucial in achieving cost-effective and affordable health care that is accessible to all. These reflect some of the original goals of Alma Ata and are potentially relevant to achieving the health targets in the more recently established Millennium Development Goals.

There are, however, substantial unanswered economic questions about how such systems should be best designed and implemented across high- as well as low- and middle-income settings. Strengthening the agency relationship with patients to reduce informational asymmetries, for example through patient enrollment, gatekeeping, and care coordination and integration, is assumed to be more efficient than providing patients with choice and competition, mainly because of market failure associated with the latter. However, the potential for supplier-induced demand may be a risk that would need to balanced either by some elements of choice and competition, or through regulation and pay-for-performance.

Co-payments reduce utilization, may increase inequalities, but have been used as a necessary source of finance in low-income countries with difficulty in raising taxes and in the absence of other funding sources. Donor aid may distort priorities, and low wages of health workers may encourage informal payments. There is the challenge of developing incentives and institutions that motivate and reward high performance without distorting allocative efficiency. Financial incentive schemes often involve other interventions to support behavior change, such as education and infrastructure support, which are necessary conditions for the financial incentives to work. Recognizing the role of these other interventions, and their relative cost-effectiveness in changing provider behavior, is a key area for further research. Research based on studies of systems-level interventions which adopt rigorous experimental designs is also much needed. This need is particularly acute in low- and middle-income settings where policies are being introduced that will shape the fundamentals of the future health system on the basis of little empirical evidence.

REFERENCES

AAKVIK, A. and HOLMÅS, T. H. (2006), "Access to primary health care and health outcomes: the relationships between GP characteristics and mortality rates," *Journal of Health Economics*, 25(6), 1139–53.

AKBARI, A., et al. (2008), "Interventions to improve outpatient referrals from primary care to secondary care," *Cochrane Database Systematic Reviews*, Issue 4, CD005471.

BÄRNIGHAUSEN, TILL and BLOOM, D. E. (2009), "Financial incentives for return of service in underserved areas: a systematic review," *BMC Health Services Research*, 9, 86.

BAZZOLI, Gloria J. (1985), "Does educational indebtedness affect physician specialty choice?" *Journal of Health Economics*, 4(1), 1–19.

BEAGLEHOLE, R., et al. (2008), "Improving the prevention and management of chronic disease in low-income and middle-income countries: a priority for primary health care," *Lancet*, 372(9642), 940–9.

BLOOR, K. and MAYNARD, A. (2003), "Planning human resources in health care: Towards an economic approach. An international comparative review." Canadian Health Services Research Foundation, Ottawa.

BORGHI, J., et al. (2005), "Economic assessment of a women's group intervention to improve birth outcomes in rural Nepal," *Lancet*, 366(9500), 1882–4.

BRIGGS, C. J. and GARNER, P. (2006), "Strategies for integrating primary health services in middle- and low-income countries at the point of delivery," *Cochrane Database of Systematic Review*, Issue 2, CD003318.

BURGESS S., et al. (2009), "Smarter task assignment or greater effort: the impact of incentives on team performance." Centre for Market and Public Organisation Working Paper No. 09/215: University of Bristol.

CHEN, L., et al. (2004), "Human resources for health: overcoming the crisis," *Lancet*, 364(9449), 1984–90.

CHOMITZ, K. M., et al. (1998), "What do doctors want? Developing incentives for doctors to serve in Indonesia's rural and remote areas." Policy Research Working Paper, The World Bank, Washington.

CHRISTIANSON, J. B., LEATHERMAN, S., and SUTHERLAND, K. (2008), "Lessons from evaluations of purchaser pay-for-performance programs: a review of the evidence," *Medical Care Research Review*, 65(6 Suppl.), 5S–35.

CLARKSON, J. E., et al. (2008), "Changing clinicians' behavior: a randomized controlled trial of fees and education," *Journal of Dental Research*, 87(7), 640–4.

CUETO, M. (2004), "The origins of primary health care and selective primary health care," *American Journal of Public Health*, 94(11), 1864–74.

DE MAESENEER, J., et al. (2008), "Funding for primary health care in developing countries," *British Medical Journal*, 336(7643), 518–19.

DONALDSON, C., et al. (2004), *Economics of Health Care Financing: The Visible Hand*, 2nd edn. (Basingstoke, UK: Palgrave Macmillan).

DORAN, T., et al. (2008a), "Effect of financial incentives on inequalities in the delivery of primary clinical care in England: analysis of clinical activity indicators for the quality and outcomes framework," *Lancet*, 372(9640), 728–36.

—— (2008b), "Exclusion of patients from pay-for-performance targets by English physicians," *New England Journal of Medicine*, 359(3), 274–84.

DUSHEIKO, MARK, et al. (2006), "The effect of financial incentives on gatekeeping doctors: Evidence from a natural experiment," *Journal of Health Economics*, 25(3), 449–78.

—— (2007), "The impact of budgets for gatekeeping physicians on patient satisfaction: Evidence from fundholding," *Journal of Health Economics*, 26(4), 742–62.

EGGLESTON, KAREN (2005), "Multitasking and mixed systems for provider payment," *Journal of Health Economics*, 24(1), 211–23.

EICHLER, R. (2006), "Can pay for performance increase utilization by the poor and improve the quality of health services?" Discussion paper for the first meeting of the Working Group on Performance-Based Incentives. 5, Center for Global Development, Washington, DC.

ELDRIDGE, C. and PALMER, N. (2009), "Performance-based payment: some reflections on the discourse, evidence and unanswered questions," *Health Policy and Plannning*, 24(3), 160–6.

ELLIOTT, R. F., et al. (2007), "Geographically differentiated pay in the labour market for nurses," *Journal of Health Economics*, 26(1), 190–212.

FORREST, C. B. (2003), "Primary care in the United States: Primary care gatekeeping and referrals: effective filter or failed experiment?" *British Medical Journal*, 326(7391), 692–95.

FOX, MARC (2003), "Medical student indebtedness and the propensity to enter academic medicine," *Health Economics*, 12(2), 101–12.

FREY, B. S. and JEGEN, R. (2001), "Motivation Crowding Theory," *Journal of Economic Surveys*, 15(5), 589–611.

GILSON, L. and McINTYRE, D. (2005), "Removing user fees for primary care in Africa: the need for careful action," *British Medical Journal*, 331(7519), 762–5.

GODDARD, M., MANNION, R., and SMITH, P. (2000), "Enhancing performance in health care: a theoretical perspective on agency and the role of information," *Health Economics*, 9(2), 95–107.

GOODMAN, DAVID C. (2005), "The physician workforce crisis: where is the evidence?" *Health Affairs*, March 15, 108–10.

GOSDEN, T., PEDERSEN, L., and TORGERSON, D. (1999), "How should we pay doctors? A systematic review of salary payments and their effect on doctor behaviour," *Quarterly Journal of Medicine*, 92(1), 47–55.

—— BOWLER, I., and SUTTON, M. (2000), "How do general practitioners choose their practice? Preferences for practice and job characteristics," *Journal of Health Services Research and Policy*, 5(5), 208–13.

—— et al. (2001), "Impact of payment method on behaviour of primary care physicians: a systematic review," *Journal of Health Services Research and Policy*, 6(1), 44–55.

GRAVELLE, H., MORRIS, S., and SUTTON, M. (2008), "Are family physicians good for you? Endogenous doctor supply and individual health," *Health Services Research*, 43(4), 1128–44.

HAINES, A., HORTON, R., and BHUTTA, Z. (2007a), "Primary health care comes of age. Looking forward to the 30th anniversary of Alma-Ata: call for papers," *Lancet*, 370(9591), 911–13.

—— —— —— (2007b), "Achieving child survival goals: potential contribution of community health workers," *Lancet*, 369(9579), 2121–31.

Hanson, K. and Jack, W. (2008), "Health worker preferences for job attributes in Ethiopia: Results from a discrete choice experiment," Georgetown University, Washington, DC.

Holmstrom, B. (1982), "Moral hazard in teams," *Bell Journal of Economics*, 13, 324–40.

Hongoro, C. and McPake, B. (2004), "How to bridge the gap in human resources for health," *Lancet*, 364(9443), 1451–6.

Horrocks, S., Anderson, E., and Salisbury, C. (2002), "Systematic review of whether nurse practitioners working in primary care can provide equivalent care to doctors," *British Medical Journal*, 324(7341), 819–23.

Hu, S., et al. (2008), "Reform of how health care is paid for in China: challenges and opportunities," *Lancet*, 372(9652), 1846–53.

Iversen, Tor and Lurås, Hilde (2000), "The effect of capitation on GPs' referral decisions," *Health Economics*, 9(3), 199–210.

Jan, S. (2003), "A perspective on the analysis of credible commitment and myopia in health sector decision making," *Health Policy*, 63, 269–78.

—— et al. (2005), "Dual job holding by public sector health professionals in highly resource-constrained settings: problem or solution?" *Bulletin of the World Health Organisation*, 83(10), 771–6.

Joshi, R., et al. (2008), "Global inequalities in access to cardiovascular health care: our greatest challenge," *Journal of the American College of Cardiology*, 52(23), 1817–25.

Kolstad, J. (2008), "How to make rural jobs more attractive to health workers. Findings from a discrete choice experiment in Tanzania." Working Paper No. 15/08, Department of Economics, University of Bergen, Bergen.

Lagarde, M. and Palmer, N. (2008), "The impact of user fees on health service utilization in low- and middle-income countries: how strong is the evidence?" *Bulletin of the World Health Organisation*, 86(11), 839–48.

Laurant, M., et al. (2004), "Substitution of doctors by nurses in primary care." Cochrane Database of Systematic Reviews, Issue 4, John Wiley & Sons, Ltd., Chichester, UK.

Lawn, J. E., et al. (2008), "Alma-Ata 30 years on: revolutionary, relevant, and time to revitalise," *Lancet*, 372(9642), 917–27.

Lewin, S., et al. (2008), "Supporting the delivery of cost-effective interventions in primary health-care systems in low-income and middle-income countries: an overview of systematic reviews," *Lancet*, 372(9642), 928–39.

Lewis, M. (2007), "Informal payments and the financing of health care in developing and transition countries," *Health Affairs (Millwood)*, 26(4), 984–97.

Macinko, J., Starfield, B., and Shi, L. (2003), "The contribution of primary care systems to health outcomes within Organization for Economic Cooperation and Development (OECD) countries, 1970–1998," *Health Services Research*, 38(3), 831–65.

Mangham, L. J. and Hanson, K. (2008), "Employment preferences of public sector nurses in Malawi: results from a discrete choice experiment," *Tropical Medicine & International Health*, 13(12), 1433–41.

Mavromaras, K. and Scott, A. (2005), "Promotion to hospital consultant in NHS Scotland," *International Journal of Manpower*, 26(7/8), 660–72.

McPake, B., et al. (1999), "Informal economic activities of public health workers in Uganda: implications for quality and accessibility of care," *Social Science & Medicine*, 49(7), 849–65.

Mills, A. (2007), "Strategies to achieve universal coverage: are there lessons from middle income countries." A literature review commissioned by the Health Systems Knowledge

Network. Health Economics and Financing Programme, London School of Hygiene and Tropical Medicine, London.

MITTMAN, D.E., CAWLEY, J.F., and FENN, W.H. (2002), "Physician assistants in the United States," *British Medical Journal*, 325(7362), 485–87.

MOONEY, G.H. and RYAN, M. (1993), "Agency in health care: Getting beyond first principles," *Journal of Health Economics*, 12(2), 125–35.

MULLEN, K, FRANK, RICHARD G., and ROSENTHAL, MEREDITH B. (2009), "Can you get what you pay for? Pay-for-performance and the quality of healthcare providers." Working Paper No. 14886: National Bureau of Economic Research.

NICHOLSON, SEAN (2002), "Physician specialty choice under uncertainty," *Journal of Labor Economics*, 20(4), 816.

NORTH, D.C. (1993), "Institutions and credible commitment," *Journal of Institutional and Theoretical Economics*, 149(1), 11–23.

OXMAN, A.D. and FRETHEIM, A. (2008), "An overview of research on the effects of results-based financing.." Norwegian Knowledge Centre for the Health Services, Oslo.

PALMER, N., et al. (2004), "Health financing to promote access in low income settings-how much do we know?" *Lancet*, 364(9442), 1365–70.

PERES, E. M., et al. (2006), "The practice of physicians and nurses in the Brazilian Family Health Programme: evidences of change in the delivery health care model," *Human Resources for Health*, 4, 25.

PETERSEN, L.A., et al. (2006), "Does pay-for-performance improve the quality of health care?" *Annals of Internal Medicine*, 145(4), 265–W71.

POWELL DAVIES, GAWAINE, et al. (2008), "Coordinating primary health care: an analysis of the outcomes of a systematic review," *Medical Journal of Australia*, 188 (8 Suppl), S65–8.

PRENDERGAST, C. (1999), "The provision of incentives in firms," *Journal of Economic Literature*, 37(1), 7.

PROPPER, CAROL, CROXSON, BRONWYN, and SHEARER, ARRAN (2002), "Waiting times for hospital admissions: the impact of GP fundholding," *Journal of Health Economics*, 21(2), 227–52.

RICHARDSON, G., et al. (1998), "Skill mix changes: substitution or service development?" *Health Policy*, 45(2), 119–32.

ROBINSON, J.C. (2001), "Theory and practice in the design of physician payment incentives," *Milbank Quarterly*, 79(2), 149.

ROHDE, J., et al. (2008), "30 years after Alma-Ata: has primary health care worked in countries?" *Lancet*, 372(9642), 950–61.

ROLAND, M. (2004), "Linking physicians' pay to the quality of care: a major experiment in the United Kingdom," *New England Journal of Medicine*, 351(14), 1448–54.

ROSENTHAL, Meredith B., et al. (2006), "Pay for performance in commercial HMOs," *New England Journal of Medicine*, 355(18), 1895–902.

RUSSELL, S. (2004), "The economic burden of illness for households in developing countries: a review of studies focusing on malaria, tuberculosis, and human immunodeficiency virus/acquired immunodeficiency syndrome," *American Journal of Tropical Medicine and Hygiene*, 71(2 Suppl), 147–55.

SAULTZ, J.W. and LOCHNER, J. (2005), "Interpersonal continuity of care and care outcomes: a critical review," *Annals of Family Medicine*, 3(2), 159–66.

SCOTT, A. (2000), "Economics of general practice," in J.P. Newhouse and A.J Culyer (eds.), *Handbook of Health Economics* (Amsterdam: North Holland).

SCOTT, A. (2001), "Eliciting GPs' preferences for pecuniary and non-pecuniary job characteristics," *Journal of Health Economics*, 20(3), 329–47.

—— and HALL, J. (1995), "Evaluating the effects of GP remuneration: problems and prospects," *Health Policy*, 31(3), 183–95.

—— and COOTE, W. (2007), "Whither divisions of general practice? An empirical and policy analysis of the impact of divisions within the Australian health care system," *Medical Journal of Australia*, 187(2), 95–9.

—— and VICK, S. (1999), "Patients, doctors and contracts: an application of principal–agent theory to the doctor–patient relationship," *Scottish Journal of Political Economy*, 46(2), 111–34.

—— et al. (2009), "The effects of an incentive program on quality of care in diabetes management," *Health Economics*, 18(9), 1091–108.

SIBBALD, B., LAURANT, M., and SCOTT, A. (2006), "Changing Task Profiles," in R. B. Saltman, A. Rico, and W. Boerma (eds.), *Primary Care in the Driver's Seat? Organisational Reform in European Primary Care* (Maidenhead: Open University Press).

SIMOENS, STEVEN and SCOTT, ANTHONY (2005), "Integrated primary care organizations: to what extent is integration occurring and why?" *Health Services Management Research*, 18(1), 25–40.

SMITH, J. and MAYS, N. (2005), "Primary care trusts: do they have a future?," *British Medical Journal*, 331(7526), 1156–57.

STARFIELD, B. (2008), "Refocusing the system," *New England Journal of Medicine*, 359(20), 2087–91.

—— and SHI, L. (2007), "Commentary: primary care and health outcomes: a health services research challenge," *Health Services Research*, 42(6, Part 1, Dec.), 2252–56.

—— —— and MACINKO, J. (2005), "Contribution of primary care to health systems and health," *Milbank Quarterly*, 83(3), 457–502.

STIGLER, G. (1971), "The theory of economic regulation," *Bell Journal of Economics and Management Science*, 2(1), 3–21.

STILWELL, BARBARA, et al. (2003), "Developing evidence-based ethical policies on the migration of health workers: conceptual and practical challenges," *Human Resources for Health*, 1(1), 8.

SUTTON, M., et al. (2010), "Record rewards: the effects of targeted quality incentives on the recording of risk factors by primary care providers," *Health Economics*, 19, 1–13.

THORNTON, J. and ESPOSTO, F. (2003), "How important are economic factors in choice of medical specialty?" *Health Economics*, 12(1), 67–73.

WAGSTAFF, ADAM (2009), "Social Health Insurance vs. Tax-Financed Health Systems. Evidence from the OECD." Policy Research Working Paper. The World Bank Development Research Group, Washington, DC.

WALKER, D. G. and JAN, S. (2005), "How do we determine whether community health workers are cost-effective? Some core methodological issues," *Journal of Community Health*, 30(3), 221–9.

WALSH, J. A. and WARREN, K. S. (1979), "Selective primary health care: an interim strategy for disease control in developing countries," *New England Journal of Medicine*, 301(18), 967–74.

WHALLEY, D., GRAVELLE, H., and SIBBALD, B. (2008), "Effect of the new contract on GPs' working lives and perceptions of quality of care: a longitudinal survey," *British Journal of General Practice*, 58(546), 8–14.

WHO (WORLD HEALTH ORGANIZATION) (1996), "Integration of health care delivery," *WHO Technical Report Series*, 861, 1–68.

—— (2008), "Primary health care now more than ever," *The World Health Report 2008* (Geneva: World Health Organisation).

WILLIS-SHATTUCK, M., et al. (2008), "Improving motivation and retention of health professionals in developing countries: a systematic review," *BMC Health Services Research*, 8(1), 247.

WORDSWORTH, S., et al. (2004), "Preferences for general practice jobs: a survey of principals and sessional GPs," *British Journal of General Practice*, 54(507), 740–46.

ZWEIFEL, PETER and MANNING, WILLARD G. (2000), "Moral hazard and consumer incentives in health care," in A. J. Culyer and J. P. Newhouse (eds.), *Handbook of Health Economics*, Vol. 1, Part 1 (Amsterdam: Elsevier), 409–59.

CHAPTER 21

....

THE GLOBAL HEALTH WORKFORCE*

....

TILL BÄRNIGHAUSEN AND DAVID E. BLOOM

21.1 INTRODUCTION

"PEOPLE deliver health" (Joint Learning Initiative 2004). The health workforce, i.e. the people who are "primarily engaged in action with the primary intent of enhancing health" (WHO 2006), diagnose illnesses, heal, care for people, monitor health outcomes, support treatment adherence, provide medical information and prevent diseases. The importance of health workers as decision-makers and service providers in health systems is obvious. The magnitude of their role is matched by their impact on health spending. WHO estimates that across countries worldwide about 50 percent of total public and private health expenditure (including capital costs) is spent on health worker wages, salaries and allowances (Hernandez et al. 2006).

In the following, we review the health economics and health systems literature on the health workforce. We organize the review according to three perspectives on health workers, which correspond roughly to chronological phases of academic publication: health workforce planning (1960s and 1970s), the health worker as economic actor (1980s and 1990s), and the health worker as necessary resource (1990s and 2000s).

A major research focus of studies on the health care workforce in the 1960s and 1970s was on models to predict future health staffing needs; many planning models developed in this period are still applied today. This research was triggered by shortages of specific types of health workers in developed countries and by reports from socialist countries that health manpower planning could aid health policymakers in ensuring an adequate supply of health workers.

* We thank Larry Rosenberg, Sherry A. Glied, and Peter C. Smith for valuable comments on an earlier version of this manuscript and Gaargi Ramakrishnan for research support.

In the 1980s and 1990s, the research focus shifted to the study of health workers' effects on allocative and technical efficiency in health systems. This research was motivated by the perception of rising health expenditures in developed countries and the belief that health workers do not always act in their patients' best interests. In this chapter, we review the literature on one research theme in this phase that is not discussed in detail elsewhere in this book (health worker licensure).

In the 1990s and continuing in the 2000s, health workers increasingly became viewed as a resource necessary to the achievement of population health goals. In developed countries, essential health care could not be delivered in rural and remote areas because the human resources for such delivery were not available. In developing countries, it became apparent that population health goals—such as the United Nations Millennium Development Goals (MDGs) to "reduce child mortality," "improve maternal health," and "combat HIV/AIDS, malaria and other diseases" (United Nations 2009)—could not be attained unless the sizes of many national health workforces were dramatically increased. Given these two major themes in this phase, we review the research on programs to increase the supply of health workers to underserved areas in developed countries and studies measuring and analyzing international health worker migration.

In separate sub-sections below, we describe the health policy backgrounds that led to each phase of research and then review relevant literature. The three perspectives are of course highly stylized; the backgrounds are reductionist descriptions of much richer policy contexts; and the periods overlap. However, the perspectives are useful in framing past research, structuring our exposition, and laying out a research agenda on the health workforce for coming years.

21.2 FIRST PHASE: HEALTH WORKFORCE PLANNING

21.2.1 Background

Three historical backgrounds gave rise to health workforce planning studies in the 1960s and 1970s. First, many developed and developing countries experienced shortages of different types of health workers (Bärnighausen and Bloom 2009b). These shortages demonstrated the insufficiency of existing systems to ensure adequate health worker supplies and led to the conclusion that "[h]ealth manpower is not a commodity whose production can be left to the imperfect functioning of laissez-faire market mechanisms" (Hall and Mejia 1978).

Second, reports from socialist countries, such as the USSR, asserted that health manpower planning could produce valid projections of future health workforce requirements, aiding policymakers in designing workforce policies to ensure sufficient supplies of health workers (Popov 1971; Daniels 1974). Third, WHO identified a number of technical difficulties that policymakers would inevitably face in ensuring adequate future supplies of health workers both in developing and developed countries, including the "longest preparatory period of all the health resources," "the rigidity of the health and education systems," and the fact that manpower cannot be stored or discarded (Hall and Mejia 1978).

WHO advocated health workforce planning as a method to overcome these difficulties (Hornby et al. 1976). The organization envisioned that health workforce planners would calculate future health worker requirements through mathematical modeling that incorporated detailed data on population projections, disease burdens, health services, and capacities of health care facilities and education institutions. The planners would prepare several health workforce scenarios and present them to policymakers, who, in turn, would select the best option for implementation.

However, WHO soon came to realize that health policymaking did not follow this rational model (Hornby et al. 1976; Hall and Mejia 1978). In 1978 the WHO thus broadened the objectives of planning to include implementation plans and communication strategies and emphasized the importance of the "political dimension," "leadership readiness for and commitment to change," "enabling legislation for planning and subsequent plan implementation," and "administrative capacity and willingness to implement the plan" (Hall and Mejia 1978).

21.2.2 Literature

Although the focus of health workforce planning by the 1970s had moved away from mathematical modeling towards management and policymaking, the initial emphasis on estimation led to the development of four main approaches—still used today[1]—to planning for national or regional health workforce requirements: the need, demand, service targets, and population ratio approaches. These approaches differ in their scientific stance and in the type of information that they utilize.

The need approach takes a normative stance. Experts use epidemiological information to estimate the future occurrence of disease cases in a population. The number and types of health workers necessary to provide the services to adequately treat all disease cases are then calculated, using information on health worker time per service. In contrast, the demand approach takes a positive stance. Future demand for health services is predicted from current demand by assuming that the relationships between demand and its determinants (such as population size and income) will remain unchanged while the level of the determinants changes. Predicted health service demand is then translated into human resource requirements.

---

[1] These approaches are defined well in the 1978 WHO book on health manpower planning by Hall and Mejia (1978). More recent reviews used similar categorizations of planning approaches (Markham and Birch 1997; O'Brien-Pallas et al. 2001; Murphy 2002; Dreesch et al. 2005).

The service targets approach usually takes a normative stance but, unlike the need approach, allows for constraints to the provision of health care in calculating future service requirements. Such constraints include health care capacity and technology on the supply side and ability and willingness to pay for health care on the demand side. Finally, the population ratio approach can either take a normative or a positive stance. Future health worker requirements are predicted using population growth predictions and health worker-to-population ratios derived from studies or deliberations among policymakers.

21.2.2.1 *First Approach: Need*

One example of an analysis following the need approach to estimating health workforce requirements is a study by Schönfeld, Heston and Falk (1972) calculating the numbers of physicians required for primary care in the United States (US). Schönfeld et al. used national data to predict the annual numbers of cases of different diseases requiring attention by two categories of primary care physicians (pediatricians and internists). They then calculated the total number of physician hours needed to adequately treat all disease cases using treatment norms. Finally, to estimate health worker need, they divided the total physician hours required in one year by the average number of hours a physician works per year. The study concluded that only about half the needed number of primary care physicians was available at the time (Schönfeld et al. 1972).

Other applications of the need approach to estimating health worker requirements in the US include the Lee-Jones report of 1933 and the "adjusted needs-based model" developed by the Graduate Medical Education National Advisory Committee (GMENAC) of 1980. In the period 1960–80, the need approach to estimating health worker requirements was further applied in the USSR (Ministry of Health 1967), in Latin America (CENDES 1965), and in Sri Lanka (Hall and Mejia 1978). A recent example is an analysis by Birch et al. (2007) who estimated the need for registered nurses in the Atlantic Region of Canada.

The need approach is appealing to health workers because it is clearly rooted in epidemiology and medicine. In addition, its underlying ethic—that care should be provided according to need and independently of other characteristics of individual patients—is often embraced by the health professions (Cookson and Dolan 2000; Bodenheimer and Grumbach 2002). However, the approach can be criticized on conceptual and practical grounds. Conceptually, as Klarman (1969) points out, "[w]hether need is a desirable standard hinges on society's willingness to accord an absolute priority to health services, regardless of cost." Some modifications of the need approach address this criticism. For example, a study may take into account only those diseases whose treatments meet certain cost–benefit criteria (Hall and Mejia 1978). Practically, the morbidity data for need projection may not be available or may be measured with considerable uncertainty in many countries. In addition, the need approach may not be robust across geographical areas, practice settings, or time periods.

Even if data and methods allowed valid estimation of health worker requirements according to health need and a country had sufficient resources and the political will to provide all the required health workers, it is unlikely that health care would be provided exactly according to policy plans. Patients may not demand needed health services and may demand unneeded ones; health workers may not supply needed services and may supply unneeded ones (Murphy 2002).

Because the treatment norms used in this approach are based on current medical practice, need-based planning may inhibit innovation. Current medical practice may be replaced by alternative means of delivery, e.g. by substituting one type of health worker with another or by increasing the use of information technology.

In sum, the need approach may only be feasible in situations where detailed data on disease prevalence and incidence are available, the health sector can draw on adequate resources to fund needed health workers, and the strength of sectoral control is such that it can be assured that most utilized health care is needed.

21.2.2.2 *Second Approach: Demand*

A 1975 study by Hall, Reinke, and Lawrence (1975) on health workforce requirements in Chile follows the demand approach. The researchers first estimated the marginal effects of geographical location, income, sex, age, insurance coverage, and education on three measures of health care demand. They then used forecasted values of these variables to estimate future demand for health services. Finally, they converted predicted demand into health worker requirements, using estimates of productivity and staffing patterns of health care facilities, which were based on field observation and expert opinion (Hall 1971). Other health manpower studies employing a demand approach were conducted for Peru, Taiwan, the US, and the UK (Bärnighausen and Bloom 2009b).

Whether the predictive nature of the demand approach is an advantage or a disadvantage depends on the intended use of estimated health worker requirements. If policymakers merely intend to adjust the status quo of health services delivery to changes in a few factors that are outside their control (such as population size and composition, economic growth, or migration), demand studies will provide sufficient information. Such studies may also provide baseline estimates for planning in countries where policymakers intend to significantly change health care utilization.

Although demand studies may thus be useful in many policy situations, they are often infeasible because the data necessary to estimate demand functions are lacking (Dreesch et al. 2005). In addition, they may not yield valid or reliable estimates of future health worker requirements. First, they commonly do not take into account that demand and supply are simultaneously determined and may thus produce biased results. Research on health worker requirements following the demand approach may benefit from increased use of economic models of health care demand (Feldstein 1967; Benham 1971; Feldstein 1971). Second, the assumption of many demand-based studies that the relationships between demand and its determinants will remain unchanged in the future is likely to be violated in many situations. Third, projected values of demand determinants may not be sufficiently accurate to yield useful demand forecasts. For instance, per-capita income may not rise to predicted levels because of an unexpected economic crisis. Fourth, the findings of demand-based studies may not be generalizable. For instance, one of the determinants commonly taken into account in demand-based studies is income. However, estimates of the income elasticity of health care demand in microeconomic studies (which are often used for demand-based forecasting) vary widely across geographic areas and time periods (Bärnighausen and Bloom 2009b).

21.2.2.3 *Third Approach: Service Targets*

Hall and Mejia (1978) describe a study deriving health worker requirements from service targets. Colombian health planners first identified "priority services" for a population of nine million people lacking access to basic health care, based on morbidity surveys, "the accumulated experience of pilot simplified medicine programs, statistics on service utilization, referral rates, and international experience." The planners then calculated the numbers of different types of health workers required to provide these services, using "normative techniques."

Many recent examples of estimations of health worker requirements follow a service target approach. For instance, Kurowski, Wyss, Abdulla, and Mills (2007) estimated the numbers of health workers required to deliver 33 "priority interventions" identified by the Commission on Macroeconomics and Health (2001) as important to achieving the MDGs. Dreesch et al. (2005) proposed a similar method to estimate the health workforce required to achieve the MDGs.

The main differences between the two normative planning approaches (service targets and need) are in the scope of health care considered and in the constraints that are taken into account. The service targets approach decides on priority interventions, assessing not only health care need but also (explicitly or implicitly) existing constraints to meeting that need; in contrast, the need approach starts by identifying health care need and assumes that all need can be met. The former approach will thus yield more realistic human resources requirements than the latter. The service targets approach has further advantages: it explicitly disaggregates need into different components, is easy to communicate, can be easily combined with other planning approaches, and facilitates the study of health worker productivity (Hall and Mejia 1978). Moreover, unlike the need and the demand approach, the service targets approach does not depend on detailed local data to yield useful estimates of health workforce requirements.

On the other hand, just like the needs approach, the service targets approach assumes that consumers demand and health workers provide precisely those services that the planners used to derive health worker requirements. In most settings, however, the overlap between the health services consumed and those planned will be imperfect. The health services approach may be most useful in countries where the government can exert substantial control over the health care sector and is willing to use this power to maximize delivery of planned services and minimize delivery of unplanned ones.

21.2.2.4 *Fourth Approach: Population Ratio*

Health worker-to-population ratios have been frequently used in determining man-power requirements. For instance, following a WHO recommendation, Thailand aimed at achieving a physician-to-population ratio of 1:5000 in the period 1972–6 (Chunharas 1998). Bahrain tried to attain a physician-to-population ratio of 1:650 in the period 1998–2005 (Ahmed et al. 2000). In the 1993 World Development Report, the World Bank stated that "[t]he public health and minimum essential clinical interventions require about 0.1 physician per 1000 population and between two and four graduate nurses per physician" (World Bank 1993); and in the 2006 World Health Report, WHO identified a "needs-based sufficiency" threshold of 2.5 health workers per 1000 population.

The popularity of the population ratio approach to health workforce planning stems from the ease and flexibility of its use. The data to estimate current health-worker-to-population ratios are available in most countries worldwide and ratio objectives are easy to communicate to policymakers.

Yet the approach suffers from many limitations. First, population ratios are nec-essarily averages across geographical regions; sub-regions may have widely differ-ent ratios. Figure 21.1 shows the quotients of urban nurse-to-population ratios divided by the rural nurse-to-population ratios for country-years for which these data were available in the WHO *Global Atlas of the Health Workforce* (2009). Figure 21.2 shows the urban-to-rural quotients for physicians based on the same data source.[2] The two figures show large differences between health worker population ratios in urban and rural areas in most countries for which data were available, sug-gesting that for many planning purposes countrywide averages—which are more widely available than rural- and urban-specific values—will not be sufficiently disaggregated.[3]

Second, unlike the other three health worker planning approaches, the popula-tion ratio approach does not require an intermediary step of estimating health serv-ices to calculate the health worker numbers. It is thus the approach least likely to lead to a focus on health worker productivity in planning future worker require-ments. Third, the approach does not explain which factors drive health worker

---

[2] The graphs show the ratios for all country-years for which data were available in the WHO *Global Atlas of the Health Workforce* with one exception: we do not show the urban-to-rural ratio for physicians for Bhutan (2004). Because the ratio is quite large (599), the differences between the other ratios in the graphs would have been difficult to discern had we included it in the display.

[3] Note that while the WHO *Global Atlas* is the most reliable dataset on health worker population ratios available (Anand and Bärnighausen 2004), it cannot be ruled out that the differences health worker population ratios between urban and rural areas shown in the two figures can be partially explained by differences in data sources and data definitions (such as definitions of physicians and nurses or rural and urban areas) (WHO 2009). However, it is unlikely that improved adjustment for these differences would alter the conclusion that rural-to-urban health worker population ratios vary widely across countries.

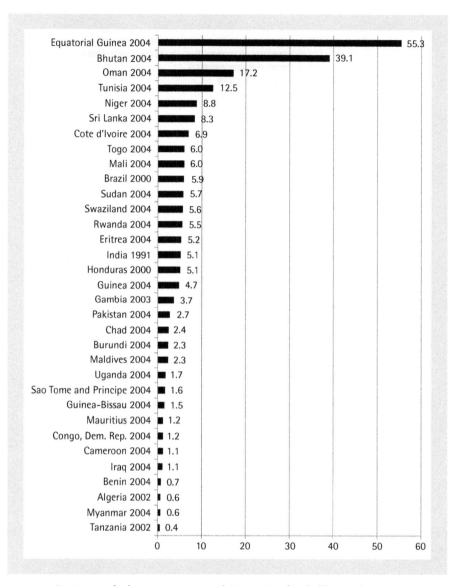

FIGURE 21.1 Quotients of urban nurse-to-population ratios divided by rural nurse-to-population ratios

requirements, except for changes in crude population size. Thus, the population ratio approach to health workforce planning is mainly useful for international comparison and as an indicator of a country's overall health human resources situation (Bossert et al. 2007), rather than as the main planning tool to estimate health worker requirements.

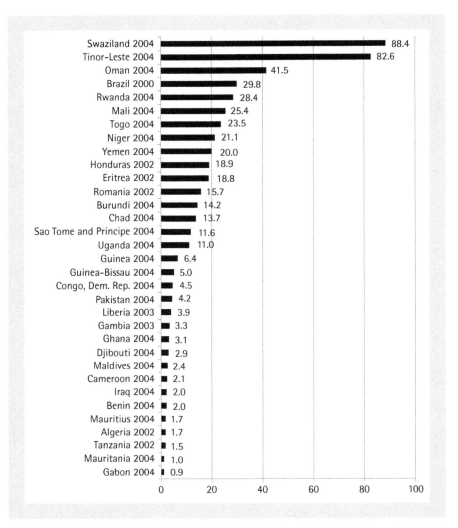

FIGURE 21.2 Quotients of urban physician-to-population ratios divided by rural physician-to-population ratios

21.3 SECOND PHASE: THE HEALTH WORKER AS ECONOMIC ACTOR

21.3.1 Background

Starting in the 1970s and continuing in the 1980s and 1990s, policymakers in developed countries became increasingly worried about rising health expenditures. The average annual growth rate of health care expenditure in real terms for eighteen countries belonging to the OECD was 3.0 percent in the period 1980–90 and 3.3 percent in the period 1990–2001 (Huber and Orosz 2003).[4] Health care expenditures throughout the developed world rose in terms of both per-capita spending on health and the proportion of per-capita gross domestic product (Huber 1999; Huber and Orosz 2003; Bärnighausen and Bloom 2009b).[5]

At the same time, the apparent health worker shortage of previous decades gave way to a perceived oversupply (Schroeder 1984; Bärnighausen and Bloom 2009b).[6] The focus of research on health workers thus shifted from planning in order to ensure future supplies to investigating the extent to which health workers contribute to increases in health expenditures (Stone 1997). Health workers came to be seen as profit-maximizing economic actors individually and as rent-seeking professional groups collectively. Much of the research in this phase was motivated by the belief that health workers do not always act in their patients' best interest, exploiting market failures in health care for their own gain and reducing social welfare in the process.

While the view of health workers as profit-maximizing economic actors was narrow (neglecting, for instance, the influence of such factors as altruism and professional ethics in guiding the actions of nurses and doctors (Le Grand 1997)),[7] the rigorous application of microeconomic theory to health worker behavior was fruitful, leading to important insights on a range of topics, such as competition among providers, health worker licensure, information asymmetry and health worker agency (Blomqvist 1991), health worker performance and productivity (Cutler and Berndt 2001), provider payment and incentives (Sloan and Kasper 2008), and medical decision-making. Other chapters in this handbook are devoted to many of these topics, including agency (Chapter 25), provider payment and incentives (Chapter 26), competition among providers (Chapter 28), performance and productivity (Chapters 29 and 30), and medical

---

[4] In this study, health care spending was adjusted for inflation using the gross domestic product deflator (Huber and Orosz 2003).

[5] While most macroeconomic studies of the income elasticity of health care expenditure estimated values greater than unity (Newhouse 1977; Gerdtham and Jonsson 1991; Milne and Molana 1991; Gerdtham et al. 1992; Hitiris and Posnett 1992; Hitiris 1997), the estimates vary substantially and some studies find income elasticities smaller than unity (Parkin et al. 1987; Selvanathan and Selvanathan 1993). Reasons for the divergent results include different datasets, econometric models, and approaches to adjusting for purchasing power in studies with cross-country data (Okunade and Suraratdecha 2000).

[6] Claims of health worker shortages or oversupplies imply that quantity standards for health workers have been set. Such quantity standards are difficult to determine and usually quite uncertain (see above) (Ginzberg 1983), making it difficult to validate claims of shortages or oversupplies. For the argument in this section, however, it is unimportant whether such claims are valid. We merely need to show that policymakers and researchers perceived an oversupply of health workers where previously they had perceived a shortage.

[7] Many recent economic models of health worker behavior take a more differentiated view of factors explaining health worker behavior (Encinosa et al. 2007; Frank and Zeckhauser 2007; Olbrich 2008; Schneider and Ulrich 2008).

decision-making (Chapter 32). In this sub-section, we thus cover only one prominent research topic in this phase that is not discussed in detail elsewhere in this volume: health worker licensure.

21.3.2 Health Worker Licensure

Health worker licensure, i.e. the authorization of health workers to practice their profession, has been introduced into national or sub-national legislation in most countries worldwide (Rowe and Garcia-Barbero 2005; Bärnighausen and Bloom 2009b). To obtain a health worker license, candidates must have completed formal training in a recognized health care education institution and must usually meet further requirements such as completion of practical training, passage of licensure examinations, proof of absence of a criminal record, and swearing of a professional oath. Licensing may be exercised by the Ministry of Health or by independent professional bodies, such as a chamber, order, college or council (Rowe and Garcia-Barbero 2005). Violations of clearly specified conditions (for instance, malpractice or substance use) can lead to revocation of a health worker license.

21.3.2.1 *Theories of Licensure*

Two types of theories explain the existence of legislation, including health worker licensure (Moore 1961; Posner 1974; Paul 1984; Noether 1986). "Public interest" theories hold that policymakers supply regulation in response to the demand of the public for the correction of a market failure. According to "interest group" theories, on the other hand, policymakers supply regulation in response to the demands of interest groups trying to increase the incomes of their members (Stigler 1971; Peltzman 1976). The two types of theories offer different explanations for the existence of health worker licensure and lead to different predictions regarding licensure effects.

"Public Interest" Theories   A common version of the "public interest" explanation for the existence of licensure is "the belief that the public interest will be best served if the poorly trained, incompetent, and unethical people are kept from practicing," because such exclusions will increase the average quality of health services (Gaumer 1984). This version is not motivated by an economic model of behavior.

Arrow (1963) developed a "public interest" theory of licensure analogous to Akerlof's (1970) classic analysis of "The market for 'lemons.'" Because consumers cannot easily judge the quality of individual health workers, the price of a health service does not differ by health worker and reflects the average quality of the service in the market. Workers know their abilities and those with above-average ability leave the health care sector to pursue higher paying employment opportunities. The withdrawal lowers the average quality of health workers and the prices of health services fall, causing those among the remaining workers whose abilities exceed the new average ability to exit the market. The process repeats itself until only the least capable health workers are left to supply health services. The market fails because of informational asymmetry between health workers and consumers of health services. Searching out information to overcome this asymmetry may be more expensive for the individual consumer than the expected gain in welfare (Leland 1979). Licensure may serve as a means of reducing the informational asymmetry between health worker and consumer by screening out those workers who do not meet defined minimum quality standards—in Arrow's words "[t]he general uncertainty about the prospects of medical treatment is socially handled by rigid entry requirements" (Arrow 1963).

However, if the only purpose of licensure is to reduce informational asymmetry between health workers and consumers, certification—which unlike licensure does not exclude anyone from practicing as a health worker—should serve that purpose at least equally well without reducing consumer choice. Several authors thus argued that the selection of health worker licensure over certification is evidence that health worker interests dominate the public interest in the regulation of health care (Moore 1961; Friedman 1962; Leffler 1978; Leland 1979). Svorny (1987) refuted this argument, holding that licensure is more effective in ensuring that health workers provide high-quality care, because a worker who loses her certification can continue to practice, while a worker whose loses her license is barred from practice and forfeits the entire premium stream derived from health care education.

"Interest Group" Theories "Interest group" explanations for the existence of health worker licensure originated in the belief that licensure was introduced in response to the demands of interest groups aiming to ensure that incumbent health workers earn economic rents (Kessel 1958; Friedman 1962; Rayack 1967; Kessel 1970). Peltzman (1976) developed a formal model of the influence of interest groups on regulation (such as licensure legislation), based on a study by Stigler (Stigler 1971). According to the model, self-interested legislators maximize the expected number of votes in their favor

$$M = n \cdot f - (N-n) \cdot h,$$

where n is the number of potential voters belonging to the interest group that is set to benefit from the regulation, f is the average probability that a member of the interest group will vote for the legislator, N is the total number of potential voters, and h is the average probability that a member of the group which incurs a loss due to the legislation (every non-n) votes against the legislator (Maurizi 1975). In this model, the probability of a supportive vote from the beneficiary group (f) is a function of the net benefit per interest group member (g) which, in turn, is a function of the total dollar amount transferred to the beneficiary group (T), the total amount of dollars spent by the group to mitigate opposition (K), and the cost of organizing the beneficiary group to support the legislator and to mitigate opposition ($C(n)$).

$$g = \frac{T - K - C(n)}{n}$$

The legislator chooses the size of the group she will benefit (n), and offers the group T in return for K. The probability of opposition h, on the other hand, increases with the rate at which the income of a member of N is taxed to pay for T and decreases with

$$z = \frac{K}{(N - n)}.$$

Note that, assuming diminishing returns to the per-capita net benefit, the legislator who maximizes M benefits both n and $(N-n)$ to some extent. Peltzman's model further predicts that the cost of interest group organization and $C(n)$ and "imperfect information about both the gains and losses of regulatory decisions" restrict the size of the group benefiting from the regulation. Furthermore, "the costs of using the political process" limit the size of the gains of the beneficiary group (Peltzman 1976).[8] Based on the "interest group" theories of regulation, we would expect health worker groups to be successful in increasing their rents through regulation, because—in comparison to many other occupational groups—they are small, well-informed, and well-organized in professional organizations (Friedman 1962; Kessel 1970; Stigler 1971; Peltzman 1989).

21.3.2.2 Literature on Health Worker Licensure

There are three general categories of health worker licensure studies. In the first, studies examined whether health care markets are competitive or monopolistic. Monopolistic market structures are taken as evidence that licensure benefited health workers and hurt consumers. Licensure studies in the second category analyzed the effects of changes in licensure regulation on health worker incomes or on the quantity, price, or quality of health services. Studies in this category infer from relationships between these outcomes and the stringency of licensure requirements whether "interest group" or "public interest" explanations of licensure hold true. The third category includes studies that investigated whether the political power of health worker interest groups determines licensure legislation. A positive relationship between interest group power and licensure legislation is taken as evidence that the interests of health workers dominated those of consumers in influencing licensure legislation.

First Category: Market Structure One approach to determining the level of competitiveness in the health care market was to estimate the return to health worker education and to compare it to the returns to education in other occupations. Studies

---

[8] Using a set-up similar to Peltzman's, Becker (1983) developed another "interest group" theory of regulation. Becker's model predicts that deadweight loss (i.e. the difference between the gains of the beneficiary group and the losses of the public) is a constraint on the gains of the beneficiary group, because deadweight loss increases at an increasing rate as regulation moves output away from the efficient level, requiring increasing marginal pressure to overcome opposition to the regulation.

employing this approach generally found significant positive returns to medical education. However, the estimated returns to education varied widely, depending on the time period of observation, the particular physician specialties, the comparison occupations, and the estimation technique (Friedman and Kuznet 1945; Wilkinson 1966; Lindsay 1973; Maurizi 1975; Leffler 1978; Leffler and Lindsay 1980; Burstein and Cromwell 1985; Marder and Willke 1991; Weeks et al. 1994). Moreover, a number of estimation problems were identified in these studies. First, the results were sensitive to the choice of discount rate and there is no consensus as to which discount rate to use to estimate returns to medical education (Leffler 1978). Second, the studies commonly failed to take into account progressive taxation (Leffler 1978) and the cost of malpractice insurance. Third, many of the earlier studies of returns to medical education did not control for differences in hours worked across occupations (Lindsay 1973). Later studies took this criticism into account. Studies since 1985 that have calculated hours-adjusted internal rates of return (IRR) suggest that for many medical specialties the stringent licensure requirements did not lead to excessive returns (Burstein and Cromwell 1985; Bärnighausen and Bloom 2009b).

Another approach to assess whether health care markets are competitive or monopolistic was to investigate the relationship between physician density per population and the price of physician services. A positive association between density and price was interpreted as evidence of a monopolistic market (Newhouse 1970) or as evidence that physicians induce demand for their services (Evans et al. 1973; Fuchs 1978; Cromwell and Mitchell 1986; Tussing and Wojtowycz 1986). However, as Sloan and Feldman (1978) and Newhouse (1978) pointed out, the inability to control for differences in quality of physician services in these studies rendered their results of little explanatory value.

A third approach was to estimate an index of market power based on comparison of marginal revenue to marginal cost in the health services industry (Bresnahan 1982; Panzar and Rosse 1987). The results from these studies were inconclusive. Wong (1996) did not find evidence that the marginal revenue exceeds marginal costs in the market for physician services in the US, while Seldon, Jung, and Cavazos (1998) observed that the price for physician services was maintained above marginal costs.

In sum, the studies of market structure do not provide decisive evidence for monopolistic structures in health care markets. Moreover, even if they had provided such evidence, the evidence would have been insufficient to rule out the possibility that monopolistic structures were serving the public interest, as none of the studies took consumer benefits into account. It is possible that consumers are better off in a less competitive market than in a more competitive one.[9] For instance, licensure legislation may restrict entry of health workers into the market and at the same time improve the quality

---

[9] Conversely, lack of evidence of monopolistic structures does not imply that licensure was established to protect the public. As Svorny (1987) points out, "there *must* have been a one-time gain to practicing physicians when restrictions on practice of medicine were imposed. As in other protected markets, entry may dissipate any rents over time."

of health care. If the outward shift in demand caused by the latter effect exceeds the inward shift in supply caused by the former, consumer welfare will increase.

Second Category: Licensure Effects A second category of licensure studies investigated the effects of changes in licensure legislation on outcomes to establish whether "public interest" or "interest group" explanations of licensure hold true. Outcomes considered in this category of studies included health worker incomes and the price, quality and quantity of health services.

A number of studies found that health workers' incomes (Friedman and Kuznet 1945; Leffler 1978; White 1978; Muzondo and Pazderka 1980; Anderson et al. 2000) or the price of health services and products (Benham and Benham 1975; Shepard 1978) increased when licensure regulations became stricter. The studies inferred from the results that licensure benefited health workers and not consumers. Yet, these studies suffer from the same fundamental weakness as the studies investigating the level of competitiveness in the health services: Their results do not rule out that the quality-improving effect of licensure legislation shifted health services demand to such an extent that aggregate consumption and consumer welfare increase despite the supply-restricting effect of the legislation (Svorny 1987). Hence the results cannot be used to determine whether licensure legislation benefited the public.

Two other approaches in this category of studies are better suited for this purpose. First, it is theoretically possible to exclude the possibility that health worker licensure benefited consumers through analysis of the quality of health services.[10] If health services quality did not improve in response to licensure regulation, it could be ruled out that the legislation benefited the consumers. If health services quality did improve, additional information would be necessary to determine whether the quality improvement was sufficient in size to compensate for a reduction in consumer welfare due to supply-restricting effects of licensure.

Three studies that investigated the effect of licensure on health service quality came to very different conclusions. Carroll and Gaston (1981) found that some licensure requirements for dentists in the US led to a reduction in the quality of dental services; Feldman and Begun (1985) found that licensure legislation in the US increased the quality of optometric services; and Haas-Wilson (1986) did not find any significant effect on optometric service quality of four state restrictions on optometric practice which, if violated, could have led to revocation of optometric license. In addition, it is highly unlikely that the quality measures used in the three studies captured all, or even the most important, dimensions of health services quality. Carroll and Gaston (1981) measured quality as waiting time for dental appointments; Feldman and Begun (1985) measured it as length and thoroughness of eye exams; and Haas-Wilson (1986) measured it as the thoroughness of eye exams. The studies thus analyzed the effect of licensure legislation on some specific indicators of process quality, while ignoring other quality dimensions (such as outcome quality).

---

[10] We use the word "quality" here to mean all possible dimensions of heath service quality as well as increases in certainty about the level of quality in the market for health services.

Second, analysis of the effect of licensure legislation on equilibrium consumption can be used to determine whether consumers benefited from such legislation. If licensure legislation caused an outward shift in the demand for health services that is greater than the inward shift in supply, equilibrium consumption would have increased and consumers would have benefited from the legislation; if, on the other hand, the outward shift in demand were smaller than the inward shift in supply, equilibrium consumption would have decreased and consumer welfare would have been reduced.[11]

Svorny (1987) investigated the effect of two particular medical licensure regulations (basic science certification and citizenship) on the consumption of physician services. She found that, controlling for a range of socioeconomic, population, and health system characteristics, more stringent licensure requirements in a US state were associated with lower numbers of physicians per population in the state, and concluded that "the interests of organized medicine dominated those of consumers in influencing the medical regulatory supply process" (Svorny 1987). Adams, Ekelund, and Jackson examined the effect of a range of variables capturing the stringency of midwife licensure and other midwifery regulations on the consumption of the services of certified nurse-midwives (CNM). They found that more stringent midwifery regulations in a US state led to lower consumption of midwifery services in the state and concluded that "supply-restricting effects dominated quality assurance in the US market for CNM services" (Adams et al. 2003).

Both studies have technical limitations that diminish the strength of the evidence that licensure reduces social welfare. Svorny (1987) assumed that her outcome variable, physician population density by US state, was a measure of the quantity of physician services consumed in the states. However, it is plausible that physicians in states with lower physician population densities provided on average more services per year than physicians in states with higher densities. The conclusion that licensure decreases equilibrium consumption of health services may thus be wrong. Adams, Ekelund, and Jackson (2003) controlled for endogeneity between their outcome variable (the quantity of midwife services) and the licensure and regulation variables using a number of instrumental variables. However, the instrumental variables (hospital charges for an uncomplicated vaginal delivery, number of CNM per-capita, physician deliveries as a percentage of total deliveries, total population in the state) are likely to have affected the outcome variable through many pathways other than the licensure and regulation variables, leading to biased coefficients in the instrumental variable regressions.

In sum, analyses of the licensure effect on health worker income or the price of health services cannot determine whether licensure served the public interest. Analyses of the licensure effect on health service quality can theoretically rule out that licensure benefited the public, but past studies were not able to demonstrate that licensure was in the

---

[11] This identification of the net effect of licensure legislation on consumer benefits is possible because we assume that such legislation never leads to an outward shift in supply. If this assumption were not met, consumer welfare could decrease when equilibrium consumption increases.

public interest (and it seems unlikely that future studies will) because of practical difficulties in measuring comprehensively all dimensions of health service quality that can
be affected by licensure legislation.

Third Category: Political Power   A third category of licensure studies analyzed the
relationship between the political power of health worker interest groups and the
passage of licensure legislation and other occupational regulation. Variables used to
proxy interest group power were found to be positively associated with passage of
licensure legislation for physicians, nurses, dentists and pharmacists (Stigler 1971),
physician assistants and psychologists (Graddy 1991), and with the stringency of
licensure regulation for dentists (Becker 1986) and optometrists (Begun et al. 1981).
The authors of these studies interpreted their results as evidence that "interest group"
explanations of licensure hold true.

   However, it is unclear whether the proxy variables really measured the political power
of health worker interest groups. For instance, Stigler (1971) and Becker (1986) used the
percentage of an occupation living in urban areas as a measure of political power because
the costs of organizing campaigns for legislation are lower for concentrated populations
(Stigler 1971). However, the concentration of health workers in cities may not matter for
political power in countries where most members of an occupation have access to communication technologies, such as mail or telephone, so that political support can be
organized independent of physical distance.

   Other proxies are equally questionable. Graddy (1991) assumed that the political
power of health worker groups (physician assistants and psychologists) increases
with the ratio of group members "belonging to the major professional association" to
the total number of employed persons, and Begun, Crowe, and Feldman (1981)
assumed that the political power of optometrists increases with the ratio of optometrists to their competitors (ophthalmologists and opticians). However, political
power may decrease in these ratios beyond some point. Ceteris paribus, the ratios
increased with group size. However, as group size increases, the cost of organizing
political support among group members may rise, reducing the group's political
power (Peltzman 1976).

   In addition, a number of variables hypothesized to proxy political power of interest
groups in these studies were found not to be associated with licensure legislation and
other regulation (for instance "the ratio of the occupation to the total labor force" in
Stigler's 1971 study and "the percentage of optometrists who belong to their state optometry association" and "whether or not the state's optometry association has a legislative
lobbyist" in the 1981 study by Begun, Crowe, and Feldman). The absence of significant
relationships between these variables and occupation regulation suggests that the variables either did not measure political power or that certain dimensions of political power
did not influence occupational regulation.

   Another problem with the above analyses is that they did not control for reverse causality.
It seems likely that in many cases the introduction of licensure or an increase in licensure
stringency reduced the costs of organizing political support by reducing the number of practitioners, increasing homogeneity in interests among these practitioners, and establishing a

central registry of licensees. Thus licensure may strengthen health workers' political power. In sum, while the literature on the relationship between political power of health worker interest groups and licensure suggests that political power does determine licensure legislation—i.e. that "interest group" explanations of the existence of licensure hold true—the studies in this category suffer from a number of shortcomings, limiting the strength of this conclusion.

Shortcomings of the Existing Literature on Health Worker Licensure An important shortcoming of the literature on health worker licensure regardless of the category into which it falls is that almost all published studies were conducted in the US, even though health worker licensure regulations exist in most developed and developing countries. The US health services market has characteristics that are rarely found in other countries, some of which are likely to influence the effect of licensure on market outcomes. For instance, in the US, health workers may already have strong incentives to provide high-quality health services because of the high costs associated with health care malpractice suits. The marginal effect that licensure can have on market outcomes may thus be lower in the US compared to settings where malpractice suits are less expensive. Future studies need to investigate causes and effects of licensure regulation in other countries.

Two further criticisms apply to studies in the first and second categories. First, the real effects of licensure may differ from the effects that legislators or interest groups intend to achieve. Changes in licensure regulation are infrequent events. Legislators and members of interest groups have few opportunities to observe the effects of licensure laws and to learn from failures. Hence, inferences about the behavior of actors in the regulatory process based on observed effects of regulation (as are made in many of the studies discussed above) may be invalid.

Second, the studies are concerned with structures and outcomes in the market for health services. Health services, however, are merely instruments to attain better health. It is therefore possible that consumers suffered a welfare loss in the market for health services, while overall consumer welfare increased.

21.4 Third Phase: The Health Worker as Necessary Resource

21.4.1 Background

In the 1990s and 2000s, the lack of health workers became a major research focus in developed and developing countries. Health worker shortages in developed countries were local rather than nationwide, occurring in so-called medically underserved areas.[12]

---

[12] A medically underserved area is an area where the number of health workers falls below a target. As described in section 21.2, such targets can be based on need, demand, or supply criteria (such as service targets or population ratios). Commonly, a mix of criteria is used (Bärnighausen and Bloom 2009d).

For instance, in 2008 Rabinowitz et al. write about the US that the "persistent shortage of physicians in rural areas continues to have a major impact on access to care for those living in small communities.... This rural physician shortage has existed for more than 80 years, despite the fact that, in general, people living in rural areas have a greater need for medical care, being older, sicker, and poorer than their non-rural peers."

In developing countries, evidence emerged that the population density of health workers affected both population health outcomes (such as child mortality (Anand and Bärnighausen 2004)) and health systems outcomes (such as childhood vaccination coverage (Anand and Bärnighausen 2007)). These findings emphasized the need to increase health worker education and retention in developing countries (Joint Learning Initiative 2004; WHO 2006). In addition, with the adoption of the MDGs by national governments and international organizations, health became a major focus of development policies (United Nations 2009). While achievement of the health MDGs does not depend on health services delivery alone, they are unlikely to be achieved without substantial increases in service coverage in developing countries. The indicators used to monitor progress towards the health MDGs include health service targets, e.g. the proportion of 1-year-old children immunized against measles, or the proportion of population with advanced HIV infection with access to antiretroviral drugs (United Nations 2009). Such health service targets could not be achieved without substantially increasing the health workforce in developing countries (Joint Learning Initiative 2004; WHO 2006; WHO 2008).[13]

The shift in perspective from regarding health workers as economic agents to viewing them as a resource necessary to improve population health led to research on means to increase health worker supplies to such underserved areas. In the following, we review two major topics in this third phase of research on the health workforce: first, programs aimed at attracting health workers to underserved areas in developed countries; and, second, health worker emigration from developing to developed countries (Aiken et al. 2004). Although the supply of health workers to underserved areas is a function not only of health worker movements, but also of education rates (Bärnighausen and Bloom 2009a), studies on health worker education are few (Eckhert 2002) and thus do not warrant a review.

21.4.2 Developed Countries: Interventions to Increase Health Worker Supply to Underserved Areas

Programs to increase the supply of health workers to underserved areas can affect health workers in different stages of their careers. Before the start of training, selective

---

[13] Of course, increases in the efficiency of health care delivery, e.g. through changes in health worker team composition and task shifting from more to less highly educated health workers, could decrease the gap between current health worker numbers and the numbers required to achieve the health MDGs. However, it is very unlikely that efficiency increases alone can eliminate the gap (WHO 2008).

admission strategies attempt to increase the number of health workers who will practice in underserved areas by selecting those individuals who—given observable characteristics—are most likely to work in these areas after graduation. During training, curricula specific to health needs in underserved areas and exposure to practice in such areas attempt to increase graduates' likelihood of choosing underserved practice by specifically preparing them for this type of service. Last, financial-incentive programs offer scholarships (during training) or loan repayments (after training) in return for service in underserved areas (Bärnighausen and Bloom 2009c). We extracted information on these programs from three recent systematic reviews of four types of programs (selective admission to medical school, medical school training for practice in underserved areas, residency training for practice in underserved areas (Brooks et al. 2002; Rabinowitz et al. 2008), and financial-incentive programs for return of service in underserved areas (Bärnighausen and Bloom 2009d)) and from studies identified through searches of the health and economics literature.

We included only those studies that compared outcomes in program participants with outcomes in non-participants. All included studies measured an outcome in either one of two categories: provision of care—if the study compared all health workers enrolled in a program to all health workers—or retention—if the study compared only those enrolled and non-enrolled health workers who at some point took up practice in an underserved area. Two types of retention outcomes can be distinguished: retention in the *same* underserved area and retention in *any* underserved area.

We identified only one study reporting the effect of selective admission to medical school without additional medical school training to prepare students for practice in underserved areas (Basco et al. 1998). The study found—unsurprisingly—that students attending medical schools with selective admission targeting future generalists were significantly more interested in primary care and in rural practice than students attending medical schools that did not have such a selective admission policy.

Other studies investigated programs that trained (future) health workers specifically for practice in underserved areas (with or without selective admission policies) either during medical school or during residency. These studies found that program participants were significantly more likely than non-participants to practice in underserved areas (Brazeau et al. 1990; Rabinowitz 1993; Fryer et al. 1994; Bowman and Penrod 1998; Rabinowitz et al. 1999b; Rabinowitz et al. 2001; Smucny et al. 2005), to intend to practice in underserved areas (Rosenthal 2000), and to remain in the *same* underserved area (Pathman et al. 1999; Rabinowitz et al. 2005). There was only one exception among these studies, which did not find any significant difference between participants and non-participants (Rabinowitz et al. 1999a).

Five of seven studies investigating the effect of participation in financial-incentive programs on retention in the *same* underserved area found that participants were significantly less likely to remain in the area (Pathman et al. 1992; Pathman et al. 1994a; Pathman et al. 1994b; Holmes 2004; Pathman et al. 2004). Another study did not report a significance level but found substantially lower retention among participants (Singer et al. 1998), and one study did not find a significant difference (Jackson et al. 2003). On the other hand, ten of the twelve studies investigating the effect of financial-incentive programs on provision of care or retention in *any* underserved area found that participants were more likely to provide care to underserved populations (Xu et al. 1997a, 1997b; Pathman et al. 2000; Rabinowitz et al. 2000; Brooks et al. 2003; Probst et al. 2003; Inoue et al. 2007; Matsumoto et al. 2008; Rittenhouse et al. 2008) and to continue to practice in some underserved area (Pathman et al. 2000; Holmes 2004). These differences were shown to be statistically significant in eight of the ten studies (Xu et al. 1997a, 1997b; Rabinowitz et al. 2000; Pathman et al. 2000; Brooks et al. 2003; Probst et al. 2003; Holmes 2004; Rittenhouse et al. 2008), while two other studies reported that participants were significantly less likely than non-participants to remain in some underserved area (Pathman et al. 1992; Matsumoto et al. 2008).

Because the (future) health workers tracked in all of the above studies chose to participate in the programs, it is difficult to distinguish whether the findings are due to true effects of program participation or merely due to selection into the programs. Selection issues are particularly apparent in the evaluation of programs with selective admission policies. As selection criteria were likely chosen because they were positively associated with practice in underserved areas, we would expect that observed differences in the likelihood to practice in underserved areas between participating and non-participating health care students can be at least partially explained by selective admission. Indeed, the one study that does not find any significant difference in the provision of care in underserved areas between participants and non-participants in a program with selective admission (and medical school training for rural practice) controlled for rural upbringing in the analysis (Rabinowitz et al. 1999a)—while the program "recruits and selectively admits medical school applicants who have grown up in a rural area and intend to practice family medicine in rural and underserved areas" (Rabinowitz et al. 1999b). Another study of the same program concluded that "the admission component … is the most important reason for its success" (Rabinowitz et al. 2001). Implicit in such a conclusion is the assumption that at least some proportion of participants would not have studied to become health workers, had they not enrolled in the program. If this assumption were not met, the program would not have increased the supply of health workers to underserved areas.

Fourteen studies controlled for additional variables in the comparison between participants and non-participants, such as sex, age, ethnicity, marital status, medical specialty (Pathman et al. 1992; Pathman et al. 1994b; Xu et al. 1997a, 1997b; Bowman and Penrod 1998; Rabinowitz et al. 1999a, 1999b; Pathman et al. 2000; Rabinowitz et al. 2000; Rabinowitz et al. 2001; Probst et al. 2003; Holmes 2004; Pathman et al. 2004; Rittenhouse et al. 2008). However, even those studies that control for factors likely to be closely related to care provision and retention in underserved areas (such as growing up in an underserved area (Xu et al. 1997a; Xu et al. 1997b; Rabinowitz et al. 1999a; Rabinowitz et al. 2000) or "strong interest" prior to medical school to practice as a doctor in an underserved area (Xu et al. 1997b; Rabinowitz et al. 2000)) cannot rule out that participants selected into the program on unobserved characteristics related to the preference of working in underserved areas.

One study of program effect attempted to control for selection on unobserved variables by using a selection model (Holmes 2004). To identify the program effect, the study used four medical school characteristics: "historical proportion of graduates specializing in primary care," "quality of the school," a "tuition index," and a "public school indicator." It seems unlikely that these characteristics affected students' probability of underserved practice only through their effect on program participation and not through other pathways. The characteristics may thus not be valid variables to identify program effects.

In sum, studies evaluating programs aimed at increasing the supply of health workers to underserved areas found that participants are more likely to provide care for underserved populations and to remain in underserved areas in the long run (even if not in the same underserved area where they were initially placed). However, because the studies to date did not convincingly control for selection effects, the evidence does not allow the inference that the programs caused increases in health worker supply to underserved areas.

21.4.3 Developing Countries: Health Worker Emigration

In the past decade, health worker migration from developing to developed countries was a common topic of editorials, policy reports, and scientific publications (Bärnighausen and Bloom 2009b; Joint Learning Initiative 2004; WHO 2006). Below, we summarize the research on international health worker migration regarding measurement (i.e. estimation of the size of migration flows from developing to developed countries or the stock of health workers who migrated), causes, welfare impact, and programs and policies to address health worker migration.

A number of studies described international migration flows or stocks of in- or out-migrated health workers for individual migration source countries (Bärnighausen and Bloom 2009b). While the data in these studies were useful to demonstrate the magnitude of health worker migration from developing to developed countries, they were insufficient for many research purposes. For one, the country-level data cannot be pooled for multi-country analyses, because different studies used different methods to estimate the size of migration flows and stocks. In addition, most of the studies covered only short periods of time. Finally, some studies measured only migration of health workers who graduated from specific institutions or regions in a country (Zijlstra and Broadhead 2007).

Four different studies published datasets of *stocks* of emigrated health workers from a number of countries (Hagopian et al. 2004; Mullan 2005; OECD 2005; WHO 2006; Clemens and Pettersson 2008).[14] Each used numbers of health workers reported in

---

[14] The data reported in WHO (2006) is extracted from OECD (2005).

recipient countries to estimate the magnitude of emigration from source countries. The stock estimates differ substantially across the datasets (see Table 21.1). These discrepancies are due to several factors, and together they demonstrate some of the difficulties in estimating international health worker migration flows.

First, the four datasets used different sources of information on the numbers of foreign physicians in recipient countries. WHO/OECD (OECD 2005; WHO 2006) and Clemens and Pettersson (2008) used national census data, while Mullan (2005) and Hagopian et al. (2004) used data from health workers' professional organizations. Second, to estimate emigration stocks different studies counted health workers in different sets of recipient countries. Third, the studies used different definitions of migrant health workers. WHO, Mullan, and Hagopian et al. defined a migrant health worker as one who was trained in another country, while Clemens and Pettersson defined a migrant health worker as one born in another country. This distinction is important, because some of the countries with the worldwide lowest population densities of health workers (such as Lesotho and Swaziland (WHO 2009)) do not have their own medical school and thus depend on physicians trained in other countries—including their own citizens (Clemens and Pettersson 2008). Last, the four datasets estimate stocks of emigrated health workers for different years (Table 21.1).

One comprehensive dataset provides physician emigration *rates* for all countries worldwide for each year in the period 1991–2004 (Docquier and Bhargava 2006; Docquier and Bhargava 2007). Figure 21.3 shows annual emigration rates (in % per year) for the year 2004 for all countries in sub-Saharan Africa covered in the dataset.

Table 21.1 Estimates of Stocks of Physicians Who Emigrated from Selected Sub-Saharan African Countries

Study	WHO 2006, OECD 2005	Clemens and Pettersson 2008	Mullan 2005	Hagopian et al. 2004
Year of data	2002	2000	2004	2002
Country				
South Africa	12136	7363	3734	3788
Nigeria	4261	4856	3921	2281
Ghana	926	1639	NR	515
Ethiopia	335	553	NR	266
Uganda	316	1837	NR	175
Zimbabwe	237	1602	NR	101
Angola	168	2102	NR	NR
Cameroon	109	845	NR	NR
Tanzania	46	1356	NR	NR
Mozambique	22	1334	NR	NR

Note: NR = not reported.

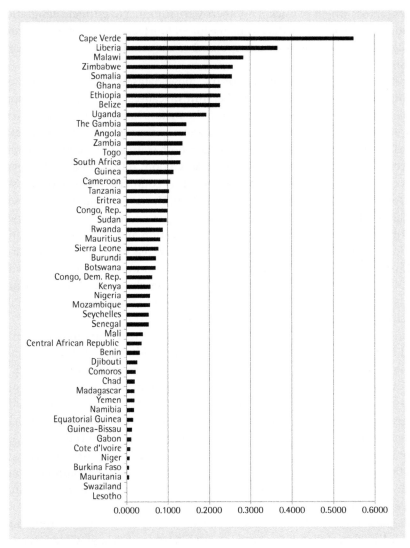

FIGURE 21.3 Estimates of health worker emigration rates in Sub-Saharan African countries, 2004

According to the dataset, in 2004 emigration rates exceeded 10 percent in seventeen countries in the region and 20 percent in eight countries. Such panel data on health worker emigration rates are extremely useful for a wide range of migration analyses. However, the dataset has a number of limitations. For one, the definition of migrant physician differed across recipient countries (a physicians born in another country, a physician with citizenship in another country, and a physician trained in another country (Clemens and Pettersson 2008)). Moreover, for only four of the sixteen recipient countries (across which physician numbers were summed to estimate emigration flows from source countries) were data available for all fourteen years. For all other recipient countries, the authors intra- or extrapolated some country-year values of emigrated physicians.

The relatively recent development of the above datasets and the fact that each has some limitations may explain why the literature on causes of health worker migration is largely descriptive and why the literature on the welfare impact of the migration is small. Studies on the causes of health worker migration investigated reasons for migration decisions through surveys of health workers in both source and recipient countries (for references to such studies, see Bärnighausen and Bloom 2009b). In these surveys, health workers consistently listed higher earnings in other countries as one of the most important reasons for migration plans or past migration. However, health workers also named a number of other factors as influencing their migration decisions, including job security, flexible leave policies, opportunities for education and training, opportunities for promotion, the management of health services, workplace safety (in particular the risk of work-related HIV infection), family welfare, and country stability (Bärnighausen and Bloom 2009b). Non-financial factors appear to be nearly as important as earnings differentials in motivating migration, but the patterns of important non-financial factors differ across countries (Bärnighausen and Bloom 2009b).

Despite a well-developed economics literature on the welfare impact of migration (Grubel and Scott 1966; Kwok and Leland 1982; Goldfarb et al. 1984; Borjas 1995), only a few studies examined the particular impact of international health worker migration on social welfare in source and recipient countries. Studies in Kenya (Kirigia et al. 2006) and Malawi (Muula et al. 2006) estimated the financial loss due to emigration of a health worker as the total costs of educating such a worker. The estimated losses of returns on investment were about US$500 thousand (year 2005 US$) for a doctor in Kenya, more than US$300 thousand for a nurse in Kenya (Kirigia et al. 2006), and between approximately US$240 thousand (at an annual interest rate of 7%) and US$26 million (at an interest rate of 25%) for a nurse or midwife in Malawi (Muula et al. 2006).

While these financial losses seem large, two studies of remittances from emigrated health workers found that the remittances (of Filipino physicians (Goldfarb et al. 1984) and Tongan and Samoan nurses (Connell and Brown 2004)) exceeded the initial investment in their human capital, suggesting that at least in some countries it may pay to train health workers for export.

Another study estimated the social net present value of a financial incentive that pays fully for a student's education as a health worker in return for a few years of service in an ART program in sub-Saharan Africa. The study found that these financial incentives are highly cost-beneficial if they are effective in reducing health worker emigration (Bärnighausen and Bloom 2009a).

A final set of publications on health worker migration discussed potential programs and policies to reduce emigration of health workers from developing countries or to mitigate negative consequences of migration. Bärnighausen and Bloom provide an overview over these interventions, which comprise both micro-level approaches (selective admission, training for practice in developing countries, increased health worker training in developed countries, compulsory service, financial incentives, and non-financial incentives) and macro-level approaches (visa restrictions, "ethical recruitment" in developed countries, and compensation payments from countries receiving health workers to countries losing them) (Bärnighausen and Bloom 2009b).

Some of these interventions have already been implemented (such as compulsory service in South Africa (Reid 2001), financial incentive in South Africa (Ross 2007), non-financial incentives in Zambia (Koot and Martineau 2005), and an "ethical recruitment policy" in the UK (Carlisle 2004)). However, studies evaluating the effect of the implemented programs and policies on health worker migration are as yet lacking.

In sum, although the recent focus of development policy on population health sparked research on health worker migration from developing to developed countries, the majority of studies were descriptive in nature, in part, because comprehensive data on international migration flows of health workers were not available. Future initiatives should emphasize further improvements in data on international health worker migration. Once validated data are available, researchers can draw on the extensive literature on migration in economics and other disciplines to further investigate the causes and consequences of health worker migration and to evaluate existing interventions to reduce migration rates.

21.5 CONCLUSIONS

Although this review of research on the health workforce since the 1960s divides the literature into chronological phases, the three research perspectives on the global health workforce are of course merely stylized descriptions of main research thrusts and do not imply that such foci were necessarily the best use of research resources during the different phases. Moreover, the three perspectives are not mutually exclusive. For instance, some of the studies of the health worker as a necessary resource use health workforce planning approaches to estimate the size of the gap between available and needed health workers. Other studies that are motivated by a perceived or measured lack of health workers clearly view health workers as economic actors who consider financial and non-financial incentives in their location decisions.

Opportunities for future research on the health workforce abound. While they are likely to include new approaches, our review suggests that the transfer of existing approaches could lead to important insights. The following transfers are examples. First, studies on health worker licensure were mostly carried out in the US. It seems likely that the strength of health worker "interest groups" relative to the power of the public differs across stages of socioeconomic development and by type of health system. Evidence on the causes and effects of health worker licensure in different developing countries is thus likely to contribute substantially to the licensure debate. Second, programs to attract health workers to underserved areas have been implemented in many developing countries. Evaluations of these programs—ideally extending the approaches used in developed countries to account fully for selection effects—would be of substantial value to policymakers. Last, researchers interested in the movement of health workers from developing to developed countries could draw on the large economics literature on migration to investigate causes and effects and develop a coherent economic model of medical migration.

REFERENCES

ADAMS, A. F., EKELUND, R., and JACKSON, J. D. (2003). "Occupational licensing of a credence good: the regulation of midwifery." *Southern Economic Journal*, 69/3: 659–75.

AHMED, A. A., FATEHA, B., and BENJAMIN, S. (2000). "Demand and supply of doctors and dentists in Bahrain, 1998–2005." *Eastern Mediterranean Health Journal*, 6/1: 6–12.

AIKEN, L. H., BUCHAN, J., SOCHALSKI, J., NICHOLS, B., and POWELL, M. (2004). "Trends in international nurse migration." *Health Affairs (Millwood)*, 23/3: 69–77.

AKERLOF, G. A. (1970). "The market for 'lemons': quality uncertainty and the market mechanism." *Quarterly Journal of Economics*, 84: 488–500.

ANAND, S. and BÄRNIGHAUSEN, T. (2004). "Human resources and health outcomes: cross-country econometric study." *Lancet*, 364/9445: 1603–9.

———— (2007). "Health workers and vaccination coverage in developing countries: an econometric analysis." *Lancet*, 369/9569: 1277–85.

ANDERSON, G. M., HALCOUSSIS, L. J., and LOWENBERG, A. D. (2000). "Regulatory barriers to entry in the healthcare industry: the case of alternative medicine." *The Quarterly Review of Economics and Finance*, 40: 485–502.

ARROW, K. J. (1963). "Uncertainty and the welfare economics of medical care." *The American Economic Review*, LIII/2: 941–73.

BÄRNIGHAUSEN, T. and BLOOM, D. (2009a). "Conditional scholarships for HIV/AIDS health workers: educating and retaining the workforce to provide antiretroviral treatment in sub-Saharan Africa." *Social Science and Medicine*, 68: 544–51.

———— (2009b). "Changing research perspectives on the global health workforce. National Bureau of Economic Research (NBER) Working Paper No. 15168." Cambridge, MA, NBER.

———— (2009c). "Designing financial-incentive programmes for return of medical service in underserved areas: seven management functions." *Human Resources for Health*, 7/1: 52.

———— (2009d). "Financial incentives for return of service in underserved areas: a systematic review." *BMC Health Services Research*, 9/1: 86.

BASCO, W. T., Jr., BUCHBINDER, S. B., DUGGAN, A. K., and WILSON, M. H. (1998). "Associations between primary care-oriented practices in medical school admission and the practice intentions of matriculants." *Academic Medicine*, 73/11: 1207–10.

BECKER, G. (1983). "A theory of competition among pressure groups for political influence." *The Quarterly Review of Economics*, XCVIII/3: 371–400.

——— (1986). "The public interest hypothesis revisited: a new test of Peltzman's theory of regulation." *Public Choice*, 49: 223–34.

BEGUN, J. W., CROWE, E. W., and FELDMAN, R. (1981). "Occupational regulation in the states: a causal model." *Journal of Health Politics, Policy and Law*, 6/2: 229–54.

BENHAM, L. (1971). "The labor market for registered nurses: a three-equation model." *The Review of Economics and Statistics*, 53/3: 246–52.

—— and BENHAM, A. (1975). "Regulating through the professions: a perspective on information control." *Journal of Law and Economics*, 18/2: 421–47.

BIRCH, S., KEPHART, G., TOMBLIN-MURPHY, G., O'BRIEN-PALLAS, L., ALDER, R., and MACKENZIE, A. (2007). "Human resources planning and the production of health: a needs-based analytical framework." *Canadian Public Policy*, 33/supplement: S1–16.

BLOMQVIST, A. (1991). "The doctor as double agent: information asymmetry, health insurance, and medical care." *Journal of Health Economics*, 10/4: 411–32.

BODENHEIMER, T. and GRUMBACH, K. (2002). *Understanding health policy: a clinical approach.* New York, Lange Medical, McGraw-Hill.

BORJAS, G. J. (1995). "The economic benefits from migration." *Journal of Economic Perspectives*, 9/2: 3–22.

BOSSERT, T., BÄRNIGHAUSEN, T., BOWSER, D., MITCHELL, A., and GEDIK, G. (2007). *Assessing Financing, Education, Management and Policy Context for Strategic Planning of Human Resources in Health.* Geneva, WHO.

BOWMAN, R. C. and PENROD, J. D. (1998). "Family practice residency programs and the graduation of rural family physicians." *Family Medicine*, 30/4: 288–92.

BRAZEAU, N. K., POTTS, M. J., and HICKNER, J. M. (1990). "The Upper Peninsula Program: a successful model for increasing primary care physicians in rural areas." *Family Medicine*, 22/5: 350–5.

BRESNAHAN, T. F. (1982). "The oligopoly solution concept is identified." *Economics Letters*, 10: 87–92.

BROOKS, R. G., WALSH, M., MARDON, R. E., LEWIS, M., and CLAWSON, A. and (2002). "The roles of nature and nurture in the recruitment and retention of primary care physicians in rural areas: a review of the literature." *Academic Medicine*, 77/8: 790–8.

—— MARDON, R., and CLAWSON, A. (2003). "The rural physician workforce in Florida: a survey of US- and foreign-born primary care physicians." *Journal of Rural Health*, 19/4: 484–91.

BURSTEIN, P. L. and CROMWELL, J. (1985). "Relative incomes and rates of return for U.S. physicians." *Journal of Health Economics*, 4: 63–78.

CARLISLE, D. (2004). "UK's 'ethical recruitment policy' needs to be strengthened." *British Medical Journal*, 328: 1218.

CARROLL, S. L. and GASTON, R. J. (1981). "Occupational restrictions and the quality of service received: some evidence." *Southern Economic Journal*, 47/4: 959–76.

CENDES (CENTER FOR DEVELOPMENT STUDIES; C. U. VENEZUELA) (1965). *Health Planning: Problems of Concept and Method.* Washington, DC, Pan-American Health Organization.

CHUNHARAS, S. (1998). "Human resources for health planning: a review of the Thai experience." *Human Resources Development Journal*, 2/2: 1–12.

CLEMENS, M. A. and PETTERSSON, G. (2008). "New data on African health professionals abroad." *Human Resources for Health*, 6: 1.

COMMISSION ON MACROECONOMICS AND HEALTH (2001). *Macroeconomics and Health: Investing in Health for Economic Development.* Geneva, WHO.

CONNELL, J. and BROWN, R. P. (2004). "The remittances of migrant Tongan and Samoan nurses from Australia." *Human Resources for Health*, 2/1: 2.

COOKSON, R. and DOLAN, P. (2000). "Principles of justice in health care rationing." *Journal of Medical Ethics*, 26: 323–9.

CROMWELL, J. and MITCHELL, J. (1986). "Physician-induced demand for surgery." *Journal of Health Economics*, 5/3: 293–313.

CUTLER, D. M. and BERNDT, E. R. (2001). *Medical Care Output and Productivity*. Chicago and London, National Bureau of Economic Research Studies in Income and Wealth, University of Chicago Press.

DANIELS, R. S. (1974). "Health planning in the U.S.S.R.: are there lessons to be learned?" *American Journal of Public Health*, 64/6: 613–5.

DOCQUIER, F. and BHARGAVA, A. (2006). "The medical brain drain: a new data set on physicians' emigration rates (1991–2004)." <http://siteresources.worldbank.org/INTRES/Resources/DataSetDocquierBhargava_Medical_BD100306.xls> June 25, 2007.

———— (2007). "A new panel data set on physicians' emigration rates (1991–2004)." <www.ires.ucl.ac.be/CSSSP/home_pa_pers/docquier/filePDF/MBD1_Description.pdf> June 25, 2007.

DREESCH, N., DOLEA, C., DAL POZ, M. R., et al. (2005). "An approach to estimating human resource requirements to achieve the Millennium Development Goals." *Health Policy and Planning*, 20/5: 267–76.

ECKHERT, N. L. (2002). "The global pipeline: too narrow, too wide or just right?" *Medical Education*, 36/7: 606–13.

ENCINOSA, W. E., GAYNOR, M., and REBITZER, J. B. (2007). "The sociology of groups and the economics of incentives: Theory and evidence on compensation systems." *Journal of Economic Behavior & Organization*, 62/2: 187–214.

EVANS, R. G., PARISH, E. M. A., and SULLY, F. (1973). "Medical productivity, scale effects, and demand generation." *Canadian Journal of Economics*, 6/3: 376–93.

FELDMAN, R. and BEGUN, J. W. (1985). "The welfare cost of quality changes due to professional regulation." *The Journal of Industrial Economics*, 34/1: 17–32.

FELDSTEIN, M. S. (1967). "An aggregate planning model of the health care sector." *Medical Care*, 5/6: 369–81.

—— (1971). "An econometric model of the Medicare system." *The Quarterly Journal of Economics*, 85/1: 1–20.

FRANK, R. G. and ZECKHAUSER, R. J. (2007). "Custom-made versus ready-to-wear treatments: behavioral propensities in physicians' choices." *Journal of Health Economics*, 26: 1101–27.

FRIEDMAN, M. (1962). *Capitalism and Freedom*. Chicago, University of Chicago Press.

—— and KUZNET, S. (1945). *Income from Independent Professional Practice*. New York, National Bureau of Economic Research.

FRYER, G. E., STINE, C., KRUGMAN, R. D., and MIYOSHI, T. J. (1994). "Geographic benefit from decentralized medical education: student and preceptor practice patterns." *Journal of Rural Health*, 10/3: 193–8.

FUCHS, V. (1978). "The supply of surgeons and the demand for operations." *Journal of Human Resources*, 12 (supplement): 35–56.

GAUMER, G. L. (1984). "Regulating health professionals: a review of the empirical literature." *The Milbank Memorial Fund Quarterly. Health and Society*, 62/3: 380–416.

GERDTHAM, U. G. and JONSSON, B. (1991). "Price and quantity in international comparisons of health expenditure." *Applied Economics*, 23: 1519–28.

—— SOGAARD, J., ANDERSON, G., and JONSSON, B. (1992). "An econometric analysis of health care expenditure: a cross-section study of OECD countries." *Journal of Health Economics*, 11: 63–4.

GINZBERG, E. (1983). "How many physicians are enough?" *Annals of the American Academy of Political and Social Science*, 468: 205–15.

GOLDFARB, R., HAVRYLYSHYN, O., and MAGNUM, S. (1984). "Can remittances compensate for manpower outflows: the case of Philippine physicians." *Journal of Development Economics*, 15: 1–17.

GRADDY, E. (1991). "Toward a general theory of occupational regulation." *Social Science Quarterly*, 72/4: 676–95.

GEMENAC (GRADUATE MEDICAL EDUCATION NATIONAL ADVISORY COMMITTEE) (1980). *Report of the Graduate Medical Education National Advisory Committee to the Secretary, Department of Health and Human Services*. Washington, DC, US Department of Health and Human Services.

GRUBEL, H. and SCOTT, A. (1966). "The international flow of human capital." *American Economic Review*, 56: 268–83.

HAAS-WILSON, D. (1986). "The effect of commercial practice restrictions: the case of optometry." *Journal of Law and Economics*, 29: 165–86.

HAGOPIAN, A., THOMPSON, M. J., FORDYCE, M., JOHNSON, K. E., and HART, L. G. (2004). "The migration of physicians from sub-Saharan Africa to the United States of America: measures of the African brain drain." *Human Resources for Health*, 2/1: 17.

HALL, T. L. (1971). "Chile health manpower study: methods and problems." *International Journal of Health Services*, 1/2: 166–84.

——and MEJIA, A. (1978). *Health Manpower Planning: Principles, Methods, Issues*. Geneva, WHO.

——REINKE, W. A., and LAWRENCE, D. (1975). "Measurement and projection of the demand for health care: the Chilean experience." *Medical Care*, 13/6: 511–22.

HERNANDEZ, P., DRÄGER, S., EVANS, D. B., TAN-TORRES EDEJER, T., and DAL POZ, M. R. (2006). *Measuring Expenditure for the Health Workforce: Evidence and Challenges*. Geneva, World Health Organization.

HITIRIS, T. (1997). "Health care expenditures and integration in the countries of the European Union." *Applied Economics*, 29: 1–6.

—— and POSNETT, J. (1992). "The determinants and effects of health expenditure in developed countries." *Journal of Health Economics*, 11: 173–81.

HOLMES, G. M. (2004). "Does the National Health Service Corps improve physician supply in underserved locations?" *Eastern Economic Journal*, 30/4: 563–81.

HORNBY, P., MEJIA, A., RAY, D., and SIMEONOV, L. A. (1976). "Trends in planning for health manpower." *World Health Organization Chronicle*, 30/11: 447–54.

HUBER, M. (1999). "Health expenditure trends in OECD countries, 1970–1997." *Health Care Financing Review*, 21/2: 99–117.

—— and OROSZ, E. (2003). "Health expenditure trends in OECD countries, 1990–2001." *Health Care Financing Review*, 25/1: 1–22.

INOUE, K., MATSUMOTO, M., and SAWADA, T. (2007). "Evaluation of a medical school for rural doctors." *Journal of Rural Health*, 23/2: 183–7.

JACKSON, J., SHANNON, C. K., PATHMAN, D. E., MASON, E., and NEMITZ, J. W. (2003). "A comparative assessment of West Virginia's financial incentive programs for rural physicians." *Journal of Rural Health*, 19 Suppl: 329–39.

JOINT LEARNING INITIATIVE (2004). *Human Resources for Health: Overcoming the Crisis*. Boston, Global Equity Initiative.

KESSEL, R. A. (1958). "Price discrimination in medicine." *Journal of Law and Economics*, 1: 20–53.

—— (1970). "The A.M.A. and the supply of physicians." *Law and Contemporary Problems*, 35/2: 267–83.

KIRIGIA, J. M., GBARY, A. R., MUTHURI, L. K., NYONI, J., and SEDDOH, A. (2006). "The cost of health professionals' brain drain in Kenya." *BMC Health Services Research*, 6: 89.

KLARMAN, H. E. (1969). "Economic aspects of projecting requirements for health manpower." *Journal of Human Resources*, 4/3: 360–76.

KOOT, J. and MARTINEAU, T. (2005). *Mid Term Review: Zambian Health Workers Retention Scheme 2003-2004.*

KUROWSKI, C., WYSS, K., ABDULLA, S., and MILLS, A. (2007). "Scaling up priority health interventions in Tanzania: the human resources challenge." *Health Policy Planning*, 22/3: 113–27.

KWOK, V. and LELAND, H. (1982). "An economic model of the brain drain." *American Economic Review*, 74: 91–100.

LE GRAND, J. (1997). "Knights, knaves or pawns? Human behaviour and social policy." *Journal of Social Policy*, 26/2: 149–69.

LEE, R. I. and JONES, L. W. (1933). *The Fundamentals of Good Medical care: An Outline of the Fundamentals of Good Medical Care and an Estimate of the Service Required to Supply the Medical Needs of the United States*. Chicago, University of Chicago Press.

LEFFLER, K. B. (1978). "Physician licensure: competition and monopoly in American medicine." *Journal of Law and Economics*, 21/1: 165–86.

—— and LINDSAY, C. M. (1980). "Markets for medical care and medical education: an integrated long-run structural approach." *Journal of Human Resources*, 16: 21–40.

LELAND, H. E. (1979). "Quacks, lemons, and licensing: a theory of minimum quality standards." *Journal of Political Economy*, 87/6: 1328–46.

LINDSAY, C. M. (1973). "Real returns to medical education." *The Journal of Human Resources*, VIII/3: 331–48.

MARDER, W. D. and WILLKE, R. J. (1991). Comparisons of the value of physician time by specialty. in H. E. Frech (ed.), *Regulating Doctors' Fees: Competition, Benefits, and Controls Under Medicare*. Washington, D.C., American Enterprise Institute.

MARKHAM, B. and BIRCH, S. (1997). "Back to the future: a framework for estimating healthcare human resource requirements." *Canadian Journal of Nursing Administration*, 10: 7–23.

MATSUMOTO, M., INOUE, K., and KAJII, E. (2008). "A contract-based training system for rural physicians: follow-up of Jichi Medical University graduates (1978-2006)." *Journal of Rural Health*, 24/4: 360–8.

MAURIZI, A. (1975). "Rates of return to dentistry and the decision to enter dental school." *Journal of Human Resources*, 10: 521–8.

MILNE, R. and MOLANA, H. (1991). "On the effect of income and relative price on demand for health care: EC evidence." *Applied Economics*, 23: 1221–6.

MINISTRY OF HEALTH (1967). *The System of Public Health Services in the USSR*. Moscow, Ministry of Health.

MOORE, T. G. (1961). "The purpose of licensing." *Journal of Law and Economics*, 4: 93–117.

MULLAN, F. (2005). "The metrics of the physician brain drain." *New England Journal of Medicine*, 353/17: 1810–18.

MURPHY, G. T. (2002). "Methodological issues in health human resource planning: cataloguing assumptions and controlling for variables in needs-based modelling." *Canadian Journal of Nursing Research*, 33/4: 51–70.

MUULA, A. S., PANULO, B., JR., and MASEKO, F. C. (2006). "The financial losses from the migration of nurses from Malawi." *BMC Nursing*, 5: 9.

MUZONDO, T. R. and PAZDERKA, B. (1980). "Occupational licensing and professional incomes in Canada." *Canadian Journal of Economics*, 13: 659–67.

NEWHOUSE, J. P. (1970). "A model of physician pricing." *Southern Economic Journal*, 37: 174–83.

—— (1977). "Medical care expenditure: a cross-national survey." *Journal of Human Resources*, 12/1: 115–25.

—— (1978). *The Economics of Medical Care*. Reading, MA, Addison-Wesley.

NOETHER, M. (1986). "The growing supply of physicians: has the market become more competitive?" *Journal of Labor Economics*, 4/4: 503–37.

O'BRIEN-PALLAS, L., BAUMANN, A., DONNER, G., MURPHY, G. T., LOCHHAAS-GERLACH, J., and LUBA, M. (2001). "Forecasting models for human resources in health care." *Journal of Advanced Nursing*, 33/1: 120–9.

OECD (2005). *Trends in International Migration*. Paris, OECD.

OKUNADE, A. A. and SURARATDECHA, C. (2000). "Health care expenditure inertia in the OECD countries: a heterogeneous analysis." *Health Care Management Science*, 3: 31–42.

OLBRICH, A. (2008). "The optimal negligence standard in health care under supply-side cost sharing." *International Journal of Health Care Finance and Economics*, 8: 73–85.

PANZAR, L. and ROSSE, J. N. (1987). "Testing for 'monopoly' equilibrium." *The Journal of Industrial Economics*, 35/4: 443–56.

PARKIN, D., McGUIRE, A., and YULE, B. (1987). "Aggregate health care expenditures and national income." *Journal of Health Economics*, 6: 109–27.

PATHMAN, D. E., KONRAD, T. R., KING, T. S., SPAULDING, C., and TAYLOR, D. H. (2000). "Medical training debt and service commitments: the rural consequences." *Journal of Rural Health*, 16/3: 264–72.

—— —— TAYLOR, D. H., JR., and KOCH, G. G. (2004). "Outcomes of states' scholarship, loan repayment, and related programs for physicians." *Medical Care*, 42/6: 560–8.

—— RICKETTS, T. C., 3rd (1992). "The comparative retention of National Health Service Corps and other rural physicians. Results of a 9-year follow-up study." *Journal of the American Medical Association*, 268/12: 1552–8.

—— —— —— (1994a). "Medical education and the retention of rural physicians." *Health Services Research*, 29/1: 39–58.

—— —— —— (1994b). "The National Health Service Corps experience for rural physicians in the late 1980s." *Journal of the American Medical Association*, 272/17: 1341–8.

—— STEINER, B. D., JONES, B. D., and KONRAD, T. R. (1999). "Preparing and retaining rural physicians through medical education." *Academic Medicine*, 74/7: 810–20.

PAUL, C. (1984). "Physician licensure legislation and the quality of medical care." *Atlantic Economic Journal*, 12/4: 18–30.

PELTZMAN, S. (1976). "Toward a more general theory of regulation." *Journal of Law and Economics*, 19: 211–40.

—— (1989). "The economic theory of regulation after a decade of deregulation." *Brookings Papers on Economic Activity: Microeconomics*, Special Issue: 1–41.

POPOV, G. A. (1971). *Principles of health planning in the USSR*. Geneva, WHO.

POSNER, R. A. (1974). "Theories of Economic Regulation." *The Bell Journal of Economics and Management Science*, 5/2: 335–58.

PROBST, J. C., SAMUELS, M. E., SHAW, T. V., HART, G. L., and DALY, C. (2003). "The National Health Service Corps and Medicaid inpatient care: experience in a southern state." *Southern Medical Journal*, 96/8: 775–83.

RABINOWITZ, H. K. (1993). "Recruitment, retention, and follow-up of graduates of a program to increase the number of family physicians in rural and underserved areas." *New England Journal of Medicine*, 328/13: 934–9.

RABINOWITZ, H. K. DIAMOND, J. J., HOJAT, M., and HAZELWOOD, C. E. (1999a). "Demographic, educational and economic factors related to recruitment and retention of physicians in rural Pennsylvania." *Journal of Rural Health*, 15/2: 212–8.

—— —— MARKHAM, F. W., and HAZELWOOD, C. E. (1999b). "A program to increase the number of family physicians in rural and underserved areas: impact after 22 years." *Journal of the American Medical Association*, 281/3: 255–60.

—— —— and PAYNTER, N. P. (2001). "Critical factors for designing programs to increase the supply and retention of rural primary care physicians." *Journal of the American Medical Association*, 286/9: 1041–8.

—— —— and RABINOWITZ, C. (2005). "Long-term retention of graduates from a program to increase the supply of rural family physicians." *Academic Medicine*, 80/8: 728–32.

—— —— and WORTMAN, J. R. (2008). "Medical school programs to increase the rural physician supply: a systematic review and projected impact of widespread replication." *Academic Medicine*, 83/3: 235–43.

—— —— VELOSKI, J. J., and GAYLE, J. A. (2000). "The impact of multiple predictors on generalist physicians' care of underserved populations." *American Journal of Public Health*, 90/8: 1225–8.

RAYACK, E. (1967). *Professional Power and American Medicine*. Cleveland, World Publishing Company.

REID, S. J. (2001). "Compulsory community service for doctors in South Africa—an evaluation of the first year." *South African Medical Journal*, 91/4: 329–36.

RITTENHOUSE, D. R., FRYER, G. E., JR., PHILLIPS, R. L., JR., MIYOSHI, T., NIELSEN, C., GOODMAN, D. C., and GRUMBACH, K. (2008). "Impact of Title VII training programs on community health center staffing and National Health Service Corps participation." *Annals of Family Medicine*, 6/5: 397–405.

ROSENTHAL, T. C. (2000). "Outcomes of rural training tracks: a review." *Journal of Rural Health*, 16/3: 213–6.

ROSS, A. J. (2007). "Success of a scholarship scheme for rural students." *South African Medical Journal*, 97/11: 1087–90.

ROWE, A. and GARCIA-BARBERO, M. (2005). *Regulating and Licensing of Physicians in the WHO European Region*. Copenhagen, WHO Regional Office for Europe.

SCHNEIDER, U. and ULRICH, V. (2008). "The physician–patient relationship revisited: the patient's view." *International Journal of Health Care Finance and Economics*, 8: 279–300.

SCHÖNFELD, H. K., HESTON, J. F., and FALK, I. S. (1972). "Numbers of physicians required for primary medical care." *New England Journal of Medicine*, 286/11: 571–6.

SCHROEDER, S. A. (1984). "Western European responses to physician oversupply. Lessons for the United States." *Journal of the American Medical Association*, 252/3: 373–84.

SELDON, B. J., JUNG, C., and CAVAZOS, R. J. (1998). "Market power among physicians in the U.S., 1983–1991." *The Quarterly Review of Economics and Finance*, 38/4: 799–824.

SELVANATHAN, S. and SELVANATHAN, A. (1993). "A cross-country analysis of consumption patterns." *Applied Economics*, 25: 1245–59.

SHEPARD, L. (1978). "Licensing restrictions and the cost of dental care." *Journal of Law and Economics*, 21: 187–201.

SINGER, J. D., DAVIDSON, S. M., GRAHAM, S., and DAVIDSON, H. S. (1998). "Physician retention in community and migrant health centers: who stays and for how long?" *Medical Care*, 36/8: 1198–213.

SLOAN, F. A. and FELDMAN, R. (1978). Competition among physicians. in W. Greenberg (ed.), *Competition in the Health Care Sector*. Maryland, Aspen Systems Corporation.

—— and KASPER, H. (2008). *Incentives and Choice in Health Care*. Boston, MIT Press.

SMUCNY, J., BEATTY, P., GRANT, W., DENNISON, T., and WOLFF, L. T. (2005). "An evaluation of the Rural Medical Education Program of the State University Of New York Upstate Medical University, 1990–2003." *Academic Medicine*, 80/8: 733–8.

STIGLER, G. J. (1971). "The theory of economic regulation." *The Bell Journal of Economics and Management Science*, 2/1: 3–21.

STONE, D. A. (1997). "The doctor as businessman: the changing politics of a cultural icon." *J Health Polit Policy Law*, 22/2: 533–56.

SVORNY, S. V. (1987). "Physician licensure: a new approach to examining the role of professional interests." *Economic Inquiry*, XXV/497–509.

TUSSING, A. D. and WOJTOWYCZ, M. A. (1986). "Physician-induced demand by Irish GPs." *Social Science and Medicine*, 23/9: 851–60.

UNITED NATIONS (2009). United Nations Millennium Development Goals. (Available from: <http://www.un.org/millenniumgoals/, 10 April 2009>.)

WEEKS, W. B., WALLACE, A. E., WALLACE, M. M., and WELCH, H. G. (1994). "A comparison of the educational costs and incomes of physicians and other professions." *New England Journal of Medicine*, 330: 1280–6.

WHITE, W. D. (1978). "The impact of occupational licensure of clinical laboratory personnel." *Journal of Human Resources*, 13/1: 91–102.

WHO (WORLD HEALTH ORGANIZATION) (2006). *World Health Report 2006: Working Together for Health*. Geneva, WHO.

—— (2008). *Task Shifting: Rational Redistribution of Tasks Among Health Workforce Teams: Global Recommendations and Guidelines*. Geneva, WHO.

—— (2009). Global atlas of the health workforce. (Available from: <http://www.who.int/globalatlas/default.asp>, 12 September 2009.)

WILKINSON, B. (1966). "Present values of lifetime earning for different occupations." *Journal of Political Economy*, 74: 556–72.

WONG, H. S. (1996). "Market structure and the role of consumer information in the physician services industry: an empirical test." *Journal of Health Economics*, 15: 139–60.

WORLD BANK (1993). *World Development Report*. Washington, D.C., World Bank.

XU, G., FIELDS, S. K., LAINE, C., VELOSKI, J. J., BARZANSKY, B., and MARTINI, C. J. (1997a). "The relationship between the race/ethnicity of generalist physicians and their care for underserved populations." *American Journal of Public Health*, 87/5: 817–22.

—— VELOSKI, J. J., HOJAT, M., POLITZER, R. M., RABINOWITZ, H. K., and RATTNER, S. (1997b). "Factors influencing physicians' choices to practice in inner-city or rural areas." *Academic Medicine*, 72/12: 1026.

ZIJLSTRA, E. E. and BROADHEAD, R. L. (2007). "The College of Medicine in the Republic of Malawi: towards sustainable staff development." *Human Resources for Health*, 5: 10.

CHAPTER 22

··

THE ECONOMICS OF THE BIOPHARMACEUTICAL INDUSTRY

··

PATRICIA M. DANZON

22.1 INTRODUCTION: KEY CHARACTERISTICS OF BIOPHARMACEUTICALS[1]

SPENDING on biopharmaceuticals has grown rapidly over the last two decades. This spending growth reflects technological advances that contribute significantly to human health but also pose novel challenges for policymakers. The US research-based biopharmaceutical industry invests 15–17 percent of sales in R&D, and the R&D cost of bringing a new compound to market is estimated at over $1bn. (DiMasi and Grabowski 2007). This research intensity underlies many of the unique features of this industry. First, regulation of the safety and efficacy of new drugs entails high costs, benefits and policy debate about the appropriate extent and structure of regulation. Second, the biopharmaceutical firm's cost structure has high, globally joint, fixed costs of R&D and low marginal costs of production. Patents are thus essential to enable innovator firms to recoup their R&D investments. But patents operate by limiting competition and enabling innovator firms to charge prices above marginal cost. Defining appropriate prices and patent terms, including criteria for post-patent generic entry, is problematic. The high price-marginal cost margin also creates strong incentives for promotion that has sometimes been viewed as inappropriate.

[1] The terms "biopharmaceuticals" and "pharmaceuticals" are used interchangeably to include both traditional pharmaceuticals and biologics, except where explicitly noted.

Alternatives to patents have been proposed (prizes, patent-buyouts, etc.) but all have implementation challenges.

Third, on the demand side consumer price sensitivity is undermined by physician prescribing, acting as agents for consumers who cannot readily evaluate the benefits and risks of pharmaceuticals, and by pervasive insurance coverage, to protect consumers against financial risk. Inelastic demand creates incentives for firms to charge higher prices than they would if consumers were informed decision-makers and faced full prices. To address the information asymmetries and insurance-induced distortions, private and public insurers in the US and other countries use a range of strategies to control patient and supplier moral hazard, including tiered formularies and patient cost sharing in the US and price or reimbursement controls in other countries. These third party payer controls significantly affect drug pricing, rates of uptake or diffusion of new products, the nature of competition between firms and ultimately profitability and incentives for R&D to supply new medicines.

Fourth, the global nature of pharmaceutical R&D raises issues of appropriate cross-national price differentials and cost sharing. National regulators have incentives to free-ride, driving domestic prices to country-specific marginal cost, leaving others to pay for the joint costs of R&D. The long R&D lead times—on average roughly twelve years from drug discovery to product approval—make the incentives for short run free-riding by individual countries particularly acute because negative effects will be delayed for years and hard to attribute. While the principle of differential pricing between the richest and poorest nations is widely accepted, consensus breaks down on appropriate price levels and differentials, particularly for middle-income countries with emerging middle classes but large poor populations. In practice, the ability of pharmaceutical firms to price discriminate is undermined by government policies that regulate domestic prices by referencing foreign prices, adoption of most-favored-nation clauses, and legalization of drug importation (also called parallel trade or international exhaustion of patent rights). These cross-national price spillovers in turn create incentives for firms to delay or not launch new drugs in low price markets, if these low prices would undermine potentially higher prices in other markets. Thus the design of each country's price regulatory system affects not only its prices and availability of drugs but also availability in other countries through price spillovers in the short run, and through R&D incentives in the long run.

Structurally, the on-patent phase of most pharmaceuticals can be viewed as oligopolistic with differentiated competitor products in the short run. In the longer run, the appropriate model for a therapeutic class is monopolistic competition, with generic entry on patent-expired older molecules and dynamic competition from newer, improved products as new therapeutic pathways are discovered. Despite high costs of drug discovery, over the last two decades thousands of small firms have been created around new R&D technologies or products. Many have exited as products fail, but new entry of firms and products continues to occur.

Although the biopharmaceutical industry is heavily regulated, the economic rationale for regulation is not structural barriers to competition. Rather, market access regulation is a response to imperfect and/or asymmetric information of consumers and physicians in evaluating the safety and efficacy of new products. Price and/or reimbursement regulations are a response to patents and insurance-related moral hazard. To the extent that market power exists, it is due in part to government-granted monopoly implied by patents. Both positive and normative analysis of product differentiation and pricing must take into account heterogeneity in patients' response to different drugs, and the roles of physician prescribing and third party payment as key determinants of demand elasticities. In this context, drawing welfare conclusions about optimal levels of R&D and product variety is complex. Most analysis to date and most discussion here is therefore positive rather than normative.

The structure of this chapter is as follows. Section 22.2 reviews R&D costs, regulation, productivity and incentives for innovation. Section 22.3 discusses market demand and pricing, effects of insurance, reimbursement regulation, alternatives to patents, and generics. Section 22.4 reviews trends in promotion, regulation of promotion and its effects. Section 22.5 discusses global issues, including differential pricing and R&D for neglected diseases. Section 22.6 concludes. The focus is on the US, as the largest single market (North America accounted for 45.9 percent of global pharmaceutical sales in 2007, compared to 31.1 percent for Europe) and the home of the largest number of multinational pharmaceutical and smaller biotech companies. Important differences in other countries' regulatory and reimbursement systems are noted, to the extent possible.

22.2 R&D: Technology, Regulation, and Costs

22.2.1 Technology

The pharmaceutical industry grew out of the chemical industry. Advances in basic science, medicine, and microbiology have enabled new generations of medicines to treat previously untreated diseases—for example, anti-ulcerants in the 1980s, antidepressants, and lipid lowering drugs (statins) in the 1990s, recombinant proteins and monoclonal antibodies more recently. The nature and potential of pharmaceutical R&D was revolutionized in the 1990s by advances in microbiology, informatics, genomics, and other sciences that are still evolving. Many of the basic science breakthroughs occurred in academic labs, often with government funding. In the US, the 1983 Bayh-Dole Act facilitated the commercialization of these discoveries, by enabling the transfer of IP rights to the private parties responsible for the innovation, subject to residual rights retained by government. This process continually spawns new start-up firms, which usually obtain venture capital and other private and public equity financing. Many are acquired by larger companies, seeking to acquire the new technologies and products. The most successful survive to become midsize and ultimately large biotech firms, such as Genentech,

Amgen, Gilead, etc. Thus the biotech revolution has revolutionized drug discovery and transformed industry structure.

22.2.2 Regulation of R&D and Market Access

Although the methods of drug discovery have changed, the process still proceeds through stages of lead identification, pre-clinical laboratory and animal testing, followed by small scale human trials to establish safety and proof of concept and ultimately large human clinical trials, often in thousands of patients, to prove safety and efficacy prior to drug approval. This process, culminating in drug approval, is regulated in the US by the Food and Drug Administration (FDA), by the European Medicines Evaluation Agency (EMEA) in Europe and by similar agencies in other countries that have evolved in similar ways. In the US, the 1938 Food, Drug and Cosmetics Act required any firm seeking to market a new chemical entity (NCE) to file a new drug application (NDA) to demonstrate that the drug was safe for use as suggested by the proposed labeling. The FDA had 180 days to reject the NDA. This Act also established jurisdiction over drug advertising and requirements that patients obtain a prescription from a physician in order to obtain retail drugs.

The 1962 Kefauver-Harris Amendments laid the ground rules of current FDA regulation. These Amendments strengthened safety requirements; added the requirement that drugs show proof of efficacy, usually by double blind, randomized controlled trials of the drug relative to placebo; removed the 180 day time limit within which the FDA could reject an NDA; extended FDA oversight of clinical testing and manufacturing; and restricted manufacturers' promotion to approved indications. Basic requirements for promotional materials include that they cannot be false or misleading; they must provide a fair balance of risks and benefits; and they must provide a "brief summary" of contraindications, side effects and effectiveness. The 2007 Amendments further strengthened the FDA's authority to grant conditional or restricted approval, subject to specified risk evaluation and monitoring systems.

The economic rationale for requiring pre-market proof of safety is that manufacturers may face suboptimal incentives to provide risk information to consumers in the absence of regulatory requirements. The requirement for pre-market proof of efficacy has been more controversial, given the high cost and launch delays associated with doing large Phase III trials required to establish efficacy and/or detect remote risks in subpopulations. The economic rationale for efficacy requirements is that imperfect information may prevent physicians and consumers from making accurate evaluations, leading to wasted expenditures on ineffective drugs and other associated costs, and possibly excessive product differentiation that undermines price competition. Firms may have incentives to exaggerate benefits and downplay risks in their promotion, given the high price-marginal cost margins. Moreover, setting standards and evaluating clinical trial evidence of efficacy and safety requires expertise and is a public good that can arguably be provided most efficiently by a single expert agency.

However, these pre-launch requirements for safety and efficacy also add significantly to the cost and delay of launching new drugs, raising concerns over barriers to entry and forgone benefits for consumers. Subsequent legislation has addressed some of these cost-increasing effects of the 1962 Amendments. The Orphan Drug Act of 1983 increased "pull and push subsidies" for drugs that receive orphan status (defined as conditions that affect less than 200,000 individuals in the US), including market exclusivity for seven years and a 50 percent tax credit for expenses accrued through clinical testing. Between 1983 and 1998, the number of orphan drugs increased five-fold, while the number of non-orphan drugs increased less than two-fold (Lichtenberg and Waldfogel 2003).

To accelerate FDA review of regulatory filings, under the Prescription Drug User Fee Act (PDUFA) of 1993[2] and subsequent renewals, pharmaceutical firms pay user fees that are used to fund additional FDA reviewers.[3] These user fees now account for about 50 percent of total processing costs at the FDA (US FDA 2005). The Priority Review system provides a six month target review time for new drugs that target unmet medical need, whereas "standard review" drugs have target review time of ten months. Fast Track status to further accelerate the approval of novel drugs that are "intended for the treatment of a serious or life-threatening condition" and "demonstrate the potential to address unmet medical needs for the condition" (US FDA 1997). Fast Track has reduced overall development times by approximately 2.5 years (Tufts Center for the Study of Drug Development 2003).

Harmonization of requirements of the US FDA and parallel agencies in the EU and Japan has enabled companies to prepare a common dossier, typically based on trials done in multiple countries, although some country-specific variations remain—for example, the EMEA typically requires comparison relative to current treatment rather than placebo and Japan requires trials on Japanese nationals—and each agency makes its own approval decision based on its evaluation of risks vs. benefits.

22.2.3 R&D Costs

The cost of developing an approved new medical entity (NME), measured as a discounted present value at launch, grew from $138 million in the 1970s to $802 MILLION in 2001 and over $1bn in 2007 (DiMasi and Grabowski 2007). This high cost per NME reflects three main factors: high input costs of discovery research, animal and human trials; high failure rates, including the great majority of preclinical candidates and over four out of five compounds that enter human trials; and the eight–twelve years required,

---

[2] This has subsequently been renewed three times as part of the Food and Drug Administration Modernization Act (1997) and subsequent legislation.

[3] The fee for review of data related to product approval was $767,400 for applications with new clinical data, $383,700 for supplemental applications or those with no new clinical data (for fiscal year 2006). There is also a fee for each manufacturing facility ($264,000) and an annual fee for the right to market products ($42,130) (FDA 2005a).

such that roughly half of the total cost per NME is forgone interest or capitalization cost. Although this capitalization cost is not an out-of-pocket expense to firms, it is an opportunity cost that must be returned to investors in order to attract capital.

Several factors have contributed to this growth in cost per NME and, inversely, to the implied declining R&D productivity. Clinical trial costs have risen, due to larger and longer trials, more procedures and higher cost per participant (DiMasi, Hansen, and Grabowski 2003). These trends reflect many factors, including: longer trials for drugs targeted at chronic diseases; higher costs of medical care and testing due to new medical technologies; higher failure rates on compounds that address novel targets (Aghazadeh, Boschwitz, Beever, and Arnould 2005); collection of economic data to satisfy payer demands for cost-effectiveness data; and heightened regulatory concerns to detect remote risks. Whether or not regulatory standards have increased is hard to distinguish from underlying changes in circumstances. As patents have expired on prior innovations, many of the mass, primary care diseases can be treated reasonably well with cheap generics, hence regulators and payers may require either high benefits or minimal risks on new drugs. Innovator firms have shifted R&D towards diseases with few existing treatment options, which are typically more complex, with less well understood biological pathways, such as Alzheimer's, cancer, obesity, and rheumatoid arthritis. Failure rates on drugs with novel mechanisms are higher than on drugs that address well-established targets, reflecting both safety and efficacy failures that sometimes are only manifest in the large scale, Phase III trials. Many of the successful innovative products are biologics, discovered by biotechnology firms. Despite rising R&D investments, large pharmaceutical firms have been unable to generate internally new drugs to replace their patent-expiring older drugs. Although large firms have aggressively acquired and inlicensed new products and technologies from biotech firms, many have seen dramatic declines in market capitalizations, and some consolidation.

22.2.4 Empirical Evidence on Costs and Benefits of Regulation

Measuring the costs and benefits of regulation requires identifying the counterfactual against which to compare actual experience. Early studies used intertemporal and cross-national comparators, which both require strong *ceteris paribus* assumptions. With that caveat, studies generally concluded that the 1962 Amendments, which raised safety standards and added efficacy requirements, increased costs for firms, added to delay in drug approval, and possibly reduced competition (for example, Grabowski, Vernon, and Thomas 1978). Peltzman's (1973) study of both benefits and costs of the 1962 Amendments concluded that the benefits were minimal and were far outweighed by the costs due to fewer new drugs. However, the methods and conclusions have been questioned (for example, Temin 1979). In particular, ascribing the 1960s decline in NCEs entirely to regulation, rather than to a short-term hiatus in scientific opportunities, may over-state the costs and under-state the safety improvements of the 1962 Amendments.

Several recent studies have examined the benefits and costs of the priority review policy introduced by PDUFA in 1992. The User Fee and Priority Review systems have clearly reduced review time: Between 1993 and 2003 the median time to approval for "priority" drugs declined from 14.9 to 6.7 months, while review times for "standard" products only decreased from 27.2 to 23.1 months (Okie 2005). At issue is whether faster review led to approval of more risky products, and hence contributed to increased post-launch adverse drug reactions and some recalls. Olson (2004a) finds that post-launch reports of adverse drug reactions were more likely for drugs that the FDA rates as "priority," but that these safety costs were outweighed by the benefits of a faster launch due to priority review, assuming Lichtenberg's (2002) estimate of gain in life expectancy due to new drugs. However, costs may be under-estimated, given subsequent evidence of under-reporting of adverse events through the FDA's post-marketing surveillance mechanisms (Brewer and Colditz 1999; Bennett, Nebeker, et al. 2005). By contrast, the General Accounting Office (US GAO 2002b) found that drug withdrawals rates differed insignificantly between the period before and after the PDUFA; however, this study did not control for other factors that may have influenced drug withdrawals rates. Philipson, Berndt, Gottschalk and Sun (2008) consider the speed-safety trade-off induced by PDUFA and conclude that net welfare effects were significantly positive.

While accelerating regulatory review plausibly has positive net effects, provided it remains adequately resourced, reducing the duration of Phase III trials raises more fundamental trade-offs between risk reduction and prompt access to new drugs. Whether this trade-off should be framed more rigorously in terms of net expected QALYs gained is a fundamental question that has not been widely addressed. However, significant progress is underway on trying to improve the trade-off by initially restricting launch to more controlled environments and by supplementing pre-launch randomized controlled trials with post-launch observational evidence. The 2007 FDA Amendments Act authorized the FDA to condition approval on risk evaluation and mitigation strategies, such as post-launch monitoring requirements through patient registries and approvals limited to patient subgroups with greatest medical need. Such restrictions may increase FDA willingness to approve new drugs earlier. In addition, advances in statistical methods for analyzing claims and other data from routine care, to adjust for possible nonrandom assignment of patients to different treatments, offers a potentially rich and relatively cheap source of information that could supplement clinical trial data, providing larger sample sizes, detail on subpopulations and evidence on long term effects without delaying access to new drugs. Such approaches are critical to efficiently detect rare safety issues and identify subpopulations at risk for adverse effects or non-response. Over time, accumulation of evidence and understanding of heterogeneity in patient response to drugs, based on genetic and other biomarkers, should eventually enhance the safety and efficacy of approved drugs, reduce R&D failure rates and costs, and advance the goal of "personalized medicine."

Although charges that the FDA is "captured" by the industry are common in popular media, standard economic models of producer vs. consumer capture of the regulatory process appear to be less relevant than current events and crises in explaining the shifting regulatory emphasis between safety and speed to market. For example, public and Congressional concerns focused on speeding up access to new drugs in the 1980s and 1990s, partly in response to the AIDS crisis. More recently, post-launch evidence on risks of some widely used drugs, including the COX-2 inhibitors for arthritis and pain (notably rofecoxib (Vioxx) and valdecoxib (Bextra)), the SNRI anti-depressants and others have led to a range of proposals and initiatives to enhance regulation of safety. Some argue that an effective oversight board should be independent of the FDA as the approving agency (for example, Okie 2005) to avoid industry capture. On the other hand, given the FDA's limited resources and vast responsibilities, there is a strong case for co-ordination of pre- and post-launch monitoring to take advantage of expertise and econ-omies of scale in reviewing data and assuring consistency.

22.2.5 Regulation vs. Markets vs. Tort Liability

Some have argued that consumers should be permitted to make their own evaluations of risks vs. benefits based on phase II trials (Madden 2004).[4] However, phase II trials are small, designed to provide proof of concept and preliminary dose-ranging evidence of safety and efficacy in select patient subgroups. Such trials lack the statistical power to provide credible results for general decision-making. A specialized agency such as the FDA accumulates expertise and provides a public good in evaluating the evidence on safety and efficacy, including requiring that minimum standards and reasonable trade-offs be met as a condition of launch. Such information would be under-provided in a free market regime and cannot be efficiently assessed from the personal experience of individual physicians or even health plans, both of which have more limited informa-tion and expertise than the FDA and may be imperfect agents, given their financial stakes, respectively, in prescribing and controlling drug spending.

The expanded range of drug therapy and growth of insurance coverage have increased the social benefit of having a regulatory agency review and establish minimum standards for marketed drugs. When consumers paid out-of-pocket and few drugs were available, the main benefit of a regulatory requirement for efficacy was to protect consumers from wastefully spending their own money on useless drugs. Given the expansion in number and complexity of drugs available, with many consumers taking multiple prescriptions for chronic diseases, the information burden of staying informed and the potential cost of being misinformed have increased, as has the potential for adverse drug reactions and interactions. The growth of insurance coverage has also undermined individual consum-er's financial incentives to avoid wasteful spending on drugs that are of low or only minor benefit. These trends increase the public good case for a regulatory agency such as the FDA to establish minimum standards of safety, efficacy, and quality as a condition of market access. Similar arguments might also be applied to limit reimbursement to approved indi-

---

[4] Post-launch efficacy trials would be required with results posted on the internet, for consumers to make their own evaluations (Madden 2004).

cations, as occurs in most countries with national or social insurance systems. By contrast, in the US both Medicare and private health plans so far generally reimburse for off-label use, provided it is supported by published studies as listed in medical compendia.

A related question is the optimal role of tort liability, given regulation. The FDA is an expert agency that relies on internal specialists and external advisory panels comprised of medical and statistical experts who review and evaluate comprehensive data on risks and benefits. Their decisions should in theory be better informed, more consistent across drugs and more able to balance societal risks and benefits than the untrained juries that decide tort claims. Moreover, tort claims focus on adverse outcome to an identified patient, who may have had competing medical and life-style risk factors, rather than average effects for patients at large. For example, if the FDA decided that a 1 percent risk of an adverse outcome from a drug was acceptable in view of its benefits, how does a jury decide whether an individual patient's adverse event is within this 1 percent, in which case the firm should not be liable, or lies outside the 1 percent, in which case the drug may be less safe than expected and the firm should be liable? More generally, notions of a "defective product" under strict product liability or "negligent product design" in a negligence claim, are problematic when applied to drugs for which it may be prohibitively costly to identify patients at risk of adverse response. Unclear standards lead to erratic and unpredictable liability rulings, in which case incentives for safety are likely to be excessive (Craswell and Calfee 1986). Moreover, tort decisions made ex post, after a drug has been on the market, are at risk of applying new information retroactively, holding a firm liable for a rare adverse effect that only emerges after widespread or long-term use of the drug, which could not reasonably have been foreseen without undue costs and delay of pre-launch testing that would deprive other patients of access. However the Supreme Court recently struck down the claim of pre-emption, that the FDA's regulatory approval protects companies against liability when the agency's instructions are followed, because the FDA has not expressly been given pre-emption by Congress.[5]

22.3 INDUSTRY STRUCTURE, COMPETITION, PRICING, AND PRICE REGULATION

22.3.1 Industry Structure and Competition

The pharmaceutical industry is structurally competitive, with relatively low overall concentration and continual entry of new firms and products. Patents constitute a government-granted barrier to generic competition for the term of the patent, in order to enable innovators to recoup R&D investments. However, over time firms are subject to both intermolecular and intra-molecular competition. Specifically, dynamic

---

[5] *Wyeth vs. Levine* (2009).

competition exploits and pushes scientific advance, such that within each therapeutic class there are typically several similar but differentiated, competing compounds that are ultimately challenged by generics and by dynamic competition from new, improved originator products. Number of competitor compounds in a class depends on the size of the market (Acemoglu and Linn 2004) but successive entry occurs increasingly rapidly. The period of market exclusivity of first entrants to a new therapeutic class fell from 10.2 years in the 1970s to 1.2 years in the late 1990s (DiMasi and Paquette 2004).

Price competition between on-patent brands (intermolecular) is muted by two institutional characteristics: physician prescribing and insurance coverage. Theory suggests that the separation of prescribing from consumption reduces demand elasticity if physicians are imperfectly informed about drug prices and/or are imperfect agents for patients (assuming no payer controls). The limited evidence from the UK and Germany suggests that placing physicians at risk for drug spending through indicative budgets increases price sensitivity, mainly through greater use of generics, but may also lead to inappropriate rationing.[6]

More fundamentally, insurance coverage undermines patients' price-sensitivity, hence makes the demand facing manufacturers more price-inelastic. This creates incentives for firms to charge higher prices and patients to use more (and/or more costly) drugs, unless payers adopt controls. Consumer cost-sharing can mitigate this tendency for insurance to induce producer and consumer moral hazard, but only by reducing financial protection for patients, which may have undesirable efficiency and equity effects unless cost-sharing is appropriately income-adjusted.

To counteract this price-increasing tendency of insurance, both private and public insurers use a range of strategies to either encourage competition or constrain prices directly. In fact, the structure of insurance reimbursement has become the major determinant of competition and pricing strategies for pharmaceuticals. Conclusions on the extent and nature of price competition may therefore be specific to particular insurance arrangements, as are estimates of demand elasticity.

22.3.2 Pricing and Reimbursement in the US

In the US, private insurers and pharmacy benefit managers (PBMs) establish three- or four-tier formularies of preferred drugs, with higher co-payments for higher tiers—for example, $5 for a generic, $25 for a preferred brand, $45 for a non-preferred brand and 25 percent coinsurance for the fourth tier. The tiered co-payments shift utilization towards drugs on lower tiers. This ability to shift market share enables PBMs to negotiate price discounts from manufacturers in return for preferred formulary placement.

---

[6] From 1993–2001, Germany had a drug spending limit with over-runs in principle to be repaid partly by physicians and the pharmaceutical industry. Physicians responded by reducing prescription volume and switching to cheaper drugs (Munnich and Sullivan 1994), and by referring patients to hospitals that were exempt from the spending limit (Schulenburg et al. 1994).

Medicare (the public program for seniors) added Part D to provide outpatient drug coverage under the Medicare Modernization Act (2003). Seniors can choose among private prescription drug plans (PDPs) that are similar to PBMs and use similar formulary structures to negotiate drug price discounts. Under the "non-interference" clause of the Medicare Modernization Act, the federal government is barred from negotiating drug prices, although this may change. Thus formulary design, whereby PBMs, PDPs, and other payers induce competitive discounting, is the main mechanism for constraining prices on pharmacy-dispensed outpatient drugs in the US. Discounts are confidential in order to preserve competitive incentives. Although comprehensive evidence on effects of formularies on drug prices is unavailable, theory and anecdotal evidence suggest that competitive discounting is effective in therapeutic classes with several, closely substitutable drugs, but that it is less effective in specialty classes, including most biologics, where clinical differences between drugs limit payers' ability to constrain physician/patient choices.

Competitive price discounting has also been constrained by the "best price" provision for Medicaid, the public program for certain low income groups. Under the 1990 Omnibus and Reconciliation Act, originator drugs must give Medicaid the lower of (a) the "best price" offered to any non-federal purchaser or (b) a 15.1 percent discount off AMP (the average manufacturer price to the retail sector), plus an "excess-inflation" rebate for price increases greater than the CPI (to deter firms from raising AMP in response to the best price provision). For 2003, the combined effect of these mandatory discounts resulted in an average 31.4 percent discount for Medicaid, relative to AMP (CBO 2005b). By tying Medicaid rebates to discounts given to private payers, the Medicaid best price provision limits the ability of manufacturers to price discriminate, which led to a decline in discounts to private payers (GAO 1993; CBO 1996). The MMA explicitly exempted discounts granted to Medicare PDPs from the Medicaid Best Price provision, to encourage deep discounts to PDPs. Duggan and Scott Morton (2006) found that drugs with larger Medicaid market share had larger price increases.[7]

Many cancer drugs and other biologics that require infusion in a physician's office are reimbursed under Medicare Part B or the medical benefit of private plans. Since 2005 Medicare pays physicians the manufacturer's volume-weighted Average Sales Price (ASP), plus 6 percent to cover storage and handling. This reimbursement approach creates perverse incentives for physicians to prefer high-priced products and hence for manufacturers to compete by charging high rather than lower prices (Danzon, Wilensky, and Means 2005). This system will also undermine potential savings from follow-on biologics, unless such follow-on products are classified under the same reimbursement code as the originator product, in which case firms may have an incentive to discount to physicians, which would in turn reduce subsequent calculations of ASPs.

---

[7] As a proxy for price to private payers, they use the average price paid by Medicaid, which is a percent of a list price. They report that, in a limited sample of drugs, the log of this price is highly correlated with the log of a better measure of transactions price to private payers.

22.3.3 Price Regulation and Competition Ex-US

In most industrialized countries with universal national health insurance schemes, the government (or a surrogate) regulates prices or reimbursement for drugs as for other medical services. Price controls generally only apply if the product is reimbursed, consistent with the view that pharmaceutical price regulation is fundamentally an insurance strategy to control potential supplier pricing moral hazard. Patient co-payments are often modest and invariant to the drug price. Firms thus have little incentive to price below the regulated price except for sales to hospitals, where tendering is common and prices are reportedly often below regulated prices.

The theoretically optimal insurance/reimbursement contract for drugs must deter both insurance-induced over-use by patients and excessive prices by manufacturers, while paying prices sufficient to reward appropriate R&D, taking into account the global scope of pharmaceutical sales. Models by Lackdawalla and Sood (2005), Garber and Romer (2006), Jena and Phillipson (2008), and Danzon, Towse and Ferrandiz (2011) address some of these issues. An important conclusion is that patient cost sharing alone cannot simultaneously provide optimal incentives for efficient use of drugs, control of patient moral hazard and optimal provider incentives for R&D. In addition, given the global nature of pharmaceutical utilization, creating optimal R&D incentives require appropriate price differentials across countries (Danzon and Towse 2003; Danzon, Towse and Ferrandiz 2011). In practice, many countries also regulate conditions of patient access and total drug spending.

In regulating drug price and/or reimbursement, most countries use some form of either *internal* or *external* benchmarking (for more detail see Danzon and Keuffel 2007, Danzon 2011).[8]

Internal benchmarking. This compares the price of the new drug to prices of other drugs in the same class, with potential mark-ups for improved efficacy, side effect profile or convenience, and sometimes for local production. An extreme variant of internal benchmarking is *Reference Price (RP) Reimbursement*. Generic RP clusters products based on the same compound, and is widely used for off-patent products. Therapeutic RP, as implemented in Germany, the Netherlands, and New Zealand, clusters products with the same or similar mode of action and/or same indication. All products in an RP group are reimbursed at the same reference price, which is usually based on a low priced product within the group. If manufacturers charge prices above the RP, the patient must pay the difference, and in practice prices usually converge to the reference price.

Internal benchmarking and, in particular, reference price reimbursement systems, differ in stringency, depending on whether reimbursement groups are broadly defined, regardless of differences in efficacy, dosing convenience and formulations, and patent

---

[8] Although some countries, including Italy, have attempted to base prices on costs, this approach is not widely used because accurate measurement of costs is problematic, particularly for R&D. R&D cost occurs over many years, should in principle include the cost of failures and forgone interest, and is largely a joint cost that must be allocated across global markets. In practice, cost-based price regulation has relied on transfer pricing rules which were designed for tax purposes, not price regulation.

status. In particular, if therapeutic reference groups disregard patent status, patent expiry on the oldest compound in a class can reduce reimbursement for later on-patent products in the group to the price of a cheap generic, effectively truncating patent life for late entrants unless patients recognize and are willing to pay surcharges for product improvements. Such reimbursement systems would significantly reduce incentives for R&D for later entrants and improved formulations of existing drugs, if applied in major pharmaceutical markets such as the US. Whether this would be welfare-enhancing, by eliminating wasteful R&D, or welfare-reducing, by eliminating potentially cost-effective new drugs and reducing competition, is probably context-specific and cannot be predicted a priori.

External benchmarking. External benchmarking caps the price of the new drug in country A to that same drug's mean, median or minimum price in specified comparator countries. For example, Italy uses an average European price, Canada uses the median of seven countries, etc. Thus external benchmarking limits the manufacturer's ability to price discriminate across countries. In cases where relatively high price countries reference lower price countries, theory and evidence suggest that such policies lead manufacturers to seek higher prices in low-price countries and delay or forgo launch, particularly in small markets, until higher prices have been established in the referencing countries (Danzon, Wang, and Wang 2005; Kyle 2005; Lanjouw 2005; Danzon and Epstein 2009). Parallel trade, which is legal in the EU, similarly creates incentives for manufacturers to seek higher prices as a condition of launch in lower-price EU markets, unless such trade can be deterred through supply limits and other mechanisms.

External referencing by high-price countries thus imposes a welfare loss in lower-price, referenced countries, contributing to launch lags and non-launch and/or higher prices. More generally, regulatory systems that induce price convergence across countries are likely to reduce social welfare. This assumes that price discrimination is welfare-increasing, compared to uniform pricing for pharmaceuticals, because utilization declines under uniform pricing as low-income countries and subgroups drop out of the market (Danzon and Towse 2003, 2005; Jack and Lanjouw 2003). Moreover, Ramsey pricing principles suggest that differential pricing also contributes to dynamic efficiency (Ramsey 1927; Baumol and Bradford 1970). Recent use of MFN clauses by some middle income countries and US proposals to legalize commercial drug importation from a broad group of countries could, if implemented, have serious negative effects on price and availability of drugs in referenced countries. Thus whereas the welfare effects of country-specific price regulation are ambiguous a priori, assuming regulators internalize (most of) the costs and benefits, welfare effects are clearly negative from regulatory systems that attempt to control one country's prices by referencing prices or importing drugs from other countries.

Drug Budgets and Expenditure Controls. Some countries have augmented price/reimbursement controls with expenditure caps on total drug spending to a target percent of health care spending—for example, France and Italy. Over-runs are recouped by price cuts or mandatory rebates from companies and/or drug classes that exceed allowed targets and/or allowed promotion guidelines.

22.3.4 Cost-Effectiveness Requirements for Reimbursement

Evaluation of the comparative effectiveness and cost-effectiveness of a new drug relative to current treatment is a condition of reimbursement in Australia, Canada, and
the UK (for most drugs) and an input to price and/or reimbursement negotiations in
many other countries. Drug cost generally includes any offsets in other medical costs,
and sometimes other societal costs such as care-giver time. Outcomes measures and
decision rules differ across countries. For example, the UK National Institute for
Clinical Excellence (NICE) generally uses cost per quality adjusted life year (QALY).
Although the CE review process is usually separate from the price control process, if
any, applying a CE threshold effectively constrains the price that can be charged for a
new drug, given its relative efficacy and cost of comparator treatment. Regulating
prices indirectly through a review of cost-effectiveness is in theory consistent with
principles of efficient resource allocation (Danzon, Towse and Ferrandiz 2011), in
contrast to other criteria used to regulate drug prices. However, many theoretical and
practical details of implementation remain unresolved, including: appropriate measurement of benefits, particularly for life-threatening treatments such as cancer; appropriate thresholds; and how to adapt decisions post-launch, as more data on costs and
outcomes accumulate.

22.3.5 Evidence of Effects of Price Regulation

Estimating effects of drug price regulation is confounded by the heterogeneity of such
systems and by other unobservable country-specific characteristics. Estimates of cross-
national drug prices indexes vary significantly, depending on the time period, sample of
drugs, the price index methodology, consumption weights and exchange rates. Many
price comparisons have been biased by focusing on small, non-random samples of
branded drugs only, and have not used standard index number methods (for example,
GAO 1992, 1994). The exclusive focus on branded drugs tends to bias comparisons in
favor of countries with strict price regulation, because more regulated markets have traditionally had lower brand prices but smaller generic market shares and higher generic
prices. Overall, countries that use direct price controls do not consistently have lower
prices than countries that use other indirect means to constrain prices (Danzon and
Chao, 2000a and 2000b; Danzon and Furukawa 2003, 2006, 2008). Drug price differences among industrialized countries are roughly consistent with differences in per capita income, which may be consistent with optimal differential pricing (see section 22.4
below).

Although theory suggests that drug price regulation may affect prices, launch timing
and R&D, measuring such effects for specific price control regimes is problematic,
because each country's regulations are different, often multidimensional and change
over time. For example, Germany adopted RP for some classes starting in 1989, but new

patented drugs were excluded from 1996 to 2004. Germany also had variants of physician drug budgets, intermittent price controls on non-referenced drugs, and changing requirements for pharmacies to substitute generics. Moreover, the effects of RP or other regulatory strategies on R&D depend on the adopting country's share of global sales, because R&D incentives depend on global expected revenues. In particular, effects of regulatory regimes on R&D have so far probably been modest, compared to the likely effects if the US were to adopt, say, therapeutic RP, given the large US share of global revenues and its low-priced generics (Danzon and Ketcham 2004).

The early literature on RP is summarized in Lopez-Casasnovas and Puig-Junoy (2000). Early evidence from Germany confirmed that brand drugs generally dropped their prices when RP was introduced. However, both theory and evidence suggest that dynamic price competition over time was weak, because firms have no incentive to reduce prices below the RP, unless other provisions make pharmacists price sensitive (Danzon and Ketcham 2004). Although RP has been compared to premium support subsidies for insurance, this analogy is imperfect because unlike premium support subsidies, RP is not risk-adjusted for patients and RP may have significant R&D effects.

22.3.6 Generics

After patent expiration of the originator brand, entry of generics can lead to intense price competition and significant savings for payers/consumers, depending on critical regulatory and reimbursement details. In the US, generics now account for almost seventy percent of all prescriptions but only about 16 percent of sales, due to their low prices. Although US prices for on-patent drugs are on average 20–40 percent higher in the US than in other industrialized countries, US generic prices are lower (Danzon and Furukawa 2008), due to US regulatory and reimbursement conditions that align to promote intense price competition. First, the 1984 Hatch-Waxman Patent Term Restoration and Generic Competition Act established the Abbreviated New Drug Application (ANDA) process, which permits generic approval on proof of same active ingredient and bio-equivalence to the originator, without new clinical trials. The generic can simply reference the originator's safety and efficacy data, once its five-year data exclusivity has lapsed.[9] Moreover, the Bolar Amendment permits generic companies to start work before expiry of the originator's patents, so generics can enter promptly once patents expire or are successfully challenged (see below). Thus the Hatch-Waxman Act dramatically reduced the time and cost required for generic entry and, by requiring bio-equivalence, established clinical conditions necessary for substitutability.

Second, all states have established default substitution rules that allow pharmacists to substitute a bioequivalent generic for the originator brand, even if the physician prescribes the brand, unless the physician specifically notes "brand required." This substitution rule makes the pharmacist the decision-maker with respect to whether and which generic to

---

[9] The EU allows ten years of data exclusivity (Kuhlik 2004).

dispense, subject to patient acceptance.[10] Since US generics are required to be bioequivalent, quality can be assumed and price is key to pharmacy choice. Public and private payers typically reimburse pharmacies a fixed amount (Maximum Allowable Cost, or MAC), regardless of which generically equivalent product is dispensed, and the MAC is based on the price of a low-price generic. Pharmacies capture the margin between their MAC reimbursement and their acquisition cost. Pharmacies therefore have strong incentives to dispense the cheapest generics, which in turn creates incentives for generic suppliers to compete on price. Generic price competition has been intensified by the consolidation of retail pharmacies into large national chains, such as Walgreens or Rite-Aid, which purchase at corporate levels. Similarly, independent pharmacies purchase through group purchasing organizations. Generic suppliers compete for the business of these high-volume customers through low prices, broad product range and prompt availability of new generics. Brand image is irrelevant for FDA-approved generics that are certified bioequivalent. Thus in the US generics companies do not invest in sales force, promotion or brand.

Finally, most health plans create strong financial incentives for patients to accept generics by placing generics on the lowest formulary tier, with a $0–$10 co-pay, while off-patent brands are on the third or fourth tier with a $40–$50 co-pay or not covered. This co-pay spread has increased over time and has contributed to generic share growth.

Whereas generics in the US are pharmacy-driven, unbranded, and cheap, generic markets in many EU and Latin American countries were traditionally physician-driven. Generics in physician-driven markets tend to be branded, heavily promoted and higher priced. These high-price, branded generics survive in markets that lack the regulatory and reimbursement conditions for price-competitive generics, specifically: bioequivalence; pharmacy substitution as the default rule; financial incentives for pharmacies to substitute low-price generics; and patient incentives to accept generics. Until recently, many European countries authorized pharmacy substitution only if the physician prescribed by generic name, which is uncommon. Moreover, countries that regulate drug prices traditionally also regulated pharmacy dispensing margins as a percent of the drug price, which creates perverse incentives for pharmacists to prefer higher priced products, even if they are authorized to substitute. Moreover, patient co-payments are often invariant to the price of the drug dispensed. In such contexts, generic companies behave like originator products, detailing their brand to physician decision-makers, competing on brand rather than price, which results in relatively high generic prices and often low generic shares (Danzon and Furukawa 2011). Several EU countries have recently changed their regulations, to encourage generic uptake and reduce generic prices. For example, German sickness funds now negotiate discounts directly from generic suppliers, and pharmacies must dispense these preferred generics.

Many middle and lower income countries that were late in adopting the World Trade Organization's Trade Related Intellectual Property (TRIP) regime grandfathered existing "copy products" that claim "similarity" but have not demonstrated bioequivalence to

---

[10] Substitution is not permitted on a few drugs for which any slight change in patient response could be critical.

the originator product. Since quality is uncertain, generic substitution by pharmacies is generally not authorized (although it may occur in practice), and generics market to physicians, competing on brand as a surrogate for reliability, rather than price. The unfortunate result is that many middle and low income countries have relatively high generic prices (Danzon and Furukawa 2008) and uncertain generic quality.

Incentives for early generic entry are greater in the US than in other countries because of the Hatch-Waxman provision, that a generic that successfully challenges the originator's patents (a paragraph IV filing), rather than waiting for the patents to expire, obtains 180 days' exclusivity as the sole generic in the market. Since the sole generic can gain significant market share and profits while shadow-pricing the brand, generic companies invest aggressively in challenging brand patents. Originator firms often issue "authorized generics" to compete during this 180-day exclusivity period. Patent challenges have spawned extensive litigation between generic and originator firms. The circumstances in which originators can legally settle with generic challengers and, more generally, optimal incentives for patent challenges, remain important issues.

Originator brands' options in responding to post-patent generic entry depends on regulatory rules and the nature of competition. In the US pharmacy-driven generic market, originator strategies to produce their own generics have been unsuccessful (other than authorized generics during the exclusivity period) because originator firms lack the major generic firms' large portfolio of products and low costs, which are essential for competing for pharmacy customers.[11] Other originator strategies include: shifting patients to a follow-on formulation (usually a delayed release version of the original drug) or a related product (such as a single isomer version); raising price to the price-inelastic brand-loyal segment (Frank and Salkever 1992); or switching the drug to over-the-counter status, if it can be shown to be safe and effective under patient self-medication.

Empirical studies of generic entry have shown, not surprisingly, that generic prices are inversely related to number of generic competitors (Grabowski and Vernon 1992); generic entry is more likely for compounds with large markets (measured by pre-expiry brand revenue), chronic disease markets (price sensitive patients) and oral-solid (pill) form (Scott Morton 1999; Scott Morton 2000). Caves, Whinston, and Hurwitz (1991) found that total volume did not increase after patent expiration, presumably because the positive effect of lower price is offset by the elimination of promotion at patent expiry, as substitutability erodes the promoter's return on investment. Scott Morton (2000) finds no significant generic deterrent effect of incumbent advertising via detailing or journal advertising from two–three years prior to generic entry. This is unsurprising, given that such advertising targets physicians, whereas pharmacists make the generic substitution decision, in response to price and other financial incentives.

For biologics, the manufacturing process involves live organisms and complex processes. The abbreviated approval process, that simply requires bioequivalence and referencing of the originator's clinical trials, is therefore not available to generic biologics.

---

[11]   The major exception is Novartis, whose Sandoz generic division is a broad scale and global generic producer.

Rather than require complete de novo clinical trials, the EMEA has adopted guidelines for an abbreviated approval pathway for follow-on biologics that relates requirements to product-specific complexity, and a similar approach was authorized in 2010 for the US. The expected outcome is that follow-on biologics will have some, albeit reduced clinical trial requirements and, in the US, originator biologics will receive a 12-year data exclusivity period compared to the five years for chemical drugs, although both types receive ten years in the EMEA. Follow-on biologics will also have higher manufacturing costs than most chemical drugs and may not be treated as substitutable by payers. Thus originator biologics are unlikely to face the almost certain and complete generic erosion faced by originator chemical drugs in the US. Moreover, whether follow-on biologics yield significant savings to payers/patients will depend on whether they are coded as substitutable by payers and by confidence of physicians and patients, which may take time. In the US, given the current perverse reimbursement incentives for dispensing physicians to prefer more costly drugs, significant savings from follow-on biologics are unlikely unless these reimbursement rules are changed to encourage use of cheaper products, given comparable quality.

22.3.7 Profitability and Rates of Return

The pharmaceutical industry is widely perceived to earn excessive profits. Accurate measurement of pharmaceutical profits has no easy solution. Available accounting data treat R&D as a current expense that offsets current, country-specific revenues, rather than as an investment in a long-lived intangible asset that may generate revenues in global markets over a ten–twenty-year product life. Adjusting accounting data to treat R&D and promotion as investments reduced accounting rates of return to levels comparable to other industries (Clarkson 1996).

As an alternative approach, Caves, Whinston, and Hurwitz (1991) estimated the Lerner index, proxied by the ratio of the price of originator drugs relative to generic prices (a proxy for marginal cost), at roughly five. However, this price-marginal cost estimate at patent expiry over-states the average Lerner index over the life-cycle because prices of originator drugs rise in the US and marginal costs decline with time since launch. More fundamentally, a one-year Lerner index based on short-run marginal production cost in one country is both theoretically and empirically inadequate as a measure of profit for global products with high and long-lived R&D investments.

A third—and conceptually more correct approach—measures the rate of return on investment in a cohort of drugs, using discounted cash flow estimates of costs and returns. Grabowski and Vernon (1990) and Grabowski et al. (2002) estimate the return on R&D for new drugs introduced in the 1970s, early 1980s and 1990s, respectively. Market sales data are used to estimate the net present value of sales over a twenty-year product life of global sales. Comparing this NPV of net revenues to the estimated average capitalized cost of R&D per NCE, at launch, Grabowski and Vernon conclude that the 1970s drug cohort on average earned a return roughly equal to its cost of capital, whereas the

1980s and 1990s cohorts show a small, positive excess return. The returns distribution is consistently highly skewed, with only the top 30 percent of drugs covering the average R&D cost. This extreme result would be mitigated if the distribution of revenues were compared to the distribution of R&D costs, rather than to a single mean R&D cost per NCE, but the overall conclusion of skewed return distribution would probably remain.

This evidence that pharmaceutical R&D investments on average earn a roughly normal rate-of-return is consistent with the theoretical prediction that, if the expected return on R&D exceeded the cost of capital, competitive entry would occur until the excess expected profit is eliminated. Such competitive adjustments are neither instantaneous nor perfect, due to the long lead times and unpredictable outcomes of R&D, and unpredictable competitive and regulatory conditions. But given the evidence of extensive competitive entry to exploit R&D opportunities, dynamic competition should reduce *expected* profits to competitive levels. This suggests that in designing policy, regulators should focus less on short run profitability measures and more on whether the resulting rate of R&D yields a level and mix of new drugs that is socially optimal. The current trend of payers to demand evidence of cost-effectiveness relative to existing drugs as a condition for reimbursement, reinforces incentives for manufacturers to target R&D towards innovative therapies and away from imitative drugs. Given R&D uncertainties, ex post realizations will still yield some "me-too" drugs, and some of these have value as a competitive constraint and in improving therapies for some subsets of patients.

22.3.8 Industry Structure and Productivity: Regulation or Technology?

Several early studies (for example, Grabowski 1976, Grabowski and Vernon 1978, Temin 1979, and Thomas 1990) concluded that regulation-induced increases in R&D cost and risk created scale economies that resulted in concentration of innovation in large firms and exit of smaller firms.

However, since the 1980s and 1990s the biotechnology revolution has apparently eliminated any advantages of size in drug discovery and shifted the balance of power in the industry to smaller firms that create innovation. Large firms have continued to grow mainly by acquiring such biotechnology firms or their products, and by large horizontal mergers with other medium and large firms. In the 1990s firms often rationalized horizontal mergers on grounds of economies of scale and scope in R&D, but the empirical evidence does not support claims for gains from mergers on average, after controlling for the condition of firms that chose to merge (Danzon, Epstein, and Nicholson 2007). Larger firms' experience does have some advantage in conducting complex phase III trials for regulatory approval (Danzon, Nicholson, and Pereira 2005). In theory, smaller firms can purchase such expertise through contract research, sales and manufacturing organizations and/or by hiring experienced personnel from larger firms. A growing number of biotechnology firms have grown to be fully-integrated firms. Thus increased regulatory requirements over the last two decades do not appear to have harmed small firms, and technological change has certainly benefited them. Moreover, competition for promising products developed by smaller discovery firms is strong and prices paid for such products have risen over the last decade, reflecting the shifting of bargaining power from large to smaller firms (Longman 2004; Longman 2006).

Theory might suggest that the high rate of new start-ups in this industry reflects excessive entry as firms compete for profits in a differentiated products oligopoly, and that such entry is welfare reducing due to the repeated initial costs associated with achieving reasonable scale. However, the great majority of new start-ups are formed around new technologies, which face great scientific uncertainty that can only resolved by preclinical and clinical testing that takes time. The rate of discovery of new technologies is driven in part by public funding of basic research and the incentives to commercialize such research that results from patent regimes and reimbursement rules, and possibly by favorable tax treatment of R&D, especially for orphan drugs. Whether or not public funding to basic research is excessive or suboptimal is an important subject for research. Thus in the current environment it does not appear that regulation of market access or endogenous investments in sunk R&D costs are major contributors to excessive product differentiation or monopoly power, with the possible exception of orphan drugs that by design receive five years of market exclusivity.

However, it is plausible that health insurance coverage for modestly differentiated on-patent drugs, when cheap generics are available for off-patent, therapeutic substitutes, contributes to product differentiation through slightly differentiated molecules and new formulations. Whether insurance structures in the US create incentives for excessive product differentiation, including extensions and new formulations, and whether this reduces cross-price demand elasticities are important subjects for future research.

22.3.9 Alternatives to Patents

The potential welfare losses entailed by patents have led to several proposed alternative mechanisms to create incentives for innovation, including direct government grants ("push" mechanisms) and government-funded prizes or rewards ("pull" mechanisms). Grants raise issues of determining optimal levels and allocation of funding, and maintaining grantees' incentives. Prizes avoid grantee performance issues but still pose huge valuation and implementation challenges, since the true social value of pharmaceuticals may not be known until several years after launch, as additional safety and efficacy data accrue for the initial and possibly additional indications. Measuring and valuing the health gain is also problematic. Of course it may be argued that a regulator's value estimates may be no more inaccurate than the prices that result under the patent system, given distortions due to insurance, promotion etc. Hollis (2005) argues that therapeutic value could be measured in incremental quality-adjusted life years (QALYs), with volume determined annually based on actual sales by competitive suppliers. Whether such a system would be superior to a patent system with prices indirectly regulated based on incremental QALYs gained (Danzon et al. 2011) or other approaches to constraining the distorting effects of insurance is an important area for future research.

22.4 Promotion

22.4.1 Regulation

The 1962 FDA Act, with subsequent Amendments, establishes the foundation for regulation of promotion in the US, subject to the US constitutional protection of freedom of speech, which includes commercial speech. The 1962 Act restricts promotional claims to facts established in clinical trials; requires that risks as well as benefits be described in brief summary; and excludes promotion of unapproved indications. The FDA's 1997 Guidance relaxed the requirement that the full product label, which includes all known risks, be displayed in broadcast ads. Rather, the requirement for a brief summary of risks and benefits could be provided by giving a website, a toll free number, or reference to a print ad with the full label, in addition to advice to "see your physician." These changes were deemed to reflect the ways in which consumers obtain information from modern media. In its oversight of promotion, as for its other activities, the FDA is required by statute to consider risks and benefits to patients. Costs and, in particular, whether promotion leads to unnecessary spending, is beyond the FDA's purview. The 1997 FDAMA permitted companies to inform physicians of potential unapproved ("off-label") uses of drugs through the distribution of peer reviewed journals.

By contrast, many other countries are more restrictive in regulating pharmaceutical promotion, on grounds of unnecessary costs and possibly that any constitutional protections of freedom of speech have been more narrowly interpreted. Countries that regulate prices often include limits or deterrents to promotion. The UK Pharmaceutical Price Regulatory Scheme (PPRS) limits the promotional expenditure that companies can deduct as a cost in calculating their return on capital. Germany's global drug budget, in effect from 1993–2001, placed the pharmaceutical industry at financial risk for budget over-runs, second in line after physicians, in order to discourage promotion. France penalizes "excessive" promotion, both directly through fines for exceeding allowed promotion limits and indirectly through penalties for over-shooting allowed sales limits. Samples are a significant component of promotion in the US, while some other countries prohibit samples; even where there is no prohibition, samples have less value to patients in countries where all patients are insured with low co-payments.

Most countries restrict DTCA to so-called "help seeking" ads, which inform consumers about the availability of treatment for a health condition but do not mention a specific product. The exception is New Zealand, which also has a commitment to freedom of commercial speech. New Zealand has no constraining statute that requires DTCA to present a "fair balance" between risks and benefits. Survey results indicate that between 82–90 percent of individuals recall benefits information in DTCA in both the US and New Zealand, but only 20–27 percent recall risk information in New Zealand compared to 81–89 percent recall for risks in the US (Hoek, Gendall, and Calfee 2004).

22.4.2 Trends in Promotion

Promotion by manufacturers is an important mechanism whereby physicians, consumers and payers learn about drugs. Promotion in the US as a percent of sales grew from 14.1 percent in 1996 to 17.1 percent in 2003 (Berndt 2005).[12] This promotion spending estimate is downward biased due to omitting promotion-related components of pre- and post-launch clinical trials, but is also is upward biased because almost two-thirds reflects free samples distributed to physicians for patient use. Samples are valued at a retail price, which significantly exceeds the economic cost of sampling to manufacturers.[13] Ignoring samples, the largest components of promotional spending are physician and hospital detailing, direct to consumer advertising, and medical journal advertising, but relative shares differ significantly across drugs.

Direct to consumer advertising (DTCA) grew rapidly, prior to and following the 1997 FDA reinterpretation of the guidelines for broadcast DTCA (Palumbo and Mullins 2002; Berndt 2005). The 1997 FDA Guidance increased the share of DTCA that is broadcast, from under 30 percent prior to 1997 to almost two-thirds in 2002 (Rosenthal, Berndt, et al. 2002, 2003). DTCA tends to be concentrated on the leading drugs in a class, and on therapeutic classes that are particularly amenable to patient awareness and choice, such as antidepressants, antihistamines, antihyperlipidemics, and antiulcerants. The industry has recently adopted voluntary promotion guidelines that, among other things, allow only those gifts to physicians that benefit patients, and limit DTCA within the first year post-launch of a new product, to enable education of physicians about new products, and as a precaution against unanticipated adverse effects.

Pharmaceutical promotion is also changing in response to the growth of managed drug benefits. The implementation of drug formularies shifts power from physician-patients to payers who design formularies. Recent cuts in pharmaceutical sales forces partly reflects this shift in influence from physicians to payers, who are more interested in evidence of comparative effectiveness and cost-effectiveness (Elixhauser, Luce, and

---

[12] For 2003, the reported promotion spending in the US is less than the spending on R&D of $34.5 billion (PhRMA 2005); however, this country-specific measure of R&D-to-sales is imprecise for multinational firms with global sales but R&D concentrated in at most a few countries.

[13] The opportunity cost of samples to firms lies between the marginal production cost and the actual ex-manufacturer selling price, which is the forgone manufacturer revenue had the patient paid for the drug.

Steiner 1995; Neumann 2004). Other factors contributing to cuts in sales force include: belief that the "medical representative arms race" had hit diminishing returns; patent expiration on many high volume products; and shift of new product approvals towards specialty products that require smaller sales forces.

Currently the US lags other countries in the use of comparative and/or cost-effectiveness as an input to reimbursement decisions. Recent increases in public funding for comparative research may change this, although so far there is no link to reimbursement. Greater focus on evidence-based comparative effectiveness may shift industry's promotion focus from detailing and DTCA towards investment in documenting health outcomes, comparative-, and cost-effectiveness.

22.4.3 Evidence on Effects of Pharmaceutical Promotion

The pharmaceutical industry's large expenditure on advertising is controversial, with policy concern over both magnitude and form. The economic literature outlines the issues and provides some evidence, but data availability has limited empirical studies and basic questions remain unresolved. The economic rationale is that promotion can provide information to physicians and consumers about the benefits and risks of drugs, which is necessary for appropriate help-seeking, prescribing, and compliance. Critics contend that much promotion is designed to persuade rather than inform; that it increases product differentiation, brand loyalty, market power, and prices; and that it leads to inappropriate use, including use of high-price, on-patent drugs when cheap generics would be equally effective.

Promotion studies pre-1997. An early proponent of the anti-competitive hypothesis, Walker (1971) argued that large promotion expenditure raises entry barriers and increases market power, by requiring new entrants to make large outlays in order to attract awareness of new products. The alternative view is that advertising may enhance competition by facilitating the introduction of new products and new firms. Telser (1975) found that new entry into a therapeutic class is positively related to promotional intensity. However, causal relationships remain questionable. Leffler (1981) finds that selling effort is related to the number of new products introduced in a class, and concludes that pharmaceutical advertising is at least partly informative. However, repeated advertising of established pharmaceutical products more likely accomplishes "reminder" and "habit-formation" purposes. Thus pharmaceutical advertising is clearly multidimensional and net effects on competition, information and appropriate usage may differ, depending on the circumstances. Berndt et al. (1995) find that promotional stocks of detailing, journal advertising, and DTCA (pre-1997) significantly affect industry-level demand for antiulcerants, but with diminishing returns, again suggesting the importance of reminder or loyalty-building promotion.

Promotion studies post-1997. The growth of DTCA has shifted the focus and the complexity of empirical studies of promotion, with important data and empirical challenges. One major empirical challenge is that DTCA is endogenously determined and just one of several types of promotion a firm may use. Ignoring the endogeneity of DTCA and its correlation with other (often unobserved) forms of promotion and managed-care contracting can lead to biased estimates of the impact of DTCA. Second, estimates of effects of promotion spending must take into account lagged and future impacts of information stocks, as physicians form prescribing habits and patients tend to stay with a particular brand for chronic medications, once they have found a drug that works for them. Third, the net effect of one firm's promotion depends on competitors' strategic responses.

Drawing welfare conclusions from the empirical evidence is particularly problematic. The economic/marketing literature generally views advertising that expands aggregate category sales as more likely to be informative, and hence welfare-enhancing, whereas advertising that simply changes market shares without affecting aggregate use is more likely to be wasteful (for a discussion see Berndt 2005; Kravitz, Epstein et al. 2005). However, in the case of heavily insured pharmaceuticals, for which consumers pay only a small fraction of the cost out-of-pocket, it is possible that even category-expanding effects could reflect unnecessary use (and/or unnecessarily costly use), even though such purchases are well-informed and rational for individual consumers, given their insurance coverage.

With these caveats, some of the main findings from the recent literature are reviewed here (for a more detailed review, see Berndt 2005). The study of promotion in the anti-histamine and antiviral categories by Narayanan et al. (2004) acknowledges the complex market environment by including data on DTCA, detailing, pricing, and other medical spending as alternative marketing mechanisms; measuring both the short and long run effects of promotion; and estimating cross-firm elasticities. All marketing mix variables are modeled as endogenous. This study finds that, of the four marketing variables, only DTCA has a positive but small effect on aggregate category sales. Each product's own DTCA also positively affects its own brand sales, but interaction effects with other brands' DTCA are negative. Own DTCA and detailing appear to be complements, rather than substitutes. The estimated return on investment is lower for DTCA than for detailing, suggesting that firms might gain by reallocating marketing budgets away from DTCA and towards detailing. This study has limited therapeutic scope and significant data limitations, but it does illustrate the importance of including the full marketing mix and controlling for endogeneity of the marketing variables.[14]

In contrast to the Narayanan et al. (2005) paper, other studies suggest that DTCA has a greater effect on category sales than on individual brand sales. Rosenthal and

[14] Narayanan et al. rely on three sets of instruments for price, DTCA and detailing. Price is instrumented with the pharmaceutical PPI interacted with product dummy variables as well as lagged (3 years total) PPI interacted with product dummies (36 instruments for 12 product categories). DTCA is instrumented with the PPI for television, radio and print advertising. Detailing was instrumented with employment data.

Berndt (2003) conclude that DTCA has a significant positive impact on class sales, with an average elasticity of roughly .1, but they find no evidence that detailing or DTCA affects product-specific market shares, controlling for product sampling.[15] The authors emphasize that failure to find brand-specific effects could reflect learning or unmeasured longer term effects. Wosinska (2002) finds that DTCA for the cholesterol reducing medications (statins) positively affects brand share only if the brand had preferred formulary status. Similarly, Iizuka and Jin (2005b) find that DTCA increases total category sales, but brand-specific share is only significantly shifted by physician promotion such as detailing and journal publications. The authors conclude that a product should hold at least 58 percent market share of its therapeutic category sales in order to recoup DTCA investment. In fact, they find that 69 percent of DTCA spending is on drugs with at least a 60 percent market share. They also find that DTCA increases the number of doctor visits at which a drug is prescribed (Iizuka and Jin 2005a), with some differences between patient types in their responsiveness to DTCA (young vs. elderly; private vs. public insurance). Donohue and Berndt (2004) find that DTCA has no significant effect on choice of product, but that it does motivate individuals to visit the physician. These findings are supported by a randomized control trial by Kravitz et al. (2005), in which standardized patients (who were not sick, but were scripted with dialog to feign depression or adjustment disorder) asked unsuspecting blinded physicians for either no medication, a generic drug or a specific brand. Patients who requested a drug were significantly more likely to receive a drug, but not necessarily the suggested drug. Even if such findings could be generalized, they do not necessarily support conclusions about appropriateness of DTCA, which would also require data on costs and medical outcomes.

International Comparisons. Cross-national evidence on effects of promotion are limited, in part because data on promotion spending is limited and sometimes inconsistent across countries. For example, the content of a detail visit to a physician can be very different, depending on time spent, messaging allowed, whether sampling is permitted, etc. Berndt, Danzon, and Kruse (2007) provide some evidence on cross-national differences in promotion and in diffusion of new drugs.

22.5 DRUGS FOR DEVELOPING COUNTRIES

Patents create the potential for static efficiency loss, if prices to consumers exceed marginal cost and result in suboptimal consumption. In most industrialized countries with comprehensive insurance coverage, this patent-induced tendency for under-consumption is roughly offset by an insurance-induced tendency for over-consumption. However, in many middle and most low income countries (LICs), insurance coverage is

---

[15] Instruments include a quadratic of the drug's remaining patent life, a post-1997 time trend and the monthly cost of TV advertising.

minimal and patients pay out-of-pocket for drugs. This raises concerns that requiring these countries to adopt standard, twenty-year product patents, under the WTO TRIPs provisions, may lead to unaffordable drug prices and suboptimal drug consumption.[16]

In theory, patents need not lead to high prices in markets/countries where patent holders perceive that demand is highly price-elastic, due to consumers' limited ability or willingness to pay. Thus for globally marketed drugs, price discrimination across countries should enable firms to recoup their R&D investments by pricing above marginal cost in high income countries while pricing close to marginal cost in LICs.[17] In practice, price differentials between high and lower income countries vary less than in proportion to average per capita income, hence prices are relatively unaffordable in middle and low income countries (MLICs), especially for the poorest subgroups in these countries. These relatively high prices in MLICs may in part reflect firms' perceived inability to maintain price differentials between countries, due to external referencing and parallel trade. They may also reflect an optimal pricing strategy of targeting only the high income subgroups, due to inability to maintain price differentials within countries, (Mulcahy and Towse 2011). Flynn et al. (2009) show that a single price monopolist would rationally charge a high price, relative to mean per capita income, in countries with highly skewed distribution of income, and that welfare losses are potentially large. Regulatory structures that protect differential pricing within as well as between countries would encourage lower pricing to low-income populations. Compulsory licensing has also been suggested (e.g. Flynn et al. 2009) and is authorized under TRIPs under certain conditions. However, whether compulsory licensing of generic producers would achieve marginal cost pricing depends on market conditions. Even marginal cost prices may be unaffordable to the poorest subgroups, in which case additional tax-financed subsidies may be appropriate. Such subsidies exist for vaccines, through the Global Alliance for Vaccines and Immunization (GAVI) and for some HIV-AIDs drugs, but not for most other drugs.

For drugs to treat diseases that occur only in developing countries, patents are an ineffective mechanism to stimulate R&D, because these consumers' ability to pay is insufficient to recoup R&D investments. Recent "push" subsidy initiatives include public private partnerships that combine government and philanthropic funds with private industry expertise and resources, to address diseases such as malaria (Medicines for Malaria Venture), tuberculosis (the Global Alliance for TB), an AIDs vaccine (the International AIDs Vaccine Initiative, IAVI), and others (Kremer 2002). "Pull" subsidies include the Advance Market Commitment (AMC) approach, which would guarantee purchase of vaccines that meet specified conditions at pre-specified prices. Pneumococcal vaccine has been selected as the first vaccine target. Thanks to these public–private partnerships, significant progress has been made, with several promising drug and vaccine candidates in late stage development.

---

[16] See Article 31 <http://www.wto.org/english/tratop_e/trips_e/t_agm3_e.htm>.

[17] For a discussion of these issues, see for example Malueg and Schwartz (1994); Danzon (1997); Dumoulin (2001); Maskus (2001); Scherer and Watal (2002); Danzon and Towse (2003, 2005, 2009); Jack and Lanjouw (2003), Danzon, Towse and Ferrandiz (2011).

22.6 Conclusions

The R&D intensity of biopharmaceuticals, their high cost and non-obvious risks and benefits has led to patents, extensive regulation of market access, promotion and pricing, and insurance coverage. These features in turn radically affect supply and demand, pricing, competition and market structure of the biopharmaceutical industry. Theoretical and empirical research has shed some light on the effects of various components of regulation but many important questions remain for future research. These include the optimal structure of market access regulation, including safety and efficacy trade-offs and integration of pre-launch clinical trial data with post-launch observational data; effectiveness and costs of promotion and promotion regulation; optimal structure of regulation and competition to constrain prices, including price differentials across and within countries; optimal patent and data exclusivities (or alternative regimes); pricing and reimbursement for biologics, in particular, physician-dispensed cancer and other drugs, for which current Medicare reimbursement systems create perverse incentives in the US and other countries debate appropriate pricing and financing systems. Generics have delivered enormous savings to consumers/payers in countries, such as the US, with regulation and reimbursement regimes that encourage generic price competition. Achieving substantial savings from follow-on biologics will require changes in current regulatory and reimbursement systems.

In summary, although there is a large and growing literature on the pharmaceutical industry that has produced valuable information and useful lessons learned, important issues remain for future research. Economic models from other industries require significant adaptation to fit this industry's peculiar characteristics—in particular, high rates of R&D and technical change, hard-to-measure but potentially life-affecting effects, patents, insurance, and physicians, consumers, payers and pharmacists as potential customers. This industry remains a fertile area for future research.

REFERENCES

ACEMOGLU, D. and LINN, J. (2004). "Market size in innovation: Theory and evidence from the pharmaceutical industry." *Quarterly Journal of Economics* 119(3): 1049–90.

AGHAZADEH, BEHZAD, BOSCHWITZ, JEFF, BEEVER, CHARELY, and ARNOULD, CATHERINE (2005). "Know thy R&D enemy: the key to fighting attrition." *Vivo* Jan. 2005: 59–64.

ANIS, A. H., GUH, D. P., and WOLCOTT, J. (2003). "Lowering generic drug prices: Less regulation equals more competition." *Medical Care* 41(1): 135–41.

——and WEN, Q. (1998). "Price regulation of pharmaceuticals in Canada." *Journal of Health Economics* 17(1): 21–38.

ATTARAN, A. (2004). "How do patents and economic policies affect access to essential medicines in developing countries?" *Health Affairs* 23(3): 155–66.

BAUMOL, W. J. and BRADFORD, D. F. (1970). "Optimal departures from marginal cost pricing." *American Economic Review* 60(3): 265–83.

BENNETT, C. L., NEBEKER, J. R., LYONS, E. A., et al. (2005). "The Research on Adverse Drug Events and Reports (RADAR) Project." *Journal of the American Medical Association* 293(17): 2131–40.

BERGMAN, M. A. and RUDHOLM, N. (2003). "The relative importance of actual and potential competition: Empirical evidence from the pharmaceuticals market." *Journal of Industrial Economics* 51(4): 455–67.

BERNDT, E. R. (2002). "Pharmaceuticals in US health care: Determinants of quantity and price." *Journal of Economic Perspectives* 16(4): 45–66.

—— (2005). "The United States' experience with direct-to-consumer advertising of prescription drugs: what have we learned?" International Conference on Pharmaceutical Innovation, Taipei, Taiwan.

—— BUI, L., REILEY, D. R. and URBAN, G. L. (1995). "Information, marketing, and pricing in the US antiulcer drug market." *American Economic Review* 85(2): 100–5.

—— PINDYCK, R. S., et al. (2003). "Consumption externalities and diffusion in pharmaceutical markets: Anti-ulcer drugs." *Journal of Industrial Economics* 51(2): 243–70.

—— DANZON, P. M. and KRUSE, G. (2007). "Dynamic competition in pharmaceuticals: cross-national evidence from new drug diffusion." *Managerial and Decision Economics* 28(4–5): 231–50.

BHATTACHARYA, J. and VOGT, W. B. (2003). "A simple model of pharmaceutical price dynamics." *Journal of Law & Economics* 46(2): 599–626.

BORRELL, J. R. (1999). "Pharmaceutical price regulation: A study on the impact of the rate-of-return regulation in the UK." *Pharmacoeconomics* 15(3): 291–303.

BREWER, T. and COLDITZ, G. A. (1999). "Postmarketing surveillance and adverse drug reactions: current perspectives and future needs." *Journal of the American Medical Association* 281(9): 824–9.

CALFEE, J. E., WINSTON, C., et al. (2002). "Direct-to-consumer advertising and the demand for cholesterol-reducing drugs." *Journal of Law & Economics* 45(2): 673–90.

CAVES, R. E., WHINSTON, M. D., and HURWITZ, M. A. (1991). "Patent expiration, entry, and competition in the United-States pharmaceutical-industry." Brookings Papers on Economic Activity, *Microeconomics* 1991: 1–66.

CHAUDHURI, S., GOLDBERG, P. K., et al. (2006). "Estimating the Effect of Global Patent Protection in Pharmaceuticals: A Case Study of Quinolones in India." *American Economic Review* 96(5): 1477–514.

CLARKSON, K. W. (1996). "The effects of research and promotion on rates of return," in Robert B Helms (ed.), *Competitive Strategies in the Pharmaceutical Industry*. Washington, DC: American Enterprise Institute Press, 238–68.

COCKBURN, I. M. (2004). "The changing structure of the pharmaceutical industry." *Health Affairs* 23(1): 10–22.

—— and HENDERSON, R. M. (2001). "Scale and scope in drug development: unpacking the advantages of size in pharmaceutical research." *Journal of Health Economics* 20(6): 1033–57.

COMANOR, W. S. (1986). "The political economy of the pharmaceutical industry." *Journal of Economic Literature* 24(3): 1178–17.

CBO (CONGRESSIONAL BUDGET OFFICE OF THE UNITED STATES) (1996). *How the Medicaid Rebate on Prescription Drugs Affects Pricing in the Pharmaceutical Industry*. Washington, DC: CBO.

—— (2004). *A Detailed Description of CBO's Cost Estimate for the Medicare Prescription Drug Benefit*. Washington, DC: CBO.

CBO (Congressional Budget Office of the United States) (2005a). *Prices for Brand Name Drugs Under Selected Federal Programs.* June 2005. Washington, DC: Congressional Budget Office of the Unites States.

—— (2005b). *The Rebate Medicaid Receives on Brand-Name Prescription Drugs.* June 21 2005. Washington, DC: Congressional Budget Office of the Unites States.

Craswell, R. and Calfee, J. (1986). "Deterrence and uncertain legal standards." *Journal of Law, Economics, and Organization* 2(2): 279–303.

Danzon, P. M. (1997). "Price discrimination for pharmaceuticals: welfare effects in the US and the EU." *International Journal of the Economics of Business* 4(3): 301–21.

—— (1998). "The Economics of Parallel Trade." *Pharmacoeconomics* 13(3): 293–304.

—— (2001). "Reference pricing: theory and empirical evidence." In *The Economics of Reference Pricing and Pharmaceutical Policy.* G. López-Casasnovas and Bengt Jonsson (eds.) Colección de Economía de la salud y Gestión Sanitaria Springer Verlag, Barcelona 2001.

—— and Chao, L. W. (2000a). "Does regulation drive out competition in pharmaceutical markets?" *Journal of Law & Economics* 43(2): 311–57.

—— —— (2000b). "Cross-national price differences for pharmaceuticals: how large and why?" *Journal of Health Economics*, 19(2): 159–95.

—— and Epstein, A. J. (2009). "Effects of regulation on drug launch and pricing in interdependent markets." NBER Working Papers 14041, National Bureau of Economic Research, Inc.

—— and Furukawa, M. F. (2003). "Prices and availability of pharmaceuticals: Evidence from nine countries." *Health Affairs* 22(6): W521–36.

—— —— (2006). "Prices and availability of biopharmaceuticals: an international comparison." *Health Affairs* (Sept.–Oct.) 25(5):1353–62.

—— —— (2008). "International prices and availability of pharmaceuticals in 2005." *Health Affairs* (Jan 10, 27(1): 221–33.

—— —— (2011). "Competition in Generic Pharmaceutical Markets: Cross-National Evidence." NBER Working Paper.

—— and Ketcham, J. (2004). "Reference pricing of pharmaceuticals for Medicare: evidence from Germany, the Netherlands and New Zealand," in D. M. Cutler & A. M. Garber (eds.), *Frontiers in Health Policy Research*, Vol. 7. Cambridge, MA: National Bureau of Economic Research and MIT Press.

—— and Keuffel, E. (2007). "Regulation of the pharmaceutical industry." In *Economic Regulation and Its Reform: What Have We Learned?* ed. Nancy Rose. Cambridge, MA: NBER Press, forthcoming. Available at: <http://www.nber.org/books_in_progress/econ-reg/danzon-keuffel9-14-07.pdf>.

—— and Percy, A. (2000). "The effect of price regulation on productivity in the pharmaceutical industry." In *Studies in Income and Productivity*, eds. A. Heston and R. Lipsey. NBER-Chicago: University of Chicago Press.

—— and Towse, A. (2003). "Differential pricing for pharmaceuticals: reconciling access, R&D, and patents." *International Journal of Health Care Finance and Economics* 3: 183–205.

—— —— (2005). "Theory and implementation of differential pricing for pharmaceuticals," in K. Maskus and J. Reichman (eds.), *International Public Goods and Transfer of Technology Under a Globalized Intellectual Property Regime.* Cambridge: Cambridge University Press.

—— Nicholson, S., and Pereira N. (2005). "Productivity in pharmaceutical-biotechnology R&D: the role of experience and alliances." *Journal of Health Economics* 24(2): 317–39.

—— PEREIRA, N. S. and TEJWANI, S. (2005). "Vaccine supply: a cross-national perspective." *Health Affairs* 24(3) (May/June): 706–17.

—— WANG, Y. R., and WANG L. (2005). "The impact of price regulation on the launch delay of new drugs: evidence from twenty-five major markets in the 1990s." *Health Economics* 14(3): 269–92.

—— WILENSKY, G. R., and MEANS, K. E. (2005) "Alternative strategies for Medicare payment of outpatient prescription drugs: Part B and beyond." *American Journal of Managed Care*, 11(3): 173–80.

—— EPSTEIN, A. J., and NICHOLSON, S. (2007). "Mergers and acquisitions in the pharmaceutical and biotech industries." *Managerial and Decision Economics* 28, 4–5: 307–28.

—— MULCAHY, A., and TOWSE, A. (2011). "Pharmaceutical prices in emerging markets." NBER Working Paper, Cambridge MA.

—— TOWSE, A., and FERRANDIZ, J. M. (2011). "Setting Optimal Absolute and Relative Prices for Pharmaceuticals Across Countries". NBER Working Paper, Cambridge MA.

DIMASI, J. A. (2001). "New drug development in the United States from 1963 to 1999." *Clinical Pharmacology & Therapeutics* 69(5): 286–96.

—— (2002). "The value of improving the productivity of the drug development process: Faster times and better decisions." *Pharmacoeconomics* 20: 1–10.

—— and GRABOWSKI, H. G. (2007). "The cost of biopharmaceutical R&D: is Biotech different?" *Managerial and Decision Economics* 28(4): 469–79.

—— HANSEN, R.W., et al. (1991). "Cost of innovation in the pharmaceutical industry." *Journal of Health Economics* 10(2): 107–42.

—— —— and GRABOWSKI, H. G. (2003). "The price of innovation: new estimates of drug development costs." *Journal of Health Economics* 22(2): 151–85.

—— —— and PAQUETTE, C. (2004). "The economics of follow-on drug research and development: Trends in entry rates and the timing of development." *Pharmacoeconomics* 22: 1–14.

DONOHUE, J. M. and BERNDT, E. R. (2004). "Effects of direct-to-consumer advertising on medication choice: The case of antidepressants." *Journal of Public Policy & Marketing* 23(2): 115–27.

DRANOVE, D. and MELTZER, D. (1994). "Do important drugs reach the market sooner?" *RAND Journal of Economics* 25(3): 402–23.

DUGGAN, MARK and MORTON, FIONA SCOTT (2006). "The distortionary effects of government procurement: evidence for Medicaid prescription drug purchasing." *Quarterly Journal of Economics* 121: 1–31.

DUMOULIN, J. (2001). "Global pricing strategies for innovative essential drugs." *International Journal of Biotechnology* 3(3/4): 338–49.

EISENBERG, R. S. (2001). "The shifting functional balance of patents and drug regulation." *Health Affairs* 20(5): 119–35.

EKELUND, M. and PERSSON, B. (2003). "Pharmaceutical pricing in a regulated market." *Review of Economics and Statistics* 85(2): 298–306.

ELIXHAUSER A, LUCE, B. R., and STEINER, C. A. (1995). *Cost Effectiveness Analysis, Medical Technology Assessment, and Managed Care Organizations.* Bethesda, MD: MEDTAP International Inc.

FINK, C. (2001). "Patent protection, transnational corporations, and market structure: a simulation study of the Indian pharmaceutical industry." *Journal of Industry, Competition and Trade* 1(1): 101–21.

FLYNN, S., HOLLIS, A. and PALMEDO, M. (2009). "An economic justification for open access to essential medicine patents in developing countries." *Journal of Law, Medicine and Ethics* Summer, 37: 2–25.

FRANK, R. G. and SALKEVER, D. S. (1992), "Pricing, patent loss and the market for pharmaceuticals," *Southern Economic Journal* 59: 165–79.

GAHART, M. T., DUHAMEL, L. M., et al. (2003). "Examining the FDA's oversight of direct-to-consumer advertising." *Health Affairs* 22(1, Suppl.): 120–3.

GANSLANDT, M. and MASKUS, K. E. (2004). "Parallel imports and the pricing of pharmaceutical products: evidence from the European Union." *Journal of Health Economics* 23(5): 1035–57.

GARBER, A., JONES, C. I., and ROMER, P. M. (2006). "Insurance and incentives for medical innovation." *Forum for Health Economics and Policy* 9(2): art. 4.

GRABOWSKI, H. (1976). *Drug Regulation and Innovation: Empirical Evidence and Policy Options.* Washington DC: American Enterprise Institute.

—— and MUELLER, D. C. (1978). "Industrial research and development, intangible capital stocks, and firm profit rates." *Bell Journal of Economics* 9(2): 328–43.

—— and VERNON, J. M. (1990). "A new look at the returns and risks to pharmaceutical R&D." *Management Science* 36(7): 804–21.

—— —— (1992). "Brand loyalty, entry and price competition in pharmaceuticals after the 1984 Drug Act." *Journal of Law and Economics* 35(2): 331–50.

—— —— (1996), "Prospects for returns to pharmaceutical R&D under health care reform," in Robert B. Helms (ed.), *Competitive Strategies in the Pharmaceutical Industry.* Washington, DC: The American Enterprise Institute Press, 194–207.

—— —— (2000). "Effective patent life in pharmaceuticals." *International Journal of Technology Management* 19(1–2): 98–120.

—— —— and THOMAS, L. G. (1978). "Estimating Effects of Regulation on Innovation: International Comparative Analysis of Pharmaceutical Industry." *Journal of Law & Economics* 21(1): 133–63.

—— —— and DIMASI, J. A. (2002). "Returns on research and development for 1990s new drug introductions." *Pharmacoeconomics* 20: 11–29.

HAUSMAN, J. A. and MACKIE-MASON, J. K. (1988). "Price discrimination and patent policy." *RAND Journal of Economics* 19(2): 253–65.

HENDERSON, R. and COCKBURN, I. (1996). "Scale, scope, and spillovers: The determinants of research productivity in drug discovery." *RAND Journal of Economics* 27(1): 32–59.

HERXHEIMER, A. (2004). "Open access to industry's clinically relevant data: Urgently needed, but when will we get it, and in what form?" *British Medical Journal* 329(7457): 64–5.

HOEK J, GENDALL, P., and CALFEE, J. (2004). "Direct-to-consumer advertising of prescription medicines in the United States and New Zealand: an analysis of regulatory approaches and consumer responses." *International Journal of Advertising* 23: 197–227.

HOLLIS, A. (2002). "The importance of being first: evidence from Canadian generic pharmaceuticals." *Health Economics* 11(8): 723–34.

—— (2005). "An efficient reward system for pharmaceutical innovation." Working paper 17.1.2005. University of Calgary, Calgary, Alberta, Canada.

HOROWITZ, J. B. and MOEHRING, H. B. (2004). "How property rights and patents affect antibiotic resistance." *Health Economics* 13(6): 575–83.

HUDSON, J. (2000). "Generic take-up in the pharmaceutical market following patent expiry: A multi-country study." *International Review of Law And Economics* 20(2): 205–21.

HURWITZ, M. A. and CAVES, R. E. (1988). "Persuasion or information: promotion and the shares of brand name and generic pharmaceuticals." *Journal of Law & Economics* 31(2): 299–320.

IIZUKA, T. (2004). "What explains the use of direct-to-consumer advertising of prescription drugs?" *Journal of Industrial Economics* 52(3): 349–79.

—— and JIN, G. (2005a). "Direct to consumer advertising and prescription choices." Working Paper: Owen Graduate School of Management (Vanderbilt University). Nashville, TN.

———— (2005b). "The effect of prescription drug advertising on doctor visits." Working Paper: Owen Graduate School of Management (Vanderbilt University). Nashville, TN.

JACK, W. and LANJOUW, J. O. (2003). "Financing pharmaceutical innovation: how much should poor countries contribute?" Working Paper No. 28: Centre for Global Development. Washington D.C.

JENA, A. B. and PHILIPSON, T. J. (2008). "Cost-effectiveness analysis and innovation." *Journal of Health Economics* 27:1224–36.

JENSEN, E. J. (1987). "Research expenditures and the discovery of new drugs." *Journal of Industrial Economics* 36(1): 83–95.

JOGLEKAR, P. and PATERSON, M. L. (1986). "A closer look at the returns and risks of pharmaceutical research-and-development." *Journal of Health Economics* 5(2): 153–77.

KRAVITZ, R. L., EPSTEIN, R. M., FELDMAN, M. D., FRANZ, C. E., AZARI, R., WILKES, M. S., HINTON, L., and FRANKS, P. (2005). "Influence of patients' requests for direct-to-consumer advertised antidepressants." *Journal of the American Medical Association* 293(16): 1995–2002.

KREMER, M. (2002). "Pharmaceuticals and the developing world." *Journal of Economic Perspectives* 16(4): 67–90.

KUHLIK, B. N. (2004). "The assault on pharmaceutical intellectual property." *University of Chicago Law Review* 71(1): 93–109.

KYLE, M. (2005). "Pharmaceutical price controls and entry strategies." *The Review of Economics and Statistics*, February 2007, 89(1): 88–99.

LACKDAWALLA, D. and SOOD, N. (2005) "Insurance and innovation in health care markets." NBER Working Paper.

LANJOUW, J. O. (2002). "A new global patent regime for diseases: US and international legal issues." *Harvard Journal of Law and Technology* 16: 85–124.

—— (2005). "Patents, price controls and access to new drugs: how policy affects global market entry." NBER Working Paper 11321. NBER, Cambridge, MA.

LEFFLER, K. (1981). "Persuasion or information? The economics of prescription drug advertising." *Journal of Law and Economics* 24: 45–74.

LICHTENBERG, F. (2002). "Pharmaceutical knowledge: capital accumulation and longevity," in J. Haltiwnager, C. Corrado and D. Sichel (eds.), *Measuring Capital in the New Economy*. Chicago: University of Chicago Press.

—— and PHILIPSON, T. J. (2002). "The dual effects of intellectual property regulations: Within- and between-patent competition in the US pharmaceuticals industry." *Journal of Law & Economics* 45(2): 643–72.

—— and WALDFOGEL, J. (2003). "Does misery love company? Evidence from pharmaceutical markets before and after the orphan drug markets." NBER Working Paper 9750.

LING, D. C., BERNDT, E. R., and KYLE, M. K. (2002). "Deregulating direct-to-consumer marketing of prescription drugs: Effects on prescription and over-the-counter product sales." *Journal of Law & Economics* 45(2): 691–723.

LONGMAN, R. (2004). "Why early-stage dealmaking is hot." *Vivo: The Business and Medicine Report*: 28.

LONGMAN, R. (2006). "The large molecule future." *Vivo: The Business and Medicine Report*: 3.

LOPEZ-CASASNOVAS, G. and PUIG-JUNOY, J. (2000). "Review of the literature on reference pricing." *Health Policy* 54(2): 87–123.

LU, Z. J. and COMANOR, W. S. (1998). "Strategic pricing of new pharmaceuticals." *Review of Economics And Statistics* 80(1): 108–18.

MADDEN, B. J. (2004). "Breaking the FDA monopoly." *Regulation* 27(2): 64–6.

MAHINKA, S. P. and BIERMAN, M. E. (1995). "Direct-to-OTC marketing of drugs: possible approaches." *Food and Drug Law Journal* 50(1): 49–63.

MALUEG, D. A. and SCHWARTZ, M. (1994). "Parallel imports, demand dispersion, and international price discrimination." *Journal of International Economics* 37: 167–95.

MASKUS, K. E. (2001). *Parallel Imports in Pharmaceuticals: Implications for Competition and Prices in Developing Countries*. Final Report to World Intellectual Property Organization: World Intellectual Property Organization, Geneva.

MUNNICH, F. E. and SULLIVAN, K. (1994), "The impact of recent legislative change on Germany", *Pharmacoeconomics* 11–16(Suppl. 1): 1.

NARAYANAN, S., DESIRAJU, R., and CHINTAGUNTA, P. K. (2004). "Return on investment implications for pharmaceutical promotional expenditures: the role of marketing-mix interactions." *The Journal of Marketing* 68(4) (Oct.): 90–105.

NEUMANN, P. J. (2004). "Evidence-based and value-based formulary guidelines." *Health Affairs*, 23(1) (Jan.–Feb.): 124–34.

—— ZINNER, D. E., et al. (1996). "The FDA and regulation of cost-effectiveness claims." *Health Affairs* 15(3): 54–71.

OKIE, S. (2005). "What ails the FDA?" *New England Journal of Medicine* 352(11): 1063–66.

OLSON, M. K. (2004a). "Are novel drugs more risky for patients than less novel drugs?" *Journal of Health Economics* 23(6): 1135–58.

—— (2004b). "Managing delegation in the FDA: Reducing delay in new-drug review." *Journal of Health Politics Policy And Law* 29(3): 397–430.

PALUMBO, F. B. and MULLINS, C. D. (2002). "The development of direct-to-consumer prescription drug advertising regulation." *Food and Drug Law Journal* 57(3): 423–43.

PELTZMAN, S. (1973). "Evaluation of consumer protection legislation: 1962 drug amendments." *Journal of Political Economy* 81(5): 1049–91.

PHILIPSON, T., BERNDT, E., GOTTSCHALK, A., SUN, E. (2008), "Cost-benefit analysis of the FDA: the case of the prescription drug user fee acts." *Journal of Public Economics* 93: 1306–25.

PhRMA (PHARMACEUTICAL RESEARCH AND MANUFACTURERS OF AMERICA) (2005). *Guiding Principles: Direct to Consumer Advertisements about Prescription Medicines*. Washington, DC: PhRMA.

PRIEGER, J. E. (1996). "Ramsey pricing and competition: the consequences of myopic regulation." *Journal of Regulatory Economics* 10: 307–21.

RAMSEY, F. P. (1927). "A contribution to the theory of taxation." *Economic Journal* 37: 47–61.

RECTOR, T. S., FINCH, M. D., DANZON, P. M., and PAULY M. V. (2003). "Effect of tiered prescription copayments on the use of preferred brand medications." *Medical Care* 41(3): 398–406.

REIFFEN, D. and WARD, M. R. (2005). "Generic drug industry dynamics." *Review Of Economics And Statistics* 87(1): 37–49.

RIDLEY, D., GRABOWSKI, H. G., and MOE, J. L. (2006). "Developing drugs for developing countries." *Health Affairs* 25(2): 313–24.

ROBERTS, P. W. (1999). "Product innovation, product-market competition and persistent profitability in the US pharmaceutical industry." *Strategic Management Journal* 20(7): 655–70.

ROSENTHAL, M. B., BERNDT, E. R., DONOHUE, J. M., FRANK, R. G., and EPSTEIN, A. M. (2002). "Promotion of prescription drugs to consumers." *New England Journal of Medicine* 345(7): 498–505.

—— —— EPSTEIN, A. M., and FRANK, R. G. (2003). "Demand effects of recent changes in prescription drug promotion." *Frontiers in Health Policy Research*. Cambridge, MA: MIT Press and National Bureau of Economic Research, 6: 1–26.

SCHERER, F. M. (1993). "Pricing, profits and technological-progress in the pharmaceutical industry." *Journal of Economic Perspectives* 7(3): 97–115.

—— (1997). "How US antitrust can go astray: The brand name prescription drug litigation." *International Journal of the Economics of Business* 4(3): 239–57.

—— (2004). "The pharmaceutical industry: Prices and progress." *New England Journal of Medicine* 351(9): 927–32.

—— and WATAL, J. (2002). "Post-TRIPS options for access to patented medicines in developing nations." *Journal of International Economic Law* 5(4): 913–39.

SCHNEEWEISS, S., SOUMERAI, S. B., et al. (2002). "The impact of reference-based pricing for angiotension-converting enzyme converting inhibitors on drug utilization." *Canadian Medical Association Journal* 166(6): 737–45.

SCHOFFSKI, O. (1996). "Consequences of implementing a drug budget for office-based physicians in Germany." *Pharmacoeconomics* 10(Suppl. 2): 81–8.

SCHULENBURG, J. M. and SCHOFFSKI, O. (1994) "Transformation of the health care system, an economic analysis of the changes in referrals and hospital admissions after the drug budget of the health care reform act of 1992," in P. Oberender (ed.), *Probleme der Transformation im Gesundheitswesen*, Baden-Baden, Nomos, 45–81.

SCOTT MORTON, F. (1997). "The strategic response by pharmaceutical firms to the Medicaid most-favored-customer rules." *RAND Journal of Economics* 28(2): 269–90.

—— (1999). "Entry decisions in the generic pharmaceutical industry." *RAND Journal of Economics* 30(3): 421–40.

—— (2000). "Barriers to entry, brand advertising, and generic entry in the US pharmaceutical industry." *International Journal of Industrial Organization* 18(7): 1085–104.

SKREPNEK, G. H. (2004). "Accounting- versus economic-based rates of return: Implications for profitability measures in the pharmaceutical industry." *Clinical Therapeutics* 26(1): 155–74.

SUH, D. C., MANNING, W. G. et al. (2000). "Effect of multiple-source entry on price competition after patent expiration in the pharmaceutical industry." *Health Services Research* 35(2): 529–47.

TELSER, L. (1975). "The theory of supply with applications to the ethical pharmaceutical industry." *Journal of Law & Economics* 18: 449–78.

TEMIN, P. (1979). "Technology, regulation, and market structure in the modern pharmaceutical industry." *Bell Journal of Economics* 10(2): 429–46.

—— (1983). "Costs and benefits in switching drugs from Rx to OTC." *Journal of Health Economics* 2(3): 187.

THOMAS, L. G. (1990). "Regulation and firm size: FDA impacts on innovation." *RAND Journal of Economics* 21(4): 497–517.

—— (1996). "Industrial policy and international competitiveness in the pharmaceutical industry," in *Competitive Strategies in the Pharmaceutical Industry*. R. Helms (ed.). Washington DC, The American Enterprise Institute: 107–29.

TUFTS CENTER FOR THE STUDY OF DRUG DEVELOPMENT (2003). "FDA's fast track initiative cut total drug development time by three years, according to Tufts CSDD." <http://csdd.tufts.edu/NewsEvents/RecentNews.asp?newsid=34> accessed 2005.

ULRICH, V. and WILLE, E. (1996). "Health care reform and expenditure on drugs." *Pharmacoeconomics* 10(Suppl. 2): 81–8.

US FDA (FOOD AND DRUG ADMINISTRATION) (1997). "Food and drug administration modernization act of 1997." USFDA, Washington, DC.

—— and DHHS (DEPARTMENT OF HEALTH AND HUMAN SERVICES) (2005a). "Food and drug administration establishment of prescription drug user fee rates for fiscal year 2006." *Federal Register* 70(146), Aug. 1.

———— (2005b). "Fast track, priority review and accelerated approval: oncology tools." Washington, DC: Food and Drug Administration.

———— (2005c). "FY 2004 PDUFA financial report." DHHS, Washington, DC, March.

US FTC (FEDERAL TRADE COMMISSION) (2002). "Generic drug entry prior to patent expiration: an FTC study." July, USFTC, Washington, DC.

US GAO (GENERAL ACCOUNTING OFFICE) (1992). "Prescription drugs: companies typically charge more in the United States than in Canada." Pub. No. GAO-HRD-92-110. US GAO, Gaithersburg, MD.

—— (1993). "Medicaid: changes in drug prices paid by HMOs and hospitals since enactment of rebate provisions." US GAO, Gaithersburg, MD.

—— (1994). "Prescription drugs: companies typically charge more in the United States than in the United Kingdom." Pub. No. GAO/HEHS-94-29. US GAO, Gaithersburg, MD.

—— (2002). "Effect of user fees on drug approval times, withdrawals, and other agency activities." US GAO, Gaithersburg, MD.

US MEDICARE (2003) "Prescription drug, improvement and modernization act of 2003." Public Law 108-173. US Medicare, Washington, DC.

WALKER, H. (1971). *Market Power and Price Levels in the Ethical Drug Industry*. Bloomington, IN, University of Indiana Press.

WARDELL, W. M. (1973). "Introduction of new therapeutic drugs in United States and Great Britain: international comparison." *Clinical Pharmacology & Therapeutics* 14(5): 773–90.

WATAL, J. (2000). "Pharmaceutical patents, prices and welfare losses: Policy options for India under the WTO TRIPS agreement." *World Economy* 23(5): 733–52.

WIGGINS, S. N. (1981). "Product quality regulation and new drug introductions: some new evidence from the 1970s." *Review of Economics And Statistics* 63(4): 615–19.

—— and MANESS, R. (2004). "Price competition in pharmaceuticals: The case of anti-infectives." *Economic Inquiry* 42(2): 247–63.

WOSINSKA, M. (2002). "Just what the patient ordered? Direct-to-consumer advertising and the demand for pharmaceutical products." Marketing Research Paper Series: Harvard Business School. Cambridge, MA.

WRIGHT, D. J. (2004). "The drug bargaining game: pharmaceutical regulation in Australia." *Journal of Health Economics* 23(4): 785–813.

Wyeth v. Levine (2009). 555U.S.

CHAPTER 23

DISEASE PREVENTION, HEALTH CARE, AND ECONOMICS

JANE HALL

23.1 INTRODUCTION

THE prevention of disease covers a wide range of activities that can occur both within and outside the health system. In the developed countries, the increased life expectancy associated with the control of infectious and many acute diseases, has resulted in an increasing prevalence of chronic and other continuing diseases. Although environmental conditions are far more prominent as a cause of disease in the developing countries (Prüss-Üstün et al. 2008), nonetheless, these countries are also dealing with the increasing burden of chronic disease, including cardiovascular disease, cancers, diabetes and depression, which become more prevalent with aging (WHO 2008). Many of these conditions and diseases are associated with risk factors or precursors which make them, in theory at least, preventable. Less disease and illness would deliver on one of the widely accepted health system goals of improving the health of the population.

Health care systems are increasingly costly, representing an average of 8.9 percent of GDP across developed (OECD) countries; and that cost is predicted to grow even more as health care has to deal with the management of more chronic disease and co-morbidities, often associated with aging populations, a greater range of possible interventions delivered by new drugs and other technologies, and workforce shortages. Despite many differences in the ways countries finance and organize their health care systems, all are faced with the same challenges of managing these pressures. Not surprisingly, health systems have developed to respond to the occurrence of illness and so many commentators have questioned whether it would be better to have a system focused on health protection rather than illness care; or the fence at the top of the cliff rather than the ambulance at the bottom. It seems that many governments now take the view that there is an under-investment in prevention within health care delivery systems. In the UK, for example, according to a recent Government White Paper, "We must re-orientate our health and social care services to focus together on prevention and health promotion. This means a shift in the centre of gravity of spending" (Department of Health 2006). And similarly in Australia, a recent report states:

> The balance of our health system needs to be reoriented. Our health system must continue to provide access to appropriate acute and emergency services to meet the needs of people when they are sick. Balancing this fundamental purpose, our health system also needs greater emphasis on helping people stay healthy through stronger investment in wellness, prevention and early detection. (Health and Hospitals Reform Commission 2009)

Although people in general are living longer and healthier lives than their forebears, the growth in obesity in many developed countries has led to predictions of falling health prospects for future generations. This possible reversal of a historical trend has further encouraged the view that something is amiss with the social arrangements that underpin changing lifestyles. These social arrangements encompass the choices made by individuals, the environments in which they live, the types of work they do, the supply of food and other health related commodities, as well as direct actions taken by governments.

The chapter attempts to take these policy issues and explore how the economic analysis of prevention can add to debate and policy development. The chapter starts by asking what is prevention, and draws on the economic concepts of human capital and utility maximization. This provides a framework for investigating why people make the decisions they do, and how they will respond if their incentives or constraints alter. This approach can yield useful insights into behavior: why do individuals keep smoking? Why are obesity levels rising? Why do health care providers miss opportunities for simple screening of their patients? Why do parents not have their children immunized? Thus economic analysis can provide a basis for designing prevention strategies. The importance of good health to many aspects of human well-being suggests there should be particular attention paid to prevention in consideration of equity of opportunity.

Section 23.3 addresses whether there is a current under-investment in prevention. For many policymakers and public health advocates, this question is about whether more prevention will save on future health care expenditure. This section repeats the argument that this is the wrong question and that the appropriate question is whether the benefits delivered justify additional spending on prevention. The answer is "it depends"; the potential benefits of prevention are broader than gains in health outcomes and thus the return on an investment in prevention can only be assessed once there is clarity about the benefits to be considered. Section 23.4 then turns to the special challenges in building an evidence base for prevention policy.

23.2 WHAT IS PREVENTION?

Traditionally prevention has been classified in three stages: primary prevention, aimed at limiting the development of risk factors; secondary prevention, aimed at reducing the development from risk factors to established disease; and tertiary prevention aimed at reducing disease progression. Alternative approaches have been based on type of risk activity (clinical, develop personal skills, strengthen community actions, create supportive environments, reorient health services, build health public policy; Rush et al. 2002); by categories of activity (prevention, detection, health programs, and education; Ungar and Santos 2002); by type of approach (clinical prevention, health promotion, health protection, and healthy public policy; Goldsmith et al. 2006).

"Prevention is better than cure" according to the old saying. But what is prevention? A recently proposed definition for England is:

> a clinical, social, behavioral, educational, environmental, fiscal or legislative intervention or broad partnership program designed to reduce the risk of mental and physical illness, disability or premature death and/or to promote long-term physical, social, emotional and psychological well-being. (Le Grand 2009)

Many of these activities lie within the domain of governments, such as regulation (banning tobacco advertising), environmental regulation (controls on pollution), fiscal measures (taxing "bads" such as tobacco and alcohol); while others lie within the scope of public health programs which are population based and non-exclusive in consumption. However, there are various activities which rely on a service provided to an individual, such as screening, immunization, and early detection. These services may be provided within or independently of other aspects of personal primary care services; for example primary care providers can provide services such as screening for risk factors, counseling for lifestyle change, early detection through physical examinations (such as cervical cancer or prostate disease) or encouraging their patients to undergo further tests (such as for bowel cancer). The ongoing management of individual risk factors, or established continuing disease relies on the activities of health care providers and their interactions with patients.

The concept of the health production function was introduced earlier (see Chapter 6 in this volume) and provides a useful starting point for consideration of prevention, just as it does for economic behavior and addiction, concepts of equity and fairness, and the determinants of health in childhood (Chapters 10, 34, and 8 of this volume, respectively). Health is a product of genetic inheritance, environmental and context factors, lifestyle choices, and the use of medical services. Prevention cannot be considered in a static framework as it takes a long-term view. Although the notion of health human capital has been a powerful conceptual tool, there has been little attempt to apply it specifically to prevention as distinct from treatment (Kenkel 2000). Prevention is an activity now that will affect future health, through changing the risk of future bad health and/or death, or promoting well-being. While prevention is generally considered as an investment, so that action taken now will have a positive effect on future health, this definition also allows for a negative, or disinvestment, effect. Thus health in the current period is a product of genetic inheritance at birth, and other inputs in all previous periods. These inputs can be actions taken by the individual, i.e. their own effort, or actions taken by others such as government regulation or intervention to change environmental or contextual factors, or services provided through the health system.

Now the individual seeks not to maximize health, but to maximize their own utility or well-being over their life-cycle. Thus they will invest in their own health promoting activities as long as their individual welfare gain from that is greater than their individual welfare loss from forgoing other activities. This results in the best outcome for the individual, as judged by the greatest lifetime utility for that individual, given the opportunities and constraints they face. Does it represent the best outcome for society? Individuals will determine their own actions, taking environmental and other context factors as given. However, societies have the opportunity to change the context: health harming products such as tobacco may be forbidden or regulated to reduce supply or increase prices; planning regulations may increase open space available for recreation; food standards may ensure essential nutrients are added such as iodine fortification in bread.

The question of whether one set of social arrangements are better than another lies within the scope of normative economics. In neoclassical welfare economics, the principle of consumer sovereignty holds, which means that social welfare is an aggregation of individual welfare utilities, and individual utility is determined by individuals' own judgments of what is good for them. If this principle is used to judge social welfare, then social interventions are warranted to correct market failures which arise due to lack of information (consumers are unable to make informed choices), externalities (such as in infectious disease where A's risk of disease is affected by B's disease status), or the moral hazard of insurance (which encourages consumers to use medical treatment at less than its full cost rather than prevention which is not subsidized). See Kenkel (2000) for a full exposition.

The importance of health to social welfare has been stressed by extra-welfarism; even proposing that, if not the only goal of health expenditure, then the most important should be the maximization of health (Culyer 1991). Most economic evaluation is based on the premise of maximizing the units of health gain achieved for health expenditure. Although individual preferences across health states are incorporated in measures such as QALYs, these are limited to aspects of health states, and do not explore trade-offs between health states, or aspects of them, with other dimensions of well-being. Yet it seems that for most people there is a trade-off between health and other things they enjoy. Therefore, restricting the social goals of health expenditure to health outcomes only is a departure from what people would choose for themselves, or the principle of consumer sovereignty.

However, a concern with fairness or equity is widespread in the stated objectives of health policymakers, and in health economics (see Chapter 34 of this volume). As Olsen describes, this can lead to different approaches depending on whether the focus is on a just distribution of health, of the achievable gains in health, or access to health care. There are criticisms of the extra-welfarist or health-only approach, by other commentators who still depart from the consumer sovereignty basis of social welfare; in general, they suggest that some form of social values can be developed through the community or policymakers as its agents (Mooney 1994; Hurley 2000; Mooney 2001; Richardson 2001; Richardson and McKie 2005).

The notion that there is something special about health and about the fairness concerns generated by the unequal chances of poor health is strong. Good health is of value not just in itself but also provides the ability to enjoy other aspects of life; a precondition for human flourishing. "Health and survival are central to the understanding not only of the quality of one's life, but also for one's ability to do what one has reason to want to do"(Sen 2002). Criticisms of welfarism and utilitarianism within health economics have been much influenced by the work of Sen (1985, 1987, 1992). Sen argues that individual well-being comprises two parts; functionings, that is what people do or achieve, and capabilities, that is what opportunities people have to achieve. However, individuals may choose freely not to achieve something which lies within their capabilities, and if this should be the case the resultant inequality is a reflection of personal preferences rather than social inequity. Extending this to health, then health status can be considered as a functioning, the level of health achieved, a measure of what people do. The capability to achieve good health (which may or may not be exercised as a result of personal decisions about smoking or other risky behavior) is the ability provided by social arrangements including income, environments and other social factors (Sen 2002). Sen himself has described the complex and multi-dimensional nature of health equity, encompassing the achievement of good health, the capability to achieve good health, and the distribution of health care. Inequalities resulting from free choice are not an inequity.

The notion of capabilities has proved an attractive approach for thinking about what equity in health/health care means; it should also prove to add further insights to understanding the economics of prevention. It could be said that the goal of prevention is to maximize the capabilities of each person to achieve good health. As those capabilities are determined by a range of factors outside the individual's control, prevention aimed at improving equity in those capabilities is an important consideration for broader issues of social justice.

23.2.1 Summary

Prevention encompasses a wide range of activities, both around individual behaviors and choices, and government interventions and social arrangements. The economic concept of the health production function provides a useful framework for considering what prevention is. The goal of prevention is to improve health, and in some arguments it is to maximize health. Health maximization relegates other sources of human well-being as less important, even though most individuals do not behave as though health is the only important goal. The importance of good health to many aspects of human well-being suggests there should be particular attention paid to prevention in consideration of health equity and social justice more broadly. Sen's capabilities framework offers a potentially valuable approach to thinking about prevention, with capabilities encompassing those factors outside the individual's control impacting on health and health risks, and achievements the result of capabilities and individual choices.

23.3 Is There an Under-investment in Prevention?

To many policymakers and public health advocates, the case for there being an under-investment in prevention seems self-evident. Prevention advocates frequently argue that prevention will reduce health care budgets and not surprisingly Health Ministers and their governments find the notion of improving the nation's health while saving health care costs not only very attractive, but the only way to address the fiscal pressures of growing health budgets (Redmond et al. 2007; Cohen et al. 2008; National Health and Hospitals Reform Commission 2009).

Economic evaluation was first systematically applied to prevention in the 1970s (Weinstein and Stason 1976). As the number of studies grew it was clear that far from saving on health spending, in general prevention increased health care costs (Russell 2009). The number of studies has increased exponentially since then. Useful resources are provided by registries of these studies; for example Health Technology Assessment Resources, the NHS Centre for Reviews and Dissemination, and the Tufts Registry. In early 2009, the NHS Centre for Reviews and Dissemination recorded over 4000 studies on its databases under the heading "prevention." A systematic review of 599 published economic analyses compared primary prevention with treatment (though this category included secondary and tertiary prevention) (Cohen et al. 2008); about 20 percent of prevention strategies will be cost saving with the other 80 percent generating additional costs, much the same as the proportion of treatment interventions which were shown to save health care costs.

The reason for this is readily explained. Those individuals need to be identified from the general population, through some screening or case finding program. And the intervention itself may require long-term therapy and monitoring. For example, universal childhood vaccination can be easily targeted—vaccination is targeted to all children at specific ages, and a single dose vaccine requires only one service. In contrast, reducing the risk of cardiovascular disease through reduction of high blood pressure is likely to require identifying those with established hypertension from across the population, and then providing pharmaceutical treatment to those individuals for their remaining lifetimes. The net costs (or savings) of prevention depend on the cost of the intervention and the proportion of the population to which it is applied, compared to the cost of treatment and the proportion of the target group who will become ill in the absence of prevention.

This general conclusion is based on the existing body of evidence from published economic evaluation studies. At least in the case of primary prevention for cardiac disease, the preventive interventions that have been assessed have been clinical interventions with pharmaceuticals, such as medications to reduce high blood pressure or high cholesterol compared with later treatment of heart disease, with very little attention paid to broader public health programs (Schwappach et al. 2007). Further, there are strong incentives for producers of such interventions to fund such research (as they are likely to benefit from adoption) and a resulting under-investment in assessing programs not based on some proprietary product (Kenkel 2000).

The economic case for prevention does not rest on its ability to generate cost savings, but rather that it represents a better, in terms of benefits to society, allocation of resources. If the purpose of health care interventions is, to use the old phrase, "to add years to life, and life to years," then value for money can only be determined by comparing the gains from prevention and their costs compared to the alternatives. This is the scope of economic evaluation; alternatives are compared in terms of their costs and benefits, defined as achievement of objectives (see Chapter 31 for discussion of this approach). The appropriate measure of outcome has to capture the benefits of both programs being compared. So for example, if two different programs which aim to prevent obesity are being compared, then weight gain would be an appropriate outcome measure. However, if the prevention of diabetes with treatment of evident disease is the comparison, then the appropriate outcome will capture the effects of mortality and morbidity. The use of cost-utility analysis is generally preferred to cost-effectiveness analysis for consideration of prevention programs, as it captures a greater range of patient relevant effects.

The case of more investment in prevention has been argued on the cost per QALY for many programs providing high economic value (Woolf 2009). This is not enough to make sensible investment decisions on prevention. Even interventions which provide health gains for a relatively low cost may be targeted to a large proportion of the population. For example in Australia, about half of the adult population are over-weight or obese (Australian Institute of Health and Welfare 2008), so that even a low cost program will have a large target group, meaning a large total expenditure. A focus on cost per QALY does not consider the impact on the total budget, and this may be beyond the capacity of the government or the willingness of the nation to pay (see Birch and Gafni 1992).

Arguments in favor of prevention often include the economy wide effects of better health. This is the gain in society's economic production due to increased labor force participation, and lower payouts for disability related income support. The argument is that reducing mortality and morbidity will increase the productive capacity of the economy by reducing sickness due to absenteeism and by increasing workforce participation. There are several problems with accepting the human capital value of prevention. These fall into two categories. First, distributional issues: health gains are valued more highly for those in the paid workforce, and potentially for some groups of workers over others; this would, for example, value gains for middle aged men over older people and women.

Second, the validity of wage rates as a measure of increased production: absenteeism may be compensated by the additional effort of other workers or the employment of new workers; and whether the marginal wage is equal to the marginal productivity of labor (see Chapter 31 on cost-effectiveness analysis for more discussion). More broadly, though, the issue of the appropriateness of production gains as the measure of benefit has to be considered against the overall objectives of investments in health care.

23.3.1 Is Health All There Is?

Although quality adjusted survival is clearly an advance on measuring only lives saved, or life-years gained, it is limited to health gains, thus implicitly determining the goal of health care expenditure to be health and only health. Health gain maximization alone is perhaps best expressed as "A QALY is a QALY is a QALY." This assumes that a QALY gain is independent of the process by which it is gained and of to whom it accrues. A QALY gained from preventive effort may not be equivalently valued to the same QALY gain from treatment (Schwappach 2007); it depends on the relative disutility of being sick and undergoing therapy, and that of the effort required for prevention. While economic evaluations of prevention have been good at capturing the relative costs, there has been less attention to the differential values of the process aspects. Similarly, the social value of a unit of health gain is generally assumed to be equally valued, irrespective of the total gain to any one individual, their initial health state, or other characteristics. Most commentators accept that there is more to be considered in the benefits of health care than units of health status gained, at least conceptually, but this is rarely implemented in practical applications (Brouwer et al. 2008; Coast 2009). Practically, decision-making in settings where economic analysis is routinely used, such as NICE in the UK, use QALY maximization as a proximate goal; but ask for consideration of other factors, such as consumer and patient autonomy, fairness in the distribution of limited resources, availability of alternative treatments, severity of the condition (National Institute for Health and Clinical Excellence 2007).

Critics of QALY maximization have pointed to the need for wider outcomes and for the inclusion of aspects of process utility (Mooney 1994); for example, individuals are often prepared to pay for extra convenience, additional comfort, and for information that has no immediate bearing on their health status. The potential importance of these extra benefits has led to renewed interest in applying cost-benefit analysis, and stated preference methods to elicit values for the benefits of health care. But what benefits should be considered? The answer to this question is generally summarized as whatever individuals who make up society value, as indicated by their willingness to pay. It helps to explore this idea in the context of particular types of prevention programs. A note of caution, though, is that eliciting willingness to pay through surveys where the decision is hypothetical and the respondent knows they will not have to pay, should not be taken as valid estimates of consumer value.

23.3.2 Screening and the Value of Information

Screening is often assumed to lead to improved health, as individuals with established risk factors or early but non-symptomatic disease can be identified and appropriate action, modification of risk exposure, or early therapy can be instituted. The conditions under which screening can be assessed to be effective in population health outcomes are well-established, and evaluation should include the cost per unit of health outcome. However, the immediate "product" of screening is information, as Cairns and Shackley (1993) point out: "screening in health care can be viewed as an investment which yields additional information." This raises the issue of whether information has value independent of its use in taking action to avoid poor outcomes, and if so how to assess it.

The value of information is generally treated as positive. Evidence to support this is drawn from studies which show a positive willingness to pay for tests which provide information but do not change outcomes, such as ultrasound in normal pregnancy (Berwick and Weinstein 1985) or prenatal screening which identifies a fetus affected by a severe condition even though the mother has already rejected the option of abortion (Mooney and Lange 1993). Even with relatively common conditions, most people screened will receive a negative (no suspicious finding) result, and these people may gain reassurance from the information. This may be particularly the case with prenatal screening. On the other hand, information can have negative effects, with a positive screening test result raising anxiety, increasing the need for that individual to change their lifestyle, or increase their use of the health system. Indeed, once individuals have had a positive result they may perceive themselves to be at risk for other conditions as well (Stone and Stewart 1996), and one study showed that identifying untreated hypertension led to an increase in the use of health services for non-related conditions.

The case of prenatal screening is particularly complex, as the "intervention" available to parents with a positive result is termination. Evaluations have frequently assessed the "cost per case prevented" which, in effect, treats the birth of handicapped child as having no value (Sadovnick and Baird 1981; Piggott et al. 1994). This is a complex ethical debate, and beyond the focus of this discussion.

Similarly, genetic screening also has some very specific implications (Hall et al. 1988), and with the increased potential for genetic screening these will become more important. The information from a genetic test has value to people beyond the individual tested. It has consequences for other family members, as even knowing there is a potentially inherited condition changes their risk status. Parents may feel guilty at having passed on an inherited condition; affected siblings may blame their parents; and unaffected siblings may also experience guilt associated with being one spared poor health. Genetic information, even the knowledge of whether an individual has been tested, or has refused a test, can determine their risk status; and this could be used by employers or insurers. Neither welfarist nor extra-welfarist approaches have to date adequately addressed the value of information issues (Hall 1996).

23.3.3 Preferences over lifestyles

The inclusion of non-health outcomes is evident in investigations of preferences for aspects of treatment, for primary care services, and for screening (Longworth et al. 2001; Gerard et al. 2003; Scott et al. 2003; Haas 2005). Primary and secondary prevention programs often target lifestyle choices, such as smoking, diet, alcohol consumption and physical activity. However, similar non-health attributes for the benefits of these types of programs have received little attention in economic studies; such attributes might be change in body shape, ability to participate in other activities, or features of the intervention such as social interaction with other program participants (see Owen et al. 2010 for an example). However, it would seem that social marketers are aware that non-health outcomes may be as or more important than health outcomes, with anti-smoking campaigns promoting social acceptability, and diet and exercise programs promising greater attractiveness and improved family life.

Individuals' choices are influenced by their perceptions of costs, risks and benefits; when an individual has to change in some way, whether it is to attend a screening clinic, take a child for an immunization, or alter their diet, they are asked to give up something they would enjoy. Participating in screening requires giving up the time to travel and wait, plus any anxiety and discomfort associated with the examination and waiting for the results. Having one's child immunized means more time, plus dealing with any side-effects of the vaccine. Changing one's diet means forgoing the pleasures of forbidden food, pleasures that can be missed even after long-term change (Brink 2009). In economic terms these are losses in consumer utility, though rarely counted in evaluations of prevention.

Indeed it is difficult to know how to count them. Standard economic theory has assumed that consumer preferences are fixed, and that what is a consumer loss today would be a loss tomorrow, next year and in several years' time. Public health and health promotion, in contrast, are prepared to change consumer preferences and social acceptability. Smoking in many countries is no longer socially acceptable, and individuals who once enjoyed tobacco can become strident in their lack of enjoyment of others' smoking. Individuals who once avoided physical activity can develop pleasure in the process of exercise (Brink 2009). There are also for many lifestyle behaviors an apparent contradiction between individuals' continued actions and their expressed preference to "kick the habit." The development of approaches which explain the effect of addiction on demand is covered in Chapter 10 of this volume.

23.3.4 Summary

Although it is frequently argued (but not by economists) that prevention will save expenditure on future treatment, the current body of evidence demonstrates that it is more likely to generate additional health care costs. However, the evaluations that have been undertaken are predominantly of clinical interventions, rather than broad public health programs. That said, the economic case for a greater investment in prevention rests on the benefits of prevention outweighing the opportunity costs of increasing preventive activities. These benefits may go beyond better health outcomes as measured by Quality Adjusted Life Years; a unit of health gained from treatment is not equivalent to the same health gained from prevention unless the (dis)utility of illness and undergoing treatment is equivalent to the (dis)utility of the effort required by prevention. Other potential benefits from prevention are the value of information, improved well-being from a different lifestyle, and lower risks of future adverse events. These have not been systematically considered in evaluations to date. The range of benefits that it is appropriate to consider depends on the concept of social welfare that is adopted.

23.4 ASSESSING PREVENTIVE STRATEGIES

This section now turns from how to assess whether there is an under-investment in prevention to the question of how to assess proposed interventions. The pattern of health service delivery and thus a nation's investment in prevention is not fixed by some central single decision. Rather it is the result of various decisions: the decisions of funders about what services to cover and how to pay for them; the decisions of providers in what services to provide; and the decisions of consumers about whether to visit health care providers, and then to follow their advice. How do individuals make those decisions? Understanding decision-making is the basis for predicting how people will change their behavior if the incentives change. For example, economic explanations for the rise in obesity demonstrate how technology has changed the costs of purchasing and preparing different foods, while increasing workforce participation outside the home has increased the opportunity costs of time spent preparing food (Cutler et al. 2003). The assessment of prevention must account for the extent to which people will actually change their behavior; for example providing free early childhood health checks will not deliver benefits unless parents take up the service.

23.4.1 Considerations for the Economic Evaluation of Prevention Programs

Economic evaluation relies on clinical studies for evidence of effectiveness. An economic evaluation is increasingly conducted alongside the clinical trial of new pharmaceuticals, and although much less often for evaluations of other medical interventions and health delivery programs, interest in doing so is growing. For acute conditions, the endpoint of the trial is the final relevant outcome of interest. Consequently for many treatments, the evidence of effectiveness and costs can be drawn from one study. This is not the case for evaluations which include a prevention, particularly a primary prevention, arm. The range of interventions being considered can be broad, so that evidence has to be drawn from a number of studies. The final relevant outcome may be distant in time from the intervention, so that the trial evidence is based on intermediate outcomes; for example, a lifestyle intervention may be evaluated in terms of changes in diet and exercise, whereas the final relevant outcome is reduction of cardiovascular disease and will not occur until many years after the initial intervention. This requires extensive and often complex modeling, with input to the model developed from a range of sources. Another type of complexity arises because several risk factors are precursors to a range of diseases. For example, smoking, alcohol consumption, illicit drug use, diet, and lack of exercise are implicated in injury and accidents, many cancers, coronary heart disease and stroke, respiratory disease, and diabetes (WHO 2002). An issue related to immunization is that the individuals who benefit are not just those vaccinated, but others whose risk of being infected will reduce as the pool of infection is reduced (Beutels et al. 2003). All this implies that generally there is much greater uncertainty in models of prevention programs.

The application of economic evaluation is focused on the incremental effect of an identifiable and separable program, for example adding a new drug into a current treatment regimen. But prevention is the outcome of many factors; what prevention happens and how is the result of a complex set of individual decisions, whether they are the decisions of individuals as consumers and patients (lifestyle, immunization, screening for common diseases or risk factors, whether and how to use health services) or as providers (workforce participation, where to locate, and what services to offer), and the way they interact. While clinical and behavioral interventions are often considered as substitutes, their maximal effect may be through their interaction.

The inclusion of additional health care costs which arise due to complications, side-effects or failure of the initial treatment are clearly directly related to the intervention and so generally accepted as good practice. Prevention programs can give rise to unrelated costs, where the improvement in longevity means an aging cohort with more cancers and chronic disease (McPherson 2008; van Baal et al. 2008). There is no agreement as to whether these should be included, and for recent contributions to the debate, see Lee (2008) and Meltzer (2008). It is worth noting that this will generally have more impact on the cost-effectiveness of prevention programs, as it raises the cost of prevention.

Another issue is the choice of discount rate. The higher the discount rate, the more that future benefits, as well as costs, are reduced in value. Prevention programs are likely to be highly sensitive to the choice of discount rate as costs are usually incurred immediately, while benefits (health gains and future treatment costs avoided) arise in the future. The approach adopted by most government and regulatory bodies is that the same discount rate should be applied to costs and benefits. Discounting costs reflects a preference for current funds over future funds; this may reflect a pure time preference for the present over the future, or the opportunity cost of capital funds. There seems to be no argument over there being a positive time preference over funds. The consistency argument is simply that if costs are discounted, then benefits should be discounted at the same rate; and that to not do so would result in constant delaying of expenditure (as the future costs are valued less than current expenditure).

Critics of this approach argue that differential discounting of costs and health gains is appropriate, with a much lower rate (or even zero) applied to health gains, to reflect the social value of future health gains compared to current gains. Differential discounting will generally make prevention programs more attractive (Brouwer et al. (2005) provide some examples). Schwappach argues that as revealed preferences demonstrate that most people do have decreasing discount rates over time, this should be incorporated in the analysis of prevention (Schwappach 2007). Indeed, the National Institute of Health and Clinical Excellence in the UK mandated differential discounting, with 6 percent applied to costs and 1.5 percent applied to benefits, until 2004. The change to using the same discount rate remains contested (Claxton et al. 2006; Gravelle et al. 2007).

In short, the economic evaluation of prevention programs presents more challenges than most therapeutic interventions. There are a number of issues which have received relatively little attention, and have not been resolved in theory. Therefore, the practice needs to be cognizant of these and their impact on the results and address them explicitly.

23.4.2 Taxes and Subsidies

There is a long history of imposing taxes on the health "bads" of tobacco and alcohol. The rationale for taxing these substances was initially based on externalities. That is, as smoking and high consumption of alcohol led to more disease, and that as costs of treatment are shared either through private insurance or public financing, smokers and drinkers were not paying their way. The imposition of taxes made private costs more aligned with social costs. The responsiveness of consumption to price increases has been well-studied, and increasing prices on tobacco and alcohol does alter consumption. Once research showed that the additional costs of health care attributable to smoking were more than covered by the revenue raised through tobacco taxes, the argument moved to much more paternalistic grounds, that it was governments' role to protect individuals from the consequences of poor choices. The extent to which government should interfere with individual choice remains controversial (Jochelson 2006).

Not surprisingly, given the success of public health in reducing tobacco consumption (through fiscal and other strategies), a similar approach has been advanced for unhealthy foods, the so-called fat tax. There is a substantial literature on the use of taxation and food choices; examples are Darmon et al. (2002); Drewnowski and Darmon (2005); Drewnowski and Specter (2004). Whereas any tobacco use is harmful, dietary change is largely concerned with a balanced diet rather than removing such foodstuffs entirely. Further, as food is essential and a higher component of household expenditure in low income groups, taxes on food have equity considerations. Against that, a diet high in fruit and vegetables is a more expensive option than one consisting of more energy dense foods, which can make healthy eating behaviors less reachable for low income groups. This makes the arguments of selective taxation of food much more complex.

Fiscal interventions can alternatively lower prices through subsidies, so that healthy choices are made cheaper choices. Many programs have removed or reduced financial barriers, such as the provision of free immunization or screening programs. Studies which have modeled changes in consumption, using actual market data, concluded that purchasing patterns respond to price, though the extent of the response should be expected to vary with incomes, availability and prices of other foods, and cultural factors (Goodman and Anise 2006). A longitudinal study from China found large and significant responses in food consumption to changing prices (Gou et al. 1999). In the US, a prospective observational study investigated the association between food prices and children's BMI, and the density of food outlets (restaurants, grocery and convenience stores); lower prices for fruit and vegetables were associated with lower increases in BMI (Sturm and Datar 2005).

Some success in increasing consumption of fruit and vegetables through free or subsidized provision has been demonstrated, but with short follow-up periods and often without measuring the effect on weight loss (Bere et al. 2005; Wall et al. 2006). Changing prices at consumption points, such as cafeterias and vending machines, does seem to increase the purchase of healthier alternatives (Sutherland et al. 2008a).

23.4.3 Direct Financial Incentives

Paying directly for good behavior rather than taxing unhealthy behavior is attracting widespread policy attention (McGinnis et al. 2002; Redmond et al. 2007; Scott and Schurer 2008; Le Grand 2009; National Health and Hospitals Reform Commission 2009). This can be for adherence to prescribed therapy, regular attendance for screening and immunization, or participating in healthy lifestyles, and is intended to reinforce change and to encourage personal responsibility for maintaining one's own health. Financial incentives have proved effective in encouraging relatively simple behaviors, and particularly those which require a once only decision; appointment keeping, immunization, extending antenatal care to low income women, ensuring completion of TB treatment in homeless or drug using populations, and screening have all been shown to be responsive to incentives (Giuffrida and Torgerson 1997; Jepson et al. 2000; Kane et al. 2004; Jochelson 2007; Sutherland et al. 2008b). As expected, the larger the incentive, the greater the change observed.

Financial incentives have also been applied to more complex behaviors such as smoking, physical activity, and diet. Rewards are effective in increasing participation in behavior change programs, but these diminish once the reward is withdrawn; they also have some effect in inducing short-term changes in behavior, but these diminish over longer periods. Incentives have been shown to have modest to no effect on short-term outcomes such as weight loss; and the evidence shows a lack of sustained change (Kane et al. 2004; Goodman and Anise 2006; Jochelson 2007; Madore 2007; Cahill and Perera 2008; Paul-Ebhohimhen and Avenell 2008; Sutherland et al. 2008a; Marteau et al. 2009). However, they may be more effective as part of multi-faceted strategies than used alone (Jochelson 2007).

23.4.4 Incentives Linked to Health Insurance and Employment

As part of the German health reforms in 2004, sickness funds (insurers) have been allowed to offer bonuses to their fund members for health promoting behavior, namely screening, immunization, check-ups, and exercise (Schmidt 2007). Bonuses may take the form of cash payments, reductions in insurance premiums, decreased co-payments on certain service use, or in kind such as sporting equipment. Those who enrolled in the program had lower health care costs than those who did not participate; but enrollment was on a voluntary basis and the analysis does not adjust for other factors, such as initial health status. A similar approach has been adopted by PruHealth, a private insurer operating in the UK and South Africa, offering lower premiums for healthy behaviors. According to the company, costs have been reduced among the health behavior adopting group (Wilkinson 2008). This is not surprising. Those who volunteer for participation in such programs are likely to be better risks than those who do not; so in effect, this scheme allows the insurer to identify a better risk group. Further it is not clear that these programs promote real change, or just encourage participants to forms of behavior that are monitored and so rewarded.

The idea that cost savings accrue from better lifestyles, healthier employees will improve productivity and reduce absenteeism costs, has also been used to advocate that employers subsidize health promotion programs for over twenty years, but with little rigorous analysis to support the assertion (Warner and Murt 1984). More recently, for example, the US Department of Health and Human Services (2003) argued that:

> Employers are becoming more aware that over-weight and obesity, lack of physical activity, and tobacco use are adversely affecting the health and productivity of their employees and ultimately, the businesses' bottom line ... with benefit-to-cost ratios, ranging from $1.49 to $4.91 (median of $3.14) in benefits for every dollar spent on the program

but did not provide the evaluations on which the claim is based. However, other economic evaluation studies of health promotion programs (as discussed above) may engender some skepticism about these claims. Health promotion at work may also be used to attract workers, by offering non-wage benefits, or to selectively attract individuals with better health expectations.

23.4.5 Problems in Rewarding Complex Behaviors

There is an inherent cost with the use of any financial instruments, and even a modest incentive will have a substantial cost if widely applied. As well as the cost of the incentive itself, there are the administrative costs associated with the program, and this can be large if the desired impact is difficult to monitor. Further, incentives may provide a gain to the group of people already engaging in the desired behavior. Consider, for example, a bonus paid to those who participate in approved exercise programs. If the group who earn the bonus have simply switched their activities from one form of exercise to another, there is no gain in terms of additional exercisers. There is a gain to those individuals who switch (windfall gain); and to the operators of the approved programs.

Although rewards and penalties may be similar in terms of their financial impact, they can have quite different psychological impacts, and so their effectiveness may vary considerably. This is particularly true in terms of unintended effects. For example, penalties may lead to a sense of failure, lowered self-esteem and may make it more difficult for a person to try again, or try an alternative approach (Jochelson 2007). Some programs have also made rewards dependent on the achievement of a goal by a group, thus attempting to enlist social support for individuals attempting to make difficult changes. While social support can be a positive reinforcer, there can be unintended effects if one person is alienated through being seen to fail and preventing the group from achieving their reward (Jochelson 2007).

There is an issue in whether incentives are intended to change the costs of the opportunities open to individuals, and hence encourage the choices they would like to make. This approach does not change the intrinsic motivation of individuals but by changing prices increases the attractiveness of the healthy alternative. Direct incentives, in contrast to price changes, may be an attempt to change motivation by providing extrinsic reinforcement. Several writers have pointed to the unintended potential effect of replacing intrinsic motivation with extrinsic rewards (Frey and Oberholzer-Gee 1997; Gneezy and Rustichini 2000; Frey and Jegen 2001). While extrinsic motivation may be powerful in prompting behavior change, the new behavior is unlikely to be maintained once the external reward is ceased. Further, it has been suggested that extrinsic motivation may reduce intrinsic motivation; the desired behavior is seen as less worthwhile so that those who were already motivated actually reduce that behavior.

An alternative view of behavior change is that complex behaviors are the result of habit; one's preference for current behavior is influenced by one's previous behavior. Under this approach the role of incentives is to reinforce the reward of changing behavior, and once the new habit is formed individuals will be self-motivated (Cameron et al. 2001; Charness and Gneezy 2008).

There is limited evidence of the impact of financial incentives across income groups. Financial incentives are likely to be effective when they remove or significantly reduce a price barrier that is militating against some desired behavior; price barriers affect lower income groups more, so removing such barriers should favor low income groups. However, incentives that reward a complex behavior are more likely to offer windfall gains to higher income groups. Under many programs, eligibility for the reward is dependent on enrollment in the program. Many of those eligible do not enroll (Bere et al. 2005) and even among those who do, many do not claim their rewards (Redmond et al. 2007). It may be that they consider the reward too trivial to claim, or it may be that the process is poorly understood. However, difficult enrollment processes are likely to disadvantage those with less education or from minority populations. Incentives that impose penalties or reduce service eligibility may have unintended effects in disadvantaged groups, by not taking into account all the factors that impinge on their behaviors, and then denying them effective care (Steinbrook 2006).

23.4.6 Changing the Health System to Focus on Prevention

The way in which health care services are funded establishes inherent incentives (see Chapter 26 in this volume). The development of third-party payments limited to "medically necessary services" has left many preventive activities in an ambiguous situation. Fee-for-service is generally associated with higher utilization, but the extent to which this encourages the use of preventive services depends on whether those services attract a fee. Out-of-pocket fees have been associated with even lower use of preventive services (Lurie et al. 1987). Capitation is associated with lower service use and costs; given that part of the risk rests with the provider, this should encourage prevention at least for services which are effective in the short term. In practice, the enrollment period is usually too short for any benefits in reduced service use to be realized. Where capitation is an alternative form of funding, such as the US Health Maintenance Organizations (HMOs), there has in practice been a stronger emphasis on primary care and on coverage for preventive services. While this may be due to the financial incentive, it is much more likely to reflect the clientele who are attracted to HMO cover who tend to be younger, healthier, and more likely to invest in their own health protection.

Of more interest is the use of targeted payments or pay-for-performance funding as a means of encouraging better health outcomes (Berwick et al. 2003; Committee on Redesigning Health Insurance Performance Measures Payment and Performance Improvement Programs Institute of Medicine 2007; Epstein 2007). In practice, the performance in pay for performance has tended to focus on specific activities, such as achieving immunization coverage, or counseling on smoking. A recent review concluded that there is still limited evidence to support the effectiveness of these financial incentives (Christianson et al. 2009). Financial incentives have been widely applied in the UK, as the basis of the general practitioner contracts and the Quality and Outcomes Framework implemented since April 2004. General practice earnings increased (Galvin 2006; Maynard 2007), but the extent to which this represents real improvement is disputed (Brown and Lilford 2006; Campbell et al. 2007; Downing et al. 2007; and see discussion in Scott and Jan, Chapter 20 in this volume). In the US, there has also been growing enthusiasm accompanied by implementation in different settings, with both Medicare and most HMOs adopting some form of incentive based payment (Rosenthal and Dudley 2007). There is speculation but little data on the unintended consequences, such as short-termism, neglecting other effective care, and crowding out intrinsic motivation. The financial incentive is only one factor among a myriad of influences on provider behavior; financial incentives do not occur in a vacuum and may interact with other factors. In sum, although prevention seems not to be actively rewarded and appropriately encouraged within most modern health care delivery, it is not clear from the existing evidence what the optimal policy response is (Dudley et al. 2004).

23.4.7 Summary

Developing the evidence base that will support a broad prevention strategy presents a number of challenges. New investments in treatment are increasingly subject to economic evaluation; consequently there is a growing expectation that the same assessment will be applied to new prevention programs. This requires sophisticated modeling techniques, and agreement on the appropriate range of benefits and costs to be included. Implementation of new programs requires individuals to change their current behaviors. There is increasing interest in the use of financial incentives to motivate such changes. Payments directed at consumers and patients have been successful in bringing about change in simple, one-off behaviors, such as attendance at ante-natal clinics, but complex behavioral changes such as eating and exercise patterns are much more difficult to effect. Payments made to providers can also effect change in the pattern of service delivery but it is not clear what type and size of payments will ensure optimal outcomes.

23.5 CONCLUSION

The economic analysis of prevention draws on the range of concepts and techniques used in health economics. The notion of health as a component of human capital is a useful framework for the consideration of prevention. Economic analysis can be used to understand and predict behavior, and to assess whether changed use of resources represents a worthwhile improvement in individual and social welfare. As societies and health systems increase their emphasis on health promotion and disease prevention, there are many opportunities for health economics to contribute to the development and implementation of policy. As yet, the body of theory and the empirical evidence does not provide a coherent framework for new approaches to prevention but it does provide promising avenues for further research.

Important topics include whether health gains from prevention are valued equivalently to health gains from treatment, the extent to which individuals value a reduction in risk of future poor health, the value of information about health risk, the non-health benefits (and consumer losses) from prevention that should be valued, and the appropriate rate of discounting benefits. There are challenges in applying the methods of economic evaluation to multi-faceted strategies where the different components interact to reinforce effect. There is ongoing debate about the appropriate objectives for health care expenditure, and whether the overall goal is to maximize health or to maximize some other concept of well-being and social welfare. This is particularly important in considering prevention, as the range of potential benefits extends beyond health outcomes. As good health is an important precondition for other aspects of human well-being, health promotion and the prevention of disease is a significant consideration for any social goals concerning equality of opportunity.

REFERENCES

AUSTRALIAN INSTITUTE OF HEALTH AND WELFARE. 2008. *Australia's Health 2008: The Eleventh Biennial Health Report of the Australian Institute of Health and Welfare.* Australian Institute of Health and Welfare: Canberra.

BERE, E., VEIERØD, M. B., and KLEPP, K.-I. 2005. The Norwegian school fruit programme: Evaluating paid vs. No-cost subscriptions. *Preventive Medicine* 41: 463–70.

BERWICK D. M. and WEINSTEIN M. C. 1985. What do patients value? Willingness to pay for ultrasound in normal pregnancy. *Medical Care* 23: 881–93.

—— DEPARLE, N. A., EDDY, D. M., et al. 2003. Paying for performance: Medicare should lead. *Health Affairs* 22: 8–10.

BEUTELS, P., VAN DOORSLAER, E., VAN DAMME, P., and HALL, J. 2003. Methodological issues and new developments in the economic evaluation of vaccines. *Expert Review Vaccines* 2: 89–100.

BIRCH, S. and GAFNI, A. 1992. Cost effectiveness/utility analyses: Do current decision rules lead us to where we want to be? *Journal of Health Economics* 11: 279–96.

BRINK, S. 2009. The diabetes prevention program: How the participants did it. *Health Affairs* 28: 57–62.

BROUWER, W. B. F., NIESSEN, L. W., POSTMA, M. J., and RUTTEN, F. F. H. 2005. Need for differential discounting of costs and health effects in cost effectiveness analyses. *British Medical Journal* 331: 446–8.

—— CULYER, A. J., VAN EXEL, N. A., and RUTTEN, F. F. H. 2008. Welfarism vs exrtra-welfarism. *Journal of Health Economics* 27: 325–38.

BROWN, C. and LILFORD, R. 2006. Cross sectional study of performance indicators for English primary care trusts: Testing construct validity and identifying explanatory variables. *BMC Health Services Research* 6: 81.

CAHILL, K. and PERERA, R. 2008. Competitions and incentives for smoking cessation. *Cochrane Database of Systematic Reviews (Online)* 3: CD004307. DOI: 10.1002/14651858.CD004307. pub3. Available at: <http://onlinelibrary.wiley.com/o/cochrane/clsysrev/articles/CD004307/frame.html>.

CAIRNS, J. and SHACKLEY, P. 1993. Sometimes sensitive, seldom specific: A review of the economics of screening. *Health Economics* 2: 43–53.

CAMERON, J., BANKO, K. M., and PIERCE, W. D. 2001. Pervasive negative effects of rewards on intrinsic motivation: The myth continues. *The Behavior Analyst* 24: 1–44.

CAMPBELL, S., REEVES, D., KONTOPANTELIS, E., MIDDLETON, E., SIBBALD, B., and ROLAND, M. 2007. Quality of primary care in England with the introduction of pay for performance. *New England Journal of Medicine* 357: 181–90.

CHARNESS, G. and GNEEZY, U. 2008. Incentives to exercise UCSB Departmental Working Paper 11–08. Department of Economics, UCSB: Santa Barbara.

CHRISTIANSON, J., SUTHERLAND, K., and LEATHERMAN, S. 2009. *Financial Incentives, Healthcare Providers and Quality Improvements: A Review of the Evidence.* Health Foundation: London.

CLAXTON, K., SCULPHER, M., CULYER, A., MCCABE, C., BRIGGS, A., AKEHURST, R., et al. 2006. Discounting and cost-effectiveness in NICE—stepping back to sort out a confusion. *Health Economics* 15: 1–4.

COAST, J. 2009. Maximisation in extra-welfarism: A critique of the current position in health economics. *Social Science and Medicine* 69: 786–92.

COHEN, J. T., NEUMANN, P. J., and WEINSTEIN, M. C. 2008. Does preventive care save money? Health economics and the presidential candidates. *New England Journal of Medicine* 358: 661–3.

Committee on Redesigning Health Insurance Performance Measures Payment and Performance Improvement Programs Institute of Medicine. *Rewarding Provider Performance: Aligning Incentives in Medicare.* National Academies Press: Washington DC, 2007.

Culyer, A. J. 1991. The normative economics of health care finance and provision. In A. McGuire, P. Fenn, and K. Mayhew (eds.), *Providing Health Care: The Economics of Alternative Systems of Finance and Delivery.* Oxford University Press: Oxford, 65–98.

Cutler, D. M., Glaeser, E. L., and Shapiro, J. M. 2003. Why have Americans become more obese? *Journal of Economic Perspectives* 17: 93–118.

Darmon, N., Ferguson, E. L., and Briend, A. 2002. A cost constraint alone has adverse effects on food selection and nutrient density: An analysis of human diets by linear programming. *Journal of Nutrition* 132: 3764–71.

Department of Health. 2006. *Our Health, Our Care, Our Say: A New Direction for Community Services.* Department of Health: London.

Downing, A., Rudge, G., Cheng, Y., Tu, Y., Keen, J., and Gilthorpe, M. 2007. Do the UK government's new quality and outcomes framework (QOF) scores adequately measure primary care performance? A cross-sectional survey of routine healthcare data. *BMC Health Services Research* 7:166.

Drewnowski, A., and Darmon, N. 2005. Food choices and diet costs: An economic analysis. *Journal of Nutrition* 135: 900–4.

—— and Specter, S. E. 2004. Poverty and obesity: The role of energy density and energy costs. *American Journal of Clinical Nutrition* 79: 6–16.

Dudley, R. A., Frolich, A., Robinowitz, D. L., Talavera, J. A., Broadhead, P., and Luft, H. S. 2004. Strategies to support quality-based purchasing: A review of the evidence. AHRQ publication no. 04–0057. Agency for Healthcare Research Quality: Rockville.

Epstein, A. M. 2007. Pay for performance at the tipping point. *New England Journal of Medicine* 356: 515–17.

Frey, B. and Jegen, R. 2001. Motivation crowding theory. *Journal of Economic Surveys* 15: 589–611.

—— and Oberholzer-Gee, F. 1997. The cost of price incentives: An empirical analysis of motivation crowding-out. *American Economic Review* 87: 746–55.

Galvin, R. 2006. Pay-for-performance: Too much of a good thing? A conversation with Martin Roland. *Health Affairs* 25: w412–19.

Gerard, K., Shanahan, M., and Louviere, J. 2003. Using stated preference discrete choice modelling to inform health care decision-making: A pilot study of breast screening participation. *Applied Economics*, 35: 1073–85.

Giuffrida, A. and Torgerson, D. J. 1997. Should we pay the patient? Review of financial incentives to enhance patient compliance. *British Medical Journal* 315: 703–7.

Gneezy, U. and Rustichini, A. 2000. A fine is a price. *Journal of Legal Studies* 29: 1–17.

Goldsmith, L. J., Hutchison, B., and Hurley, J. 2006. *Economic evaluation across the four faces of prevention: A Canadian perspective.* McMaster University: Hamilton.

Goodman, C. and Anise, A. 2006. *What is Known About the Effectiveness of Economic Instruments to Reduce Consumption of Foods High in Saturated Fats and Other Energy-dense Foods for Preventing and Treating Obesity?* WHO Regional Office for Europe: Copenhagen.

Gou, X., Popkin, B., Mroz, T., and Zhai, F. 1999. Food price policy can favourably alter macronutrient intake in china. *Journal of Nurtrition* 129: 994–1001.

Gravelle, H., Brouwer, W. B. F., Niessen, L. W., Postma, M. J., and Rutten, F. F. H. 2007. Discounting in economic evaluations: Stepping forward towards optimal decision rules. *Health Economics* 16: 307–17.

HAAS, M. 2005. The impact of non-health attributes of care on patients' choice of GP. *Australian Journal of Primary Health*, 11: 40–6.

HALL, J. 1996. Consumer utility, social welfare and genetic testing. A response to "Genetic testing: An economic and contractarian analysis." *Journal of Health Economics* 15: 377–80.

—— VINEY, R., and HAAS, M. 1988. Taking a count: The evaluation of genetic testing. *Australian and New Zealand Journal of Public Health* 22: 754–8.

HURLEY, J. 2000. An overview of the normative economics of the health sector. In A. J. Culyer, and J. P. Newhouse (eds.). *Handbook of Health Economics*. Volume 1a. Elsevier Science, North-Holland: Amsterdam, 55–118.

JEPSON, R., CLEGG, A., FORBES, C., LEWIS, R., SOWDEN, A., and KLEIJNEN, J. 2000. The determinants of screening uptake and interventions for increasing uptake: A systematic review. *Health Technology Assessment (Winchester, England)* 4: i–vii, 1–133.

JOCHELSON, K. 2006. Nanny or steward? The role of government in public health. *Public Health* 120: 1149–55.

—— 2007. *Paying the Patient: Improving Health Using Financial Incentives*. King's Fund: London.

KANE, R. L., JOHNSON, P. E., TOWN, R. J., and BUTLER, M. 2004. A structured review of the effect of economic incentives on consumers' preventive behavior. *American Journal of Preventive Medicine* 27: 327–52.

KENKEL, D. S. 2000. Prevention. In A. J. Culyer and J. P. Newhouse (eds.), *Handbook of Health Economics*. Amsterdam: Elsevier, 1675–720.

LE GRAND, J. 2009. *Incentives for Prevention: Health England Report No. 3*. Health England: London.

LEE, R. H. 2008. Future costs in cost effectiveness analysis. *Journal of Health Economics* 27: 809–18.

LONGWORTH, L., RATCLIFFE, J., and BOULTON, M. 2001. Investigating women's preferences for intrapartum care: Home versus hospital births. *Health and Social Care in the Community*, 9: 404–13.

LURIE, N., MANNING, W. G., PETERSON, C., GOLDBERG, G. A., PHELPS, C. A., and LILLARD, L. 1987. Preventive care: Do we practice what we preach? *American Journal of Public Health* 77: 801–4.

MADORE, O. 2007. The impact of economic instruments that promote healthy eating, encourage physical activity and combat obesity: Literature review issue prb 06–34e <http://www.parl.gc.ca/information/library/PRBpubs/prb0634-e.htm> accessed April 12, 2007.

MARTEAU, T. M., ASHCROFT, R. E., and OLIVER, A. 2009. Using financial incentives to achieve healthy behaviour. *British Medical Journal* 338: b1415.

MAYNARD, A. 2007. Is doctors' self-interest undermining the NHS? *British Medical Journal* 334: 224.

McGINNIS, J. M., WILLIAMS-RUSSO, P., and KNICKMAN, J. R. 2002. The case for more active policy attention to health promotion. *Health Affairs* 21: 78–93.

McPHERSON, K. 2008. Does preventing obesity lead to reduced health-care costs? *PLoS Medicine* 5/2: e37.

MELTZER, D. 2008. Response to future costs and the future of cost-effectiveness analysis. *Journal of Health Economics* 27: 822–4.

MOONEY, G. 1994. What else do we want from our health services? *Social Science and Medicine* 39: 151–4.

—— 2001. Communitarianism and health economics. In J. B. Davis (ed.), *The Social Economics of Health Care*. Routledge: London and New York, 40–60.

Mooney, G. and Lange, M. 1993. Ante-natal screening: What constitutes "benefit?" *Social Science & Medicine.* 37: 873–8.

National Institute for Health and Clinical Excellence. 2007. *Behaviour Change at Population, Community and Individual Levels: NICE Public Health Guidance 6.* National Institute for Health and Clinical Excellence: London.

—— 2009. *A Healthier Future for all Australians. Interim Report.* Commonwealth of Australia: Canberra.

Owen, K. M., Pettman, T. L., Haas, M. R., Viney, R. C., and Misan, G. M. 2010. Individual preferences for diet and exercise programs: Changes over a lifestyle intervention and their link with outcomes. *Public Health Nutrition* 13/2: 245–52.

Paul-Ebhohimhen, V. and Avenell, A. 2008. Systematic review of the use of financial incentives in treatments for obesity and overweight. *Obesity Reviews* 9: 355–67.

Piggott, M., Wilkinson, P., and Bennett, J. 1994. Implementation of an antenatal serum screening programme for Down's Syndrome in two districts. *Journal of Medical Screening* 1: 45–9.

Prüss-Üstün, A., Bos, R., Gore, F., and Bartram, J. 2008. *Safer Water, Better Health: Costs, Benefits and Sustainability of Interventions to Protect and Promote Health.* World Health Organisation: Geneva.

Redmond, P., Solomon, J., and Lin, M. 2007. *Can Incentives for Healthy Behavior Improve Health and Hold Down Medicaid Costs?* Center on Budget and Policy Priorities: Washington.

Richardson, J. 2001. Empirical ethics versus analytical orthodoxy: Two contrasting bases for the reallocation of resources. In J. Bridges (ed.) *Economics and Health: 2000: Proceedings of the Twenty-second Australian Conference of Health Economists.* University of New South Wales, School of Health Services Management: Sydney, 227–42.

—— and McKie, J. 2005. Empiricism, ethics and orthodox economic theory: What is the appropriate basis for decision-making in the health sector? *Social Science & Medicine* 60: 265–75.

Rosenthal, M. B. and Dudley, R. A. 2007. Pay-for-performance: Will the latest payment trend improve care? *Journal of the American Medical Association* 297: 740–4.

Rush, B., Shiell, A., and Hawe, P. 2002. A census of economic evaluations of primary prevention interventions in population health. Centre for Health and Policy Studies, University of Calgary, Calgary, Canada.

Russell, L. B. 2009. Preventing chronic disease: An important investment but don't count on cost savings. *Health Affairs* 28: 42–5.

Sadovnick, A. and Baird, P. A. 1981. A cost-benefit analysis of prenatal detection of Down Syndrome and neural tube defects in older mothers. *American Journal of Medical Genetics* 10: 367–78.

Schmidt, H. 2007. Personal responsibility for health—developments under the German healthcare reform 2007. *European Journal of Health Law* 14: 241–50.

Schwappach, D. L. 2007. The economic evaluation of prevention—let's talk about values and the case of discounting. *International Journal of Public Health* 52: 335–6.

—— Boluarte, T. A., and Suhurcke, M. 2007. The economics of primary prevention of cardiovascular disease: a systematic review of economic evaluations. *Cost Effectiveness and Resource Allocation* 5:5.

Scott, A. and Schurer, S. 2008. *Financial Incentives, Personal Responsibility and Prevention.* Commonwealth of Australia: Canberra.

—— Watson, M. S., and Ross, S. 2003. Eliciting preferences of the community for out of hours care provided by general practitioners: A stated preference discrete choice experiment. *Social Science and Medicine* 56: 803–14.

SEN, A. K. 1985. *Commodities and Capabilities*. Elsevier Science: Amsterdam.

—— 1987. *On Ethics and Economics*. Basil Blackwell: Oxford.

—— 1992. *Inequality Reexamined*. Oxford University Press: Oxford.

SEN, A. 2002. Why health equity? *Health Economics* 11: 659–66.

STEINBROOK, R. 2006. Imposing personal responsibility for health. *New England Journal of Medicine* 355: 753–6.

STONE, D. H. and STEWART, S. 1996. Screening and the new genetics: A public health perspective on the ethical debate. *Journal of Public Health Medicine* 18: 3–5.

STURM, R. and DATAR, A. 2005. Body mass index in elementary school children, metropolitan area food prices and food outlet density. *Public Health Monograph* 119: 1059–68.

SUTHERLAND, K., and CHRISTIANSON, J. B., and LEATHERMAN, S. 2008a. Impact of targeted financial incentives on personal health behavior: A review of the literature. *Medical Care Research and Review* 65: 36S–78.

—— LEATHERMAN, S. and CHRISTIANSON, J. 2008b. *Paying the Patient: Does it Work? A Review of Patient-targeted Incentives*. The Health Foundation: London.

UNGAR, W. J. and SANTOS, M. T. 2002. *The Paediatric Economic Database Evaluation*. Canadian Coordinating Office for Health Technology Assessment: Ottawa.

US DoHaH (DEPARTMENT OF HEALTH AND HUMAN SERVICES). 2003. Prevention makes common "cents." *Services*. UDoHaH: Washington, DC.

VAN BAAL, P., POLDER, J. J., DE WIT, G. A., HOOGENVEEN, R. T., and FEENSTRA, T. L. 2008. Lifetime medical costs of obesity: Prevention no cure for increasing health expenditure. *PLoS Medicine* 5(2): e29.

WALL, J., MHURCHU, C. N., BLAKELY, T., RODGERS, A., and WILTON, J. 2006. Effectiveness of monetary incentives in modifying dietary behavior: A review of randomized, controlled trials. *Nutrition Reviews* 64: 518–31.

WARNER, K. E. and MURT, H. A. 1984. Economic incentives for health. *Annual Review of Public Health* 5: 107–33.

WEINSTEIN, M. C. and STASON, W. B. 1976. *Hypertension: A Policy Perspective*. Harvard University Press: Cambridge, Mass.

WILKINSON, E. 2008. Can you pay people to be healthy? *The Lancet* 371: 1325–6.

WOOLF, S. H. 2009. A closer look at the economic argument for disease prevention. *Journal of the American Medical Association* 301: 536–8.

WHO (WORLD HEALTH ORGANISATION). 2002. *Reducing Risks, Promoting Healthy Life: The World Health Report 2002*. WHO: Geneva.

—— 2008. *Primary Health Care: Now More Than Ever*. WHO: Geneva.

CHAPTER 24

LONG-TERM CARE

JOSE-LUIS FERNANDEZ, JULIEN FORDER, AND MARTIN KNAPP

24.1 INTRODUCTION

24.1.1 What is Long-term Care?

LONG-TERM care has been defined by the US Department of Health and Human Services (2009) as "the range of medical and/or social services designed to help people who have disabilities or chronic care needs." The description is very similar to that offered by the European Commission (2009) of "a range of medical and social services for persons who are dependent on help with basic activities of daily living, caused by chronic conditions of physical or mental disability."

Long-term care therefore differs from health care as conventionally defined in that its primary goal is not to cure or prevent ill-health but to allow individuals to achieve and maintain optimal levels of personal functioning (in the context, of course, of their living circumstances and their personal abilities and preferences). Promotion of quality of life—in general, not just health-related—is consequently a core aim. Although long-term care therefore includes provision of medical care, the term tends to be more closely used to describe an array of group and individual care and support arrangements for providing help with domestic tasks (such as shopping, cleaning, preparing meals), personal care tasks (dressing, bathing), personal concerns (safety) and social engagement. Care and support of this kind could be provided by paid staff, family or other carers (usually unpaid). Specialist housing, employment support, training, leisure services and some health care might be included under the long-term care umbrella, depending on country and context. We use the abbreviation LTC to refer to long-term (social) care.

24.1.2 Challenges of Economic Analysis in Long-term Care

Although the potential contribution of economic analysis to the pursuit of equity and efficiency in LTC is as relevant as in a health system or in other areas of public policy, there are some challenges. For example, the full assessment of the impact of social care services requires measurement of changes in a wide range of well-being dimensions for people who use service and their carers. The ASCOT tool (Netten et al. 2009), for instance, covers eight such dimensions (social participation and involvement, control over daily living, food and nutrition, safety, cleanness and accessibility of accommodation, occupation and dignity). Evaluating social care outcomes also requires sophisticated methodologies for attributing changes along each dimension to the effect, not only of services, but to a number of non-service related factors.

Indeed, to a greater extent than is generally the case in health care, LTC outcomes are known to be co-produced by factors other than formal care and support inputs. In particular, needs-related characteristics (such as an individual's degree of physical disability, sensory impairment and cognitive functioning), and situational features (such as the built environment and the nature of family and social support) are major drivers of variations in outcomes. Consequently, the evaluation of service productivities and system efficiency, for example, requires careful adjustment for the effects of these non-service factors (which we can identify as "non-resource inputs"; Knapp 1984). Furthermore, because individual abilities and functioning tend to deteriorate in old age and with some congenital disabilities and conditions, needs can appear to grow (and outcomes to worsen) despite the potential beneficial effects of services.

In addition to their direct effects on this "production of welfare" process, needs-related factors and non-resource inputs affect outcomes indirectly through their mediating effects on service productivities. The marginal effect of community-based services on older people's welfare, for instance, depends significantly on factors such as physical and mental health, the availability of informal support, and attitudinal characteristics of older people and their carers (Davies et al. 2000).

On the supply side, factors associated with intrinsic personal characteristics of paid carers, such as emotional warmth towards the individuals they support, critically affect the qualities of the support provided and thus potentially the outcomes achieved (Donabedian 1980; Davies and Knapp 1981). Moreover, given the quintessentially personal and relational nature of most LTC, individuals will have their own preferences about what support is required or how it is delivered, varying with personal characteristics such as their self-confidence and desire for autonomy. In fact, as we discuss below, tailoring support arrangements to the expressed wishes of individuals is one of the core values of LTC, even if not properly implemented in practice.

The fluidity and intrinsic inter-individual variability of LTC arrangements implies a limited degree of technological determinacy in the production of welfare process, and complicates the analysis of the relationship between inputs and outcomes. It means, for instance, that it is difficult to know *ex ante* what would be the optimum care package for a particular individual. Indeed, the experiential nature of LTC means that individuals require first-hand contact with care and support arrangements to fully evaluate their appropriateness, and—given the outcome dimensions distinguished above—also their effectiveness. To add to the complexity from an analytical standpoint, some of these important influences on LTC outcomes are hard to measure, such as the degree of self-confidence, personality traits affecting the carer/user relationship and the level of risk generated by the physical environment. Combined with the challenge of measuring outcomes, this can make it hard to evaluate LTC policies and practices.

Only a relatively modest economic literature has accumulated on LTC. In part, this reflects a certain reluctance among front-line professionals and strategic decision-makers to embrace economic analytical methods as applied to care and support arrangements. Nevertheless, rapidly growing demand for LTC (see below) and resulting pressures on public finances mean that governments across the globe are increasingly recognizing the need to get a better understanding of how to finance and allocate LTC resources, how to achieve individual and societal outcomes cost-effectively, and how to pursue equity in the distribution of benefits and burdens.

In sections 24.3, 24.4, and 24.5 of this chapter we discuss provision, financing and governance, respectively. First, we need to understand the consequences of aging populations on the need for and cost of LTC.

24.2 Population Aging: Implications for Long-term Care

24.2.1 Demography and Need

> Population aging will increase spending further, mainly through long-term care needs of the frail elderly. In 2005, long-term care expenditure accounted for just over 1% of GDP across OECD countries. We project that such spending will reach between 2% and 4% of GDP by 2050. Improving the efficiency of health care systems is thus imperative to accommodate future pressures (Gurría 2009).

This statement from the OECD Secretary-General is typical of many now being heard across the world. Advances in public health, medicine and other areas over the past few decades have contributed to the aging of the world population, but they have brought new challenges for health and long-term care. The main driving force for future LTC expenditure will almost certainly be the number of older people in need of care and support. There will be significant increases in the absolute and relative numbers of older people in society, as well as changes in the age-specific prevalence of disability (Robine et al. 2005). Whether the prevalence of disability among successive cohorts of older people will increase or not is particularly important, because the effect on service demand of the predicted growth in the number of older people could be more than offset by a significant reduction in this prevalence (Fries 1989; Doblhammer and Kytir 2001). The key question is how many of the extra years of life predicted for successive cohorts of older people will be disability-free. Currently there is no consensus on this "compression of morbidity" hypothesis, and consequently more evidence is required to predict with confidence likely future trends in the needs of older people.

The other main influences on future LTC needs and costs, and on the balance between public and private expenditure, are informal care supply, unit cost inflation, and changes in wealth holdings.

24.2.2 Informal Care Supply

Family members and friends are key frontline providers of LTC, and the time devoted to unpaid caring is often considerable. In England, for instance, whereas 70 percent of carers provide care for less than twenty hours per week, more than 20 percent of carers living in the same household as the dependent person provide 100 or more hours of care per week (Wanless et al. 2006). The supply of such support varies significantly across countries and cultures. Availability responds to a range of influences. Some countries are experiencing a reduction in the number of households shared across generations, with fewer older people living with their children and more marriages ending in divorce. This decrease in the rate of co-habitation is particularly important because co-resident carers are typically those providing the most intensive levels of support.

There are marked inter-country differences in social and cultural expectations about the role of family and community in supporting people in need (Eurobarometer 2007). Whereas it is still the case in many Southern European countries, for example, that the family is expected to provide the bulk of the support required by older people with care needs, in recent times in many countries there has been a fall in the expressed and observed willingness to provide informal care. In contrast, the reduction in the life expectancy gap between men and women means that some countries are seeing increases in the levels of support provided by older males to their dependent spouses (Pickard et al. 2000).

Informal care is important because of its buffering effect on demand for formal services, thus reducing collective expenditure. But it can have considerable knock-on effects on carers' opportunities in the labor market, and consequently for their ability to prepare themselves financially for their *own* old age (e.g. by contributing to a pension scheme). Moreover, very intensive levels of informal care have been linked to increased risks of health problems, including depression and high levels of stress (Molyneux et al. 2008).

24.2.3 Unit Costs of Services

People with physical and mental disabilities may need support with "everyday" activities such as feeding, dressing, or washing which involve significant levels of human input. The labor-intensive nature of LTC means that the unit costs of services tend to increase through time in line with wages, rather than with general price levels. In the UK for instance, predictions of future LTC expenditure have assumed yearly unit cost increases that are 2 percent above general price inflation, equivalent (other things equal) to an approximately 50 percent increase in real expenditure levels over a twenty-year period (Wittenberg et al. 2004; Wanless et al. 2006).

In addition to this relative price effect, there could be further pressure on LTC unit costs due to rising expectations about the quality of care demanded by future cohorts of older people (who will often have enjoyed better standards of living during their "working years" and who are likely to be more engaged, more assertive).

24.2.4 Availability of Financial Resources

A society's capacity to meet the future demand for LTC will depend on its wealth, reckoned in terms of both individuals' abilities to pay for their own care, and society's ability to fund a collective care system. Internationally, there is evidence that newer cohorts of older people are wealthier, for instance through indexation of their pensions to earnings, and through ownership of housing assets (Boreham and Lloyd 2007). As a result, it is possible that future generations of older people will be better placed financially (on average) to face some of the costs of care, and that this in turn will lessen the burden on the public purse.

At a broader societal level, however, the picture is more challenging. Most countries rely on the working age population as the primary funding source for LTC, through taxes or social insurance contributions, but many are faced with a relatively (and in some cases absolutely) shrinking working age population (Figure 24.1). This increase in the old-age dependency ratio would place considerable and probably unsustainable funding

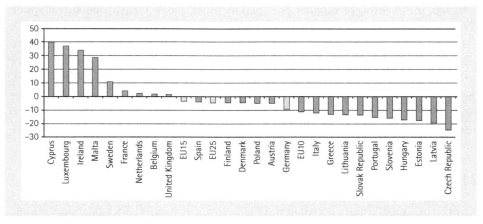

FIGURE 24.1 Projected changes in employment (% change of employed people aged 15–64 between 2003 and 2050), EU 25

burdens on younger groups. Added to other financial pressures, such as the need for those individuals to contribute to pension schemes, this could prove politically very difficult, and could undermine public support for a collective care system. In addition, of course, marginal tax increases for working age groups could reduce incentives to work.

24.3 PROVISION

While there are relatively few types of long-term care services (certainly when compared with the range of health care technologies), they tend not to be standardized across countries or over time. Nevertheless, across every high-income country over recent decades it is clear that there has been substantial growth in "formal" provision of many service types.

24.3.1 Health vs. Social Care Services

The provision of LTC can be described along a series of key dimensions, the first of which relates to the nature of the care provided, and particularly whether services belong to the health or social care system. The boundaries between the two systems vary between countries in line with differences in, for example, local funding arrangements, professional training and preferences. In general, however, health-related services are essentially the nursing and other health care inputs required to deal *directly* with physical and/or mental health problems, and in particular with long-term health conditions such as diabetes and heart disease. In contrast, long-term *social* care services relate mostly to non-medical inputs which support individuals with the impact on their daily functioning and broader well-being of their mental or physical health problems. Through time, this distinction has become more problematic in many industrialized countries, as budgetary pressures have tended gradually to pull health care professionals away from assisting individuals with activities of daily living such as bathing, feeding and dressing (Twigg 1997).

Given that in a majority of countries, health and social care services are governed through different funding and administrative arrangements, it is unsurprising that their effective coordination is shared internationally as a key policy objective (Lewis 2001a). There are particular concerns regarding the negative effect on the health care system of shortages in social care services, which it is argued result in avoidable admissions to, and unnecessarily long stays in inpatient beds, in particular for older people. As a result, financial incentives have been introduced in some countries with some apparent success, whereby the social care system compensates the acute health sector for delays in hospital discharges linked to a lack of social care support (Andersson 2000).

Overall, there is growing evidence of the interrelationship in the performance of the two systems (Fernandez and Forder 2008; Forder 2009). Although more research would be helpful, the results confirm a significant degree of substitutability between health and social care.

24.3.2 Provider Sector

Another highly relevant parameter for dissecting provision is the balance between sectors, with some LTC systems heavily reliant on public services and others dominated by for-profit (referred to as "private" in the UK) and non-profit (voluntary, charitable, third sector) providers. Changes in the sectoral balance have been very marked in some countries (see Figure 24.2 for an illustration of the recent English evolution). Across *all* countries, however, there are debates about the efficiency and equity consequences of "commissioning" (purchasing, contracting and allocation) of services from the different sectors (Kendall et al. 2006). Commissioning is the process of purchasing, but also includes some wider tasks: assessing population needs, specifying services that could meet those needs, contract negotiation with providers (and eventual contract termination), performance monitoring, and then reconsideration of the consequences for strategic decision-making.

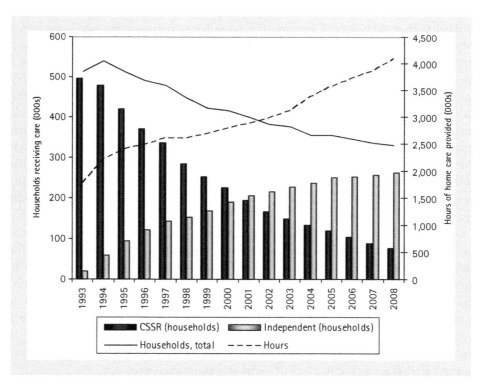

FIGURE 24.2 Changes in the targeting of community care services for older people by sector of provision, 1993–2008

From a cost perspective, non-state, and particularly for-profit providers often outperform the state sector. In England, for instance, the hourly cost of home care provided directly by municipalities in 2007/8 was more than 80 percent higher than the service provided by for-profit and non-profit bodies (Health and Social Care Information Centre 2008). However, lower unit costs in these latter sectors are usually at least partly linked to inferior working conditions for front-line staff, including poorer pensions, holiday entitlements, and training opportunities (Robinson and Banks 2005). This can translate into higher turnover of staff, poorer continuity of care, and more frequent coordination failures in service provision. It is also worth noting that the differential in unit costs in favor of the non-state sectors is partially offset by the increased transaction costs for the state because of the regulatory and commissioning frameworks needed.

A consideration here is provider motivation. Indeed, given the information asymmetries and difficulties in performance monitoring, the delivery of services by providers who are solely motivated by financial reward could lead to poor welfare outcomes for service users, and could even expose them to unacceptable levels of risk. In fact, recent research examining the intrinsic motivations of residential care providers suggests that the majority, regardless of sector, are not primarily motivated by pecuniary rewards (Matosevic et al. 2007). Classifying non-state providers on the basis of expressed motivations into three broad groups ("empathizers," "professionals," and "income prioritizers"), Kendall et al. (2003) found that most had primarily empathic motives, while the second largest group were "professionals," motivated primarily by "mercantile" considerations linked to a desire for autonomy and control over one's business. Clearly, commissioning structures and arrangements need to respond to provider motivations, and build especially on their empathetic and mercantile aspects.

24.3.3 Community vs. Institutions

The locus of care is one of the most important policy issues in LTC, particularly whether services are provided "in the community" or in institutions. Services in the community include support provided in an individual's own home (such as personal care, meals on wheels, and sitting services) and services provided outside it, such as in day care centers and social clubs. Institutional care is sometimes divided between residential care and nursing care, the latter catering for people with higher levels of mental or physical disability.

There is a high degree of substitutability between types of formal (and informal) services, and between support in the community and in institutions (Davies et al. 2000). In part, the potential for substitutability reflects the relatively low skills required to provide support with tasks such as bathing, dressing, and feeding. This fact also limits the potential for efficiency improvements in the provision of such support. In contrast, considerable policy attention is being placed on understanding the possible cost-effectiveness of tele-care and tele-health, which exploit technological advances in areas such as the monitoring of health conditions, and personal risk.

The vast majority of service recipients prefer to receive long-term care support in their own home, or in other community settings. Residential care is thus often seen as a service of last resort. In England, for instance, the median length of stay in residential care is approximately twelve months, and most residents either move on to inpatient care or die in the care facility. The service is therefore commonly targeted on the most dependent people, often those with significant levels of physical, cognitive and other health problems.

However, services in the community and institutions provide a different balance of outcomes. In some cases, residential services can actually achieve better outcomes for dependent users than community-based services, in particular when issues of safety are important. In addition, the cost of the two types of care can differ a great deal. The direction of the difference depends crucially on two factors: the level of need and therefore of support required, and whether accommodation costs are taken into account consistently in the two settings.

It is commonly assumed that the costs of community-based care are lower (and therefore that it is possible to save money by substituting community for residential care). However, when accommodation costs in the community are taken into account, especially for people with high levels of dependency, residential care can be significantly less expensive than the equivalent care in the community because of the potential to exploit scale economies. A key factor is the amount of supervision required, given its perhaps prohibitive cost when provided in the community.

New service models are being developed which attempt to merge features of the "home" (domestic) environment whilst providing enhanced care levels. Hence, provision of sheltered accommodation and in particular assisted living apartments and "extra care" facilities has grown significantly in recent times. Although highly valued by users, these new services have tended to target people with low or moderate levels of disability (Darton and Callaghan 2009: 284).

24.4 FINANCING

There are many pressing economic issues relating to the funding of long-term care services. Following Fernandez et al. (2009), we first examine the rationale for (private and/or public) collective funding mechanisms for LTC. After reviewing the equity and efficiency implications of alternative arrangements, we then consider some of the main "families" of funding systems adopted internationally. Finally, we discuss some of the key implementation decisions likely to drive significantly the performance of the funding system.

24.4.1 The Rationale for Collective Funding Arrangements

Market failures mean that private funding solutions, through informal care or through unregulated markets, do not offer effective protection against the consequences of long-term dependency. Many dependent older people have no or only limited family support, and out-of-pocket payments for intensive support packages would be unaffordable for a large proportion of people. (The average cost of a residential care home for older people in England, for instance, exceeds £500 per week.)

Voluntary insurance against long-term care dependency also presents difficulties. Few people consider it an option because of low risk perception, risk neglect (low willingness to pay for insurance coverage), moral hazard, and adverse selection (see Johnson and Uccello 2005; Finkelstein and McGarry 2006: Gleckman 2007; Brown and Finkelstein 2008a and 2008b). In addition, private insurers have found it difficult to calculate care costs associated with long-term dependency, and thus to price their products accurately. Internationally, only France, the US, Israel, and a few other countries have developed non-negligible private insurance markets.

Collective funding systems allow resources to be targeted on the most vulnerable groups in society, and have therefore been justified on equity grounds. Equity considerations are particularly relevant because of the effect of funding arrangements on service demand: consumption of LTC services responds to the level of charges at the point of use (Wanless et al. 2006). In other words, funding arrangements do not just impact on "who *pays* for what service" but also "who *gets* what service," and therefore have potentially major implications for the distribution of burdens and benefits.

Of course, collective funding systems also achieve the important objective of pooling risks. During their lifetime, a large majority of the population will spend a considerable period of time with limited capacity to care for themselves due to illness, disability or aging. For example, Kemper et al. (2006) suggest that 69 percent of all people turning 65 in 2005 in the US would experience some LTC need during their lifetime, with 20 percent of people overall and 28 percent of women requiring more than five years of care. Lifetime costs can be very substantial, especially for the tail of the distribution of individuals who need support over long periods. Current estimates in England, for instance, suggest that average lifetime social care costs for people reaching the age of 65 exceed £30,000 (Forder and Fernandez 2009). In the US, Spillman and Lubitz (2000) estimate that lifetime LTC expenditures in nursing home care for people turning 65 in 2000 will average $44,000 (in 1996 dollars), with home care expenditures increasing the figure by a third. Similarly, Kemper et al. (2006) calculate that the average present discounted value of lifetime LTC expenditures for people turning 65 in 2005 is approximately $47,000, with 28 percent of non-zero expenditures exceeding $100,000.

Collective funding models also have their drawbacks. One familiar problem is moral hazard: individuals take greater personal and/or financial risks in the knowledge that the system would help them with the cost of potential disabilities developed as a result. Another familiar problem when scheme membership is not compulsory is adverse selection: the people most interested in taking part in the scheme will be those whose expected care costs exceed their expected financial contributions to the scheme.

24.4.2 Equity and Efficiency in Funding Arrangements

Several criteria have been proposed for evaluating the performance of funding systems (Hirsh 2006; Wanless et al. 2006). Three are given almost universal emphasis: equity, efficiency, and sustainability.

24.4.2.1 *Equity*

A widely promoted criterion is that a funding system should promote horizontal equity, ensuring that individuals with equal needs (but potentially different levels of wealth) have equal access to support. Charging policies should protect the dignity of service users by making sure they are left with sufficient resources to afford their normal daily expenses. Equally, funding arrangements should promote personal and family responsibility, while not penalizing people who have made sacrifices to make their own financial provision. The arrangements should recognize and value the roles played by informal carers. Partly because of the difficulty in specifying written eligibility criteria relating to informal care, insurance-based funding models typically operate *carer-blind* entitlements to services, and thus do not take into account the availability of informal care for determining levels of state support. (We return to this issue below.) Finally, it is argued that eligibility rules for financial support should be transparent in order to facilitate the public auditing of the allocation process, and therefore allow public views to be fed into the system. Transparency would also allow individuals to plan better for their old age, by making explicit the level of state support they can expect. Of the main groups of funding arrangements, means-tested systems tend to be more complicated, as they require elaborate rules specifying the relationship between state support and individuals' income and assets.

24.4.2.2 *Efficiency*

Funding arrangements, it is argued, should also promote efficiency in the use of care resources. Hence, they should create incentives to use of the right mix of services, and support diversity in supply to ensure that a range of services is available to respond to individual circumstances, needs, and preferences. They should encourage efficient interaction between public services, especially between health and social care. In many countries, for instance, differences in funding rules for health and social care have led to service retrenchment and cost shunting, usually to the detriment of the weaker, social care, partner (Lewis 2001; Wanless et al. 2006). It is also recommended that funding arrangements allow the effective pooling of risks across individuals, thereby generating significant insurance benefits, and covering in particular the so-called "catastrophic" financial risk of very prolonged use of services.

24.4.2.3 *Sustainability/Acceptability of Funding Arrangements*

In terms of sustainability, the ideal funding system would attract a high degree of public support, ensure affordability for the public purse, and offer flexibility. Public support will vary depending on whether the financial contributions required of different groups in society are perceived to be worthwhile. In turn this depends on whether individuals believe that (i) the system will help them when they need support; (ii) the public subsidy is targeted on the "right" care for the "right" people; and (iii) contributions are affordable. The sense of affordability will vary with whether financial contributions are due at one point in time or spread over a period, and whether contributions are raised from non-users as well as users.

In general, *pay-as-you-go* systems, which do not imply a direct link between individuals' financial contributions and expected payoffs, are more affordable in the short run. They do not require financial "war chests" to be accumulated up front, and contributions can be spent as they are received. However, in the context of an aging society, they can imply a significant redistribution of resources across generations.

24.4.3 Policy Options for Funding Long-term Care

Since it is not possible to achieve success by every one of these criteria simultaneously, policymakers—working within their own socio-demographic, cultural, economic, and political contexts—will likely aim to select funding arrangements which yield a "preferred" combination of effects on equity, efficiency, and sustainability.

Internationally, funding systems can be broadly clustered into three groups: those providing a minimum safety net, those offering universal benefits, and those that combine universal and wealth-targeting.

24.4.3.1 *Minimum Safety-net Systems*

Exemplified by countries such as England and the US, the first cluster of systems corresponds to those which minimize state intervention, concentrating their support on individuals lacking the financial ability to meet the costs of services. These *safety-net* systems are characterized by relatively low levels of state expenditure, and are usually funded through a combination of general (central and/or local) taxation and charges levied at the point of use, calculated on the basis of means-tested rules.

These arrangements can polarize the population in need into three groups: low-wealth individuals who receive services funded by the state; wealthy individuals who can self-insure and fund services out of pocket; and a third group of dependent people with moderate assets who struggle to afford the services they require, or simply go without (Wanless et al. 2006). As a result, means-tested systems can generate significant unmet need.

The decrease in state support with people's wealth can be perceived as unfair as it penalizes financially prudent individuals who save during their lifetime to enjoy a more comfortable lifestyle in their old age. From an (in)efficiency point of view, means-tests can create incentives for individuals to deplete their assets in order to increase the state subsidy they receive. Restricting public support to people with low means can also lead to the stigmatization of people who receive such support as "poor" or "feckless."

24.4.3.2 *One System for All*

An increasing number of countries have recently developed universal funding systems. Such models imply significantly greater levels of state expenditure, but they ensure greater equality and social cohesion. Whether these gains are worth the increased fiscal pressures is ultimately a political judgment.

In tax-funded, universal systems, exemplified by Denmark and Sweden, and more recently by Scotland, LTC is funded by the public sector, with no or small co-payments from service users at the point of use. Because total state expenditure is budget-constrained, tax-funded systems have a degree of flexibility in matching resources to needs, through a redefinition of eligibility criteria, or through waiting lists.

In contrast, social insurance systems are funded through earmarked contributions, usually levied through a payroll tax on earnings. Typically, eligibility is assessed on the basis of clear, algorithm-driven rules linking disability levels to entitlements to specified levels of state support. They offer a more transparent allocation process than care-managed systems, and provide greater assurances about "rights" to support. As a result, social insurance expenditure is need-driven, rather than budget-constrained. However, such arrangements can lack flexibility in the way they match care to individual needs, because of the use of overly simple rules for defining eligibility. A co-payment is generally required from the service user, normally means-tested. The German and Japanese systems fall largely into this category.

24.4.3.3 *Progressive Universalism*

The third family of funding systems combines universal entitlements to state help with a means-tested element so that those in greater financial need receive greater state support. Progressive universalism of this kind aims to minimize state financial commitments while retaining an element of universality, in order to promote social cohesion, provide some insurance benefits to all, while limiting (relative to universal schemes) state expenditure. Progressive universalism is exemplified by the French system, with the needs-tested and means-tested universal entitlement associated with the Allocation Personnalisée d'Autonomie introduced in 2002.

24.4.4 Implementation Factors

Seldom is the saying that the devil lies in the detail more appropriate than when applied to the analysis of LTC funding systems. Sometimes apparently innocuous implementation choices can generate very different incentives for key stakeholders and affect system performance.

24.4.4.1 *Revenue-raising Mechanism*

One such implementation issue is the choice of revenue-raising mechanisms, potentially from direct or indirect taxation, earnings-related social insurance contributions, private insurance premiums, or user charges. Different revenue sources create different incentives, and imply different degrees of income redistribution. Higher user charges at the point of need, for instance, might deter not only unnecessary but also necessary consumption, and so can lead to unmet need.

24.4.4.2 *Defining Eligibility*

Another important implementation decision concerns the process for defining eligibility for support, and more specifically whether algorithms are used, or whether entitlement is evaluated by front-line professionals (e.g. by care managers). Means-tested systems are usually associated with "care-managed" systems, where front-line professionals use their professional experience to assess a potentially quite wide range of factors when deciding entitlement. Although potentially more efficient in matching needs to services, care-managed systems have been criticized for lacking transparency. Conversely, algorithm-based eligibility systems typically used in social insurance systems (such as the French, Austrian, German, Japanese, and new Spanish arrangements) are more transparent, but can lead to naive allocation patterns which ignore needs not amenable to inclusion in the algorithm.

24.4.4.3 *Carer-blind or Carer-sighted*

Whether or not levels of informal care are taken into account when assessing levels of state support can affect the equity, efficiency and sustainability of a care system, the key aspect being whether eligibility for support is reduced when informal (unpaid) carers provide support (as in England, the so-called "carer-sighted" option) or whether informal care activity is ignored (as in Japan, "carer-blind").

In fact, formal care systems can interact very differently with the informal care sector (Twigg 1989; Twigg and Atkin 1994). At one extreme, carers are perceived purely as resources, and entitlement to state support is denied to people with informal support. Or formal services treat carers as co-workers, providing them with support and encouragement so that they can continue fulfilling their caring role. Dependent people with informal carers are still entitled to (reduced levels of) state support, with funding also made available for services aimed at reducing carer stress, such as respite care. In a more extreme form of this model, formal services aim to meet the needs of carers per se, hence treating carers as co-users of services. Finally, in models in which carers are superseded by formal services, the state aims to replace fully their caring activities. Providing the same amount of formal care to someone with no informal support as to someone with equal needs but with significant family support might not be regarded as unequivocally fair. But neither might it be fair to leave carers to provide, unsupported, all the burden of looking after dependent older people.

24.4.4.4 *Interactions with Other Systems*

Account should also be taken of the implications for contiguous systems, such as health, housing and welfare benefits. The interaction between health systems that offer treatment that is free at the point of use and means-tested social care systems, for instance, can lead to situations where individuals with very similar needs but different underlying clinical causes (e.g. stroke and cognitive impairment) are provided with very different levels of state support depending on whether they are considered to have social or health needs. These boundary issues can lead to cost-shunting between budgets.

24.5 GOVERNANCE

Working under a range of fiscal and political pressures, public authorities in many countries have taken steps to improve how scarce public resources are allocated to long-term care and other public services. Attention is most often focused on what types of services and support people should be offered, but another important area of inquiry is in how LTC systems are organized and managed.

24.5.1 Market Reforms

The long-term care systems of many countries have undergone significant organizational reform in recent years. Approaches have included the introduction of competition into hitherto public bureaucratic care systems, contracting out, the adoption of "hard" contracts with providers, and the use of fixed-price payment systems, notably in the Netherlands, France, Israel, Australia, and England (Propper 1993; Knapp et al. 1994; Lyons 1994; Roberts et al. 1998; Knapp et al. 2001; Schmid 2003).

While some countries (such as Denmark and Finland) still retain high levels of public hierarchical organization in long-term care, we now see a substantial use of market-like arrangements supplanting the traditional public model. Other countries, particularly the US, have a much longer history of market arrangements, most notably in the nursing home sector. Regardless of the starting point, a key LTC policy goal is to strike the right balance between markets and hierarchies. Policy questions include the degree to which provision should be separated from commissioning, where non-public sector providers are in competition; how transactions between providers and public sector commissioners should be organized; the sort of contracts to use; and whether the use of non-profit rather than for-profit providers should be promoted.

There is a general theoretical literature relevant to these points, but relatively little is specifically developed for LTC. The main arguments are relevant, nonetheless: markets appear to coordinate resources better than hierarchies, especially when there is high competition, investment to develop production technology does not tie providers to specific purchasers, and/or when few scale economies apply (Hart 1995; Hart 2003). However, markets are susceptible to information problems when services are complex, as they often are in LTC (Milgrom and Roberts 1992). Also, the more formal contracting in markets will mean higher transaction costs than for hierarchies (Williamson 1986; Forder et al. 2005).

The empirical evidence is rather sparse. The main lines of inquiry in LTC have been about the effects of competition in the nursing home market; the use of different forms of contract or reimbursement arrangements; and the market implications of non-profit rather than for-profit nursing home ownership.

A mostly US literature has looked at the effects of competition on the quality of nursing home care. A number of studies have assessed how regulation in the US such as certificate-of-need laws and construction moratoria can act as barriers to entry and so push up prices. Nyman (1994) found evidence that these regulations can confer providers with market power and so increase prices. His earlier work also suggested that these regulations were associated with lower quality when there is excess demand (Nyman 1988) and this is supported by more recent studies (Starkey et al. 2005). Forder and Netten (2000) also found a negative relationship between price and competition in the UK residential care market.

Contract design—specifically the degree of case-mix contingency of US nursing home reimbursement under Medicaid—has also been shown to have significant effects on access to care and, in some instances, quality of care (Grabowski 2001; Grabowski 2002). The use of high-powered incentives in Medicaid reimbursement (e.g. prospective payments) is associated with lower quality when the market is experiencing excess demand (Nyman 1985). There is also some evidence that cost-reimbursement contracts are associated with higher nursing home prices in England (Forder 1997; Forder and Netten 2000). Similar results were found in the domiciliary care sector in England (Forder et al. 2004).

Ownership of provider organizations also leads to differential behaviour in the nursing home sector (Spector et al. 1998). A large meta-analysis in the US suggests that non-profit nursing homes delivery higher quality (process measured) than for-profit homes (Comondore et al. 2009). Grabowski argues, nonetheless, that there are positive spillover effects on quality between sectors and this endogeneity needs to be accounted for in comparative analyses (Grabowski and Hirth 2003). The effect is argued to stem from information-limited consumers taking signals from non-profit home behaviours. Many of the above studies have indicated the negative effects of information asymmetries in markets (Forder 1997; Christensen and Arnould 2005).

On the question of whether quasi-markets out-perform public hierarchical arrangements, there is some work relating to residential care for older people in England. This found that transaction costs of market-based mechanisms were higher than for hierarchical arrangements but (net) production costs were lower, so that the total costs of market governance arrangements overall were (slightly) lower (Forder 2005). Further equity considerations would apply. Lunt et al. (1996) have argued that the concepts of transaction cost economics are particularly appropriate to the analysis of LTC, emphasizing the social context of transactions, but do not develop an empirical analysis.

24.5.2 Integration

Much of our consideration of marketization and market-like governance concerns the degree of *vertical* integration between purchaser and provider. There is also the question of the degree of *horizontal* integration between social care and related services, particularly health care.

A systematic review found a number of specific programs that combined health and social care for older people in an integrated and coordinated fashion (Johri et al. 2003). Programs were reviewed from the US (Program for all-inclusive care for the elderly, PACE, and social HMOs), Canada (SIPA), Italy and the UK (the Darlington case management project).

The results were positive, indicating that for the specific projects, acute hospitalization rates, in particular, were significantly reduced with greater use of preventative community-based care (e.g. intensive use of day health centers, care at home). LTC institutionalization rates were also reduced, and outcomes and satisfaction often improved. There was also evidence of overall cost savings in a number of these programs. Although downward service substitution was a key feature, better coordination and case-management of services between health and social care drove many of the beneficial results. In one study in Italy, decreases were reported in the use of both institutional (including hospital) and community-based services. In other words, good integrated case-management prevented apparently inappropriate/excessive use of all service types: i.e. not only downward substitution, but real needs prevention.

There have been (limited) attempts to integrate the entire range of health and social care for all enrollees (not just a targeted, high-risk population) in the form of "social HMOs" in the US. An early evaluation, however, found mixed results and suggested that s/HMOs are less effective than specific programs (Kodner and Kyriacou 2000).

In Sweden, in the early 1990s, much of the (community) health and social care system was reorganized so that it was integrated at the local government level. In addition, a system of cross-charging was put in place. Sweden subsequently experienced a significant fall in acute hospital bed numbers (from 6/1000 in 1988 to 3.5/1000 in 1998). In geriatric care this reduction was greatest (Pederson 1998).

In 1997 the Australian government implemented a *coordinated care* trial to run for two years. This approach has much in common with the PACE program in the US. The first phase (to 1999) demonstrated that integration was feasible for a range of scenarios. However, whilst being very popular with users, the first phase did not result in a reduction of intensive service use; if anything hospital utilization was greater than for the control group. The second phase, which targeted much more closely the very frail, appeared to be much more successful (Temkin-Greener et al. 2008).

A number of studies shed light on the potential of better integration to improve resource allocation by looking at rates of substitution between health and social care services. High rates of substitution underline the need for high degrees of coordination between social care and health care organizations to ensure that resources are efficiently allocated across the interface between sectors (Forder 2009).

The *Evercare* program in the US combines care-management (by specialist nurses) with provision of long-term nursing care. This combination might be described as "intermediate care" in the UK and some other countries. Nurse practitioners identify and manage users in nursing homes believed to be at increased risk of hospitalization. This management involves attempting to avoid hospital admission using a short-term burst of intensive service (intermediate care) within the nursing home (called intensive service days, ISDs). The evaluation of the Evercare demonstration program (Kane et al. 2002) showed a minor preventative effect (a small reduction in the events that led to a need for hospitalization), and a large substitution effect: many people stayed in the nursing home rather than going to hospital. When they did go, they stayed for less time. Average admissions per 100 enrollees were at 50 percent compared with controls; hospital length of stay (LoS) was at 80 percent compared with controls, although adding the average intensive service days (ISDs) of those "admitted" brings the total LoS to about the same as the control. ISDs are however significantly cheaper and easier to implement. Since outcome differences were negligible, Evercare represented a cost-effective program.

In the English case, studies have found that an increase in care home and/or home care provision had the effect of reducing rates of delayed discharge, average length of stay (all ages) and total hospital bed-day use (Fernandez and Forder 2002; Fernandez and Forder 2008).

In conclusion, governance matters considerably in determining how resources in the LTC sector are deployed, affecting how efficiently outcomes are achieved for service users. LTC systems show a significant mix of governance arrangements with pure market transactions, quasi-markets, public hierarchies, and networks all in operation. There is some evidence on specific policy questions, such as the impact of nursing home ownership, but rather less on whether market forms per se outperform alternatives such as public bureaucracies. It remains unclear whether many of these "market reforms," reducing vertical integration, have been beneficial by economic criteria. As regards horizontal integration, there is evidence that better coordination of resources between social care and health care sectors can lead to improved efficiency, but the results suggest that full structural integration may be a step too far.

24.6 Conclusions

Long-term care services are used by people with chronic health and related conditions, most of whom are older people. Because of population aging—a worldwide phenomenon—increasing attention is being focused on the economics of LTC and in particular on issues such as how to organize, fund, and deliver care and support to meet the significant future growth in demand for LTC. Applying economic analysis to LTC, however, is fraught with a series of particular challenges.

There are first issues of input mix efficiency. In most countries, health and social care services are subject to different funding and governance arrangements. This can lead to service coordination failures, and raises issues of joint service optimization. LTC is provided either "in the community" or in institutions, but given the low skills requirements and its labor-intensive nature there is limited potential for efficiency improvements. Individuals in need usually prefer to remain in community settings, and policy often focuses on helping older people live at home. However, for higher need individuals, institutional care can sometimes achieve better outcomes at lower cost (if the opportunity costs of accommodation in the community are taken into account); new service models combining a home environment with high levels of care are being developed to address this challenge. Implementation of some care arrangements relies on providers from a range of sectors (public, for-profit, and "non-profit"); the balance between provider sectors varies considerably between different countries, with implications usually for prices and transaction costs.

Informal care provides a buffer on demand for formal services, thus reducing short-term expenditure on formal services. Co-resident carers often provide intensive levels of support, with considerable impact on their emotional/physical health and ability to provide financially for their own old age. The balance between informal and formal care varies significantly between cultures and countries, and LTC systems are increasingly needed to respond to evolving household structures and a decline in the willingness of family and community to provide informal care.

Evaluation of social care outcomes is complex due to the wide range of well-being dimensions for service users and the need to adjust for the impact of non-service related factors. Needs-related characteristics and situational features are particularly important drivers of variations in outcomes, and ongoing age-related deterioration can mask the beneficial effects of services. Furthermore, some influences on outcomes are hard to measure, such as the influence of user personality traits and, on the supply side, the emotional user–carer bond. These factors, combined with the intrinsic heterogeneity of user preferences, all complicate the design of an individual's optimum care package and the analysis of the relationship between inputs and outputs. Nevertheless, economic analytical methods offer scope for the development of better outcome measures in order to improve the allocation of LTC resources.

There is a wide range of funding models for LTC, each with its strengths and weaknesses. Newer cohorts of older people tend to be wealthier on average, but market failures of private funding solutions and the limited take-up of voluntary insurance support the rationale for collective funding arrangements. Such systems target resources on the most vulnerable and achieve risk pooling, albeit with the challenge of moral hazard and adverse selection. Equity, efficiency, and sustainability criteria are all strongly emphasized in comparisons of competing funding arrangements. There is also a lot of discussion of the promotion of personal and family responsibility while not penalizing those who make their own financial provision; encouragement of efficient interaction between health and social care systems, and fairness across generations.

The choice of funding system is broadly between three approaches: systems that provide a minimum (means-tested) safety net; those offering universal benefits (either tax-funded or social insurance); and the "progressive universalism" model that combines universal entitlements with a means-tested element. The degree of state involvement (organization and expenditure) varies across these models. In all cases, implementation rules need to be carefully constructed to avoid unmet need, unintended incentives, and the potential to "game" the system. One important parameter is whether the availability of informal care affects the level of state support.

The type of governance structure within which a LTC system operates will influence whether resources are deployed efficiently. The widespread introduction of competition and "contracting out" of service provision has resulted in market-like arrangements in which the means of provision and purchasing are separately owned, and contracts negotiated by both parties. This is a very different framework to the public hierarchical organization of LTC, commonly with unified ownership and decision-making vested in one party. Non-profit LTC organizations fall somewhere in between, operating in some respects as networks based on trust and co-operation. A key issue is to strike the right balance between markets and hierarchies, in particular in how contract-based transactions between providers and public sector commissioners are organized. Since an important goal of these market reforms is greater efficiency and quality, it would be useful to build on the sparse empirical evidence about the impact of provider structures on price, quality and access to care. For now, it remains unclear whether market forms per se outperform the alternatives on key criteria, and across all countries there is debate about the efficiency and equity consequences of commissioning services from different provider sectors.

In addition to these challenges, a modern LTC system must also accommodate the growing policy emphasis of giving older and disabled people greater control over their lives. Mechanisms for "self-directed" support are being introduced that allocate a monetary care budget to an individual, who then decides what care and support to purchase (Knapp 2007). The budget can be transferred in a variety of ways, including voucher-like arrangements and cash payments. This approach potentially encourages innovative care arrangements, but also requires new governance frameworks. Information asymmetries and potential market vulnerability of frail or cognitively impaired budget holders can be quite challenging. Services users (and their carers) have little bargaining power relative to providers (compared to, say, large purchasers such as a municipality or social insurance fund) and may face exploitation by service providers. In practice, the "empowerment" of the user may be limited by heavy reliance on brokerage (advisory, support) services. At the heart of the trend towards self-directed support is the belief that user empowerment can improve the quality of care while being cost-effective. It may also help break down barriers between sectors and budgets, because users need and want to bridge the gaps between health, social care, and housing.

The degree to which any LTC model achieves its policy outcomes is highly sensitive to the detail of the arrangements. Given demographic trends and the pressures on public finances, the economics of LTC will clearly remain a significant political challenge for the foreseeable future.

REFERENCES

ANDERSSON, G. (2000) Integrated care for the elderly. The background and effects of the reform of Swedish care of the elderly. *International Journal of Integrated Care*, 1 (Nov.), 1–124.

BOREHAM, R. & LLOYD, J. (2007) Asset accumulation across the life course. A report of research carried out by the National Centre for Social Research on behalf of the International Longevity Centre, UK, London, International Longevity Centre.

BROWN, J. R. & FINKELSTEIN, A. (2008a) The interaction of public and private insurance: Medicaid and the long-term care insurance market. *The American Economic Review*, 98, 1083–102.

———— (2008b) Why is the market for long-term care insurance so small? *Journal of Public Economics*, 91, 1967–91.

CHRISTENSEN, E. & ARNOULD, R. (2005) The impact of asymmetric information and ownership on nursing home access. *International Journal of Health Care Finance and Economics*, 5, 273–97.

COMONDORE, V. R., DEVEREAUX, P. J., ZHOU, Q. et al. (2009) Quality of care in for-profit and not-for-profit nursing homes: systematic review and meta-analysis. *British Medical Journal*, 339, b2732–.

DARTON, R. & CALLAGHAN, L. (2009) The role of extra care housing in supporting people with dementia: Early findings from the PSSRU evaluation of extra care housing. *Journal of Care Services Management*, 3, 284–94.

DAVIES, B. & KNAPP, M. (1981) *Old People's Homes and the Production of Welfare*, London, Routledge and Kegan Paul.

—— FERNÁNDEZ, J. L. & NOMER, B. (2000) *Equity and Efficiency Policy in Community Care*, Aldershot, Ashgate.

DOBLHAMMER, G. & KYTIR, J. (2001) Compression or expansion of morbidity? Trends in healthy-life expectancy in the elderly Austrian population between 1978 and 1998. *Social Science and Medicine*, 52, 385–91.

DONABEDIAN, A. (1980) *The Definition of Quality and Approaches to its Assessment*, Michigan, Health Administration Press.

EUROBAROMETER (2007) *Special Surveys. Health and long-term care in the European UnionFieldwork: May–June 2007*, Geneva, Eurobarometer.

EUROPEAN COMMISSION (2009) Available at: <http://ec.europa.eu/health-eu/care_for_me/long_term_care/ms_se_en.htm>.

FERNANDEZ, J.-L. & FORDER, J. (2002) The importance of social care in achieving an efficient health care system: the case for reducing hospital delay discharge rates. London, LSE Health and Social Care, London School of Economics.

—— —— (2008) Consequences of local variations in social care on the performance of the acute health care sector. *Applied Economics*, 40, 1503–18.

—— —— TRUKESCHITZ, B., ROKOSOVÁ, M. & McDAID, D. (2009) *How Can European States Design Efficient, Equitable and Sustainable Funding Systems for Long-term Care for Older People?*, Copenhagen, World Health Organization.

FINKELSTEIN, A. & McGARRY, K. (2006) Multiple dimensions of private information: evidence from the long-term care insurance market. *The American Economic Review*, 96, 938–58.

FORDER, J. (1997) Contracts and purchaser–provider relationships in community care. *Journal of Health Economics*, 16, 517–42.

—— (2005) *The Organisation of Social Care in England: Markets, Hierarchies and Contract Choices in Residential Care for Older People*, London, London School of Economics.

—— (2009) Long-term care and hospital utilisation by older people: an analysis of substitution rates. *Health Economics*, Online print.

—— & FERNANDEZ, J. L. (2009) Analysing costs and benefits of social care funding arrangements in England: technical report, Canterbury, PSSRU discussion paper 2644.

—— & NETTEN, A. (2000) The price of placements in residential and nursing home care. *Health Economics*, 9, 643–57.

—— KNAPP, M., HARDY, B., KENDALL, J., MATOSEVIC, T. & WARE, P. (2004) Prices, contracts and motivations: institutional arrangements in domiciliary care. *Policy and Politics*, 32, 207–22.

—— ROBINSON, R. & HARDY, B. (2005) Theories of purchasing. In J., Figueras, R. Robinson, & E. Jakubowski (eds.), *Purchasing to Improve Health Systems Performance*, Maidenhead, Open University Press.

FRIES, J. F. (1989) The compression of morbidity: near or far? *The Milbank Quarterly*, 67, 208–32.

GLECKMAN, H. (2007) The role of private insurance in financing long-term care. *Center for Retirement Research at Boston College*, 7, 13.

GRABOWSKI, D. C. (2001) Medicaid reimbursement and the quality of nursing home care. *Journal of Health Economics*, 20, 549–69.

—— (2002) The economic implications of case-mix Medicaid reimbursement for nursing home care. *Inquiry*, 39, 258–78.

—— & HIRTH, R. (2003) Competitive spillovers across non-profit and for-profit nursing homes. *Journal of Health Economics*, 22, 1–22.

GURRÍA, A. (2009) Strategic options to finance pensions and healthcare in a rapidly aging world. Opening remarks by Angela Gurría, OECD Secretary-General at the Davos Meeting, Industry Partners' Session, January 30.

HART, O. (1995) *Firms, Contracts and Financial Structure*, Oxford, Oxford University Press.

—— (2003) Incomplete contracts and public ownership: remarks, and an application to public–private partnerships. *Economic Journal*, 113, C69–C76.

HEALTH AND SOCIAL CARE INFORMATION CENTRE (2008) *Personal Social Services Expenditure and Unit Costs England, 2007–08*, London, Health and Social Care Information Centre.

HIRSH, D. (2006) *Facing the Cost of Long-term Care: Towards a Sustainable Funding System*, York, Joseph Rowntree Foundation.

JOHNSON, R. W. & UCCELLO, C. E. (2005) Is private long-term care insurance the answer? *Center for Retirement Research at Boston College*. Available at: <http//:urban.org/url.cfm?ID=1000795>.

JOHRI, M., BELAND, F. & BERGMAN, H. (2003) International experiments in integrated care for the elderly: a synthesis of the evidence. *Journal of Geriatric Psychiatry*, 18, 222–35.

KANE, R., KECKHAFER, G. & ROBST, J. (2002) Evaluation of the Evercare demonstration program: final report. University of Minnesota, Minnesota.

KEMPER, P., KOMISAR, H. L. & ALECXIH, L. (2006) Long-term care over an uncertain future: what can current retirees expect? *Inquiry*, 42, 335–50.

KENDALL, J., MATOSEVIC, T., FORDER, J., KNAPP, M., HARDY, B. & WARE, P. (2003) The motivation of domiciliary care providers in England: new concepts, new findings. *Journal of Social Policy*, 32, 489–512.

—— KNAPP, M. R. J., & FORDER, J. (2006) The third sector and social care in the Western developed world, in W. W. Powell & R. Steinberg (eds), *The Nonprofit Sector: A Research Handbook*, 2nd edn. Connecticut: Yale University Press, 415–31.

KNAPP, M. (1984) *The Economics of Social Care*. London: Macmillan.

—— (2007) Social care: choice and control, in John Hills, Julian Le Grand, and David Paichaud (eds), *Making Social Policy Work: Essays in Honour of Howard Glennerster*. Bristol: Policy Press, 147–72.

—— HARDY, B. & FORDER, J. (2001) Commissioning for quality: ten years of social care markets in England. *Journal of Social Policy*, 30, 283–306.

—— WISTOW, G., FORDER, J. & HARDY, B. (1994) Markets for social care: opportunities, barriers and implications. In W., Bartlett, C., Propper, D. Wilson, & J. Le Grand (eds.), *Quasi-markets in the Welfare State*, Bristol, SAUS Publications.

KODNER, D. & KYRIACOU, C. (2000) Fully integrated care for the frail elderly: two American models. *International Journal of Integrated Care*, 1(1): 1–24.

LEWIS, J. (2001) Older people and the health–social care boundary in the UK: half a century of hidden policy conflict. *Social Policy and Administration*, 35, 343–59.

LUNT, N., MANION, R. & SMITH, P. (1996) Economic discourses and the market: the case of community care. *Public Administration*, 74, 396.

LYONS, M. (1994) The privatisation of human services in Australia: Has it happened? *Australian Journal of Public Administration*, 53, 179–89.

MATOSEVIC, T., KNAPP, M., KENDALL, J., HENDERSON, C. & FERNANDEZ, J.-L. (2007) Care home providers as professionals: understanding the motivations of care home providers in England, *Aging and Society*, 271, 103–26.

MILGROM, P. & ROBERTS, J. (1992) *Economics, Organization and Management*, New Jersey, Prentice-Hall.

MOLYNEUX, G. J., MCCARTHY, G. M., MCENIFF, S., CRYAN, M. & CONROY, R. M. (2008) Prevalence and predictors of carer burden and depression in carers of patients referred to an old age psychiatric service. *International Psychogeriatrics*, 20, 1193–202.

NETTEN, A., BURGE, P., MALLEY, J., POTOGLOU, D., BRAZIER, J., FLYNN, T. & FORDER, J. (2009) *Outcomes of Social Care for Adults*, Canterbury, PSSRU.

NYMAN, J. A. (1985) Prospective and cost-plus Medicaid reimbursement, excess Medicaid demand and the quality of nursing home care. *Journal of Health Economics*, 4, 237–59.

—— (1988) Excess demand, the percentage of Medicaid patients, and the quality of nursing home care. *Journal of Human Resources*, 23, 76–92.

—— (1994) The effects of market concentration and excess demand on the price of nursing home care. *Journal of Industrial Economics*, 42, 193–204.

PEDERSON, L. (1998) Health and social care for older people in Denmark: a public solution under threat? In C. Glendinning (ed.), *Rights and Realities: Comparing New Developments in Long-term Care for Older People*, Bristol, Policy Press.

PICKARD, L., WITTENBERG, R., COMAS-HERRERA, A., DAVIES, B. & DARTON, R. (2000) Relying on informal care in the new century? Informal care for elderly people in England to 2031. *Aging and Society*, 20, 745–72.

PROPPER, C. (1993) Quasi-markets, contracts and quality in health and social care: The US experience. In J. Le Grand & W. Bartlett (eds.), *Quasi-markets and Social Policy*. Basingstoke, Macmillan.

ROBERTS, J., LE GRAND, J. & BARTLETT, W. (1998) Lessons from experience of quasi-markets in the 1990s. In W. Bartlett, J. Roberts, & J. Le Grand (eds.), *A Revolution in Social Policy: Quasi-market Reforms in the 1990s*, Bristol, Policy Press.

ROBINE, J. M., JAGGER, C., VAN OYEN, H. E. C., ROMIEU, I., CLAVEL, A., BARKER, G. & LE ROY, S. (2005) Are we living longer, healthier lives in the EU? EHEMU Technical report 2.

ROBINSON, J. & BANKS, P. (2005) *The Business of Caring: King's Fund Inquiry into Care Services for Older People in London*, London, King's Fund.

SCHMID, H. (2003) Rethinking the policy of contracting out Social Services to non-governmental organizations. *Public Management Review*, 5, 307–23.

SPECTOR, W. D., SELDEN, T. M. & COHEN, J. W. (1998) The impact of ownership type on nursing home outcomes. *Health Economics*, 7, 639–54.

SPILLMAN, B. C. & LUBITZ, J. (2000) The effect of longevity on spending for acute and long-term care. *New England Journal of Medicine*, 342, 1409–15.

STARKEY, K., WEECH-MALDONADO, R. & MOR, V. (2005) Market competition and quality of care in the nursing home industry. *Journal of Health Care Finance*, 32, 67–81.

TEMKIN-GREENER, H., BAJORSKA, A. & MUKAMEL, D. B. (2008) Variations in service use in the program of all-inclusive care for the elderly (PACE): is more better? *The Journals of Gerontology Series A: Biological Sciences and Medical Sciences* 63, 731–8.

TWIGG, J. (1989) Models of carers: how do social care agencies conceptualise their relationship with informal carers? *Journal of Social Policy*, 18: 53–66.

—— (1997) Deconstructing the "social bath": help with bathing at home for older and disabled people. *Journal of Social Policy*, 26, 211–32.

—— & ATKIN, K. (1994) *Carers Perceived: Policy and Practice in Informal Care*, Buckingham, Open University Press.

US DEPARTMENT OF HEALTH AND HUMAN SERVICES (2009) Glossary of terms. Available at: <http://aspe.hhs.gov/daltcp/diction.shtml#LTC>.

WANLESS, D., FORDER, J., FERNANDEZ, J.-L., POOLE, T., BEESLEY, L., HENWOOD, M. & MOSCONE, F. (2006) *Securing Good Care For Older People: Taking A Long Term View*, London, Kings Fund.

WILLIAMSON, O. (1986) *Economic Organisation: Firms, Markets and Policy Control*, Brighton, Wheatsheaf Books.

WITTENBERG, R., COMAS-HERRERA, A., PICKARD, L. & HANCOCK, R. (2004) Future demand for long-term care in the UK: a summary of projections of long-term care finance for older people to 2051, *Health and Aging* 11: 2–4.

CHAPTER 25

....

PHYSICIAN AGENCY AND PAYMENT FOR PRIMARY MEDICAL CARE*

....

THOMAS G. MCGUIRE

25.1 INTRODUCTION

....

THIS chapter reviews the theoretical and empirical literature on physician agency, emphasizing empirical research appearing since 2000. The review is directed to consideration of a policy common to many health care systems: paying for primary care in a way that encourages efficient and patient-oriented care. In the US, much of this discussion is currently centered on the idea of providing a "medical home" for patients, but the issues are hardly confined to the US. Health care systems in many countries structure payment systems to primary care doctors to make use of physician agency and encourage doctors to take responsibility for their patients.

I use the term "agency" to refer first to the regard a physician may have for the welfare of her patient, a form of altruism. I also use the term to refer to the ability a physician may possess to act on behalf of the patient.[1] Under this second meaning falls the issue of physician-induced demand, one of the long-standing concerns of health economics.[2] Both are relevant for designing a payment system for primary care.

* Thanks are due to Randy Ellis, Jacob Glazer, Sherry Glied, Bruce Landon, and Peter Smith for helpful comments on an earlier draft. Zach Yoneda provided first-rate research assistance.
[1] Physicians as gatekeepers to health care resources are sometimes regarded as also being agents of third-party payers, or even of society. At the time a person buys insurance, he wants physicians in the plan to constrain moral hazard in use, even though at the time he is a patient, he would like the physician to accommodate his insured demand.

[2] For a more extensive theoretical treatment of physician objectives and review of the literature before 2000, see McGuire (2000).

A medical home is premised on patient enrollment with primary care physicians, a feature of primary care in the UK and many other countries. Norway (Grytten and Sorensen 2007) and Netherlands (Exter et al. 2004) have explicit enrollment-based payment systems. Germany (Busse and Riesberg 2004) has a fee structure that indirectly amounts to the same thing. Our analysis of payment systems to support the medical home has applications in these countries as well.

25.2 A Policy Application: Paying for the Medical Home

The medical home has been advanced in the field of pediatrics as a method for organizing practices for the care of children with special needs (Barr and Ginsburg 2006). The idea took root as a more broadly applicable basis for thinking about the role of the primary care practitioner. As the American College of Physicians defines it, "The advanced medical home acknowledges that the best quality of care is provided not in episodic, illness-oriented, complaint-based care—but through patient-centered, physician-guided, cost-efficient, longitudinal care that encompasses and values both the art and science of medicine" (Barr and Ginsburg 2006: 5). The medical home is organized around the patient's individual, personal physician, in most cases the primary care doctor, who oversees the patient's treatment and who "leverages the key attributes of the advanced medical home to coordinate and facilitate the care of patients and is directly accountable to each patient" (Barr and Ginsburg 2006: 5). The concept establishes the primary care physician as the chief coordinator and patient advocate to help the patient navigate an increasingly complex medical system. Proponents of medical homes advocate for what is seen as the "traditional" physician/patient relationship, when third-party payment incentives interfered less, and quality concerns and professionalism guided physician actions (Larson 2003). Though empirical studies have yet to be done on the impact of a medical home, quality primary care and effective patient management has been shown to lower morbidity and mortality in both cross-national and international studies (Starfield et al. 2005), demonstrating, at least in principle, that better primary care may improve health outcomes.

From the physician perspective, current methods of health care delivery and organization of practice leave much to be desired, particularly in the realm of primary care. Patients, physicians, and hospital officials all report lower rates of coordination among specialties, lower rates of patient involvement, decreased patient face time and higher rates of duplicate/redundant visitation due to lack of communication (Roter and Hall 1989; Forrest et al. 2000; Schillinger et al. 2003; Schoen et al. 2004; Gandhi 2005; Gandhi et al. 2005; Gottschalk and Flocke 2005; Pham et al. 2007). Furthermore, despite the recommendations of the American College of Physicians highlighting the importance of time as an element of "high quality clinical care," "effective communication," and "resource stewardship," physicians report having too little time to spend with patients (Yarnall et al. 2003; Braddock and Snyder 2005; Ostbye et al. 2005). The typical primary care visit lasts 12–16 minutes, covering 6–8 distinct medical topics (Tai-Seale et al. 2007).[3]

In addition to the presumed health quality benefits for individual patients enrolled in a medical home, some have speculated that the medical home model could reduce costs. Starfield and Shi (2004) argue that personal knowledge of the patient and transformation to "longitudinal" as opposed to "complaint-based" care should decrease resources spent on any given patient due to long term case management. Demand for expensive specialty care might decrease, as preventative measures may decrease eventual need for more expensive acute care. It seems unrealistic, however, to expect that system savings associated with medical homes will free up resources.

The structure of payment to a primary care physician expected to provide the medical home is an open area of research. Davis (2007a) argues that neither a pure capitation nor a pure fee-based system are good ways to support the care management required in a medical home. Capitation puts primary doctors too much at risk, and a fee-based system has well-known drawback by not emphasizing high quality of care. Elsewhere (Davis 2007b), she argues that a system mixing prospective and fee-based components (as well as some performance-related payments) is the sensible way to support a medical home.[4]

Goroll et al. (2007) propose to pay for a medical home by per patient risk-adjusted capitation intended to cover costs of comprehensive treatment of patients. (The authors prefer not to use the term "capitation," but this nonetheless accurately describes their form of payment.) The intention is to strip physician payment of quantity-related financial incentives, and pay the physician generously enough to finance infrastructure, quality care, and build incentives to please and attract patients. Goroll et al. would also

---

[3] One direction of evolution in the US is physicians restructuring their practices as "retainer" or "concierge" medical practices (Brennan 2002; Scandlen 2005). The retainer refers to a premium paid by the patient over-and-above the fees the physician receives as part of the patient's regular insurance. In exchange, the physician spends more time with patients, provides more comprehensive services, and reduces the practice size to one half or less of a typical practice, thus increasing the availability and access to the physician enjoyed by the patients deciding to remain and pay the retainer fee. Essentially, advocates of the medical home seek to bring what is now on the high-end fringe of private medical care into mainstream payment public and private insurance systems in a way that does not require infusions of funds into health care and is accessible to all patients, not just those who can afford to pay additional retainers to their physician.

[4] Physicians have advocated for reform of payments to improve care/reduce costs and support the idea of a medical home. To move away from procedure-based incentives in US Medicare's Resource-Based Relative Value Scale based payment system, Goldfield et al. (2008a) advocate transition to a visit-level payment partly based on the patient's case mix (rather than what is done in terms of procedures). The inspiration for this reform is the hospital episode Medicare makes to hospitals in the form of diagnosis-related groups (DRGs) and the payment system based on them. In the context of a medical home, Schoenbaum et al. (2008) point out that physicians can control visits not just procedures, and the per-visit payment might not achieve the desired efficiencies.

include some pay-for-performance.[5] Though they acknowledge that in the short term such a system is unlikely to be financially "neutral" (i.e. physicians must be given enough in capitated compensation to want to switch payment systems), the long run incentives to increase efficiency are thought to offset initial losses. Physicians' willingness to act on behalf of their patients is fundamental to a capitation payment for primary care.

The purpose of this chapter is to consider the implications of the theoretical and empirical literature on physician behavior and payment for design of a payment system to finance a medical home. To preview, analysis of physician behavior implies primary care physicians should be paid by a combination of an enrollment-based prospective payment, and fees related to procedures. As in many areas of health economics designing such a system involves issues of moral hazard and adverse selection. We will be mostly concerned here with the moral hazard component: designing a payment system to convey appropriate incentives to supply care. Since these will require some prospective payment, after developing this argument we make some preliminary comments on the implications for dealing with selection in the upfront enrollment payment associated with the medical home.

25.3 AGENCY AND PHYSICIAN INDUCED DEMAND

The basic idea of "agency" in the health care context is that physicians act partly out of concern for the welfare of their patients. While this is certainly not a bizarre idea to anyone outside of the economics profession, it goes against the grain of conventional approaches to seller behavior in which profit maximization guides decisions. The early literature in health economics reflected a physician's altruism in the concept of a "target income." This was later supplemented by approaches in which physicians balance income or profit against welfare of the patient in a utility-based framework. In this later literature physicians are regarded as having a direct concern for their patient's health.

25.3.1 Target Income and Physician Utility

In one early study, Fuchs (1978) found that an increased supply of surgeons, controlling for demand factors, *increased* market price. To explain these findings, Fuchs and others proposed that physicians pursue a "target income."[6] In contrast to more recent papers, the original target income (TI) hypothesis was not about fees, but was used to explain

---

[5] There are obviously many difficult practical problems to work out in paying physicians by some form of prospective payment, either visit or person-based. These are outside the scope of this chapter. Ellis and Miller (2008) review the various bases of payment, including procedure, visit and person, with discussion of how these would play out in physician payment.

[6] Speculation about a target income held by doctors can be traced back to Feldstein (1970).

why higher physician-to-population ratios (presumably a measure of supply in relation to demand) were associated with a *higher* price of physician services, not a lower one, as simple price theory would suggest. The idea was this: Suppose physicians only set a price high enough so as to attain some target. Physicians could make more by charging a higher price, but choose not to, perhaps because of concern for patient welfare. As more physicians appear in a market and patients are spread more thinly among the available suppliers, physicians must raise prices to maintain the target income. TI behavior, in the 1970s, reflected *restraint* in pricing, presumably from a concern for their patients. Physicians were "humanitarian" in Farley's (1986) term, not fully exploiting their price-setting power unless they were forced to by competitive pressures.[7]

In the 1980s, when direct fee-setting replaced increased supply as the mechanism used by regulators to limit physician prices, TI theory was recycled to explain another empirical anomaly, the negative correlation between fees and the quantity supplied, as was found, for example, by Rice (1983). During the 1980s, writers proposing TI explanations around fee responses linked it to physician induced demand (PID). Physicians could set quantity because they could induce demand. Interestingly, TI behavior was no longer a sign of benevolence. TI behavior frustrated policies designed to contain health care costs. Physicians were using their power to influence patient utilization in their own (the physicians') interests in order to counter well-intentioned fee regulation. The altruistic interpretation of TI was gone, and the link forged between TI and physician induced demand.

The negative relation between p and q is obvious if the physician sets q to maintain a target where $T = p \times q$. If the price falls, q must go up to maintain the target. The most obvious problem with the TI theory is that it does not explain how the "target" is set. What income is "just right" for doctors? Why should it differ across individuals and change over time?

The TI theory also suffers from a fundamental logical flaw. If there is only one good price then $p \times q = T$, and TI theory associates a unique quantity with any price. If, however, as is obviously the case, many prices and quantities contribute to a physician's income target from different procedures and different payers, there is no unique solution for quantities as a function of prices. Mathematically, the TI theory consists of one equation and many unknowns. The equation $p1q1 + p2q2 = T$ cannot be solved for $q1$ as a function of prices. When there are many (say n) quantities, as in the case of Medicare fee reform, and Medicare reduces $p1$, even if physicians behave according to the TI theory, it does not mean that $q1$ needs to go up. Any of $q2 \ldots qn$ could change to keep income at the target.

The target income equation is thus incapable of predicting what would happen to quantities following a price change. The TI objective needs a model of how a physician makes choices about what combination of quantities to set to achieve a target income.

---

[7] There are many problems with this theory from a conceptual standpoint. For example, it implies that if physicians have the same target income, but face different levels of demand, they will charge different prices.

Integrating the concept of TI within a model of physician utility accomplishes this objective, as, for example, in the utility-based balancing of income versus the disutility of inducement in Evans (1974) or McGuire and Pauly (1991). The fundamental idea in the many approaches to physician utility is that the two objectives of physicians are net income (or profit) and patient health. A formal model of this idea can be traced back to Ellis and McGuire (1986) and carries forward to many papers in the interim,[8] including the recent analysis of pay-for-performance in the UK (Gravelle, Sutton, and Ma 2008). The utility function looks like this: $V(B, \pi)$, where B is patient benefit, and π is net practice income. In many papers, the form of utility is further simplified to be linear in both arguments so physician utility could be written as $V = bB + \pi$. The weight on patient benefit, b, in relation to the weight (1) on profit, is a measure of agency. This form of utility is used in Gravelle, Sutton, and Ma (2008), and in Ellis and McGuire (1986). We will employ this model below to analyze payment for a medical home within the context of physician agency as represented by a two-argument utility function. Before doing so, it is important to introduce consideration of a concept related to physician agency, physician-induced demand.

25.3.2 Physician-Induced Demand

The physician-induced demand (PID) hypothesis, formulated first by Evans (1974), is essentially that physicians engage in some persuasive activity to shift the patient's demand curve in or out according to the physician's self-interest. At a conceptual level there is agreement about what constitutes PID:[9] "Physician-induced demand (PID) exists when the physician influences a patient's demand for care against the physician's interpretation of the best interest of the patient." It is important to keep two distinctions in mind when applying this definition. The first is the distinction between useful agency and inducement. Fuchs (1978) defined demand inducement as above, in relation to the consumer's optimal consumption point, leaving open scope for influence in the interest of the patient distinct from inducement. Thus, if a physician influenced a patient to move towards the consumer's optimal point this would not be inducement, only useful agency. Pauly (1980) makes use of the same concept in his definition of a "perfect agent": The physician assists the patient to demand "exactly those quantities of care of various types that the patient would have chosen if he had the same information and knowledge the physician has" (Pauly 1980: 5). The upshot of these definitions is that showing influence (as many studies in the health economics literature do) is not enough to establish "inducement."

It is important to keep two distinctions in mind when applying this definition. The first is the distinction between useful agency and inducement. Fuchs (1978) defined

[8] See McGuire (2000) for review.
[9] Some of the more prominent discussions of PID consonant with this definition are Fuchs (1978); Pauly (1980); Eisenberg (1986); Culyer (1989); and Williams (1998).

demand inducement as above, in relation to the consumer's optimal consumption point, leaving open scope for influence in the interest of the patient distinct from inducement. Thus, if a physician influenced a patient to move towards the consumer's optimal point this would not be inducement, only useful agency. Pauly (1980) makes use of the same concept in his definition of a "perfect agent": The physician assists the patient to demand "exactly those quantities of care of various types that the patient would have chosen if he had the same information and knowledge the physician has" (Pauly 1980: 5). The upshot of these definitions is that showing influence (as many studies in the health economics literature do) is not enough to establish "inducement."

The second distinction is between utilization and demand, a distinction that has become more salient with the growth in supply-side cost sharing and managed care, rationing devices that do not rely on controlling costs by decreasing quantity demanded. A physician can influence *utilization* (quantity) without influencing *demand* (the schedule). Patients treated in a managed care plan paid by capitation may receive less treatment than comparable patients in a fee-based plan. This could be interpreted as a PID-type mechanism—a decrease in demand caused by the physician. At the price they were paying and with a fully informed demand patients would have exhibited moral hazard and demanded the extra treatment but the physician influenced them otherwise and lowered their demand. Alternatively, it could be evidence of rationing—the plan physicians simply ration the care, not allowing patients to have all they want. The managed care plan patients have the same demand as the fee-based plan patients, it is simply unsatisfied.

A physician with a utility function of the type $V(B, \pi)$ discussed above will do some inducement if she is able to influence patient demand. Consider the position of a physician valuing both profit and patient health. If the physician supplies completely accurate and unbiased information to the patient, the patient would use the quantity that maximizes the patient's benefit. Around this level of use, a small modification of information would have very small impact on consumer welfare, because the consumer is at a point where the marginal benefit of health care is zero (this is how the optimum is defined). The physician, by contrast, may gain or lose money (depending on the payment incentives) from inducing the patient to demand more or less. Some inducement will then certainly take place by optimization of the V utility function.

Regarding the physician as valuing both profit and patient benefit puts a limit on the degree of demand inducement. More inducement may make money for the physician, but coming at a cost in patient health benefit, at some point inducement would be limited. Any seller gains from a higher demand, and unless there is some cost to inducement, a doctor pursuing net income would induce demand indefinitely. Other approaches to limiting inducement have appeared in the literature. Stano (1987) assumes that inducement has a real resource cost (like advertising) and is limited by the profit calculations of doctors in the presence of diminishing returns. Dranove (1988) proposes that patients can detect inducement with error, limiting the degree a profit maximizing physician would want to induce. Most theoretical approaches to limiting inducement follow Evans (1974), where inducement is limited by the psychic costs the physician bears when she gives advice to the patient slanted toward her own self-interest (McGuire and Pauly 1991; Zweifel and Breyer 1997). This conception of the cost of inducement fits well with the utility-based approach to physician behavior.

McGuire and Pauly (1991) formalized the ideas of Evans and Fuchs in a model intended to draw the implications of PID for physician response to fee changes when there were multiple payers or multiple fees. Inducement was limited by physician dis-utility. A general model of physician utility with income effects can encompass pure profit maximization (when the marginal utility of income is constant) and target income (when the derivative of the marginal utility of income is minus infinity at the target). The approach can be used to interpret the effects of a change in the number of patients per doctor as a result of, say, increasing the number of physicians, or a change in fees, that is, a change in the margins.

A change in the number of physicians per capita changes physician income, but if fees remain the same, incurs no price or substitution effect. The income effect of fewer patients per doctor increases the marginal utility of income. The amount of inducement necessary to bring the return to inducement into equality with this new value must therefore increase. Many papers test this "availability" effect.[10] A recent study applying this methodology to France is Delattre and Dormont (2003) who find evidence consistent with an availability effect.

Consider next fees. Suppose only one payer (imagine this to be US Medicare) reduces its fee. The effect of this can be thought of in two parts, an income effect and a substitution effect. The income effect of the fee fall increases the marginal utility of income, tending to increase inducement for all services.[11] There is also a substitution effect which comes about because a reduction in one fee reduces the return to inducement for that service. This effect will tend to reduce inducement for the service whose fee has fallen and increase it for other services. Thus, the effect of a fee reduction for service on inducement for that service is ambiguous, depending on income and substitution effects. The net effect, however, is unambiguous for other services—inducement should increase—because income and substitution effects work in the same direction.

Some papers have applied the income and substitution effect framework to physician behavior, such as Nguyen and Derrick (1997), Tai-Seale et al. (1998), and Yip (1998). Gruber, Kim, and Mayzlin (1999) studied Cesarean section rates in Medicaid and found that substitution effects dominated any income effects. Reductions in the higher pay physicians received for C-sections compared to normal deliveries reduced the rate of C-sections. Mitchell, Hadley, and Gaskin (2002) found strong cross-price effects for ophthalmologists in Medicare, but no income effects. Nassiri and Rochaix (2006) use income and substitution effect ideas to organize findings about physician response to expenditure caps in Quebec. Physicians anticipate hitting ceilings and adjust their

---

[10] See particularly Dranove and Wehner (1994); and Gruber and Owings (1996).

[11] Even if the income effect was completely dominant and the physician pursued a target income, the TI model does not imply that all income will be recovered from the service experiencing the fee reduction. In general it will be distributed among all the services a physician supplies.

intensity recommendations in ways consistent with income effects. Cockx and Brasseur (2003) use the income and substitution effect idea to study a natural experiment in fee changes in Belgium.

Empirical studies in health economics continue to document the effect of reimbursement changes on health care delivered to patients without interpreting the results in any particular theoretical framework. Reductions in marginal payment to doctors lead to reductions of services used by patients (Rosenthal 2000). Giuffrida and Gravelle (2001) suppose primary care physicians experience disutility from either positively or negatively inducing demand, and decide to induce based on whether fees for after-hours visits are favorable or not. Jacobson et al. (2006) find that higher payments to physicians for providing chemotherapy to Medicare patients leads to proscribing more intensive therapy. The relative fees for breast-conserving surgery and radical mastectomy as treatment for breast cancer affected the rates of these two surgeries received by women in Medicare (Hadley et al. 2003).[12]

Returning to the Fuchs/Pauly definition of PID, two things must be established for evidence on physician behavior to support the PID hypothesis. First, the exercise of control must be in the interest of the physician, not the patient. This criterion seems to have been met by the studies reviewed here. Adding up the evidence, on obstetricians doing more C-sections, surgeons doing more bypass operations, physicians referring more frequently to their own labs, and other studies, makes a convincing case that doctors can influence quantity and sometimes do so for their own purposes.

The second criterion from the Fuchs/Pauly definition is that the physician exercise quantity control by influencing the patient's demand, not by quantity setting through rationing. Some studies have attempted to isolate the quantity setting effect and find some evidence for it, including Chalkley and Tilley (2005) among dentists in the UK and Lien, Ma, and McGuire (2004) among substance abuse counselors in the US. Most studies though do not distinguish the mechanism of quantity control. It could be induced demand in the Fuchs/Pauly sense, quantity setting, or a reaction of the provider in setting "effort" affecting demand for the paid-upon quantity of care (McGuire 2000).

25.4 PAYING FOR PRIMARY CARE BY A MIXED SYSTEM

Now consider payment for primary care in the context of three fundamental features of the market for physician services. First, physicians have some ability to induce demand and do so partly in their own interest. Second, physicians are concerned about the health of their patients and this is reflected in their treatment decisions. Third, physician services are largely paid for by third parties—private or public programs—and patients face no or

---

[12] Papers finding no evidence of any inducement include Madden, Nolan, and Nolan (2005); and Grytten and Sorensen (2001).

small out-of-pocket costs at the time they use services. We have not heretofore discussed this third feature but it obviously characterizes health care payment systems in higher-income countries, and underlies the concern about moral hazard in demand for health care.

25.4.1 Physician Fees and Incentives

Fee-based payment to physicians, including those in primary care, is the dominant form of payment in the US, Germany, Canada, France, and many other countries. In the US, even when a physician is a member of a group and the group is paid by capitation, individual physicians are generally paid by fees (Rosenthal et al. 2002). Fees are the prices paid for physician services, but these prices are not chosen by the individual seller. In public programs in the US and elsewhere, fees are set administratively by reported procedures; in Medicare, for example, about 7000 procedures have their own fees. Private payers also decide fees, often scaling up or down the prices set by Medicare. Large physician groups may negotiate fees with private payers. In the UK, primary care physicians are paid mainly on the basis of the number of patients enrolling in their practice, though some services are paid by fees. The new pay for performance, now accounting for 25 percent of the income of UK primary care physicians, relates physician pay to procedures performed, sharing some features of a fee system.

Pure fee-based payment systems, although highly prevalent, have come under widespread criticism. Because fees reward physicians for each thing they do, fees may encourage too much treatment (Ginsburg and Grossman 2005). While this is certainly true in many cases, it is not fees that inherently cause over-use; rather, fees above marginal costs create such incentives. A very low fee would lead to too little care provided. This observation leads to the natural conception of an "optimal" fee that is just right, or "neutral," neither being to high and encouraging too much care, or too low and discouraging necessary care.

Current fee structures prevailing in the US can be traced to the work of Hsiao and his colleagues during the 1980s. The purpose of the fee reform was to use fees to match revenues and "cost," where cost was defined to include physician skill, time, and effort along with material cost. Hsiao undertook to measure how much time physicians spent conducting various procedures, using physician expert panels to rate the complexity and effort involved in the work, and supplementing this with survey data on physicians' practice costs (Hsiao et al. 1988). The Resource Based Relative Value Scale (RBRVS) was promoted as setting fees for procedures based on their relative "cost," taking account of time, subjective effort, and other medical resources. Medicare adopted the RBRVS in modified form and still uses it as a basis for payment, though many changes have been made over the years.[13] Medicare's fee schedule is, in turn, employed by some private insurers and Medicaid programs.

A "neutral" payment system pays the physician just cost; in other words, creates no opportunities for higher profit by providing more or fewer services. An economically

---

[13] See MedPAC (2006) for discussion of relative and absolute levels of physician fees, and the processes used to update and modify these.

neutral payment system takes physician self-interest out of the picture by paying exactly cost (including the physician's opportunity cost of time), so from the standpoint of her own financial welfare, a physician is indifferent about how much treatment takes place. Then, the only thing left for her to worry about is patient welfare, and her choice about treatment would be guided only by what is best for the patient.

Suppose as we have referred to above that physician utility depends on two arguments, the benefit the patient receives as a function of the quantity of treatment, $B(x)$, and the profit the physician receives, also a function of the quantity of treatment $\pi(x)$: $V(B(x), \pi(x))$. The presence of the $B(x)$ in physician utility is the representation of physician agency. Maximizing V with respect to choice of quantity leads to the following first-order condition:

$$V_B B' + V_\pi \pi' = 0, \tag{1}$$

where subscripts on V represent partial derivatives with respect to the arguments of utility and B' and π' are derivates with respect to quantity. Both V_B and V_π will be positive, meaning the physician values both patient health benefit and net income for herself. The solution to (1) in general terms involves relative preferences of the physician for patient welfare and profit, as well as patient benefit itself (the B'). The term π' depends on the relation between costs and revenues in the payment system.

Economic neutrality of a fee system can be defined as a payment system that sets marginal revenue equal to marginal cost. Neutrality means profit is invariant to the choice of quantity, and $\pi' = 0$. Therefore, in the case of economic neutrality, (1) reduces to:

$$B' = 0 \tag{2}$$

Since profit is unaffected by choice of quantity, the physician, with some concern for the patient, would choose the quantity to maximize patient benefit, where $B' = 0$.

Maximizing patient benefit is not the standard for economic efficiency, which requires that costs be considered along with benefits. Economic neutrality leading to marginal benefit $B' = 0$ implies an excess utilization of health care. Setting the marginal benefit of health care to zero could be understood as the physician choosing quantity to maximize patient health or her accommodation to the patient's demand, subsidized by health insurance.

At an empirical and practical level, administered fees have also been subject to harsh critique by health economists. Newhouse's *Pricing the Priceless* (2002) covers the history and economic research on administered pricing for physicians, hospitals and health plans, including the problems with an RBRVS-type approach. In this discussion, we deal with what I regard to be the most fundamental issue in a fee-based approach: in the context of insured patients, neutral fees do not lead to an economically efficient physician choice of health care for patients.

Against this background we now consider alternatives to a straight fee-based system. The basic conclusion of what is to follow is this: Physicians should be paid by a two-part payment or mixed system including a prospective and a fee-based component. The fee-based component should *discourage* (not be neutral towards) services at the margin. There are a series of good reasons for this, some stemming from the concept of physician agency.[14] The prospective component called for in these analyses is readily interpreted as the payment for a "medical home."

25.4.2 Argument I: Physician Agency Implies Fees Should be Lower than Marginal Cost and There Should be a Prospective Component of Payment

Equation (1) describes the physician's choice of quantity of treatment x. We want this choice to be at a level of treatment where the marginal benefit of treatment, B' equals the marginal cost of treatment which we designate by c. For simplicity assume marginal cost is constant. Since $V_B > 0$ (i.e. agency is present), and the physician values profit, $V_\pi > 0$, for (1) to have a solution where $B' > 0$, it must be that $\pi'(x) < 0$ at that solution.

What payment policy creates a profit function that has a negative derivative of profit with respect to quantity? Profits *falling* with quantity implies simply that marginal revenue is less than marginal cost. Call marginal revenue the fee, f. Thus, for (1) to hold at an efficient x, fee must be *less than* marginal cost.

A fee set at less than (constant) cost also implies that if such a fee were the only revenue the physician receives, the practice would lose money. To be feasible and acceptable to physicians, payments must at least cover costs. If we are going to have $f < c$, this means we have to pay physicians over and above fees. Call the non-fee-based component of payment F. Think of F as a per person payment to the physician independent of the services the person receives. In the presence of both elements of a payment system, total revenue per patient to the physician is $F + fx$. The requirement (formally referred to as a participation constraint) that revenues cover costs can be expressed as:

$$F + fx - cx \geq 0, \tag{3}$$

A payment system that has a prospective component, F, and a fee (or cost-based) component, f, is referred to as a "mixed system" (Ellis and McGuire 1986).

This simple model gives us the elements we need to design a physician payment system that includes the feature of payment for a medical home. Figure 25.1 shows this diagrammatically. The figure includes two constructs, physician "indifference curves" derived from (1), and payment systems. Both net revenues, π, and x are goods in physician utility. Quantity x is a good because it benefits the patient. The slope of a physician's indifference curve in (x,π)–space is $-V_B B'/V_\pi$. A "neutral" payment system in which the

[14] The analysis here draws on and summarizes some of the points made in work I have done with Randy Ellis, Jacob Glazer and Albert Ma: Ellis and McGuire (1986, 1990, 1993); Ma and McGuire (1997); Glazer and McGuire (2002).

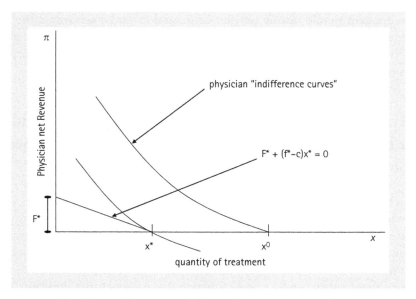

FIGURE 25.1 Physician preferences and choice of treatment in mixed payment systems

physician was paid just cost would be coincident with the horizontal axis in Figure 25.1, that is, where $\pi = 0$ for any x. The physician, with any degree of agency, would maximize utility by choice of quantity where $B' = 0$, and the slope of the indifference curve and revenue line are equated at 0. We call this quantity x^0 in the Figure. Designate x^* to be the optimal quantity where $B' = c$. We find the optimal payment system as the one that leads the physician to maximize utility by choice of x^* leaving profits at zero. The payment system line accomplishing this is shown in the figure. F^* is the (optimal) payment for the medical home, $f^*(<c)$ is the optimal level of fees.

At this optimal solution, the slope of the physician's indifference curve, $-V_B B'/V_\pi$, is equated to the marginal profit on x, f^*-c. Interestingly, the greater the degree of physician agency V_B, the lower f^* must be, and the more payment is weighted towards F. Intuitively this makes sense. The more the physician values patient health benefit, the more the physician must be discouraged by the payment system from providing more care. As first noted by Ellis and McGuire (1986), when the physician is a "perfect agent" and $V_B = V_\pi$, (1) implies $f^*= 0$ at efficiency and a fully prospective payment system is optimal. In general though, we expect physicians to be imperfect agents, valuing their own net revenue above benefits to others, and the optimal payment system would include the mix of prospective and fee-based payments.

25.4.3 Argument II: Physician Ability to Induce Demand Implies Fees Should be Set at Less than Marginal Cost

Physicians can affect quantity by influencing patient valuation of services. In the nota-tion we have been using here, physicians can affect the $B(x)$ function in their own interest. The physician would induce demand in the direction in which she profits, leading the patient to overvalue and demand more than they otherwise would if the physician profits by more services, and conversely, leading the patient to demand less than they otherwise would if the physician would profit by the patient demanding fewer services.

The ability of the physician to affect patients' demand can be used to counter demand-side moral hazard. For this to work, the physician should move to the left (*reduce*, rather than *in*duce demand). Models of demand inducement portray the physician as trading off profit against the discomfort of distorting patient preferences or away from those the physicians believes would be the most accurate. The optimal fee, f^*, would have to be less than marginal cost to move the physician to reduce patient demand. Ideally, the fee would be enough less than marginal cost to convince the physician to shift patient demand to the left just enough to counter the quantity increasing effects of health insurance.

25.4.4 Argument III: Demand Side Moral Hazard Implies Fees Should be Less than Marginal Cost

The analysis so far has regarded patients as completely passive, with physicians making the determination of treatment. Patients have a role in deciding quantity in many cases. Because they do not pay for care directly, patients tend to demand too much health care, referred to as "moral hazard." Interpreting a fee-based payment system coupled with insured patients as driving quantity to where $B' = 0$ (x^0 from Figure 25.1), as being due to patient decisions rather than physician decisions is an easy translation. Both the physician agent and the self-interested patient would seek x^0. Patient incentives cannot be counteracted without introducing copayments, thereby undermining the financial protection conferred by insurance. The payment system to physicians can be used to counter demand-side moral hazard by imposing marginal losses on physicians around the optimal level of treatment. Figuring the optimal f^* in this context would require assessment of the relative roles of the physician and patient, as well as the degree of agency. In any case, we can be sure that the answer implies a fee less than marginal cost coupled with a positive prospective payment F.

25.4.5 Argument IV: Physician Marginal Cost is Less than Average Cost Implying Fees Should be Less than Average Cost

Physician fees as figured by US Medicare include elements to pay for necessary equipment, malpractice costs, office expenses, and other items that do not vary in proportion to the number of procedures a physician undertakes. Our arguments that fees should be less than neutral, i.e. less than marginal cost, apply also therefore with respect to average cost. It would be preferable to pay physicians with a component of revenue, F, independent of service volume, and reduce fees below average cost so as to avoid unde-sirable incentives for too high a quantity.

25.4.6 Argument V: Fees Do Not Pay for Everything Physicians Should do, and a Prospective Component of Payment Encourages Supply of the Otherwise Unreimbursed Activities

It goes without saying that quality of physicians' services is a major issue in health policy, and the "quality" typically referred to does not mean the number of procedures per-formed for which physicians get paid by fees. Fees pay for the quantity of things done, not the quality with which they are done. How can the payment system for primary care encourage the many things that physicians must do to provide high quality care that are not recognized in fees?

Some literature in health economics (Ma 1994; McGuire 2000) regards "quality" as a "non-contractible" input into the production of health for the patient. Non-contractibility means the input cannot be used as a basis of payment (cannot be part of the "contract" for payment, or paid by "fees"). Non-contractibility is distinct from observability. Some things a physician can do to improve the quality of a visit are to spend an adequate amount of time with the patient, or pay careful attention to the patient's symptom reports. These activities may be observable to a patient, but too ill-defined to be able to use as a basis of payment. (How is "time" counted? From the time the patient enters the examining room? The amount of time the physician and patient are together in the room? Less time the physician is on the phone with other matters?) One can think con-cretely about the "time" a physician puts into an exam or other procedure as the non-contractible input. Some physicians (e.g. psychiatrists) report time-based procedures, but generally physicians are not paid on an explicit report of time. Yet time certainly matters to the quality of most of what a doctor does, and is, furthermore, observable to patients. McCall (1996: 52), a physician, writes in his advice book for patients, "the amount of time a doctor spends interviewing you, examining you, and explaining things reflects how genuinely concerned that doctor is for your welfare." While "time" is one concrete candidate for what we mean by non-contractible quality as an input into patient health, others—diligence, responsiveness, attentiveness—can be thought of in the same category as well.

The analysis around Argument I is relevant here. The physician with a high utility weight on patient benefits will be willing to supply all activities needed by a patient, whether contractible or not. In a mixed system, it is the prospective component that plays this role. There is a second way a mixed system can induce physician quality, related to profit incentives. Physicians will be interested in pleasing profitable customers. The F or prospective component can do this. This is the precise idea behind concierge medi-cine. The monthly payment is attractive enough to the doctor to induce her to spend the time and attention required to more fully address a patient's demand for care. Ma (1994) shows that by setting the prospective payment high enough, incentives due to demand response can be used to elicit effort (quality) from the provider.

25.4.7 Argument VI: Practical Considerations

I want to mention briefly some practical arguments for paying primary care by a combination of enrollment-based prospective payment and a fee-based component. Prospective payment, the per-patient F specified above and referred to as payment for the medical home, should ideally vary by health care needs of the patient. For physicians to be paid fairly and be willing to accept and serve sicker patients, the total revenue they expect for these patients should cover expected costs. Some "risk adjustment" of the F portion of payment is called for. Individual or small groups of physicians have limited tolerance for financial risk (Robinson 2001). If the enrollment fee is only supposed to cover, say, 30 percent of physician practice costs, the burden of coming up with the case-mix adjuster to accurately capture differences in expected costs by patient is much reduced. A simple risk adjusted formula combined with fees for 70 percent of costs might provide enough protection against cost risk for physicians and, by the arguments I–V above, confer desirable incentives to treat and take patients, guarding against both incentives to under-treat as well as to overtreat. Keeping a fee-based payment active allows for policy calibration of the mix between the upfront and fee-based component. What is the right mix? The precise answer to this is not known, but if both an upfront and a fee-based component are maintained within the payment system, policy could start with 30 percent upfront–70 percent fee-based, and adjust as monitoring provides evidence for physician and patient response.

25.5 Discussion: Movements in the Right Direction

Physician agency, encompassing ideas related to physician concern for their patients and physician ability to affect patients' demand and utilization, has implications for reform of physician payment in primary care. The series of arguments laid out above all imply that physician fees should be set where possible at a level *below* the marginal cost of the services, where marginal cost is understood to include the cost of physician time. This requires part of payment in primary care be made independent of procedures performed. These arguments apply directly to establishing a payment to primary care physicians for providing a "medical home" for their patients.

Implementing a payment system with a prospective part and a fee-based part—a "mixed system"—raises a number of practical problems. It is worthwhile noting, however, that physician payment systems with these features have emerged in a number of contexts. Primary care physicians in the UK traditionally have been paid according to the number of patients enrolling with them, the prospective part of the mix in a mixed system. Quality indicators in the UK pay for performance system fall into four areas, one being services provided, for example, whether certain tests were run or prenatal care provided for pregnant women (Gravelle, Sutton, and Ma 2008). The marginal reward the primary care doctor gains by conducting these procedures is less than the marginal cost, but consistent with the idea of a mixed system.

Norway introduced a primary care partial capitation system to "improve the quality of primary physician services" in 2001 (Grytten and Sorensen 2007). Patients enroll with a primary care physician and the physician gets a capitation payment that averages about 30 percent of their income. Physicians are also reimbursed by fees for procedures. The Netherlands pays primary care physicians with a combination of capitation for public patients and fees for private patients (Exter et al. 2004), which, in the presence of common quality decisions at the practice level as has been found, for example, by Glied and Zivin (2002), to yield similar incentives to a mixed system for each patient.

In Germany, the mandatory health insurance system covering 90 percent of the population pays physicians with what amounts to a two-part payment (Busse and Riesberg 2004). Patients may enroll with a primary care physicians, and there is a "fee" associated with this "procedure." Israel also features mandatory enrollment in health plans, some health plan payment to community-based physicians has features of a mixed system.

There is some evidence that market forces in the US would support the kind of mixed payment to physicians. During the 1990s, competition among managed care organizations (MCOs) and among medical groups accepting risk in contracts with these MCOs radically transformed the market for health insurance in California (Casalino and Robinson 1997). Some of these contracts gave physician groups nearly full risk for all of health care services, but more common was some risk sharing with the MCO over services, such as hospital care, provided outside the medical group. Over the middle part of the decade, health insurance premiums in California were essentially flat, largely due to sharp declines in rates of hospitalization. A similar experience of a drop in use of hospitalization followed the introduction of primary care fundholding in the UK (Dusheiko et al. 2006). Although some of the California medical groups, organized as Independent Practice Associations (IPAs), subsequently failed after health care costs resumed an upward track at the close of the decade (Bodenheimer 2000), it is instructive to observe the form of the contracts that emerged in this "market" between the MCOs and the medical groups and between the medical groups and the physicians working in the group or as part of the IPA. Shared risk was an important part of both sets of contracts. Initially, medical groups were eager for straight capitation contracts (Casalino and Robinson 1997), but during the 1990s the contracts evolved to include more risk sharing in the form of targets and bonuses, and explicit risk sharing over expenditure limits. The contracts between the groups and the physicians also transmitted some but not all of the financial risk to the affiliated physicians (Rosenthal et al. 2002). Contracts with mixed system features emerged between MCOs and medical groups and between the groups and the physicians.

In sum, theoretical and empirical evidence on physician behavior and agency imply that neither pure procedure-based physician payment nor pure capitation systems should be the basis of medical home finance in health care. The prospective enrollment component in a mixed system gives physicians the financial support for infrastructure and the incentive to attract and accept patients. The (small) fee-based payment protects the physician against financial risk and confers incentives in-between those with a fee-based system (tending toward oversupply) and capitation (tending toward undersupply). Mixed systems are clearly feasible, as evidenced by US and more extensive international experience. The medical home pairs naturally with a mixed payment system.

BIBLIOGRAPHY

BARR, M. and GINSBURG, J. (2006). *The Advanced Medical Home: A Patient-Centered, Physician-Guided Model of Health Care*. American College of Physicians Policy Monograph.

BODENHEIMER, T. (2000). "California's beleaguered physician groups: will they survive?" *The New England Journal of Medicine*, April 6, 324/14: 1064–8.

BRADDOCK, C. H. and SNYDER, L. (2005). "The doctor will see you shortly: the ethical significance of time for the patient–physician relationship." *Journal of General Internal Medicine*, 20: 1057–62.

BRENNAN, T. A. (2002). "Luxury primary care: market innovation or threat to access?" *The New England Journal of Medicine*, 346: 1165–8.

BUSSE, R. and RIESBERG, A. (2004). *Health Care Systems in Transition: Germany*. Copenhagen: WHO Regional Office for European on behalf of the European Observatory on Health Systems and Policies.

CASALINO, L. P. and ROBINSON, J. C. (1997). *The Evolution of Medical Groups and Capitation in California*. Menlo Park, CA: Henry J. Kaiser Foundation and California HealthCare Foundation.

CHALKLEY, M. and TILLEY, C. (2005). "The existence and nature of physician agency: Evidence of stinting from the British National Health Service." *Journal of Economics & Management Strategy*, 14/3: 647–64.

COCKX, B. and BRASSEUR, C. (2003). "The demand for physician services: Evidence from a natural experiment." *Journal of Health Economics*, 22/6: 881–913.

CULYER, A. J. (1989). "The normative economics of health care finance and provision." *Oxford Review of Economic Policy*, 5: 34–58.

DAVIS, K. (2007a). "Paying for care episodes and care coordination." *The New England Journal of Medicine*, 356: 1166–8.

—— (2007b). "Making payment reform in the US healthcare system possible." *Medscape General Medicine*, 9/4: 63.

DELATTRE, E. and DORMONT, B. (2003). "Fixed fees and physician-induced demand: A panel data study on French physicians." *Health Economics*, 12/9: 741–54.

DRANOVE, D. (1988). "Demand inducement and the physician/patient relationship." *Economic Inquiry*, 26: 251–98.

—— and WEHNER, P. (1994). "Physician-induced demand for childbirths." *Journal of Health Economics*, 13: 61–73.

DUSHEIKO, M., GRAVELLE, H., JACOBS, R., and SMITH, P. (2006), "The effect of budgets on doctor behaviour: evidence from a natural experiment," *Journal of Health Economics*, 25: 449–78.

ELLIS, R. P. and MCGUIRE, T. G. (1986). "Provider behavior under prospective reimbursement." *Journal of Health Economics*, 5: 129–51.

—— —— (1990). "Optimal payment systems for health services." *Journal of Health Economics*, 9: 375–96.

—— —— (1993). "Supply-side and demand-side cost sharing in health care." *Journal of Economic Perspectives*, 7: 135–51.

—— and MILLER, M. M. (2008). "Provider payment methods and incentives." In Kris Heggenhougen and Stella R. Quah (eds), *International Encyclopedia of Public Health*, 6 vols. London: Elsevier.

EISENBERG, J. M. (1986). "Doctors' decisions and the cost of medical care." *Health Administration Press*. Ann Arbor, MI: Health Administration Press.

EVANS, R. (1974). "Supplier-induced demand: some empirical evidence and implications," in M. Perlman (ed.), *The Economics of Health and Medical Care*. London: Macmillan, 162–73.

EXTER, A., HERMANS, H., DOSLJAK, M. and BUSSE, R. (2004), *Health Care Systems in Transition: Netherlands*, Copenhagen, WHO Regional Office for Europe on behalf of the Europena Observatory on Health Systems and Policies.

FARLEY, P. J. (1986). "Theories of the price and quantity of physician services." *Journal of Health Economics*, 5/4: 315–33.

FELDSTEIN, M. (1970). "The rising price of physicians' services." *Review of Economics and Statistics*, 52/2: 121–33.

FORREST, C. B., GLADE, G. B., BAKER, A. E., BOCIAN, A., VON SCHRADER, S. and STARFIELD, B. (2000). "Coordination of specialty referrals and physician satisfaction with referral care." *Archives of Pediatrics and Adolescent Medicine*, 154: 499–506.

FUCHS, V. R. (1978). "The supply of surgeons and the demand for operations." *The Journal of Human Resources*, 13: 35–56.

GANDHI, T. K. (2005). "Fumbled handoffs: one dropped ball after another." *Annals of Internal Medicine*, 142: 352–8.

—— SITTIG, D. F., FRANKLIN, M., SUSSMAN, A. J., FAIRCHILD, D. G., and BATES, D. W. (2005). "Communication breakdown in the outpatient referral process." *Journal of General Internal Medicine*, 142: 352–8.

GINSBURG, P. B. and GROSSMAN, J. M. (2005). "When the price isn't right: how inadvertent payment incentives drive medical care." *Health Affairs*, 24/5: W5376–84.

GIUFFRIDA, A. and GRAVELLE, H. (2001). "Inducing or restraining demand: the market for night visits in primary care." *Journal of Health Economics*, 20: 755–79.

GLAZER, J. and MCGUIRE, T. G. (2002). "Setting health plan premiums to ensure efficient quality in health care: minimum variance optimal risk adjustment." *Journal of Public Economics*, 84: 153–73.

GLIED, S. and ZIVIN, J. (2002) "How do doctors behave when some (but not all) of their patients are in managed care?" *Journal of Health Economics*, 22(2): 337–53.

GOLDFIELD, N., AVERILL, R., VERTREES, J., FULLER, R., MESCHES, D., MOORE, G., WASSON, J., and KELLY, W. (2008). "Reforming the primary care physician payment system: eliminating E & M codes and creating the financial incentives for an 'advanced medical home.'" *Journal of Ambulatory Care Management*, 31/1: 24–31.

GOROLL, A.H., BERENSON, R.A., SCHOENBAUM, S.C., and GARDNER, L.B. (2007) "Fundamental reform of payment for adult primary care: comprehensive payment for comprehensive care." *Journal of General Internal Medicine*, 22: 410–15.

GOTTSCHALK, A. and FLOCKE, S. A. (2005). "Time spent in face-to-face patient care and work outside the examination room." *Annals of Family Medicine*, 3: 288–93.

GRAVELLE, H., SUTTON, M. and MA, A. (2008). "Doctor behavior under a pay for performance contract: further evidence from the quality and outcomes framework." *Centre for Health Economics*. <www.york.ac.uk/inst/che/publications/index.htm>.

GRUBER, J., and OWINGS, M. (1996). "Physician financial incentives and Cesarean section delivery." *RAND Journal of Economics*, 27: 99–123.

—— KIM, J., and MAYZLIN, D. (1999). "Physician fees and procedure intensity: the case of cesarean delivery." *Journal of Health Economics*, 18/4: 473–90.

GRYTTEN, J. and SORENSEN, R. (2001). "Type of Contract and Supplier-induced Demand for Primary Physicians in Norway," *Journal of Health Economics*, 20/3: 379–93.

—————— (2007). "Primary physician services: list size and primary physician's service production." *Journal of Health Economics*, 26/4: 721–41.

HADLEY, J., MANDELBLATT, J. S. et al. (2003). "Medicare breast surgery fees and treatment received by older women with localized breast cancer." *Health Services Research*, 38/2: 553–73.

HSIAO, W. C. et al. (1988). "Estimating physicians' work for a resource-based relative-value scale." *New England Journal of Medicine*, 319/13: 835–41.

JACOBSON, M., O'MALLEY, A. J. et al. (2006). "Does reimbursement influence chemotherapy treatment for cancer patients?" *Health Affairs*, 25/2: 437–43.

LARSON, E. B. (2003). "Medicine as a Profession—Back to Basics: Preserving the Physician–Patient Relationship in a Challenging Medical Marketplace." *The American Journal of Medicine*, 114: 168–72.

LIEN, H., MA, C. A. and MCGUIRE, T. G. (2004). "Provider–client interactions and quantity of health care use." *Journal of Health Economics*, 23/6: 1261–83.

MA, C. A. (1994). "Health care payment systems: cost and quality incentives." *Journal of Economics & Management Strategy*, 3/1: 93–112.

—— and MCGUIRE, T. G. (1997). "Optimal health insurance and provider payment." *American Economic Review*, 87/4: 685–704.

MADDEN, D., NOLAN, A., and NOLAN, B. (2005). "GP Reimbursement and Visiting Behaviour in Ireland," *Health Economics*, 14/10: 1047–60.

MCCALL, T. B. (1996). *Examining Your Doctor*. Seacaucus, NJ: Citadel Press.

MCGUIRE, T. G. (2000). "Physician agency," in A. Culyer and J. P. Newhouse (eds.), *Handbook of Health Economics*. Amsterdam: North Holland.

—— and PAULY, M. V. (1991). "Physician response to fee changes with multiple payers." *Journal of Health Economics*, 10/4: 385–410.

MedPAC (Medicare Payment Advisory Commission) (2006). "Report to Congress: Medicare payment policy." Washington, DC: MedPAC. Available at: <http://www.medpac.gov/documents/Mar06_EntireReport.pdf>.

MITCHELL, J. M., HADLEY, J., and GASKIN, D. J. (2002). "Spillover effects of Medicare fee reductions: evidence from ophthalmology." *International Journal of Health Care Finance and Economics*, 2/3: 171–88.

NASSIRI, A. and ROCHAIX, L. (2006). "Revisiting physicians' financial incentives in Quebec: a panel system approach." *Health Economics*, 15/1: 49–64.

NEWHOUSE, J. P. (2002). *Pricing the Priceless: A Healthcare Conundrum*. Cambridge, MA: MIT Press.

NGUYEN, N. X. and DERRICK, F. W. (1997). "Physician behavioral response to a Medicare price reduction." *Health Services Research*, 32: 283–98.

OSTBYE, T., YARNALL, K. S. H., KRAUSE, K. M., POLLAK, K. I., GRADISON, M. and MICHENER, J. L. (2005). "Is there time for management of patients with chronic diseases in primary care?" *Annals of Family Medicine*, 3: 209–14.

PAULY, M. V. (1980). *Doctors and Their Workshops: Economic Models of Physician Behavior*. Chicago, IL: University of Chicago Press.

PHAM, H. H., SCHRAG, D., O'MALLEY, A. S., WU, B., and BACH, P. B. (2007). "Care patterns in Medicare and their implications for pay-for-performance." *The New England Journal of Medicine*, 356: 1130–9.

RICE, T. (1983). "The impact of changing Medicare reimbursement rates on physician-induced demand." *Medical Care*, 21: 803–15.

ROBINSON, J. (2001). "Theory and practice in the design of physician payment incentives." *The Milbank Quarterly*, 79/2: 149–77.

ROSENTHAL, M. B. (2000). "Risk sharing and the supply of mental health services." *Journal of Health Economics*, 19/6: 1047–65.

—— FRANK, R. G., BUCHANAN, J. L. and EPSTEIN, A. M. (2002). "Transmission of financial incentives to physicians by intermediary organizations in California." *Health Affairs*, 21/4: 197–205.

ROTER, D. L. and HALL, J. A. (1989). "Studies of doctor–patient interaction." *Annual Reviews in Public Health*, 10: 163–80.

SCANDLEN, G. (2005). "Consumer-driven health care: just a tweak or a revolution?" *Health Affairs*, 24: 1554–8.

SCHILLINGER, D., PIETTE, J., and GRUMBACH, K. (2003). "Closing the loop: physician communication with diabetic patients who have low health literacy." *Archives of Internal Medicine*, 163: 83–90.

SCHOEN, C., OSBORN, R., and HUYNH, P. T. (2004). "Primary care and health system performance: adults' experiences in five countries," *Health Affairs*, Web Exclusives W4: 487–503.

SCHOENBAUM, S. C., BERENSON, R. A., GARDNER, L. B., and GOROLL, A. H. (2008). "Commentary on Goldfield et al.'s 'Reforming the Primary Care Physician Payment System.'" *Journal of Ambulatory Care Management*, 31/2: 151–3.

STANO, M. (1987). "A further analysis of the physician inducement controversy." *Journal of Health Economics*, 6: 229–38.

STARFIELD, B. and SHI, L. (2004). "The medical home, access to care, and insurance: a review of evidence." *Pediatrics*, 113: 1493–8.

—— SHI, L., and MACINKO, J. (2005). "Contribution of primary care to health systems and health." *The Milbank Quarterly*, 83: 457–502.

TAI-SEALE, M., et al. (1998). "Volume responses to Medicare payment inductions with multiple payers: a test of the McGuire–Pauly model." *Health Economics*, 7: 199–219.

—— McGUIRE, T. G., and ZHANG, W. (2007). "Time allocation in primary care office visits." *Health Services Research*, 42/5: 1871–94.

WILLIAMS, A. (1998). "Medicine, economics, ethics and the NHS: a clash of cultures?" *Health Economics*, 7: 565–8.

YARNALL, K. S. H., POLLAK, K. I., OSTBYE, T., KRAUSE, K. M., and MICHENER, J. L. (2003). "Primary care: is there enough time for prevention?" *American Journal of Public Health*, 93: 635–41.

YIP, W. (1998). "Physician responses to medical fee reductions: changes in the volume and intensity of supply of Coronary, Artery Bypass Graft (CABG) surgeries in the medicare and private sectors." *Journal of Health Economics*, 17: 675–700.

ZWEIFEL, P., and BREYER, F. (1997). *Health Economics*. New York: Oxford University Press.

CHAPTER 26

··

PROVIDER PAYMENT
AND INCENTIVES*

··

JON B. CHRISTIANSON AND DOUGLAS CONRAD

26.1 INTRODUCTION

ANY payment arrangement, irrespective of its design, creates incentives that can affect the decisions of individuals or organizations receiving the payment. The use of financial incentives to influence the behavior of another party is common in all areas of commerce. The design of incentives and the evaluation of their impact has been examined in the research literature at many different levels. For example, in the economics literature, the principal–agent relationship has been studied with the goal of specifying optimal financial incentives in contracts under different assumptions (see, for instance, Pratt and Zeckhauser 1985; Eisenhardt 1989; Sappington 1991; Milgrom and Roberts 1992; Prendergast 1999). The literature on employee compensation examines use of different payment approaches to encourage desired behaviors on the part of workers (for example, Gerhart and Rynes 2003; Rynes, Gerhart, and Parks 2005), while the marketing literature addresses consumer responses to targeted incentive programs. An empirical, "applied" literature on the impact of financial incentives on behavior can be found pertaining to each sector of the economy, including health care, and related conceptual issues are addressed in several academic disciplines, such as psychology and decision-making, in addition to economics (see, for instance, Rynes, Gerhart, and Parks 2005).

  * Dr. Christianson gratefully acknowledges support from the Quality Enhancing Interventions (QEI) Project of the Health Foundation, United Kingdom. Portions of this chapter are also available, with greater detail, in Christianson, Leatherman, and Sutherland, *Financial Incentives, Health Care Providers, and Quality Improvements: A Review of the Evidence*, the Health Foundation, UK (2009). Dr. Conrad is appreciative of support from the National Institutes of Health and from the Robert Wood Johnson Foundation Health Care Financing and Organization (RWJ-HCFO) Initiative for research on paying for quality.

Within health care, there has been a longstanding interest in how the type and amount of payment to health care providers affects the type and amount of services received by consumers and, ultimately, the costs of health care to individuals, employers, insurers, and governments. Researchers have devoted less attention to the impact of financial incentives on the quality of services either offered by providers or sought by consumers.

In this chapter, we first provide background and a conceptual framework relating to the effects of payment incentives on the behavior of health care providers. We then summarize the empirical literature on the effect of financial incentives in health care, relying primarily on the findings of review articles. Specifically, we address: the effect of general provider payment incentives on the amount and type of care provided; the evidence that general payment incentives have indirectly affected quality of care; and the impact of payment incentive programs that attempt specifically to reward providers for improving quality of care, or for achieving specific benchmark levels of quality.

26.2 Background: Provider Payment Incentives

As a general matter, financial incentives in payment arrangements between payers and providers are intended by payers to influence the utilization of health care services by consumers. The utilization of health care services typically is modeled as the result of the joint decisions of providers and consumers. In an economic paradigm, consumers demand medical care and providers supply it. However, an unusual characteristic of this exchange is that patients expect their providers to play the role of trusted patient "agent" in the decision process. Providers possess better information about the consequences of treatment alternatives, and the consumer trusts the provider to convey that information in an unbiased manner, typically accompanied by a treatment recommendation.

Financial incentives have the potential to influence the recommendations of providers in their role as agents for their patients. Indeed, the intent of different payment arrangements often is to alter the interaction of providers with consumers in reaching a decision about the utilization of services. For example, if a primary care physician is "at risk" for the cost of referrals to specialists (e.g. through a capitation payment that includes both primary and specialty services), the primary care physician may be more likely to suggest to patients that she/he can provide the service (specialty care is not needed) or to recommend that the patient seek specialty care from a relatively low cost provider. The degree to which either physician response is observed depends on many factors in addition to the amount of financial reward at stake, including the ability of primary care physicians to reconcile their recommendations with their role as patient advocate or agent for the patient's best interest. In any event, if either action were taken, it might, or might not, have an impact on costs or quality. Providing services in the primary care physician's office could result in lower costs and have no effect on quality. Or, the lower cost specialist may, in fact, provide higher quality care than delivered by more expensive specialists who might otherwise receive the referral. And, of course, patients do not always accept the recommendations of their primary care physicians.

Economic theory suggests that different types of payment approaches can lead to different types of provider behaviors, with each payment approach having its own strengths and drawbacks. In assessing approaches to paying physicians, Robinson (2001: 149) observes that "There are many mechanisms for paying physicians; some are good and some are bad. The three worst are fee-for-service, capitation, and salary." Nevertheless, historically these approaches have been the most commonly used by health care payers.

26.2.1 Capitation

Under capitation payment, the provider agrees to deliver a specified list of health services to a predetermined group of individuals for a fixed amount per person per time period. The provider bears financial risk in situations where the actual cost of these services exceeds that fixed amount. Conversely, the provider retains at least a portion of monies that accrue when the cost is less than the predetermined reimbursement. The most frequently voiced concern about capitation is that the provider entity receiving the payment might act too aggressively in constraining service use, eliminating some "necessary" as well as some "unnecessary" services. The result could be lower quality of care for patients. This is especially true, it is thought, if there is no sharing of risks or surpluses, if the capitated contract is short-term in nature, and if contract renewal does not depend on measures other than costs.

Also, providers under capitation are bearing *underwriting risk*. Unless the capitation payment is adjusted for the health status (and, therefore, the expected cost) of the provider's panel of enrollees, the provider organization is at risk for higher costs of sicker enrollees, while revenues per enrollee are fixed. In that sense, the provider organization under capitation is assuming the risks normally underwritten by insurers. The provider's potential incentive to select favorable risks from the population is thus an unintended consequence that must be managed by the payer through risk adjustment and other contracting terms. Larger provider organizations are better positioned to assume this underwriting risk; that is, the "law of large numbers" (Morrisey 2007) works in their favor.

It can be argued that if provider organizations, reimbursed by capitation payments, care for an enrolled population over a period of time, they have an incentive to provide services that maintain or improve the health of that population, as this health maintenance and health promotion will, over the longer term, yield financial benefits. However, if individuals remain in a provider panel of patients for only a limited time period, this incentive is weakened. Moreover, because an increase in the number of enrollees for whom the provider earns a positive margin would increase net income, other things equal, capitation payment also creates incentives to compete on quality to attract patients (Conrad and Christianson 2004).

26.2.2 Fee-for-Service

Fee-for-service payment in medical care is essentially the counterpart to "piece-rate" payment in other sectors of the economy. Providers are rewarded for providing more services to patients. Robinson (2001) has noted that this form of payment for services is not common outside of medical care, because it contains such a powerful incentive for "over-provision" of services (more services provided than an informed consumer would desire) on the part of the "agent" and therefore necessitates monitoring on the part of the payer, which can be expensive when output cannot be measured easily. In some respects, it seems intuitive that more medical care would benefit patients in most cases, and therefore that fee-for-service payments would be associated with higher quality of care and better patient outcomes. However, there is research suggesting that more care does not necessarily imply higher quality or better outcomes. Provider incomes increase whether or not the services they provide are needed, or are of dubious worth, and there may be a risk to patient health associated with "over-treatment" or "inappropriate treatment," just as there is with "under treatment" (see Institute of Medicine 2001).

26.2.3 Prospective Payment per Admission or Episode of Care

To modify the incentives under fee-for-service, reimbursement based on payment per episode or, for institutions, payment per admission has been introduced. For, example, the United States' Medicare program uses this approach to pay for inpatient care ("DRG" payments). Under prospective payment, services are bundled for payment purposes, creating incentives for providers to limit the services they provide in response to a specific event or illness episode. However, unlike capitation, providers receive more revenues the greater number of events or episodes they treat. They are not responsible for providing all needed services to a defined population. There are various efforts underway to craft prospective payment approaches that would apply in non-institutional settings (e.g. see Prometheus 2006).

26.2.4 Salary

Under salary arrangements, the provider is paid a fixed amount per time period. There is no incentive to deliver unnecessary services, nor is there an incentive for "under-provision," except to the degree that providers may "shirk" under salaried arrangements. That is, they may attempt to provide fewer services—work less hard—than expected under the contractual arrangement. There is no particular incentive under a pure salary method of payment for providers to deliver high quality care, so there typically is a heavy reliance by payers on enforcement of rules and procedures thought to enhance quality. The result could be quality-enhancing or, to the degree that rule enforcement limits provider ability to bring professional judgment to bear in treatment decisions, lower quality of care.

26.2.5 Budgets

At the organizational or institutional level, providers may be reimbursed through a negotiated budget process. The nature of the incentives in this payment arrangement can resemble capitation, when the number of individuals served in a given period is fixed, and the organization is at risk for budget over-runs and can keep savings. Alternatively, the incentives can resemble those of salaried providers when the organization serves patients who seek care, but does not assume responsibility to provide care to a fixed number, or enrolled group, of individuals for a specified time period.

In reality, any payment arrangement, whatever its accompanying incentives, will seldom be observed without some modification when applied to the reimbursement of medical care providers. Terms such as fee-for-service or capitation are employed commonly by policymakers and researchers as a "short-hand" for what they view as the "essential core" of the payment arrangement.

However, in most cases, providers are paid using some manner of "blended" approach. Robinson (1999) describes some uses of blended payment approaches in the US. For instance, physicians may receive a base salary, with additional compensation for achieving targets relating to productivity, cost minimization, and/or attainment of quality benchmarks or goals for improvement. These blended payment arrangements are intended to achieve the best balance of provider behavior—for example, by combining capitation incentives for provider cost control per enrollee (a form of "supply-side cost-sharing") with fee-for-service incentives for provision of services. Also, as Jack (2005) points out, offering a menu of incentive arrangements allows the payer to achieve increased provider participation at lower costs.

The general literature on payment arrangements suggests that, even under the best designed payment scheme, desired outcomes are not likely to be achieved through financial incentives alone; measurement and monitoring activities are required as well. The greater the cost of these activities, the less likely that use of financial incentives, all else equal, will be a cost-effective approach to changing provider behaviors. In particular, incentive designers must face the problem of "multi-tasking," in which providers may "treat to the test"—that is, target their quality improvement efforts on the performance measures explicitly rewarded, while downplaying other care dimensions of equal or potentially even greater importance for health outcomes (Eggleston 2005; Frolich et al. 2007).

Equally important, the effectiveness of any financial incentive scheme in eliciting changes in provider behaviors depends not only on the amount and type of payment, but also on the characteristics of providers themselves (e.g. their preferences for monetary versus other rewards, such as autonomy, security, etc.) and of the context in which they practice. For instance, whether the risks associated with a particular incentive scheme are borne by the individual provider or shared within a provider group could have an important impact on provider responses (Town et al. 2004), as could the existence of multiple payment arrangements across different purchasers, which dilutes the impact of any specific incentive on provider behavior.

26.3 CONCEPTUAL MODEL FOR PREDICTING EFFECTS OF SPECIFIC INCENTIVE PROGRAMS

In this section we offer a conceptual model of the provider's choice of the quantity and quality of output as a means of organizing our thinking about the effects of specific provider payment incentives. The model, adopted from Conrad and Christianson (2004), generates a set of testable hypotheses. We focus on the provider's choice of quantity of services (output) and quality per unit of service.

26.3.1 Choice of Quantity and Quality of Output

Providers offer differentiated services in local markets. The customization of services to individual patients with idiosyncratic preferences and physical and mental health needs, coupled with asymmetric information, confers a degree of pricing power on the individual medical provider (Pauly and Satterthwaite 1981; McGuire 2000), and we assume that the provider seeks to maximize net income by choosing the optimal quantity of services and quality per unit of service.

First, we discuss the effect of quality incentives under a fee for service (FFS) payment approach. The market-determined price "mark-up" function per unit of quality captures the quality incentive, and specific hypotheses are derived concerning the effect of small changes in exogenous variables (factors beyond the medical provider's control) on the provider choice of quality and quantity. These hypotheses ultimately should be tested in *reduced-form* equations that address the total effect of a small change in an exogenous variable—such as the price mark-up for higher quality—on the levels of quantity and quality.

26.3.2 Hypothesis 1 (Quality Effects of Quality-Based Financial Incentives)

The *direct* effect of an increase in the market price mark-up for quality is to induce the provider to increase the level of quality per unit of output, holding constant the marginal cost of quality and the level of exogenous variables that shift the demand for and cost of services (such as income and health insurance coverage). This is intuitive and is precisely the reasoning behind private and public policymakers' use of financial incentives to encourage improved quality. However, there is more to the story.

Indirectly, the increased price mark-up also affects quality per unit of output by raising the marginal revenue per unit of quantity. This indirect effect will reinforce the positive direct effect of the price mark-up on quality if total costs rise less than proportionately as the provider's quantity of output increases. Put differently, if there are economies of scale in the production of services, the marginal quality incentive will spur increased quality through an indirect "quantity" effect.

Figure 26.1, Panel A, displays the marginal costs and marginal revenue per unit of quantity. The increase in price mark-up for quality (indirectly) raises the marginal revenue per unit of quantity, thus shifting the quantity marginal revenue curve in Panel A from $MR(0)$ to $MR(1)$. The marginal cost per unit of quantity also shifts in Panel A from $MC(0)$ to $MC(1)$, which reflects the increased cost per unit from increased quality per unit of output.

Figure 26.1, Panel B, illustrates the marginal costs and marginal revenue per unit of quality (z). The direct effect of an exogenous increase in the market price mark-up for quality is to shift the quality marginal revenue curve from $MR(0)$ to $MR(1)$ along $MC(0)$. At the higher equilibrium output, $q(1)$, the marginal cost of quality is now shifted to $MC(1)$ in Panel B because increased quality per unit is now applied to a larger number of quantity units. In Figure 26.1, Panel B, we have diagrammed the case where the new equilibrium quality is higher, i.e., $z(1) > z(0)$.

Pope and Burge (1992: 159) remark that, in light of the mixed results of econometric studies of provider production, "...a hypothesis of *roughly* (emphasis added) constant returns to scale is not unreasonable." To the extent this generalization is valid, indirect effects on quality through induced quantity changes will be small.

26.3.3 Hypothesis 2 (Quantity Effects of Quality-based Financial Incentives)

The *direct* effect of an exogenous increase in the market price mark-up for quality, through a shift in the level of $r(z)$, leads to increased quantity (q), holding other exogenous variables constant (e.g. demand price and cost shifters). If the price mark-up for incremental quality, $r(z)$, is sufficiently large relative to the marginal cost of quality and if the diminution of the price mark-up, $r'(z)$, is relatively small, then the *indirect* effect on quantity of the increase in quality reward also will be positive. This indirect effect operates through the increase in the marginal net income per unit of quantity as providers enhance the quality per unit in response to the quality incentive, $r(z)$.

Moreover, as shown in the Appendix, if the production of services is roughly constant in returns to scale ($s \approx 1$), the indirect effect will be negligible, and one

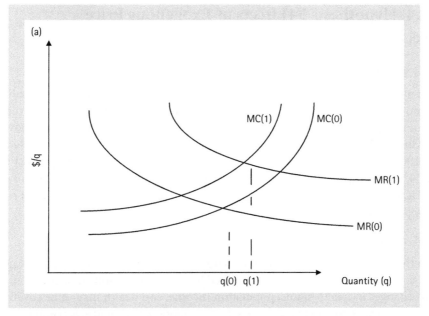

FIGURE 26.1A Panel A—marginal revenue (MR), marginal cost (MC) of quantity

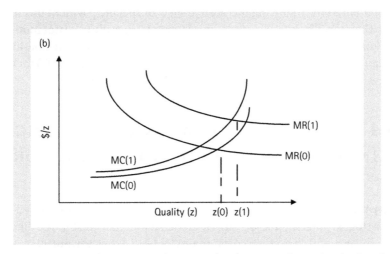

FIGURE 26.1B Panel B—marginal revenue (MR), marginal cost (MC) of quality

would unambiguously predict increased equilibrium quantity as the result of increased *quality-based* price mark-up. Panel A of Figure 26.1 illustrates this case, where the quality incentive-induced shift in quality leads to larger shifts in marginal revenue than in marginal cost—resulting in a higher level of equilibrium output.

26.3.4 Hypothesis 3 (Effects of Exogenous Price Level Changes)

26.3.4.1 *Quality Effects*

In this model exogenous increases in price level (p) do not *directly* influence quality. The exogenous price level, p in our model, does not directly influence either the marginal revenue of quality or marginal cost of quality expressions. However, it can be shown that the indirect effect of exogenous price increases on quality depends exclusively on the cost-elasticity of quantity (s). If cost rises more than in proportion to the quantity of output ($s1$), then exogenous price increases not explicitly tied to quality per unit of output would lead to *lower* quality as providers trade-off increased output levels against reduced quality per unit of service.

26.3.4.2 *Quantity Effects*

Other things equal, by increasing the marginal profitability of output, an exogenous increase in price level will result in increased level of output. Shifts in willingness to pay due to changes in health status, population income, and health insurance coverage are illustrative of exogenous demand factors (h in our model) that could give rise to such shifts.

This formal model and its specific hypotheses might serve as a guide to further research on the effects of specific payment incentives on quality of care. It is best viewed as a complement to the following literature review of specific payment incentive effects on quality. The prevailing studies of specific payment generally have not motivated their empirical analyses with formal models, and the microeconomic model outlined here is similar in spirit to the behavioral model developed by Frolich et al. (2007) for organizing their review of clinician responses to specific quality incentives.

26.4 Assessing the Impact of Financial Incentives on Provider Behavior

The greater the effect of new financial payment arrangements, or of revised incentives within existing arrangements, on provider behavior, the greater the likelihood of detectable, meaningful changes in costs, quality, or both. However, not all research studies are designed to capture both cost and quality impacts of utilization changes. This may reflect a lack of data related to quality of care. Or, the research may focus, by design, on a specific outcome to the exclusion of others. Given the sometimes dramatic increases in health care costs experienced by private health plans, public payers, and other organized health care purchasers, the impact of payment systems on costs often has been the primary, or only, focus of research. However, in many studies the analysis has been content to stop at documenting and explaining utilization changes, assuming that decreases in utilization of the service in question will ultimately mean lower costs.

(The obvious flaw in this reasoning is that use of other services may increase as a consequence of lower use of the service targeted by the change in incentives, with uncertain consequences for overall costs.)

When investigating the literature on the impact of financial incentives on providers, the first challenge frequently is to understand the nature of the financial incentives in question. In experimental studies, clear, simple financial incentives often are employed. However, incentives in practice are likely to be much more complicated and nuanced. The provider payment incentives in observational studies reflect the more complicated reimbursement arrangements that exist in the "real world," which is a strength of these studies. However, in observational studies it often is difficult to sort out the effect of financial incentives from other factors that influence provider behavior. And, researchers may not take the time to construct a fully nuanced view of the incentives faced by providers in their study, opting instead to characterize incentives using the capitation/fee-for-service/salary shorthand.

26.4.1 Evidence on Effects of Provider Payment Incentives on Type and Amount of Care

There are six published literature reviews addressing the impact of financial incentives on utilization and costs. McCleary, Asubonteng, and Munchus (1995) reviewed the early literature on the effect of financial incentives on physician behavior in Health Maintenance Organizations. (HMOs are insurance arrangements, common in the United States, in which enrollees agree to seek services from a limited network of providers, typically receiving in return more comprehensive coverage and/or a lower premium.) They found that service utilization was generally less for enrollees in HMOs, where physicians are often, but not always, reimbursed by salary or by capitation payments. They also observed that little research addressed the impact of financial incentives on quality of care, and that more research is needed in this area. Like McCleary, Asubonteng, and Munchus (1995), Hellinger (1996) reviewed the impact of financial incentives on physician behavior in managed care plans (a term used in the literature to encompass HMOs and other arrangements with limited provider networks and/or procedures that constrain provider decision-making). He found that financial incentives were a key element in the success of managed care plans in reducing utilization of services, but also identified several sources of bias in prior studies.

A literature review by Aas (1995) assessed changes in behavior resulting from changes in inpatient payment policies for hospitals and physicians. The author concluded that physicians paid by capitation had lower admission rates than physicians paid fee-for-service, that payment of hospitals on a per-day basis resulted in longer lengths of stay (compared to other payment methods), and that salaried physicians used fewer diagnostic procedures than physicians paid fee-for-service.

Flynn, Smith, and Davis (2002) reviewed the literature regarding different approaches used to manage health care utilization, describing the different types of financial incentives employed to influence provider behavior. The authors concluded that the studies assessing the impact of payment approaches on provider behavior generally have not been satisfactory. They found no conclusive evidence of behavior impacts, with the exception that fee-for-service payment tended to be associated with the delivery of more primary care services by physicians.

Rice (1997) assessed the impact of changes in financial incentives in the US Medicare program in the context of a theoretical model. He concluded that the literature on fee-for-service payment provided evidence that physicians often respond to payment changes, sometimes increasing volume of services provided in response to payment reductions. A sixth paper, by Mitchell (1996), reviewed the evidence on the relationship between physician ownership of facilities and their referral patterns, concluding that ownership was associated with increased utilization of services.

In summary, the relatively large number of published studies that assess the impact of provider financial incentives on medical care utilization and costs have found, with very few exceptions, that providers will take steps to reduce utilization or costs when rewarded to do so. However, the usefulness of this literature for decision makers in the future is limited in many respects. For instance, the exact nature of the financial incentives often was not explained by study authors and, as a consequence, possible causal linkages were not clear. Many of the studies used datasets with very small numbers of providers or practice settings. In these cases, it was difficult to adequately control for the context in which the financial arrangements were implemented. In general, more information about context would have been helpful in drawing conclusions regarding the generalizability of study findings. None of the authors described a systematic approach for identifying the studies included in their reviews.

Finally, except in a small number of studies, the empirical analysis was not carefully linked to an explicit theory of provider decision making. This left the results open to a variety of ad hoc interpretations, especially where information on context was lacking. The strength of this body of research lies in the consistency of its findings that providers do respond to financial incentives rather than in the insights it provides for the design of effective incentive arrangements.

26.4.2 Evidence on Indirect Effects of Provider Payment Incentives on Quality of Care

The effectiveness of financial incentives at reducing utilization raises questions regarding whether the lower levels of utilization compromise quality of care and has stimulated research on this issue. This research can be difficult to conduct because of variation in the way in which the concept of "quality" is understood and used. In one widely cited definition, quality of care is seen as "the degree to which health services for individuals and populations increase the likelihood of desired health outcomes and are consistent with current professional knowledge" (Lohr and Schroeder 1990). However, this is only one of many different possible definitions of "quality."

In its early stages, the development of this line of research was limited by the rate of progress in the development of process measures of quality that (1) had a clear scientific basis, (2) could be collected in a consistent manner across different types of payment approaches, and (3) were likely to be sensitive to changes in financial incentives over the (typically) restricted time period encompassed by most studies. At times, the measures used to indicate differences in quality across payment arrangements were controversial. For example, some studies assumed that higher rates of apparently overused procedures, such as cesarean sections, indicated poorer quality care. In other instances, questions can be raised regarding whether quality measures were constructed in the same way under different reimbursement schemes. For instance, researchers frequently have pointed out that, when providers were not paid fee-for-service, they may not have been as diligent at recording the care that they provided. This could result in an incomplete assessment of care received by patients under capitated arrangements and erroneous conclusions regarding the impact of capitation on quality of care. Similarly, fee-for-service-based preventive incentives may result in improved documentation, but not increased preventive services per se (Fairbrother et al. 1999; Fairbrother et al. 2001; Roski et al. 2003).

Measurement of patient outcomes often was limited to comparisons of mortality rates under different payment arrangements or, when inpatient care was the focus, hospital readmission rates. More recently, as the field of quality measurement has progressed, so has the breadth and sophistication of the measures used to assess the impact of financial incentives on quality.

In this section, we discuss the evidence of the impact of financial incentives on quality, where the incentives were not structured specifically to reward providers for improving quality or meeting quality goals or benchmarks. Instead, the financial incentives considered in these studies typically were designed to influence other outcomes, most commonly utilization of services or costs. Most authors incorporated quality measures alongside measures of cost and utilization in their study designs, but some focused on measuring only quality impacts. This literature has a number of strengths. It addresses impacts of financial incentives on quality of care in a wide variety of settings, for a range of medical services, and over a substantial period of time. Most studies are tied closely to public policy concerns of the time period in which they were conducted. Specifically, in virtually all of the studies of this type, the framing of the question concerns whether payment arrangements that place providers at some degree of financial risk have a negative impact on quality of care.

Thirteen literature reviews have addressed the relationship between financial incentives and quality of care, where the incentives were not designed to reward quality directly. Three of these reviews investigated the impact of payment reforms in the United Kingdom, eight addressed the impact of managed care on quality in the United States, and two focused on how moving to prospective payment for hospitals in the US affected quality of care. These reviews generally were completed in the 1990s and all considered a variety of outcome measures, some related to quality of care and others related primarily to cost and utilization. In this respect, they reflected the structure of individual studies, which typically included other measures, along with quality indicators, in their analyses. None of the reviews covered studies published after 2000.

In 1996, Silcock and Ratcliffe summarized the evidence concerning the impact of payment changes instituted in 1990 in the UK on services provided by general practitioners. The authors concluded that the "small but growing" body of evidence was not sufficient to draw definitive conclusions. Smith and Wilton (1998) examined the impact of NHS reforms designed to create an "internal market" for services, with GPs purchasing care on behalf of their patient populations. They concluded that the evidence was incomplete or mixed and suggested that procedural aspects of care delivery seemingly had improved, but there was little evidence regarding impacts on the health of patients. Mays, Mulligan, and Goodwin (2000) also reviewed studies relating to this topic. They concluded that few studies attempted to measure quality directly but that GP fund holders probably had used their funds to make services more accessible and waiting times shorter. These are not clinical measures of quality, nor of health status, but do suggest more timely service provision for patients. In summary, these three reviews find little evidence regarding impacts of UK payment reforms for GPs on quality of care.

The eight reviews of the impact of managed care in the US on quality reached similar conclusions. Five of these reviews were conducted by Luft and, for the last three, co-authors (Miller and Luft 1994; Miller and Luft 1997; and Dudley et al. 1998). In his first review, Luft (1980) compared quality of care in HMOs versus fee-for-service arrangements and concluded that HMOs compared favorably on structure and process measures of quality. With respect to outcome measures, he concluded that HMO enrollees did as well as, and in some cases better than, enrollees in fee-for-service plans. However, he also noted that data were limited and that the studies focused on well-established HMOs, leading him to observe that the issue was largely "unresolved."

Luft (1988) updated his review eight years later, with similar conclusions. At that time, Luft cautioned that these findings might not hold up because the insurance industry in the United States was moving into a new era of competition between HMOs and other plans, and new forms of HMOs were proliferating. Miller and Luft (1994) published a further review of this literature in 1994, concluding that quality of care in HMOs and fee-for-service indemnity plans was "roughly comparable." In fourteen of seventeen studies, quality measures were better or equivalent in HMOs. Three years later, Miller and Luft (1997) found "... equal numbers of statistically significant positive and negative results" on quality measures for HMOs compared to non-HMO plans. They observed that results unfavorable to HMOs were found for populations with chronic illnesses and suggested that more research was needed that addressed quality of care for this group.

One year later, Dudley et al. (1998) reviewed the entire literature from 1980 through 1997 that compared quality of care in HMOs versus other insurance arrangements. Their innovation was the use of a scoring system to evaluate the relative strength of the evidence. They found no clear pattern favoring better or worse quality of care in HMOs versus fee-for-service plans. Dudley et al. (1998) noted the relative lack of studies that examined the link between explicit incentives for quality and measures of quality of care.

Two other authors conducted literature reviews on the same topic at approximately the same time, reaching conclusions similar to those of Luft and colleagues. Cangialose et al. (1997) found no differences in clinical quality or outcomes in patients in managed care plans versus traditional insurance arrangements. Steiner and Robinson (1998), based on a systematic review of the literature, found that managed care increased the use of screening and had a neutral impact on patient outcomes.

Hodgkin and McGuire (1994) reviewed of the impact of Medicare's movement to prospective payment for hospitalized beneficiaries based on diagnosis related groups (DRGs). In general, they concluded that the strength of hospital responses to prospective payment was related to the percent of hospital revenue derived from Medicare.

Since the publication of the review papers summarized above, there have been several published studies investigating the impact of provider payment incentives on quality of care (Christianson, Leatherman, and Sutherland 2008). Studies contrasting the delivery of services by physicians under managed care versus fee-for-service found results similar to the findings reported in the previous review articles. Relating to the impact of financial incentives on institutional care, two studies by Volpp and colleagues (2003, 2005) are of note in that they found a significant negative impact associated with a change in hospital payment arrangements. The state of New Jersey (US) replaced a regulated "all payer" system for hospital payment with a system in which insurers could selectively contract with hospitals. The authors hypothesized that, under the rate setting system, hospitals would compete for patients by providing more services, while in the contracting system hospitals would compete by offering lower rates, creating negative pressures on quality. They found some evidence of slower decreases in in-hospital mortality rates in New Jersey, relative to trends in a comparison state.

In general, the findings of studies in this area, taken together, provide little compelling evidence that financial incentives designed to reduce or control costs or utilization have had a negative impact on quality of care. There are several possible explanations. First, the incentives studied were designed, for the most part, to reduce utilization of services. Generally, the link between service reduction and quality in the studies is not clear. This would be the case, especially, if utilization was excessive prior to the introduction of different payment arrangements. Second, the literature reports results for a wide range of quality and outcome measures, making it difficult to detect patterns in the findings. And, the most commonly used outcome measure—mortality—may not be sensitive to the relatively modest changes in financial incentives found in many studies. Also, mortality can be influenced by a host of factors, many unrelated to medical care, making it difficult to isolate the marginal effects of provider incentives.

The exact nature of provider payment arrangements often is not clearly described in the studies. This is true in particular for comparisons of quality of care under different insurance arrangements. Because the relationships between payment arrangements and quality are likely to be more subtle than the links between payment and service utilization, the absence of a description of provider payment incentives makes interpretation of findings even more difficult. How incentives are transmitted to the level at which decisions about treatment are actually made also is not clear in most studies. And, information typically is lacking concerning other efforts at the health plan, hospital or physician practice level relating to quality management. It seems likely that these efforts would interact with financial incentives for providers to influence quality of care. Most studies do not control for quality management efforts at the care delivery level when drawing conclusions about the impact of financial incentives.

26.4.3 Evidence on Effects of Specific Payment Incentive Programs on Quality of Care

In this section, we summarize the research relating to financial incentives employed by payers with the specific intent of improving quality of care and patient outcomes. These incentives typically are "layered on" existing fee-for-service, capitation or salary payment arrangements, creating a "blended" payment scheme. Recently, incentives with this objective have been labeled "pay-for-performance," or P4P. Compensation based in part on product or service quality is commonplace in other industries, but the rapid expansion in its use by health care purchasers over the last five years is noteworthy.

At the conceptual level, some authors have pointed out that paying for performance can diminish the intrinsic satisfaction present in carrying out "work" (e.g. Berwick 1995; Gagné and Deci 2005), although all do not agree on the potential significance of this effect (e.g. Eisenberger and Cameron 1996). The argument is thought to apply especially well to medical care providers, who are believed to be motivated to a substantial degree by an intrinsic desire to help their patients and a duty of professionalism. This being the case, paying providers for achieving standardized metrics relating to care processes risks trivializing the nonfinancial motivations of providers and could lead them to resist adopting care practices believed to improve quality. Moreover, previous research raises the concern that the effects of pay for performance will be short term, and that—if the extrinsic financial incentive is removed—performance may revert to levels even inferior to the pre-incentive baseline (cf. Deci and Ryan 1985).

There are nine articles that reviewed literature on the relationship between financial incentives directed at physicians and quality of care, where the incentives were intended to improve quality. Seven of these review articles had a broad focus in their search strategies, including all types of care, while two limited their scope to specific types of care: immunizations (Achat, McIntyre, and Burgess 1999) and preventive care (Town et al. 2005).

In the earliest review, Scott and Hall (1995) identified studies that examined changes in general practitioner reimbursement, observing that this literature lacked linkages between reimbursement and actual patient outcomes. They cited one study done in the UK in 1991 that reported that general practitioners were more likely to reach some quality targets if paid specifically to do so, but noted that the research design was weak. Achat, McIntyre, and Burgess (1999) followed with a systematic review of the literature assessing the impact of financial incentives for patients and providers on immunization rates. The review focused on two provider studies published in the early 1990s—Kouides et al. (1998) and Ritchie et al. (1992)—that evaluated experiments in which primary care physicians were rewarded for improving levels of immunizations or achieving targets. Both studies indicated improvement that apparently was associated with the use of financial incentives. Armour and colleagues' (2001) review of the literature also found few studies relating to the impact of financial incentives on quality of care. In four studies where quality metrics were used as outcome measures, there were mixed results. The authors noted the very limited amount of research that had been done to assess the impact of financial incentives on quality of care.

In a selective review of the literature, Conrad and Christianson (2004) concluded that studies of explicit financial incentives and their impact on quality are directed almost entirely at preventive care, with inconclusive results. They also observed that these studies provided little insight into the role of market and organizational factors as mediators of the effects of financial incentives on quality.

Dudley et al. (2004) required that articles use random assignment to be included in their review. Of the eight studies they identified that used randomized trials, four had incentives directed at individual providers. There were significant improvements in quality for five of the seven quality indicators used in these studies. Across all studies in the Dudley et al. (2004) review, it appeared that significant quality improvements were more likely to be observed when the physician incentives modified a fee-for-service payment, as compared to taking the form of a bonus payment. Dudley et al. (2004) note that seven of the eight randomized trials involved preventive care. Town et al. (2005) addressed the impact of financial incentives exclusively on preventive care. His search process, which focused on literature published between 1966 and 2002, identified six studies involving eight different uses of financial incentives and concluded that only one incentive was associated with a greater provision of preventive care on the part of physicians. However, Town et al. (2005) cautioned that the incentives generally were weak, suggesting only that small rewards are unlikely to motivate significant improvements in use of preventive services.

In a review published in 2006, Petersen et al. searched the literature from 1980–2005, identifying seventeen relevant studies. Thirteen of the studies focused on process of care measures, mostly relating to preventive care. Petersen et al. (2006) found that five of six studies with physician level incentives, and seven of nine with provider group incentives, had some positive effect on quality. In four cases there was evidence of unintended side effects. As in the other reviews, the authors noted that there were relatively few studies in the literature that assessed the impact of financial incentives on quality of care. In another review published in 2006, Rosenthal and Frank found seven empirical studies addressing the effects of paying for quality of care. They reported two positive findings in these studies, with studies that had stronger research designs reporting no impacts of financial incentives. They also noted the focus of these studies on preventive care.

All of the reviews above commented on the relative lack of rigorous research on the impact of paying providers for quality improvements on quality of care. The few published studies meeting the inclusion criteria of the review authors mostly addressed preventive care. The most reasonable conclusion, based on these reviews, is that the evidence base for both justifying and designing physician pay-for-performance schemes to improve quality of care is thin.

In their review of more recent published evaluations of purchaser P4P efforts, Christianson, Leatherman, and Sutherland (2008) observed that most evaluations reported improvement in selected outcome measures. However, in purchaser P4P initiatives directed at physicians, financial incentives often were combined with other quality improvement efforts, making it impossible to determine the incremental contribution of the incentives in achieving the reported results, and the lack of a contemporaneous control group in most of these evaluations further complicated interpretation of the findings.

There have been fewer evaluations of P4P initiatives related to hospitals and long-term care facilities (e.g. see Grossbart 2006; Nahra et al. 2006; Glickman et al. 2007; Lindenauer et al. 2007). As with physician P4P arrangements, there is evidence suggesting improved quality, but the role of financial incentives is not always clear (Christianson, Leatherman, and Sutherland, 2009). Evaluations of both physician and institutional P4P initiatives do suggest several implementation issues such as questionable communication of program incentives to providers, payment for improved documentation rather than improved quality, and the need to monitor actions of physicians in constructing panels of patients used in measuring performance.

Since the publication of the literature reviews summarized above, several additional evaluations of physician P4P programs in the US have been published (Christianson, Leatherman, and Sutherland 2009). Their findings were generally consistent with the findings reported by Christianson, Leatherman, and Sutherland (2008); improvements in some measures occur over time, but evidence of the relationship between those improvements and the introduction of financial incentives often is not compelling. Recent studies also have explored various aspects of the P4P program in the UK (Christianson, Leatherman, and Sutherland, 2009). Most of this research addressed the impact of the program on subgroups of patients and on physician attitudes and beliefs regarding P4P and its effectiveness. One important finding was that concerns about possible physician manipulation of the rules regarding elimination of patients from performance measurement (so-called "exception reporting") appear less important than suggested by earlier analysis (Doran et al. 2006; Doran et al. 2008).

26.5 Conclusions

This chapter has sought to provide conceptual background for assessing the impacts of provider payment incentives, and then to synthesize the empirical evidence in three domains: the direct effects of general payment incentives on the utilization and cost of health services, the indirect effects of general payment incentives on quality of care, and, finally, the direct effects of specific performance-based incentives on quality. The conceptual background highlights the potential complementary effects on quality that are likely to result from payment incentives aimed primarily at utilization and cost, and posits that capitation, budgets, salary, fee-for-service, and episode-based payment arrangements will have different effects on use and cost. Moreover, theory suggests that there can be unintended consequences such as favorable selection ("cream-skimming") and "treating to the test" by providers. Because of these and other possible effects of incentives, mixed payment mechanisms may perform better than pure schema such as capitation or fee-for-service.

Our literature review demonstrates that general incentives targeting utilization and cost typically have produced changes consistent with theoretical expectations: that is, fewer hospital admissions and lower costs under capitation, longer hospital length of stay under per diem reimbursement, fewer diagnostic tests under salary compared to fee-for-service, more primary care services under fee-for-service, and higher rates of use of physician services (e.g. imaging) in physician-owned facilities.

In general, HMOs (and the capitation mechanisms in place at the time studies were executed) and fee-for-service settings appear to produce roughly comparable quality—more recent studies being almost equally divided between evidence favorable to HMOs and findings favorable to non-HMO settings, with a few studies suggesting poorer quality in HMOs for chronically ill and the frail elderly. In our judgment, the most appropriate conclusion is that there is not consistent evidence of meaningful quality differences between HMOs and fee-for-service settings. By extension, one cannot conclude that tight payment constraints, such as capitation, lead to diminution in quality of care. Also, it is important to note that HMOs use a variety of different payment schemes (including salary and fee-for-service) to reimburse physicians and institutional providers, and that they also employ rules and policies to influence provider behavior. Therefore, the comparisons of HMOs to fee-for-service settings in these studies do not simply reflect differences in payment schemes.

Published empirical studies of the effects of payment incentives that specifically target quality are modest in number and in the scope of their inquiry. Most studies, and almost all randomized trials, have concentrated on preventive services—with equivocal results regarding quality. The nature of both the randomized trials and the observational studies does not allow inferences regarding the dose-response relationship between size of incentive and either the scope or intensity of provider behavior change. That is, existing studies do not reveal a "tipping point" or a gradient of behavioral response. While the results of observational studies suggest that paying for better performance often is associated with positive results, the importance of financial incentives typically is not clear, because the incentives are implemented concurrently with other components of an overall quality improvement effort. The studies do encourage incentive designers and implementers to be wary of unintended consequences and hint at particular provider adjustments to look for: favorable risk selection by providers and multi-tasking in favor of the rewarded dimensions of performance.

Overall, the research literature underscores how difficult it is to design and carry out studies (of the impact of financial incentives) that yield unambiguous findings with clear guidance for policymakers. Most of the studies to date have been "point in time" evaluations. Studies that track the effects of financial incentives over longer periods of time have the potential to address some, but not all, of the shortcomings in the existing literature. A good example of this is the developing body of research addressing the UK's pay-for-performance initiative (see Christianson, Leatherman, and Sutherland, 2009), which includes multiple studies, using different methodological approaches, that address the diverse impacts of that payment scheme over time.

APPENDIX

PHYSICIAN PRACTICE EQUILIBRIUM

To simplify the comparative statics, while retaining the essence of the firm's problem, consider the following practice demand and cost functions:

(1) Physician Practice Demand: Price $= p(q, h) + r(z)z$ (inverse demand function in terms of price)

(2) Total Cost: Cost $= z^c q^s \cdot i$

(3) Net income: $\pi = [p(q, h) + r(z)z]q - z^c q^s \cdot i(m')$

where terms are defined as follows: q = quantity of output, z = quality per unit of quantity, r = the market-determined price mark-up ("marginal reward") for quality per unit of service above that implied by the reservation demand price (p), c is the quality elasticity of total cost, z is the measure of quality per unit of service, and h and i are vectors of exogenous demand (price) and cost shifters, respectively. This functional form of cost implies a flexible total cost elasticity of quantity, with $s > 1$ ($s = 1$) indicating rising (constant) marginal costs with increasing quantity of output. Assuming downward sloping demand for quantity and quality, $p'(q)$ and $r'(z)$ are both negative. The quality reward function, $r(z)$, is a positive function of quality.

In this model, the monopolistically competitive physician firm (practice) has some indirect influence over price through choice of quality (z) and the quantity of output (q). The firm is assumed to maximize net income by choice of z and q, subject to the demand constraint.

The maximization problem is presented in equations A1 through A3:

(A1) Physician Practice Demand: $P = p(q, h) + r(z)z$

(A2) Total Cost: $C = z^c q^s \cdot i(m')$

(A3) Net income: $\pi = [p(q, h) + r(z)z]q - z^c q^s \cdot i(m')$

Necessary First Order Conditions (NFOC): first partial derivatives written as primes, ', second and cross-partials written as double primes, ", and the arguments following in parentheses ()

(A4) Quantity: $\pi'(q) = 0 = p(q, h) + r(z)z + p'(q)q(h) - z^c \cdot i \cdot s \cdot q^{s-1}$

(A5) Quality: $\pi'(z) = 0 = q(h) \cdot [r(z) + r'(z)z - c \cdot i q^{s-1} z^{c-1}]$

Sufficient Second Order Conditions for a Maximum (SSOC):

(A6) $\pi''(q) = p'(q) + p'(q) + p''(q) \cdot q - s(s-1)q^{s-2}z^c i$

$= 2p'(q) + p''(q) \cdot q(h) - s(s-1)q^{s-2}z^c i < 0$, assuming downward sloping demand ($p'(q) < 0$); and $p''(q) > 0$ but sufficiently small and/or s is sufficiently greater than 1 (diseconomies of scale in quantity of output), that $\pi''(q)$ is < 0

(A7) $\pi''(z) = r'(z)q + r''(z)zq + r'(z)q - c(c-1)q^s \cdot z^{c-2} \cdot i = q[2r'(z) + r''(z)z - c(c-1)q^{s-1} \cdot z^{c-2} \cdot i]$
< 0, assuming $c > 1$,

which implies that the marginal cost of quality is increasing with quality (holding constant the quantity of output), and that the absolute value of $r''(z)z$, which has a positive sign by concavity of the price mark-up function ($r(z)$), is sufficiently small compared to $r'(z)$ that the SSOC inequality, $\pi''(z) < 0$, holds.

(A8) The Hessian determinant (order $k = 2$, for the 2 endogenous variables):
$$H = \pi''(q) \cdot \pi''(z) - \pi''(q, z) \cdot \pi''(z, q) > 0$$

The key cross-partial derivatives are:

(A9) $\pi''(q, z) = \pi''(z, q) = r(z) + r'(z)z - c \cdot i \cdot sq^{s-1}z^{c-1}$

Since the right-hand side of (A5) must equal zero and $\pi''(q, z) = \pi''(z, q) = r(z) + r'(z)z - c \cdot i \cdot sq^{s-1}z^{c-1}$ differs from that first order condition only by the multiplier s after the minus sign, we can determine the sign for $\pi''(q, z)$, conditional on assumptions regarding the magnitude of s (returns to scale in physician production. If $s > 1$, then $\pi''(q, z) < 0$. If $s = 1$, then $\pi''(q, z) = 0$. If $s < 1$, $\pi''(q, z) > 0$.

(A9') $\pi''(q, r) = z$

(A9") $\pi''(z, r) = q$

Comparative Statics:
Applying Cramer's rule (Silberberg 1990), we solve for the total derivatives of the change at equilibrium in each of the two endogenous variables for small changes in the primary exogenous parameter of interest, $r(z)$, which denotes the market-determined mark-up of price for a unit change in quality above the reservation level:

Quantity Effects

(A10) $q'(r) = \{-\pi''(q, r) \cdot \pi''(z, z) - (-1)\pi''(z, r) \pi''(q, z)\}/H$

Substituting the values of $\pi''(q, r), \pi''(z, z), \pi''(z, r)$, and $\pi''(q, z)$ into equation (A10),

(A10') $q'(r) = -zq\{2r'(z)+r''(z)z - c(c-1)z^{c-2} \cdot sq^{s-1} \cdot i\} - (-1)q[r(z) + r'(z)z - csq^{s-1}z^{c-1} \cdot i]/H$.

The first term in {} on the right-hand side of (A10') is negative by SSOC condition (A7). When multiplied by $-zq$, the first half of the equation $\{-\pi''(q, r) \cdot \pi''(z, z)\}$ is therefore positive. The first half of the equation can be interpreted as the *direct* effect of an increase in the $r(z)$ reward function on the marginal net income attributable to increased quantity—$\pi''(q, r)$—weighted by the rate of diminution in the marginal net income of quality as quality increases—$\pi''(z)$.

The second half of the equation captures the *indirect* effect of an increase in the level of the reward function $r(z)$ on the marginal net income of quality—$\pi''(z, r)$—weighted by the cross-effect of quality on the marginal net income of quantity—$\pi''(q, z)$. As discussed above, the sign of this indirect effect depends totally on the cost elasticity of quantity (i.e., returns to scale, or s). If returns to scale are decreasing ($s > 1$), the effect will be to dampen the rise in quantity induced by an increase in the price mark-up. Under constant returns the indirect effect is zero, and for increasing returns the indirect effect will be to *reinforce* the direct effect of quality rewards.

Similar reasoning and application of Cramer's rule (Silberberg 1990) yields:

Quality Effects

(A11) $z'(r) = \{\pi''(q) \cdot (-1)\pi''(z, r) - \pi''(z, q) \cdot (-1) \pi''(q, r)/H$

Substituting and collecting terms yields the following expression:

(A11′) $z'(r) = \{[2p'(q) + p''(q) \cdot q(h) - s(s-1)q^{s-2}z^c i] \cdot [-q]/H\} + \ldots \{[r(z) + r'(z)z - c \cdot i \cdot sq^{s-1}z^{c-1}]$ $z/H\}$

The first term of this expression in {} before the $+ \ldots$ is unambiguously positive for positive output (q) given the SSOC for $\pi''(q) < 0$. This first term is larger the *less* price-elastic is demand, i.e., the greater is $p'(q)$ in absolute value, and the less rapidly price-elasticity rises with increased quantity, i.e., the smaller is $p''(q)$. This first term will decline with increases in the cost-elasticity of quality and quantity—c and s, respectively—and with higher levels of input cost shifters (i). This first term captures the *direct* marginal effect of increased reward on the marginal net income from increased quality—$\pi''(z, r)$—weighted by the rate of diminution in the marginal net income from increased quantity as quantity increases—$\pi''(q)$.

The second term, after {} $+ \ldots$ balances the marginal revenue from increased quality per unit of quantity, which equals $[r(z) + r'(z)z]$, against the marginal cost of quality multiplied by the cost elasticity of quantity, s. Both marginal revenue and marginal cost of quality are then multiplied by the level of quality (z). The second term reflects the *indirect* effect of increasing the level of the reward function, $r(z)$, which then increases the marginal net income from quantity increases—as reflected in $\pi''(q, r) = z$.

In turn, the induced increase in quantity exerts a cross-effect on quality through the cross-partial, $\pi''(z, q)$. Thus, as shown earlier, the direction of the indirect effect will depend solely on the cost elasticity of quantity (s) factor.

Higher cost elasticity of quality (larger c), higher cost elasticity of quantity (larger s), and higher levels of exogenous input cost shifters (i) are negatively related to $z'(r)$. The negative relation between $z'(r)$ and cost shifters, i, reflects the cost shifters' effect of reducing quantity, which thereby results in higher marginal costs of quality *per unit* of quantity.

By similar reasoning, we can derive the total effect on equilibrium quality of an exogenous increase in the price level (p). Since price level does not enter the first order condition for quality (Equation A5), the total derivative of quality with respect to price level simplifies to:

(A12) $z'(p) = r(z) + r'(z)z - cisq^{s-1}z^{c-1} /H$

The numerator of right-hand side of this equation, $\pi''(q, z)$, reflects the *indirect* effect of increased price level on quality—through its effect on quantity. Except for the factor s after the minus sign, the numerator is identical to the right-hand side of the first order condition (A5).

Thus, in this model, the (indirect) effect of increased price level on quality will be positive, zero, or negative depending on whether the cost elasticity of quantity (s) is less than 1 (increasing returns to scale), equal to 1 (constant returns to scale), or greater than 1 (decreasing returns to scale).

References

AAS, I. H. M. (1995). "Incentives and Financing Methods." *Health Policy*, 34/3: 205–20.

ACHAT, H., P. McINTYRE, and M. BURGRESS (1999). "Health Care Incentives in Immunization." *Australian and New Zealand Journal of Public Health*, 23/3: 285–8.

ARMOUR, B. S., M. M. PITTS, R. MACLEAN, C. CANGIALOSE, M. KISHEL, H. IMAI, and J. ETCHASON (2001). "The Effect of Explicit Financial Incentives on Physician Behavior." *Archives of Internal Medicine*, 161/10: 1261–6.

BERWICK, D. M. (1995). "The Toxicity of Pay for Performance." *Quality Management in Health Care*, 4/1: 27–33.

CANGIALOSE, C. B., S. J. CARY, L. H. HOFFMAN, and D. J. BALLARD (1997). "Impact of Managed Care on Quality of Healthcare: Theory and Evidence." *The American Journal of Managed Care*, 3/8: 1153–70.

CHRISTIANSON, J. B., S. LEATHERMAN, and K. SUTHERLAND (2008). "Lessons from Evaluations of Purchaser Pay-for-Performance Programs: A Review of the Evidence." *Medical Care Research and Review*, 65/6 Suppl.: 5S–34S.

―― ―― ―― (2009). *Financial Incentives, Health Care Providers, and Quality Improvements: A Review of the Evidence*. London: The Health Foundation.

CONRAD, D. A. and J. B. CHRISTIANSON (2004). "Penetrating the 'Black Box': Financial Incentives for Enhancing the Quality of Physician Services." *Medical Care Research and Review*, 61/3 Suppl: 37S–68S.

DECI, E. L. and R. M. RYAN (1985). *Intrinsic Motivation and Self-Determination in Human Behavior*. New York: Plenum.

DORAN, T., C. FULLWOOD, H. GRAVELLE, D. REEVES, E. KONTOPANTELIS, U. HIROEH, and M. ROLAND (2006). "Pay-for-Performance Programs in Family Practices in the United Kingdom." *The New England Journal of Medicine*, 335/4: 375–84.

―― ―― D. REEVES, H. GRAVELLE, and M. ROLAND (2008). "Exclusion of Patients from Pay-for-Performance Targets by English Physicians." *The New England Journal of Medicine*, 359/3: 274–84.

DUDLEY, R. A., R. H. MILLER, T. Y. KORENBROT, and H. S. LUFT (1998). "The Impact of Financial Incentives on Quality of Health Care." *The Milbank Quarterly*, 76/4: 649–86.

―― A. FROLICH, D. L. ROBINOWITZ, J. A. TALAVERA, P. BROADHEAD, H. S. LUFT, and K. McDONALD (2004). "Strategies to Support Quality-Based Purchasing: A Review of the Evidence." Technical Review Number 10. AHRQ Publication No. 04-0057, Rockville, MD: Agency for Healthcare Research and Quality.

EGGLESTON, K. (2005). "Multitasking and Mixed Systems for Provider Payment." *Journal of Health Economics*, 24: 211–23.

EISENBERGER, R. and J. CAMERON. (1996). "Detrimental Effects of Reward. Reality or Myth?" *American Psychologist*, 51/11: 1153–66.

EISENHARDT, K. M. (1989). "Agency Theory: An Assessment and Review." *Academy of Management Review*, 14: 57–74.

FAIRBROTHER, G., K. L., HANSON, S. FRIEDMAN, et al. (1999). "The Impact of Physician Bonuses, Enhanced Fees, and Feedback on Childhood Immunization Coverage Rates." *American Journal of Public Health*, 89: 171–5.

—— M. J., SIEGEL, S. FRIEDMAN, et al. (2001). "Impact of Financial Incentives on Documented Immunization Rates in the Inner City: Results of a Randomized Controlled Trial." *Ambulatory Pediatrics*, 1: 206–12.

FLYNN, K. E., M. A. SMITH, and M. K. DAVIS (2002). "From Physician to Consumer: The Effectiveness of Strategies to Manage Health Care Utilisation." *Medical Care Research and Review*, 59/5: 455–81.

FROLICH, A., J. A., TALAVERA, P. BROADHEAD, and R. A. DUDLEY (2007). "A Behavioral Model of Clinician Responses to Incentives to Improve Quality." *Health Policy*, 80: 179–93.

GAGNÉ, M. and E. L. DECI (2005). "Self-Determination Theory and Work Motivation." *Journal of Organizational Behavior*, 26: 331–62.

GERHART, B. and S. L. RYNES (2003). *Compensation. Theory, Evidence, and Strategic Implications.* Thousand Oaks, CA: Sage Publications.

GLICKMAN, S. W., F. S., OU, E. R. DELONG, et al. (2007). "Pay for Performance, Quality of Care, and Outcomes in Acute Myocardial Infarction," *JAMA* 297/21: 2373–80.

GROSSBART, S. R. (2006). "What's the Return? Assessing the Effect of 'Pay for Performance' Initiatives on the Quality of Care Delivery." *Medical Care Research and Review*, 63 (Special Supplement): 29S–48S.

HELLINGER, F. J. (1996). "The Impact of Financial Incentives on Physician Behavior in Managed Care Plans: A Review of the Evidence." *Medical Care Research and Review*, 53/3: 294–314.

HODGKIN, D. and T. G. MCGUIRE (1994). "Payment Levels and Hospital Response to Prospective Payment." *Journal of Health Economics*, 13/1: 1–29.

INSTITUTE OF MEDICINE (2001). *Crossing the Quality Chasm: A New Health System for the 21st Century.* Washington, DC: National Academy Press.

JACK, W. (2005). "Purchasing Health Care Services from Providers with Unknown Altruism." *Journal of Health Economics*, 205/24: 73–93.

KOUIDES, R. W., N. M. BENNETT, B. LEWIS, J. D. CAPPUCCIO, W. H. BARKER, and F. M. LAFORCE (1998). "Performance-Based Physician Reimbursement and Influenza Immunization Rates in the Elderly. The Primary-Care Physicians of Monroe County." *American Journal of Preventive Medicine*, 14/2: 89–95.

LINDENAUER P. K., D. REMUS, S. ROMAN, et al. (2007). "Public Reporting and Pay for Performance in Hospital Quality Improvement." *New England Journal of Medicine*, 356/5: 486–96.

LOHR, K. and S. SCHROEDER (1990). "A Strategy for Quality Assurance in Medicare." *The New England Journal of Medicine*, 322/10: 707–12.

LUFT, H. S. (1980). "Assessing the Evidence on HMO Performance." *Milbank Memorial Fund Quarterly*, 58/4: 501–36.

—— (1988). "HMOs and the Quality of Care." *Inquiry*, 25/1: 147–56.

MAYS, N., J.-A. MULLIGAN, and N. GOODWIN (2000). "The British Quasi-Market in Health Care: A Balance Sheet of the Evidence." *Journal of Health Services Research & Policy*, 5/1: 49–58.

MCCLEARY, K., J. ASUBONTENG, and G. MUNCHUS (1995). "The Effect of Financial Incentives on Physicians' Behaviour in Health Maintenance Organizations." *Journal of Management in Medicine*, 9/1: 8–26.

McGuire, T. G. (2000). "Physician Agency." In A. J. Culyer and J. P. Newhouse (eds.), *Handbook of Health Economics*, Vol.1A. Amsterdam: Elsevier, 461–536.

Milgrom, P. and P. Roberts (1992). *Economics, Organization, and Management*. Englewood Cliffs, NJ: Prentice Hall.

Miller, R. H. and H. S. Luft (1994). "Managed Care Plan Performance Since 1980: A Literature Analysis." *The Journal of the American Medical Association*, 271/19: 1512–9.

—— and H. S. Luft (1997). "Does Managed Care Lead to Better or Worse Quality of Care?" *Health Affairs*, 16/5: 7–25.

Mitchell, J. M. (1996). "Physician Joint Ventures and Self-Referral: An Empirical Perspective," in R. G. Spece, D. S. Shimm, and A. E. Buchanan (eds.), *Conflicts of Interest in Clinical Practice and Research*. New York: Oxford University Press, 299–317.

Morrisey, M. (2007). *Rating and Underwriting in Health Insurance*. Chicago: Health Administration Press/AUPHA Press, 63–4.

Nahra, T. A., K. L. Reiter, R. A. Hirth, J. E. Shermer, and J. R. C. Wheeler (2006). "Cost-effectiveness of Hospital Pay-for-performance Incentives." *Medical Care Research and Review*, 63/1 (Suppl., Feb.): 49S–72S.

Pauly, M. V. and M. A. Satterwaite (1981). "The Pricing of Primary Care Physicians Services: A Test of the Role of Consumer Information." *The Bell Journal of Economics*, 12/2: 488–506.

Petersen, L. A., L. D. Woodard, T. Urech, C. Daw, and S. Sookanan (2006). "Does Pay-for-Performance Improve the Quality of Health Care?" *Annals of Internal Medicine*, 145/4: 265–72.

Pope, G. C. and R. T. Burge (1992). "Inefficiencies in Physician Practices." *Advances in Health Economics and Health Services Research*, 13: 129–64.

Pratt, W. and R. J. Zeckhauser. (1985). *Principals and Agents: The Structure of Business*. Cambridge, MA: Harvard University Press.

Prendergast, C. (1999). "The Provision of Incentives in Firms." *Journal of Economic Literature*, 37: 7–63.

Prometheus (2006). "Provider Payment for High Quality Care." Prometheus Payment, Inc., Washington, DC, April.

Rice, T. (1997). "Physician Payment Policies: Impacts and Implications." *Annual Review of Public Health*, 18: 549–69.

Ritchie, L. D., A. F. Bisset, D. Russell, V. Leslie, and I. Thomson (1992). "Primary and Preschool Immunisation in Grampian: Progress and the 1990 Contract." *British Medical Journal*, 34/6830: 816–19.

Robinson, J. C. (1999). "Blended Payment Methods in Physician Organizations under Managed Care." *Journal of the American Medical Association*, 282/13: 1258–63.

—— (2001). "Theory and Practice in the Design of Physician Payment Incentives." *The Milbank Quarterly*, 79/2: 149–77.

Rosenthal, M. B. and R. G. Frank (2006). "What is the Empirical Basis for Paying for Quality in Health Care?" *Medical Care Research & Review*, 63/2: 135–57.

Roski, J., R. Jeddeloh, L. An et al. (2003). "The Impact of Financial Incentives and a Patient Registry on Preventive Care Quality: Increasing Provider Adherence to Evidence-Based Smoking Cessation Practice Guidelines." *Preventive Medicine*, 36: 291–9.

Rynes, S. L., B. Gerhart, and L. Parks (2005). "Personnel Psychology: Performance Evaluation and Pay for Performance." *Annual Review of Psychology*, 56: 571–600.

Sappington, D. E. M. (1991). "Incentives in Principal–Agent Relationships." *Journal of Economic Perspectives*, 5: 45–66.

SCOTT, A. and J. HALL (1995). "Evaluating the Effects of GP Remuneration: Problems and Prospects." *Health Policy*, 31/3: 183–95.

SILBERBERG, E. (1990). *The Structure of Economics. A Mathematical Analysis.* New York: McGraw-Hill.

SILCOCK, J. and J. RATCLIFFE (1996). "The 1990 GP Contract: Meeting Needs?" *Health Policy*, 36/2: 199–207.

SMITH, R. D. and P. WILTON (1998). "General Practice Fundholding: Progress to Date." *British Journal of General Practice*, 48/430: 1253–7.

STEINER, A. and R. ROBINSON (1998). "Managed Care: US Research Evidence and Its Lessons for the NHS." *Journal of Health Services Research and Policy*, 3/3: 173–84.

TOWN, R., R. KANE, P. JOHNSON, and M. BUTLER (2005). "Economic Incentives and Physicians' Delivery of Preventive Care. A Systematic Review." *American Journal of Preventive Medicine*, 28/2: 234–40.

—— D. R. WHOLEY, J. KRALEWSKI, and B. DOWD (2004). "Assessing the Influence of Incentives on Physicians and Medical Groups." *Medical Care Research and Review*, 61/3: 80S–118S.

VOLPP, K. G., J. D. KETCHAM, A. J. EPSTEIN, and S. V. WILLIAMS (2005). "The Effects of Price Competition and Reduced Subsidies for Uncompensated Care on Hospital Mortality." *HSR: Health Services Research*, 40/4: 1058–77.

—— S. V. WILLIAMS, J. WALDFOGEL, J. H. SILBER, J. S. SCHWARTZ, and M. V. PAULY (2003). "Market Reform in New Jersey and the Effect of Mortality from Acute Myocardial Infarction." *HSR: Health Services Research*, 38/2: 515–33.

CHAPTER 27

....

NON-PRICE RATIONING AND WAITING TIMES

....

TOR IVERSEN AND LUIGI SICILIANI

27.1 INTRODUCTION

....

WITH small patient co-payments, health care has to be rationed in one way or another at the point of use. A positive waiting time may be considered as one such rationing device. This chapter reviews recent contributions on the waiting-time phenomenon. We concentrate on the literature published after the Elsevier *Handbook on Health Economics* (Cullis, Jones, and Propper 2000), which reviews the literature up to the late 1990s. Their review discusses theoretical issues, empirical and policy issues and the meaning of an optimal waiting time. The theoretical part includes theories concentrating on the demand side (waiting time as a rationing device) and the supply side (extra-funding of long waits may encourage long waits, consultant behavior, and private sector). The empirical part contains studies on the implied cost of waiting from market data and from contingent valuation methods, and estimates of demand and supply elasticities. The section about policy options concludes that increased funding per se is less likely to reduce waiting than using funds to create direct incentives to reduce waiting. Subsidies to those who leave the waiting list and buy private treatment, indices for prioritization and internal markets are all considered with pros and cons. The chapter states that "In the absence of an over-arching welfare analysis both empirical work and policy recommendations are inevitably piecemeal and open to debate. Given the inherent weaknesses of applied welfare economics, the challenge is to find a framework which would attract a broader consensus."

We think that some of the recent normative literature has started to see the waiting time problem from a perspective that may attract a broader consensus. Section 27.2 reviews such literature and analyzes waiting times as a rationing device in relation to alternatives such as co-payments and explicit criteria. It also describes the relationship between waiting times and the private sector. Section 27.3 reviews recent contributions to dynamic modeling and estimates of demand and supply elasticities. Section 27.4 investigates the effectiveness of different policy instruments. Section 27.5 sums up and suggests issues for future research.

27.1.1 Waiting Time Measurements

Statistics on waiting times are available from both administrative and survey data. In many OECD countries, waiting times from administrative sources are collected at patient level and then aggregated at provider, region, county, or country level. When looking at waiting times across providers or countries, it is crucial that waiting times are comparable. Two common measures of waiting times are: (1) *the waiting time of patients selected for treatment*: this figure measures the period between the time the patient is added to the waiting list and the date of treatment; (2) *the waiting time of patients on the list at a census date*: differently from the first measure which refers to the complete waiting of the patients, the second measure is "incomplete," as the figure refers to the time that patients on the list have been waiting until a certain census date (Don, Lee, and Goldacre 1987; Sanmartin 2001; Siciliani and Hurst 2004).

Both figures are measured either by taking the *average* waiting time across all the patients within a certain surgical procedure, specialty or provider, or by taking the *median* waiting time. The empirical evidence suggests that the distribution of waiting across patients is generally skewed, with a relatively small proportion of patients having a long wait. As a result, the average waiting time tends to be higher than the median waiting time.

Note that the average (or median) waiting time of patients admitted is not necessarily higher than the average (or median) waiting time of patients on the list. On the one hand, the full length of waiting of any patient measured under the "waiting time of patients admitted" always exceeds the partial length of any patient measured under the "waiting time of patients on the list." This is often referred to as the "interruption bias" (Salant 1977: 40–1). On the other hand, it is patients with longer waiting who are more likely to be included when the "waiting time of the patients on the list" is measured. This is known as "length bias" (Salant 1977: 40; Don, Lee, and Goldacre 1987).

Evidence from England suggests that the average and median waiting time of patients admitted was approximately fourteen and seven weeks during 1989–99. The average and median waiting of patients on the list was generally higher over the same period, respectively above fifteen and ten weeks (Siciliani and Hurst 2005), suggesting that the "length bias" is bigger than the "interruption bias."

Waiting can occur in many settings: inpatient waiting (between specialist visit and treatment), outpatient waiting (between family doctor visit and specialist visit), waiting for a general practitioner (family doctor) visit, waiting for a nursing home bed and so on. Below, our analysis focuses mainly on inpatient waiting.

Waiting times differ markedly across procedures and across specialties. Waiting times for elective procedures (like cataract, hip and knee replacement), tend to be higher than for more serious conditions (like coronary bypass or PTCA). Similarly, waiting times for Ear, Nose, and Throat tend to be higher than for Cardiology (Hurst and Siciliani 2003:

annex 2). Waiting times might also differ within procedures if providers differ in the criteria used to classify urgent versus non-urgent patients, and in rules about when a patient is added or removed from the waiting list.

27.1.2 Overview of Waiting Times Across Countries

Waiting times vary substantially across countries. For some countries, like Austria, Belgium, France, Germany, Japan, Luxembourg, Switzerland, and the United States, waiting times are negligible and are not a policy issue. In contrast, waiting times are a serious policy issue in Australia, Canada, Denmark, Finland, Ireland, Italy, Netherlands, New Zealand, Norway, Spain, Sweden, and United Kingdom. Evidence from administrative data suggests that the countries with highest average waiting times of patients admitted for treatment were in 2000 the United Kingdom and Finland, followed by Denmark, Norway, Australia, and Spain. The country with the shortest waiting times was the Netherlands. There is great variability across countries. Average waiting times for cataract, hip and knee replacement were respectively 206, 244, 281 days in England, while they were 63, 133, 160 days in Norway (Siciliani and Hurst 2004).

Limited evidence on international data exists also from survey data. Blendon et al. (2002) measure for five English-speaking countries the percentage of respondents to a phone survey in 2001, who waited longer than four months. They find that 38 percent had been waiting for at least four months in the United Kingdom, 27 percent in Canada, 26 percent in New Zealand, 23 percent in Australia, and 5 percent in the United States (see also Blendon et al. 2004).

27.1.3 Willingness to Pay (WTP) for Wait Reductions and Contingent Evaluation

Some authors have suggested that the population's or the patients' valuation of a reduction in hospital waiting time can be estimated by asking them about their willingness to pay. Propper (1990, 1995) uses a stated-preferences methodology to infer what people are willing to pay for a reduction in waiting. Based on a representative sample of the English population she finds that the value of a reduction of a month on a waiting list for non-urgent treatment is £35–40 (at 1987 prices). As expected, willingness to pay increases with income. While Propper uses a representative sample of the population, in Bishai and Lang (2000) patients are asked about how long they waited for cataract surgery in three different countries. They estimate that an average cataract patient would be willing to pay between $24 and $107 (at 1992 prices) for a reduction in waiting time of one month.

Johannesson et al. (1998) estimate from Swedish survey data the demand for private insurance. They show how the results may depend on the alternatives offered and find figures in the same range as Propper. This is surprising as while Propper's respondents were faced with a hypothetical choice between immediate treatment and treatment after some positive wait, Johannesson's respondents based their purchase decision on their perceived chances of making use of insurance. Thus one would expect Johannesson's respondents to have a lower average WTP.

An approach consistent with a revealed-preference approach (which does not provide a WTP) is to study the observed trade-off between waiting time and travel time. The costs generated by travel time should be interpreted more broadly than just the costs of travel for the patient. Choosing a distant hospital may involve rather high accommodation and travel costs for family, relatives and friends, or simply discomfort for being far from home. Monstad et al. (2006) estimate the trade-off between waiting time and distance from observations of patients having total hip replacements in Norway during 2001–3. With free choice of hospital, patients have the option of reducing the wait by travelling a longer distance. The authors find that both waiting time and distance reduce the probability of choosing a particular hospital. Patients are willing to wait a considerable length of time to avoid travelling. The reluctance to travel increases with age and decreases with educational attainment.

27.2 TYPES AND ROLE OF NON-PRICE RATIONING IN ECONOMIC THEORY

In this section we review alternative rationing mechanisms. The main criterion that is used to evaluate the relative merits of such mechanisms is the utilitarian criterion, i.e. the difference between the sum of the benefits for the patients and the costs to the provider.

27.2.1 Rationing by Waiting Time

Many OECD countries with a national health service or public health insurance combine the absence of co-payments with the presence of capacity constraints. In such countries an excess demand arises. One way to bring the demand for and the supply of health services in equilibrium is to rely on waiting times as a rationing device. As argued by Lindsay and Feigenbaum (1984), Iversen (1993, 1997), and Martin and Smith (1999), waiting times tend to discourage demand: this arises because patients with low expected benefit give up the treatment, because some patients with high expected benefit opt for treatment in the private sector or because patients become too sick to obtain the treatment after a while or die. Waiting times may also influence positively the supply of health services: altruistic providers may exert greater effort and treat a larger volume of patients when waiting times are higher. Also, waiting times are often used as performance indicators for healthcare providers (for example in the United Kingdom). Hospital managers have a higher probability of losing their job when waiting times are higher, and may therefore exert a higher effort.

27.2.2 Threshold Rationing

Suppose that a patient's benefit is observable to the provider and that patients differ in expected benefit. Then the provider could treat all the patients with highest expected benefit compatibly with its capacity constraint, and refuse treatment (or dump) patients with low expected benefit. We name this method "threshold rationing" (Gravelle and Siciliani 2008a). For a given capacity, the same number of patients receive treatment under threshold rationing and waiting-time rationing. Also, under both methods it is the patients with highest expected benefit who receive treatment. However, under waiting-time rationing, patients need to "wait" which reduces utility. Therefore, waiting-time rationing is inferior to threshold rationing. Given this intuitive result, it is surprising that threshold rationing is not more widespread. This might be due to the difficulty in perfectly observing patients' expected benefit.

It could be argued that in practice providers are able to observe a patient's benefit only imperfectly so that some dimensions of benefit are observable while others are not (i.e. some dimensions are private). Gravelle and Siciliani (2008a) show that even in this imperfect setting, threshold rationing is likely to be superior. Expected welfare across all patients will be higher when patients with higher observable benefit receive treatment while the patients with low observable benefit are refused the treatment (and waiting time is zero for all patients receiving treatment). This result is second best. Since the observable benefit is only an imperfect measure of benefit, there are some patients with high unobservable benefit who do not receive treatment and some patients with low unobservable benefit who do receive treatment. Some misallocation of patients therefore arises under threshold rationing. But the aggregate benefit for the patients treated from having zero waiting time is always greater than the cost from such misallocation of patients, and therefore welfare is higher under threshold rationing.

Interestingly, most of the theoretical literature assumes that either waiting-time rationing or threshold rationing is used (but not both). For example Lindsay and Feigenbaum (1984), Iversen (1993, 1997), and Martin and Smith (1999) assume that patients are rationed only through waiting-times. In contrast De Fraja (2000), Boadway, Marchand, and Sato (2004), and Malcomson (2005) assume that only rationing by dumping is used. Siciliani (2007) shows that a mix of waiting-time rationing and threshold rationing might be optimal when dumping patients generates disutility to the doctors. This assumption is justified on the ground that patients within publicly-funded health systems might feel that they are entitled to public treatment. If a patient is dumped, she might argue against the specialist, insisting she needs treatment or might make a formal complaint to the hospital, the health authority or other institutions. In summary, rationing only by waiting times generates an excessive disutility for the patients.

Rationing only by dumping (or threshold rationing) generates an excessive disutility for the providers.

Another argument in favor of, at least some, waiting-time rationing is that waiting times might reduce providers' costs by reducing the probability of idle capacity (Iversen 1993; Goddard, Malek, and Tavakoli 1995; Iversen 1997; Olivella 2003). If demand is stochastic, some waiting times reduce the probability that hospital's capacity remains unused. This argument is likely to hold when waiting times are low. However, as suggested by Iversen (1993) there might be a point over which higher waiting times increase costs, which may be due to the higher costs of managing the waiting list (for example increased resources needed for repeated examinations of the patients). The empirical evidence on the impact of waiting times on hospitals' cost is limited. Preliminary evidence from the UK suggests that at the sample mean of about three months, a marginal increase in waiting either has no effect or increases providers' costs (Siciliani, Stanciole, and Jacobs 2009).

27.2.3 Rationing by Price vs. Non-price Rationing

Above we have argued that waiting-time rationing is inefficient compared to threshold rationing when patient's benefit is observable or imperfectly observable. If patient's benefit is not observable, then threshold rationing cannot be implemented anymore: if the provider cannot observe benefit, patients with low benefit cannot be dumped. Gravelle and Siciliani (2008b) argue that even when patient's benefit is unobservable, waiting-time rationing might be inefficient compared to other forms of rationing, like rationing by co-payments, a policy instrument used in several countries. They show that a utilitarian government can obtain a higher welfare by introducing a positive co-payment and by setting waiting time to zero as opposed to setting a positive waiting time and zero co-payment, or a combination of positive co-payment and positive waiting time (Felder 2008 obtains a similar result). The intuition is the following. A co-payment reduces the utility of the patients because of the lower net income but simultaneously increases the revenues for the healthcare provider. In contrast, waiting-time rationing reduces utility of the patients through a postponed benefit, but has no effect on providers' revenues. A sufficient condition for a co-payment to dominate is that the marginal disutility of waiting is higher for patients with higher benefit, which seems plausible.

27.2.4 Waiting-time Prioritization

In some countries where waiting times are common, policymakers have encouraged the development of waiting-time prioritization, the idea being that patients with higher benefit should wait less. Schemes can have a limited number of priority categories, as in Spain and Sweden, and Australia and Italy (recommended admission within thirty days, ninety days, and twelve months). More elaborate priority scoring systems in New Zealand and Canada assign points to patients and patients with higher scores have shorter waits (Noseworthy and McGurran 2001; Siciliani and Hurst 2005: section 3.2.1). Different priority scoring systems have been recently investigated by Testi et al. (2007, 2008) in an Italian public university hospital.

This policy is usually justified on equity grounds. If patients with higher benefit have a higher disutility from waiting than patients with lower expected benefit, reducing waiting time for patients with high benefit and increasing waiting time for patients with low benefit might reduce the total disutility from waiting. However, there might also be an efficiency argument in favor of prioritization. Gravelle and Siciliani (2008a) suggest that even if the marginal disutility of waiting is constant across patients with different benefit, waiting-time prioritization is welfare increasing under weak regularity conditions of the distribution of the benefit. In a related paper, Gravelle and Siciliani (2009) suggest that waiting time should be lower for patients with higher disutility from waiting and lower elasticity of demand.

Askildsen, Kaarbøe, and Holmås (2010) study the effects of waiting-time thresholds in the hospital sector in Norway. Regional health authorities have made guidelines for waiting-time prioritization. The guidelines define priority groups that depend on the characteristics of the diseases. The authors study whether or not the policy of waiting time prioritization can be traced in the observed waits. The results are mixed. They find that patients in the highest priority groups wait shorter than the patients in lower priority groups. But they also find that the probability of experiencing a wait longer than the one recommended is higher for the high priority groups than for the low priority groups.

27.2.5 Waiting Times and the Private Sector

In most countries public and private provision of care exist in parallel. An important distinction between the sectors is that access to the private sector requires private insurance or direct payment when treated while public treatment often entails a wait before being treated. Hence, for the patient there is a trade-off between paying and waiting.

Besley, Hall, and Preston (1999) study to what extent the demand for private health insurance is influenced by hospital waiting lists in the UK. They find that a rise in the long-term waiting list (number of patients on the list waiting more than twelve months) by one person per thousand, initiates a 2 percent increase in the probability that an individual with mean characteristics would buy private insurance.

In the political debate it is often claimed that the private sector causes a shorter waiting time because fewer patients are cared for in the public sector. Iversen (1997) argues that if the demand for a public treatment is sufficiently elastic with respect to the waiting time, the introduction of a private sector will result in a longer waiting time in the public sector. In the model the public sponsor is supposed to determine the hospital's budget by balancing marginal benefits against marginal costs. An elastic demand for a public treatment makes possible a large reduction in public expenditures by increasing the waiting time in the public sector. Olivella (2003) shows that this effect is reinforced if private treatment fees are regulated, since regulation of the fees adds to the elasticity of demand with respect to waiting time.

Hoel and Sæther (2003) study the optimal length of the waiting time in the public sector when a private alternative exists. Their normative results depend strongly on the society's concern for equity. If perfect lump-sum taxation is feasible, equity concerns can be fully taken care of through the tax system and the optimal waiting time equals zero. If distributional objectives are sufficiently strong and lump-sum taxation is not feasible, it may be optimal to have a positive waiting time for public treatment. The favorable distributional effect is caused by the high-income persons choosing to be treated privately instead of accepting the waiting time in the public sector.

Marchand and Schroyen (2005) analyze the adverse effects of waiting on labour market decisions and sickness insurance. They study whether the welfare gains from redistribution (the rich pay taxes while buying treatment in the private sector) may outweigh the deadweight loss of waiting in a mixed system. From numerical simulations on their model they find that the welfare gains of a mixed system relative to the best pure system depend on the parameter choices that are made. Especially for bell-shaped distributions that are skewed to the right the welfare gains are found to be quite low. The conclusion implies that policy measures that aim at reducing waiting times in publicly-funded health systems do not necessarily override any redistribution in society. According to the authors it also invites investigation of whether cost-reducing measures, such as lower quality of amenities in the NHS, are cheaper sorting devices.

An important policy debate is related to whether or not a physician who is employed by the public sector also could be engaged in the private sector, i.e. having a dual practice. The concern is that his or her private interests may impact negatively on the performance of the public sector, for instance with regard to waiting time. There are some theoretical contributions to this debate. Barros and Olivella (2005) study the allocation of patients between the public and the private sector in a system with physician dual practice. For a range of rationing policies they find that full cream skimming (all the mildest conditions are treated in the private sector) is unlikely to occur because the patients in mild conditions are not willing to pay the price for being treated in the private sector.

González (2005) studies the problem of cream skimming when the public sector considers transferring some patients to the private sector in order to attain a reduction in the waiting time. She shows that a problem of cream skimming arises which reduces the incentives of the public authority to implement the policy because of the cost increase that occurs.

While Barros and Olivella (2005) and González (2005) are both limited to positive theory, Biglaiser and Ma (2007) also consider consumer welfare. They study dual job incentives with a focus on public-service physicians referring patients to their private practices, which is called moonlighting. They find that unregulated moonlighting may be detrimental to consumer welfare when it leads to adverse behavioral reactions such as moonlighters shirking more in the public system, and dedicated doctors abandoning their sincere behavior.

27.3 Why Does Waiting Time Occur?

27.3.1 Waiting Time as a Dynamic Phenomenon: Long-run Equilibrium and Steady State

Waiting times are a dynamic phenomenon. Waiting times tend to increase when demand for treatment is higher than the supply of treatment. An excess demand at a point in time increases the waiting list, which then increases waiting times. Similarly, an excess supply reduces the waiting list and waiting times. Worthington (1987, 1991) was among the first to introduce the time component directly into the analysis, describing the waiting time's phenomenon in terms of a dynamic system, i.e. stocks and flows. The stock is given by the waiting list (the queue) and increases when demand flow outweighs the supply flow.

Van Ackere and Smith (1999) and Smith and van Ackere (2002) further explore system dynamics. They integrate econometric results on the responsiveness of demand for and supply of health care into a dynamic model that illustrates the path taken over time by policy-relevant variables in the National Health Service. Their approach allows modelling several state variables (beds, doctors, waiting list, waiting time) and allows for many interactions and feedback effects. Due to the analytical complexity, the model can only be exploited through numerical simulations. For example, starting with an initial waiting time of three months, they can simulate the effect of a 10 percent increase in resources in the English National Health Service.

Using a differential-equation approach Siciliani (2008) shows that if potential demand grows faster than supply, both waiting time and waiting list increase over time in the long run. However, if supply grows faster than demand but the difference in growth rates is small, then a solution with decreasing waiting time but increasing waiting list may arise, at least over certain time intervals. If the difference in growth rates is large, then both waiting time and waiting list reduce in the long run. Overall, the dynamics of waiting time is driven by the difference in the growth rates between demand and supply, while the dynamics of the waiting list is more complex.

27.3.2 Empirical Evidence on Demand and Supply Elasticity

The literature estimating the responsiveness of the demand for and the supply of health-care treatments is extensive. However most of the studies focus on the UK, probably due to data availability. Recently, other countries like Denmark, Norway and Portugal have been systematically collecting waiting time information. Future studies might shed light on whether the elasticities estimated in the existing studies also hold for other countries.

The unit of observation is either a local geographical area (such as an electoral ward or district health authority) or a health care provider (hospital). Typically, cross-sectional evidence across UK providers suggests that the demand for treatment is inelastic. Lindsay and Feigenbaum (1984) find that the elasticity of inpatient demand with respect to the waiting time is between −0.55 and −0.64 for medical conditions with low waiting-time decay rate, while it is between −0.65 and −0.70 for conditions with high decay rate. Martin and Smith (1999) find an elasticity of inpatient demand of about −0.21. They both assume equilibrium between supply and demand.

More recent studies have extended the above work by using panel data, therefore controlling for unobserved heterogeneity, and also by collecting separate data on additions to the list (demand) and patients treated (supply), therefore relaxing the requirement of equilibrium between demand and supply. Gravelle, Dusheiko, and Sutton (2002), Gravelle, Smith and Xavier (2003) and Martin, Jacobs, Rice, and Smith (2007) find a demand elasticity in the range −0.1 to −0.2, which confirms the cross-sectional results.

The evidence on the elasticity of supply is less clear cut. Lindsay and Feigenbaum (1984) find an elasticity of 1.3. Martin and Smith (1999, 2003) also suggest that the elasticity is large, respectively equal to 2.93 and 5.29. These studies assume equilibrium between demand and supply (i.e. only data on patients treated is available). When this assumption is relaxed (i.e. both data on patients treated and admissions to the list are available), the elasticity is substantially lower: indeed Gravelle, Smith, and Xavier (2003), Martin, Jacobs, Rice, and Smith (2003), and Martin, Rice, Jacobs, and Smith (2007) find that the elasticity is in the range 0.07 to 0.18. In summary, when the equilibrium between demand and supply is assumed (only patients treated is measured), the elasticity of supply is rather elastic, while when equilibrium is not assumed (there is separate measurement of patients treated and patients added to the list), the elasticity of supply is rather inelastic.

The above studies are either cross-sectional or make use of short panel data (up to seven years). Iacone, Martin, Siciliani, and Smith (2007) use instead time-series data from the English National Health Service over the period 1952–2003. They find that the short-run supply elasticity is 0.12, which is consistent with cross-sectional and panel-data studies that do not assume equilibrium. However, they find that the implied demand elasticity is equal to −1.1 which is substantially larger compared to previous studies. This may be due to the fact that referral practices from general practitioners or specialists tend to be sluggish, i.e. it may take some time for providers to change their referral practice in response to a variation in waiting times. This will ultimately result in a smaller demand responsiveness in the short-run compared to the long-run.

There is an older literature which focuses on the association between waiting list, rather than waiting time, and activity. This literature finds that there is no significant (or seldom a positive) association between the waiting-list size of hospitals and the number of treatments supplied from both cross-sectional evidence (Buttery and Snaith 1980; Culyer and Cullis 1976, p. 248; Frankel 1989; Nordberg et al. 1994; Newton et al. 1995) and time-series evidence (Goldacre et al. 1987; Henderson et al. 1995; Culyer and Cullis 1976: 249). However, it is worth emphasizing that this literature mainly examines associations between the variables rather than focusing on the causal relationship between activity, waiting time and its determinants, which is the focus of the more recent literature reviewed above.

Finally, rather than focusing only on the responsiveness of demand and supply with respect to waiting times, some studies provide estimates of the effect of exogenous supply and demand shifters on waiting times. Martin and Smith (1999) suggest that in England the elasticity of waiting time with respect to the number of beds is −0.24. Using an international sample from OECD, Siciliani and Hurst (2004) estimate that a marginal increase of 0.1 acute care beds (per 1000 population) and of 0.1 practicing physicians (per 1000 population) is associated with a marginal reduction of mean waiting times of respectively 5.6 days and 8.3 days.

All the above studies use administrative data. In contrast Fabbri and Monfardini (2009) make use of survey data to estimate the demand elasticity for specialist consultations in the Italian health care system with respect to both waiting times and co-payments. Using count data models, they find that demand elasticity with respect to the co-payment is −0.3, while with respect to waiting time is −0.04.

27.4 Are There Effective Instruments for Reducing Waiting Times?

27.4.1 Temporary Increase in Activity

In many countries, governments have tried to reduce waiting times by adding temporary and limited amounts of resources to hospital budgets to encourage extra activity (and eliminate the waiting list backlog). These temporary increases in resource ignore the dynamic nature of waiting times and waiting lists. At best, a temporary increase in activity will lead to a temporary reduction in waiting times.

27.4.2 Increase Allocative Efficiency: Activity-based Funding

A more structural reform to increase the efficiency of the providers is to replace payment systems based on fixed budgets with activity-related payments where more activity is rewarded with higher revenues. Activity-based funding has replaced fixed budgets arrangements in many European countries. The theory predicts, as intuitive, that the introduction of prices should lead to an increase in activity, as driven by the higher marginal revenue. However, the empirical evidence on the effects of activity-based funding is mixed.

In Norway, the government introduced partial activity-based remuneration from 1997. Biørn, Hagen, Iversen, and Magnussen (2003) suggest that this policy led to a rise in the annual growth rate of activity from 2 percent between 1992 and 1996 to 3.2 percent between 1997 and 1999. Kjerstad (2003) finds that after 1997 activity increased by 4 percent in hospitals that were paid with an activity-based funding method, while the increase was only 2 percent in hospitals that were not (control group). He therefore suggests that the activity-based funding contributed to an extra increase in activity of 2 percent.

For England, Farrar et al. (2006) suggest that the introduction of "Payment by Results," a system which replaces a payment scheme for hospitals based on fixed budgets with one based on tariffs per patient treated, had little or no effect on the volume of patients treated, although the policy seems to have generated a small reduction in length of stay. Street and Miraldo (2007) suggest that the policy might have complemented the target-setting regime (discussed below) which led to a reduction in waiting times.

In Denmark, an initiative with activity-based funding was introduced in 2004 between the counties and the hospitals. An evaluation study showed that the policy might have contributed to increased activity as well as decreased waiting times (Vallgårda et al. 2001; Street, Vitikainen, Bjorvatn, and Hvenegaard 2007).

27.4.3 Demand Containment

One policy option available to policymakers is to reduce waiting times by encouraging other forms of rationing, like threshold rationing (discussed above). An increase in the clinical thresholds for making patients eligible for treatment in the public sector will reduce demand and the number of patients on the waiting list, which will ultimately reduce waiting time for the patients receiving treatment. In practice, this policy encourages doctors to prioritize patients more systematically with the help of clinical guidelines, which will help them to add to the list only patients with higher need.

In New Zealand a system was introduced in 1999 under which patients are classified according to three possible categories: (a) scheduled for surgery/booked, (b) given certainty of treatment within six months, and (c) put under active care and review. This system aims at improving predictability for patients and "fairness" (the level of need will be considered). According to Gauld (2004), when the policy was introduced there was an expectation that the development and the use of scoring systems would be an objective process. He argues that the booking system was hastily introduced and raises several issues, for instance that specialists and patients could potentially distort the scoring process through misrepresentation.

27.4.4 Choice and Competition

Siciliani (2005) studies to what extent substitutability among hospitals has an impact on the number of treatment and waiting time offered within a duopolistic market structure.

Substitutability is influenced by hospital density and the regulation of patient choice. The more substitutability there is, the more of an increase in supply of hospital 1 is offset by an increase in demand from hospital 2. Due to this externality, hospital 1 cannot fully internalize the benefits, in terms of lower waiting times, from its increase in supply. The main result is that an increase in substitutability lowers supply and increases waiting time. The increase in waiting time is smaller the higher is the payment per treatment relative to the fixed budget component. For a given level of substitutability, a higher payment per treatment is always associated with a higher supply and a lower waiting time, since a higher payment per treatment implies less externality.

Xavier (2003) obtains quite similar results in a modified Hotelling framework in which time, money and distance are determinants of the demand for hospital care. A main mechanism that drives the results in both these models is that hospitals consider the waiting time as the main instrument that regulates the number of patients who demands treatment from the hospital.

Brekke, Siciliani, and Straume (2008) model hospital competition within a Salop framework. Two types of patients are introduced; high benefit patients and low benefit patients. Hospitals compete on the segment of demand with high benefit, while they are local monopolists on the demand segment with low benefit. They find that introducing competition, by allowing previously regulated monopolies to compete for patients, leads to an increase in equilibrium waiting times only if the competitive demand segment is sufficiently large relative to the monopoly segment.

While the theoretical literature predicts an uncertain effect of choice and competition on waiting times, the empirical studies tend to show a negative relationship. Siciliani and Martin (2007) estimate the effect of choice on waiting times using a panel of 120 English publicly funded hospitals with quarterly data during the period 1999–2002. The results show that, at the sample mean, more choice has a negative impact on waiting times. The economic importance of the result is modest: an extra hospital in a catchment area will only reduce waits by, at most, a few days with more choice. The analysis also suggests that the impact of choice on waits is not linear and that, once a certain degree of choice is reached (between eleven and fourteen hospitals), further increases in choice can have a deleterious effect on waits, which may be consistent with the theory provided by Siciliani (2005).

Dawson et al. (2007) estimate the impact of the London Patient Choice Project on ophthalmology waiting times. Patients at risk of breaching inpatient waiting-time targets were offered the choice of an alternative hospital with a guaranteed shorter wait. Using a difference-in-differences approach with hospitals outside London as controls, the authors find both a modest reduction in waiting times, and a reduction in variation in waiting times within London.

Propper, Burgess, and Gossage (2008) exploit a policy change by the UK government to identify the impact of competition on quality and waiting times. The UK government introduced and encouraged competition in the National Health Service between 1991–6. But since 1997, when the government changed, competition was strongly discouraged. Areas where providers are monopolists (for example rural areas) are used as control group, since competition is absent before and after the policy change. Quality is measured through mortality from Acute Myocardial Infarction (AMI). They find that competition leads to a reduction in waiting times but also to a reduction in quality (higher mortality rates).

27.4.5 Targets and Waiting-time Guarantees

Hanning (1996) reports on a policy initiative that introduced a maximum waiting-time guarantee for twelve procedures in Sweden in 1992. Patients who waited for these procedures were guaranteed a waiting time no longer than three months from the physician's decision to treat/operate. The results show a reduction in waiting lists and waiting times, at least during the first two years. Reductions seem to have been achieved mainly by increased production, improved administration of the waiting lists, and a change in attitudes toward waiting lists. It is not quite clear how much additional resources added to the favorable result.

Propper et al. (2008) make use of a "natural experiment" to test whether or not a waiting time-target combined with sanctions for hospital managers result in a reduction of hospital waiting times. While this regime was implemented in England beginning in 2000, it was not implemented in other parts of the UK. A difference-in-differences methodology is used to test whether or not the policy had an effect on the waiting time. Scotland was used as control. The study finds that "targets and terror" policy significantly reduced the number of patients waiting over six and twelve months by 20 percent and 60 percent respectively.

Reductions in waiting times might have been obtained by increasing activity, reducing demand (i.e. refusing treatment to some patients) or by giving priority to patients who were close to hitting the maximum waiting-time target, at the expense of a higher waiting of other patients. Dimakou, Parkin, Devlin, and Appleby (2009) show that the hazard rate (the probability of exiting the waiting list, i.e. of being treated) indeed increases when the waiting time is closer to the maximum waiting-time target, and decreases when it is above the target.

27.4.6 Primary Care and Waiting Times

The introduction of the GP fundholding scheme in the UK in 1991 (terminated in 1999) gave the GPs the opportunity to buy elective treatments from hospitals on behalf of their patients. GPs who shop around may be able to achieve a reduction in the waiting time their patients are likely to experience. A related question is then whether or not this reduction in waiting time is accompanied with an increase in the waiting times for GPs who choose not to be a fundholder. Propper, Croxson, and Shearer (2002) study the effect of fundholding on hospital waiting times using a difference-in-differences methodology. The results indicate that when fundholding GPs paid for their patients' care, they were able to secure a reduction in waiting times of about 8 percent for their patients relative to all other patients. However, where they could only choose hospitals, but not pay for the care, they were rarely able to reduce the time their patients had to wait for treatment. Hence, it seems like the ability of GPs to pay for the care, rather than to choose hospital, determines shorter waits.

Dusheiko, Gravelle, and Jacobs (2004) use the opportunity offered by the abolition of the voluntary fundholding regime and its replacement by the compulsory Primary Care Trust (PCT) scheme to examine the effect of budgetary regimes on waiting times. Similar to Propper, Croxson, and Shearer (2002) they distinguish between the elective hospital treatments that fundholders are supposed to pay for out of their practice budget (chargeable admissions) and the hospital treatments they are not supposed to pay for (non-chargeable). Under the PCT scheme practice budgets are abolished and none of the hospital treatments are paid for by the individual practice. A national dataset with data for the two years before and the two years after fundholding was abolished is employed. Since fundholding was voluntary, fundholders are likely to differ from non-fundholders with regard to observable and unobservable characteristics. In the econometric analysis the authors correct for potential selection bias by several methods. They find a significant non-trivial negative effect on waiting times for chargeable elective treatments and also for some non-chargeables. They argue that their results provide estimates of the negative effect of fundholding status on waiting times for all types of elective admissions. Hence, the authors seem to find a more extensive effect of fundholding on hospital waiting times than Propper, Croxson, and Shearer (2002).

27.5 THE MAJOR GAPS IN KNOWLEDGE AND CHALLENGES FOR FUTURE RESEARCH

27.5.1 Studies of Demand and Supply Elasticities

The cross-sectional and panel data studies have confirmed results from previous literature of an inelastic demand. Estimates of the elasticity of supply show mixed results depending on whether equilibrium is assumed or not. So far all published empirical studies apply data from the UK. It seems desirable, with recent data made available from other countries, to estimate the demand and supply elasticities under different institutional settings. Some methodological issues remain. One main challenge in the estimation of the demand equation is the availability of "need" variables which can control for the health status of the catchment area served by the provider (to minimize the risk of spurious regression or omitted variable, if for example providers in areas with higher need have higher waiting times). A second econometric challenge remains the endogeneity between waiting times and activity. Unbiased estimates rely on the use of valid instruments, which can often be challenged. Some recent studies in the UK have made use of separate measurements for demand (number of referrals) and supply (number of treatments). But these measures are unlikely to be available for other countries. Finally, it remains a matter of concern that supply elasticities vary to a great extent even within the same country across different studies. This might be due to detailed institutional settings which might vary over time (within a country). Future research across different countries might investigate which institutional settings (gatekeeping system, activity-based funding, fee-for-service) favor a more elastic supply with respect to a marginal variation in waiting times.

27.5.2 Demand Containment: Rationing and Prioritization

In the presence of excess demand, health care has to be rationed in one way or another at the point of use. Important rationing devices are threshold (or explicit) rationing, co-payments, waiting times, and combinations. Recent normative literature has started to see these rationing devices in relation to each other. As long as some dimensions of benefit are observable to the clinicians, threshold rationing generally provides the highest welfare. Only patients whose benefit is above cost are treated without delay, while the others receive no treatment. If health benefit is non-contractible, an optimal co-payment is typically positive and trades off the need of insurance with the need to contain health care expenditure (moral hazard). Welfare in this case is lower than under threshold rationing. Finally, waiting times rationing provides even lower welfare than under rationing by co-payments. Both waiting times and co-payments ration demand, but while higher co-payments are recovered by the provider as higher revenues, imposing waiting times generates a deadweight loss which is not recovered by anyone else.

Future work might analyze why rationing by waiting is so frequently observed in practice despite being a relatively inefficient way of rationing. One possible explanation is that political constraints might inhibit policymakers from implementing threshold rationing or introducing co-payments. Threshold rationing requires the explicit refusal of treatment to patients, while under waiting-time rationing everyone is added to the list and therefore seemingly treated "equally." Similarly, the introduction of co-payments may appear to undermine the solidarity principles on which many publicly funded health systems are based (provision should not be based on ability to pay). For future research, a political-economy approach might be better suited to understand such issues. On the normative side, future work might investigate the scope of combining different rationing mechanisms simultaneously, as opposed to analyzing them in isolation or as alternatives to each other. It might also be worth investigating the role of equity concerns in the determination of the optimal rationing mechanism.

When waiting-time rationing is the chosen form of rationing, some governments have encouraged the use of prioritization guidelines to reduce waiting times for patients with high benefit at the cost of increased waiting times for patients with low benefit. Since clinicians prioritize patients even without the use of guidelines, future empirical research might test whether such policies do actually encourage prioritization, or, at least, reduce variations across clinicians in prioritization practices.

27.5.3 Hospital Financing

Activity-based funding has replaced fixed budgets arrangements in many countries. The empirical evidence suggests that, following these initiatives, activity increases in Norway and Denmark, but not in England. However, the research is scattered. Moreover, existing studies focus either on the effect of activity-based funding on the volume of activity or on the effect on waiting times, but rarely on both. Future research should focus on the joint estimation of both effects, which will allow disentangling whether reductions in waiting times are obtained thanks to increases in supply rather than reductions in demand. Ideally, the effect of activity-based financing should be tested within a "natural experiment" set up. However, natural experiments are rare, as often policies are introduced at a point in time and are common to all providers. In the lucky cases where the policy is introduced only for a sub-group of providers, it is often the case that the decision to participate to the "treatment group" (i.e. to adopt the new policy) is voluntary, which might generate biased results. Nevertheless, econometric techniques like matching estimators may to some extent address this issue.

27.5.4 The Role of Choice and Competition in Reducing Waiting Time

Recent literature has contributed to our understanding of the role of choice and competition under excess demand. While the theoretical literature concludes that more competition may either increase waiting time or have, at most, an indeterminate effect, depending on the assumptions made, the limited amount of empirical literature finds shorter waiting times, at least for moderate degrees of competition, and convergence of waiting times across hospitals. It is sometimes difficult to distinguish the effect of more choice from the effect of deploying more resources. Again, the empirical studies use UK data, and it is likely to add to our understanding if also empirical studies from other countries would be developed.

27.5.5 The Waiting Time and the Private Sector

When a private sector exists in parallel with the public sector, a positive waiting time may be an efficient sorting mechanism when equity concerns are strong and lump-sum taxation is not possible. We have shown that theoretical work shows mixed results with regard to the strength of this argument. Policy-relevant recommendations seem to require empirical studies. Since empirical studies require variation in health care institutions, studies that compare several (national) health care systems seem to be necessary.

There are no studies on the effect of physician dual practice on public sector waiting time. Physicians with dual practice may attract patients to their private practice by offering shorter waiting time in their private practice compared with the public hospital. Theoretical and empirical studies of this phenomenon both seem to be needed. A challenge in doing empirical studies is both to acquire sufficient variation in regulation regimes and to account for that physicians in dual practice may have unobservable characteristics that are different from those who work solely in one of the sectors.

The literature might also gain from future work that takes normative considerations into account and that aims at developing optimal regulation and payment schemes for physicians.

27.5.6 The Role of Waiting-time Targets

While in the past providers with long waiting times were more likely to attract more resources, it now seems to be more common that providers who do not meet waiting-time targets are penalized (or providers with low waiting are rewarded). The existing studies find that the imposition of waiting-time targets is effective in reducing waiting times. It seems that what is rewarded gets done. There is not much knowledge of potential unintended effects, as manipulation of lists and dumping of patients. In other words, it is not quite clear whether waiting-times reductions are obtained through an increase in supply or a reduction in demand.

27.5.7 The Role of the General Practitioner

The introduction of the GP fundholding scheme in the UK opened up for studies of the role of informed purchasing in reducing waiting times. Published studies agree that GP purchasing of elective hospital treatments on behalf of their patients results in reduced waiting times. Results disagree about whether this reduction also includes hospital treatments that are not paid for by the GP.

Hence, it is not clear what the effect of GP agency is in addition to the one of purchasing. In particular, there are gaps in understanding what role GPs may have in regulating access to specialist care. On the one hand, gatekeeping adds the cost of one extra consultation. On the other hand, the GPs' rationing decisions may relieve hospital doctors from some of the burden of rationing, reduce the pressure on the specialist health care sector and perhaps reduce hospital waiting times. A surprise is then that countries with a gatekeeping system often show longer waiting times than countries with direct access to specialist care. Theoretical and empirical studies of how gatekeeping may influence GP agency and hospital waiting times seem to be of interest.

REFERENCES

ASKILDSEN, J. E., HOLMÅS, T. H., and KAARBOE, O. (2010). "Monitoring Prioritisation in the Public health-care sector by use of medical guidelines. The case of Norway." *Health Economics*, DOI: 10.1002/hec.1659.

BARROS, P. and OLIVELLA, P. (2005). "Waiting lists and patient selection." *Journal of Economics and Management Strategy*, 15: 623–46.

BESLEY, T., HALL, J., and PRESTON, I. (1999). "The demand for private health insurance: do waiting times matter?" *Journal of Public Economics*, 72: 155–81.

BIGLAISER, G. and MA, C.-T. A. (2007). "Moonlighting: public service and private practice." *RAND Journal of Economics*, 38/4: 1113–33.

BIØRN E., HAGEN T. P., IVERSEN T., and MAGNUSSEN J. (2003). "The effect of activity-based financing on hospital efficiency. A Panel Data Analysis of DEA Efficiency Scores 1992–2000." *Health Care Management Science*, 6: 271–83.

BISHAI, D. M. and LANG, H. C. (2000). "The willingness to pay for wait reduction: the disutility of queues for cataract surgery in Canada, Denmark, and Spain." *Journal of Health Economics*, 19: 219–30.

BLENDON, R. J., et al. (2002). "Inequities in health care: a five-country survey." *Health Affairs*, 21/3: 182–91.

—— et al. (2004). "Confronting competing demands to improve quality: a five-country hospital survey." *Health Affairs*, 23/3: 119–35.

BOADWAY, R., MARCHAND, M., and SATO, M. (2004). "An optimal contract approach to hospital financing." *Journal of Health Economics*, 23: 85–110.

BREKKE, K., SICILIANI, L. and STRAUME, O. R. (2008). "Competition and waiting times in hospital markets." *Journal of Public Economics*, 92/7: 1607–28.

BUTTERY, R. B. and SNAITH, A. H. (1980). "Surgical provision, waiting times and waiting lists." *Health Trends*, 12: 57–61.

CULLIS, P., JONES, J. G., and PROPPER, C. (2000). "Waiting and medical treatment: analyses and policies." In A. J. Culyer and J. P. Newhouse (eds.), *North Holland Handbook on Health Economics*, Amsterdam: Elsevier, 1201–49.

CULYER, A. and CULLIS, J. (1976). "Some economics of hospital waiting lists in the NHS." *Journal of Social Policy*, 5: 239–64.

DAWSON, D., GRAVELLE, H., JACOBS, R., MARTIN, S., and SMITH, P. C. (2007). "The effects of expanding patient choice of provider on waiting times: evidence from a policy experiment." *Health Economics*, 16: 113–28.

DE FRAJA, G. (2000). "Contracts for health care and asymmetric information." *Journal of Health Economics*, 19/5: 663–77.

DIMAKOU, S., PARKIN, D., DEVLIN, N., and APPLEBY, J. (2009). "Identifying the impact of government targets on waiting times in the NHS." *Health Care Management Science*, 12: 1–10.

DON, B., LEE, A., and GOLDACRE, M. J. (1987). "Waiting list statistics. III. Comparison of two measures of waiting times." *British Medical Journal*, 295: 1247–8.

DUSHEIKO, M., and GRAVELLE, H., and JACOBS, R. (2004). "The effect of practice budgets on patient waiting times: allowing for selection bias", *Health Economics*, 13/10: 941–58.

FABBRI, D. and MONFARDINI, C. (2009). "Rationing the public provision of healthcare in the presence of private supplements: evidence from the Italian NHS." *Journal of Health Economics*, 28/2: 290–304.

FARRAR, S., YI, D., SCOTT, A., SUTTON, M., SUSSEX, J., CHALKLEY, M., and YUEN, P. (2006). "National evaluation of Payment by Results interim report: quantitative and qualitative analysis." Report to Department of Health, Health Economics Research Unit, University of Aberdeen, Aberdeen.

FELDER, S. (2008). "To wait or to pay for treatment? Restraining ex-post moral hazard in health insurance." *Journal of Health Economics*, 27/6: 1418–22.

FRANKEL, S. (1989). "The natural history of waiting lists: some wider explanations for an unnecessary problem." *Health Trends*, 21: 56–8.

GAULD, R. (2004). "Health care rationing policy in New Zealand: Development and lessons." *Social Policy & Society*, 3/3: 235–42.

GODDARD, J., MALEK, M., and TAVAKOLI, M. (1995). "An economic model of the market for hospital treatment for non-urgent conditions." *Health Economics*, 4/1: 41–55.

GOLDACRE, M.J., LEE, A., and DON, B. (1987). "Waiting list statistics I: relation between admissions from waiting lists and length of waiting list." *British Medical Journal*, 295: 1105–8.

GONZÁLEZ, P. (2005). "On a policy of transferring public patients to private practice." *Health Economics*, 14: 513–27.

GRAVELLE, H. and SICILIANI, L. (2008a). "Is waiting time prioritisation welfare improving?" *Health Economics*, 17/2: 167–84.

—— ——(2008b). "Optimal quality, waits and charges in health insurance." *Journal of Health Economics*, 27/3: 663–74.

—— (2009). "Third degree waiting time discrimination: optimal allocation of a public sector health care treatment under rationing by waiting." *Health Economics*, 18/8: 977–86.

—— DUSHEIKO, M. and SUTTON, M. (2002). "The demand for elective surgery in a public system: time and money prices in the UK National Health Service." *Journal of Health Economics*, 21: 423–49.

—— SMITH, P. C., and XAVIER, A. (2003). "Performance signals in the public sector: the case of health care." *Oxford Economic Papers*, 55: 81–103.

HANNING, M. (1996). "Maximum waiting time: an attempt to reduce waiting lists in Sweden", *Health Policy*, 36: 17–35.

HENDERSON, J., NEWTON, J., and GOLDRACE, M. (1995). "Waiting list dynamics and the impact of earmarked funding." *British Medical Journal*, 311: 783–5.

HURST, J. and SICILIANI, L, (2003). "Tackling excessive waiting times for elective surgery: a comparison of policies in twelve OECD countries." OECD Health Working Paper, 6: 1–216 <www.oecd.org/health>.

HOEL, M. and SÆTHER, E. M. (2003). "Public health care with waiting time: the role of supplementary private health care." *Journal of Health Economics*, 22: 599–616.

IACONE, F., MARTIN S., and SMITH P. C. (2007). "Modelling the dynamics of a public health care system: evidence from time-series data." CHE Research paper, RP29, Centre for Health Economics, University of York.

IVERSEN, T. (1993). "A theory of hospital waiting lists." *Journal of Health Economics*, 12: 55–71.

—— (1997). "The effect of private sector on the waiting time in a National Health Service." *Journal of Health Economics*, 16: 381–96.

JOHANNESSON, M., JOHANSSON, P.-O., and SÖDERQVIST, T. (1998). "Time spent on waiting lists for medical care: an insurance approach." *Journal of Health Economics*, 17: 627–44.

KJERSTAD, E. M. (2003). "Prospective funding of general hospitals in Norway: incentives for higher production?" *International Journal of Health Care Finance and Economics*, 4: 231–51.

LINDSAY, C. M. and FEIGENBAUM, B. (1984). "Rationing by waiting lists." *American Economic Review*, 74/3: 404–17.

MALCOMSON, J. M. (2005). "Supplier discretion over provision: theory and an application to medical care." *RAND Journal of Economics*, 36/2: 412–32.

MARCHAND, M. and SCHROYEN, F. (2005). "Can a mixed health care system be desirable on equity grounds?" *Scandinavian Journal of Economics*, 107/1: 1–23.

MARTIN, S. and SMITH, P. C. (1999). "Rationing by waiting lists: an empirical investigation." *Journal of Public Economics*, 71: 141–64.

—————(2003). "Using panel methods to model waiting times for National Health Service surgery." *Journal of the Royal Statistical Society*, 166/Part 2: 1–19.

—— JACOBS, R., RICE, N., and SMITH, P. C. (2003). "The UK evidence on waiting for health care." Mimeo, CHE, University of York.

—— RICE, N., JACOBS, R., SMITH, P. C. (2007)., "The market for elective surgery: joint estimation of supply and demand." *Journal of Health Economics*, 26/2: 263–85.

MONSTAD, K., ENGESÆTER, L. B., and ESPEHAUG, B. (2006). "Patients' preferences for choice of hospital." Working Paper 05/06. Health Economics Bergen, Bergen, Norway.

NEWTON, J., HANDERSON, J., and GOLDRACE, M. (1995). "Waiting list dynamics and the impact of earmarked funding." *British Medical Journal*, 311: 783–5.

NORDBERG, M., KESKIMAKI, I., and HEMMINKI, E. (1994). "Is there a relation between waiting list length and surgery rate?" *International Journal of Health Planning and Management*, 9: 259–65.

NOSEWORTHY, T. and MCGURRAN, J. (2001). "From chaos to order: making sense of waiting lists in Canada." Final report. Western Canada Waiting List Project. <www.wcwl.org>.

OLIVELLA, P. (2003). "Shifting public-health-sector waiting lists to the private sector." *European Journal of Political Economy*, 19: 103–32.

PROPPER, C. (1990). "Contingent valuation of time spent on NHS waiting lists." *Economic Journal*, 100/400: 193–200 (Conference Suppl., April).

—— (1995). "The disutility of time spent on the United Kingdom's National Health Service waiting lists." *Journal of Human Resources*, 30: 677–700.

—— CROXSON, B., and SHEARER, A. (2002). "Waiting times for hospital admissions: the impact of GP fundholding." *Journal of Health Economics*, 21/2: 227–52.

—— SUTTON, M., WHITNALL, C., and WINDMEIJER, F. (2008). "Did 'targets and terror' reduce waiting times in England for hospital care?" *The BE Journal of Economic Analysis & Policy*, 8/2 (Contribution), Article 5.

—— BURGESS, S., and GOSSAGE, D. (2008). "Competition and quality: evidence from the NHS internal market 1991–9." *The Economic Journal*, 118/525: 138–70.

SALANT, S., (1977). "Search theory and duration data: a theory of sorts." *The Quarterly Journal of Economics*, 91/1: 39–57.

SANMARTIN, C. (2001). "Toward standard definitions of waiting times." Western Canada Waiting List Project, Final Report.

SICILIANI, L. (2005). "Does more choice reduce waiting times." *Health Economics*, 14/1: 17–23.

—— (2007). "Optimal contracts for health services in the presence of waiting times and asymmetric information." *BE Journal of Economic Policy and Analysis*, 7/1 (Contribution), article 40.

—— (2008). "A note on the dynamic interaction between waiting times and waiting lists." *Health Economics*, 17/5: 639–47.

—— and HURST, J. (2004). "Explaining waiting-time variations for elective surgery across OECD countries." *OECD Economic Studies*, 38/1: 96–122.

—————(2005). "Tackling excessive waiting times for elective surgery: a comparison of policies in twelve OECD countries." *Health Policy*, 72: 201–15.

SICILIANI, L. and MARTIN, S. (2007). "An empirical analysis of the impact of choice on waiting times." *Health Economics*, 16/8: 763–79.

—— STANCIOLE, A., and JACOBS, R. (2009). "Do waiting times reduce costs?" *Journal of Health Economics*, 28/4: 771–80.

SMITH, P. and VAN ACKERE, A. (2002). "A note on the integration of system dynamics and economic models." *Journal of Economic Dynamics and Control*, 26/1: 1–10.

STREET, A. and MIRALDO, M. (2007). "The impact of the reform of hospital funding in England." Paper presented at: Evaluating Health Policy: New Evidence from administrative Data. University of York, York.

—— VITIKAINEN K., BJORVATN, A., and HVENEGAARD, A. (2007). "Introducing Activity-Based Financing: A Review of Experience in Australia, Denmark, Norway and Sweden." CHE Research Paper no. 30, Centre for Health Economics, University of York, York.

TESTI, A., TANFANI, E., and TORRE, G. (2007). "A three-phase approach for operating theatre schedules." *Health Care Management Science*, 10: 163–72.

—— VALENTE R., ANSALDO, L., and TORRE, G. C. (2008). "Prioritizing surgical waiting lists." *Journal of Evaluation in Clinical Practice*, 14: 59–64.

VALLGÅRDA, S., KRASNIK, A., and VRANGBÆK, K. (2001). Health *Systems in Transition, Denmark*. Copenhagen: European Observatory on Health Systems and Policies.

VAN ACKERE, A. and SMITH, P. C. (1999). "Towards a macro model of National Health Service waiting lists." *System Dynamics Review*, 15/3: 225–52.

WORTHINGTON, D. J. (1987). "Queuing models for hospital waiting list." *Journal of Operational Research Society*, 38/5: 413–22.

—— (1991). "Hospital waiting list management models." *Journal of Operational Research Society*, 42/10: 833–43.

XAVIER, A. (2003). "Hospital competition, GP fundholders and waiting times in the UK internal market: the case of elective surgery." *International Journal of Health Care Finance and Economics*, 3: 25–51.

CHAPTER 28

....

INCREASING COMPETITION BETWEEN PROVIDERS IN HEALTH CARE MARKETS: THE ECONOMIC EVIDENCE*

....

CAROL PROPPER AND GEORGE LECKIE

28.1 INTRODUCTION

....

OVER the past two decades the extent of competition between hospital providers in health care markets, both in the US and elsewhere, has changed substantially. In the US, the growth of managed care has led to the introduction of price competition between health care providers while in Europe, England, Denmark, Sweden, Norway, and Holland are all seeking to increase competition by increasing the extent of patient choice. Whatever the nature of the health care markets, those promoting competition make an appeal to a simple economic argument. Competitive pressure helps make private firms more efficient. They cut costs and improve their goods and services in order to attract consumers, and this continual drive for improvement is good for the economy. Firms that are unable or unwilling to become more efficient will be priced out of the market while new, more efficient, firms will enter the market. It seems easy to transfer this logic to the provision of health services. Giving purchasers or service users the ability to choose applies competitive pressure to health care providers and, analogously with private markets, they will raise their game to attract business.

The aim of this chapter is to subject this assumption to the scrutiny provided by the theoretical and empirical economic evidence on competition between providers in

* We would like to thank the ESRC for financial support provided through its Centre funding of CMPO.

health care provider markets. Does either economic theory or the empirical evidence suggest that greater competition will decrease prices, raise quality and improve health outcomes? What is the impact of centrally fixed prices on competition? Will all patients gain, or are some likely to lose? The rest of the chapter is structured as follows. Section 28.2 discusses the impact of competition in health care markets, section 28.3 examines the role of information in increasing competition, section 28.4 examines the effects of using centrally set prices, and section 28.5 offers some concluding comments.

28.2 Competition between Hospitals

This section examines the theoretical and empirical economic evidence on the effect of greater competition between providers in health care markets. Most of the evidence focuses on a narrow set of outcomes, primarily the effect of competition on prices and quality of health care, sometimes with a focus on winners and losers. The majority of studies provides evidence only on positive questions, such as "does competition increase quality?" Few of these studies allow normative analysis, which would assess whether greater competition is beneficial overall. Most of the evidence comes from the United States and the little evidence from elsewhere is dominated by that from England or the UK.

28.2.1 The Impact of Competition on Health Care Markets: What Economic Theory Predicts

Health care markets are usually thought to differ from textbook competitive markets in a number of important ways. These include: the fact that the product is differentiated (due, for example, to hospital's different geographical location or different styles of health care), that information is imperfect and that government regulation is extensive as a response to these departures from the textbook competitive market. In addition, many firms, even in a system like that of the USA, are not-for-profit (Dranove and Satterthwaite 2000). In these types of complex markets, economic theory fails to provide strong guidance as to whether competition is optimal.

In particular, where there is product differentiation, competition can provide too little quality or variety, too much, or just the right amount. The intuition is as follows. Competition may "under-provide" variety since competitive firms cannot capture the consumer surplus from additional variety. A monopolist may provide more variety as it is the only seller in the market and can capture the consumer surplus. Alternatively, competition may produce too much variety since in a competitive market part of the profit from new variety will come from "stealing demand" from other firms. A firm deciding to offer a new variety will not take account of this external effect so there will be excessive product variation relative to the socially optimal level of variation (Gaynor and Vogt 2000).

Analyses that take account of the multi-product nature of hospital production and the imprecision of measures of both quality and price have shown that the impact of competition between hospitals on price and quality is ambiguous (Dranove and Satterthwaite 2000). The impact of competition will depend on the responsiveness of the buyer of health care to both quality and price. This will depend on how precisely price and quality can be observed. If price and/or quality cannot be measured and reported well, this will make the buyer less responsive to changes in price or quality. If quality is observed accurately but price is observed poorly, then demand becomes less responsive to price, allowing providers to raise their prices, but also giving the provider an incentive to increase and possibly "over-produce" quality. If price is observed accurately but quality is observed poorly, then the levels of quality supplied will be too low. Finally, if quality has several attributes, one of which is easier to observe than another (for example, clinical quality and patient amenity), then competition may lead to over-production of the one that is easily observed and under-production of the others that are less easy to observe. (It is worth noting that the over- and under-production are relative to the socially optimal levels of production. In practice, if regulators also cannot observe dimension of quality, it is not clear whether competition or regulation will be preferred.)

There may also be an interaction between the nature of the market and the method of price setting. First, this interaction will affect the general level of prices. In a market in which buyers of health care are covered by generous health insurance and there is no centralized price setting (as in the United States before the 1980s), buyers will not be sensitive to price, but will be responsive to differences in quality. So price may be high, but quality will also be high. In markets where buyers have "harder" budget constraints (as in the UK during the 1990s internal market, see section 28.2.3.1), price may be more important and hospitals will compete on prices, leaving quality to fall below efficient levels. Where a single price is fixed for all providers for a treatment (as in prospective payment systems), there will also be no price competition. In this case, all competition will be in terms of quality. Competition may lead to excessive levels of quality and excessive product differentiation (Gaynor 2004), but if government reimbursement for a treatment is too low, competition may lead to the quality of this treatment being too low.

Second, this interaction will affect patients differentially. As individuals differ in the severity of their illnesses, any regime that sets a single price for all patients of a certain type—for example, a single price for the treatment of a certain condition—will set up incentives to treat the less costly patients and to avoid treating or "under-treat" the more costly patients. Such regimes include the diagnosis-related group (DRG) system used in the United States by the government (and most private insurers in the US as well) and any kind of prospective payment system, in which reimbursement is set in advance of treatment. These incentives exist regardless of whether there is competition or not, but the introduction of competition into a previously monopolistic market may sharpen them, resulting in differential treatment of patients. So, for example, patients who are more expensive to treat may get worse quality care or remain untreated (known as "skimping" and "dumping") while hospitals compete for lower cost patients by offering them better quality ("creaming") (Ellis 1998). Differential treatment might also arise in markets where patients are covered by insurers who differ in the generosity with which they reimburse hospitals.

There are other aspects of quality patients might care about: notably, in systems with long waiting lists, the impact of hospital competition on waiting times. In such systems, Brekke et al. (2008) argue that a limited amount of patient choice allows semi-altruistic providers to compete to attract high-benefit patients and that this leads to a reduction in waiting times. However, if the health care market is sufficiently competitive, the incentive for hospitals to "compete" to avoid treating the sickest and most unprofitable patients will dominate this first effect, leading to longer waiting times for these patients.

28.2.2 The US Evidence on Competition and Health System Outcomes

Almost all the evidence comes from the US market, and much of this comes from one—albeit very large—market, California. Some of the early evidence is difficult to interpret because of the methods of analysis used. In early studies, hospital markets were not well-defined and there was no recognition of the fact that the measure of competition might be affected by the outcomes that were being studied. Later studies tend to have paid more attention to these issues, and are more reliable indicators of outcomes.

The results of these studies show impact of competition depends on the "rules of the game": the institutional features of the health care market. Three regimes can be identified in the US health care market (Dranove and Satterthwaite 2000). In the first, which operated in the 1960s and 1970s, consumers were covered by generous insurance and hospitals were reimbursed retrospectively for their full costs. In the second, which began in the early 1980s, government payers (Medicare) introduced prospective payment schemes and utilization review. Private insurers followed their lead. Prospective payment schemes (PPS) reimburse hospitals according to the average cost for a procedure or treatment group. Under these schemes, if treatment costs exceed reimbursement rates, the hospital absorbs the loss. Thus, PPS give two incentives: to lower costs and to avoid treating high cost patients. The third regime began in the 1980s, took hold in the 1990s, and is known as managed care. Payers created preferred provider organizations (PPOs), which contracted with hospitals to obtain discounted prices. This system limits the number of hospitals that can be chosen by the health care users. Alongside preferred provider organizations have grown up managed care organizations (known as health maintenance organizations or HMOs), in which the insurer enrolls the individual for a set period for a fixed fee. Managed care organizations have an incentive to be concerned about price and have also been very active in seeking information on quality. However, in the mid-to-late 1990s there was a "backlash" against managed care. Many consumers reported problems with managed care, disliked the restrictions on their care plans and their limited choice of providers and feared that their plans might not be able to provide or pay for the care they will need when they are very sick. As a result HMOs have relaxed the constraints on consumer choice and made their plans more flexible.

28.2.2.1 *The Effects on Prices and Quality of Competition*

Most studies suggest that the switch to both prospective payment and managed care increased price competition and lowered costs (or lowered the growth in costs) (e.g. Zwanziger and Melnick 1988; Feldman et al. 1990; Robinson 1991; Melnick et al. 1992; Gaskin and Hadley 1997; Keeler et al. 1999; Baker and Phibbs 2002; Heidenreich et al. 2002; Bundorf et al. 2004). There is also evidence that hospitals in competitive markets decreased the amount of uncompensated care (care for which they did not get paid for) they provided in response to the introduction of increased price competition (Gruber 1992; Dranove and Satterthwaite 2000; Gaynor and Vogt 2000). However, Dranove et al. (2008) suggest that the managed care backlash of the mid-1990s weakened MCOs ability to play competitive hospitals off against one another to secure price discounts. Thus, the backlash made demand less sensitive to price.

In terms of the effect on quality, it is the generally accepted view (though the empirical support is quite weak) that the first regime resulted in a "medical arms race" (Robinson and Luft 1985). As buyers were not sensitive to price, hospitals competed on quality, both to attract buyers and to attract physicians to practice at their hospitals. This had the impact of raising both price and quality in areas with more hospitals (Joskow 1980). More recently, attention has focused on the impact of managed care on quality. An influential early study focused on the treatment of elderly patients admitted to hospital with a heart attack. All these patients, because of their age, were covered by government insurance (Medicare), which generally paid above the marginal costs of care for AMI. This shows that higher competition was associated with lower AMI death rates post-1990 (Kessler and McClellan 2000). Similar findings are reported by Rogowski et al. (2007), who look at deaths across a broader range of medical conditions, and Sari (2002), who measures quality of health care by number of in-hospital complications. However, other studies show more mixed results (Shortell and Hughes 1988; Ho and Hamilton 2000; Mukamel et al. 2001; Gowrisankaran and Town 2003; Volpp et al. 2003).

Incentives for hospitals to increase quality when operating in competitive markets may depend on the precise mix of payers that the hospitals have. There is evidence that HMOs have preferences for higher quality hospital care (Schulman et al. 1997; Chernew et al. 1998; Escarce et al. 1999; Gaskin et al. 2002; Young et al. 2002; Rainwater and Romano 2003). This leads to both price reductions and quality improvements in competitive environments where HMO penetration is high. Mukamel et al. (2001), Sari (2002), and Rogowski et al. (2007) all find higher HMO penetration is associated with higher quality. However, not all the evidence supports this view; Kessler and McClellan (2000) find no association between the two and Shortell and Hughes (1988) and Shen (2003) both find higher HMO penetration to be negatively associated with hospital quality of care. Where reimbursement rates are set by Medicare (or another government insurer) that sets relatively low rates, hospitals may respond to competition for patients by reducing quality

(Gowrisankaran and Town 2003). The argument is that the hospital has no control over reimbursement rates and, if they are too low, the hospital may not have an incentive to compete for these patients by supplying better quality. If this is the case, the outcome of competition will depend on the precise mix of payers. Gowrisankaran and Town (2003) examine the treatment of both Medicare and HMO patients and find that competition reduced death rates for HMO patients but increased those of Medicare patients.

The more competitive market conditions of the 1990s also led to harsher financial conditions. Bazzoli et al. (2008), who look at the impact of financial performance on quality, find some limited evidence that hospital financial condition (measured as cash flow as a proportion of total revenue) is negatively associated with the number of in-hospital complications, medical errors and deaths.

28.2.2.2 Evidence on Hospital Mergers

Over the last twenty years, the US market for hospital care has seen a substantial rise in hospital mergers (Gaynor and Haas-Wilson 1999). Mergers have been offered as a means to achieve cost reductions through reduced non-price competition, increased patient base (economies of scale) and decreased administrative costs. However, a recent empirical study by Harrison (2007) argues that the primary reason for the mergers during this period was actually due to competitive pressures to increase market power (via a reduction in the number of hospitals providing substitute products) rather than to decrease productive inefficiencies through cost savings. This argument is consistent with a large body of evidence that demonstrates that hospital mergers lead to higher prices but few if any cost savings (Connor et al. 1998; Noether 1988; Melnick et al. 1992; Dranove and Ludwick 1999; Keeler et al. 1999; Dranove and Lindrooth 2003; and Gaynor and Vogt 2003). Further, Ferrier and Valdmanis (2004)—who study the short run effects of hospital mergers on hospital efficiency and productivity—find no evidence that merged hospitals perform better than similar hospitals that did not merge.

Until recently, mergers between not-for-profit hospitals have been tolerated, as it was viewed that their not-for-profit status would mean that mergers would not have anti-competitive effects. Indeed, the not-for-profit hospitals themselves claimed that their principal objective was to maximize the community's welfare rather than to maximize profit or shareholder wealth. In some cases this argument has been accepted by the courts (Gaynor and Vogt 2000). One court judgement stated: "The Board of University Hospital is simply above collusion." Recent studies have challenged this view. Mergers by not-for-profits have been found to decrease competition and have an equally negative impact on outcomes as mergers by for-profits (Abraham et al. 2007). The evidence seems to indicate no significant differences between the pricing behavior of for-profit and not-for-profit hospitals (Sloan 2000). Not-for-profit hospitals use their market power in a way similar to for-profits: studies of not-for-profit mergers find that mergers lead to price increases (Gaynor and Vogt 2003). This implies that the for-profit/not-for-profit status of hospitals that wish to merge should not be considered a factor in predicting whether a merger is likely to be anti-competitive (Federal Trade Commission and Department of Justice 2004).

Mergers do not always lead to increased market concentration via a reduction the number of firms providing substitute products. For highly specialized complex procedures (e.g. cardiac surgery) that tend to be provided by only a small number of hospitals, mergers will typically leave the effective number of hospitals unchanged as typically at most one of the merging parties will carry out the procedure. However, these mergers are likely to alter the allocation of consumers across hospitals ("business stealing") and as hospitals are differentiated in terms of quality and cost, this has welfare implications. However, Huckman (2006), who examines the effect of mergers on the average cost and quality of major cardiac procedures in New York, finds these mergers have little effect on the average cost and quality of cardiac care.

28.2.2.3 *Differential Treatment of Patients and Differential Responses by Hospitals*

Competition may also lead to differential treatment of different types of patients, although this outcome has been less studied. Kessler and Geppert (2005) examine the treatment given to elderly Medicare patients admitted to hospital following a heart attack. They investigate the extent to which (lack of) competition has an impact on patients who are otherwise sicker compared with those who are otherwise healthier. They find that in more competitive markets there was greater variation in medical care. Furthermore, this variation was on average beneficial. Healthy patients in more competitive markets received less intensive treatment than those in more concentrated markets, without any significant difference in health outcomes. Sick patients in more competitive markets received more intensive treatment than similar patients in more concentrated markets, with the former having better health outcomes. The effect of competition is that there is more appropriate treatment, with greater variety in treatment styles across hospitals in more competitive areas and that neither patient group loses.

A related issue is whether price-based competition changes the type of services provided. Mukamel et al. (2000) examine whether hospitals in more price-competitive environments will shift resources from activities related to clinical service, which are not easily observed and evaluated by patients, into hotel services, which are easily observed. They study the change to selective contracting in California in the early 1980s and find some evidence to support resource shifting. In not-for-profit hospitals, resource use declined more in clinical services than in hotel services.

28.2.3 Evidence on Competition and Health Outcome from Outside the United States

The evidence on competition between hospitals outside the United States is extremely limited, mainly because such competition has been extremely rare. In addition, some of this evidence is less about competition per se than about the effect of changes to the payment mechanisms that have accompanied policies to increase competition.

28.2.3.1 *Evidence from the UK*

The primary non-US evidence on competition comes from the UK internal market in hospital care that operated between 1991 and 1997. This internal market encouraged competition between NHS hospitals for contracts for hospital care from two sets of buyers: the geographically based district health authorities and the smaller GP fundholders. Prices could be negotiated between hospitals and the buyers, and price lists (though not including any discounts) were supposed to be publicly available. Information on quality was very limited. The evidence suggests that greater competition was associated with lower costs (Söderlund et al. 1997). The bargaining power of district health authorities was lower than that of GP fundholders, and hospitals that had greater business from fundholders had lower posted prices (Propper et al. 1998; Propper 1996). On the other hand, two large-scale studies of the association between competition and quality suggest that quality—as measured by deaths of patients admitted to hospitals with heart attacks—fell during the internal market (Propper et al. 2004, 2008). This combination of falls in price and a drop in quality fits with the predictions of economic theory: where demanders are sensitive to price and quality information is weak, both prices and quality are likely to fall as competition increases.

There is a considerable body of evidence to suggest that the two types of purchasers were differentially able to reap the benefits from provider competition. Compared to district health authorities, GP fundholders were able to secure shorter waiting times for their patients, were more able to move contracts and generally appeared to be more responsive to patients' wishes and more willing to exploit competition between hospitals for their business (Le Grand 1999; Croxson et al. 2001; Propper et al. 2002; Dusheiko et al. 2004). This may in part be due to their smaller size: district health authorities were concerned that if they removed their business the whole hospital would fail. It is also likely to be due to self-selection among GPs of fundholding status. So there is some evidence of differential treatment of patients from different buyers. There has been no systematic study of whether "skimming", "creaming", or "dumping" occurred. Case study evidence suggests that fundholders did not engage in patient dumping, even though they had the incentive to do so (Matsaganis and Glennerster 1994).

Two recent UK studies have considered the effect of competition on waiting times. Dawson et al. (2007), who analyze the impact of a London-based initiative to increase patient choice, find that this led to shorter average waiting times in the London region and a convergence in waiting times amongst London hospitals. Siciliani and Martin (2007), who look at hospital density and waiting times, find a modest negative relationship between the two; hospitals in more competitive markets have shorter waiting times.

28.2.3.2 *Other Evidence*

The Nordic countries have NHS-type systems where care is provided by the public sector and finance is provided through taxation. In Norway, Denmark, and Sweden some elements of patient choice driven competition has been introduced, primarily to decrease waiting times. In all three countries, it has been accompanied by a move towards output-related (DRG-type) payments. A review of Denmark and Sweden concluded that the incentives for hospitals to accept patients from outside their area have been weak and, perhaps unsurprisingly, only a small proportion of patients went out of area under these schemes (Williams and Rossiter 2004). The evidence does not support a strong reduction in waiting times in Denmark. In Sweden there is some evidence that the move to output-related payments in the late 1980s and early 1990s initially increased productivity (Gerdtham et al. 1999) and reduced waiting times, but at the expense of increased total costs (Kastberg and Siverbo 2007). In the mid-1990s, adjustments were made to control costs, but this led to longer waiting times and the initial productivity increases ceased (Håkansson 2000). There appears to be little assessment of the impact of output-related payments on provider competition or outcomes in Norway. Another country with an NHS system also attempted to increase competition. New Zealand, in 1993, pursued a "big-bang" policy change whereby they pushed through a radical set of market orientated reforms designed to improve efficiency via increased competition between providers (Gauld 2000). However, these reforms failed to bring about the improvements in performance that were hoped for and also had several adverse consequences. Ashton and Press (1997) measure the degree of market concentration pre- (1992) and post-reform (1994) and find little change over the two year period. In response to this lack of improvement, the reforms were restructured in 1996 and the government sought a softer approach of "incremental" change.

In summary, the evidence makes it clear that "institutions matter"; the effects of competition depend on the features of the market. Important features include: whether prices are set centrally or not, who makes the choice of provider, and the availability of information on quality and prices. Where buyers care about price, competition between hospitals has led to lower costs or lower cost growth, both in the US and in the UK. The relationship between competition and quality has been less studied but the best US evidence suggests that quality is higher where markets are more competitive (though this was not the case in the English internal market). Not-for-profit hospitals appear to respond to competition in very similar ways to for-profit hospitals.

28.3 The Use of Information in Health Care Markets

The provision of information on provider performance is a prerequisite for choice driven competition between providers. However, the evidence—mainly from the United States—suggests that such information does not necessarily improve outcomes.

28.3.1 The Use of Information

A comprehensive review (Marshall 2002) suggests very different use of information on provider performance by consumers, buyers, and health care providers. Although consumers state they want more information, published data has only a small impact on consumer decision-making. For example, only one in nine coronary artery bypass graft patients from four Pennsylvania hospitals were aware of the Pennsylvania report cards on cardiac surgeons. Less than one-quarter of these patients said it had any significant impact on their choice of surgeon. Furthermore, there was a low willingness to pay for the report cards. Lack of interest in, and lack of use of, performance data appears to be due to difficulties in understanding the information, lack of trust in the data, problems with timely access to the information, and lack of choice.

Purchasers use information on providers to a greater extent than patients, but there is evidence that they find it inadequately packaged and targeted. Providers are more responsive to performance data than consumers or purchasers (or individual doctors). Unsurprisingly, organizations shown in a positive light by performance reports are more likely to use the information for benchmarking and internal performance monitoring. Those identified as poor performers are more likely to criticize the validity of the data (Propper and Wilson 2003).

28.3.2 The Impact of Information on Health Outcomes

Public reporting of performance may engender positive responses by providers, but it may also have unintended consequences. This stems from the fact that outcomes, particularly quality, are very difficult to measure in health care (Propper and Wilson 2006). Information on performance gives providers the incentive to do well according to the criteria that are published: the problem is that they will do this by increasing efforts to improve the published criteria, which is not necessarily the same thing as improving actual outcomes. Possible responses include the improvement of performance and the exodus of poor performers but also, less positively, the selection of patients, differential treatment of patients and manipulating the data to appear to do better (Propper and Wilson 2003). Examples of manipulation of the data from the UK include the re-categorization of patients during the 1990s to reduce published inpatient waiting lists. Smith (1995) provides a list of some of the less positive responses of providers to the publication of information in health care.

Report cards have been introduced in the United States to provide information, at the level of individual surgeons in hospitals, on the quality of outcomes. There are relatively few studies of their impact and the studies have come to rather different conclusions. Studies of the impact of the mandatory New York coronary artery bypass graft surgery report cards, which were introduced in the late 1980s, concluded that mortality decreased. Possible explanations include: the exodus of low volume, high mortality surgeons, a marked improvement in the performance of non-low volume surgeons, and improvement in the performance of surgeons new to the system (Hannan et al. 1994). But Dranove et al. (2003) use the same data to examine the impact of report cards on appropriate matching of patients to hospitals, on the quality and incidence of intensive cardiac treatments and on the resource use and health outcomes that determine the net consequences of report cards on social welfare. They find that report cards led to substantial selection by providers of patients, increased sorting of patients to providers on the basis of severity of their illness, and significant declines in the use of intensive cardiac procedures for sicker patients. Treated patients in the two states (New York and Pennsylvania) that had report cards were less ill than those treated in states without report cards. Patients within a hospital were more similar in terms of severity and those who were sicker were more likely to go to teaching hospitals. The introduction of report cards also altered the treatments given so that both healthier and sicker patients received more treatment, but while this improved the outcomes for healthier patients, it worsened outcomes for sicker ones, because hospitals avoided performing intensive surgical therapies that were monitored for sicker patients and instead used less effective medical therapies. Overall, Dranove et al. (2003) conclude that these cards reduced patient welfare, though the longer-term effects might be more positive. For example, the increased patient sorting that report cards engender might lead to more accurate and effective treatment as hospitals become more specialized in the treatment of certain types of patients.

In summary, while consumers have access to more information, information in health care markets is often too complex for direct use by consumers. It is often in a form that is of limited use for buyers of health care. It is most widely used by providers themselves and they appear to respond quickly to the incentives given by the information. In these responses they will focus on improving measured outcomes; this may or may not improve actual outcomes and there is considerable evidence of "gaming the system".

28.4 THE IMPACT OF CENTRALLY SET PRICES

The United States led the way in introducing prospective prices for treatment. In 1983, Medicare implemented a prospective payment system and private payers followed suit. Under the prospective payment system, the amount a hospital receives for treating a patient is based on the diagnosis-related group (DRG) for the episode of hospitalization. Each DRG has a payment weight assigned to it, based on the average cost of treating patients in that DRG. Hospitals receive this predetermined amount regardless of the actual cost of care. In the UK, the current government has introduced centrally set fixed prices as part of its "payment by results" system. Such systems are intended to give incentives to bring down costs, as providers can keep the difference between actual expenditure and the DRG payment, but it is important that prices correctly reflect the economic costs of the activity. Paying too much wastes resources, while paying too little reduces both output and capacity, lowers the quality of the services that are provided, and diminishes the incentives for innovation (Cookson and Dawson 2006).

US research suggests that in the presence of competition, providers are extremely responsive to signals given by centrally set prices. For example, prior to the adoption of the prospective payment system, the average length of stay in hospital had been stable for around seven years. Once the prospective payment system went into effect, the average length of stay began an immediate decline, the number of certain procedures performed on patients dropped precipitously and others rose by well over 100 per cent (Federal Trade Commission and Department of Justice 2004). Medicare's administrative pricing system, albeit inadvertently, made some services very lucrative and others unprofitable. The results of the pricing distortions are that some services are more or less available than they would be based on the demand for the service. An example is provided by cardiac care. Medicare reimbursement rates in the early 2000s make this type of care very profitable. Hospitals use this profit to subsidize the provision of less profitable or unprofitable services, but this pricing distortion also creates a direct economic incentive for specialists in cardiac care to enter the market. In response, general hospitals in the United States have tried to find ways to limit the expansion of competition (Federal Trade Commission and Department of Justice 2004) for example by mergers or agreements between hospitals.

Single prices may also encourage differential treatment of patients. As noted above, they give incentives to over-provide services to patients with expected costs below the fixed price ("creaming"), to offer lower quality ("skimping") or to simply under-provide services ("dumping") to patients with expected costs above the fixed price (Ellis 1998). Setting a single price does not necessarily encourage high quality. The US Medicare system has been argued to be "largely neutral or negative towards quality" (Federal Trade Commission and Department of Justice 2004). The reasons are as follows. All providers meeting basic requirements are paid the same regardless of the quality they provide. At times, providers are paid more when complications occur as a result of error (for example, if a patient is pushed into a better rewarded DRG as a result of medical complications), thus actually providing an incentive for poorer quality.

28.5 Discussion

We conclude by raising some issues that seem to be pertinent for policymakers interested in increasing competition in their health care systems.

First, it is clear that the impact of competition on outputs depends on the exact nature of the health care market. The institutional structures matter. Important aspects of the market include: who makes the choice of provider (payer or patient), the availability of information on quality and prices, and whether prices are set centrally or not. Competition between hospitals appears to be associated with lower costs. However, the relationship between competition and quality has not been studied as extensively. The evidence suggests that generally quality is higher where hospital markets are more competitive, though there are exceptions.

Second, it is important to distinguish between payer choice and patient choice, as they are not the same thing. If one is to operate well, the other may have to be restricted. In resolution of this conflict, most systems are characterized by payer choice and limited direct patient choice. Outcomes will therefore depend on the behavior of—and so the incentives facing—the purchasing agents.

Third, the provision of information is a prerequisite for informed choice and therefore needed to increase competition and to make health care markets work. But such information is generally partial and so gives the providers opportunities to "game the system."

Fourth, centrally set fixed prices are used by policymakers to encourage providers to compete in terms of quality rather than price. These prices are generally set at average cost, giving providers incentives to bring down costs. But they also give incentives to select into treatment those patients that are cheaper to treat than the fixed price ("creaming"), to under-treat, conditional on selection into treatment, those with expected costs above the fixed price ("skimping") or simply to treat the most severely ill patients ("dumping"). These incentives are present whether or not competition exists, but are intensified when hospitals are subject to either actual competition or competition based on league tables. Clearly, these incentives will also be sharpened the larger the component of providers' income that is based on prospective fixed price per case payments. Centrally fixed prices may also encourage entry of specialist providers who concentrate only on the well-reimbursed activities, and penalize providers who currently cross-subsidize between activities.

Finally, if it is accepted that payer-driven competition is broadly beneficial, then the logic is that it should be promoted. This is likely to require regulatory intervention. Competition is intended to increase pressure on hospitals, something that hospitals, just as other firms in a market, are likely to want to avoid. In the US, hospitals have tried to reduce this pressure by entering into preferential pricing agreements, negotiating access rights to selected buyers or by merging. Many not-for-profit providers have merged and where they have done so they often appeal to the fact that their principal motivation is to serve local communities and—in some cases—this argument has been accepted by the courts. However, the US experience suggests that the benefits of mergers between either for- or not-for-profits may well be exaggerated and so regulatory policy will be needed to promote competition.

References

ABRAHAM, J. M., GAYNOR, M., and VOGT, W. B. (2007) Entry and competition in local hospital markets. *Journal of Industrial Economics*, 55, 265–88.

ASHTON, T., and PRESS, D. (1997) Market concentration in secondary health services under a purchaser-provider split: The New Zealand experience. *Health Economics*, 6, 43–56.

BAKER, L. C., and PHIBBS, C. S. (2002) Managed care, technology adoption, and health care: the adoption of neonatal intensive care. *RAND Journal of Economics*, 33, 524–48.

BAZZOLI, G. J., CHEN, H. F., ZHAO, M., and LINDROOTH, R. C. (2008) Hospital financial condition and the quality of patient care. *Health Economics*, 17, 977–95.

BREKKE, K. R., SICILIANI, L., and STRAUME, O. R. (2008) Competition and waiting times in hospital markets. *Journal of Public Economics*, 92, 1607–28.

BUNDORF, M. K., SCHULMAN, K. A., STAFFORD, J. A., GASKIN, D., JOLLIS, J. G., and ESCARCE, J. J. (2004) Impact of managed care on the treatment, costs, and outcomes of fee-for-service medicare patients with acute myocardial infarction. *Health Services Research*, 39, 131–52.

CHERNEW, M., SCANLON, D., and HAYWARD, R. (1998) Insurance type and choice of hospital for coronary artery bypass graft surgery. *Health Services Research*, 33, 447–66.

CONNOR, R. A., FELDMAN, R. D., and DOWD, B. E. (1998) The effects of market concentration and horizontal mergers on hospital costs and prices. *International Journal of the Economics of Business*, 5, 159–80.

COOKSON, R., and DAWSON, D. (2006) Hospital competition and patient choice in publicly funded health care. *The Elgar Companion to Health Economics*. Cheltenham: Edward Elgar.

CROXSON, B., PROPPER, C., and PERKINS, A. (2001) Do doctors respond to financial incentives? UK family doctors and the GP fundholder scheme. *Journal of Public Economics*, 79, 375–98.

DAWSON, D., GRAVELLE, H., JACOBS, R., MARTIN, S., and SMITH, P. C. (2007) The effects of expanding patient choice of provider on waiting times: Evidence from a policy experiment. *Health Economics*, 16, 113–28.

DRANOVE, D., and LINDROOTH, R. (2003) Hospital consolidation and costs: another look at the evidence. *Journal of Health Economics*, 22, 983–97.

—— and LUDWICK, R. (1999) Competition and pricing by nonprofit hospitals: a reassessment of Lynk's analysis. *Journal of Health Economics*, 18, 87–98.

—— and SATTERTHWAITE, M. A. (2000) The industrial organization of health care markets. In A. J. Culyer and J. P. Newhouse (eds.), *Handbook of Health Economics*. Amsterdam: North Holland.

—— KESSLER, D., MCCLELLAN, M., and SATTERTHWAITE, M. (2003) Is more information better? The effects of "Report cards" on health care providers. *Journal of Political Economy*, 111, 555–88.

—— LINDROOTH, R., WHITE, W. D., and ZWANZIGER, J. (2008) Is the impact of managed care on hospital prices decreasing? *Journal of Health Economics*, 27, 362–76.

DUSHEIKO, M., GRAVELLE, H., and JACOBS, R. (2004) The effect of practice budgets on patient waiting times: allowing for selection bias. *Health Economics*, 13, 941–58.

ELLIS, R. P. (1998) Creaming, skimping and dumping: provider competition on the intensive and extensive margins. *Journal of Health Economics*, 17, 537–55.

ESCARCE, J., VAN HORN, R. L., PAULY, M. V., WILLIAMS, S. V., SHEA, J. A., and CHEN, W. (1999) Health maintenance organizations and hospital quality for coronary artery bypass surgery. *Medical Care Research and Review*, 56, 340–62.

FEDERAL TRADE COMMISSION and DEPARTMENT OF JUSTICE (2004) *Improving Health Care: A Dose of Competition*. Washington, DC: Federal Trade Commission and Department of Justice.

FELDMAN, R., CHAN, H. C., KRALEWSKI, J., DOWD, B., and SHAPIRO, J. (1990) Effects of HMOS on the creation of competitive markets for hospital services. *Journal of Health Economics*, 9, 207–22.

FERRIER, G. D., and VALDMANIS, V. G. (2004) Do mergers improve hospital productivity? *Journal of the Operational Research Society*, 55, 1071–80.

GASKIN, D. J., and HADLEY, J. (1997) The impact of HMO penetration on the rate of hospital cost inflation, 1985–1993. *Inquiry—the Journal of Health Care Organization Provision and Financing*, 34, 205–16.

—— ESCARCE, J. J., SCHULMAN, K., and HADLEY, J. (2002) The determinants of HMOs' contracting with hospitals for bypass surgery. *Health Services Research*, 37, 963–84.

GAULD, R. D. C. (2000) Big bang and the policy prescription: Health care meets the market in New Zealand. *Journal of Health Politics Policy and Law*, 25, 815–44.

GAYNOR, M. (2004) Competition and quality in health care markets: what do we know, what don't we know? Paper commissioned by the Federal Trade Commission. Mimeo, Department of Public Policy, Carnegie Mellon University, Pittsburgh.

—— and HAAS-WILSON, D. (1999) Change, consolidation, and competition in health care markets. *Journal of Economic Perspectives*, 13, 141–64.

—— and VOGT, W. B. (2003) Competition among hospitals. *RAND Journal of Economics*, 34, 764–85.

—— (2000) Antitrust and Competition in Health Care Markets. In A. J. Culyer and J. P. Newhouse (eds.), *Handbook of Health Economics*. Amsterdam: North Holland.

GERDTHAM, U. G., LOTHGREN, M., TAMBOUR, M., and REHNBERG, C. (1999) Internal markets and health care efficiency: A multiple-output stochastic frontier analysis. *Health Economics*, 8, 151–64.

GOWRISANKARAN, G., and TOWN, R. J. (2003) Competition, payers, and hospital quality. *Health Services Research*, 38, 1403–21.

GRUBER, J. (1992) The effect of price shopping in medical markets: hospital responses to PPOs in California. NBER Working Paper 4190, Cambridge, MA.

HÅKANSSON, S. (2000) Productivity changes after introduction of prospective hospital payments in Sweden. *Casemix*, 2(2), 47–57.

HANNAN, E. L., KILBURN, H., RACZ, M., SHIELDS, E., and CHASSIN, M. R. (1994) Improving the outcomes of coronary-artery bypass-surgery in New York State. *Journal of the American Medical Association*, 271, 761–6.

HARRISON, T. D. (2007) Consolidations and closures: An empirical analysis of exits from the hospital industry. *Health Economics*, 16, 457–74.

HEIDENREICH, P. A., MCCLELLAN, M., FRANCES, C., and BAKER, L. C. (2002) The relation between managed care market share and the treatment of elderly fee-for-service patients with myocardial infarction. *American Journal of Medicine*, 112, 176–82.

HO, V., and HAMILTON, B. H. (2000) Hospital mergers and acquisitions: does market consolidation harm patients? *Journal of Health Economics*, 19, 767–91.

HUCKMAN, R. S. (2006) Hospital integration and vertical consolidation: An analysis of acquisitions in New York State. *Journal of Health Economics*, 25, 58–80.

JOSKOW, P. L. (1980) The effects of competition and regulation on hospital bed supply and the reservation quality of the hospital. *Bell Journal of Economics*, 11, 421–47.

KASTBERG, G., and SIVERBO, S. (2007) Activity-based financing of health care: experiences from Sweden. *International Journal of Health Planning and Management*, 22, 25–44.

KEELER, E. B., MELNICK, G., and ZWANZIGER, J. (1999) The changing effects of competition on non-profit and for-profit hospital pricing behavior. *Journal of Health Economics*, 18, 69–86.

KESSLER, D. P., and GEPPERT, J. J. (2005) The effects of competition on variation in the quality and cost of medical care. *Journal of Economics and Management Strategy*, 14, 575–89.

—— and MCCLELLAN, M. B. (2000) Is hospital competition socially wasteful? *Quarterly Journal of Economics*, 115, 577–615.

LE GRAND, J. (1999) Competition, cooperation, or control? Tales from the British National Health Service. *Health Affairs*, 18, 27–39.

MARSHALL, M. (2002) The publication of performance data in the National Health Service. NHS research paper. <http://www.chi.nhs.uk/eng/ratings/academic_papers/index.shtml>.

MATSAGANIS, M., and GLENNERSTER, H. (1994) The threat of cream skimming in the post-reform NHS. *Journal of Health Economics*, 13, 31–60.

MELNICK, G. A., ZWANZIGER, J., BAMEZAI, A., and PATTISON, R. (1992) The effects of market-structure and bargaining position on hospital prices. *Journal of Health Economics*, 11, 217–33.

MUKAMEL, D. B., MUSHLIN, A. I., WEIMER, D., ZWANZIGER, J., PARKER, T., and INDRIDASON, I. (2000) Do quality report cards play a role in HMOs' contracting practices? Evidence from New York State. *Health Services Research*, 35, 319–32.

—— ZWANZIGER, J., and TOMASZEWSKI, K. J. (2001) HMO penetration, competition, and risk-adjusted hospital mortality. *Health Services Research*, 36, 1019–35.

NOETHER, M. (1988) Competition among Hospitals. *Journal of Health Economics*, 7, 259–84.

PROPPER, C. (1996) Market structure and prices: The responses of hospitals in the UK National Health Service to competition. *Journal of Public Economics*, 61, 307–35.

—— and WILSON, D. (2003) The use and usefulness of performance measures in the public sector. *Oxford Review of Economic Policy*, 19, 250–67.

—— —— (2006) The use of performance measures in health care systems. *The Elgar Companion to Health Economics*. Cheltenham: Edward Elgar, 326–34.

—— —— and SODERLUND, N. (1998) The effects of regulation and competition in the NHS internal market: the case of general practice fundholder prices. *Journal of Health Economics*, 17, 645–73.

—— CROXSON, B., and SHEARER, A. (2002) Waiting times for hospital admissions: the impact of GP fundholding. *Journal of Health Economics*, 21, 227–52.

—— BURGESS, S., and GREEN, K. (2004) Does competition between hospitals improve the quality of care? Hospital death rates and the NHS internal market. *Journal of Public Economics*, 88, 1247–72.

—— —— and GOSSAGE, D. (2008) Competition and quality: Evidence from the NHS internal market 1991–99. *Economic Journal*, 118, 138–70.

RAINWATER, J. A., and ROMANO, P. S. (2003) What data do California HMOs use to select hospitals for contracting? *American Journal of Managed Care*, 9, 553–61.

ROBINSON, J. C. (1991) HMO market penetration and hospital cost inflation in California. *Journal of the American Medical Association*, 266, 2719–23.

—— and LUFT, H. S. (1985) The impact of hospital market-structure on patient volume, average length of stay, and the cost of care. *Journal of Health Economics*, 4, 333–56.

ROGOWSKI, J., JAIN, A. K., and ESCARCE, J. J. (2007) Hospital competition, managed care, and mortality after hospitalization for medical conditions in California. *Health Services Research*, 42, 682–705.

SARI, N. (2002) Do competition and managed care improve quality? *Health Economics*, 11, 571–84.

SCHULMAN, K. A., RUBENSTEIN, L. E., SEILS, D. M., HARRIS, M., HADLEY, J., and ESCARCE, J. J. (1997) Quality assessment in contracting for tertiary care services by HMOs: A case study of three markets. *Joint Commission Journal on Quality Improvement*, 23, 117–27.

SHEN, Y. C. (2003) The effect of financial pressure on the quality of care in hospitals. *Journal of Health Economics*, 22, 243–69.

SHORTELL, S. M., and HUGHES, E. F. X. (1988) The effects of regulation, competition, and ownership on mortality-rates among hospital inpatients. *New England Journal of Medicine*, 318, 1100–7.

SICILIANI, L., and MARTIN, S. (2007) An empirical analysis of the impact of choice on waiting times. *Health Economics*, 16, 763–79.

SLOAN, F. A. (2000) Not-for-profit ownership and hospital behavior. In A. J. Culyer and J. P. Newhouse (eds.), *Handbook of Health Economics*. Amsterdam: North Holland.

SMITH, P. (1995) On the unintended consequences of publishing performance data in the public sector. *International Journal of Public Administration*, 18, 277–310.

SÖDERLUND, N., CSABA, I., GRAY, A., MILNE, R., and RAFTERY, J. (1997) The impact of the NHS reforms on English hospital productivity: an analysis of the first three years. *British Medical Joural*, 315, 1126.

VOLPP, K. G. M., WILLIAMS, S. V., WALDFOGEL, J., SILBER, J. H., SCHWARTZ, J. S., and PAULY, M. V. (2003) Market reform in New Jersey and the effect on mortality from acute myocardial infarction. *Health Services Research*, 38, 515–33.

WILLIAMS, J., and ROSSITER, A. (2004) *Choice: the evidence*. London: Social Market Foundation.

YOUNG, G. J., BURGESS, J. F., and VALLEY, D. (2002) Competition among hospitals for HMO business: Effect of price and nonprice attributes. *Health Services Research*, 37, 1267–89.

ZWANZIGER, J., and MELNICK, G. A. (1988) The Effects of Hospital Competition and the Medicare PPS Program on Hospital Cost Behavior in California. *Journal of Health Economics*, 7, 301–20.

CHAPTER 29

....

MEASURING ORGANIZATIONAL PERFORMANCE

....

JAMES F. BURGESS JR. AND ANDREW STREET

29.1 Conceptual Framework

29.1.1 Introduction

ORGANIZATIONS that operate in regulated settings, such as the health sector, are not free to do as they please. But it would be naïve to expect them to do exactly as they are told. Performance measurement in the health sector has developed largely to assess whether organizations are, indeed, acting in accordance with what is desired of them.

But the analytical task is not at all straightforward, for some fairly fundamental reasons—none of which is unique to the health sector, but all of which have health care contextual nuances. First, health care organizations usually serve many "masters." For instance, while hospitals will be answerable to their shareholders or stakeholders, they will also have to satisfy regulatory requirements established by different tiers of government, contractual requirements agreed with third-party payers, obligations to professional and voluntary oversight bodies, and the needs of the patients they serve. These "masters" will have different expectations about what the organization is supposed to achieve and, therefore, different conceptions of what constitutes good performance. It would seem obvious that measurement of organizational performance requires a clear statement about the standards under which the organizational units are to be evaluated. But, while inevitably standards will be context-specific, in analytical practice and particularly in the organizational performance literature, these standards are rarely made explicit. In what follows, for expository purposes we shall consider the evaluation of organizations operating in a regulated context, so that they face a single "master" (or principal), this being a regulatory authority charged with maximizing social welfare. A general form of this principal's objective function will be discussed in section 29.1.2.

Second, health care organizations are charged with pursuing many different objectives. This means that performance cannot be readily reduced to a single dimension, such as "profit" or "rate of return" that is the common for-profit metric. Financial performance may well be important, but health care organizations also are concerned about how many and which patients they treat, that patients are treated with dignity and respect, the morale and coordinated effort of their staff, and their standing in the local community, among a host of other things. These concerns are likely to be inter-related but in a complex manner: while some objectives may be complementary, others may be subject to trade-off. For example, while treating more patients may enhance the regard with which the organization is held locally, staff morale and quality may suffer in the face of resource constraints. Moreover, organizations may have different views to their principals about the relative importance to be placed on each objective.

Third, the amount of effort required to meet these objectives will be a source of contention between the principal and organizations tasked with meeting them. Organizations would prefer to limit their effort because it is costly to work harder or seek ways of becoming more efficient, possibly balanced by their degree of altruism which will moderate effort minimization. But the principal would like organizations to maximize their effort consistently regardless of the degree of altruism, because this will contribute directly to higher performance for all. Moreover, in a way that is specific, though not unique, to the health care context, teamwork in organizational performance is required to meet the principal's objectives. It is not a matter of simply making physicians, nurses, managers, and others work harder, but to work smarter and in a more coordinated manner. This issue is considered more in a companion chapter (Barros and Olivella Chapter 19, this volume), so here we simply observe that to motivate organizations to exert more effort than they otherwise would, the principal needs to reward them in some way. One option would be to link rewards directly to the amount of effort exerted. The general problem that effort is unobservable or, at least, extremely costly to observe is augmented by the difficulty in measuring effort in coordination. The alternative is to link rewards to the level of performance achieved. The problem here is that observed performance is a function not only of how much effort is exerted but also of the environment in which the organization operates. The techniques to measure organizational performance have been developed specifically in an attempt to disentangle the relative contributions of effort and environment to observed performance and to find the right level within the organization at which to focus the incentives. The trade-off here is between trying to motivate performance at the organizational level while realizing that this might distort incentives within the organization especially in view of the complexities of trying to motivate performance of staff working within the organization (Bokhour et al. 2006; Barros and Olivella 2009).

We approach organizational performance measurement by first formulating a principal–agent model in which a regulator (principal) delegates responsibility to health care organizations (agents) to advance a subset of overall health sector objectives. The performance of these organizations is then assessed in relation to the objectives that have been set. But the measurement of performance is complex, not least because it is intimately bound up with effort which, as noted above, is difficult to observe. In what follows we use the term "efficiency" in a fairly narrow economic sense whereby the level of achievement is related to the resources employed in the production process. Both effort and efficiency have to be estimated indirectly, after taking account of measurable phenomena, such as inputs, outputs, and constraints on the production process. We consider four issues fundamental to the development of an efficiency model in an economic context, asking what the appropriate unit of analysis is, what the relevant system outputs are, what inputs are used in the production of these particular outputs are and what constraints on the production process are faced. We emphasize again that these answers must be specific to a particular objective or set of objectives. This is followed by a review of the main analytical techniques used to assess efficiency in that context, namely stochastic frontier analysis and data envelopment analysis. We conclude that, despite the challenges in measuring and comparing organizational performance, considerable analytical advances allow greater confidence to be placed in the results of analysis. Applying these results in a policy context in such a way that improvements in organizational performance will be engendered requires design of a suitably powered incentive regime.

29.1.2 The Evaluative Context

A simple principal–agent framework can be employed to describe the relationship between the principal (regulator, insurance company, or other body with organizational oversight) and health care organizations (as agents). Let us assume that the principal acts benevolently, aiming to further those objectives that improve social welfare. In the health sector, the primary objective may be to improve the health of the population, but other concerns may be relevant. For instance, regulators are often concerned with both the level of population health and with the distribution of health among the population. Similarly the principal may be concerned both with benefits enjoyed by those that make use of the health system (consumer surplus) and those that work for it (producer surplus). Meeting distributional concerns and pursuing overall social welfare may have implications on how organizational performance should be assessed, issues to which we shall return in due course.

Assume for the moment that the principal is concerned about the amount of health care output produced from finite resources. We shall consider the nature of outputs in more detail in section 29.2.2, but for the sake of exposition we suppose output consists of the number of patients treated and the quality of their treatment. The principal contracts with health care organizations, specifying the output required and the payment arrangements. This means that the principal does not need to be directly concerned with the production process itself. Instead it is left to these health care organizations to organize production in such a way that they meet their contractual obligations subject to the payment schedule faced. The principal's problems, though, are first to design an optimal contract and second to monitor whether it has been fulfilled. This is not straightforward because the principal is likely to suffer two informational disadvantages relative to health care organizations (Laffont and Tirole 1993).

First, the principal will be less well-informed than the health care organization with respect to the production function. This is because the organization will have private information about how best to organize production, such as the optimal labor and capital mix and the appropriate scale of production. The organization also will be better informed about the nature and influence of environmental (or exogenous) factors on the cost of production. Specifically to the health care example, the costs of coordinating across the factors of production, especially as they address widely varying patient complexity and needs, will be among the most difficult to assess. Second, the principal will be unable to observe accurately the endogenous actions of the organization, notably the level of effort expended, again both by specific individuals and in teamwork or coordination across staff.

One way for the principal to reduce its information deficit is, obviously, to gather information (Laffont and Tirole 1993). But, in addition to information about the agent's characteristics, this demand extends to information about other organizations in similar circumstances. The value of comparative information has long been established. Holmström demonstrates that it is always optimal to make pay contingent upon information about common or industry variations, as it reduces the chance of wrongly rewarding poor effort and wrongly penalizing high effort (Holmström 1979). Holmström suggests that an average of the correlated measures of similar firms will be a sufficient summary of the relevant information for the firm's contract, allowing common uncertainty shared with other firms to be filtered out of each firm's contract (Holmström 1982).

A similar argument underpins Shleifer's proposal for "yardstick competition"—or relative performance evaluation—of organizations that face limited competitive pressure (Shleifer 1985). Shleifer presents yardstick competition as a form of price regulation designed to enable regulators of local monopolies to exert downward pressure on costs by simulating the incentives of competition in situations where actual competition is unlikely to emerge. Under this proposal, the regulated price is based on costs observed in all organizations within the same industry, not just on each individual organization's costs because this information allows the principal to infer more about the conditions within the industry and about the level of effort behind each particular organization's cost level. To be able to reduce information asymmetry in this way, either organizations must be identical (which is extremely unlikely) or differences in their operating conditions must be taken into account systematically. If not, differences in observed costs will not be a good signal of effort but may well be related to exogenous idiosyncratic factors over which the organizations have little control. Where organizations or their environments are heterogeneous, Shleifer argues for "reduced-form" regulation using regression analysis to control for exogenous characteristics. In essence, this is analogous to the approach taken to measuring organization performance by economists. This involves defining the organization, what it produces, what inputs it employs, and what production constraints it faces. We turn to these matters in the next section.

29.2 MODELING THE PRODUCTION PROCESS FOR ORGANIZATIONAL PERFORMANCE OR "EFFICIENCY"

29.2.1 Unit of Analysis

The boundaries of any organizational performance or efficiency analysis must be clearly defined. A fundamental question to ask is: what is the unit of organization in which we are interested? Any efficiency analysis should be examining a single analytically defined entity in a straightforward manner, while also recognizing that its achievements are likely to be influenced by the actions or constraints imposed by other organizations or factors beyond its immediate control. When multiple agencies or organizations are involved in joint production these concerns are especially likely to affect analytical choices. Three criteria should guide the choice of analytical unit:

- First, the unit of analysis should capture the entire production process of interest.
- Second, their function should be to convert inputs into outputs using some measurable definition of those terms, and they should have discretion about the technological process by which this conversion takes place.
- Third, the units comprising the analytical sample should be comparable, particularly in the sense that they are seeking to produce the same set of outputs as defined by the analyst.

The complexity of the production process in health care, as modeled by the choices of the analyst, does not make defining this comparative set of units straightforward. The production of the majority of health care outputs rarely conforms to a production-line type technology, where a set of clearly identifiable inputs are used to produce a standard type of output. Rather than a production line, the majority of health care is tailor-made to the specific needs of the individual recipient (Harris 1977). Thus, the analytic process and variables must be defined concretely within a varying set of perceived outputs and production processes as seen by the organization.

29.2.2 Outputs

Defining, measuring, and valuing the outputs of the health sector and its constituent organizations is a challenge for three main reasons.

First, health care is not demanded for its own sake but for its contribution to health. This contribution is not measured on a routine basis, except through the use of mortality data. The instruments available to measure the change in health status resulting from contact with the health system are usually applied only in clinical trial settings, with organizations rarely collecting information for (the much greater majority of) patients not enrolled in trials. There are some exceptions, and signs that routine health status measurement may become a feature of future health policy (Vallance-Owen et al. 2004, Department of Health 2007), which may allow such information to feature in efficiency analyses.

In the absence of this information, intermediate measures of output are adopted, but these should be related to positive health outcomes in a plausible manner. The obvious candidate output measure is some count of the number of patients. This measure is consistent with hospital reimbursement policy which, in most countries, has moved toward activity-based funding, whereby payments are made in line with the number of patients treated making allowance for expected differences in care requirements by differentiating patients using Diagnosis Related Groups (DRGs) or variants thereof. Consistent with these funding arrangements, more efficient hospitals are those that treat more DRG-weighted patients for a given amount of input.

Describing and categorizing patients who receive care in non-hospital settings is more difficult. This is largely because such patients are highly heterogeneous, defying classification in the face of diagnostic uncertainty or multiple diagnoses, non-medical factors that drive care requirements, and chronic or terminal conditions for which care is likely to be required for an indefinite period. As a consequence, funding of such services on the basis of activity is uncommon, with population- or capitation-based funding of services being a common alternative. Unsurprisingly, efficiency analysis of providers of these services are often constrained by a lack of data on what funds are used for, but there are some notable exceptions (Alexander et al. 1998; Giuffrida 1999; Farsi et al. 2005).

The second challenge to assessing the efficiency of health care organizations in producing output is that they rarely act in isolation. Much of the output of the health system is the result of joint production, with different service providers assuming responsibility for the patient at different stages of the (sometimes lengthy) care pathway. Transfer of responsibility at the requisite time probably has more to do with the altruistic desire of providers to act in the patient's interest than to the financial incentives they face, but poorly designed funding arrangements can thwart such altruism by encouraging cost shifting. Efficiency analyses need to be aware of this possibility in order to avoid drawing false conclusions. Is a short length of stay evidence of better organization within the hospital or the result of "quicker and sicker" discharging of patients that shifts costs onto the next set of providers along the care pathway? Hence our recommendation that the unit of analysis should capture the entire production process of interest.

The third challenge arises because organizations often produce various types of output as they pursue multiple objectives, which may be imposed by the organization's stakeholders, and which were summarized as the quantity and quality vectors in the principal's objective function in section 29.1.2. This is a general problem and various solutions have been proposed. The balanced scorecard, for instance, has proven particularly appealing to commercial organizations wishing to assess how progress against intermediate objectives advances their ultimate objective (to maximize profit) as a way of focusing limited managerial attention time to priorities (Kaplan and Norton 1992). Non-profit organizations typically lack such an obvious ultimate objective and have to decide what weight (value) to attach to different objectives and which should take priority should they be in conflict. Even for-profit health care organizations are unlikely to pursue profit maximization to the exclusion of other considerations. What types of output should take precedence and what objectives prioritized will depend on a complex interplay of factors, most notably the incentives the organization faces (e.g. how it is paid and what public reporting requirements it faces) and the internal balance of power, particularly between managers and clinicians (Newhouse 1970; Harris 1977; Crilly and Le Grand 2004).

One way to prioritize different objectives would be according to their respective contributions to enhancing health outcomes but, as noted, this information is not routinely available. Or the weights might reflect the principal's values, when these are available, such as in the form of regulated prices (which are usually based on production costs). But these values are not always made explicit either.

In the absence of an externally generated set of weights with which to establish priorities, the vast majority of efficiency analyses instead infer values from observed organizational behavior. Indeed, some see this as an attractive feature of the methods (Cooper et al. 2000). This means that such analyses are limited to evaluating the differential effort that organizations exert in the pursuit of objectives and do not explore whether there is divergence between principal and agent in their respective values.

29.2.3 Inputs

Classical formulations of the production function consider two inputs, labor and capital. Labor inputs to the production of health care take many forms, with the likes of paramedics, receptionists, doctors, nurses, porters, cleaners, administrators, and even alternative medicine providers such as acupuncturists and chiropractors all contributing in various ways to the care process. If there is interest in evaluating the contribution of specific types of labor to the production process or in exploring substitution possibilities among types of labor these inputs can be entered as distinct categories in the efficiency model. For instance, there may be debate surrounding the effectiveness of particular health providers and ability may well vary by individual. The individual variation may be the most important factor in determining health status outcomes as well, as one-size-fits-all standards of care may be easy to measure, but not social welfare maximizing. Determining individual contributions is further complicated because some labor inputs contribute directly to services and health while others operate in supporting roles. Understanding the underlying production process is the key to solving these conundrums.

There also is a price to such a disaggregated formulation, the dangers being under-estimation of the full resource commitment and biased estimates of organizational efficiency. Under-counting of the staffing complement is more likely for organizations that rely more heavily on agency staff or sub-contract from other providers than for those that employ staff directly. When organizations have adopted different contractual arrangements, a single measure of input in the form of total expenditure may be preferable.

Accounting for most non-labor inputs into the production process is reasonably straightforward, and many organizations have information systems that capture the resource use for individual patients, particularly if this information is required for billing purposes. However, allowing for capital, which is usually defined as having a useful life of more than one year, brings with it an additional challenge: how to attribute its use to any particular period. This challenge holds irrespective of whether capital is measured in terms of physical stock or by using a measure of rental cost. Imprecise attribution can lead to incorrect inferences about relative efficiency, particularly if some organizations draw more heavily on their inheritance while others make more substantial current investments in their capital stock in the hope of boosting future output.

29.2.4 Political and Environmental Constraints

In many health systems the constituent organizations face restrictions about where they can locate and what they can do, which means they cannot reduce costs simply by relocating to an area with lower input prices or by being selective about which types of patient they treat. These constraints might limit the amount of output that can be produced for a given level of input. In effect, the production possibility frontiers for some organizations will lie inside those of organizations operating in more favorable circumstances. Other constraining effects include mission (e.g. teaching obligations), community environmental standards (e.g. pollution), and varying jurisdictional political attitudes toward the balance between regulation and competition. There are three ways to account for these constraints.

First, comparisons can be limited to organizations operating in similar circumstances. This is at the expense of a reduced sample size and means that insights that might have been gained from considering a more heterogeneous sample will be lost and analytical power may be lacking. For example, this is frequently done by considering analytic units in one region at a time or by considering (e.g.) teaching and non-teaching facilities separately, but even analyzing the entire population of existing units may be too limited a sample size to make sound conclusions.

Second, variables could be subject to some form of conditioning or risk adjustment prior to their inclusion in the efficiency model. This is commonly applied when considering the different types of patients that hospitals treat. Rather than a separate variable for patients in each DRG, for instance, a single composite variable is constructed by weighting patients according to their expected resource requirements (Harper et al. 2001).

Third, the constraining factors can be entered directly into the efficiency model, in a fashion analogous to control variables in standard econometric practice. These constraints should be entered directly into the production process in a single stage estimation (Battese and Coelli 1995). There is a long-standing—but mistaken—tradition of going about this as a two-stage process, with some form of production function first estimated in order to derive organizational estimates of "efficiency." The "efficiency" estimates are then regressed against the set of constraining factors. As well as being mislabeled, these "efficiency" estimates are not independent observations, which means that second stage estimates will be biased.

29.3 ANALYTICAL TECHNIQUES

Analysis of the efficiency with which organizations convert inputs into outputs is not straightforward because the optimal production process is unobservable to the analyst. Indeed, the organizations themselves may not know the best way to organize production, and in the short term may have to "make do" with their current staffing structure and capital configuration, occasionally changing processes and effort allocations in the hope that this will improve matters. These alterations may involve re-specifying staff contracts, investing in new equipment, refocusing effort into a particular process, or wholesale departmental restructuring. In some sectors, changes to working practices or the working environment seem to be a perpetual state of affairs, suggesting that organizations are "muddling through" rather than having a clear idea of what constitutes their optimum strategy or "best practice." However, it should be noted that if the contextual issues we have emphasized are really important, true best practice only would be transferrable between quite similar organizations and environments. This makes identification of what needs to be transferred difficult, especially for heterogeneous health care organizations.

As well as being more ignorant than the organizations themselves about the optimal production process, the analyst also lacks information about the specific arrangements in each organization. Instead, information is usually limited to what inputs are employed in the production process and what outputs are produced. But, crucially, this information is often available for a number of organizations in the same line of business, which allows the analyst to undertake comparative analysis. The analyst's supposition is that organizations that produce a higher level of output for a given amount of input are more productive: they have a higher ratio output to input than other organizations. Organizations are defined as being "technically efficient" if they produce the maximum level of output that can be produced for a given amount of input under the prevailing technological process. In addition, an organization is "allocatively efficient" if it produces the maximum level of output possible using the cheapest mix of inputs given their relative prices.

The most commonly used forms of comparative analysis are data envelopment analysis (DEA) and stochastic frontier analysis (SFA). These differ in two fundamental respects: first, in how they position and shape the (unobservable) best practice production frontier and, second, in how they interpret deviations from this frontier. These differences are illustrated in the two figures below for an industry employing a single type of input (measured along the x axis) to produce a single type of output (on the y axis). The points indicate the input–output combinations for each organization in the industry.

The DEA frontier representation of best practice in Figure 29.1 is positioned by the organizations with the highest observed output : input ratios, so that the frontier "envelops" the other organizations in the sample. The inefficiency of each organization is measured by its vertical distance from the frontier.

Many regard this highly deterministic interpretation of the distance as problematic and prefer SFA because it acknowledges the possibility of measurement or modeling error in individual observations. The history of the DEA method comes out of an engineering perspective that assumes accurate measurement while the SFA approach was devised by econometricians attempting to extend error distribution theory. The SFA frontier (Figure 29.2) then is shaped according to an econometric model specifying the nature of the production process and is positioned after incorporating classical error assumptions. This means that the production frontier may not pass through the extreme uppermost observation(s) and that the vertical distance of each organization from the frontier captures a mixture of inefficiency and error.

We do not attempt to exhaustively review the literature, which others have done (Worthington 2004; Hollingsworth 2008; Rosko and Mutter 2008), but instead draw attention to various advances made in applying these techniques. We describe four particularly

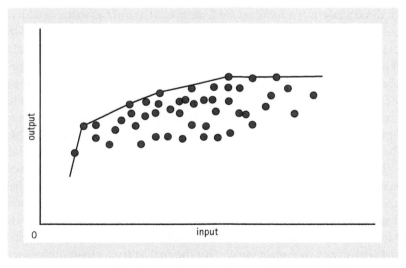

FIGURE 29.1 Production frontier: data envelopment analysis

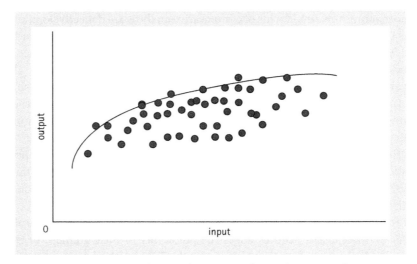

FIGURE 29.2 Production frontier: stochastic frontier analysis

important innovations for this context: analysis of efficiency change over time; allowance for quality; consideration of multiple objectives; and use of patient-level data.

A long-standing comparative advantage of DEA over SFA has been the relative ease with which it has been possible to analyze efficiency change—conditional, of course, upon having robust, measurable data generating processes about organizations over several time periods. The Malmquist index is used to measure the distance the DEA frontier moves from one period to the next and attributes some of this change to general technical improvements and the remainder to changes in efficiency (Malmquist 1953; Caves et al. 1982).

Longitudinal analysis is a more recent feature of SFA and has witnessed an evolution over three generations of models. The first generation of SFA models applied the standard panel data model but, instead of simply supposing that the organizational (fixed or random) effect captured unobservable organizational characteristics, interpreted this effect as being entirely due to a level of inefficiency that did not vary over time (Pitt and Lee 1981; Schmidt and Sickles 1984). The second generation of models allowed for changes in efficiency for the industry as a whole (Greene 1993) and for each organization (Kumbhakar 1990; Battese and Coelli 1992), analogous to the DEA Malmquist index. The third generation of models separates the organizational effects into unobservable characteristics and efficiency, and are thereby true to the original motivation behind standard panel data models (Farsi et al. 2005; Greene 2004, 2005). These "true" models tend to be hard to estimate, though, as they rely on substantial temporal variation and sufficient local data density which is often lacking in the data. This feature of progress in this field, where increased model complexity requires exponential increases in local data density, creates great tension for the analyst trying to optimize method and dimensionality against the limitations of the data.

The next innovation is to recognize that both quantity and quality matter. While there have been a number of important theoretical expositions that explore organizational behavior in relation to the quantity and quality of health care (Pope 1989; Hodgkin and McGuire 1994; Chalkley and Malcomson 2000), empirical analyses have been limited by inadequate data on quality. This is changing as information about the quality of output becomes more readily available. A number of studies have considered in-hospital mortality and readmissions as markers for quality (Carey and Burgess 1999; Rosko 2001; McKay and Deily 2008), others have used process measures such as waiting times (Yaisawarng and Burgess 2006). Such studies are welcome because improvements in quality are likely to be an increasingly important driver of patient utility and to overlook these contributions would be to underestimate productivity gains in health care (Cutler and Huckman 2003; Castelli et al. 2007). Models that incorporate quality measures are likely to feature more prominently in future.

DEA holds a comparative advantage over SFA in being able to incorporate multiple outputs in a straightforward manner. Even so, despite heroic efforts to do so (Olesen and Petersen 2002) the great diversity of activities in the health care sector generally prohibits each output being individually specified, even if patients can be classified in some way. This rules out using these frontier techniques for price setting purposes (Newhouse 1994). Not that this would be sensible anyway, because the output weights/parameter estimates would merely reflect "most favorable" weights (in DEA) or sample averages (in SFA), neither of which have a particular claim as a basis for price setting (Smith and Street 2005). Many jurisdictions that have adopted activity based funding regimes have well-established price setting processes, and these prices can be used as weights to aggregate multiple outputs into a single index capturing the quantity of patients treated, adjusting for differences in case-mix (Burgess and Wilson 1998; Harper et al. 2001).

But as well as treating patients, health care organizations are often tasked with pursuing other objectives, such as offering short waiting times prior to hospital admission, enhancing patient experience, and exercising cost control. Unlike DEA, SFA models have struggled to analyze simultaneous pursuit of these multiple objectives. However, the use of seemingly unrelated regression (SUR) techniques is a promising way forward, where a set of performance equations is estimated simultaneously allowing for covariance across equations. The SUR approach models covariance by incorporating a latent variable which can be interpreted as an unmeasured organizational effect on performance (Jacobs 2001; Hauck and Street 2006).

The use of hierarchical (especially patient-level) data is probably where most significant analytical gains are to be made, and in this respect SFA beats DEA hands down in being able to exploit such information. Unlike many industries, but like the education sector, most health systems collect detailed information about each and every member of the public they serve and about the nature of the service provided. Rarely has this wealth of information been used in efficiency analyses, which tend to rely on summarized information aggregated at the unit of analysis. This means that a great deal of salient detail about what each organization is doing is lost to the analyst, information which may be pertinent in making sound comparisons across organizations. Moreover, as noted above, if all patients are different to one degree or another and case mix adjustment has built-in limitations, then capturing and allowing for that variation may be one of the most important goals of an organizational performance model. Most obviously it is possible to control for characteristics of each patient that may have a bearing on costs over and above that recognized by whatever output classification is in use (Olsen and Street 2008). The use of patient-level data also permits robust comparisons to be made when there are a small number of organizations, which is a common problem in many contexts (Olsen and Street 2008). These models interpret the organizational effect as a measure of organizational performance in a manner analogous to first generation panel data models.

A further advantage is that, rather than being forced to use the legal entity (e.g. hospital) as the unit of analysis, patient-level data enables consideration of specific "production lines," where there is likely to be greater standardization in the types of patients treated and activities undertaken. These production lines might be defined as hospital departments or by disease type or condition. The challenge for such analysis is in ensuring correct identification of the significant relative resources devoted to the activity, but as clinical costing systems become more widely adopted and cost allocation processes become more standardized this should become less of a barrier to analysis. Further econometric advances, most likely employing hierarchical methods that correct standard errors for provider, that allow for facility-level clustering or that employ quantile regression techniques (Liu et al. 2008), are already emerging.

29.4 Discussion

29.4.1 Policy Conclusions

Much of the blame for the lack of greater policy use of these methods surely lies with the analysts, who frequently have over-claimed the robustness of their methods in ways that have not helped convince policymakers of their efficacy (Hollingsworth and Street 2006). But this is beginning to change. Recent efforts in the Netherlands (Agrell et al. 2007) and the UK (Jacobs et al. 2006) illustrate that analysts in this area are learning from their previous policy mistakes, trying to account for the balance between analytical effectiveness and simplicity with which policymakers are acutely concerned, and becoming more effective at communicating what these analyses can and cannot do. As we have asserted, though, the main remaining problem is the difficulty in managing multiple goals that policymakers are trying to balance, which is especially difficult when those policymakers are either unwilling or unable to specify detailed loss functions that can be optimized directly.

One way to take the wide ranging set of issues we have raised would be pessimistically, as if there is no hope of producing sound analysis that incorporates all these concerns. But, more optimistically, we believe that awareness of the scope of these concerns allows the analyst to pay careful attention to the context of the needs for measuring and evaluating organizational performance in order to perform nuanced and useful policy analysis. The way to accomplish this task is to exert the analytical effort necessary to understand the true production process in the organizations we are studying by specifying the right inputs, outputs and valuations that reflect their actual locus of control.

Accomplishing these goals requires careful attention to the process of analysis itself. We recommend a structure that moves from conceptual framework, to analytical techniques, to conclusions (Worthington 2004; Jacobs et al. 2006). It also recognizes that there are inherent uncertainties in all of the choices that are made, so sensitivity analysis is essential. After all, when comparing health service organizations, each operating within a unique context, no measurement is ever going to be exact. Using Bayesian, resampling, or other techniques, especially those that explicitly state the loss function from inaccuracy or error, it is possible and desirable to form carefully crafted confidence statements regarding conclusions that are drawn (Fernández et al. 2000; Gravelle et al. 2003). These will reflect an understanding that most managers already possess, that they can alter the moving course of their ships to some degree, but they just do not have the control and property rights over the factors of production to change course instantaneously. Another useful approach, that has been employed in some circumstances, but would benefit policymakers and analysts if they used it more, is to sort or group organizations into more homogeneous groups or clusters using these techniques and measures. Another outcome of the uncertainty, that is analogous to similar issues raised more explicitly in the general health care quality measurement literature, is that true "ranking" of organizations is not stable or supportable statistically (Giuffrida et al. 1999; Huang et al. 2005; Roy and Mor 2005). Many websites and other public reporting of organizational performance measures break facilities into as few as three groups (exceptional, average, low) and admit when power is too limited to make robust comparative statements. This approach frequently has been ridiculed by researchers too enamored of their sophisticated techniques, but there is much folk wisdom and logic in the concept that these methods could vastly improve in execution by having grouping as a goal rather than ranking.

29.4.2 Back to the Principal

As we conclude, it is useful to reflect on the property rights of the organization and the full set of possible multiple objectives that the principal may be considering in regulating or evaluating those health care organizations. For example, if we think of an organization as an entity exerting property rights over factors of production in health services then, as in all property rights models, the key features for social welfare valuation are those that distort the excludability, divisibility and transferability of those factors of production. Variation in professionalism or effort by health professionals is an example. Although sometimes professionals are not even directly employed by the organization, even when they are directly employed they may not view the fruits of their efforts or the process by which they provide services as being under the control of the organization. These sorts of difficulties in evaluating the specific efforts and efficiency of health service organizations themselves are pervasive, complex, and seldom discussed or understood.

Technical efficiency has been the main focus of the preceding discussion and allocative efficiency incorporates the concept of optimization subject to the relative price of inputs. These are concepts where understanding and agreement are relatively widespread, at least among economists.

Less appreciated in analytical treatments is that organizations operate in dynamic contexts, drawing on past investments and planning for the future. Technical change, innovation, and growth in the health sector are ubiquitous, some of which decreases costs, but most of which increases costs with often uncertain and variable effects on health. If we value the role of health service organizations in generating and facilitating these advances and having them as a laboratory for their economic evaluation, we need to take them into account when evaluating performance. Techniques for evaluating dynamic efficiency are not easy to employ and they are heavily dependent on measuring the realization of health benefits when these typically have long and uncertain lags. Nevertheless, evaluation of units with an organizational mandate for researching and testing these advances, such as teaching institutions, must account for balancing these goals.

The potential that equity might be compromised by blind pursuit of efficiency has long been recognized by economists (Wagstaff 1991), though debate has not permeated the literature on performance measurement to any great extent. This is probably because it is rare for the principal to delegate responsibility for pursuing equity objectives down to the organizational level. If these concerns are articulated to organizations, they usually appear in terms of constraints on their behavior. For example, the principal may specify that organizations are to treat patients on the basis of health need instead of ability to pay and that they are not to exercise discriminatory admission policies among patients. But if the principal is concerned with (say) geographical equity it may try to ensure an appropriate geographical spread of health care resources across its jurisdiction—which may involve decisions about where organizations ought to be located when contemplating new capital investments or about which existing organizations it contracts with. Indeed, the principal may tolerate some under-utilization of resources, such as hospitals in remote areas having higher costs because they are required to serve a small catchment population, where economies of scale cannot be realized. This requirement might be controlled for in the assessment organizational performance by including some measure of "remoteness" to capture this environmental constraint.

29.4.3 Incentives

Finally, we turn to the incentive theories that principals need to take account of in considering specific options to achieve particular objectives or combinations of objectives. In essence, all discussion of organizational performance comes back to theories of regulation and control. There are two salient concerns. First, Laffont and Tirole emphasize that we need to choose carefully between high-powered and low-powered incentives (Laffont and Tirole 1993). When quality or other products are measured imperfectly, when we are worried about crowding out individual initiative, or when there are high levels of innovation that are difficult to motivate directly then low-powered incentives are preferred. Each of these conditions is part of the environment we have asserted represents the health care industry in this essay. Second, though, any efforts to resolve these uncertainties and sharpen up the incentive structure have two further effects. First, improving the specificity of the measurement process might itself distort the production process (e.g. imagine what the impact would be of videotaping all clinician–patient encounters and having third parties assess them for payment and efficiency; the first research-oriented looks at this are not encouraging (Tai-Seale et al. 2007). Second, it adds to the dimensionality of a process that ultimately reflects an individual health services delivery experience for each patient (e.g. one of the key choices that must be made by a principal is whether to be provider or patient focused where attempting to be both adds considerable complexity). The final approach to incentives must be balanced, but it must assess unintended consequences of goal setting in focusing too closely on a subset of the universe of goals for patients and principals.

29.4.4 Concluding Comments

Though the balance between regulation and competition in health care markets differs country by country, we have postulated an environment for measuring organizational performance anchored by public goals of improving social welfare. We have emphasized that social welfare has multiple components that may vary in their weights when measuring the performance of particular organizations. Methods currently employed to assess these organizations vary substantially in their data requirements, sensitivities to measurement and the data generating processes, and methodological properties. While the picture we have painted of the measurement process is complex in ways not easily simplified by modeling, we recognize the analytical advances that have been made in this area and remain optimistic about further advances that exploit the wealth of data available in the health sector and that are likely to generate policy-relevant insights into organizational performance.

REFERENCES

AGRELL, P. J., BOGETOFT, P., HALBERSMA, R. & MIKKERS, M. C. (2007) *Yardstick Competition for Multi-product Hospitals: An Analysis of the Proposed Dutch Yardstick Mechanism*, Utrecht, Nederlandse Zorgautoriteit.

ALEXANDER, J. A., WHEELER, J. R. C., NAHRA, T. A. & LEMACK, C. H. (1998) Managed care and technical efficiency in outpatient substance abuse treatment units. *Journal of Behavioural Health Services and Research*, 25, 377–96.

BATTESE, G. & COELLI, T. (1992) Frontier production functions, technical efficiency and panel data: with application to paddy farmers in India. *Journal of Productivity Analysis*, 3, 153–69.

—— —— (1995) A model for technical inefficiency effects in a stochastic frontier production function for panel data. *Empirical Economics*, 20, 325–32.

BOKHOUR, B. G., BURGESS, J. F., HOOK, J. M., et al. (2006) Incentive implementation in physician practices: A qualitative study of practice executives perspectives on pay for performance. *Medical Care Research and Review*, 63, 73S–95.

BURGESS, J. F. & WILSON, P. W. (1998) Variation in inefficiency among US hospitals. *INFOR Canadian Journal of Operational Research and Information Processing*, 36, 84–102.

CAREY, K. & BURGESS, J. F. (1999) On measuring the hospital cost/quality trade-off. *Health Economics*, 8, 509–20.

CASTELLI, A., DAWSON, D., GRAVELLE, H. et al. (2007) A new approach to measuring health system output and productivity. *National Institute Economic Review*, 200, 105–17.

CAVES, D. W., CHRISTENSEN, L. R. & DIEWERT, W. E. (1982) The economic theory of index numbers and the measurement of input, output and productivity. *Econometrica*, 50, 1393–414.

CHALKLEY, M. & MALCOMSON, J. M. (2000) Government purchasing of health services. In A. J. Culyer & J. P. Newhouse (eds.), *Handbook of Health Economics*. Amsterdam, North Holland.

COOPER, W. W., SEIFORD, L. M. & TONE, K. (2000) *Data Envelopment Analysis: A Comprehensive Text with Models, Applications, References and DEA-solver Software*, Boston, Kluwer Academic Publishers.

CRILLY, T. & LE GRAND, J. (2004) The motivation and behaviour of hospital Trusts. *Social Science and Medicine*, 58, 1809–23.

CUTLER, D. M. & HUCKMAN, R. S. (2003) Technological development and medical productivity: the diffusion of angioplasty in New York state. *Journal of Health Economics*, 22, 187–217.

DEPARTMENT OF HEALTH (2007) *Guidance on the Routine Collection of Patient Reported Outcome Measures (PROMs)*, London, Department of Health.

FARSI, M., FILIPPINI, M. & KUENZLE, M. (2005) Unobserved heterogeneity in stochastic frontier models: an application to Swiss nursing homes. *Applied Economics*, 37, 2127–41.

FERNÁNDEZ, C., KOOP, G. & STEEL, M. (2000) A Bayesian analysis of multiple-output production frontiers. *Journal of Econometrics*, 98, 47–79.

GIUFFRIDA, A. (1999) Productivity and efficiency changes in primary care: a Malmquist index approach. *Health Care Management Science*, 2, 11–26.

—— GRAVELLE, H. & ROLAND, M. (1999) Measuring quality of care with routine data: avoiding confusion between performance indicators and health outcomes. *British Medical Journal*, 319, 94–8.

GRAVELLE, H., JACOBS, R., JONES, A. & STREET, A. (2003) Comparing the efficiency of national health systems: econometric analysis should be handled with care. *Applied Health Economics and Health Policy*, 2, 141–7.

GREENE, W. H. (1993) The econometric approach to efficiency analysis. In H. O. Fried, C. A. K. Lovell & S. S. Schmidt (eds.), *The Measurement of Productive Efficiency: Techniques and Applications*. New York, Oxford University Press, 68–119.

—— (2004) Distinguishing between heterogeneity and inefficiency: stochastic frontier analysis of the World Health Organization's panel data on national health care systems. *Health Economics*, 13, 959–80.

—— (2005) Reconsidering heterogeneity in panel data estimators of the stochastic frontier model. *Journal of Econometrics*, 126, 269–303.

HARPER, J., HAUCK, K. & STREET, A. (2001) Analysis of costs and efficiency in general surgery specialties in the United Kingdom. *European Journal of Health Economics*, 2, 150–7.

HARRIS, J. E. (1977) The internal organisation of hospitals: some economic implications. *Bell Journal of Economics*, 8: 467–82.

HAUCK, K. & STREET, A. (2006) Performance assessment in the context of multiple objectives: a multivariate multilevel analysis. *Journal of Health Economics*, 25: 1029–108.

HODGKIN, D. & MCGUIRE, T. G. (1994) Payment levels and hospital response to prospective payment. *Journal of Health Economics*, 13, 1–29.

HOLLINGSWORTH, B. (2008) The measurement of efficiency and productivity of health care delivery. *Health Economics*, 17, 1107–28.

—— & STREET, A. (2006) The market for efficiency analysis of health care organisations. *Health Economics*, 15, 1055–9.

HOLMSTRÖM, B. (1979) Moral hazard and observability. *Bell Journal of Economics*, 10, 74–91.

—— (1982) Moral hazard in teams. *Bell Journal of Economics*, 13, 324–40.

HUANG, I.-C., DOMINICI, F., FRANGAKIS, F., DIETTE, G. B., DAMBERG, C. L. & WU, A. W. (2005) Is risk-adjustor selection more important than statistical approach for provider profiling? Asthma as an example. *Medical Decision Making*, 25, 20–34.

JACOBS, R. (2001) Alternative methods to examine hospital efficiency: data envelopment analysis and stochastic frontier analysis. *Health Care Management Science*, 4, 103–15.

—— SMITH, P. C. & STREET, A. (2006) *Measuring Efficiency in Health Care: Analytical Techniques and Health Policy*, Cambridge, Cambridge University Press.

KAPLAN, R. S. & NORTON, D. P. (1992) The balanced scorecard: measures that drive performance. *Harvard Business Review*, 70: 71–9.

KUMBHAKAR, S. C. (1990) Production frontiers, panel data, and time-varying technical efficiency. *Journal of Econometrics*, 46, 201–11.

LAFFONT, J.-J. & TIROLE, J. (1993) *A Theory of Incentives in Procurement and Regulation*, Cambridge, Massachusetts, The MIT Press.

LIU, C., LAPORTE, A. & FERGUSON, B. S. (2008) The quantile regression approach to efficiency measurement: insights from Monte Carlo simulations. *Health Economics*, 17, 1073–87.

MALMQUIST, S. (1953) Index numbers and indifference surfaces. *Trabajos de Estatistica*, 4, 209–42.

McKAY, N. L. & DEILY, M. E. (2008) Cost inefficiency and hospital health outcomes. *Health Economics*, 17, 833–48.

NEWHOUSE, J. P. (1970) Toward a theory of non-profit institutions: an economic model of a hospital. *American Economic Review*, 60, 64–74.

—— (1994) Frontier analysis: how useful a tool for health economics? *Journal of Health Economics*, 13, 317–22.

OLESEN, O. B. & PETERSEN, N. S. (2002) The use of data envelopment analysis with probabilistic assurance regions for measuring hospital efficiency. *Journal of Productivity Analysis*, 17, 83–109.

OLSEN, K. R. & STREET, A. (2008) The analysis of efficiency among a small number of organisations: how inferences can be improved by exploiting patient-level data. *Health Economics*, 17, 671–81.

PITT, M. M. & LEE, L. F. (1981) The measurement and sources of technical efficiency in the Indonesian weaving industry. *Journal of Development Economics*, 9, 43–64.

POPE, G. C. (1989) Hospital nonprice competition and Medicare reimbursement policy. *Journal of Health Economics*, 8, 147–72.

ROSKO, M. D. (2001) Cost efficiency of US hospitals: a stochastic frontier approach. *Health Economics*, 10, 539–51.

—— & MUTTER, R. L. (2008) Stochastic frontier analysis of hospital inefficiency. *Medical Care Research and Review*, 65, 131–66.

ROY, J. & MOR, V. (2005) The effect of provider-level ascertainment bias on profiling nursing homes. *Statistics in Medicine*, 24, 3609–29.

SCHMIDT, P. & SICKLES, R. C. (1984) Production frontiers and panel data. *Journal of Business and Economic Studies*, 2, 299–326.

SHLEIFER, A. (1985) A theory of yardstick competition. *RAND Journal of Economics*, 16, 319–27.

SMITH, P. C. & STREET, A. (2005) Measuring the efficiency of public services: the limits of analysis. *Journal of the Royal Statistical Society: Series A*, 168, 401–17.

TAI-SEALE, M., McGUIRE, T. G. & ZHANG, W. (2007) Time Allocation in Primary Care Office Visits. *Health Services Research*, 42, 1871–94.

VALLANCE-OWEN, A., CUBBIN, S., WARREN, V. & MATTHEWS, B. (2004) Outcome monitoring to facilitate clinical governance: experience from a national programme in the independent sector. *Journal of Public Health*, 26, 187–92.

WAGSTAFF, A. (1991) QALYs and the equity-efficiency trade-off. *Journal of Health Economics*, 10, 21–41.

WORTHINGTON, A. C. (2004) Frontier efficiency measurement in health care: a review of empirical techniques and selected applications. *Medical Care Research and Review*, 61, 135–69.

YAISAWARNG, S. & BURGESS, J. F. (2006) Performance-based budgeting in the public sector: an illustration from the VA health care system. *Health Economics*, 15, 295–310.

CHAPTER 30

....

HEALTH SYSTEM
PRODUCTIVITY

....

JACK E. TRIPLETT[1]

30.1 INTRODUCTION

....

PRODUCTIVITY is the ratio of outputs to inputs, and productivity growth is the growth of the ratio—that is, it is a shift in a production function. In concept, health system productivity differs little from productivity in any other industry or sector. Though the economics of medical care may in some respects appear unique, production in the sector is still described by a production function, a relation between medical care inputs and output. Productivity change in medical care is a shift in that medical care production function.

However, productivity in the medical care sector has behaved very differently from other industries, even other services industries: Measured productivity growth in medical care has typically been negative. Murray (1992) reported negative labor productivity growth in Swedish hospitals. Triplett and Bosworth (2004, 2007) found negative productivity growth in US medical care between 1987 and 2005, at a rate of about one percent per year, a finding confirmed by Harper et al. (2008). When the UK statistical office added the output of medical care to the country's national accounts, the negative productivity growth implied by the new measure provoked an outcry in Parliament and the appointment of a special commission on public sector services productivity measurement (Atkinson 2005) to determine what was wrong.

Few industries have experienced more innovation, so medical care's negative productivity growth is highly suspect. Economists generally believe that measured productivity growth in the sector is biased downward because of difficulties in measuring medical care output accurately and also that measurement errors are pervasive in some of the inputs, particularly in pharmaceuticals and medical devices and in the high-tech

[1] I appreciate valuable comments from Joseph P. Newhouse, Mary O'Mahoney, and the editors.

portions of medical equipment. In all productivity measurement, the most essential tasks are getting the data right, which provides the agenda for section 30.3 of this chapter. Data on inputs and outputs—indeed, economic data generally—for the health care sector are much less well-developed than for many other sectors of the economy, which is bizarre considering the size of health care in most industrialized countries and the importance of the sector. Many studies of medical care productivity employ data from the national accounts (which are described in Commission of the European Communities et al. 1993), but micro-data studies face the same measurement problems.

Medical care is not the only determinant of health. In section 30.4, I discuss some of the economic implications of the fact that medical care, though it is demanded to improve health, does not, *by itself*, produce health.

30.2 CONCEPTS OF PRODUCTIVITY CHANGE

The conventional framework for any measurement of productivity rests on the production function, in this case for the output of medical care services. The inputs are conventionally notated as KLEMS: capital services, labor services (the vector of all labor inputs, from surgeons to janitors), energy, intermediate or purchased materials (which in this sector includes pharmaceuticals used in hospitals and clinics, stents, and so forth), and purchased services. That is:

$$\text{medical services} = f(\text{K,L,E,M,S}) \tag{1}$$

In equation (1.1) all the variables, including output, should be understood as vectors,[2] the elements of which, however, are usually aggregated for analysis.

The medical care production function in equation (1) implies:

Productivity change (medical care) = growth of medical services/growth in $f(\cdot)$ (2)

Equation (1.2) is known as "multifactor productivity" (MFP) growth. It is also called TFP (total factor productivity), which is a synonym.[3] Productivity change is usually interpreted as a measure of changing efficiency in production, or of technological change, though in practice measurement errors and other inconsistencies limit the validity of this interpretation.

A *partial* productivity measure is "labor productivity" (LP). LP growth is usually calculated as the growth in medical services over the growth in the labor input, which implies the growth of the average product of labor. Properly, LP growth in the medical care sector is:

---

[2] So the usual mathematical convention properly would have: $0 = g(\text{medical services, K,L,E,M,S})$.

[3] The term MFP was introduced in National Research Council (1979) to avoid the implication that equations such as (2) have necessarily enumerated all the inputs. *Measured* productivity change also reflects inputs that have not been accounted for, or not accurately or fully measured.

$$\text{LP (medical care)} = \partial \text{ (medical services)}/\partial \text{ L,} \qquad (3)$$

using equation (1.1), that is, it is the growth of the marginal product of labor. I say little about LP in this chapter because MFP is the more comprehensive measure.

For an alternative perspective, recast the numerator in the productivity ratio to measure the welfare gain that an economic activity produces (Hulten (2001) contrasts the two perspectives). In health *system* productivity, the welfare gain is the improvement in health; it may also encompass aspects of the patients' medical experiences, such as the painfulness of medical procedures, length of waiting times, pleasantness of their encounters with health system personnel, quality of food and amenities in hospitals and so forth. In the rest of this chapter we neglect for brevity elements of the patients' medical encounters, without suggesting that they are unimportant.

The alternative perspective requires an expanded notion of the inputs and resources that contribute to improved health. We posit a relation between a measure of health and the inputs that produce health, or to put it alternatively, the determinants of population health. Thus, in parallel with equation (1), we can write the "health production function":

$$\text{health} = h(\text{medical care, time, consumption, R\&D, environment, etc}). \qquad (4)$$

The inputs in equation (4) include medical care services, the output in equation (1).[4] The non-medical inputs include time spent by people investing in their own health (for example, exercise), as well as consumption items that have health implications (some food, plus tobacco and alcohol, for example), research and development, the quality of the environment, and other influences.

This way of thinking about health—and the relation between medical care and health—was introduced into economics by Grossman (1972), but it is a formalization of relations long known in epidemiology. For example, McKeown (1976) showed that most long-term improvements in health could not be accounted for by medical interventions. Grossman explained that the loss of utility from abstaining from the consumption of pleasurable activities today that (like smoking) have deleterious long-term consequences for health was comparable to individuals' investing in health (Chapter 6, by Bolin).

---

[4] If national accounts *industry* data are used to estimate equation (1), the output domain would normally include the public and private medical care sectors, and therefore the drugs and medical devices provided by those institutions.

The domain would exclude, however, expenditures for drugs and medical devices purchased as final consumption by households (even though those expenditures are included in GDP), because the SNA excludes household production. Equation (1) could be made to match total health care spending in GDP if a household "industry" were added to the domain of equation (1), and households were treated as an additional sector that contributes to the production of medical care. There are other reasons for adding nonmarket production to the national accounts—see Jorgenson, Landefeld, and Nordhaus (2006).

Equation (4) implies an alternative productivity measure, one for the production of health:

$$\text{MFP change (health)} = \text{change in health/change in } h\,(\cdot) \qquad (5)$$

In this case, productivity change can be interpreted as a measure of the efficiency of all of society's resources that are used to produce health. The resources include utility forgone in desisting from the consumption of unhealthy goods and from abandoning the pursuit of unhealthy lifestyles.

A major question in health economics is the value of national expenditures on medical care, which are increasing in nearly all countries (see Chapter 14 by Chernew and May). The proper way to estimate the *productivity of the medical care resources used to improve health* is to make use of equation (4). This task implies a partial productivity measure, which can be expressed as (using Z as the partial measure of productivity, and substituting equation 1 into 4):

$$Z = \partial\,(\text{health})/\partial\ \text{medical care}$$
$$= \partial\,(\text{health})/\partial\ [f\,(\text{KLEMS})] \qquad (6)$$

As with any partial derivative, the value of Z will depend on the values of the other variables in the equation, particularly in the case of health the life style, diet, and environmental variables.

Thus, a nation's health is not a straightforward function of its per capita expenditures on medical care. The contribution of medical services to improved health cannot be established without considering non-medical determinants of health.

For example, substantial US expenditures for blood pressure medication intended to reduce the amount of salt in patients' bodies may just be offsetting the excessive salt added by the US food processing industry, so there may be no net gain in health, relative to societies that consume less salt and fewer medications. And one cannot judge the performance of the UK National Health System by a naïve examination of trends in NHS expenditures and vital statistics. UK health may change because of the other variables in $h(\cdot)$, variables that perhaps have more influence on health than does the National Health Service. Philipson and Posner (2008) present another example when they suggest that the inverse relation between obesity and income is a consequence of a fall in the price of consuming calories and a rise in the cost of exercise (once a costless by-product of manual labor), which the higher-income groups can better afford: Expenditures on medical care then partly offset the negative health impacts of obesity.

One often hears statements such as: The US medical care system must not be efficient or productive because the US does not have the highest health level in the world, even though it has the highest per capita spending on health care. This is a non sequitur, because it does not take into account any other variables in the health function of equation (4). More healthful diets or lifestyles in Japan or Mediterranean countries may give inhabitants of those countries better health with lower inputs of medical care than in the

US. Similarly, regressions of cross-country expenditures on medical care (or similar variables, such as consumption of pharmaceuticals) and levels of health are of little value unless they control for the dependence of health on health-determining factors other than medical care.

30.3 ESTIMATING MEDICAL CARE PRODUCTIVITY

Equation (1.2) can be estimated in a number of ways. One option is econometric (see any standard textbook that covers production function estimation), or by some type of envelopment method (Fare et al. 1994). Because the form of the function $f(\cdot)$ implies an index number formula, a frequently employed alternative is to estimate it by a ratio of index numbers (see section 30.3.3). Hulten (2001) reviews the relative advantages of econometric and index number approaches and Schreyer (2001) presents a comprehensive review of methods for estimating productivity change. Regardless of the method of estimation—econometric or index numbers—the measurement issues are the same.

30.3.1 Estimating Productivity of the Medical Care Sector: Output

The greatest difficulty in measuring medical care productivity is measuring output. Both conceptual and practical problems arise. Alternative approaches compete in the literature.

30.3.1.1 *Treatment for an Illness*

A growing number of health economists have endorsed an episode of treatment for a disease or illness as the unit of output for measuring medical care. Authors who proposed, developed, or supported the treatment-based approach include Scitovsky (1964, 1967); Newhouse (1989, 1992); Cutler, McClellan, Newhouse, and Remler (1996); Berndt, Busch, and Frank (1999); Berndt et al. (2000); Shapiro, Shapiro, and Wilcox (2001); Cutler and Berndt (2001); Triplett (2001); and Dawson et al. (2005). Atkinson (2005), in his review of methods for estimating medical care productivity, writes: "Ideally, we should look at the whole course of treatment for an illness...." If the treatment is the unit, then the products of medical care are treatments classified by disease, so the approach demands grouping medical care expenditures by a disease classification, such as the International Classification of Diseases, published by the World Health Organization.

It is useful to state the rationale for the treatment-based approach. On the one hand, one can proceed from the consumer side. What people ultimately want from medical care is improved health. The medical care system pursues this through treatment of ailments and diseases. Doctors' appointments, hospital patient days, drugs—things that have typically been treated as outputs in past measurements of medical care—are, from a consumer perspective, more accurately viewed as inputs used in the production of treatments, or (perhaps better) as intermediate stages to the ultimate goal of obtaining a treatment. Medical care is only one determinant of health, but that does not change the fact that the consumer is seeking better health when deciding to visit a health care establishment.

A second rationale starts from equation (4). The medical care system's contribution to health is:

$$\text{contribution to health} = \partial\,(\text{health})/\partial\,(\text{medical care}) \tag{7}$$

other variables in equation (4) constant. An increment to medical care is an intervention. Most interventions are disease-specific (though some might directly affect overall health). The effect of an intervention, its contribution to health, also manifests itself on a disease-specific element of health. For example, one might want to determine the effect on health from treatment of a heart condition. The effect comes from either reduction in mortality from heart disease or reduction of disabling effects of the heart condition. Both the treatment and the effect (measured by QALY, for example[5]) are disease-specific.

This rationale provides a concept for measuring the medical care *input* to the production of health, and one might object that measuring the *output* produced by the medical care sector should reflect an output concept. However, there is no very strong case for any alternative concept from the output side. In a famous exchange with Griliches, Gilbert (1961) contended that units such as a visit to a doctor or a day's stay in the hospital were the appropriate units because, he argued, those were the transaction units, the units for which medical care suppliers charged their customers.[6] Even if this were true in Gilbert's day, compensation schemes have increasingly been shifting toward Diagnostic Related Group (DRG) systems, where the unit is clearly the treatment of an illness, not a day in the hospital.

Implementing an illness-based output concept is greatly facilitated by the International Classification of Diseases (WHO 1977), which provides a well-developed classification system that can be used for medical expenditures, and by DRG systems. DRG systems fit into the ICD system at the chapter level. DRG systems render collecting data by illness groups more feasible because providers already have the data in their records. However, DRG systems are not currently completely comparable across countries (Schreyer 2009).

As well, much other medical information, information that an analyst would use in conjunction with medical care data and health accounts, is collected, tabulated, and

---

[5] For a discussion of QALY and similar measures of health outcomes, see Chapter 33.

[6] Griliches' response was repeated in his collected essays, among other places (Griliches 1988). The debate is best interpreted as an example (of which there are many) of the difference between output and input measurement concepts for economic data.

organized on similar principles. Scientific advances also fit into the system: Research on new treatments takes place, obviously, at the level of a specific disease, so it can be fitted naturally into the ICD. This is important for developing methods to deal with treatment improvements in output measures for medical care (considered in a subsequent section).

Thus, using a disease-based classification system such as ICD for measuring medical care output makes the economic classifications line up with the classifications that are used for other scientific work, and with the classification used for payments. This is a great advantage.

Several reservations are routinely expressed. First, not all medical expenditures fit into a disease-based system. Much preventative care (routine physical examinations, for example) cannot be attributed to a chapter of the ICD. Some part of nursing home and other rehabilitative care may not be explicitly related to any particular illness, even though some medical event—a stroke, for example—may have precipitated the nursing home admission. Additionally, the problem of co-morbidities must be allowed for in some way in assigning costs to chapters or subchapters of the ICD.

These frequently-voiced reservations must, however, be put into context: Cost-of-illness (COI) accounting has been carried out for many years, starting in the US with Rice (1966)—see also Rice, Hodgson, and Kopstein (1985). Hodgson and Cohen (1999) allocated 86 percent of US medical expenditure to the ICD classification; most of the unallocated amounts were caused by data deficiencies and had nothing to do with co-morbidities or other conceptual problems. Heijink et al. (2008) present data from COI accounts across a group of other countries. The challenge is not "Can it be done?" The challenge is to improve on what has been done in the past (improved methods for distributing the costs of co-morbidities, for example).

It will also be necessary to shift the orientation from one-time snapshots of illness costs—the traditional focus—to time series, which are necessary for productivity analysis, and indeed for much other analysis of medical care. A start toward the appropriate time-series focus is Roehrig et al. (2009), which appears to be the first such study. Several previous studies compute rates of expenditure change by disease grouping by linking together COI estimates carried out independently for two or more years: Polder and Achterberg (2004) for the Netherlands, 1994 to 1999, Heijink et al. (2008), for several countries and pairs of dates, and Triplett (2001), who links a number of mental health studies in the US. Linking COI studies that have been done separately creates error because of methodological non-comparability in the base studies, so is inferior to a study that applies a consistent methodology through time. OECD (IHAT 2009) recommends constructing time series.

Statistical agencies in several countries have adopted the cost-of-illness approach, which has made great improvements in the data. Among these, prominent milestones are the hospital price indexes in the US Producer Price Indexes (Catron and Murphy 1996), which have from the early 1990s collected the cost of a sample of diagnoses (extension of this concept to other medical care providers has been announced), the Eurostat Manual for services output in national accounts (Eurostat 2001), which specified that medical care output should be estimated on a cost-of-illness basis, the North

American Product Classification System (NAPCS, which guides collection of industry product data in the US, Canada, and Mexico), which adopted a version of the ICD as the "product codes" for medical care industries,[7] and the forthcoming OECD manual for health care and education output in national accounts (Schreyer 2009).

Finally, researchers working on international comparisons of medical care costs have adopted cost-of-illness as the appropriate empirical framework (OECD 2003; Busse, Schreyogg, and Smith 2008). Indeed, constructing data on expenditure trends at the cost-of-illness level provides essential information for any analysis of medical care costs. It is astonishing that so much discussion has taken place about the rising cost of medical care, in so many countries, with minimal information (or concern) about the illnesses whose medical care are experiencing rising costs. Generating data on trends in the cost of disease is important not just for productivity analysis, but also for the analysis of medical care costs.

Arraying medical expenditures by a disease classification is only the first step in implementing a treatment-based output concept. It is also necessary to separate trends in medical care expenditures into trends in quantities of treatments and prices or costs of treatments. Before discussing this in section 30.3.2, I consider in the next subsection an alternative concept for medical care output.

30.3.2 Medical Outcomes as the Output Measure: A Treatment Index or an Outcomes Index?

Equation (1.4) suggests valuing medical care interventions by their incremental contributions to health, that is, the contribution of each intervention is its medical outcome measure. If so, why form an index of treatments? Why not measure medical outcomes directly, disease-by-disease, and combine them into a weighted measure? Indeed, Dawson et al. (2005) proposed exactly that—to ignore the intervention entirely and look only at its effect on health. Their preferred basic measure of the output of the National Health Service is a weighted index of QALYs, by disease classifications, where one QALY is valued at £30,000 (see their equations 12 and 111).[8]

Among reasons for preferring the medical outcome measure is the general knowledge that not all treatments are effective. Errors and mistakes, misprescriptions and misdiagnoses (patients still receive antibiotics for viral infections, for example), botched operations, and variance across areas in modes of treatment are well-known. Inter-area differences in medical practice may be errors or may be differences of opinion about best practice, but even if the latter, presumably more knowledge will eventually show that some treatments that were thought to be best practice were not. This evidence suggests that some interventions are not making a positive incremental contribution to health. For these cases, bypassing the treatment measure would bring us closer to an output measure that measures the incremental contribution to health that the medical care system makes.

---

[7] Although it appears that only the US will implement this portion of NAPCS at this time.

[8] A summary report by a subset of the same authors is Castelli et al. (2007).

However, similar phenomena occur in other parts of the economy and are not adjusted out of the productivity measures for other sectors. Botched and inappropriate car repairs, for example, occur with some frequency; sometimes, they are corrected by the original repairer so the corrections do not result in new output, but sometimes the customer seeks out a new shop, so that repairing the botched job actually increases GDP (and is included in the numerator for the estimate of car repair productivity). We do not subtract such "re-dos" from GDP, even though they hardly contribute to consumers' welfare, nor do we adjust for defective manufactured products that are also not infrequently produced.

Whether appropriate or not, treatments are still produced in the medical care sector and they still use resources in the medical care sector. By that standard, they are outputs of the medical care sector.

Another reason for preferring treatments as the output measure for medical care arises from the distinction between output and welfare that is embodied in equations (1) and (4). Medical care services are an input in equation (4). The output is health. One never wants to measure an input by its output (nor an output by an input). If the output of the medical care sector were measured as a health outcome, and that measure then used as an input in the equation for the determinants of health, the possibility of productivity change in the health equation is largely eliminated by convention. One of the things we need to know is the productivity of the medical care sector in the production of health. To estimate that, the measure of medical sector output must be independent of the output of health. It must in principle be possible that the output effect of a change in an input quantity differs from the change in the input.[9]

A final, pragmatic, reason also has great weight: A health output measure that is based on disease treatments is grounded on a more precise statistic than an output measure that is based entirely on medical outcome measures. Measuring health output by treatments may not be that far along at present. Nevertheless, more information is available on expenditure by disease, on numbers of treatments by disease, and even on health care prices by disease than on medical outcome measures, and treatment information is inherently more concrete and therefore more precisely measured information. Measuring medical care output by treatments is not that different from the way we measure car repair in national accounts (Triplett 2001), and can readily be understood within the usual framework of economic statistics. In contrast, even health economics professionals raise difficulties, both conceptual and practical, with existing medical outcomes measures (Meltzer 2001). A sound measurement principle is to minimize the use of undeveloped and potentially controversial measures, using them only where they are necessary and not where alternatives exist.

In summary, measuring medical care output by health outcomes, though seemingly appealing, mixes concepts from two different types of measurement—the measure of production and productivity in the medical care sector and the measurement of the determinants of health. In the absence of a system for estimating equation (4)—that is,

---

[9] To avoid confusion, it is not inconsistent to make the quality adjustment for a changed treatment depend on the ratio of medical outcomes for the new and old treatments, suggested in section 30.3.3.3.

in the absence of a "health account"—it might be tempting to attain a partial measure of the impact of the medical care sector on the determinants of health by using health outcomes to estimate the output of medical care. But mixing concepts in an economic measurement always provokes confusion. Better to estimate both equations (1) and (4) than to inter-mingle and confound separate conceptual systems.

30.3.3 From Expenditures on Treatments to Quantities of Treatments

Collecting expenditures on treatments, by disease classification, is necessary but not sufficient to measure output. From section 30.3.1.1, output for medical care is measured by the quantities of medical care treatments, which we will alternatively designate *medical care services*. Expenditures on, for example, heart attacks equal the price or cost of treating heart attacks times the quantity of medical care services for the treatment of heart attacks. Both price (medical care inflation) and quantity information are necessary, but the quantity of medical care services is the most crucial measure, because the services quantities are the outputs of the medical care sector, and they are one of the inputs into the production of health.

Two methodologies exist for obtaining estimates of quantity changes of medical treatments: deflation and direct quantity indexes.

30.3.3.1 *Deflation*

The first, "deflation," is the conventional methodology of national accounts: The change in expenditures for some category of goods and services is divided by a price index (a measure of inflation) for that category to obtain the quantity measure. For example, expenditures on treating heart attacks would be divided by a price index for treating heart attacks. Generally accepted procedures for deflation in national accounts are presented in the SNA handbook (Commission of the European Communities—Eurostat et al. 1993: ch. 16).

Because medical care services are heterogeneous, both their price and their quantity are expressed as index numbers. Index numbers most commonly employed in productivity measurement are the Törnqvist index and the Fisher index (Caves, Christensen, and Diewert 1982), both of which are termed "superlative index numbers."[10]

Suppose the deflating price index is a Fisher index (the Fisher index number is the geometric mean of Paasche and Laspeyres index numbers). Then, for periods 0 and 1:

$$(\Sigma P_1 Q_1 / \Sigma P_0 Q_0) / \{[\Sigma P_1 Q_0 / \Sigma P_0 Q_0][\Sigma P_1 Q_1 / \Sigma P_0 Q_1]\}^{\frac{1}{2}} =$$
$$\{[\Sigma P_0 Q_1 / \Sigma P_0 Q_0][\Sigma P_1 Q_1 / \Sigma P_1 Q_0]\}^{\frac{1}{2}} \quad (8)$$

[10] The modern concept of the superlative index number was developed by Diewert (1976), though the term itself was in use much earlier. The Fisher index number appears in the text. The Törnqvist (quantity) index is: $I(T_{01}) = \Pi\{(q_1/q_0)^s\}$, where $s = (\frac{1}{2}[P_0 q_0 / \Sigma P_0 q_0 + P_1 q_1 / \Sigma P_1 q_1])$, for each of the *ith* quantities. In this expression, and in equation (1.8), the subscript i, designating the ith quantity, is suppressed.

The terms in square brackets on the left-hand side are Laspeyres and Paasche price indexes, and the term in curly brackets is the Fisher price index. Deflation yields, on the right-hand side, a Fisher quantity index number (in parallel, the geometric mean of Laspeyres and Paasche quantity indexes, each of which is shown inside a square bracket); the Fisher quantity index measures the change in the quantities of treatments for (in the example) heart attacks. To give it an alternative interpretation, the quantity index on the right-hand side of equation (8) shows the rate of growth in medical services for this medical ailment. The quantity index takes account of differences in severities and of variations in treatment; it is not just a count of the number of heart attack treatments.

The theoretically correct way to aggregate outputs is by marginal cost (MC) weights (Fisher 1993). By the usual competitive assumption, MCs are proportional to prices, which are the weights in the quantity index (the right-hand side of equation (8)). Thus, deflation preserves (approximately) the theoretical aggregation condition.

However, the assumption that prices and MCs are proportional is especially problematic in medical care, where many prices have remote connections to costs. Even in the United States, where prices charged for medical care treatments are routinely collected and medical care price indexes published (in the Producer Price Index), the usual national accounts deflation methodology is therefore questionable when applied to medical care, because the prices–MCs proportionality assumption is untenable. In other countries, government-provided medical care means a price index for medical care has no relevance. For this reason, medical care output in most countries' national accounts is not estimated by deflation.

30.3.3.2 *Direct Quantity Index*

The alternative method is to aggregate the quantities directly—that is, to compute directly the right-hand side of equation (8). As an example, one could compute an index of the quantity of heart attack treatments. This computation requires data on quantities of treatments, classified by case severity, type of treatment and so forth; the weights for the index are the costs (not the prices or consumer valuations) of the various treatments. The correct weight for each treatment is its marginal cost (MC); in practice, average cost (AC) is more likely to be obtainable, so AC provides an approximation to MC.

Several European and Oceanic countries are experimenting with direct quantity indexes of medical care. Schreyer (2009) lists: Australia, Finland, France, Germany, Netherlands, New Zealand, Norway, Sweden, and the UK. In some of these cases, however, the indexes are not computed on a disease basis, and not all of them are based on completed treatments.[11] In principle, countries with government-provided health care would have the treatment quantities and costs by disease in their health care management systems; in practice, most do not, either for obscure political or bureaucratic

---

[11] For example, Schreyer (2009) says that the health measure in the UK national accounts is "a cost weighted activity index." However, these UK "activities" are not completed treatments, they are a mix of mostly intermediate functions (see the description in Dawson et al. 2005). The UK measure is not an adequate output index.

reasons (in a few countries) or because managing governmental health care systems has not been done very effectively.

30.3.3.3 *When Treatment Characteristics Change*

The major methodological problems with either the deflation method or the direct quantity index method arise because of (a) improved treatments, generally but not necessarily in the same facility, and (b) treatments that move between facility types or that cross industry lines, so that the equivalent treatment (measured by medical outcomes) is available at lower cost.

Improved Treatments When improved treatments for a disease are introduced, they create the infamous price index "quality change" problem. If the better treatment is introduced at higher cost, and the new one is compared directly with the old (either its cost or its quantity), it will show up inappropriately as medical care inflation, instead of (as it should) an increase in the quantity of medical services, unless some "quality adjustment" is made. Even if the new, improved treatment is cheaper (yet better) than the old (so that comparing the new and the old will record a drop in cost), direct comparison still understates the true cost decline because an allowance or adjustment should also be made for the value of the improvement.

The best way to do it is to adjust the prices or quantities by a measure of the medical outcome, even though outcomes do not, strictly speaking, concord with the theory that underlies the measurement of output. Considering two treatments used for the same diagnosis, and letting m_a and m_b be the value of medical outcome measures corresponding to treatments a (the old one, used in period 1) and b, while p_2 and p_1 are the prices of treatments in periods 2 and 1, respectively, then the quality-adjusted price measure (η_{21}) is:

$$\eta_{21} = p_2/(p_1(m_b/m_a)) \tag{9}$$

Expenditures on this treatment are $p_1\,q_1$ and $p_2\,q_2$ in the two periods, so that the deflated quantity change in treatments (λ_{21}) is:

$$\lambda_{21} = (q_2(m_b/m_a))/q_1 \tag{10}$$

Notice that the adjustment makes the improvement in outcomes part of the quantity change in medical care. Thus, if the new treatment is 20 percent better by the medical care outcome measure, it should be recorded (whether the adjustment is made in the price index used for deflation or in the direct quantity measure) as approximately 20 percent more output.[12]

---

[12] This is an oversimplification because m_a and m_b are valuations, and the value of improvements in medical outcome measures will usually not be linear; as with everything else, diminishing marginal utility sets in. A 20 percent improvement in the medical outcome measure itself would normally be valued at less than 20 percent.

Where the direct quantity index method is used to measure the output of medical care, the same result would be obtained through a parallel adjustment to the quantities, equivalent to equation (10). In this case, no price index adjustment is needed. The implicit, quality-adjusted change in the price of the treatment is obtained by dividing the expenditure change by equation (10)—refer back to equation (8).

Whether deflation or direct quantity index method is used, the great difficulty is the lack of sufficient medical care outcome measures to facilitate an adjustment.[13] The medical outcome measure should, of course, refer to the specific change in treatment and only to that change. Other changes (e.g. hospital meals and amenities) should be held constant, to avoid the danger of double-counting. An outcome measure obtained from a medical trial is an example where other influences are held constant; an outcome measure from a hospital patient survey may not do so.

An Equivalent Treatment (Judged by a Medical Care Outcome Measure) Becomes Available at Lower Cost in a Different Facility The archetypal example is cataract surgery (Shapiro, Shapiro, and Wilcox 2001), once done in a hospital with a lengthy recovery period and now performed as an outpatient procedure, often in a non-hospital facility. If deflation is employed, any price reduction will be missed because prices are gathered by repeat visits to the same facility; in consequence, output increase is understated (refer to equation 8), and so is productivity change. If the direct quantity index is computed, the quantities from both providers may be recorded, but the change in the cost weights will be missed or misinterpreted, and again, output increase and productivity change are understated.[14] The solution to this problem is again to obtain a medical outcome measure, which will tell, when the treatment moves to a new, lower cost facility, whether or not it is an equivalent treatment.

The major work on these two problems has been done in the deflation context, and includes: Cutler et al. (1996) on heart attacks, Berndt, Busch, and Frank (1999) on depression, Shapiro, Shapiro, and Wilcox (2001) on cataract surgery, and several other similar studies summarized in Cutler (2004). They show that true inflation in medical care in the United States was substantially lower than had been thought. Consequently, the output growth of medical services was greater and productivity growth was also understated in the available government data (consequently, the medical care productivity estimates in Triplett and Bosworth 2004 are biased downward). The studies also hint that policy measures to slow the growth of medical costs may impact medical care services, rather than (as most policymakers have hoped) simply slowing the growth of medical care inflation.

[13] On medical outcome measures, see Chapter 33 in this volume. The quality change problem in economic statistics generally is discussed in Triplett (2005); for the link between medical outcome measures and traditional index number quality adjustments, see Triplett (1999).

[14] The first facility has a decline in quantities (say), with relatively high cost weights; the second facility we suppose has an increase in quantities of treatments, with relatively low cost weights. Then, the shift between the two will be recorded as a decline in a (weighted) quantity index, when the quantities should not decline. Instead, a decline in medical inflation (the reduction in cost) should be recorded.

It has sometimes been thought that one can circumvent the twin change-in-treatment problems noted above by collecting data from insurance company claims, rather than from medical care providers. One advantage of claims data is their large sample size. However, even though in principle claims data could be fitted into either side of equation (8)—that is, they could be used to calculate a weighted price index or a weighted quantity index—in practice, researchers have calculated a unit value index:

$$\text{unit value index} = (\Sigma P_1 Q_1/n_1)/(\Sigma P_0 Q_0/n_0) \qquad (11)$$

where n_0 and n_1 are the numbers of treatments in periods 0 and 1, respectively, and of course, P and Q are prices and quantites of treatments. Deflation by the unit value index gives:[15]

$$\text{output change} = \{(\Sigma P_1 Q_1/\Sigma P_0 Q_0)\}/\{(\Sigma P_1 Q_1/n_1)/(\Sigma P_0 Q_0/n_0)\} = n_1/n_0 \qquad (12)$$

Thus, the unit value index implies a quantity index of medical care services that is just a count of the number of treatments. Even though a researcher can subdivide the data to achieve more homogeneous groupings (to calculate separate indexes for types of heart attacks, for example), it is hard to accept the idea that any grouping of medical treatments can be regarded as homogeneous. The extreme heterogeneity in treatments, therefore, is simply assumed not to matter, but the assumption is tenuous, at best.

All the research cited above has focused entirely on estimating improved price indexes, to get better measures of inflation in the provision of medical care. This reflects the special character of the US system, and even in the US the use of deflation for estimating the growth in medical care services is problematic, as indicated earlier. Too little work on the change-in-treatment problems has been done from the direct quantity measurement side, that is, by estimating outcome-adjusted direct quality indexes of medical care (direct estimation of the right-hand side of equation 8 and of equation 10). Such future work will presumably originate from researchers in countries outside the United States (and its unique deflation environment for the measurement of medical care output). Some of the data required for the research, especially costs and quantities of treatments, should be (but may not be) in the files of government health care programs. However, the detailed information on health outcomes that is required is scarce. Schreyer (2009) presents information on current research and development activities on medical care output measurement within OECD countries' statistical agencies.

30.3.4 Estimating Productivity: Inputs to Medical Care

Of the inputs to medical care listed in equation (1), *capital* poses the most troublesome problems. The contribution of capital to current output is the flow of capital services

---

[15] See also Balk (1999, 2008), who presents the same result.

provided by the industry's stock of capital goods—physical capital such as buildings and equipment, and also intangible capital.[16] The flow of capital services is derived from the stock. The price of capital services, in concept, is the charge for the use of a capital good for a unit of time. Estimating the price and quantity of capital services is complex, because estimation requires (except when the capital good is rented or leased, when the lease payment provides the price measure) determining the capital stock, estimating deflators for the stock, and measuring depreciation, all of which pose major empirical difficulties. However, medical capital goods pose no problems that are not already familiar in work on measuring capital services in other sectors of the economy. The methods, accordingly, will not be reviewed here (for a summary, see Schreyer 2001).

However, few countries publish much data on the detailed types of capital equipment used by the medical care sector. Where information is available, the fundamental measurement problem is quality change.

For many years, economists have known that quality change poses serious price measurement problems. Among the many relevant references that could be cited are Stigler et al (1961); Griliches (1994); and Boskin et al. (1996). Quality change measurement errors are likely when goods and services experience rapid technological change. Medical care industries purchase a range of very highly technological equipment, which is importantly linked with technical change in treatments, and it is hard to measure accurately.

For example, a scanner is essentially an imaging device coupled to a computer. We know that imaging has made vast strides in recent years, and computers have declined in price at the rate of 20–30 percent *per year* for more than fifty years (Triplett 2005). Moreover, the only research study of scanner prices that exists (Trajtenberg 1990) found that CT scanner prices fell at a rate not too dissimilar from those of computers. Few countries even have a price index for scanners in their investment goods price indexes, and the US Producer Price Index for diagnostic equipment (which includes scanners) shows only a relatively modest (by computer standards) decline. If scanner prices are declining more rapidly than government price indexes indicate, then investment in scanners (the quantity of scanners) is under-estimated (refer to equation 8), and accordingly so is the capital input in equation (1). More accurate measurement of high-tech medical equipment is an urgent need. Methods that have been used for computers and other technological goods, such as hedonic indexes (Triplett 2006), are also appropriate to scanners.

A similar point applies to some *materials* inputs, including pharmaceuticals and medical devices such as stents. Much recent technological change in medicine has proceeded through materials inputs that are unique to the medical care sector. It is not clear how

---

[16] A long history of debate over concepts of capital in production analysis spilled over into national accounts measurement. The debate is now settled, on the lines suggested in Jorgenson, Gollop, and Fraumeni (1987). See, in particular, the OECD handbook on productivity measurement by Paul Schreyer (2001), which records the consensus and makes recommendations for the measurement of capital stocks and capital services in national accounts that are wholly consistent with the methods now generally accepted in production analysis. See also Hulten (2001). From the *conceptual* view, medical care presents no unique problems in the measurement of capital.

well these intermediates are represented in the national statistics of most countries—the data are suspect because of problems of coverage, of detail, of the quality of information on inter-industry flows, and again, quality change errors in the measured deflators are paramount. Some good work on pharmaceuticals can be cited (see the summary in Berndt et al. 2000), but it is not nearly comprehensive. No similar research on medical devices has appeared, despite their importance in some recent improvements in medical treatments.

Of course, some intermediate materials inputs to the medical sector present no unique problems. Hospitals consume paper products and cleaning supplies, like any other business.

In medical care industries, *services* include purchased medical services from other medical establishments (which present the same measurement concerns already covered in section 30.3.2), and other services, such as accounting, business services, communications and so forth. Triplett and Bosworth (2004) suggest substantial measurement issues for these and similar services; the discussion applies as well to their roles as inputs to the production of medical care.

Most economists probably believe that measuring the *labor* input is much easier than measuring capital, but problems persist. Though the basic unit of measurement is labor hours, human capital is a major contributor to output, in all industries, but especially in medical care. Jorgenson, Gollop, and Fraumeni (1987) provide methods for incorporating labor quality, or human capital, in industry accounts and productivity analysis. Dawson et al. (2005) present information on medical human capital in the UK. However, the traditional human capital measures distinguish mainly years of schooling or levels of educational attainment; they need extending to take account of the unique sets of skills and training in modern medicine.

Unpaid volunteer labor in hospitals, hospices and so forth, and time spent caring for ill relatives and friends, is an important input into producing medical care. For productivity measurement of medical care, there is no reason to conform to all the conventions of national accounts (where unpaid labor is excluded), even if the measure of medical care output retains the market output boundary of the national accounts. Estimates of unpaid labor belong in a study of medical care productivity.

Implications: Most, though probably not all, measurement errors in the inputs to the medical care sector imply that measured input growth is too low. For example, if the technical change in scanners is imperfectly captured in the data, then the growth of capital inputs to medical care is understated, and similarly for the growth of medical devices such as stents and for pharmaceuticals, where there is in fact evidence of understatement. Moreover, the growth of human capital in medicine is greater than the growth of labor hours, so to the extent that human capital is not accounted for in medical care industries, growth in the labor input is also understated.

Since productivity growth estimates have the inputs in the denominator, understatement of input growth has the effect of *overstating* productivity growth. We have already noted in the Introduction, however, that most empirical estimates of productivity growth in medical care have reported negative growth. Putting those two facts together suggests the size of the likely bias to output measures: The measurement error in output growth therefore must be large enough to eliminate negative productivity growth indicated by the current statistics (provided we are right in our priors that medical care productivity growth should not be negative) and also additionally large enough to nullify the effects of understatement of input growth. That suggests a very large error indeed in measured output growth in the medical care sector.

30.3.5 A Conceptual Error

A relatively minor slip in the Atkinson (2005) report opened a hole that the UK health and education bureaucracies initially exploited for their own ends. Atkinson noted that services such as health and education are valued more highly by a society with a higher income. This is quite correct. If one is doing a cost–benefit analysis, for example, the increased valuation that is associated with income growth should be factored in, and this increased valuation, relative to cost, would lead to production of more of the services.

In the UK, the Atkinson suggestion induced government agencies to add to their productivity numbers "wealth" adjustments (some quite substantial) to incorporate a presumed increased willingness to pay for their outputs. These adjustments have in several cases converted negative agency productivity growth estimates into putative positive ones.

For productivity measurement, willingness-to-pay adjustments are quite wrong. The agencies have muddled the P's and the Q's.

Productivity is the ratio of outputs to inputs, the quantities. When a society is willing to pay more for a service, it is an increase in its price. The quantity of the service is whatever the quantity is, the quantity is not increased by a presumed increase in its value.

One way to see this is to consider productivity change from the standpoint of the dual. Duality theory tells us that one can compute productivity in two alternative and equivalent ways: as the ratio of the quantity of outputs to the quantity of inputs or as the ratio of output prices to input prices.[17] In a competitive economy, those two calculations yield the same result (one can hardly presume that this applies to a government agency, of course, but leave that aside for present purposes). Productivity increases as the quantity ratio *increases* and as the price ratio *decreases* (greater efficiency makes it possible to lower the price of output relative to the cost of inputs). Thus, an increase in the price of output relative to inputs is a sign of decreasing productivity. Making a positive adjustment to government productivity numbers when their output valuation rises relative to their input costs turns the signal of prices on its head.

The UK Office for National Statistics has now rescinded the adjustment for presumed increased willingness to pay for government services (ONS 2008). This willingness-to-pay adjustment should not be mimicked elsewhere.

---

[17] Calculating MFP from the price side is not done very often, but it has a long history. One of the first ever MFP calculations compared growth in output price indexes and input price indexes (Copeland and Martin 1938).

30.4 HEALTH, ITS DETERMINANTS, AND THE PRODUCTIVITY OF PRODUCING IT

Grossman's (1972) approach to the analysis of health has become the standard for economists' thinking about the subject (see Bolin, Chapter 6). It is a bit surprising, then, that attempts to implement the Grossman model empirically are few. The difficulties in doing so are evident from equation (4): Analysis of the production of health requires measuring health (which is multi-dimensional), identifying and measuring the determinants of health and then finding an appropriate way to summarize them, analogous to the index number formula for inputs in equation (2). Representing the $h(.)$ function in equation (4) may be complicated because of the heterogeneity in the units in which the variables in it are expressed.

Abraham and Mackie (2005: ch. 6) suggest constructing a "health account." The health account would provide a welfare-oriented measure as a counterpart to the market-oriented measures of the System of National Accounts, or SNA (Commission of the European Communities et al. 1993), and would link the change in health to the inputs that determine health, of which medical care is but one. Thus, it would be structured by analogy to the familiar national accounts that record economic activity, but would be built around the functional relation and the variables in equation (4).

Output in such an account requires measuring health. QALY is one empirical possibility, so the health account would benefit from the substantial ongoing research to improve this and similar measures (these are reviewed in Chapter 33).

As inputs for the health account, the Abraham–Mackie report lists: medical care (the output of the medical care account), time invested in one's own health (in principle, based on time-use surveys, which are conducted in a number of countries, though the report lists several conceptual problems in using these data in a health account), "other consumption items" (discussed below), research and development (R&D data are also compiled in many industrialized countries), and environmental and "disease state" variables, with pollution mentioned specifically.

Presumably, environmental effects would encompass such things as improved public health and sanitation measures and changes in working conditions, a greatly neglected contributor to historical health improvements. The Sheffield Industrial Museums Trust, South Yorkshire, UK, has a display of the appalling working conditions that prevailed in UK steel production even as late as the 1930s. Leaving aside the distressing number of industrial accidents that must have accompanied the lack of even rudimentary safety precautions, working long hours in the searing heat (workers tied wet rags around their faces to protect their lungs) undoubtedly exacted a frightful toll on life expectancy and on the morbidity of workers who survived to old age. Employees in some industries were literally worked to death.[18]

---

[18] The same was true in the United States. Costa (2000) found that at least a quarter of the decline in respiratory ailments among US elderly men over the twentieth century can be attributed to employment shifts out of occupations associated with the highest risks for such diseases.

The list of inputs into equation (4) is no doubt long. In many instances, a virtuous circle appeared: For example, part of the increase in income over time was taken in improved working conditions, which led to improved health, which in turn (since the link between improved health and greater earnings is well-established) led to further income increases which fed back to greater improvements in working conditions. For some purposes, taking account of the feedbacks matters, even though it greatly complicates the modeling because it suggests that the single equation representation in equation (4) is too simple.[19]

Cutler and Rosen, in an ongoing project, are estimating disease models and combining them with economic data (see their proposal in Cutler and Rosen 2007). Their research uses the perspective of the Grossman model (and the related epidemiological perspective), so one can think of it as estimating equation (4), on a disease-by-disease basis. They have selected disease categories that account for a large portion of national health care expenditures and are working toward determining the factors—including of course medical care—that affect changes in mortality and morbidity. At present, they have eschewed the more complicated task of aggregating their disease models into an overall accounting for health. A second effort along similar lines, but for cancer and circulatory diseases in the UK, is reported in Martin, Rice, and Smith (2008). Their work is directed toward making comparisons of the determinants of health costs in different countries.

More research on the determinants of health, especially the non-medical determinants, is vital. Statistical agencies should be encouraged to develop data to enable such research.

Does putting the data into an SNA-type economic *accounting* structure further the objective? Abraham and Mackie and their co-authors start from "holes" or "gaps" in the existing national accounts that arise because the accounts do not measure welfare, and because their measures of outputs (and inputs) are incomplete—only market inputs and outputs are included. For example, uncompensated labor expended on the care of the ill is excluded from the SNA, by convention. If the task is filling SNA holes or gaps then it seems reasonable to work out an expanded accounting system that meshes with, or is patterned after, the traditional national accounts structure. Many of the details have yet to be worked out.

Data requirements for an economic welfare account for health go beyond the database for research on health determinants. For example, Abraham and Mackie list diet among health determinants, certainly an important consideration. The report of the World Cancer Research Fund/American Institute for Cancer Research (2007) summarizes evidence connecting dietary factors to different types of cancer—consumption of red and processed meats raises the risk of colorectal cancers, and excessive consumption of salt for stomach cancer, while on the other hand, consumption of fresh fruits and

---

[19] Actually, equation (4) oversimplifies Grossman's (1972) model. He implies time subscripts on some variables to incorporate delayed effects of current life style and consumption on future health. The time subscripts have been suppressed for present purposes.

vegetables reduces risks of a number of digestive system cancers. A research model for cancers might be designed in which dietary data are employed in conjunction with medical care data to determine the relative impacts of diet and medical care on cancer death and incidence rates. If the objective is to estimate determinants of health, then information on consumption of the foods of interest (data which are readily available) is the main requirement.

Fitting dietary (and lifestyle) influences on health into an SNA-type accounting structure is more difficult. In the Grossman (1972) model, and from a welfare perspective, it is necessary to compute the *net* gain—the value of the increment to health, less the loss in utility from abstaining from steak and ham, or from eating vegetables when the individual does not like them.[20] One can conceive of a research project to measure such utility losses, and, though more difficult, perhaps putting them into an aggregate welfare estimation. It is much less clear, however, how utility losses should be fitted into an *accounting* structure.

One possible parallel is with environmental accounting. Some production processes (electricity generation, for example) produce both goods and "bads" (the "bad" in this case is pollution). In an environmental account, one subtracts the values of the bads from the goods to get a net welfare measure. In the health case, the bads are utility losses from pursuing more healthy life styles,[21] so equation (4) should be rewritten as:

$$(\lambda \text{ (health, utility loss)}) = h \text{ (medical care, time, consumption, R\&D,}$$
$$\text{environment, etc.)} \tag{13}$$

In the structure implied by equation (1.13),[22] the net output (the value of welfare gains from improved health less the value of utility losses from dietary and behavioral changes) is the relevant measure for welfare, and therefore for the SNA-analog health account. The net measure, however, is not the measure that is useful for research on health. For that task, only the gross measure, health, is wanted.

The difference between gross and net is reduced the larger is the proportionate contribution of medical care to the change in health. Though it is clear from the historical record that medical care was not the main determinant of past health improvements (McKeown 1976), Cutler (2004) contends that medicine has been the main factor over the last half century, particularly if one adds in the contribution of medical research to the information that has led to changed life styles. Even so, he suggests that the utility losses from life style changes subtract approximately half the utility gain from improved health (Cutler 2004: 139–40). Thus, the net output measure is still likely to differ substantially from the gross.

---

[20] "[Nonmarket accounts] should address the major conceptual issues by measuring income and output in ways that best correspond to net economic welfare" (Nordhaus 2006: 143).

[21] This is not the definition of "bads" used in Chapter 33, where bads are things that contribute to current utility, but have negative long-term influences on health. Here, bads are things that subtract from current utility.

[22] Or, to be more general: $0 = \eta$ (health, utility losses, medical care, time, consumption, R&D, environment, etc.).

In programs to generate data choices must be made, so priorities must be established. It is not premature to recommend collection of more information about the determinants of health. It may be premature to recommend that statistical agencies organize health data to accommodate a welfare-oriented health account: The effort to estimate the utility losses from behavorial changes will likely steal resources away from the generation of data on the determinants of health. For most purposes, it seems clear that developing data on the determinants of health should receive priority.

As was true of the development of national accounts in the 1930s, health accounts have not evolved very far. The situation will change with more work on their conceptual underpinnings and practical needs.

30.5 Conclusion

The main limitation on the analysis of health system productivity lies in deficiencies in data. For the medical care sector, the major needs are not only better input data but also expenditures data that are arrayed by disease or illness classification and better methods for separating expenditure changes on health care into increases in price or cost and increases in the quantity of medical services.

Though they are needed for productivity research, these data are needed primarily for other, more important purposes. Nearly all industrialized countries are concerned with advancing medical care expenditures. Yet, they have very little information on what their medical expenditures buy. The National Health Accounts produced in many countries have become nearly irrelevant to the current policy debates on medical care costs because they show only who provides the money for health care (consumers, governments, insurance companies) and who gets it (hospitals, doctors, pharmaceutical companies). They do not show what is bought for health care expenditures—treatments for disease.

It is naïve to think that expenditures across all types of disease are growing at the same rate: Are expenditures growing more rapidly for treatments of circulatory diseases, or for mental health care, or for cancer? How many countries have this information? How can one make sensible policy decisions on medical expenditures without knowing where the increases originate?

And of course, just knowing which disease categories have advancing expenditures is not enough: We also need to know whether the more rapidly increasing sectors have growing expenditures because of rapidly increasing treatment costs or rapidly increasing numbers of treatments. Again, there is no reason to believe that treatment costs are advancing at the same rates across medical conditions. In the US Producer Price Indexes for hospitals (which are published by ICD categories), the past inflation rate for blood and blood forming organ diseases is *two and a half times* the inflation rate for treating infectious diseases. These are hospital costs, not total costs of treating the disease, but they suggest strongly that the costs of treating different diseases are not advancing at the same rate. How can anyone design intelligent policy on advancing medical care expenditures without knowing where costs are rising? And why? It is commonly alleged, for example, that costs are rising because of technological advance; but do the diseases that have the most innovations in new treatments have the greatest cost increases? Little data exist to answer that question. Information on price or cost growth by disease is sadly not available in most countries that have had debates about medical care expenditure containment.

If expenditure growth is contained, is the effect to reduce medical care inflation? Or is it, instead, to reduce the growth of medical care services? We don't really know. Only after determining this can we move to the next stage and ask whether the growth in the number of medical care services is worth it, a question that has too often been "answered" with a minimal amount of relevant data.

Improving the database for the analysis of medical care productivity deserves high priority. It deserves high priority, not so much because productivity analysis is necessarily that important, but because vital questions of health care policy demand exactly the same data.

REFERENCES

ABRAHAM, KATHARINE and CHRISTOPHER MACKIE, eds. 2005. *Beyond the Market: Designing Nonmarket Accounts for the United States*. Washington, DC: The National Academies Press.

ATKINSON, TONY. 2005. *Atkinson Review: Final Report: Measurement of Government Output and Productivity for the National Accounts*. Basingstoke and New York: Palgrave McMillan.

BALK, BERT M. 1999. On the Use of Unit Value Indices as Consumer Price Subindices. In Walter Lane, ed., *Proceedings of the Fourth Meeting of the International Working Group on Price Indices*. Washington, DC: US Department of Labor, pp. 112–20.

—— 2008. *Price and Quantity Index Numbers: Models for Measuring Aggregate Change and Difference*. Cambridge: Cambridge University Press.

BERNDT, ERNST R, SUSAN BUSCH, and RICHARD G. FRANK. 1999. Price Indexes for the Treatment of Depression. In Jack E. Triplett, ed., *Measuring the Prices of Medical Treatments*. Washington, DC, Brookings Institution Press, 71–102.

BERNDT, ERNST R. DAVID M. CUTLER, RICHARD FRANK, ZVI GRILICHES, JOSEPH NEWHOUSE, and JACK E. TRIPLETT. 2000. Medical Care Prices and Output. In Anthony J. Cutler and Joseph P. Newhouse, eds., *Handbook of Health*, Vol. 1A. Amsterdam: Elsevier, 119–18.

BOSKIN, MICHAEL J., ELLEN R. DULBERGER, ROBERT J. GORDON, ZVI GRILICHES, and DALE JORGENSON. 1996. Toward a More Accurate Measure of the Cost of Living. Advisory Commission to Study the Consumer Price Index. Interim Report to the Senate Finance Committee, December.

BUSSE, REINHARD, JONAS SCHREYOGG and PETER C. SMITH. 2008. Variability in Healthcare Treatment Costs Amongst Nine EU Countries: Results from the Healthbasket Project. *Health Economics*, 17/S1: S1–8.

CASTELLI, ADRIANA, DIANE DAWSON, HUGH GRAVELLE, and ANDREW STREET. 2007. Improving the Measurement of Health System Output Growth. *Health Economics*, 16: 1091–107.

CATRON, BRIAN and BONNIE MURPHY. 1996. Hospital Price Inflation: What Does the New PPI Tell Us? *Monthly Labor Review*, July, 120/7: 24–31.

CAVES, DOUGLAS W., LAURITS R. CHRISTENSEN and W. ERWIN DIEWERT. 1982. The Economic Theory of Index Numbers and the Measurement of Input, Output, and Productivity. *Econometrica*, 50/6: 1393–414.

COMMISSION OF THE EUROPEAN COMMUNITIES: EUROSTAT, INTERNATIONAL MONETARY FUND, ORGANISATION FOR ECONOMIC COOPERATION AND DEVELOPMENT, UNITED NATIONS AND WORLD BANK. 1993. *System of National Accounts, 1993*. Paris: Commission of the European Communities: Eurostat, International Monetary Fund, Organisation for Economic Cooperation and Development, United Nations and World Bank.

COPELAND, MORRIS A. and EDWIN M. MARTIN. 1938. The Correction of Wealth and Income Estimates for Price Changes. Conference on Research in Income and Wealth, *Studies in Income and Wealth* 2: 85–119 and 131–5.

COSTA, DORA L. 2000. Understanding the Twentieth Century Decline in Chronic Conditions Among Older Men. *Demography*, Feb., 37/1: 53–72.

CUTLER, DAVID M. 2004. *Your Money or Your Life: Strong Medicine for America's Health Care System*. Oxford: Oxford University Press.

—— and ERNST R. BERNDT, eds. 2001. *Medical Care Output and Productivity. Studies in Income and Wealth*, Vol. 62. Chicago: The University of Chicago Press for the National Bureau of Economic Research.

—— and ALLISON B. ROSEN. 2007. Measuring Medical Care Productivity: A Proposal for US National Health Accounts. *Survey of Current Business*, June, 87: 54–8.

—— MARK MCCLELLAN, JOSEPH P. NEWHOUSE, and DAHLIA REMLER. 1996. Are Medical Prices Declining? Evidence from Heart Attack Treatments. *Quarterly Journal of Economics*, 113/4: 991–1024, November.

DAWSON, DIANE, HUGH GRAVELLE, MARY O'MAHONEY, ANDREW STREET, MARTIN WEALE, ADRIANA CASTELLI, ROWENA JACOBS, PAUL KIND, PETE LOVERIDGE, STEPHEN MARTIN, PHILIP STEVENS, and LUCY STOKES. 2005. Developing New Approaches to Measuring NHS Outputs and Productivity: Final Report. Unpublished report. Centre for Health Economics, University of York and the National Institute for Social and Economic Research, York and London.

DIEWERT, W. ERWIN. 1976. Exact and Superlative Index Numbers. *Journal of Econometrics*, May 4/2: 115–45.

EUROSTAT. 2001. Handbook on Price and Volume Measures in National Accounts. March. Luxembourg: Eurostat.

FARE, ROLF, S. GROSSKOPF, B. LINDGREN, and P. ROOS. 1994. Productivity Developments in Swedish Hospitals: A Malmquist Output Index Approach. In A. Charnes, W. W. Cooper, A. Lewin, L. Seiford, eds., *Data Envelopment Analysis: Theory, Methodology and Applications*. New York: Kluwer Academic Publishers, 253–72.

FISHER, FRANKLIN M. 1993. *Aggregation: Aggregate Production Relations and Related Topics*. Cambridge, MA: MIT Press.

GILBERT, MILTON. 1961. Quality Changes and Index Numbers. *Economic Development and Cultural Change*, April, 9: 287–94.

GRILICHES, ZVI. 1988. *Technology, Education, and Productivity*. Oxford: Basil Blackwell.

—— 1994. Productivity, R&D, and the Data Constraint. *American Economic Review*, March, 84/1: 1–23.

GROSSMAN, MICHAEL. 1972. *The Demand for Health: A Theoretical and Empirical Investigation. National Bureau of Economic Research, Occasional Paper 119*. New York: Columbia University Press.

HARPER, MICHAEL J., BHAVANI KHANDRIKA, RANDAL KINOSHITA, and STEVEN ROSENTHAL. 2008. Multifactor Productivity Contributions of US Non-Manufacturing Industry Groups: 1987–2005. Unpublished paper presented at the World Congress on National Accounts and Economic Performance Measures for Nations, Arlington, Virginia, US, May 13–18.

HEIJINK, R., M. NOETHEN, T. RENAUD, M. KOOPMANSCHAP, and J. J. POLDER. 2008. Cost of Illness: An International Comparison of Australia, Canada, France, Germany and The Netherlands. *Health Policy*, 88/1: 49–61.

HODGSON, THOMAS A. and ALAN J. COHEN. 1999. Medical Care Expenditures for Major Diseases, 1995. *Health Care Financing Review*, Winter, 21: 119–64.

HULTEN, CHARLES R. 2001. Total Factor Productivity: A Short Biography. In Charles R. Hulten, Edwin R. Dean and Michael J. Harper, eds., *New Developments in Productivity Analysis. Studies in Income and Wealth*, Vol. 63. Chicago: University of Chicago Press for the National Bureau of Economic Research.

IHAT, OECD-Eurostat-WHO. 2009. Notes on Improving the Quality of the Estimation of Capital Formation in the SHA. Document code SHA-REV-A1001. OECD, Paris, October 7.

JORGENSON, DALE W., FRANK M. GOLLOP, and BARBARA M. FRAUMENI. 1987. *Productivity and US Economic Growth*. Cambridge, MA: Harvard University Press.

—— J. STEVEN LANDEFELD, and WILLIAM D. NORDHAUS. 2006. *A New Architecture for the US National Accounts. Studies in Income and Wealth*, Vol. 66. Chicago: University of Chicago Press.

MARTIN, S., N. RICE, and P. SMITH. 2008. Does Health Care Spending Improve Health Outcomes? Evidence from English Programme Budgeting Data. *Journal of Health Economics*, 27: 826–42.

McKEOWN, THOMAS. 1976. *The Role of Medicine: Dream, Mirage, or Nemesis?* London: Nuffield Provincial Hospitals Trust.

MELTZER, DAVID. 2001. Theoretical Foundations of Medical Cost Effectiveness Analysis: Implications for the Measurement of Benefits and Costs of Medical Interventions. In David M. Cutler and Ernst R. Berndt, eds., *Medical Care Output and Productivity. Studies in Income and Wealth*, Vol. 62. Chicago: The University of Chicago Press for the National Bureau of Economic Reseach.

MURRAY, RICHARD. 1992. Measuring Public-Sector Output: The Swedish Report. In Zvi Griliches, ed., *Output Measurement in the Service Sector, Studies in Income and Wealth*, Vol. 56. Chicago: University of Chicago Press for the National Bureau of Economic Research, 517–42.

NATIONAL RESEARCH COUNCIL. 1979. *Measurement and Interpretation of Productivity. Report of the Panel to Review Productivity Statistics*. Washington, DC: National Academy of Sciences.

NEWHOUSE, JOSEPH P. 1989. Measuring Medical Prices and Understanding Their Effect: The Baxter Prize Address. *Journal of Health Administration Education*, 7/1: 19–26.

—— 1992. Medical Care Costs: How Much Welfare Loss? *Journal of Economic Perspectives*, 6/3: 3–21.

NORDHAUS, WILLIAM D. 2006. Principles of National Accounting for Nonmarket Accounts. In D.W. Jorgenson, J. S. Landfeld and W. D. Nordhaus, eds., *A New Architecture for the US National Accounts: Studies in Income and Wealth*, Vol. 66. Chicago: University of Chicago Press, 143–60.

OECD (ORGANIZATION FOR ECONOMIC COOPERATION AND DEVELOPMENT). 2001. *Measuring Productivity, OECD Manual: Measurement of Aggregate and Industry-Level Productivity Growth*. Paris: OECD.

—— 2003. *A Disease-Based Comparison of Health Systems: What is Best and at What Cost?* Paris: OECD.

ONS (OFFICE FOR NATIONAL STATISTICS, UK). 2008. Public Service Productivity: Health Care. ONS UK Centre for the Measurement of Government Activity, London, January.

PHILIPSON, TOMAS and RICHARD POSNER. 2008. Is the Obesity Epidemic a Public Health Problem? A Decade of Research on the Economics of Obesity. NBER Working paper no. 14010. National Bureau of Economic Research, Cambridge, MA, May.

POLDER, J. J. and P. W. ACHTENBERG. 2004. *Cost of Illness in the Netherlands*. Bilthoven, The Netherlands: Centre for Public Health Forecasting, National Institute for Public Health and the Environment.

PRICE STATISTICS REVIEW COMMITTEE. 1961. *The Price Statistics of the Federal Government. Government Price Statistics, Hearings, Part 1. 87th Congress, 1st Session, 1961*. Washington, DC: US Congress, Joint Economic Committee. Also published as: National Bureau of Economic Research, General Series, Number 73.

RICE, DOROTHY P. 1966. Estimating the Cost of Illness. Health Economic Series No. 6. DHEW Publication No. (PHS) 947-6, US Department of Health, Education, and Welfare, Rockville, MD.

—— THOMAS A. HODGSON, and ANDREA N. KOPSTEIN. 1985. The Economic Cost of Illness: A Replication and Update. *Health Care Financing Review*, Fall, 7/1: 61–80.

ROEHRIG, CHARLES, GEORGE MILLER, CRAIG LAKE and JENNY BRYANT. 2009. National Health Spending by Medical Condition. *Health Affairs*, 28/2: 358–67.

SCHREYER, PAUL. 2001. *Measuring Productivity, OECD Manual: Measurement of Aggregate and Industry-Level Productivity Growth*. Paris: OECD.

—— 2009. Towards Measuring the Volume of Health and Education Services: OECD Draft Handbook. Paris: Organisation for Economic Co-operation and Development. Paper STD/CSTAT/WPNA(2008)12.

SCITOVSKY, ANNE A. 1964. An Index of the Cost of Medical Care: A Proposed New Approach. In Solomon J. Axelrod, ed., *The Economics of Health and Medical Care*. Ann Arbor: Bureau of Public Health Economics, University of Michigan.

—— 1967. Changes in the Costs of Treatment of Selected Illnesses, 1951–65. *American Economic Review*, 57/5: 1182–95.

SHAPIRO, IRVING, MATTHEW D. SHAPIRO and DAVID W. WILCOX. 2001. Measuring the Value of Cataract Surgery. In D. M. Cutler and E. R. Berndt, eds., *Medical Care Output and Productivity. Studies in Income and Wealth*, Vol. 62. Chicago: The University of Chicago Press for the National Bureau of Economic Research, 411–37.

STIGLER, G. J. et al. 1961. *The Price Statistics of the Federal Government. Government Price Statistics, Hearings, Part 1. 87th Congress, 1st Session, 1961*. Washington, DC: US Congress, Joint Economic Committee. Also published as: National Bureau of Economic Research, General Series, Number 73.

TRAJTENBERG, M. 1990. *Economic Analysis of Product Innovation: The Case of CT Scanners*. Cambridge, MA: Harvard University Press.

TRIPLETT, JACK E. 1999. Accounting for Health Care: Integrating Price Index and Cost-Effectiveness Research. In Jack E. Triplett, ed., *Measuring the Prices of Medical Treatments*. Washington, DC: Brookings Institution Press, 220–50.

—— 2001. What's Different About Health? Human Repair and Car Repair in National Accounts and in National Health Accounts. In D. M. Cutler and E. R. Berndt, eds., *Medical Care Output and Productivity. Studies in Income and Wealth*, Vol. 62. Chicago: The University of Chicago Press for the National Bureau of Economic Research, 15–94.

TRIPLETT, JACK E. 2004. Performance Measures for Computers. In Dale W. Jorgenson and Charles Wessner, eds., *Deconstructing the Computer*. Washington, DC: National Academies Press, 99–139.

—— 2005. *Handbook on Hedonic Indexes and Quality Adjustments in Price Indexes: Special Application to Information Technology Products*. Paris: OECD Publishing.

—— and BARRY P. BOSWORTH. 2004. *Productivity in the US Services Sector: New Sources of Economic Growth*. Washington, DC: Brookings Institution Press.

—— —— 2007. The Early 21st Century US Productivity Expansion is *Still* in Services. *International Productivity Monitor*, Spring, 14: 3–19.

WORLD CANCER RESEARCH FUND / AICR (AMERICAN INSTITUTE FOR CANCER RESEARCH). 2007. *Food, Nutrition, Physical Activity and the Prevention of Cancer: A Global Perspective*. Washington, DC: AICR.

WHO (WORLD HEALTH ORGANISATION). 1977. *Manual of the International Classification of Diseases, Injuries and Causes of Death (ICD-9)*. Geneva: WHO.

CHAPTER 31

....

THE METHODS OF COST-EFFECTIVENESS ANALYSIS TO INFORM DECISIONS ABOUT THE USE OF HEALTH CARE INTERVENTIONS AND PROGRAMS

....

SIMON WALKER, MARK SCULPHER, AND MIKE DRUMMOND

31.1 INTRODUCTION

....

THE developed world is faced with rising real health care costs. An important driver of increased cost pressure is the arrival in the market of new medical technologies such as pharmaceuticals and devices. The question facing health care systems is whether these new technologies should be funded by collectively funded health care systems and made available to patients. A range of other resource allocation decisions face health systems, including whether to invest in new equipment and buildings and the appropriate organization of services.

In standard economic theory, the supply and demand for new technologies and health services in perfectly competitive markets would result in efficient outcomes (so called "market clearing" prices and quantities). However, health and healthcare have many characteristics which, taken together, limit the functioning of markets (Arrow 1963). These include significant uncertainty (about both the occurrence and recovery from illness); limits to effective individual choice arising from asymmetries of information between healthcare professionals and patients and individuals not facing the full cost of their care at the point of delivery; and the presence of significant ineradicable monopoly characteristics among providers. As a result health care markets, without government intervention, are unlikely to produce efficient solutions. Furthermore, unregulated markets for health care raise a number of profound distributional issues as individuals' use of services is necessarily governed by their willingness and ability to pay rather than medical need. Private insurance is a partial market-based response to this but insurance itself is characterized by potential inefficiencies (such as moral hazard; Nyman 2006) and fails to address equity concerns if cover is unavailable or prohibitively expensive for those with pre-existing or chronic health conditions.

The basic economic problem is often described as a problem of unlimited wants but with limited resources to satisfy them. This applies as much to health care as to any other market, but the shortcomings of free markets in health care, on the basis of efficiency and equity, means that alternative ways of allocating resources need to be established—that is, choices must be made about which health care interventions to provide and which not to provide within a health care system. The methods of economic evaluation have been developed to help to inform these choices.

Economic evaluation can be defined as "the comparative analysis of alternative courses of action in terms of both their costs and consequences" (Drummond et al. 2005). The economic evaluation of health care technologies has become a central policy tool in many health care systems (Tam and Smith 2004). These methods have most notably been adopted to inform decisions about the funding of expensive new medicines—for example, by the National Institute for Health and Clinical Excellence (NICE 2008) in the UK. However, they have also been applied to inform decisions as disparate as investment in workplace health (Tompa et al. 2008) and safety programs and incentivizing family doctors to change practice (Mason et al. 2008). This chapter seeks to explain the theoretical foundations of these methods and their implementation in practice.

Health care systems around the world are not homogenous. Each exhibit their own features and nuances which imposes constraints on the appropriate way to analyze interventions and make decisions about their implementation. This chapter will, in the main, focus on a budget constrained health care sector, where implementing a new technology with additional costs will result in other health care services being displaced hence forgoing health improvement elsewhere. While not all health care systems operate under such a "hard" budget constraint in the long run, in the short run they must make trade-offs within the health care sector. This simplification also makes easier the exposition and interpretation of what is presented in this chapter.

31.2 PRINCIPLES OF CHOICE IN HEALTH CARE

Although all economic evaluation methods have formal links to the principles of micro-economic analysis, there are several different normative viewpoints present in the field—that is, alternative frameworks for judging whether one allocation of resources should be judged socially preferable to another. The choice of normative viewpoint has an impact on analytic methods and the types of recommendation likely to flow from the analysis. These normative viewpoints can be classified broadly as either "welfarist" or "non-welfarist" as described briefly below.

31.2.1 Welfarism

Welfarism is based on orthodox neo-classical welfare economics, the central principles of which are: (i) the welfare of society is based on the utility (well-being) of the individuals in the society; and (ii) individuals are the best judges of their own well-being (Broadway and Bruce 1984). In principle, interpersonal comparisons of utility are not permitted. Instead improvements in societal welfare can only come about when a change (for example, a change in policy) results in at least one individual being better off and no individual being made worse off (a so-called "Pareto" improvement). However, policy decisions which produce winners but no losers are likely to be few and far between.

For this practical reason the welfarist framework has been extended using the concept of "potential Pareto improvement." Developed by Kaldor (1939) and Hicks (1939) the idea is that if the "gainers" from a policy change, those individuals made better off by a change, can *potentially* compensate the "losers," those made worse off, such that no individual would be worse off and therefore such a change would result in an increase in social welfare. Note the emphasis on "potential compensation": if compensation was actually paid this would be equivalent to a Pareto improvement. The Kaldor–Hicks compensation test forms the normative basis for a widely used approach to economic evaluation (known as cost-benefit analysis) as used, for example, in most appraisals of new transport investments (Mishan 1971).

The welfarist approach is open to criticism (Sen 1979). For many people the assumptions underpinning it are too restrictive and the notion that social welfare is only a function of individual utilities too narrow (Sen 1979; Culyer 1991). Welfarism has also been criticized because of the mechanisms needed to employ it as a method for economic evaluation. In general, utilities are expressed through individuals' willingness to pay; that is, the largest amount an individual would be willing to pay for a change in policy. Willingness to pay is often calculated from market prices (if these are prices arising in competitive markets) or imputed using other methods if market prices are not available ("shadow prices"), but these methods raise major issues in healthcare. First, an individual's willingness to pay is likely to be closely related to their ability to pay, but when individuals' incomes are widely dispersed the sum of willingness to pay values may not actually reflect aggregate utility. This is because those with higher income are prepared to pay higher prices but they are likely to derive less utility from their last unit of income (termed a lower marginal utility of money). One response is to give greater weight to a pound spent by a poor person than by a rich person—but all attempts to reweight these "pound votes" are likely to prove controversial (Lerner 1944).

Second, as a result of problems in the functioning of the market for healthcare (e.g. asymmetries of information) consumer sovereignty may be compromised, and this raises still further issues about whether the willingness to pay of individuals actually reflects the utility they derive. Applications of welfarism are also usually based on the assumption that we are in a "first best" world, one in which markets are perfectly competitive and result in efficient outcomes. In such a world, at the market clearing price the marginal social benefit is equal to the marginal social cost. Thus the price represents the opportunity cost in terms of both demand and supply and as such the market price can be used to value both the outcomes and the resources used (where the opportunity cost represents the value of the next best alternative forgone). Several authors (Sculpher et al. 2005; Claxton et al. 2007) have argued that this first best world does not exist, for example as a consequence of the existence of externalities whereby individuals do not incur the full cost of their actions, and as such making decisions based on prices that are assumed to be derived in a first best world may actually reduce social welfare (Diamond and Mirrlees 1971a and 1971b).

31.2.2 Non-welfarist approaches

Non-welfarist approaches, which can take several forms such as extra-welfarism or social decision-making, exchange the notion of the objective being the maximization of some aggregation of individual utilities for another set of objectives. When considering decisions in health care this generally involves maximizing some target measure of health, though this does not necessarily have to be the case. Some would argue that the non-welfarist approach has been influenced by Sen's capability theory (Sen 1993). The theory emphasizes functional capabilities, i.e. what a person can do or can be, instead of the more standard welfarist emphasis on utilities. However, in its general use in the economic evaluation of health care, adopting a non-welfarist approach has led to a focus on a much narrower objective, i.e. health alone, rather than the wider ranging measures of well-being implicit in Sen's theory.

When making decisions in health care, the use of an objective function under which health is maximized may be controversial given that this would appear to negate individuals' preferences and can thus appear paternalistic. However, if such objectives arise from some form of legitimate process, for example from the decisions of a democratically elected government, or through the voluntary purchase by a consumer of an insurance plan which makes decisions on the basis of such an objective function, then it is more difficult to interpret the function as paternalistic. Although such functions clearly involve strong assumptions and social value judgments, Claxton et al. (2007) argue that these value judgments can be seen as explicit.

31.3 MAKING CHOICES

In selecting a welfarist or a non-welfarist approach to making resource allocation decisions in health care, a series of value judgments are effectively being made about what should matter in terms of both outcomes and opportunity costs. In either approach an objective function is being maximized, whether that be the summation of individual utilities or, for example, the health of the population, subject to one or more constraints. Different choices may be made under each approach as both the outcome and the opportunity cost could be valued very differently by the methods associated with each of the approaches.

Although rarely used in health care, cost-benefit analysis (CBA) is an approach to economic evaluation which has its roots in the welfarist normative framework (Sugden and Williams 1979). Although there are many variants, in general CBA quantifies the costs of interventions in terms of their impact of resources and takes market prices where possible to value these. In principle, all outcomes would be included with valuation based on the willingness to pay of individuals who stand to gain or lose from a new policy. These methods rarely explicitly consider the constraints imposed by finite budgets.

The non-welfarist paradigm predominates in the economic evaluation used by most health care systems to inform resource allocation. NICE in the UK, for example, seeks to make decisions which are consistent with maximizing health subject to a fixed NHS budget using a set of tools called cost-effectiveness analysis (CEA)(NICE 2008). This is illustrated in Figure 31.1 below which shows the comparison of a new intervention (which could be generalized to any particular new policy) compared with existing practice. The y-axis shows the additional cost of the new intervention when it is priced at 3 alternative levels (P*, less than P* or greater than P*). The x-axis shows the gain in health

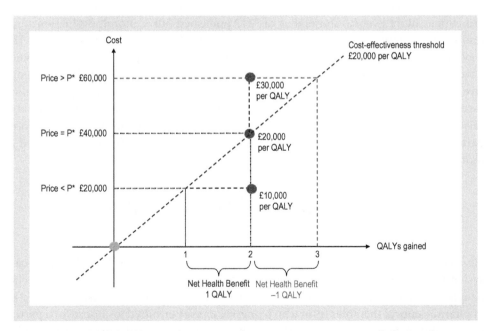

FIGURE 31.1 Assessing the cost-effectiveness of an intervention given an objective of maximizing health subject to a fixed budget

Source: Claxton et al. 2008.

generated by the new technology in terms of individuals' survival duration adjusted for the quality of life they experience—so called quality-adjusted life-years (QALYs) which are discussed in more detail below.

Consider first the situation where the new intervention generates two QALYs per patient but at an additional cost of £20,000 per patient (based on a price <P*). Given the fixed budget, to fund this new intervention another existing service must be displaced elsewhere in the health system (possibly in a quite different clinical area). This displacement generates an "opportunity cost": forgone health for another group of patients who no longer receive the service. The cost-effectiveness "threshold" reflects the estimate that, for every £20,000 generated through displacement of one or more existing service, the opportunity cost is 1 QALY. In this first scenario, then, the additional cost of the new intervention has an opportunity cost of 1 QALY but itself generated two QALYs, hence its introduction would be cost-effective as there is a net gain in health of one QALY from the same fixed budget. In contrast, Figure 31.1 shows that, if the additional cost of the new intervention is £40,000 (due to a higher price = P*), then the benefit of the new treatment is exactly offset by that lost elsewhere; the health system gains nothing from funding the new intervention. If the additional cost per patient is £60,000 (with a price >P*) then the opportunity cost, resulting from the displacement of existing services to fund the new intervention, is greater than the additional health it generates (3 QALYs versus two QALYs); this could not be considered cost-effective as there is a net loss in health.

CEA (or its variant, cost-utility analysis) is the most widely used form of economic evaluation in health care. The NHS Economic Evaluation Database (See <http://www.crd.york.ac.uk/crdweb/>) shows that, of 7212 published full economic evaluation studies in the database, over 98 percent used some form of cost-effectiveness analysis. The way these studies are used to inform decisions varies. For example, some systems do not have a "hard" budget constraint so the opportunity cost of funding new (more expensive) interventions may fall, in part at least, outside the health system (e.g. additional insurance premiums or taxation, or reduced expenditure elsewhere). The methods also raise a number of issues including which existing services new interventions are compared with, how health is measured and what costs are included. These are discussed in more detail below.

31.4 Defining the Decision Problem

Healthcare revolves around choices. These choices occur at all levels of the healthcare system: for example, a physician must decide which treatments to give to a specific patient with a particular condition; a hospital formulary committee must decide the set of pharmaceutical therapies from which physicians are permitted to choose for a particular condition; managers must decide whether it is worth investing in expensive equipment with large upfront cost, for example magnetic imaging machines—the list of points of choice is almost endless.

Any explicit approach to making these types of choices needs to specify the decision problem being addressed which involves two key questions. These are described below in the context of choosing between alternative medical interventions, but this can be readily generalized to the other types of choice summarized above.

31.4.1 Who is the Choice Directed At?

This typically takes the form of the patient group which is the intended recipient of, for example, a new therapeutic or diagnostic intervention. This will often need to be quite specific—for example, in making decisions about whether to give patients access to new pharmaceuticals, the recipient group of patients will usually be tightly defined by the product's license. There may be a series of sub-groups of recipients which are distinguished in the decision problem—for example, the cost-effectiveness of a new treatment for ischemic heart disease may be considered separately for sub-groups of patient defined in terms of the severity of their current condition.

31.4.2 What is the Choice Between?

It is necessary to define the options being compared. Economic evaluation is often used to assess new medical technologies, so these need to be specified together with the options against which the new intervention will be compared. In principle, comparators should reflect all the existing ways in which the recipient group is currently (or could be) managed. This may include a "do nothing" option or a sequence of possible interventions. More generally, the aim of a study might be to identify the most cost-effective way of managing a particular group of patients from a number of existing interventions. Again, the principle is to include all possible options in the analysis.

31.5 A Clinical Scenario

The chapter so far is intended to provide a grounding in the policy motivation for economic evaluation and the underlying normative issues in undertaking studies. We now further develop the key elements of undertaking economic evaluation in practice.

Box 31.1 outlines a simple scenario regarding the comparison of chemotherapy treatments for breast cancer. This example will be used throughout the remainder of the chapter to illustrate some of the conceptual issues raised in this chapter. This clinical scenario is also used as part of Chapter 32 by Griffin and Claxton on uncertainty in economic evaluation.

Box 31.1 A Clinical Scenario to Illustrate the Methods of Economic Evaluation: Introduction

---

You are in control of a central budget from which the healthcare services for a specific population must be paid for. For example, you may be an insurance company or an institute with the remit to assessing health care interventions and programs for possible reimbursement or coverage within a national health care system.

You must decide which chemotherapy (if any) to make available to patients presenting with early breast cancer, while being mindful of your obligation to provide healthcare to patients with other diseases from your finite budget.

The regulatory body with the remit for licensing drugs lists three approved regimens for use in patients with early breast cancer:

- First generation chemotherapy (FGO);
- Second generation chemotherapy (SGO);
- FGO in combination with SGO (COMB).

31.6 MEASURING OUTCOMES

The assumed objective, in terms of the outcomes of health care programs and interventions, is central to economic evaluation. As shown in Figure 31.1 above the focus of outcome measurement in most evaluations is on health. Let us consider the treatment of a single disease. If there are a set of mutually exclusive treatment options, where the set of treatment options includes all relevant treatments for the disease (perhaps including a "no treatment" option), how should we decide which treatment is the "best"? If we are treating a single disease, and making decisions only within that disease area, a key source of evidence on the comparative effect of different treatments will be randomized controlled trials (RCTs), if available. The main results of such trials are typically clinical measures of outcome—for example, in a transitory illness, time with symptoms or, in cancer, overall survival. If the objective of the decision-maker is simply to choose the treatment from the mutually exclusive interventions which the trials suggest gives the best result for the clinical measure of outcome then it is generally a straightforward choice.

However, things can become rather more complicated if we have two different clinical measures within a disease area, which are not perfectly correlated—for example, severity of symptoms and duration with symptoms. Or, similarly, we may be trying to make decisions across disease areas which have different clinical measures of outcome. For example, a choice may be faced between funding a new drug for a cancer which gives an extra eight weeks of progression free survival or a new drug for the treatment of flu symptoms which reduces the time with symptoms by two days. In these circumstances we need to be able to establish a trade-off between the two measures, but how would this be addressed?

It would be helpful to have some "generic" (non-disease specific) unit of health measurement which could allow us to make choices between treatments across disease areas.

The reason for this should be clear from Figure 31.1: it is necessary to compare the health gained from a new intervention, relative to an existing comparator, with the health decrement associated with displacing existing services (typically from quite different clinical areas) to fund the additional cost of the new technology. One unit of health outcome that has a degree of comparability across disease areas is overall survival duration, the estimated mean time until death. One issue that arises from using overall mean survival duration is that, while it is a clinical measure of outcome, results from trials will generally not provide this information. This is because, for many diseases, trials do not have a long enough follow-up to estimate mean survival with any degree of accuracy and are often not large enough to estimate differences between interventions with any degree of precision. This raises an issue of how to link other "intermediate" endpoints, such as time to progression in cancer, which clinical randomized controlled trials are powered to find differences in between treatments, and the overall survival. We will return to this later in the extrapolation and modeling section of this chapter.

Overall survival clearly has benefits over disease specific units of health by facilitating comparison across treatments in different disease groups where the change in survival is considered one of the key impacts of health care interventions on health. However, few would argue that health improvement is purely about extending survival. If, for example, we have a choice between two cancer drugs, one of which has minimal side effects and the other has significant side effects, is it inevitable we would select the latter just because it had very marginally higher overall survival? There are also disease areas where treatments have no effect on overall survival but instead lead to improvements in health-related quality of life (HRQoL), for example some treatments for mental illnesses or most interventions in dermatology. By only considering overall survival we would clearly ignore the health gain generated by interventions in such clinical areas.

There are arguments, therefore, for measuring health in such a way that it captures both changes in the *quantity* of life (overall survival) as well as the HRQoL (morbidity). The most commonly used and well-known measure, which jointly encompasses both the quantity and quality of life, is the quality adjusted life year (QALY), although other measures have been proposed (Murray et al. 2002). QALYs are generated by the summation across all health states of the length of time in a particular health state multiplied by a weight representing the HRQoL attached to that health state (see Box 31.2). These weights are often referred to as "utility" although this has a quite different meaning to the same term used by the neoclassical economist. The HRQoL weights are based on a scale where 1 represents perfect health and 0 represents death. Negative values are also permitted (i.e. health states considered worse than death).

There are various approaches for deriving the HRQoL weights (See Box 31.3). Importantly, these weights represent preferences and an important issue is whose preferences should be used in estimating the weights. The main contending sources of preferences are the general public (who are typically the ultimate payers) and patients. There are arguments for and against both groups, and the choice is essentially a political rather than scientific one (Brazier et al. 2005). The HRQoL weights should satisfy three requirements. First, more desirable health states should receive higher weights. Second, they should be anchored on perfect health and death, as these two states are relevant if we are

Box 31.2 Quality-adjusted life-years from an Intervention

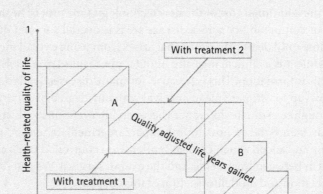

With treatment 1 the patient's HRQoL would deteriorate along the lower path and they would die at time X. However, with treatment 2 the patient would maintain a higher quality of life and would live longer and would instead die at time Y. The area below treatment path 1 represents the QALYs associated with treatment 1 and the area below treatment path 2 represents the QALYs associated with treatment 2. The area between the two paths is the QALYs gained by treating the patient with treatment 2 instead of treatment 1. This can be separated into 2 parts: area A represents the QALY gain as a result of quality improvement and area B the QALY gain as a result of quantity improvement (figure based on Gold et al. 1996).

to make comparisons between all possible interventions. Finally, they should be measured on an interval scale, such that an increase from 0 to 0.2 is considered equivalent to an increase from 0.8 to 1.

There are now a number of measurement instruments that facilitate the measurement of individuals' health states in a way that can be expressed in terms of HRQoL weights. One of these measures is the EuroQol (EQ)-5D (Kind 1996) which is used widely in RCTs and other clinical studies (See Box 31.4).

QALYs have been widely criticized (Nord and Kamlet 2009). For many they lack sensitivity to actual changes in health, in part due to their generic nature. Another criticism is that QALYs provide a crude representation of how individuals would make the trade-off between length and quality of life—for example, the assumption of constant

Box 31.3 Deriving Health–related Quality of Life Weights

Two most common widely used methods for establishing the health related quality of life weights are time trade-off (TTO) and standard gamble (SG). Time trade-off involves asking an individual to make a choice between living the rest of his/her life, for time t, in a given health state, which has an as yet unknown quality of life value of h_i, and living a shorter period, for time x, in perfect health, which has a quality of life value of 1. Time x is varied until the individual is indifferent between the two alternatives. At this point the quality of life weight attached to the state is equal to x/t.

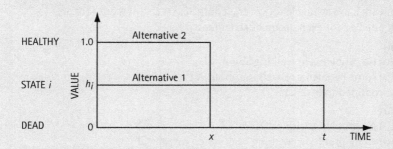

With standard gamble, an individual is asked to make the choice between the certainty of remaining in a given health state, with an as yet unknown quality of life x, or an alternative with two possible outcomes, perfect health and death. The probability of the outcome perfect health in the alternative, p, is then varied until the individual is indifferent between remaining in the state with certainty or taking the gamble between perfect health and death. At this point the health related quality of life weight for the state x is equal to p.

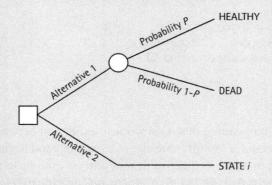

Source: Drummond et al. 2005

Box 31.4 Euroqol (EQ)–5D

Getting all patients in a clinical trial to value their health states using the TTO or SG would be very time consuming. Instead values using these techniques have been placed on health states through the use of questionnaires. An example of such a questionnaire is the EQ-5D which is a standardized instrument for use as a measure of health outcome. Applicable to a wide range of health conditions and treatments, it provides a simple descriptive profile and a single index value for health status. Individuals are asked 5 questions about various aspects of their health (mobility, self-care, usual activities, pain/discomfort, and anxiety/depression) on which there are 3 levels to choose from (no problem, moderate problems, severe problems). The states described by the instrument are linked to existing preference weights which are available for several countries (see <www.euroqol.org>).

Tick one box for each group of statements:

Mobility

I have no problems in walking about ❑

I have some problems in walking about ❑

I am confined to bed ❑

Self-Care

I have no problems with self-care ❑

I have some problems washing or dressing myself ❑

I am unable to wash or dress myself ❑

Usual Activities

I have no problems with performing my usual activities (e.g. work, study, housework, family, or leisure activities) ❑

I have some problems with performing my usual activities ❑

I am unable to perform my usual activities ❑

Pain/Discomfort

I have no pain or discomfort ❑

I have moderate pain or discomfort ❑

I have extreme pain or discomfort ❑

Anxiety/Depression

I am not anxious or depressed ❑

I am moderately anxious or depressed ❑

I am extremely anxious or depressed ❑

proportional trade-off assumes that if someone is indifferent between, say, ten years in a particular (dysfunctional) health state and five years in good health, they will also be indifferent between one year in that health state and six months in good health. There has also been concern that while QALYs focus on individuals' health, they can be a poor reflection of individuals' preferences regarding the distribution of health improvement between different types of patient. Alternatives to the QALY such as the healthy-years equivalent and the patient trade off (Drummond et al. 2005) have been suggested to address these problems, but there are very few examples of their use in applied economic evaluation studies.

Despite these criticisms, QALYs are now widely used in economic evaluations supporting decision-making in health care. For example, NICE requires their use in studies undertaking to inform its decisions about whether to recommend new technologies for use in the NHS (NICE 2008); similar agencies internationally recommend QALYs, at least as an element in studies submitted to them (Tam and Smith 2004). The QALY, then, is an extensively used and understood measure of health in cost-effectiveness analyses. For example, they were recommended as the appropriate unit for health measurement by the Panel on Cost-Effectiveness in Health and Medicine, a US panel with expertise in cost-effectiveness analysis, clinical medicine, ethics, and health outcomes measurement, which was convened by the US Public Health Service (Gold et al. 1996).

Box 31.5 A Clinical Scenario to Illustrate the Methods of Economic Evaluation: Measuring and Valuing Outcomes

Published studies indicate FGO offers an improvement in survival when compared to no treatment, while the second generation regimen SGO offers an improvement in survival when compared to FGO, and the combination regimen of FGO and SGO offers an improvement in survival when compared to SGO alone. However, the side effect profile of COMB is considered to be worse than the side effect profile of FGO alone and SGO alone.

Patients will receive chemotherapy for three months. Patients on COMB experience a health-related quality of life (HRQoL) score (in terms of a 0 to 1 "utility") of 0.5 while on treatment, those on SGO a score of 0.6 and those on FGO 0.7.

Following treatment and until progression all patients have a HRQoL score of 0.75. Patients who receive FGO are expected to have a cancer recurrence four years after the end of treatment, those who receive SGO have a recurrence five years after the end of treatment and those who receive COMB have a cancer recurrence six years after the end of treatment.

Following progression, all patients have the same expected survival of two years with a HRQoL score health-related quality of life of 0.6.

Those patients who receive no chemotherapy treatment are expected to receive four QALYs.

Treatment	QALYs generated during treatment	Expected QALYs accumulated post-treatment during progression free survival	Total expected QALYs accumulated per patient
No treatment			4 QALYs
FGO	$0.7 \times 0.25 = 0.175$	$4 \times 0.75 = 3$	$3.175 + (2 \times 0.6) = 4.375$
SGO	$0.6 \times 0.25 = 0.15$	$5 \times 0.75 = 3.75$	$3.9 + 1.2 = 5.1$
COMB	$0.5 \times 0.25 = 0.125$	$6 \times 0.75 = 4.5$	$4.625 + 1.2 = 5.825$

How would the effects of alternative options on outcomes be captured in CBA within a welfarist paradigm? Given the general absence of unregulated markets in health, the focus would be on estimating the shadow price of the health outcomes— that is, the price at which the health outcome would be valued if a market for them existed and all market distortions were removed. There are two approaches which have been used to find this shadow price: revealed preference and contingent valuation (see Box 31.6). Revealed preference involves finding real life situations where individuals trade health and wealth, and then estimating an implicit value based on the individuals' behavior in these circumstances. An example of this method is the use of wage premiums for more dangerous jobs as a measure of how much the individual is willing to accept in return for increased risk of loss of life or injury (Johanesson 1995). Contingent valuation attempts to calculate the shadow price of health by creating hypothetical markets where tradeoffs between health and wealth are investigated in a sample of individuals (Drummond et al. 2005). Discrete choice experiments have also been used to value different treatments, based on the premise that any treatment can be described based on its characteristics and the extent to

---

Box 31.6 Examples of Revealed Preference and Contingent Valuation

Revealed preference: the value of a statistical life

"Suppose jobs A and B are identical except that workers in job A have higher annual fatal injury risks such that, on average, there is one more job-related death per year for every 10,000 workers in job A than in job B, and workers in job A earn $500 more per year than those in job B. The implied value of statistical life is then $5 million for workers in job B who are each willing to forgo $500 per year for a 1-in-10,000 lower annual risk" (Fisher et al. 1989).

Contingent valuation: road safety

"Suppose that you are buying a particular make of car. You can choose to have a new kind of safety feature fitted to the car at an extra cost. The risk of a car driver being killed in an accident is 10-in-100,000. You could choose to have a safety feature fitted to your car which would halve the risk of the car driver being killed, down to 5-in-100,000. Taking into account how much you can personally afford, what is the most that you would be prepared to pay to have this safety feature fitted to the car?" (Jones-Lee et al. 1985).

Hypothetical example

Current risk of death without safety feature: 10-in-100,000
New risk with safety feature: 5-in-100,000
Reduction in risk (dR): 5-in-100,000
Example maximum premium willing to pay (dV): $100
Implied value of life = $dV/dR = \$(100/5) \times (10^5) = £2,000,000$

which individuals value the treatment depends on its level of these characteristics (Ryan and Gerard 2003).

The use of contingent valuation and discrete choice methods is not confined to valuing health outcomes. Indeed, one of the suggested advantage of these methods is that they enable a wider set of outcomes to be incorporated into studies (e.g. effect of interventions on other areas of individuals' well-being such as convenience and the value they attach to information). These allow the comparison of benefits across different fields although it is unclear how decisions can be made, particularly when transfers between different sectors are not possible.

31.7 Costs

It is not the money costs of resources that we are directly interested in, but instead the opportunity costs, i.e. what is the next best thing we could do with the resources we use to provide a course of treatment. However, the most direct way to estimate the opportunity cost is, first, to estimate the resource costs associated with an allocation and then transform this into the opportunity costs (whether they be in terms of health or utilities). Which resources will be included depends on the perspective taken, e.g. whether we should include productivity costs if the focus is on health and there is a fixed budget, where productivity costs are any gain in output as a result of the health care intervention. The transformation into opportunity costs also depends on the view we take on prices, i.e. do we accept that prices reflect opportunity cost or do we instead need to calculate shadow prices?

Costs associated with different health care programs and treatments can be split into several groups: costs arising from the use of resources within the health care sector; costs relating to resource use by patients and their families; costs arising from resource use in other sectors of the economy; and costs stemming from productivity changes.

31.7.1 Which Costs Should Be Included?

The range of the above costs considered in an economic evaluation is likely to be based upon the consideration of four points (Drummond et al. 2005). First, what is the perspective of the analysis? This is perhaps the most essential, as it is determined by the budget constraint imposed on the decision-maker and also on specific judgments that we are making. If the perspective is that of the healthcare sector, we are unlikely to be interested in the costs imposed on patients or their families. However, these costs would clearly be of importance if we took a broader societal perspective, i.e. an all-encompassing perspective whereby changes in costs and productivity are all included. Many health care systems use economic evaluation methods to inform resource allocation decisions within that sector—as a result, they take a perspective reflecting their own budget constraint (e.g. NICE's technology appraisal program in the UK). Other agencies take a wider cost perspective because they are responsible for a wider set of budgets or have no direct budget responsibility at all (e.g. the TLV, which makes decisions about the use of new pharmaceutical products in Sweden).

Second, is the comparison restricted to two or more programs immediately under study? If the comparison relates to set of specific options with specific costs being common to all the interventions being compared, then these costs need not be considered as they would not affect the choice between interventions. However, if it is thought that, at some later stage, a wider comparison of interventions may be considered, including some interventions not considered in the original evaluation, it would be wise to include costs which are common. Third, are some costs merely likely to confirm a result that would be obtained by consideration of a narrower range of costs? If it is felt that the costs are unlikely to affect the balance of costs between the various interventions it may not be worth the extra resource use required to collect them. Finally, what is the relative order of magnitude of costs? Similarly to the last point, if it is considered that some costs will be very small and unlikely to change the balance of costs between different interventions then it may not be worth considering them given the cost of collecting information on them.

31.7.2 Measuring and Valuing Costs

Once the costs to be included in the evaluation have been decided upon, then the method for valuing the costs is based on the measurement of two components. First, the physical quantities of the resources consumed (e.g. days in hospital, doctors' visits, etc.) must be estimated. Second, the value of these resources in money terms must be estimated (i.e. the prices).

The measurement of the physical quantities of the resources consumed will often depend upon the context for the economic evaluation. If the economic evaluation is being undertaken as part of a randomized controlled trial, data on the resource use may be collected as part of the study's case record forms. This could be supplemented by patient questionnaires for resource use not easily captured from routine clinical notes (e.g. patients' use of community care services). If there is no trial (or similar clinical study) providing a vehicle for the collection of resource use data, these could be collected from patients' clinical notes, hospital data systems, or through patient questionnaires.

For many resources, market prices may be available. Theoretically the proper price for a resource is its opportunity cost (the value of the forgone benefits given the resources use in its next best alternative). However, the pragmatic approach to costing is to take existing market prices which would reflect the opportunity cost in a "first best" world (Drummond et al. 2005). However, there are many reasons why the market price may not reflect the true cost of the resource—for example, some prices may be subsidized or set under government issued monopoly patents. If a health system perspective is taken, then the financial costs falling on the system is the sole focus. Here the opportunity cost is in terms of health (see Figure 31.1).

If we take a societal perspective we may also need to value productivity costs if there are productivity gains or losses associated with the health care interventions being assessed, for example due to the patient or one of their relatives being unable to work. These are commonly valued using one of two approaches: the human capital approach or the friction cost method, with the latter only being used to assess productivity losses. More discussion of these approaches and their strengths and weaknesses can be found in Sculpher (2001).

Once resource use and prices have been collected, the total resource cost of a patient can then be calculated by the summation of the resources included multiplied by their price. Box 31.7 considers the measurement and aggregation of costs in our clinical scenario.

31.8 How Do We Make Decisions Based on Costs and Outcomes?

Earlier we briefly touched upon how costs and outcomes can be combined for the purpose of decision-making (see Figure 31.1). We will now examine this further. Let us consider a decision-maker allocating resources across the health system. Ideally, with

---

Box 31.7 A Clinical Scenario to Illustrate the Methods of Economic Evaluation: Dealing With Costs

The published pricing lists indicate that SGO is the most expensive chemotherapy regimen simply in terms of purchasing the drugs, followed by COMB, with FGO being the cheapest. Due to the more serious side effects associated with COMB patients will require more treatment than those on SGO, and similarly those on FGO will require less treatment than those on SGO. Each year of progression free survival costs $250 in medical care resources. Following progression, care costs $5000 until death.

	Chemotherapy cost	Cost of treating side-effects	Cost of care during progression free survival	Cost of care following progression	Total cost of care
No treatment					$7500
FGO	$5000	$500	$1000	$5000	$11,500
SGO	$10,000	$1000	$1250	$5000	$17,250
COMB	$7500	$5000	$1500	$5000	$19,000

a fixed budget, the decision-maker would select from all available treatments, which includes all possible treatments in all disease areas, the subset that maximizes health benefits for the entire patient population subject to the given budget constraint. This approach could be achieved using mathematical programming (Epstein et al. 2007). However, in practice such an approach is not possible: there is no single decision-maker deciding on all treatments, nor is there enough information about the effectiveness and cost of all services to be able to formulate such a problem. Instead, when making decisions using economic evaluation, decision rules are used which attempt to proxy this ideal solution.

31.8.1 Decision Rules for CEA

Let us first consider the decision between a set of mutually exclusive interventions/programs before extending our analysis to consider independent interventions/programs. We consider two interventions for a disease, A and B, from a health system perspective where the relevant unit of output is a QALY. Figure 31.2 shows the cost-effectiveness plane which represents the incremental costs and effects of one of the treatments compared to the other. Note that the north east quadrant is what we illustrated in Figure 31.1. The origin represents the comparator treatment, in this case let it be B. If treatment A lies to the right of the origin it is more effective (has more QALYs than B), or if is to the left it is less effective. If treatment A lies above the x-axis then it is more costly than B, and vice versa.

If intervention A is less costly and more effective, then A is said to dominate B. Similarly if A is more costly and less effective than B, then it is dominated by B. In both cases the choice between A and B is obvious: the dominant option is clearly preferable. In practice, however, it is rare that costs and outcomes lend themselves to the dominance rule. Usually A will be both more costly and more effective than B or vice versa, i.e. in the

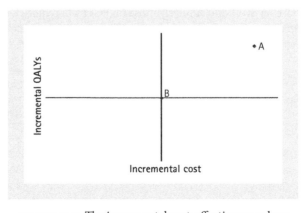

FIGURE 31.2 The incremental cost-effectiveness plane

north-east or south-west quadrant. The critical issue in these cases is whether the additional (incremental) cost of the intervention is worth paying for its incremental benefits, or similarly if it is worth making the cost saving given the lower outcomes which are associated with it. The decision rules developed to address this issue generally focus on the incremental cost-effectiveness ratio (ICER) which is defined:

$$ICER_{AB} = \frac{Costs_A - Costs_B}{QALYs_A - QALYs_B}$$

The ICER defines the amount that must be paid, per extra QALY, for the more expensive, but more effective, intervention. Whether to implement A given an ICER of a particular value will depend on the perspective the analysis is taking, with the key being what is displaced at the expense of the extra expenditure, i.e. the opportunity cost. If we define the threshold that we are willing to pay per extra QALY as λ, then if the ICER is greater than this we would not fund A, if it is less than λ we would fund A; if it is equal to λ we are indifferent between funding A and not funding A. This takes us back to the principles we covered earlier as illustrated in Figure 31.1. But where does λ come from? In general the choice is between a λ which represents the opportunity cost under a fixed budget (i.e. the ICER of the displaced treatment) or some measure of societal willingness to pay under an adjustable budget (also see McCabe et al. 2008).

An ICER compares two alternatives. However, when there are a number of mutually exclusive alternatives, then a number of comparisons can be made which will generate a series of possible ICERs. Table 31.1 looks at a number of hypothetical alternative interventions. Treatment X is dominated by all other treatments, it is both more expensive and less effective. Therefore, as discussed previously, it can be ignored. The choice is then between W, Y, and Z. These should be ranked in order of cost. The ICERs for each of these non-dominated options is then calculated relative to the next cheapest as shown in Table 31.2.

Figure 31.3 represents the cost-effectiveness plane for these three treatments where the origin is Z. As can be seen from the figure, there is a combination of Z and Y (e.g. if we give 50% of the patients Z and 50% of the patients Y), whereby the combination dominates W. Therefore, W is said to be subject to "extended dominance," and can be

Table 31.1 Costs and QALYs of Mutually Exclusive Alternatives

Treatment	Cost	QALYs
W	$8000	7
X	$10,000	5
Y	$9000	8
Z	$4000	6

Table 31.2 Incremental Costs and QALYs of Mutually Exclusive Alternatives

Treatment	Cost	QALYs	Incremental cost	Incremental QALYs	ICER
Z	$4,000	6			
W	$8,000	7	$4,000	1	$4,000
Y	$9,000	8	$1,000	1	$1,000

removed from consideration. Extended dominance can also be found from the ICERs. Once all dominated treatments are removed and the treatments ranked in order from least to most costly and the ICERs calculated, then if the ICER of the next most effective and expensive treatment is less than the ICER for the treatment compared to the next less effective and expensive treatment, then the treatment is subject to extended dominance.

All dominated and extended dominated strategies should be removed from the option decision set before making decisions about which treatment should be used. A failure to do so will lead to comparisons not with the next best treatment but with clearly inferior alternatives. Consequently, the ICERs will be underestimated and we will not ensure we select the optimum treatment. Box 31.8 considers decision rules in the context of the hypothetical clinical scenario.

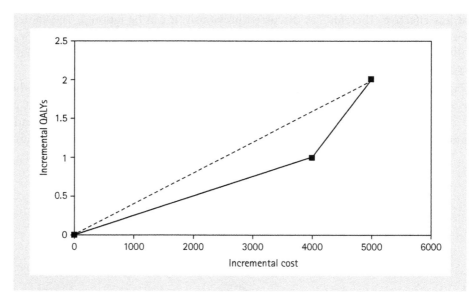

FIGURE 31.3 Top right quadrant of the cost-effectiveness plane for options *Z*, *W*, and *Y* as defined in Tables 31.1 and 31.2

It should be noted that decision rules outlined above are based on several assumptions, notably constant returns to scale, perfect divisibility and non repeatability, which may not always hold. A critique can be found in Birch and Gafni (1992). While extended dominance may not hold, in that a combination of two programs may not be possible in practice, its implications for decision-making still holds as long as λ is constant no matter how expensive a new treatment is. This is based on the argument that if you were willing to pay for the extendedly dominated treatment you must also be willing to pay for the next more expensive and more effective treatment. The largest criticism of ICER decision rules is related to the argument above in that ICERs only give us information about the cost per unit, not the total cost of the program. With perfect divisibility and constant returns to scale this does not matter. However, when this is not the case the size of the project does matter as it can alter the cost per QALY on the marginal project which will be displaced, or the societal WTP (Birch and Gafni 1992).

31.8.2 Decision Rules for CBA

Decision rules for CBA are rather different to those of CEA. Both costs and benefits of health care interventions are expressed in monetary terms using appropriate prices (or shadow prices), and the "net present value" of an intervention (the difference

---

Box 31.8 A Clinical Scenario to Illustrate the Methods of Economic Evaluation: Decision Rules

You must now make a decision about which treatment, if any, to make available to patients with early stage breast cancer. The incremental costs and QALYs are presented in the table below:

	Incremental cost	Incremental QALYs	Incremental cost per additional QALY
FGO vs. No treatment	$4000	0.375	$10,667
SGO vs. FGO	$5750	0.725	$7931
COMB vs. SGO	$1750	0.725	$2414
COMB vs. No treatment	$11,500	1.825	$6301

As can be seen from the ICERs, both FGO and SGO are subject to extended dominance by a combination of No treatment and COMB. Assuming we accept the exclusion of treatments based on extended dominance, this leaves us with a choice between two options: No treatment or COMB.

Consider how you would now choose between No treatment and COMB, and what additional information you would need to know.

between its aggregate benefit and its aggregate cost) is assessed. Any project with a positive net present value should be considered as a potential Pareto improvement using the welfarist principle discussed above. When selecting between mutually exclusive alternatives then the alternative with the highest net present value should be selected. The simplicity of this rule relies upon the assumption that budget constraints can typically be ignored. If budget constraints are recognized under CBA by health system decision-makers then, similarly to ICER decision rules, it would be necessary to compare the net present value of the treatment with the net present value of the treatments which would be displaced to fund it. If a broader view of public sector decisions is taken, CBA methods can be used to compare policies across sectors, although such decisions would typically be outside the remit of health system decision-makers.

31.9 Vehicles for Economic Evaluation

A large proportion of economic evaluations are conducted based on the information of a single randomized controlled trial (Sculpher et al. 2006). However, relying on a randomized trial as a single vehicle for economic evaluation has a number of key limitations (Sculpher et al. 2006). As a result of these limitations, economic evaluation for decision-making would normally need to draw upon a range of sources for evidence, including RCTs, but also cohort studies, quality of life surveys, etc.

Economic evaluation is not only concerned with the *measurement* of costs and effects but also with the appropriate synthesis of relevant evidence to inform resource allocation *decisions* within healthcare. It should be noted, therefore, that RCTs and decision analytic models are not competing alternatives (Drummond et al. 2005). Instead, RCTs are focused on different types of measurement whilst decision models are concerned with informing specific decisions.

All relevant comparators must be considered for the correct calculation of ICERs. However, many RCTs will fail to compare all the relevant options that might be considered by decision-makers, for example in RCTs drugs will typically just be compared to one other treatment which may not even be an active intervention but instead a placebo. To compare all the relevant options it is probable that evidence from a number of RCTs will be required to be synthesized through a meta-analysis (Egger et al. 1993). A decision analytic model will allow the results of the meta-analysis to be combined with other types of evidence, such as costs and utilities.

As was described in the outcomes section of this chapter, clinical trials often compare interventions in terms of intermediate endpoints rather than final outcomes, for example in cancer trials, time in remission. However, as discussed previously, the economic evaluation may require outcomes to be in QALYs. Decision models can be used to link intermediate outcomes with the outcomes required for decision-making.

Decision analytic modeling provides a framework for the synthesis of the data from all of the relevant sources. It also allows for the consideration of decision-making under uncertainty (see Chapter 32).

Decision analytic modeling provides a framework for decision-making which can satisfy the important objectives of economic evaluation (Drummond et al. 2005), namely:

1. Structure. It can provide a structure which appropriately reflects the prognoses of patients and how the treatments will impact on these prognoses.
2. Evidence. It can provide a framework within which all relevant evidence can be synthesized.
3. Assumptions and scientific value judgments. It provides an *explicit* way of bringing to bear the assumptions and judgments that are inevitably needed in making decisions based on uncertainty evidence.
4. Evaluation. It provides a structure which allows the translation of the relevant evidence into the outcomes of interest, namely costs and effectiveness, so that decisions can be made.

There are many types of decision models that can be used in economic evaluation, with perhaps the most common being decision trees and Markov models. However, two features that they all have in common are probabilities and expected values (Drummond et al. 2005). Probabilities represent the strength of belief that an event will happen; this may be based on prior evidence when available, but this may not always be the case and such values could be elicited from expert opinion if required. The other key feature is expected values; given a treatment it is still uncertain what the patient's outcome will be, for example, with a cancer drug there will be probabilities that they will progress or not progress. The expected costs and outcomes are a weighted sum of the possible costs and outcomes dependent on what occurs, with the weight based on the probability that those events will occur. The expected values represent the best estimate of the endpoints of interest for decision-making. More detailed discussion of decision modeling can be found in Drummond et al. (2005).

31.10 Summary

Resources are finite but wants are infinite. The scarcity of resources will always lead to decisions about which competing treatments to choose in health care. Methods for the economic evaluation of health care interventions facilitate a formal joint consideration of costs and outcomes for the purpose of decision-making. They allow for a decision over whether one allocation of resources is more preferable to another, not just within disease areas but also across them.

Two broad principles of choice have been proposed for economic evaluation, welfarist, based on orthodox welfare economics, and non-welfarist, which changes the objective from utility maximization to another set of objectives. The latter is more prominent in policy, but the choice between the two has key implications for some aspects of methodology including the types of outcomes and costs that should be included in any analyses.

This chapter has discussed the approaches that have been taken to quantify outcomes and costs from health care interventions. Perhaps the most predominant measure of outcome used in economic evaluations in health care is the QALY. The choice of costs to use depends on the decision-making context and the perspective taken. Incremental cost-effectiveness ratios can then be compared to cost-effectiveness thresholds to allow for efficient decision-making. It should be clear that using solely the results of individual trials to conduct such analyses has significant drawbacks, and that it is more appropriate to synthesize all the relevant evidence to allow economic evaluations to meet the needs of decision-makers. A useful tool for doing this is decision analytic models.

REFERENCES

ARROW, K. (1963) Uncertainty and the welfare economics of medical care. *American Economic Review*, 53, 941–73.

BIRCH, S. and GAFNI, A. (1992) Cost effectiveness/utility analyses: do current decision rules lead us to where we want to be? *Journal of Health Economics*, 11, 279–96.

BRAZIER, J., AKEHURST, R., BRENNAN, A., DOLAN, P., CLAXTON, K., McCABE, C., SCULPHER, M., and TSUCHYIA, A. (2005) Should patients have a greater role in valuing health states? *Applied Health Economics and Health Policy*, 4, 201–8.

BROADWAY, R. and BRUCE, N. (1984) *Welfare Economics*. Oxford, Blackwell.

CLAXTON, K. and AKEHURST, R. (2005) It's just evaluation for decision making: recent developments in, and challenges, for cost-effectiveness research. In Smith, P., Ginnelly, L., and Sculpher, M. (eds.) *Health Policy and Economics: Opportunities and Challenges*. Oxford, Oxford University Press.

—— SCULPHER, M., and CULYER, A. (2007) Mark vs Luke? Appropriate methods for the evaluation of public health interventions. Centre for Health Economics Paper 31, University of York.

—— BRIGGS, A., BUXTON, M., CULYER, A., McCABE, C., WALKER, S., and SCULPHER, M. (2008) Value Based Pricing for NHS drugs: an opportunity not to be missed? *British Medical Journal*, 336, 251–4.

CULYER, A. (1991) The normative economics of health care finance and provision. In McGuire, A., Fenn, P., and Mayhew, K. (eds.) *Providing Health Care: The Economics of Alternative Systems of Finance and Delivery*. Oxford, Oxford University Press.

DIAMOND, P. and MIRRLEES, J. (1971a) Optial taxation and public production: I. Production efficiency. *American Economic Review*, 61, 8–27.

—— —— (1971b) Optimal taxation and public production: II. Tax rules. *American Economic Review*, 61, 261–78.

DRUMMOND, M. F., SCULPHER, M. J., O'BRIEN, B. J., STODDART, G. L., and TORRANCE, G. W. (2005) *Methods for the Economic Evaluation of Health Care Programmes*. Oxford: Oxford Medical Publications.

EGGER, M., DAVEY-SMITH, G., SONG, F., and SHELDON, T. (1993) Making sense of meta-analysis. *Pharmacoepidemiology and Drug Safety*, 2, 65–72.

EPSTEIN, D., CHALABI, Z., CLAXTON, K., and SCULPHER, M. (2007) Efficiency, equity and budgetary policies: informing decisions using mathematical programming. *Medical Decision Making*, 27, 128–37.

FISHER, A., CHESTNUT, L., and VIOLETTE, D. (1989) The value of reducing risks of death: A note on new evidence. *Journal of Policy and Management*, 8, 88.

GOLD, M. R., SIEGEL, J. E., RUSSELL, L. B., and WEINSTEIN, M. C. (1996) *Cost-Effectiveness in Health and Medicine*. New York, Oxford University Press.

HICKS, J. (1939) Welfare propositions in economics and interpersonal comparisons of utility. *Economic Journal*, 49, 696–712.

JOHANESSON, P. (1995) *Evaluating Health Risks*. Cambridge, Cambridge University Press.

JONES-LEE, M., HAMMERTON, M., and PHILIPS, P. (1985) The Value of Safety: Results of a National Sample Survey. *Economic Journal*, March, 95/377, 49–72.

KALDOR, N. (1939) Welfare propositions and interpersonal comparisons of utility. *Economic Journal*, 49, 549–52.

KIND, P. (1996) The EuroQoL instrument: an index of health-related quality of life. In Spilker, B. (ed.) *Quality of Life and Pharmacoeconomics in Clinical Trials*. 2nd edn. Philadelphia, Lippincott-Raven.

LERNER, A. (1944) *The Economics of Control*. New York, Macmillan.

MASON, A., WALKER, S., CLAXTON, K., COOKSON, R., FENWICK, E., and SCULPHER, M. (2008) The GMS quality and outcomes framework: Are the quality and outcomes framework (QOF) indicators a cost-effective use of NHS resources? Quality and Outcomes Framework. Joint executive summary. Reports to the Department of Health from the University of East Anglia and the University of York.

MCCABE, C., CLAXTON, K., and CULYER, A. (2008) The NICE cost-effectiveness threshold: what it is and what that means. *Pharmacoeconomics*, 26, 733–44.

MISHAN, E. (1971) *Cost–Benefit Analysis*. London, Allen and Unwin.

MURRAY, C., SALOMON, J., MATHERS, C., and LOPEZ, A. (2002) *Summary Measures of Population Health: Concepts, Ethics, Measurement and Applications*. Geneva, WHO.

NICE (NATIONAL INSTITUTE FOR HEALTH AND CLINICAL EXCELLENCE) (2008) *Guide to the Methods of Technology Appraisal*. London, NICE.

NORD, E. and KAMLET, M. (2009) QALYs: some challenges. *Value in Health*, 12 (Suppl. 1), S10–S15.

NYMAN, J. (2006) The value of health insurance. In Jones, A. (ed.) *The Elgar Companion to Health Economics*. Cheltenham, UK, Edward Elgar.

RYAN, M. and GERARD, K. (2003) Using discrete choice experiments to value health care programmes: current practise and future research reflections. *Applied Health Economics and Health Policy*, 7, 373–8.

SCULPHER, M. J. (2001) The role and estimation of productivity costs in economic evaluation. In Drummond, M. F. and McGuire, A. E. (eds.) *Theory and Practice of Economic Evaluation in Health*. Oxford, Oxford University Press.

—— CLAXTON, K., DRUMMOND, M., and MCCABE, C. (2006) Whither trial-based economic evaluation for health care decision making. *Health Economics*, 15, 677–87.

SEN, A. (1979) Personal utilities and public judgments: or what's wrong with welfare economics. *Economic Journal*, 89/355, 537–58.

—— (1993) Capability and well-being. In Nussbaum, M. and Sen, A. (eds.) *The Quality of Life*. Oxford, Clarendon Press.

SUGDEN, R. and WILLIAMS, A. H. (1979) *The Principles of Practical Cost–Benefit Analysis*. Oxford, Oxford University Press.

TAM, T. and SMITH, M. (2004) Pharmacoeconomic guidelines around the world. *ISPOR Connections*, 10, 4–5.

TOMPA, E., CULYER, A., and DOLINSCHI, R. (2008) *Economic Evaluation of Interventions for Occupational Health and Safety: Developing Good Practice*. Oxford, Oxford University Press.

CHAPTER 32

....

ANALYZING UNCERTAINTY IN COST-EFFECTIVENESS FOR DECISION-MAKING

....

SUSAN GRIFFIN AND KARL CLAXTON

32.1 INTRODUCTION

....

DECISION-MAKERS within the health care sector are faced with the choice between numerous competing health care interventions and programs, of which only a proportion can be provided with the resources available. The expected health benefits and costs of these interventions will inevitably be estimated with some uncertainty. Nevertheless a choice must be made given the quantity and quality of the evidence currently available. Therefore any decision made will necessarily be uncertain. The type of decision-maker may vary, incorporating insurance providers, government departments or independent institutes, but in all cases a formal assessment of the evidence that is transparent, repeatable and defensible is a constructive aid to decision-making. Chapter 31 demonstrated how cost-effectiveness analysis can be used as a tool to identify health care programs that, if funded, would be compatible with the decision-maker's objective. In this chapter we explore how uncertainty in cost-effectiveness can be characterized and how an understanding of uncertainty can inform adoption and research decisions. The primary focus in this chapter is on the social decision-making approach (Sugden and Williams 1979) (see Box 32.1—CEA and net benefits) where the decision-maker's objective is assumed to be the maximization of health gains subject to a given budget constraint. However, the principles underlying the analysis of uncertainty extend to other approaches, such as cost–benefit analysis.

In cost-effectiveness analysis the available evidence relating to alternative healthcare interventions is gathered and collated to provide a unified assessment of the health gains

Box 32.1 Cost–effectiveness Analysis

The available evidence is gathered and combined to calculate the costs and health outcomes associated with each alternative. Health outcomes can be measured in terms of quality-adjusted life years (QALYs), a generic measure that combines quantity of life with the quality of life. If one of the comparators is expected to produce greater health benefits at a lower cost, that intervention is the most cost-effective. However, where one comparator is expected to produce greater health benefits at a greater cost than the next best alternative, then a decision rule must be applied to identify the most cost-effective alternative. With a fixed budget, the decision to provide a more costly intervention will displace other activities that would have produced health gains. To assess whether the more costly intervention represents a better use of healthcare resources it is necessary to compare the value of the health gains displaced to the value of those gained by switching. This can be achieved by comparing the cost per QALY gained with the new intervention (incremental cost-effectiveness ratio (ICER)) to a cost-effectiveness threshold, λ, which represents the opportunity cost of displacing other treatments. Alternatively, the cost-effectiveness threshold can be used to convert the incremental cost of the new treatment into the incremental amount of health displaced, in order to calculate incremental net health benefit (NHB). Equally the threshold can be used to convert the incremental health benefits of the new treatment into the incremental benefit in terms of costs, in order to calculate net monetary benefit (NMB). If the new treatment has a positive incremental NHB or NMB it is cost-effective.

$$ICER = \frac{Costs_B - Costs_A}{QALYs_B - QALYs_{A<\lambda}}$$

$$incNHB = (QALYs_B - QALYs_A) - \frac{Costs_B - Costs_A}{\lambda}$$

$$incNHB = (QALYs_B - QALYs_A)\lambda - (Costs_B - Costs_A)$$

and opportunity costs associated with providing those treatments. The evidence available to inform a cost-effectiveness analysis, such as the results of clinical trials, and the way in which the evidence is analyzed and interpreted are all subject to uncertainty. Uncertainty is thereby inherent to decisions about resource allocation in health care. To understand why uncertainty matters, it is important to consider the questions to be answered by decision-makers faced with the choice between alternative health care interventions.

The chapter begins with the rationale for presenting a full characterization and analysis of uncertainty within any cost-effectiveness analysis. An overview of methods that can be used to conduct a cost-effectiveness analysis that accounts for uncertainty is provided, including the means to present and interpret the results. The benefits and limitations of the methods for analyzing uncertainty are considered in the context of providing information to decision-makers in a timely fashion. The chapter concludes by discussing the additional questions that arise when we consider the need for further research to support those decisions. Throughout the analysis presented in this chapter cost-effectiveness is summarized as the net health benefit of each of the interventions considered (see Box 32.1). During the chapter a clinical scenario is utilized to further illustrate the application of some of the key concepts covered (see Boxes 32.2–32.5).

32.2 Why Uncertainty Matters

As a consequence of uncertainty the true values of the costs, health outcomes, and overall net health benefits for the interventions under assessment are unknown. Instead, the expected net health benefits are estimated with uncertainty. It is important to distinguish this uncertainty from variability and heterogeneity. Variability refers to the natural

Box 32.2 Clinical Scenario: Introduction

Throughout this chapter we will illustrate some of the concepts with a clinical scenario in which you are a decision maker in control of a central fund of money from which the healthcare services utilized by members of that fund must be paid for. For example, you may be an insurance company or an institute with the remit to approve health care interventions and programs for reimbursement within a national health care system.

You must decide which chemotherapy (if any) to make available to patients presenting with early breast cancer, while being mindful of your obligation to provide healthcare to patients with other diseases. You must also decide whether it would be worthwhile gathering further evidence to inform your decision.

The regulatory body with the remit for licensing drugs lists three approved regimens for use in patients with early breast cancer:

- First generation chemotherapy regimen, FGO;
- Second generation chemotherapy regimen, SGO;
- A combination of first and second generation chemotherapy, COMB.

Thus there are four mutually exclusive treatment options for patients: no chemotherapy, FGO, SGO or COMB. The licensed regimens emerged over time, with each successive regimen offering an improvement in survival when compared to the previous regimen, but at a cost of increased toxicity and side effects. Each successive regimen was more costly to deliver in comparison to the previous regimen. The evidence on these various clinical outcomes and costs can be used to inform an overall assessment of the total costs and benefits associated with each treatment option, but this assessment may be uncertain. To reduce the decision uncertainty it may be possible to initiate further research.

Box 32.3 Clinical Scenario: Searching and Synthesis

Table S1 shows the evidence base in terms of the existing randomized controlled trials of treatments for early breast cancer.

What does this evidence base tell us about the relative efficacy of the treatment options we wish to compare?

One way to synthesize the evidence is to conduct a series of pair-wise meta-analyses. This would result in six distinct treatment effect estimates, one for each of the pairs compared in the evidence base. However, in order to inform the cost-effectiveness analysis we must compare each treatment with all of the other relevant alternatives simultaneously, in terms of which is more effective and by how much and with what level of certainty. Is it possible to compare COMB with FGO on the basis of this analysis?

Another option might be to conduct a meta-analysis using SGO as the common comparator, and the hazard ratio as the outcome measure. This would allow us to compare SGO with FGO and COMB, but would not incorporate the no chemotherapy option and would exclude half of the studies reporting evidence on the effectiveness of FGO, SGO, and COMB.

To allow a comparison between any of the four treatment options, a mixed treatment comparison can be conducted, using the hazard ratio as the common outcome. To do so it is necessary to assume "transitivity" of treatment effects, i.e. the assumption would be that if COMB is more effective than SGO in study 9, and if SGO is more effective than FGO in study 5, then had COMB been included in study 5 it would have appeared more effective than SGO. The results of this mixed treatment comparison could be reported in terms of any pair-wise comparison of the four relevant comparators, quantifying the relative effectiveness and the associated uncertainty.

To incorporate all of the available studies, a generalized evidence synthesis could be conducted by making an assumption about the pattern of the survival function (in addition to an assumption of transitivity); this would allow the median weeks survival in study 3 to be related to the hazard ratios reported in the other studies. This method of synthesis offers the same reporting options as the mixed treatment comparison.

Note that if a systematic review is used to identify the existing studies, the search criteria will determine which of the studies are located. If the scope of the review is to identify all studies that include FGO, SGO, or COMB then only studies 1–9 would be identified. However, in both the mixed treatment comparison and the generalized evidence synthesis study 10 would provide indirect evidence on the treatment effects of FGO, SGO, and COMB even though none are included directly in that trial.

Box 32.3 Continued

Table S1 Summary of randomized controlled trials of treatments for early breast cancer

Evidence base	Comparators					Outcome measure for treatment effect	Method for synthesis		
Study	No chemo	FGO	SGO	ULR	COMB		Meta-analysis with common comparator	Mixed treatment comparison	Generalized evidence synthesis with multiple outcomes
1	✓	✓				Hazard ratio		✓	✓
2	✓	✓				Hazard ratio		✓	✓
3		✓	✓			Median weeks survival			✓
4		✓	✓			Hazard ratio	✓	✓	✓
5		✓	✓			Hazard ratio	✓	✓	✓
6			✓	✓		Hazard ratio		✓	✓
7			✓		✓	Hazard ratio	✓	✓	✓
8			✓		✓	Hazard ratio	✓	✓	✓
9				✓	✓	Hazard ratio		✓	✓
10	✓					Hazard ratio		✓	✓

Notes: FGO = first generation chemotherapy; SGO = second generation chemotherapy; ULR = unlicensed chemotherapy regimen; COMB = combination of first and second generation chemotherapy regimens

Box 32.4 Clinical Scenario: Probabilistic Sensitivity Analysis

A decision analytic model was constructed to estimate the expected lifetime costs and health outcomes associated with each chemotherapy regimen and for no treatment. The effects of toxicity and any adverse events are captured in the estimated costs and health related quality of life while receiving chemotherapy. The input parameters, sources of evidence to inform the estimates and the probability distributions assigned to those parameters are listed in Table S2.

Ten thousand Monte Carlo simulations were used to propagate the parameter uncertainty through to the model results and a selection of the output is presented in Table S3. Thus, for each plausible set of values for the input parameters, θ, there is a corresponding estimate of total costs and total quality-adjusted life years (QALYs) for each chemotherapy regimen and no treatment. By specifying a cost-effectiveness threshold, in this case $50,000 per QALY, the net health benefits can be calculated. Table S4 summarizes the expected costs and health outcomes for each alternative and shows the incremental cost-effectiveness ratios, and the probability that each is cost-effective.

How can this output help to inform the decisions of which treatment to provide to patients with early breast cancer, and whether further research should be conducted to inform that decision?

On the basis of current evidence, averaging across the uncertainty in value of the inputs, it appears that COMB in the most cost-effective, offering the greatest net health benefit or equivalently the highest ICER below the threshold of $50,000 per QALY. However, the result is not certain, as the probability that COMB is the most cost-effective option is only 60%, giving an error probability of 40%. In other words the analysis indicates that there is a 40% probability that providing COMB to all patients is not the most cost-effective use of health care resources. Is this level of uncertainty enough to justify the initiation of further research? To assess the value of the health benefits that could be achieved in the absence of all input uncertainty we can look to the final column of Table S3. By comparing this to the net health benefits we expect to achieve by basing our decision on the current information, we can calculate the expected value of perfect information: 16.7–16.44 = 0.26 units of net health benefit (equal to 0.26*$50,000 = $13,000 per patient). The information has value every time the decision is taken, and so to calculate the population value of information it is necessary to estimate the number of patients for whom the information would be used. This itself necessitates some assessment of how long the information will be of use, accounting for the fact that technologies change over time such that information generated now may have little relevance to the treatments and characteristics of patients in the future. The population expected value of information can be compared to the expected costs of additional research to see whether there is any potential value in initiating further research. If the costs of research exceed the population value of perfect information, then investing in further research will not be worthwhile.

Box 32.4 Continued

Table S2 Inputs to the decision analytic model

Parameter	Source of evidence	Properties	Distribution
Treatment effects on progression-free and overall survival.	Generalized evidence synthesis of randomized controlled trials (RCTs).	Expressed as mean and standard deviation of log hazard ratio. Continuous and unbounded.	Normal.
Baseline hazard of progression and death with no chemotherapy.	Large observational study with 10-year follow-up.	Expressed as mean and standard deviation of probability of surviving each year. Bounded between zero and one.	Beta.
Health related quality of life (HRQoL) while receiving chemotherapy.	Regression analysis of individual patient data from RCTs.	Coefficients for incremental HRQoL with chemotherapy compared to no chemotherapy. Continuous and unbounded.	Normal (implied by regression analysis).
HRQoL for health states of progression-free, and recurrent breast cancer.	Single RCT that incorporated generic HRQoL measure.	Expressed as mean and standard deviation of HRQoL. Upper bound at one.	Gamma for (1 − HRQoL).
Cost of chemotherapy.	Resource use from generalized evidence synthesis of RCTs, unit costs from national pricing databases.	Expressed as mean and standard deviation of number of cycles of chemotherapy received. Lower bound at zero.	Gamma for resource use. No uncertainty in unit costs as true values known.
Costs for health states of progression-free, and recurrent breast cancer.	Cohort study.	Expressed as mean and standard deviation of health care costs per year. Lower bound at zero.	Gamma.
Increased risk of death compared to general population after 10 years without recurrence.	No published studies available. Expert opinion elicited to express likelihood of risk returning to population norms or remaining elevated.	Mean and standard deviation of relative risk of death compared to general population.	Lognormal distribution.

Box 32.4 Continued

Table S3 Output of the probabilistic sensitivity analysis of the decision analytic model

	No chemotherapy			FGO			SGO			COMB			Best choice	Max NHB
	Costs ($,000)	QALYs	NHB	Costs ($,000)	QALYs	NHB	Costs ($,000)	QALYs	NHB	Costs ($,000)	QALYs	NHB		
θ_1	30	15	14.4	32	16	15.36	38	17	16.24	75	20	18.5	COMB	18.5
θ_2	34	14	13.32	37	16	15.26	41	17	16.18	80	17	15.4	SGO	16.18
θ_3	29	14	13.42	31	15	14.38	35	15	14.3	78	18	16.44	COMB	16.44
θ_4	30.5	17	16.39	33	17	16.34	38	17	16.24	73	18	16.54	COMB	16.54
...	...	...	...	...	...	...	...	...	...	...	...	...	...	...
$\theta_{9,999}$	28	13	12.44	30.5	14	13.39	45	15	14.1	79	17	15.42	COMB	15.42
$\theta_{10,000}$	35	16	15.3	38	18	17.24	41	18	17.18	82	18	16.36	FGO	17.24
Mean	31	15	14.38	34	16	15.32	38	17	16.24	78	18	16.44	COMB	16.7

Notes: QALYs = quality adjusted life years; NHB = net health benefits.

Box 32.4 Continued

Table S4 Summary results of the probabilistic sensitivity analysis

	Expected costs ($,000)	Expected QALYs	ICER ($)	NHB	Probability cost-effective
No chemo	31	15	–	14.38	0
FGO	34	16	3,000	15.32	0.15
SGO	38	17	4,000	16.24	0.25
COMB	78	18	40,000	16.44	0.60

Box 32.5 Clinical Scenario: Approval, Delay, or Coverage with Evidence

The decision about what treatment to provide to patients on the basis of current evidence may have an impact on the prospect of generating additional evidence. Approving a treatment for widespread use can prevent further randomized trials to determine efficacy being conducted, by making recruitment impossible or unethical. On the other hand if access to cost-effective treatments is delayed in order to complete additional research, this imposes an opportunity cost on current patients, albeit with the aim of improving expected outcomes for future patients. Gathering evidence in non-randomized study designs is feasible and may even be easier after a treatment has been approved for widespread use.

The decision analytic model results shown in Box 32.3 indicated that COMB was the most cost-effective treatment with an expected net health benefit of 16.44 compared to current practice SGO with 16.24 units of net health benefit per patient. The results also indicated that the expected value of perfect information was 0.26 units of net health benefit per patient, and with 30,000 patients per year over a period of 5 years this gives a population expected value of information of $1.7bn (using a discount rate of 3.5% per annum).

Given the size of the opportunity costs of decision uncertainty, further analysis is warranted to calculate expected value of information associated with each parameter in the model. The results were that the opportunity cost of uncertainty in the treatment effect of COMB compared to SGO is valued at 0.2 units of net health benefit per patient, and the opportunity cost of eliminating uncertainty in the health related quality of life associated with patients who receive COMB is valued at 0.05 units per patient. The remaining parameters were not associated with any value of information. A randomized trial could reduce the uncertainty surrounding the relative efficacy of COMB compared to SGO. Such a trial would cost $10m (200 units of net health benefit) to conduct, would recruit for two years and take three years to report. An observational study could reduce the uncertainty around the health related quality of life impacts of treatment with COMB. Such a trial would cost $1m and take one year to report.

A range of decisions are available, and the following three are evaluated in Table S5:

1. Approve COMB for immediate use, which would prevent the conduct of further randomized trials.

Box 32.5 Continued

2. Delay introduction of COMB for two years to allow an RCT to be conducted comparing COMB to SGO, during which additional information about health related quality of life would also be gathered. During this two-year period, half of all patients would receive COMB but the other half would be randomized to current practice of SGO. After two years of recruitment, a further one year would be required for follow-up and analysis before the results were available.

3. Approve COMB for use with the condition that additional information be gathered on health related quality of life. Patients would immediately benefit from the introduction of COMB, and after one year would benefit from the additional information on health related quality of life.

The option that would maximize net health benefits is to delay the introduction of COMB to allow a randomized controlled trial to be conducted. The increase in expected net health benefits from the additional information more than offsets the opportunity cost of delaying the introduction of COMB by two years. The benefits from the earlier introduction of COMB in options 1 and 3 are not enough to justify forgoing the valuable information that is expected from the randomized trial.

Table S5 Evaluating approval, delay and coverage with evidence

Year	1	2	3	4	5	
Number of patients (discounted at 3.5% per annum)	30,000	28,986	27,058	24,405	21,268	
Expected gain in net health benefit relative to current practice SGO	Population gain in net health benefit					Total
A. Provide COMB on the basis of current evidence = 16.44 – 16.24	6000	5797	5412	4881	4254	
B. Provide COMB with perfect information on efficacy = (16.44 + 0.20) – 16.24	12,000	11,594	10,823	9762	8507	
C. Provide COMB with perfect information on HRQoL = (16.44 + 0.05) – 16.24	7500	7246	6765	6101	5317	
D. Provide COMB with perfect information on efficacy and HRQoL = (16.44 + 0.05 + 0.20) – 16.24	13,500	13,043	12,176	10,982	9570	
1. Provide COMB on the basis of current evidence, with no further research	A	A	A	A	A	26,343
2. Three year RCT to determine efficacy and HRQoL	0.5*A – 200	0.5*A	A	D	D	31,663
3. One year observational study to determine HRQoL	A – 20	C	C	C	C	31,409

Note: HRQoL = Health related quality of life

Table 32.1 Uncertainty in Population Net Health Benefits

	Population net health benefits	
Possible value for θ	Intervention A	Intervention B
θ_1	100	120
θ_2	80	105
θ_3	60	55
θ_4	40	30
θ_5	20	10
Average	60	64

variation between patients in their response to treatment and the costs they incur, even when they have the same observed characteristics. Additional evidence cannot reduce this natural variability. Heterogeneity refers to differences between patients in terms of identifiable characteristics such as age, gender and severity of disease, which may imply different expected costs, outcomes and treatment decisions. Uncertainty refers to the fact that we can never know for certain what the mean (expected) costs and effects would be if the treatment is provided for a particular population of patients even if they have the same observed characteristics. Additional evidence can reduce uncertainty and provide more precise estimates. If the purpose of the health care system is to maximize health gains from available resources then it is the expected effects and costs, and the uncertainty in estimating them that will be of primary interest.

Consider the choice between two mutually exclusive alternative interventions. For ease of exposition suppose that the expected costs and health outcomes associated with both alternatives can be calculated on the basis of a single parameter, θ, and so we can determine the net health benefits (NHB) of alternative j as, $NHB_j = f(\theta)$. There is uncertainty about true value of θ, and the current evidence indicates that it could take any of five possible values with equal probability. Table 32.1 describes the range of possible values for the net health benefits of the two interventions being compared, and the expected[1] net health benefit for each. Intervention A represents current practice, and intervention B represents a new competing health technology.

32.2.1 Which Intervention is Most Cost-effective Given Current Evidence?

Based on what is currently known (the available evidence), the decision-maker must choose which intervention to reimburse. The current evidence indicates that

---

[1] The expected value of an uncertain variable can be calculated by summing each possible value multiplied by the probability of observing that value.

intervention B has the highest expected net health benefits. Approving intervention B for widespread use in the health care sector would therefore appear compatible with the decision-maker's objective to maximize health gains subject to their budget constraint. The choice between interventions is subject to uncertainty though, because for some possible values of θ intervention A would provide greater net health benefits. Intervention B is cost-effective for two out of the five possible values of θ, and so the probability it is cost-effective is 0.4 and choosing to reimburse intervention B carries an error probability equal to 0.6. For three out of the five, equally likely, possible values of θ intervention A would have been better, and so the probability that A is cost-effective is 0.6.

So how does this uncertainty influence choice between alternative interventions? If intervention A were selected patients would on average be expected to forgo four units $(64 - 60)$ of net health benefits that they could have expected to achieve with intervention B. To choose A rather than B and incur this opportunity cost would imply that the decision-maker valued more certainty (A has a higher probability than B) to the extent that they would be willing to forgo improvements in health. Such a decision-maker could be described as risk averse. If decisions are made on behalf of a large public or private institutions, any risks associated with the cost of the interventions are able to be spread among a large number of taxpayers or shareholders, rendering the financial risk inconsequential (Arrow and Lind 1970). However, health risks cannot be spread in this manner because these are borne by specific patients. If individual attitudes to risk are deemed to be an important aspect of outcome then measures of health outcome which reflect these preferences are needed so they can be incorporated in the estimate of expected net health benefit (see for example Cher et al. 1997). In these circumstances net health benefit would capture all aspects of value to the health care decision-maker and by evaluating expected costs and health gains they could simply choose the alternative with the highest expected net benefit. Such decisions, based only on expected cost-effectiveness, would be appropriate so long as there are no irreversible aspects of the decision, e.g. an investment cost which can not be recovered, costs associated with reversing the decision later or opportunity costs associated with the impact on prospects of further research (Palmer and Smith 2000; Eckermann and Willan 2008; Griffin et al. 2010).

Therefore, assuming an appropriate measure of health gain is used and there are no significant costs associated with reversing any decision, the most cost-effective intervention given current evidence is the one with the greatest expected net health benefit, irrespective of the amount of decision uncertainty (Claxton 1999).[2] So, does it follow that once an intervention has been identified as cost-effective on the basis of current evidence, it should be reimbursed? The evidence available to inform any decision is not static. The decision-maker may take a passive role and wait for additional information

---

[2] A characterization of the uncertainty around the value of the inputs is still required to obtain unbiased estimates of net health benefit when it is a non-linear function of those inputs. In a non-linear model the expected value of the output is not obtained if the calculation is performed using only the expected values of the inputs (for example mean $[x]^2 \neq$ mean $[x]^2$).

to appear, or choose to initiate actions to acquire further evidence to support the decision. New information may affect the assessment of which intervention is viewed as most cost-effective, precipitating a change or reversal of a decision that may have resource implications. Furthermore the conditions under which new information is collected are altered by the decision to reimburse an intervention. Thus the resource allocation decision is not simply which intervention to reimburse on the basis of current evidence, but also whether it is worthwhile gathering additional information to support that decision and whether it is worthwhile delaying the introduction of a new intervention until that additional information is available. These questions are addressed in the following sections.

32.2.2 Is the Current Evidence Sufficient?

The degree of uncertainty in the estimated net health benefits is relevant when we wish to address questions about the sufficiency of the current evidence base, and whether resources should be allocated to fund further research. When a reimbursement decision is made on the basis of uncertain information, there is a possibility that subsequent evidence will indicate that the intervention selected did not in fact have the highest net benefits. When this happens, patients will have been receiving a sub-optimal intervention and population health will not have been maximized. A decision supported by a greater evidence base would be less uncertain, with less chance that later evidence could alter the estimated net benefits to the extent that one of the alternative interventions would appear cost-effective. In cost-effectiveness analysis we wish to make an informed assessment about whether current evidence is sufficient by taking account of the opportunity costs imposed on patients as a result of uncertainty. This opportunity cost is simply the health forgone as a result of misidentifying the most cost-effective alternative.

Table 32.2 shows the comparison between interventions A and B with additional columns that indicate the intervention and associated net health benefits that could be achieved if the value of the parameter θ were known with certainty. Averaging across the maximum net health benefits associated with each possible value of θ indicates the net health benefits we would expect to achieve if all uncertainty could be resolved with additional evidence. Comparing this to the expected net health benefits for the decision based on current, uncertain evidence provides the expected opportunity cost of uncertainty, equal to five (69 – 64) units of net health benefit. This is also known as the expected value of perfect information, and this represents the maximum possible gain from reducing decision uncertainty.

Additional information is expected to reduce uncertainty. In this case from an error probability of 0.6 associated with intervention B to zero if all the uncertainty is resolved (the value of θ is known). The value of this reduction in uncertainty is the opportunity costs which are avoided. In Table 32.2 there are opportunity costs of 5, 10, and 10 associated with θ_3, θ_4, and θ_5 respectively, but no opportunity costs associated with θ_1 and θ_2 (B is the best choice for these value of θ). The expected opportunity cost of uncertainty

Table 32.2 Uncertainty in Net Health Benefits

Possible value for θ	Net health benefits		Maximum achievable if know value of θ	Choice if know value of θ
	Intervention A	Intervention B		
θ_1	100	120	120	B
θ_2	80	105	105	B
θ_3	60	55	60	A
θ_4	40	30	40	A
θ_5	20	10	20	A
Average	60	64	69	

is therefore five (25/5) which is also equal to the expected value of perfect information. Indeed additional information is valuable insofar as it reduces the expected opportunity cost of uncertainty surrounding a decision. Where the value of additional information exceeds the expected costs of research, the decision-maker could improve population expected net health benefits by investing in further research (Claxton and Posnett 1996). When the value of additional information does not exceed the costs of acquiring it, the current evidence may be described as sufficient. Additional information would still be expected to reduce any decision uncertainty, but the resources expended to obtain that information would exceed any expected gain in health benefits that would result from that reduction in uncertainty.

32.2.3 What are the Consequences of Decision-making Under Uncertainty?

If the decision about which intervention to reimburse could be changed, instantaneously and without cost, as new information arrived, then a comparison of the expected costs and health outcomes for each intervention as they would be implemented would be sufficient. However, this may not be the case in practice, and revising decisions may be impossible (irreversible) or costly. For example, suppose intervention B is a new treatment for breast cancer that requires a novel means of administration. In order to provide the new treatment the decision-maker must invest in a large, one-off training program to teach staff the administration technique (a sunk cost). The time and resources used to provide the training program displace two units of net health benefits that could have been produced by an alternative use of those resources. If new evidence later indicated that B was in fact inferior to previous chemotherapy regimens and it was discontinued earlier than expected, the money invested in training would be irrecoverable and would not have generated the expected improvement in health benefits. In contrast, the decision to invest in the chemotherapy drugs themselves is not irreversible, because at the point at which the new treatment is discontinued the health service stops purchasing those drugs and invests the money elsewhere. By estimating the scale of any sunk costs and the costs of reversing a decision and combining it with the probability of incurring those costs, we can make sure the decision about which intervention to reimburse on the basis of current evidence accounts for those potential losses.

Option value and option pricing is a way of understanding the impact of irreversibility and sunk costs on an uncertain decision (Palmer and Smith 2000). By deferring the decision an option is retained to avoid an irreversible commitment of resources in the event that the most cost-effective intervention was misidentified. Suppose the figures in Table 32.2 represent the net health benefits accruing to the relevant patient population over a period of one year. Let us assume that there is a trial underway to reveal the true value of θ that will report in two year's time. The decision-maker must choose whether to adopt intervention B now, gaining four units of net health benefit per year at a one-off cost of two units of net health benefit invested in the training program, or to wait two years and then take the decision. After two years the decision-maker would only reimburse intervention B and undertake the training program if the true value of θ were θ_1 or θ_2, and so would have a 0.2 probability of gaining twenty units of net health benefit and a 0.2 probability of gaining twenty-five units of net health benefit per year as well as incurring the one-off cost of two units of net health benefit. The difference between the net present value of deferring the decision and the net present value of immediate reimbursement of intervention B represents the option value. This is equivalent to the value of perfect information deferred for two years (Palmer and Smith 2000). Option-pricing techniques often consider the arrival of new information as uncertain and outside of the decision-maker's control. The arrival of new information could be part of the choice set for the decision-maker where the decision to undertake further research is taken at the same time as the reimbursement decision (Eckermann and Willan 2006). In this example the decision-maker could choose between reimbursing intervention B and undertaking further research to determine the true value of θ, deferring the decision to reimburse intervention B while undertaking further research on the value of θ, or reimbursing B without collecting additional information and thus avoiding the costs of research but forgoing the value of further information.

Much of the trial evidence to support clinical interventions is produced in order to gain a license for use in the health care sector, for example in order to gain approval from a body such as the Food and Drugs Administration in the US. Further evidence is then gathered in order to persuade potential users of the technology to switch to the new intervention. In some countries (for example the UK, Canada, and New Zealand) a formal analysis of cost-effectiveness is required before a new intervention will be recommended for widespread use. By approving an intervention for widespread use in the health care sector, the decision-maker removes the incentives for manufacturers to produce any further supporting evidence. In addition, once an intervention becomes widely used it may mean that further research will be viewed as unethical and, once patients have access to a new technology, they may be unwilling to enroll in clinical trials. Hence the decision to approve a new intervention may diminish the prospect of gaining additional information that would reduce uncertainty in the estimated net health benefits. If the value of that information would have exceeded the costs of acquiring it, then this can be viewed as an opportunity loss of approving an intervention for widespread use. Regarding Table 32.2, if the decision to approve treatment B for widespread use prevented the conduct of research to determine the true value of θ, the gain in four units of net health benefit from reimbursing B instead of A $(64 - 60)$ is less than the opportunity cost of five units of net health benefit due to forgoing the research $(69 - 64)$. In these circumstances the decision to adopt a technology cannot be separated from the question of whether the evidence to support such a decision is sufficient. The decision-maker must consider whether the benefits of immediate access to a technology exceed the value of the evidence that may be forgone. If not, adoption and reimbursement decisions may undermine the evidence base for future clinical practice and reduce expected net health benefits for the population of future patients. In section 32.4.4 further consideration is given to the choice set available to decision-makers who wish to provide access to a technology but also gather further evidence, for example with the issue of a coverage with evidence decision.

32.3 How Can We Evaluate Decision Uncertainty?

Two important reasons why uncertainty matters have been discussed above: (i) to assess whether the current evidence is sufficient; and (ii) to assess the consequences of an uncertain decision in terms of sunk costs and evidence that may be forgone. However, it should also be noted that when costs and outcomes are evaluated using a decision model in which there is a non-linear relationship between inputs and net benefit, e.g. Markov process, the correct calculation of expected effects and costs will require the uncertainty around all the parameters to be expressed (see footnote 2). In this next section we will describe methods that can be used to characterize the various sources of uncertainty.

32.3.1 Characterizing the Current Evidence and Uncertainty

First, it is necessary to identify the current available evidence in order to assess how much information this provides about the costs and health outcomes of the interventions to be compared. The available evidence will comprise randomized trials, observational studies and any other source of information about the values of interest and the manner in which they should be analyzed. These can be identified using methods of systematic review (Sutton et al. 1998) to search databases and other sources of published and unpublished evidence. Where there are multiple sources of information about a particular value the information must be brought together. The process of pooling data from multiple sources to provide a single unified estimate is known as generalized synthesis of evidence (Prevost et al. 2000). Before synthesizing data it is necessary to make a judgment about the quality and relevance of each source of evidence and whether it provides useful information about the value being estimated.

The process of identifying potential sources of evidence is rarely exhaustive. Increasing the scope of a search to identify a wider selection of evidence incurs a penalty in terms of the time taken to complete the systematic review. Limiting the scope to make the analysis achievable within a timeframe that is of use to the decision-maker will result in some studies remaining unidentified and therefore excluded from the analysis. The relevance of each identified source of evidence is assessed based on characteristics such as how well the study sample represents the patient population for whom the decision will be made, the potential bias incorporated in the study design, the generalizability of the information to the healthcare setting in which the interventions will be provided and whether the outcomes reported are defined and measured appropriately. Where identified studies are reviewed and assumed to provide no information relevant to the decision problem these too are excluded from the analysis. Those studies that have been identified and included represent the current evidence to be used to inform a decision analysis.

A common method for evidence synthesis is the meta-analysis of a set of randomized trials (Sutton et al. 2000). In standard meta-analysis, those trials that are judged to be sufficiently homogenous in terms of characteristics such as the interventions compared and the definition of the reported outcome measure are weighted according to sample size (variance) and pooled to produce a single estimate of treatment efficacy that reflects the combined uncertainty. A mixed treatment comparison extends standard meta-analysis to consider a network of trials that need not contain a common comparator by assuming that if A>B and B>C, then by implication A>C (Hasselblad 1998). A standard meta-analysis of randomized controlled trials would assume that study designs outside the inclusion criteria provide no information about the treatment effect being estimated. This assumption is relaxed in generalized evidence synthesis to recognize that other designs, for example observational studies, provide us with some information about the treatment effect, but that it is estimated with less precision due to the greater level of expected bias. The judgment is that data from observational studies can be combined with data from randomized trials so long as an estimate of the additional imprecision caused by bias inherent to an observational study design is incorporated. In addition, methods for generalized evidence synthesis relax the need to restrict the synthesis to a single outcome measure by enabling the synthesis of information on multiple outcomes and functions of parameters (Prevost et al. 2000; Sutton and Abrams 2001; Ades and Cliffe 2002).

32.3.2 Evaluating Parameter Uncertainty

Reported estimates of treatment effects, resource use, quality of life weights and other parameters which are based on sample data commonly report summary sufficient statistics (e.g. mean and standard error) which provides information on the range of values those parameters may take, and the likelihood of observing any particular value. Each different value would imply a different estimate of the expected costs and health outcomes for the interventions under comparison. In order to reflect our uncertainty around the parameter values included in the model, we need to describe the range of values the parameter could take, and the likelihood of it taking each particular value. One-way and multi-way sensitivity analyses have been used to show the impact of varying parameter values within some plausible range, but these fail to quantify the likelihood of any particular combination of parameter values.

To characterize uncertainty parameters can be represented by distributions instead of single values. This characterization of parameter values as random variables relies on a Bayesian interpretation of probability (Luce and O'Hagan 2003). If we have aggregate or secondary data in the form of the results from previously published studies, it is possible to assign to it a probability distribution based on the characteristics of the parameter we wish to describe and using the available information on for example the mean, standard error and any covariance with other parameters. Among the characteristics to consider is the range of possible values the parameter could take, the pattern that the distribution of likely values would take, the correlation between the value of the parameter and other model inputs and the way in which the reported results were estimated. Some sources of secondary data provide only partial information to inform an appropriate probability distribution, in which case some assumptions may be necessary. These assumptions provide another source of uncertainty as discussed in section 32.3.3. If the evidence to inform a parameter consists solely of individual patient-level data then the analyst can determine the requisite information to assign a distribution, or a non-parametric alternative for describing the distribution can be achieved through the use of bootstrapping (Briggs et al. 1997). Once distributions have been assigned to all the parameters the uncertainty can be propagated through the decision model in order to provide a unified assessment of the combined parameter uncertainty. This process is known as a probabilistic sensitivity analysis (Briggs 2000). One of the most common methods used to conduct a probabilistic sensitivity analysis is Monte Carlo simulation. This process involves repeatedly selecting random values for each parameter (from the assigned distribution), and for each set of random values calculating the associated net health benefits. The output is a distribution of estimated net health benefits for each intervention. Probabilistic sensitivity analysis is currently recommended as the appropriate way to reflect parameter uncertainty in several guidelines for cost-effectiveness analysis (CCOHTA 2003; NICE 2004).

Model parameters maybe correlated (related to each other in some way) and although early examples of probabilistic sensitivity analysis in the literature often assumed independence between parameters this is not necessary. For example, where a regression analysis has been used to estimate model parameters, the relationship between those parameters can be estimated from the covariance matrix so that the correlation between regression coefficients is reflected in the multivariate normal case. Similarly methods of evidence synthesis, which are increasingly used to estimate the relative effect of interventions, generate correlated outputs. Again these correlations can be fully captured in sensitivity analysis by sampling from or directly using the output of such syntheses in the decision model. If there is no evidence from statistical analysis that parameters are correlated it is generally not necessary to impose it. Of course any logical relationship between parameters should be reflected in the model structure, e.g. the probability of an event occurring (p) is clearly related to the probability that the event does not occur ($1-p$). This and other types of logical relationship (e.g. transition probabilities in a Markov model) should be reflected in the model structure rather than imposing correlation.

32.3.3 Evaluating Other Sources of Uncertainty

In addition to parameter uncertainty there will be uncertainty in the choice between alternative assumptions and judgments which could be made about the approach to analysis, including the choice between statistical models, structures for decision analytic models and how to define the set of evidence that is considered relevant. These judgments will be informed by the analytical framework underlying the cost-effectiveness analysis, the characteristics of the evidence and the disease process that the models seek to represent, but while these may rule out some assumptions and judgments that are inappropriate, they may not point to a single best alternative. Performing probabilistic cost-effectiveness analysis for each of set of plausible assumptions (scenarios) will provide a range of values that the net benefits could take. However, as with parameter uncertainty we need to know not only the range of values, but the likelihood of each. If each of the scenarios were equally likely to be appropriate, then we could simply average across the set of results. If some assumptions were considered to be more appropriate than others then a weighted average that reflects the plausibility of each would be more appropriate (Hoeting et al. 1999).

In some cases, differences between alternative assumptions and judgments can be expressed in the form of an additional parameter in the model (Bojke et al. 2005). Suppose for example that we were uncertain as to whether the benefits from treatment were sustained beyond the period observed in the available trials. Alternative modeling assumptions could be that the benefit from treatment ceased as soon as the trials ended, that the benefit from treatment was sustained but diminished over time, or that the benefits from treatment observed in the trial continued over the remaining lifetime of the patients. Instead of calculating the model results for each scenario, we could include a parameter in the model that described the proportion of the treatment effect that was sustained over time. The possible range of values for this parameter would be 0 to 100 percent but not all values in this range may be equally plausible. Therefore a distribution which represents the likelihood of the parameter taking any particular value must be assigned.

This requires explicit judgments to be made about the value of, and the uncertainty surrounding, a parameter or relative weights of alternative scenarios, for which no direct evidence is available (O'Hagan et al. 2006). Formal methods for eliciting distributions to represent the beliefs of relevant experts have been developed in the risk analysis field more widely, but have only recently begun to be applied in cost-effectiveness analysis (Leal et al. 2007). The use of formal elicitation poses a number of important questions: who should provide the judgments (which experts or decision-makers); which particular methods of elicitation should be used; how should the quality of judgments be calibrated (tested) and weighted; and should more than one expert be used? If so, then how should judgments be combined and if not combined how should we choose which one is most credible? Elicitation is also time and resource intensive and for these reasons it is more common to present these other sources of uncertainty as a series of probabilistic scenarios. However, it is then left to the decision-maker to implicitly assess the credibility and plausibility of each.

32.3.4 Presenting Uncertainty

The uncertainty that needs to be presented is the uncertainty about which intervention should be reimbursed, that is the decision uncertainty. We might be highly uncertain about the true value of the net health benefits associated with a particular intervention but at the same time not uncertain at all about the fact that it does not represent the most cost-effective use of health care resources. When there are only two alternatives being compared, the decision uncertainty could be adequately described by assessing the distribution of the incremental net benefit for one alternative compared to the other. A confidence interval would describe the range of values that the incremental net benefit could take given the specified confidence level. If the range included zero this would indicate that there were plausible values for the incremental net benefit that would support different decisions. However, the interval would not indicate the likelihood of observing those values. Alternatively, Figure 32.1 shows an incremental cost-effectiveness plane, which graphically shows the joint distribution of incremental costs and health benefits for one intervention compared to another. By observing the proportion of points that fall below a cost-effectiveness threshold, the decision-maker can assess the likelihood that the new intervention is cost-effective.

Presenting uncertainty in terms of an incremental analysis does not extend to a comparison of more than two alternatives because the next best comparator against which the incremental benefit should be calculated can vary. Where the probabilistic sensitivity analysis has been conducted by means of Monte Carlo simulation, the analyst can note, for each set of randomly drawn parameter values, which treatment would provide the maximum net health benefits. By plotting the proportion of times each treatment provides the maximum net benefit across the whole simulation on the y-axis and the threshold value used to calculate net benefits on the x-axis, a cost-effectiveness acceptability curve is produced, as shown in Figure 32.2 (Fenwick et al. 2001). This provides a visual depiction of the probability that each intervention is cost-effective for a range of values for the cost-effectiveness threshold. It is not always the case that the alternative

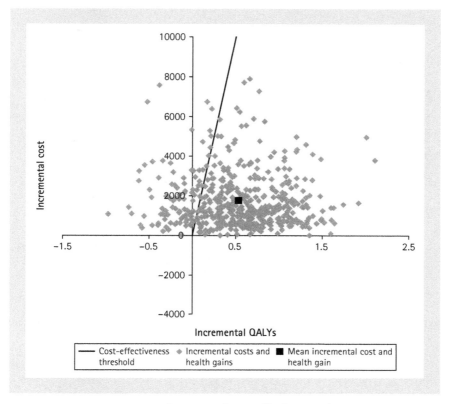

FIGURE 32.1 Incremental cost-effectiveness plane

with the highest expected net benefit has the highest probability of being cost-effective. This occurs when the distribution of net benefits is skewed so that the mean or expected value diverges from the median (the central value). This is shown in Table 32.2, where intervention B is cost-effective for two out of five possible values of θ despite having the greater expected net health benefit. Thus it is not possible to tell from viewing a cost-effectiveness acceptability curve which alternative represents the best use of available resources given current evidence. In order to provide this information in the graph we discard the treatments that do not have the maximum expected net benefits for each threshold value, leaving a cost-effectiveness acceptability frontier (Figure 32.3) that depicts the probability that the treatment that would maximize expected net benefit is cost-effective at each threshold value (Fenwick et al. 2001).

32.3.5 Value of Information

As discussed in section 32.2, the opportunity cost of decision uncertainty can be calculated and this is useful in answering questions about the sufficiency of the current

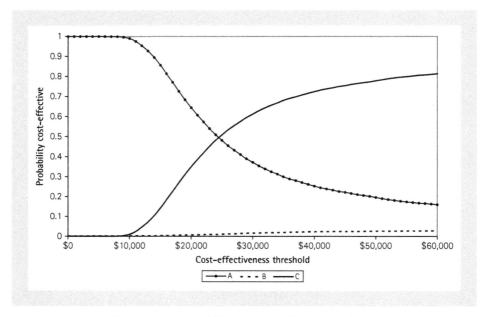

FIGURE 32.2 Cost-effectiveness acceptability curves for three mutually exclusive interventions

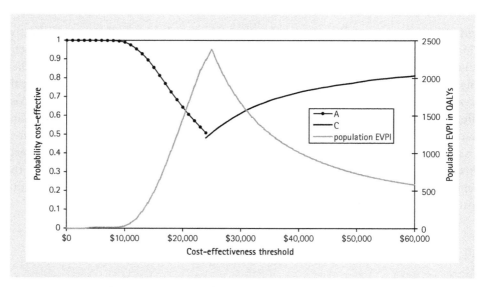

FIGURE 32.3 Cost-effectiveness acceptability frontier and population EVPI for three mutually exclusive alternatives

evidence and the need for further research. The difference, in Table 32.2, between the expected maximum net health benefits if all uncertainty was resolved (69) and the expected net health benefits for a decision based on current evidence (choose intervention B with expected net health benefit 64) describes the expected value of perfect information about θ for an individual patient. However, information can inform treatment choice for all current and future patients. Therefore population EVPI requires estimates of this current and future patient population. This requires a judgment to be made about the time over which additional evidence that can be acquired in the near future is likely to be useful and relevant. Generally, fixed time horizons of ten, fifteen, and twenty years have been used in the health literature as well as the environmental risk and engineering literature (Yokota and Thompson 2004). However, any fixed time-horizon is really a proxy for a complex and uncertain process of future changes, all of which impacts on cost-effectiveness and the future value of evidence (Phillips et al. 2008). The population expected value of perfect information can be calculated for a range of threshold values and plotted, either separately or on the same graph as the cost-effectiveness acceptability frontier, as shown in Figure 32.3. If they are plotted on the same graph, the relationship between the incremental cost-effectiveness ratio, the threshold and the value of information becomes clear. When the threshold is equal to the ICER the expected incremental net benefit is zero and the decision-maker is indifferent between two alternatives. At this point the choice between A and C is most uncertain and any additional information that would allow us to differentiate between the alternatives will be valuable, so the expected value of information reaches a maximum. When the threshold is much lower than the ICER, A has the highest expected net benefit and there is little decision uncertainty associated with this choice (the error probability is low), therefore the EVPI is also very low.

32.4 Evaluating the Need for Evidence and the Consequences of Uncertain Decisions

The characterization of uncertainty is required to enable the value of additional research to be quantified. Parameter uncertainty is reducible through further investigation: a larger sample will provide more information about the true underlying values in the population of interest. The other sources of uncertainty described in 32.3.3 may also be reducible through further investigation. For example, if we consider the need to extrapolate beyond existing data, the uncertainty in the choice of model could be reduced by data from an additional trial with a longer period of follow-up. There are a series of questions to be asked if a cost-effectiveness analysis is to be used to inform a decision-maker who is concerned with the need for additional research.

32.4.1 Is the Evidence Sufficient?

The expected value of perfect information represents the upper bound for the value of additional research to reduce parameter uncertainty. If the population EVPI does not exceed some minimum expected cost of research then we may say that the current evidence is sufficient as the health gains forgone by devoting resources to further research would be greater than those achieved by the resultant expected reduction in decision uncertainty. In this manner, the upper bound for the value of additional information can be used to identify cases where further research is not required. However, if the population EVPI exceeds the expected cost of research then further investigation is potentially worthwhile but further analysis will be required to indicate what type of evidence may be most valuable and how further research might be designed.

32.4.2 What Type of Evidence is Needed?

Some parameters, though estimated with uncertainty, may have little impact on the decision, and hence make little contribution to the decision uncertainty. Further evidence to reduce the uncertainty in these parameter values will be of little value. In order to know what type of evidence would be most valuable, it is necessary to identify those parameters that contribute to the decision uncertainty. This is achieved by calculating the expected value of perfect information associated with single parameters or groups of parameters. The expected value of the decision taken with perfect information about the parameter(s) of interest but with the uncertainty in the remaining parameters unaltered is compared to the expected value of the decision based on current information. This is often referred to as the expected value of partial perfect information. The study design appropriate for providing the additional information will differ according to the parameter of interest. For example, the gold standard for obtaining further information about efficacy is a properly controlled randomized trial. In contrast an observational design may be appropriate to acquire further information about the health related quality of life associated clinical events or the natural history of disease (Welton et al. 2006).

32.4.3 How Should Research be Designed?

Additional information generated by further research will in general reduce, but not eliminate, uncertainty. To assess the value of further research it is necessary to calculate the expected value of this "imperfect" sample information. The expected value, in terms of the reduction in decision uncertainty, and the expected costs of research will differ both between parameters and for a given parameter in terms of the study design, the size of the sample, the length of follow-up and other characteristics. To calculate the expected value of sample information (EVSI) it is necessary to predict the reduction in uncertainty that would result from the additional information, and to incorporate the imprecision in this prediction (Ades et al. 2004). The value of the expected reduction in the opportunity costs of decision uncertainty can be compared to the expected costs of the particular study design. This has been referred to as the expected net benefit of sample information, and if it is positive this would imply that conducting the study would be a worthwhile use of health care resources that would be expected to lead to an increase in net health benefits.

The computational time required to calculate the expected value of sample information in cost-effectiveness analyses that rely on simulation can be burdensome and in many cases not feasible within the time constrains of some decision-making processes. In addition the number of possible research designs and combinations of studies that might be possible makes the full evaluation of this research decision space even more computationally challenging. While methodological work continues to reduce the computational burden in identifying the optimal research designs using EVSI (see for example Brennan and Kharroubi 2007) the current methods can be used to establish whether a particular proposed research design represents an efficient use of healthcare resources. Thus the expected value of sample information has an important role to play in informing the allocation of research funds between competing proposals.

32.4.4 The Consequences of Approving an Intervention

Where value of information analyses indicate that an improvement in health gains may be achieved by investing in further research, this has implications for how and when the decision-maker approves a new intervention. As mentioned in section 32.2, once an intervention is in widespread use this can limit the ability to conduct research by removing incentives for manufacturers to undertake research, undermining the ethical basis of clinical trials and reducing the pool of patients willing to enroll.

By delaying the approval of a new intervention until additional evidence has been gathered the decision-maker can ensure that the prospects for conducting experimental research are unaffected. However, this delay imposes an opportunity costs on patients who must wait to receive an expected improvement in net health benefits. Regarding Table 32.2, for every year that intervention B is delayed, patients requiring treatment will forgo four units of net health benefit. If this delay ensures that additional information is acquired, patients presenting after the information is available will benefit from up to five additional units of net health benefit. If intervention B is assumed to have a lifetime of ten years before it becomes obsolete, then, ignoring discounting, delaying the introduction of B any more than five and half years would result in an overall loss of expected net health benefits. Therefore there are circumstances in which the approval of a technology that is expected to be cost-effective should be withheld until further evidence is provided, i.e. when an "only in research" decision is suitable (Chalkidou et al. 2007).

In other circumstances additional evidence may be provided by the manufacturer or by publicly funded research, while at the same time the apparently cost-effective technology is approved for widespread use. In principle, this seems an efficient solution to the problem—some patients get early access to an apparently cost-effective technology but the evidence is also generated so that this decision can be reconsidered when cost-effectiveness as well as potential harm can be reassessed. If reimbursement or approval decisions are made conditional on evidence being provided, i.e. coverage with evidence development (Hutton et al. 2007), it will be necessary to consider the type of evidence required and whether this can or will be gathered once the technology is approved for use. For example, the type of observational registry data that are often envisaged will be unable to provide more precise estimates of relative treatment effect because a comparable control group will not be available. Therefore, setting aside the question of whether manufacturers or the public sector should the bear the costs of research, the decision to approve a technology will depend, not only on the overall value of information for the decision, but also on whether the value is associated with types of evidence that will require particular research designs.

Cost-effectiveness, uncertainty, the need for evidence and the price of a technology are closely related. For example, if additional evidence is required but cannot be gathered once approval is granted then an "only in research" recommendation can be made (full market access will only be granted once the required research has been conducted and if the results confirm the cost-effectiveness of the intervention). To avoid being presented with such a recommendation the manufacturer may be able to reduce the price of the product to the point where the benefits of early access exceed the value of any evidence that would be forgone by granting immediate market access. Where "coverage with evidence" is possible (partial or full market access is granted while further evidence is gathered) some incentive may be required to ensure that the additional evidence will be collected once approval is granted. One way to do this is to reimburse at an initially lower price but reconsider price and coverage once the research has been conducted. Such flexible pricing schemes linked to evidence have recently been adopted by the UK Department of Health. Other "risk sharing" or "conditional coverage" schemes effectively reduce acquisition costs by making reimbursement or price conditional often on some measure of outcome. Depending on their design such schemes may also generate additional evidence but more commonly they are simply a means of offering a discount while preserving a world price of a product. However, an explicit consideration of the value of evidence in reimbursement and approval decisions provides an incentive for investment in evaluative research. Those manufacturers who are able to support claims of cost-effectiveness with more relevant evidence at launch will tend to be able to claim higher prices than those who do not due to the lower level of decision uncertainty surrounding the cost-effectiveness of their product.

32.5 SUMMARY

It should be apparent that the decision about which treatment to approve for use is inextricably linked to the question of whether further evidence is required to support that decision. Both impact on the amount of net health benefits the decision-maker expects to achieve for their population of patients. The decision to approve an intervention for widespread use affects the prospects of acquiring additional evidence, and that additional evidence in turn affects the assessment of which intervention should be reimbursed. A cost-effectiveness analysis that did not incorporate an assessment of decision uncertainty would not reflect the consequences of uncertainty in terms of irreversibility and sunk costs, and the ability to increase the expected net health benefits for the population by investing in additional research.

There are limits to the ability to reflect uncertainty in cost-effectiveness analyses, and one of these is the timeframe within which the information provided by the analysis will be of use. The need to produce results in a timely fashion can be expressed in terms of the opportunity costs to patients of delaying the introduction of new interventions while the analysis is conducted. However, this must be balanced against the potential opportunity losses imposed by introducing interventions early when the evidence base is insufficient and as a consequence losing out on valuable additional research. Searching for sources of evidence to inform cost-effectiveness analyses and using computer intensive methods to acquire estimates of expected outcomes and the value of additional information are time consuming. In addition, methods for describing modeling uncertainty and eliciting expert opinions are not widely used, which means that most published cost-effectiveness analyses limit the exploration of decision uncertainty to that attributable to parameter uncertainty. Nevertheless, even if the analysis of decision uncertainty is limited to estimating the expected value of partial perfect information about parameters it can be a useful tool in prioritizing research and indicating what type of evidence is required (Claxton and Sculpher 2006; Welton et al. 2006; Colbourn et al. 2007).

This chapter has described the principles underlying the evaluation of decision uncertainty and presented an analytical framework that corresponds to those principles. The range of methods described is by no means comprehensive. The explicit nature of the assumptions and value judgments used to evaluate decision uncertainty can at first glance make a formal approach unappealing. However, once it is recognized that it is impossible to avoid such assumptions when basing a single decision on the information provided by a body of evidence, the advantages of a formal approach become apparent. The explicit and quantitative nature of cost-effectiveness analysis makes it transparent, accountable and able to be applied consistently across different decision problems. By presenting the available evidence and the assumptions used in combining that evidence to decision-makers they can assess the extent to which the analysis meets their objectives.

REFERENCES

ADES, A. E. and CLIFFE, S. (2002) Markov Chain Monte Carlo estimation of a multi-parameter decision model: consistency of evidence and the accurate assessment of uncertainty. *Medical Decision Making*, 22, 359–71.

—— LU, G., and CLAXTON, K. (2004) Expected value of Sample Information Calculations in Medical Decision Modeling. *Medical Decision Making*, 24, 207–27.

ARROW, K. and LIND, R. (1970) Uncertainty and the evaluation of public investment decisions. *The American Economic Review*, 60, 364–78.

BOJKE, L., CLAXTON, K., SCULPHER, M., and PALMER, S. (2005) Characterising structural uncertainty in decision-analytic models: a review and application of methods. *Value in Health*, 12: 739–49.

BRENNAN, A. and KHARROUBI, S. (2007) Expected value of sample information for Weibull survival data. *Health Economics*, 16/11, 1205–25.

BRIGGS, A. H. (2000) Handling uncertainty in cost-effectiveness models. *Pharmacoeconomics*, 17, 479–500.

—— WONDERLING, D. E., and MOONEY, C. Z. (1997) Pulling cost-effectiveness analysis up by its bootstraps: a non-parametric approach to confidence interval estimation. *Health Economics*, 6, 327–40.

CCOHTA (CANADIAN COORDINATING OFFICE FOR HEALTH TECHNOLOGY ASSESSMENT) (2003) Guidelines for Authors of CCOHTA Health Technology Assessment Reports. Ottawa, CCOHTA.

CHALKIDOU, K., HOY, A., and LITTLEJOHNS, P. (2007) Making a decision to wait for more evidence: when the National Institute for Health and Clinical Excellence recommends a technology only in the context of research. *Journal of the Royal Society of Medicine*, 100, 453–60.

CHER, D., MIYAMOTO, J., and LENERY, L. A. (1997) Incorporating risk attitude into Markov-process decision models. *Medical Decision Making*, 17, 340–50.

CLAXTON, K. (1999) The irrelevance of inference: a decision-making approach to the stochastic evaluation of health care technologies. *Journal of Health Economics*, 18, 342–64.

—— and POSNETT, J. (1996) An economic approach to clinical trial design and research priority-setting. *Health Economics*, 5, 513–24.

—— and SCULPHER, M. (2006) Using value of information analysis to prioritise health research: Some lessons from a recent UK experience. *Pharmacoeconomics*, 24, 1055–68.

COLBOURN, T., ASSEBURG, C., BOJKE, L., PHILLIPS, Z., WELTON, N. J., CLAXTON, K., ADES, A. E., and GILBERT, R. E. (2007) Preventitive strategies for group B streptococcal and other bacterial infections in early infancy: cost-effectiveness and value of information analyses. *British Medical Journal*, 335, 665–2.

ECKERMANN, S. and WILLAN, A. (2006) Expected value of information and decision making in HTA. *Health Economics*, 16, 195–209.

—— —— (2008) The option value of delay in health technology assessment. *Medical Decision Making*, 28, 300–5.

FENWICK, E., CLAXTON, K., and SCULPHER, M. (2001) Representing uncertainty: the role of cost-effectiveness acceptability curves. *Health Economics*, 10, 779–89.

GRIFFIN, S., CLAXTON, K., PALMER, S., and SCULPHER, M. (2010) Dangerous omissions: the consequences of ignoring decision uncertainity. *Health Economics*, 20/2: 212–24.

HASSELBLAD, V. (1998) Meta-analysis of multitreatment studies. *Medical Decision Making*, 18, 37–43.

HOETING, J. A., MADIGAN, D., RAFTERY, A. E., and VOLINSKY, C. T. (1999) Bayesian model averaging: A tutorial with discussion. *Statistical Science*, 14, 382–417.

HUTTON, J., TRUEMAN, P., and HENSHALL, C. (2007) Coverage with evidence development: an examination of conceptual and policy issues. *International Journal of Technology Assessment in Health Care*, 23, 425–35.

LEAL, J., WORDSWORTH, S., LEGOOD, R., and BLAIR, E. (2007) Eliciting expert opinion for economic models: an applied example. *Value Health*, 10, 195–203.

LUCE, B. and O'HAGAN, A. (2003) *A Primer on Bayesian Statistics in Health Economics and Outcomes Research*. Bethesda, Medtap International.

NICE (NATIONAL INSTITUTE FOR HEALTH AND CLINICAL EXCELLENCE) (2004) *Guide to the Methods of Technology Appraisal*. London, NICE.

O'HAGAN, A., BUCK, C. E., DANESHKHAH, A., EISER, J. E., GARTHWAITE, P. H., JENKINSON, D. J., OAKLEY, J. E., and RAKOW, T. (2006) *Uncertain Judgements: Eliciting Expert Probabilities*. Chichester, Wiley.

PALMER, S. and SMITH, P. C. (2000) Incorporating option values into the economic evaluation of health care technologies. *Journal of Health Economics*, 19, 755–66.

PHILLIPS, Z., CLAXTON, K., and PALMER, S. (2008) The half-Life of truth: What are appropriate time horizons for research decisions? *Medical Decision Making*, 28, 287–99.

PREVOST, T. C., ABRAMS, K. R., and JONES, D. R. (2000) Hierarchical models in generalized synthesis of evidence: an example based on studies of breast cancer screening. *Statistics in Medicine*, 19, 3359–76.

SUGDEN, R. and WILLIAMS, A. (1979) *The Principles of Practical Cost–Benefit Analysis*. Oxford, Oxford University Press.

SUTTON, A. J. and ABRAMS, K. R. (2001) Bayesian methods in meta-analysis and evidence synthesis. *Statistical Methods in Medical Resaerch*, 10, 277–303.

—— —— JONES, D. R., SHELDON, T. A., and SONG, F. (1998) Systematic reviews of trials and other studies. *Health Technology Assessment*, 2/19.

—— —— —— —— —— (2000) *Methods for Meta-analysis in Medical Research*, London, John Wiley.

WELTON, N. J., ADES, A. E., CALDWELL, D. M., and PETERS, T. J. (2006) Research prioritisation based on expected value of partial perfect information: a case study on interventions to increase uptake of breast cancer screening. *Journal of the Royal Statistical Society Series A*, 171, 807–41.

YOKOTA, F. and THOMPSON, K. M. (2004) Value of information literature analysis: a review of applications in health risk management. *Medical Decision Making*, 24, 287–98.

CHAPTER 33

···

HEALTH UTILITY
MEASUREMENT

···

DONNA ROWEN AND JOHN BRAZIER

33.1 INTRODUCTION

···

ECONOMIC evaluation using cost utility analysis (CUA) is increasingly being used to inform resource allocation decisions, such as through the establishment of bodies such as the National Institute for Health and Clinical Excellence (NICE) in England and Wales (NICE 2004, 2008), and similar agencies in Australia (Commonwealth Department of Health and Aging 2002), and the Netherlands (Health Insurance Council 1999). CUA measures health outcomes using the Quality Adjusted Life Year (QALY). The QALY combines both quantity and quality of life into a single measure of health outcome by adjusting life years using a quality weight. This quality adjustment weight is often referred to as health utility as the number represents a valuation not simply a measurement of health. The utility value is measured on an interval scale, with an upper anchor at one for full health and a lower anchor at zero (assuming it is equivalent to dead).

Measuring and valuing health is a major component of economic evaluation, meaning that health utility measurement has been growing in popularity in recent years due to the increasing demand for health state values in economic models and evaluations. Yet generating health state values is often a complex and sometimes contentious issue (Brazier et al. 2007). The main issues in health utility measurement are how to describe health states, how to value the health state description (including how to model the health state values to estimate values for all possible states) and whose values should be used. This article briefly outlines these main issues and then focuses on recent methodological developments in health utility measurement.

33.2.1 OVERVIEW OF ISSUES

33.2.1 Describing Health and Quality of Life

The purpose of health utility measurement is to provide the quality adjustment weight, known as the "Q," for the QALY. One of the main benefits of the QALY is that it can be used across all health care interventions for all patient groups (see Chapter 31 for an overview of the QALY). This suggests that the health state description and the corresponding quality adjustment weight used to generate the QALY should be comparable across different interventions and patient groups. Two broad approaches are typically used to describe the health state. The first approach is to construct a bespoke description of the condition and/or its treatment, often referred to as a vignette. This can take a variety of forms from a text narrative or structured text description using bullet points to other formats such as videos or simulation.

The second approach is to use preference-based measures that consist of a self-complete patient questionnaire (that can be completed by proxies), a health state classification system and preference weights for all states defined by the classification system. Each patient self-completes the questionnaire and their responses are used to assign them to a unique health state from the health state classification system. The utility score for that health state is then obtained using existing preference weights. The EQ-5D is the most commonly used measure and the classification system has five dimensions: mobility, self-care, usual activities, pain/discomfort, anxiety/depression. Each dimension has three levels: no problems, some problems, extreme problems. The classification system defines 243 health states and the corresponding utility score is generated using existing preference weights based upon general population preferences (for UK weights, see Dolan 1997). Other widely used generic preference-based measures include: Quality of Well-being (QWB) scale (Kaplan and Anderson 1988), HUI1, HUI2 and HUI3 (Torrance et al. 1982; Torrance et al. 1996; Feeny et al. 2002), 15D (Sintonen and Pekurinen 1993), AQoL (Hawthorne et al. 1999), and SF-6D (Brazier et al. 2002; Brazier and Roberts 2004), a six-dimensional classification system derived from the SF-36 and SF-12. In recent years the use of vignettes has fallen as the second approach of preference-based measures of health-related quality of life has become increasingly popular because it provides a direct empirical link to the experiences of patients.

Preference-based measures can be condition specific but are more usually generic, meaning they are appropriate for measuring health across different patient groups and interventions. Generic preference-based measures have been advocated for providing comparability across all conditions and treatments and are recommended by agencies such as NICE (2004, 2008). The self-complete questionnaires used to collect health state data are easily included in clinical trials or routine data collection systems with little respondent burden, and the existing scoring algorithms are quickly and easily used to generate the health state utility value. The most commonly used generic measures are summarized in Table 33.1. These measures are all designed for adults (>16), except for

Table 33.1 Classification Systems of Generic Preference–Based Measures of Health

Instrument	Dimension	Levels	Health states
QWB	Mobility, physical activity, social functioning	3	945
	27 symptoms/problems	2	
HUI2	Sensory, mobility, emotion, cognition, self-care, pain	4–5	24,000
	Fertility	3	
HUI3	Vision, hearing, speech, ambulation, dexterity, emotion, cognition, pain	5–6	972,000
EQ-5D	Mobility, self-care, usual activities, pain/discomfort, anxiety/depression	3	243
15D	Mobility, vision, hearing, breathing, sleeping, eating, speech, elimination, usual activities, mental function, discomfort/symptoms, depression, distress, vitality, sexual activity	4–5	31bn
SF-6D	Physical functioning, role limitation, social functioning, pain, energy, mental health	4–6	18,000 (SF-36 version) 7500 (SF-12 version)
AQoL	Independent living (self-care, household tasks, mobility), social relationships (intimacy, friendships, family role), physical senses (seeing, hearing, communication), psychological well-being (sleep, anxiety and depression, pain)	4	16.8mn

Source: Brazier et al. (2007). By permission of Oxford University Press.

the HUI2 that was designed for children. Other preference-based measures are being developed for use in children including the EQ-5D-Y (Wille and Ravens-Sieberer 2006) and the CHU-9D (Stevens 2010).

Generic measures of health have been found to be inappropriate or insensitive for some medical conditions (Brazier et al. 2007) including chronic obstructive pulmonary disease (COPD; Harper et al. 1997) and over-active bladder (Kobelt et al. 1999). Clinicians and researchers often include condition specific measures in trials to measure quality of life rather than generic preference-based measures. An important development in the literature has been the use of technique for mapping between non-preference-based condition specific and preference-based measures.

33.2.2 Valuing Health and Quality of Life

For use in cost utility analysis health state values must be valued on a common scale with an upper anchor of one at full (or perfect) health and a lower anchor at zero that is assumed equivalent to "dead." Health states valued as being worse than dead are given a value below zero. In recent years new techniques for valuing health states have been examined, but traditionally the main techniques used to value health states are standard gamble (SG), time trade-off (TTO) and visual analog scale (VAS).

The foundations for SG come from expected utility theory, which assumes that individuals faced with a choice between options will choose the option that maximizes their "expected" utility. For states better than dead, the SG task provides respondents with a choice between (a) a certain health state, h, or (b) the uncertainty of a gamble with two possible health states, full health or the other with zero (or low) utility (Figure 33.1). The probability of full health, P, in the uncertain gamble is varied to determine the point at which the respondent is indifferent between the two options, and this probability P is the utility value for the certain health state, h. SG has been found to be feasible and acceptable amongst many patient groups and conditions and studies using SG to collect health state values typically have completion rates over 80 percent and some as high as 95–100 percent. Due to its foundations in expected utility theory SG is often portrayed as the gold standard (Torrance 1986) and is often chosen as it mimics the uncertainty that is frequently faced in medical decisions (Mehrez and Gafni 1993), albeit in an unrealistic way (Richardson 1994). However SG comes under criticism as the values it generates not only represent the respondents' valuation of the health state but are likely to also incorporate attitudes to risk and other non-health considerations such as loss aversion (Bleichrodt 2002). Furthermore some researchers raise doubts regarding respondents', understanding of the SG task due to the complexities of explaining probabilities to respondents.

TTO was developed to overcome the difficulty of explaining probabilities to respondents (Torrance et al. 1972). For health states considered to be better than dead, the TTO task provides respondents with a choice between (a) health state h for t_h years, after which they will die, or (b) full health for x years ($x \le t_h$), after which they will die. Typically t_h remains fixed and years in full health, x, is varied to determine the point where the respondent is indifferent between the two options. The utility for health state h is x/t_h. As for SG, a variety of variants of TTO exist, including different props, different titration methods to reach the point of indifference and different modes of administration that have been shown to have important implications for the values obtained.

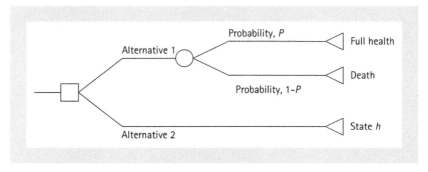

FIGURE 33.1 Standard gamble for a chronic health state valued as better than dead

Research has found TTO to be more practical and reliable than SG (Dolan et al. 1996). For health states considered to be better than dead, the TTO task provides respondents with a choice between (a) health state h for t_h years, after which they will die, or (b) full health for x years ($x \leq t_h$), after which they will die (Figure 33.2). TTO relies on the assumption that individuals will be prepared to sacrifice years of life to improve their quality of life, regardless of how many years of life are remaining. Yet the valuation of a health state may be affected by the duration of a state, for example individuals may not be willing to trade to avoid a poor health state with short duration, or may regard severe states as having a maximum possible endurance time. This can mean that responses are sensitive to time t in health state h where different responses would be found if t, for example, was set at ten weeks or ten years. In contrast to SG, TTO has come under criticism as it does not measure attitudes to risk, whereas health care is often characterized by its uncertainty. Furthermore, TTO assumes constant proportional trade-off between quality and quantity of life, but given time preference and other factors like maximal endurable time this is not likely to hold (Sutherland et al. 1982; Dolan and Gudex 1995; Dolan et al. 1996).

VAS is typically represented using a vertical line with well-defined endpoints and respondents are asked to draw a horizontal line that best represents their value of or feelings about a health state. A conventional VAS scale asks respondents to rate a health state on a scale from 0 to 100 using a vertical line on a page, where 0 is the "worst imaginable health state" and 100 is the "best imaginable health state" (Figure 33.3). The scale should have interval properties where the difference between 10 and 20 should be the same as a difference between 90 and 100. In order to rescale VAS values onto a scale anchored at zero for dead the respondent must also rate "dead" on the same scale. VAS has high response and completion rates and is quick, cheap and easy to administer. However the VAS task is not choice-based, meaning that many researchers remain skeptical over its ability to reflect preferences. Furthermore there are concerns that VAS suffers from response spreading, where if respondents are asked to value multiple health states they

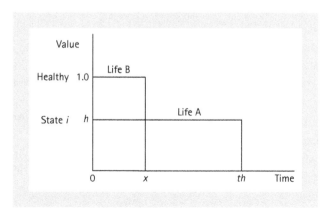

FIGURE 33.2 Time trade-off for a chronic health state valued as better than dead

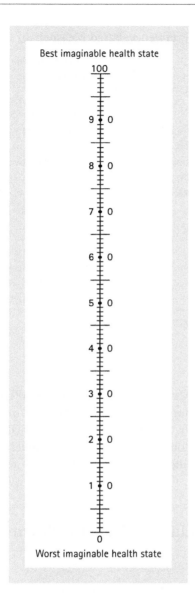

FIGURE 33.3 Visual analog scale

Best imaginable health state

100

9 0

8 0

7 0

6 0

5 0

4 0

3 0

2 0

1 0

0

Worst imaginable health state

spread their values across the scale. This suggests that VAS does not provide an interval scale and is prone to context effects and endpoint bias. There has therefore been recent interest in mapping VAS values to SG or TTO rather than using VAS values directly, but there are doubts about the stability of these functions (Dolan and Sutton 1997; Feeny et al. 2002; Stevens et al. 2006).

The main generic measures use a variety of valuation techniques to obtain their health state utility values, as summarized in Table 33.2. This is an important cause for concern, since SG, TTO, and VAS have been shown to generate different values for the

Table 33.2 Valuation Methods of Generic Preference-Based Measures of Health

Instrument	Country	Valuation technique	Modeling to obtain tariff preference weights
QWB	USA	VAS	Statistical: additive, except for symptom/problem complexes
HUI2	Canada, UK	VAS transformed into SG	MAUT: multiplicative
HUI3	Canada, France	VAS transformed into SG	MAUT: multiplicative
EQ-5D	Belgium, Denmark, Finland, Germany, Japan, Netherlands, Slovenia, Spain, UK, USA, Zimbabwe	TTO, VAS, ranking	Statistical: additive, with interaction term
15D	Finland	VAS	MAUT: additive
SF-6D	Australia, Brazil, Hong Kong, Japan, Portugal, Singapore, UK	SG, ranking	Statistical: additive, with interaction term
AQoL	Australia	TTO	MAUT: multiplicative

Source: Brazier et al. (2007). By permission of Oxford University Press.

same states (Green et al. 2000; Salomon and Murray 2004). Furthermore different variants of SG and TTO in terms of mode of administration, props and procedure for finding the point of indifference have been shown to produce different values (Dolan and Sutton 1997; Lenert et al. 1998). One study found that differences in values obtained using different variants were larger than differences between valuation techniques (Dolan and Sutton 1997).

33.2.3 Modeling Health State Valuation Data to Obtain Preference Weights

Valuation studies are undertaken to obtain health state utility values for a variety of health states. However due to the large number of health states described by the classification system of most generic measures it is infeasible to obtain directly observed values for all states. Only a selection of health states is valued and subsequently utility values for all states defined by the classification system are estimated using modeling techniques.

Two approaches are used to estimate utility values for all states: the decomposed approach and the composite approach. The decomposed approach uses multi-attribute utility theory (MAUT) to select states to be valued and the functional form (usually multiplicative or additive) of the statistical model. This involves three stages: valuing each dimension separately to estimate single dimension utility functions; valuing "corner states," where for example one dimension has extreme problems and all other dimensions have no problems; and valuing a selection of non-corner states and solving a system of equations to generate preference weights for each dimension and any interactions specified in the model. This approach was used to estimate utility values for HUI2, HUI3, and AQoL.

The composite approach involves the valuation of a sample of states chosen using a statistical design such as orthogonal array. Typically regression techniques are then used to estimate a variety of models on the data, to estimate utility values for all health states valued. The standard model is defined as:

$$h_{ij} = f(\mathbf{X}_i \, \boldsymbol{\beta}) + \varepsilon_{ij} \tag{1}$$

Where $i = 1,2,\ldots, n$ represents individual health states and $j = 1,2,\ldots, m$ represents respondents. The dependent variable h_{ij} is the value for health state i valued by respondent j and $\mathbf{X}_i$ is a vector of dummy explanatory variables for each level λ of dimension δ of the health state classification where level $\lambda = 1$ acts as a baseline for each dimension. ε_{ij} is the error term which is subdivided $\varepsilon_{ij} = u_j + e_{ij}$, where u_j is the individual random effect and e_{ij} is the usual random error term for the ith health state of the jth individual.

33.2.4 Comparing the Generic Measures

The common scale of health state values anchored at one for full health and zero for "dead" should mean that all preference-based measures are comparable to each other, where the value of a health state for a patient is identical regardless of the instrument used. However, many studies have illustrated that different generic preference-based measures may assign different index scores to the same patients (see for example Longworth and Bryan 2003; O'Brien et al. 2003; Barton et al. 2004; Brazier et al. 2004; Espallargues et al. 2005). This is unsurprising given the differences in the coverage of each measure as indicated by the large variety of dimensions and levels (see Table 33.1), and the variety of valuation techniques used (see Table 33.2). The criteria for selecting the most appropriate measure is to compare the instruments in terms of practicality, reliability and validity of the classification system, valuation study and modeled preference weights. Although some measures perform better than others for certain conditions (Brazier et al. 2007), no measure has been found to be better across all conditions. This presents problems for policymakers who need to make comparisons across conditions.

33.2.5 Whose Values?

Health state values can be obtained from a variety of sources including patients, carers, health professionals, and the general public. The choice of whose values should be used may affect the values elicited, as different groups provide different values. Typically the general population gives lower health state values than patients actually in the state or a similar state. For example patients with colostomies valued their own health at 0.92 whereas the general public valued the same health states at 0.80 (Boyd et al. 1990). This large difference in values can have a substantive impact on cost per QALY estimates, and hence the choice of whose values to use is important. NICE (2004, 2008) and the Washington Panel (Gold et al. 1996) recommend the use of general population values. The main arguments in favor of using general population values are that public funding is often used to provide health care so public preferences should be used, and that general population values have no vested interests (unlike patient values) as they are obtained via a "veil of ignorance" where individuals do not know the future health states they will experience. This debate will be examined further later.

33.2.6 Policy Implications

The analyst has a wide choice of approaches to generating health state utility values in terms of the way health is described, the way it is valued and who provides the values. All these factors have been shown to have an important impact on the values generated on a given sample of patients. While there are some important theoretical considerations as to the right choice (such as the best method for modeling preference data), there are also major normative issues, such as whose values should be used. To assist policymakers undertaking comparisons across programs, the Washington panel on Cost Effectiveness in Health and Medicine (Gold et al. 1996) and some public agencies (such as NICE 2004, 2008) have used the notion of a reference case that has as a default one or other of the generic preference-based measures. While this may be helpful for policymakers, this leaves an important range of methodological questions around the most appropriate generic descriptive system, what to do when data from the chosen preference-based measure is not available, what to do when the chosen generic measure is not appropriate, better ways to elicit preferences from respondents, better ways to model preference data and the potential role of experience-based measures of utility (a.k.a. direct utility assessment). The rest of this chapter describes some of the recent methodological developments addressing these issues.

33.3 METHODOLOGICAL DEVELOPMENTS

33.3.1 Mapping

Many clinical studies do not use preference-based measures, as their preferred condition specific (or generic) measure is not preference-based and so does not generate health state values. This may be a response to the requirements of licensing authorities that do not accept generic measures or due to lack of space. To limit the evidence base to those using the favored generic preference-based measure would be to exclude potentially important evidence. Mapping is one solution that is gaining popularity as it enables health state utility values to be estimated when no preference-based measure was included in the study. Recent developments in mapping can also enable comparisons across studies using different measures on the same patient population for the purpose of evidence synthesis.

Mapping, sometimes referred to as "cross-walking," is most commonly used to estimate health state utility values when utility data is unavailable as no preference-based measure was included in the study. Typically mapping by statistical association has involved a separate dataset that contains respondents' self-reported scores for their own health using two or more measures. Regression methods are used to estimate a statistical relationship between the indices generated by the measures or their descriptive systems and the regression results are then applied to the study dataset.

Suppose a clinical trial is conducted that records the health related quality of life of their patients using the SF-36, a commonly used profile measure of health, but researchers wish to estimate health state utility values using the EQ-5D. The first step is to obtain an external dataset containing responses from the measures you want to map from (SF-36) and to (EQ-5D), preferably using a patient sample that is similar to the sample used in the clinical trial. If there is no appropriate external dataset, the researcher can design and implement a study to collect the appropriate data. Second, regression techniques are used to estimate the relationship between the preference-based measure (EQ-5D) and the chosen subset of variables (SF-36) using the external dataset. Third, the regression results are applied to the trial dataset to predict the required utility scores. Alternatively, many mapping algorithms already exist that map the SF-36 onto the EQ-5D (for example Franks et al. 2004; Gray et al. 2006; Sullivan and Ghuschyan 2006; Ara and Brazier 2008; Rowen et al. 2009a).

Mapping can be applied using a variety of measures to map from: non-preference-based condition specific quality of life measures, non-preference-based generic quality of life measures, measures of disease severity and these can complemented by other clinical and socio-demographic measures. These measures are usually mapped onto a single index utility value, but can alternatively be mapped onto levels on individual domains to generate a health state description which can then be converted into a utility score using the usual preference weights (see Gray et al. 2006).

A recent review of mapping studies (Brazier et al. 2010) found that the SF-12 and SF-36 were the most common measures to map from and the EQ-5D was the most commonly used measure to map to. The most popular regression technique was ordinary least squares (OLS) estimation using the preference-based index as the dependent variable and dimension or item scores as independent variables. More complex specifications of models, the inclusion of non-health variables and different methods of estimations did not have a large impact on results. Reported R-squared ranges from 0.17 to 0.71 and root mean squared error ranges from 0.08 to 0.2, though this is not usually reported. Typically the performance of models mapping from a condition specific measure to a generic preference-based index was found to be more variable than mapping from a generic measure to a generic preference-based index.

Mapping is quick and easy to apply and can even be used when only mean cohort scores are available (Ara and Brazier 2008). However some mapping studies have high errors in their estimated utility values and some studies have found a relationship between error and severity, where error increases for more severe health states, see for example the results of using the SF-36 to predict the EQ-5D index in Figure 33.4. This may in part be due to a difference in the dimensions covered by the two measures, as important dimensions may not be present in both measures. For example, vitality typically has an insignificant coefficient when SF-36 dimension scores are mapped onto EQ-5D as it only appears in the SF-36. Currently the literature does not examine uncertainty around the estimates or provide guidance on the estimated values for use in probabilistic sensitivity analysis (PSA), and this will be an area for future research. It should be noted that mapping to a generic preference-based measure will only be appropriate if that measure is appropriate for that patient population. Generic measures are not appropriate in all conditions, and in these cases mapping will not solve this problem; it may be better instead to directly value the content of the condition specific non-preference-based measure as discussed later. The use of mapping functions is always a second best solution to using a preference-based measure in the first place, but

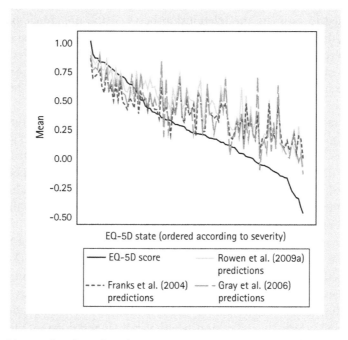

FIGURE 33.4 Observed and predicted EQ-5D scores using a variety of models mapping the SF-36 and SF-12 onto EQ-5D

Source: Rowen, Brazier, and Roberts 2009a.

can be used as a pragmatic solution to enable health state utility values to be estimated when no utility data is available. Mapping can also be used to estimate utility values for a preferred preference-based measure, for example mapping is one option recommended by NICE (2008) to estimate EQ-5D utility data when EQ-5D data is unavailable in the study dataset.

33.3.1.1 *Mapping Using Preferences Rather Than Statistical Association*

Mapping by statistical association assumes it is appropriate to use different measures on the same population, which may not be the case for all preference-based measures for use across all patient groups and conditions. "Preference-based mapping" is another solution to map between different preference-based measures (Rowen et al. 2009b). Preference-based mapping uses general population values for states defined by the descriptive systems of different measures using the same valuation method, with the same anchor points. It is argued that this generates a common yardstick for conversion between measures, while also preserving the advantages of the descriptive system of each measure. The relationship between the preference-based measures is determined directly by people's preferences for different states and not by associations in self-reported scores. This enables researchers and policymakers to estimate EQ-5D utility values using available data from other generic preference-based measures. The extent to which this genuinely achieves comparability raises the same concerns as those described in the next section in relation to the comparability between preference-based condition specific measures.

33.3.2 Using the Most Appropriate Descriptive System: The Role of Condition Specific Measures

Generic preference-based measures have been shown to perform poorly in some conditions, such as visual impairment in macular degeneration (Espallargues et al. 2005), hearing loss (Barton et al. 2004), leg ulcers (Walters et al. 1999), and urinary incontinence (Haywood et al. 2008). For these types of conditions, mapping from the measures used in the study onto a generic preference-based measure does not offer a solution since any mapping function is limited by the degree of overlap between the descriptive systems. There has been increasing interest in the development of condition specific preference-based measures (Brazier and Dixon 1995). This has been achieved either by the development of entirely new measures (e.g. Revicki et al. 1998a and 1998b; Torrance et al. 2004), or from existing non-preference-based condition specific measures (Brazier et al. 2005a; Stevens et al. 2005; Brazier et al. 2008; Ratcliffe et al. 2009; Yang et al. 2009; Young et al. 2009). There are three stages in the development of a preference-based measure from an existing health status measure (Brazier et al. 1998; 2002). The first stage is to develop a set of health states amenable to valuation from the health status measure. Typically a range of psychometric techniques such as factor analysis and Rasch analysis are used to determine the dimensions to be included in the health state classification, to inform the selection of items that will be used in the descriptions of each dimension and to determine the number of levels (see Young et al. 2009 for an example). The second stage is to undertake a survey to value the health states or at least a sample of them. Finally where only a sample of the states are valued the health state valuation data are modeled in order to value all possible health states derived from the condition specific measure.

There remain some fundamental concerns as to whether values from different descriptive systems can be used to make comparisons between interventions for different conditions (Gold et al. 1996; NICE 2008; Dowie 2002). It has been argued that the only way to achieve cross-program comparability is to use the same generic preference-based measure. Using one instrument in all studies is the only way to ensure that different patient groups are being judged in terms of the same dimensions of health, using the same valuation methods and the values are obtained from the same sample.

Another alternative view is that comparability can be achieved by the use of a common numeraire like money or a year in full health. Provided the values are obtained using the same tightly specified valuation "protocol" in terms of the valuation technique (and variant), procedures, common anchors (full health and death), visual aids and the same type of respondents (such as a representative sample of the general population), it could be argued that a common measuring stick is being used and so comparisons can be made between quality adjustment weights estimated using different descriptive systems. It seems to have been an implicit assumption in the willingness to pay literature and the early QALY literature of the 1970s and 1980s that this is the case. Indeed there is no other area of applied economics where the description of benefit has to be standardized across programs.

However, there are a number of obstacles to achieving comparability when using different descriptive system that have been identified in the literature (Brazier and Tsuchiya 2010). The failure to capture important side-effects of treatment is the rationale in clinical research for using a generic measure alongside the condition specific measure (CSM) in a trial. The problem for economic evaluation is that it needs a single measure of effectiveness. Even assuming there are no side-effects, the achievement of comparability between specific instruments requires an additional assumption, namely that the impact of different dimensions on preferences is additive, whether or not they are included in the descriptive system. The impact of breathlessness on health state values, for example, must be the same whether or not the patient has other health problems not covered by the descriptive system, such as pain in joints. Some degree of preference interaction has been shown to exist with generic instruments (Dolan 1997; Feeny et al. 2002) and these interactions may be larger for CSMs since they focus on a narrower range of health dimensions (though the problem will also exist for generic health measures, since they too exclude many important dimensions). For the decision-maker, these concerns need to be weighed against the limitations of their chosen generic measure failing to reflect important differences in health. An alternative approach is to add specific dimensions to generic measures in an attempt to make them more relevant and this is currently being explored by researchers.

33.3.3 States Worse Than Dead

Historically most valuation studies that have been conducted have used SG and TTO to elicit health state utility values. Yet both SG and TTO values can be criticized for their different protocol for valuing states worse than dead and states better than dead. Here we focus on TTO, since this problem has so far received more attention with this technique, but the same issues arise with SG. This is an important issue as all responses, including worse than dead responses, inform the preference weights for each classification system. In the case of the EQ-5D the UK utility weights range from 1 to -0.594 (Dolan 1997), meaning that many states have preference weights that are considered worse than dead due to the large number of worse than dead responses in the valuation study (Measurement and Valuation of Health (MVH) study; Dolan 1997).

The most common TTO protocol for valuing states worse than dead is shown in Figure 33.5 and was used in the Measurement and Valuation of Health (MVH) study (Dolan 1997). The TTO task for states worse than dead provides respondents with a choice between (a) health state h for y years followed by full health for x years, after which they will die, or (b) immediate death. The sum of years in health state h and years in full health are fixed at t, $x + y = t$, meaning that this choice differs from the choice for states better than dead where years in health state h are fixed at t_h (typically $t_h = 10$ and $t = 10$). Years in the health state, y, and years in full health, $x = t - y$ are varied to determine the point where the respondent is indifferent between the two options. It is evident to the respondent during the preference elicitation procedure that the protocol has changed, as the respondent is introduced to a new task and usually a different TTO prop is used. The ordering of the states in choice (a) is problematic as respondents may view the prospect of returning to full health following a severe health state as unrealistic, yet reversing the ordering of full health and the severe health state (see Torrance et al. 1982) has other problems, for example individuals may believe they can commit suicide following their years in full health.

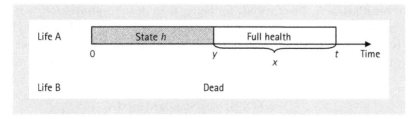

FIGURE 33.5 Time trade-off for a chronic health state valued as worse than dead

The utility for health state h can then be generated using a variety of methods. The formula that is consistent with the theory is $-x/y$. However when using the TTO protocol where $t = 10$ this produces values bounded at -39 for the minimum possible value for any health state, where $y = 0.25$ and $x = 9.75$ meaning that the respondent is indifferent between (a) health state h for three months, followed by full health for nine years and nine months, and (b) immediate death. This creates problems for the use of TTO values in the regression model used to estimate preference weights for all states defined by the classification system, as worse than dead responses have a larger impact on the model predictions than better than dead responses.

One alternative is to rescale TTO values for states to -1 using either $-x/t$ (Dolan 1997) or $\frac{-x/y}{-z}$ (Shaw et al. 2005) where z is the worst value produced using the formula $-x/y$. Although it is convenient to transform or bound the valuations of states worse than dead to -1, there is little empirical evidence for why this should be the case. Transforming the values in this way means that these transformed scores can no longer be interpreted as utility values measured on the same utility scale as states better than dead (Patrick et al. 1994).

Recent developments in the literature have taken two alternative approaches to deal with the issue of states worse than dead: to change the modeling techniques used to estimate utility values for all states, or to change the protocol used to elicit values for health states that are valued as being worse than dead.

33.3.3.1 Solution (1): Developments in Modeling Existing TTO Preference Data

One approach to deal with worse than dead TTO responses is to use different modeling techniques to estimate preference weights on TTO values elicited using the MVH TTO protocol. Craig and Busschbach (2009) use an "episodic random utility model (RUM)" that changes the way TTO responses are modeled and the contribution of the model is in its analysis of worse than dead responses. Simply, if the standard model and episodic RUM were estimated on a dataset containing only better than dead responses the predicted values would be identical, but the specification of the model would be different.

The standard regression model earlier defined in equation (1) is $h_{ij} = f(\mathbf{X}_i\beta) + \varepsilon_{ij}$ where h_{ij} is the value for health state i valued by respondent j and $\mathbf{X}_i$ is a vector of dummy explanatory variables for each level λ of dimension δ of the health state classification for health state h_{ij}. The formula for better than dead responses is $h_{ij} = x_{ij}/t_h$ where x_{ij} represents years in full health and t_h represents years in the health state h_{ij}, typically fixed at 10 years. Substituting this into equation (1) provides the model specification for better than dead responses using the standard model and the episodic RUM model:

$$x_{ij}\big/t_h = f(\mathbf{X}_i\beta) + \varepsilon_{ij} \text{ Standard model} \tag{2}$$

$$x_{ij} = f(t_h \mathbf{X}_i \boldsymbol{\beta}) + \eta_{ij} \text{ Episodic RUM model} \tag{3}$$

The standard formula for worse than dead responses as outlined above is $h_{ij} = {}^{y_{ij}-t}\!/\!_{y_{ij}} = {}^{-x_{ij}}\!/\!_{y_{ij}}$ where x_{ij} represents years in full health ($t-y$ in the earlier discussion) and y_{ij} represents years in the health state h_{ij}. Substituting this into equation (1) provides the model specification for worse than dead responses:

$$-x_{ij}\!/\!_{y_{ij}} = f(\mathbf{X}_i \boldsymbol{\beta}) + \varepsilon_{ij} \text{ Standard model} \tag{4}$$

$$-x_{ij} = f(y_{ij} \mathbf{X}_i \boldsymbol{\beta}) + \eta_{ij} \text{ Episodic RUM model} \tag{5}$$

Craig and Busschbach (2009) argue that the error component in the standard model differs for better than dead responses and worse than dead responses, whereas the episodic RUM model assigns the same error component thus producing consistent results. Figure 33.6 shows the difference in predicted health state utility values for both models (Craig and Busschbach 2009) using the UK MVH dataset (Dolan 1997) that was used to estimate the UK EQ-5D preference weights. For the standard model (referred to in Figure 33.6 as the instant RUM TTO) the unadjusted estimates are estimated as described above and the adjusted estimates rescale worse than dead responses using $h_{ij}=x_{ij}/t$ as used to produce the UK EQ-5D preference weights (Dolan 1997). In this dataset the episodic RUM produces higher predictions than the standard model for severe states.

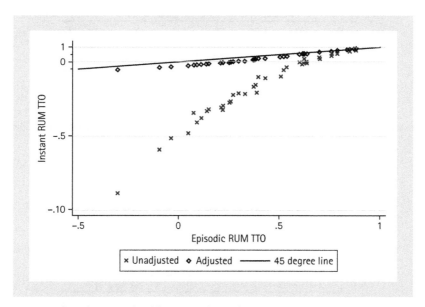

FIGURE 33.6 Predicted EQ-5D health state utility values using the standard and episodic RUM models

Source: Craig and Busschbach 2009.

The main contribution of the episodic RUM model is that all TTO responses are treated identically in the model specification. Yet this does not resolve the problems outlined earlier that the TTO choice tasks are different for states valued as better than or worse than dead. This approach is an alternative approach to model existing TTO data, but a better approach for future valuation studies may be to use the same TTO task to value all states.

33.3.3.2 Solution (2): The Lead Time TTO

A TTO procedure has been proposed that introduces a "lead time" whereby a period in full health is added to the start of the usual TTO, meaning that states worse than dead can be valued by cutting in to the lead time. This task, developed by Devlin et al. (2010) out of work by Robinson and Spencer (2006), is illustrated in Figures 33.7 and 33.8.

The "lead time" TTO task provides respondents with a choice between (a) full health for f years followed by health state h for $t-f$ years, after which they will die, or (b) full health for g years, after which they will die. Figures 33.7 and 33.8 indicate that the only difference in protocol is that $g > f$ for states better than dead and $g < f$ for states worse than dead. Years in full health, g, is varied to determine the point where the respondent

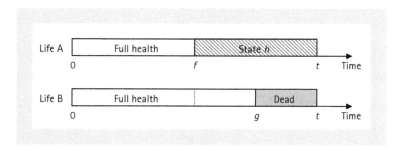

FIGURE 33.7 "Lead time" time trade-off for a health state valued as better than dead

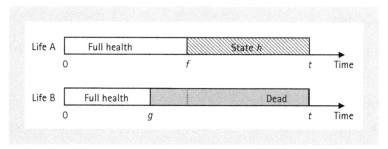

FIGURE 33.8 "Lead time" time trade-off for a health state valued as worse than dead

is indifferent between the two options and the utility for health state h is calculated using $(g-f)/_{(t-f)}$. The same method, props, and formula to calculate the TTO value are used for all states, where the value is negative for states worse than dead and positive for states better than dead. This approach has the advantage that it does not draw attention to the fact that respondents are valuing a state as worse than dead, yet this may mean that respondents are not fully aware of what their responses indicate. This method makes a strong assumption of additive separability where the value of state h should not be affected if it is preceded by full health for period f, and may suffer from the problem of ordering effects in moving from full health to a poor health state. Due to the long overall time period the lead time approach may be unrealistic for older respondents, and some respondents exhausted the lead time in pilot work. This new procedure is the subject of further methodological research being undertaken by members of the EuroQol group and elsewhere.

33.3.4 Ordinal Measures

Given the concerns with conventional cardinal methods of health state valuation, there has been increasing interest in using ordinal tasks that require the respondent to rank one or more states (Kind 1996; Salomon 2003; McCabe et al. 2006). The ability to derive cardinal health state values from ordinal information comes from the assumption that a respondent's selection over a set of states will be related to a latent variable. It allows for the fact that individuals make errors of judgment and sometimes may choose the health state with a lower value. The proportion of occasions on which such an error is made is related to the distance between the mean values of the states. There will be more agreement in preferences the further apart the mean values for two states are in terms of the latent variable. This has been the basis for the more general use of discrete choice experiments. The application of a logistic function provides a means of modeling the latent utility value from ordinal data (Luce 1959; McFadden 1974). By making additional assumptions it is possible to "explode" ranking data into discrete choice data, whereby the ordering of X states is seen as a sequence of discrete choices, although this requires an assumption about the irrelevance of alternative options in the task that has been shown to be violated (McCabe et al. 2006).

In this chapter, we focus on the problem of anchoring the values estimated by logistic models onto the full health to dead scale required for calculating QALYs, where full health is one and dead is zero. There have been three solutions to this problem applied in the literature to date. One has been to anchor the lowest scoring state on zero (Coast et al. 2008), but this does not allow for the fact that the worst state may be better or worse than being dead and so this does not provide a means of combining health state values with survival in a way that is required to calculate QALYs. The second has been to use the TTO or SG value of one of more health states, usually the worst state, to anchor the latent variable on the required zero to one scale (Ratcliffe et al. 2009). This offers a practical solution, but it does not get away from the concerns with the cardinal methods mentioned earlier. Furthermore if the transformation is not linear this requires more than one health state to be valued and a mapping function to be estimated.

The third approach has been to include being dead in the choice of states, either in the ranking task (McCabe et al. 2006) or the discreet choice experiment (DCE) (Brazier et al. 2009) and so the standard regression model in equation (1) is adapted as follows:

$$h_{ij} = f(\mathbf{X}_i\boldsymbol{\beta} + \phi D) + \varepsilon_{ij} \tag{6}$$

where ϕD is a dummy variable that takes a value of one for the dead state. The regression can be estimated using a conditional logistic or rank-ordered logit model. By dividing the coefficients on the dimension levels by the coeficient for dead, it is possible to rescale the latent variable onto the zero to one scale. This has been successfully applied using rank data (Salomon 2003; McCabe et al. 2006) and DCE data (Brazier et al. 2009). However, it has been strongly criticized for not providing a link for respondents who do not feel that any states are worse than dead (Flynn et al. 2008). The distance between the worst state and dead cannot be estimated for these respondents, and while it is possible to generate mean values across a sample of respondents, a large proportion of respondents have been disenfranchised. This is a major problem for descriptive systems concerned with milder health states and a significant one for generic measures like EQ-5D that cover a broader range of severity.

Another approach has been proposed that includes survival as an attribute (Johnson et al. 2007; Bansback et al. 2009). This to some extent overcomes the problem of nontrading associated with the approach of using a dead state or at least significantly reduces it. The resultant DCE has some similarity to TTO since it effectively involves varying the length of time spent in each state. The difference is that length of life is varied for all states and is not limited to the better states as it is for TTO. The design and modeling of this DCE is rather more complex since the relationship between health and length of life is multiplicative rather than additive. The appropriate equation for modeling such data has been proposed by Bansback et al. (2009) as follows:

$$h_{ijk} = \alpha + \beta_1 t_{ijk} + \mathbf{X}_{ik}\boldsymbol{\beta}_2 t_{ijk} + \varepsilon_{ij} \tag{7}$$

where utility h_{ijk} from health state i is derived by individual j in scenario $k = 1,\dots,K$ (each scenario will involve two or more states). The difference here from equation (1) is that equation (7) includes variable t for survival, so that if someone lives for t years in a perfect state then this represents the utility gain. Furthermore interaction terms between health dimensions and survival are included to reflect the mutiplicative relationship. However, note that there is no place for the standard health dimension dummies as main effects, since these have no value without a time variable.

The task of anchoring the values on the full health–dead scale requires a further step and one proposed solution involves solving a hypothetical choice problem at a point of indifference between two alternatives in a way that is analogous to TTO (Bansback et al. 2009). This does not get away from some of the concerns with TTO, such as the assumption of constant proportional trade-off, although this can be tested within this approach and the consequences for health state values demonstrated. Research on this method is currently being undertaken.

33.3.4 Experience vs. Preferences

Much of the health state valuation literature has been concerned with respondents valuing hypothetical states to obtain preference or decision-based utility. There has been increasing interest, however, in the use of experience-based measures of utility in economics (Dolan and Kahneman 2008). There is an analogy to the debate about whose values: whether to use general population values that are preference-based; or patient values that can be preference-based or based on their current states, and so experience-based.

The main argument for the use of general population preferences is that they pay for the service. However, whilst members of the general population want to be involved in health care decision-making, it is not clear that they want to be asked to value health states specifically. At the very least, it does not necessarily imply the current practice of using relatively uninformed general population values.

33.3.4.1 Why Patient Values?

The main argument for using patient experience-based values is the fact that patients understand the impact of their health on their well-being better than someone trying to imagine it. It avoids having to describe the health state to respondents and all the limitations of the classification systems of current generic or even condition specific measures of health. There is ample evidence that we are poor at predicting our utility from future experiences (Dolan and Kahneman 2008). In the context of health, members of the general public seem to be unable to take sufficient account of their future adaptation to ill health. Respondents are only providing the disutility of the state from their current perspective and not their perspective once they are experiencing the state. Assuming patients do adapt, then this accounts for the finding that patients tend to give higher values to the same state. The adaptation hypothesis seems to hold for many physical conditions, but this may not be the case for all conditions (e.g. some mental health problems), although this does not change the essential argument about using patient values.

To use patients' experience-based values requires a value judgment that society wants to incorporate all the changes and adaptations that occur in patients who experience states of ill health over long periods of time. It can be argued that some adaptation may be regarded as "laudable," such as skill enhancement and activity adjustment, whereas cognitive denial of functional health, suppressed recognition of full health and lowered expectations may be seen as less attractive from a policy perspective. Furthermore, there may be a concern that patient values are context based, reflecting their recent experiences of ill health and the health of their immediate peers and so incorporate existing inequalities in society.

There are some important practical problems in asking patients to value their own health, many of whom will by definition be quite unwell. In addition, to obtain values on the conventional zero to one scale required for QALYs valuation techniques requires a patient to compare their existing state to full health, which they may not have experienced for many years. For patients who have lived in a chronic health state like chronic obstructive pulmonary disease or osteoarthritis, for example, the task of imagining full health is as difficult as a healthy member of the general population trying to imagine a poor health state.

33.3.4.2 *A Middle Way*

It has been argued that it seems difficult to justify the exclusive use of patient values or the current practice of using values from relatively uninformed members of the general population (Brazier et al. 2005b). Existing generic preference-based measures already take some account of adaptation and response shift in their descriptive systems, but whether this is sufficient is ultimately a normative judgment. If it is accepted that the values of the general population are required to inform resource allocation in a public system, it might be argued that respondents should be provided with more information on adaptation. There have been some attempts to do this, showing that the general public may change their values in the face of information about adaptation (McTaggart-Cowan et al. 2010), but this requires further research.

33.4 SUMMARY

Health state utility measurement is a key part of the economic evaluation of health care. There are three key questions to address in deciding how to generate health state values: what it is we are trying to value (i.e. description), how we should value health (i.e. the valuation technique and methods of modeling preference data) and whose values we should use. There have been important developments in each of these areas over the last two decades and the availability of alternative methods has grown. This creates problems for policymakers, since these methods generate different values on the same patient population.

This chapter has reviewed key developments in the field. Given the growing number of preference-based and non-preference-based measures an important development has been the estimation of mapping functions between these measures and a favored target generic measure to provide a firmer basis for synthesizing evidence for use in cost effectiveness models. These mapping functions are not always successful and another approach has been to value the content of generic or condition specific measures, but this runs into concerns about comparability.

A central problem with the QALY has been how to value states on the full health–dead scale. The lead time TTO has been developed to overcome the problem of states worse than dead that are currently dealt with in an inconsistent manner. There are also new modeling approaches to deal with this problem. Concerns with cardinal methods for valuing health states have led to an exploration of ordinal methods of valuation. A number of alternative methods have been developed for placing the latent variable on the full health–dead scale that are being explored by researchers around the world.

Finally the question of whose values remains and whether experience utility should be used rather than conventional preference-based utility raises important issues about perspective and the role of factors such as adaptation. This is a reminder that some of the key parameters in an economic model involve normative as well as technical judgments.

REFERENCES

ARA, R. and BRAZIER, J. (2008). Deriving an algorithm to convert the eight mean SF-36 dimension scores into a mean EQ-5D preference-based score from published studies (where patient level data are not available). *Value in Health* 11: 1131–43.

BANSBACK, N., BRAZIER, J., TSUCHIYA, A., and ANIS, A. (2009). A comparison of a discrete choice experiment to the time-trade-off to value health states for QALYs. Paper presented to the Health Economics Study Group, University of Sheffield, Sheffield, July.

BARTON, G. R., BANKART, J., DAVIS, A. C., and SUMMERFIELD, Q. A. (2004). Comparing utility scores before and after hearing aid provision: Results According to the EQ-5D, HUI3 and SF-6D. *Applied Health Economics and Health Policy* 3: 103–5.

BLEICHRODT, H. (2002). A new explanation for the difference between time trade off utilities and standard gamble utilities. *Health Economics* 11(5): 447–56.

BOYD, N. F., SUTHERLAND, H. J., HEASMAN, Z. K., TRICHTER, D. L., and CUMMINGS, B. J. (1990). Whose values for decision making? *Medical Decision Making* 10: 58–67.

BRAZIER, J. E. and DIXON, S. (1995). The use of condition specific outcome measures in economic appraisal. *Health Economics* 4, 255–64.

—— and ROBERTS, J. (2004). The estimation of a preference-based index from the SF-12. *Medical Care* 42: 851–9.

—— and TSUCHIYA, A. (2010). Preference-based condition specific measures of health: what happens to cross programme comparability? *Health Economics* 19: 125–9.

—— HARPER, R., THOMAS, K., JONES, N., and UNDERWOOD, T. (1998). Deriving a preference based single index measure from the SF-36. *Journal of Clinical Epidemiology* 51(11): 1115–29.

—— ROBERTS, J., and DEVERILL, M. (2002). The estimation a preference-based single index measure for health from the SF-36. *Journal of Health Economics* 21(2): 271–92.

—— —— TSUCHIYA, A., and BUSSCHBACH, J. (2004). A comparison of the EQ-5D and SF-6D across seven patient groups. *Health Economics* 13: 873–84.

—— —— PLATTS, M., and ZOELLNER, Y. (2005a). Estimating a preference-based index for a menopause specific health quality of life questionnaire. *Health and Quality of Life Outcomes* 3: 13.

—— AKEHURST, R., BRENNAN, A., et al. (2005b). Should patients have a greater role in valuing health states? *Applied Health Economics & Health Policy* 4: 201–8.

—— RATCLIFFE, J., TSUCHIYA, A., and SOLOMON, J. (2007). *Measuring and Valuing Health for Economic Evaluation*. Oxford: Oxford University Press.

Brazier, J. E., Czoski-Murray, C., Roberts, J., Brown, M., Symonds, T., and Kelleher, C. (2008). Estimation of a preference-based index from a condition specific measure: the King's Health Questionnaire. *Medical Decision Making* 28(1): 113–26.

—— Rowen, D., Yang, Y., and Tsuchiya, A. (2009). Using rank and discrete choice data to estimate health state utility values on the QALY scale. Health Economics and Decision Science Discussion Paper 09/10, University of Sheffield, Sheffield.

—— Yang, Y., Tsuchiya, A., and Rowen, D. (2010). A review of studies mapping (or cross walking) from non-preference based measures of health to generic preference-based measures. *European Journal of Health Economics* 11: 215–25.

Coast, J., Flynn, T., Natarajan, L., et al. (2008). Valuing the ICECAP capability index for older people. *Social Science and Medicine* 67: 874–82.

Commonwealth Department of Health and Aging (2002). Guidelines for the pharmaceutical industry on the submission to the Pharmaceutical Benefits Advisory Committee. Australian Publications Production Service, Canberra.

Craig, B. M. and Busschbach, J. J. V. (2009). The episodic random utility model unifies time trade-off and discrete choice approaches in health state valuation. *Population Health Metrics* 7: 3.

Devlin, N., Tsuchiya, A., Buckingham, K., and Tilling, C. (2011). A Uniform Time Trade Off Method for States Better and Worse than Dead: Feasibility Study of the "Lead Time" Approach, *Health Economics* (forthcoming).

Dolan, P. (1997). Modelling valuations for EuroQol Health States. *Medical Care* 35(11): 1095–108.

—— and Gudex, C. (1995). Time preference, duration and health state valuations. *Health Economics* 4: 289–99.

—— and Kahneman, D. (2008). Interpretations of utilities and their implications for the valuation of health. *Economic Journal* 118: 215–34.

—— and Sutton, M. (1997). Mapping visual analogue scale health state valuations on to standard gamble and time trade-off values. *Social Science and Medicine* 44: 1519–30.

—— Gudex, C., Kind, P., and Williams, A. (1996). Valuing health states: a comparison of methods. *Journal of Health Economics* 15: 209–31.

Dowie, J. (2002). Decision validity should determine whether generic or condition-specific HRQOL measure is used in health care decisions. *Health Economics* 11: 1–8.

Espallargues, M., Czoski-Murray, C., Bansback, N., et al. (2005). The impact of Age Related Macular Degeneration on Health Status Utility Values. *Investigative Ophthalmology and Visual Science* 46: 4016–23.

Feeny, D., Furlong, W., Torrance, G.W., et al. (2002). Multi-attribute and single-attribute utility functions for the Health Utilities Index Mark 3 system. *Medical Care* 40(2): 113–28.

Flynn, T. N., Louviere, J. J., Marley, A. A. J., Coast, J., and Peters, T. J. (2008). Rescaling quality of life values from discrete choice experiments for use as QALYs: a cautionary tale. *Population Health Metrics* 6: 6.

Franks, P., Lubetkin, E. I., Gold, M. R., Tancredi, D. J., and Haomiao, J. (2004). Mapping the SF-12 to the EuroQol EQ-5D Index in a National US Sample. *Medical Decision Making* 24: 247–54.

Gold, M. R., Siegel, J. E., Russell, L. B., and Weinstein, M. C. (1996). *Cost-effectiveness in Health and Medicine*. Oxford: Oxford University Press.

Gray, A. M., Rivero-Arias, O., and Clarke, P. M. (2006). Estimating the association between SF-12 responses and EQ-5D utility values by response mapping. *Medical Decision Making* 26: 18–29.

GREEN, C., BRAZIER, J., and DEVERILL, M. (2000). Valuing health-related quality of life. A review of health state valuation techniques. *Pharmacoeconomics* 17: 151–65.

HARPER, R., BRAZIER, J. E., WATERHOUSE, J. C., WALTERS, S. J., JONES, N. M. B., and HOWARD, P. (1997). A comparison of outcome measures for patients with chronic obstructive pulmonary disease (COPD) in an outpatient setting. *Thorax* 52: 879–87.

HAWTHORNE, G., RICHARDSON, J., and OSBOURNE, R. (1999). The Australian quality of life (AQoL) instrument: a psychometric measure of Health-Related Quality of Life. *Quality of Life Research*, 8: 209–24.

HAYWOOD, K. L., GARRATT, A. M., LALL, R., SMITH, J. F., and LAMB, S. E. (2008). EuroQol EQ-5D and condition-specific measures of health outcome in women with urinary incontinence: reliability, validity and responsiveness. *Quality of Life Research* 17: 475–83.

HEALTH INSURANCE COUNCIL (1999). Dutch Guidelines for Pharmacoeconomic research. CVZ, Amstelveen, Netherlands: Health Insurance Council.

KAPLAN, R. M. and ANDERSON, J. P. (1988). A general health policy model: update and application. *Health Services Research* 11: 478–507.

KIND, P. (1996). Deriving cardinal scales from ordinal preference data: the analysis of time trade off data using pairwise judgement models. Paper presented to the Health Economists Study Group, Brunel University, July.

KOBELT, G., KIRCHPERGER, I., and MALONE-LEE, J. (1999). Quality of life aspects of the over active bladder and the effect of treatment with tolterodine. *British Journal of Urology* 83: 583–90.

LENERT, L. A., CHER, D. J., GOLDSTEIN, M. K., BERGEN, M. R., and GARBER, A. (1998). The effect of search procdures on utility elicitations. *Medical Decision Making* 18: 76–83.

LONGWORTH, L. and BRYAN, S. (2003). An empirical comparison of EQ-5D and SF-6D in liver transplant patients. *Health Economics* 12: 1061–7.

LUCE, R. D. (1959). *Individual Choice Behavior: A Theoretical Analysis*. New York: John Wiley & Sons, Inc.

McCABE, C., BRAZIER, J., GILKS, P., TSUCHIYA, A., ROBERTS, J., O'HAGAN, A., and STEVENS, K. (2006). Using rank data to estimate health state utility models. *Journal of Health Economics* 25/3: 418–31.

McFADDEN, D. (1974). Conditional logit analysis of qualitative choice behavior. In P. Zarembka (ed.) *Frontiers in Econometrics*. New York: Academic Press, 105–42.

McTAGGART-COWAN, H. M., TSUCHIYA, A., O'CATHAIN, A., and BRAZIER, J. E. (2010). The impact of disease adaptation information on general population values for rheumatoid arthritis states. Health Economics and Decision Science Discussion Paper, University of Sheffield, Sheffield.

MEHREZ, A. and GAFNI, A. (1993). HYEs versus QALYs: in pursuit of progress. *Medical Decision Making* 13: 287–92.

NICE (2004). Guide to the methods of technology appraisal <http://www.nice.org.uk/pdf/TAP_Methods.pdf>.

—— (2008) Guide to the methods of technology appraisal. NICE, London. <http://www.nice.org.uk/aboutnice/howwework/devnicetech/technologyappraisalprocessguides/guidetothemethodsoftechnologyappraisal.jsp>.

O'BRIEN, B. J., SPATH, M., BLACKHOUSE, G., SEVERENS, J. L., and BRAZIER, J. E. (2003). A view from the Bridge: agreement between the SF-6D utility algorithm and the Health Utilities Index. *Health Economics* 12: 975–82.

PATRICK, D. L., STARKS, H. E., CAIN, K. C., UHLMANN, R. F., and PEARLMAN, R. A. (1994) Measuring preferences for health states worse than death. *Medical Decision Making* 14(1): 9–18.

RATCLIFFE, J., BRAZIER, J., TSUCHIYA, A., SYMONDS, T., and BROWN, M. (2009). Using DCE and ranking data to estimate cardinal values for health states for deriving a preference-based single index from the sexual quality of life questionnaire. *Health Economics*, 18: 1261–76.

REVICKI, D. A., LEIDY, N. K., BRENNAN-DIEMER, F., THOMSON, C., and TOGIAS, A. (1998a). Development and preliminary validation of multi-attribute rhinitis symptom utility index. *Chest* 114: 693–702.

——— ——— ——— SORENSON, S., and TOGIAS, A. (1998b). Integrating patients preferences into health outcomes assessment: the multiattribute asthma symptom utility index. *Chest* 114: 998–1007.

RICHARDSON, J. (1994). Cost-utility analysis: what should be measured. *Social Science & Medicine* 39: 7–21.

ROBINSON, A. and SPENCER, A. (2006). Exploring challenges to TTO utilities: valuing states worse than dead. *Health Economics* 15: 393–402.

ROWEN, D., BRAZIER, J., and ROBERTS, J. (2009a). Mapping SF-36 onto the EQ-5D index: how reliable is the relationship? *Health and Quality of Life Outcomes* 7: 27.

——— ——— TSUCHIYA, A., and HERNANDEZ, M. (2009b). The simultaneous valuation of states from multiple instruments using ranking and VAS data: methods and preliminary results. Health Economics and Decision Science Discussion Paper 09/06, University of Sheffield.

SALOMON, J. A. (2003). Reconsidering the use of rankings in the valuation of health states: a model for estimating cardinal values from ordinal data. *Population Health Metrics* 1: 12.

——— and MURRAY, C. J. L. (2004). A multi-method approach to measuring health state valuations. *Health Economics* 13: 281–90.

SHAW, J. W., JOHNSON, J. A., and COONS, S. J. (2005). US valuation of the EQ-5D health states: development and testing of the D1 valuation model. *Medical Care* 43(3): 203–20.

SINTONEN, H. and PEKURINEN, M. (1993). A fifteen-dimensional measure of health-related quality of life (15D) and its applications. *Quality of Life Assessment: Key Issues in the 1990s*. Dordrecht, Netherlands: Kluwer Academic Publishers, 185–95.

STEVENS, K. J. (2010). Working with children to develop dimensions for a preference-based, generic, pediatric health-related quality-of-life measure. *Qualitative Health Research* 20: 340–51.

——— BRAZIER, J., MCKENNA, S., DOWARD, L., and CORK, M. (2005). The development of a preference-based measure of health in children with atopic dermatitis. *British Journal of Dermatology* 153: 372–7.

——— MCCABE, C. J. and BRAZIER, J. E. (2006). Mapping between Visual Analogue Scale and Standard Gamble data: results from the UK Health Utilities Index 2 valuation survey. *Health Economics* 15: 527–33.

SULLIVAN, P. W. and GHUSHCHYAN, V. (2006). Mapping the EQ-5D Index from the SF-12: US general population preferences in a nationally representative sample. *Medical Decision Making* 26: 401–9.

SUTHERLAND, H. J., LLEWELLYN, T. H., BOYD, D., and TILL, J. E. (1982). Attitudes towards quality of survival: the concept of maximum endurable time. *Medical Decision Making* 2: 299–309.

TORRANCE, G. W. (1986). Measurement of health state utilities for economic appraisal: A review. *Journal of Health Economics* 5: 1–30.

——— THOMAS, W. H., and SACKETT, D. L. (1972). A utility maximisation model for evaluation of health care programs. *Health Services Research* 7(2): 118–33.

——— BOYLE, H. B., and HORWOOD, S. P. (1982). Application of multi-attribute utility theory to measure social preferences for health states. *Operations Research* 30(6): 1043–69.

—— FEENY, D. H., FURLONG, W. J., BARR, R. D., ZHANG, Y., and WANG, Q. (1996). A multi-attribute utility function for a comprehensive health status classification system: Health Utilities Mark 2. *Medical Care* 34: 702–22.

—— KERESTECI, M. A., CASEY, R. W., ROSNER, A. J., RYAN, N., and BRETON, M. C. (2004). Development and initial validation of a new preference-based disease-specific health-related quality of life instrument for erectile function. *Quality of Life Research* 13: 349–59.

WALTERS, S. J., MORRELL, C. J., and DIXON, S. (1999). Measuring health-related quality of life in patients with venous leg ulcers. *Quality of Life Research* 8: 327–36.

WILLE, N. and RAVENS-SIEBERER, U. (2006). Age-appropriateness of the EQ-5D adult and child-friendly version: testing the feasibility, reliability and validity in children and adolescents. In X. Badía (ed.) *23rd Scientific Plenary Meeting of the EuroQol Group in Barcelona, Spain: September 14–16*. Barcelona: IMS Health, 217–29.

YANG, Y., BRAZIER, J. E., TSUCHYIA, A., and COYNE, K. (2009). Estimating a preference-based index from the Over Active Bladder questionnaire. *Value in Health* 12(1): 159–66.

YOUNG, T., YANG, Y., BRAZIER, J., TSUCHIYA, A., and COYNE, K. (2009). The first stage of developing preference-based measures: constructing a health-state classification using Rasch analysis. *Quality of Life Research* 18: 253–65.

CHAPTER 34

....

CONCEPTS OF EQUITY AND FAIRNESS IN HEALTH AND HEALTH CARE

....

JAN ABEL OLSEN

VARIOUS concepts of fairness are a central concern of many health policy makers, not least because a fair distribution of resources is often considered a prerequisite of public support for publicly funded health care. This chapter will describe the various concepts of equity and fairness that have been developed by economists in health and health care.

34.1 INTRODUCTION

....

The interest among health economists in equity and fairness can be explained by the simple facts that health inequalities, and hence inequalities in *needs* for health care, exist in all countries. Furthermore, health policy objectives in most countries with a publicly funded health sector share two key equity concerns: first, "equal access for equal need," and second, reduction in health inequalities. These twin equity objectives can be found in health policy documents in Norway, the UK, and most likely your own country (check it out). Interestingly, the same twin equity objectives were emphasized by the latest World Health Assembly, following the report from the WHO Commission on Social Determinants of Health (<www.who.int/social_determinants/en/>). Thus, equity focused health policies reflect value judgments that are widely agreed upon, way beyond the social values of Northern European welfare states.

The concern of "equal access for equal need" reflects the ideology behind a universal coverage National Health Service, that no one should be deprived of health care because of their inability to pay for it (see Williams 1988). Note that this objective of *equal access (to health care) for equal (health) needs* reflects the socialist distributive principle: "from each according to his ability, to each according to his needs." No wonder therefore that some politicians in some countries use the rhetorical concept "socialized medicine" when referring to countries with national health schemes. However, no matter its ideological label, there is a surprisingly wide political support in favor of this distributive principle for health care in countries which have chosen it.

The second concern reflects a view that some important types of health inequalities are considered unfair. Policy documents in some countries, including the report from the WHO Commission on Social Determinants of Health, are often referring to an aim of reducing *avoidable* health inequalities. It is not clear, however, what is meant by *avoidable* in this context: technologically infeasible; too costly; against the law of natural variations; or, an acknowledgement of the fact that preferences for health-related lifestyles will always differ across people?

Equity-related policy objectives have some important implications for health economic models and analytical approaches, which in many ways differ from the paradigm of neo-classical economics. First, rather than (subjective) preferences, the focus lies on (more objective) *needs*. While strength of preferences is usually measured by willingness to pay, needs are usually measured in terms of some concept of *health*. Thus, measuring health becomes paramount. The focus on *access* to health care leads us towards two different issues. One issue is that of access as opposed to utilization, i.e. differences in health care utilization may not be an appropriate measure of differences in access, because of cultural diversity in health care use (see Mooney 2007). The other issue relates to health care *finance*. By logic, the dictum of equal access requires that one's contribution to the financing of health care is divorced from one's needs for health care. Wagstaff and van Doorslaer (2000) distinguish between divorcing payment from utilization (delivery), and divorcing payment from ability to pay (finance). When health care finance is included as a non-earmarked tax, the level of financial equity is essentially a matter of the level of progressivity in the tax system as a whole, an issue that lies outside the discretion of health policy makers. An important implication for health economists, though, is to unravel the stated distributive principle for health care *before* we start searching for the optimal health care financing model.

Frequently, both health policy makers and health economists are imprecise in the meaning they attach to the concepts of equity and fairness. Not only are health policy objectives on equity and fairness hard to interpret, but there is conceptual overlap in the scientific literature between "equity," "equality," "fairness," and "justice." In her paper "The concepts and principles of equity and health," Margaret Whitehead emphasizes the importance of focusing on the *cause* of an inequality when judging the extent to which it is unfair: "The term 'inequity' has a moral and ethical dimension. It refers to differences which are *unnecessary* and *avoidable*, but in addition are considered *unfair* and *unjust*. So, in order to describe a certain situation as inequitable the *cause* has to be examined and *judged* to be unfair in the context of what is going on in the rest of society" (Whitehead 1992, italics in original).

This chapter, therefore, starts with a background framework on the principal *causes* of inequalities in health and health care. Section 34.3 attempts to clarify the concept of equity, and its interrelations with equality, fairness, and justice. The remainder of the chapter is concerned with how equity issues and theories of distributive justice are being integrated into health economic models. In section 34.4, equity and efficiency are brought together when discussing the "paradigm of the health frontier." Sections 34.5 and 34.6 enquire into the key question "equality of what?," first in terms of which "stream of health" (health gains, expected health without treatment, total lifetime health) that is the focus of attention, and second, whether we are concerned with equality of opportunities or equality of outcomes, an issue strongly related to the intricate issue of "personal responsibility." The renewed interest in the literature on the distinction between equality of opportunity and equality of outcomes, as well as in the notion of responsibility, represents an attempt to clarify the reasons why one type of inequality can be labeled fair, while another be unfair. The final section draws some implications.

34.2 Inequalities in Health and Health Care: A Background Framework

Before any consideration of health *care*, inequalities in *health* arise because of variations in the three classes of *determinants* of population health (Evans et al. 1994; Olsen et al. 2003). The first determinant of population health, *genetics* explains inherited diseases through natural variations in human biology. Second, the physical and social *environment* includes working conditions, pollution, cultural norms and position in the social hierarchy. Third, health-related *lifestyle* refers to people's behavior regarding diet, exercise, and substance use.

The three classes of determinants differ in the extent to which individuals have control over them. Genetic endowments are health *preconditions* and reflect a "biological lottery" over which we have no control. The environment in which people happen to live represents their *opportunities* that—at least for children—reflect a "social lottery" over which they may have little control. Lifestyle is the determinant over which we have most discretion, but precisely how much of that reflects sovereign consumer preferences and how much reflects social conditioning is a very contentious issue.

Figure 34.1 gives a graphical representation of the determinants of population health—along an "outside–inside own control" continuum. Health-related *lifestyle* is emphasized within this map of causation because this variable is associated with the issue of responsibility that will be elaborated by the end of the chapter. Note that variations in "lifestyle-diseases" are explained not by variations in preferences alone, but also by mental or biological responses to the environment in which people happen to live.

The relative importance of these three sets of population health determinants for explaining real world inequalities in underlying health will of course vary between countries. The differences in physical and social environments are obvious.

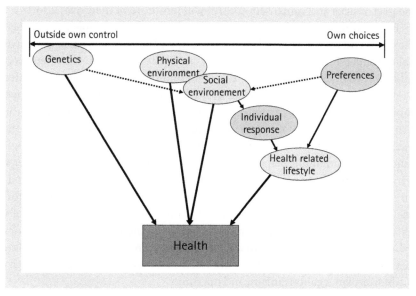

FIGURE 34.1 The determinants of ill health

In an era of increasingly effective medical strategies for the prevention and treatment of adverse health conditions, health care utilization can also be a determinant of health inequalities. For example, when people in ill health are denied access to health care, the initial health inequalities will be reinforced. If health care is being rationed by market prices, inequalities in ability to pay may explain the major differences in utilization. If rationed in terms of needs and waiting time, inequalities in utilization may be explained by different preferences or cultural norms, and/or by supply side variations in quality and regional distribution of providers.

When concerned with reducing these inequalities, two types of policy interventions exist. First, there are policies for the distribution of health *care*, either on the basis of "equal access for equal needs," or on the basis of a compensation to those affected by what is considered unfair determinants, e.g. allocating more health care to socially deprived groups (see e.g. Hauck et al. 2002). Second, there are policies targeted at the initial determinants (genetics, environment, preferences), something which calls for the involvement of other sectors beyond the health service.

Within the framework of Figure 34.1, we can understand why some social inequalities in health are very difficult to avoid no matter how strong policy interventions are implemented. This is due to the existence of underlying variables that have an impact on both one's social position as well as one's health. First, natural variations from birth imply that the biological preconditions for social success (shown as the dotted arrow from genetics to social environment), as well as good health later in life will differ (see e.g. Case et al. 2005). Second, there are variations in health-related preferences across social classes (see e.g. Balia and Jones 2008). People have different personality traits: ambitious people with low time preferences and much self-control will put more of their own efforts into both their social standing as well as their health. To the extent that people choose their social class, they may end up where health-related habits and culture best correspond with their personality traits (shown as the dotted arrow from preferences to social environment). Later adaption to social norms, or the social conditioning, will thereby reinforce our health-related choices. Given that some health inequalities are so difficult to overcome, policy objectives often refer to a *reduction*—not elimination—of health inequalities.

Health inequalities are not necessarily inequitable. Whitehead (1992) holds that there is a consensus view in the literature that health differences determined by biological variation and health damaging behavior would not normally be classified as *inequities* in health. Interestingly, these types of causes refer to the determinants genetics and preferences in Figure 34.1. Hence, it follows that *inequitable inequalities* would be those that are caused by environmental factors. However, rather than consider the *cause* of a health inequality to be the distinguishing issue on whether an inequality is equitable or *inequitable*, what may be considered *equitable inequalities* can be analyzed with reference to the three distributive principles that have been most widely applied by health economists: utilitarianism, egalitarianism, and maximin.

34.3 CONCEPTS OF EQUITY IN HEALTH AND THREE DISTRIBUTIVE PRINCIPLES

In the Elsevier *Handbook of Health Economics*, Alan Williams and Richard Cookson (2000) held that: "In economics the term 'equity' is usually taken to refer to fairness in the distribution of a good (in this case 'health'), and 'fairness' is taken almost unthinkingly to mean reducing inequalities". In one of his many papers on equity, Tony Culyer held that: "Plainly, there is no single, universal theory of equity, but it is widely agreed that *equity* implies *equality*. Unfortunately, there is no accord concerning *what* should be equal" (2001, italics in original). Theories of justice have in various ways been applied in the analysis of equity in health and health care (see e.g. Olsen 1997; Dolan 1998). Thus, there appears to be quite strong overlap in how health economists have come to use the concepts of "fairness," "justice," "equity," and "equality." If "equity implies equality," "fairness means reducing inequalities," and theories of justice are applied in the analyses of equity, what then distinguishes these concepts?

So, when do we think that an observed inequality in health or health care is fair, just, and equitable? Initially, most people seem to interpret equality as the default position associated with fairness and justice. Not only is this a widely held connotation in everyday language, but *equality* is the initial reference state in most theories of justice, whether they are concerned with procedures or distributions. According to Elster (1992): "The task of the major theories of justice can be stated as *justifying deviations from equality*...the burden of proof is on the advocate of an unequal distribution" (italics in original).

Based on Aristotle's famous principle of justice that "equals should be treated equally and unequals unequally," a distinction has been drawn between horizontal vs. vertical equity. Horizontal equity requires the like treatment of like individuals, and vertical equity requires the unlike treatment of *unlike* individuals. The crucial issue then is to identify the morally relevant characteristics that would justify that individuals become unlike in terms of their entitlements to health care.

34.3.1 Equality = Equal Shares

Equality means equal division of the distribuendum (the entity to be distributed) or equalisandum (the entity of which we want an equal distribution). Admittedly different authors have not always been very precise regarding what the entity is. It might be income, wealth, utility, well-being, primary goods, opportunities, circumstances, basic capabilities, or—for the current context—health or health care. Some of these entities are hard to measure, and some of them have an instrumental purpose in that they are believed to be important for the good we are seeking, which most likely is some sort of well-being. Good health makes people capable of flourishing in other important walks of life (Sen 1985, 1992, 2002; Culyer 1989). There are positive side effects from improved health in terms of wealth (through labor force participation), and social relations including wider participation in communal life. Hence, aiming for equality in health seems partly to be motivated by aiming for equal opportunities to flourish.

Equality of health care is normally expressed as "equal access (to health care) for equal need." Note the two provisos: (i) *access*, as opposed to utilization, means that inequalities in health care use due to variations in preferences would normally be acceptable (see Mooney et al. 1991; Culyer et al. 1992), and (ii) *equal need* means that health care should *not* be distributed independently of variations in needs, i.e. "unequals should be treated unequally." The concept of *need* therefore becomes crucial in health economics. In everyday language, need is often taken to express the degree of urgency for health care, i.e. "need as ill health" in terms of the expected no-treatment profile or severity of a patient's illness. However, amongst health economists *need* is a concept that refers to the degree of potential benefits from treatment, i.e. "need as capacity to benefit" (see e.g. Culyer 1989, 2001). Hence, in order to reconcile these contrasting interpretations, the slogan "equal access for equal need" must mean equal capacity to benefit, given an equal initial state of ill health (see Olsen 1997).

34.3.2 Equity = Not Necessarily Equal Shares

Two decades ago Le Grand (1987, 1991) argued that inequalities in health care use are not inequitable if they result from different choices or preferences. More recently Dolan and Tsuchiya held that "an inequality only becomes an inequity if an individual cannot be held responsible for his disadvantage" (Dolan and Tsuchiya 2003). It follows from this line of reasoning that those inequalities in health that emerge from an equal "choice set," or can be ascribed to different degrees of responsibilities, would be referred to as *equitable inequalities*.

While the concept of *responsibility* is being used at the *individual* level (i.e. the view that people should be held responsible for their own health-related behavior), the concept of *avoidability* is used at the *societal* level (i.e. the view that society has a duty to reduce inequalities in health that are avoidable). The WHO Commission on Social Determinants of Health suggested that the distinguishing issue is the extent to which an inequality is *avoidable* or not: "Not all health inequalities are unjust or inequitable. If good health were simply unattainable, this would be unfortunate but not unjust. Where inequalities in health are avoidable, yet are not avoided, they are inequitable." So, from this line of reasoning, unavoidable inequalities would be referred to as *equitable inequalities*.

The concept of equity is also closely intertwined with fairness. According to various health economics glossaries, equity is defined as: "fairness in the allocation of resources, treatments or outcomes among different individuals or groups" (<http://www.worldbank.org/hsr/class/module1/glossary.htm>), or: "the degree to which some distribution or other is judged to be 'fair'" (<http://www.nlm.nih.gov/nichsr/edu/healthecon/glossary.html>).

34.3.3 Fairness—Some Diverse Interpretations

Fairness is a word with seemingly only positive connotations. It refers to what is intuitively right, acceptable[1] or just. Within health economics the concept of fairness has primarily been used in relation to equity, in terms of fairness in the *distribution* of health or health care.

However, a completely contrasting perception of fairness in the health economics literature is the concept of "actuarial fairness," in which one's health insurance premium is equal to the expected health care costs, something which differs across risk groups. Thus, it is considered unfair to force people to make a higher contribution to the financing of health care than their individual expected health care costs. Interestingly, this particular view of "actuarial fairness" was translated into an eloquent marketing expression in an advertisement for private health insurance: "Healthy people shouldn't have to pay unhealthy premiums."[2] To the extent that this conception of fairness conforms to any theory of justice, it resembles the *libertarian* idea of people's right to the fruit of their own labor, implying that any forced redistribution is considered unfair.

Another conception of fairness in the economics literature is the criterion "fairness as non-envy": when no agent wishes to hold any other agent's final bundle, this is an equitable allocation (Varian 1975). Note that the distribuendum is no longer

---

[1] Kahneman et al. (1986) report from a survey in which the various statements were labeled "Acceptable" vs. "Unfair."

[2] Heading in a PRU advertisement appearing in UK newspapers October 2007.

unidimensional (e.g. income), but multiple (e.g. leisure and income). Applied in a health economics context this could be presented as a choice between bundles of health and wealth: A [80 QALYs, €60,000 annual income] and B [70 QALYs, €80,000 annual income]. If Ann prefers A and Betty prefers B, then it is fair—simply because they would not swap. However, this concept of "fairness as non-envy" has received little attention in the health economics literature, in which much of the concern for equity and fairness has dealt with partial distributions of a unidimensional good, like number of QALYs.

In a most seminal paper entitled "Justice as Fairness," Rawls (1958) held that "the fundamental idea in the concept of justice as fairness" is: (i) equal rights to the most extensive liberties (the liberty principle), and (ii) any inequalities are unacceptable unless they work to everyone's advantage (the difference principle). The liberty principle deals with *procedural justice*, the difference principle deals with *distributive justice* and leads to the maximin solution, discussed further below.

34.3.4 Justice = Just Procedures + Just Distributions

While the concept of fairness may give a broad set of connotations reflecting the many situations in everyday life for which it is being used, the concept of justice is somewhat more "professional" and often associated with the disciplines of philosophy, law and political science, which perhaps primarily are concerned with *procedural justice*. Except for a few health economics papers addressing procedural justice (see e.g. Wailoo and Anand 2005; Dolan et al. 2007), health economists have primarily applied theories of *distributive justice*, and particularly those that can ascribe solutions identified as points on a health possibility frontier.

34.3.4.1 *Utilitarianism as Health Maximization*

The health maximizing paradigm inherent in cost-effectiveness analysis (CEA) is founded on classical utilitarianism. Rather than utility or happiness, health is the maximand, and the utilitarian "greatest happiness principle" is translated to "the greatest (total) health principle." Utilitarianism appears in a modified and simplified version when maximizing health: (i) as opposed to the measurement of utility, there are widely accepted methods for cardinal measurement of health states, and QALYs are being used as a "sophisticated measure of health"; (ii) individual differences in relative strengths of preferences for health are disregarded by assigning the same finite end points [0–1] on the cardinal health scale; and (iii) interpersonal comparisons of health gains are made from the normative judgment that a given health gain is assigned the same social value no matter the characteristics of the patients involved, i.e. "a QALY is a QALY is QALY."

The more general application of utilitarianism would be to allocate health care for the purpose of maximizing utility, in contrast to health only. However, when utility is measured within a welfarist tradition of willingness-to-pay (WTP), it bears on the question of inequality in the distribution of health care, simply because WTP depends on *ability* to pay.

34.3.4.2 *Egalitarianism*

Strong egalitarianism involves everybody getting an identical share. Elster (1992) refers to this type of egalitarianism as "strongly envious" and distinguishes it from the Rawls-type egalitarianism of maximin, in which inequalities are accepted as long as they benefit the worst-off. While strong egalitarianism may appear to be an extreme distribution rule, it is not absurd. Reinhardt (1998) provides a great example of bringing home chocolate bars to two siblings, where clearly a Pareto-inferior combination [2, 2] is better (in terms of peace and harmony) than a combination [3, 4] which adheres to the assumption of monotonicity ("more is better"). Abásalo and Tsuchiya (2004) explored the existence of such preferences for strong egalitarianism in health, providing results that suggested people violate the assumption of monotonicity.

34.3.4.3 *Maximin: Rawls' Difference Principle*

In his theory of justice, Rawls (1971) is egalitarian at the outset, but accepts inequality as long as it is not possible to further the improvement of the better off. Rawls' distribuendum is a composition of so-called "primary goods," among which health is surprisingly not included. The key issue for the maximin criterion is the severity of the worst off. As long as it is feasible to improve the health of the worst off, resources would be directed to this individual irrespective of the forgone improvements for the others. Norman Daniels (1985) contends that Rawls' theory does not apply to health, because "the theory is idealized to apply to individuals who are 'normal, active and fully cooperating members of society over the course of a complete life' (...) In effect, *there is no distributive theory for health care because no one is sick*" (italics in original). While the need for Rawls' primary goods, e.g. food and clothing, are more or less the same for all, there is a much more unequal distribution of the need for health care and education, reflecting the "natural lottery." There are consequently much wider variations in the resources required to meet such unequal distribution of needs. Applying the maximin principle to health would therefore be a commitment to "the futile goal of eliminating or 'levelling' all natural differences between persons" (Daniels 1985). Independently of the suggested inapplicability of Rawls' theory to distributive justice in health and health care, still, the maximin principle represents one possible decision rule in our context. It implies always to give priority to the one with the worst severity, or non-treatment profile, provided of course that the expected outcome is positive.

34.4 THE HEALTH FRONTIER: EQUITY–EFFICIENCY TRADE-OFF

From an economic perspective, the theories of justice outlined above have been more formally analyzed within the framework of the health frontier, especially when considering health services. Their prescribed solutions can be identified as points on the frontier. Trade-offs between health-related objectives have been analyzed in terms of social welfare functions.

Health policy objectives on equity and fairness must be integrated with key objectives on effectiveness and efficiency: effective use of health care resources and "value for money."[3] In the health economics literature, *cost-effectiveness* refers to costs per unit of health outcome, i.e. the cheaper it is to produce a QALY, the more cost-effective is the intervention. In his seminal paper on the equity–efficiency trade-off, Wagstaff (1991) referred to *efficiency as health-maximization*: the most efficient allocation of health care resources is that specific point on the health frontier that maximizes the total sum of health. However, in accordance with standard welfare economics, the collection of *all* frontier points are referred to as being *Pareto-efficient*.

Bearing in mind that an efficient allocation of resources crucially depend on the maximand, Reinhardt (1998) used the parable that choosing the most efficient route to drive depends on where you want to go: "The word 'efficiency' in health economics has meaning only against a well-defined set of social goals. In abstracting from such goals, the term usually is meaningless." Hence, *allocative efficiency* refers to that allocation which maximizes the maximand! This maximand could be any multiple objective, but it is often a dual objective involving a trade-off between health maximization and equal distribution of health. The approach to finding the optimal distribution follows standard welfare economics: first establish the constraints in terms of what is technologically and economically feasible (the health frontier), and then choose the best point in accordance with the objective function.

34.4.1 The Paradigm of the Health Frontier

There are three key assumptions in the approach behind the health frontier:

1. Fixed total health care budget to be distributed between two (groups of) patients, A and B.
2. The health production functions for each group are positive, but diminishing.
3. The health outcomes are measurable on a cardinal scale, e.g. as QALYs, and interpersonally comparable.

If the health production functions were similar, the frontier would be symmetric around the 45-degree equality line from the origin, and, thus, the health maximizing allocation would be identical with the egalitarian, as well as the maximin, solutions. However, the purpose with this frontier is to illustrate the different solutions that emerge when the production functions differ, i.e. when the two groups of patients have different capacities to benefit from health care. If health maximization were the only policy objective, then the point U in Figure 34.2 becomes the efficient allocation, with which the situation E with equal health can be compared. When the objective is a combined one of achieving

[3] According to the British NHS constitution, "The NHS is committed to providing best value for taxpayers' money and the most effective, fair and sustainable use of finite resources" (<www.dh.gov.uk/en>).

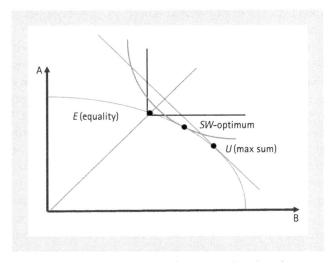

FIGURE 34.2 Equality, efficiency, and trade-offs

as much total health as possible, and the most equal distribution as possible, there is a trade-off between the two points on the frontier, often referred to as "the equity–efficiency trade-off," leading to point *SW* that maximizes social welfare (see Wagstaff 1991).

The shape of the frontier is concave, and hence includes Pareto-efficient distributions only, i.e. improving one group's health would imply a reduction in the other group's health. While this shape is something that has very strong appeal to economists, it reflects a rather restrictive setting: (i) the assumption of a fixed health care budget available like "manna from the sky," something which is relevant in the context of a national health service receiving its budget like "manna from the Treasury" where people's right to a slice of the budget is *independent* of their contribution to it; and (ii) the size of the budget is independent on how it is being distributed between the groups, i.e. there are no production gains from any of the patient groups that would be channeled back to the health service in terms of increased tax revenues as a consequence of having received health care. An implicit restriction in this health frontier is that maximin and equality yield the same solution. In order to have a frontier which distinguishes the maximin from the egalitarian point, the frontier would have to include an increasing part, which requires that the first of the above assumptions has to be relaxed.

An explanation for the upward sloping section, from the vertical axis to point *R*, in Figure 34.3 would be that the treatment of A enables him to increase production, which would mean that some of his output could be deployed to the provision of more health care, thereby benefiting the less productive B. In other words, the upward sloping section illustrates negative net health care costs of treating A, i.e. he would more than "pay his way" in terms of health care.[4] In Figure 34.3, the total health care budget will increase up to point *R*.

---

[4] For an elaboration of this argument, see the model presented in Olsen and Richardson (1999).

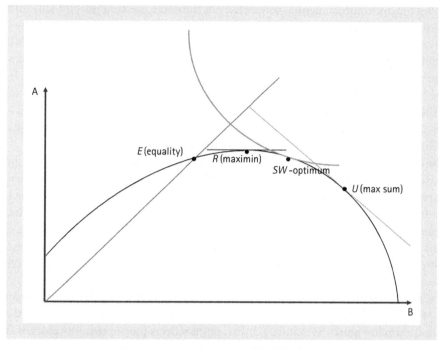

FIGURE 34.3 A more general health frontier

Figure 34.3 illustrates a more general health frontier that will distinguish the three theories of distributive justice with each respective unique distribution: *E* involves equal health for A and B, *R* is the maximin, and *U* is the max total health. Most economists would more or less instinctively focus on the Pareto-section [*R–U*]. However, if equality per se is part of the health policy objectives, the section [*E–R*] may also become relevant. Points *outside* [*E–U*] would not be consistent with any of the above theories of justice.[5]

34.4.2 The Social Welfare Function for Health

The works of most importantly Wagstaff (1991), Culyer and Wagstaff (1993), Dolan (1998), Williams and Cookson (2000), and Abásalo and Tsuchiya (2004) have more formally put the above theories of distributive justice in the context of a health-related social welfare function (HRSWF), with various degrees of restrictions, from the extreme egalitarian which maximizes total health subject to the constraint of *equal* distributions, to the opposite end of maximizing health with *no* constraints on distributions. The standard SWF that most economists would be familiar with is an isoelastic function

---

[5] For an even more generalized health frontier with a backward bending part that illustrates the elitist point of maximax, see Olsen (1997).

yielding the optimum tangential somewhere in the Pareto section $[R–U]$.[6] This function includes two key parameters: the *inequality aversion* parameter ranging from the value of -1, indicating distribution neutrality, i.e. no preferences for how total health is being distributed (point U), to the infinity value indicating that only the group whose health is worse would matter (point R), i.e. the L-shaped maximin. The higher the value in this range $[-1, \infty]$ of this parameter, the more inequality averse preferences would it reflect, and the lower is the social value of increasing health gains for one group relative to the other. In other words, it involves diminishing value to increasing QALYs and represents a deliberate departure from the idea that QALYs should be weighted equally.

The other parameter in the standard HRSWF is the *relative weights of the two groups*. This weight might be used to reflect principally any characteristic that is considered to have relevance for their relative entitlements to health care, e.g. differences in their social class. Interestingly, the simplest version of the HRSWF is the one used in cost-effectiveness analyses whereby all patient groups have the same relative weights, and there is distribution neutrality, i.e. "a QALY is a QALY is a QALY" regardless of any differences in non-health characteristics, and no matter how many QALYs one group receives relative to the other group.

The point at which the *iso-welfare curve* is tangential to the health frontier represents the optimal distribution of health gains across the two groups of patients, indicated as the SW-optimum in Figures 34.2 and 34.3. This point reflects the opportunity costs of equity in terms of health benefits forgone for patient B for an additional unit of health gain for patient A: the more equality prone you are, the higher the opportunity cost of equity.

Most of the literature on the health frontier and the HRSWF has considered *prospective health gains* as the distribuendum. It is implicitly, and sometimes explicitly, assumed that all other *streams of health* are identical, such as the expected health without treatment and age. This is surprising given the interest in the severity level (Nord 1995; Ubel 1999), and the "fair innings" issue (Williams 1997; Tsuchiya 2000). Thus, it becomes important to extend the analysis of alternative distribuenda, i.e. turn to the issue "equality of what."

34.5 Equality of What I: Health Gains, Prospective Health, Total Health, or What?

In the context of health equality, there are principally *four* different entities of which we may seek an equal distribution. They reflect a taxonomy of four different *streams of health*, depending on two distinguishing issues: prospective vs. retrospective health;

---

[6] For an alternative HRSWF version that includes a backward bending part that may yield the optimum tangential in the section $[E–R]$, see Abásalo and Tsuchiya (2004).

and health gained from health care vs. health gained "free," i.e. without health care (see Dolan and Olsen 2001). The first represents the equal prospective health *gains* line that can be seen in Figures 34.2 and 34.3. However, if the two patients have different prospects *without* treatment, i.e. their "need as ill health" differs, the health frontier will be located in a prospective health space where the equal prospective health line is different from the equal prospective *gains* line. Hence, if inclined to reduce inequalities in prospective health, i.e. considering their no-treatment profile *plus* their potential gains, one would be drawn towards an equal prospective health line.

A quite different concern would be to consider not only the prospective health, but in addition the *retrospective* health, i.e. the total expected lifetime health. This is the issue in the "fair innings" argument. Then finally, something which may appear as one strange consideration, namely equality in *total* health gains, i.e. not only the prospective gains, but the retrospective gains as well. The paper in which this particular stream of health was formally analyzed (Dolan and Olsen 2001) suggested that the potential relevance of *past* health gains from health care when distributing *current* health care deals with the *cause* of ill health (an issue discussed in section 34.6 below).

Of course, the only health stream that decisions on health care resource allocation can influence is the prospective gains. The question is *which other streams* of health are relevant to bring into consideration? These other streams may be relevant when we seek answers to the following questions: What will happen without treatment? How old are the patient groups (or how much health have they already had)? How much of their previous health can be ascribed to past health care use? Which of these (combination of) streams are considered relevant, or towards which equality line society would be most strongly drawn, remain empirical questions.

Table 34.1 provides a numerical example of four patient groups who are similar in every respect except for the QALY-numbers associated with the four different streams of health. The exercise for the reader is to prioritize *one* patient group on the basis of the partial information provided in each line and the previous ones as you move sequentially down the rows. In other words, ignore information listed below each row.

If the only information that distinguishes the four patients is their prospective health gain (first row), I assume you would prioritize A. Note that there is no trade-off involved. With the additional information on the no-treatment profile (second row), you notice a trade-off between maximizing health (i.e. opt for A) *or* reduce inequalities in

Table 34.1 Differences in Health Streams Across Patients (Figures in Terms of QALY)

Patient group	A	B	C	D
Streams of health				
Prospective gains	9	8	8	8
No-treatment profile	3	1	3	3
Age	60	60	30	30
Previous health gained from health care	0	0	3	0

prospective health (i.e. opt for *B*). There certainly is no correct answer here, it depends on your preferences vis-à-vis maximizing health or *reducing inequalities in prospective health*. However, if you are like most of my students who have faced this numerical exercise, you would opt for *B*.

Then, with the additional information about their age (retrospective health), if you would like to *reduce inequalities in total lifetime health* you would be drawn from *B* towards *C* (or *D* who is similar on these three streams). Note that the health gains are similar for *B* and *C*, so there is a trade-off between severity and age here. If you are concerned with equalities in *prospective* health, you would be drawn towards *B*; if you are concerned with equalities in *total* health, you would be drawn towards *C*. Dolan and Tsuchiya (2005) report a recent empirical study on preferences for equal prospective health vs. equal total health.

With the final information about previous health gains (bottom row), note that *C* and *D* are identical, except that *C* has previously consumed health care resources while *D* has not. This is not straightforward, but if you would like to *reduce inequalities in total health gains*, you would opt for *D*. Dolan and Olsen (2001) argue that the equity relevance of this stream depends on the *causes* of the need for health care, and in particular the extent to which the need for health care reflect risky behavior or unhealthy lifestyle, i.e. the extents to which people could be held responsible for their past—and current—needs for health care.

The identification of these four separate health streams relates to an important issue in the analyses of equity, namely "equality of what?," or more specifically: which stream(s) of health is the equalisandum. The analyses disclosed a health stream that may be of particular relevance when discussing equal opportunities vs. equal outcomes.

34.6 Equality of What II: Outcomes vs. Opportunities

In general, cost-effectiveness methodologies have a prospective focus on outcomes when comparing resources and health gains. Why then, in this context of fair distributions of health care that is intended to yield health outcomes, consider the *cause* of the need for health care? What makes equal *opportunities* more relevant than equal *outcomes*?

Equal opportunities lead to unequal outcomes when people choose to use their opportunities differently. Improvements in health depend not only on health care, but on patients' health-related behavior, something which can be formalized in terms of heterogeneous health production functions, including health care, and patient efforts. A given intervention may therefore yield more health outcomes in patients who adhere, comply and make their own efforts, than in patients who don't: For example, some interventions have proven to yield less health *outcome* in smokers than in non-smokers.

Hence, in a *prospective* evaluation including sub-group analyses, it is not the unhealthy behavior per se that is being condemned or blamed. Rather it is the lower health outcome that is being acknowledged.

What about a *retrospective* consideration? Figure 34.1 illustrates that variations in preferences and choices lead to variations in ill-health, and hence variations in needs for health care. Should then the fact that people have *had* equal opportunities for choosing their health-related behavior have any influence on their entitlements to health care?

Le Grand (1987) has argued for a principle called "equity of choice": "if an individual's ill health results from factors beyond his or her control then the situation is inequitable; if it results from factors within his or her control then it is equitable." Note that this argument involves retrospective consideration: "if (. . .) ill health *results* from."

An editorial in *Health Economics* concluded on the basis of a discussion of the World Development Report 2006 (WDR) that "equality of opportunity should be given a *fair innings* in health economics" (Dias and Jones 2007). This WDR held that the works of scholars like Rawls, Dworkin, Sen, and Roemer have all contributed to shifting the focus of social justice from outcomes to opportunities; Rawls (1971) with his concept of "primary goods" including opportunities; Dworkin (1981) with his argument that we should be compensated for aspects of the "circumstances" over which people have no control, or for which we could not be held responsible; Sen (1985) with his suggestion that the entity to be equalized is the "capability sets," i.e. the set of functionings from which a person might be able to choose; and Roemer (1998) with his distinction between circumstances vs. efforts, and argument for an "equal opportunity policy."

Much influenced by these scholars there is a literature trying to merge a radical *principle of equalization* with a liberal *principle of responsibility*—referred to as liberal egalitarianism: "Liberal egalitarian theories argue that society should eliminate inequalities in health that arise from factors outside individual control, but not inequalities that arise from differences in choices" (Cappelen and Norheim 2005). This appears to be quite similar to the "responsibility-sensitive egalitarian ethics" discussed by Devooght (2004). Another telling attempt at merging these two principles is the title "Equality and responsibility" of a book (Lake 2001) and of a journal article (Fleurbaey 1995).

The tricky issue springs out of the widely held ethical view that people can only be held responsible for what has been chosen voluntarily: "knowingly, consciously and freely." There are different views on the dividing line between which choices stem from free will and which don't, something known as "Dworkin's cut" or more generally the "responsibility cut" (Devooght 2004), implying that there are some causes of ill health we should be held responsible for—in that they reflect own choices, as opposed to those causes we can *not* be held responsible for—because we could not influence them. Within the framework of Figure 34.1, where would we locate this "responsibility cut" on the "outside–inside own control" continuum? The more "liberal egalitarian" you are, the further to the right end would you cut. Should people only be held responsible for the health-related lifestyle that *solely* reflect preferences; should they be held responsible for all health-related lifestyle choices; or do you hold the more extreme view that people choose their physical and social environment and so you might cut further to the left?

At the left end of the figure, biological variations are unavoidable—at least in the short run. The extent to which the inequalities they cause are considered fair or unfair is a contentious issue. Devooght (2004) holds: "Nature as such cannot be normative. The distribution of nature's fortune is neither just or unjust, good or bad." Daniels (1985) was referred to above suggesting it was futile to try to eliminate "natural differences." Still, we might feel a duty to compensate those who have been unlucky in the biological lottery, e.g. people with born handicaps or inherited diseases. Such health states are by definition completely without own fault.

At the right end of Figure 34.1 is the (health-related) preference variation. The more of the health-related lifestyle that can be explained by well-informed sovereign consumer preferences, i.e. "free will," the more can we claim that people should be held *responsible* for their behavior. There is still an important causational issue to bear in mind before we can hold individuals fully responsible for the health states in which they've ended up. Most chronic diseases such as cardio-vascular diseases and cancer have a *multifactoral* causation, which include not only one's health-related lifestyle. Bad genes and an unhealthy environment impact on the immune system, and make people more susceptible to diseases. However, risk seeking behavior, e.g. motor cycling, parachuting, is different in that an adverse event is clearly due to the particular risky choice. Hence, the *ex post* blame or culpability issue becomes more straightforward when unlucky in risk seeking events than for events following a multifactoral causation.

So why this disapproval of unhealthy behavior? Is unhealthy behavior per se considered sinful and of a lower moral order than healthy behavior? Or is it the financial burden imposed on others, i.e. that the health care costs associated with treating the ill health *exceed* one's contribution in terms of health care financing? The former reflects moralistic "healthism," something which has little appeal to economists with an affinity to sovereign preferences. The latter reflects an externality, something which in principle can be solved via indirect taxation.

Schokkaert and Devooght (2003) argue that responsibility sensitive fair compensation include two sets of characteristics, those for which individuals are to be kept responsible, and those for which they can be compensated. Compensation means community rating whereby high risk sub-groups are being cross-subsidized by low risk sub-groups.

Which risks should be community rated, and which should be individually rated then? The further we are to the left of the "outside–inside own control" continuum of Figure 34.1, the less influence we have on our risks. Given equal probabilities in the *biological lottery*, there appears to be a strong case for community rated health insurance related to the probability of "nature's misfortune." The second type of risks is those related to the physical and social environment. If variations in such risks reflect a *social lottery* involving unequal circumstances or unequal opportunities, there is an admittedly highly normative argument for a community rated health insurance that would not punish people for the increased health care costs associated with their "social misfortune." While social variation in health might in theory be avoidable, it is certainly in practice much easier to avoid that people face ("actuarially fair") premiums that correspond with their social class's risk level.

The third type of risk is that related to lifestyle, something which lies towards the other end of the continuum. If it is the case that individuals have control over these risks in that they can influence through their chosen behavior, why shouldn't this set of risks be individually rated? The contentious issue is whether people really have control and discretion over their health-related behavior: Do people have full information about the expected health-related consequences following the alternative options in their "choice set," and do they exercise free will and have complete self control? Or, is it rather so that people's health-related behavior corresponds with the habits of their peers and group identity, reflecting social conditioning?

No matter how many of our health-related choices are made by active sovereign consumers *or* by passive social animals, the fundamental issue remains: to what extent should healthy people have to cross-subsidize unhealthy people? The simple economic solution to unhealthy choices is to seek to internalize externalities, i.e. to levy an indirect tax equal to the expected health-related costs associated with such choices (Cappelen and Norheim 2006). Tobacco taxes represent a prime example. Note that the rationale for indirect taxation on unhealthy behavior in this context would be to cover the associated health care costs, in order to avoid forced redistribution of health care financing. If the indirect taxes were set *higher* than the expected associated health care costs, such a policy would have an additional paternalistic rationale, something which has nothing to do with equity or fairness as such.

The key issue in the current context is the extent to which it is considered fair to take the costs associated with health-related behavior into account when prioritizing. The *ex post* policy would be one in which people's entitlements to health care depend on their previous healthy behavior, which is more contentious in that it evokes blame and punishment. A quite different approach is an *ex ante* policy, in which people have the same entitlements when ill, but those with an unhealthy behavior have contributed more to the financing of health care. This latter approach implies that different fairness concerns are taken into account when dealing with the three classes of risks. For the biological and social lotteries, *community rating* is considered fair, while for the behavioral risks, *individual rating* is considered fair.

34.7 Conclusion

The above discussion has revealed strong conceptual overlaps in how health economists have come to use the words "equality," "equity," "fairness," and "justice." The concept of equity appears to be the one with the least precise inherent definition, in that it deals with equality *and* fairness. The default seems to be that "equity implies equality," but when an *unequal* distribution is considered fair, it represents an *equitable inequality*. Hence, any distribution could in principle be classified as *equitable* as long as people have considered it to be fair. However, the literature appears to distinguish between equitable vs. inequitable inequalities with reference to the issue of "individual responsibility" for own health and the issue of "societal avoidability."

But how do we know if people consider a distribution to be fair? Richardson and McKie (2005, 2006) have argued convincingly for "empirical ethics," which is described as an iterative process whereby researchers elicit the views of representative population samples, and these views are then subjected to ethical analysis. The results from the ethical analysis are then fed back to the samples, and their values are reassessed, and so on. Note that this repeated process requires "deliberation, clarification and careful reflection" among respondents, something which calls for a qualitative research approach.

The issue of *avoidability* has received much attention in policy documents as well as by some scholars in the field, suggesting that if an inequality is avoidable, it is inequitable. Within our framework on causes of inequalities in health, it appears that biological variations are *un*avoidable, while variations in the social environment are more avoidable. This may explain the health policy objectives on reducing social inequalities in health, as well as a growing literature on this topic (see e.g. Marmot 2005; Marmot and Wilkinson 2006). Future studies based on "empirical ethics" may reveal the extent to which this issue of *avoidability* is something that representative population samples also find important.

This chapter was influenced by the argument that whether an inequality can be judged equitable, the *cause* has to be examined. While biological variation is a cause, it was argued that since "nature's fortune is neither just nor unjust," this type of health inequality is not inequitable. However, although ethical theories may not label such inequalities as inequitable, people may still hold preferences in favor of compensating those who are victims of nature's misfortune (see e.g. Charny et al. 1989).

One cause of health inequalities that people appear to be more reluctant to compensate for is that following variations in *health-related lifestyle*. While the principle of "equal access for equal need" neglects any differences in the efforts made to reduce one's needs, there is increasing concern for developing ways in which people should be held responsible for their own health-related choices. The ethical justification for this can be found in the principle of *equal opportunities* within "choice sets": an inequality in health outcomes that follows from equal opportunities to make well-informed choices across a range of health-related options would be considered a fair inequality. The principle of "equity of choice" (Le Grand 1987) has led to an increased focus on individual *responsibility* for own health, and what is referred to as "responsibility-sensitive egalitarian ethics" (Devooght 2004).

Compensating for inequities takes place through redistributive health policy interventions. Note that while *health care* is tradable and therefore can be redistributed across individuals, *health* cannot be redistributed (except through organ transplantations). So, after a fair distribution in health *care* has been achieved, further reductions in health inequalities can only be achieved through interventions in the *determinants* of health.

Health economists' approach to the analysis of fairness in the distribution of health has to a large extent been analyzed within the paradigm of a health frontier and a health-related social welfare function (HRSWF). The purpose with the HRSWF is to identify the preferred point on the health frontier, which represents a trade-off between efficiency, in terms of maximum total health, and equality, usually in terms of *equal gains* (assuming all other health streams are identical for the two groups). The preferred point would then represent the equitable one, or a fair inequality. Thus, rather than an "equity vs efficiency trade-off," it would have been more precise to refer to this as an *"equality vs. health maximization trade-off."*

While there has been much recent work on measuring *equity weights* based on different functional forms of the HRSWF, relatively little attention has been given to streams of health other than the prospective gains stream. This is particularly surprising given that the no-treatment profile is a relevant stream when concerned with reducing inequalities in prospective health, and past health (age) is relevant when concerned with reducing inequalities in lifetime health, or the "fair innings" approach to fairness in health.

Equity weights imply that we turn away from the principle of "a QALY is a QALY is a QALY" to a situation where a QALY is valued differently depending on which value is assigned to a particular group characteristic, e.g. its social class. The challenge then is first to identify which characteristics of a patient group are morally relevant to assign a weight different from unity (see Olsen et al. 2003), and then estimate the magnitude of these weights (for a recent report, see Dolan et al. 2008).

The standard health frontier is applicable in a quite restrictive policy context: a given health care budget whose size is independent of its distribution between the two groups. A more generalized frontier including an upward sloping part is more relevant when there are net production gains from interventions.

The health frontier is not meaningful in the context of private health insurance systems with individual contracts. In such systems, one's *ex post* right to health care resources depends on having paid insurance *ex ante* for one's expected use of these resources. There is no "collective health care budget" but an aggregation of individual budgets based on insurance customers' individual ratings.

Furthermore, the health frontier is meaningful only within a national jurisdiction, where entitlements usually depend on citizenship. As opposed to an NHS (National Health Service), there is no such thing as a "GHS" (global health service). When studying international health inequalities, other analytical approaches and norms are useful, such as the idea of a "universal basic health norm" (Acharya 2004). It is a sad fact, though, that the existing international inequalities in health and access to health care bring no associations to the concepts of "equity" and "fairness."

References

ABÁSALO, I. and TSUCHIYA, A. (2004) Exploring social welfare functions and violation of monotonicity: an example from inequalities in health, *Journal of Health Economics* 23(2): 313–29.

ACHARYA, A. (2004) Towards establishing a universal basic health norm, *Ethics & International Affairs* 18(3): 65–78.

BALIA, S. and JONES, A. M. (2008) Mortality, lifestyle and socio-economic status, *Journal of Health Economics* 27(1): 1–26.

CAPPELEN, A.W. and NORHEIM, O. F. (2005) Responsibility in health care: a liberal egalitarian approach, *Journal of Medical Ethics* 31: 476–80.

———(2006) Responsibility, fairness and rationing in health care, *Health Policy* 76(3): 312–9.

CASE, A., FERTIG, A., and PAXSON, C. (2005) The lasting impact of childhood health and circumstance, *Journal of Health Economics* 24(2): 365–89.

CHARNY, M. C., LEWIS, P. A., and FARROW, S. C. (1989). Choosing who shall not be treated in the NHS, *Social Science and Medicine* 28: 1331–8.

CULYER, A. J. (1989) The normative economics of health care finance and provision, *Oxford Review of Economic Policy* 5: 34–58.

—— (2001): Equity: some theory and its policy implications, *Journal of Medical Ethics* 27: 275–83.

—— and WAGSTAFF, A. (1993) Equity and equality in health and health care, *Journal of Health Economics* 12: 431–57.

—— VAN DOORSLAER, E., and WAGSTAFF, A. (1992): Comment: "Utilisation as a measure of equity" by Mooney, Hall, Donaldson and Gerard, *Journal of Health Economics* 11: 93–8.

DANIELS, N. (1985) *Just Health Care*. Cambridge: Cambridge University Press.

DEVOOGHT, K. (2004) On responsibility-sensitive egalitarian ethics, *Ethics and Economics* 2(2): 1–21.

DIAS, P. R. and JONES, A. M. (2007) Giving equality of opportunity a fair innings, *Health Economics* 16(2): 109–12.

DOLAN, P. (1998), The measurement of individual utility and social welfare, *Journal of Health Economics* 17: 39–52.

—— and OLSEN, J. A. (2001) Equity in health: the importance of different health streams, *Journal of Health Economics* 20, 823–34.

—— and TSUCHIYA, A. (2005). Health priorities and public preferences: the relative importance of past health experience and future health prospects, *Journal of Health Economics* 24: 703–14.

—— EDLIN, R., TSUCHIYA, A., and WAILOO, A. (2007) It ain't what you do, it's the way that you do it: Characteristics of procedural justice and their importance in social decision-making, *Journal of Economic Behavior and Organisation* 64(1): 157–70.

——————— et al. (2008) The relative societal value of health gains to different beneficiaries, Health Technology Assessment Programme Journal Series Report RM03/JH11/PD, University of Birmingham, Birmingham, UK.

DWORKIN, R. (1981) What is equality? Part 2: Equality of resources, *Philosophy and Public Affairs* 10: 283–345.

ELSTER, J. (1992) *Local Justice: How Institutions Allocate Scarce Goods and Necessary Burdens.* New York: Russell Sage Foundation.

EVANS, R. G., BARER, M., and MARMOR, T. (eds.) (1994) *Why Are Some People Healthy and Others Not? The Determinants of Health of Populations.* New York: A. de Gruyter.

FLEURBAEY, M. (1995) Equality and responsibility, *European Economic Review* 39: 683–9.

HAUCK, K., SHAW, R., and SMITH, P. C. (2002) Reducing avoidable inequalities in health: a new criterion for setting health care capitation payments, *Health Economics* 11: 667–77.

KAHNEMAN, D., KNETSCH, J. L., and THALER, R. H. (1986) Fairness as a constraint on profit seeking: Entitlement in the market, *American Economic Review*, 76(4): 728–41.

LAKE, C. (2001) *Equality and Responsibility*. Oxford: Oxford University Press.

LE GRAND, J. (1987) Equity, health and health care. *Social Justice Research* 1: 257–74.

—— (1991) *Equity and Choice*. London: Harper Collins.

MARMOT, M. G. (2005) Social determinants of health inequalities, *The Lancet* 365(9464): 1099–104.

—— and WILKINSON, R. G. (eds) (2006) *Social Determinants of Health*, 2nd edn. Oxford: Oxford University Press.

MOONEY, G. (2007) Equity in the context of diversity of culture and diversity of economic systems, in D. McIntyre and G. Mooney (eds.), *The Economics of Health Equity*. Cambridge: Cambridge University Press.

—— HALL, J., DONALDSON, C., and GERARD, K. (1991) Utilisation as a measure of equity weighing heat? *Journal of Health Economics* 10: 475–80.

NORD, E. (1995) The person-trade-off approach to valuing health-care programs. *Medical Decision Making* 15(3): 201–8.

OLSEN, J. A. (1997) Theories of justice and their implications for priority setting in health care, *Journal of Health Economics* 16: 625–40.

—— and RICHARDSON, J. (1999) Production gains from health care: What should be included in cost-effectiveness analyses? *Social Science and Medicine* 49: 17–26.

—— RICHARDSON, J., DOLAN, P., and MENZEL, P. (2003) The moral relevance of personal characteristics in setting health care priorities, *Social Science and Medicine* 57: 1163–72.

RAWLS, J. (1958) Justice as fairness, *Philosophical Review* 67(2): 164–94.

—— (1971) *A Theory of Justice*. Cambridge, MA: Harvard University Press.

REINHARDT, U. E. (1998) Abstracting from distributional effects, this policy is effective, in M. L. Barer, T. E. Getzen, and G. L. Stoddart (eds.), *Health, Health Care and Health Economics: Perspectives on Distribution*. Chichester, UK: John Wiley.

RICHARDSON, J. and McKIE, J. (2005) Empiricism, ethics and orthodox economic theory: what is the appropriate basis for decision-making in the health sector? *Social Science and Medicine* 60: 265–75.

—— —— (2006) Economics, political philosophy and ethics: the role of public preferences in health care decision-making, in R. Ashcroft, A. Dawson, H. Draper and J. McMillan (eds.), *Principles of Health Care Ethics*, 2nd edn. Chichester, UK: John Wiley & Sons.

ROEMER, J. (1998) *Equality of Opportunity*. Cambridge, MA: Harvard University Press.

SCHOKKAERT, E. and DEVOOGHT, K. (2003) Responsibility-sensitive fair compensation in different cultures, *Social Choice and Welfare* 21: 207–42.

SEN, A. (1985) *Commodities and Capabilities*. Amsterdam: North-Holland.

—— (1992) *Inequality Re-examined*. Oxford: Oxford University Press.

—— (2002) Why health equity? *Health Economics* 11: 659–66.

TSUCHIYA, N. (2000) QALYs and ageism: philosophical theories and age weighting, *Health Economics* 9(1): 57–68.

UBEL, P. A. (1999) How stable are people's preferences for giving priority to severely ill patients? *Social Science & Medicine* 49(7): 895–903.

VARIAN, H. (1975) Distributive justice, welfare economics, and the theory of fairness, *Philosophy and Public Affairs* 4: 223–47.

WAGSTAFF, A. (1991) QALYs and the equity–efficiency trade-off, *Journal of Health Economics* 10: 21–41.

—— and VAN DOORSLAER, E. (2000) Equity in health care finance and delivery, in A. J. Culyer and J. P. Newhouse (eds.), *Handbook of Health Economics*. Amsterdam: Elsevier.

WAILOO, A. and ANAND, P. (2005) The nature of procedural preferences for rational health care decisions, *Social Science and Medicine* 60: 223–36.

WHITEHEAD, M. (1992) The concept and principles of equity and health, *International Journal of Health Services* 22(3): 429–45.

WILLIAMS, A. (1988) Priority setting in public and private health care: a guide through the ideological jungle, *Journal of Health Economics* 7: 173–83.

—— (1997) Intergenerational equity: an exploration of the "fair innings" argument, *Health Economics* 6(2): 117–32.

—— and COOKSON, R. (2000) Equity in health. In A. J. Culyer and J. P. Newhouse (eds.), *Handbook of Health Economics*. Amsterdam: Elsevier.

CHAPTER 35

....

MEASURING INEQUALITY AND INEQUITY IN HEALTH AND HEALTH CARE[*]

....

EDDY VAN DOORSLAER AND TOM VAN OURTI

35.1 INTRODUCTION

....

THE health economics literature on the measurement of equity in health care and health inequality is relatively young. Le Grand (1978) was one of the early contributions before Wagstaff et al. (1989, 1991) proposed the use of concentration curves and indices to measure socioeconomic inequalities in the health care sector. Since then, the literature on measurement of inequalities in the health sector has steadily evolved to become almost a sub-field within health economics.

With the exception of a limited number of contributions (Le Grand 1978; Le Grand 1987; Wagstaff and van Doorslaer 2004), the measurement and explanation of *total* inequalities in health and health care has received relatively little attention and most emphasis is placed on *socioeconomic* inequalities in the health care sector, i.e. inequalities in the health care sector related to socioeconomic status. This does not mean that inequalities related to other dimensions—for example demographics—are deemed irrelevant, and indeed in a few recent theoretical publications these issues are explored (Gravelle et al. 2006; Fleurbaey and Schokkaert 2009). But up to now, the majority of empirical measurement applications have focused on socioeconomic inequalities.

* We are grateful for financial support from the NETSPAR funded project "Income, health and work across the life-cycle." We thank Adam Wagstaff, Owen O'Donnell, Peter Smith, Sherry Glied, Esen Erdogan Ciftci, and Hans van Kippersluis for very helpful comments on an earlier version of this chapter, and Guido Erreygers and Philip Clarke for discussion on specific topics in this chapter. The usual caveats apply and all remaining errors are the authors' responsibility.

The measurement tools used by economists differ from those used in public health and epidemiology, although they are clearly related (Wagstaff et al. 1991). The literature has been dominated by the application of so-called "rank-dependent" inequality tools that were mostly developed in the income inequality literature for analysis of the univariate income distribution (Lambert 2001). In the context of socioeconomic inequalities in the health care sector, these measures were adapted to the bivariate distribution of health[1] or health care with income, and have been used to measure inequalities in many outcomes worldwide (see e.g. O'Donnell et al. 2008b).

Within the scope of this chapter we cannot provide an exhaustive review of the entire literature on measurement of socioeconomic inequalities in the health sector and have restricted coverage in four respects. First, we take the Elsevier *Handbook of Health Economics* chapter by Wagstaff and van Doorslaer (2000) as a starting point and discuss new developments since 2000. Second, the existing literature can be subdivided into that concerned with inequalities in: (i) health; (ii) health care; and (iii) health care payments. We focus on the first two since advances made in the third relate mostly to the measurement of financial protection in low-income settings, a distinct issue from health equity. Readers interested in the literature on inequalities in the financing of health care should consult Wagstaff and van Doorslaer (2000), who deal with the progressivity of health care finance in *developed* countries, and an update of this work by De Graeve and Van Ourti (2003). Some of the relevant issues for *developed* countries are also discussed in Chapters 12 ("public sector health care financing"), 13 ("voluntary private health insurance"), and 15 ("user charges") of this book. For readers interested in inequalities in the financing of health care in *developing* countries, the literature has become more focused on the catastrophic and impoverishing consequences of out-of-pocket payments. We refer to Wagstaff and van Doorslaer (2003); Wagstaff (2005b); van Doorslaer et al. (2007); Wagstaff and Lindelöw (2007); Flores et al. (2008); O'Donnell et al. (2008a); Wagstaff (2009a); and to Chapters 13 ("voluntary private health insurance") and 15 ("user charges") of this Handbook. Third, this chapter is concerned with the association between income, on the one hand, and health and health care, on the other. Where necessary, we discuss the potential underlying causal pathways of this association, but for a more extensive discussion of the causal/structural relationships between income, health and health care, we refer to Chapter 7 ("socioeconomic determinants of health: dimensions and mechanisms") of this Handbook. In section 35.2.1.1, we explain in detail that a significant association or causal effect is a necessary but not sufficient condition for the presence of inequalities. Fourth, we take a static viewpoint and do not discuss life-cycle inequality. We refer interested readers to Chapter 36 ("intergenerational aspects of health care") for issues related to life-cycle inequality in health care consumption and financing. For readers interested in how socioeconomic inequalities in health evolve over the life-cycle, we refer to van Doorslaer et al. (2008). Finally, we restrict the discussion to *economics*

---

[1] Throughout this chapter, health will be used as shorthand for any health-related variable, including health care use or expenditures.

approaches of measuring socioeconomic inequalities in health and health care. For details on the computational and statistical issues (using STATA) we refer to O'Donnell et al. (2008b).

The remainder of this chapter contains three sections. The next section gives some methodological underpinnings to the measures of socioeconomic inequalities in health and health care that are applied in the empirical literature reviewed in section 35.3. The final section concludes.

35.2 Measurement and Decomposition of Socioeconomic Inequality in Health and Health Care

In this section, we discuss the measurement tools developed and used by health economists to analyze socioeconomic inequalities in health and health care.

35.2.1 Measurement

After presenting the essentials of the concentration index, which is the workhorse of socioeconomic inequality measurement in most of the health economics literature, we describe the recently developed decomposition techniques of the concentration index. We describe all measurement tools for the bivariate health–income distribution, but obviously these are by extension equally valid for indicators of health care use.

35.2.1.1 *The Concentration Index*

The measurement of socioeconomic health inequalities has a longstanding tradition in public health and epidemiology. The range (often implemented as odds ratios or relative risk ratios resulting from regression analysis), and the index of dissimilarity have been frequently applied (Wagstaff and van Doorslaer 2000: 1851–2).

Wagstaff et al. (1991) proposed the concentration index as an alternative to these measures. Their basic argument was that the concentration index simultaneously

(i) reflects the socioeconomic dimension to inequalities in health, while the index of dissimilarity does not;

(ii) reflects the experiences of the entire population, while the range—that compares the top and bottom socioeconomic groups—might "overlook what is going on in intermediate groups" (ibid.: 545);

(iii) reflects changes in the distribution of the population across socioeconomic groups, while the range "takes no account of the sizes of the groups being compared" (ibid.: 545).

In addition, the concentration index has a long tradition in economics to measure distributional issues related to taxation, and thus its properties are reasonably well understood (Lambert 2001).

An intuitive understanding of the concentration index is most easily obtained from a graphical presentation. Figure 35.1 presents two hypothetical examples of concentration curves. Both curves plot the cumulative proportion of health against the cumulative proportion of the population ranked by socioeconomic status, starting with the lowest socioeconomic position. Several points are worth noting. First, inequalities can be "in favor" of the worse- or better-off. They are in favor of the better-off if the concentration curve lies underneath the line of equality (here curve 1), and in favor of the worse-off if the opposite configuration applies (here curve 2). For example, concentration curve 1 shows that the 60 percent worst-off have only 40 percent of total health, while concentration curve 2 shows that 10 percent of the worst-off have thirty percent of total health. Second, socioeconomic equality applies if the concentration curve coincides with the diagonal (i.e. "line of equality"). Third, concentration curves might have inflection points and only need to be monotonically increasing, unlike Lorenz curves which are by definition always convex and increasing. Fourth, concentration curves measure relative inequalities implying that equiproportionate health changes leave socioeconomic inequality unchanged.

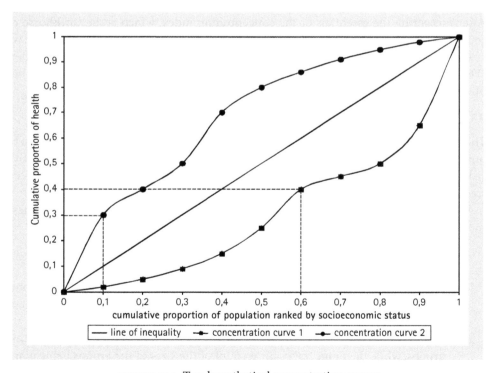

FIGURE 35.1 Two hypothetical concentration curves

The concentration index—denoted as $CI(h)$—equals twice the area between the concentration curve and the diagonal, and reflects offsetting inequalities in different parts of the distribution in case the concentration curve crosses the diagonal. It can be computed as:

$$CI(h) = \frac{2\sum_{i=1}^{n} h_i R_i^y}{\sum_{i=1}^{n} h_i} - 1 = \frac{1}{n}\sum_{i=1}^{n}\left[\left(\frac{h_i}{\bar{h}}\right)(2R_i^y - 1)\right] \tag{1}$$

where h_i denotes health of individual i, $\bar{h}$ is the average of h_i, and $R_i^y = n^{-1}(i-0.5)$ is the fractional rank of socioeconomic status y_i (say income). In calculating equation (1) it is assumed that individuals are ranked from low to high socioeconomic status. The bounds of this measure are $n^{-1}(1-n)$ and $n^{-1}(n-1)$ with a negative (positive) value representing pro-worse-off (pro-best-off) inequality. Equation (1) shows that the concentration index is related to the covariance of health and the fractional rank of socioeconomic status. This idea has been exploited by Kakwani et al. (1997) who show that the concentration index equals α_1 in the so-called convenient OLS-regression:

$$2\sigma_{R^y}^2 \frac{h_i}{\bar{h}} = \alpha_0 + \alpha_1 R_i^y + \varepsilon_i \tag{2}$$

where $\sigma_{R^y}^2$ is the variance of R_i^y, ε_i is an error term with mean zero, α_0 and α_1, are parameters to be estimated. For more details on the statistical issues underlying equation (2), one should consult Kakwani et al. (1997). O'Donnell et al. (2008b) discuss statistical inference and ways to deal with more complex sample design features.[2]

Koolman and van Doorslaer (2004) provided an intuitive interpretation. They show that the concentration index can be given a redistribution interpretation, i.e. $0.75 \times CI(h)$ equals the proportion of total health that should be redistributed from the richest half to the poorest part of the population in order to reduce the concentration index to zero. In addition, they highlight that the concentration index is conceptually different from a correlation coefficient as it is the product of (i) the variability of health, measured by the coefficient of variation of health, (ii) the correlation coefficient of health and the fractional rank, and (iii) an "almost constant" term.

$$CI(h) = \frac{\sigma_h}{\bar{h}} \times \rho(h_i, R_i^y) \times 2\sigma_{R^y} \tag{3}$$

In other words, two countries might have the same concentration index because one has a high coefficient of variation of health but a low correlation coefficient, and the other has a low coefficient of variation of health and a high correlation coefficient. For

---

[2] O'Donnell et al. (2008b) also discuss statistical inference for concentration curve dominance checks.

example, Koolman and van Doorslaer (2004) report the same correlation coefficients between income rank and the number of dental visits in Italy and Finland, but a much higher coefficient of variation in the number of dental visits in Italy. Another way of making the difference clear is that adding a constant to all health observation leaves the correlation coefficient unchanged, but changes the coefficient of variation.

Although these findings add to the intuitive understanding obtained from studying Figure 35.1, it is feasible to arrive at a more complete notion by identifying the axioms that define the concentration index. Bleichrodt and van Doorslaer (2006) provide such a welfare economics foundation and show that the *CI condition* is the most crucial axiom underlying the concentration index. The *CI condition* is a restricted version of the more intuitive *principle of socioeconomic related health transfers* which imposes that "a transfer of health from someone who is better-off in terms of socioeconomic status to someone who is worse-off in terms of socioeconomic status does not lead to a reduction in social welfare provided the transfer does not change the ranking of the individual in terms of socioeconomic status" (Bleichrodt and van Doorslaer 2006: 952). The *CI condition* in addition gives conditions for the amount of health one might be willing to forgo by transferring health from the person who is best-off in terms of socioeconomic status to any other person. Bleichrodt and van Doorslaer (2006) note that the plausibility of this condition might be contestable and provide the example of a health transfer "from a person with high living standards to a person with lower living standards when the person with high living standards is in poor health and differences in living standards are small" (Bleichrodt and van Doorslaer 2006: 955). While some might challenge the principle of socioeconomic related health transfers on the grounds that one cannot trade health (see for example, Chapter 34, "Concepts of equity and fairness in health and health care"), this is not warranted since "what matters is that more equal health profiles are preferred to less equal health profiles" (ibid.: 950).

An alternative illustration of the *CI condition* emerges from interpreting equation (1) as a weighted sum of health shares with the weights declining linearly from $2R_n^y-1 = n^{-1}(n-1)$ to $2R_1^y-1 = n^{-1}(1-n)$. These weights illustrate the very specific ethical stance underlying the concentration index. Pereira (1998) and Wagstaff (2002) were alerted to this point and proposed an extension of the concentration index that allows for varying "attitudes to inequality aversion" by generalizing the weights much along the lines of the extended Gini coefficient (Yitzhaki 1983), i.e.

$$CI(h,v) = \frac{1}{n}\sum_{i=1}^{n}\left\{\left(\frac{h_i}{\bar{h}}\right)\left[1-v(1-R_i^y)^{v-1}\right]\right\} \tag{4}$$

where each $v > 1$ represents another "attitude to inequality aversion" with higher v's resulting in more aversion to inequality.[3] Varying the value of v thus allows one to

---

[3] There are two special cases, i.e. when $v = 1$, every person gets the same weight and there is no inequality aversion, i.e. $CI(h,1)\equiv 0$; and if $v = 2$, we get the standard concentration index. Also note that the bounds of the extended concentration index are only symmetric in case of $v = 2$, i.e. $1-v \le plimCI(h, v) \le 1$.

analyze how socioeconomic inequalities in health depend on the degree of inequality aversion. Despite this attractive feature, Erreygers et al. (2010) argue that caution should be exercised in applying the extended concentration index. They show that the extended concentration index with $v \neq 2$ might assign non-zero socioeconomic inequality to distributions in which the chances of having high or low health levels are symmetrically distributed over the rich and the poor (i.e. a situation where there is no systematic bias in favor of the rich or the poor). They propose an alternative 'symmetric' index that allows for varying attitudes towards inequality *and* that will always indicate zero socioeconomic inequality when health levels are symmetrically distributed over the rich and the poor. Its weighting scheme is inversely symmetric and monotonously increasing in the fractional rank. The symmetric index can be calculated as follows:

$$SI(h, \alpha) = \frac{1}{n} \sum_{i=1}^{n} h_i \left\{ (1 + \alpha) 2^{2(1+\alpha)} \cdot \left[\left(R_i^y - \tfrac{1}{2} \right)^2 \right]^\alpha \cdot \left(2 R_i^y - 1 \right) \right\} \tag{5}$$

with the inequality aversion parameter $\alpha > -1/2$. Values of $-1/2 < \alpha < 0$ put more emphasis on those with a fractional rank close to the middle (i.e. $R_{iy} = 1/2$), while taking $\alpha > 0$ puts more emphasis on those at the upper and lower end of the income distribution.[4]

Another noteworthy extension is the framework of Wagstaff and van Doorslaer (2004) that unifies the measurement of total and socioeconomic inequalities in health by analyzing the difference between the concentration index that measures socioeconomic health inequalities and the Gini index of health that measures total health inequalities. The Gini index is calculated by replacing the rank of socioeconomic status in equation (1) by the health rank. If socioeconomic status is measured as a categorical variable, the sub-group decomposition of Lambert and Aronson (1993) is applicable, where the sub-groups are defined by the categorical indicator of socioeconomic status. We refer to section 35.2.1.3 for a description of this sub-group decomposition method.

Finally, policymakers might also be interested in overall performance involving the trade-off between socioeconomic health inequalities and the average health level. Wagstaff (2002) has exploited an analogy with abbreviated social welfare functions used to analyze this trade-off for average income and income inequality (Lambert 2001) to propose the so-called achievement index:

$$A(h) = \overline{h}[1 - CI(h)] \tag{6}$$

The achievement index is defined as the product of average health and one minus the concentration index of heath. The value of $A(h)$ is higher/lower than $\overline{h}$ if the socioeconomically worst-off have better/worse health, i.e. $CI(h)$ is negative/positive.

---

[4] To illustrate, consider the case where the poorest individual gets one-third of total health and the richest gets two thirds of total health, and the other individuals have zero health. The standard concentration index in equation (1) indicates that inequalities favor the rich, i.e. $CI(h) = CI(h, 2) \cong 1/3$. Increasing the inequality aversion parameter v to 3 reveals no inequalities, i.e. $CI(h, 3) \cong 0$; and further increasing v to 4, indicates pro-poor inequalities, i.e. $CI(h, 4) \cong -1/3$. In addition, the index proposed by Erreygers et al. (2010) also satisfies the so-called mirror property (see also section 35.2.2). The value of the symmetric index coincides with the value of the Erreygers index for $\alpha = 0$.

35.2.1.2 *Factor Decomposition of the Concentration Index*

While a concentration index can be used to compare socioeconomic inequalities in health across countries or across time, it provides little or no guidance on the factors associated with these inequalities. A better understanding of these factors may help to unravel the origins of these health inequalities, and to standardize estimates of socio-economic inequality for confounders. In addition, it should help distinguishing between total inequalities and those that truly matter, i.e. those that can be considered inequitable. Wagstaff et al. (2003) have proposed a method to "decompose" the con-centration index into contributing factors.[5] It starts from the linear regression equa-tion (7) that links health to a set of K factors x_i—say demographics, income, education and so on—, i.e.

$$h_i = \beta_0 + \sum_{j=1}^{K} \beta_j x_{ij} + e_i \tag{7}$$

where $\beta_0, \ldots, \beta_K$ are coefficients and e_i is an error term with mean zero. Next Wagstaff et al. (2003) show that combining equation (1) and (7) results in

$$CI(h) = \sum_{j=1}^{K} \left[\left(\beta_j \frac{\overline{x}_j}{\overline{h}} \right) CI(x_j) \right] + \frac{2\text{cov}(e_i, R_i^y)}{\overline{h}} \tag{8}$$

which shows that socioeconomic health inequality is a weighted sum of the socioeco-nomic inequalities in its factors/determinants, where the weights are defined as the "average elasticities" $\eta_j = \overline{h}^{-1}(\beta_j \overline{x}_j)$; and a final term corresponding to the covariance between the unexplained part in equation (7) and the fractional income rank. In other words, in order for a factor to contribute to socioeconomic health inequalities, two con-ditions should be satisfied. First, the factor should be associated with health, as revealed through a non-zero "average elasticity." Second, the factor should be unequally distrib-uted across socioeconomic status.

Apart from identifying factors associated with socioeconomic health inequalities, the factor decomposition in equation (8) offers other advantages. First, it is common in pub-lic health and epidemiology (Coggon et al. 1997), but also in earlier health economics contributions (Wagstaff and van Doorslaer 2000) to standardize estimates of socioeco-nomic inequality for confounders using a direct or indirect method. Equation (8) can be reinterpreted as an indirect standardization method by including the standardizing variables—say age (a_i) and sex (s_i)—among the other factors in equation (7), i.e.

$$h_i = \beta_0 + \beta_a a_i + \beta_s s_i + \sum_{j=1}^{K} \beta_j x_{ij} + e_i \tag{9}$$

and next to rewrite equation (8) as

---

[5] Both Clarke et al. (2003) and Gravelle (2003) have noted that this is similar to a factor decomposition of the Gini index (Rao 1969).

$$CI(h) - [\eta_a CI(a) + \eta_s CI(s)] = \sum\nolimits_{j=1}^{K} \eta_j CI\,(x_j) + \bar{h}^{-1}\,[2\,\mathrm{cov}\,(e_i, R_i^y)] \qquad (10)$$

The main advantage of this approach over the typical indirect standardization approach is that it does not suffer from an obvious omitted variables bias. The typical indirect standardization only includes age and sex in equation (7). Consequently η_a and η_s are biased if there are other correlated variables relevant to explain health. Second and similarly, it has been common practice in the literature on inequalities in *health care* to compute so-called "horizontal inequity indices" where horizontal equity is understood to mean that individuals with the same need for health care should end up receiving the same amount of health care (Wagstaff and van Doorslaer 2000). Measuring socioeconomic inequality in health care consumption is not enough to assess "equity performance." Any socioeconomic inequalities that are due to the factors related to "need of health care" should not be considered inequitable. An inequity index can then be constructed by putting the terms related to these need factors to zero in equation (8). The subdivision of the factors into "need" and "non-need" is a moral stance and should be the outcome of a public debate, but let's for the sake of the argument assume that in an analysis on equity in the number of visits to a GP, health status is considered a "need" variable and health insurance a "non-need" one. It is commonly found that individuals with lower socioeconomic status report more visits to the GP, are less likely to have health insurance and have lower health status. The proposal here would be to calculate equation (8) and next remove the term related to health status, and only use the remaining term on health insurance to analyze the "equity performance."

While the factor decomposition of the concentration index offers interesting opportunities to unravel the components of measured inequality, it is important to draw attention to a number of issues.[6] First, equation (8) only holds if equation (7) is linear, but this might in some instances be contestable. For example, in the empirical literature on the determinants of health care utilization, non-linear regression methods are common to deal with the skewed and/or count data nature of the dependent variables. But also linear methods with interaction effects are sufficient to jeopardize the linear decomposition, especially in the case of horizontal equity measurement. Any violation of additive separability between the "need" and "non-need" factors makes it impossible to isolate the effect of "need" and "non-need" variables and thus makes it impossible to apply the linear decomposition procedure (see Schokkaert et al. (1998) for an earlier illustration in risk adjustment). Several procedures have been proposed to deal with non-linear models. For interested readers, we refer to Gravelle (2003), van Doorslaer and Gerdtham (2003), and van Doorslaer et al. (2004a). Second, the factor decomposition is a descriptive tool that sheds light on the association between the socioeconomic

---

[6] In a recent contribution, Fleurbaey and Schokkaert (2009) propose a general framework based on social choice theory to analyze "unfair" inequalities in the health care sector. While it encompasses many of the issues discussed in section 35.2.1, it is not included here since it has not yet been applied empirically.

inequality in—and elasticity of—each factor and socioeconomic health inequality. It only delivers guidance on the underlying causal relationships if equation (7) has a causal interpretation.

35.2.1.3 *Decomposition of the Concentration Index: Extensions*

The factor decomposition in equation (8) disentangles the factors associated with socio-economic health inequality for a given country or at a given point in time, but does not convey how the importance of these factors evolves over time or differs between countries. In other words, it does not decompose *changes* in socioeconomic health inequalities. Similar issues have received a great deal of attention in the labor economics literature (Blinder 1973; Oaxaca 1973; Oaxaca and Ransom 1994), and Wagstaff et al. (2003) have adapted and extended these methods to the health setting by expressing the change in socioeconomic health inequality into changes in socioeconomic inequality in each of the K factors *and* into changes in the "average elasticities" as follows.[7]

$$\Delta CI = \sum_{j=1}^{K} \eta_{jl} \left[CI_l(x_j) - CI_m(x_j) \right] + \sum_{j=1}^{K} CI_m(x_j) \left[\eta_{jl} - \eta_{jm} \right] + REST \qquad (11)$$

where ΔCI denotes the difference between the index for h^l (say the health distribution in country l) and the one for h^m (say the health distribution in country m), and $REST$ is a residual term. While equation (11) only allows for discrete changes, the method is very general as the subscripts l and m may refer to different countries or to different time periods. An alternative decomposition method was proposed by Wagstaff et al. (2003) by taking the total differential of equation (8) which also allows for the decomposition of the "average elasticities" into changes in their determinants, i.e. the coefficients, the average of the determinants, or average health. O'Donnell et al. (2006) discuss the decomposition methods for changes in socioeconomic health inequalities in more detail. In addition, they provide an example of an Oaxaca-like decomposition of mean health (i.e. the difference between the poor and the rich) taken from Wagstaff and Nguyen (2004) and a decomposition of changes in the entire health distribution taken from O'Donnell et al. (2009). Finally, Van Ourti et al. (2009) develop an *exact* decomposition technique for changes in the concentration index that explicitly accounts for the non-linear relationship between income and health.

While these decompositions can be used to evaluate changes in socioeconomic inequality over time, they do not move beyond the static cross-sectional nature of the concentration index. Starting from the framework set out by Shorrocks (1978), Jones and López-Nicolás (2004) have proposed a decomposition technique that distinguishes between concentration indices based on short-run and long-run measures of socioeconomic status and health. The crucial question then becomes whether socioeconomic

---

[7] An equivalent decomposition weighs with the "average elasticities" of country m and the concentration indices of country l, i.e.

$$\Delta CI = \sum_{j=1}^{K} \eta_{jm} \left[CI_l(x_j) - CI_m(x_j) \right] + \sum_{j=1}^{K} CI_l(x_j) \left[\eta_{jl} - \eta_{jm} \right] + REST_{lm}.$$

inequalities measured using long-run indicators differ from inequalities measured with short-run indicators. They show that this occurs if "there are systematic differences in health between those individuals who are upwardly mobile [in socioeconomic status] and those who are downwardly mobile" (Jones and López-Nicolás 2004: 1016). Obviously, this comes at a cost, i.e. the requirement of repeated observations on the same individuals, whereas two independent cross-sections can be used to calculate the decomposition in equation (11). The complications of this long-run perspective are easily inferred from the long-run concentration index:

$$CI^{LR}(h) = \frac{2\sum_{i=1}^{n}\bar{h}_i R_i^{\bar{y}}}{\sum_{i=1}^{n}\bar{h}_i} - 1 = \sum_{t=1}^{T} w_t CI_t(h) - \frac{2\sum_{t=1}^{T}\sum_{i=1}^{n}(h_{it}-\bar{h}_t)(R_{it}^y - R_i^{\bar{y}})}{\sum_{t=1}^{T}\sum_{i=1}^{n}h_{it}} \quad (12)$$

where an upper bar with subscript i indicates the average for individual i across time, an upper bar with subscript $t = 1,\ldots,T$ indicates an average across individuals in time period t and w_t denotes the share of health in each period t.[8] Equation (12) shows that long-run socioeconomic inequality is a weighted sum of short-term concentration indices and a second term summarizing whether there are systematic health differences between individuals that are upwardly and downwardly mobile in terms of socioeconomic status. Long-run inequalities are larger (smaller) than short-term inequalities if upwardly (downwardly) mobile individuals are healthier.[9]

A final decomposition method links the Gini index of health to the concentration index of health, and thus allows to measure and compare total and socioeconomic health inequalities.[10] Following Rao (1969) and Lambert and Aronson (1993), Wagstaff and van Doorslaer (2004) have shown that the Gini index of health can be written as:

$$G(h) = CI^B + CI^W + R \quad (13)$$

where a finite (or limited) number of socioeconomic groups has been assumed. Equation (13) shows that the Gini of health can be written as the sum of "between-group"

---

[8] Consequently, $\bar{y}_t = n^{-1}\sum_{i=1}^{n} y_{it}$; $\bar{h}_t = n^{-1}\sum_{i=1}^{n} h_{it}$; $\bar{y}_i = T^{-1}\sum_{t=1}^{T} y_{it}$ with $\bar{y}_1 \le \bar{y}_2 \le \ldots \le \bar{y}_n$; $\bar{h}_i = T^{-1}\sum_{t=1}^{T} h_{it}$; and $w_t = \left(\sum_{t=1}^{T}\sum_{i=1}^{n} h_{it}\right)^{-1}\sum_{i=1}^{n} h_{it}$.

[9] Jones and López Nicolás (2004) also present a health-related socioeconomic status mobility (M(h)) index that focuses on the second term and is expressed as the percentage change between long-run inequalities and the weighted sum of short-term inequalities, i.e. $M(h) = \left[\sum_{t=1}^{T} w_t CI_t(h)\right]^{-1}\left[\sum_{t=1}^{T} w_t CI_t(h) - CI^{LR}(h)\right]$ The latter can also be decomposed along the lines of the decomposition in equation (8).

[10] This decomposition method is related to—but different from—the sub-group decomposition of the concentration index (Clarke et al. 2003; Wagstaff 2005b).

inequalities (CI^B), "within-group" inequalities (CI^W) and a residual term (R) that reflects the fact that the rank of socioeconomic status need not correspond with that of health. "Between-group" inequality is calculated as the concentration index of the average health levels per group. "Within-group" inequality is calculated as the concentration index of individual health where individuals are first rank by socioeconomic group and within group by individual health level. The residual term reflects the overlap between the rank of health and the rank of the socioeconomic groups, and will only be zero if both ranks coincide.

35.2.2 Properties of Health Variables

In section 35.2.1, we discussed the concentration index but did not pay attention to the properties of the underlying variables, i.e. socioeconomic status and health. For socio-economic status, we can be brief: only an ordinal scaling is required to be able to rank individuals (or groups) by some indicator of socioeconomic status. For further details on measuring socioeconomic status—including the choice of the indicator: income, consumption, wealth or something else—see e.g. Wagstaff and Watanabe (2003); Lindelöw (2006); or O'Donnell et al. (2008b: ch. 6). In the remainder of this section, we discuss the consequences for measures of inequality of the properties and the measurement scale of health which have received some attention recently (Clarke et al. 2002; Wagstaff 2005a, 2009b; Erreygers 2009a, 2009b; Erreygers and Van Ourti 2010).

35.2.2.1 *Mirror, Bounds, and Measurement Scale*

In section 35.2.1, we have implicitly assumed that health is measured with ratio scale properties and that its bounds are [0, + ∞], but these assumptions are unrealistic in some cases. Erreygers and Van Ourti (2010) distinguish health variables by their measurement scale and boundedness and show that the most relevant difference is between cardinal and ratio scale variables.[11] In addition, the range of the health variable can be either bounded or unbounded; in the first case health varies between a finite lower limit h^{min} and a finite upper limit h^{max}. For such a bounded health variable, we can construct a corresponding ill health variable by calculating the shortfall with regard to the maximum, i.e. $s_i \equiv h^{max} - h_i$.[12] This distinction between health variable types is not just a matter of semantics but corresponds to examples of variables encountered in health inequality studies. For example, health care expenditures and life expectancy are both measured on a ratio scale, but the former is unbounded while the latter is obviously bounded. The health utility index (Furlong et al. 2001; Feeny et al. 2002) is an example of a bounded

---

[11] For completeness, we mention that a cardinal scale makes differences between individuals meaningful, and a ratio-scale implies that ratios between individuals have meaning and that 0 corresponds to a situation of complete absence.

[12] We also assume that the lower limit of bounded and unbounded ratio scale health variables is zero, which means that it takes non-negative values only.

health variable measured on a cardinal scale, and the predicted linear (latent health) index from an ordered probit model for self-assessed health (van Doorslaer and Jones 2003) is—due to the properties of the ordered probit model—unbounded and its zero point is arbitrarily fixed at zero.

The measurement scale and boundedness have important implications for the concentration index. To start with the former, measuring relative inequality by computing a concentration index is only meaningful for variables measured on a ratio scale since, the index must remains unchanged under a positive proportional transformation of the health variable. For cardinal variables, the value of the concentration index depends upon the chosen cardinalization since it is not invariant to positive linear transformations (Kakwani 1980; van Doorslaer and Jones 2003; Erreygers 2009a, 2009b).[13]

The assumption of unboundedness is even more important for the applicability of the concentration index. Wagstaff (2005a) observed that many empirical studies use binary health indicators and showed that this affects the theoretical bounds of the concentration index. This result was generalized to any bounded health variable by Erreygers (2009a), who showed that the bounds of the concentration index depend upon the lower and upper limit and the mean value of health.[14] In other words: the bounded nature of the relevant health variable complicates the comparison of populations with different mean values (and/or limits) of health. This is a general result that holds for any rank-dependent inequality index and for this reason we also urge for caution when applying the achievement index to health variables with a bounded range.[15] A second consequence of the finite upper limit was highlighted by Clarke et al. (2002). They argued that it seems natural to assume that the informational content of a bounded health variable—for example, SF-36 scores lying between 0 and 100 (Ware and Gandek 1998)—is identical to that of the related ill health variable, i.e. upper limit minus SF-36 score. Nevertheless, they show that the concentration index of health might differ from that of ill health. Erreygers (2009a) discusses this issue in more detail and argues that "since health and ill health are mirrors of one another, it seems reasonable to expect that the two concentration indices provide mirror images of the degree of inequality" (ibid.: 5). This will, however, only occur if health and ill health have the same mean.[16] The bottom line is that for bounded health variables the concentration index is unattractive because it does not satisfy the condition of "mirror images."

35.2.2.2 *Alternatives to the Concentration Index for Bounded Variables*

Several variants of the concentration index have been proposed to address the mirror, bounds, and measurement scale issues. Following Wagstaff et al. (1991), Clarke et al.

---

[13] The concentration index is not invariant to positive linear transformations since $CI(\tilde{h}) = (c + d\bar{h})^{-1}(d\bar{h})\,CI(h)$ for $\tilde{h}_i = c + dh_i$ with $d > 0$.

[14] i.e. $-B \leq CI(h) \leq B$ with $B = \left[\left(h^{max} - \bar{h}\right)\left(\bar{h} - h^{min}\right)\right] / \left[\bar{h}(h^{max} - h^{min})\right]$.

[15] Clarke and Hayes (2009: 560–1) also discuss other properties of the achievement index.

[16] This is easily seen from $CI(s) = [-\bar{h}(h^{max} - \bar{h})^{-1}]CI(h)$.

(2002) propose the use of the generalized concentration index $GCI(h)$—defined as the concentration index multiplied by mean health—to solve the mirror issue.[17]

$$GCI(h) = \overline{h} CI(h) = \frac{1}{n} \sum_{i=1}^{n} h_i \left(2R_i^y - 1 \right) \qquad (14)$$

While providing a solution to the mirror issue, the generalized concentration index is not invariant to positive linear transformations and thus fails to be independent from the chosen cardinalization. Wagstaff (2005a) proposes to divide the concentration index by its upper bound to overcome the dependence of the concentration index on the mean value of a binary health variable. Erreygers (2009a) generalizes this normalized concentration index $NCI(h)$ to any bounded variable

$$NCI(h) = \frac{\overline{h} \left(h^{\max} - h^{\min} \right)}{\left(h^{\max} - \overline{h} \right)\left(\overline{h} - h^{\min} \right)} CI(h) = \frac{1}{n} \sum_{i=1}^{n} \left\{ \left[\frac{h_i \left(h^{\max} - h^{\min} \right)}{\left(h^{\max} - \overline{h} \right)\left(\overline{h} - h^{\min} \right)} \right] \left(2R_i^y - 1 \right) \right\} \quad (15)$$

and shows that this index resolves the mirror issue and does not depend on the chosen cardinalization. In addition, the normalized concentration index has a fixed range, i.e. the minimum and maximum bounds are always −1 and +1. Using an axiomatic approach, Erreygers (2009a) defines a "corrected" concentration index:

$$CCI(h) = \left(\frac{4\overline{h}}{h^{\max} - h^{\min}} \right) CI(h) = \frac{1}{n} \sum_{i=1}^{n} \left[\left(\frac{4h_i}{h^{\max} - h^{\min}} \right) \left(2R_i^y - 1 \right) \right] \qquad (16)$$

Similar to the normalized concentration index, the corrected concentration index resolves the mirror issue and is not dependent on the chosen cardinalization.

A crucial property of both the normalized and corrected concentration index relates to the distinction between absolute and relative inequality. For unbounded variables, these concepts are distinct and no inequality index exists that measures both simultaneously.[18] This is crucially different for bounded variables; inequality indices can never be purely relative or purely absolute if one believes the mirror issue should be solved since "depending on whether you look at one side (health) or the other (ill health), the same change may be seen as relative inequality preserving or as relative inequality changing" (Erreygers 2009b: 2).[19] It follows that neither the normalized concentration index nor the corrected concentration index are pure relative inequality indices.

---

[17] This index has traditionally been used to measure absolute inequalities for unbounded variables such as income (Lambert 2001).

[18] Absolute inequality measurement implies that adding a constant to everyone's level of health should leave inequality unchanged, while relative inequality measurement assumes that equiproportionate changes should leave inequality unchanged.

[19] More exactly, Erreygers and Van Ourti (2010) show that an index that is invariant to positive linear transformations and that solves the mirror issue can never be a relative inequality index.

The main difference between these indices is the way they deal with the dependence on mean health (and its bounds). From equations (15) and (16), it is easily inferred that both indices are equal for $\bar{h} = 0.5(h^{max} - h^{min})$, i.e. when mean health is exactly halfway between the upper and lower limit of health. As soon as mean health moves away from this point, the indices start to diverge: setting out from an unequal health distribution, and next gradually decreasing mean health—which in the limit implies a perfectly equal situation where everyone has minimal health or maximal ill health (depending on the mirror image)—makes the corrected concentration index tend to zero inequality, while the normalized index does not show this tendency. For further details, we refer to Erreygers (2009a, 2009b), Erreygers and Van Ourti (2010), and Wagstaff (2009b).

35.2.2.3 *Implications for Health Inequality Measurement*

The consequences of the measurement scale and boundedness for the concentration index led Erreygers and Van Ourti (2010) to suggest guidelines on the suitability of the alternative rank-dependent inequality indices to deal with these problems.[20,21] These guidelines follow directly from the discussion in sections 35.2.2.1 and 35.2.2.2 and are summarized below.

First, the concentration index should only be used for *unbounded* variables measured on a *ratio scale* since it is not invariant to positive linear transformations. If these measurement properties of the health variable are satisfied, then the concentration index measures relative socioeconomic health inequalities.[22] Second, while both the normalized and corrected concentration indices can be used with *cardinal* and *ratio scale bounded* variables, we recommend the latter since it has the advantage of indicating a perfectly equal distribution when one pushes mean health of an unequal health distribution to the limit.

A remaining concern is the applicability of the factor decomposition in section 35.2.1.2. For *unbounded ratio-scale* variables, the factor decomposition in equation (8) is unaffected. Our advice against applying the concentration index to *unbounded cardinal* variables is only a recent insight. Hence, the existing literature has applied the factor decomposition to unbounded cardinal health variables. While the magnitude of the factor contributions will depend on the chosen cardinalization, van Doorslaer and Jones (2003) show that the factor decomposition can be rescued by focusing on the *percentage* factor contributions since these remain unchanged under different cardinalizations of

---

[20] Note also that, except for the extended concentration index, all indices in this chapter—equations (1), (14), (15), and (16)—are weighted sums with linearly declining weights. They only differ in terms of the normalization of h_i.

[21] The discussion in Erreygers and Van Ourti (2010) has wider appeal as they consider a general class of rank-dependent inequality indices, and also nominal, ordinal, and absolute measurement scales. They also introduce a modified concentration index that can be applied to unbounded variables with cardinal scale.

[22] Absolute socioeconomic health inequalities can only be meaningfully measured for unbounded variables with an *absolute* scale using the generalized concentration index (Erreygers and Van Ourti 2010).

health.[23] For *bounded cardinal* and *ratio scale* variables, Erreygers (2009a) shows that the values of the coefficients in equation (7) depend on the particular cardinalization and therefore suggests replacing equation (6) by

$$\frac{h_i - h^{\min}}{h^{\max} - h^{\min}} = \beta_0^* + \sum_{j=1}^{K} \beta_j^* x_{ij} + e_i^* \tag{17}$$

such that the coefficients (and the error term) are invariant to positive linear transformations of health. Combining equations (8), (16), and (17) gives the factor decomposition of the corrected concentration index:

$$CCI(h) = 4\left[\sum_{j=1}^{K} \beta_j^* GCI\left(x_j\right) + GCI\left(e_i^*\right) \right] \tag{18}$$

Comparing equations (8) and (18) reveals that the differences between the decomposition of the concentration index and the corrected concentration index are subtle, and we therefore expect the use of the "corrected" concentration index to mainly affect estimates of socioeconomic health inequality itself, rather than its factor decomposition.

A final concern is how to proceed when faced with ordinal health variables. Since these are incompatible with rank-dependent inequality indices, researchers have responded by projecting cardinal scales onto ordinal variables. For example, van Doorslaer and Jones (2003) mapped the cardinal HUI scale on the ordinal self-assessed health categories (see also section 35.3.2). Another example is the widespread use of binary 0/1 variables (with 0 indicating the absence and 1 the presence of a certain condition, e.g. immunization against measles), that one might interpret as a projection into 0 and 100 percent (see also section 35.3). Alternatively, one might resort to other measurement approaches that take the ordinal nature of the variable of interest explicitly into account (Allison and Foster 2004; Apouey 2007; Abul Naga and Yalcin 2008; Zheng 2008).

35.3 EMPIRICAL APPLICATIONS AND POLICY IMPLICATIONS

A large and rapidly growing number of papers have used the tools outlined in the previous sections to analyze issues of inequity and inequality. Again, in our review of the literature since 2000, we do not aim to be exhaustive but rather to highlight some of the more interesting empirical applications and the policy relevance of their findings. We

---

[23] Start by taking a positive linear transformation of health: $\tilde{h}_i = c + dh_i$. Rewrite equation (7) accordingly — $\tilde{h}_i = (\beta_0 + c)d + d\sum_{j=1}^{K}\beta_j x_{ij} + de_i$ — and apply the decomposition in equation (8). Dividing by the concentration index leads to the percentage contributions: $1 = \left[(\bar{\tilde{h}})CI(\tilde{h})\right]^{-1}\left\{d\sum_{j=1}^{K}\left[(\beta_j\bar{x}_j)CI(x_j)\right] + 2\mathrm{cov}(de_i, R_i^y)\right\}$. After some algebra, this further reduces to equation (8).

start with the literature on health care inequity, as this is less affected by the measurement issues for bounded scales like health.

35.3.1 Horizontal Inequity in Health Care Use

The main innovation in this literature since 2000 was the use of a variety of decomposition methods outlined in section 35.2.1.2.[24] This has shifted attention from the mere *measurement* of inequity as inequality in need-standardized use to an *explanation* of measured socioeconomic inequality. In a linear context, the correction for need differences can then easily be left to a second stage of the analysis. This is the main reason why several recent empirical studies (e.g. van Doorslaer et al. 2006; Lu et al. 2007) have used linear (OLS) regression methods to decompose observed inequality into its contributing factors. van Doorslaer et al. (2004a) have attempted to extend the approach to a non-linear setting by adopting a "partial effects" representation of non-linear count models to assess the degree of horizontal inequity in health care use in 12 European countries. This representation has the advantage of preserving a linear additive model of actual utilization, but it only holds by approximation, and its error term includes, in addition to the estimation error, an approximation error which depends on the choice of estimation method for the partial effects.

For the purpose of illustrating the policy relevance of these methods, we draw on some of the empirical findings that were recently obtained from a large cross-country comparative study of the inequalities in medical care use by income in 21 countries commissioned by the OECD (van Doorslaer et al. 2004b; van Doorslaer et al. 2006). In general, they find relatively few violations of the horizontal equity principle for doctor visits and hospitalizations and a very high degree of pro-rich inequity for dental care use. However, when doctor utilization is separated into general practitioner (GP) and medical specialist visits, and into the probability of a contact versus the conditional number of visits, some important differences in inequity patterns emerge. While GP utilization tends to be fairly equitably and in some countries even significantly pro-poor distributed, the picture that emerged for specialist utilization was very different, with the great majority of OECD countries showing clear pro-rich inequity patterns. This is especially the case for the probability of a visit during a year, but also for the total number of visits during the same year.

The diagram in Figure 35.2 presents the estimated horizontal inequity indices and their confidence intervals for years around 2001 for the probability of a specialist visit. It can be seen that in all countries, after standardizing for need through the decomposition method, the horizontal inequity index is significantly positive. This implies that, given

---

[24] All studies assume that the average relationship observed between need (health) and health care use is an appropriate vertical norm. Attempts to measure vertical inequity in the use of health care have been very rare, but a notable exception is Sutton (2002) who studied both vertical and horizontal inequity in the use of GPs in Scotland.

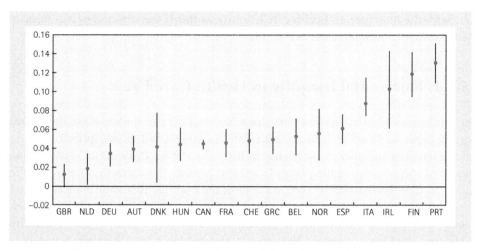

FIGURE 35.2 Horizontal inequity indices for probability of a specialist visit, by country (with 95% confidence interval)

Source: van Doorslaer et al. 2004b.

the same need, in all countries those on higher incomes are more likely to see a specialist (or those on lower incomes less likely). But there are also important differences between countries and the decomposition unravels to what extent the unequal distribution of various factors that co-determine health care contribute to this finding. Recall from section 35.2.1.2 that for any factor to be able to affect the unequal distribution of medical care by income, two requirements need to be met: (i) after controlling for other covariates, it needs to have an effect on use (i.e. a non-zero (partial) use elasticity), and (ii) it has to be unequally distributed by income (i.e. a non-zero concentration index). Each factor's contribution to the measured inequality in medical care use is defined as simply the product of its elasticity and its concentration index and the sum of all such contributions equals the concentration index of (predicted) health care use. These contributions to the horizontal inequity index—which can be positive or negative—are presented in the bar chart in Figure 35.3 for the probability of a specialist visit. These are inequity (not inequality) contributions because the contributions of the need-related variables (which are always negative because need induces higher use and tends to be more concentrated among the lower incomes) have been deleted from the chart. We can observe that, in spite of the near universal and largely publicly funded cover for these types of care, the partial contribution of income is still substantial in most countries, but especially large in Portugal and Finland. For policy purposes, most interesting are the contributions of the variables related to the insurance system. Two examples—France and Ireland—are of particular policy interest here because of the public–private mix adopted.

In France, about 85 percent of the population used to buy (complementary) private health insurance coverage to cover public sector copayments (about 30% of doctor fees). In 2000, the government introduced the *Couverture Maladie Universelle (CMU)* to

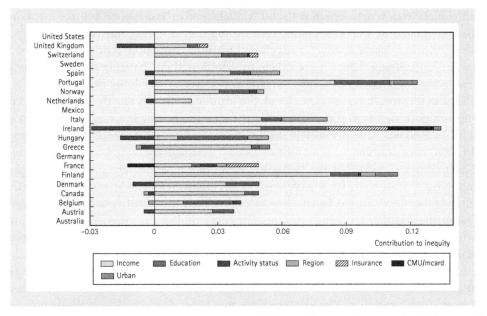

FIGURE 35.3 Decomposition of inequity in the probability of a specialist visit (excluding need contributions)

Source: van Doorslaer et al. 2004b.

basically waive the copayments for the 10 percent least well off in the population. It can be seen that the pro-poor contribution of the fee waiver for about 10 percent of the French population compensates almost entirely for the pro-rich contribution of the private cover of 85 percent of the population. The situation bears some similarity but is nonetheless different in Ireland. There, 30 percent of the population with an income below a threshold qualifies for a *medical card* which essentially provides an entitlement for free GP and other care. All others are required to pay fee-for-service for GP consultations and some outpatient and inpatient care. However, about 50 percent of the Irish population purchased private cover for inpatient and outpatient care. Also in Ireland, the unequal distribution of such private coverage contributes to the pro-rich distribution, but, unlike in France, the unequal distribution of the *medical card* seems to add to this. While the fee waiver does have a pro-poor contribution to GP utilization in both countries (not shown), in Ireland it leads to a substitution away from specialist visits, but not in France. This may be related to the very low mean use of specialists in Ireland generally (van Doorslaer et al. 2006).

While examples such as the one above are helpful in drawing attention to potentially important policy amenable determinants of the distribution of health care, they are not directly useful for policy evaluation or simulation, as this requires a causal interpretation of the identified effects. To the extent, for instance, that the individual decision to purchase private health insurance is voluntary, it is likely to be influenced by unobservable individual characteristics, such as the individual's level of "risk." As a result, the insurance effect estimated in a cross-sectional relationship may not only consist of a utilization effect but also a degree of adverse selection (by insured) or risk selection (by insurers). If the entire insurance "effect" were driven by selection, then changing the availability of private insurance coverage would not alter the degree to which the use of specialists is related to income. If, on the other hand, the insurance effect is mostly a direct effect on consumption, then expansion or reduction of access to private insurance (through taxes or incentives) will have an effect on the distribution of specialist care by income. Jones et al. (2006) have examined this for four countries (Ireland, Italy, Portugal, and the UK) and their findings suggest that the utilization effect of supplementary private coverage is important. Private cover is often obtained as an employment benefit, resulting in positive selection, but once insured, beneficiaries are more likely to consult a medical specialist. As a result, they claim that private insurance does not simply act as a marker of a higher propensity to consume such care, but also induces additional use over and above what would be used in the absence of such cover.

Comparative findings on horizontal inequity in three Asian countries are reported in an analysis by Lu et al. (2007) for Hong Kong, South Korea, and Taiwan. They include licensed traditional (non-Western) medicine practitioners and find a significant pro-rich inequity in its use in all three countries. In addition, a large number of country-specific studies have emerged. Of particular interest is Morris et al. (2005) because they illustrate that testing for instances of unequal treatment for equal need associated with other characteristics than income, like ethnicity, employment status or education is feasible. Tests of horizontal equity using the rank based indices presented in section 35.2, however, require a natural ranking order, which does not exist for characteristics like marital status or gender.

If the aim is not to decompose the inequality or inequity but merely to measure it, the linear setting can be abandoned and non-linear methods can be used to model health care utilization more appropriately. One example is Van Ourti (2004), who used eight waves from the Panel Study of Belgian Households to estimate random effects count data models. While these highly non-linear models no longer allow for the decomposition technique to be applied, the estimates can still be used to obtain estimates of the horizontal inequity indices. It does require making assumptions about the nature of the unobserved heterogeneity in order to be able to include the individual effects among the need or non-need factors in the computation. Similarly, Bago d'Uva et al. (2007, 2009) use latent class hurdle models on the eight waves of the European Community Household Panel data to estimate short and long run indices of inequality and horizontal inequity for ten EU member states using the methods of section 35.2.1.3. In the need adjustment procedure, they also partition the individual time invariant unobserved heterogeneity into a need-related and a non-need-related part, thereby distinguishing between the conventional approach (i.e. that all use variation *not* explained by need variables reflects inequity) and a more conservative approach (i.e. that inequity is only that portion of the total systematic variation with income which is explained by non-need variables). In almost all cases, this expanded approach to the need versus non-need partitioning of explained variation leads to higher (i.e. less pro-poor or more pro-rich) index values. They argue that "this suggests that much of the variation associated with income that remains unexplained in cross-sectional models not accounting for hetero-geneity derives from unobserved need heterogeneity" (Bago d'Uva et al. 2009: 9). As can be seen from Figures 35.4 and 35.5, the general pattern of findings of pro-poor inequity in GP visits in most (seven out of ten) EU countries and pro-rich inequity in specialist utilization in all countries studied largely confirms earlier cross-country comparative work based on a single cross-sections by van Doorslaer et al. (2004a). But while the rank-ings of countries are fairly robust to these variations in the approach, the results do sug-gest that better control for need, adoption of a longer run perspective and even using an arguably more conservative index all lead to more pro-rich estimates for specialist care and less pro-poor inequity in GP care.

Also the empirical literature describing and evaluating (changes in) the distribution of health services use in the developing world has grown rapidly over the last decade. A use-ful resource is the collection of studies contained in the Reaching the Poor volume (Gwatkin et al. 2005) which presents five such studies in Asia, three in Africa, and three in Latin America. Many of these case studies use several of the tools discussed in section 35.2. A great variety of interventions were studied—ranging from the use of contracting to improve equity in primary health care delivered in Cambodia to expanding access to

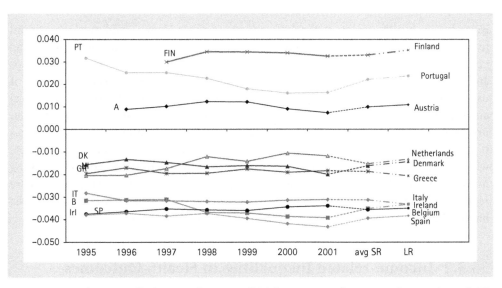

FIGURE 35.4 Short-run (SR) versus long-run (LR) "conservative" inequity for number of GP visits, by country

Source: Bago d'Uva et al. 2007.

Note: "avg(SR)" refers to $\sum_{t=1}^{T} w_t CI_t(h)$ in equation (11) and "LR" refers to $CI^{LR}(h)$ in equation (11)

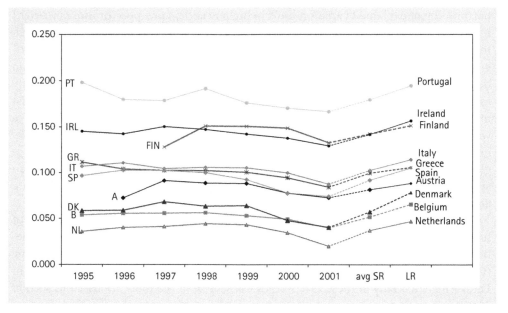

FIGURE 35.5 Short-run (SR) versus long-run (LR) "conservative" inequity for number of specialist visits, by country

Source: Bago d'Uva et al. 2007.

Note: "avg(SR)" refers to $\sum_{t=1}^{T} w_t CI_t(h)$ in equation (11) and "LR" refers to $CI^{LR}(h)$ in equation (11).

reproductive health services through the private sector in Kenya—and most were found to favor the poor, either by achieving higher coverage among the poor or by producing greater coverage increases among disadvantaged than among more privileged groups and thereby reducing disparities. While these are just a handful of selected examples of useful case studies, we tend to agree with the conclusion of the editors that "technical analyses like those produced through the Reaching the Poor program (RPP) can make an important contribution to policy development. (…) Without accurate empirical information about the distribution of program benefits, even ardently pro-poor policymakers with strong political support can too easily go astray. This seems to have been happening in the health field because of reliance on the incorrect assumption that programs are reaching disadvantaged groups. Technical information can also be useful tools in the hands of those wishing to increase political commitment" (Gwatkin et al. 2005: 14–15).

35.3.2 Income-related Inequalities in Health Outcomes

The economic literature on the measurement and comparison of health disparities using rank-based measures has expanded rapidly in the last decade. A large number of health indicator variables have been used in analyses on socioeconomic health inequalities, including mortality rates (e.g. Wagstaff 2000; Hosseinpoor et al. 2006), survival (e.g. van Doorslaer and Gerdtham 2003), (quality-adjusted) life expectancy (e.g. Gerdtham and Johannesson 2000; Burström et al. 2005), anthropometric measures (e.g. Wagstaff and Watanabe 2000; Van de Poel et al. 2007; Zhang and Wang 2007; Van de Poel et al. 2008) as well as dummy variables for the presence of chronic conditions (e.g. Hernández-Quevedo et al. 2006).

One of the most popular measures is self-assessed health (SAH) as derived from answers to the question "how is your health in general?" with the responses typically being "very good," "good," "fair," "bad" and "very bad." SAH is popular as it is available in most general survey datasets and is known to be a very good predictor of other health outcomes (Idler and Benyamini 1997). The most important drawback of SAH is that the responses (1 to 5) are ordinal and therefore cardinal or ratio-scales need to be projected onto these variables to apply the indices described in section 35.2 (see also section 35.2.2.3).

Van Doorslaer and Jones (2003) used ordered probit regression to model the ordinal SAH variable, much along the lines of equation (7). But instead of estimating these thresholds alongside the regression coefficients, they impose these thresholds from external data and use interval regression. Their external thresholds were obtained from the McMaster Health Utility Index (HUI) and the predicted values of the interval regression model can then be used to compute the concentration index. They also showed that the interval regression approach had greater internal validity than alternative approaches for measuring concentration indices and curves in the Canadian dataset for which the individual HUI values were available. Van Doorslaer and Koolman (2004) used this interval regression to estimate and decompose income-related inequalities in self-assessed health in thirteen EU countries using data from the 1996 wave of the ECHP. Significant inequalities in health (utility) favoring the higher income groups emerged in all countries, but were particularly high in Portugal and (to a lesser extent) in the UK and in Denmark. By contrast, relatively low health inequality was observed in the Netherlands and Germany, and also in Italy, Belgium, Spain, Austria, and Ireland.[25] There was a positive correlation with income inequality but the relationship was much weaker than in the van Doorslaer et al. (1997) comparison. The decomposition analysis shows that the (partial) elasticities of the explanatory variables are generally more important than their unequal distribution by income in explaining the cross-country differences in income-related health inequality. They also employ the Oaxaca-type decomposition analysis explained in section 35.2.1.3 to decompose the "excess" inequality compared to the country with the lowest CI (the Netherlands) and find that, ceteris paribus, especially the health and income of non-working Europeans like the retired and disabled show the greatest contributions. This begs the question to what extent income-related inequality in SAH for adult populations is as much a consequence of reverse causation (i.e. falling

---

[25] These results were based on the concentration index but prove to be robust to the corrected concentration index, which in this particular case only amounts to multiplying the CI(h)s by 4 times the mean.

incomes as a result of withdrawal from the labor force) as of income advantages leading to better health. To the extent that the decompositions are not based on causal underlying models, these questions cannot be answered.

Lindeboom and van Doorslaer (2004) have analyzed reporting heterogeneity of SRH using an ordered response model on Canadian data and examined whether reporting behavior differs depending on individual characteristics. They found no evidence of reporting heterogeneity for income, education, and language (French–English), but strong effects for sex and age, i.e. females and older individuals report better health for the same true health status. Bago d'Uva et al. (2008) have analyzed reporting behavior in Indonesia, India, and China combining an ordered response model with a vignette approach (see e.g. Tandon et al. 2003). They tend to confirm the finding of Lindeboom and van Doorslaer (2004), i.e. there is evidence of significant (but relatively small) reporting bias for income, region (urban/rural) and age, but its consequences for the measurement of socioeconomic health inequalities seem relatively mild.

Cross-country comparisons have not been limited to OECD member states. Wagstaff (2000) used standard concentration indices and curves to compare socioeconomic inequalities in child mortality estimated from *Living Standards Measurement Study* (LSMS) surveys across nine developing countries while Webster et al. (2005) examined equity in coverage of two of the most powerful interventions for the prevention of childhood mortality in twenty-six African countries: insecticide-treated bed nets and vaccinations. Van de Poel et al. (2008) have used the Erreygers (2009a) corrected concentration index to compare socio-economic inequalities in stunting and mortality of children under 5 using *Demographic and Health Survey* (DHS) data from forty-seven developing countries. Zhang and Wang (2008) recently used the concentration index to document trends in socioeconomic inequality in overweight in the United States in the period 1971–2000. The World Bank has documented inequalities in a large number of health, nutrition, and population indicators by wealth status across virtually all countries with DHS data available (Gwatkin et al. 2000) and time trends in these (Gwatkin et al. 2007).[26]

As highlighted in section 35.2.2, the choice of health indicator—i.e. good or bad health, bounded or unbounded health, etc.—has implications for the use of the standard concentration index as a measure of inequality. Using the results obtained by Van de Poel et al. (2008), Erreygers (2009a) illustrates the changes in country results and rankings obtained when employing the different inequality measures. In the example of a binary variable for stunting rates that he uses, the normalized concentration index simply equals the standard concentration index divided by one minus the mean prevalence of stunting and the corrected concentration index equals four times the standard concentration index multiplied by the mean prevalence of stunting. He finds that the correlation between the concentration index used (i.e. standard, normalized, or corrected) and the mean prevalence of stunting varies substantially with the type of index used. In particular, he notes that this correlation is not only positive for the concentration index

---

[26] These overviews, as well as the country-specific reports are available at <www.worldbank.org/povertyandhealth>.

measuring stunting and negative with the concentration index measuring lack of stunting, but is also of the opposite sign for the two measures which are invariant with respect
to positive (stunting) or negative (lack of stunting) measurement (i.e. a positive correlation for the corrected and a negative for the normalized index). As we explained in section 35.2.2.2, this finding can be attributed to the fact that the normalized concentration
index does not manage to indicate a perfectly equal distribution when one pushes the
mean prevalence of stunting to the limit, i.e. in countries with very low prevalence of
stunting the normalized and corrected concentration index will reveal substantially different degrees of socioeconomic inequalities in stunting.

Recently, a number of studies have also adopted some of the methods described in
section 35.2.1 for distributional impact analyses.[27] These aim to assess not only the mean
impact of an intervention or a reform on a certain health or health care outcome, but
also its impact on the socioeconomic distribution of the outcome characteristic of interest. This is typically more straightforward to do in a setting where there is a universal
need for an intervention with proven effectiveness.

A good example is Masanja et al. (2005) who examined the impact of the Integrated
Management of Childhood Illness (IMCI) strategy on inequality of health outcomes
and access across socioeconomic gradients in rural Tanzania using a difference-in-differences approach. They compare changes in concentration indices between 1999 and
2002 in two districts with and two districts without IMCI for three indicators of child
health (underweight, stunting, wasting) and eight indicators of access to appropriate
treatment (like measles and DPT immunization, use of treated and untreated nets, and
appropriateness of caretaking and careseeking). Table 35.1 reports the differences in
before–after differences in both the means and the concentration indices that they
obtained for the IMCI and the non-IMCI districts for four of their indicators. We can see
from the first column that the difference-in-differences for the ill health indicators
(underweight and stunting) was negative for stunting (i.e. indicating greater improvement for the IMCI group) but positive for underweight. The two vaccination coverage
differences-in-differences are both negative, indicating greater improvements among
the non-IMCI groups for both. The second column shows the changes in the concentration indices of these measures. They show an improvement for the first three indicators
(i.e. underweight and stunting have become less concentrated among the poor and measles coverage less concentrated among the non-poor) but a deterioration for DPT coverage (i.e. has become more concentrated among the non-poor in IMCI group compared
to non-IMCI).

However, we have mentioned in section 35.2.2 that the standard concentration index
for a bounded—here binary [0,1]—variable does not satisfy the mirror condition. In
such cases, it is better to use the corrected concentration index and to assume that the
binary variable can be interpreted as the prevalence of a health outcome. An important
advantage is that the results are then identical to the ones obtained using their mirror

---

[27] Several good examples are also included in Gwatkin et al. (2005) and Yazbeck (2009).

Table 35.1 Changes in inequality With and Without Integrated Management of Childhood Illness (IMCI) in Rural Tanzania

		Mean	Standard concentration index	Corrected concentration index
Underweight				
No IMCI	before	0.27	−0.1360	−0.1469
	after	0.19	−0.1660	−0.1262
	difference	−0.08	−0.0300	0.0207
IMCI	before	0.30	−0.0710	−0.0852
	after	0.23	−0.0570	−0.0524
	difference	−0.07	0.0140	0.0328
Diff-in-diff		0.01	0.0440	0.0120
Stunting				
No IMCI	before	0.51	−0.1220	−0.2489
	after	0.40	−0.1330	−0.2128
	difference	−0.11	−0.0110	0.0361
IMCI	before	0.59	−0.1020	−0.2407
	after	0.43	-0.0320	-0.0550
	difference	−0.16	0.0700	0.1857
Diff-in-diff		−0.05	0.0810	0.1496
Measles coverage				
No IMCI	before	0.89	0.0120	0.0427
	after	0.93	0.0080	0.0298
	difference	0.04	−0.0040	-0.0130
IMCI	before	0.88	0.0150	0.0528
	after	0.89	-0.0120	-0.0427
	difference	0.01	-0.0270	-0.0955
Diff-in-diff		−0.03	−0.0230	−0.0826
DPT coverage				
No IMCI	before	0.86	0.0340	0.1170
	after	0.95	-0.0110	-0.0418
	difference	0.09	-0.0450	-0.1588
IMCI	before	0.87	0.0110	0.0383
	after	0.83	0.0300	0.0996
	difference	−0.04	0.0190	0.0613
Diff-in-diff		−0.13	0.0640	0.2201

Source: First two columns from Masanja et al. (2005)

concept (i.e. *not* underweight, stunted, or vaccinated). This was done in column three and it is clear from the differences that these corrections may lead to different conclusions. While they will never change the sign of the concentration index itself, they may change the sign of the difference in two index values. An example of such sign reversals can be observed in the non-IMCI groups for stunting.

35.4 Conclusion

The literature on measuring equity in health and health care since 2000 has been characterized by three clear trends: (a) a rapidly expanding empirical application of the basic tools of the concentration indices and curves to a wide range of situations, (b) the development and application of various types of decomposition methods aimed at explaining the measured inequalities and inequities, and (c) the further development of the the theoretical underpinnings and properties of the basic inequality measurement tools.

The review reveals the now widespread dissemination of concentration indices and curves in both the economic and non-economics literature on inequalities. Increasingly, the methods have also gained acceptance from policy advisors around the world and international organizations like the World Bank (Gwatkin et al. 2000; Gwatkin et al. 2007; Yazbeck 2009), WHO (Van de Poel et al. 2008) or the OECD (van Doorslaer et al. 2004b) who have started using these tools in comparative studies.

Second, the various decomposition methods that were developed over the past decade or so have been adopted in a wide variety of situations to enhance understanding of differences or changes in situations. Advances made with respect to dealing with health reporting biases, with correction for unobserved heterogeneity in needs and the use of more complex non-linear econometric models to deal with these have often confirmed the robustness of earlier findings. While the decompositions have proven useful in shedding further light on a large number of cross-country or other comparisons, and enhancing our understanding of the sources of inequality, the lack of causal interpretation of the underlying relationships does limit their usefulness for policy prescription. It is expected that the next phase of development may address some of these perceived limitations.

Finally, it is envisaged that further work is required on the theoretical and welfare basis of the tools. Several recent papers (Fleurbaey 2006; Fleurbaey and Schokkaert 2009) have drawn attention to some of the crucial assumptions underlying the measures of socioeconomic inequality, which are sometimes perceived as very restrictive and undesirable. It is not impossible that ways to overcome these perceived deficiencies will require trading off improvements along more than one dimension. This might lead to an exploration of multi-dimensional indices of inequality, perhaps along the lines of Abul Naga and Geoffard (2006), who consider under which circumstances an income transfer from a healthy to an unhealthy person may be welfare improving even if the unhealthy person is wealthier. Similarly, it seems worthwhile to consider in further detail which (potential) health transfers from wealthier to poorer persons are welfare improving, and which are not.

Much has also been learned about the relevance of the measurement properties of the underlying health and health care variables for the measurement of socioeconomic inequality. For unbounded variables—such as health expenditures—the distinction between cardinal and ratio measurement scale is important: the standard concentration index has its usual desirable properties for ratio scale measures, but no rank-dependent index exists that can be used meaningfully with unbounded cardinal variables. If the health variable is bounded—for example the health utility index (HUI) has lower bound 0 and an upper bound of 1—this distinction is irrelevant. We then advise to use the corrected concentration index which is not dependent upon the mean health level and the bounds of the health variable and solves the mirror issue: measuring health positively or negatively—i.e. as the shortfall with respect to maximal health—then leads to identical results.

Overall, the contributions of economists to the measurement of equity and inequality in health and health care have clearly been accumulating over the last decade, and there is no sign of this trend weakening. On the contrary, we feel that the field is alive and kicking and further substantial advances can be anticipated in the next decade.

References

ABUL NAGA, R. and GEOFFARD, P.-Y. (2006). "Decomposition of bivariate inequality indices by attributes." *Economics Letters*, 90/3: 362–7.

—— and YALCIN, T. (2008). "Inequality measurement for ordered response health data." *Journal of Health Economics*, 27: 1614–25.

ALLISON, R. A. and FOSTER, J. E. (2004). "Measuring health inequality using qualitative data." *Journal of Health Economics*, 23: 505–24.

APOUEY, B. (2007). "Measuring health polarization with self-assessed health data." *Health Economics*, 16/9: 875–94.

BAGO D'UVA, T., JONES, A. M., and VAN DOORSLAER, E. (2007). "Measurement of horizontal inequity in health care utilization using European Panel data." Tinbergen Institute discussion paper, 2007-059/3, Erasmus University Rotterdam.

—— VAN DOORSLAER, E., LINDEBOOM, L., and O'DONNELL, O. (2008). "Does reporting heterogeneity bias the measurement of health disparities?" *Health Economics*, 17/3: 351–75.

—— JONES, A. M., and VAN DOORSLAER, E. (2009). "Measurement of horizontal inequity in health care utilization using European Panel data." *Journal of Health Economics*, 28/2: 280–9.

BLEICHRODT, H. and VAN DOORSLAER, E. (2006). "A welfare economics foundation for health inequality measurement." *Journal of Health Economics*, 25: 945–57.

BLINDER, A. (1973). "Wage discrimination: reduced form and structural estimates." *Journal of Human Resources*, 8: 436–55.

BURSTRÖM, K., JOHANNESSON, M., and DIDERICHSEN, F. (2005). "Increasing socio-economic inequalities in life expectancy and QALYs in Sweden 1980–1997." *Health Economics*, 14/8: 831–50.

CLARKE, P. M. and HAYES, A. J. (2009). "Measuring achievement: changes in risk factors for cardiovascular disease in Australia." *Social Science and Medicine*, 68: 552–61.

—— GERDTHAM, U.-G., JOHANNESSON, M., BINGEFORS, K., and SMITH L. (2002). "On the measurement of relative and absolute income-related health inequality." *Social Science and Medicine*, 55: 1923–8.

—— —— and CONNELLY, L. B. (2003). "A note on the decomposition of the health concentration index." *Health Economics*, 12: 511–16.

COGGON, D., ROSE, G., and BARKER, D. J. P. (1997). *Epidemiology for the Uninitiated*, 4th edn. London: BMJ Publishing Group.

DE GRAEVE, D. and VAN OURTI, T. (2003). "The distributional impact of health financing: a review." *The World Economy*, 26: 1459–79.

ERREYGERS, G. (2009a). "Correcting the concentration index." *Journal of Health Economics*, 28/2: 504–15.

—— (2009b). "Correcting the concentration index: A reply to Wagstaff." *Journal of Health Economics*, 28/2: 521–4.

—— and VAN OURTI, T. (2010). "Measuring socioeconomic inequality in the health, health care and health financing by means of rank-dependent indices: a recipe for good practice." Tinbergen Institute discussion paper, 2010-076/3, Erasmus University Rotterdam.

—— CLARKE, P., and VAN OURTI, T. (2010). "Mirror, mirror, on the wall, who in this land is fairest of all? Revisiting the extended concentration index." Research paper no. 2010-015, Faculty of Applied Economics, University of Antwerp, Antwerp.

FEENY, D., FURLONG, W., TORRANCE, G. W., GOLDSMITH, C. H., ZHU, Z., DEPAUW, S., DENTON, M., and BOYLE, M. (2002). "Multi-attribute and single-attribute utility functions for the health utilities Index Mark 3 System." *Medical Care*, 40/2: 113–28.

FLEURBAEY, M. (2006). "Health, equity and social welfare." *Annales d'Economie et de Statistique*, 83/84: 21–59.

—— and SCHOKKAERT, E. (2009). "Unfair inequalities in health and health care." *Journal of Health Economics*, 28/1, 73–90.

FLORES, G., KRISHNAKUMAR, J., O'DONNELL, O., and van DOORSLAER, E. (2008). "Coping with health care costs: implications for the measurement of catastrophic expenditures and poverty." *Health Economics*, 17/12: 1393–412.

FURLONG, W. J., FEENY, D. H., TORRANCE, G. W., and BARR, R. D. (2001). "The Health Utilities Index (HUI) system for assessing health-related quality of life in clinical studies." *Annals of Medicine*, 33/5: 375–84.

GERDTHAM, U.-G. and JOHANNESSON, M. (2000). "Income-related inequality in life-years and quality-adjusted life-years." *Journal of Health Economics*, 19/6: 1007–26.

GRAVELLE, H. (2003). "Measuring income related inequality in health: standardization and the partial concentration index." *Health Economics* 12: 803–19.

—— MORRIS, S., and SUTTON M. (2006). "Economic studies of equity in the consumption of health care," in A. M. Jones (ed.), *Elgar Companion to Health Economics*. Cheltenham: Edward Elgar, 193–204.

GWATKIN, D., RUTSTEIN, S., JOHNSON, K., PANDE, R., and WAGSTAFF, A. (2000). "Socioeconomic differences in health, nutrition and population." Health, Nutrition and Population Discussion Paper, The World Bank, Washington, DC.

—— WAGSTAFF, A., and YAZBECK, A. (eds.) (2005). *Reaching the Poor with Health, Nutrition, and Population Services: What Works, What Doesn't, and Why?* Washington DC: The World Bank.

GWATKIN, D., RUTSTEIN, S., JOHNSON, K., SULIMAN, E., WAGSTAFF, A., and AMOUZOU, A. (2007). *Socio-Economic Differences in Health, Nutrition and Population Within Developing Countries: An Overview.* Washington DC: The World Bank.

HERNÁNDEZ-QUEVEDO, C., JONES, A. M., LÓPEZ-NICOLÁS, A., and RICE, N. (2006). "Socioeconomic inequalities in health: a comparative longitudinal analysis using the European Community Household Panel." *Social Science and Medicine*, 63: 1246–61.

HOSSEINPOOR, A. R., VAN DOORSLAER, E., SPEYBROECK, N., et al. (2006). "Decomposing socioeconomic inequality in infant mortality in Iran." *International Journal of Epidemiology*, 35/5: 1119–22.

IDLER, E. L. and BENYAMINI, Y. (1997). "Self-rated health and mortality: a review of twenty-seven community studies." *Journal of Health and Social Behavior*, 38: 21–37.

JONES, A. M. and LÓPEZ-NICOLÁS, A. (2004). "Measurement and explanation of socio-economic inequality in health with longitudinal data." *Health Economics*, 13: 1015–30.

—— KOOLMAN, X., and VAN DOORSLAER, E. (2006). "The impact of supplementary private health insurance on the use of specialists in selected European countries." *Annales d'Economie et de Statistique*, 83/84, 251–7.

KAKWANI, N. C. (1980). *Income Inequality and Poverty: Methods of Estimation and Policy Applications.* Oxford: Oxford University Press.

—— WAGSTAFF, A., and VAN DOORSLAER, E. (1997). "Socioeconomic inequalities in health: measurement, computation, and statistical inference." *Journal of Econometrics*, 77: 87–103.

KOOLMAN, X. and VAN DOORSLAER, E. (2004). "On the interpretation of a concentration index of inequality," *Health Economics*, 13/7: 649–56.

LAMBERT, P. J. (2001). *The Distribution and Redistribution of Income: A Mathematical Analysis*, 3rd edn. Manchester: Manchester University Press.

—— and ARONSON, J. R. (1993). "Inequality decomposition analysis and the Gini coefficient revisited." *Economic Journal*, 103/420: 1221–7.

LE GRAND, J. (1978). "The distribution of public expenditure: the case of health care." *Economica*, 45: 125–42.

—— (1987). "An international comparison of health inequalities." *European Economic Review*, 31: 182–91.

LINDEBOOM, M. and VAN DOORSLAER, E. (2004). "Cut-point shift and index shift in self-reported health." *Journal of Health Economics*, 23: 1083–99.

LINDELÖW, M. (2006). "Sometimes more equal than others: how health inequalities depend on the choice of welfare indicator." *Health Economics*, 15: 263–79.

LU, R. J., LEUNG, G. M., KWON, S., TIN, K. Y. K., VAN DOORSLAER, E., and O'DONNELL, O. (2007). "Horizontal equity in health care utilization—evidence from three high-income Asian economies." *Social Science and Medicine*, 64: 199–212.

MASANJA, H., SCHELLENBERG, J. A., DE SAVIGNY, D., MSHINDA, H., and VICTORA, C. G. (2005). "Impact of integrated management of childhood illness on inequalities in child health in rural Tanzania." *Health Policy and Planning*, 20/Suppl. 1: i77–i84.

MORRIS, S., SUTTON, M., and GRAVELLE, H. (2005). "Inequity and inequality in the use of health care in England: an empirical investigation." *Social Science and Medicine*, 60/6: 1251–66.

OAXACA, R.L. (1973). "Male–female wage differentials in urban labor markets." *International Economic Review*, 14: 693–709.

—— and RANSOM M. R. (1994). "On discrimination and the decomposition of wage differentials." *Journal of Econometrics*, 61/1: 5–21.

O'DONNELL, O., VAN DOORSLAER, E., and WAGSTAFF, A. (2006). "Decomposition of inequalities in health and health care," in A. M. Jones (ed.), *The Elgar Companion to Health Economics*. Cheltenham: Edward Elgar, 179–92.

—— —— RANNAN-ELIYA, R. P., et al. (2008a). "Who pays for health care in Asia." *Journal of Health Economics*, 27: 460–75.

—— —— WAGSTAFF, A., and LINDELÖW, M. (2008b). *Analyzing Health Equity Using Household Survey Data: A Guide to Techniques and Their Implementation*. Washington DC: The World Bank.

—— LÓPEZ NICOLÁS, Á. and VAN DOORSLAER, E. (2009). Growing richer and taller: explaining change in the distribution of child nutritional status during Vietnam's economic boom. *Journal of Development Economics*, 88/1: 45–58.

PEREIRA, J. A. (1998). "Inequality in infant mortality in Portugal 1971–1991," in P. Zweifel (ed.), *Health, the Medical Profession, and Regulation: Developments in Health Economics and Public Policy*, Vol 6. New York: Springer-Verlag, 75–93.

RAO, V. M. (1969). "Two decompositions of a concentration ratio." *Journal of the Royal Statistical Society. Series A (General)*, 132/3: 418–25.

SCHOKKAERT, E., DHAENE, G., and VAN DE VOORDE, C. (1998). "Risk adjustment and the trade-off between efficiency and risk selection: an application of the theory of fair compensation." *Health Economics*, 7: 465–80.

SHORROCKS, A. F. (1978). "Income inequality and income mobility." *Journal of Economic Theory*, 19: 376–93.

SUTTON, M. (2002). "Vertical and horizontal aspects of socio-economic inequity in general practitioner contacts in Scotland." *Health Economics*, 11/6: 537–49.

TANDON, A., MURRAY, C. J. L., SALOMON, J. A., and KING, G. (2003). "Statistical models for enhancing cross-population comparability." In C. J. L. Murray and D. B. Evans (eds.), *Health Systems Performance Assessment: Debates, Methods and Empiricisms*. Geneva: World Health Organization, 727–46.

VAN DE POEL, E., O'DONNELL, O. and VAN DOORSLAER, E. (2007). "Are urban children really healthier? Evidence from 47 developing countries." *Social Science and Medicine*, 65: 1986–2003.

—— HOSSEINPOOR, A. R., SPEYBROECK, N., VAN OURTI, T., and VEGA, J. (2008). "Socioeconomic inequality in malnutrition in developing countries." *Bulletin of the World Health Organisation*, 86/4: 282–91.

VAN DOORSLAER, E. and GERDTHAM, U.-G. (2003). "Does inequality in self-assessed health predict inequality in survival by income? Evidence from Swedish data." *Social Science and Medicine*, 57/9: 1621–9.

—— and JONES, A. M. (2003). "Inequalities in self-reported health: validation of a new approach to measurement." *Journal of Health Economics*, 22: 61–87.

—— and KOOLMAN, X. (2004). "Explaining the differences in income-related health inequalities across European countries." *Health Economics*, 13/7: 609–28.

—— WAGSTAFF, A., BLEICHRODT, H., et al. (1997). "Socioeconomic inequalities in health: some international comparisons." *Journal of Health Economics*, 16/1: 93–112.

—— KOOLMAN, X., and JONES, A. M. (2004a). "Explaining income-related inequalities in health care utilisation in Europe." *Health Economics*, 13/7: 629–47.

—— MASSERIA, C., and THE OECD HEALTH EQUITY GROUP (2004b) "Income-related inequality in the use of medical care in 21 OECD countries." In OECD (ed.), *Towards High-performing Health Systems*. Paris: OECD Health Policy Studies, 109–41.

VAN DOORSLAER, E., MASSERIA, C., KOOLMAN, X., and THE OECD HEALTH EQUITY GROUP (2006). "Inequalities in access to medical care by income in developed countries." *Canadian Medical Association Journal*, 174: 177–83.

——— O'DONNELL, O., RANNAN-ELIYA, R. P., et al. (2007). "Catastrophic payments for health care in Asia. *Health Economics*, 16/11: 1159–84.

——— VAN KIPPERSLUIS, H., O'DONNELL, O., and VAN OURTI, T. (2008). "Socioeconomic differences in health over the life cycle: evidence and explanations." *Netspar Panel Paper*, Vol. 12. Tilburg: Netspar.

VAN OURTI, T. (2004). "Measuring horizontal inequity in Belgian health care using a Gaussian random effects two part count data model." *Health Economics*. 13/7: 705–24.

——— VAN DOORSLAER, E., and KOOLMAN, X. (2009). "The effect of income growth and inequality on health inequality: theory and empirical evidence from the European Panel." *Journal of Health Economics*, 28/3: 525–39.

WAGSTAFF, A. (2000) "Socioeconomic inequalities in child mortality: comparisons across nine developing countries." *Bulletin of the World Health Organization*, 78/1: 19–29.

——— (2002). "Inequality aversion, health inequalities and health achievement." *Journal of Health Economics*, 21: 627–41.

——— (2005a). "The bounds of the concentration index when the variable of interest is binary, with an application to immunization inequality." *Health Economics*, 14: 429–32.

——— (2005b). "Inequality decomposition and geographic targeting with applications to China and Vietnam." *Health Economics*, 14/6: 649–53.

——— (2009a). "Measuring financial protection in health," in P. Smith, E. Mossialos, and S. Leatherman (eds.), *Performance Measurement for Health System Improvement: Experiences, Challenges and Prospects*. Cambridge: Cambridge University Press, 114–37.

——— (2009b). "Correcting the concentration index: a comment." *Journal of Health Economics*, 28/2: 516–20.

——— and LINDELÖW, M. (2007). "Progressivity in the financing of decentralized government health programs: a decomposition." *Health Economics*, 16/11: 1271–5.

——— and NGUYEN, N. (2004). "Poverty and survival prospects of Vietnamese children under Doi Moi," in P. Glewwe, N. Agrawal, and D. Dollar (eds.), *Economic Growth, Poverty and Household Welfare in Vietnam*. Washington, DC: World Bank, 313–50.

——— and WATANABE, N. (2000). "Socioeconomic inequalities in child malnutrition in the developing world." Policy Research Working paper, 2434, World Bank, Washington, DC.

——— ——— (2003). "What difference does the choice of SES make in health inequality measurement?" *Health Economics*, 12/10: 885–90.

——— and VAN DOORSLAER, E. (2000). "Equity in health care finance and delivery," in A. J. Culyer and J.P. Newhouse (eds.), *Handbook of Health Economics*, Vol. 1. Amsterdam: North Holland, 1803–62.

——— ——— (2003). "Catastrophe and impoverishment in paying for health care: with applications to Vietnam 1993–1998." *Health Economics*, 12/11: 921–33.

——— ——— (2004). "Overall versus socioeconomic health inequality: a measurement framework and two empirical illustrations." *Health Economics*, 13: 297–301.

——— ——— and PACI, P. (1989). "Equity in the finance and delivery of health care: some tentative cross-country comparisons." *Oxford Review of Economic Policy*, 5: 89–112.

——— PACI, P., and VAN DOORSLAER, E. (1991). "On the measurement of inequalities in health." *Social Science and Medicine*, 33/5: 545–57.

—— VAN DOORSLAER E., and WATANABE N. (2003). "On decomposing the causes of health sector inequalities with an application to malnutrition inequalities in Vietnam." *Journal of Econometrics*, 112: 207–23.

WARE, J. E. and GANDEK, B. (1998). "Overview of the SF-36 health survey and the international quality of life assessment (IQOLA) project." *Journal of Clinical Epidemiology*, 51: 903–12.

WEBSTER, J., LINES, J., BRUCE, J., ARMSTRONG SCHELLENBERG, J. R. M., and HANSON, K. (2005). "Which delivery systems reach the poor? A review of equity of coverage of ever-treated nets, never-treated nets, and immunization to reduce child mortality in Africa." *Lancet Infectious Diseases*, 5: 709–17.

YAZBECK, A. (2009). *Attacking Inequality in the Health Sector: A Synthesis of Evidence and Tools.* Washington, DC: The World Bank.

YITZHAKI, S. (1983). "On an extension of the Gini index." *International Economic Review*, 24/3: 617–28.

ZHANG, Q. and WANG, Y. (2007) "Using concentration index to study changes in socio-economic inequality of overweight among US adolescents between 1971 and 2002." *International Journal of Epidemiology*, 36: 916–25.

ZHENG, B. (2008) "Measuring inequality with ordinal data: a note." *Research on Economic Inequality*, 16: 177–88.

CHAPTER 36

....

INTER-GENERATIONAL
ASPECTS OF HEALTH CARE

....

LOUISE SHEINER

THE physical process of aging means that the use of health services varies significantly by age. This association between age and health care consumption raises a number of issues related to inter-generational equity. In particular, how do society's resources get allocated across age groups, and how will increases in health spending affect this distribution over time? To what degree will the aging of the population increase public sector health care burdens? And, finally, what are the inter-generational implications of public sector health care spending and financing?

36.1 HEALTH SPENDING BY AGE

....

In all developed countries, health spending systematically increases with age (with the exception of the high level of spending on infants.) Figure 36.1 plots the age distribution of health spending in the United States in 2004.[1] The data show that health spending increases gradually through middle age, before accelerating sharply at older ages. Much of this sharp acceleration is accounted for by expenditures on home health and nursing home care, which are very highly concentrated on those 85 years and older. However, even without these long-term care expenditures, health spending increases markedly with age.

---

[1] The graph uses the data on health spending by age (CMS 2004) reported at the bottom of Figure 36.1. The x values are simply the middle age in the age range of each group, with ninety chosen as the plotting point for the 85+ age group.

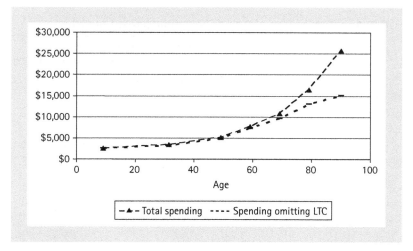

FIGURE 36.1 Health spending by age group, US, 2004
Source: CMS (2004)

Table 36.1 Age Distribution of Health Spending, United States, 2004

Age Group	0–18	19–44	45–54	55–64	65–74	75–84	85+
Spending	$2,650	$3,370	$5,210	$7,787	$10,778	$16,389	$25,691
Spending omitting LTC	$2,569	$3,240	$4,934	$7,405	$9,684	$13,032	$15,116
LTC	$80	$130	$276	$382	$1,094	$3,357	$10,575

Source: CMS (2004)

36.1.1 Cross-country Comparisons of the Age Distribution of Health Spending

While this general relationship is a characteristic of health spending in most countries, the exact relationship between age and health spending varies considerably (Sheiner 2004; EC 2006; OECD 2006). This cross-country variation is likely the product of both differences in the age profile of health needs (i.e. differences in the relative health of the population by age) as well as institutional factors that affect prices seen by the consumer or access to technology.

It is useful to examine both total health spending and spending excluding long-term care.[2] Countries differ substantially on whether long-term care is provided formally or informally (EC 2006), and there may be differences in the extent to which formal long-term care services are deemed health expenditures versus other non-health social

---

[2] The OECD (2006) and the EC (2006) long-term projections analyze long-term care spending separately from other types of health care spending.

Table 36.2 Age Distribution of Health Spending across Countries

	US (1999)	Canada (1999)	Germany (1998)	Netherlands (2000)	Australia (1998)	New Zealand (1998)	UK (1998)	Belgium (1998)
Ratios of per capita health spending								
1. >65/<65	3.9	5.2		4.9	4.1	4.7	3.9	4.5
2. 75–84/65–74	1.4	1.9		2.2		1.9	2.3	1.7
3. 85+/75–84	1.7	2.2		2.3		2.0	2.0	1.9
4. 75+/65–74	1.7	2.4		3.8	2.0	2.3	2.9	2.1
Ratios of per capita health spending excluding long-term care								
1. >65/<65	3.7	4.1	3.1	2.9	3.2	4.2	3.1	3.5
2. 75–84/65–74	1.2	1.6	1.3	1.3		1.3	1.7	1.4
3. 85+/75–84	1.0	1.6	1.1	1.0		1.5	1.6	1.2
4. 75+/65–74	1.4	1.8	1.3	1.3	1.4	1.5	2.0	1.5

Source: Sheiner (2004)

services. Furthermore, long-term care services are, in many ways, different from other forms of health care. In particular, spending on long-term care is less likely to be affected by technological change than other forms of health care, and thus is less relevant in thinking about how future technological advances might affect the age distribution of health spending[3] (Cutler and Sheiner 2001).

Table 36.2 reports various measures of health spending gradients across countries from Sheiner (2004).[4] According to her data, the ratio of total health spending of the elderly relative to the non-elderly ranges from 3.9 in the UK and the US to 5.2 in Canada; that is, health spending per elderly person is about four times as high as health spending per non-elderly person in the UK, and about five times higher in Canada. With the exception of the Netherlands, the pattern across countries is similar for spending excluding long-term care, with Canada and New Zealand allocating relatively large shares of spending to the elderly, and the UK and Australia allocating relatively small shares.

Perhaps a more interesting comparison is the relationship between health spending and age *within* the elderly population. The elderly have different sources of health insurance coverage than the non-elderly in a number of countries, and may also have different access to certain types of services. In the US, for example, the elderly are covered by Medicare, whereas the non-elderly are covered by a mixture of private and public insurance. Because

[3] Of course, to the extent that advances in technology prolong life in such a way as to increase the demand for long-term care, technological advances will indirectly affect such spending.

[4] Cross-country comparisons of the age distribution of health spending are difficult because each country gathers data and estimates age distributions in different ways. Recently, the OECD and the EC have undertaken efforts to compile such data on a more standardized basis, but nevertheless, countries still differ on the accuracy and comprehensiveness of their data. See OECD (2006) and EC (2005).

Medicare sets the prices it pays to providers, differences in spending between the elderly and the non-elderly may reflect differences in prices, rather than differences in actual health services. Furthermore, if the differential use of high technology accounts for the variation in the distribution of spending across countries, such differences are likely to be more apparent in comparisons of the relatively young old and the oldest old. Increases in life expectancy make these differences particularly germane to forecasts of future health expenditures, as the oldest old will comprise an increasing share of the elderly.

The bottom two rows of the table report results from Sheiner (2004) on the age distribution of acute health spending within the elderly population. Relative to 65–74-year-olds, average spending on 75–84-year-olds varies from a low of 1.2 times as much in the US to a high of 1.7 times as much in the UK. Relative spending on the oldest old shows similar variation: in the US and in the Netherlands, spending on those 85 and over is about the same as on those 75–84, whereas in Canada and the UK, spending on those 85 and over is about 60 percent higher than on those 75 to 84.

There are several possible explanations for these differences. Sheiner points out that the countries with the highest ratios of spending of the oldest old relative to the younger old are those countries that use new technologies less intensively. She hypothesizes that, because new technologies tend to be used on the younger old before they diffuse to the older old, a faster rate of technology adoption could account for the differences in the relative spending by age.

However, these differences could be the result of a host of other factors as well, including differential access to health services, arising out of differences in the ratio of coinsurance to income, as well as differences in the pricing and composition of services used by the oldest old relative to the younger old. A deeper understanding of the source of these differences across countries would be helpful in projecting future age/health profiles and also in analyzing the potential effects of different health reforms.

36.1.2 Changes in the Age Profiles of Health Spending over Time

An important question in forecasting future health care costs for the elderly is whether the distribution of health spending by age will change over time. Analysts have identified a number of reasons why the relationship between health spending and age might not be stable.

36.1.2.1 *Effects of Technological Growth*

Technological advances in the treatment of illness might affect the distribution of health spending by age. For example, it is clear that advances in the treatment of premature babies have led to a significant concentration in spending on the youngest young. Similarly, technological advances that allow for better treatments for the very ill might lead to an increased concentration of spending on the elderly, and technological advances that are focused on prevention or treatment of chronic conditions might lead to a less concentrated spending distribution.

Cutler and Meara (1998) used a series of national medical expenditure surveys to document the distribution of health spending in the United States by age over time. Their analysis showed an increasing concentration of spending on the elderly between 1963 and 1987, which was accompanied by an increase in the intensity of service use by the sickest elderly patients. Their results suggested that increased use of high technology in medicine could lead to a more highly concentrated distribution of spending.

However, as noted above, differences in the health spending of the elderly and the non-elderly in the US are difficult to interpret because of the different sources of insurance coverage. In particular, the rate of growth of Medicare reimbursements has differed from the growth rate of private sector reimbursements, and so the changes in nominal spending might not reflect differences in real health expenditures. It would not be reasonable to attribute the changes in the age/health profiles to technology if changes in nominal spending reflect differences in prices of services rather than differences in quantity of services.

To address the problem with the US data, Sheiner examined the trends in the distribution of health spending in Canada and Japan over the 1980s and 1990s (Figures 36.2 and 36.3; reproduced from Sheiner 2004). She finds no evidence of an increasing concentration of spending on the elderly in Canada between 1980 and 2000—either for total health spending or spending excluding long-term care, suggesting that technological innovation has not had a disproportionate effect on the spending of the elderly. Similarly, the distribution of spending between the elderly and non-elderly in Japan was relatively stable.

Sheiner (2004) also examines the distribution of health spending for the elderly of different ages in the US during the 1990s. This comparison is not subject to the same

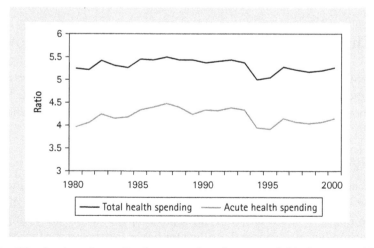

FIGURE 36.2 Distribution of spending by age in Canada: Ratio of elderly to non-elderly health spending

Source: Sheiner (2004)

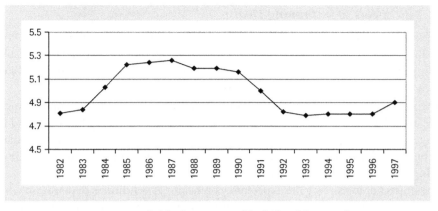

FIGURE 36.3 Ratio of elderly to non-elderly health spending, Japan
Source: Sheiner (2004)

problems as the comparison of the elderly and non-elderly because Medicare is the primary insurance coverage for virtually all persons 65 or older in the United States. Her results show no evidence of an increase in concentration of health spending on the oldest old (Figure 36.4).

This finding was reinforced by the results of Meara, White, and Cutler (2004), who found that the earlier trend toward increasingly concentrated spending on the elderly had reversed itself. They attributed the reversal to reforms to Medicare's physician, hospital, and home health payment systems and to the differential coverage of prescription drugs between Medicare and the private sector.

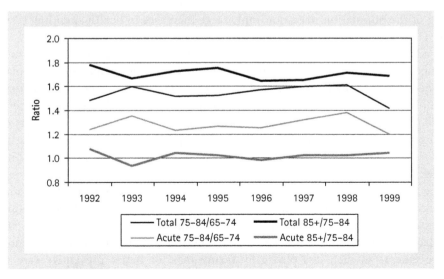

FIGURE 36.4 Distribution of US health spending by age group
Source: Sheiner (2004)

36.1.2.2 *Effects of Improving Health*

While average health spending increases with age, age is not a good predictor of health spending at the individual level. Health spending is far better explained by measures of health status (OECD 2006). A key question in assessing how age profiles are likely to shift over time is how the health of the population will evolve.

The most easily measured indicator of health improvements is the ongoing increase in life expectancy. Over the past twenty-five years, life expectancy has increased by an average of almost 1 percent per year in the US, and projections of future populations assume that life expectancy will continue to increase over time.[5] Predictions for other developed countries are for similar increases.[6]

The impact of increasing life expectancy on health expenditures depends on whether the additional years of life are spent in poor health or in good health. In the past, most projections of health expenditures assumed that the age distribution of health expenditures would remain constant. The 85-year-olds of tomorrow, for example, were assumed to have the same health status as the 85-year-olds of today. Under this assumption, increases in life expectancy raise total health spending because they increase the number of old people and because the increase is concentrated in the oldest old—those with the highest health expenditures.

The assumption of constant age distribution of health spending has been criticized as overly pessimistic. It is well-documented that, across many countries, health expenditures climb sharply as a person approaches death and that time until death is a better predictor of health spending than is age (Sabelhaus, Simpson, and Topoleski 2004; EC 2005; Gray 2005; OECD 2006). The relationship between spending and proximity to death means that increases in longevity, which lower proximity to death at any given age, are likely to reduce health spending at any given age, and that the aging of the population need not imply large increases in health spending (Zweifel et al. 1999).

In addition to the ongoing increases in life expectancy, researchers have documented an ongoing reduction in disability in a number of countries (Jacobzone, Cambois, and Robine 2000). As noted by Cutler and Sheiner (2001), even when proximity to death is accounted for, measures of disability are good predictors of health spending. They estimated that including both proximity to death and projected declines in disability could lower projected medical expenditures by about 15 percent by 2050. However, the recent steep rise in rates of obesity threatens to reverse the trend of declining disability (Sturm, Ringel, and Andreyeva 2004).

The relationship between disability and longevity and health expenditures may be more complicated than has often been acknowledged by this strand of the literature. To the extent that increases in longevity and reductions in disability arise from factors unrelated to contemporaneous health spending—for example, reductions in smoking, improvements in diet, less physically taxing jobs, or better preventive care when

---

[5] Social Security Administration (2008).
[6] OECD (2006).

young—then age-specific health spending for the elderly should decline over time. However, if the reductions in disability and increase in longevity are attributable to improved and more costly medical care, then the relationship between improved health and the age distribution of health spending is more ambiguous, as the increased spending that produces these health benefits might outweigh the reductions in spending associated with improved health. Indeed, several studies find that increased use of technology increases life expectancy and lowers disability, but also increases health spending (Jacobzone 2003; Chernew et al. 2005; Goldman et al. 2005; Holly 2005; Lubitz 2005).

Nonetheless, in recent years, many official projections of future health spending have incorporated some effects of likely improvements in health over time. For example, the Congressional Budget Office now incorporates "death costs" in their long-term Medicare projections.[7] Using their methodology, including the effects of time-to-death has a relatively small effect on projected Medicare expenditures, reducing them by about 5 percent by 2080. The European Commission projections include death costs as well as other improvements in health in their long-range projections (EC 2006). On average, their preferred scenario assumes that improvements in health lower health spending by about 25 percent by 2050.

36.2 Implications of Demographic Change for Aggregate Health Spending

The age composition of the population in most developed nations will undergo dramatic changes in the next few decades. In the US, for example, the population over age 65 is projected to rise from 12 percent today to 20 percent by 2035.[8] In Japan and many European countries, the elderly share of the population is already significantly higher than in the US and it is projected to continue rising. For example, in Germany, the elderly share of the population is already 20 percent and it is projected to rise to 30 percent by 2035.[9]

Population aging stems from two sources: increases in life expectancy and reductions in fertility. The previous section addressed how increases in life expectancy and other improvements in health might affect per capita health spending of the elderly. A more important source of aging has to do not with increases in life expectancy, but with past reductions in fertility. The dramatic decline in fertility following the post-war baby boom (in the US, from a peak of 3.7 in 1957 to roughly 1.7 by 1977) means that the ratio of elderly to non-elderly in the population will increase substantially over the next twenty years or so. As noted by Cutler, Poterba, Sheiner, and Summers (1990) most of the increase in the elderly share of the population between now and 2030 stems from past reductions in fertility, rather than gains in life expectancy.[10]

---

[7] See Sabelhaus, Simpson, and Topoleski (2004) for a description of CBO's methodology.

[8] Intermediate Scenario, Social Security Trustees Report 2007.

[9] Eurostat Population projections 2008.

[10] Most projections assume that fertility rates stabilize but that life expectancy continues to increase over time. Thus, over the long run, life expectancy increases are the primary cause of population aging.

The reduction in fertility has two effects on health spending as a share of GDP—one direct and one indirect. The direct effect stems from the fact that the elderly spend substantially more on health care than the non-elderly. Thus, an increase in the share of elderly in the population raises average health spending per capita.

The indirect effect stems from the relationship between fertility and per capita GDP. Given its capital stock, a nation's output is determined by the size of its labor force and the productivity of its workers. A reduction in fertility eventually translates into a decline in the working age population and, barring major changes in labor force participation or immigration, in a lower ratio of workers to population, thus lowering GDP per capita even as GDP per worker is unaffected.[11]

A simple overlapping generations model demonstrates these effects:

- There are two generations, young and old.
- There are N_y young and N_o old.
- The elderly share of the population is α.
- The average health spending of the old, HC_o, is β times the average health spending of the young, HC_y, with $\beta > 1$.
- The labor force participation of the young and the old are L_y and L_o, respectively.
- GDP is equal to output per worker, P, times the number of workers, $L_y N_y + L_o N_o$.

Then, aggregate health spending can be written as:

$$HC_T = N_y HC_y + N_o HC_o = HC_y(N_y + \beta N_o)$$

Per capita health care is

$$PCH = \frac{HC_T}{N_y + N_o} = \frac{HC_y(N_y + \beta N_o)}{N_y + N_o} = HC_y((1-\alpha) + \alpha\beta) = HC_y(1 + \alpha(\beta - 1))$$

Given that $\beta > 1$, per capita health care spending increases with α, the elderly share of the population. Per capita health spending also increases with β, the ratio of elderly to non-elderly health spending.

The effect of aging and improving health on β is ambiguous. Holding constant relative health needs by age, aging leads to an increase in β as the share of the very old increases.[12] However, an improvement in the health of the elderly lowers β. Depending on how much improvements in health lower age-specific health spending, β may increase or decrease over time.

---

[11] See Elmendorf and Sheiner (2000) for an overview of the macroeconomic effects of aging on GDP and living standards.

[12] As the baby boomers enter retirement, the share of the oldest old in the elderly population declines a bit. However, as the baby boomers age, the share of the oldest old climbs significantly (Jacobzone, Cambois, and Robine 2000).

To calculate health care spending as a share of GDP, we write GDP per capita as:

$$P\frac{Workers}{Population} = P\frac{L_y N_y + L_o N_o}{N_y + N_o} = P((1-\alpha)L_y + \alpha L_o) = P(L_y - \alpha(L_y - L_o))$$

As long as the labor force participation of the young, L_y, exceeds that of the old, L_o, then an increase in the elderly share of the population, α, lowers per capita GDP. Just as the improving health of the elderly can lower the relative health spending on the elderly, β, it is also plausible that the improving health of the elderly might increase the labor force participation of the elderly, thereby offsetting some of the effects of aging on per capita GDP.[13]

Putting these two pieces together, we can write health spending as a share of GDP as the ratio of per capita health care spending to per capita GDP:

$$\frac{HC_T}{GDP} = \frac{HC_y}{P}\frac{(1+\alpha(\beta-1))}{(L_y - \alpha(L_y - L_o))}$$

This equation includes all the important factors underlying the relationship between aging and health care spending as a share of GDP—the elderly share of the population, the relative health of the elderly, and the relative labor force participation of the elderly.[14] As can be seen, population aging increases health spending as a share of GDP because (1) the elderly spend relatively more on health care and (2) they are less likely to participate in the labor force.

In addition, the first term, $\frac{HC_y}{P}$, which is the ratio of per capita spending on the young relative to output per worker, measures the relative cost of health spending.[15] If per capita health spending rises with productivity, then this term is a constant. If per capita health spending rises faster than productivity, then this ratio increases over time, boosting the health care spending share of GDP.

The growth rate of $\frac{HC_y}{P}$ is generally referred to as "excess cost growth" and assumptions about how this term will evolve over time are key to long-term projections of health spending.[16] In most countries, the relative cost of health care has been growing

---

[13] See Sheiner, Sichel, and Slifman (2007) for a discussion of the magnitude of the increase in labor force participation necessary to offset the macroeconomic effects of aging.

[14] These are the factors considered in the OECD (2006).

[15] The health care of the young in this model can be thought of as the age and sex adjusted health spending that is typically used in exercises measuring the relative cost of health spending.

[16] Excess cost growth is typically defined as the excess of health spending per capita over GDP per capita, instead of GDP per worker (implicitly, this definition implies that the income elasticity of spending is one, so that any growth in the ratio of spending to income is "excess" of what can be explained). In steady state, the ratio of workers to population is constant, and there is no difference between the two concepts. During the demographic transition, however, the ratio of workers is declining and thus per capita income is increasing more slowly than productivity. The EC (2006) report discusses which of these measures of cost growth is more reasonable as a baseline—if health care demand grows with income, than the income concept is appropriate. However, to the extent that health care is a labor-intensive industry, increases in economy-wide productivity can increase the relative cost of health care.

significantly faster than productivity. As noted in OECD (2006), age-adjusted per capita health spending in OECD countries grew, on average, one percentage point faster than per capita GDP between 1981 and 2002, and one and a half percentage points faster than GDP between 1970 and 2002, with the slowdown in health spending growth during the latter period reflecting cost cutting measures taken by OECD countries. In the US, per capita health spending increased at a rate of about two percentage points faster than per capita GDP between 1970 and 2005 (CBO 2007). However, analysts have found that roughly half of this increase is attributable to changes in administrative costs, the structure of insurance, and relative prices, and demographics, with the remaining roughly one and a quarter percentage point increase attributable to "excess cost growth" (Newhouse 1992; Cutler 1995; Smith, Heffler, and Freeland 2000; Follette and Sheiner 2008).

There is a great deal of uncertainty surrounding the likely path of future health care spending. On the one hand, health spending has continued to grow faster than GDP for decades; on the other hand, health spending growth must slow to the rate of GDP growth eventually or else it would eventually comprise 100 percent of GDP growth. Most long-term projections assume that health spending growth will slow gradually to the rate of per capita GDP growth, although the pace of that slowdown differs significantly between projections.[17]

36.3 IMPLICATIONS OF DEMOGRAPHIC CHANGE FOR GOVERNMENT BUDGETS

Much of health care spending is publicly financed. The average public share of health spending is about 75 percent in the OECD countries, ranging from a high of 90 percent (Luxembourg) to a low of about 45 percent (the United States and Greece) (OECD 2007). This substantial government involvement in health care financing means that macroeconomic challenges are also budgetary challenges.

Incorporating government financing into our simple model is easy:

Let S_y be the share of the young's health spending that is government financed and let $S_y + \lambda$ be the share of the old's health spending that is government financed.

---

[17] For example, the Medicare Trustees (2007) assume that per capita health spending grows one percentage point faster than per capita GDP on average over the next seventy-five years, with faster growth in the near term and slower growth further out. OECD (2006) presents two scenarios—one where per capita health spending continues to grow at a rate one percentage point faster than per capita GDP, and another where cost controls gradually bring the growth of health spending in line with GDP growth.

Then, public spending on health care is equal to

$$S_y HC_y N_y + (S_y + \lambda) HC_y \beta N_o$$

Per capita public health spending on health care is:

$$S_y HC_y + (1 + \alpha(\beta - 1)) + \lambda \alpha \beta HC_y$$

and public health spending as a share of GDP is

$$\frac{HC_y}{P} \frac{S_y(1 + \alpha(\beta - 1)) + \lambda \alpha \beta}{L_y - \alpha(L_y - L_o)}$$

36.3.1 Government Financing by Age

If the government financed an equal share of the per capita spending of the young and the old, then $\lambda = 0$, and government health spending as a share of GDP would be a constant fraction of total health spending as a share of GDP. But if the government finances more of the health care of the elderly than of the non-elderly, then $\lambda > 0$, and aging has an additional impact on government health spending over and above its impact on national health spending—as the share of the elderly increases, the share of health spending financed by the government also increases.

This is clearly the case in the US, where all the elderly are covered by Medicare, but only some of the non-elderly receive publicly-financed care through Medicaid or other low-income programs. In 2004, for example, 67 percent of the health spending of the elderly was publicly financed, compared with 33 percent of the health spending of the non-elderly. Because Medicare is financed by the federal government whereas Medicaid is jointly financed with the states, the federal government's health spending is even more skewed toward the elderly than total government spending. In 2004, the federal government financed roughly 60 percent of the health spending of the elderly but only 20 percent of the health spending of the non-elderly.[18] The increased public financing of health spending arising from the increased elderly population share accounts for most of the increase in projected federal health spending over the next thirty years (CBO 2008).

While other countries do not have such a stark distinction between spending for the non-elderly and the elderly, the public share of health spending tends to be higher for the elderly than the non-elderly (Colombo and Tapay 2004). In Canada, for example, the average public share of health spending in 2001 was 65 percent for the non-elderly but 79 percent for the elderly. Some of this difference is attributable to programmatic differences—the Canadian government provides the elderly larger subsidies for prescription drugs and dental visits than the non-elderly, and some is due to differences in the

---

[18] All of these calculations are based on CMS (2004).

composition of spending. In particular, spending on prescription drugs and non-physician professionals is mostly privately financed. These two categories of spending represent a smaller share of the total health spending of the elderly than the non-elderly, thus raising the publicly financed share of the health spending for the elderly relative to the non-elderly.[19]

36.3.2 Endogenous Changes in Public Financing

As noted above, recent long-term projections of health spending have attempted to adjust for the improving health of the elderly, likely changes in labor force participation, and rates of growth of health spending.

However, one factor that is typically treated as a constant is the share of health spending that is government financed. As already discussed, to the extent that the government finances a larger share of the health spending of the elderly, this will understate the government's likely future burden and budgetary effects.

In addition, if per capita health spending continues to increase more rapidly than per capita GDP, there may be another reason to anticipate changes in the public financing of health benefits. As health spending increases as a share of income, the costs of private insurance and out-of-pocket payments can become prohibitive, particularly for those with low income and relatively large health expenditures. This increased private burden of health spending may prompt changes in government policy.

Follette and Sheiner (2005) studied the evolution of public financing of health expenditures in the United States. They found that the share of health spending in the United States that is publicly financed has been increasing over time, particularly for those with low income. Because of this increased public role, health spending as a share of income has increased much more slowly for the low income groups than has overall health spending as a share of GDP. For example, if the public share of health care had remained at the level it was in 1970, by 2008, the elderly in the lowest income quintile would have been spending 38 percent of their income on private insurance premiums and out of pocket payments; instead, Follette and Sheiner estimate that the share in 2008 would be just 25 percent.[20] Looking forward, they note that, under the assumption of 1 percentage point excess cost growth, without changes in the share of health spending that is publicly financed, health spending for the lowest quintile of elderly would reach about 30 percent of income by 2030 and 40 percent of income by 2050. Under the assumption of two per-

---

[19] Author's calculations from data in Statistics Canada (2001).

[20] The income share of health spending for the lowest-income quintile elderly climbed to almost 39 percent by 2004, as prescription drugs (which were not covered by Medicare at the time) consumed a larger share of health spending. Subsequently, Medicare was expanded to provide subsidized prescription drug coverage, with the largest subsidies for those with low income. Follette and Sheiner (2008) point to this expansion of public funding as an example of the public reaction function.

centage point excess cost growth, these shares would be 40 percent and 60 percent, respectively. To the extent that the government continues to expand low-income subsidies so as to prevent such increases in private health spending and the consequent family budget pressures, current projections of government health spending likely understate the demands on public budgets.

It is very difficult to find data on private health spending by age and income in other countries. However, given that, in most countries, a significant share of health spending is private and the fact that the health spending of the elderly is so much higher than that of the non-elderly, the private health expenses of the elderly most likely exceed those of the non-elderly. In this case, if per capita health spending continues to increase faster than income, then, as in the US, private health spending will likely become unacceptably burdensome for the low-income elderly, and there will be demand for increased public subsidies. Thus, projections that assume that the public share of health spending is constant will likely understate the budgetary challenges faced by governments with developed health systems.

36.4 Inter-generational Transfers in Public Health Spending

Health spending has two attributes that raise the question of inter-generational transfers.[21] First, health care spending varies by age. Second, health care is heavily subsidized by government. If health care, paid either directly out-of-pocket or through insurance, were privately purchased, then there would be little scope for inter-generational transfers—people would simply choose what to spend their money on, and it would not matter whether it was health care or something else.[22] People would either consume less

---

[21] It is important to distinguish between the question of fairness and the calculations of inter-generational transfers. The existence of the transfers reflects, at least in part, the societal viewpoint that unequal access to appropriate health care is in itself unfair, and, thus the existence of inter-generational transfers does not necessarily imply that the health system is inequitable. Van Doorslaer and Ourti (Chapter 35, this volume) and Olsen (Chapter 34, this volume) discuss the various approaches to defining and measuring inter-generational equity in health care.

[22] Government can induce inter-generational transfers through regulation. For example, insurance market regulations that require community rating can lead to implicit subsidies for those with higher expected health spending. In addition, there is the possibility that, even with private health insurance, there is some inter-generational redistribution. Sheiner (1999) explores whether employer-provided insurance implicitly subsidizes older workers. If the wage offset for the value of employer-provided insurance doesn't vary by age, then younger workers would be subsidizing the insurance premiums of older workers. However, she finds evidence that wages do vary based on the expected value of health expenditures, and thus, there is no inter-generational redistribution. The possibility that retiree health benefits are financed by current workers also seems plausible, but it has not been examined empirically.

when young in order to finance health care when older, or they would spend more on health care and less on other goods when they were older.[23] However, the fact that health care spending is government subsidized raises the question of whether certain cohorts receive government subsidies at the expense of others.

This question has been heavily analyzed for public pensions, particularly the social security system in the United States. Most public pensions are largely pay-as-you-go; that is, current benefits are financed by taxes on current workers. This system has well-known characteristics. In particular, the system depends on the ratio of workers to beneficiaries—as this ratio falls, benefits need to be cut or taxes increased. In order to assess inter-generational fairness, analysts examine rates of return on pension contributions (generally payroll taxes) and the net present values different cohorts receive from the system over their lifetimes.[24] Early cohorts—those who received benefits without paying much in taxes—tend to have the highest rates of return, while rates decline for older cohorts. In steady state, the rate of return in any pay-as-you-go system must equal the growth of aggregate income.[25]

The public provision of health care has the same basic inter-generational structure as public pensions—the taxes on workers exceed their current benefits, while the dollar value of benefits to the elderly exceeds their taxes. However, because much of government health insurance is financed through general revenues rather than payroll taxes, the link between taxes paid and benefits received is less clear cut than for public pensions. In addition, public pensions provide cash whereas public health programs provide health insurance, which can be hard to value, particularly at the individual level. Nonetheless, the dollar flows between generations provide a reasonable measure of the inter-generational impacts of publicly provided health insurance.

[23] As discussed in Elmendorf and Sheiner (2000), whether health care is substitutable for other forms of contemporaneous consumption or whether it should be treated separately affects the way health spending affects saving. Martins, de la Maisonneuve, and Bjornerud (2006) suggest that private health care spending should be viewed as substitutable for other consumption, whereas public health care spending needs to be treated differently.

[24] As noted by Steuerle and Bakija (1994) in reference to social security, calculations of rates of returns and net present values can yield different conclusions about the distribution of benefits by income. For example, the rates of return on social security contributions for lower-income workers might be higher than for high-income workers, but because the contributions of high-income workers are larger, they might receive a larger dollar value of subsidy when calculated in net present value terms. This is not likely to be an issue with Medicare, however, as the benefits received do not vary as much by income.

[25] The steady state rate of return from a pay-as-you-go system is equal to the rate of growth of the economy's wage bill, or $(1+n)(1+g)-1$, where n and g are the rates of labor force and productivity growth, respectively. This rate of growth is believed to be less than the interest rate, r, so that payroll contributions earn less than they would if they were invested. The loss from the system experienced by later cohorts is the product of their contributions and the difference between r and $(1+n)(1+g)-1$. The larger are the benefits paid to earlier cohorts, the larger are the payroll contributions and the larger the net present value loss for later cohorts.

36.4.1 Measures of Inter-generational Transfers

The parallel between public health care and public pensions is clearer in the United States than in other countries: the United States provides public health insurance to its elderly through Medicare, and part of Medicare spending is financed explicitly through payroll taxes. But, even in countries with universal health systems, the health systems typically involve significant inter-generational transfers. As noted by Corak, Lietz, and Sutherland (2005), taxes paid in Europe are heavily weighted toward the working-age population, while benefits are weighted toward the elderly. Thus, the health system can be viewed as having the same structure as the pension system, with the working age population paying "net taxes" equal to taxes paid less health benefits received, and the elderly receiving "net benefits" equal to health benefits received less taxes paid.

Cutler and Sheiner (2000) analyzed the rates of returns received by different cohorts from the Medicare program.[26] Their results, reproduced in Table 36.3 and Figure 36.5, illustrate the patterns of redistribution (but not the magnitude) implicit in the health systems of most developed countries. The first line of Table 36.3, labeled baseline, presents the internal rates of return realized by different cohorts under the assumption that per capita health growth slows to the rate of per capita GDP growth over twenty-five years.[27] As expected, the early cohorts experienced very high rates of return from the Medicare program. For example, the rate of return on the taxes paid by the cohort born in 1910—whose members turned 65 in 1975, just a few years after Medicare's inception—was about 28 percent. Subsequent generations receive lower returns, but, because

Table 36.3 Internal Rates of Return to Medicare

	Cohort Born In							
	1910	1920	1930	1940	1950	1960	1970	1980
Baseline	27.6%	12.1%	7.0%	4.6%	3.4%	2.8%	2.5%	2.2%
Reforms to close deficit								
Raise payroll tax 2 pct pts	27.6	12.1	7.0	4.5	3.0	2.2	1.6	1.3
Cut benefits 38 percent	27.6	11.6	5.5	3.0	2.1	1.7	1.4	1.3
Social Security Rate of Return	8.4	5.7	4	2.7	2.2	1.8	1.9	1.9

Source: Cutler and Sheiner (2000)

[26] Medicare is separated into three parts—Part A, which mostly covers hospital care, Part B, which finances physician expenses, and the new part D, which covers prescription drugs. Part A is funded by payroll taxes, whereas Parts B and D are funded by general revenues. Cutler and Sheiner used the age distribution of income taxes to allocate the burden of the general revenues required to fund Medicare Part B.

[27] This was the Medicare Trustees' basic assumption at the time the research took place.

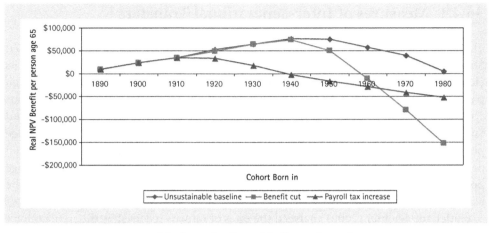

FIGURE 36.5 Net benefits from Medicare, by cohort
Source: Cutler and Sheiner (2000)

of the rapid growth of health costs, the rates of return are still substantially higher than those received on social security contributions (noted in the bottom line of the table).[28] These relatively high rates of return will be a characteristic of all countries where health spending is increasing faster than income.

It is important to distinguish between rates of return and net benefits. As health spending increases, the net present value benefit from the system can increase even as the rates of return are decreasing, so long as the rates of return remain above the long-run level. Figure 36.5 plots the net present value received by different cohorts under the US Medicare program, assuming a 3 percent discount rate. According to this measure, the generation born in 1940 will receive the largest net transfer from the Medicare program.

Of course, under this baseline the Medicare system would be running substantial long-run deficits.[29] As noted above, in steady state, the rate of return on any pay-as-you-go system must equal the growth rate of aggregate income, which the social security actuaries expect to be about 1½ percent per year. The fact that the projected Medicare returns are above that reflects the fact the system is not in long-run actuarial balance. Cutler and Sheiner analyzed two different possibilities for closing the Medicare deficit—raising taxes or cutting benefits. As can be seen from the table and figure, which of these reforms is chosen has important inter-generational consequences. Raising

---

[28] If per capita health spending is growing at a rate z percentage points faster than per capita GDP, then, under a pure pay-as-you-go system, the rate of return is $(1+n)(1+g)(1+z)$, using the terminology from above. To sustain this rate of return requires tax payments also be increasing at a rate faster than per capita GDP. Eventually, these taxes become too burdensome (in the limit, they comprise all of wages) and then rates of return must fall back to the sustainable level of $(1+n)(1+g)$.

[29] Cutler and Sheiner assume that benefits financed by general revenues are fully paid for each year, but that the payroll taxes used to finance Medicare Part A are constant, as under current law.

payroll taxes has much greater effects on younger cohorts, whereas cutting benefits also affects older cohorts.[30]

While this analysis is specific to the Medicare system in the US, the findings can be generalized to all other countries with rapid health spending growth and financial imbalances. All of these countries will need to eventually close their financing gaps. How they do so can have significant inter-generational consequences.

36.5 CONCLUSIONS

The distribution of health spending by age has important effects on inter-generational transfers, the private burden of health spending, and government budgets. There remains much to be learned about how each of these attributes of the health system will evolve over time. The aging of the population, particularly combined with continued rapid increases in health spending, will bring to the fore difficult issues related to the inter-generational distribution of societal resources. While increased pressures on private budgets will no doubt increase the demand for larger subsidies, increased pressures on government budgets and the tax burden faced by workers will create pressures to limit such subsidies. It is important to have a good understanding of the factors affecting the inter-generational distributions implicit in health systems when addressing these potential generational conflicts.

REFERENCES

CBO (CONGRESSIONAL BUDGET OFFICE) (2007). *The Long-term Outlook for Health Care Spending, November.* Washington, DC: CBO.

CHERNEW, MICHAEL E., DANA P. GOLDMAN, FENG PAN, and BAOPING SHANG (2005). "Disability and Health Care Spending Among Medicare Beneficiaries." *Health Affairs* 24/2: W5-R42–W5-R52.

[30] As noted, in keeping with the assumption used by the Medicare Trustees at the time, Cutler and Sheiner assumed that per beneficiary Medicare spending would slow to the rate of per capita GDP after twenty years. Since then, the assumptions used by the Trustees have changed significantly. In particular, the Trustees now assume that the growth rate of per capita Medicare spending slows to the growth rate of per capita GDP only very slowly, so that by the end of the eighty-year projection period, per capita Medicare spending is still increasing a little faster than per capita GDP. In addition, a prescription drug benefit was introduced in 2006; according to the Trustees, the Medicare drug benefit raises Medicare outlays by about 15 percent in 2008 and by about 20 percent by 2030 (CMS Report 2008).

The rates of return from Medicare under these new assumptions have not been analyzed. However, the implications are clear. The combination of the different assumptions about the trajectory of health spending and the enactment of the prescription drug benefit will result in significantly higher rates of return for all cohorts save the ones turning 65 near the end of the projection period—that is for all cohorts born before 2015. Of course, the faster pace of assumed growth would also require a more substantial tax increase or benefit cut to make the system sustainable.

CMS (CENTER FOR MEDICARE AND MEDICAID SERVICES) (2004). *US Health Spending by Age*. Washington, DC: CMS, Office of the Actuary, National Health Statistics Group.

COLOMBO, FRANCESCA and NICOLE TAPAY (2004). "Private Health Insurance in OECD Countries; The Benefits and Costs for Individuals and Health Systems." OECD Health Working Paper 15, Paris.

CORAK, MILES, CHRISTINE LIETZ, and HOLLY SUTHERLAND (2005). "The Impact of Tax and Transfer Systems on Children in the European Union," IZA (The Institute for the Study of Labor) discussion Paper no. 1589. May.

CUTLER, DAVID (1995). "Technology, Health Costs and the NIH." Paper presented at the National Institutes of Health Economics Roundtable on Biomedical Research, Cambridge MA.

—— and ELLEN MEARA (1998) "The Medical Costs of the Young and Old: A Forty Year Perspective." In David Wise (ed.), *Frontiers in the Economics of Aging*. Chicago: University of Chicago Press, 215–46.

—— and LOUISE SHEINER (2000). "Generational Aspects of Medicare." *American Economic Review* 90, May: 1–12.

—— —— (2001). "Demographics and Medical Care Spending: Standard and Non-Standard Effects," in Alan Auerbach and Lee Ronald (eds.), *Demographic Change and Fiscal Policy*. Cambridge: Cambridge University Press, 253–91.

—— JAMES POTERBA, LOUISE SHEINER, and LAWRENCE SUMMERS (1990). "An Ageing Society: Opportunity or Challenge?" *Brookings Papers on Economic Activity* 21/1990–1: 1–74.

EC (EUROPEAN COMMISSION) (2005). *The 2005 EPC Projection of Age-related Expenditure: Agreed Underlying Assumptions and Projection Methodologies*. Brussels: EC.

—— (2006). *The Impact of Ageing on Public Expenditure: Projections for the EU25 Member States on Pensions, Health Care, Long-term Care, Education and Unemployment Transfers (2004–2050)*. Brussels: EC.

ELMENDORF, DOUGLAS and LOUISE SHEINER (2000). "Should America Save for Its Old Age?" Federal Reserve Boards FEDS Working Paper 00-03, Washington.

FOLLETTE, GLENN, and LOUISE SHEINER (2005). "The Sustainability of Health Spending Growth," Federal Reserve Working Paper, FEDS 2005-60, Washington.

—— —— (2008). "An Examination of Health Spending Growth in the United States," in Franco Daniele (ed.), *Fiscal Sustainability: Analytical Developments and Emerging Policy Issues*. Rome, Italy: Banca D'Italia, 443–64.

GOLDMAN, DANA P., BAOPING SHANG, JAYANTA BHATTACHARYA, et al. (2005). "Consequences of Health Trends and Medical Innovations for the Future Elderly," *Health Affairs*, 24/Suppl. 2: W5-R5-W5-R17.

GRAY, ALASTAIR (2005) "Population Ageing and Health Care Expenditure," *Ageing Horizons*, Spring–Summer, 2: 15–20.

HOLLY, ALBERTO (2005). "Health-based Predictive Models: How to Extrapolate Existing Medical Information into the Projections of Future Health Care Expenditure?" Prepared for the Workshop organized by the European Commission, the Working Group on Ageing and the OECD, Brussels, February 21 and 22.

JACOBZONE, STEPHANE (2003). "Healthy Ageing and the Challenges of New Technologies: Can OECD Social and Healthcare Systems Provide for the Future?" *Geneva Papers on Risk and Insurance: Issues and Practice*, April 28/2: 254–74.

—— E. CAMBOIS, and J. M. ROBINE. (2000). "Is the Health of Older Persons in OECD Countries Improving Fast Enough to Compensate for Population Ageing?" OECD Economic Studies 30/1, Paris.

LUBITZ, JAMES (2005). "Health, Technology, and Medical Care Spending," *Health Affairs*, 24/ Suppl. 2: W5-R81-W5-R85.

MARTINS, JOAQUIM OLIVEIRA, CHRISTINE DE LA MAISONNEUVE and SIMON BJORNERUD (2006). "Projections of OECD Health and Long-term Care Public Expenditures." Banca D'Italia Research Department Public Finance Workshop, Fiscal Indicators, Perugia, 751-93, Rome, Italy, March 30 to April 1.

MEARA, ELLEN, CHAPIN WHITE, and DAVID M. CUTLER (2004). "Trends in Medical Spending by Age, 1963–2000," *Health Affairs* 23/4: 176–83.

NEWHOUSE, JOSEPH P. (1992). "Medical Care Costs: How Much Welfare Loss?," *Journal of Economic Perspectives*, Summer, 6/2: 3–21.

OECD (2006). "Projecting OECD Health and Long-Term Care Expenditures: What are the Main Drivers?" OECD Economics Department Working Papers, no. 477, OECD Publishing, Paris.

—— (2007). *Health at a Glance 2007*. Paris: OECD.

SABELHAUS, JOHN, MICHAEL SIMPSON, and JULIE TOPOLESKI (2004). "Incorporating Longevity Effects into Long-term Medicare Projections," Congressional Budget Office Technical Paper Series, January 2004–2, Washington, DC.

SHEINER, LOUISE (1999). "Health Care Costs, Wages, and Aging," Federal Reserve Working Paper FEDS 99-19, Washington, DC.

—— (2004). "The Effects of Technology on the Age Distribution of Health Spending: A Cross-Country Perspective," Federal Reserve Working Paper, FEDS 2004-14 (April), Washington, DC.

—— DAN SICHEL, and LARRY SLIFMAN (2007). "A Primer on the Macroeconomic implications of Population Aging," Federal Reserve Working Paper, FEDS 2007-01, Washington, DC.

SMITH, SHEILA, STEPHEN K. HEFFLER, and MARK S. FREELAND. (2000). "The Impact of Technological Change on Health Care Cost Increases: an Evaluation of the Literature." Unpublished Working Paper, Office of the Actuary, CMS, Baltimore.

SOCIAL SECURITY ADMINISTRATION (2008). *The 2008 Annual Report of the Board of Trustees of the Federal Old-Age and Survivors Insurance and Federal Disability Insurance Trust Funds*. Social Security Administration: Office of the Actuary.

STATISTICS CANADA (2001). *Health Expenditures in Canada by Age and Sex, 1980–81 to 2000–01*. Ottawa: Statistics Canada.

STEUERLE, C. EUGENE and Jon M. BAKIJA (1994). *Retooling Social Security for the 21st Century: Right and Wrong Approaches to Reform*. Washington DC: Urban Institute Press.

STURM, R., J. RINGEL, and T. ANDREYEVA (2004). "Increasing Obesity Rates and Disability Trends." *Health Affairs*, March/April, 23/2: 1–7.

ZWEIFEL, P., S. FELDER and M. MEIERS (1999). "Ageing of Population and Healthcare Expenditure: A Red Herring?" *Health Economics*, 8/6: 485–96.

CHAPTER 37

....

ECONOMETRIC
EVALUATION
OF HEALTH POLICIES*

....

ANDREW M. JONES AND NIGEL RICE

37.1 THE EVALUATION PROBLEM

....

37.1.1 Counterfactuals and Treatment Effects

THE narrow goal of evaluative research is to identify the causal impact of an intervention on outcomes of interest. The broader goal is to understand the mechanisms underlying this impact. In evaluating the cost-effectiveness of medical technologies, randomized controlled trials (RCTs) are often regarded to be the gold standard in identifying internally valid estimates of causal effects. In health policy research, randomized experiments are less prevalent and researchers are more often faced with identifying causal relationships from observational, or non-experimental, sources of data where the assignment of individuals to treatment or control group is beyond the control of the researcher.[1]

* We gratefully acknowledge funding from the Economic and Social Research Council (ESRC) under the Large Grant Scheme, reference RES-060-25-0045. We are also grateful to Anirban Basu, Bill Greene, Rodrigo Moreno Serra, John Mullahy, Karen Mumford, Silvana Robone, Pedro Rosa Dias, Jo Swaffield, Ranjeeta Thomas, and Pravin Trivedi for their comments on an earlier version.

[1] In the context of development economics, Banerjee and Duflo (2008) review the advantages of randomized experiments, which allow the assignment of treatment to be isolated and controlled by researchers, in providing internally valid estimates of effectiveness. They also seek to address some of the common criticisms of randomized experiments: whether the results of an experiment are dependent on the specific environment where it is carried out, limiting their replicability and generalizability to other contexts; whether there are problems with compliance in experimental studies; whether randomization itself may affect outcomes (for example, through Hawthorne effects); whether experiments only reflect partial equilibrium effects and fail to capture general equilibrium or spillover effects that may occur when policies

In such circumstances, the identification of causal effects is often less than straightforward and econometric tools are often called into play.

The evaluation of a treatment, in its broadest sense, refers to the measurement of the impact of an intervention on specified outcomes of interest. In the clinical context, this frequently means identifying the effect of a particular treatment or treatment technology on health outcomes, where the treatment is compared to no-treatment, a placebo, or, more commonly, an existing treatment or technology. For public health and health policy research we might be interested in the evaluation of a particular treatment, but we might also be interested in the evaluation of a broader policy intervention or program, such as a ban on smoking in public places or a reform of provider reimbursement. Throughout the chapter we use the terms policy intervention, program, or treatment interchangeably, using treatment as shorthand for all three. Similarly, we refer to individuals as the target of the policy interventions. In practice the unit of analysis may be organizations or groups such as hospitals or other health care providers.

Heckman (2008) argues that the evaluation problem consists of three distinct steps: definition (which relates to policy analysis and relevant theory); identification (which relates to what, in principle, can be learned from the whole population); and inference (which relates to what, in practice, can be estimated from sample data). Angrist and Pischke (2008) pose these steps as questions: what is the causal relationship of interest (which, they argue, can often be clarified by asking what experiment would ideally be used to capture the effect); what is the identification strategy to isolate this effect; and what is the mode of inference to estimate and test the effect with sample data? The analogy between causal effects and experimental design is highly influential in the evaluation literature and shapes much of the language and conceptual framework that is used, although Heckman (2008) strikes a note of caution and stresses the danger of confusing definition of an underlying causal mechanism with a particular identification strategy, such as randomization. In practice, policy effects are typically defined by the agenda of policymakers, coupled with theory from economics or other disciplines that helps to define the relevant outcomes and their relationship to the treatments. This theory may help to shape the identification strategy. Most applied health economics is not concerned with pure testing of scientific hypotheses; instead it focuses on estimating economically relevant magnitudes of policy effects and on providing evidence to inform decision-making.[2]

The search for a convincing identification strategy usually boils down to finding a source of variation in the treatment that is independent of other factors that influence

---

are implemented on a larger scale; and issues that arise when there is heterogeneity in treatment effects. The drawbacks of a mechanical reliance on the experimental approach, and of "quasi-experimental" approaches that use instrumental variables, with instruments selected to mimic a randomized experiment rather than being drawn from a structural model, are reviewed by Deaton (2008). He is critical of the use of these methods to evaluate projects per se and favours their use as tools to aid our understanding of the underlying theoretical mechanisms that drive behaviour.

[2] This explains the prominence of statistical decision analysis in the recent economic literature on health technology assessment (see e.g. Claxton 1999) which has parallels with the work of Manski (2005) in the general program evaluation literature.

outcomes. Randomizing the assignment of treatment, in the context of a social experiment, is one such source of independent variation. While randomized trials are the norm in the evaluation of new clinical therapies, and despite the precedent set by the RAND Health Insurance Experiment, their use for the evaluation of broader health and social programs remains relatively rare (e.g. Björkman and Svensson 2009; Gertler 2004; Miguel and Kremer 2004). In non-experimental settings the identification strategy may mean appealing to a rich enough set of observed confounders so that any remaining variation in treatment is effectively randomized. Often this raises the challenge of finding variation over time or across groups that can be used to convincingly mimic the features of a randomized experiment, so that the analysis can be interpreted as a quasi-experimental design, or "natural experiment" (see e.g. Meyer 1995; Rosenzweig and Wolpin 2000). A neat example of the analogy between a designed experiment and a natural experiment is the work of Stillman et al. (2009) who make use of a random ballot of Tongans who applied to emigrate to New Zealand to identify the effects of migration on mental health.

The recent health economics literature contains many examples of proposed natural experiments and these are reviewed in more detail in Jones (2009). For example, to try to identify independent variation in individual health Almond (2006) uses the 1918 influenza pandemic while Doyle (2005) uses severe traffic accidents. To identify independent variation in the use of prenatal care Evans and Lien (2005) use the impact of the 1992 Port Authority Transit (PAT) strike in Pennsylvania on access to health care. Lindahl (2005) proposes lottery winnings as a source of exogenous variation in income in a study of the income–health gradient. Broader macroeconomic shocks have been used as natural experiments: for example, Frijters et al. (2005) use the reunification of Germany in 1990; Jensen and Richter (2004) use the 1996 crisis in the public pension system in Russia; Duflo (2000) uses reform of public pension provision for black African women at the end of the Apartheid era in South Africa. Natural experiments may call on historical data: Van Den Berg et al. (2006) use the state of the Dutch economy at the end of the nineteenth century to study long-term consequences for mortality rates during the twentieth century. Institutional and policy reforms are often the source of natural experiments. Lleras-Muney (2005) uses state-level reforms the US educational system to provide variation in educational attainment that is independent of individual decisions. Health policies and reforms are of particular relevance for health economics: for example, Bleakley (2007) focuses on a program aimed at the eradication of hookworm in the Southern US, while Pop-Eleches (2006) uses the 1966 ban on abortion and family planning under the Ceausescu regime in Romania.

To put these identification strategies into practice, natural experiments are often used to support estimation approaches such as instrumental variables (IV), regression discontinuity (RD) and difference-in-differences (DD). The problem of inference focuses on the assumptions required to implement a given identification strategy with a particular sample or samples of data. In recent years there has been a heavy emphasis on keeping parametric assumptions to a minimum. The literature has favored methods such as matching, non-parametric regression, and control function approaches and on making inferences that are robust to functional form and distributional assumptions.[3] Similarly computation of standard errors needs to take account of sampling methodologies and data structures and make appropriate adjustments for features such as clustering of observations and heteroscedasticity.

In defining the evaluation problem, a fundamental problem arises in attempting to derive inference of a causal relationship between a treatment, denoted d, and an outcome, denoted y. The treatment effect of interest, Δ, is the change in potential outcome for individual, i, when exposed to the intervention compared to an alternative (referred to as the control) and can be defined as:

$$\Delta_i = y_i^1 - y_i^0 \tag{1}$$

where superscript 1 denotes treatment and 0 denotes the control. The evaluation problem is that an individual cannot be observed to be under treatment and under the control at the same time. At any particular point in time only one of the potential outcomes can be observed (Roy 1951; Rubin 1974). This framework, which emphasizes unobserved potential outcomes, is often referred to as the Rubin Causal Model (Holland 1986). Methods to define and estimate the counterfactual outcome lie at the heart of all attempts to identify causal relationships between treatment assignment and the outcomes of interest.[4]

37.1.2 Average Treatment Effects

A common approach to addressing the evaluation problem is to focus on average treatment effects (ATE). For example the population average treatment effect (PATE) is the difference in the average potential outcomes in the treated and control groups for the population as a whole:

$$PATE = E[y^1 - y^0] = E[y^1] - E[y^0] \tag{2}$$

For a particular sample of data the analog of the PATE is the sample average treatment effect (SATE):

$$SATE = \frac{1}{n}\sum_{i=1}^{n} y_i^1 - \frac{1}{n}\sum_{i=1}^{n} y_i^0 \tag{3}$$

---

[3] However, it is notable that applications of one the most commonly adopted approaches in health economics—difference-in-differences—rely on a heavily parametric approach, using linear models (see Jones 2009).

[4] In this sense the evaluation problem can be seen as a particular brand of missing data problem and many of the methods used to evaluate treatment effects, such as those based on propensity scores, are used in that more general context as well.

where $n = n^1 + n^0$ and n^1 and n^0 are the numbers of treated and controls in the sample.

More often, the relevant concept is the treatment effect for the subset of the population who would actually be assigned to treatment (e.g. Heckman, LaLonde, and Smith 1999). This is the treatment effect on the treated (ATT, or sometimes ATET or TT). The population average treatment effect on the treated (PATT) is:

$$PATT = E[y^1 - y^0 \mid d = 1] = E[y^1 \mid d = 1] = E[y^0 \mid d = 1] \qquad (4)$$

The PATT represents the expected gain from the intervention for an individual randomly selected from the treated population, rather than for any individual in the general population. For example, the PATT would be applicable to a study of an area-based intervention where the area is chosen on the basis of certain characteristics or for any interventions where those who self-select into treatment respond differently from those who do not. The sample analogue of the PATT is the sample average treatment effect (SATT).

It is worth emphasizing that the fundamental treatment effect of interest, Δ_i, is individual specific and that there may be considerable heterogeneity in treatment effects across individuals. While much of the evaluation literature focuses on average treatment effects, the broader impact on the full distribution of treatment effects is also of interest. Heckman, Smith, and Clements (1997) note that while randomized experiments can identify average treatment effects, due to the additivity of the expectations operator as seen in equation (2), they may not identify other features of the distribution without further assumptions being imposed. They discuss other measures of the impact of a treatment such as the proportion of people receiving the treatment who benefit from it, $P(\Delta > 0 \mid d = 1)$; the proportion of the total population that benefits, $P(\Delta > 0 \mid d = 1)P(d = 1)$; selected quantiles of the distribution of treatment effects, such as median treatment effects; and the distribution of gains from treatment at selected values of covariates.

37.1.3 Selection Bias

Selection bias arises in situations where assignment to the treatment is correlated with observed or unobserved factors ("confounders") that are also correlated with the outcome. Where evaluative research relies on observational data, obtained from non-experimental study designs, the effects of selection are likely to be more pronounced than those found in experimental settings where the study design aims to remove confounding effects. If sufficient characteristics that determine the assignment of treatment are observed, then methods based on *selection on observables* can be used to consistently estimate the treatment effect. These methods include regression analysis, matching estimators, and inverse probability weighted estimators. If, however, selection into treatment is based on characteristics that are unobservable to the researcher then methods that allow for *selection on unobservables* are appropriate. These approaches are mostly based on finding factors that predict treatment assignment but, crucially, that do not have a direct effect on the outcome of interest. Methods include instrumental variables, control functions, and the joint estimation of the outcome and treatment in a structural approach. Longitudinal data may provide a way of dealing with unobservables as in the difference-in-differences approach and panel data regression methods.

To illustrate, consider Figure 37.1 which presents a stylized view of the potential outcomes for the treated (y^1) and controls (y^0) plotted against time. For simplicity, these are shown to follow a common linear trend over time. Treatment is assigned at the point shown by the dotted vertical line and, in this example, sample data may be observed before treatment ($t − 1$) and after treatment (t). Notice that there is a gap between the potential outcomes prior to treatment, which may be due to observed (x) or unobserved (u) confounders. In the example the treated have better outcomes whether or not they receive the treatment, so selection bias is positive, as shown by the vertical distance $\{x, u\}$. The challenge for the analyst is to identify the causal effect of the treatment, allowing for the confounding effect of selection bias.

Now consider the kinds of data that might be available to evaluate the treatment. First we may have cross-section data collected after treatment at time t. Then a simple comparison of the (mean) outcomes for the treated and untreated will equal the distance CD. This over-estimates the true treatment effect, which equals CC', by the amount of selection bias $C'D$. If the selection bias is fully accounted for by observable confounders x, then methods such as regression or matching may be used to deal with the problem, effectively adjusting the counterfactual outcomes (y^0) so that they are comparable to y^1. Graphically this would eliminate the vertical gap between the two lines prior to treatment so that both potential outcomes were observed to have equivalent pre-treatment trajectories. If the selection bias is due to unobservables u, then other methods, such as instrumental variables, should be considered.

Now consider a before and after comparison of the outcomes for the treated cases. In this case using the vertical difference in (mean) outcomes before and after, CA, will over-estimate the true treatment effect CC' by the vertical distance $C'A$. This bias reflects

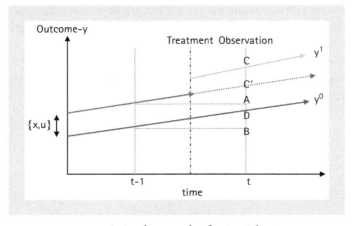

FIGURE 37.1 A simple example of potential outcomes

the underlying trend in outcomes and has nothing to do with the treatment itself. One way to account for the trend, and also for fixed differences due to x and u, is to take the difference in differences. This estimates the treatment effect by taking the difference between the change over time for the treated (CA) and the change over time for the controls (DB). So long as the two groups share the same trend ("parallel trends"), the resulting difference equals the true treatment effect CC'. The difference-in-differences approach will work as long as the common trend assumption holds. Differences in the trend that are attributable to observables can be captured by controlling for those covariates, through regression or matching. Differences due to unobservables that vary over time are more problematic.

To define selection bias more formally, consider the difference between the population means of the outcome y for the treated and controls, which can be decomposed as follows (see Heckman, Ichimura, Smith, and Todd 1998):

$$
\begin{aligned}
&E[y \mid d = 1] - E[y \mid d = 0] \\
&= E[y^1 \mid d = 1] - E[y^0 \mid d = 0] \\
&= E[y^1 - y^0 \mid d = 1] + \{E[y^0 \mid d = 1] - E[y^0 \mid d = 0]\} \\
&= PATT + Bias
\end{aligned}
\tag{5}
$$

In this case the simple difference in population means equals the average treatment effect on the treated plus a selection bias that captures the underlying difference in potential outcomes, in the absence of treatment, between those assigned to treatment and those assigned to the control. This selection bias may be attributable to observables or to unobservables. The bias term can be further decomposed (Heckman, Ichimura, Smith, and Todd 1998; King and Zeng 2007). Bias can arise due to: failing to control for relevant confounders (*omitted variable bias*); inclusion of covariates that are themselves affected by the treatment (*post-treatment bias*); failure to adequately control for covariates within the observed range of data, for example when applying a linear model to a non-linear relationship (*interpolation bias*); or failure to adequately control for covariates when extrapolating to areas outside the observed range of the data, for example if a linear approximation holds within the sample but not beyond it (*extrapolation bias*). For a well-designed experiment, where randomization fully determines assignment to treatment, $E[y^0 \mid d = 1] - E[y^0 \mid d = 0] = 0$, eliminating the bias.

The sources of selection bias can be illustrated further by expressing the potential outcomes as regression functions. Using some fairly general notation, let the potential outcomes be (additive) functions of observable (x) and unobservable (u) confounders (e.g. Heckman, Ichimura, and Todd 1997):

$$
\begin{aligned}
y^0 &= \mu^0(x) + u^0 \\
y^1 &= \mu^1(x) + u^1
\end{aligned}
\tag{6}
$$

Then, by definition:

$$
y = (1 - d)y^0 + dy^1
$$

So:

$$y = y^0 + d(y^1 - y^0)$$
$$= \mu^0(x) + d(\mu^1(x) - \mu^0(x)) + u^0 + d(u^1 - u^0) \tag{7}$$

In this formulation the "treatment regression" (7) of y on d consists of an "intercept," $\mu^0(x)$, which reflects the way in which baseline (pre-treatment) outcomes depend on x. Then the treatment effect is $(\mu^1(x) - \mu^0(x))$ which may vary with observable characteristics (captured by interactions between d and x). The error term reflects unobservable baseline differences in the outcome, u^0, as well as unobservable idiosyncratic differences in the benefits of the treatment, $(u^1 - u^0)$. Treatment assignment is likely to be influenced by both of these terms, creating selection bias on unobservables. For example a doctor may take account of their personal assessment of a specific patient's capacity to benefit when deciding which treatment regime to adopt.

The model can be augmented by a model of treatment assignment/participation:

$$d = 1 \quad if \quad d^* = \mu_d(z) + u_d > 0 \tag{8}$$

where z are covariates that influence assignment to treatment and where u_d may be correlated with $u^0 + d(u^1 - u^0)$. Using linear functions for the regressions (6) coupled with (8), gives Roy's (1951) model:

$$y = x'\beta_j + u_j, \ j = 0,1 \tag{9}$$

where the regression coefficients can differ by treatment regime.

37.2 SELECTION ON OBSERVABLES

37.2.1 Regression Analysis

In situations where selection into treatment is based only on observables, we can use outcome data from a set of potential comparison individuals for whom observed characteristics are comparable to those of the treated individuals, so that like is compared with like. This is the idea behind the use of standard regression analysis and the use of matching (Cochran and Rubin 1973; Rubin 1973a; Heckman, Ichimura, and Todd 1997; Deheija and Wahba 1999) and inverse probability weights (e.g. Hirano, Imbens, and Ridder 2003).

The key assumption of the selection on observables approach is that, conditional on the chosen set of covariates x, selection into treatment is independent of the outcomes of interest (Heckman and Robb 1985). Recall equation (5), which can now be rewritten conditional on the set of observed covariates x:

$$E[y \mid d = 1, x] - E[y \mid d = 0, x]$$
$$= E[y^1 - y^0 \mid d = 1, x] + \{E[y^0 \mid d = 1, x] - E[y^0 \mid d = 0, x]\} \tag{10}$$
$$= PATT_{\mid x} + Bias$$

This implies that a minimal assumption to eliminate the bias term, and therefore for the identification of the PATT, is *unconfoundedness*, *ignorability*, or *conditional independence* (Rosenbaum and Rubin 1983):

$$y^0 \perp d \mid x \tag{11}$$

Condition (11) states that, conditional on x, the assignment of treatment d is independent of the potential outcome y^0 and, hence, would make the bias term in (10) disappear. In estimating (10) a weaker version of this condition can be expressed in terms of expected values, but this is not invariant to transformations of y (Heckman, Ichimura, and Todd 1997). Note that assumptions about the distribution of y^1 among the treated are not required for identification of the PATT as this is identified from the observed data.

In practice, and in particular if covariates are well-balanced between the treated and controls, analysts may be willing to assume the parametric structure implied by a regression model. Given the unconfoundedness assumption, (11), a simple way to estimate average treatment effects is the standard linear regression framework. To see this consider the definition of the PATT:

$$PATT_{\mid x} = E[y^1 - y^0 \mid d = 1, x]$$
$$= E[y^1 \mid d = 1, x] - E[y^0 \mid d = 1, x]$$
$$= \tau(.) \tag{12}$$

This implies:

$$E[y^1 \mid d = 1, x] = E[y^0 \mid d = 1, x] + \tau(.) \tag{13}$$

Then, the basic identifying assumption for estimation of the PATT using a linear regression model is:

$$E[y^0 \mid d = 1, x] = E[y^0 \mid d = 0, x] = x'\beta_0 \tag{14}$$

This combines unconfoundedness (11) with the assumption that the conditional mean of y^0 is a linear function of the covariates. In this context, as noted by Hirano and Imbens (2001: 263), it can be argued that "linearity is not really restrictive, as we can include functions of the original covariates in the vector x."

Then, by definition:

$$E(y \mid d, x) = d \cdot E(y^1 \mid d, x) + (1 - d) \cdot E(y^0 \mid d, x) \tag{15}$$

Then, using (13) and (14):

$$E(y \mid d, x) = d\{x'\beta_0 + \tau(.)\} + (1 - d)\{x'\beta_0\}$$
$$= x'\beta_0 + \tau(.)d \tag{16}$$

So the linear regression estimate of the ATT is the coefficient $\tau(.)$ on the treatment indicator d. This can be estimated by least squares. The simplest version of this model treats $\tau(.)$ as a fixed coefficient, but the treatment effect need not be constant. To allow for heterogeneity in the treatment effect d could be interacted with the x variables or it could be treated as a random parameter. The model with a full set of interaction terms gives Roy's model (9) but, given the unconfoundedness assumption (11), the regression models can be estimated independently for the treated and controls. The ATT can then be estimated as the difference in the average of the predicted values of the two regressions, estimated for the sample of treated individuals:

$$\hat{\tau}_{LR} = \frac{1}{n^1} \sum_{i \in \{d=1\}} (x_i'\hat{\beta}_1 - x_i'\hat{\beta}_0) = \overline{x}_1'(\hat{\beta}_1 - \hat{\beta}_0) \tag{17}$$

Notice that the counterfactual outcome $E(y^0 \mid d = 1, x)$ is estimated by:

$$\frac{1}{n^1} \sum_{i \in \{d=1\}} (x_i'\hat{\beta}_0) = \overline{x}_1' \hat{\beta}_0 = \overline{x}_0' \hat{\beta}_0 + (\overline{x}_1 - \overline{x}_0)' \hat{\beta}_0 \tag{18}$$

While the regression model for the controls may do a good job of estimating β_0 for the observed sample of controls, if $\overline{x}_0$ and $\overline{x}_1$ are far apart, the model may do a poor job of extrapolating to the sample of treated observations. This makes it clear that, for linear models, it is balancing of the means of the covariates that is important, but this is contingent on the linear specification being correct. For non-linear specifications other facets of the distribution will be important (Ho et al. 2007; Basu, Polsky, and Manning 2008).

37.2.2 Matching

The method of matching avoids the need to make parametric assumptions such as those implied by the linear regression model (16). The idea behind matching estimators is that if a suitably matched group of individuals can be identified, then the average outcome across these individuals provides the counterfactual for the mean outcome for treated individuals in the absence of treatment (Cochran and Rubin 1973; Rubin 1973a; Heckman, Ichimura, and Todd 1997; Deheija and Wahba 1999). For matching to provide a non-parametric estimate the unconfoundedness assumption (11) has to be coupled with the requirement of weak overlap:

$$P(d = 1 \mid x) < 1 \tag{19}$$

so that it is possible to find controls who share the same x values as each treated case. Otherwise regression models are required to extrapolate counterfactual outcomes to areas outside the range of common support,[5] meaning that estimates of the counterfactual are *model dependent*.

A number of alternative methods for defining the matched group of individuals have been proposed. Exact matching consists of finding a match to a treated individual, from the pool of controls, based on the set of observed characteristics of the individual. Individuals can then be compared to their matched counterparts. The choice of observed characteristics is important and should be based on all factors that affect both treatment assignment and outcomes of interest but are not affected by the treatment itself (to avoid *post-treatment bias*). Where this is not the case, matching fails to control for treatment selection. Accordingly, matching is based on pre-treatment characteristics of individuals. It is assumed that for each combination of values of x among the treated, an untreated individual can be found. This ensures common support over x. Individuals with characteristics only observed within those treated, or indeed, only within comparison cases, may be ignored as appropriate matches are not available. But in doing so, the population of interest and, hence, the relevant treatment effect is redefined to the area of common support.

The method of exact matching is most practicable when the number of observed characteristics is reasonably small and where characteristics are measured as discrete variables. In such circumstances, the ability to locate matched cases is enhanced. However unconfoundedness is unlikely to hold if the list of observables is short. For the majority of empirical problems, where matches are sought over a larger number of covariates, or for continuous variables, finding exact matches is more difficult and alternative methods are usually required.

37.2.3 Propensity Scores

Where there are many covariates exact matching is often impracticable and other methods of matching are required. The leading method is propensity score matching (Rosenbaum and Rubin 1983). Rosenbaum and Rubin (1983) show that the curse of dimensionality can be overcome by using a balancing score.[6] They show that unconfoundness in terms of the full set of covariates implies unconfoundedness in terms of a balancing score $b(x)$:

$$y^0 \perp d \mid x \Rightarrow y^0 \perp d \mid b(x) \tag{20}$$

---

[5] Common support requires that for each level of $p(x)$, the probability of observing a non-treated individual is positive. Accordingly, the PATT is identified by restricting attention to comparative non-treated individuals that fall within the support of the propensity score distribution of the treatment group. In the case if the PATE the required overlap condition is stronger: $0 < P(d = 1 \mid x) < 1$.

[6] Hahn (1998) established that the value of conditioning on the propensity score, rather than on the elements of x directly, stems from the reduction in dimensionality rather than a gain in efficiency for semiparametric estimators.

There are many balancing scores, including x itself, but the one that is most commonly used is the propensity score:

$$p(x) = E(d \mid x) = P(d = 1 \mid x) \tag{21}$$

which is the population conditional expectation of d given x. Then, rather than conditioning on the full set of the covariates, the propensity score approach conditions only on the propensity score.[7] For example the PATT may be redefined as:

$$PATT_{PS} = E_{p(x),\, d\, =\, 1}\{E(y^1 \mid d = 1, p(x)) - E(y^0 \mid d = 1, p(x))\} \tag{22}$$

Matching is just one way in which the propensity score can be used to estimate (22). Other methods include blocking (Rosenbaum and Rubin 1983), inverse probability weighting (Hirano, Imbens, and Ridder 2003) and regression on the propensity score using semiparametric regression models such as series approximations or local linear regression (Hahn 1998; Heckman, Ichimura, and Todd 1998).

Blocking (*stratification* or *interval matching*) divides the region of common support into "blocks" of pre-defined width (Rosenbaum and Rubin 1983, 1984). Each block contains both treated individuals and their corresponding controls based on the propensity scores and the criterion used to define the common support (for example, a radius criterion). The treatment effect is then computed separately for each block and the overall ATT as the weighted average of the individual block effects, with weights defined by the number of treated individuals within each block. This can be seen as a simple form of non-parametric regression using a step function (Imbens 2004). For example, Dehejia and Wahba (1999) define the intervals on the basis of treatment and controls failing to exhibit a statistically significant difference in estimated propensity scores (Becker and Ichino 2002).

A general expression for the propensity score matching estimator of the PATT is:

$$\hat{\tau}_{PS} = \frac{1}{n^1} \sum_{i \in \{d=1\}} \left(y_i - \sum_{j \in \{C(p_i(x))\}} w_{ij} y_j \right) \tag{23}$$

where w_{ij} is a weight applied to the contribution of comparison individual, j, as an appropriate counterfactual for treated individual, i, and is determined by the distance between their respective propensity scores. $C(p_i(x))$ represents the set of comparable neighbors for each treated individual, i, where closeness between the propensity scores of the multiple js for each i is defined by some appropriate criterion. Notice, that the final outcome of the matching process is to compare the sample mean for the treated with sample mean

---

[7] In practice matching on the propensity score may be combined with exact matching on specific covariates or matching within subgroups of the sample defined by the covariates. The Mahalanobis metric, which scales differences in x by the inverse of their covariance matrix, is often used for exact matching of covariates.

for an appropriately selected and weighted set of control observations. In this sense the fact that particular treated cases are paired with particular controls during the matching process is irrelevant and matching is simply a way of restricting the sample that is used for comparisons. This leads Ho et al. (2007) to suggest that the use of term matching is unfortunate and could be a source of misunderstanding. They suggest that the approach would be better labeled as "pruning" rather than matching.[8]

Empirical implementation of the propensity score approach involves estimating the individual's propensity to receive treatment, most commonly using either a probit or logit regression when the treatment is binary, and matching treated individuals to controls with a similar propensity for treatment. Again, it is important that there is common support over the estimated propensities for both treatment and control groups, even if their respective densities are different.

Two concerns are relevant in the application of propensity score matching techniques: first, whether matching is performed with or without replacement, and, second, the number of matches to use in the control group. Matching without replacement means that an individual in the control group is matched to only the closest individual in the treatment group. This can result in poor matches between control and treated individuals unless there are sufficient individual observations in the potential control group to ensure that close matches are obtained for all individuals. Poor matches occur where propensity scores are not close, resulting in bias in the matching estimator of the treatment effect. Matching with replacement avoids this problem by allowing each control individual to be matched to multiple treated individuals, again selected on the basis of closest propensity score match. Accordingly, matching with replacement is helpful in reducing bias since comparison individuals can be used more than once if they happen to be the closest match to more than one treated individual. However, the variance of the propensity score matching estimator is likely to be greater than the corresponding estimator without replacement due to greater reliance on a smaller number of comparison individuals. Allowing multiple matches for each treated individual tends to reduce the variance of the propensity score matching estimator of the treatment effect due to the increased information used to obtain the counterfactual. The choice of the number of controls to match to each treated individual, however, involves a trade-off between bias and variance. By including only the closest match bias is reduced, however, the variance of the estimator can be reduced by including more matches, but at the expense of increasing the bias if the additional matched controls are not close matches to the treated individual.

An often neglected point is that matching only requires information on the treatment and on the covariates, not on the outcomes. Good practice in empirical analysis is to conduct the matching exercise without access to the outcome data to avoid them influencing the results (Rubin 2006: 3). Repeated specification searches, aimed at improving

---

[8] Note that this argument applies for the estimation of average treatment effects, that rely on additivity, but does not apply to other measures such as quantile treatment effects.

the balance of treated and controls, only involves the covariates and will not bias subsequent analysis of the treatment effects.

The simplest form of propensity score matching is *nearest-neighbor* (NN) matching, which seeks to match each treated individual to the closest untreated individual, based on their estimated propensity scores. Matching may be performed with or without replacement. This form of matching can lead to substantial bias if the nearest-neighbors turn out to be poor matches, in the sense that the propensity scores are not close. In addition, given that, when sampling without replacement, each control individual is matched to at most one treated individual, the order in which matches are sought may influence the resulting estimator of the PATT.

The methods of *caliper* and *radius matching* offer a compromise between the bias and variance of the propensity score matching estimator. The methods define a tolerated radius or neighborhood around the propensity score for treated individuals beyond which matched controls are excluded. The caliper method only uses the nearest neighbor if it lies within the radius, while the radius method uses all of the matches that lie within the radius (Cochran and Ruben 1973; Deheija and Wahba 2002). The choice of the radius is subjective and involves a compromise between the desire to obtain a small bias by having a small radius and to exclude as few treated individuals as possible (excluded due to failing to find an appropriate match). Common support is often invoked by the requirement for at least one comparison individual to be within the defined propensity score radius criterion.

Kernel density matching provides a further way to construct the counterfactual for treated individuals (Heckman, Ichimura, and Todd 1997). For each treated individual the counterfactual is the kernel weighted average of the multiple comparison individuals. The contribution of a potential match to the counterfactual will depend on the distance of the propensity score to that of the treated individual, together with the chosen bandwidth for the kernel function. Silverman (1986) provides guidance on the choice of bandwidth. The closer the match, in terms of propensity scores, the greater the weight placed on the match.

Empirical research has often used bootstrap methods for conducting inference with matching estimators (for example, Heckman, Ichimura, and Todd 1997, 1998; Heckman, Ichimura, Smith, and Todd 1998). Abadie and Imbens (2008), however, describe situations where the validity of the bootstrap is not justified and in the context of nearest neighbor matching suggest the use of analytical estimators of the asymptotic variance as an alternative (Abadie and Imbens 2006).

To assess the degree of common support kernel density estimators can be used to obtain smoothed estimates of the densities of the propensity score for the treated and constructed control groups which can then be plotted against each other to identify areas where common support breaks down. Also it is important to check whether the covariates are successfully balanced between the treated and controls.

The success of matching methods relies on the ability of the chosen set of covariates to induce unconfoundedness in terms of the balancing score (20). This can be appraised using various methods that assess the degree to which matching has improved covariate balance between the treated and controls. One commonly used measure to assess the difference in the means of the covariates, used before and after matching, is the normalized difference (Rosenbaum and Rubin 1983; Lalonde 1986):

$$\frac{\bar{x}^1 - \bar{x}^0}{\sqrt{(Var(x^1) + Var(x^0))}} \tag{24}$$

Also t-tests for the difference in means are often proposed as a way of checking for balancing. This approach is criticized by Ho et al. (2007) and Imbens and Wooldridge (2008): for example, "the critical misunderstood point is that balance is a characteristic of the observed sample, not some hypothetical population. The idea that hypothesis tests are useful for checking balance is therefore incorrect" (Ho et al. 2007). They argue that this is compounded by the fact that pruning affects the statistical power of the hypothesis tests and that it is therefore misleading to use tests, such as t-ratios for the difference in means, as a guide to the quality of matching.

Analysts are often tempted to stop after checking for balance in the sample means of the covariates but the balancing condition relates to the full empirical distribution and it is wise to check higher moments (variance, skewness, kurtosis) and cross-moments (such as the covariance). Ho et al. (2007) suggest that non-parametric density plots and quantile–quantile (QQ) plots for each covariate and their interactions should be compared for the treated and controls.

Perfect balancing is unlikely to be achieved in practice and that, rather than simply comparing means after matching, running parametric regression models on the matched sample is likely to improve causal inferences (Rubin 1973b, 1979, 2006; Heckman, Ichimura, and Todd 1998; Imbens 2004; Abadie and Imbens 2006; Ho et al. 2007). In this sense, matching can be used as a non-parametric pre-processing of the data to select observations prior to parametric modelling. Alternatively, Indurkhya et al. (2006) suggest conditioning regression models on the propensity score as a means of achieving balance and lessening reliance on the parametric assumptions underlying the specification of a model conditioned on all the confounding variables. Similarly, propensity score weights may be combined with regression models in a weighted least squares approach (see e.g. Robins and Rotnitzky 1995). Robins and Ritov (1997) argue that this provides a *doubly robust* estimator as it is consistent so long as either the propensity score or the regression model is correctly specified.

37.3 SELECTION ON UNOBSERVABLES

37.3.1 Structural Models and Control Functions

The use of standard regression models, such as equation (16), to estimate treatment effects relies on the unconfoundedness assumption (11). This implies that, conditional on the observed covariates, treatment assignment is uncorrelated with any unobservable factors that are captured by the error term in the simple treatment regression model (ε):

$$y = x'\beta + \tau d + \varepsilon \tag{25}$$

Now consider estimating this regression model when the treatment variable, d, is correlated with the error term, even after conditioning on the set of observed covariates, x. This reflects selection on unobservables and, due to omitted variable bias, OLS estimation would be a biased and inconsistent estimator of the treatment effect parameter τ. One approach to identifying the treatment effect in this case involves specifying a model to determine treatment assignment and estimating this jointly with the outcome equation of interest. Often this approach involves strong distributional assumptions and is fully parametric.[9] For example, consider the following specification for the treatment equation:

$$d^* = x'\gamma + z'\theta + \eta_i \tag{26}$$

where d^* is a latent variable with the following observation mechanism:

$$d = \begin{cases} 1 & \text{iff} \quad d^* > 0 \\ 0 & \text{otherwise} \end{cases} \tag{27}$$

The set of variables, z, provide a source of independent variation in d (independent from y) and, due to the fact that it does not enter the outcome equation directly, is referred to as an exclusion restriction. While these variables should be correlated with treatment assignment, they should be uncorrelated with the outcome, y, except through their effect on d.

By assuming a joint distribution for the two error terms ε and η the model can be estimated by full information maximum likelihood (FIML) estimation. For example it may be assumed that they are bivariate normally distributed with zero mean and covariance matrix given by:

$$\Sigma = \begin{bmatrix} \sigma_\varepsilon^2 & \sigma_{\varepsilon\eta} \\ \sigma_{\varepsilon\eta} & 1 \end{bmatrix} \tag{28}$$

In (28) the covariance terms, $\sigma_{\varepsilon\eta}$ reflect the endogeneity of the treatment variable. The restriction that the variance of the error for treatment assignment is unity is a requirement for the probit model for the binary treatment. In practice identification may be fragile due to the assumption of joint normality which may not be appropriate. Furthermore, finding appropriate variables to include in z might prove difficult, or they

---

[9] The strong assumptions that are often required to achieve identification of point estimates for treatment effects, in the presence of selection on unobservables, lead Manski to focus on partial identification and to propose estimates of the bounds for treatment effects (e.g. Manski 1990).

might only be weakly related to treatment assignment or correlated with the error in the outcome equation of interest.

An alternative to estimating the model as a system is to take a control function approach. This focuses on estimating the outcome equation (25) on its own and captures selection bias by including estimates for the terms $E(\varepsilon \mid x, d = 1) = E(\varepsilon \mid x, \eta > -x'\gamma - z'\theta)$ and $E(\varepsilon \mid x, d = 0) = E(\varepsilon \mid x, \eta \leq -x'\gamma - z'\theta)$ as controls. In the case of bivariate normal error terms this corresponds to the Heckman (1979) two-step estimator, which uses the inverse Mills ratio from a probit model for the control function. For more general versions of the index models the control functions can be written as functions of the propensity score $P(d = 1 \mid x, z)$ (Heckman and Robb 1985).

The example of a structural model used here is very simple, involving a single outcome and a single binary treatment with a linear equation for the outcome. In practice applications in health economics may involve multiple outcomes and treatments and these may be binary, count data or multinomial variables. The FIML approach can be extended to specify a complete system of equations for the outcomes and treatments and estimates them jointly, allowing for common unobservable factors and identifying the model through exclusion restrictions. Estimation can be done by maximum likelihood (MLE), maximum simulated likelihood (MSL), Bayesian MCMC, discrete factor models (DFM) or using copulas (see e.g. Aakvik et al. 2003; Geweke et al. 2003; Aakvik et al. 2005; Deb and Trivedi 2006; Deb et al. 2006a, 2006b; Zimmer and Trivedi 2006). See Jones (2009) for a full discussion of these methods and applications.

37.3.2 Instrumental Variables

The idea of instrumental variables estimators is to find one or more variables that are predictive of treatment assignment but which are not directly correlated with the outcome. For a linear regression equation like (25) this implies finding a set of variables, z, that are correlated with d, but uncorrelated with ε. Formally, these conditions can be written $E(z'\varepsilon) = 0$ and $E(z'd) \neq 0$. The variables, z, are referred to as instruments and can be used to derive consistent estimators of the treatment effect. Where the two conditions are met, the set of instruments form exclusion restrictions on the model.

The IV approach is often motivated by the analogy with randomized experiments and the notion that randomization is a perfect instrument. If subjects were randomized, say, by the toss of a fair coin then when z takes a value 1 (heads) the subject would be allocated to treatment and when it takes a value 0 (tails) they would be allocated to the control. The value of z perfectly predicts the assignment of treatment and, ordinarily, there would be no reason to expect that its value would be associated with outcomes. The challenge for researchers is to find natural instruments that mimic the process of randomization. In the absence of randomization it is unlikely that an instrument will be found that perfectly predicts treatment assignment for all individuals. Coupled with the fact that there are likely to be unobservable differences in the magnitude of the treatment effect across individuals and that these differences will often influence the assignment of treatment (recall equation (7)) this creates a fundamental difficulty with the IV approach that the treatment effect identified in sample data by the IV estimator will be contingent on the instruments used. This has been addressed through the concept of local average treatment effects (LATE) which is introduced below.

Conceptually, the mechanics of the IV estimator are best explained as a two-part process reflected in two-stage least squares (2SLS). In the first part, the treatment variable, d, is regressed on the set of instruments, z, and the set of included regressors in the outcome equation, x.[10] From this regression a prediction of treatment assignment can be obtained which replaces the treatment variable in the second stage regression of the outcome of interest. The estimated coefficient on this variable is the IV estimator of the treatment effect. Note, however, that since the treatment variable in the second stage is replaced by its predicted value from the first stage regression (with the corresponding uncertainty surrounding these estimates), OLS standard errors in the second stage will be biased and require correction. This correction is automatically implemented in 2SLS routines in standard econometric software packages.

Standard IV estimators such as 2SLS are consistent in the presence of heteroscedastic errors. Standard errors, however, will be biased leading to invalid inference. Further corresponding diagnostic tests, and importantly, tests of over-identifying restrictions will also be invalid if the errors are heteroscedastic. A potential solution is to use "robust" estimators of the covariance matrix. More commonly, however, is the use of generalized method of moments (GMM) estimators (Hansen 1982). The GMM IV estimator exploits the set of l (number of instruments) moment conditions to derive a consistent and efficient estimator of the treatment effect in the presence of arbitrary heteroscedasdicity (Baum et al. 2003).

While IV estimators offer a potential solution to the problem of selection on unobservables, they are biased in finite samples. Accordingly, they are best employed when dealing with large samples where one can appeal to the consistency properties of the estimators. The credibility of the IV approach and the extent of bias rely on the assumptions outlined above. These assumptions are ultimately untestable. But, to gauge their credibility, a number of tests should be performed prior to reporting the estimated treatment effect and it is considered good practice to report tests for the: endogeneity of the treatment variable; instrument validity; model identification (relevance); the problem of weak instruments; and model specification. We cover each of these briefly.

There is no direct test of the validity of an instrument set, $E(z'\varepsilon) = 0$ since ε is unknown. However, if there are more instruments than endogenous regressors a test of over-identifying restrictions is available which should be routinely reported for any practical application of instrumental variables. For IV where the errors are homoscedastic, the appropriate statistic is provided through the Sargan (1958) test. This can be viewed as nR^2 of a regression of the estimated IV residuals on the set of instruments, where n is the

---

[10] If any of the set of exogenous explanatory variables, x, are omitted from the first stage, then this might induce correlation between the omitted variables and the second stage residuals, potentially leading to an inconsistent estimator of the treatment effect.

sample size and R^2 is the uncentered r-squared (see Baum et al. 2003). For heteroscedastic errors, the GMM alternative is the J statistic of Hansen (1982). This is essentially a test of a function of the corresponding moment conditions derived from minimizing the GMM criterion function. Under the assumption of homoscedasticity the J statistic and Sargan statistic coincide. Both provide tests of the null hypothesis that the instruments are uncorrelated with the error term (that they are *valid*) and that they are therefore legitimately excluded from the outcome equation. The statistics are distributed as chi-squared with degrees of freedom equal to the number of over-identifying restrictions (number of instruments, l, minus the number of endogenous regressors, k). Rejection of the null hypothesis implies that the orthogonality conditions do not hold and the approach to defining instruments should be reviewed. The test is only applicable to situations where there are more instruments than endogenous regressors and hence the model is said to be over-identified. Where this is not the case, and further instruments are not available, higher order terms of the instruments or interactions with exogenous regressors, x, might be used to obtain appropriate over-identifying restrictions.

Identification and weak instruments refer to related concepts, although the implication of each is different. Identification refers to the strength of the relationship between the instruments, z, and the endogenous regressor, d, that is $E(z'd) \neq 0$ and is often referred to as the *relevance* of the instruments. Tests of identification are often tests of the rank of $E(z'd)$. Where there is more than one endogenous regressor, the rank test refers to the ability of the set of instruments to induce independent variation in the endogenous regressors. Test statistics, such as those suggested by Anderson (1984) and Cragg and Donald (1993), provide tests of whether at least one endogenous regressor has no correlation with the set of instruments.

A further problem arises, however, even where we are satisfied that both the conditions, $E(z'\varepsilon) = 0$ and $E(z'd) \neq 0$ hold. If some elements of $E(z'd)$ are close to zero, that is if one or more of the endogenous regressors are poorly correlated with the set of instruments, then we face a problem of *weak instruments*. A consequence of weak instruments is an increase in IV bias (Hahn and Hausman 2002). To illustrate consider the simple case where there is a single treatment d and instrument z. Then the probability limit of the IV (2SLS) estimator is:

$$\hat{\tau}_{IV} \xrightarrow{p} \tau + \frac{Cov(z,\varepsilon)}{Cov(z,d)} \tag{29}$$

If $Cov(z, \varepsilon) = 0$ the IV estimator is asymptotically unbiased. But so long as there is some residual correlation between the instrument and the outcome, as is likely to be the case in practice, then weak instruments, implying a small value for $Cov(z,d)$, may lead to explosive bias. In the extreme, weak instruments would result in a bias in the IV estimate equivalent to the bias observed in simple OLS in the presence of an endogenous regressor. Accordingly, IV regression would offer no improvement over OLS. The test statistic of Cragg and Donald (1993) has been suggested as providing a test for weak instruments. For a single endogenous regressor this statistic is equivalent to an F-test of the joint significance of the set of instruments in the first-stage regression of 2SLS. In these circumstances, Staiger and Stock (1997) suggest as a rule of thumb that a first-stage F statistic of less than 10 is cause for concern. Moreover, Stock and Yogo (2002) provide critical values for the Cragg and Donald statistic that limit the IV bias to a given percentage of the bias of OLS. If the chosen instruments are suspected to be weak, then a search for alternative instruments should be undertaken. This might include consideration of transformations of the existing instruments. A further concern is that IV bias is an increasing function of the number of instruments and hence, caution should be used in selecting over-identifying instruments.

The fundamental problem we are attempting to resolve through the use of IV is that the treatment variable, d, is endogenous, that is it is correlated with the error, ε. A simple test of whether treatment is endogenous follows the two-stage approach to estimation outlined above. As before, the first stage consists of the regression of d, on the set of instruments, z, and the set of included regressors in the outcome equation, x. From this regression compute the predicted error, $\hat{\eta} = d - \hat{d}$. This can then be included in the second stage regression of y on d, x and $\hat{\eta}_i$. A test of significance of the estimated coefficient on $\hat{\eta}_i$ is a test of endogeneity of the treatment variable. Further, for this model, the estimated coefficient on d is the IV estimator of the treatment effect.

Finally, it is good practice to apply tests of model specification. A general test of specification is provided through the use of Ramsey's (1969) reset test adapted for instrumental variables (see Pagan and Hall 1983; Pesaran and Taylor 1999). The test is more properly thought of as a test of a linearity assumption in the mean function or a test of functional form restrictions and omitted variables (see for example Wooldridge 2002) and can be useful as a general check of model specification. For OLS the test simply consists of computing the predicted values from a regression, $\hat{y}$, and inserting powers (for example, $\hat{y}^2$, $\hat{y}^3$ and $\hat{y}^4$) of the predictions into the regression and re-estimating the model. A Wald test of the joint significance of these terms provides a test of specification under the null hypothesis of no neglected non-linearities. The test can be adapted for IV regression by forming the predictions based on x and $\hat{d}$, the predicted value of the endogenous regressor from the first-stage regression (Pesaran and Taylor 1999). Alternatively, the Pagan and Hall (1983) version of the test forms the predictions from a reduced form regression of y on the set of instruments, z, and exogenous regressors, x.

As mentioned above, if there is heterogeneity in the response to treatment the IV estimator identifies a local average treatment effect, or LATE (Imbens and Angrist 1994; Angrist, Imbens, and Rubin 1996). This is the average treatment effect over the subgroup of the population that are induced to participate in the treatment due to variation in the instrument.[11] The fact that IV estimates only identify the LATE and that the results are therefore contingent on the set of instruments explains why different empirical studies can often produce quite different estimates, even though they examine the same outcomes and treatments. The fact that the definition of the LATE involves the values of the instrument is criticized by Heckman (2008) who argues that the definition of treatment

---

[11] The definition of the LATE relates to instruments that are monotonically related to treatment assignment.

effects should be kept distinct from the particular strategy used to identify and make inferences about the effect. Heckman and Vytlacil (1999, 2007) have extended the analysis of local treatment effects by specifying a latent index model for the assignment of treatment and using it to identify those individuals who are indifferent between treatments. The method is applied by Basu et al. (2007) in a study of treatments for breast cancer. This approach defines the marginal treatment effect (MTE): the treatment effect among those individuals at the margin of treatment. The MTE is the building block for the LATE; average treatment effect on the treated (ATT); and average treatment effect (ATE). It can be identified using Local-IV methods or by specifying multiple equation models with a common factor structure (e.g. Aakvik et al. 2005; Basu et al. 2007).

37.3.3 Regression Discontinuity

The regression discontinuity (RD) design exploits situations where the assignment to treatment changes discontinuously with respect to a threshold value of one or more exogenous variables (the *forcing variables*). For example, eligibility for free prescription drugs may be a deterministic function of an individual's age. The contrast between individuals on either side of the discontinuity is used to identify the treatment effect. In a sense it can be seen as an IV strategy, in that the forcing variable predicts assignment of the treatment. But rather than excluding a direct effect of the forcing variable on the outcome, identification relies on the discrete jump in the outcomes at the point of discontinuity. In a "sharp" regression discontinuity design, passing the threshold completely determines the allocation of treatment. In a "fuzzy" design, which is more likely in practice, the allocation of treatment is stochastic and the threshold creates a discontinuity in the probability of treatment. The discontinuity design relies on a comparison of observations "before and after" the threshold and does not have a separate control group. For this reason, applications typically use a narrowly defined neighborhood around the discontinuity, to try and ensure that the treated and untreated observations are comparable in other respects, and often exploit graphical and non-parametric methods to identify any discontinuity. This approach is yet to be used widely in health economics (see for example Card and Shore-Sheppard 2004; Lleras-Muney 2005; Ludwig and Miller 2007; Card, Dobkin, and Maestas 2008; Carpenter and Dobkin 2009).

37.3.4 Difference-in-differences

In applied economics one of the most commonly used methods of evaluating the effect of a policy intervention is the difference-in-differences, or double differences (DD), approach (Ashenfelter 1978; Ashenfelter and Card 1985; Heckman and Robb 1985) DD, is essentially a before-and-after design with controls and there are many recent examples of its use in the health economics literature, typically used in the context of "natural experiments" (see Jones 2009). The basic method requires data in both a pre-treatment and post-treatment period, $t = 0,1$, on the treated $(g = 1)$ and control $(g = 0)$ groups. These may be constructed from longitudinal data on the same individuals or from repeated cross sections (Heckman, Ichimura, and Todd 1997). DD is often used to estimate treatment effects in the context of randomized social experiments, especially if blocked randomization is used and regression analysis is still required to adjust for imbalance in covariates post-randomization. As an illustration, for the stylized example depicted in Figure 37.1, the DD treatment effect is the quantity $(CA) - (DB)$. Given a "parallel trends" assumption $(DB) = (C'A)$ and therefore the treatment effect is the quantity: CC'.

Consider again the definition of the PATT, now expressed in terms of the indicators t and g:

$$\begin{aligned} PATT\big|_x &= E[y^1 - y^0 \mid d = 1, x] \\ &= E[y^1 - y^0 \mid t = 1, g = 1, x] \\ &= E[y^1 \mid t = 1, g = 1, x] - E[y^0 \mid t = 1, g = 1, x] \\ &= \tau(.) \end{aligned} \tag{30}$$

This implies:

$$E[y^1 \mid t = 1, g = 1, x] = \tau(.) + E[y^0 \mid t = 1, g = 1, x] \tag{31}$$

Then, the basic identifying assumption of linear DD is:

$$E[y^0 \mid t = 1, g = 1, x] = x'\beta + \alpha t + \gamma g \tag{32}$$

In (32) the time effect (α) is common to both treated and controls ("parallel trends"). The group effect γ captures any fixed (time-invariant) difference between the treated and controls, whether this is due to observable or unobservable confounders. The covariates x are included to account for any time-varying confounders.

By definition:

$$E(y \mid t, g, x) = dE(y^1 \mid t, g, x) + (1 - d)E(y^0 \mid t, g, x) \tag{33}$$

Then, using (32) gives:

$$\begin{aligned} E(y \mid t, g, x) &= d\{\tau(.) + x'\beta + \alpha t + \gamma g\} + (1 - d)\{x'\beta + \alpha t + \gamma g\} \\ &= \tau(.)d + x'\beta + \alpha t + \gamma g \end{aligned} \tag{34}$$

So the DD estimate of the PATT is the coefficient on the interaction term $d = t.g$ in a model that includes main effects for time (t) and group (g). As with the standard linear regression estimator, $\tau(.)$ need not be constant. To allow for heterogeneity in the treatment effect d could be interacted with the x variables or it could be treated as a random parameter.

The DD approach is applicable to repeated cross-sections of data as long as it can be assumed that the composition of the observations in the two cross-sections has not changed over time. It further assumes that it is possible to identify individuals in the first period who are eligible for treatment. This would be straightforward if, for example, a policy was implemented in a given area only, or directed at individuals with certain characteristics (for example, young smokers).

An important assumption of the DD method is the common time trend for both the treated and control group. This assumes that in the absence of treatment, the average change in the outcomes would be the same for treated individuals as for untreated individuals. Failure of this assumption would confound the estimated treatment effect with a natural time trend producing biased inference. An example of the assumption failing to hold is when there is a pre-treatment dip in outcomes for the treated cases (known in the labor economics literature as an *Ashenfelter dip*).

For identification, the closer the control and treatment group in terms of both observable and unobservable characteristics, the greater the credibility of the DD approach in recovering the treatment effect. To enhance comparability between treatment and control group, the approach can be combined with matching. Accordingly, pre-treatment controls can be matched with treated individuals to ensure that the characteristics of treated and controls are close and hence are more comparable.

An advantage of combining the DD approach with matching, for example using propensity scores, is that the method of matching relies on the assumption that selection into treatment is based on observable measured characteristics (Heckman, Ichimura, Smith, and Todd 1998). Where this assumption is untenable, inference will be contaminated with omitted variable bias through a failure to control for important but unobserved or unobservable characteristics. Combining matching with the DD approach further allows control for unobserved time-invariant components and accordingly, increasing the credibility of the identification of the treatment effect.

Given sufficient information on both controls and treated individuals prior to treatment, it is possible to test the credibility of the parallel trend assumption. An example of this is Galiani et al.'s (2005) evaluation of the impact of the privatization of local water services on child mortality in Argentina. They estimate a *placebo regression* using only data from the pre-treatment period, but including an indicator of those cases that would go on to be treated. Also they include measures of deaths from infectious and parasitic diseases and from causes unrelated to water quality. The fact that they detect a reduction for the former but not for the latter creates confidence in their identification strategy.

Equation (32) shows that linearity is central to the standard DD approach. Athey and Imbens (2006) propose a more general approach, labeled changes-in-changes (CC), that relaxes the additivity assumption required for DD. Their approach allows pre-treatment outcomes to be general function of unobservables, with the restrictions that outcomes are strictly monotonic in the unobservables and that the unobservables are time invariant within groups. Let F_{gt} denote the distribution function for y for group $g\,(0,1)$ at time $t\,(0,1)$. The CC approach uses the distribution F_{01}, for the controls after treatment, to construct the counterfactual. The counterfactual value of an observed outcome for a treated individual, y, is given by $F_{01}^{-1}(F_{00}(y))$, where $F_{00}(y)$ is the probability corresponding to y in the distribution of outcomes for the controls before treatment and $F_{01}^{-1}(.)$ gives the quantile of that probability in the post-treatment distribution for the controls.

37.3.5 Panel Data Models

Where repeated observations are available on individuals we can extend the linear DD model, (34), to a panel data regression model that includes error components:

$$y_{it} = \tau d_{it} + x'_{it}\beta + \alpha_t + \gamma_i + \varepsilon_{it} \tag{35}$$

where $i(i = 1,...n)$ indexes individuals and t time $(t = 1,...,T)$. This is a two-way fixed effects specification (2FE) where the time effects (α_t) capture the common trend, usually measured by including a dummy variable for each wave of the panel, and each individual has their own fixed effect (γ_i) to capture their time-invariant characteristics.

With individual panel data an individual's own history, prior to treatment is used to construct the counterfactual. In effect, they are used as their own control group. But there may be other "natural control groups" that can be used to form the counterfactual. For example, variation within families can be used to control for shared environmental and genetic traits: this can involve using information on parents or grandparents (Auld and Sidhu 2005); information on siblings (Currie and Stabile 2006); or on twins (Behrman and Rosenzweig 2004; Almond et al. 2005; Black et al. 2007).

In this context, the estimate of τ is a difference-in-differences estimator. The consistency of this estimate relies on a particular variant of the unconfoundedness or conditional independence assumption (11):

$$E(y_{it}^0 | d_{it}, x_{it}, t, \gamma_i) = E(y_{it}^0 | x_{it}, t, \gamma_i) \tag{36}$$

The individual effect in (35) can be removed from the equation by transforming the variables to represent deviations from their within individual means:

$$y_{it} - \overline{y}_i = \tau\left(d_{it} - \overline{d}_i\right) + \left(x'_{it} - \overline{x}'_i\right)\beta + (\alpha_t - \overline{\alpha}) + (\varepsilon_{it} - \varepsilon_{it-1}) \tag{37}$$

with $\overline{y}_i = 1/T\sum_{t=1}^{T} y_{it}$ etc. Alternatively, first differencing the data has the same desired effect:

$$y_{it} - y_{it-1} = \tau\left(d_{it} - d_{it-1}\right) + \left(x'_{it} - x'_{it-1}\right)\beta + (\alpha_t - \alpha_{t-1}) + (\varepsilon_{it} - \varepsilon_{it-1}) \tag{38}$$

Note, however, that in both approaches not only is the unobserved individual effect removed but also all time-invariant regressors. A further approach is to specify fixed effects by including dummy variables for each individual.[12] This approach becomes burdensome where the number of individuals is large.[13]

The credibility of the conditional independence assumption used above in equation (36) may be strengthened when the panel data model conditions on lagged values of the regressors and, more importantly on lagged outcomes. For example, with a one-period lag of the outcome this gives the dynamic specification:

$$y_{it} = \tau d_{it} + \delta y_{it-1} + x'_{it} \beta + \alpha_t + \gamma_i + \varepsilon_{it} \tag{39}$$

which implies a modified version of the conditional independence assumption:

$$E(y^0_{it} \mid d_{it}, y_{it-1}, x_{it}, t, \gamma_i) = E(y^0_{it} \mid y_{it-1}, x_{it}, t, \gamma_i) \tag{40}$$

For models like (39), that include dynamics as well as an individual effect, the usual fixed effects estimators such as within-groups or first differences break-down. This is because the transformations induce correlation with the error term ε_{it}. Arellano and Bond (1991) proposed generalized method of moments (GMM) estimators for these kinds of dynamic panel data models. Instruments are created within the model by first taking differences of the equation to sweep out the individual effect and then using lagged levels or differences of the regressors as instruments. The validity of this approach rests on the degree of autocorrelation in the error term.

Bover and Arellano (1997) extended the use of GMM to dynamic specifications for categorical and limited dependent variable models, where it is not possible to take first differences or deviations as the latent variable y^* is unobserved. Contoyannis et al. (2003) consider the determinants of a binary indicator for functional limitations using seven waves of the British Household Panel Survey (BHPS). Their models allow for persistence in the observed outcomes due to state dependence, unobservable individual effects and persistence in the transitory error component. These are estimated by Maximum Simulated Likelihood using the GHK simulator. In related work Contoyannis et al. (2004) explore the dynamics of self-assessed health (SAH) in the BHPS. In this kind of application it is quite likely that the unobserved individual effect will be correlated with the observed regressors including indicators of treatment. Also, it is well-known that dynamic specifications raise the issue of how to treat the initial observations, y_{i0}, often referred to as the *initial conditions problem*. To deal

---

[12] Excluding one individual to represent the baseline case against which the effects of others can be contrasted.

[13] Inferences concerning the estimate of τ depend on the assumptions made about the error term ε_{it} and it may not be reasonable to assume serial independence. Bertrand, Duflo, and Mullainthan (2004) have suggested that standard errors should be adjusted to allow for clustering within individuals in applications of DD.

with the problem of initial conditions an attractively simple approach suggested by Wooldridge (2005) can be used. This specifies the distribution of the individual effects as a linear function of the outcome at the first wave of the panel and of the within-individual means of endogenous regressors.

37.4 Ex Ante Evaluation and Micro-simulation

The techniques outlined above offer approaches to the ex post evaluation of treatment effects by comparing outcomes across suitably constructed treatment and control groups. Clearly, ex post evaluation is crucial in understanding the true impact of a treatment or policy. There may be situations, however, where the likely impact of the introduction of a policy or treatment is required, but where experimental approaches to ex post evaluation are not feasible, for example due to cost, or perhaps ethical or political concerns. In such circumstances, the ability to simulate the effects of a policy that currently does not exist but potentially could be implemented has become the focus of recent research. Ex ante approaches to evaluation have been used in the field of labor economics, where simulation of the labor supply response to changes in aspects of the tax-benefit system is of interest (for example Blundell and MaCurdy 1999; Creedy and Duncan 2002). In development economics ex ante evaluation has been used to investigate the effects of conditional cash transfer programs for stimulating improved social outcomes (see for example Todd and Wolpin 2006, 2009).

While ex post evaluation uses data on both the treated and non-treated, for ex ante evaluation the treatment group is simulated to represent the population characteristics of interest as they would appear under the hypothetical policy change. Ex ante evaluation can be based on either structural estimation or reduced form estimation, built on behavioral models (Todd and Wolpin 2006, 2009). For example, this might involve changing household budget constraints to reflect the impact of wage subsidies, income support or conditional cash transfers (CCTs), as in Todd and Wolpin (2009), who evaluate Mexico's PROGRESA experiment. They adopt a reduced form approach that avoids the use of structural estimation and specific functional forms. They show that, if the impact of the policy reform can be captured wholly through changes in the budget constraint, a fully non-parametric approach can be used and they derive a matching estimator to identify the treatment effects. This places ex ante evaluation within the potential outcomes framework and constructs counterfactuals by matching untreated individuals with other untreated individuals. The matching is based on functions of observable variables that are generated by the model, reflecting the impact of the policies on shadow prices and full income in the budget constraint. For example, if the impact of a proposed policy would be to increase a household's income by $500, that household would be matched with another that has an income $500 greater than theirs but that is comparable in terms of other relevant characteristics.

Micro-simulation has been suggested as an instrument for ex ante evaluation (Bourguignon and Spadaro 2006). Micro-simulation models consider the changes, at a micro level, in the economic circumstances brought about by a policy and the corresponding imputed behavioral responses and outcomes. Typically micro-simulation models consider representative samples of agents such as individuals or households and assess the impact of policy on these samples. An advantage of the micro-simulation approach is that the imputed consequences of a policy change can be made over various time horizons. Further, since imputed changes can be made at the individual level, evaluation of the distributional impact of policies can be undertaken (Spadaro 2005).

Micro-simulation is an established and widely used tool for analyzing the impact of policies and has been developed in areas outside the health sector, most commonly focusing on the impact of fiscal policies on population income and welfare distributions. The approach, however, has yet to be used widely in health economics. Micro-simulation models can be arithmetical or behavioral and static or dynamic (Bourguignon and Spadaro 2006). Arithmetical models are simply concerned with the gainers and losers from a policy and ignore any behavioral responses that might be brought about by the reform. In this sense, arithmetic models estimate the immediate impact of a policy. Behavioral micro-simulation, in contrast, accounts for the behavioral response of individuals to the policy intervention often achieved through the use of structural behavioral models based on a utility maximizing framework subject to a budget constraint. The approach has the benefit of allowing policy evaluation to be assessed on the basis of corresponding social welfare functions (Spadaro 2005). The various parameters of the utility function are estimated using appropriate data, for example, a household survey. Once estimates of the parameters are known, simulating outcomes of interest under alternative policy regimes can be undertaken.

Static micro-simulation models offer a snap-shot of the impact of a policy reform at a particular point in time. The simulated population is the same as the reference population with the exception that relevant characteristics (income, consumption, health, etc.) are updated. This approach is appropriate if there are few long-run behavioral responses to the policy. Dynamic models, in contrast, project samples of individuals over time. Often this is achieved by creating a synthetic panel that simulates individual or household trajectories. The approach incorporates relevant life-course events such as changes in demographics, household composition, educational attainment and labor market transitions using what are termed dynamic aging techniques. Once the synthetic panel is constructed simulations of the impact of an intervention or policy reform can be computed. More ambitious approaches incorporate dynamics with behavioral responses to policy reforms. This adds an additional layer of complexity to the simulation whereby transition probabilities are assumed to be endogenous to the budget constraint requiring further estimation of more sophisticated structural models (Bourguignon and Spadaro 2006).

37.5 FURTHER READING

This chapter has skimmed the surface of a large and ever-growing literature. Comprehensive recent reviews are provided by: Angrist and Pischke (2008); Blundell and Costa-Dias (2008); Frölich (2004), who pays particular attention to multiple treatments; Heckman and Vytlacil (2007); Heckman (2008); Imbens and Wooldridge (2008), who give a general review and history of evaluation methods in econometrics and statistics and provide a formal treatment of some of the most recent technical developments; Lee (2005); and Todd (2008), who provides examples from development economics. Imbens (2004) concentrates on methods that apply under the assumption of unconfoundedness. Rubin (2006) collects together his contributions on the subject of matching. Caliendo and Kopeining (2008) focus on the practical application of propensity score matching. Auld (2006) discusses the pros and cons of the instrumental variable approach in the context of health economics. Heckman and Smith (1995), Banerjee and Duflo (2008), and Deaton (2008) debate the pros and cons of randomized social experiments. Bourguignon and Spadaro (2006) discuss micro-simulation techniques as a tool for the evaluation of public policies.

Jones (2009) provides a detailed review of the health econometrics literature since 2000 and focuses on the identification strategies that have been adopted in recent work with health data.

Cameron and Trivedi (2009) provide a comprehensive guide to the use of Stata for micro-econometrics including many of the approaches discussed in this chapter. Jones, Rice, Bago d'Uva, and Balia (2007) illustrate the use of Stata for applied health economics, with a particular emphasis on panel data regression. Becker and Ichino (2002) and Nichols (2007) provide guidance on the application of estimators for treatment effects, especially matching approaches, in Stata.

REFERENCES

AAKVIK, A., T. H. HOLMAS, and E. KJERSTAD (2003). "A low-key social insurance reform-effects of multidisciplinary outpatient treatment for back pain patients in Norway." *Journal of Health Economics*, 22: 747–62.

—— J. J. HECKMAN, and E. J. VYTLACIL (2005). "Estimating treatment effects for discrete outcomes when responses to treatment vary: an application to Norwegian vocational rehabilitation programs." *Journal of Econometrics*, 125: 15–51.

ABADIE, A. and G. IMBENS (2006). "Large sample properties of matching estimators for average treatment effects." *Econometrica*, 74: 235–67.

—— —— (2008). "On the failure of the bootstrap for matching estimators." *Econometrica*, 76: 1537–57.

ALMOND, D. (2006). "Is the 1918 influenza pandemic over? Long term effects of in utero influenza exposure in the post 1940 US." *Journal of Political Economy*, 114: 672–712.

—— K. Y. CHAY, and D. S. LEE (2005). "The costs of low birth weight." *Quarterly Journal of Economics*, 120: 1031–83.

ANDERSON, T. W. (1984). *Introduction to Multivariate Statistical Analysis*. 2nd edn. John Wiley & Sons.

ANGRIST, J. and S. PISCHKE (2008). *Mostly Harmless Econometrics: An Empiricist's Companion*. Princeton: Princeton University Press.

—— G. IMBENS, and D. RUBIN (1996). "Identification of causal effects using instrumental variables." *Journal of the American Statistical Association*, 91: 444–72.

ARELLANO, M. and S. BOND (1991). "Some tests of specification for panel data: Monte Carlo evidence and an application to employment equations." *Review of Economic Studies*, 58: 277–97.

ASHENFELTER, O. (1978). "Estimating the effect of training programs on earnings." *Review of Economics and Statistics*, 60: 47–57.

—— and D. CARD (1985). "Using the longitudinal structure of earnings to estimate the effect of training programs." *Review of Economics and Statistics*, 67: 648–60.

ATHEY, S. and G. W. IMBENS (2006). "Identification and inference in nonlinear difference-in-differences models." *Econometrica*, 74: 431–97.

AULD, M.C. (2006). "Using observational data to identify the causal effects of health-related behaviour." In A. M. Jones (ed.), *The Elgar Companion to Health Economics*. Cheltenham: Edward Elgar.

—— and N. SIDHU (2005). "Schooling, cognitive ability and health." *Health Economics*, 14: 1019–34.

BANERJEE, A. V. and E. DUFLO (2008). "The experimental approach to development economics." NBER Working Paper w14467.

BAUM, C. F., M. E. SCHAFFER, and S. STILLMAN (2003). "Instrumental variables and GMM: estimation and testing." *Stata Journal*, 3: 1–31.

BASU, A., J. HECKMAN, S. NAVARRO, and S. URZUA (2007). "Use of instrumental variables in the presence of heterogeneity and self-selection: an application to treatments of breast cancer patients." *Health Economics*, 16: 1133–57.

—— D. POLSKY, and W. G. MANNING (2008). "Do propensity score methods suffer from the curse of dimensionality? Finite sample evidence from non-linear response models." HEDG Working Paper 08/11, University of York.

BECKER, S. and A. ICHINO (2002). "Estimation of average treatment effects based on propensity scores." *The Stata Journal*, 2: 358–77.

BEHRMAN, J. R. and M. R. ROSENZWEIG (2004). "Returns to birthweight." *Review of Economics and Statistics*, 86: 586–601.

BERTRAND, M., E. DUFLO, and S. MULLAINATHAN (2004). "How much should we trust differences-in-differences estimates?" *The Quarterly Journal of Economics*, 119: 249–75.

BJÖRKMAN, M. and J. SVENSSON (2009). "Power to the people: evidence from a natural randomized field experiment on community-based monitoring in Uganda." *The Quarterly Journal of Economics*, 124: 735–69.

BLACK, S., P. DEVEREUX, and K. SALVANES (2007). "From the cradle to the labour market ? The effect of birth weight on adult outcomes." *The Quarterly Journal of Economics*, 122: 409–39.

BLEAKLEY, H. (2007). "Disease and development evidence from hookwork eradication in the Americal South." *The Quarterly Journal of Economics*, 122: 73–117.

BLUNDELL, R. and M. COSTA-DIAS (2008). "Alternative approaches to evaluation in empirical microeconomics." CEMMAP working paper CWP26/08.

BLUNDELL, R. and T. MACURDY (1999). "Labour supply: A review of alternative approaches." In O. Ashenfelter and D. Card (eds.), *Handbook of Labor Economics*, Vol. 3A. Amsterdam: Elsevier.

BOVER, O. and M. ARELLANO (1997). "Estimating dynamic limited-dependent variable models from panel data." *Investigaciones Economicas*, 21: 141–65.

BOURGUIGNON, F. and A. SPADARO (2006). "Microsimulation as a tool for evaluating redistribution policies." *Journal of Economic Inequality*, 4: 77–106.

CALIENDO, M. and S. KOPENEINIG (2008). "Some practical guidance for the implementation of propensity score matching." *Journal of Economic Surveys*, 22: 31–72.

CAMERON, A. C. and P. K. TRIVEDI (2009). *Microeconometrics Using Stata*. College Station, Texas: Stata Press.

CARD, D. and L. D. SHORE-SHEPPARD (2004). "Using discontiunous eligibility rules to identify the effects of the federal medicaid expansions on low-income children." *Review of Economics and Statistics*, 86: 752–66.

—— C. DOBKIN, and N. MAESTAS (2008). "The impact of nearly universal insurance coverage on health care utilization: evidence from Medicare." *American Economic Review*, 98: 2242–58.

CARPENTER, C. and C. DOBKIN (2009). "The effect of alcohol consumption on mortality: regression discontinuity evidence from the minimum drinking age." *American Economic Journal: Applied Economics*, 1: 164–82.

CLAXTON, K. P. (1999). "The irrelevance of inference: a decision making approach to the stochastic evaluation of health care technologies." *Journal of Health Economics*, 17: 341–64.

COCHRAN, W. and D. RUBIN (1973). "Controlling bias in observational studies: a review." *Sankhya*, 35: 417–46.

CONTOYANNIS, P., A. M. JONES, and N. RICE (2003). "Simulation-based inference in dynamic panel probit models: an application to health." *Empirical Economics*, 28: 1–29.

—— —— —— (2004). "The dynamics of health in the British household panel survey." *Journal of Applied Econometrics*, 19: 473–503.

CRAGG, J. G. and S. G. DONALD (1993). "Testing indentifiability and specification in instrumental variables models." *Econometric Theory*, 9: 222–40.

CREEDY, J. and A. DUNCAN (2002) "Behavioral micro-simulation with labor supply responses." *Journal of Economic Surveys*, 16: 1–39.

CURRIE, J. and M. STABILE (2006). "Child mental health and human capital accumulation: the case of ADHD." *Journal of Health Economics*, 25: 1094–118.

DEATON, A. S. (2008). "Instruments of development: randomization in the tropics, and the search for the elusive keys to economic development." NBER Working Paper 14690.

DEB, P. and P. K. TRIVEDI (2006). "Specification and simulated likelihood estimation of a nonnormal treatment-outcome model with selection: application to health care utilization." *Econometrics Journal*, 9: 307–31.

—— C. LI, P. K. TRIVEDI, and D. M. ZIMMER (2006a). "The effect of managed care on use of health care services: results from two contemporaneous household surveys." *Health Economics*, 15: 743–60.

—— M. K. MUNKIN, and P. K. TRIVEDI (2006b). "Bayesian analysis of the two-part model with endogeneity: application to health care expenditure." *Journal of Applied Econometrics*, 21: 1081–99.

DEHEIJA, R. and S. WAHBA (1999). "Causal effects in nonexperimental studies: re-evaluating the evaluation of training programs." *Journal of the American Statistical Association*, 94: 1053–62.

—— —— (2002). "Propensity score matching methods for nonexperimental causal studies." *Review of Economic Studies*, 84: 151–61.

DOYLE, J. J. (2005). "Health insurance, treatment and outcomes: using auto accidents as health shocks." *Review of Economics and Statistics,* 87: 256–70.

DUFLO, E. (2000). "Child health and household resources in South Africa: evidence from the old age pension program." *American Economic Review,* 90: 393–8.

EVANS, W. N. and D. S. LIEN (2005). "The benefits of prenatal care: evidence from the PAT bus strike." *Journal of Econometrics,* 125: 207–39.

FRIJTERS, P., J. P. HAISKEN-DENEW, and M. A. SHIELDS (2005). "The causal effect of income on health: evidence from German reunification." *Journal of Health Economics,* 24: 997–1017.

FRÖLICH, M. (2004). "Programme evaluation with multiple treatments." *Journal of Economic Surveys,* 18: 181–224.

GALIANI, S., P. GERTLER, and S. E. SCHARGRODSKY (2005). "Water for life: the impact of the privatization of water services on child mortality." *Journal of Political Economy,* 113: 83–120.

GERTLER, P. (2004). "Do conditional cash transfers improve child health? Evidence from PROGRESA's control randomized experiment." *American Economic Review,* 94: 336–41.

GEWEKE, J., G. GOWRISANKARAN, and R. J. TOWN (2003). "Bayesian inference for hospital quality in a selection model." *Econometrica,* 71: 1215–38.

HAHN, J. (1998). "On the role of the propensity score in efficient semiparametric estimation of average treatment effects." *Econometrica,* 66: 315–31.

—— and J. HAUSMAN (2002). "Notes on bias in estimators for simultaneous equation models." *Economics Letters,* 75: 237–41.

HANSEN, L. (1982). "Large sample properties of generalized method of moments estimators." *Econometrica,* 50: 1029–54.

HECKMAN, J. J. (1979). "Sample selection bias as a specification error." *Econometrica,* 47: 153–62.

—— (2008). "Econometric causality." CEMMAP working paper CWP1/08.

—— and R. ROBB (1985). "Alternative models for evaluating the impact of interventions." In J. J. Heckman and B. Singer (eds.), *Longitudinal Analysis of Labor Market Data.* Cambridge: Cambridge University Press.

—— and J. A. SMITH (1995). " Assessing the case for social experiments." *Journal of Economic Perspectives,* 9: 85–115.

—— and E. VYTLACIL (1999). "Local instrumental variables and latent variable models for identifying and bounding treatment effects." *Proceedings of the National Academy of Sciences,* 96: 4730–4.

—— —— (2007). "Econometric evaluation of social programs." In J. J. Heckman and E. Leamer (eds.), *Handbook of Econometrics,* Vol. 6B. Amsterdam: Elsevier.

—— J. A. SMITH, and N. CLEMENTS (1997). "Making the most out of programme evaluations and social experiments: accounting for heterogeneity in programme impacts." *Review of Economic Studies,* 64: 487–535.

—— H. ICHIMURA, and P. E. TODD (1997). "Matching as an econometric evaluation estimator: evidence from evaluating a job training programme." *Review of Economic Studies,* 64: 605–54.

—— —— —— (1998). "Matching as an econometric evaluation estimator." *Review of Economic Studies,* 65: 261–94.

—— —— J. A. SMITH, and P. E. TODD (1998). "Characterizing selection bias using experimental data." *Econometrica,* 66: 1017–98.

—— R. J. LALONDE, and J. A. SMITH (1999). "The economics and econometrics of active labor market programs." In O. Ashenfelter and D. Card (eds.), *Handbook of Labor Economics Volume III.* Amsterdam: Elsevier.

HIRANO, K. and G. W. IMBENS (2001). "Estimation of causal effects using propensity score weighting: an application to data on right heart catheterization." *Health Services & Outcomes Research Methodology*, 2: 259–78.

—— —— and G. RIDDER (2003). "Efficient estimations of average treatment effects using the estimated propensity score." *Econometrica*, 71: 1161–89.

HO, D. E., K. IMAI, G. KING, and E. A. STUART (2007). "Matching as nonparametric preprocessing for reduced model dependence in parametric causal inference." *Political Analysis*, 15: 199–236.

HOLLAND, P. W. (1986). "Statistics and causal inference." *Journal of the American Statistical Association*, 81: 945–60.

IMBENS, G. W. (2004). "Nonparametric estimation of average treatment effects under exogeneity: a review." *Review of Economics and Statistics*, 86: 4–29.

—— and J. ANGRIST (1994). "Identification and estimation of local average treatment effects." *Econometrica*, 62: 467–75.

—— and J. M. WOOLDRIDGE (2008). "Recent developments in the econometrics of program evaluation." NBER Working Paper 14251.

INDURKHYA, A., N. MITRA, and D. SCHRAG (2006). "Using propensity scores to estimate the cost-effectiveness of medical therapies." *Statistics in Medicine*, 25: 1561–76.

JENSEN, R. T. and K. RICHTER (2004). "The health implications of social security failure: evidence from the Russian pension crisis." *Journal of Public Economics*, 88: 209–36.

JONES, A. M. (2009). "Panel data methods and applications to health economics." In T. C. Mills and K. Patterson (eds.) *Palgrave Handbook of Econometrics*. Vol. II: *Applied Econometrics*. Basingstoke: Palgrave MacMillan.

—— N. RICE, T. BAGO D'UVA, and S. BALIA (2007). *Applied Health Economics*. London: Routledge.

KING, G. and L. ZENG (2007). "When can history be our guide? The pitfalls of counterfactual inference." *International Studies Quarterly*, 51: 183–210.

LALONDE, R. J. (1986). "Evaluating the Econometric Evaluations of Training Programs with Experimental Data." *American Economic Review*, 76: 604–20.

LEE, M.-J. (2005). *Micro-econometrics for Policy, Program, and Treatment Effects*. Oxford: Oxford University Press.

LINDAHL, M. (2005). "Estimating the effect of income on health and mortality using lottery prizes as exogenous source of variation in income." *Journal of Human Resources*, 40: 144–68.

LLERAS-MUNEY, A. (2005). "The relationship between education and adult mortality in the United States." *Review of Economic Studies*, 72: 189–221.

LUDWIG, J. and D. L. MILLER (2007). "Does Head Start improve children's life chances? Evidence from a regression discontinuity design." *Quarterly Journal of Economics*, 122: 159–208.

MANSKI, C. F. (1990). "Nonparametric bounds on treatment effects." *American Economic Review Papers and Proceedings*, 80: 319–23.

—— (2005). *Social Choice with Partial Knowledge of Treatment Response*. Princeton: Princeton University Press.

MEYER, B. (1995). "Natural and quasi-experiments in economics." *Journal of Business and Economic Statistics*, 12: 151–61.

MIGUEL, E. and M. KREMER (2004). "Worms: Identifying impacts on education and health in the presence of treatment externalities." *Econometrica*, 72: 159–217.

NICHOLS, A. (2007). "Causal inference with observational data." *The Stata Journal*, 7: 507–41.

PAGAN, A. R. and D. HALL (1983). "Diagnostic tests as residual analysis." *Econometric Reviews*, 2: 159–218.

PESARAN, M. H. and L. W. TAYLOR (1999). "Diagnostics for IV regressions." *Oxford Bulletin of Economics and Statistics*, 61: 255–81.

POP-ELECHES, C. (2006). "The impact of an abortion ban on socioeconomic outcomes of children: evidence from Romania." *Journal of Political Economy*, 114: 744–73.

RAMSEY, J. B. (1969). "Tests for specification errors in classical linear least squares regression analysis." *Journal of the Royal Statistical Society Series B*, 31: 350–71.

Robins, J. M. and Y. RITOV (1997). "Towards a curse of dimensionality appropriate (CODA) asymptotic theory for semi-parametric models." *Statistics in Medicine*, 16: 285–319.

—— and A. ROTNITZKY (1995). "Semiparametric efficiency in multivariate regression models with missing data." *Journal of the American Statistical Association*, 90: 122–29.

ROSENBAUM, P. R. and D. B. RUBIN (1983). "The central role of the propensity score in observational studies for causal effects." *Biometrika*, 70: 41–55.

—— —— (1984). "Reducing the bias in observational studies using subclassification on the propensity score." *Journal of the American Statistical Association*, 79: 516–24.

ROSENZWEIG, M. R. and K. I. WOLPIN (2000). "Natural 'natural experiments' in economics." *Journal of Economic Literature*, XXXVIII: 827–74.

ROY, A. (1951). "Some thoughts on the distribution of earnings." *Oxford Economic Papers*, 3: 135–46.

RUBIN, D. B. (1973a). "Matching to remove bias in observational studies." *Biometrics*, 29: 159–83.

—— (1973b). "The use of matched sampling and regression adjustments to remove bias in observational studies." *Biometrics*, 29: 185–203.

—— (1974). "Estimating causal effects of treatments in randomized and non-randomized studies." *Journal of Eductational Psychology*, 66: 688–701.

—— (1979). "Using multivariate matched sampling and regression adjustment to control bias in observational studies." *Journal of the American Statistical Association*, 74: 318–28.

—— (2006). *Matched Sampling for Causal Effects*. Cambridge: Cambridge University Press.

SARGAN, J. D. (1958). "The estimation of economic relationships using instrumental variables." *Econometrica*, 26: 393–415.

SILVERMAN, B.W. (1986). *Density Estimation for Statistics and Data Analysis*. London: Chapman and Hall.

SPADARO, A. (2005). "Micro-simulation and normative policy evaluation: an application to some EU tax benefit systems." *Journal of Public Economic Theory*, 7: 593–622.

STAIGER, D. and J. H. STOCK (1997). "Instrumental variables regression with weak instruments." *Econometrica*, 65: 557–86.

STILLMAN, S., D. MCKENZIE, and J. GIBSON (2009). "Migration and mental health: Evidence from a natural experiment." *Journal of Health Economics*, 28: 677–87.

STOCK, J. H. and M. YOGO (2002). "Testing for weak instruments in linear IV regression." NBER Technical Working Paper No 284. <http:www.nber.org/papers/T0284>.

TODD, P. E. (2008). "Evaluating social programs with endogenous program placement and selection of the treated." In T. P. Schultz and J. A. Strauss (eds.) *Handbook of Development Economics*, Vol. 4. Amsterdam: Elsevier.

—— and K. I. WOLPIN (2006). "Assessing the impact of a school subsidy program in Mexico: using a social experiment to validate a dynamic behavioural model of child schooling and fertility." *American Economic Review*, 96: 1384–417.

TODD, P. E. and K. I. WOLPIN (2009) "Ex ante evaluation of social programs." *Annales d'Economie et de Statistiques*. ADRES, 55–56.

VAN DEN BERG, G. J., M. LINDEBOOM, and F. PORTRAIT (2006). "Economic conditions early in life and individual mortality." *The American Economic Review*, 96: 290–302.

WOOLDRIDGE, J. M. (2002). *Econometric Analysis of Cross Section and Panel Data*. Cambridge, MA: MIT Press.

—— (2005). "Simple solutions to the initial conditions problem in dynamic nonlinear panel data models with unobserved heterogeneity." *Journal of Applied Econometrics*, 20: 39–54.

ZIMMER, D. M. and P. K. TRIVEDI (2006). "Using trivariate copulas to model sample selection and treatment effects: application to family health care demand." *Journal of Business & Economic Statistics*, 24: 63–76.

....

CHAPTER 38

HEALTH ECONOMICS AND POLICY: THE CHALLENGES OF PROSELYTIZING

....

ALAN MAYNARD AND KAREN BLOOR

THE preceding chapters have revealed the breadth of scope and the complexity of health economics. In this concluding chapter we review the state of the sub-discipline. What are its successes and what are its failures? Has health economics informed and improved decision-making in health policy and practice, or do the products of the profession remain esoteric and inaccessible to health professionals and the policy community? What lacunae remain to be addressed, and what are prospects for the future?

Health economics is concerned with analyzing the production and distribution of health, and health care is one input into these processes. Its economic significance in terms of its level and growth rate in relation to GDP makes it an important area of policymaking and a large market for the employment of economists. As with all areas of scientific endeavor there is a need for health economists to focus not only on the production of new knowledge but also on the translation of evidence into practice. To term this as "proselytizing" is perhaps provocative but nonetheless highlights the need not only to add to the evidence base about what works at what cost in the markets for health and health care, but also to advocate the use of this knowledge to policymakers and practitioners. When seeking to convert others to the economist's path, it is always useful to bear in mind the dictum of the late Alan Williams: "Be reasonable! Do it my way!" (Culyer 1997).

While the sub-discipline has been relatively successful in engaging with clinicians, some economists remain reluctant to engage with policy. Policy can be defined in many ways e.g. "political sagacity; prudent conduct, craftiness, and a course of action adopted by government or a party" (*Concise Oxford Dictionary*). Many policymakers have limited experience in interpreting statistical analysis, but they are also often unfamiliar with the sometimes esoteric language of economics. This means that participation in the policy process often requires simplification and repetition. Furthermore tenure in many political posts may be short-lived requiring economic proselytes to reinforce continually their arguments to new incumbents in strategic policy posts.

Key characteristics in advancing knowledge from the ivory tower to the policy environment are timeliness and relevance, as seen by the users of health economic advice. This may require purveyors of that advice to be sensitive to fluctuations in policy priorities, to be patient and opportunistic, and where appropriate to repackage their wares appropriately without compromising scientific integrity and quality of research. This is not an easy balance to maintain.

38.1 Global Health Policy Goals

The ranking of policy goals fluctuates over time, and there are trade-offs to be confronted in the pursuit of each. But three objectives remain central to most if not all health policy reforms: efficiency, equity, and expenditure control.

38.1.1 The Pursuit of Efficiency

Efficiency in health care, broadly defined, means maximizing "health" within available budgets, so it combines clinical priorities (to improve the health of patients and populations and to improve the quality of health care) with economic priorities (to achieve this while minimizing opportunity costs). For decades the efficiency of public and private health care systems has been constrained by a weak evidence base about the clinical and cost-effectiveness of therapies used in everyday medical practice. This has contributed to a marked propensity for clinicians to deliver very different amounts and types of health care, to patients with similar health care needs and personal characteristics. Other persistent efficiency failures include an apparently universal reluctance to benchmark and reduce avoidable medical errors and a lack of focus on regulation of health care that focuses on outcomes, especially patient reported outcome measures (PROMs), rather than structure and process (Wennberg, Freeman, and Culp 1987; Committee on Quality Health Care in America 1999; Kohn, Corrigan, and Donaldson 1999; Maynard 2008). These failures to deliver what is cost-effective to patients and to give both insurees and taxpayers "value for money" have also fuelled expenditure inflation and thwarted attempts by policymakers to improve equity in health care and health.

The market for health care is beset with market failures and perverse incentives, which mean that inefficiencies are difficult to address. In insurance based systems, market failures including moral hazard, asymmetry of information, and supplier induced demand mean that, instead of tackling inefficiency, the purchasing insurance companies are able to pass on cost inflation to insurees and their employers in increased insurance premia. The impact of this expenditure inflation could in principle be mitigated by tax breaks, but in practice these may even have exacerbated failures as they tend to be inequitable and have substantial opportunity costs, in terms of public finance forgone and possible distortions in the broader economy.

In public health care systems similar perverse incentives exist, influencing both patients and providers, and often leading to inefficient resource allocation. Whilst the purchasers in such systems may find it more difficult than insurance companies to raise expenditure, depending on the time in the electoral cycle, they also generally lack the instruments to engineer change. Thus in the English NHS, the strategic purchaser (the Primary Care Trust) has to remunerate provider Trust hospitals according to a fixed tariff price, and they have little or no control over volume or process and outcome quality. Thus inefficiency in both public and private systems is a necessary product of the incentive structure. Without reform of payment and monitoring systems (e.g. comparative cost, activity, and outcome data at the practitioner level) waste is institutionalized in health care systems.

38.1.2 The Pursuit of Equity

Both economists and policymakers are concerned not only with the efficient production of "health" but with its distribution. While there have been advances over recent decades in life expectancy, these have not been distributed evenly throughout populations. The main rationale for the development of public health care systems and for much of the public intervention in private markets, was altruistic concern about the health of the poor. This, in combination with more self-interested concerns about public health risks (e.g. the externalities created by infectious disease) and the economic benefits of keeping the workforce healthy, justifies public intervention in health care. Equity concerns are epitomized by the creation of health insurance in Germany by Bismarck in the late nineteenth century, and by Lloyd George in Britain in the early twentieth century. In more recent times such concerns remain, but are still supplemented by public health and externality arguments. Concern for equity is illustrated by civil disturbance protests around the inadequacy of health care in rural China, and by the tardy attempts of the USA to deal with forty-six million citizens lacking insurance coverage. Public health and externality concerns are epitomized by the threats to public health arising from severe acute respiratory syndrome (SARS) and, more recently, the threats of an influenza pandemic. Health care reforms tend to be promoted as altruistic and equity-driven, but almost always contain a component of political and personal self-interest.

Whilst equity concerns often precipitate health care reform, the evaluation of the success of reforms, in terms of improvements in health and utilization of health care of the poor has been generally poor. Health inequalities are persistent (Townsend and Davidson 1982; Becker 1991; van Doorslaer et al. 1997; Wagstaff et al. 1999), and sporadic policy attempts to reduce them tend to focus on access to, and utilization of, health care, for example by reducing price barriers to consumption and reallocating funds to deprived communities. The actual and relative health gain acquired from these investments, and their cost-effectiveness as means of improving and equalizing population health, often remains unclear. There are, of course, many more important determinants of health than the provision of health care. Economists are emphasizing, for example, the role of genetics and investments in preschool children as key determinant of health over the life cycle. The implication is that investments to improve cognitive and non-cognitive skills in the early years of life may produce better life chances and health than investing "downstream" in remedial health care (Becker 1991; Heckman 2006). This economic approach may produce insights and evidence that can be used to reform social processes, supplementing the existing dominant epidemiological literature (Marmot 2005; Wilkinson and Pickett 2009).

38.1.3 The Pursuit of Macro-economic Expenditure Control

The remarkable characteristic of health care expenditure is its unswerving upward path in most developed countries. The causes of this increase are numerous, and include wage increases in this highly labor-intensive industry, and price increases resulting from improvements in health care technology, often higher than are clearly justified by the health gain that they create. As Reinhardt emphasized thirty years ago (Reinhardt 1981) income and expenditure in health care is an identity: provider income is derived entirely from households, whether through taxation, insurance premia or out of pocket payments. While in purely economic terms, expenditure control is not a goal in itself if the expenditure is valued by households, there are dead weight losses associated with transactions costs of insurance systems and revenue raising under taxation. More importantly, market failures in health care all tend to be inflationary: information asymmetry and supplier induced demand all mean that health care expenditure tends to be higher than it would be if consumers were perfectly informed. This is one of the contributors to expenditure inflation in health care, which is a concern in tax funded systems and, because of competitiveness in the general economy, in privately dominated systems too.

In most health care systems, individuals do not face the costs of health care at the point of use, and therefore decisions about planning and commissioning health care are devolved to agents. Both public and private health care systems are characterized by weak purchasing agencies which tend to be passive price and quality takers rather than evidence based price and quality makers. The passivity of purchasers is a product of perverse incentives, weak information systems that fail to demonstrate performance of practitioners in relation to relative costs, activities and outcomes, and soft budget constraints. Whilst single payer public health care systems have the necessary conditions to control expenditure inflation, political advantage may result from increasing funding. Furthermore when governments choose to increase health care funding significantly, as happened in the UK during the last decade, local and national management systems may be so weak that significant amounts of the funding are absorbed into pay and price increases (Maynard and Sheldon 2002; Wanless et al. 2007).

Private health care systems suffer from similar weaknesses. An OECD study concluded that premium levels tend to inflate worldwide at rates in excess of increases in local inflation (Colombo and Tapay 2004). As in public health care systems, the focus of management in the insurance industry has been on financial issues, particularly probity, rather than on value for money for households who fund health care either directly or through reduced wages.

38.2 THE RESPONSE OF HEALTH ECONOMISTS

Given the ubiquitous nature of these objectives, and the stubborn nature of market failures in health care, what do economists in this sector do and how well do they contribute to greater understanding of health and health care, and the mitigation of inefficiency, inequity, and expenditure inflation in health care systems?

Alan Williams described health economics in his "plumbing diagram" (Figure 38.1; Williams 1987). This system is made up of eight areas of activity, linked by interactive flows. Various attempts have been made to divide up the work of health economists amongst these areas. Comparing an analysis of journal articles in the period up to 2000 (Maynard and Kanavos 2000; Table 38.1) with the topics dealt with in this volume (Table 38.2) gives an impression of how health economists have allocated their own scarce resources—time, effort and energy—over recent decades.

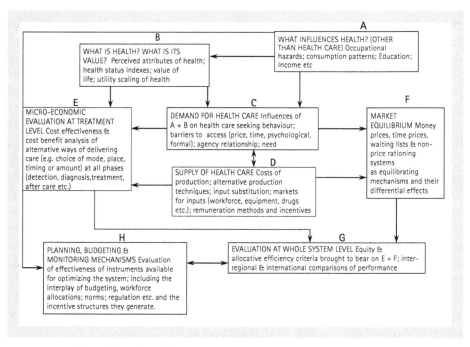

FIGURE 38.1 Williams' plumbing diagram
Source: Williams 1987.

Table 38.1 Percentage of Articles Falling in Each of Williams' Categories in the Two Leading Health Economics Journals up to 2000

Williams' category	Number of articles	Articles as a percentage of total
A: what influences health (other than health care)?	84	11
B: what is health? What is its value?	57	8
C: demand for health care	96	13
D: Supply of health care	152	21
E: Microeconomic evaluation at treatment level	108	15
F: Market equilibrium	57	8
G: Evaluation at whole system level	76	10
H: Planning, budgeting and monitoring mechanisms	90	12
Overview articles	16	2
Total	736	100

Source: Maynard and Kanavos 2000.

The content of this volume (Table 38.2) is rather different to the content of health economics journals between the 1980s and 2000 (Table 38.1), perhaps reflecting some rebalancing of the sub-discipline from microeconomic evaluation at treatment level towards more macro-level input into the evaluation of health systems, and demand for, supply of, and equilibrium in, health care markets. In addition, the persistence of health inequalities despite the existence of universal access to health care in most developed countries, along with emerging "epidemics" of behavior-related health problems such as obesity and alcohol-related illness, has resulted in a resurgence of interest in Williams' box A (what influences health, other than health care?). The rebalancing partly reflects the huge success of health economists in raising awareness of the importance of economic evaluation of health care interventions, and the "mainstreaming" of this into health services research. While progress is still being made in terms of methodological development in this area, as described in Chapters 31 and 32, it seems that health economists are increasingly directing their efforts into the policy field.

38.3 HEALTH ECONOMICS AND ITS IMPACT ON POLICY: SUCCESSES AND ISSUES REMAINING TO BE ADDRESSED

There are many areas where health economics has made a substantial impact on policy processes, including the four we focus on here: health technology assessment, tariffs for hospital care, outcome measurement and incentivizing health care delivery.

Table 38.2 Contributions from this Volume to Each of Williams' Categories

Category	Chapters
A: What influences health (other than health care)?	5: The promise of health 6: Health production 7: Socioeconomic status and health 8: Determinants of health in childhood 9: Economics of infectious diseases 10: Economics of health behaviors and addictions 11: Economics and mental health 23: Disease prevention, health care, and economics
B: What is health? What is its value?	33: Health utility measurement
C: Demand for health care	12: Public sector health care financing 13: Voluntary private health insurance 15: User charges 16: Insurance and the demand for medical care 17: Guaranteed access to affordable coverage in individual health insurance markets
D: Supply of health care	11: Economics and mental health 14: Health care cost growth 18: Managed care 19: Hospitals: teaming up 20: Primary care 21: The global health care workforce 22: The economics of the biopharmaceutical industry 24: Long term care 25: Physician agency and payment for primary health care 26: Provider payment and incentives
E: Microeconomic evaluation at treatment level	31: The methods of cost-effectiveness analysis 32: Analyzing uncertainty in cost-effectiveness for decision-making
F: Market equilibrium	27: Non-price rationing and waiting times 28: Increasing competition between providers in health care markets
G: Evaluation at whole system level	2: Health systems in industrialized countries 3: Health systems in low- and middle-income countries 4: The political economy of health care 34: Concepts of equity and fairness in health and health care 35: Measuring inequality and inequity in health and health care 36: Intergenerational aspects of health care
H: Planning, budgeting and monitoring mechanisms	29: Measuring organizational performance 30: Health system productivity

Nevertheless, even in these "success stories," problems remain to be addressed by the health economics community.

38.3.1 Health Technology Assessment

In most developed economy health care systems, perhaps with the exception of the United States (Singer 2009) it seems that the fundamental inevitability of health care rationing has been largely accepted by policymakers. The policy question has become not whether to ration care, but how? Systems of health technology assessment (HTA) involve rationing health care on the basis of comparative cost-effectiveness, often with the use of a "cut-off" cost per quality adjusted life year (QALY) criterion which may facilitate progress towards efficiency and cost containment objectives.

After US innovation in 1972 with the Office of Technology Assessment (Congress of the United States 1972), it was left to the Australians to introduce health technology assessment with legislative power, with their inclusion in 1993 of economic evaluation into the process of reimbursement decisions through the Pharmaceutical Benefits Advisory Committee (Henry, Hill, and Harris 2005). In the last decade the UK has also included HTA into reimbursement decisions, with the sophisticated and rigorous systems of the National Institute of Health and Clinical Excellence (NICE) and partner agencies in Scotland and Northern Ireland, which review the clinical and cost-effectiveness of new technologies. Similar agencies exist now in many other European countries and in Canada.

NICE has been a particularly vigorous advocate of HTA and is regarded by many as an example of good practice, in particular with regard to transparency in its processes. Without doubt, NICE, PBAC, and other agencies are transparent and largely rigorous in their practices but there remain some challenges for health economists and policymakers in the area of HTA.

First, there is a balance between rigor of analysis and its timeliness. NICE has been criticized for taking too long to appraise new interventions and perhaps even being "too" rigorous in comparison to other similar agencies (House of Commons Health Committee 2008). There may be scope for improving timeliness of these kinds of decisions by incorporating economic theories of decision-making under uncertainty (see Chapter 32), for example by conditional pricing or value based pricing schemes. However, the quality of NICE and other agencies' appraisal of new technologies is often dependent on the evidence that pharmaceutical companies present, which can be variable. In general, and unlike the Australian PBAC, NICE has so far operated as a price taker with no power to negotiate lower prices with industry and no responsibility to minimize NHS expenditure. If the cost-per-QALY threshold is interpreted by industry as a maximum price, this has potential to create or at least maintain cost inflation in health care.

Next, HTA agencies are necessarily selective in terms of which health care interventions they subject to appraisal. These organizations appear very proficient at adding to the therapies available to patients, even when they are of marginal cost-effectiveness, but they are poor at removing redundant or relatively cost ineffective interventions. This is needed especially when health service funding is likely to be relatively static, such as in a period of economic recession. The opportunity cost of accepting some new technologies with high costs per QALY may be that existing services, perhaps of superior cost-effectiveness, will be sacrificed. This highlights the issue of the appropriate cost-per-QALY "cut-off" or range, which is another area where health economists can contribute substantially. The utility basis of QALYs is an area of continuing methodological development (see Chapter 33), and there is evidence that local strategic purchasers in England use a lower cut off for routine services than the arbitrary and relative generous rationing criteria of NICE (Martin, Rice, and Smith 2007).

Thus, while it is clear that HTA has been a health economics success story, policy issues and methodological issues undoubtedly remain.

38.3.2 Pricing Hospital Care

Many countries throughout the world have emulated the initiative of US Medicare twenty-five years ago, and introduced tariffs for hospital care based on diagnostic related groups (DRGs). This created substantial improvements in efficiency in some systems, for example German sickness funds switched from per diem payments to DRGs at the beginning of the decade and this had the immediate effect of reducing length of stay, leading to underused beds and the closure of hospitals. As in the USA, Australia, and many other DRG-using countries there have been considerable benefits in reducing length of stay with no evident and significant effect on patient outcomes. Again this is a health economics success story, with the economists' views on opportunity cost, efficiency, and incentive structures contributing to a policy improvement.

Now that DRG-type tariff pricing has become accepted, there is a developing role in how to manipulate tariffs without damaging outcomes for patients. Inflating tariff rates by less than the rate of growth of general prices is intended to put further downward pressure on costs, and incentivize providers to be more efficient. The common practice in DRG systems is to fix tariffs in relation to the average cost of procedures. But why use the average? Why not fix them in relation to the cheapest quartile, or in relation to the most efficient providers? Some health care systems now relate the tariffs to the average cost of day case management of patients, with the intention of penalizing and altering the behavior of providers using inpatient stays (Street and Maynard 2007).

In future, it may be that rather than to use tariffs as a passive accounting tool, they can be used to incentivize change in hospital practices, for example to increase day case surgery. Similarly "never events" (things which should never happen in a well-run hospital; Rosenthal 2007) such as medication errors, wrong site surgery, patient trips and falls, and hospital acquired infections can be benchmarked and managed down by manipulating prices (for example by refusing to reimburse events which should not have happened). In any evaluation of such policies careful attention to patient outcome effects, opportunity costs and potential unintended consequences is essential.

38.3.3 Improving Incentive Structures in Health Care Provision

The discipline of economics in general has an inherent belief in the potentially beneficial effects of well-designed incentives. Nonetheless, in health care, policies to mitigate poor incentives, particularly those faced by individual practitioners, are only recently beginning to emerge, and economic questions remain.

In the UK, an interesting experiment in manipulating incentive structures faced by primary care doctors has been introduced in the quality and outcomes framework (QOF), part of the renegotiated contract for general practitioners (GPs) in 2004 (see Chapter 20). This incentivization of health care processes such as monitoring hypertension had noticeable effects on GP behavior and reduced variations in clinical compliance with guidelines (Doran et al. 2008; Campbell et al. 2009) However, it was costly and the relationship between some of its performance targets and likely population health improvements was questionable (Fleetcroft and Cookson 2006).

Incentive experiments are emerging at organizational as well as individual level. An example of this is the Centers for Medicare and Medicaid Services (CMS), Premier healthcare alliance Hospital Quality Incentive Demonstration (HQID) in the USA (Premier Healthcare Alliance 2010) which is being emulated in regions of the English NHS (Department of Health 2008). This program sets largely process or guideline parameters in five clinical areas: hip and knee replacements, coronary artery bypass graft surgery (CABG), heart failure, pneumonia, and acute myocardial infarction. Each hospital benchmarks its compliance with these parameters and reports annually on its progress, resulting in a "league table" of performance. The top 10 percent of performers, as measured by a "composite quality score," are then rewarded by an additional 2 percent quality incentive payment on their annual Medicare tariff payments, whilst the second best 10 percent performers gain a 1 percent quality payment reward. After three years, any hospitals which did not achieve a quality score above the ninth and tenth decile thresholds established in year one were threatened with a reduction in their tariff payments of 1 and 2 percent respectively.

Evidence of the effectiveness of the US incentives scheme is weak, as there has been no randomized controlled trial and most published reports lack any control group. Studies with non-equivalent control groups have reported modestly improved quality of care scores in the participating hospitals compared with non-participants (Grossbart 2006; Lindenauer et al. 2007) They also report converging hospital performance, with improvement of only 1.9 percent in the highest performing hospitals but 16.1 percent in the lowest, presumably as they strove to avoid the financial penalties (Lindenauer, Remus, Roman, Rothberg, Benjamin, Ma, and Bratzler 2007). The improvements were however based only on process measures, not on the outcome indicators, and a further study found no evidence of effect on mortality or on costs (Ryan 2009). A systematic review of all hospital pay for performance schemes found little formal evaluation, and methodological flaws in most of the eight published studies they located (Mehrotra et al.

2009). The conclusions from this overview of the evidence offer only modest encouragement for would-be reformers.

Incentive programs raise three significant economic questions. First, which is the more efficient policy focus, targeting individuals or teams of practitioners, as in the GP-QOF, or targeting institutions and organizations, as in the Premier scheme, in the hope that they in turn can alter the practices of clinicians and ensure the delivery of safer, more efficient care? Harris (1977; and see Chapter 19) argued that hospitals are two separate firms, each with separate objectives, managers, resourcing, and constraints. The demand side firm is managed by medical staff and the supply side is run by non-clinical managers and administrators. Harris argues that regulatory policy has been predominately targeted at the latter, and what is needed is the transfer of cost-minimizing incentives to medical firms within the hospital. This plausible logic implies that incentivization should be focused on practitioners rather than institutions, although actual choice of focus is an empirical issue. However this logic appears to have had little impact on the design of incentive reforms where the focus still tends to be on institutions.

Second, what is the relative role of rewards or bonuses for good performance compared with penalties or fines for poor performance, and what is the appropriate size of incentive either way? Prospect theory suggests that a small penalty will have a greater effect than a larger bonus (Kahneman and Tversky 1979). Is there evidence of this in health care? It seems that fines were never actually levied in the Premier/CMS alliance program, as the threat of them drove poor performers to change rapidly. What would have been the effect of their imposition, and if they are not levied, will behavior changes persist over time?

Finally, there is a general lack of information on the costs of significant quality improvement, and their value (cost-effectiveness) in terms of patient outcomes generated. To assess this may require further investment in improving patient reported outcome measures.

38.3.4 Development of Patient Reported Outcome Measures (PROMs)

The measurement of broad health outcomes, as reported by patients and valued by representative samples of the population, rather than narrow clinical measures of the success of interventions (see Chapter 34), has undoubtedly been a success story for health economics. The RAND health insurance experiment (Newhouse 1993) produced a quality of life measure (SF36) nearly forty years ago, and European parallels (in particular EQ-5D) have also been developed and used over several decades. These measures have been translated into dozens of languages and used in thousands of clinical trials and other forms of health services research, but the extension of their use into routine medical care has been remarkably slow.

Patient reported outcome measures (PROMs) are however now beginning to emerge in routine delivery of health care. In particular, the English NHS is making large investments

in PROMs. From April 2009 data has been collected before and after a number of procedures in routine NHS practice, starting with hip and knee replacement surgery, groin hernia repair and varicose vein procedures. In each of these interventions, patients are asked
to complete a condition-specific measure of benefit and also a generic outcome measure,
EQ-5D (EuroQol Group 2010). Some US centers and a British insurer, the British United
Provident Association (BUPA), have used variants of SF36 (<sf36.org>, accessed March
12, 2010) similarly, but no large public or private health care system has invested in PROMs
the way the English NHS is currently doing. There are plans in the NHS to collect PROMs
from patients in all surgical procedures in English public and private hospitals that treat
NHS patients. Over the next few years, hospital performance as rated by these measures
will be benchmarked and monitored, with rewards and financial penalties. In time it is also
planned to extend PROMs to six chronic conditions and subsequently to all care.

This substantial policy experiment generates equally substantial evaluative issues for
economists and others. Routine collection of patient reported outcomes will generate a
large volume of data reporting health gain in terms of the difference in physical and psychological functioning after compared to before treatment. It is to be hoped that evaluation will be appropriately funded to exploit this large and engaging body of data. The
economic issues around this work are numerous. What are the opportunity costs of this
initiative, in terms of administration and staff and patient time? In some treatment areas
(e.g. hernia repair and removing asymptomatic cancer growths) the patient is likely to
feel worse for some time after the procedure and may report negative outcomes. How
will this be reported to patients and the public? How will clinicians react if their patients
report are poorer outcomes than those of their peers? And perhaps most urgently, how
will the data be appropriately risk adjusted to avoid misleading inferences and the inevitable backlash from clinicians if this occurs?

38.4 CONCLUSIONS

This stimulating volume, and many of the authors of the preceding chapters, contribute
to and continue to develop a greater understanding of the evidence base informing
health policy. In general, the sub-discipline has progressed in a crab-like fashion, making some significant inroads to the policy process in some areas and but less so in others.
A sharp focus of the profession on policy issues must be maintained, and may improve
funding success during a period of recession. Faced with public sector financial constraints, policymakers are likely to turn increasingly to the economics profession for
solutions. We must be ready to help.

In retrospect, the lack of a clearer focus on incentives, outcome measurement in routine health care delivery and the determinants of health may be a product of how the
profession has been funded. In Europe, most funding in health economics has been
directed towards the economic evaluation of health technologies, in order to inform
rationing bodies like NICE. By collaborating with clinicians, economists have developed

a rich stream of funding both for methodological and applied work associated with the rise of HTA. Methodological and practical developments have been numerous and substantial in this field, and the importance of economics as part of the process of regulating reimbursement of new health technologies has become generally accepted in Europe. In the USA an analogous funding stream has been associated with the health insurance industry. It may be that the historical balance in terms of development of the sub-discipline has been affected perhaps too much by the availability of funding, rather than the priorities of society.

With developing research designs and an improving evidence base for health policy, the importance of proselytizing to ensure continued research funding and continued improvements in the efficient delivery of population health care remains. This work has to campaign for policymaking that is well-evidenced, cautious in its implementation and accompanied wherever possible by rigorous evaluation. The propensity of decision-makers to absorb ideas in a naïve fashion is ubiquitous, as illustrated by the burgeoning interest in financial incentive systems. Incentives will doubtless have an effect, but without careful design, implementation, and evaluation they may produce unintended consequences, incompatible with the health policy goals of efficiency, equity, and expenditure control.

This overview has highlighted a number of success stories from health economics, but also areas where we need to continue to develop improve the evidence base. We hope that the trademarks of economics, measurement, and incentivization, will continue to facilitate improved efficiency, equity, and macroeconomic expenditure control in future years, and that the proselytizing of health economists will continue.

References

BECKER, G. S., 1991, *A Treatise on the Family*, Harvard University Press, Cambridge, MA.

CAMPBELL, S. M., DREEVES, D., KONTOPANTELIS, E., SIBBALD, B., and ROLAND, M., 2009, Effects of pay for performance on the quality of primary care in England. *New England Journal of Medicine*, 361, 368–78.

COLOMBO, F. and TAPAY, N., 2004, *Private Health Insurance in OECD Countries: The Benefits and Costs for Individuals and Health Systems*, OECD, Paris.

COMMITTEE ON QUALITY HEALTH CARE IN AMERICA, 1999, *To Err Is Human: Building a Safer Health System*, Institute of Medicine, Washington, DC.

CONGRESS OF THE UNITED STATES, 1972, The Technology Assessment Act. Public Law 92-484, 92nd Congress: HR 10243.

CULYER, A. J., 1997, *Being Reasonable About the Economics of Health: Introduction*, Edward Elgar, Cheltenham, UK.

DEPARTMENT OF HEALTH, 2008, *Using the Commissioning for Quality and Innovation (CQUIN) Payment Framework*, Department of Health, London.

DORAN, T., FULLWOOD, C., KONTOPANTELIS, E., and REEVES, D., 2008, Effect of financial incentives on inequalities in the delivery of primary clinical care in England: analysis of clinical activity indicators for the quality and outcomes framework, *Lancet*, 372/9640, 728–36.

EUROQOL GROUP, 2010, *EuroQol Group*, Rotterdam, The Netherlands.

FLEETCROFT, R. and COOKSON, R., 2006, Do the incentive payments in the new NHS contract for primary care reflect likely population health gains?, *Journal of Health Services Research and Policy*, 11/1, 27–31.

GROSSBART, S., 2006, What's the return? Assessing the effect of "pay for performance" initiatives on the quality of care delivery, *Medical Care Research and Review*, 63, 29S–48.

HARRIS, J., 1977, The internal organization of hospitals: some economic implications, *The Bell Journal of Economics*, 8/2, 467–82.

HECKMAN, J. J., 2006, Skill formation and the economics of investing in disadvantaged children, *Science*, 312, 1900–2.

HENRY, D. A., HILL, S. R., and HARRIS, A., 2005, Drug prices and value for money: the Australian pharmaceutical benefits scheme, *Journal of the American Medical Association*, 294, 2630–2.

HOUSE OF COMMONS HEALTH COMMITTEE, 2008, *National Institute for Health and Clinical Excellence (NICE): Report on an Investigation by the Select Committee on Health*, House of Commons, Westminster.

KAHNEMAN, D. and TVERSKY, A., 1979, Prospect Theory:An analysis of decision under risk. *Econometrica*, 47/2, 263–92.

KOHN, L. T., CORRIGAN, J. M., and DONALDSON, M. S., 1999, *To Err is Human: Building a Safer Health System*, Institute of Medicine, Washington, DC.

LINDENAUER, P. K., REMUS, D., ROMAN, S., et al. 2007, Public reporting and pay for performance in hospital quality improvement, *New England Journal of Medicine*, 356/5, 486–96.

MARMOT, M., 2005, Social determinants of health inequalities, *Lancet*, 365, 1099–104.

MARTIN, S., RICE, N., and SMITH, P.C., 2007, Further evidence on the link between health care spending and health outcomes, Centre for Health Economics, University of York, York, CHE Research Paper 32.

MAYNARD, A., 2008, *Payment for Performance (P4P): International Experience and a Cautionary Proposal for Estonia*, WHO, Paris.

—— and KANAVOS, P., 2000, Health economics: an evolving paradigm, *Health Economics*, 9/3, 183–90.

—— and SHELDON, T., 2002, Funding for the National Health Service, *Lancet*, 360/9332, 576.

MEHROTRA, A., DAMBERG, C. L., SORBERO, M. E. S., and TELEKI, S. S., 2009, Pay for performance in the hospital setting: what is the state of the evidence? *American Journal of Medical Quality*, 24, 19–28.

NEWHOUSE, J. P., 1993, *Free for all? Lessons from the RAND Health Insurance Experiment.* Harvard University Press, Cambridge, MA.

PREMIER HEALTHCARE ALLIANCE, 2010, CMS/Premier Hospital Quality Incentive Demonstration (HQID). Premier, Charlotte, NC.

REINHARDT, U. E., 1981, Table manners at the health care feast, in D. Yaggy and W. G. Anlyan, eds., *Financing Health Care: Competition versus Regulation*, Ballinger Publishing Company, Cambridge, MA.

ROSENTHAL, M. B., 2007, "Nonpayment for performance? Medicare's new reimbursement rule," *New England Journal of Medicine*, 357/16, 1573–5.

RYAN, A. M., 2009, Effects of the Premier Hospital Quality Incentive Demonstration on Medicare patient mortality and cost, *Health Services Research*, 44, 821–42.

SINGER, P., 2009, Why we must ration health care, *New York Times*, July 15.

STREET, A. and MAYNARD, A., 2007, Activity based financing in England: the need for continual refinement of payment by results, *Health Economics, Policy and Law*, 2/0404, 419–27.

TOWNSEND, P. and DAVIDSON, N., 1982, *Inequalities in Health: The Black Report*, Penguin, Harmondsworth.

VAN DOORSLAER, E. V., WAGSTAFF, A., and BLEICHRODT, H., 1997, Income-related inequalities in health: some international comparisons, *Journal of Health Economics*, 16/1, 93–112.

WAGSTAFF, A., VAN DOORSLAER, E., VAN DER BURG, H., et al., 1999, Equity in the finance of health care: some further international comparisons, *Journal of Health Economics*, 18, 263–90.

WANLESS, D., APPLEBY, J., HARRISON, A., and PATEL, D., 2007, *Our Future Health Secured? A Review of NHS Funding and Performance*, The King's Fund, London.

WENNBERG, J. E., FREEMAN, J. L., and CULP, W. J., 1987, Are hospital services rationed in New Haven or over-utilised in Boston, *Lancet*, May 23, 1(8543): 1185–8.

WILKINSON, R. and PICKETT, K., 2009, *The Spirit Level: Why More Equal Societies Almost Always Do Better*, Allen Lane, London.

WILLIAMS, A. H., 1987, "Health economics: the cheerful face of the dismal science?" in A. Williams, ed., *Health Economics*, Macmillan, Basinstoke, UK.

INDEX

Lightning Source UK Ltd.
Milton Keynes UK
UKOW05f1258100915

258403UK00004B/6/P

9 780199 675401